STATES, DEBT, AND POWER

States, Debt, and Power

'Saints' and 'Sinners' in European History and Integration

Kenneth Dyson

OXFORD
UNIVERSITY PRESS

OXFORD
UNIVERSITY PRESS

Great Clarendon Street, Oxford, OX2 6DP,
United Kingdom

Oxford University Press is a department of the University of Oxford.
It furthers the University's objective of excellence in research, scholarship,
and education by publishing worldwide. Oxford is a registered trade mark of
Oxford University Press in the UK and in certain other countries

First Edition published in 2014

Impression: 2

Published in the United States of America by Oxford University Press
198 Madison Avenue, New York, NY 10016, United States of America

British Library Cataloguing in Publication Data
Data available

Library of Congress Control Number: 2014931571

ISBN 978–0–19–871407–1

Printed and bound by
CPI Group (UK) Ltd, Croydon, CR0 4YY

With thanks and love to my son Charles George,
for reminding me of what is most important in life.

The writer today should be not so much the mouthpiece
of a community (for then he will only tell it what it
knows already) as its conscience, its critical faculty, its generous
instinct. Louis MacNeice (1938), *Modern Poetry: A Personal Essay*
(Oxford: Oxford University Press), preface, iii.

Never take a risk that you cannot afford to lose.
Unattributed 'golden rule' of investing.

Acknowledgements

Paraphrasing the French poet Paul Valéry, a book is never finished, only abandoned. Nevertheless, this sense of incompleteness and loss has its compensations. It provides me with the opportunity to thank all those who have contributed, in their various ways, to helping make this book possible. My debts are numerous, many contracted in long discussions with kind and patient colleagues.

The stimulus to work on the book came from the Sixth Framework Programme of the European Union (EU), Priority 7, Citizens and Governance in a Knowledge-Based Society (CIT3-CT-2005-513421). This research project grant helped me to undertake the initial, exploratory research. In writing *European Economic Governance and Policies* (Oxford University Press, 2010), with Lucia Quaglia, I unearthed a number of historical documents that highlighted the significance of creditor-debtor state relations in shaping European macroeconomic governance. Study of neglected Bank of England and HM Treasury documents of 1931–1932, alongside the much-better-known Keynes' documents of 1933–1944, led me to rethink longer-term patterns in European macroeconomic governance. Looking back at the role of creditor-debtor state relations in European history posed the question of how far these relations have been reframed and formalized within a 'new Europe'. The book began life as an exercise in pattern detection, in tracing and teasing out continuities and changes in European macroeconomic governance over time.

I benefitted from scores of elite interviews in Amsterdam, Brussels, Berlin, Frankfurt, London, Luxembourg, Paris, and elsewhere, conducted on terms of anonymity and confidentiality. They led me to identify and examine the informal 'creditor-state club' at the heart of European macroeconomic arrangements. I came to recognize the significance of this informal club in imparting substance to negotiating the foundations of European macroeconomic arrangements, in setting its historic trajectories of path-dependent behaviour, and in exercising disproportionate influence on crisis management. This book would have been much weaker without the frankness, patience, and good will of these interviewees.

In writing a book that grounds historical and political analysis in a great deal of economic and technical argument and detail, I have accumulated many debts of gratitude. Very often, friends and colleagues, in and outside academia, will be unaware of just how helpful they have been. They have not just supplied me with papers, documents, and historic data sets. They have forced me to clarify my thinking. Above all, they have bolstered my confidence in crossing disciplinary boundaries and in reassuring me about the value of history in enlightening policy-makers. They have also shown me the importance of engaging with the moral and emotional aspects of debt. Debt evokes complex and powerful sentiments of guilt, shame, fear, humiliation, resentment, and anger. Popular emotions, and their manipulation by governing elites, complicate the politics of sovereign debt crises. They give it a fragile and indeterminate nature that macroeconomic modelling cannot internalize. This interest was stimulated by colleagues at Cardiff University, notably Paul Crosthwaite, Kate Griffith, Bruce Haddock, and Martin Kayman, as well as by Noel O'Sullivan at Hull University. In their own individual ways, friends and colleagues have helped to shape and correct my thinking. However, they are not accountable for errors of fact and judgement that may affect this book. These errors remain entirely my own responsibility.

I am hugely indebted to those who have helped me to track down historical debt data. On Belgium and the Netherlands, I was assisted by Ivo Maes (Catholic University of Leuven and National Bank of Belgium); on France, by Guillaume Daudin (University of Lille 1 and Sciences Po, Paris) and Nicolas Jabko (Sciences Po); on Germany, by Klaus Deutsch (Deutsche Bank); on Greece, by George Pagoulatos (Athens University of Economics and Business); on eighteenth-century Ireland, by Aidan Kane (NUI Galway); on Italy, by Maura Francese (Bank of Italy) and Francesco Stolfi (Exeter University); on the Ottoman Empire, by Şevket Pamuk (London School of Economics); and on Spain, by Francisco Comín (University of Alcalá, Madrid). My insights into the history of public debt were greatly enriched by the advice of Erik Buyst (Catholic University of Leuven), Jack Hayward (Hull University), Scott Newton (Cardiff University), and Helen Nicholson (Cardiff University).

With respect to the complex relations between public debt, macroeconomic theories, and financial markets, my debts are again too numerous to catalogue. However, a few people deserve special mention. Ivo Maes has been enormously generous with his time. Hanspeter Scheller (formerly the European Central Bank and the Bank for International Settlements) helped me greatly in shaping my thinking. On a more practical level, I remain indebted to the research officers who worked on the two-volume *European Economic Governance and Policies*—Ruth Mullineux, Martin Pasiak, Marc Pollentine, and Katja Seidel. My invaluable guides to research on financial journalism were Gary Merrill (Goldsmiths College London) and Damian Tambini (London School of Economics). More generally, Graham Bishop, Michael Moran (Manchester University), and Lucia Quaglia (York University) offered helpful guidance on financial markets and public debt.

Dealing with the complex relationships between law, debt, and statecraft was made much easier by the good advice I received from Dorothee Bohle and Bela Greskovits (both at the Central European University, Budapest). The subtleties of the law were unravelled for me by Ioannis Glinavos (Reading University), Jiri Priban (Cardiff University), and Michael Waibel (Cambridge University).

My work on sub-national fiscal governance benefitted hugely from the advice of Massimo Bordignon (Catholic University of Milan), Alistair Cole (Cardiff University), Mark Donovan (Cardiff University), Kyle Hanniman (University of Madison Wisconsin), Michael Keating (Aberdeen University), and Wolfgang Renzsch (Magdeburg University).

Through the complex writing and revision process I have once again been supported by the patient guidance and practical support of Dominic Byatt and his colleagues at Oxford University Press. As with my previous books on the history and politics of the euro, they have helped steer this book from its early beginnings to final production. Dominic has been throughout a source of great reassurance as well as excellent technical advice. In addition, I have benefitted inestimably from the anonymous reviewers for Oxford University Press. As only they will know, their influence has been considerable.

Inevitably, the greatest pleasure of all resides in expressing my most personal thanks. Colleagues at Cardiff University have been a source of continuing intellectual stimulation and congenial company. They have provided me with the happiest years of my academic life.

Above all else, however, my family remains the firm, loving foundation on which this book and my academic career have been built. As a young academic, my parents, Arthur and Freda, were always there to support me. The joy of my life has been to share it with my wife Ann and with our two wonderful boys, Charles and Thomas. They have enriched my life beyond measure. We three have been beneficiaries—along with all our friends—of Ann's unfailing love, affection, and kindness.

Kenneth Dyson
Cardiff University
November 2013

Contents

Part III State Liability and Territorial Control

Part IV Sovereign Creditworthiness and European Integration

List of Tables

List of Abbreviations

AFME	Association for Financial Markets in Europe
AFT	*Agence France Trésor*
AMECO	Annual Macroeconomic Database (EU)
A1P1	Article 1 of Protocol 1 of the European Convention for the Protection of Human Rights and Freedoms
ARC	Accounting Regulatory Committee (EU)
BCBS	Basel Committee on Banking Supervision
BEPGs	Broad Economic Policy Guidelines
BIO	*Banque impériale ottomane*
BIS	Bank for International Settlements
BITs	Bilateral Investment Treaties
CACs	Collective-Action Clauses
CAP	Common Agricultural Policy
CCPs	Central Counterparties
CDE	Coercive Debt Exchange
CDOs	Collateralized Debt Obligations
CDS	Credit Default Swap
CDU	Christian Democratic Union (Germany)
CEBS	Committee of European Banking Supervisors
CiU	*Convergència i Unió* (Catalan political party)
CPD	Cumulative Probability of Default
CSU	Christian Social Union (Germany)
DDAs	Deficit-Debt Adjustments
DM	Deutsche Mark
EACH	European Association of CCP Clearing Houses
EAF	Exceptional Access Framework
EBA	European Banking Authority
EBF	European Banking Federation
EBRD	European Bank for Reconstruction and Development
EC	European Community
ECA	Economic Cooperation Administration (US)
ECB	European Central Bank
ECHR	European Court of Human Rights

ECJ	European Court of Justice
ECOFIN	Council of Economic and Finance Ministers
ECSC	European Coal and Steel Community
ECU	European Currency Unit
EDP	Excessive Deficit Procedure
EEA	European Economic Area
EEC	European Economic Community
EFC	Economic and Financial Committee (EU)
EFO	Economic and Financial Organization
EFSF	European Financial Stability Facility
EFTA	European Free Trade Association
EMCF	European Monetary Cooperation Fund
EMI	European Monetary Institute
EMS	European Monetary System
EMU	Economic and Monetary Union
EPDA	European Primary Dealers Association
EPSAS	European Public Sector Accounting Standards
EPU	European Payments Union
ERF	European Reserve Fund
ERM	Exchange-Rate Mechanism
ERM II	Exchange-Rate Mechanism II
ESA	European System of Integrated Economic Accounts
ESM	European Stability Mechanism
ESMA	European Securities and Markets Authority
ESRB	European Systemic Risk Board
EU	European Union
Eurostat	Statistical Office of the European Union
FCL	Flexible Credit Line
FDI	Foreign Direct Investment
FSAP	Financial Sector Assessment Programme
FSB	Financial Stability Board
FSF	Financial Stability Forum
G7	Group of 7
G8	Group of 8
G10	Group of 10
G20	Group of 20
GDP	Gross Domestic Product
GFMA	Global Financial Markets Association
GVA	Gross Value-Added
HIPCs	Highly Indebted Poor Countries
IASB	International Accounting Standards Board
ICSID	International Centre for the Settlement of Investment Disputes
IDDC	International Debt Discount Corporation
IFRS	International Financial Reporting Standards
IGC	Intergovernmental Conference
IIF	Institute of International Finance

IMF	International Monetary Fund
INSEE	*Institut de la statistique et des études économiques*
IOSCO	International Organization of Securities Commissions
IPSAS	International Public Sector Accounting Standards
IPSASB	International Public Sector Accounting Standards Board
IRAP	Imposta Regionale sulle Attivita Produttive
ISDA	International Swaps and Derivatives Association
ISLA	International Securities Lending Association
JEDH	Joint External Debt Hub
LTCM	Long-Term Capital Management
LTV	Loan-To-Value
MAB	Mexican, Argentinean, and Brazilian
MAP	Mutual Assessment Process
MIP	Macroeconomic Imbalance Procedure
NAB	New Arrangements to Borrow
NPRF	National Pensions Reserve Fund (Republic of Ireland)
NRSRO	Nationally Recognized Statistical Rating Organization
NTMA	National Treasury Management Agency (Republic of Ireland)
OCA	Optimum Currency Area
OECD	Organization for Economic Cooperation and Development
OEEC	Organization for European Economic Cooperation
OMT	Outright Monetary Transactions
OPEC	Organization of Petroleum Exporting Countries
OTC	Over-The-Counter
PDM	Public Debt Management
PFI	Private Finance Initiative
PLL	Precautionary and Liquidity Line
PR	Public Relations
QE	Quantitative Easing
RWA	Risk-Weighted Assets
SDRM	Sovereign Debt Restructuring Mechanism
SDRs	Special Drawing Rights
SEC	Securities and Exchange Commission (US)
SGP	Stability and Growth Pact (EU)
SIFIs	Systemically Important Financial Intermediaries
SIFMA	Securities Industry and Financial Markets Association
SLS	Standard Levels of Service
SNP	Scottish National Party
SPD	Social Democratic Party (Germany)
SSCI	Social Science Citation Index
SSM	Single Supervisory Mechanism
STRIPS	Separate Trading of Registered Interest and Principal Securities
SWFs	Sovereign Wealth Funds
VAR	Value at Risk
VAT	Value-Added Tax
VLD	Flemish Liberal Party
WPDM	Working Party on Debt Management (OECD)

Archival Sources

The book has benefitted from access to various indispensable data sources. The single richest general historical source remains the monumental reference work of Angus Maddison, *The World Economy*, in two volumes (OECD 2006). However, it is more useful for GDP statistics than for national debt. More relevant for historical data is the European State Finance Database, which was originally created by Professor Richard Bonney (http://esfdb.websites.bta.com). There are also some useful, more time-limited data sources. They include the League of Nations Archive in the United Nations Office, Geneva, as well as the more complete and consistent European time series data available in the European Commission AMECO database (http://ec.europa.eu/economy˙finance/ameco/user/serie/SelectSerie.cfm).

The data bank HISTAT of the GESIS-Lebnitzinstitut für Sozialwissenschaften is an indispensable source of historical data on public debt for the nineteenth and twentieth centuries. Schremmer (1994) is an additional useful general source on public debt in Britain, France, and Germany before 1914; Comín (1996, 2012) provides data on Spanish public debt since 1850; whilst Güran (2003) is invaluable for Ottoman fiscal data. The UK Office for National Statistics has a data series for Britain's national debt as percentage of GDP going back to 1855 (Government Statistical Service 1999: 46). Various sources on Italian public debt have been traced back to unification (1861) and consolidated in Francese and Pace (2008). They identify its central and local, and short- and long-term components. Although they present Italian public debt in absolute figures, they make some attempt to relate public debt to GDP. The Bundesbank (1976) provides German data on public debt from 1877 to 1945, breaking it down into its various components (federal and state, long and short term). However, the German data is expressed either in monetary terms (like Italian) or in per capita terms. Hence it is not readily comparable with British data which is expressed as percentage of GDP.

I have made use of the copious post-1945 statistical series available from the French *Institut de la statistique et des études économiques* (INSEE), the German *Statistisches Bundesamt*, the Italian Banca d'Italia, the UK Office of National Statistics, and the US Congressional Office for the Budget. The 1997–1998 East Asian and Russian debt crises were important in highlighting the interconnectedness and the opacity of creditor-debtor relations. In their wake the Bank for International Settlements (BIS), the International Monetary Fund (IMF), and the World Bank worked to introduce greater consistency, transparency, and comparability into data on external debt. In Europe, Economic and Monetary Union (EMU) was a major catalyst for the European Commission, the Statistical Office of the European Communities, and later the European Banking Authority (EBA), to pursue the same objectives, notably the annual *Public Finances in EMU*. The statistical series of these bodies enabled a more complete picture of European public debts to emerge. Similarly, the annual reports on sovereign bond outlook produced by the Organization for Economic Cooperation and Development (OECD) are invaluable for data on sovereign bond issuance and regional breakdown. The EU bank stress test also generated new data on exposure of banks to sovereign debt, especially in cases like Greece (e.g. Committee of European Banking Supervisors (CEBS), Aggregate Outcome of the 2010 EU Wide Stress Test Exercise, 23 July 2010).

Other useful data sources on contemporary debt figures include the various national debt management offices. They include *L'Agence France Trésor*, the Irish National Treasury Management Agency (NTMA), the Italian *Dipartimento del Tesoro*, the Portuguese IGCP, and the Spanish *Tesoro Público*. Other helpful sources include the German Federal Finance Ministry *Monthly Report*; the Greek Ministry of Finance, *Hellenic Republic Debt Bulletin*; the Bank of Canada *Banking and Financial Statistics*; and the US Treasury *Monthly Statement of the Public Debt*.

However, when one wishes to look at the interactions between public debt and the broader national accounts, corporate and household, the situation is less satisfactory. Until the first decade of the twenty-first century, creditor and debtor state data on gross, and especially net, external debt have been variable. On balance, as the 1997–1998 East Asian and Russian debt crises demonstrated, the frequency and timely availability of data has been better from creditor than from debtor states (Bank for International Settlements 2002). Analysts lacked a fully comprehensive and consistent measure of total external debt, especially of short-term debt in total external financing. Gaps included direct investment, inter-company lending, and domestically issued debt securities held by non-resident non-banks. The figures contained discrepancies. Data was limited on external borrowing by the non-bank private sector (companies and households), especially with liberalization of exchange controls; on foreign holdings of debtor state debt securities; and on the short- and long-term maturity distribution of bank debt.

The East Asian and the Russian sovereign debt crises of 1997–1998 and the huge, coercive Argentinean default of 2001 proved turning points. The IMF (1999, 2002) and the Institute of International Finance (IIF) (2006) began to concern themselves with 'principles of fair debt restructuring' and 'good faith debtor behaviour'. The World Bank Global Development Finance Team concerned itself more systematically with sovereign debt restructuring. Even if inadequate for the purpose of offering an early-warning system on systemic risks, the new Financial Stability Forum (FSF) began to concern itself with monitoring financial risk (Brown 2010). The three major US-based credit rating agencies expanded their capacity in sovereign bond ratings and in examining default issues.

Not least, the key international financial institutions—the BIS, the IMF, the OECD, and the World Bank—sought to draw lessons about the dangers of excessive foreign debt, especially short-term external debt. They developed the Joint External Debt Hub (JEDH). Launched in 2006, it replaced an earlier joint exercise begun in 1999. JEDH provides more comprehensive, detailed, and consistent external debt data so that meaningful comparisons can be made. However, for the purpose of this book it offers only a very short historical picture. The quality and comparability of data diminishes as one goes back in time. This difficulty is serious because it is important to try to set contemporary events in a longer-term time frame. The book has had to make cautious use of the past data available to us, for instance for Greece and Spain, if only to get a sense of how external debt has developed over time in different domestic settings.

The situation with respect to data on public debt has been better within EU Member States and EU accession states because of EMU. EMU was associated with new data requirements for the purpose of the excessive deficit procedure (Article 104c and the Protocol on the Excessive Deficit Procedure, the Treaty on European Union, 1992), and consequent on the creation of ESA 95 (the European System of National and Regional Accounts). They provided an opportunity structure within which the European Commission and the Statistical Office of the European Communities (Eurostat) could develop common standards for presenting budgetary accounts (Savage 2005).

However, even in the EU, there is greater consistency in the treatment of gross public debt than net public debt, notably due to different treatment of assets (International Monetary Fund 2010c: 15). More seriously, some very important data remained for long publicly unavailable, for instance on the share of public debt that is held by non-residents (external public debt). Earlier historical data on gross public debt suffers from cross-national and temporal variations in scope and methodology so that again one has to treat data with caution.

Similarly, historical data on foreign exchange reserves are incomplete, for instance the ratio of reserves to short-term debt. The IMF sought to strengthen transparency requirements on central bank reserves, particularly their currency composition. However, especially outside Europe, reserve accumulation shifted to sovereign wealth funds (SWFs) in many states with large current account surpluses, especially commodity exporters. The governance reforms of SWFs under the Santiago Principles of October 2008—agreed under the auspices of the IMF—improved their transparency. Since April 2009 coordination was also strengthened with the new International Forum of Sovereign Wealth Funds. Nevertheless, the minimum disclosure requirements on SWFs remained low. The Norwegian SWF was in this respect one of the most virtuous in the world.

Finally, this book has benefitted from considerable advances in theoretical and empirical research on the history of sovereign debt defaults and restructuring. Reinhart and Rogoff (2008) remains an indispensable starting point in accessing sources of historical data. Tomz and Wright (2007, 2012) have examined the economic and political sources of surges and the costs of defaults in the 1820s, 1870s, 1890s, 1930s, and 1980s. I have supplemented these sources in two ways. First, this book provides more detailed historical public debt data on key European states. Secondly, it draws on sources that highlight the specific domestic social and political contexts as well as the international contexts of sovereign debt defaults. Domestic context helps understand why, for ideological or opportunistic reasons, some governments are more disposed than others to resort to default or financial repression. International context shows that coercive behaviour towards creditors is more likely when global 'bad times' of stagnating or falling economic output affect creditor as well as debtor states. States face the unavailability of credit when it is most needed.

Prologue: The Perils of Sleepwalking

> When the past speaks, it always speaks as an oracle.
>
> Friedrich Nietzsche, *Untimely Meditations* (1876: 93)

This book examines the problem of debt and its relationship to political power over a much longer historical period than that of the post-2007 crisis and its post-1960s' antecedents. Its time frame stretches from Ancient Greece to the euro area. It deals with changing representations of debt and their complex relationship with economic and political realities. This time frame helps bring out the roots of the problematic nature of this relationship. Its problematic nature stems from a proclivity to illusion, hubris, and complacency, leading governing elites, financial markets, and households to sleepwalk into sovereign, corporate, and personal debt crises. The value of this approach lies in placing current debates about the sustainability of the euro area in an historical perspective. It helps to see what is contextually specific to these debates and what is consistent with long-standing patterns. It also avoids the temporal problem of trying to assess a crisis that is far from over and that does not offer an opportunity to look back from an historical distance.

The Problem of Debt

One of the most striking developments in early twenty-first-century Europe has been the shift of debt to the centre of political discourse. This trend was evident in the European Union (EU), the euro area, and their Member States. In fact, well before the prolonged and existentially threatening post-2007 financial and economic crisis, public finances were being represented as in a condition of continuing crisis. The state's capacity to make political choices seemed to be increasingly constrained by accumulated implicit as well as explicit liabilities in pensions, health, and social care (Pierson 2001). These liabilities derived from heightened expectations of social entitlements, political competition to satisfy these expectations, and powerful demographic changes, above all population ageing. Accumulating liabilities were not matched by political willingness to be taxed or to make higher insurance contributions or by rates of economic growth that ensured sustainable financing. The perception of crisis in public finances was heightened by greater opportunities for tax avoidance and evasion. These opportunities grew with international and European moves to capital liberalization. They were also related to the size of the underground or grey economy.

Even before 2007–2008, governing elites seemed sleepwalkers, caught up in discourses of 'tax crisis', and increasingly of 'debt crisis', over which they seemed to have little control. Generational accountancy researchers calculated that in 2012 Germany had an implicit public debt/GDP ratio of 147 per cent, mainly resulting from unfunded social security liabilities (Moos and Raffelhüschen 2013). Taken together with explicit public debt, total German liabilities were estimated at 227 per cent of GDP and as equivalent to an increase of 11 per cent in taxes and contributions or a fall of 9.4 per cent in public expenditure. The estimates were even more alarming for Belgium, Britain, France, and the Netherlands.

The post-2007 financial and economic crisis served as a tipping point in helping to privilege the narrative of 'debt crisis'. It also confirmed an impression that the scope for political action in the EU, the euro area, and Member States was narrowing further towards vanishing point. European states and institutions faced the simultaneous impacts of three interconnected crises: banking crisis, sovereign debt crisis, and macroeconomic crisis. They were caught up in the potentially deadly embrace of the sovereign-debt and banking-crisis nexus. Shaky bank balance sheets threatened the solvency of their sovereigns, whilst banks risked being brought down by sovereigns, to whose debt they were overexposed. Public finances became further impaired by bank bail-out costs and by contingent liabilities within the financial system. In addition, fiscal balances registered the negative effects of credit contraction and macroeconomic crisis. Sharply contracting tax revenues coincided with heightened pressures on public spending from unemployment. Political and electoral arguments abounded about the irresponsibility of banks, about growing economic and social inequality, and about threats to social justice. Nevertheless, the dominant policy discourse identified the crisis as one of public debt. It was seen as requiring massive deleverage by European states, including the institutionalization of fiscal austerity.

The economic, social, and political consequences proved enormous, potentially alarming, for European states and for more recent, hard-won gains from European integration. The asphyxiation of political power was symbolized in the continuing benefits enjoyed by asset-rich, wealthy elites. They benefitted from the impact of central bank quantitative easing on asset prices far more than the real economy. Inequalities of wealth and income grew. The crisis witnessed the further concentration of financial power in a few systemically significant mega-banks, the re-emergence of a weakly regulated world of 'shadow' banking, and the visible disciplinary role of volatile financial markets through the impact of sovereign bond yields on public finances.

An early outcome of the crisis was the institutionalization of austerity. The euro area fiscal compact treaty of 2012 embedded the balanced-budget rule in the higher domestic law of the Member States with the aim of making fiscal consolidation an automatic process. The crisis of the 'debt state' found its political expression in a reframing of the nature and role of the European state, and of the EU and the euro area, on terms that left centre-Left discourse on the defensive (Streeck 2013). The state and the EU were redesigned around the twin principles of fiscal consolidation and structural reform. In contrast, there was little evidence of institutionalization of the concept of the developmental or entrepreneurial state, mobilizing productive investment in public infrastructure. The fiscal compact treaty was not matched by a European Social Stability Pact, laying down basic numeric rules of social provision, like the percentage of GDP spent on education and child care, and basic standards in minimum wages.

Good Debt, Bad Debt: The Developmental State, the Self-Binding State

Historically, the problem of debt and its relationship to political power has been represented in terms of opposed narratives of good and bad debt. Narratives of good debt focus on its functions in enabling the state to undertake productivity-enhancing investment, to provide collective insurance against risk, to build social integration and identity, and to share burdens across generations. Wisely-used public debt can be part of a model of sustainable economic growth, creating a self-reinforcing capacity to finance debt at low cost.

In contrast, narratives of bad debt stress its encouragement of extravagant and wasteful public expenditure on current consumption, diverting otherwise productive resources; its inducements to moral hazard and profligate rent-seeking behaviour; and its imposition of burdens on future generations. Reducing public debt is seen as a precondition for sustainable economic growth. However, the narrative of bad debt can also be directed at the financial sector. The financial sector endangers debt sustainability when it grows at a rate beyond GDP growth. This danger arises from bank lending to property and other asset markets rather than for the production of goods and services, for support to small businesses that help create jobs, and for investment in long-term infrastructure.

In these opposed narratives, images of debt and of the state are elided. The narrative of good debt is associated with a positive image of the state; that of bad debt with a negative image of the state. The first narrative celebrates the developmental and entrepreneurial role of the state as an engine of innovation. It is represented as possessing the superior capacity to take on the huge uncertainties, long time spans, and enormous costs associated with fundamental innovations that the private sector does not have. Mazzucato (2013) illustrates this role with respect to microelectronics, the Internet, global positioning systems, and energy technologies. The narrative of bad debt emphasizes the crowding-out of private investment by the state and the atrophy of private entrepreneurship. The state is represented as the source of 'crony' capitalism, which negates the vitality of free and open markets. It is seen as the root cause of a dependency culture, subordinating policies to the interests of *rentiers* and/or to recipients of state benefits. Public debt becomes symbolic of the state's role as obstacle to economic and social progress. This narrative advocates the self-binding state, imposing on itself clear, firm fiscal rules, independent monitoring mechanisms, and sanctions.

The contrast comes out starkly in the narratives of public debt in the German historical and institutional school of economics and in the British classical school of economics. Each offers not just a different conception of debt and state but also a keen insight into the practical challenges that debt poses. On the one hand, there is Lorenz von Stein's statement: 'One has to judge as undeveloped every fiscal authority that does not know how to make use of its credit' (1885–1886, Volume 3: 2). In this view, the challenge is to use public credit to undertake productivity-enhancing investment. This type of debt financing enables the state to augment its future revenues, service its debts, and ensure its solvency; to build social solidarity; and to achieve intergenerational justice. On the other hand, as David Hume argued in *Of Public Credit* (1759), states need a substantial fiscal buffer or safety margin to deal with emergencies. In his view, governing elites are too myopic, short-sighted, and vain to be trusted to be sufficiently prudent in managing public finances.

In the final analysis, judgements about debt are contingent on whether it is used to strengthen the capability of the state, understood as the ability of those who represent it to deliver outcomes valued by its citizens and to credibly embody principles of good conduct. There is no single 'correct' level of public investment. Big variations in returns are to be expected, depending on when, where, and on what money is spent, and on state capacity to deliver. Judgements about debt are also contingent on consistency with the virtue of prudence in safeguarding against security threats and war, financial and economic shocks, and contingent liabilities that are associated with entrenched social and economic entitlements. These judgements are path-dependent, bound up in experiences with, and legacies of, previous choices.

States need 'fiscal space' to ensure that they possess discretion to act in the public interest. This space is contingent on their vulnerabilities. The more exposed they are to security threats, to financial shocks, and to long-term contingent liabilities in social provision, the bigger the fiscal buffer needs to be. In this respect the attempt to apply a universal rule—like the EU 60 per cent public debt/GDP rule—makes little sense. Prudence requires risk assessment. For instance, a state with high structural dependence on the financial sector is likely to need a bigger fiscal buffer to insure it against systemic risks. Similarly, designing fiscal rules has to pay attention to the value of infrastructural and social investment. The optimal value for public debt/GDP ratio could be higher or much lower than 60 per cent, depending on such factors as exposure to geo-strategic and financial shocks, the quality of public expenditure, and tax capacity.

These different insights into public debt open a Pandora's Box of questions which bedevil judgement about the relationship of debt to political power. The answers are highly context-specific, grounded in different constellations of vulnerability to shocks and in different conceptions of the state, and thus contestable. When, and to what degree, is debt used to finance expenditure on current consumption rather than on investment? When is investment productivity-enhancing? What is the trade-off with 'crowding out' private-sector investment? What is an adequate fiscal safety margin? On which factors is this safety margin most contingent—external security threats, risks from banking crisis, economic shocks, or adverse demographics of welfare-state development? In thinking about debt financing, how should we reconcile considerations of collective insurance, social integration, and identity-building with avoidance of moral hazard and rent-seeking? Just how prudent does one need to be? The answers to these questions highlight the complex and multifaceted character of debt. They show why a single, coherent account of a state is so difficult to sustain as credible.

The striking feature of late-twentieth-century and early-twenty-first century narratives of debt and public power was the intellectual dominance of eighteenth-century Anglo-centric views. The insights of the late-nineteenth-century German historical and institutional school were marginalized (Dietzel 1855; Stein 1885–1886; Wagner 1863). Belief in the entrepreneurial state as an engine of innovation, undertaking risks that the private sector was reluctant to bear, suffered atrophy (Mazzucato 2013). In the United States the discourse of Thomas Jefferson on states and debt triumphed over that of Alexander Hamilton's developmental state. In Europe German Ordo-liberal ideas informed the foundational institutional arrangements and rules of Economic and Monetary Union (EMU) in the Maastricht Treaty of 1993 and in the Stability and Growth Pact (SGP) of 1997 (Dyson and Featherstone 1999). These ideas bore a closer affinity to the thinking of Hume, Jefferson, Adam Smith, and David Ricardo than to any notion of a developmental state.

The Key Arguments

Three arguments thread through this book. They do so in a way that is sufficiently flexible to encompass the enormous diversity of European experience across space and over time. The first is the centrality of creditor-debtor state relations for an understanding of the history of political rule in Europe. Their importance needs to be contextualized. The interests of states are far from unitary. The framing of creditor and debtor state interests is nested within larger political issues of state security in Europe, within their conditioning by historical memory, with the extent to which past guilt and fear of isolation play a role, and within more general perceptions of financial and economic vulnerability. It is also conditioned by factors of political ideology, particularly the value that domestic actors place on the appropriate balance between encouraging self-responsibility and showing solidarity and between insisting on fundamental creditor-state principles and practising reciprocity. Hence neither creditor nor debtor state interests are exogenous and timeless givens.

Nevertheless, the distinctive historically and ideologically coloured forms of creditor-debtor state relations should not obscure a fundamental pattern. Creditor-debtor state relations are asymmetric both in arguing and in bargaining power. Power gravitates towards creditor states, like Germany and the Netherlands in European monetary union. Despite their lack of numbers in comparison with debtor states, they possess an aura of power. Power gravitates above all to creditor states with systemic significance, endowing them with network capital. Their arguing power stems from their capacity to frame how policy issues, like coordination and liquidity provision, are debated. They set the normative standards of policy evaluation. They gain power over agenda-setting, bringing forward proposals around which other states negotiate.

The bargaining power of creditor states derives primarily from their capacity to make or break efforts to construct new institutional arrangements and rules. They have a lower intensity of preference for an agreement compared to retaining the status quo (Moravcsik 1998: 62). In short, they have the power to shape the outcomes of negotiated agreements through the threat of exit.

At the same time, creditor-state power varies with negotiating context (cf. Aspinwall and Schneider 2001; Naurin 2009). It is greater during negotiations of foundational institutional arrangements and rules, like the Maastricht Treaty of 1993 and the SGP of 1997, than during later negotiations about reforms to these arrangements. The threat of exit by creditor states has greater credibility as a bargaining resource in the former negotiating context than in the latter context (cf. Dyson and Featherstone 1999; Fuchs 2013). In particular, the combination of European monetary union with a single market in financial services provided a powerful catalyst for creating—across both creditor and debtor states—a perception of shared risks from contagion and from a disorderly unravelling of the euro area. This change of context had major implications for power over negotiating outcomes on euro area reforms to manage banking and sovereign debt crises.

Creditor-state power also faces the persistent challenge of matching the assumption of joint liability with external control of debtor states. Its exercise seems to follow a law of external control: the more peripheral a debtor state, the greater the degree of interference by creditor states. The corollary of this law is the incentive for this type of debtor state either to adapt *ex ante* to creditor states, leading to convergence; or to seek alternative economic arguments and to find allies to renegotiate foundational arrangements; or to seek protection from its creditors through a variety of instruments. These features of creditor-state and debtor-state power weave through the book.

Creditor-debtor state relations and political rule are associated in complex ways. Creditor-debtor state relations mirror changes in political rule and in the structures of social interests and cultural conceptions of entitlement that underpin political rule. Attitudes to debt prove most problematic—most prone to foster illusion—in certain cultural contexts: those that prize elite magnificence and display, that celebrate hedonistic consumption, and that emphasize welfare protection through patronage. These contexts sustain forms of political rule that exploit state resources for partisan interests, that generate 'crony' capitalism, and that intensify inequality. In thinking about attitudes to, and practices of, debt one needs to be alert to underlying structures of social interests. As Chapter 9 shows, each structure of social interests, and its associated economic culture and ideology of debt, breeds its own illusions about debt sustainability.

At the same time, creditor-debtor state relations challenge and expose deficiencies in domestic political will and state capacity to act. They trigger often polarizing debate about domestic reforms within debtor states. The parameters of their domestic political interaction are changed by how creditor-state elites define appropriate fiscal and monetary policies and by how they use their own policy instruments. In turn, the smart use of domestic policies to strengthen domestic growth trajectory can help shift the dynamics of creditor-debtor state relations. The German historical and institutional school emphasized how important the state can be in mobilizing and directing credit into productive investment. States can reshape their context.

The second argument centres on the importance of context. It shows how changing domestic representations of what constitutes appropriate or normal debt have been bound up with the unstable European and international contexts that rulers and governing elites have faced. External threats, war, and conquest, and their representation and use by ambitious and often insecure governing elites, were central to redefinitions of appropriate debt and to the development of debt financing practices. A discourse of external 'emergency' changes attitudes to sustainable debt. It is amenable to elite manipulation and to fostering fiscal illusion. At the same time the discourse of security threat and war proved to have an impact beyond its encouragement of sleepwalking into debt crisis. Once changes in technologies and scale led to 'total' war and reliance on mass mobilization, warfare acted as a political catalyst for development of new forms of social welfare provision by the state (Tilly 1975, 1990).

The rise of welfare states, and the social interests and structures of entitlement bound up with this process, have played a major role in changing representations of appropriate debt. However, this phenomenon came much later in European history. In the post-1945 period, especially from the 1960s, welfare-state development was important in reframing debates about sustainable debt. It helped privilege social democratic politics and the development of the 'tax state'. However, in the wake of the oil crises and exchange-rate crises of the 1970s and early 1980s, and especially with the post-2007 crisis, newly influential representations of acceptable debt began to reframe debates about the welfare state. They drew on projections of the costs of an ageing population and entrenched social entitlements. This reframing suggested that the illusion of the welfare state had been to make decisions about individual policies without taking account of long-term implications for fiscal deficits and public debt (Pierson 2001). States seemed to be sleepwalking into fiscal crises as their commitments were not aligned with political will and state capacity to deliver. The resulting 'institutionalization of fiscal austerity' placed social democratic politics on the defensive (Beckert and Streeck 2012). This discursive shift highlighted the need for tough and controversial political choices in economic and social policies that would define the character of early-twenty-first-century politics. They involved some combination of raising taxes, increasing contributions and payments, tightening eligibility requirements, cutting benefits, and expanding labour-market participation, including immigration. The nature of these choices will tell us much about power in society, specifically how much inequality we are prepared to tolerate. The choices promised to be tougher still if there was a further discursive shift towards defining external security threats.

The third argument highlights the limitations of formal economic reasoning about sovereign creditworthiness and sustainable debt. The book reveals the context-specific and constructed nature of debt. Despite the claims made for formal modelling and probabilistic reasoning, the relationship between debt and political rule remains pre-eminently a realm of subjective knowledge, conveyed by storytelling. Stories perform vital functions. They offer a compass in navigating radical economic and political uncertainty, as well as a sanctuary for retreat in the face of sheer complexity and passionate contestation. Stories also have a moral function. They distribute praise and blame amongst European states. However, stories also serve as distorting prisms through which responsibility is evaded. They function as prisons that screen out much of reality.

The corollary of this context-specific and constructed nature of debt is that belief in a single universal theory of optimal debt, from which precise and firm fiscal rules can be derived, is an illusion. The limitations of formal economic reasoning are also manifest in the representation of credit provision to households and companies as a series of transactions, in which risks were securitized and sold on to investors. The representation of credit as a commitment to the welfare of the client, involving personal judgement and trust by lenders, suffered atrophy. The US sub-prime mortgage crisis testified to the illusion engendered by faith in impersonal, transaction-based financial engineering.

These three arguments point to the central theme of the book—illusion, the mismatch of appearance and reality in representations of debt, and the transience of creditor-state power. Illusion does not mean that beliefs about sovereign creditworthiness and optimal debt cease to be real for governing elites and participants in financial markets. It refers to commitment to beliefs that combine wish-fulfilment as a prominent motivation in holding them with their insusceptibility to proof (Freud 1927: 31). Illusions are valued and retained for various reasons, even when they are shown to rest on faulty assumptions that collide with reality. They economize in dealing with radical complexity and uncertainty. They offer the promise of intellectual control. Not least, they provide a convenient way to attribute praise and blame to states. Holding certain beliefs about sovereign creditworthiness and optimal debt promotes the interests of particular financial and governing elites. It plays to their self-esteem and vanity. However, narrative constructions of sovereign creditworthiness and optimal debt are not necessarily accurate or consistent. They are imperfect models of reality. They contain unconscious biases. They filter information, typically endowing specific financial variables with more significance than environmental, social, and governance standards. They induce myopic behaviour.

Moreover, narrative constructions of sovereign creditworthiness and optimal debt attribute blame to individual states or rulers in ways that, however cognitively convenient, neglect the deeper social and cultural contexts that condition the form and content of these narratives. They foster the illusion that the state is, or can become, master of its own creditworthiness. The illusory nature of this belief becomes evident in the face of the ongoing mismatch between liability and control. Narrative constructions of sovereign creditworthiness are predominantly shaped by forces and actors external to governing elites.

The book contextualizes economic modelling and formal economic reasoning by stressing the complex interplay between the moral, imaginative, and rational faculties in discourses and practices of debt. At its heart is a critique of the dangers of intellectual entrapment within formal economic reasoning about sustainable public debt. This type of reasoning assumes that sustainable debt is amenable to scientific method, calculation, and probabilistic reasoning. The book argues that sovereign creditworthiness is a realm of subjective and highly imperfect knowledge, one that is more properly amenable to narrative reasoning. Formal economic reasoning has an important part to play in exposing errors and fallacies in narrative reasoning about debt. However, it also gives rise to small, artificial worlds of modelling that have an ambiguous relationship to economic institutions and behaviour (Morgan 2012). Modelling generates its own illusions of control. Moreover, constructing persuasive narratives requires an engagement with cultural, social, and political issues that transcend narrow economic reasoning. One of the dominant issues is the political and policy dangers of entrapment within 'crony' capitalism as financial and banking elites capture politics and policy. With it comes the erosion of standards of governance, deepening of economic and social inequality, and degradation of environmental standards.

The long-term historical relationship between states and debt exposes the pervasiveness of illusion and the negative qualities to which it gives rise—complacency, hubris, and vanity. Their pervasiveness serves to subvert simple faith in the objective quality of official data; in statistically-grounded technocratic formulae for assessing long-term debt sustainability; in regulatory reliance on banks' own models of risk and what they tell us about the health of their balance sheets; and, more generally, in the idea of an impartial, neutral arbiter of sustainable debt.

However, pervasiveness is not inevitability. Governing elites can prove enlightened and reflective in debt financing. They can use public debt to support bold structural reforms that enhance economic and fiscal capacity and to promote science-based innovation through both research and development spending and an active entrepreneurial role in taking risks. As key figures in the late-nineteenth-century German school of historical and institutional economics argued, debt can be employed to finance productive investment in public infrastructure and in building social solidarity and political inclusivity (Dietzel 1855; Stein 1885–1886; Wagner 1863). This insight retains a contemporary resonance. Mazzucato (2013) argues for the importance of the developmental or entrepreneurial state as fundamental science and innovation become ever more expensive and risky in fields like energy. Modern theories of endogenous growth show how debt can strengthen long-term growth potential and debt sustainability (Aizenman, Kletzer, and Pinto 2007; Vandenbroucke 2012). By taking on a bold entrepreneurial role, allied with good fortune in avoiding too many costly failures, some states succeed in climbing the ladder from debtor state to creditor state.

Much depends on whether governing elites believe that the state can make a positive difference. Belief that the state is an obstacle deprives the state of the will and capacity to take entrepreneurial risks. Correspondingly, fiscal consolidation that leads to deterioration in productive investment in infrastructure, environmental quality, governance standards, and social cohesion has serious, negative long-term implications for public debt/GDP ratio and debt sustainability.

In addition, sovereign debt and banking crises and macroeconomic shocks can serve as cathartic moments when fiscal illusion, hubris, and complacency are exposed. However, this promise of a new realism can be subverted by their perverse effect in strengthening incentives to conceal and manipulate financial data and to resort to various forms of fiscal gimmickry. Crisis management can, in short, foster new illusion, hubris, and complacency. As this book shows, talk of European convergence around 'sound' money and 'sound' finances is overdone. It ignores historical path dependencies, the powerful forces of inertia in economic cultures, and the dynamics of opportunistic political behaviour.

The key to sovereign creditworthiness does not lie in placing simple faith in compliance with the logic of macroeconomic debt sustainability models. It resides in three factors: the quality of moral judgement of governing elites; their culturally and ideologically conditioned political will; and state capacity, including net household financial assets as a percentage of GDP (see Chapter 13). Much hangs on the 'character' of governing elites and their publics. This character is exemplified in their engagement with questions of reciprocity and social justice and in their internalization of prudence as a moral virtue. The history of European states, debt, and power is testament to pervasive character weakness, evasion of responsibility, and moral failure. It is marked by hypocrisy. There is the hypocrisy of debtor-state elites who hide from their own policy mistakes by cultivating victimhood. There is also the hypocrisy of 'virtuous' creditor-state elites who harbour and protect banks which have lent recklessly and contributed to imprudent borrowing.

Character weakness is exhibited in another form. Sovereign creditworthiness is bound up with fiscal and banking gimmickry (Morgenstern 1950). It is a story of creative accounting and image management, using concealment, mendacity, and trickery. Examples include the misvaluation of their assets by banks, government use of off-balance-sheet budgeting, and window-dressing fiscal accounts by using complex, opaque derivatives. These practices make financial and fiscal transparency and compliance with bank capital adequacy requirements and with firm fiscal rules highly problematic. The firmness of fiscal rules—like those in the EU SGP and the so-called fiscal compact treaty—proves illusory for another reason. They rest on slippery concepts like structural fiscal balance that are open to varying interpretations and thus leave governing elites with considerable room for manoeuvre. Placing reliance on official data and on fiscal rules can add to the illusion, hubris, and complacency of financial and governing elites. Sovereign debt crises are about reckless creditors, feckless borrowers, opacity, and statistical information of dubious quality.

More tragically still, the history of European states, debt, and power testifies to pervasive moral complacency about the innocent, the semi-innocent, and the financially illiterate and gullible. Their experiences are extraneous to formal top-down models of sovereign debt sustainability and to banks' own risk models. The poor and the deprived are reduced to sullen silence as powerful, incestuous governing and banking elites evade responsibility for their excessive risk-taking. Only when they engage in social protest or in populist forms of political mobilization do the poor gain media and political attention. Social and political reasoning about sustainable debt is much more amenable to bottom-up models that stress inclusivity, reciprocity, and social justice.

The moral sense of injustice felt by the innocent and the gullible expresses itself in strongly-held sentiments of resentment, humiliation, despair, and anger. Characteristically marginalized or silenced in dominant narratives of sovereign debt crisis, they carry a disproportionate share of the harsh consequences of the activities of reckless creditors and feckless borrowers. The efforts of banks and states at deleverage, and to protect creditors, result in loss of real income and economic opportunity for the poor and dispossessed. Their sufferings are catalogued in unemployment, wage cuts, diminished savings, higher taxes, reduced benefits, housing eviction, family breakdown, mental health, and suicide. Historically, sovereign creditworthiness is predominantly a top-down narrative. However, this narrative poses serious political legitimacy problems. These problems relate to what sovereign debt policies tell us about the nature of social cooperation and about distributive justice between various types of creditors, debtors, taxpayers, and those with pressing social needs (cf. Sen 1993).

The problem of sovereign creditworthiness is institutional as well as moral. The historical examination of states and their debts highlights the issue of state capacity. The proneness of governing elites to illusion, hubris, and complacency is exposed—and sovereign creditworthiness compromised—by the mismatch between liability and control. Mismatch between the ease with which liability can be assumed and control over capacity to meet obligations shows how tough moral judgements are inextricably bound up with questions about institutional feasibility. These questions plagued the European Union and the euro area, as well as modern democracies in general. They also figured as a constant, if contextually varying, feature of European history.

A series of other questions arise as soon as we attempt an answer to this question about the relationship between states, debt, and power. In what ways are creditor-debtor relations important? Are creditor-debtor relations essentially a material phenomenon?

Or, are they politically constituted? Which interests and principles inform the behaviour of creditor states and debtor states? To what extent are the effects of creditor-debtor relations shaped by domestic and European governing structures of rule and the opportunities that they offer to statecraft? Or, are they grounded in 'mentalities', in economic cultures and prevailing ideologies of debt, at elite and public levels? Do creditor-debtor relations vary over time with whether the negotiating context is one of 'good' or 'bad' times at international level? Do they alter synchronically with the size and systemic significance of states? Do they vary with institutional and legal contexts? How do states contend with the fundamental political problem of matching liability with control?

There are libraries of books, journal articles, and working papers about sovereign debt defaults and restructurings, mostly grounded in economics. However, the concepts and frameworks of analysis that they employ touch on only some aspects of the questions that I wish to address, and then only partially. They are, on the whole, averse to thinking about creditor-debtor relations as politically constituted. They are also, on the whole, disposed to underplay historical contexts. Their reliance on very short historical time frames of analysis relegates key variables to the shadows.

This book opts for a wide historic canvas and a broad-brush, cross-disciplinary approach, using selective historical examples to illustrate how 'mentalities' of debt have changed. The chapters are thematically structured around the different interconnected questions highlighted previously. At the same time, each chapter is informed by an historical approach, which helps to bring out the dynamics of the complex relationship of states, debt, and power. It is important to understand what the book is not. It is not a narrative economic history. It is not an analysis grounded in a particular theory of political economy. It is not another history of the post-2007 crisis. The book is for those who like to reflect on the bigger historical picture, who are interested in the contextual variability of behaviour, and who are fascinated by the complexity of the human.

The Euro Area Sovereign Debt Crises: The Shrinking Creditor-State Club

The contemporary relevance and value of a more historically informed debate is enhanced by the shift of sovereign debt crisis from its association with developing economies and emerging markets to EU and euro area Member States. In 2005 eight euro area Member States held the coveted triple-A credit rating from all three leading credit rating agencies. They represented 75.5 per cent of euro area GDP. By the end of 2012 this informal creditor-state club had shrunk to just four—Finland, Germany, Luxembourg, and the Netherlands, accounting for 36.4 per cent of euro area GDP. Caught up in a home-grown house-price bubble, even the virtuous Netherlands began to look vulnerable. Euro area Member States figured in the top five biggest credit rating downgrades between 2007 and 2012: Greece, Cyprus, Spain, Portugal, and Ireland. They occupied seven of the top ten places. Only Turkey figured in the top ten credit rating upgrades. The rest were Latin American and Asian states. In consequence, the value of euro area sovereign bonds as collateral had significantly diminished. The share of euros in the reserves of central banks in developing states fell from 31 per cent in 2009 to 24 per cent in 2012. The share of the US dollar held steady at about 60 per cent. Also, the shrinkage of the informal creditor-state club in the euro area had significant implications for relative state power, the visibility of that power, and creditor-debtor state relations within the currency area.

From 2007 public debate about the sources, the nature, and the implications of the financial and economic crisis pushed the problem of debt to the centre of Europe's political agenda. It posed the question of how this problem should be represented. Was it a crisis of debt? Was it a crisis of growth? Was it a moral crisis? Should it be defined on creditor terms or debtor terms? Was there an independent standard by which it could be represented and managed impartially?

The crisis also begged the question of whether states possess the capacity to manage the huge financial risks associated with market-based credit creation. Do they have the political will as well as the state capacity to deflate mortgage and public finance credit bubbles in a timely fashion? Have they the will and capacity to restructure and recapitalize big, powerful banks? Are they too caught up in 'crony', 'insider' capitalism, granting inordinate privileges to financial elites? Do they possess the will and capacity to mobilize net household financial assets where they comprise a very high percentage of GDP? Doubts about this will and capacity heighten voter fears that governing elites lack a clear moral compass and cannot be trusted to responsibly promote public interests. They also heighten investors' fears that states will resort to some combination of default, coercive financial repression, and inflation, leading to the renationalization of financial systems. Both risks—popular disillusionment with, and rejection of, governing elites and collapse of creditor confidence—were noticeably high in the EU because of the imperfectly constructed institutional construction of the euro area. By 2013 it still lacked the indispensable infrastructure of banking, fiscal, and political union to help sustain its monetary union. The euro area faced the existential challenge of having a strongly bank-based financial system and increased reliance on effectively functioning cross-national financial markets in the absence of an effective bank resolution mechanism and common deposit insurance.

The post-2007 crisis offers an opportunity to situate the problems of debt in a much longer time frame than that of current or recent debt data series. This book addresses the historical—and essentially political—question of how important debt and relations with creditors have been in shaping the character of European states and the European integration process. Political science has conspicuously neglected this key question, ceding the territory to economics, which is less well equipped for this purpose. The book argues that creditor-debtor relations have major implications for how we conceive of European states, how we represent their power as 'strong' or 'weak' and their virtue as 'saints' or 'sinners'. In this and other ways, debate about the rights and wrongs of debt reveals theological traces.

The Concept of Sovereign Creditworthiness

The concept of sovereign creditworthiness is fundamental to the complex relationship between states, debt, and power. It is used to frame, hedge, and differentiate state power. Sovereign creditworthiness defines standards of appropriate behaviour for states.

It creates opportunities for certain kinds of action and constrains others. It empowers certain elites and certain types of argument over others. Not least, sovereign creditworthiness differentiates 'strong' and 'virtuous' from 'weak' and 'venal' states. It is a signifier of state power and virtue.

Sovereign creditworthiness is not simply an economic and material phenomenon. It has moral, emotional, and psycho-dramatic characteristics. At times of maximum fiscal stress, it lays bare the fundamental realities of state power. It reveals the moral dilemmas that beset the use of state power, the complex emotions of guilt, resentment, shame, and humiliation that debt arouses, and the vulnerability to the non-rational, herd-like, fear and panic that infects financial market behaviour. At the most fundamental level, states are caught between their duty to honour contracts and their right to revise what has become socially and politically intolerable. They can claim the right to insist that the vested interests that have a privileged role in the 'private governance of public debt' should share in carrying the burdens of adjustment to excessive indebtedness, by their 'bail-in' to crisis management (cf. Keynes 1923: 56).

How this dilemma is resolved, and with what consequences, illustrates the tragic gap between the potential and the actual power of states. It testifies to the significance of state capacity, to the practical difficulties in building it, and to the dangers of ignoring it in favour of reliance on macroeconomic models, formal rules, and official financial data. State capacity is expressed in the ability to enforce contracts, to extract tax revenues efficiently, to spend productively on infrastructure, to control fiscal balances, and thus to service debts. From the late eighteenth century northern and central European states began to strengthen this capacity. These improvements made possible large economic returns that, in turn, enhanced states' claims to sovereign creditworthiness (Besley and Persson 2011; Dincecco and Katz 2012). State-capacity building helped these European states to manage better the dilemma between, on the one hand, the duty to honour their debts and, on the other, the loss of popular legitimacy in their efforts to appease their creditors. State capacity was expressed in strengthened fiscal accountability and transparency, in disincentives to rent-seeking behaviour by governing and financial elites, in effective tax extraction, and in productive investment in infrastructure and building social solidarity. States were prepared to shoulder entrepreneurial risk in pursuing fundamental innovation.

State capacity is historically contingent and far from the norm. It has proved notably elusive in southern and in eastern Europe, the traditional 'arc of default'. It depends on a cluster of complementary characteristics. They include inclusive, accountable, transparent, and efficient governing structures, as well as an economic culture that supports sound finances and stability-oriented growth. Its fragility is exposed, above all, in international 'bad times' when economic output falls, fiscal imbalances increase, and borrowing costs threaten to become prohibitive. These circumstances make more visible the resistance of powerful, entrenched institutional actors to reforms. State capacity—and, by extension, EU and euro area capacity—reveals the central problem at the heart of the politics of sovereign creditworthiness: the balancing of liability with control. The obligation to pay has to be matched by inspiring confidence that someone is in control of the capacity to pay. Word has to be matched by deed.

How the dilemma between honouring contracts and revising what has become intolerable is resolved reveals as much about the willingness of states to pay as their capacity to pay. Incentives to comply with obligations to creditors can prove weak in the face of claims to sovereign immunity and the various practices of statecraft that are available to debtor-state elites to avoid or evade compliance (Eaton, Gersovitz, and Stiglitz 1986; Ritschl 2012b). The limits of enforceability are defined by dominant domestic economic cultures and ideologies, along with party and electoral competition and the opportunistic behaviour that they induce. In large part because of differences in governing structures and mentalities, France paid hefty war reparations promptly after 1871. Germany systematically evaded them after 1918.

Sleepwalking into Crisis: Virtue, Illusion, and Transience

> In however small a circle we may live, we are either debtors or creditors before we have had time to look around.
>
> Johann Wolfgang Goethe, *Elective Affinities* (1809: 22)

Goethe reminds us that the relations between creditor states and debtor states are intrinsic to European political life. They are decisive in moulding its character and in forming an informal hierarchy amongst its states. They are intrinsic because a capitalist economy is a credit-based economy. It is characterized by two features. First, there are imbalances in the distribution of credits and liabilities amongst states. Secondly, there are domestic differences in bank size, in quality of banking supervision, in incentives to credit creation, and thus in vulnerability to bank crises consequent on asset-price booms and busts. The health of a capitalist economy is fundamentally dependent on the capacity of states to ensure the continuing flow of credit (Stein 1885–1886; Wagner 1863). It requires prudent allocation by creditors, responsible and productive use of credit by debtors, and the avoidance of excessive and persisting external imbalances. Moreover, it requires structures of governance that foster efficiency, inclusiveness, fairness, and trust, including the confidence that contracts will be honoured. It also needs supportive economic cultures and ideologies of debt. States that approximate to these conditions are deemed virtuous and are exceptional rather than the norm.

The author of *Faust*, and former financial adviser to the Court of Weimar, was all too aware that the conditions of virtue are more honoured in the breach than in the observance. European history and integration provides abundant material to feed stories of imprudent creditors, reckless debtors, and delusional governing elites. It is a tale of the corrosion of creditor-debtor relations by complacency about excessive and persisting external imbalances; by unsustainable domestic credit creation and asset-price bubbles; and by imprudent governing elites and their resort to concealment, mendacity, and various forms of fiscal gimmickry. History also shows how the asymmetries in the power of creditor and debtor states spill over into moral and highly emotive controversies about fair burden-sharing and the use of state power.

These tales are given an added twist by certain less attractive features of human behaviour. Debt problems are aggravated by the political exploitation of the state's resources for personal and partisan gains, so-called 'rent-seeking'. They are made more difficult to manage by dominant forms of economic culture and debt ideology. Especially by the twentieth century, governing elites faced powerful political, financial, and commercial incentives to indulge citizens in the hedonistic pleasures of consumption. The effects were to induce complacency about credit risks. Debt problems are further magnified by the internal dynamics of financial markets. They are sites of avarice, greed, and cunning, with the potential to unleash waves of extraordinary panic and self-destruction. As Goethe noted in *Faust Part II*, financial alchemy—in various forms—retains an enduring attraction (Krennbauer 1949). The outcome is a deep-seated difficulty at the heart of the politics of sovereign creditworthiness: how to balance liability with control. This difficulty attests to the significance of state capacity, the limits of enforceability, and the willingness to pay. Governing structures and 'mentalities' are central to the politics of sovereign creditworthiness.

The world of sovereign creditworthiness becomes all the more confusing because it contains wise as well as reckless and ruthless creditors, prudent as well as foolish and venal debtors, and public-spirited as well as corrupt governing elites. It offers space for great variation in how problems of debt are represented and managed. Instruments of statecraft cover a wide spectrum between privileging and coercive financial repression of creditors. Practising statecraft entails immense moral challenges. On the one hand, there is the challenge of compliance with legal contract, of state reputation, and of ensuring the future flow of credit on which economic and social opportunities depend. On the other, there is the risk of collusion with financial elites. Governing elites can collude in benign neglect of the exploitation of financial illiteracy, including the mis-selling of complex financial products. They can collude in tolerating major collateral damage to the innocent when crisis occurs.

Sovereign debt crises reflect fundamental structural characteristics of financial capitalism. They tear away its rational and technocratic economic face to expose politically painful moral and cultural issues of social justice and shared identity, including sense of victimhood. They reveal the powerful role of sentiments in how problems of debt are represented. The associated emotions range from pleasure, through embarrassment, to guilt, shame, and humiliation. Sentiments infect financial markets, which shift from exuberance, via anxiety and fear, to panic. These characteristics are intrinsic to capitalist economies. However, they are inadequately captured in conventional macroeconomics and political economy, with their narrow and heroic assumption of rational individual behaviour. They are also not reflected in formal legal theories that rest on the naïve assumption of compliance with fiscal and financial rules. Formal economic and legal theories ignore the imperfections of financial markets and fiscal rules, reflecting pervasive opacity and gimmickry in banks' own risk models and in the availability of fiscal data. Their faith in 'clear' and 'firm' fiscal rules founders on the slippery character of the concepts on which they are based, like cyclically adjusted structural budget balance. These deficiencies were built into the Maastricht Treaty on Economic and Monetary Union of 1993 and the fiscal compact treaty of 2012.

> Lo, all our pomp of yesterday
> Is one with Nineveh and Tyre!
> Judge of the Nations, spare us yet,
> Lest we forget—lest we forget!
>
> Rudyard Kipling,
> *Recessional*, 17 July 1897

This quotation from Rudyard Kipling alerts us to a second theme: the precariousness and historical transience of creditor-state power. Part of the explanation for assuming liabilities without accompanying strengthening of external control is to be found in the susceptibility of financial and political elites and publics to illusion, hubris, and complacency. The German philosopher Friedrich Nietzsche highlighted this susceptibility as a mark of the human condition, above all with respect to debt, in his *Human, All too Human* (1879) and his *Twilight of the Idols* (1895). The relationship between states and their debts risks ensnarement in illusion and self-destructive vanity. As Angela Merkel, the German Federal Chancellor, stressed, debtor states ask more of creditors than they can prudently deliver; creditor states risk overestimating their own capacity.

The evolutionary biologist Robert Trivers (2011) attempted to provide a more scientific basis for understanding the systematic human bias to illusion, hubris, and complacency. People continually paint distorted pictures of the world in their efforts to persuade others to approve their policies and behaviour. They then become entrapped within their own illusions. Psychoanalysis offers further insights into the pathologies associated with imaginative constructs of identity. In particular, governing elites and publics of creditor states are prone to believe in their own 'exceptionality'. They fall victim to the illusion that they occupy a special position at the centre of events, that they enjoy immunity, and that they have little or no need to take account of others' viewpoints. Self-deception includes the belief that creditor states possess a special capability to improve the lot of others by making available their superior knowledge, wisdom, and moral insight. There is a thin line between what they see as virtue and those in debtor states regard as 'tyranny'. Similarly, governing elites in debtor states are prone to define their position as one of victimhood, diverting blame from their own policy mistakes. The history of sovereign debt is littered with examples of how readily governing elites and publics are seduced into illusion, and self-destructive behaviour, by self-regarding beliefs about their own exceptional virtues.

Explanations of the pervasiveness of illusion, hubris, and complacency and of the historical transience of creditor-state status need to go beyond biological and psychological factors to consider political and economic conditions. Joseph Schumpeter (1943: 261–2) suggests that moral standards like prudence relax once one moves beyond the level of the family and the business. At the level of the state, Europe, and international institutions, there is a reduced sense of reality. The sense of fiscal responsibility and what can credibly be achieved suffer as a consequence. Debt becomes too complex and too opaque to understand. In short, Schumpeter identifies a generic problem of fiscal transparency. However, this generalization requires qualification. Fiscal transparency problems are very much greater in Cyprus, Greece, Hungary, and Romania than in Britain, France, the Netherlands, and Sweden (Alt, Lassen, and Wehner 2012). Cultural, institutional, and negotiating contexts matter. Also, the problem of fiscal transparency is not the only factor inducing illusion, hubris, and complacency at the level of the state. In addition, the electoral cycle creates powerful political incentives to promise more than can be delivered and to conceal and to manipulate fiscal data.

Economically, sovereign creditworthiness sits uncomfortably on a bed of dynamite. Relations between creditors and debtor states are shaped by the underlying external imbalances in trade and financial flows and by asymmetry in domestic credit creation. Abundant, easily available credit serves to generate illusion, hubris, and complacency.

It helps form hedonistic, consumption-based economic cultures that place low priority on thrift, saving, and long-term investment. Creditors are able to make substantial short-term returns by investing in debtor states. Debtor states benefit from the growth effects of inward capital flows, notably into property, construction, and 'prestige' investment projects. This reciprocal illusion and complacency burst when the sustainability of the debts comes into question. Capital flows dry up. Creditors nurse substantial losses. Debtors have to make sudden, painful adjustments under external pressure. Symmetry of rewards in the international political economy of good times gives way to asymmetric burdens in bad times. Economic shocks have paradoxical effects. They serve to expose past illusion, hubris, and complacency. However, this effect is offset by their tendency to reinforce incentives to conceal and manipulate fiscal data and resort to fiscal gimmickry (Alt, Lassen, and Wehner 2012).

Risks of social and political explosion mount when governing elites fail to grasp the vulnerability that comes from excessive dependence on external debts and from expanding domestic private and public debt. They escalate once exponential growth in the size of financial assets is matched by lax, complacent supervision and regulation, allied to the exotic credit-creating skills of banks. Control becomes illusory as states become enmeshed in a living, pulsating, opaque, and inscrutable world of debts. The world of debt keeps changing shape, with toxic assets migrating across public and private boundaries and potentially entrapping states and banks in a deadly mutual embrace. Its nature stems, in part, from the powerful inducements to reckless, feckless, and volatile behaviour in complex, esoteric financial markets. Greed, fear, and temptations to 'game' supervisory and regulatory authorities are endemic. The nature of the world of debt also derives from the inducements to fiscal gimmickry. They are provided by domestic political structures, notably electoral timetables; by evading blame at times of economic shock; and by lack of fiscal transparency (Alt, Lassen, and Wehner 2012).

The ephemeral nature of sovereign creditworthiness and transience of creditor-state power reflect their vulnerability to shocks that originate in external and internal factors and in policy errors and accidents of history. On a macroeconomic level, creditworthiness and creditor-state power are exposed to potentially huge, negative shocks from external factors, notably crises precipitated by unsustainable external trade and financial imbalances and, above all, by wars and conquest. Creditor-state elites may generate punitive reactions from elites in distressed debtor states who resent the politically and socially intolerable burdens of asymmetric adjustment into which they feel forced. Shocks can also derive from the accumulation of domestic and European policy mistakes, characteristically related to illusion, hubris, and complacency. Policy-makers may neglect timely productivity-enhancing investment in infrastructure, perhaps because of an unwillingness to make the case for taxes or because of an undifferentiated application of cuts to public expenditure. Financial market supervisors may tolerate oversize, undercapitalized, and overleveraged banking systems, leading to financial shocks. Central banks may fail to counter the mispricing of risks and asset-price bubbles, for instance in housing and property. It is possible to fall victim to one's own imprudent financial, fiscal, and monetary policies, grounded in illusory but politically convenient assumptions about growth and debt. To all these factors are added world-historic changes in the distribution of economic power, undermining once-prized comparative advantages of states.

On a very different macro-historical level, the transience of creditor-state power is highlighted by larger world-historic changes in the distribution of economic power, undermining once-prized comparative advantages of states. Over the previous millennium, the major shift—from the fifteenth century onwards—was the gradual rise of a North Atlantic-based world economy. It had profound asymmetric effects on the trading and financial prowess of European city states and territorial states. This world-historic process of change enriched the merchants and financiers of the United Provinces and England. It privileged their role in shaping the institutional attributes of the fiscal state and public debt financing (Acemoglu, Johnson, and Robinson 2005). The new millennium suggests an ongoing shift away from the Atlantic-based world economy towards an Asia-Pacific world economy. The corollary is a radical shift of creditor-state power away from a Europe that lost its dominance of triple-A credit ratings and became externally debt-dependent. These larger, world-historic shifts underline the risk of attributing creditor-state status simply to deliberate policies. The fortune of being in the right place at the right time plays an important role.

The symbiotic relationship between public and private debt exposes a dilemma in retaining sovereign creditworthiness. On the one hand, there is an inbuilt bias for the sum total of debt claims to become greater than the worth of what is explicitly or implicitly pledged against the debt—whether GDP growth of a state, the value of a bank's assets, or the price of a house. Sovereign creditworthiness cannot avoid being enmeshed in wider developments in national accounts. States are exposed when overleveraged banks are major holders of newly risky public debt and are simultaneously burdened by household and corporate defaults. On the other hand, in seeking to tame financial market excesses, states encounter serious collective-action problems. They encounter a mismatch between their actual and potential liabilities and their territorial and institutional control. This mismatch bedevils efforts to sustain state image as creditworthy.

Why Europe?

The choice of Europe as the geographic focus of this book has a number of justifications. Most obviously, it rests on the author's own interests and expertise in European macroeconomic governance. However, three other factors are more important in justifying the choice of Europe. First, Europe can lay claim to be special in the historical origins and development of public debt and the notion of sovereign creditworthiness. It originated the central features of the modern state (Dyson 2010). The emergence of the 'fiscal' state was bound up, in part, in the dynastic and territorial ambitions of rulers and in war. It also reflected the efforts of creditors to hold rulers to account through more representative, if oligarchic, forms of government (cf. Tilley 1990; Stasavage 2012). The historical outcome was a territorial shift from fiscal fragmentation to centralization. New and powerful government bureaucracies professionalized tax extraction and debt financing. They helped build national assets through more efficient spending on education, training, the judiciary, transport, and communications (Besley and Persson 2011). From the late eighteenth century, effectiveness in state capacity building increasingly differentiated 'strong' from 'weak' states, notably those in northern and central from those in southern Europe (Dincecco and Katz 2012).

Also, in Europe 'relationship' banking, based on intimate contacts and personal trust between professional bankers and rulers, took its first recognizable form from the thirteenth century. The Ricciardi family of Lucca was followed by the Bardi and Peruzzi—and later Medici—families of Florence, and by the Fugger family of Augsburg and the various Genoese families. This type of banking was characteristic of the 'court Jews' of eighteenth-century Germany and the Rothschild family across nineteenth-century Europe. Bankers like Gersten von Bleichröder and Samuel Oppenheim were close to Otto von Bismarck in Prussia and the newly unified Germany. The idea of the modern, impersonal European fiscal state was slowly born out of this highly personalized power. In sovereign debt it retained certain traces of this 'gentlemanly' culture. Governing elites and certain financial elites were understood to be bound together on the basis of trust in each other's honour and propriety.

In its earliest manifestations, the conception of sovereign creditworthiness was defined sociologically by a very narrow *rentier* class of inherited wealth. Its members saw in fixed income from state-guaranteed bonds a relatively safe asset that—through political engagement—they sought to secure. Their economic interests depended on ensuring accountability and transparency of governing elites. They looked to automatic mechanisms like the gold standard to discipline elites. They also relied on the professional reputation of certain banks and bankers to 'brand' states as creditworthy. The rise of the modern fiscal state saw major improvements in accountability and transparency. Nevertheless, the complex inheritance of personalized power with oligarchic *rentier* power remained visible in the 'private governance of public debt'. The 'private governance of public debt' took the form of an incestuous relationship between a few big national banks and their governments, along with a residual lack of transparency about banking and government balance sheets. *Rentier* power retained a powerful grip on how sovereign creditworthiness was defined, even if its axis shifted from individuals to big powerful insurance and pension funds.

Secondly, relations between creditor and debtor states have been central to the historically novel processes of post-1945 European integration. An informal creditor-state club was at the heart of the European Payments Union (EPU), the Exchange-Rate Mechanism (ERM), and the birth and operation of the euro area. The ambivalent nature of sovereign debt crises was highlighted by Cyprus, Greece, Ireland, and Portugal, and by threats to Italy and Spain. They served as catalysts for institutional capacity building in European integration process. They also revealed acute internal tensions and conflicts over the terms, pace, and sequencing of reforms and tested the limits of creditor-state and debtor-state tolerance for the implications of living in a European monetary union.

Not least, evolving sovereign debt crises in Europe made visible the power asymmetry between creditor and debtor states. Germany was the pre-eminent creditor within the EU, but within a diminishing informal creditor-state club. Norway and Switzerland were pre-eminent outside the EU. Central and eastern Europe and southern Europe represented debtor states. Iceland was the most distressed debtor state in the European Economic Area (EEA). This pattern in creditor-debtor state relations offers a lens with which to examine European integration and the euro area. It brings out the disparity between north and west Europe (minus Iceland and Ireland) and eastern and southern Europe.

Thirdly, because of the historical distinctiveness of cross-national monetary integration and union, Europe offers a unique opportunity to examine continuity and change in the politics of sovereign creditworthiness. Has European integration given birth to a 'new Europe', transforming the politics of sovereign creditworthiness? Has it generated endogenous processes of preference formation? These two questions assume a topicality and significance in the context of the enormous changes in European macroeconomic governance over recent decades, including the 2012 European Stability Mechanism (ESM) treaty and the fiscal compact treaty. The EU also initiated new mechanisms for mutual surveillance of excessive deficits, excessive imbalances, and structural reforms in areas like product, services, capital, and labour markets. The question remains—just how much have relations between creditor and debtor states changed?

Europe became important for three reasons. First, sovereign debt crisis shifted from being represented as a developing state phenomenon to one that involved supposedly advanced states. Between 2007 and 2013 the biggest losers in sovereign credit ratings were to be found in the euro area. The biggest gainers were in emerging markets, notably Latin America. IMF attention and resources shifted accordingly.

Secondly, the creation of the euro area in January 1999, and its growth from eleven to eighteen EU Member States by 2014, was an historic milestone. There was a new powerful supra-national actor, the European Central Bank (ECB), with crisis management instruments. Thirdly, the contagious sovereign debt crises that began to unfold from 2007 demonstrated to euro area Member States their vulnerability. Systemic risks from contagion had shifted from exchange rates to sovereign bond markets. The euro area had rescued Member States from exchange-rate shocks. The question was—could it, and should it, rescue them from sovereign bond market shocks? However this question is answered, it demanded major institutional capacity building at supra-national and domestic levels. The euro area faced an institutional and a legitimacy crisis. It faced the challenge of creating a European fiscal, banking, and political union on terms that would match the assumption of joint liability with external control on Member-State sovereignty (Bini Smaghi 2010c). The early gainer was the ECB, which expanded its mandate into financial stability and banking union. In contrast, the European Commission was put on the defensive. Under the impact of crisis, the Heads of State and Government in the forms of the European Council and the new euro summit sought to carve out enhanced roles in European economic governance.

The core problem in redesigning the euro area to rescue its Member States from sovereign bond market shocks was the absence of independent democratic legitimacy for European banking and fiscal union. The euro area was caught up in a tortuous progression of banking and sovereign debt crises, from Ireland to Cyprus. Governing parties in France, Greece, Ireland, and Spain suffered heavy electoral defeats. Populist political mobilization, in creditor states like Finland and the Netherlands, as well as distressed debtor states, threatened solidarity on EU policies. After the 2012 French elections, even the traditional Franco-German 'motor' of EMU lacked unity of core beliefs and a sense of purpose. There was a lack of political consensus about the nature, form, and temporal synchronization of economic, banking, fiscal, and political union. This lack of consensus, and the unwillingness to give powers to supra-national institutions, reflected the very different economic self-interests, policy preferences, and principles of creditor and debtor states. Above all, the creditor-state elites, led by Germany, which provided the guarantees of euro area creditworthiness, wished to limit their liabilities. They sought to ensure that strict supra-national controls over debtor states preceded joint liability. The ESM remained an intergovernmental body with a de facto German veto power on its future decisions.

The Wider Global Context

This focus on Europe should not obscure the extent to which the politics of sovereign creditworthiness has a global character. The implications of excessive external imbalances for creditor-debtor state relations occupy the resources and skills of the Bank for International Settlements (BIS), the IMF, and the World Bank. These international financial institutions are central to debates about how to correct external imbalances; how to deal with the complex political and legal issues of creditor protection; and how to avert risks from contagion and threats of retaliatory measures. The Asian, Latin American, and Russian sovereign default crises of 1998–2000, the Argentinean default in 2001, and the government-backed Dubai World default in 2009 highlighted this larger global dimension. Their scale was huge. The Argentinean default amounted to $82.3 billion; the Russian default in 1998 to $73.4 billion; the Ecuadorian default in 1999 to $6.6 billion; the Peruvian default in 2000 to $4.9 billion; and the Ukrainian defaults in 1998 and 2000 to $1.4 and $1.1 billion (Packer 2003: 59). However, they were eclipsed by the size of the Greek debt restructuring in 2012 and by the size of the IMF contribution to the Greek bail-out as part of the Troika that monitored Greek compliance (along with the European Commission and the ECB).

By the beginning of the new millennium the central global dynamic had become the imbalance between China as the creditor and the United States as the debtor. It touched on larger macro-historical questions about shifting power in the world economy, on fundamental geo-strategic interests, and on the sustainability of the United States' global leadership role. China accounted for 21 per cent of the world's combined surpluses in 2008. Earlier, in the 1980s, the problem of global external imbalances had centred on Japan and the United States, with Japan representing a huge 42 per cent of the world's combined surpluses in 1986. The Plaza Accord of 1985 was a US-led multilateral attempt to coordinate an exchange-rate appreciation of the yen in order to set in process a 'policy-induced surplus reversal' (International Monetary Fund 2010). Subsequently, the US Omnibus Trade and Competitiveness Act of 1988 offered the basis for retaliation against states that were assessed as 'manipulating their currencies'.

The historic shift away from Europe (or rather Germany) as part of the central dynamic of global external imbalances had occurred by the 1980s. In the late 1960s the problem of global external imbalances had focused much more on Germany and Japan, each of which had accounted for 20 per cent of the world's combined surpluses (International Monetary Fund 2010: 14–15). The challenge from Germany and Japan was the context for President Richard Nixon's imposition of a tax of 10 per cent on all US imports in August 1971 until they re-valued their currencies against the dollar.

Despite this global scale, the politics of sovereign creditworthiness has a regional concentration. In the period 1820–1913, the most sensitive issues of sovereign default and restructuring centred on Latin America, and to a lesser extent North Africa. Measured by years in default between 1825 and 1940, the league table was topped by Honduras (79 per cent), Mexico (57 per cent), and Colombia (49 per cent) (della Paolera and Taylor 2012: 42). Eight Latin American states defaulted after the crisis of 1873, which saw a massive collapse in commodity prices. Latin America also spawned the first major, Bank of England-coordinated, 'bail-out', with harsh conditionality, precipitated by the imminence of an Argentinean default and the Baring Crash of 1890–1891. Latin America figured prominently in the 1980s and again in the Argentinean default of 2001.

Despite this concentration in the formerly colonial periphery, Europe has its own history of sovereign defaults. In a longer historical perspective, the politics of sovereign creditworthiness has been central in the development of European states, above all their rise and fall. It permeates narratives about Florence and Venice in Renaissance Italy, the Spanish and the Hapsburg Empires, the Ottoman Empire, the French *ancien régime*, the Napoleonic Wars and their aftermath, as well as post-1918 and post-1945 Europe. Post-2010, the politics of sovereign creditworthiness assumed once again a European focus.

This book has two omissions. It does not deal directly with the Latin American debt crises of the 1980s, the Mexican debt crisis of 1995, the Asian and Russian debt crises of 1997–1998, let alone the huge Argentinean crisis in 2001. There is already a large specialized literature on these cases. Equally, the book does not examine China-US creditor-debtor state relations. These examples are important in their own right. They have also led to important lesson-drawing about how to manage the politics of sovereign creditworthiness. For instance, the 1997–1998 crises heightened awareness of the risks of excessive reliance on short-term external debt, especially in generating roll-over problems. They demonstrated the value of accumulating big buffers of foreign-exchange reserves, as well as of improving processes for negotiating debt restructurings. Leading emerging market economies took radical action to mitigate risks. The heavy costs to creditors from the Argentinean crisis led to a new resort to bilateral investment treaties (BITs) and to collective-action clauses (CACs). They sought to better protect creditor interests in the continuing absence of an international regime for orderly sovereign insolvency that could constrain the potentially coercive behaviour of debtor-state elites.

The global dimension of the politics of sovereign creditworthiness and the lesson-drawing from sovereign debt crises elsewhere form the context of this book. They are not the objects of investigation. Nevertheless, the global dimension of the politics of sovereign creditworthiness remains important. Sovereign creditworthiness in Europe is bound up in larger global external imbalances because of the intimate, often opaque interconnectedness of trade and financial markets. The scale of this interconnectedness was evident in the post-2007 banking and financial crisis. European banks proved enmeshed in the US sub-prime mortgage market and vulnerable to the collapse of Lehman Brothers in 2008. For this and other reasons, European governments were drawn into hugely costly bank bail-outs, with negative implications for sovereign creditworthiness. Moreover, a group of emerging market economies emerged as new creditor states, potentially playing a major role with respect to Europe, for instance through their asset purchases. They included Brazil, China, India, Russia, and Singapore, alongside oil-rich Arab and Gulf states. They had limited collective-action capacity. Nevertheless, their good will was important in ensuring a strong IMF role in euro area crisis management. International institutions, above all the IMF, G20, the Financial Stability Board, and the BIS, played vital roles in discussions about improved EU and euro area crisis prevention and management. The IMF was also a key player in the Troika arrangements put in place to deal with the sovereign debt crises in Cyprus, Greece, Ireland, and Portugal. By 2012–2013 it was taking a more critical and independent stance on euro area reforms, partly under pressure from emerging market economies, partly consequent on the illusions that had attended the earlier Greek 'bail-out', and partly as the IMF technical staff gained a stronger internal voice. This external hard-line position was evident over the restructuring of Greek debt and over the Cyprus banking crisis.

Disclaimers

This book has an ambitious purpose. It seeks to examine the complex relations between states, debt, and power and the centrality of the idea of sovereign creditworthiness in the making of modern Europe. The approach rests on a belief in the value of interdisciplinary insights and, in particular, of history as tools of policy analysis. A broad macro-historical perspective can help to throw fresh light on current debates about sovereign debt crisis. It opens them to a more independent, critical, and judicious assessment that goes beyond 'here-and-now' reporting, reliance on limited and questionable official data, and those whose representation of the problem is limited to the confines of macroeconomic modelling and formal legal analysis.

Historical research helps to uncover forgotten facts. It broadens the range of evidence beyond that which informs conventional public debt sustainability analysis. It shows how the way in which society represents problems of debt changes over time. It helps to sharpen contextual understanding of present conditions. In these ways historical evidence and arguments about the past are relevant to enhancing the quality of debate about contemporary sovereign debt problems.

Inevitably, however, the book rests on a set of choices and exclusions and requires certain academic disclaimers. First, it does not claim to provide an authoritative account of the evolution of the post-2007 financial and sovereign debt crises that rocked the euro area, the wider EU, and the EEA, spreading from their periphery into their core. As these crises unfolded, they remained initially the territory of journalists and economic commentators. Instead, the book uses historical research and analysis, including new longer-term historical debt data, to examine how far the evolving crises reveal underlying patterns in the relations between creditor and debtor states. The importance of this cleavage has been neglected both in studies of European macroeconomic governance and, more generally, of European integration. The evolving and deepening post-2007 crises forced these underlying relations to the surface, unmasking asymmetries of power and generating polarization and differentiation. They exposed the failure to construct adequate institutional capacity in three core areas of European economic governance. There was inadequate capacity to correct excessive and destabilizing intra-European imbalances; to secure cross-national financial stability; and to ensure a 'lender of last resort' to Member-State governments faced by extreme emergencies. This capacity was needed not just to provide time and support for painful structural reforms and fiscal consolidation but also to ensure the cohesion, integrity, and irreversibility of European monetary union.

This neglect and failure reflected the short-term and very particular historical context in which European monetary union had been forged. Its context was threefold: the desire of Member States to shed their past vulnerability to asymmetric exchange-rate shocks; memories of the high inflation of the 1970s; and, not least, the absence of experience of sovereign debt default in the process of European integration. The tacit assumptions were that defaults were an emerging market phenomenon and that clear and firm fiscal rules would prevent them. Defaults were undesirable, unnecessary, and unexpected in advanced market economies. Illusion and complacency were induced by the belief that EU governments could be trusted to honour their commitments, subject to peer pressure. There was no serious attention to institutional capacity and economic culture or to the scope for concealment, mendacity, and gimmickry in fiscal policies. Illusion and complacency were compounded by a dominant teleological understanding of the European integration process, above all in the so-called 'monetarist' approach to monetary union. It followed its own logic, with monetary integration driving economic convergence and political union. The indeterminacy of European politics fits uncomfortably with this type of thinking.

A longer European historical perspective underlines the precarious nature of sovereign debt dynamics and recurring collective-action problems. States face an imperfect match between their liabilities (explicit and implicit) and their territorial control. The more imperfect is this match, the greater the risk that construction of their sovereign creditworthiness will become negative. This problem was at the heart of currency debasements in Imperial Rome, monarchical financial repression in late medieval and early modern Europe, the debt problems that plagued the birth and development of modern European states, and the 'arc of default' in nineteenth- and early-twentieth-century Europe. The sovereign debt crisis that gathered pace in 2010–2011 posed the question of how much had changed. Was there a 'new Europe'? Or, was Europe just 'dancing to the music of time'?

The second disclaimer relates to the nature of the book. It will not be read with sympathy by those who seek the intellectual order and discipline of theory-driven research rooted in an individual discipline or branch of a discipline. They will miss the carefully tested hypotheses of much political economy in the US tradition (e.g. Enderlein, Trebesch, and von Daniels 2010; Tomz 2007). The book crosses disciplinary boundaries and is historically-minded and empirically-driven. It is the product of long, detailed, and patient immersion in different types of empirical and theoretical material on debt and what it tells us about power. In particular, the book seeks out new historical sources and data to illuminate how representations of sovereign debt have changed. The aim is to see whether themes and patterns across space, and over time, can be teased from this complex material. The book is not confined to a specific body of theory, or even narrowly to political economy. Instead, it ranges across disciplines that are relevant to understanding how problems of debt have been represented. The book's coherence lies in its sensitivity to contextual spatial and temporal understanding and in the themes and patterns that it identifies. As befits the subject matter, the themes are complex, and the patterns are kaleidoscopic. It can be read as a series of interconnected essays.

To the extent that the book can claim a theoretical home, it is closest to 'strategic constructivism' (cf. Jabko 2012). In this approach, sovereign creditworthiness has two dimensions. It rests on culturally- and historically-anchored representations of credit and debt and of appropriate standards in managing debts. Sovereign creditworthiness embodies a notion of what constitutes fiscal 'normality'. Governing elites become entrapped within these representations. At the same time, sovereign creditworthiness provides a powerful strategic resource. It is appropriated and used in various ways, principally by actors in, and close to, the financial markets on which states depend for their debt financing. This strategic dependency means that certain actors are able to use sovereign creditworthiness to advance and legitimate a particular political and policy agenda. They frame appropriate standards of fiscal normality and mobilize coalitions of sometimes strange bedfellows in their support. For this reason sovereign creditworthiness is vulnerable to 'crony' capitalism and discursive capture.

Sovereign creditworthiness has various uses. It is employed as a norm by which the quality of states and their governments is assessed. It provides a constraint on what governing elites can do. It serves as a discipline on their fiscal, economic, and social policies. It functions as a beacon that differentiates certain states as 'saints' and reduces the costs of financing for their governments. It offers a space in which financial markets can benefit from 'risk-free' assets and states can benefit from access to ample, low-cost credit. In short, sovereign creditworthiness is a political concept that frames, hedges, and differentiates state power.

Consistent with its interdisciplinary treatment of states, debt, and power, and its focus on the politics of sovereign creditworthiness, the book's methodology is essentially qualitative and plural. It is grounded in historically-informed political science. It also borrows eclectically from other disciplines that can shed light on states, debt, and power. The focus on long-term contextual understanding of the politics of sovereign creditworthiness makes less relevant, and practical, the employment of a single set of objective indicators and replicable coding, for instance of financial repression or defaults. The book is not for those who seek the rigour and precision of time-limited comparisons of a large number of contemporary cases. However, there are gains. A longer-term focus offers insights into patterns in creditor-debtor relations that are hidden by data that cover just a few decades. It also shows how, and why, power over ideas of creditworthiness has changed over time, along with ideas about how power should be used.

The patterns that emerge are multiple, kaleidoscopic, shifting, and far from consistent. Size and systemic significance of banking sectors clearly matter, as in Cyprus, Iceland, and Ireland. However, much also depends on the efficiency of the supervisory system, the nature of bank liabilities, and health of bank balance sheets. Luxembourg was a different case from Cyprus. Size and systemic significance also matter for state power. However, they are not coterminous with the attribution of sovereign creditworthiness. Additionally, 'good' governance matters. Governance that is both inclusive and protects creditor interests can be seen as a precondition of sovereign creditworthiness (Stasavage 2011). However, too close a penetration of financier interests into political rule leads to oligarchic rule, 'crony' capitalism, state capture, *rentier* regimes, and the 'hollowing out' of the notion of representative government. The resultant atrophy of social and political trust risks negative consequences for sovereign creditworthiness.

Similarly, creditor-state power varies with negotiating context. It is at its most evident when foundational institutional arrangements and rules are being negotiated, like the IMF in 1944, European monetary union in 1988–1991, the SGP in 1995–1997 and later, post-2010, European fiscal and banking union. Debtor states depend on creditor-state participation for these foundational agreements to be credible, and creditor states have stronger incentives to favour the status quo. In consequence, creditor states have the power to shape outcomes by resorting to the key bargaining resource of threat of exit from negotiations. The challenge for others is to keep them at the negotiating table. In subsequent negotiations creditor states continue to benefit from the path-dependent character of behaviour within the asymmetrically designed institutional framework. However, in later negotiations about reforms to these arrangements, especially in crisis conditions, the new reality of being locked into cooperation, fears about contagion, and the power of numbers play a larger role in influencing outcomes. Creditor-state power becomes more circumscribed once the threat of exit loses credibility. Debtor states have higher prospects of influencing negotiated outcomes. They can employ their knowledge of how best to use institutional frameworks; they can seek to deploy new expert legal and technical arguments for reforms; and they can exploit their knowledge of other states' policy positions, especially the constraints facing creditor states in pursuing their positions (Beach 2005; Fuchs 2013; Naurin 2009; Tallberg 2008).

In addition, the search for patterns confronts problems of reification and of unit-of-analysis. The distinction between creditor and debtor states has value in showing how and why certain kinds of economic argument come to be privileged in domestic discourse. However, the ascription of unitary interests to creditor or debtor states is problematic. Creditor states do not necessarily share the same geo-strategic interests. Their historical experiences of security threats are different. Creditor states have interests that do not necessarily coincide with those of private creditors. Bailing-out creditors places costs on their taxpayers, who are likely to feel resentment. The same problem arises in ascribing unitary interests to debtor states. They are positioned differently in international structures of power. Cyprus is very different from Ireland or Portugal. Equally, creditor states vary in their distinctive historical memories, shaping their attitudes to the nature and to the use of their power. For these reasons, Germany, the Netherlands, Norway, and Switzerland cannot be understood solely by reference to their creditor status. Germany is reluctant to be represented as coercively asserting its power in EU and euro area negotiations. It fears attribution of German hegemony to the euro area. In specific configurations of international circumstances, geo-strategic interests and historical lesson-drawing, notably the fear of isolation in Europe, may prevail over economic interests.

In addition, size is a significant variable. Some creditor states and some debtor states are more systemically significant: Germany more than Luxembourg or Norway; Italy more than Cyprus. The creditor-debtor state dimension also ignores differences in domestic political and economic incentive structures. Governing elites face different configurations of institutional veto points, notably legislative, judicial, and territorial. They vary in the tightness of electoral constraints. Economically, states differ in their degrees of structural dependency, notably on banking. Germany and Luxembourg were both creditor states in 2013, but the latter had a vastly bigger banking system relative to its GDP. Similarly, Portugal and Cyprus were both debtor states, but the latter had in 2013 a much greater dependency on its banking sector. The Luxembourg government found itself defending the Cypriot government in 2013 against Dutch and German demands. This example illustrates the limits on the capacity of the informal creditor-state club to behave as a unitary actor.

Additionally, the interests of creditor-state elites and private creditors may not be wholly the same. Private creditors tend to be more bellicose than their 'protector' states in enforcing the honouring of debt contracts. For governing elites, unlike private creditors, the test of strategic acumen is much more complex and challenging. They have to take account of geo-strategic interests and threats, the burden of historical memory, and the complex web of economic and financial interdependence, as well as their taxpayers and their electorates. For this reason, they may favour the 'bail-in' of private-sector creditors at time of banking or sovereign debt crisis. Germany and the Netherlands led the way in pressing for bank 'bail-ins' as the sovereign debt crisis intensified, above all over Cyprus in 2013.

Perhaps the clearest pattern over the period since the mid-twentieth century has been the formalization of creditor-debtor state relations. The period has witnessed a shift away from the pure legal doctrine of sovereign immunity and an institutionalization of arrangements to ensure debt sustainability. A second pattern is the persistence of acute collective-action problems, which constrain the scope and depth of this formalization, even within the euro area. Sovereign creditworthiness retains its irreducibly political character. A third pattern is the problematic matching of joint liabilities and territorial control. This problem was particularly acute in larger territorial units—as opposed to city states—in the process of state building. It remains serious in federal states and, above all, in cross-national monetary unions like the euro area. Finally, illusion, hubris, and complacency are recurrent. The incentives and constraints vary. At times of crisis the prospects for a 'new realism' may seem brighter. However, factors of fiscal opacity, electoral and party competition, and economic shock ensure that these character weaknesses keep a firm foothold in political life. These four patterns weave through the book.

The broad historical sweep of the book rests on the assembly of evidence from a wide range of seemingly unconnected episodes and events from many centuries. They include Athens, the Delian League, and the first recorded defaults; the innovative use of annuity debt financing by Italian city states and other continental cities in late medieval Europe; individual private lending by Luccan and Florentine merchant bankers to English kings and by the German Fugger family to the Hapsburgs; the resort to alchemists by King Henry VI of England and by Electors of the Holy Roman Empire; techniques of financial repression, including the expropriations of church and monastic lands and properties by King Philip IV of France and by King Henry VIII of England; syndicated bank loans by Genoese merchant bankers to King Philip II of Spain; the role of 'court Jews' (*Hofjuden*) within the Holy Roman Empire after 1648; and the legacy of John Law and of the Revolution's *assignats* for French attitudes to money and credit. In post-1815 European history, the book covers the Europe-wide role of the Rothschild family; Camille de Cavour's creative use of British and French debt financing to realize Piedmont's ambition to hegemony within the Italian peninsula; the role of Gerson von Bleichröder in financing Otto von Bismarck's policy for unifying Germany; Greek and Ottoman debt crises; hyperinflation as an instrument for reducing debt in post-1918 Hungary and the German Weimar Republic; and credit as an instrument in West German-Soviet *Ostpolitik* during the post-1945 Cold War. These events and episodes in the history of political rule and debt are interesting in their own right. More importantly perhaps, they provide the historical prologue to the distinctive configuration of modern sovereign bond markets. They also provide the essential raw material for thinking about patterns.

A book of this type inevitably raises many more questions than it can hope to answer, especially relating to the dynamics of creditor and debtor states. It makes some suggestions about the conditions under which certain states may make the transition from debtor to creditor states. However, the book does not treat this as its central question and the extent to which this transition is attributable to accident or to deliberate policies. The basic question relates to long-term patterns in creditor-debtor state relations and in representations of sovereign creditworthiness. The search for these patterns draws attention to how strategic choices are embedded in social forces and to the underlying structures of power that shape ascendant ideas of sovereign creditworthiness.

Though patterns are discernible over time, the constellation of creditor states and debtor states changes. They can be pictured in terms of different types, moving on a continuum from creditors through lapsed creditors and illusory creditors, to chronic debtors, and vice versa. In the late 1920s and early 1930s, for instance, Germany was a chronic debtor, and France was a creditor. Britain, which had been the major creditor state before 1914, struggled to accommodate its political ambitions to its new debtor status. This dynamics of change in the constellation of creditor and debtor states was, as so often in European history, bound up with cataclysmic events. It reflected the ruinous costs of war, hyperinflation and currency debasement, property price crashes, bank insolvencies, and deep, protracted, and synchronized recession. Shocks, for instance from unsustainable household debts, can suddenly rob a state of its creditor status. The adjustment burden is easier to manage when shocks take place in a benign, expansionary world economic context. The severe financial crises of Finland and Sweden in 1990–1993 provide examples of states that were able to rapidly retrieve their creditor status. Similarly, Ireland went from debtor in the 1980s to creditor in the first decade of the euro, only to lose that status in the post-2007 crisis.

Perhaps most strikingly of all, the book differs from standard macroeconomic theorizing in highlighting the strongly moral, emotional, and libidinal qualities that attach to relations between states and their creditors and between creditor and debtor states. These qualities are very much the subject matter of political philosophy, fictional literature, critical cultural theory, and psychoanalytic theory. Critical engagement with states, debt, and power involves exploring the hidden corners and silent places of financial markets and states, and the deeper sources of potentially self-destructive behaviour. The book's adoption of the terms 'saints' and 'sinners' is an ironic play on the nature of power relations. It serves as a warning that one must treat the conventional picture of creditors as 'saints', and debtors as 'sinners', with great caution. This metaphor reflects and induces a pronounced bias to binary argument about debt. Its use can be dangerously misleading and intensify sovereign distress and systemic instability.

Creditor-debtor state relations are a three-way moral challenge. They involve a huge ongoing challenge to the exercise of prudent judgement. The challenge is to reconcile the avoidance of moral hazard in rewarding reckless behaviour; to prevent contagion and systemic crisis and the shared costs to which they give rise; and to establish governance processes that facilitate consensus between creditors and debtors and build mutual trust and common identity around fairness in sharing often painful burdens of adjustment. Prudence involves making reckless creditors as well as feckless debtors assume responsibility for the consequences of their behaviour; safeguarding taxpayers; and, most pressing of all, protecting innocent victims from shouldering excessive costs, consequent on the mistakes of others. It also means having strategic acumen in averting the danger of isolation for a state like Germany by recognizing that her interests and those of Europe are inextricably bound together through the single European market and monetary union.

The difficulties of meeting this complex moral challenge are magnified by several factors: incomplete knowledge about the balance sheets of states (their total assets as well as liabilities); the size and the opacity of banking systems; deep-seated structural asymmetries of power over policies; the short, intense timescales of crisis management; and, not least, the emotional intensity that accompanies crisis. Narrow, partial perspectives and short-term myopia in crisis management contribute to high emotional temperature. The problems are compounded by the spatial and temporal blinkers of nation states and their governments. They face incentives to prioritize short domestic political timetables over considerations of domestic and European long-term sustainability and distributive justice.

Above all, structural asymmetries are apparent in ascendant ideas about sovereign creditworthiness and who has power over issue-framing and agenda-setting. This power is expressed in the 'branding' and the disciplining role of financial markets, which are volatile, 'news-driven', and often 'herd-like'. It is also apparent in the privileged role of creditor states, whose interest is to protect their taxpayers from having to bail out 'irresponsible' debtors.

Elites and publics in creditor states picture themselves as confronted by pervasive *incivisme* in chronic debtor states, like Cyprus, Greece, Hungary, and Romania. Their governing elites and publics are accused of evading fiscal responsibility, using concealment, manipulation, and tricks in reporting fiscal data, and pursuing rent-seeking and personal self-aggrandisement at the expense of the public interest. Conversely, governing elites and publics in chronic debtor states are prone to populist attacks on the imperialist pretensions of creditor states, which are pictured as subjecting them to the status of colony or protectorate.

These moral, emotional, and temporal challenges of crisis management expose reformers, whether those in debtor states who argue for deep-seated structural reforms and fiscal consolidation or those in creditor states who argue for collective responsibility for debts and greater symmetry in burden-sharing. Under the pressure of crisis domestic support for their agendas proves fragile. Initial enthusiasm for the technocratic government of Mario Monti in Italy gave way to his weak performance in the February 2013 elections. The German Social Democrats and Greens veered closer to the position of the Merkel government as the September 2013 federal elections neared. The fragility of support for reform agendas highlights just how deep-seated are collective-action problems in creditor-debtor state relations.

Difficulties: The Shadowy World of Debt

Writing about states, debt, and power poses a number of difficulties. We are dealing with a complex, arcane, and shadowy world of debt, infected with illusion, shaped by gamesmanship, subterfuge, and image management, and presenting a 'hall of mirrors' to observers. Despite great efforts to improve fiscal transparency, what official data there is cannot be assumed to be reliable (Morgenstern 1950). Moreover, sovereign debt has evolved from a 'gentlemanly' culture of social rank and long-term personal financial relationships into a highly technocratic culture of quantitative experts, statistical modelling, and obscure financial instruments, like derivatives. Even the informed observer can find this highly technical world difficult to negotiate. To help the general reader, the book provides a glossary of technical terms.

The complexity, opacity, and technicality of the world of credit and debt are the reason why it represents such a serious political problem for liberal democratic societies. It evades pressures for accountability and transparency, 'games' the public and its representatives, and encourages profligate and self-seeking behaviour. The opportunities for creative accounting are legion. They stem in part from the absence of consolidated balance sheets and rigorous reporting discipline. In addition, shareholder and voter incomprehension and the semi-informed nature of professional commentary create an environment in which concealment, manipulation, and trickery can thrive. Governing elites succumb to temptation to gain a favourable impression by selective presentation of fiscal data, by exploiting technical loopholes, and by hiding toxic assets 'off balance sheet'.

Insiders—not just outsiders—have only very imprecise knowledge of what 'whole-of-government' balance sheets look like—what they owe and own. They face deficient accounting disclosure and financial management practices. Carrying out valuations, whether of pensions or heritage assets, is costly and difficult. Public debt accounts provide a poor measure of the liabilities of a government.

This book seeks to provide general readers with a political analysis of this deeply problematic technocratic world of debt, which is a 'systemically significant' process for both liberal democracy and capitalism. Even if deterred by the statistics and by the technical language, resort to the glossary and persistence with the statistical tables should pay rich dividends. The reader will identify connections and implications that have eluded the author.

One aspect of this shadowy world of debt is the complex gamesmanship in the relations between states, private creditors, and international financial institutions. States seek to strengthen their negotiating power vis-à-vis private creditors by exploiting information asymmetries. They are unwilling to share fiscal and financial data, other than on a selective basis, for instance about off-balance-sheet liabilities, exposures of their banks, debt arrears, or the size of foreign-exchange reserves. At the same time, international financial institutions—led by the International Accounting Standards Board (IASB) and the IMF—have attempted to embed the principle of transparency and the notion of fair dealing with private creditors in state behaviour. However, like investment banks with respect to financial market supervision and regulation, states are tempted to game the system, if only to play for time in making necessarily painful and politically costly adjustments.

A particular difficulty confronts this book. It stems from the paradox between, on the one hand, the availability of large amounts of national historical statistical data on public debt in various sources and, on the other, the lack of comparability in coverage, scope, and methodology. Lack of consistency in the measurement of public finances and in cross-national information about their levels and composition makes comparison problematic. This difficulty still affects contemporary fiscal data. For instance, social benefits may or may not be taxed; different financing mechanisms for health, pensions, and unemployment benefits make headline figures very different; whilst the size of contingent liabilities may not always be reflected in the same ways in public finance figures. Additionally, recording of external debt liabilities faces the problem that often only the direct purchaser, not the actual holder of the debt, is recorded. Hence tracing regional breakdowns in external debt liabilities is fraught with hazards and uncertainties. These limitations compound the risk of illusion, even for the most cautious and scrupulous analyst.

Moreover, in some instances, like Greece and Ottoman Turkey, compiling historical public debt data is complicated because it was not always serviced. Also, it is technically difficult to define what constitutes servicing, especially when official foreign creditors are involved. In addition, there were often no consolidated accounts of public expenditure. For this reason, historical debt data are easier to collect in some states, like Belgium and the Netherlands, than in others. Historians of debt are reliant on surviving sources. Unlike social scientists, they cannot design a questionnaire to elicit standardized data. However, these difficulties are not sufficient excuse for ignoring a rich array of primary sources, including official government and specialist archives, as well as secondary sources in which historians have examined in detail key documents relating to debts. The label 'unbiased' is difficult for even contemporary, technically more proficient sources to deny. Fiscal data obscure as much as they reveal.

A third difficulty relates to the way in which sovereign creditworthiness and creditor-debtor state relations lend themselves to a moralizing and often emotionally charged discourse, namely the binary opposition of 'saints' and 'sinners'. The metaphor is in some sense instructive. In the manner of St Augustine, sinners can—by their exertions—become saints. Redemption can be found through the productive use of debt. Conversely, saints may be led into sin. Unless one believes in predestination, the lesson is that we should beware of thinking about states and sovereign creditworthiness in fixed, non-historical categories.

However, the crude binary opposition of saints and sinners risks obscuring the moral ambiguity that surrounds debt. Not all debt is sinful. Wisely and productively used, it can serve as an instrument of human betterment through collective insurance, social integration, and intergenerational burden-sharing (Stein 1885–1886). Moreover, the reckless behaviour of creditors can contribute to the misery of debtors. Saints may find themselves confronted with morally questionable outcomes from their choices about how best to handle sinners. In particular, intervening in ways that fail to discriminate between punishing those responsible and avoiding injury to the innocent can undermine moral authority. Collateral damage is one of the chief moral challenges that confront private creditors and creditor states. It negatively affected the images of the euro area and Germany, notably in the Cypriot crisis of 2013. The unexamined misuse of the language of saints and sinners is part of the problem of creditor-debtor state relations. It can lead, for instance, to populist mobilization of resentment in creditor states and amongst private creditors at what is represented as the lazy and feckless behaviour of Greeks compared to Germans. However, official data on hours worked and on retirement age of Germans and Greeks does not corroborate this image.

A fourth difficulty with which the book grapples is the narrowing of intellectual horizon that comes from the colonization of debate about sovereign creditworthiness. Debate has been dominated by investment banking and its close, incestuous relationships to the macro- and financial economics profession, to financial public-relations consultancies, and to financial journalism and media. The book seeks to offer a more critical and independent perspective by a cross-disciplinary and historical approach that captures the politics of sovereign creditworthiness. It argues that focusing on investor preferences, and the test of market credibility, does not adequately address the moral questions at the heart of sovereign creditworthiness.

The issue is whether financial markets are right in their branding of states. There are legitimate grounds to entertain serious doubts about faith in the reliability of markets. Investors use quantitative risk indicators to assess debt sustainability. Their views about sovereign creditworthiness change in the light of new data and of technical refinements to their models. However, in the final analysis these assessments remain highly qualitative. They are based on subjective images of state strength, governing competence, and public responsibility. They rest on imagined projections of state fiscal behaviour. Selective use is made of indicators, and different data sets are open to interpretation in ways that create openings for subjectivity. In particular, faith in the notion of efficient markets creates space for serious errors in assessing the economic fundamentals of states and currencies. The disciplinary power of the instruments at the disposal of financial market actors, like sovereign credit ratings, makes these errors into matters of grave public concern.

Not least, reliance on the opinions of professional financial journalists risks narrowing the horizons of public debate. They are close to investment banks and their financial public relations consultancies, on which they depend for access, sources, and future newsworthy stories. Sometimes journalists are located in financial media that rely on investment banks for subscription and advertising revenues and as ongoing sources of information, news, and comment. This incestuous media context heightens the danger that financial journalism fails to play an independent investigative role. There is a risk of serious and unacknowledged conflicts of interests in public debate. The effect is to accentuate herd-like behaviour in branding states.

In this inhospitable context, the book reasserts the value of historically and politically grounded understanding of sovereign creditworthiness. It differentiates types of state and looks into the 'black box' of sub-national fiscal governance. It also examines the behaviour of the various participants and elucidates the reflexive character of the relations of states to financial markets. It explores the imbalance between 'branding' states and 'taming' markets and the distinctive configurations of power in sovereign bond markets. Not least, it teases out longer-term patterns and contingencies in the relations of European states, debt, and power. In this way, the book seeks to move outside the frenetic 'here-and-now' of the post-2007 financial and economic crisis. It dives behind vivid events to deeper structural patterns.

1

Contextualizing Debt: History, Morality, and the Triple Structural Dimension

> It was his characteristic bias to shrink from the moral stupidity of... missing blindly in his own life of to-day the crises which he recognized as momentous and sacred in the historic life of men.
>
> George Eliot, *Daniel Deronda* (1876: 568)

The fraught debates that accompanied the mounting European sovereign debt crises after 2007 illustrated the perils of intellectual amnesia and of faith in universally valid fiscal and financial rules. Time horizons proved strikingly narrow. Financial market practitioners, financial journalists, and economic commentators were immersed in online, real-time financial and political data. They inhabited a world of 24-hour news. Political economists, macroeconomists, and public intellectuals preferred to work within the parameters of their models, endlessly perfecting them to cope with the new 'unexpected'. They generalized from very limited historical data. Debate was constrained by the ceaseless pressure of the 'here-and-now' in a media-saturated world. Its quality was further diminished by the erosion of the capacity of financial journalists for independent and critical scrutiny. They became over-dependent on the superior resources of investment banks for privileged access to newsworthy stories and for background information and knowledge. The casualties of 'crony' capitalism were accountability, balanced argument, and public-interest considerations.

Professional debate about sovereign creditworthiness amongst economists and financial experts was blinkered by reliance on forms of abstract reasoning that presumed scientific mastery and that led to closure in participation. It benignly neglected the lessons of history as irrelevant to a new, enlightened world. Scientific, self-referential academic debates about sovereign creditworthiness worked with narrow financial accounting. They neglected historical financial dynamics and their linkages to the real economy of output and jobs. Above all, debate failed to engage critically with the big historical themes of war, banking, and financial crisis, with socio-cultural and ideological change, and with the moral issues that attended sovereign debt crisis. An underlying faith in universally valid rules and policy prescriptions marginalized context-specific thinking and expertise.

The cultivation of historical sensibility and reflexive understanding has become more important, just as the conditions for its practice have deteriorated. This need for overcoming intellectual amnesia is vital in considering the complex relationships between states, debt, and power. There have, of course, been enormous changes over time in fiscal instruments of rule and in the parameters of their deployment. Coercive financial repression is less easy to practise as demands for accountability and transparency of rule have grown. Financial markets have hugely expanded opportunities to escape states' territorial control. European integration and the rise of international financial institutions have altered the governance context in which states manage their debts. Demands for fiscal transparency and accountability have grown, narrowing the scope for fiscal gimmickry.

Nevertheless, some fundamental issues about power and its use recur. They reflect the paradoxical nature of debt. Debt serves both to enable and to constrain state power. On the one hand, there is an enduring incentive for governing elites to resort to debt financing in order to augment their scarce resources and build viable states. Debt provides firepower to states to pursue their cherished purposes. On the other hand, debt offers an incentive for governing elites to indulge illusion and hubris. It leaves them sitting on a bed of dynamite and exposes the limits of their territorial control. To add to these problems, debt is bound up in moral dilemmas. Governing elites face hard moral choices, which are inherently political. The problems arise when they are seen as amenable to an overarching single philosophy. They have to be resolved on a case-by-case basis, so that in some contexts more value may be placed on the 'duty to pay debt', whilst in others the emphasis may fall on securing 'freedom from debt'. Practical wisdom resides in recognizing the importance of specific historical contexts.

Examined over the long term, the relationship between states, debt, and power exposes the ease with which governing elites and publics fall into the grip of illusion, hubris, and complacency. The tendency of modern democracies to pile up debt by making unaffordable promises to voters—and to resort to statistical manipulation to improve appearances—is just one manifestation of this phenomenon. The failure of governing elites to use 'good' times in order to build up fiscal 'buffers' to withstand the shocks that accompany 'bad' times has long historic pedigree. Similarly, illusion, hubris, and complacency led to the inadequate design of the euro area and its vulnerability to shocks. It lacked the rudiments of banking and fiscal union, not least the supra-national discretionary authority to act in supreme emergency. Legal frameworks and institutional structures of governance can help make a difference. However, strengthened fiscal accountability and transparency can at best mitigate the proneness of governing elites and publics to indulge in illusion, hubris, and complacency.

Some systems of governance are more inclusive and more disciplinarian than others. Nevertheless, there remains an underlying unwillingness either to address awkward questions about the sustainability of financial behaviour or to do the hard moral thinking about fair burden-sharing. This unwillingness is apparent amongst creditors as well as debtors. It is exposed in the recurrent phenomenon of the 'illusory' creditor and the 'chronic' debtor. The longer historical view shows how state power has been bound up with the reckless and the feckless and with heavy collateral damage to innocents from sovereign debt crises. Recurrent themes include the mismatch between liability and control and the unreliability of debt payments. In contracting debt, private individuals, corporate executives, and governing elites are prone to underestimate risk, to exploit new financial instruments and technical loopholes in opaque ways, and—when faced with debt crisis—to attempt to offload their liabilities to others.

Why the History of Public Debt?

This book seeks to make the case for a historically-minded political economy. Political economy needs to rediscover its capacity to help us to think afresh about the role of debt in political rule and to awaken our sensitivity to continuity and change. Its eighteenth-century roots were planted in a view of history as a laboratory that can help broaden and enrich our understanding of what debt tells us about states and their power. History offers insight into the historically contingent, subjective, and contestable character of notions of what constitutes fiscal 'normality' and sovereign creditworthiness. It reveals sovereign creditworthiness as subjective knowledge.

History illustrates the precariousness of sovereign creditworthiness because of the radical uncertainties attached to public debt dynamics and the pervasive incentives to fiscal illusion, hubris, and complacency on the parts of both creditors and debtors—the 'reckless' and the 'feckless'. It also bears witness to the seemingly intractable political problems of limiting collateral damage to the innocent in debt crises. History also helps question Anglo-centric and state-centric views on the origins of public debt. Above all, the historic 'arc of default' in Europe testifies to persisting governance problems. These problems are manifest in weak state capacity to build assets—and thus reputation—by productive investment in infrastructure and in building social solidarity (Dietzel 1855; Stein 1885–1886; Wagner 1863). They are also apparent in weak capacity to extract taxes to service debts, above all when, as in Italy in 2007, net financial household wealth stands at over 200 per cent of GDP, well ahead of Germany. The debt financing of this historic 'arc of default' is associated with a relatively low rate of return on public investment (cf. Checherita-Westphal, Hughes Hallett, and Rother 2012).

An historical approach highlights the different social forces that help shape the choices between strategies for making public debt sustainable—whether to prioritize fiscal consolidation, economic growth, inflation, default, or various forms of financial repression. It shows the financial creativity of states in engineering stealth subsidy of public debts to finance themselves at below-market rates and in hiding debts off-balance-sheet. Historical data also illustrate how conceptions of fiscal 'normality', including what constitutes excessive and sustainable debt, have altered over time. European states managed to avoid defaults in the past when their public debt/GDP ratios exceeded the Maastricht Treaty's 60 per cent for very long periods. More strikingly, they did so when these ratios stayed above 100 per cent, even 200 per cent, for decades. Conceptions of fiscal normality have changed over time in ways that reveal shifts in the balance of social forces, notably the varying fortunes of *rentier* power.

An historical approach helps also to illustrate how dependency of states on creditors for financing debt helps create privileged stakeholders. In the thirteenth century the ambitions of Popes were underpinned by the Bonsignori of Siena, whilst the Ricciardi of Lucca attracted various rulers (Blomquist 2005). They were followed by the Bardi and later the Medici of Florence. The rise of Hapsburg power was intimately connected to the Fugger of Augsburg. Barings and the House of Rothschild were dominant players in early nineteenth-century Europe, whilst J.P. Morgan and then Goldman Sachs assumed iconic significance in twentieth-century Europe.

Sovereign debt rests on an inbuilt asymmetry of power that is readily disguised by abstract economic models and legal principles. These models and principles serve to camouflage the gap between, on the one hand, the ideology of free, competitive markets and formal legal contract and, on the other, 'crony' capitalism in which wealthy financial and banking elites collude in the exercise of state power, gaining tax and regulatory privileges. Sovereign creditworthiness is a function of reputation—but with whom? In public-interest terms, the reference groups would be not just a privileged set of creditors. They would embrace taxpayers, the unemployed, and the poor and underprivileged. If sovereign debt is to be reconciled with representative government, then it has to be managed in a way that sustains reputation with both. Ideally, fairness in burden-sharing would place emphasis on 'reckless' creditors as well as 'feckless' debtors'. Above all, it would shield the innocent and ensure that the least advantaged were enabled to fully participate in society (Sen 1989, 1993: 30). However, historical experience shows how elusive this ideal of fair burden-sharing is in the face of privileged creditor power. The challenge of meeting contractual obligations to creditors has to be seen in a wider context of supporting a system of social cooperation based on distributive justice. Otherwise, 'crony' capitalism is in danger of hollowing-out representative government, competitive markets, and legal impartiality and producing populist politics, fuelled by anger at elites.

An historical overview of states, debt, and power shows how doctrines about sovereign immunity and the rules of the game have changed. Nevertheless, beneath the surface, similarities can be discerned over time. They are hidden from view by new forms of representative government, with their stricter accountability and transparency. The tricks of feckless financing, as practised by late medieval rulers, find parallels in modern 'off-balance-sheet' devices and private-finance initiatives. Earlier currency debasements foreshadow modern printing of money and 'inflation taxing' of creditors. There are affinities between the power of medieval and early modern merchant-financiers and twenty-first-century Primary Dealer investment banks. The nineteenth-century 'arc of default' across eastern and southern Europe embraces states that were in the eye of the European sovereign debt storm in the early twenty-first century. Fiscal illusion and hubris recur over time. Their roots are to be found in the political pride that Thomas Hobbes characterized as vainglory and Jean-Jacques Rousseau as *amour-propre*. The incentive to fall victim to these traits is in turn shaped by the political characteristics of regimes, above all in those that are based on authoritarian and charismatic rule. In addition, history shows how, in 'good' times, rulers are disposed to public borrowing and/or to encourage private borrowing on a scale that exceeds capacity to service debt in 'bad times'.

In macroeconomics, public debt is characteristically understood in terms of a narrow, one-dimensional assumption of a material world, comprised of rational, utility-maximizing individuals responding to measureable indicators of sovereign creditworthiness. This book examines what history and political science can teach us about changing temporal contexts of public debt, the underlying power structures in sovereign debt markets, and different ideologies of debt. In doing so, it draws on other social science and humanities disciplines, each of which in its own way challenges the dominant assumptions in macroeconomics and its claim to offer a 'master science' of credit and debt.

Anthropology goes beyond the material character of credit and debt to examine the contrasting cultural constructions of sovereign creditworthiness and assumptions about risk. Corpus linguistics teases out linguistic patterns in discourse about debt over time, whilst critical discourse analysis focuses on the socio-cultural, ideological, and psychological contexts in which these discourses operate. Cognitive psychology stresses how attitudes to debt and the reputations of states are shaped by inferences from government behaviour, as well as from data. It shows how, in order to resolve the cognitive uncertainties associated with debt dynamics, individuals rely on short cuts and heuristics to arrive at conclusions about sovereign creditworthiness and to guide their action. Neuroscience emphasizes the significance of non-rational thinking about debt. Psychiatry delves into personality disorders, like narcissism and psychopathic traits, as roots of the antisocial behaviour that can characterize creditors and debtors. Imaginative literature uncovers through vivid characterization the complex human motives and experiences that shape representations of debt. It fleshes out how emotions like guilt, shame, despair, and humiliation shape identity formation in creditor-debtor relations.

Notwithstanding their many differences, these disciplines serve to highlight the sources of illusion that come to characterize thinking about credit and debt. They provide material and insights that cast doubt on the belief in sovereign creditworthiness as quantifiably determinable and in risk management as a precise science. They help give weight to a more nuanced understanding of debt, as a phenomenon to which individuals assign social meanings. These meanings are bound up with identity. Critical discourse theory adds the additional insight that power and knowledge presuppose each other (Fairclough 1989). Notions about debt, fiscal normality, and sovereign creditworthiness are bound up in shifting constellations of social forces. These notions are used to legitimate power and as tools of power. As such, ideas about sovereign creditworthiness help us to understand where power lies in European history and integration, and how it changes.

A long-term historical perspective highlights the intimate association of the reputation of European rulers and states with their debts. Reputation for reliability and good faith in fulfilling one's obligations on time is a resource of power in managing relations with creditors. However, if forfeited, it casts a shadow over the future (cf. Tomz 2007). The reputation of many European rulers suffered from association with an unmanageable burden of debt payments to revenues and a disastrous fiscal legacy. The list includes the English Kings Edward II and Henry VI; the Spanish Bourbons; the French Kings Henry III, Louis XIV, and Louis XVI; the Bavarian King Ludwig II; and Ottoman Sultans from the sixteenth century. Sovereign debt defaults in the period 1820–1913 secured enduring images of the Hapsburg Empire, Greece, Portugal, Serbia, Spain, and Ottoman Turkey as chronically weak states with incompetent rulers. Greece, Serbia, and the Ottoman Empire ended up in the hands of foreign debt administrations (Suter 1992).

Even the reputation of certain rulers as 'strong' sits uncomfortably alongside their resort to instruments of coercive financial repression, including expropriation and pillage, to coinage debasement, and to debt default, as well as the onerous debts that they bequeathed. This problem haunts assessments of English kings like Richard I, Henry V, Edward I, Edward III, and Henry VIII; King Philip II of Spain; Frederick the Great of Prussia; and King Louis XIV and the Emperor Napoleon of France.

Most problematic is 'odious' debt, associated with corrupt regimes, in which governing elites borrowed, squandered, and stole the proceeds. Despite reputational loss with creditors, their successors may choose to write off all or certain odious debts on the moral grounds that the innocent and past victims of repression should not be required to shoulder responsibility. This stance was taken by the post-Czarist Soviet Russia and by post-Ottoman Turkey.

European history exemplifies the high fiscal price paid for the pursuit of glory. The boundary between bold political ambition and fiscal illusion and hubris is soon crossed, often imperceptibly. Even victory in war breeds illusion and hubris. It tends to leave public finances in a parlous state: for instance, Britain after the Napoleonic Wars and after the First and Second World Wars. Napoleon's 'Hundred Days' in 1815, before the Battle of Waterloo, proved the most expensive in the history of France. War financing deepens the shadowy world of debt opacity and resort to fiscal trickery, for instance in the US Civil War. Periods of stability prove precarious. King Henry II of France was highly creditworthy in 1555–1557, only to default. Conversely, the government of Raymond Poincaré stabilized the franc at an undervalued exchange rate. France made a rapid transition from a major debtor state in 1919–1926 to become the leading European creditor by 1928–1929 with enormous gold reserves.

An historical perspective helps to show how these notions of sovereign creditworthiness change over time. It highlights continuities and changes in who defines debt sustainability and how. It highlights the normative background of meanings that they attach to debt, as well as the relationship of these meanings to shifting constellations of social forces. History also helps to draw out how this agency and subjectivity is set within international and domestic structures. These structures generate opportunities and constraints that privilege certain meanings over others. Typically, the history of public debt is written by creditors. They make history in their own image and create serviceable, enduring myths about creditworthiness and the hierarchy of states. The image of states, their rulers, and publics, is intimately associated with these myths.

Why Does Sovereign Creditworthiness Matter?

Sovereign creditworthiness involves the belief that the public debt is sustainable; that the state is solvent; and that it complies with the prevailing notion of fiscal 'normality'. These beliefs are politically laden and historically contingent and contestable When is public debt 'unsustainable'? When is a state insolvent? What are the appropriate limits on sovereign debt? Given that notions of sustainability, solvency, and normality are contentious, the capacity of certain actors to pin them down in precise, technical definitions signals who possesses power.

Sovereign creditworthiness is intrinsic to the image of state strength. In particular, it serves as a great differentiator between 'core' and 'periphery' states. Tomz (2007) distinguishes between 'stalwarts', who honour commitments to creditors in all circumstances; 'fair-weather' states, whose reliability in 'bad times' is questionable; and 'lemons', which may resort to default even in 'good' times. The difficulty lies in classifying a state as a 'stalwart'. States that seem to fit this category may not have been tested in 'all circumstances': and, if they have, amnesia may be at work. Technically, the United States engaged in partial defaults in 1898 (over Cuba after the Spanish–American War) and in 1933 (after the departure from gold).

Loss of creditworthiness is manifested in sovereign debt distress and ultimately in default. It shakes confidence in the state, undermines its reputation, and casts a shadow over future relations with creditors. In such circumstances creditors are disposed to draw negative inferences from the behaviour of its governments, politicians, and banks and to be unwilling to lend, other than at penalty interest rates. The consequences are adverse for images of state power, of the governing competence of its elites, and of the virtue of its public.

At stake is the very character of the state: the trust that its creditors, its own citizens, and the governing elites of other states have in its words and its deeds. Loss of creditworthiness forces an existential choice on states. Its elites can focus on rebuilding credibility. This requires clearly acknowledging the nature and scale of fiscal problems; making transparent the balance sheet of assets and liabilities and the revenue streams to service debts; building political processes that constructively engage in finding solutions, including with creditors; and generating persuasive, tangible, and deliverable plans of action. Elites can opt to climb the 'reputational ladder' and become 'stalwarts' by firmly signalling a change in preferences and behaviour through costly commitments to change policies (Tomz 2007). Conversely, loss of sovereign creditworthiness may force governing elites to recognize that the fundamental duty of the state is to save itself. In this case they shelter behind the idea of sovereign immunity and resort to the coercive face of the state. The result is damaging effects on creditors, risks of financial contagion, and deterioration in the climate of international and intra-European relations.

The history of sovereign creditworthiness highlights the inherent tension between the sovereign claims of states—expressed in the concept of sovereign immunity—and their need to raise finance by entering the debt market. The difficulties in managing this tension help explain variations in the extent to which states waive their right to immunity in selected jurisdictions, the absence of supra-national legal authority to adjudicate on contracts, and the problematic character of reputation—with whom, the markets or citizens? It makes questionable the credibility of international and European rules of the game in constraining sovereign behaviour. Sovereign debt restructuring and default emerge as implicit, contingent outcomes. Sovereign debt is ultimately a field of contractual hazard and ongoing renegotiations between states and their creditors (cf. Kletzer and Wright 2000: 621). This insight was ignored in the rules governing Economic and Monetary Union (EMU) in Europe before 2010. The incentives to negotiate cooperatively are considerable. Nevertheless, state allegiance to collective arrangements remains conditional. *In extremis* distressed debtor-state elites can resort to systemically damaging statecraft.

Sovereign creditworthiness is inseparable from questions about responsibility: who is responsible for debt crisis; and who should and does bear the burdens of adjustment? Answering these questions is made more difficult because debt is a shadowy and opaque world, whose nature and functioning is dimly understood. Its nature enables political, official, and, above all, financial elites to evade responsibility and to displace costs onto others. The victims are all too often the innocent poor, who suffer disproportionately from wage, benefits, and public-service cuts, and the middle classes who find themselves squeezed by tax rises and entitlement cuts. Sovereign creditworthiness is, consequently, at risk from destabilizing populist mobilization, driven by a deeply-felt sense of injustice and outrage at inequities in burden-sharing.

Sovereign creditworthiness matters because it contains a potentially fateful paradox. On the one hand, it is systemically central to capitalism and state finances and to the capacity of governing elites to gain and retain reputation for acting responsibly with respect to both their creditors and their citizens. On the other hand, sovereign creditworthiness rests on a bed of dynamite. This precariousness derives from multiple, often interconnected sources. They include the systemic risks associated with excessive external imbalances; the number and diversity of international creditors (official and non-official); the asymmetry of creditor information in contracting and their heterogeneity of interests in pursuing claims; the vulnerability to domestic banking and financial crises; the asymmetry between the power of states to tame financial markets and the power of markets to brand states; the illusion, hubris, and complacency that infect both markets and states; the differences in state capacity to adjust to external imbalances and banking crises; and the absence of supra-national legal authority to adjudicate in cases of sovereign debt distress and to open questions about terms of debt repayment. At the heart of the fateful paradox is the impossibility of separating legal questions about creditor protection from larger, morally and politically contentious questions about social justice, about what responsibility entails, and about with whom one most needs to secure reputation.

Sovereign Creditworthiness: The Triple Structural Dimension

The idea of sovereign creditworthiness is structurally embedded in a triple sense. First and foremost, it reflects the structural realities of external imbalances and their consequences for asymmetry of power over how this idea is understood. The configuration of external imbalances shapes whose ideas about sovereign creditworthiness resonate most strongly in public policies. It privileges the ideas of creditor over debtor states and the kind of ideas that serve creditor interests, above all limiting liabilities incurred in offering collective financial support to debtors. This sensitivity of ideas to structure is apparent in the speed with which ascendant ideas about how best to secure sovereign creditworthiness change once states shift from debtor to creditor, or creditor to debtor, status.

Secondly, the idea of sovereign creditworthiness is historically nested in the principle of sovereignty and the intergovernmental structures that reflect and support this principle. The corollary of the EU or euro area not being a fiscal state was a striking historical continuity in forms of statecraft. It did not issue its own debt, mutualize Member-State debts, and possess independent revenue streams to ensure debt servicing. In consequence, patterns recur over time. In a painting by Nicolas Poussin, alluded to by Anthony Powell in his novel *A Question of Upbringing*, the four allegorical figures of wealth, industry, poverty, and pleasure are depicted as moving in rhythm to the music played by Old Father Time. Similarly, creditor-debtor state relations can be seen as a revolving 'Dance to the Music of Time'.

However, the idea of sovereign creditworthiness in Europe has become newly structurally embedded in a third sense. It is caught up in the *sui generis* processes of post-1945 European integration, in its specific and evolving institutional structures (some supra-national) and rules, and in the bold political ambition to build a 'new Europe' and forge 'ever closer union'. EU Member States have been increasingly bound together through the single European market, monetary union (17 of its 28 Member States by 2013), and deepening financial market integration. Complex, interdependent webs of legally contracted, often implied, liabilities heightened their vulnerability to banking and bond market contagion. The legally contracted liabilities included large shares of Greek, Irish, Italian, Portuguese, and Spanish debt held by French and German banks. Swedish banks were similarly heavily implicated in Baltic State debts, whilst much Hungarian debt was denominated in euros (and in Swiss francs). The implicit liabilities followed from the commitment to underwrite the sovereign debt of fellow Member States facing severe difficulties in bond markets. It took the forms of the balance sheet of the European Central Bank (ECB) and the temporary European Financial Stability Facility (EFSF) and the permanent European Stability Mechanism (ESM).

The complex effects of this triple structural embedding are manifest in the internal tension within the EU, and especially the euro area, between two conceptions of its nature as a community. On the one hand, the EU is pictured as a *Stabilitätsgemeinschaft* ('stability community'). It embodies the 'sound' money and finance values of its most powerful creditor state, Germany. In its extreme formulation, it is a 'no-bail-out' community, dedicated to averting moral hazard. The EU is not a 'transfer union'. Its solidarity is one of individual effort by Member States to comply with rules that are designed to ensure long-term debt sustainability. Solidarity has to be earned.

On the other hand, the EU is viewed as a *Schicksalsgemeinschaft*, a community that shares a common destiny or fate. This conceptualization derives from an historical obligation to change the quality of inter-state relations in order to secure peace. This obligation is realized through aligning fundamental national interests around the mutual gains from economic and political integration. A 'community of shared destiny' opens the way to a 'fiscal transfer' union and to strong supra-national institution building, with the ECB as a leading example. This unresolved tension between two conceptions of community manifests itself in an EU bias towards 'constructive ambiguity' in managing sovereign debt problems. Economic governance reforms are pursued by stealth (Dyson and Quaglia 2010a).

By common consent, the evolving post-2007 financial and economic crisis exposed the weaknesses and tensions at the heart of EU and euro area crisis prevention and crisis management mechanisms. It highlighted a paradox. On the one hand, the highly institutionalized, regularized processes of European integration offered a more fertile ground for fleshing out new ideas for institutional and policy reforms than the global level of the

International Monetary Fund (IMF). Seen historically, the scope and pace of European economic governance reforms to shore up sovereign creditworthiness was unprecedented.

On the other hand, the crisis made more explicit the asymmetrical power within the European integration process (Zartmann and Rubin 2000). It gave statecraft a more coercive face and a more top-down form, intervening deeply into state sovereignty. The trajectory, scope, and nature of European economic governance reforms were overwhelmingly shaped by creditor-state power. Managing sovereign debt crisis showed just how far the process of shaping European integration was from being neutral between creditor and debtor states.

The Third Structural Dimension: Managing Sovereign Debt Crisis in Europe

Managing sovereign debt crises of Member States was institutionally encumbered by absence of an EU or euro area fiscal state. It lacked independent discretionary tax, spending, and debt-issuance authority. The EU and the euro area were essentially governed by rules. It did not have the features of a macroeconomic union, able to stabilize the European economy. There was no supra-national 'lender of last resort', other than the ECB with respect to the euro area banking system. The European Council and the Council of Ministers proved hesitant and irresolute in embarking on a coordinated European recovery programme in 2008–2009 and again in 2012–2013. They behaved similarly with respect to developing a collective financial assistance mechanism in 2010–2012. Member States retained a formidable capacity to play the sovereignty game to avert sharing risks or to avert fiscal compliance. Where they pooled or delegated sovereignty, it was on terms that privileged creditor-state power. This privileging was most evident in the negotiating context of designing foundational institutional arrangements and rules and in the resulting path-dependent behaviour.

The underdevelopment of sovereign debt crisis management capacity at the euro area level had its corollary in the lonely, exposed role of the ECB. It was induced to cross the boundary of monetary and fiscal policies and to expand its balance sheet with potentially weak collateral. Scope opened for a potentially dangerous game of chicken between the two key creditors, the ECB and the German federal government, about which might defect—at a moment of supreme emergency—from acting as lender of last resort to Member States. Measured in terms of a fiscal union, a 'new Europe' was only tentatively apparent. It was expressed in the hope that the ESM would evolve into the 'European Monetary Fund'; that the euro area would acquire its own finance minister; and that the euro area would have the power to veto Member-State budgets. These hopes rested on the provision of a political legitimacy that the EU lacked.

Managing sovereign debt crises in the EU and the euro area was also encumbered by a narrow conception of fiscal policy governance. The EU Stability and Growth Pact (SGP) had been fixated on EU rules rather than on strengthening Member-State capacity for surveillance and monitoring. The fiscal compact treaty of 2012 represented a shift towards greater emphasis on tougher domestic discipline, bringing national courts into the process. The narrow conception of fiscal governance was also apparent in the EU concentration on 'excessive deficits', stressing nominal fiscal deficit rules. Prior to the economic governance reforms of 2011–2012, and the fiscal compact treaty (Article 4), the public debt ratio had been relegated to a secondary role. The focus moved to domestic 'debt brakes' and to domestic judicial review. However, Article 3(3) of the fiscal compact treaty still provided for 'exceptional circumstances'.

Perhaps most seriously of all, the SGP had underestimated the significance of developments in corporate and household balance sheets for budget deficit and public debt dynamics. The fiscal rules took insufficient account of the risks from banking and external shocks to trend GDP growth rates and thus to structural deficits and to debt projections. European economic governance reforms in 2011–2012, notably the new Macroeconomic Imbalance Procedure (MIP), attempted to address these weaknesses. However, asymmetry was built into the MIP, placing the onus on debtor states.

In addition, the weak management of sovereign debt stemmed from the neglect of the complex, highly qualitative, but core issues of Member-State state capacity. This neglect was evident in EU accession processes and in euro area entry conditions, specifically the Maastricht Treaty convergence criteria which focused on indicators of nominal fiscal and monetary performance. The convergence criteria did not directly address the institutional capacity, other than central bank independence, or the cultural and ideological willingness to sustain the commitments of European monetary union. Capacity to extract taxes, spend productively, control fiscal balances, provide reliable and timely data, and undertake structural reforms was essential to sustaining these commitments.

The case of Greece offered graphic illustration of this failure to address state capacity building and the underlying features of economic culture and ideological attitudes. Perversely, both EU structural funds and euro area low interest rates had served to empower traditional structures of political patronage and corruption. EU banks had funded Greece's public-sector mismanagement and accumulated serious risks on their own balance sheets. Greece's sovereign creditworthiness invited comparisons with the Latin American states of the 1980s, Russia and Asian states in 1997–1998, and the notorious case of the Argentinean default. The 'junk' rating of Greek sovereign bonds was followed by the biggest debt restructuring to private creditors in post-1945 history. In 2012 Greek voters flirted with rejection of the harsh terms of international and European bail-outs. By 2013 it was clear that the euro area harboured at least two 'failed' states—Cyprus and Greece—and a number of 'failing' states, including Italy.

At a deeper level, weak management of sovereign debt crisis in the EU and the euro area was linked to discomfort with German creditor-state power. Germany was a classic 'reluctant hegemon'. Its governing elites and public were unhappy both with the visibility of German power and with the negative historical stereotyping of Germany that followed, above all across southern Europe after 2011. Nevertheless, German governing elites had national interests to protect, interests that they saw as coterminous with ensuring the long-term sustainability of the euro and the EU. Its negotiators sought cover in an informal creditor-state club. This club was central in framing debates, in setting agendas, and in shaping outcomes. Its ideas and interests prevailed in the redesign of European economic governance around new arrangements for banking and fiscal union. Mutualization of debts was resisted. Veto power was retained over collective financial assistance through the ESM. Creditor-state power was also evident 'within' the negotiating process. The informal creditor-state club retained the presidency of the Euro Group of finance ministers. The key documents around which other Member States negotiated were either German-generated or European Commission-generated in close association with the creditor states. The axis of power in the Franco-German relationship shifted towards Germany, all the more so when in 2012 France lost its triple-A credit rating. It was not the 'power of numbers'. The number of creditor states was dwarfed by debtor states. Creditor-state elites proved better able to engage in collective action, whereas debtor-state elites sought to differentiate themselves from each other.

Fundamentally, German power within European integration had a structural basis in external imbalances and in economic performance. The structural powerlessness of debtor states can be offset, to a limited extent, by pursuing strategies that 'borrow' power from external sources (Betzold 2010). These strategies are easier to pursue within the EU. Debtor-state elites can appeal to shared moral principles of solidarity and norms of reciprocity as independent standards of legitimacy for collective financial assistance. This type of appeal has resonance within the European Commission. They can also seek to forge common interests with creditor states around mitigating shared risks from contagion, for instance by European banking and fiscal union. In addition, debtor-state elites can look to external, third-party bodies like the European Commission and IMF staff reports and to respected macroeconomists and financiers for intellectual support. They can also play negotiation processes skilfully by building alliances and by seeking 'first-mover' advantage (cf. Pfetsch and Landau 2000; Zartman and Rubin 2000). This last strategy typically involves differentiation of the debtor state as exceptional in its adjustment and creative energy.

These four strategies offer ways to open up room for manoeuvre to debtor-state elites and to provide them with extra leverage. Yet, however strategically skilful they are, debtor-state elites face an uphill battle against creditor states. Their governing elites remain in principle unwilling to bear the high economic costs of supporting debtor states and avoid incurring the wrath of their taxpayers.

Ultimately, sustainable sovereign debt management in the euro area depends on institutional arrangements and policies that serve to reduce the sharpness of asymmetrical power and to ameliorate its more coercive aspects (Zartmann and Rubin 2000). The EU offered a uniquely favourable environment. Its well-established, dense institutional structures, their supra-national component, its rules, and the repeated and nested character of negotiations led to historically formed norms of intense cooperation and reciprocity amongst its Member States. These norms provided a negotiating context within which—once foundational institutional arrangements and rules had been set—the exit option became a less attractive and credible bargaining resource for creditor-state elites. It involved potentially prohibitively high reputational costs. Mutual dependencies of creditors and debtors and shared vulnerabilities to contagion forced themselves on the attention of negotiators. They helped to shape outcomes towards consensus, on terms that remained asymmetrical and extremely difficult to achieve politically, above all when they asked creditor-states to cross earlier negotiating red lines.

Nevertheless, sovereign debt management within the euro area and the EU remains far from neutral. Structural power continues to favour creditor-state over debtor-state elites, above all in the negotiating context of creating new institutional and policy arrangements for monetary and later fiscal and banking union and in later path-dependent behaviour (Dyson and Featherstone 1999). Negotiated outcomes express this asymmetry of power, for instance the Maastricht Treaty of 1993 and the SGP of 1997. Creditor-debtor state relations entrench certain standards of appropriate conduct. They come to be embedded in particular governing ideas that legitimize and substantiate creditor-state power. Based on the primacy of avoidance of moral hazard, the ascendant idea of sovereign creditworthiness continues to rest on the notion of the limited liability of creditor states. Their limited liability serves as guarantor of their own sovereign creditworthiness and of their continuing structural power.

Events in the euro area from 2007 showed how the structural face of creditor-state power becomes more visible as banking, sovereign debt, and macroeconomic crises deepen. In this context the exit option surfaces as a potentially viable alternative for some debtor-state elites. Their discomfort as events force them to learn about the economic, social, and political implications of living in a European monetary union may become too great to bear. Debtor-state elites in the euro area found themselves in an ambiguous position. Once creditor-state elites recognized that the institutional status quo was not viable, and reform essential, debtor-state elites had more opportunities to exercise leverage. They could more effectively deploy their information about creditor-state negotiating positions, their substantive knowledge of policy issues, and their knowledge of how to use institutional frameworks to strengthen their influence (Beach 2005; Naurin 2009; Tallberg 2008). In doing so, debtor-state elites felt more secure that, locked into cooperation through fears of contagion, creditor-state elites—notably Germany—would find it more difficult to credibly threaten exit as a bargaining resource (Fuchs 2013).

On the other hand, a powerful element of path dependency was embedded in euro-area institutional arrangements, institutionally protected by the ECB. In addition, the fiscal compact treaty, which uploaded to the euro area the so-called German 'debt brake', showed that German willingness to commit to collective financial assistance through the ESM was conditional. The institutional arrangements and rules of the euro area remained asymmetrical.

2

The Nature of Sovereign Creditworthiness: Hierarchy, Sovereignty, and Responsibility

Our tales are spun, but for the most part, we don't spin them; they spin us.
Daniel Dennett, *Consciousness Explained* (1991: 418)

'Credit' derives from the Latin word *credere*—to believe. Public credit rests on belief about the future, what creditors imagine is likely to happen. In *The Spirit of the Laws* (1751), Book 19, Chapter 27, the Baron de Montesquieu (1689–1755) wrote of the conversion of *crédit* into *confiance*. The creation of public credit led to the state being placed at the mercy of investor confidence in the future. Governing elites, and their ideologists, had to build and sustain investor faith in a political economy of continuing economic growth, in social and political progress that would ensure future repayments, and in the willingness of rulers to honour debts.

The challenge facing ideologists of the state founded on public credit was to find ways of controlling the imaginary hopes, passions, fears, and potential hysteria of investors. The birth of eighteenth-century political economy was, in part, associated with the search for economic rationalization of investor behaviour. It sought to transform—if imperfectly—hope and passion into hard-headed calculation (Pocock 1985: 112–13). The birth of political economy was inseparable from this historical revolution in public credit and its profound impact on the social and political relations that underpinned states, potentially subverting public virtue.

Sovereign creditworthiness involves the belief that a state, more precisely those who act on its behalf, possesses the will and the capacity to service its debts and honour its contracts, at any point in time. Investor confidence and state reputation with investors are at its heart. So too is the incentive to give numeric expression to the probability of sovereign default. Power gravitates towards those in investment banks and credit rating agencies who can 'objectify' sovereign creditworthiness and endow investor confidence with expert authority.

However, sovereign creditworthiness remains inherently political, bound up in moral judgements that are at once ongoing, contestable, contextual, and practical. It expresses fundamentally non-compatible beliefs about what states should do, and how; about the basis on which costs and benefits should be distributed; and about where, and whether, to draw the moral line on economic reasoning. These beliefs are grounded in different economic cultures, political ideologies, institutional interests, and competitive party and electoral politics. The obligation on the state to balance social interests, and to avoid intolerable outcomes for its inhabitants, proves exceedingly difficult to discharge once sovereign creditworthiness is in serious doubt.

The difficulty stems from the 'objective' authority and apparent precision of indicators of sovereign creditworthiness that focus on macroeconomic and financial indicators. They gain closer attention than 'softer' indicators of environmental degradation, poor quality of governance, and social deprivation, notably poverty, unemployment, educational attainment, and health (Sen 1989). In consequence, long-term state capacity to repay debts, based on a self-sustainable quality of life for future generations, tends to be peripheral to conventional measures of sovereign creditworthiness. 'Tipping points' that define the limits of state power are clearer with respect to investor standards than to environmental, social, and governance standards. Using this wider set of measures in 2012, China, India, and Russia appeared much riskier than conventional macroeconomic and financial indicators suggested, along with Bulgaria, Hungary, Latvia, Lithuania, and Romania.

The reputation of a state as creditworthy depends on both liquidity and solvency, two analytic concepts that are difficult to disentangle in practice. Creditworthy states have governments that are able to maintain access to financial markets, in the short term, for the purpose of refinancing maturing debt. They are judged to have state capacity to ensure that future fiscal policies cover the costs of servicing longer-term debts, as well as the willingness to pay. Liquidity and solvency are interrelated in that a liquidity squeeze can tip into an insolvency crisis, in that higher interest-rate premiums to cover perceptions of heightened risk can turn into a vicious circle in which confidence in debt sustainability collapses. However, given the complex determinants of solvency, reasonable people can often disagree about whether particular states are solvent. Such judgements involve the level of private as well as public debt, the strength of the banking sector, whether banking and sovereign risks are separable, future GDP growth and market interest rates, the ability to raise finance through privatizations, the ability to extract private-sector wealth through taxation, whether the fiscal multiplier is producing self-reinforcing and contagious growth or deflation, and whether liquidity support and official fiscal transfers are reliable.

For these reasons, sovereign creditworthiness goes to the heart of state power and is a matter of highly complex and contested judgement. It is bound up with state capacity to service debts by raising taxes and controlling expenditures; with the financial assets held by governments, which can be sold or liquidated; and with the willingness to pay. In the words of the Tommaso Padoa-Schioppa Group (2012), 'sovereignty ends when solvency ends'.

The Career of Concepts

The process of agreeing meanings about sovereign creditworthiness and its related concepts owed most to the practices of measurement and quantification by economists and financial experts. They became essentially technical concepts, whose elaboration provided the glue that held together an international network within an ideology of de-politicization and political neutrality. The International Monetary Fund (IMF) saw itself as an objective arbiter of claims to sovereign debt sustainability. The concepts also served as a political tool. They privileged certain interests on the basis of technocratic arguments about economic logic and political necessity. The technical content was provided by leading economists and financial experts. They acted as spokespersons for the concept and as the leading agenda-setters and gatekeepers in debates about public finances. They generated the key texts that contained authoritative definitions, manufactured relevant knowledge, and prescribed scripts for action.

However, sovereign creditworthiness and its related concepts gained conceptual life not just from within academic macroeconomics and finance. Their evolution was also conditioned by the contributions of international financial institutions like the IMF and the World Bank, credit rating agencies, sovereign bond specialists in investment banks and asset management, central banks, and law firms. They invested their careers, as well as finance, expertise, and time in developing and using these concepts. An example was Lee Buchheit of the law firm Cleary Gottlieb and active in major European debt restructurings in Greece (2011–2012), Iceland (2010), and Russia (1996–1999). He championed proposals for collective-action clauses (CACs) in sovereign bond contracts. Following the Greek debt restructuring in 2011–2012, and the huge profits earned by so-called 'hold-outs', Buchheit campaigned for reviving aspects of the IMF's earlier statutory scheme for a Sovereign Debt Restructuring Mechanism. He played a key role in championing the imposition of losses on creditors, including expansion of the list of government assets immune from seizure by 'hold-out' hedge funds.

The Social Science Citation Index (SSCI) indicates that 'debt' generated three times more citations than 'public' debt and ten times more than 'sovereign debt'. In contrast, citations under 'sovereign creditworthiness' were less than one percentage of those for 'debt'. Analysis of the SSCI suggests that, in all three cases, academic interest followed practitioner engagement with a time lag. During the Bretton Woods system, with its limited international capital flows, states had little incentive to default (Tomz and Wright 2012: 10). Hence sovereign creditworthiness elicited little academic interest. The SSCI also shows that economics, business finance, management, and law journals provided the seminal texts. Anthropology, history, sociology, international relations, and political science played a peripheral role, except in the case of 'debt'. The birth of interest in 'sovereign creditworthiness' was essentially a post-Latin American crises phenomenon, concentrated in area studies and development economics in the 1990s. Serious academic interest gathered momentum only as late as 2011. 'Creditworthiness' received much more academic attention. However, its main growth came in 1992–1996, against the background of the financial crises, and again in 2011.

'Debt' had a longer pedigree, going back to 1956. Its main citations' growth occurred in 1987–1992, in the wake of US and then British financial market liberalization (with the highest citations' figure in 1990). This period accounted for over 20 per cent of total citations of debt between 1956 and 2012. It grew again in 2007–2012, when it accounted for almost 20 per cent of total citations. The top ten citations were dominated by the *Journal of Political Economy*, notably Olivier Blanchard (1985) and Robert Barro (1979), the *Journal of Finance*, and the *American Economic Review*, particularly Guillermo Calvo (1988).

'Public debt' citations went back to 1956, 'sovereign debt' to the 1980s. The first spurt of growth in 'public debt' citations occurred in 1959–1961, coinciding with the end of the European Payments Union. It peaked again in 1965–1966. The Maastricht Treaty and Economic and Monetary Union (EMU) generated further growth. However, the main turning point was 2007–2008. Some 40 per cent of total citations for 'public debt' since 1956 occurred in the period 2007–2012. 'Sovereign debt' citations dated back to 1973. However, they only grew appreciably in the 1980s, reflecting the Latin American crises. 'Sovereign debt' citations accelerated once more in 1993–1996 and 1998, with the 1992–1993 Exchange Rate Mechanism (ERM) crises and as the third stage of EMU approached. They peaked again after the crisis of the EU Stability and Growth Pact (SGP) in 2003. As with 'public debt', over 40 per cent of the citations were post-2007. The striking feature of 'public debt' and 'sovereign debt' citations was the dominance of Anglo-American economics, finance, and law journals. The citation lists were headed by Robert Barro (1979), Alberto Alesina and Roberto Perotti (1995), and Kenneth Kletzer and Brian Wright (2000). Kenneth Rogoff had three in the top ten citation list for 'sovereign debt'. Alesina and Rogoff had worked for the IMF, and both at Harvard University. Their academic work was especially influential in giving greater precision to the usage of these concepts.

The key post-1945 historical turning point was the collapse of the Bretton Woods exchange-rate system in 1971–1973 and its aftermath of capital liberalization. Before sovereign creditworthiness had not been a pressing public policy challenge. The post-1973 environment provided an opportunity for the IMF and the World Bank—as well as European Economic Community (EEC) institutions—to redefine their roles and widen their mandates. It also offered opportunities for the credit rating agencies to extend their business into sovereign debt issues. Seizing these opportunities was facilitated by greater academic precision and widening academic engagement in usage of the relevant concepts. The practical involvement of the IMF and the World Bank in Latin American and later Asian debt crises led to the search for justificatory arguments from academic economists, business and financial market economists, and legal scholars. They became privileged interlocutors of these international financial institutions, and to a lesser extent of the European Commission as it sought economic rationale to support the drive for EMU in Europe. They helped provide the all-important models of sovereign debt sustainability.

The core question for the IMF and the World Bank was how best to provide collective financial assistance, initially to emerging markets, and notably to Latin America. At the same time, the use of conditionality to restore sovereign creditworthiness drew attention to the need to devote more resources to investigate the *inside* of these states' local specificities. However, area studies remained the weaker link in the academic chain of policy advice. Anthropologists, historians, political scientists, international relations specialists, and sociologists were largely peripheral to this process of academic co-option.

The concept of sovereign creditworthiness became more open to contestation once, with the post-2007 EU sovereign debt crises, it became a problem for advanced market economies. The IMF proved more reluctant to speak out forcefully, at least up till the bitter experience of the first Greek bail-out and the Cypriot crisis in 2012–2013. Some of the affected economies were major shareholders and entrenched on its executive board. The IMF was also the junior partner in European bail-outs. The interface with the EU and with national sovereignty in the European context proved politically difficult for the IMF to negotiate. To add to the problems, sovereign creditworthiness threatened to mutate into a systemic crisis to one of the main achievements of the post-1945 world, European economic and political integration. In tackling the problems in Cyprus, Greece, Ireland, and Portugal, and facing heightened risks in Italy and Spain, the IMF was entering a bitterly contested and contestable area. It had to engage in a new interface with the ECB and the European Commission in the Troika arrangements and with wider and urgent issues of reforms to European economic governance. This engagement raised questions about the IMF's role as the central spokesperson on matters of sovereign creditworthiness and about its claims to be an objective arbiter.

In addition, the evolving post-2007 sovereign debt crises were intimately linked to banking and financial crisis. Banks, the shadow banking sector, and credit rating agencies began to be seen as constitutive parts of the problem of sovereign debt crises. Bailing-in creditors became a newly controversial issue in crisis management. Moreover, it became less plausible to continue representing sovereign creditworthiness narrowly as an economic problem. It was also a moral problem about fair burden-sharing, a sociological problem about shared identity, and a strategic and an institutional problem about European political, fiscal, and banking union. Sovereign creditworthiness became more open to ontological contestation, related to its use in legitimizing external intervention in fiscal and financial sovereignty. The discipline of economics was no longer so secure in its authority over sovereign creditworthiness. Space opened for a more critical debate about 'official' discourse on debt and about how best to defend the rights of marginalized individuals and groups and those suffering collateral damage from debt management.

The Nature of Sovereign Debt

The analysis of what debt tells us about states and their power must begin by identifying the narrower and the broader conceptions of debt. In its narrowest sense, debt refers to sovereign borrowing. It encompasses various sovereign debt instruments and practices. They include credit facilities, treasury notes, promissory notes, lifetime or perpetual annuities, syndicated loans, and—perhaps best known—sovereign bonds. A state, like Greece by 2009, may become insolvent in this narrow sense. However, its sovereign borrowing might look sustainable in this sense, whilst it proves insolvent because of the balance sheets of its household and banking sectors, as with Cyprus, Ireland, and Spain.

A further analytical refinement is necessary. The distinction between gross and net debt remains fundamental to examining sovereign debt and its implications for creditworthiness. Net public debt takes account of the value of the assets that are held by a state and that contribute to its sovereign creditworthiness. By 2012 France and, on a more ambitious scale, Britain, led Europe in drawing up consolidated, 'whole-of-government' balance sheets. They followed the international financial reporting standards (IFRS) of the London-based International Accounting Standards Board (IASB).

Although consolidated balance sheets give a clearer idea about net public debt and sovereign debt risk, they remain weakly developed, because complex to construct. One problem is the difficulties and costs of valuing many public assets, for instance heritage sites. Moreover, financial assets are more relevant for sovereign creditworthiness than non-financial assets. The highest immediate value attaches to the most liquid financial assets, ones readily available for privatization. In 2011 only three euro area Member States had financial assets whose value exceeded their liabilities: Estonia, Finland, and Luxembourg. For the euro area as a whole, the market value of government financial assets represented more than one-third of the value of their liabilities, which stood at 92.9 per cent of GDP (European Central Bank 2012b: 65). The difficulties of compiling net public debt figures underline the extent to which debate about sovereign creditworthiness rests on shaky foundations of knowledge, opening up space for highly subjective and contestable judgements.

Sovereign borrowing is a key mechanism through which the state finances its activities, alongside taxation, money creation, and revenue from the operation of enterprises. It has three purposes that are central to state power. At its most basic, sovereign borrowing serves to manage short-term cash imbalances, which are consequent on public revenues and expenditures flowing in and out at different times. As David Hume pointed out in *On Public Credit* (1759), given the undulations in government spending, it is wiser to engage in smoothing by borrowing than by attempting to fine-tune tax rates in step.

Secondly, according to John Maynard Keynes, sovereign borrowing helps to smooth the economic cycle. In particular, it sustains aggregate demand and maintains public services during an economic downturn. This purpose of economic stabilization is less relevant for sub-national borrowing. Incentives for prudence are stronger for sub-national governments to the extent that they can rely on national governments to run fiscal deficits in times of recession.

Finally, sovereign borrowing serves the purpose of financing public investment, for instance in education, training, child care, health, urban renewal, communications, transport, and defence. By borrowing, the state distributes the costs in debt servicing across the generations that benefit. Sovereign borrowing is a form of deferred taxation in that it requires future tax revenues to service and to amortize the debt. Hence sovereign borrowing endows fiscal policies with an important temporal dimension. It poses basic political questions about intergenerational equity in the distribution of costs and benefits. For instance, sovereign borrowing raises the issue of whether it involves the exploitation of future taxpayers by current taxpayers.

In its broadest sense, the analysis of what debt tells us about power is bound up with the larger balance sheets of assets and liabilities that accrue to states. These balance sheets are the result not just of their own behaviour but also that of financial institutions and non-financial corporations and of households. They are acutely vulnerable to banking crises and household debt. Moreover, macroeconomic balance sheets are located within external trade and financial imbalances. They reflect changes in competitiveness and real exchange rates, as expressed in unit labour costs and current account divergences, and evident in international trade and financial flows. External imbalances are also affected by differences in household propensity to save and by the financial and economic policies of governments, for instance the scale and speed of financial liberalization and its effects on lending practices.

Private-sector debts, including leveraging and deleveraging by households, the financial sector, and non-financial corporations, interact in complex and important ways with public-sector balance sheets. Sovereign creditworthiness is embedded in these larger balance sheets. Public- and private-sector debts are symbiotically related, with banks serving as the main mechanism through which debt problems migrate across their borders. This process was evident in Finland and Sweden in 1990–1994 and in Britain, Cyprus, Ireland, and Spain from 2007. Banks are vulnerable to their toxic loans to non-financial corporations, for instance in construction; to households, notably as mortgages and as credit card overdrafts; and to governments, as in the euro area periphery. Once governments assume responsibility for these liabilities, unsustainable debts in the private sector undermine sovereign creditworthiness. In turn, loss of sovereign creditworthiness weakens banks, which hold sovereign bonds. Through tightening credit conditions, the effects spread to the rest of the private sector. For this reason, debate about the shift to banking and fiscal union in Europe hinged on breaking the potentially deadly mutual embrace of bank and sovereign debts.

The complex channels of transmission become apparent from analysis of total debt as a percentage of GDP (see McKinsey Global Institute 2012: 5). In the second quarter of 2011, Ireland had total debts at 663 per cent of GDP. Debts of Irish financial institutions represented the largest component at 259 per cent of GDP. It was followed by Britain, for which the respective figures were 507 per cent and 219 per cent. In the case of Spain (in third place), the figure for total debt was 363 per cent, with debts of households the largest component at 134 per cent of GDP. Italy had total debts of 314 per cent of GDP, with debts of government the largest component at 111 per cent of GDP. The comparable figures for Greece were 267 per cent and 132 per cent. In contrast, German total debts were 278 per cent of GDP, with financial institutions the main component at 87 per cent of GDP. These figures highlighted different sources of state vulnerability.

Though sovereign creditworthiness tends to be viewed in these financial accounting terms, it is ultimately about more than just total debts as a percentage of GDP. These figures appear alarming. Sometimes—as with Britain—they are. However, they need qualification. In the first place, total debt to GDP data ignore the significance of the financial assets at the disposal of households, which for instance is high in Italy. They also do not take into account the quality of bank lending practices and of supervisory mechanisms. Strikingly, by 2012 the high debt/GDP ratio in Britain had yet to produce serious concerns about sovereign creditworthiness.

Secondly, such factors as the robustness of export-led economic growth, reputation for 'good' governance, clear and firm fiscal rules, and accountable and transparent fiscal institutions affect how data on total debt to GDP are interpreted. At the height of its financial and economic crises in 1990–1994, Sweden had a lower total debt to GDP ratio (198 per cent in 1992) than in 2008 (302 per cent). The difference could be explained by the reputation that Sweden had gained from the speed and duration of its deleveraging after 1992 (cf. McKinsey Global Institute 2012). It scored highly in exports, 'good' governance, firm fiscal rules, and accountable and transparent fiscal institutions.

Total-debt-to-GDP ratio does not take into account the cultural and social prestige that attaches to the economic, social, and political institutions of a state, along with its rich heritage. Properly seen, sovereign creditworthiness is set within the context of the often intangible assets of a country: its universities, education system, cultural and scientific infrastructure, communication and transport infrastructure, and civil service. In its broadest sense, the national balance sheet is qualitative. Many European states are in this respect better placed than figures on total debt might suggest.

The complex dynamics that underpin sovereign creditworthiness have led historically to an ongoing, changing pattern of differentiation of power within European and international political economies. By 2013 differentiation based on creditworthiness was raising newly contentious questions about state power within the EU and the euro area. They related to the appropriate rules of engagement between creditor and debtor states, to responsibility and fair burden-sharing, and to whose interests the rules should serve. This differentiation is typically understood in terms of a hierarchy. There is a small core of 'creditworthy' states—in modern, narrow credit-rating parlance, 'triple A-rated'. There is a periphery of states, which are closely linked by trade and financial flows to this core. However, they are in actual or potential debt distress because of weak competitiveness and/or undercapitalized banks. Finally, there is a 'super-periphery'. It is weakly connected to world credit markets, has low capital inflows and labour export, and is typically scarred by domestic political turmoil, sharp ethnic and regional fragmentation, and a catastrophic economic situation (Sokol 2001). Fear of slipping down this hierarchy from periphery to super-periphery haunted Greek and above all Cypriot elites and publics. It generated a deep sense of despair and acute resentment and anger directed at the 'core'.

Key Dimensions of Sovereign Creditworthiness

As we have seen, sovereign creditworthiness remains a deeply problematic concept because of the difficulties in calculating net public debt and the implicit liabilities that follow from private-sector indebtedness. Its problematic character stems also from the complex and variable origins of credit booms and busts, in domestic banking and in capital inflows and outflows. Sovereign creditworthiness is linked to domestic credit conditions and the health of bank balance sheets. It is also bound up with external imbalances, above all when current account flows involve high proportions of bank and debt flows, as opposed for instance to foreign direct investment flows. The nature of external imbalances serves to open up or close down narratives about creditworthiness. External imbalances are structural, given differences in productivity growth, wage bargaining mechanisms, and unit labour cost development. They are destabilizing once big and persisting current account deficits and surpluses emerge. Deficit states become dependent on capital inflows from surplus states. They face high risks of painful fiscal retrenchment, deflation, and unemployment when confidence ebbs and inflows cease.

At the heart of creditor-debtor state relations are two difficulties: credit crises that originate in domestic financial systems; and external imbalances. Some states are structurally imbalanced, with financial sectors that form a high proportion of, or even far exceed, their GDP size. The post-2007 crisis threw up the striking examples of Britain, Cyprus, Iceland, and Ireland. This dependency relationship induces 'crony' capitalism, in which financial elites become privileged insiders in the exercise of state power and extract tax, regulatory, and other advantages. In these circumstances governing elites indulge the financial sector. Under the rationale of being a public good, requiring special treatment, the financial sector builds up unsustainably large credit exposures. The other source of difficulty in creditor-debtor state relations stems from some states having surpluses on their current accounts in goods and services. They accumulate net external assets, and receive net interest payments. Other states run deficits, become net external debtors, and must make net interest payments.

Difficult and contentious questions arise. What are the proper limits on the size, structure, and power of the financial sector? When is its power 'excessive'? How is sustainable credit provision best achieved? When do external imbalances become 'excessive' and 'unsustainable'? Who defines when they are 'excessive' and 'unsustainable'? How are external imbalances best corrected? Above all, who should bear the costs of adjustment—creditors, taxpayers, or benefit recipients and users of public services? In what proportions?

These questions are political and normative. The process of addressing them can benefit from impartial arbitration, but the answers are not amenable to objective determination. The attempts to find answers highlight differences of interest. They involve difficult judgements in the face of contending principles. They generate powerful and complex emotions, including identity issues, at times of sovereign debt crises. Not least, they pose severely practical problems of governance and consent. Notwithstanding its esoteric technical language, creditor-debtor state relations are inexorably bound up with contentious questions about how best to manage the implications of 'excessive' and 'unsustainable' financial-sector power and external imbalances.

This contention, and the ambiguities and compromises that it throws up, reflects the enduring collective-action problems that beset a policy area of the highest systemic importance for both European states and capitalism. How the contending principles and complex trade-offs are managed illustrates the distinctive, and changing, character of each state and where power lies. In domestic fiscal and financial governance, and within creditor-debtor state relations, governing elites strike their own distinctive balances that reflect differences in legal frameworks, economic cultures, and ideologies of debt. In various ways, reflecting their particular contexts, the balance is based on more or less accountability to creditors, taxpayers, and citizens; more or less transparency; more or less autonomy in making tax and spending choices; more or less efficiency in resource allocation; and more or less equity across, and within, borders.

Secondly, sovereign creditworthiness involves the arts of statecraft. Their practice is in the hands of a narrow set of political and technical elites. Sovereign creditworthiness is central to their reputation for governing competence in negotiating and managing external imbalances and domestic credit provision. This reputation is in turn essential to retaining elected or appointed office. It has to be fashioned with reference to domestic publics, to key stakeholders (notably creditors), and to the 'rules of the game'. Governing elites require skills in crafting an appropriate discourse and in selecting supportive policy instruments. Statecraft manoeuvres within a constricted, asymmetrically configured space. It attempts to tame financial market power, whilst seeking to gain a favourable branding by these same financial markets. States are in the paradoxical power position of being both regulators and clients of the financial markets. Considerations of systemic stability, social justice, accountability, transparency, and consent induce governing elites to try to minimize state vulnerability to predatory, profit-seeking market activity. Their reputation for governing competence depends on showing this capacity. At the same time, statecraft faces powerful inducements to satisfy financial market expectations. This two-dimensional game complicates problems of signalling clear intentions and resolve. However, branding states tends to trump taming financial markets.

Which face is most visible—states taming financial markets, or markets branding states—reveals where power lies. Governing elites can resort to various instruments of shelter. They can, for instance, build huge foreign-exchange reserves, practise overt or covert financial repression, print money, or restructure debts. They can impose strict regulatory and supervisory frameworks on financial markets, for instance capital adequacy or remuneration requirements. However, the practice of statecraft is severely constrained by collective-action problems amongst states in supervising and regulating financial markets. It also encounters the powerful instruments that are available to financial markets and the power that stems from their capacity to brand states as creditworthy or not. Moreover, as the financing requirements of states grow, and publics' expectations of consumer affluence rise, governing elites face stronger incentives to placate the markets by satisfying their expectations. The modern fiscal state has strengthened incentives to prioritize financial market credibility. It is confronted with demographic pressures of an ageing population, attachment to welfare-state entitlements, consumer expectations, the global reach, speed, and dexterity of financial markets, and the ever-present risks of banking and financial crises.

Thirdly, the practice of statecraft in pursuit of sovereign creditworthiness varies across space and over time. It depends on the currency in which debt is denominated (domestic or foreign), sovereign debt law, fiscal institutions, rules and norms, and economic cultures. Statecraft takes on a situation-specific character. It depends on whether a state has control of the currency in which its debt is issued; on whether the definition of sovereign immunity is absolute or less restrictive; on whether a state is embedded in inclusive international and European institutional structures that foster trust and concern for reputation; and on whether it shares in an economic culture of stability. Statecraft varies with negotiating context. When foundational institutional arrangements and rules are being negotiated, the power of creditor states to influence outcomes is at its greatest. Their leverage stems from the threat that they can exit negotiations. This power diminishes once all are embedded within those arrangements and come to recognize the need for their reform (cf. Fuchs 2013).

The practice of statecraft shows diachronic as well as synchronic variation. It registers longer-term changes in the international political economy. Its form is different in eras of plentiful, cheap capital from that in times of financial austerity. The political economy of good times contrasts with that of hard times. Above all, statecraft illustrates the big, overarching, long-term historic shifts in the distribution of power within the European and the international political economies. The shadows of world history hang over the practice of statecraft, expressed in both structural and cyclical shifts. These structural and cyclical shifts underline the role of accident and fortune as opposed to deliberate policies in influencing which states become creditors and which debtors.

Fourthly, sovereign creditworthiness is forced to the top of domestic, European, and international political agendas by crisis management (cf. Enderlein, Trebesch, and von

Daniels 2010). Dramatic events, like the post-2007 Cypriot, Greek, Icelandic, Irish, and Portuguese sovereign debt crises, catapult this esoteric 'technocratic' concept into the public sphere, along with the elites who are concerned with it. Crisis highlights the fundamentally political character of claims to expert and moral authority by banks, credit rating agencies, international financial institutions, and economists. It reveals the underlying asymmetrical power relationships and hierarchies of control amongst states. Sovereign debt crisis serves to re-energize internal 'battles of knowledge' within debtor states and within international financial institutions like the IMF. These battles focus around competing representations of the sovereign debt problem, around what should be done and by whom, and around the uses and abuses of creditor power (cf. Clegg 2010).

However, sovereign debt default at times of crisis is only one of a range of strategic options in statecraft. Once a state joins a monetary union, and issues public debt in a currency over which it has no control, it becomes more vulnerable to a forced default from the financial markets (De Grauwe 2011). This loss of control over capacity to issue sovereign debt was experienced by a number of euro area Member States in 2009–2013. They lacked the variety of policy instruments to avert default that remained available to states like Britain that issued their debt in their own currency. States outside the monetary union could use exchange-rate adjustment to reduce the external costs of debt and depend on central bank liquidity to the state. In the process, they could potentially inflate away the debt burden.

Because of their dramatic character, sovereign debt crises tend to attract greatest attention. They generate powerful narratives about debtor states like Cyprus and Greece, as well as about official creditors like the IMF and Germany and about private creditors like Russian depositors. However, the urgent short-termism of crisis management, focused on shrinking balance sheets by reducing liabilities, risks driving out longer-term action to strengthen productive assets that contribute to output growth potential. Action to restore sovereign creditworthiness faces a time consistency problem, consequent on the strength of the incentives to pursue short-term solutions that are liability-focused.

Fifthly, sovereign creditworthiness is about more than the size of gross liabilities. Correctly seen, in a longer-term perspective, risks of liquidity and solvency crises of states are a matter of the consolidated balance sheet: liabilities relative to assets. An increase in liabilities that is accompanied by a larger increase in assets reduces risks of liquidity and solvency crises. The difficulty is twofold. Financial market-based indicators tend to be short-term in focus. Also, many assets of a state are hard to value because they are not marketed. However, this second difficulty does not make them valueless.

Sovereign creditworthiness is, properly speaking, about building up assets through 'productive' debt. This can be achieved through public investment, or incentivizing private investment, in economic infrastructure, yielding a high economic rate of return (Checherita-Westphal, Hughes Hallett, and Rother 2012). Productive debt was central to the political economy of Alexander Hamilton in the United States and of Saint-Simon in France, as well as to that of the German historical school (Stein 1885–1886; Wagner 1863). Hamilton's thinking was reflected more in the practice of the US developmental state than in US political rhetoric (Chernow 2005; Mazzucato 2013). Saint-Simon's thought was influential within the Second Empire of Napoleon III, with its lavish mobilization of credit, usually off-balance-sheet, to finance public works and urban renewal

(Price 2001). Credit serves not just to finance recurrent expenditures. More importantly from the point of view of debt sustainability, it serves to build infrastructure and to promote social and political inclusivity and trust. Debt makes a positive contribution to growth by social investment in education, training, child care, and health (Vandenbroucke 2012). It also enhances long-term productive capacity through investment in public goods like energy, transport, communications, education, research and development, technology transfer, defence, finance, and the judiciary (Helm 2010). Increasing public debt through productive investment amounts to a rearrangement of the public-sector balance sheet rather than to an increase in net indebtedness. The problem is for governing elites to persuade financial markets that 'productive' debt is prima facie at least as important as gross debt levels in assessments of sustainability. It adds to the future tax base and thus helps generate higher prospective tax revenues. It can also improve governance standards.

Conversely, capital imports become problematic when they flow into financing consumption rather than investment in productive capacity. At the core of the creditworthiness problems of Cyprus, Greece, Italy, Portugal, and Spain within the euro area was the continuing scale of capital imports that had not been used for this type of investment. It raised questions about their long-term solvency. The problem for Europe's 'super-periphery', notably the western Balkans, was that it lacked the domestic conditions to make capital imports possible, let alone the capacity to use them to build long-term assets.

Sixthly, sovereign creditworthiness is not primarily about the level of interest rates payable on public debt. More importantly, it depends on the margin, negative or positive, between these interest rates and economic growth. Higher economic growth makes high interest rates tenable; low growth, as in the EU after 2007, may make even low interest rates hard to sustain. For this reason, claims to sovereign creditworthiness are easier when debt dynamics are economic-growth-driven. When interest rates far exceed growth, debt problems spiral out of control.

Fiscal contraction is counterproductive for creditworthiness because the adverse effects on tax revenues and on benefit payments mean only limited reductions in fiscal deficits. Moreover, when it leads to reduced public capital investment, future growth prospects are diminished. The result is a debt-deflation spiral that inhibits the capacity to repay debts (Fisher 1933; cf. also Tobin 1980). This effect is magnified when states in an integrated economic bloc, like the EU, practise simultaneous fiscal contraction. For this reason, collective international commitments to economic growth through coordinated demand and supply policies are a vital component in restoring individual sovereign creditworthiness.

Seventhly, the asymmetry of power between financial markets and states privileges market-based processes of constructing sovereign creditworthiness. The economic theory of signalling suggests that, faced with the problem of asymmetric information, statecraft is a matter of building reputation and confidence by credibly conveying information to creditors about 'good' intentions and 'firm' resolve (classically Spence 1973). Signalling theory comes closer than most academic economics to capturing key political dynamics of sovereign creditworthiness. It pictures creditors as seeking 'hard' evidence about policy successes that reveals 'type' of state. This evidence is embodied in the quantifications of sovereign risk by investment banks and credit rating agencies. It is also supplied by the outcomes of EU and IMF surveillance, monitoring, and compliance mechanisms. This 'positive' feedback cycle between creditors, credit rating agencies, and international financial and EU institutions underlines the strength of the incentives for states to talk and to act to differentiate themselves from 'bad types'.

Eighthly, sovereign creditworthiness is in the powerful grip of measurement and probabilistic reasoning. They are the dominant methods of structured thinking about risk. Creditor power is projected through their mastery, which becomes a badge of competence. The sovereign ratings of the Economist Intelligence Unit (2011) provide snapshots of the company that states find they are keeping. In Europe, in January–February 2011, only Norway managed AAA. The bottom positions were occupied by the 'super-periphery': Bosnia and Herzegovina, Moldova, Serbia, and Ukraine, each with CCC. Within the EU the spectrum ran from AA (Finland, Germany, the Netherlands, and Sweden) to B (which put Greece, Hungary, and Latvia on a par with Croatia and Macedonia, not to mention Cameroon and Pakistan). The city of Athens found itself on a par with a number of Mexican and Russian cities (Moody's 2011).

As Scott argues (1998: 27), 'every act of measurement is an act marked by the play of power relations'. Market-based, technocratic constructions of sovereign creditworthiness are socially, culturally, and historically anchored. They serve as instruments of creditor power. They are not simply statistical exercises in applying objective indicators of performance (Blyth 2002: 150; Breslau 2003). Measurements of sovereign risk remain potentially powerful. They are simplifying tools that help to order thinking and to legitimize and substantiate conclusions. They endow international financial institutions and EU institutions with expert and moral authority to intervene in the policy space of debtor states and to narrow their freedom of manoeuvre in taxing, spending, and borrowing. Moreover, they differentiate a core from a periphery and both from a 'super-periphery' (Sokol 2001).

Credit rating scales, and the probabilistic reasoning that underpins them, induce confidence and trust because of the precision of hard numbers. However, reliance on them begs a question about their value given the idiosyncratic nature of states and the radical uncertainty in their political and economic dynamics. In these conditions, wisdom lies in establishing confidence in the persuasiveness of a particular evidence-based narrative of sovereign creditworthiness. Narrative reasoning is intrinsically more relevant than probabilistic reasoning.

A more fundamental political question is whether credit ratings can measure the intrinsic value of a state. Ratings are in danger of being no more than a pale and potentially distorted reflection of state capacity to service its debts in full and on time. More seriously, they offer even less insight into the *willingness* of governing elites to service its debts, given the assets at their disposal. The apparent precision of finely graduated ratings conceals the views of a tiny number of officials about the state and its government. It reflects their judgemental selection of variables, notably related to institutional and socio-political factors, and their interpretation of data and events. Their judgements and interpretations are influenced by sovereign reputation.

Reputation is established in part on the basis of objective data, for instance about past fiscal performance in generating high primary surpluses to avert debt restructuring or default. This factor would help to sharply differentiate Belgium from Greece. Data can also be accumulated about the past record of government stability, efficient tax collection, structural reforms, and political consensus. However, the effort to base sovereign reputation on measurement and probabilistic reasoning is difficult to disentangle from acquired, stylized, and subjective representations of states, their publics, and the capacity of governing elites to implement 'sensible' policies. Sovereign creditworthiness is constructed by credit rating agencies and investment banks on the basis of probabilistic reasoning that camouflages subjective knowledge.

Ninthly, beneath this quantitative façade, formal assessments of sovereign creditworthiness are anchored in a dominant conception of economic culture. This conception is used to entrench certain standards of appropriate 'civilized' conduct for creditors and debtors. It involves compliance on terms of creditor power. It favours the use of the rule of law to protect investor rights and enforce avoidance of moral hazard. It seeks transparency in public accounts. It stresses government predictability in honouring contracts and complying with commitments. These standards underpin the formation of positive or negative images of state strength, public responsibility, and governing competence. In the process states acquire an anthropomorphic form as 'saints' and 'sinners'.

Finally, the process of branding of states is shaped, or at least mediated, by complex, feedback effects amongst a powerful group of actors. They include credit rating agencies, which anchor market beliefs about states; financial journalists, who serve as self-assigned watchdogs but are caught up in the promotional cultures cultivated by investment banks and their public relations consultancies; and the distinctive power configuration of the sovereign bond markets, which revolve around the teamwork of national debt management offices and their Primary Dealers, the selected investment banks that operate in a unique context of privileges and obligations. The sovereign bond markets have the all-important instruments to discipline states through the underwriting fees of Primary Dealers and through bond yield spreads. Notions about critical thresholds in yield spreads or in credit default swap spreads become embedded in market behaviour. In the opportunistic search for returns, market behaviour has an incentive to focus on contingent liabilities, which are seen as representing burdens on society, rather than on longer-term productive debt, in which borrowing is used to strengthen future infrastructure.

Above all, constructions of sovereign creditworthiness highlight the intimate interconnection between knowledge and power. They reflect ruling paradigms and constraining knowledge structures in political and economic thought. By the twentieth century macroeconomic theories had acquired power through their instrumental, legitimizing, and substantiating value to investment banks. This process was strengthened by the 'ego-involvement' of theorists and practitioners and the professional incentives to share in 'groupthink' and thereby gain credibility. The search for a professional status of macroeconomics as the 'queen' of social sciences produced a new manifestation of illusion and hubris, reinforced by its proximity to powerful market actors. Prevailing ideas in professional macroeconomic thought helped define dominant notions of fiscal normality, notably of 'excessive' fiscal deficits and public debt, of what constituted financial 'repression' by governments, and of the sources and barriers to systemic risk. International financial institutions like the IMF, central banks, finance ministries, financial media, and macroeconomists functioned within a context of knowledge structure and ideational power that ultimately privileged investment banks.

In the twenty-year period prior to the 2007 crisis, labelled later the 'Great Moderation', conventional wisdom centred on the capacity of monetary policy to deliver price stability and sustainable growth. It retained a core belief in financial market self-correction, including through financial innovation, as the means to mitigate risks and tame volatility. The conventional wisdom neglected key market-based sources of risk. It failed to define financial stability as a public good that required proactive prudential supervision and regulation. There was an underestimation of the complexity, opacity, scale, and interconnectedness of risks from financial market credit creation (International Monetary Fund 2011).

Hierarchy and Status Anxiety

The attributes of sovereign creditworthiness find expression in its central role in establishing and in legitimating a hierarchy in relations amongst European states. The discursive framing of policy issues, agenda-setting in bringing forward proposals around which others negotiate, and bargaining power over outcomes of negotiations reveal an informal, usually hidden and 'taken-for-granted', hierarchy. One or a very few creditor states assume a leadership role, based on their creditworthiness and on dependence on their good will to make possible, and sustain, cooperation and integration. The largest creditworthy state acquires shaping influence over the 'rules of the game', in return for underwriting the system and for the compliance of debtor states.

The power asymmetries in creditor-debtor state relations create incentives for debtor-state elites to prefer informal forms of hierarchy that do not depend on signing over formal authority to the leading creditor state (cf. Lake 2011). Informal hierarchy involves signing over sovereignty to European or international institutional arrangements. These institutional arrangements bear the imprint of the ideas of the leading creditor state. However, they institutionalize a norm of sharing power and set in train learning processes that creditor states may find difficult to control. Although designed on German terms, the euro area was better than bilateral dependence on German monetary and fiscal decisions under the earlier Exchange-Rate Mechanism (ERM). Similarly, the IMF was preferred to bilateral dependence on the United States. In this way, acceptance of informal hierarchy is camouflaged in the formal terms of the joint loss of sovereign authority. The imprints of German power were discernible in all the key foundational agreements on EMU: the Maastricht Treaty, the EU Stability and Growth Pact (SGP), the treaty on the European Stability Mechanism (ESM), the so-called fiscal compact treaty, and European banking union. The construction of the euro area showed the pervasive tendency for informal hierarchy to form in inter-state relations, based around constructions of creditworthiness. However, these manifestations of informal hierarchy also unleashed domestic contestation, resentment, and anger. They were a reminder that political conditionality attaches to domestic acceptance of how power is used in this hierarchy.

The hierarchy that is defined by sovereign creditworthiness is associated with status anxiety. It serves to fuel anxieties amongst governing elites and publics about relative position. These status anxieties were apparent between Prussia and the Hapsburg Empire after 1815, between France and Prussia after 1866, and between France and Germany in the context of European monetary union. Status anxieties induce governing elites to look for instruments of statecraft that can improve relative position. In doing so, they face difficult choices and trade-offs. Governing elites may select—perhaps under strong peer pressure—instruments that promise to strengthen overall collective performance, even if they do little or nothing to improve their relative position. Alternatively, they may seek to improve their relative position, even at the expense of collective performance. Whatever choices are made, status anxieties and relative positioning represent a central feature of creditor-debtor state relations.

Responsible Sovereigns

Creditworthiness rests on the notion of responsible sovereigns and poses the question of how this notion is defined (Beaulac 2004). It challenges the idea that sovereignty offers justification for fiscal and financial indiscipline. In short, creditworthiness binds and hedges sovereignty. However, 'responsible' sovereignty remains a complex, multidimensional, and controversial concept, creating space for considerable hypocrisy (Krasner 1999).

Responsible sovereigns can be expected to have responsibilities that go beyond the single principle of honouring contracts and protecting creditor interests. They must act to safeguard social justice and solidarity, to protect the innocent from 'predatory' creditors, and to avert intolerable demands on their citizens. States require discretionary authority to act resolutely at times of crisis on behalf of fundamental public interests and national identity (cf. Keynes 1923: 56–7). In supreme emergencies, they must obey the dictates of necessity, which may know no rules.

These complex expectations, along with the passions aroused by debt and the psycho-drama of sovereign debt crisis, underline the difficult balancing acts and 'judgement calls' that define the politics of sovereign creditworthiness. The problem is that, because of its derivation, creditworthiness tends to be defined narrowly in terms that enable creditors to enjoy exorbitant privileges. Once responsibility is seen in this restrictive sense, states risk capture within the private governance of public debt. Their governing elites avoid creditor 'haircuts' in sovereign debt bail-outs and 'bail-in' of bank creditors. The costs fall on taxpayers, benefit recipients, and wage earners. By 2012–2013 the EU and the euro area were widening their definition of sovereign creditworthiness in the wake of mistakes made in the Greek and Irish crises. In particular, bank 'bail-ins' were becoming a favoured tool. Moreover, it was clear that one set of 'senior' creditors—official creditors like the ECB, the ESM, and the IMF—took precedence over private creditors. All creditors were not necessarily equal.

Responsible sovereignty is difficult to define in part because of this complexity of contending principles and interests. In addition, the structure of international and European law that regulates state behaviour in managing sovereign debt, including debt rescheduling, is weakly developed. The politics of sovereign creditworthiness is distinctive because of the contrast with domestic laws relating to the insolvencies of companies and individuals. EU Member States differ in the extent to which—like Germany and the Scandinavian states—their domestic legal traditions emphasize creditor protection. Even within the EU, with its stress on sharing and limiting sovereignty, Member States remain deeply averse to ceding authority and power to external courts or commissions. They appeal to the principle of sovereignty to hide the primacy of domestic interests and power.

Creditor-state elites and international financial institutions have little compunction in placing constraints on the sovereignty of debtor states. In turn, debtor-state elites have in historical practice shown a willingness to accept the conditionality of international financial institutions as a price for pacifying creditors. It enables their governing elites to buy time, during which they can choose to act, procrastinate, or subvert reforms. The experience of bondholder committees and international financial commissions testifies to the complex and often unanticipated nature and outcomes of this collusion in abridging the principle of sovereignty. Appeals to responsible sovereignty in managing sovereign debts are multifaceted and highly political.

The situation is further complicated in the case of states that are historically allergic to the notion of becoming a 'protectorate' within an 'empire'. Their governing elites and publics are prone to a sense of victimhood, attributing blame to a dominant creditor power which is seen as usurping their sovereignty. Examples include Greece with reference to the Ottoman past and German occupation in the Second World War; Cyprus and Italy with their various historic forms of foreign rule; and Hungarians with respect to the Hapsburg 'dual monarchy' and to the Soviet Union. In these instances the EU, and above all Germany, took on the connotations of empire, colonizing their periphery. Victimhood can become a constitutive feature of national identity.

The responsible use of sovereign power in managing debt is made all the more difficult because of the fundamental precariousness of sovereign creditworthiness. It rests on a bed of dynamite. The combustible elements include the historical frequency of financial market mania and panic; the opacity of debt; the lack of synchronization between financial market and political timetables; the lack of macroeconomic understanding of governing elites and publics; weaknesses of political leadership in the face of domestic veto players; and variable state fiscal capacity to raise taxes and control expenditures. In seeking to use sovereign power responsibly, governing elites face the risk of populist mobilization of citizens, who feel alienated from elite-driven processes that seem divorced from widely-held conceptions of democratic legitimacy and from culturally-anchored conceptions of fairness in burden-sharing. The politics of sovereign creditworthiness becomes embroiled in questions about whether power has been used responsibly to protect 'innocent victims'; to preserve cherished cultural identities and social practices; and to avert the rise of political extremism and violence.

Ultimately, the notion of responsible sovereignty cannot be divorced from underlying interests and power. It offers a smokescreen that conceals the asymmetries of power between creditors and debtor states. Asymmetrical power structures mean high risks of morally objectionable outcomes. The likelihood is that the innocent and the most socially and economically marginalized and vulnerable will be punished more than those responsible for accumulating unsustainable debt. Characteristically, fiscal consolidation and structural reforms in the name of debt sustainability bear down disproportionately on those with low incomes. They are disadvantaged socially and politically as well as economically and face deeper entrapment in poverty and deprivation. The failure to address this moral complacency was testament to the illusion and hubris that infected debate about sovereign creditworthiness. It also highlighted the hypocrisy that could shelter behind claims to responsible sovereignty in debt management.

De-Politicization and the Politics of Sovereign Creditworthiness

The hidden subjectivities, historical idiosyncrasies, and emotional sensitivities in the politics of sovereign creditworthiness are conducive to arguments for its 'de-politicization'. Independent authorities, whether courts of law or fiscal councils, should have the power to enforce firm fiscal rules. Independent supervisory and regulatory authorities should enforce high capital requirements on banks. The argument for de-politicization is related to the belief that sovereign creditworthiness is a world of specialized, esoteric arts and expert knowledge, in which primacy should be given to professional consensus. The scope for policy decisions based on political passions, like resentment and indignation, should be diminished. In philosophical terms, the argument can be supported by Plato's belief in rule by a governing elite with the rigorous training, knowledge, and virtue necessary to ensure social harmony and political order. Its wide appeal lies in the notion of a superior judgement that comes with economic reasoning.

Arguments for institutional autonomy and automatic mechanisms are attractive to technical elites for reasons of self-interest and principle. They find ready reception within the IMF, the euro area, and the EU, as well as in central banks, fiscal policy commissions, and audit offices. Institutional autonomy and automaticity are seen as essential preconditions for averting systemic banking and sovereign debt crises and ensuring financial stability. This argument for de-politicization finds intellectual support in neo-classical economic beliefs about the virtue of discipline and pre-commitment. It can also draw on normative political theories about intergenerational and international justice, as well as on political science theories about state capacity. Institutional autonomy and automaticity 'lock-in' the willingness to comply with obligations. They involve pre-commitment to external rule-based discipline by political leaders, a form of 'self-binding' of state power. The risk is diminished that sovereign creditworthiness will fall victim to ideological and short-term, electorally-driven, fiscal and economic policies that ignore the requirements of long-term debt sustainability. Also, autonomous and mandatory debt restructuring mechanisms help induce a more risk-sensitive approach by creditors. They are obliged to shoulder responsibility for their reckless lending by bearing 'bail-in' costs.

The case for de-politicization is reinforced by the argument in normative political theory that an impersonal standard is needed to ensure that the interests of future generations and of those beyond a state's borders are not discounted in current, state-centred fiscal policy-making. Institutional autonomy offers particular benefits to states that are in the grip of domestic rent-seeking interests. Distributional justice needs to be safeguarded against 'insiders', who benefit disproportionately from fiscal profligacy, tax avoidance, and public employment and contracts, and who can veto reforms. In political science terms, institutional autonomy and automaticity favour state capacity building.

Two types of discourse about sovereign creditworthiness can be used to justify de-politicization: moral and contractual. The appropriate moral discourse is Platonic. It values rule on the basis of knowledge, wisdom, and virtue and conversely fears rule on the basis of the passions. Virtue requires rule by a disinterested, highly trained intellectual elite, endowed with appropriate freedom of action. However, the question arises of whether this elite can ever be disinterested. Also, where, if at all, should the limits on their action be drawn by requirements of institutional accountability and transparency?

Contractual discourse about debt is a variant of moral discourse and principally the concern of the law. Debt is associated with the language of contract and the rights and the obligations that it entails. Debate about compliance with contractual obligation is moral. However, contractual discourse is also about incentives for compliance. De-politicization is a mechanism for strengthening these incentives.

The problem is that what seems virtuous in moral and contractual discourses about de-politicizing sovereign creditworthiness can be experienced and interpreted by others as 'authoritarian' and destructive of valued cultural patterns and identities. Their perceived authoritarian character stems from the 'top-down' emphasis on accepting external discipline and acquiring self-discipline on terms defined by others. The aims are self-evidently right to their advocates: to ensure that contracts are honoured and that values of social responsibility are safeguarded in contracting debt. The outcome can prove surprising: the mobilization of counter-ideologies that demand greater democratic inclusiveness and social solidarity and that press the superior claims of national identity.

The difficulties in the agenda of de-politicization are formidable. They derive from the nature of the politics of sovereign creditworthiness. Its arts are essentially those of Aristotle's 'practical wisdom'. They are about dealing with the moral dilemmas and hidden contradictions that arise in trying to balance creditor protection, social solidarity, and systemic stability. 'Practical wisdom' involves ensuring the continuous flow of credit, avoiding moral hazard, averting contagious risks, securing social justice, and retaining solidarity. In short, the politics of sovereign creditworthiness requires hugely difficult, case-by-case, 'judgement calls'. There are huge political risks in believing that it is amenable to economic reasoning alone or to any one overarching philosophy.

At the level of practical politics, creditor-state elites have a vested interest in resisting certain proposals for new forms of institutional autonomy and automaticity at the European and international levels. Their concern is to avoid any open-ended pre-commitment to bail-out debtor states, citing the moral hazard argument. This resistance is strengthened by the 'number problem'. Characteristically, there are many more debtor states than creditor states. Independent, supra-national collective financial assistance mechanisms, like the ESM or any future European bank resolution mechanism, pose a high risk that they will cease to be agents of creditor states. Hence creditor-state elites seek to build into their design strong institutional safeguards for their own hard-won sovereign creditworthiness. They have limited self-interest in surrendering their authority to international financial institutions, except on the strictest conditions of limited liability. The ESM was designed as an intergovernmental institution. Germany had de facto veto power on the use of its instruments and on increases in its 'firepower'.

The political difficulties are compounded because de-politicization on creditor-state terms, with strict, detailed conditionality and monitoring, encounters resistance from governing elites in debtor states. They fear the 'hollowing out' of their sovereignty in fiscal and economic affairs and the abridgement of cherished notions of national independence. Above all, they fear populist mobilization around a narrative that the state has become a 'protectorate' in the hands of official creditors like the IMF, the ECB, the European Commission, and, potentially more problematic still, Germany.

3

Moralizing Credit: Bad Debt, Good Debt, and the Troubled Conscience

A wise man should have money in his head, but not in his heart.
Jonathan Swift (1812: 88)

The intellectual amnesia that surrounds sovereign creditworthiness reflects more than just the limited historical context in which it is debated. It stems also from linguistic, moral, and emotional complacency about credit and debt, public and private. Both aspects of this amnesia stem from the dominance of contemporary debates about sovereign creditworthiness by the formal concepts and abstract modelling of standard macroeconomics and by contract law. Situating these concepts and models historically, sociologically, and politically helps highlight the narrow terms in which formal macroeconomics and law represent and debate problems of debt. It brings out the underlying troubled conscience in thinking about credit and debt and the unavoidable moral judgements about what constitutes good and bad debt.

In order to examine the linguistic, moral, and emotional attributes of sovereign creditworthiness it is necessary to turn to anthropology, normative political theory, and imaginative literature, as well as to a more historically-minded political economy. These disciplines highlight the ultimately subjective basis of the knowledge that frames the way in which creditor-debtor relations are represented and debated. Credit and debt are more than just rational material exchanges within a market economy. They are socially constructed around representations of credit and debt. They involve the imaginative faculty (Moore 2010; Pocock 1985). Credit and debt are matters of hard moral judgements about character, equity, and 'good conscience'. These judgements are, in turn, bound up with powerful emotions of resentment, shame, and humiliation that attach to credit and debt. They engage emotional energy. The power and welfare of states is deeply affected by changing and conflicting representations of personal credit and debt and the emotional value attached to these representations.

The moral basis of creditor-debtor relations fascinated such diverse thinkers as Aristotle and Friedrich Nietzsche, David Hume and Adam Smith, Lorenz von Stein and Adolph Wagner, Anton Chekhov and William Shakespeare, Honoré de Balzac and Benito Pérez Galdós. The focus of their work on the morality of personal credit and debt remains relevant to representations of sovereign creditworthiness. Public and private debt is different in nature because of the sovereign character of states. However, in a practical sense they are bound together in national balance sheets. They bear jointly on sovereign creditworthiness. For satirists like Jonathan Swift or Voltaire, and novelists like Henry Fielding, there was a more intimate structural overlap between public and private debt (Moore 2010). Private and public debts were inextricably entangled in the larger financial revolution, which involved the proliferation of new credit instruments. They saw the novel or satire as an ideal way of examining the fictional character of the new credit economy, in which the seemingly 'real' value of contracts was an imaginative construct. Private and public debt was an imaginative world of promises and expectations, replete with illusion, hubris, and complacency.

The contributions of these thinkers largely pre-dated the modern engagement of macroeconomics and the law of contract with sovereign creditworthiness. Reading this literature helps not just in awakening the capacity for critical thinking about credit and debt but also in stimulating imaginative insight and compassion. It aids in unravelling the sheer complexity of the human in creditor-debtor relations. It brings out the 'internal dialogues' to which credit and debt give rise as individuals struggle with how to reconcile internalized social norms with their own deepest personal desires and hopes. Agency is revealed as deeply problematic, wish-fulfilment as an ongoing source of illusion. Not least, wider disciplinary reading beyond formal economics and law offers insights into the deeper pathologies that infect creditor-debtor relations. It shows how the climate of these relations, not least mutual trust, is governed by complex emotions and passions. This 'depth' serves as antidote to the simplistic, two-dimensional, 'surface' picture of rational creditors and debtors. The world of credit and debt is properly a realm of narrative reasoning.

Sovereign creditworthiness emerges as a multifaceted phenomenon. Anthropology and the history of political economy offer a reminder that, though historical context differs, the nature of argument about debt has in certain respects changed remarkably little over time. Linguistic analysis examines more closely continuity and change in how credit and debt are represented, notably its association with gratitude and guilt. Normative political theory reveals the rich insights that are to be gained from past thinkers who have devoted hard thinking to the moral complexities, paradoxes, and dilemmas of creditor-debtor relations. Imaginative literature casts light on the pathologies that result from the illusion, vanity, and the hypocrisy of creditors and from the imprudence, self-delusion, and venality of debtors. What emerges is a picture of how creditor-debtor relations inhabit a psychological space whose dynamics are shaped by different imaginative constructs, contending moral principles, and complex emotions of resentment, shame, humiliation, and anger.

Normative political theory shows that the question at the heart of creditor-debtor relations remains: 'what do we owe to each other?' The difficulty in answering is that the business of constructing and maintaining a normative consensus is never complete. It faces pervasive mutual distrust between creditors and debtors, opposed preferences, contending arguments from principle, passionate commitments, and radical uncertainty. Nevertheless, achieving conditional cooperation—as in the euro area—depends on some shared notion of reasonableness, fair play, and identity. Above all, it requires processes of conflict resolution and identity building that foster inclusiveness and shared ownership. Such processes seemed distant from much of the crisis management post-2007.

Novels and plays reveal that qualities of imagination, magnanimity, and compassion, as well as analytical flair, count if we are not to restrict unduly the scope of our thinking about credit and debt. They show how notions of conventional morality and folk belief, which call for endurance in 'living within one's means', conflict with individual ambitions, hopes, and expectations. The outcome is great personal anguish, even despair and suicide. In highlighting this conflict, writers like Balzac, Charles Dickens, Pérez Galdós, Joseph Roth, and Émile Zola sought to engage in contemporary debates about credit and debt. Their aim was to reframe how these debates were constructed.

The Socio-Linguistic Context of Debt: Guilt, Freedom, and Bondage

Examination of the socio-linguistic context of debt illustrates the complexity and diversity of meanings attached to debt and how its representation changes over time. They highlight its irreducibly subjective character. Later chapters analyse in greater detail the specific and differing historical and socio-political contexts in which debt is understood, how it is framed culturally and ideologically, and how it is used to affirm particular beliefs.

Certain patterns recur in lexical selections surrounding the term 'debt'. In various European languages debt co-occurs with 'bondage', 'freedom', 'gratitude', and 'honour', as in 'freedom from debt', 'debt of gratitude', and 'debt of honour'. The fundamentally moral nature of these linguistic associations suggests its power, its flexible usage, and the dilemmas to which it gives rise. Linguistic usage highlights the deep and widespread moral ambiguity and cultural discomfort attached to debt. Language matters because it complicates and troubles the relationship between states and their debts and how sovereign power is exercised when creditworthiness is at stake.

On the one hand, the historical frequency of debt amnesties or cancellations attests to a deep moral aversion to the 'enslavement' of debtors by creditors. Debt is associated with a fundamental asymmetry of power, the obligation of the weak to the strong. As such, it provokes a sense of moral concern, even outrage, one apparent in the post-2007 sovereign debt crises (Graeber 2011). For this reason, the writing-off of 'odious debts', contracted by corrupt or repressive governments, attracts moral approval (Buchheit, Gulati, and Thompson 2007). More broadly, the notion that creditors must share culpability with debtors, at least other than when borrowers have deceived them, has moral weight. Debt 'forgiveness' is consistent with the notion that there should be limits on property rights. It should be possible to benefit from generous debt restructuring procedures and from early discharge from bankruptcy. Seen in this perspective, debtors' prisons, 'pay-day' lenders, and 'loan sharks' take on an odious character.

On the other hand, debt 'default' suggests that the appropriate moral attitude of the debtor is gratitude to the creditor. There is an obligation to honour one's debts and to be prudent in contracting them. There is a moral injunction to 'live within one's means', to 'make ends meet', and to 'pay one's debts'. On this basis, the creditor should rightly enjoy the legal security of contract. Successor rulers should commit to honouring the debts of their predecessors. Moreover, debt 'forgiveness' risks precipitating widespread collateral damage. It depletes bank capital and thus lending, and it adversely affects pension funds.

In certain linguistic spaces debt takes on a powerful resonance. In Dutch and German the word *Schuld* means both debt and guilt. This linguistic association of debt with guilt is also found in the Hebrew word *Chayav*. It illustrates the deep-seated cultural anxiety that attaches to debt and the powerful feeling of shame that debt can provoke. For Germans, the fabled Swabian housewife serves as the traditional cultural icon of virtuous economic conduct: one should 'live within one's means'. This icon was appropriated by German Federal Chancellor Angela Merkel in justifying her policies on the post-2010 euro area sovereign debt crises. In doing so, she might have been appropriating John Stuart Mill (1806–1873), who wrote:

> The prudence of a nation should dictate the same conduct as the prudence of the individual; to submit to as much privation immediately, as can easily be borne, and only when any further burthen would distress or cripple them too much, to provide for the remainder by mortgaging their future income. (1848, Book V, Chapter 7.5: 'Of a National Debt')

Moral aversion to debt is not simply a Germanic or a Hebrew preoccupation. Nor is it to be solely attributed to Roman Catholic, Lutheran, and Islamic hostility to usury. Severe strictures against debt pre-dated Christianity. They had their roots in traditional folk belief that equates political rule with the virtuous household. This belief is traceable in Europe to Classical Greece and to the Roman association of excessive debt with *infamia*. Anthropologically, 'living within one's means' has the status of a common-sense principle of good conduct. William Shakespeare has Polonius say: 'Neither a borrower nor a lender be... borrowing dulls the edge of husbandry' (*Hamlet*, Scene III). Sociologically, it can be argued that associating debt with the vernacular language of 'making ends meet' forms the basis for exercising social and political power by winning the battle of ideas (cf. Bourdieu 1991; Fairclough 1989).

Reflecting his German context, Friedrich Nietzsche offered an anthropological account of the historical association of guilt with indebtedness (*das Schuldgefühl*). He stressed how debt was bound up with the moralization of concepts of duty, honour, self-esteem, and standing. In the *On the Genealogy of Morals* (1887), Second Essay, Sections 8–21, Nietzsche looked back to the 'oldest and most primitive' personal relationship between creditor and debtor as the origin of how 'one person first *measured himself* against another'. He contrasted the primordial wrath of the disappointed creditor with the bad conscience of the debtor. Driven by appetite, the creditor seeks to inflict punishment and misery on the debtor.

However, Nietzsche noted that societies have evolved in ways that create more complex socio-psychological motives. The appetite, vainglory, and hubris of creditors are contained by greater emphasis on self-esteem, honour, standing, and the pursuit of security. According to Nietzsche:

> As the power and self-confidence of a community increase, the penal law always becomes more moderate; every weakening or imperilling of the former brings with it a restoration of the harsher forms of the latter. The 'creditor' always becomes more humane to the extent that he has grown richer; finally, how much injury he can endure without suffering from it becomes the actual *measure* of his wealth. It is not unthinkable that a society might attain such a *consciousness of power* that it could allow itself the noblest luxury possible to it—letting those who harm it go *unpunished*... mercy remains the privilege of the most powerful man. (1887: 87)

This moral status of debt has been revisited in later anthropological research. Graeber (2011) points out that credit and debt pre-dated money. They took the form of favours amongst friends and neighbours, creating personal moral obligations. Later, the creation of money provided a unit of account for keeping track of debts. More importantly, it led to a depersonalization of creditor-debtor relations in economic and legal terms, making commercial society possible. This evolution in creditor-debtor relations was bound up with posting and exacting collateral in ways that strengthened the relative position of the creditor in hard times. In this way debt became bound up with the threat, and often reality, of erosion of freedom, not just for individuals but for entire families. They found themselves in a condition of 'debt slavery'.

Debt slavery was common practice in Ancient Greece and the early Roman Republic. Later, debt's connotation of a 'master–slave' relationship was repeatedly condemned. For instance, Leo Tolstoy attacked the 'debt enslavement' of Fiji in the nineteenth century by external creditors. Because of this connotation of enslavement, revolutionary changes of power, or the accession of new rulers, were frequently followed by debt cancellations and destruction of debt records. The first recorded example of debt cancellation appears to be in 2400 BC by the King Enmetena in the Sumerian city state of Lagash in Mesopotamia.

The origin of the concept of freedom was bound up with release from debt and the protection of borrowers. Debt cancellation was freedom from debt 'bondage' or 'slavery'. The association of debt with bondage endured in the Old Testament, for instance Proverbs 22.7: 'The rich rules over the poor, and the borrower is servant to the lender.' It was used to justify the cancellation of 'odious' debts after regime change. It also influenced hostility to debtors' prisons, for instance in the work of Charles Dickens. By the eighteenth century debtors were the largest proportion of the British prison population. They were housed in so-called 'mansions of misery' (Finn 2003: 109–51). Similarly, controversy was aroused by the aggressive activities of corporate and consumer debt collection and recovery agencies. From the mid-nineteenth century the debt collection departments of British guardian societies and trade associations played an increasing role in pursuit of litigation against debtors. Their activities offended against socially prevalent notions of equity and 'good conscience', especially with respect to working-class consumers and to women (Finn 2003: 278–316).

The position of debtors was ameliorated. Debtors' prisons were eliminated in 1867 in France, 1868 in the North German Confederation, 1869 in Britain, and 1879 in Sweden. Similarly, the notion of commercial freedom was associated with the birth and spread of the limited-liability company. It served to protect borrowers. The court protection of companies was extended in the United States Chapter 11 insolvency procedure and in variants across English-law-based states. Its influence in continental Europe was apparent in the German insolvency reforms of 1999 and 2011.

Despite this association with freedom, debt cancellation remains a morally ambiguous act. Lax insolvency laws, for example reducing bankruptcy discharge periods, are represented as promoting moral hazard. They are seen as stimulating 'insolvency tourism' or 'forum shopping', making the task of uncovering hidden assets more difficult. Moreover, when debts are owed to banks that operate in highly complex credit systems, debt cancellation risks widespread credit restrictions, insolvencies, and punishment of the innocent.

Bad and Good Debt in Historical Political Economy

From the eighteenth century onwards there were two main catalysts for rethinking notions of debt. The first was the rise of a new commercial society. It was associated with attachment to property rights and with the multiplication of contractual relations, encouraged above all by the use of collateral to expand credit (Pocock 1985; Riles 2011). Supported by favourable regulatory treatment, collateral use became entrenched and multiplied sources of risk. Its use was an important source of endogenous—internally generated—liquidity. Parties normally ineligible to borrow were able to enter into credit transactions. The consequence was a society in which creditor-debtor relations assumed central social and political significance. It was represented by an aspiring merchant-financier class, by *rentiers*, and by newly self-confident professions of accountancy and law. These professions provided legitimacy for the proliferation of collateral arrangements.

The second catalyst for rethinking debt was the birth and huge increase in public debt. This transformation opened up the question of whether this development was a force for good or ill. Was public debt wasting national wealth and subverting public virtue? Was it essential in order to increase the productivity of the whole economy, provide collective insurance and social integration, and ensure intergenerational burden-sharing? In Britain this question pitted Daniel Defoe (*c.*1660–1731) and Baron Bernard de Mandeville (1670–1733) against Hume and Smith; in France, Jean-François Melon (1675–1738) and Voltaire (1694–1778) against Montesquieu (1689–1755); in Germany, adherents of the school of historical and institutional economics like Lorenz von Stein (1815–1890) and Adolph Wagner (1835–1917) against the heirs to the Cameralist thinking of Johann Heinrich Gottlob von Justi (1717–1771); and in the newly independent United States, Alexander Hamilton (1755–1804) against Thomas Jefferson (1743–1826).

Historically-minded political economists and public intellectuals sought to reflect systematically on these two developments. The background was a wider cultural discomfort about debt. Already, in *The Six Books of the Commonwealth* (1577), the French lawyer Jean Bodin (1530–1596) had attacked interest-bearing loans as 'the Ruin of Princes and their Finances'. Bodin had in mind the onerous debt legacy of King Francis I and, above all, the default of King Henry II on the 'Great Loan' (*Grand Parti*) of 1555. However, later Melon, the Dutch financier Isaac de Pinto (1715–1787), and Voltaire took a much more positive view of French public debt, seeing in public expenditure a catalyst of national prosperity (Melon 1738: 329; Pinto 1771: 60; Rossel 1909). De Pinto was a main investor in the Dutch East India Company and a financier of William IV of Orange.

The ruinous French royal finances in the eighteenth century, and the crash precipitated by John Law's innovatory techniques for financing French royal debts, had a profound effect on French political economy. Montesquieu expressed his anxiety in Chapter 18, Book 22, of *The Spirit of the Laws* (1751):

> It is necessary that there should be a proportion between the state as creditor and the state as debtor. The state may be a creditor to infinity, but it can only be a debtor to a certain degree, and when it surpasses that degree the title of creditor vanishes.

In Chapter 18, Book 22, he brings out the implications for power:

> As the class of creditors is always the most exposed to the projects of ministers, and always in their eye, and under their immediate inspection, the state is obliged to give them a singular protection, that the part which is indebted may never have the least advantage over that which is creditor.

Montesquieu goes on to highlight the implications for justice in Chapter 17:

> It (public debt) takes the true revenue of the state from those who have activity and industry, to convey it to the indolent: that is, it gives facilities for labour to those who do not work, and clogs with difficulties those who do work.

The German Cameralist thinkers, led by Johann Heinrich Gottlob von Justi, took a different view of public debt. In his *Natur und Wesen der Staaten* (1760), von Justi argued that revenues should be generated primarily from state enterprises and lands. Borrowing was an instrument of *extraordinary* public finance. His ideas continued to be influential into the nineteenth century across the German-speaking world, notably in Bavaria, Prussia, Saxony, and Württemberg. They found a later echo in Joseph Schumpeter's *The Crisis of the Tax State* (1918). He was closer to Adam Smith than to von Justi in arguing that taxation should be the sole source of public revenue. However, Schumpeter followed von Justi in viewing borrowing as merited in exceptional circumstances, like the contemporary debt crisis that faced Austria after the First World War.

David Hume (1711–1776) and Adam Smith (1723–1790) produced tracts on public debt that were to prove hugely influential, forming the basis of the British classical school of economics. Their work has to be seen against the historical background of the huge increase in British public debt over the eighteenth century and its association with empire, war, and parliamentary patronage. Public debt grew from four shillings per capita in 1688 to £13 five shillings in 1766, at the time of the Spanish–Austrian War. By 1785, the American War of Independence had driven the figure to £29 fifteen shillings (Fisk 1921: 116).

In the case of eighteenth-century Ireland, as the Anglo-Irish satirist Jonathan Swift (1667–1745) recognized, the growth of public debt suggested English exploitation to support her foreign wars and imperial ventures (Moore 2010). In 1707–1715 Ireland had zero public debt. It grew to £200,000 by 1749, followed by explosive growth between 1761 and 1789, when it reached £2,200,000 (Clarendon 1791). By 1732 Swift was arguing in

A Proposal to Pay Off the Debt of the Nation that the Irish national debt was excessive with respect to trade restrictions, the great remittances to absentee English landlords, and the costs of supporting English regiments. A debate was unleashed about whether poor Ireland was being overtaxed to support an Anglo-Irish debt that was being incurred by English overseas ambitions.

Hume and Smith welcomed the opportunities for improving manners that were created by the new commercial society. However, they feared that the seductions of public debt were corrupting states and generating a politics of illusion and hubris. Public debt financing facilitated ruinous wars in Europe and underpinned the vain pursuit of empire in the Atlantic, the Mediterranean, and India. It also enlarged political patronage, creating a mutual dependence between states and creditors that led to oligarchy and factionalism and risked the collapse of public virtue. Hume and Smith, and later Jefferson, drew on copious historical cases in order to underline the importance of restoring the moral virtue of prudence. They were united in their fear that public debt would subvert property rights, which provided the foundation of virtue.

In *On Public Credit* (1759) Hume emphasized the risks when governments have overseas creditors, referring to British dependence on the Dutch. Servicing these debts requires a trade surplus, which may force governments into socially painful lowering of the real exchange rate. Here Hume anticipates the connection between debts, external imbalances, and social and political protest. He sees indebtedness to foreign creditors as the ruin of the state, which transfers away its power, and as the death of political community. Credit dependency brings either an 'easy death', in which a state resigns itself to permanent insolvency, or a 'violent death', in which it throws off dependency by repudiating its debts. Above all, like Montesquieu, Hume fears that dependence on debt interest 'gives great encouragement to a useless and inactive life'. It will lead to a reduction in the labour supply and in the flow of capital to productive activities. Either way, credit dependency was the route to political crisis.

Hume also distrusts the myopia and the imprudence of politicians with respect to debt:

> It is very tempting to a minister to employ such an expedient (borrowing) as enables him to make a great figure during his administration, without overburdening the people with taxes, or exciting any immediate clamour against himself...
> Contracting debt will almost infallibly be abused in every government. It would scarcely be more imprudent to give a prodigal son a credit in every banker's shop in London, than to empower a statesman to draw bills upon posterity. (1759: II, IX: 5)

Politicians cannot be relied on to amass reserves against emergencies during 'good' times. Hume sought to restore prudence to the head of the cardinal moral virtues. In *A Treatise of Human Nature* (1739: IV 'Of Natural Abilities') he wrote:

> It is impossible to execute any great design with success, where it is not conducted with prudence and discretion, nor will the goodness of our intentions alone suffice us to procure a happy issue to our enterprises.

In particular, Hume dwells on the random event of war and its ill-effects. War means that both allies and enemies will simultaneously engage in extra borrowing, driving up bond interest rates for all. The possibility of defeat adds a further risk premium to emergency borrowing as creditors come to anticipate default. The best insurance lies in building up a fiscal 'war chest'.

Likewise, Smith resorted to historical illustrations to illuminate his arguments against public debt in *An Inquiry into the Nature and Causes of the Wealth of Nations* (1775), Book V, Chapter III, 'Of Public Debts'. He takes up Hume's theme:

> The transfer from the owners of these two great sources of revenue, land and capital...to another set of persons (the creditors of the public, who have no particular interest), the greater part of the revenue arising from either must, in the long run, occasion both the neglect of land, and the waste or removal of capital stock...Its ruin may in some cases be unknown to him, and cannot directly affect his interest.

Smith was pessimistic about the long-term implications of the discovery of perpetual funding through debt for state power. His case rested on the affinity of states with private individuals and on the lessons from the trickery practised, and panic unleashed, by John Blunt's South Sea Company. The South Sea Bubble was linked to the promise of gains consequent on converting government debt into the equity of a company that had been given a monopoly of trade with the Spanish Empire in South America.

> The progress of the enormous debts which at present oppress, and will in the long-run probably ruin, all the great nations of Europe has been pretty uniform. Nations, like private men, have generally begun to borrow upon what may be called personal credit, without assigning or mortgaging any particular fund for the payment of the debt...The practice of funding has greatly enfeebled every state which has adopted it.

In Smith's view, taxation should be the sole source of state revenue. Despite his strictures, the Napoleonic Wars were to drive Britain's public debt levels even higher. By 1817 public debt per capita had reached £50 (Fisk 1921: 116). In his *Principles of Political Economy and Taxation* (1817), David Ricardo took an even more extreme position on public debt. Debt promoted public profligacy. He argued that future wars should be financed solely from taxation and that the existing British public debt should be totally redeemed from a once-off capital levy on the nation's property.

The debate about whether public debt promoted the virtues of commerce or the vice of profligacy was at the heart of the acrimonious dispute between Alexander Hamilton and Thomas Jefferson in the wake of the US War of Independence. In the name of virtue, Jefferson attacked Hamilton's pursuit of public debt financing, commercial empire, and executive patronage. He argued that the priority should be to freeing the new nation of debt. In a letter to Albert Gallatin (1809), Jefferson claimed:

> There does not exist an engine so corruptive of the government and so demoralizing of the nation as a public debt. It will bring on us more ruin at home than all the enemies from abroad against which this army and navy are to protect us. (*The Papers of Thomas Jefferson: Retirement Series*, Volume 1: 599)

Referring to the ruinous English practice of perpetual funding, Jefferson spelt out the principles in a series of letters. He wrote to his son-in-law, John Wayles Eppes (June 1813):

It is a wise rule, and should be fundamental in a government disposed to cherish its credit . . . 'never to borrow a dollar without laying a tax in the same instant for paying the interest annually, and the principal within a given term, and to consider that tax as pledged to the creditors on the public faith.'

. . .

The natural right to be free of the debts of a previous generation is a salutary curb on the spirit of war and indebtment, which, since the modern theory of the perpetuation of debt, has drenched the earth with blood, and crushed its inhabitants under burdens ever accumulating. (*The Papers of Thomas Jefferson: Retirement Series*, Volume 1: 337)

Jefferson was concerned, above all, to avoid future generations becoming debt slaves of the present generation. As he put it in a letter of December 1820 to the French Enlightenment thinker Antoine Destutt, Comte de Tracy:

It is incumbent on every generation to pay its own debts as it goes. A principle which if acted on would save one-half the wars of the world; and justifies, I think, our present circumspection. (*The Papers of Thomas Jefferson: Retirement Series*, Volume 1: 262)

In the prescient words of Pocock (1985: 273): 'though the American future might belong to Hamiltonian practice, it belonged to Jeffersonian ideology'.

From the mid-nineteenth century the emerging German historical and institutional school of economics took a very different view of public debt from that of Montesquieu, Hume, Smith, Ricardo, and Jefferson. They were united in the view that public debt was an integral part of national economies. Karl Dietzel (1829–1884) and Lorenz von Stein believed that the state had a positive role to play in balancing the economy, above all by financing productivity-enhancing investment in infrastructure and public provision. Public debt was not simply an instrument to deal with exceptional circumstances like war. It promoted capital accumulation. Dietzel argued that, in conditions of good management of the economy as a whole and focus on productivity-enhancing investment:

A nation is so much the richer and its national economy so much more blossoming and progressing, the greater the ratio of interest payments on government bonds in total government outlays is. (1855: 200–1)

He went on to comment, in contradiction of Ricardo:

The levy of high taxes for the purpose of the redemption of public debt can never be approved of. The pleasure of being able to say we are debt-free would be all too dearly bought. (1855: 218)

Stein (1886: 226) also stressed the role of public debt as collective insurance, above all in helping provide for old age, and thus in promoting social and political integration. However, he became aware that public debt could be politically abused to finance current consumption rather than productivity-enhancing investment. Hence Stein called for a constitutional safeguard against this misuse, a form of 'golden rule' in public finances later taken up in the Basic Law of the German Federal Republic (Holtfrerich 2013: 18).

Prudence and Social Welfare

Adolph Wagner's (1863: 1) 'Law of Growing State Needs' and belief that revenue would adjust to expenditure seemed to triumph over the aversions of Montesquieu, Hume, Smith, Jefferson, and Ricardo. Levels of public debt over 100 per cent of GDP were far from exceptional in the nineteenth and twentieth centuries. As Wagner argued, the historical context of political economy changed profoundly as new social forces entered the political arena. Public debt grew also with radical transformation in the technology, scale, and conduct of war (so-called 'total' war). Aided by new communication technologies, cross-nationally mobile credit offered opportunities to mobilize large-scale external credit. Concentration in the structure of financial markets made public balance sheets more vulnerable to big banking crises. This vulnerability grew with new private-sector technologies of credit creation, notably through the use of collateral (Riles 2011). In addition, inhibitions about public debt weakened as the spread of universal suffrage eroded *rentier* power and led to an economic culture of social welfare and entitlement. The secularization of society eroded attachment to inherited religious and folk beliefs about debt. It was accompanied by new belief in the scientific management of public finances, including creative financial engineering. These factors combined to facilitate the emergence of new, less constraining ideologies of debt.

These changes in political economy found echo in social and political thought. Intellectually, the dominant role of prudence or practical wisdom in reasoning about virtuous private and public conduct had acted as an inhibition on debt. In Aristotle's sense of *phronesis*, prudence is the ability to foresee what is needed for one's continued existence (*The Ethics*, Book Six, Chapters 5–8). It involves detailed 'knowledge of the ultimate particular thing', acquired only through practical experience. Translated into contemporary terms, Aristotle suggests that prudence does not follow from knowledge of the general principles of macroeconomics or political economy. It requires not so much the top-down application of universal truths as intimate familiarity with individual circumstances. Practical wisdom in managing public debt has only a limited amount to do with science-based, textbook prescriptions. The world of debt constitutes a variable subject matter. It is not amenable to a single overarching philosophy.

Those trained in the Aristotelian tradition continued to view prudence as connecting the other moral virtues, like consent and justice, to economic, political, and institutional realities. Debt posed difficult political questions of moral judgement, including what was feasible in particular circumstances. Following Den Uyl (1991), it can be argued that changing public and political attitudes to debt have been reflected in the relative decline of prudence as a moral virtue in modern political and economic thought. By the twentieth century, prudence seemed to have evolved into a value within instrumental rationality. It had been dethroned from its role in classical thought as the noblest of virtues, as an intrinsic aspect of practical wisdom. Prudence was less central in new ideologies of debt that celebrated elite display and public magnificence, mass consumer culture, and social welfare.

The dethronement of prudence was intimated in the writings of François Rabelais (*c.*1494–*c.*1553), the French humanist scholar, as well as of Mandeville, the widely-read Dutch-born émigré to London. In the face of condemnation from the Sorbonne, Rabelais revelled in the joys of ordinary life and in attacking prevalent hypocrisy. His *Gargantua and Pantagruel* (1653), III, 3 uses the figure of Pantagruel to celebrate the debtor.

> And what had I created? So many good, fine creditors... The man that lends nothing is an ugly, wicked creature... And what had I made? Debts. Rare and excellent things!... If you judge of the perfection of debtors by the multitude of their creditors, you will not be far out in your practical arithmetic... Not everyone is a debtor who wishes to be; not everyone who wishes to be a creditor becomes one.
>
> ...
>
> You can hardly imagine how glad I am, when every morning I perceive myself environed and surrounded with brigades of creditors—humble, fawning, and full of their reverences... which makes me verily think that the supreme height of heroic virtue... consists in being a debtor.

Mandeville delighted in outraging moralists of debt by celebrating luxury (Goldsmith 1985). In Remark Q of *The Fable of the Bees* (1714), he examined the lessons from Dutch history. Mandeville argued for a more differentiated, situational understanding of debt and mocked supposed Dutch virtues like thrift as humbug. In his view, the famed frugality of the United Provinces rested not on piety and Calvinism. It was rooted in material conditions, above all 'the hardships and calamities of war' and the lack of abundant natural resources. Once these conditions were relaxed, the Dutch became extravagant consumers. Mandeville argued that, given her different context of ample natural resources and freedom from invasion, Britain had an unparalleled opportunity to indulge private vices for public benefit. Luxury consumption could function as the engine of economic progress. The model of a virtuous household of thrift and frugality might seem appropriate to the United Provinces. It was inappropriate for Britain, where it would produce unnecessary misery. Mandeville's caustic comments on civic hypocrisy caused considerable shock. In 1723 a Middlesex grand jury convicted the book as a nuisance. Later, Hume and Smith took issue with Mandeville's approach.

The French public intellectual François de Voltaire was close to Mandeville and Melon on luxury and its connection to public and private debt. However, he agreed with Hume and Smith about the dangers from external debts. In contrast to other Enlightenment figures, Voltaire was a highly successful entrepreneur and investor, able to write on the basis of his experience in providing loans to various rulers and their families, like the Duchess of Saxe-Gotha (Rossel 1909). In 1752 Voltaire lent the substantial sum of 150,000 *livres* to the Duke of Württemberg, who was considered risky, followed by large loans to the Elector Palatine in Mannheim and, in 1753 and 1757, to the Prince-Elector of Bavaria. Both the Duke and the Prince-Elector defaulted on payments, causing Voltaire serious financial worries (Kózmiński 1929). The combination of this experience with his reading of political economy led Voltaire to conclude that creditors should be very cautious about external borrowing and that external debts were potentially a major drain on national economies.

Conversely, he agreed with Melon, who had served as secretary to John Law and who like Mandeville extolled the virtues of luxury consumption. In the view of Voltaire: 'Any state that borrows from its own people is no poorer for it... these debts even serve as an encouragement to industry' (Kózmiński 1929). Voltaire saw in domestic debt servicing and repayment a means to put cash in the hands of consumers and investors. Domestically-held public debt offered a virtuous circle in which 'confidence and the circulation of wealth are sufficient to ensure repayment' (Kózmiński 1929). It would also serve to stimulate the desirable growth of commercial society, in which England had eclipsed France.

Rabelais, Mandeville, and Voltaire can be seen as representative figures of a steep decline in the significance attached to prudence in discourse about debt. This decline paralleled the growing prestige of science as the basis for social and political organization, the financial revolution of the eighteenth century, and the explosion of private and public credit. Henri Saint-Simon (1760–1825) illustrated how science could be used to reframe debate about debt. He sought to overcome the post-Revolution conflicts of legitimacy in France by advocating a new form of state that was dedicated to social improvement on the basis of enlightened technocratic management. Saint-Simon's technocratic approach to public finances involved a shift from wasteful public expenditure and from measures that privileged idle property owners to socially useful, productive investment. According to Prosper Enfantin (1796–1864), a founder of Saint-Simonism and former banker, credit was the instrument for bringing together, peacefully and progressively, property, producers, and workers (Weill 1896). Banks were at the core of this new hierarchical social order, replacing the former guilds. The new social order centred on a new enlightened banking elite and a state that mobilized credit (Saint-Simon 1975). Saint-Simon's ideas were influential not just within French socialism. They also inspired reformers within the French Second Empire of Napoleon III. In the 1850s Saint-Simonian ideas were used to justify new bold and creative debt-financed investments in infrastructure (Price 2001). By 1860–1861 traditional French bankers were beginning to mount a strong counteraction against the resulting fiscal excesses.

A key aspect of the financial revolution and changing attitudes to debt was the increasingly abstract nature of money. Saint-Simonians like Enfantin believed that the total elimination of metal money was possible and desirable on grounds of social utility. It was essential for the mobilization of credit and for preventing 'dead, inactive capital in bank coffers' (Weill 1896). Johann Wolfgang von Goethe gave dramatic expression to the loosening sense of guilt that was associated with the move to fiat currency. In *Faust Part Two*, Mephistopheles advises the Holy Roman Emperor:

> Such paper, in the place of actual gold, is practical: we know just what we hold...But wise men will, when they have studied it, place infinite trust in what is infinite.

In institutional and technological terms, the erosion of prudence in thinking about debt can be attributed to three main factors. In the first place, it can be seen as an outcome of the establishment of property rights. When property is registered, and can be transferred, it can be posted as collateral to secure credit. Collateral represents a legal fiction. It is supposed to serve as protection against default. However, it also provides a private technology of endogenous credit creation that makes possible rapid growth in debt and in the shadow banking system (Riles 2011). The invention of collateral transformed creditor-debtor relations, creating new sources of moral hazard and risk of financial distress.

Secondly, in his novel *L'Argent* (*Money*, 1891), Zola attributed the erosion of prudence to the growing significance of the nineteenth-century stock exchange. It provided an institutional setting within which transactions could be fictitious and endlessly augmented. Zola sought to show that unsustainable debts were founded on the creation of illusion in new institutional settings.

Finally, by the late twentieth century, the loosening of the sense of constraint and guilt attached to debt took a radically new form. Consumers and investors could make use of electronic money. The combination of ever-increasing computer and communication power with deregulation created a new phase in the financial revolution. The age of 'cyber-finance' reshaped attitudes to credit: 'Money is now endless, capable of infinite multiplication and completely unreal' (Das 2011). There seemed to be no constraint on virtual credit (Graeber 2011). It also created a widespread sense of confusion, unease, and alarm about the implications for the behaviour of banks and for how central banks managed money, for instance quantitative easing.

The implications of decline in prudence became ever-more serious with the huge growth in the scale of financial assets, with the size, complexity, and opacity of the financial institutions managing these assets, and with the proliferation of ever-more exotic credit instruments, like securitization and collateralized debt obligations (cf. Borio and White 2004). The new age of cyber-finance was accompanied by the growing significance of sophisticated mathematics-trained graduates within the corporate structures of financial institutions. They developed new quantitative model-based bond trading, including securitization and derivatives. Their science-based models induced the illusion that credit risks were better controlled. The problem became one of who could control the originators and custodians of these esoteric models. The ease of credit creation enabled hubris to thrive on a historically new scale. Politically, this new dynamic rested on the privileged and collusive relations of investment banks with financial public relations consultancies in generating support for deregulation of credit.

Changes in attitudes to debt and risk were also bound up with new discourses about social entitlement. These discourses emerged with extension of the electoral franchise and with the emergence of consumer culture and the economic nexus that supported it. Expectations of state provision of benefits grew, notably in education, health, and pensions. In addition, notions of social entitlement were changed by the emergence of credit-fuelled consumer culture and high levels of household indebtedness. Consumer expectations of ever-higher living standards were fuelled by more lenient and readily available bank lending, the subsequent booms in construction and property market sectors, and the expansion of retail sectors, modern advertising, and marketing. Social status and identity became closely associated with consumption, in particular with the concept of luxury. Identifying oneself with the good life meant being able to live beyond traditional understandings of basic needs. Debt was the price paid for the joys of being part of a hedonistic consumer culture. Being unable to participate fuelled the sense of relative deprivation. In short, debt was part of a new consumer culture of social entitlement. Its denial had the potential to foster a deep sense of loss, despair, social protest, and riot.

Against this long-term background, it seems perverse to attribute the decline of the centrality of prudence to Keynesianism. The basis of this attribution comes from the questioning by Keynesian macroeconomics of the equation of public finances with the virtuous household in classical economic theory, including in the work of John Stuart Mill. Keynesians rejected the notion of public debt as simply a special case of private debt. John Maynard Keynes argued that the principles of sound finances that apply to individuals, companies, and banks do not apply in the same way at the level of the state (Skidelsky 1992). The application of truisms like 'making ends meet' from households to states involves a logical error, the 'fallacy of composition'. The explanation lies in the 'paradox of thrift': thrift may be individually desirable but, if adopted by everyone, will bring the economy to ruin. The state has a distinctive responsibility for sustaining aggregate demand. By varying its taxes, spending, and borrowing over the economic cycle, it ensures the flow of spending in the economy. Moreover, public borrowing is justifiable not just to deal with asymmetric economic shocks. It is also vital for bold and risky investment in infrastructure that seeks to yield macroeconomic and social welfare benefits, including higher trend real GDP growth.

However, a more precise reading of Keynes shows that his attitude to fiscal deficits and public debt was more complex, cautious, and differentiated. He remained convinced that fiscal policies must reconcile three social interests: investors, business, and employees. Keynes (1923) sought to correct contemporary imbalance in representing these interests. His attitudes to this imbalance were rooted in his social liberalism, which reflected a wider societal shift towards a discourse of social inclusion. The state's function was to promote social cohesion. The difficulties in interpreting Keynes' thinking on public debt stem from the complex and uncomfortable persistence of his own *rentier* social background, alongside an acute awareness of how the concept of sovereign creditworthiness must take account of wider social interests.

Ultimately, however, the key to Keynes' view of statesmanship remained prudence in the face of radical uncertainty (Skidelsky 1992). He questioned reliance on formal modelling and probabilistic reasoning. Keynes was also never an advocate of unrestrained public borrowing. He was acutely aware of the risks of long-term, harsh social sacrifice for the pursuit of short-term gains. In putting the level of aggregate demand at the centre of debate, he remained aware that accumulating a high stock of public debt created new problems and constraints. It created risk of a rise in real interest rates and painful deleverage. The result would be the loss of the confidence which, for Keynes, was the key to the 'animal spirits' that drove economic growth. His *How to Pay for the War* (1940) illustrated his concern about fiscal deficits and debt even at a time of supreme emergency. Managing public finances involved dilemmas of a kind that later Keynesians were often slower to recognize.

By the twentieth century the complex forms of discourse about debt illustrated the profound moral ambiguities associated with debt and the associated difficulties in framing and using state power. On the one hand, the various discourses of social entitlement, market society, hedonistic consumer culture, and neo-Keynesian economics suggested the dethronement of prudence. They could be linked to the erosion of a clear sense of the overall scale and meaning of debt, public and private, providing a context in which fiscal and money illusion and hubris could thrive.

On the other hand, the notion that the state is 'the household writ large' retained a continuing hold on popular imagination. The portrayal of political leaders and parties as feckless in managing public finances, as presiding over excessive public debt, and as in collusion with over-powerful bankers, invited electoral punishment. Aligning oneself with debt reduction is not in itself electorally damaging. Evidence suggests that it attracts broad public support (Alesina, Carloni, and Lecce 2010). Despite neo-Keynesian macroeconomic insights, and modern consumer, financial, and promotional cultures, states occupy a political world in which folk beliefs about debt retain a strong hold on how leaders behave and constrain their behaviour. The more practical problem stems from the paradox that, while voters want action to tackle debt in the aggregate, few are ready to accept the particular consequences. At the heart of this paradox are financial illiteracy, compounded by the incentives for political elites to pursue short-term populist politics, the tension between collective and individual interests, and assignment of responsibility for carrying the burden to others.

Morality and Debt

The politics of sovereign creditworthiness inhabits a realm that weaves together moral ambiguity with emotional attachments and passions. Sovereign creditworthiness is bound up in the normative concerns of political theory. It raises a whole set of questions about the nature of the creditor-debtor relationship. How far, and in what ways, is debt 'bad'? What is the appropriate behaviour of both parties? What is the proper balance between, on the one hand, systemic stability and collective solidarity and, on the other, avoidance of moral hazard in managing sovereign debt? Who are the innocent victims and who, in the interests of fairness, should bear the fiscal pain of macroeconomic adjustment? How far should institutional feasibility define and, if necessary, restrict conceptions of responsibility? Institutional feasibility relates to what is legally permissible. It is also about the availability of processes of dialogue and negotiation between creditors, official and private, and debtor-state elites. Institutional feasibility defines what is judged possible in given circumstances.

This moral ambiguity stems from the way in which creditor-debtor relations form a dyad, which can be represented as the master–slave dialectic in Friedrich Hegel's *Phenomenology of Mind* (1807). There cannot be creditors without debtors, any more than 'surplus' states without 'deficit' states in trade. In short, creditors need debtors, and vice versa. The relationship is unequal, but each needs the other. Indeed, the master can become enslaved by dependence on the debtor. Creditor-debtor relations exhibit features of a 'dance to the music of time'. They display recurrent patterns of behaviour. Creditor-debtor relations can be understood in terms of Hegel's 'struggle for recognition'. The debtor seeks to escape from a condition of disrespect, from sentiments of guilt, shame, and blame that attach to the role, and to gain a position of honour. Recognition is a matter of being ascribed some positive status. Punishment does not provide an adequate basis for recognition. The master–slave dialectic is about relative positioning. The debtor can aspire to freedom by gaining recognition and honour. Its denial diminishes the quality of the creditor-debtor relationship.

Moral ambiguity—and the absence of easy political solutions—originates from the problem of balancing the claims of creditors to superior virtue and uniqueness with those of debtors for recognition and honour. The conundrum is how to endow both creditors and debtors with dignity (cf. Taylor 1994). It can in principle be addressed by procedural rules that promote open dialogue and inclusiveness (Sen 1989). Procedural rules offer a way of bridging different moral positions and overcoming power differentials. In their absence, there is high risk that an atmosphere of grievance, harassment, despair, and victimhood will envelop creditor-debtor relations.

Credible commitment to such procedural rules depends on recognition by creditors that adjustment cannot be made by debtors alone. This recognition is impeded by the tendency for creditors to fear pollution of their own uniqueness—and creditworthiness—from costly bail-outs of debtors and the liabilities that they entail. As with the post-2007 euro area sovereign debt crises, the difficulty with this politics of recognition is that certain values—those associated with creditor states—are seen as having a fundamental status, so that logically not all claims should be respected. On these terms, recognition involves assimilation into a particular dominant economic culture. The freedom of a state to hold different values implies exit from shared arrangements. The politics of sovereign creditworthiness is, in consequence, troubled by an atmosphere of harassment, resentment, and victimhood. It is captured graphically in Nietzsche's contrast of 'master morality' and 'slave morality' in the First Essay of his *Genealogy of Morals*.

The political difficulties lie in how to get each to face up to the implications of this mutual, asymmetric dependence of creditor and debtor states. Their relationship has features of a prisoners' dilemma, in which neither side can defect without causing serious damage to the other. Managing this dilemma is easier when the institutional conditions are in place to help sustain an evolutionary, stable pattern of conditional cooperation. Incentives to defect are reduced by the heightened risk of widespread and shared collateral damage to creditors and debtors. As with the euro area, a set of rules of the game that encourage repeated interaction provide a 'super-game', inducing cooperation (cf. Axelrod 1984). However, risks remain. Creditor-state elites retain a paramount interest in limiting their liability. Moreover, one, or both parties, faced by deeply unpalatable choices, may choose to pursue a game of chicken, in which the bluff of the other is called. Miscalculation can have high costs for all.

The politics of creditor-debtor relations are exacerbated by a moralizing language of 'saints' and 'sinners', which is laced with feelings of pride in national virtue, on the one side, and of shame, humiliation, and resentment, on the other (Smith 2012). Esoteric technical vocabulary and efforts to construct inclusive processes of debate and negotiation cannot hide the extent to which the idea of sovereign creditworthiness is a world of identities and symbolism, to which powerful, historically grounded, and often idiosyncratic feelings are attached.

In its concern with concepts like justice, political theory highlights the normative character of creditor-debtor relations and sovereign creditworthiness. It should be about seeking opportunities to build more civilized and nuanced understandings of the interdependence between creditors and debtors, free from the notion of debt as sin. These opportunities depend on constructing orderly processes of negotiation that protect both creditors and taxpayers and that retain the dignity of debtors, enabling them to pluck substantial gain from their subordinated position. Qualitative advancement in thinking about creditor-debtor relations and sovereign creditworthiness depends on strengthening their ethical dimension and promoting cultural change in two ways.

First, analysis of sovereign creditworthiness needs to move beyond a narrow, utilitarian, and financial view of balance sheets, the realm of accountants and financial markets. It must also examine outcomes from longer-term and societal-wide perspectives. This more expansive view involves taking account of wider expectations with respect to governance, social welfare, and environmental quality. The critical re-examination of sovereign creditworthiness poses ethical questions about the operation and power of financial markets. These questions include the net social value of financial innovations like derivatives and securitization. They focus on the agenda-setting power of mega-large investment banks and the associated cluster of economists, specialist journalists, and public relations consultants. They deal with the potential conflicts of interest that stem from their power to shape public macroeconomic debates about sovereign creditworthiness. Media commentary on sovereign creditworthiness is saturated with bank analysts and advisers to financial institutions. Public debate risks distortion from the potential conflicts of interest that arise between their corporate profit-seeking positions and their public policy analysis and recommendations. This privileging in public debates offers scope for bank analysts to use an information advantage to influence markets and public opinion. The outcome may help corporate profits but threaten systemic stability (Bini Smaghi 2010b). In short, debate about sovereign creditworthiness highlights the gap between the discourse of the free market, which legitimates bank and business power, and the grubby realities of 'crony' capitalism in which these elites capture politics and policy.

This type of normative analysis suggests changes in the functioning of financial markets, including credit rating agencies, to reduce conflicts of interest, to increase transparency, and to avert excessive risk-taking through financial instruments of questionable net social value. One option is to rely on improvements in internal governance within financial markets. Examples include changes within credit rating agencies and greater accountability of managers for long-run performance, notably by changes to bank bonus practices. However, 'turkeys do not vote for Christmas'. External pressure from supervisors and regulators is required. The vexing question remains whether they can escape capture by the lobbying power of the financial sector, the enormous information advantages that it possesses, and its capacity for arbitrage between rival jurisdictions.

Secondly, the ethical dimension of creditor-debtor relations and sovereign creditworthiness requires measures to correct the political short-sightedness that so often bedevils—and raises the costs—of debt crises. Political leaders of creditor states have great difficulties in persuading their domestic political elites and publics to make short-term sacrifices as taxpayers for long-term gains from avoidance of debt default and the systemic risks that follow. This problem is greater when it involves rescuing states, like Greece and Cyprus, that are judged to be plagued by endemic corruption and failing governance capacity. It arose in 1995 when the US Congress refused to support IMF financial assistance to Mexico, though this blockage was circumvented by the US Administration.

Within the euro area, the German federal government hesitated over the Greek bail-out for some four months from January/February 2010, till after key *Land* elections. The German media was littered with images of lazy, corrupt, and featherbedded Greeks, enjoying much earlier pensions than Germans. They portrayed a bloated, privileged Greek public sector of unknown dimensions. These images ignored the reckless lending by German and other EU banks to Greece. The uncertainties that German hesitation generated contributed to higher final costs of the euro area/IMF bail-out in May 2010. Political leadership is a tough call when it seeks to reframe the moral arguments in terms that judiciously apportion blame and that are conducive to mutual respect and cooperation. As the Greek crisis gathered momentum in 2011–2012, German political leadership resorted to dramatization of the existential threat to the euro area and the EU in order to overcome the deep reluctance of elite and public opinion to shoulder the costs of further financial assistance. This kind of reframing is difficult once the psycho-drama of debt crisis has infected domestic discourse.

Normative political theory shows that managing sovereign debt crises raises issues that go to the heart of the functioning of liberal democracies. It highlights the risks of disconnection between, on the one hand, domestic political competition and electoral choices and, on the other, policies to restore sovereign creditworthiness that are negotiated or imposed internationally. Disconnection is revealed in the growth of popular alienation from conventional forms of politics. Politics comes to be seen as a meaningless activity, other than in terms of the career interests of politicians and their clients. In this context, space opens for populist political mobilization against external 'diktat', benefitting far Left and far Right parties. This phenomenon was apparent in the electoral performance of the National Front in the French Presidential and Assembly elections of 2012, of Syriza in the two Greek elections of 2012, and of the Five-Star Movement in the Italian elections of 2013. Reconnecting policy and politics posed difficult challenges in reforming the governance of the euro area. It suggested some form of supra-national European government, directly accountable to the European Parliament. In its absence it was difficult to provide democratic political legitimacy for European fiscal and banking union.

However, resistance to supra-national reforms is powerful. It arises because quasi-automatic crisis prevention and management mechanisms at the supra-national level appear to further strengthen technocratic governance at the expense of politics. Alternatively, legitimizing supra-national governance through its politicization at the European level is rejected as threatening domestic political leadership, which shelters behind sovereignty claims. Continuing to entrust the management of sovereign debt crises to intergovernmental forums, like the European Council, and the European Stability Mechanism, privileges the discourse of sovereignty. Appeals to sovereignty serve, in turn, as camouflage for the pursuit of domestic interests and power. They provide space within which the contrasting cultural and political sensitivities of creditor- and debtor-state elites about sovereign creditworthiness are sharply articulated.

The problem stems from the high trade and financial interdependence, risks of contagion, and vulnerability to sovereign bond markets in a European monetary union. The lack of legitimacy for supra-national mechanisms to act decisively in emergency exposes European states to politically and economically dangerous crises of sovereign creditworthiness over which they risk losing control. This risk of loss of control further threatens the foundations of liberal democracy and of European integration.

Sovereign Creditworthiness and Sentiments

The politics of sovereign creditworthiness cannot be effectively captured by the efficient market hypothesis and narrowly constructed models of rational, utility-maximizing creditor behaviour. In making this claim, it should not be forgotten that Keynes' notion of 'animal spirits' and his critique of probability theory stimulated behavioural economics. This branch of economics provides rich insights into how people think about debt and sovereign creditworthiness. It shows how, and why, the plethora of information, the pervasive ambiguity, and the radical uncertainty that surrounds debt and sovereign creditworthiness induces behaviour that is governed by sentiments like confidence, sociability, and feelings about fairness. They find expression in storytelling about the future (cf. Akerlof and Shiller 2009). People make decisions because they 'feel' they are right. They are influenced by what is salient, and by events and news that grab their attention, rather than by what is probable. There is, in short, some recognition of the superiority of narrative over probabilistic reasoning within economics.

Behaviourally sensitive political economy offers an important means of understanding how the politics of sovereign creditworthiness functions. Its key insight is that, in order to gain financial market confidence, governing elites must be able to construct a persuasive story about their sovereign creditworthiness. This story is about the will to honour contracts and the capacity to extract taxes, spend wisely and productively, and control fiscal balances. It offers a convincing narrative about governing competence and future economic security and prosperity.

However, the politics of sovereign creditworthiness has aspects that are not adequately captured in standard or non-standard macroeconomics or in political economy. First, it has an irreducibly moral and historical aspect. Understanding the politics of sovereign creditworthiness requires attention to the self-understanding of their roles within a narrow governing and financial elite. It is about their conceptions of proper or acceptable behaviour and fairness in particular contexts. Assessing sovereign 'character' as virtuous or not involves moral judgement. It reflects the dominant conception of fiscal normality in a specific historical context. Notions of what constitutes 'sustainable' public debt have changed over time, notably in the shadow of war. Between 1916 and 1963 British gross public debt remained over 100 per cent of GDP. It peaked at over 200 per cent, without formal sovereign debt default. By 2010, British figures well below these levels were regarded as unsustainable.

Secondly, certain biases are introduced into the politics of sovereign creditworthiness by the prestige that attaches to quantification as the basis for economic modelling of sustainable debt. 'Productive' debt that strengthens infrastructure and future economic potential tends to be relatively neglected in constructing sovereign creditworthiness because it is more difficult to capture quantitatively. This neglect reflects in part the difficulty in measuring future asset values and in part the market bias towards maximizing short-term returns over long-term outlooks.

However, perhaps the trickiest problem in understanding the politics of sovereign creditworthiness is how to incorporate emotions in constructing the meanings attached to debt and in explaining creditor and debtor behaviour. Rational political economy analysis takes us a certain way. It offers important insights into the psychology of bond markets, above all self-reinforcing panics in times of crisis. It suggests that incentives to panic may increase once states join a monetary union and lose the capacity to borrow in their own (floating) currency. This incentive is reinforced when the monetary union lacks robust collective-action capacity, whether by mutualizing debts or by executive discretion to act in supreme emergency (De Grauwe 2011; Dyson 2013). However, anthropology, cognitive psychology, psychoanalysis, philosophy, and imaginative literature offer deeper insights into the complex emotional world of debt. They show how moral thinking about debt is bound up with a range of often powerful emotions: despair, envy, fear, guilt, indignation, ingratitude, pride, resentment, shame, sympathy, and wish-fulfilment.

The notion that emotions are an essential aspect of the cultivation of moral personality goes back to Aristotle (Wallace 1994). It was taken up by Adam Smith in his *The*

Theory of Moral Sentiments (1759). He argued for the importance of certain emotions—sympathy, pity, and compassion—that are consistent with propriety, benevolence, and prudence. Smith would not approve of the creditor's contempt or of the debtor's anger. He discriminated between base passions and those consistent with dignity and honour. He would counsel that the creditor should sympathize with the conditions that gave rise to the debtor's anger. The notion of the impartial spectator was central. In Smith's view, the impartial spectator could justifiably feel indignation when shown that the innocent were bearing the costs of a sovereign debt crisis, whilst those responsible escaped lightly. Section 3, Chapter 3 of *The Theory of Moral Sentiments* dealt with 'the corruption of our moral sentiments that comes from the disposition to admire the rich and the great, and to despise or neglect the downtrodden and poor'.

As Smith would recognize, emotions pose serious problems for the politics of sovereign creditworthiness. Emotions can impede moral judgement; they can make actors partial and inconsistent in the attention that they give to moral issues; they can lead them into illusion and hubris; and they can suggest immoral goals and projects (Solomon 1976). Questions about the value and the role of emotions led philosophers to very different accounts. Those in the Stoic tradition, like Immanuel Kant and Friedrich Nietzsche, argued that emotions should play a subordinate role in moral judgements. However, this argument fits poorly with modern neurological research, which highlights just how important the non-rational mind is in all forms of decision-making. It also sits awkwardly alongside the insights of Keynes and of Akerlof and Shiller (2009) on 'animal spirits'. The weight of empirical research would seem to confirm that emotions inform and are inextricably interwoven with beliefs about debt and sovereign creditworthiness, within markets as well as politics. This insight suggests that, whatever claims may be made to the contrary, sovereign creditworthiness is a realm of narrative rather than probabilistic reasoning.

Creditor-Debtor Relations in Imaginative Literature

The literary production of short stories, novels, and plays features as a dynamic, constitutive component of historical experience of credit and debt through its representations of the financial revolution and its impact. The new credit economy that gained momentum from the late seventeenth century deeply affected literary production. The two worlds had in common their fictional character. This commonality derived from the way in which the seemingly 'real' value of credit and debt was bound up in promises and expectations about the future. It was vulnerable to the manipulation of imagination and hence provided fertile ground for literature (Pocock 1985). Literature examined diverse representations of the new forms of credit and debt and their reflection in social relationships.

Though imaginative literature focused on personal credit and debt, the economic and political phenomenon of escalating public credit remained a potent factor in its background. Literary works provided powerful symbolic images, icons, and points of cultural reference. Above all, they offered insights into the fluid and complex nexus between character, family, and social connections, and fortune in matters of credit and debt. Imaginative literature showed how they had been experienced and represented differently over time. It drew out very different and contestable conclusions about the relationship between debt and virtue.

Literary works offered portraits of the intensely psychological and emotional world of creditor-debtor relations. They exposed the affectation, cunning, vanity, and hypocrisy beneath the formal surface of legal and economic concepts of contract. Imaginative literature sought to delve behind simplifying, abstract economic and legal assumptions about individual motive and chains of causation. It focused on offering realist accounts that were rooted in the every-day life of creditors and debtors. Their characters were rarely viewed as one-dimensional or as socially determined, flat, and passive. They were enmeshed in dense networks of social relations that shaped attitudes and practices of credit and debt in ways independent of formalized market models and contractual relations (Finn 2003). Credit retained its traditional link to 'character' through association with establishing and retaining respectability, honour, and recognition. This association favoured debtors who could display and draw on their cultural and social capital.

Prior to the mid-nineteenth century, the misfortune of debtors was a dominant theme. Its dominance reflected, in part, the extent to which for many authors their insights into the human anguish, helplessness, humiliation, and despair of debtors was directly grounded in their personal experience of the social marginalization consequent on debt. Anton Chekhov, Charles Dickens, Henry Fielding, Henrik Ibsen, William Shakespeare, and Anthony Trollope shared the ignominy of debt-ridden fathers and families. Miguel de Cervantes (1547–1616) began to write *Don Quixote* in debtors' prison. Balzac, Charles Baudelaire, Daniel Defoe, Fielding, and Joseph Roth were encumbered by debts for most or all of their lives. With the exception of Defoe, they narrowly escaped debtors' prison.

Their writing registered the personal, family, and professional dishonour and emotional turmoil inflicted by carelessly contracted debts and rapacious, unsatisfied creditors. Above all, however, it stressed how the law and the penal system mistook the misfortune of debtors for their misbehaviour, asserting property rights over personal freedom. In particular, debt exposed the vulnerability of women in ways that threatened their moral and sexual degradation. Magnanimity was typically shown to be in scarce supply in the relations of creditors and debtors.

From the eighteenth century, the emergence of the British novel coincided with new controversies about the fast-growing phenomenon of public and private credit. Debt was acquiring a central role in social, economic, and political life, and in its background were a succession of continental European wars and imperial ventures. A key theme in the novel was the moral implications of the rise of a new breed of 'moneyed' men, financial speculation, and a more dynamic commercial and consumer culture. The advocates of the new political economy of credit celebrated the world of contract as synonymous with virtue. The law and the penal system became more closely engaged with debtors. Moreover, regular financial and fiscal crises exposed the risks associated with debt (Pocock 1985). Debtors represented the largest single category of prisoners in English goals (Finn 2003: 189). The novel opened a new space for a more assertive authorial voice, directly engaging with the controversial cultural and moral questions of debt in terms beyond the narrowly economic and legal.

The new world of credit was not only socially significant; it was the great generator of illusion, hubris, complacency, and all manner of social ills. Samuel Richardson's *Pamela;*

or, Virtue Rewarded (1740) provided a cultural icon, Pamela, who was to inspire later writers. Like Fielding, a fellow Whig, he endorsed the new world of public credit, in contrast to the Old Tories like Viscount Bolingbroke. However, whilst sympathetic to the new 'moneyed' men of the City, Richardson condemned the rigid enforcement of contracts on 'unfortunate' personal debtors. It advanced immoral purposes, above all with respect to women. Richardson refused to dichotomize the moral virtue of the creditor and the debtor (Finn 2003: 26–34).

Henry Fielding picked up on Pamela's distress and her example of moral probity in *Joseph Andrews* (1742). The new impersonal world of credit and debt is seen as changing traditional notions of honour and virtue. On the one hand, it retains older attributes. Credit is based on character, which in turn rests on social connections and status. On the other hand, credit transforms character and lowers moral standards. Fielding bemoaned the lack of magnanimity that infects the relations of creditors and debtors. He shows how imprudence in personal as well as public debt leads to illusion, folly, and personal ruin. Virtue was attributed to those who practised traditional moral notions of gift and reciprocity over purely individualist legal conceptions of property and contract.

An aspect of this changed world of commercial contract was the transformation of the publishing industry. Authors were caught up in the expansion of publishing as a market-oriented commercial enterprise, in which they could lose as well as make fortunes (Haynes 2010). In consequence, many of them became personally involved in issues of credit and debt. They experienced its implications for authorial freedom. Balzac, Dickens, and Fielding became intimately familiar with the law of contract and its potentially ruinous effects.

Imaginative literature helped to expose the purported political neutrality of legal forms and the harshness of punishment attached to debt. It focused on the limitations of contractual obligations. The representation of the morally culpable debtor was far from absent. However, literary work focused at least as much on the character flaws of creditors. It drew out their crude self-interests, vanity, and hypocrisy. Ingratitude was exhibited as a shared characteristic of creditors and debtors. The harsh creditor emerged as a representative social figure, oppressing the poor, causing personal distress and family breakdown, and threatening social cohesion. At the highest levels of society, creditors and debtors were represented as engaged in sordid mutual exploitation. Men married to gain access to money to pay off their debts. They exploited their wives. According to Finn (2003: 48), 'Women's wealth and bodies function as the common coin of debt repayment in the English novel.'

In broad terms, despite shifts of emphasis, the image of the 'unfortunate' debtor dominated over that of the morally culpable debtor. In the works of Galdós, Roth, and Zola, debtors faced the relentless march of large, encompassing historical forces that entrapped them. These forces of debt entrapment included the lure of entrepreneurial and financial speculation, conspicuous consumption as society becomes more commercialized, and the mismatch between money and status.

The literary treatment of credit and debt pursues a strikingly similar set of themes across Europe. A dominant theme is the juxtaposition of the antisocial and merciless greed of creditors with the self-hatred, humiliation, and dishonour of debtors. It is powerfully evoked in Joseph Roth's *The Radetzky March* (1932). Debt leads to the loss of personal, family, and professional honour. It symbolizes the larger collapse of the values on which the Hapsburg Empire had been founded. The grandson of the 'hero of Solferino', who had gained imperial rank for his family from saving the life of the Emperor, becomes ensnared in the accumulating unpaid gambling debts of his fellow officers to the obscure financier Kapturak. He degenerates into helpless self-pity. In a reference to the Hapsburg Empire, Kapturak is described as a man of the sort that 'started to circle like those cowardly black birds that can see someone dying from an enormous distance...They are the feathered brothers of mysterious Death, his heralds, his companions and his camp-followers' (1932: 188). The father of the disgraced officer, District Commissioner Herr von Trotta, views the son's dishonour as 'worse than a calamity'. He rescues his son by personal appeal to the Emperor. Though disgrace is averted, and Kapturak expelled, the District Commissioner recognizes that the old code of honour has vanished and with it the glue that holds the Hapsburg Empire together.

However, Roth notes that even Herr von Trotta was not immune.

> He had always insisted on appearing richer than he was. He had the instincts of a gentleman. And in those times (and who knows, perhaps even today), there are no costlier instincts. Men laden with such a curse know neither what they earn, nor what they spend. They draw from an invisible well. They don't calculate. They are convinced that their fortune cannot possibly amount to less than their liberality. (1932: 292–3)

The Trotta family is caught up in the mismatch between money and status. It is trapped in illusion and complacency.

This theme of the mismatch between status and power is strongly represented in Spanish literature, going back to Cervantes' *Don Quixote* (1605/1615). Narratives were typically framed around the tensions between creditors who had money, but lacked status, and debtors who possessed status, but not money. Like the Don, they had a habit of not paying their debts. This Spanish phenomenon was accentuated by the granting of noble titles (*hidalguía*), with associated tax privileges, creating an expanding group of non-productive aristocrats whose money did not match their status.

In the four-volume Torquemada novels (1889–1895) of Pérez Galdós (1843–1920) the hardened creditor is renowned for his cruelty to the poor. Faced by personal family tragedy, Torquemada resolves to reform and offers a debtor an interest-free loan, which—to his surprise—is refused. However, he proves incapable of genuine charity. The old maid-servant accuses him of trying to bribe God. Soon Torquemada returns to his old uncharitable ways, inflicting vengeance on others. He seeks to buy status through marriage into the indebted Aguilas family. In consequence, he finds himself a prisoner of polite society, driven to lavish expenditure. Creditor and debtor are bound together in a relationship that diminishes each other's ideals. Torquemada dies an uncomfortable and unhappy man.

The literary output of Henry Fielding was characterized by contempt for the way in which personal debt corrupts English aristocratic society. It is represented as creating a gulf between the superficial veneer of polite society and the underlying reality of cunning, duplicitous, and venal behaviour. A similarly bleak picture of English high society, addicted to conspicuous consumption, dependent on credit, and populated by predatory, greedy, and gullible creditors, emerges in Anthony Trollope's *The Way We Live Now* (1875). Credit is extended to the mysterious international financier, Augustus Melmotte, based on the semblance of his wealth rather than attention to his moral character or any substantive knowledge of his financial affairs. Money is shown to have a corrupting influence on creditors and debtors alike. It corrodes social bonds. Trollope paints a grim picture of the hypocrisy, dishonesty, and lack of integrity that came to deface the relations of creditors and debtors in nineteenth-century London. Moral decline culminates in dishonour and in Melmotte's disgrace and suicide.

Some of the bleakest literary portrayals of debt as a source of personal guilt, shame, and anguish relate to provincial society. In Ibsen's play *A Doll's House* (1879), Torvald Helmer affirms in Act 1: 'There can be no freedom and beauty about a home life that is founded on borrowing and debt.' Nora incurs debt in order to make possible travel away from the provincial life that so oppresses her individuality. However, her attempt to hide this debt from her banker husband places her in the power of the morally corrupt creditor, Krogstad. Nora's secret debts prove corrosive of personal relations and tragic in their consequences. Ibsen points the finger squarely at conventional morality as the source of this personal tragedy. This theme is paralleled by Gustav Flaubert's *Madame Bovary* (1856). She incurs not only financial debts for similar motives but also a metaphorical debt to bad novels from which she borrows inappropriately.

George Eliot's *Middlemarch* (1874) offers a psychologically subtle portrait of the ironies, illusions, complacency, and hypocrisy that characterize the relations of creditor and debtor in the narrow confines of English provincial life. The banker Nicholas Bulstrode, who believes that his success depends on divine providence, is finally exposed as a moral hypocrite. He pursues the idealistic young doctor Tertius Lydgate with lack of pity. In turn, Lydgate is shown as a naive, proud, and self-delusional debtor. He becomes ensnared in debt to appease his young, acquisitive, and narcissistic wife. Both Bulstrode and Lydgate finally choose exile.

The possibility of redemption is a theme that figures in the plays and short stories of Anton Chekhov. They are preoccupied with the personal anguish and family tragedies occasioned by debt in a society increasingly governed by money. His world of debt is somewhat less bleak than that of Ibsen. In *The Cherry Orchard* (1904), debt is associated with an aristocratic family living on past illusions. It becomes dependent on those it despises. The loss of the cherry orchard to the creditor symbolizes the loss of family honour. This loss of family honour is the focus of the short story *A Problem* (1887), in which the debts of Sasha cause grief to his mother and lead to a humiliating family council. Sasha consoles himself that it is usual for the young to be in debt. However, he ends up agreeing that he is profligate and a 'criminal'.

The possibility of redemption binds together Chekhov's play *The Bear* (1888) and his short story *The Bet* (1889). In *The Bear*, the merciless creditor Smirnov seeks repayment of a dead husband's debts by threatening the grieving widow. However, he learns to admire and love her. Smirnov is redeemed, proving capable of sympathy and mercy. In *The Bet*, the banker fears financial ruin on the eve of losing a wager. He decides to murder his would-be creditor before he leaves solitary confinement. However, the would-be victor has reappraised his life in prison. After years of immersion in imaginative literature, he has become contemptuous of money. Intent on forgiving debts, he escapes from his confinement so that he will lose the bet. The banker is not only freed from murdering him but also forced to reconsider his own values. Chekhov pictures a world of debt that is emotionally and morally bleak. However, he believes that imaginative literature and the practice of natural virtue can help make it better.

The possibility of redemption is also present in Johann Wolfgang von Goethe's *Faust Part II* (1831). Goethe drew on his first-hand experience of financial diplomacy at the Court of Weimar and his memories of the ruin inflicted by the currency debasements of Frederick the Great and of the French Revolution. Faust is minister of a debt-ridden Emperor, who is pleasure-loving, greedy, and gullible. He serves as the conduit through which the devilish Mephistopheles is able to exploit these weaknesses. Faust offers illusory cures for the ills of the empire, above all printing money using the gold under the Emperor's lands as collateral. However, the return to a life dedicated to pleasure proves short-lived before civil disorder breaks out. Faust is offered salvation through the love of a virtuous woman.

The theme of inner impoverishment pervades Thomas Mann's *Buddenbrooks* (1901). It provides the most famous German portrait of the character flaws of both creditors and debtors. Mann shows how these flaws combine in the financial decline of a merchant family, which was modelled on his own. The indebted and unscrupulous Bendix Grünlich is victim to his self-delusion that he is shrewd and resourceful. He marries into the Buddenbrook family in order to borrow on its credit with the banks. Grünlich is pursued by the merciless banker Kesselmeyer. However, he is refused rescue by his father-in-law, Johann Buddenbrook, and loses his wife. Johann's son, Christian, becomes a serial debtor, addicted to a life of pleasure. The one seemingly solid centre of the family firm's credit is the other son, Thomas. He leads a life dedicated to work, thrift, piety, and propriety. However, Mann highlights the self-disgust, inner emptiness, and fear that sap the vitality of Thomas Buddenbrook. His 'existence was no different from that of an actor...All this made of his life...a constant irritating pretence' (1901: 474). Thomas Mann is represented in the novel by the doomed Hanno, whose cold eye penetrates the glittering surface of the patrician creditor to reveal the 'inward impoverishment' (Part Ten, Chapter One).

The themes of endurance and magnanimity recur in Charles Dickens' portraits of credit and debt. The experience of debtors' prisons, and the power that creditors acquire over the persons of debtors, is central in *Pickwick Papers* (1837), *David Copperfield* (1850), and *Little Dorrit* (1857). Dickens reproduced his father as the debtors Wilkins Micawber and William Dorrit, both well-intentioned but naïve and incompetent men. *Little Dorrit* explored the indignity and shame associated with the Marshalsea debtors' prison, where Dickens' father had been incarcerated. Debt was associated with the stigma of family descent into a lower social class and with proximity to the world of criminality. Dickens shows how difficult it is to escape from this stigma.

Dickens highlighted the bleak loneliness of debtors in an increasingly material world, where traditional social bonds of support were dissolving. Their survival depended on sheer endurance and on the magnanimity of 'unheroic heroes', like the benefactor Arthur Clennam who serves as friend to William Dorrit in the Marshalsea. In *Little Dorrit*, Dickens reflected on the social power of money. It was represented by unscrupulous financiers, like Mr Merdle, who corrupted society, with the connivance of the complacent 'Circumlocution Office'. Debt, imprisonment, the corrupting power of money, and loneliness haunt the pages of *Little Dorrit*. Debt is the source and the symptom of deep unfairness, causing terrible collateral damage to families. The final marriage of Clennam with Little Dorrit offers a message about the redemption that can follow endurance.

The theme of the creative force of credit and its ambivalent moral effects is central to the work of Émile Zola, whose father's life had ended early in financial failure. Zola focused on the economic and social context of debt. Whilst acutely aware of the morally reprehensible aspects of financial speculation and credit expansion, he differed from Dickens in being less willing to condemn them. Zola saw them as an intrinsic part of human nature, eternally binding together creditors and debtors. The novel *La Curée* (*The Kill*, 1871) introduces the speculator Aristide Saccard, who values his wife chiefly in utilitarian terms. She is a means to open credit lines for him. Saccard reappears in *L'Argent* (*Money*, 1891) as the outcast bankrupt, hostile to Jewish bankers, who sets up his own bank, engages in fraudulent practices, and is eventually brought down by a Jewish banker. If often horrific and heartless, Saccard is equated by Zola with progress, energy, and fertility, even with a capacity for altruistic charity. He is charismatic and not without pity, paying off the debts of one of his employees. *L'Argent* also explores what debt does to the poor, reducing them to beggary, suicide, and prostitution. However, at the core of the book is the confrontation of two economic arguments, represented by the battle between two different kinds of financiers. The expansionist, credit-driven speculator is French. His arch-rival, who plots, calculates, and advises prudence, is Prussian. The Prussian wins. Nevertheless, the novel closes with the return of the Frenchman, who starts another speculative venture.

Zola was distinctive amongst novelists. He drew out the moral ambiguity in Saccard and the cyclical nature of creditor-debtor relations. Saccard rose, fell, and re-emerged. The personal sufferings of poor people in debt form a major theme in *Germinal* (1885), in which the miners buy food on credit. Their wives later kill the shopkeeper for his cruelty and the sexual payments he seeks from their daughters. In Zola's work, debt is at the root of the despair, sufferings, and indignation of the dispossessed. However, in contrast to Dickens, Zola presents these martyrs as the inevitable, tragic counterpart to the dynamic of social progress, of which greedy creditors like Saccard are a constituent part (Hemmings 1965).

In contrast, the theme of the ingenuity of the debtor was captured by Honoré de Balzac (1799–1850). His prolific writing on creditors and debtors reflected his own huge personal debts, which acted as a spur to his literary output. He was pursued for years by creditors, and only narrowly escaped debtors' prison. In Balzac's words: 'To be in debt means that you no longer belong to yourself. Other men call me to account for my life' (quoted in Robb 1994: 141). Balzac wrote from debt, about debt, and as a means to get out of debt, leaving a huge body of work.

The theme of 'money as power' was central to his multi-volume *La Comédie Humaine* (1830–1854), notably *Illusions Perdues* (*Lost Illusions*, 1843). The implications of debt for various young provincials were pictured as not just financial. They were, above all, moral. Debt sapped one's vital energy and ability to compete in a 'dog-eats-dog' world. Balzac's own life was mirrored in the contrast between greedy, unsympathetic creditors and suffering debtors. However, his debtors—unlike those of Dickens—were proud and ingenious. He took particular note of the message in the poet Charles Baudelaire's *How to Pay your Debts when You're a Genius* (Robb 1994: 47). Baudelaire too was enmeshed in debts, consequent on a flamboyant bohemian life style, and was the subject of continuous family censure.

The theme of the connection between generosity, gratitude, honour, and obligation binds together Shakespeare's treatment of credit and debt. Perhaps the most complete account of the ethical issues at the heart of the emotionally dramatic relations between creditors and debtors is to be found in Shakespeare's *The Merchant of Venice* (1596) and *Timon of Athens* (1605–1606). Shylock's painful progression from the proud creditor to shame and humiliation is used to point out the deep cynicism and lack of generosity that pervades Venetian society. It has grown wedded to the formal obligations of legal bonds. Shylock is a man of legal bonds. Shakespeare contrasts this merciless, impersonal world with the world of reciprocity and honour, in which gifts are given without conditions. Generosity expresses a spontaneous, worthy moral life. This life is strangled in a world of contracts, where it comes to appear naïve and innocent.

Timon of Athens explores this 'grace-gratitude' nexus in relation to the claims of monetary justice, again represented by legal bonds. The exiled and friendless Timon rages at the ingratitude of creditors who have, in the past, benefitted from his unconditional generosity. His creditors are 'devils'. They, and the Athenian law on debt under which he suffers, are shown as pitiless. Timon's faithful servant, Flavius, emerges as the one honest man, the moral spectator. He is the exploder of illusion, the truth-teller on debts, to whom Timon has not listened. Flavius proves, above all, capable of pity. The aftermath is bitter, for Timon and for Athens. Shakespeare seems to be suggesting that a voluntary suspension of legal obligations by creditors can, without inconsistency, be compatible with ethical obligation when motivated by generosity. He shows how the relations between creditors and debtors generate irreparable damage when just confined to enforcement of legal bonds. They require grace from the creditor and gratitude from the debtor. Shakespeare refuses to concede that Timon is simply naïve or foolish. His gaze is fixed on the sickness of society.

Sovereign Debt Crisis as Psycho-Drama

Adam Smith stressed that the baser emotions were more evident in adversity than in prosperity. Sovereign debt crisis is soon caught up in a chain reaction, starting with creditor concern, escalating into fear, and culminating in panic. The tipping point comes when fear shifts to panic, and events run out of control. The post-2010 Greek sovereign debt crisis and the Cypriot crisis from 2013 illustrated this process, with its attendant baser emotions, reflected for instance in Golden Dawn's extreme-Right politics and caricatures of Chancellor Merkel as Adolf Hitler. Similar chain reactions were apparent in post-1918 debates about German reparations and inter-Allied war debts. They figured dramatically in the unfolding post-1931 banking and sovereign debt crises (Ahamed 2010).

At such times state 'character' and national identity are at stake. Sovereign debt crises soon lead the main protagonists to attribute blame to each other, including as in Iceland using the courts. They camouflage their own failures. Accusations fly about 'improvident' and 'spendthrift' borrowers, 'reckless' lenders, 'careless' and 'complacent' regulators and supervisors, and 'cruel' foreign official creditors. Each protagonist seeks sympathy. Each provokes the anger and contempt of others. Resentment and threats of retribution mount.

Despite the image of rationality and technical prowess in which sovereign creditworthiness is enveloped, sovereign debt crises expose it as a world of raw emotions and intense psycho-dramas. They throw up powerful, emotionally charged politics. Scapegoats and vendettas figure in this process. The sovereign debt crises in the euro area's southern periphery from 2009 were associated with indignation towards Germany.

Sovereign debt crises provoke feelings of despair, fear, guilt, shame, and humiliation. The baser emotions spill over into populist, demagogic politics, which invokes images of 'colonization' and 'occupation' to characterize the process by which creditors impose conditionality on debtor states (Smith 2012). This language was common to the US South after 1865 and Greece after 2009. At the same time, governing elites in creditor states make increased efforts to differentiate themselves from fiscal and economic 'sinners'. This process helps to further poison inter-state relations. It also extends to intra-state relations. For instance, Lombardy distances itself from Sicily and Campania. Emotionally charged binary argument accompanies worsening economic times. A first casualty is Adam Smith's notion of the impartial spectator, who is able to sympathize and move debate onto a ground in which virtue can re-flourish.

The intense psycho-drama at times of sovereign debt crisis is bound up with national identity and pride. Jay Cooke's sales of huge amounts of 'national' bonds to help finance the Union cause in the US Civil War of 1861–1865 brought new popular pride in, and identity with, the Union (Oberholtzer 1907). In the immediate aftermath, Southern Democrats campaigned in highly emotional terms against honouring the new huge Union debt. They depicted Republican policy as the expression of *rentier* power at the expense of the poor. Post-war Republican campaigning focused successfully on the issue that electing the Democrats would lead to repudiation (Noll 2012: 6–8). For the Republicans the Union debt was 'sacred'. Its repudiation would be a 'national crime' (Foner 2002; Noll 2012). This post-Civil War debate about the public debt was a vital component in forging Union identity.

Emotionally charged politics is not just confined to sovereign debt crises. Governing elites use narratives about public debt to exploit powerful emotional attachments to symbols of shared public identity or to forge counter-identities. In eighteenth-century Ireland the new public debt became associated with the formation of an Anglo-Irish identity, based on who held Irish bonds. It was also linked to an Irish counter-narrative that Ireland was being 'overtaxed' to support costly English imperial ventures and the Anglo-Irish elite (Moore 2010).

The symbolic politics of sovereign debt crisis displays common features. Those on whom the costs of adjustment are inflicted seek agents to blame, domestic and foreign. The phenomenon of 'indignation' spread across the euro area's southern periphery from 2010, from Lisbon and Madrid to Athens and Nicosia. It was variously directed against the bond markets, the EU, the IMF, bankers, property and construction companies, and accountants and lawyers. Trust was eroded not just in national democratic capacity to manage debts but also in international financial institutions, EU institutions, and financial markets (European Social Survey 2013).

At the same time, this symbolic politics was historically conditioned in idiosyncratic ways. It was grounded in individual historical memories. Symbolic politics played out differently in Greece from Ireland; in Cyprus from Spain. They had their own specific historical reference points. In creditor states emotionally charged narratives revolve around claims to national 'exceptionalism'. In debtor states they concentrate on memories of colonial exploitation and national resistance. Greeks look back to Ottoman and German occupation, Germans to their own past sacrifices to re-establish their creditworthiness. Emotional reactions are bound up in perceived threats to cultural identity and pride.

These differences in symbolic worlds highlight the huge political difficulties associated with formalizing creditor-debtor relations within the EU. It is readily depicted as a twofold threat: the institutionalization of German power and the renunciation of domestic sovereignty and national identity. The political difficulties surfaced in the French elections and in the Greek elections of 2012, as well as in the Italian elections and in the Cypriot domestic crisis of 2013. Levels of political trust and satisfaction with democracy declined markedly in France, Ireland, Slovenia, and Spain. The decline reached alarming proportions in Greece. Britain, Belgium, Denmark, and Finland were also significantly affected (European Social Survey 2013).

Investors, financial journalists, and economic commentators are caught up in the emotions and psycho-dramas that infect the politics of sovereign debt crisis. Their incentive to form highly subjective 'character' judgements about states stems in part from radical uncertainty. They have to make immediate sense of confusing streams of data, fast-changing events, and news reporting. Interpreting crisis is made difficult by the opacity of debt, the lack of clarity about balance-sheet exposure, the vulnerability to manipulation of data, and the political uncertainties that surround the rise of social protest and political extremism.

The highly subjective character of market and journalist attitudes is captured in neurological and social cognition research on the significance of the unconscious mind. It suggests that behaviour is highly susceptible to imitative, herd-like behaviour. This type of research unmasks the illusions of rational control over attitudes and behaviour. It reveals the differences between what we think and what we do, between how we justify behaviour and what actually motivates behaviour.

As Chapter 2 shows, the deeper psychological world of credit and debt is more fully revealed in other literatures. Imaginative literature fleshes out the despair, indignity, dishonour, guilt, and humiliation associated with debt. In his psychoanalytical theory Sigmund Freud (1856–1939) examined how beliefs become illusory when motivated by wish-fulfilment and insusceptible of proof. His famous observation on religion might be applied to financial markets and to debt:

> Illusions commend themselves to us because they save us pain and allow us to enjoy pleasure instead. We must therefore accept it without complaint when they sometimes collide with a bit of reality against which they are dashed to pieces. (Freud 1927: 31)

Psychology went further in suggesting the attraction of this world of credit and debt to psychopaths. Hare (1993) argued that their 'mask of financial sanity' hides a lack of moral conscience, remorse, and empathy, a grandiose sense of self-worth, and crudely manipulative behaviour. Critical cultural theory, and the post-Freudian analysis on which it drew, focuses on the subversive impulses at work in financial markets, notably the death drive. Its exponents see financial markets as part of the 'libidinal' economy. Traders experience a powerful adrenalin rush from the sheer excitement of being caught up in reckless financial gambles and destruction. They take masochistic delight in waste, loss, and sacrifice (Crosthwaite 2010).

Many of these insights are deeply problematic and controversial, especially those that evade empirical substantiation. Even those that are empirical—like studies of psychopaths—encounter contestation about the clarity of their diagnostic criteria and about their appropriate use. Nevertheless, despite these problems, they attest to a 'shadow side' of credit and debt that remains hidden, secretive, difficult to access, and consciously disavowed. Credit-debtor relations possess a disposition to illusion and a pathological tendency that is not captured in economic and financial modelling.

The Reckless, the Feckless—And the Innocent

Creditors are prone to be seen as 'saints', debtors as 'sinners'. Virtue is attached to the former (prudence, hard work), vice to the latter (fecklessness, laziness). This kind of language puts at stake dignity, honour, and mutual respect. It arouses base as well as noble emotions, including resentment, grievance, and rage. The moral and emotional dimensions of debt are intimately intertwined.

Managing sovereign debt crisis has to be acutely sensitive to this powerful psychological dimension. Otherwise, those on the receiving end of punitive adjustments will mobilize in various ways to express their outrage. Building credibility in sovereign bond markets became mainstream in macroeconomic theory after the 1970s: what mattered for sovereign creditworthiness was management of market expectations (Kydland and Prescott 1977). A key element in this equation was always financial market psychology. States had to restore their credibility by increases in taxation, reductions in public-sector employment and wages, and benefit cuts. They had to align themselves with the technocratic nostrums of unelected bodies: central banks, international financial institutions, and financial market lobbies.

However, credibility in this narrow sense is only part of a much bigger and more complex political story about how states best sustain their reputation and power. The politics of sovereign creditworthiness is about the capacity to distinguish the legal contract governing creditor-debtor relations from the wider social contract on which governance is supposed to rest. Reputation in this broadest sense is lost once policies are seen to fail a wide range of social interests and any plausible connection to the notion of 'public' interest. The indicators of loss of creditor confidence are higher interest rates on debt. The indicators of loss of public confidence are social protest in its various forms, electoral gains for extremist parties, and the drift of centrist parties towards embrace of extremist positions. The demands of responsible statecraft in such circumstances are extremely onerous. They rest on constructing a convincing political discourse about the fair sharing of burdens and about investing in a better future. Organizing solidarity, making debt more productive, and taming financial market power remain the most difficult and elusive challenges facing states as they grapple with sovereign debt crisis. The solutions involve much more than the standard macroeconomic nostrums of 'credibility' and the 'quantitative engineering' of fiscal-deficit and public-debt reduction. They require the 'practical wisdom' advocated by Aristotle, the exercise of moral judgement that is contextual and proceeds in a case-by-case manner. Rigour resides in being able to make distinctions rather than in a single overarching way of thinking about debt problems.

Talking about creditors and debtors without implicit judgements about moral worth is very difficult. Creditor-state elites are open to harsh moral critique for their failure to act as responsible stewards of the system from which they benefit disproportionately. They risk hypocrisy in overlooking the role that their own reckless bankers play in creating moral hazard, for instance in mis-selling credit to the financially illiterate. Creditor-state elites can also be blamed for exposing debtor states to high risks of 'adjustment fatigue'. They can be held responsible for states becoming locked in a 'debt trap', in which lack of economic growth offers them no escape from their debt burdens. Above all, creditors need debtors.

Serious issues of fair burden-sharing arise when creditors are complicit in debtor-state problems. Their claims to a privileged position in determining domestic structural reforms and fiscal consolidation can provoke a sense of injustice. Creditors become further caught up in issues of fair burden-sharing as it becomes clear that innocent victims are bearing disproportionately the costs of adjustment. Sentiments of victimhood, indignation, and anger arise when individuals recognize that they are paying heavily for mistakes made by others and for which they bear no personal responsibility. Collateral damage to individuals and societies can be observed in statistics of poverty and deprivation, emigration, homelessness, chronic depression, and suicide.

Judgements about moral worth are even more complex in debtor states. Their governing elites and publics express resentment and anger about unfair burden-sharing. They also experience feelings of guilt and shame. Moreover, they face stigmatization by creditors as feckless, improvident, lazy, and lacking realism. Crisis makes visible the predatory and rent-seeking behaviour of their governing elites, which are accused of appropriating the wealth created by other people. The sovereignty of debtor states is abridged in the interests of their acquiring the virtues of thrift, industriousness, and responsibility that are attributed to creditor states. Institutional reforms are required to limit the scope for predatory behaviour. The very qualities that are attributed to debtor states make creditors unwilling to finance debtor-state adjustment, other than by official credits that enable them to buy time.

Managing sovereign debt crisis is, in consequence, a political problem of weighing the appropriate burdens to be born by 'the reckless', 'the feckless', and 'the innocent'. The problem is exacerbated in several ways. It is difficult to delineate who are the reckless, the feckless, and the innocent. They also have highly differential access to state power, which shapes what is done to whom. Those adversely affected differ in their capacity to escape the territorial boundaries of the state, by capital flight or by migration. Dealing with the problem of fair burden-sharing is made more difficult by the entrenched power of rent-seekers. It is compounded by the lack of clear, agreed boundaries between the 'predatory' and the 'productive' activity of creditors. Against this background, the loss of sovereign creditworthiness has the capacity to radically destabilize states and the weak institutional infrastructure of European and global economic governance.

Part I

Debt and Political Rule in European History

4

The Evolution of Public Debt

Men can do nothing without the make-believe of a beginning.
George Eliot, *Daniel Deronda* (1876: 1)

The complex historical shift from personal creditworthiness of the ruler to sovereign creditworthiness was integral to European state building. It was associated with the development of the idea and practice of the impersonal, professionalized 'fiscal state', in particular 'public' debt. In the larger territorial states of the late-medieval and early-modern periods, debt financing principally took the form of short-term, opportunistic borrowing by rulers from a narrow circle of international merchant-financiers. However, at an earlier date, debt financing evolved into new forms in the city states of Europe, gradually spreading to the larger territorial states. Rulers sought to establish more secure, longer-term borrowing from a broader social stratum of *rentiers*. They came to depend on the professional management of a consolidated public debt.

A defining feature of personal creditworthiness was high interest rates for rulers. Merchant-financiers feared currency debasement, coercive financial repression, and default by dynastically ambitious, avaricious, and often fearful territorial rulers. In contrast, public debt was associated with lower interest rates. They reflected greater confidence that debt contracts would be honoured. How, why, and when did this shift in the relationship between debt and political rule occur? What insight does it shed on 'who writes debt history'?

Creditor-debtor relations became more depersonalized and formalized as a widening social stratum of *rentiers* sought institutional reforms that would diminish the scope for financial repression by rulers. The process took the form of building state capacity through the professionalization of public finances. This professionalization involved robust tax regimes that ensured predictable revenues to service debts; more efficient and effective centralized spending controls; and, not least, new mechanisms for fiscal accountability and transparency. Sovereign creditworthiness came to be seen as dependent on strengthening state capacity to legally enforce contracts, to extract taxes, to manage investment in infrastructure, and to retain legitimacy through consent.

The history of the idea and practice of public debt reveals the limitations of both territorial state-centric and Anglo-centric accounts. Its history looks very different from the angle of a critical questioning of teleological narratives of debt history. It is important to ask: who writes debt history? The history of public debt reveals the importance of the sub-national angle and of continental European developments. It also uncovers the uncertainties and the multiple possible trajectories and outcomes within debt history. The development of public debt was bound up with the deeply entrenched and widespread nature of rent-seeking behaviour. It shows the protracted hostility to the professionalization of public finances.

At the same time, it is possible to discern connecting threads in European history. In late-medieval continental Europe city states were showcases of the rising power of the *rentier* class and the use of new debt financing instruments. Similarly, sub-national fiscal governance remained a key issue in European sovereign debt in the twenty-first century. The privileges and power of early city-based merchant-financier families—like the Ricciardi, the Bardi, the Medici, and the Fugger—were echoed in the House of Rothschild in the nineteenth century and in global investment banks like Barclays, Deutsche Bank, and BNP Paribas in the early twenty-first century. Perhaps most striking of all, the fast-changing forms of debt financing coexisted with the continuity of a small world of social connections: the private governance of public debt.

Borrowing Capacity: The Archimedes' Principle that Drives the World

> Finances are the nerves of the state... [this] is the Archimedes' principle that drives the world.
>
> Cardinal-Duc de Richelieu (1585–1642), *Testament politique* (Bonney 1981: vii), translated by the author.

From the Greek city states to modern state building, borrowing capacity has remained fundamental to political rule in Europe. It has shaped the way in which institutional structures of rule have evolved. Both governing competence and political legitimacy are bound up with the capacity to borrow, on favourable terms, above all to strengthen external security and to realize bold foreign policy ambitions. Borrowing capacity marks out certain rulers as 'special' in national and European histories. They include King Edward I and King Edward III of England; the Holy Roman Emperor Charles V; King Francis I of France; King Philip II of Spain; Augustus II the Strong, Elector of Saxony and King of Poland; and Frederick the Great of Prussia (cf. Bell, Brooks, and Moore 2009; Hunt 1990; Carande 1987; Ehrenberg 1963; Hamon 1994; Alvarez-Nogal and Chamley 2011; Bürgelt 2007). Each was, in his own way, and if only temporarily, a European master of creditworthiness.

A common thread bound together such unlikely bedfellows as Edward I of England, fifteenth-century Florence, Philip II's Spain, the seventeenth-century Papacy, pre-Revolutionary France, eighteenth-century Britain, and the Hapsburg Empire in the nineteenth century. Their annual debt servicing costs amounted to some 40–60 per cent of tax revenues or more. This type of ratio was above those incurred by the European states at the epicentre of the early twenty-first-century sovereign debt crisis (Bell, Brooks, and Moore 2009; Molho 1971; Carboni 2012; Alvarez-Nogal and Chamley 2011; Bonney 1981;

Brewer 1989). In 1427, on the verge of Renaissance greatness, Florence had debt servicing costs that equalled its total annual revenues. This burden was well in excess of the approximately 60 per cent borne by France on the eve of its Revolution in 1789 (Molho 2006: 37; Keyder 1985: 309). The greater creditworthiness of the Florentine Republic, the seventeenth-century Papacy, and eighteenth-century Britain shows that comparisons of objective debt data hide a more important story about stronger and weaker state capacity and about variations in political willingness and incentives to comply.

Otto von Bismarck, Prussian and later Imperial German Chancellor, based his strategy for securing Prussian leadership of German unification on securing a creditworthiness that exceeded that of the Hapsburg Empire. Careful and detailed fiscal planning, above all the financial support of leading banks, preceded Prussian military victories over the Hapsburg Empire in 1866 and over France in 1870. Bankers were intimately involved in laying the foundations of the new German Empire in 1871 (Stern 1978). A model was at hand in the reputation of the British 'fiscal-military' state. British engagement in successive, hugely costly wars and empire-building in the eighteenth century, and then against Napoleon's France, had demonstrated the vital importance of capacity to raise huge public debts, without provoking investor fears of default (Brewer 1989).

As the Roman Senator Cicero had written in his *Philippics*: 'endless money forms the sinews of war' (Bonney 1981; Hamon 1994). This insight was not lost on Cardinal Richelieu, France's Chief Minister (1624–1642) and architect of her rise to power after the destructive sixteenth-century wars of religion. It also inspired King Francis I of France (r. 1510–1547) in fighting his costly Italian wars against Charles V. Like the Emperor Charles V, Francis I and Richelieu—and later Bismarck—strove to be the European masters of debt financing. Francis I sought to use Crown loans at high interest rates to build up Lyon as a European financial centre. He aimed to rival the Hapsburg Emperor's Antwerp by attracting rich Italian and south German merchant-financiers (Hamon 1994). Using debt financing as an instrument for building French financial power promised a new, if elusive, virtuous circle of cheap, plentiful credit and tame merchant-financiers.

Conversely, Prince Metternich's cautious balance-of-power policy of working with and through a 'Concert of Europe' was influenced by the catastrophic fiscal position of the Hapsburg Empire after the Napoleonic Wars. With a public debt almost ten times annual revenues in 1825, it was unable to field a credible army. Even without a major international crisis over the previous 30 years, some 25 per cent of the Austrian budget was accounted for by debt servicing in 1847. The combination of Metternich's sophisticated diplomacy with huge financial support from the Rothschild Vienna office could not disguise the vulnerability of the Hapsburg Empire. It lacked the fast-growing state capacity of Prussia.

The Contingency of Creditworthiness: The Economy, War, and Social Connections

Historical reputation as 'strong' or 'weak', 'virtuous' or 'vice-prone', is intimately associated with the reputation of political rulers as creditors or debtors. Kings Philip II

Augustus (r. 1179–1223) and Louis IX (Saint Louis, r. 1226–1270) continue to be linked with the image of a fiscally virtuous France. Their virtue derives from simultaneously leading Crusades to liberate the Holy Land, avoiding onerous forced loans, and strengthening the currency (Baldwin 1986; Goff 1996). In contrast, the image of the fiscally 'harsh' France of King Philip IV (r. 1285–1314) and King Henry III (r. 1574–1589) is associated with profligate debts, currency debasements, and punitive financial repression (de la Torre 2010; Bonney 1981).

This difference in images of France draws out the close historical association of creditworthiness with benign economic circumstances. They facilitate social peace and the strengthening of state capacity. Conversely, economic 'hard' times contribute to weakening of state capacity and willingness to pay. Economic distress is linked with threats to social peace and prolonged, often indeterminate wars. It increases incentives for rulers to engage in fiscal opportunism and repression of creditors and to forge dubious social connections with ambitious and unscrupulous lawyers and financiers for this purpose. It brings out the less pleasant underlying realities of power.

Hence creditworthiness helps define the character and reputation of political rulers as trustworthy and virtuous and their places in history and in the hierarchy of European states. First and foremost, it is bound up with underlying economic structure and dynamics, over which rulers have little or no control. Their room for manoeuvre is defined by relative economic size and growth; by position in international trade routes; by access to natural resources, like fertile land and precious commodities; and by the condition of household and corporate balance sheets. Rulers are embedded in long- and short-run economic cycles. They are differentially exposed to external shocks that have profound implications for their fiscal capacity and creditworthiness. The state capacity and willingness to pay on which creditworthiness hinges is in this sense contingent rather than an historical given.

The contingency of creditworthiness is further apparent in war. Historically, war has proved the major driver of resort to huge debt financing, whilst success in war—if not bought at too high a cost—has been the major determinant of effective state building and creditworthiness. The Richelieu-inspired French wars against Hapsburg Austria and Spain saw an almost twentyfold increase in royal loans between 1635 and 1645. Their size contracted in the wake of subsequent French victories, which served to enable French state-capacity building (Bonney 1981, 1999).

However, war is also fraught with risk of setbacks, defeat, and crippling war indemnities. The legacy of Louis XIV's involvement in the War of the Spanish Succession (1701–1714) was French bankruptcy and loss of the material basis for French super-power ambitions in Europe. The French government resorted to desperate expedients to raise money, handing power to financiers and royal contractors who ran the fiscal system to their own advantage (Rowlands 2012). More dramatically still, hefty indemnities were suffered by Austria and Prussia in 1805–1807; France in 1817–1818 and in 1871; and Germany after 1918. Conversely, military victories can generate creditworthiness. Bismarck's military successes against the Hapsburg Empire and the French Second Empire radically transformed Prussian creditworthiness between 1860 and 1871 (Stern 1978).

The contingencies of almost continuous war marked Napoleonic France. Because of the lack of credibility of the earlier Revolutionary governments, Napoleon lacked a strong inherited financial capacity to raise long-term credit. Banking panic broke out in Paris in 1805 after defeat in the Battle of Trafalgar. It created fear that the new Banque de France would be forced into liquidation. The mood was suddenly reversed once news arrived that the Emperor Napoleon Bonaparte had prevailed against Austria and Russia at the Battle of Austerlitz. This episode confirmed Napoleon's hostility to financiers. He used the large Austrian war indemnity to bolster the capital of the Banque de France. The central bank was brought firmly under the umbrella of the state so that it could better facilitate the state's ability to borrow (Plessis 2002). Nevertheless, up to his disastrous Russian campaign in 1812, Napoleon relied on victories to prevent financial troubles, along with arrears in making payments. Public debt grew only from 40 million *rentes* in 1799 to 63 million in 1814.

The 'Hundred Days', following Napoleon's return from exile in 1815, and ending in defeat at the Battle of Waterloo, proved the most expensive in French history (Branda 2007). Faced by creditors who had lost confidence consequent on payment arrears, Napoleon turned—as a last expedient—to a forced loan, as well as to issuing bonds and Treasury bills. The outcome of the short glory of the 'Hundred Days' was an increase of more than fivefold in French public debt (Cyr 2010). The creditworthiness of France in 1815 was radically different from that in 1805–1812. Waterloo, and the Allied occupying army in 1815–1818, can be seen as a structural break in French public finances, forcing domestic reforms by an elite that sought to emulate British practices (Oosterlinck, Ureche-Rangau, and Vaslin 2013).

The reputation of rulers is also bound up with the character of the creditors, and intermediaries to creditors, with whom they associate and on whom they depend. Henry VIII of England was less creditworthy to German and Italian bankers than the Emperor Charles V. His employment of the English merchant, Stephen Vaughan, as his financial agent in the Low Countries was decisive for English royal finances (Richardson 1953: 50). Vaughan's reputation stemmed from his central role in the important English wool and cloth trade. Because Antwerp was part of the Empire, Vaughan—like later Thomas Gresham under Elizabeth I—had to reassure the Hapsburg Emperor that English borrowing would not negatively affect his own credit. The skills of Gresham and Vaughan in combining finance, diplomacy, and political intelligence-gathering were vital for the creditworthiness of Tudor monarchs. Similarly, in the fifteenth and sixteenth centuries Ottoman Sultans and Pashas exploited to their advantage the expulsion of Jews, above all from Spain. They brought with them, above all to Salonica, family and business connections that extended across the Mediterranean. The Nasi-Mendes family became the most important financiers to Ottoman Sultans and Pashas in the sixteenth century (Epstein 1980).

Conversely, sovereign creditworthiness suffers from dubious connections. The Salonica-based merchant John 'Jackie' Abbott earned the nickname 'King of the Leeches'. During the mid-nineteenth century, this Levantine businessman with British nationality became chief money lender to Sadik Pasha, whose total income was estimated at less than half the annual interest he owed (Mazower 2005: 155). The result was large-scale extortion and plunder under the Salonica governor. Salonica's Greek Metropolitan, leading military figures, as well as landed estates and villages, were caught up in Abbott's web of extortionate credit. The reputation of the Ottoman government suffered accordingly, at a time when foreign creditors were beginning to demand major fiscal and economic reforms.

Another notorious example was the mysterious Swedish 'Match King', Ivar Kreuger, who had a reputation for manipulating balance sheets and for his forgery of Italian bonds. Nicknamed 'Saviour of Europe', he emerged in the 1920s as a prolific financier of less creditworthy states, in return for being granted highly lucrative privileges of match monopoly (Partnoy 2009). This association reflected badly on the character of the beneficiaries. They included Greece (1926 and 1931), Hungary (1928), Poland (1925 and 1930), Romania (1930), Turkey (1930), and Yugoslavia (1928). Kreuger's biggest loans went to the French government in 1927 and the German government in 1929. They reflected the dire financial circumstances of these states (Ahamed 2010: 340–1). By 1932 Kreuger's loans to European states amounted to some \$6 billion, in 1998 prices. He committed suicide in 1932, leaving huge undisclosed losses and precipitating a financial crisis in Sweden.

In contrast, loan negotiations with Thomas Lamont of the House of Morgan, the post-1918 US financial emissary par excellence, conferred a superior branding on European states. He had served on the US reparations team at the Paris Peace Conference, was a major figure in the Dawes Plan and the Young Plan, and provided Benito Mussolini with legitimacy by arranging a large loan to Italy in 1926 (Chernow 1990). In a similar way, past rulers derived prestige by securing loans from the Ricciardi in the thirteenth century, the Bardi and the Peruzzi in the fourteenth century, the Medici when banker to the Papacy in the fifteenth century, the Fugger and the Genoese bankers in the sixteenth century, Hope and Co. of Amsterdam in the eighteenth century, and the House of Rothschild in the nineteenth century. The prestige of the Hapsburgs in Germany, Bohemia, and Hungary was linked to Jacob and Anton Fugger to such an extent that the period 1490–1560 has been labelled 'the Age of the Fugger'. They financed the election of Charles V as Holy Roman Emperor and of his brother Ferdinand I of Austria as King of Hungary and Bohemia and King of Rome (Carande 1987; Ehrenberg 1963).

Connections remain the lifeblood of debt finance and creditworthiness. Rulers continuously seek prestige by association with elite bankers, just as financiers pursue social recognition, status, and related commercial and financial advantages from their proximity to rulers. It is a symbiotic, even incestuous relationship. Bankers stand to suffer when they lose the confidence of rulers. They lose commercial and financial privileges as well as the allure that attaches to proximity to power. The Emperor Charles V severed contacts with the Welser merchant house of Augsburg over their association with large loans to King Francis I of France in Lyon (Ehrenberg 1963: 144–6). He contributed to their eventual collapse in 1614 (Häberlein and Burckhardt 2002).

Other, more dubious financiers and intermediaries succeeded in surviving repeated malpractice and scandal because of their value to rulers. Henry VII of England relied on his intimate relationship to the lawyer Edmund Dudley to manage his contacts to merchant-financiers in the City of London, notably to the Frescobaldi of Florence and the Grimaldi of Genoa. These Italian financiers were central to the conduct of his expensive financial diplomacy, which was designed to place his new Tudor dynasty at the heart of European politics through an Anglo-Hapsburg alliance (Penn 2011: 159–70). Domestically, Dudley evolved the complex arts of coercive financial repression, employing his legal expertise on sovereign prerogative to pursue 'extraordinary justice'. Evidence of wrongdoings, often based in informers, was used to bind individuals to the king through onerous financial bonds as a form of punishment (Penn 2011: 261–3).

Dudley remained a loyal servant, attuned to royal avarice and insecurity. However, rapid revenge was exacted on him on the king's death.

Similarly, the Italian Gaspar Ducci was the most important financial agent of the Emperor Charles V in Antwerp, working for the Brussels court. Charles V protected Ducci, who was deeply unpopular in Antwerp, because of his repeated success in raising large, low-cost loans. However, his protection ended once Ducci became implicated in helping raise finance in Lyon to support the French King Francis I, the Emperor's enemy (Carande 1987). Connections, their perpetuation, and their abrupt termination, illustrated the capacity of rulers to invoke their authority to define tolerable behaviour in debt financing. They could use financial repression to set boundaries.

Why Public Debt Financing?

The development of public debt, and the associated professionalization of public finances, stemmed from the combination of new incentives to mobilize large-scale debt financing with the perennial extravagance of rulers in their egoistic, often vain pursuit of fame, glory, and magnificence. Debt financing offered opportunities to indulge illusion and hubris. The incentives to develop public debt operated on the 'pull' and 'push' sides of public finances.

On the 'pull' side, there was the growth in expectations of political rule as a wider range of social forces entered public life. This change began with the spread of inherited wealth and the claims of *rentiers* to share in political power. It spread as industrialization opened up new demands for welfare and further claims to share in political power through franchise extension. In the wake of industrialization, rulers were beset with new fiscal challenges of maintaining social peace, notably in provisioning fast-growing urban centres. Another 'pull' factor was the increasing costs of new military technologies and maintaining large, permanent armies. In addition, inter-state competition for power began to focus on the rising resource requirements of infrastructure provision and industrial development. It became essential to establish a strong position in long-distance trade. Place in the hierarchy of European states depended on capacity to mobilize and employ credit on a new, huge scale.

On the 'push' side, a growing class of merchant-financiers were creative in devising new credit instruments. Also, rulers could make use of new, more expensive transport and communication technologies to enhance their capacity to extend fiscal control over greater geographic distances. Larger territorial states were better able to reduce and eliminate their comparative disadvantage over smaller city states in financing debts.

The combination of these incentives with the lure of public display and magnificence highlighted a paradox of power. On the one hand, it exposed the limitations of taxation as an instrument of political rule. On the other, it highlighted the vital importance of efficient tax collection and predictable tax revenues for servicing debt and securing creditworthiness. In the late-medieval and early-modern periods, taxation posed difficult political challenges. Rulers operated in highly decentralized, fragmented fiscal systems. However absolutist their claims to rule, they depended on the consent of powerful, often recalcitrant nobles, clergy, city burghers, and provincial elites, each with their own vested financial interests. This paradox made debt financing both more attractive and more difficult. It created an incentive to escape from the paradox through reforms to embed fiscal centralization and professionalize public finances.

Securing creditworthiness was inherently problematic in the face of the proliferation of rent-seeking and its negative effects on state capacity and willingness to pay creditors. In sixteenth-century France and Spain, and in the Ottoman Empire, the privatization of tax collection through 'tax farming' meant dependence on privileged private interests. They pursued their own personal profit in venal, often corrupt ways and deprived the central treasury of much tax revenue (Bonney 1981; Drelichman 2005; Karaman and Pamuk 2010: 609). Low state taxation capacity translated into limited creditworthiness and vulnerability to military defeats and internal rebellions, illustrated in the Ottoman Empire from the 1760s and in nineteenth-century Spain. Tax farming was converted into a form of domestic borrowing. Tax revenues were used as collateral by rulers, so that—perversely—rulers paid interest on public funds. Hence tax revenue itself became a short-term credit system for rulers.

Tax policies had further perverse effects on state capacity, willingness to pay, and sovereign creditworthiness. In Spain the Crown combined the raising of taxes to pay large, short-term debts with the granting of tax and other privileges. In consequence, hard-pressed merchants resorted to the courts to obtain an *hidalguía*. They fabricated evidence and bribed judges and witnesses for the purpose. *Hidalgos* possessed a lower nobility title, gained exemption from direct taxes, and enjoyed various legal, political, and social privileges (Drelichman 2005). The result was perverse in two ways: the burden of higher taxes to service debts was borne more unequally; and commercial activity lost social and economic status. In the Ottoman Empire, gaining access to government tax revenues through lifetime tax farming under the *malikane* system (1695–1840s) became more lucrative than investing in agriculture, trade, or manufacturing (Pamuk 2009: 23). Tax farming remained at the roots of the endemic weaknesses of the Ottoman Empire up to its demise. It lacked the capacity to service its debts.

A key inducement to reliance on debt financing was the volatility of tax revenues. They varied not just with economic wealth but also cyclically with phases of economic expansion, stagnation, and decline. As we saw earlier, tax revenues were influenced by whether rulers governed fertile land, had secure access to valuable commodities (including gold and silver), and occupied a favourable spatial location in European and global trade routes. In the case of the Emperor Charles V, these advantages offered financiers like the Fugger evidence of creditworthiness. However, crises of tax revenue emerged when the ambitions of rulers, and perceived threats to security, were not synchronized with an expansionary phase in the economic cycle. In seeking to wage wars in 1294–1297, Edward I of England was confronted by an economic downturn that adversely affected his existing creditors, above all the Ricciardi of Lucca (Blomquist 2005). He was forced to pay much higher rates of interest to new moneylenders (Bell, Brooks, and Moore 2009).

This combination of the uncertain, volatile, and privatized character of taxation with new pressures to increase expenditures and the ambitions, fears, and paranoia of rulers created strong inducements to resort to innovations in debt financing. Initially, rulers sought to manage their cash-flow problems by turning on an ad hoc, private basis to rich, cross-nationally active merchant-financiers. They were concentrated in northern

Italy, south Germany, Antwerp, and Holland: the Ricciardi, the Bardi, the Peruzzi, the Medici, the Fugger, and the Welser. However, rulers sought to reduce this external debt dependency when confronted with some combination of economic distress, rising costs of war, and weakened state capacity. They turned to strategies for cultivating domestic sources of private debt financing, including large annuity loans contracted with their cities. Alternatively, they engaged in currency debasements and other means of punishing creditors, including seizure of assets. King Henry VIII of England resorted flexibly to all these strategies at one time or another.

More importantly for the long term, territorial rulers began to experiment with developing consolidated, longer-term 'public' debt. They used as models the north Italian, Flemish, and Dutch city states. A milestone was the 'Great Loan' of 1555 by King Henry II (r. 1548–1559) of France, negotiated in Lyon. Based on the principle of public subscription, this innovation created a wider range of stakeholders in the efficacy of political rule. Financing 'public' debt by the larger territorial states laid the basis for the emergence of a set of new powerful financial centres across Europe: Antwerp, Lyon, Amsterdam, and London. Above all, the development of public debt was rooted in the evolution of a *rentier* class. Its members represented inherited wealth. They had a vested interest in secure long-term rates of return on sovereign investment and the honouring of debt contracts. They pursued this interest by advocating new forms of political representation, institutional accountability, transparency, and professionalized public finances. This shift in the balance of social forces changed the character of European states and the institutional forms of political rule.

The Changing Relationship between Debt and Political Rule

Historical analysis of the rise of public debt faces the problem that it is not possible to fix definitively 'the' date of its birth. Different dates have been assigned to individual states: for instance, 1689 for England and 1789 for France. However, fixing these dates is more symbolic than very helpful in capturing the complex dynamics. It is about the need for the make-believe of a beginning.

In reality, a variety of old and new political, institutional, and social arrangements coexisted awkwardly in eighteenth-century Britain and the United Provinces, as well as in nineteenth-century France. Moreover, European history provides a vast, evolving kaleidoscope of evolving fiscal forms. Hence, it is more useful to speak of the histories rather than 'the' history of European public debt.

Writing historically about public debt faces the added danger of teleological explanation, in which rulers are understood to be motivated by a purpose or to serve a function. Teleological explanation assumes a design at work in the development of debt financing. It tends to take the present as the fixed point of reference from which to offer 'the' authoritative reading of how public debt evolved. The consequence is underestimation of the historically complex relationship of debt to political rule. Insufficient attention is paid to the constraints posed by vested interests and to the multiple possibilities at any point in time.

The varying ways in which debt has been constructed and managed across space and over time reflects complex, ongoing changes in the balance between various social and political interests: rulers, their central bureaucracies, intermediary bodies like cities and provincial elites, merchant-financiers (later professional bankers), and other influential social groups like lawyers. The idea of the abstract, impersonal state, and earlier of absolute monarchy or republican city government, conceals much more complex social worlds. These worlds comprised personal networks, patronage relationships, and private negotiations. Public debt has not one, but multiple histories, each with its own paradoxes. Perhaps the most striking paradox is continuity in the 'private management of public debt'. It has provided a cloak for 'crony' capitalism and rent-seeking, for the atrophy of public virtue, and for debasement of the ideals of the abstract, impersonal state and representative democracy.

Geo-strategic, technological, economic, social, and political changes have shaped and complicated the long and complex history of the role of debt in political rule. History offers a fascinating insight into how these factors have led to differences in representations and practices of debt across space and over time. They have had profound effects on conceptualizations of creditworthiness. External threat was a major factor in why what was considered 'appropriate' public debt levels were much higher in fifteenth-century Florence and in European states from the First World War to the 1960s than in early-twenty-first-century European states. History reveals the power of context to change notions of 'normal' debt. It helps us to step outside the limitations of absorption in the present, including highly time-limited contemporary debt sustainability analysis. History offers the possibility of teasing out longer-term patterns by examining Classical Greece and Rome, Carolingian Europe, late-medieval and early-modern Europe, and nineteenth-century Europe. Above all, it illustrates how thin the line is between, on the one hand, political ambition and, on the other, illusion, hubris, and vanity in public affairs.

Historical changes in the relationship between debt and political rule reflect the complex interplay of four key factors: the widening territorial scale of capacity for fiscal control; professional and institutional innovation, growth, and maturity; changing social forces; and longer-term shifts in economic structure and in economic cycles. Each has in its own way affected state capacity, willingness to pay, and creditworthiness. Rulers and governing elites operated with more or less imperfect knowledge and understanding of these processes and how to master them. Yet, however fallible their grip on these structural dynamics, they often possessed more awareness of the significance of money and debt finances for political rule than many professional historians.

Overcoming Distance

There has been a slow historic shift in comparative fiscal advantage in mastering distance and thereby in strengthening state capacity, willingness to pay, and creditworthiness. This shift led to the gradual displacement of fiscal power from the European city states of late-medieval and early-modern Europe to the larger territorial states. Public debt financing techniques evolved more rapidly in the city states of northern Italy, Flanders, and the Hanseatic League. At the root of their comparative fiscal advantage were the enormously high transaction costs of transport and communications (Stasavage

2010). Covering distances was expensive in time and energy. It involved slow unreliable transport, local barriers to travel and, not least, risks from armed gangs and from plague. Transaction costs privileged smaller geographically compact states over larger territories. It explains the superior creditworthiness of Athens in the Ancient World, of Venice over the Byzantine Empire, and later of Holland over France.

Capacity for control of fiscal policies to ensure debt servicing was initially easier to establish in geographically compact city states, where creditors were able to establish powerful positions in city parliaments (Stasavage 2011). For this reason the most creditworthy states in late-medieval Europe were the north Italian city states like Florence, Genoa, and Venice, the cities of Flanders and northern France, and Hanseatic cities such as Hamburg. Similarly, the provincial estates of France sought to discipline the public finances of the royal court, which lacked effective national accountability and transparency. Distance proved a much greater problem for securing fiscal accountability and transparency in larger territorial states like France, the Hapsburg Empire, and Russia. They were also more likely than city states to practise serial, aggressive currency debasements and defaults (Chilosi and Volckart 2010).

From the thirteenth century onwards centralizing territorial rulers sought to offset their comparative fiscal disadvantage by borrowing from their cities. They used the superior creditworthiness of cities to issue debt and raise taxes for debt servicing. Rulers emulated the north Italian city states in France, Hapsburg Spain, the Burgundian and Hapsburg Low Countries, and many German principalities of the Holy Roman Empire. They employed their own cities as creditworthy intermediaries in the sale of lifetime, or perpetual, redeemable annuities (*rentes, juros*) (Boone, Davids, and Jannssens 2003; Ehrenberg 1963: 41–6). Similarly, the eight city *parlements* of early modern France proved more effective instruments of fiscal control than the royal administration (Stasavage 2003).

By substantially lowering transaction costs, technological changes in communications and transport reduced the comparative fiscal advantage of city states. They enabled larger territorial states, empires, and later multilateral institutions to increase their capacity to control public finances (cf. Innis 1950; Stasavage 2010). Road building had been decisive for the more integrative fiscal capacity of the Roman Empire than its Hellenistic imperial predecessors. Similarly, the invention of printing in the 1460s started a process of the financial, fiscal, and political integration of larger geographic spaces. It facilitated the wider distribution of financial information, the spread of financial literacy, the dissemination of new accountancy practices, and the gradual emergence of pan-European financial centres like Antwerp and Amsterdam (Chilosi and Volckart 2010).

By the eighteenth century larger territorial states, led by Britain, were able to evolve more effective institutional structures to exert control over public finances, including parliamentary assumptions of responsibility for public debts. It became possible to erect bigger, more expensive fiscal-military states, whilst simultaneously enjoying higher borrowing, lower interest rates, and reduced risk of sovereign default. The precondition was that states either stayed out of wars or emerged as military victors and empire builders.

From the middle of the nineteenth century steamships, railways, and later the telegraph and cable transformed the capacity of bankers to rapidly mobilize larger-scale cross-national borrowing. These developments enabled banks like the House of Rothschild to manage efficient, cross-national letter and courier services, which gave them and their clients a crucial information advantage (Gille 1965). In the twentieth century, automobiles, air transport, telephone communications, and later digital communications, via cable and satellite, offered opportunities for an even more radical conquering of distance. The 'space-time' world of European central bankers like Montagu Norman, Émile Moreau, and Hjalmar Schacht in the 1920s was very different from that of Mervyn King at the Bank of England and Mario Draghi at the European Central Bank in the 2000s. At the same time, this new age of electronic money and cyber-finance opened up new challenges to state capacity and creditworthiness. There was an increasing mismatch between the still-protracted domestic and European timescales of fiscal policy and the extreme 'space-time' compression in financial markets. Governing elites were acutely sensitive to twenty-four-hour, digitally transmitted 'news' that impacted on sovereign creditworthiness.

Gradually, from the nineteenth century, this overcoming of distance facilitated the emergence of a more formalized and depersonalized system of European and international creditor-debtor state relations. An early manifestation was the integration of financiers like the Barings and the House of Rothschild into European congress diplomacy after 1815. They became intimately involved in financing war indemnities, notably those of France in 1817 and 1871. They also helped manage the financial aspects of the 'Eastern Question', above all Ottoman, Greek, and Bulgarian debts (Ziegler 1988; Clay 2000; Stern 1978; Wynne 1951). This period witnessed the emergence of ad hoc, case-by-case bondholder committees and, later, permanent bondholder organizations. They became highly active in lobbying states for action to protect creditors against sovereign defaults (Esteves 2007; Wynne 1951). However, the interwar League of Nations and, from 1930, the Bank for International Settlements (BIS) lacked the institutional and financial capacity to play an active role in managing the wave of sovereign defaults and to act as lender of last resort as the Great Depression took hold. A more robust—if still imperfect—multilateral infrastructure emerged from 1944 onwards. Continuing progress in communication and transport technologies were enormously important in facilitating the work of the International Monetary Fund (IMF), the World Bank, and the evolving structures of European financial and monetary integration.

The most important consequence of improvements in communication and transport technologies was the capacity of banks to increase the scale, depth, and complexity of their operations. They made possible the emergence of global mega-conglomerates, universal both in geographic spread and in range of services. On the one hand, states gained from the increased capacity of bankers to mobilize rapidly cross-national syndicated loans. The beginnings of this process were apparent with the House of Rothschild. Its organizational mastery of communication services, allied to networks of local agents, was vital in establishing intimate and privileged 'relationship' banking with a range of European states. European states could borrow on a new, continent-wide scale (Gille: 187). On the other hand, states faced higher stakes in retaining their credibility with bankers. Their incentives to build state fiscal capacity grew. Also, the issue of bank size dwarfing the gross domestic product (GDP) of European states posed new challenges. In their efforts to attract financial assets through light-touch regulation and low taxes, states faced the risk of becoming trapped within an unsustainable business model. This risk was evident in Iceland and Ireland in 2008 and in Cyprus in 2013.

Professional and Institutional Capacity

The capacity to extend territorial mastery of debt financing and to develop public debt was closely linked to the gradual growth and dissemination of professional public accountancy from the fifteenth century. Public accountancy offered to centralizing rulers a new social technology of knowledge, power, and control in state capacity building (Miller 1990).

Late-medieval financial accounts had taken the rudimentary form of single-entry book keeping. This technique suited simple financial operations, involving low volumes of borrowing activity. Single-entry book keeping allowed only limited centralized fiscal control. Its advantage for monarchs and merchant-financiers was the ease with which financial transactions and data could be omitted, the difficulties in checking for errors, and the opportunity to conceal illicit operations, theft, and corruption (Jones 2010). For this reason, monarchs like Henry VII of England sometimes took a detailed personal interest in the 'management' of their accounts (Penn 2011: 156–7). Single-entry book keeping was staunchly defended by private tax farmers and receivers, who benefited financially from fiscal opacity, for instance in France (Bonney 1981). Its continued use in large territorial states well into the eighteenth century, and beyond, reflected the social and political power of these vested interests. Single-entry book keeping was adapted to revenue collection as a private business and to widespread financial and fiscal concealment, mendacity, and trickery (Lemarchand 2010).

In contrast, double-entry book keeping required that each financial transaction be recorded twice: as credit and as debit. It provided a superior, more transparent error-detection accounting system and instrument of financial control. Double-entry book keeping evolved from the early fourteenth century in the north Italian city states, where it was first professionally codified by the end of the fifteenth century. Its use spread to Antwerp and to the United Provinces, and from there to England and Sweden in the seventeenth century. This process of dissemination coincided with a displacement of power from private tax collectors to professional centralized fiscal administrations, staffed by trained competent public officials. The spread of double-entry book keeping coincided with the rise to political power of a new *rentier* class, which demanded an accountable and transparent fiscal state.

France illustrates the importance of these conditions. From the Paris brothers (1716–1726) to Jacques Necker (1776–1788), successive financial reformers failed to securely establish double-entry book keeping in royal finances (Lemarchand 2010). The catalyst for the adoption of double-entry book keeping between 1791 and 1808 was the Revolution and the First Empire. In 1807 professional public accountancy was institutionalized in the new Court of Accounts (*Cour des comptes*). Its final codification in the General Regulation of Public Accounting in 1838 reflected the political power of the *rentier* class under the 'July Monarchy' of Louis-Philippe.

More broadly, increased state capacity to manage public debt, willingness to pay creditors, and strengthening of sovereign creditworthiness depended on the evolution of increasingly sophisticated and inclusive representative, governing, and bureaucratic institutions. It required institutions that could legitimately claim to act on behalf of public interests. They included the establishment of parliamentary sovereignty over public finances; the assumption that state debt is 'national' or 'public'; the foundation of central banks to ensure the professional management of debt financing; the shift to longer-term, consolidated public debt; and the development of a professional and accountable fiscal administration, to which taxes were directly paid.

The United Provinces, England, and Sweden were the pacesetters, though they drew inspiration from Italian city states like Genoa and Venice (cf. Brewer 1989). Above all, sovereign creditworthiness was linked to the legal, political, and intellectual authority of autonomous, professional, and accountable fiscal institutions. Their authority underpinned state capacity to combine high levels of public debt with willingness to pay, and thus credible guarantees of creditworthiness. However, this credibility depended on their perceived competence in mastering the public finances of an enlarging geographic space, in supervising and regulating a hugely expanding banking sector and an accelerating pace of financial change, and in averting costly wars. Professional and institutional competence was a necessary but by no means sufficient condition for achieving fit between liability and control.

Changing Social Forces

Professional and institutional developments to underpin public finances were intimately related to the changing involvement of social forces in structures of political rule. The emergence of state fiscal capacity depended on the political ascendancy of the *rentier* class in oligarchic structures of rule. In Sweden, the 'Great Reduction' of King Charles XI (r. 1660–1697) curbed the power of the landed aristocracy. He sought to build a structure of political rule that would support the development of a professional fiscal administration. The aims were to ensure that Sweden could pay its debts and to secure Sweden's great power status.

In England the rise of the *rentier* class to political power is associated with the 'Glorious Revolution' of 1688. The French '*âge des petits rentiers*' is linked to the 1789 Revolution, especially the aftermath of the great sovereign bankruptcy of 1792. Its symbol was the *franc germinal*, which was created by the Emperor Napoleon I in 1803 and which retained its fixed value against gold till 1919. France undertook major reforms to public finances and its financial sector in 1815–1818, repaying arrears to creditors (Oosterlinck, Ureche-Rangau, and Vaslin 2013). It avoided currency debasement and debt default, despite successive revolutions, regime changes, and the war indemnities after 1815 and after the Franco–Prussian War of 1870. The Ottoman Empire offered a stark contrast. Power was retained by a central bureaucracy, which negotiated with provincial elites to safeguard privileges. This nexus of power constrained the economic, social, and political opportunities for domestic merchant-financiers. It provided the main source of domestic conspicuous consumption (Pamuk 2009).

Economic Structure and Cycles

The evolution of state fiscal capacity and creditworthiness was also caught up in deeper structural dynamics and the different opportunities and constraints that they created. European states were either privileged or disadvantaged by their spatial location in European and global trade routes. In the late-medieval and early-modern periods the key beneficiaries were the city states of northern Italy. They dominated the lucrative routes to the East. Their merchant-financier families emerged as the most powerful creditors of English, French, and Spanish monarchs. Lyon grew as a financial centre with a powerful Italian presence. Antwerp, Amsterdam, and Bruges benefitted from lying at the crossroads of this trade with the Baltic trade.

From the sixteenth century, as the trade axis shifted towards the Atlantic, Antwerp and Amsterdam merchant-financiers gained greater significance. This shift was reflected in the sources of debt finance. As early as the reign of Edward III, the Hull merchant William de la Pole was raising royal loans in Antwerp (Fryde 2004). The English merchant Stephen Vaughan, a protégé of Thomas Cromwell, served as the first formally appointed royal financial agent in Antwerp. His task was to establish 'the sound credit of the King'. Vaughan negotiated various loans to help pay for the ruinous double war of King Henry VIII in France and Scotland (1543–1545). This war led to huge budget deficits (Cunich 1999). His main success was gaining large loans from the Fugger and the Welser families of Augsburg, although on harsh terms (Richardson 1953: 66–7). Later Thomas Gresham performed the same services for Edward VI in Antwerp, paying off all Crown debts. He performed the same role for Queen Mary and Queen Elizabeth I, raising a big loan from the Fugger (Ehrenberg 1963: 252–5, 274–6).

Again reflecting the underlying realities of trade, by the eighteenth century the Amsterdam-based Hope and Co. was the great creditor of European rulers. It financed the wars of Catherine the Great of Russia against the Ottoman Empire. Dutch credit flowed to England, France, German principalities, Hanseatic cities, as well as Russia (Riley 1980). The flight of Hope and Co. to London in the face of the French revolutionary armies led to a major increase in the financial capacity of Barings. Barings emerged as the major financier of British war debts against Napoleon. Spurred on by the Duke of Wellington, Alexander Baring organized the loan to pay the French war indemnity in 1818 (Longford 1972; Ziegler 1988). The long-term effects of the shift of the trade axis to the Atlantic were fully felt in the nineteenth century as the London-based bankers, Baring and Nathan Rothschild, carved out leading roles in financing European state debts.

Alongside longer-term structural shifts, creditworthiness was shaped by cycles of macroeconomic expansion and contraction. Against a favourable background of macroeconomic expansion, King Louis IX of France was able to finance and lead two expensive Crusades without incurring huge debts and risking default (Goff 1996; Jordan 1979). In contrast, King Edward III (r. 1327–1377) of England financed his wars with Scotland and France by accumulating large, unsustainable debts to the Bardi and Peruzzi merchant-financiers of Florence (Hunt 1990). Much earlier in the second century AD, the increasing resort of Roman Emperors to currency debasements reflected the effects of a slowing down in macroeconomic development. Sovereign creditworthiness has always been cyclically sensitive.

Debt and Political Rule in Ancient Greece and Rome

The Classical world of Greece and Rome is less a history of the emergence of public debt than one of the emerging use of new instruments to strengthen or defend creditworthiness. Debt financing in the Classical world was most strongly associated with the city states of Greece and with the emergence of empire. Control of public finances was facilitated in the geographically highly compact world of city states, which were adapted to the high costs of communication and travel. These constraints were relaxed by the new naval technologies of the Athenians and later by the major road-building programmes of the Romans. However, it was in the city states that it was most possible to evolve institutional mechanisms to control and police public finances and evolve new forms of debt financing. These mechanisms were much less effective once republics evolved into empires. Armies and officials were then much more difficult to hold to account.

Athenian Imperialism, the Delian League, and Domestic Borrowing

The Delian League in Ancient Greece provides the first recorded evidence of emerging creditor-debtor city-state relations and use of debt default. In the fourth century BC ten out of thirteen member city states owed debts to the treasury of the temple of Apollo in Delos and defaulted (Sturzenegger and Zettelmeyer 2007: 3; Winkler 1933). In 478 BC, after repulsing the Persian invasion under Xerxes I, Athens had chosen Delos as the seat of its newly founded maritime confederacy and imperial bank because it occupied a geographically and symbolically central position in the Cyclades.

The purpose of the Delian League was to achieve coordinated action by Greek cities against the Persian enemy. However, it soon faced threats of defection. In consequence, the Athenians tightened their authority over the Delian sanctuary, especially over the financial management of its newly gained sacred funds. They also intervened directly in the affairs of member cities. Under Cimon they employed coercion, notably against Naxos and Thasos. The sanctuary received substantial tributes from member city states, which they often resented. It benefitted from interest on its loans to these cities, and used its funds to invest in the regional economy of the Cyclades. Under increasingly overt Athenian leadership, it acted—unlike other sanctuaries—as a regular bank (Chankowski 2008).

Control over Apollo's sanctuary in Delos endowed Athens with prestige and a basis for its imperial ambitions in the Aegean. The culmination of Athenian ambition was the transfer of the treasury of the maritime league to the temple of Athena in Athens in *c.*454 BC, for 'security' reasons. The treasury was used under Pericles to finance a massive public works programme.

The history of the Delian League illustrated the shift from Athenian use of persuasive instruments to establish a fiscal confederacy to coercive instruments in order to maintain the confederacy. This early example of creditor-debtor city-state relations combined elements that were to recur in European history: imperial ambition, resentment at external discipline, default, and coercion. Threat of exit from the Delian League led to Athenian garrisons and interventions in the affairs of member cities.

Debt financing in Ancient Greece grew to support war, alliance building, and vital grain purchases. However, it was not linked to the rise of bankers as public financiers or to the growth of pan-Hellenic financial centres. City-state borrowing took two forms, sacred and secular. Cities borrowed, at interest, from the sacred funds of temples like Delphi, Olympia, and Delos, not just for emergencies but also on a regular, ongoing basis. Temples provided city states with a floating debt. Preparations for war were, however, a major catalyst for seeking temple financing. For instance, in 432 BC, just before the long Peloponnesian War (431–404), Sparta and its allies sought to borrow from the temples of Delphi and Olympia to equip a fleet (Migeotte 1984).

City states also resorted to loans—either agreed or forced—from their own citizens, appealing to civic loyalty and to its patron god or goddess as a source of authority (Migeotte 2006). However, whilst the temples provided a form of floating debt, citizen loans to Greek city states are not to be confused with public debt. Greek city states did not develop anything comparable to a single, consolidated public debt. They lacked the fiscal capacity to issue and manage long-term debt in a form that paid regular interest and was transferable. Moreover, the overwhelming preference was for internal city-state borrowing, sacred and secular.

Coinage and Debasement

The major financial innovation of the Classical Greek world was coinage and the stimulus that it gave to more depersonalized and formalized debt financing. The role of Athens as the motor of financial innovation derived from her improved access to precious metals for coinage. This access was bound up with her imperialistic activity. The rise of Athenian bankers was associated with their creation of commercial credit beyond the available supply of precious metals (Cohen 2008: 77). By the fourth century BC debt was part of the lifeblood of the economy of Athens and its allies. Through a combination of maritime trade and imperialist ventures, Athenian coinage was promoted as a common currency amongst her allies.

The invention of coinage is usually attributed to Lydia in *c.* 625. Its importance to city states grew as it took on new roles. Coinage served not just as a facilitator of trade and prosperity but also as an ambassador for the individual virtues of a city state. It symbolized its heroic character. By the period of Macedon royal power, common coins had also begun to evolve as symbols of confederacy against tyranny, notably in the Achaean League in the third century BC.

As the use of coinage spread, currency debasement emerged as a central instrument for managing problems of debt. Its practice was widespread under Roman Emperors. Currency debasement was achieved by one or more of three techniques: reduction in fineness (the ratio of precious to base metal); reduction in weight; or increase in the nominal value of the coin. However, it only became a viable instrument once civic authorities gained a monopoly over the production and supply of coins. They had to be able to establish, by agreement or coercion, common weight standards so that coins could be used as an inter-city money supply. This monopoly position was not fully secured till the Roman Empire.

The increasing importance of coinage for the image and prosperity of city states induced greater interest in access to sources of precious metals as the basis for gaining creditor city-state power. They became, in consequence, more imperialistic. Athens had an early comparative advantage from its possession of rich silver mines. It used its role within the Delian League to extend its access to other sources. The power of Athens as a creditor city state was also exemplified in its decree requiring her allies to use her silver coins and weight standards. Similarly, Corinth sought to extend its trade and empire by standardization. However, prior to Macedon royal rule, Greek coins continued to lack common weight standards.

Fine-quality gold coins first circulated widely in the fourth century BC under King Philip II of Macedon (r. 359–336 BC) as a symbol of royal authority. He also exploited his annexation of gold mines to establish control of minting as a source of power, a practice that was followed in Ptolemaic Egypt *c.* 320 BC. Philip's imperialistic Hellenic Alliance expressly prohibited debt defaulting and established a Macedon-controlled system of public arbitration to settle inter-city disputes. In the footsteps of the Delian League, this second Pan-Hellenic period was governed by a new militaristic creditor kingdom, Macedon. Its coercive power was used to rule out defaults *ex ante* and to impose currency standardization.

Ancient Rome: Aversion to Public Borrowing

In contrast to the Greek city states, the Roman Republic and Empire remained officially hostile to public borrowing. Though both Republic and Empire were regularly at war, they resorted to public borrowing only exceptionally, in extreme emergencies. Between the fifth century BC and 30 BC the Republic used this instrument only twice. In 242–241 BC, in the final stage of the first Punic War, it borrowed from rich citizens to provide a fleet to attack Carthage. During the second Punic War (218–202 BC) the Republic turned to Syracuse for loans as well as to its own citizens. As earlier in the Greek city states, Roman citizens were not paid interest.

However, outside the territory of Rome, commanders like Scipio and Mark Anthony practised widespread plundering and exacted forced loans from cities under their control. Temple treasures were seized by Sully in Greece, Julius Caesar in Gaul, and Octavian in Egypt. Competition amongst commanders for military prowess and public triumph created incentives for external financial repression.

Pre-Christian Rome retained a firm belief in the autonomy and distinctiveness of the *res publica*. Public figures, above all senators, were understood to be under a moral obligation to ensure their personal creditworthiness by remaining detached from debt. This injunction was laid down in the Lex Claudia of 218 BC and reaffirmed by the Emperor Augustus. The greatest moral danger was *infamia* (Harris 2008: 180). The moral opprobrium attached to debt in Roman Stoic ideas predated Catholic social teaching. In practice, senators were far from averse to dabbling in tax farming and to lending at interest. Nevertheless, the aversion to the idea of the republic or empire becoming dependent on private financing remained (Andreau 2006). Emperor Augustus stressed that Provincial Governors must limit borrowing by cities in both East and West. In particular, sound municipal finance was to be enforced on Greek cities.

The Roman Empire was distinguished from the earlier world of the Greek city states by its monopoly of coinage issue. War acted as the stimulus for Roman coinage. The third Samnite War led to bronze coins (the *as*) in *c.*289 BC. The second, hugely costly Punic War saw the introduction of the silver *denarius* in *c.*214, which borrowed on Greek models of heroic symbolism. 'Hannibal's War' led in turn to early debasements of the *denarius*. However, Roman victory was followed by rapid spread in the use of its coins to form the basis of a united Italian currency system. Later they provided the anchor of the first Mediterranean-wide metrological system. Gold mines in Dalmatia and Spain were used to supply the Imperial mint and to strengthen the Empire's control over the minting process. Re-mintage of coins was a further source of profits. The subsequent growth of a Rome-focused trade and banking system was characterized by pervasive debt financing. Cities, temples, and bankers became major providers of credit money for commercial purposes (Harris 2008: 184).

Above all, Roman coins evolved as potent symbols of Imperial authority. For this reason, the prestige of individual Emperors, and more generally of the Empire itself, was linked to the perceived quality of Roman coins. Equally, currency debasements were associated with the gathering image of imperial decline. Debasement of silver coinage began in earnest with Nero (r. 54–68 AD), especially in 64 AD. It gathered speed under Septimus Severus (r. 193–211 AD) and Caracalla (r. 212–217 AD). During the third century AD both gold and silver coinage was radically debased, leading to a gathering loss of confidence across the Empire and the dissolution of the Roman monetary system (Harris 2008: 205).

Conversely, under Aurelian (r. 270–75 AD) and Diocletian (r. 284–305 AD), a period of economic recovery was associated with currency reforms. In 274 Aurelian deprived the Senate and the cities, with the exception of Alexandria, of the right to issue coinage and restored confidence in gold and bronze coins. Under Diocletian in 294 new weights and denominations were introduced, whilst in 311 Constantine (r. 306–337) created the gold *solidus*, which became the anchor currency for trade. Roman Emperors led the way in showing that re-coinage could serve as a bold instrument for restoring prestige. Later it was used by English monarchs. The re-coinage under Queen Elizabeth I in 1560 was part of the transformation of image of the Tudor state. The so-called 'Great Re-coinage' of 1696 followed the 'Great Revolution'. However, successful re-coinage depended on executive capacity to effectively ban and demonetize previous coin issues. The Roman re-coinages offered no more than temporary respite in a long-term currency debasement that accompanied imperial decline.

Rome's successor in the East, the Byzantine Empire, illustrates the institutional problems of fiscal accountability and control over far-flung territories. From the eleventh century onwards, notably under Alexios Comnenos (r. 1081–1118), its emperors conducted a convoluted diplomacy, which included currency debasements, financial repression, and financial and trade concessions to allies. Its purpose was to finance and augment its mercenary armies and to appease its allies in the face of multiple enemies. Byzantium's bullion reserves were exhausted by external challenges from Normans and Seljuk Turks and by internal challenges from Slav principalities. Alexios Comnenos expropriated the treasures of the churches of Constantinople, debased the coinage, and required additional taxes to be paid in the old coinage. In particular, in 1082 he granted to Venetian merchants unrestricted rights to trade free of customs dues, except in the Black Sea. In return, he gained the aid of their powerful naval fleet. However, in 1204 the Venetians were to divert the Crusade to the capture of Constantinople, with catastrophic consequences for the Byzantine Empire. A geographically small but wealthy and institutionally sophisticated creditor city state displayed its mastery over a once-mighty empire.

Who Writes Debt History? Continental Cities and the Emergence of Public Debt

Either the debt will destroy Florence or Florence will destroy the debt.
Francesco Guicciardini, *Storie Fiorentine 1378 al 1509*
(Molho 2006: 37). He referred to Florence in 1427.

Both territorial state-centric and Anglo-centric interpretations of the history of public debt and its role in strengthening creditworthiness miss the central role that continental European cities played in developing and refining instruments of debt financing, including annuities, accountancy, and fiscal control. The term *rentier* derives from the French word for annuity (*rente*). Continental city states, enjoying autonomy over their own affairs, were the classic site of *rentier* power in late-medieval and early-modern Europe. They pioneered annuity financing.

The comparative fiscal advantage of cities over larger territorial states resided in their superior mastery of distance; in their oligarchic structures of rule that privileged *rentier* power; and in their subsequent capacity to better match liability and control. The golden age of continental European city-state power stretched from the eleventh to the sixteenth centuries. They were located mainly around the Rhine-Rhône corridor, which connected northern Italy, south Germany, eastern and northern France, and Flanders to the Hanseatic League around the Baltic. These cities linked western Europe to the riches of the East (Braudel 1984). They included Bologna, Florence, Genoa, Lucca, Pisa, and Venice in Italy; Lyon and Paris in France; Augsburg, Nuremberg, Cologne, and Hamburg in Germany; Antwerp, Bruges, Amsterdam, and other cities in Flanders and the Low Countries; and Danzig, Lübeck, and Rostock in the Baltic.

These cities were major trade and financial centres. They were self-confident in their economic strength and political autonomy, determined to extend and defend their rights and privileges, and governed by a prosperous merchant class. They possessed strong financial institutions and systems of internal control, including in some instances, like Genoa and Venice, national banks. They spawned an infrastructure of bankers, lawyers, and, in some cases, universities (Pirenne 1971). Their merchant class evolved a concept of citizenship around essentially oligarchic structures of rule and mobilized popular support through myths of urban patriotism (Le Galès 2002). The sophisticated city debt financing that evolved illustrated the close intertwining of private and commercial interests with public interests. It also sharpened internal economic, social, and political inequalities. These inequalities led to growing problems of matching liability with control.

At the root of this European urban renaissance was the creditworthiness that followed from the intimate interconnections of trade, finance, and debt and from the political ascendancy of a powerful *rentier* class. The economic prowess, political self-confidence, aesthetic quality, and intellectual and cultural splendour of many continental European cities owe much to their early innovations in debt financing and their effects on the urban fabric. The catalyst for innovation in debt financing was the search for solutions to two problems. The first problem was how to protect cities in war, when merchants resisted direct taxes and resented forced loans. The second was how to remain compliant with theological doctrine on usury. Finding solutions became more urgent as the ambitions of territorial rulers grew, notably Holy Roman Emperors and French kings. Their ambitions put the political autonomy of proud cities under threat.

The solution was the issue of lifetime or perpetual annuities. They involved a transfer of capital by citizens, whilst avoiding its association with 'credit'. Annuities were paid through assignment of specific indirect taxes, like the salt tax. They were not understood as loans bearing interest, thereby circumventing usury doctrine. Various cities emerged as the chief sellers of annuities. Annuities were mostly held by rich citizens and charitable institutions of the city. As in the city states of Ancient Greece, they were not externally held. However, annuities were politically charged as they were serviced by taxes that disproportionately hit the poor and that increased as the debt grew. The result was mounting social and political strife.

By the fifteenth and sixteenth centuries territorial rulers were increasingly attracted to the idea of trying to secure their own short-term loans on the basis of the annuities and taxes of the cities. Alternatively, they sought to get the cities to issue annuities on their behalf. Their dynastic and territorial ambitions posed increasing threats to the political autonomy of cities, which increasingly sought reassurance by paying for large mercenary armies to protect themselves. The result was increasing external threat, rising resort not just to annuities but also to voluntary loans from citizens, and increases in indirect taxes on staple products to service debt. City states faced in consequence mounting and interconnected internal problems of debt servicing, taxation, and governance, fuelled by rising inequality and insurrection. Their capacity for matching liability and control was increasingly challenged.

Inclusion of annuities in dowries was a key factor in the development of tightly intertwined city oligarchies, based on intermarriage of families and the accumulation of inherited wealth into an early *rentier* class (Molho 2006). By the fifteenth century the escalation of this public debt and the heightened risk of insurrection from the poor acted as a further spur to fiscal innovations in debt financing (Isaacs and Prak 1996). It produced serious debt crises in cities like Genoa and Venice, not least in Florence where by 1427, according to Guicciardini, debt servicing costs exceeded revenues.

The fiscal tool of lifetime or perpetual annuities was developed in the city states of northern Italy. They were consolidated into the *monti*, which in turn became an instrument for cities to lend. It soon spread to cities in Flanders, France, and south Germany. The *monti* then became a building block in the efforts of territorial rulers in Flanders and France, as well as of the Papacy, to establish their own creditworthiness and raise larger loans at lower cost. In Flanders rulers depended on the cities as intermediaries in the sale of their own annuities (Ehrenberg 1963: 41). This process was evident in France. Louis IX turned to his *bonnes villes* for finance. By 1473 Louis XI was demanding forced loans from Lyon and other cities. In 1522 Francis I instituted the issue of annuities by cities, especially Paris, on behalf of the Crown.

From the mid-fifteenth century the Papacy was forced to turn to temporal revenues and debt financing in the face of costly wars and the fall in 'spiritual' revenues from across Europe. It displayed an extraordinary ability to borrow on a huge scale in the second half of the seventeenth century, at half the cost of English and French monarchs. This ability rested on the creditworthiness and revenue streams provided by local city elites, above all in Ancona, Bologna, Cesena, Imola, and Ravenna. By the 1670s debt servicing rose to account for some two-thirds of Papal revenues. Papal debt more than tripled between 1526 and 1599 and had repeated this rate of growth by 1678 (Carboni 2012).

Similarly, Philip II of Spain depended on the annuities of 18 Castilian cities, notably Burgos, Toledo, and Seville. He was able to use their creditworthiness to enhance his credibility with Italian and south German merchant-financiers, from whom he sought short-term loans (Ehrenberg 1963; Goff 1996; Hamon 1994; Alvarez-Nogal and Chamley 2011). However, Philip II was forced to conduct complex, parallel negotiations with his cities. Paradoxically, raising large loans for territorial state-building depended on the creditworthiness and good will of the cities.

Annuities came to serve key social and economic functions in binding the leading merchant families to the city. Economically, they provided an instrument to increase liquidity in an economy that was otherwise limited by its reliance on metal coinage. Annuities represented a form of surrogate money, providing security for various commercial transactions. Their possession was also a badge of family honour and social and economic status. Annuities were fundamental to the intricate linkages, notably through marriage, between leading city families. They circulated within a narrow financial oligarchy, especially through dowries. In this respect annuities lacked a key attribute of modern public debt. They were traded privately. Organized annuity trading on an exchange was pioneered by Antwerp in the seventeenth century. Politically, the combination of annuity financing with oligarchic structures of rule helped continental European city states secure a match of liability and control that eluded the larger territorial states.

Strikingly, late-medieval and early-modern England missed out on this type of urban fiscal development. It lacked royal patronage of the 'good' cities, seen in France under Louis IX and later under Henry II, who sought to develop Lyon, Paris, Rouen, and Toulouse as financial centres by promoting their role in royal borrowing (Conklin 1998; Ehrenburg 1963). Later, a myth evolved of England as the home of local self-government, and of less intrusive state centralization. However, England did not see the evolution of the civic brilliance, glory, and pride that annuity financing made possible across much of continental Europe. In the Netherlands by contrast, long-term public debt was pioneered by its cities and provinces. There was no Dutch national debt till the Napoleonic Wars (Carlos and Neal 2011: 29). In its pattern of evolution of public debt the Netherlands was closer to Italy and Spain than to England.

Who Writes Debt History? Anglo-Centric Narratives

The aphorism that creditors write history raises the question—which creditors? Historians have tended to neglect the early innovations of continental European cities and their emulation in territorial state-building in continental Europe. They have preferred to attribute a privileged historical role to post-1688 England as the source of the 'financial revolution' that created the notion and practice of modern public debt financing. Anglo-centric narratives of financial revolution focus on the English triumph in developing long-term borrowing, organized around a privileged group of City bankers. These narratives stress English exceptionality in building an institutional capacity to sustain increasingly high levels of sovereign debt, without default (see Table 4.1).

Table 4.1 British National Debt, 1702–1920

	National Debt	2009 Values
	£	£
1702	12,767,225	Not available
1757	77,817,182	10.9 billion
1763	132,120,664	20.4 billion
1776	130,451,006	16.7 billion
1786	243,206,140	29.8 billion
1793	244,720,976	27.7 billion
1815	834,262,726	57.9 billion
1914	649,770,091	58.5 billion
1920	7,831,744,300	273.0 billion

(*Source*: Hargreaves 1966: 291. 2009 values are calculated using the Bank of England Inflation Calculator)

The pivotal event is usually identified as the accession of a Dutchman as King William III (r. 1689–1702), accompanied by his many Dutch advisers. Assertion of Parliamentary sovereignty over public finances, including borrowing, was reinforced by the huge costs of William's unpopular ongoing war with France. The 1690s emerge as decisive in the establishment of the public debt. In 1694 the Bank of England was founded as the banker to the state. In 1696 Exchequer or Treasury bills were introduced as a flexible credit instrument to bridge the difficult period between contracting expenditure and collecting revenue. They were followed in 1749–1757 by 'Pelham's Conversion', which created the 'Consolidated Stock of the Nation'. In the 1790s William Pitt the Younger began the shift from placing loans through patronage to competitive contracting for loans. His first introduction of income tax in 1799 helped strengthen sovereign creditworthiness against the background of the huge financing requirements of the war with France (Fisk 1921). At the centre of this narrative is the argument that Parliamentary guarantees proved superior to monarchical promises as an instrument of creditworthiness (Brewer 1989; Dickson 1967).

John Law and Eighteenth-Century France

Anglo-centric narratives gain support from comparison with seventeenth- and eighteenth-century France. Through the notorious Scottish-born financier and gambler John Law, France imported financial revolution from Amsterdam. It took the form of a public bank on the Dutch model, recast as all-powerful, in terms suitable for an absolute monarchy rather than a Dutch republic. The bank would issue paper money, receive all tax payments as guarantee, and consolidate the public debt. The ministers of Louis XV were looking for a way to contain the scale of default after the ruinously expensive wars of Louis XIV. They wished to rebuild confidence in the French state and to finance imperial ambitions in the New World to match the English (Murphy 2006). In 1718 the private General Bank (*Banque Générale*) became the public Royal Bank (*Banque Royale*) and pursued an expansion of the money supply.

Meanwhile, Law's Mississippi Company rapidly secured more privileges, culminating in control of the collection of direct taxes, the lease of the indirect tax farms, the right to tobacco revenue collection, and the profits from the 26 royal mints. In return, in 1719 Law agreed to pay off the entire royal debt. The scheme was financed by a huge increase in share issues, supported by the Royal Bank, which provided borrowing facilities for this purpose. Law's crowning moment was his brief appointment as Controller-General of Finances, following which the Mississippi Company took over the Royal Bank. The scheme was supported by various measures of financial repression, including the reduction of the use of metal coins in favour of banknotes and support for the shares of the Mississippi Company. However, by the end of 1720 Law and the Royal Bank had been brought down by a combination of inflation, public anger at financial repression and losses, and collapse of confidence in the Mississippi Company.

The short, disastrous Law experiment blunted French enthusiasm for financial revolution. Despite the best efforts of reformers like Jacques Necker to borrow British and, above all, Swiss ideas, the debt problems of the French monarchy remained intractable. Attempts to manage these problems were preoccupied with establishing the Sinking Fund (*Caisse d'amortissement*). This device had been pioneered by Robert Walpole in 1716. It sought to reassure creditors by assigning revenue to debt reduction. However, sinking funds failed to prevent the accumulation of new debts. The history of French public debt became a catalogue of sinking funds. Following five attempts in the eighteenth century, they were used in 1816, 1858, 1866, and 1926. In the wake of Law, France's reputation as a 'pre-modern' fiscal state was sealed. It appeared unable to moderate its appetite for debt and for financial secrecy and subterfuge. The word 'budget', with its implications of estimates and control, did not appear in France till about 1764 (Grenier 2006).

Dutch and North Italian Pacesetting

Despite this favourable Anglo-French comparison, dominant Anglo-centric accounts of the history of public debt err in two ways. First, they underestimate earlier developments. Under King Charles II, and even earlier under Oliver Cromwell, reforms sought to centralize fiscal management on terms very different from the provincial models of the Netherlands and Spain (Braddick 1996). The corollary is overestimation of the scale of change in eighteenth-century Britain. The Civil War permanently put control of taxes in the hands of Parliament. During the post-1660 Restoration period, Sir George Downing, Teller of the Exchequer till 1684, initiated interest in emulating the successes of Dutch cities and provinces in strengthening their creditworthiness (Barbour 1950). The scale of change is also exaggerated. Eighteenth-century Britain was far from being an honest, law-abiding country with a professionalized fiscal state. It was riddled with nepotism, venality, and corruption in public office. British political life was characterized by riot, disorder, and distrust of the state.

Secondly, the focus on eighteenth-century Britain neglects the earlier innovations of north Italian city states in developing public debt, notably lifetime and perpetual redeemable annuities. These instruments were widely emulated by cities in France, Spain, the Low Countries, and across the Holy Roman Empire (Ehrenberg 1963). By the end of the eighteenth century, even the Ottoman Empire sought to address its financial weaknesses by a device similar to the lifetime annuity. The *esham* was designed to broaden the base of domestic state borrowing. However, the Ottoman Empire lacked the state capacity to control and limit the market that it had created (Pamuk 2009: 24).

In many ways the 'Great Loan' of 1555 by King Henry II in Lyon was the great symbolic moment when a major European territorial state adopted north Italian ideas and practices of public subscription. The Great Loan proved enormously popular with a wide range of investors, both socially and from across Europe, including Ottoman Turkey (Ehrenberg 1963). The existing floating loans were combined into a large new loan. However, Henry II's default in 1557 ruined several noble families. It precipitated a fiscal crisis in 1561, when the clergy had to bail-out the king.

Above all, the United Provinces had led the way in bringing down the interest rates on government loans. They fell almost continuously from a high point of 20 per cent in 1574 to 5 per cent by 1640, dropping to a low point of 2.5 per cent in 1747 (Hart 1999). Even in the eighteenth century the United Provinces continued to play a central role in European sovereign lending and in disseminating the notion of 'public' debt across continental Europe. As early as 1531, the Antwerp exchange had become the leading international market for European annuities, especially Spanish *juros*. The Amsterdam exchange took over this role in the seventeenth century, followed by the London exchange in the eighteenth century. However, Britain was a late comer in developing this key debt financing instrument (Munro 2011).

Also, central banks did not originate in England. Public banks can be traced back to Genoa in 1148, when the *Casa di San Giorgio* was founded as an association of city-state creditors. Renamed the *Ufficio di San Giorgio* in 1407, it continued as a 'state within a state', making loans to the city till 1736. In Venice the *Banco della Piazza del Rialto*, established in 1584, and the *Banco del Giro*, from 1619, played similar roles. Milan followed the same path in 1593. The foundation of the Bank of Amsterdam in 1609, the first year of the truce with Spain, was motivated by the search for a public guardian of probity in currency management and for insurance against default, counterfeit, and fraud. Hamburg established its own public bank in 1619. The innovative role of mercantile city states in central banking reflected the interests of their rich merchants in insuring themselves against their highly risky commercial activities. They also sought to protect their interests as creditors of their city state by institutionalizing professional management of the public debt.

Anglo-centric narratives of the history of public debt have to be set against this evidence of the pioneering role of continental European cities. They were quicker than not just continental European territorial states like Castile, France, and Russia but also Britain in developing institutional arrangements that secured sovereign creditworthiness and realized gains from lower interest rates. Their oligarchic structures of rule entrenched creditor power and enabled them to combine highly asymmetric forms of consent for taxes with large public borrowing. By the 1760s Britain had succeeded in putting in place its own oligarchic political structures that helped her achieve a scale of sovereign borrowing that dwarfed her rivals. She had become the pre-eminent 'fiscal-military' state (Brewer 1989). Nevertheless, Britain was a late arrival as a *rentier* society.

Despite British claims as a financial innovator, the Amsterdam-based bank Hope and Co. remained the richest and most powerful European bank till the end of the eighteenth century. It organized large syndicated loans to Bavaria, Portugal, Russia, Spain, and Sweden. In the process Hope and Co. acquired hugely profitable trade concessions in Portuguese diamonds and in Russian wheat and timber.

Moreover, in the eighteenth century new sovereign bond market practices spread from Amsterdam, rather than from London, across the Holy Roman Empire. Bankers in Frankfurt am Main, notably the Bethmann brothers, worked with Amsterdam bankers on bond issuance for Austria. The Frege merchant-financiers in Leipzig placed bonds for Sweden, Saxony, Prussia, and other German principalities (Holtfrerich 1999). This new role for German bankers in financial intermediation gathered pace by the late eighteenth century. They earned substantial commissions from bond issuance and trading. There were political implications amongst German principalities. They had a stronger incentive to embrace fiscal transparency and efficiency as they became much more dependent on market trust. However, this dissemination of new ideas and practices in debt financing remained Dutch-based.

Seventeenth-century Dutch banking served as the model on which English reformers built during the Restoration period under King Charles II and after the 1688 'Glorious Revolution' (cf. Roseveare 1991). The notion of 'national' or 'public' debt was already firmly embedded in the seventeenth-century Dutch United Provinces and was taken up by English fiscal reformers, notably Sir George Downing (Barbour 1950). Only later was the development of public debt constructed as a story of English institutional genius. In fact, as late as 1672, Charles II defaulted—'the Stop of the Exchequer'—to finance the war with the United Provinces (Fisk 1921). His action ruined many London goldsmiths, who had made huge fortunes as dealers in bullion, become deposit bankers for City merchants, and served as moneylenders to the king (Duncombe 2001).

Despite these major qualifications, the dominant narrative of the history of public debt remains staunchly Anglo-centric. However, the notion of a post-1688 English 'financial revolution' conceals a much more complex, slow-moving, and diffuse evolution. The notion of a national or public debt emerged gradually as a superior tool to legitimate and secure the creditworthiness of states that were heavily committed to war. It also reflected growingly powerful *rentier* interests. It was not simply bound up with the tax and borrowing requirements of the increasingly expensive fiscal-military state (cf. Tilly 1975, 1990; Brewer 1989). Nevertheless, the requirements of the fiscal-military state help to explain the English privileging of public debt. In the eighteenth century this privileging took the form of measures of financial repression, notably tightening usury laws and placing interest-rate and other restrictions on private lending (Drelichman and Voth 2008).

France in European Sovereign Debt Markets

A further weakness of Anglo-centric accounts of sovereign debt is its underestimation of France's role in European sovereign debt from the 1850s to 1914 and after the stabilization of the franc in 1926. By 1914, and again by 1931, the Banque de France had accumulated gold reserves far in excess of those of the Bank of England.

The relative size of British and French public debt changed dramatically during the nineteenth century. In relation to the total public debt of what Leroy-Beaulieu (1888: 593) called the 'civilized states', Britain's share fell from 58 per cent in 1820 to 12.7 per cent in 1886. By contrast, France's share increased from 9 per cent in 1820 to 22 per cent in 1886. The United States represented only 0.65 per cent in 1820 and 6 per cent in 1886. In 1914 France had the highest public debt in Europe. This development was presented as a virtue (Schremmer 1994). It reflected *l'âge des petits rentiers*, a thrifty France whose citizens trusted their state.

From the mid-nineteenth century, France became the leading player in financing European sovereign debt, especially to Russia, Spain, Portugal, Austro-Hungary, Romania, and Ottoman Turkey (Moulton and Lewis 1925: 335). Strategic interests and ambitions played a significant part in shaping the geographic distribution of French foreign loans. These loans were typically tied to requirements to buy French military equipment, as with Serbia, and to specific projects of strategic significance, like Russian railway development to aid military mobilization (Feis 1930; Clark 2013). Britain remained Europe's largest capital exporter. However, British financing of European sovereign debt declined appreciably from the mid-1870s in favour of her Empire (Feis 1930). In 1870–1874 four European states figured in the top five recipients of British financing. Between then and 1914 only Russia, Greece, and Italy made occasional appearances in the British top five (Stone 1999: 383). France's Crédit Lyonnais and Germany's Disconto-Gesellschaft overshadowed British banks in lending to European governments.

However, in the period 1918–1926, the Bank of England stepped into the breach opened by France's post-war debt problems to play the leading role in organizing central bank stabilization in Austria, Hungary, Italy, Belgium, and Norway. By 1928, Émile Moreau, governor of the Banque de France, reasserted French leadership in east and central Europe. He was stung into action by British claims to help stabilize Romania and accused the Bank of England of 'imperialism' (Ahamed 2010: 301–2). By then Moreau was beginning to enjoy the advantage of France's post-1926 re-emergence as a creditor power, accumulating huge gold reserves.

The Imperfect Matching of the Idea and the Practice of the Fiscal State

The rise of the concept and practice of public debt illustrates a paradox at the heart of the modern European state tradition. Public debt is a central, essential attribute of any structure of political rule that lays credible claim to being an autonomous, impersonal state, resting on the distinctiveness of public power (cf. Dyson 2010). The claim to impersonality requires the existence of legal-rational authority and professional bureaucratic organization in fiscal matters, dedicated to the public interest. It is incompatible with privatized fiscal administration through tax farming or through hidden transfers between state enterprises and governments. On this basis, pre-1789 France, post-1815 Prussia, the Ottoman Empire for all its history (despite periodic efforts at reform), and post-independence Greece fell well short of the central attributes of the European state tradition (cf. Bonney 1981, 1989; Clay 2000; Levandis 1944; Schremmer 1994; Wynne 1951).

However, there was a basic tension between normative claims to the autonomy and the distinctiveness of the state and the power that was accorded to narrow social elites of private merchant-financiers and the 'private government of public debt'. This tension was already apparent in the city states of northern Italy in the late-medieval and early-modern periods, as well as in the cities of Flanders and Germany that subsisted on financing through lifetime or perpetual annuities (Migeotte 1984, 2006; Molho 2006). The concept of public debt disguised the grip of a small social oligarchy on fiscal government (Stasavage 2011).

The moral aversion of the Roman Republic and the early Emperors to private debt financing had been linked to this belief in the autonomy and distinctiveness of the public power (Andreau 2006). The return to this Roman belief in the idea of the autonomous and impersonal state fitted with a new notion of 'public' debt. However, some awkward questions remained about the compatibility of the privileges that were accorded to certain banks as providers of, and intermediaries for, public debt financing with the notion of the autonomous, impersonal state. Public and private interests were enmeshed in debt financing in ways that undermined claims to the inclusivity of public power and that threatened 'crony' capitalism. The idea that the state was supervising, regulating, and taxing financial markets in the public interest was compromised. The gains from professional forms of fiscal administration were offset by extractive rather than inclusive structures of rule. The claims to the autonomy and distinctiveness of public power were placed in question by the 'private government of sovereign creditworthiness'.

A further historical paradox stems from the leading roles of the United Provinces, Sweden, and England—and, earlier, the north Italian city states—as pacesetters in developing the institutional framework and mechanisms for public debt. They were not central to the evolution of the idea of the autonomous, impersonal state. The development of this intellectual tradition was associated with France and Prussia (Dyson 2010). As early as 1710, the English author Daniel Defoe provided a picture of the impersonal, public character of the new British debt in *An Essay upon Publick Credit*.

Despite its identification with the continental European state tradition, France's evolution of the institutional characteristics of the fiscal state remained highly incomplete before the French Revolution and the Napoleonic period (Lemarchand 2010). Thereafter, after public finance reforms in 1815–1818 in the shadow of the defeat at Waterloo and Allied occupation, France began to emerge as a leader in European public debt financing. However, till after 1918 *rentier*-centred arguments about tax justice triumphed. They emphasized protecting the individual from arbitrary state power and resisted the idea of direct income tax. Instead, France depended on an increasingly unwieldy system of profit taxes and indirect taxes. Proliferating special budgets made French public finances opaque well into the twentieth century. The process of constructing a unified tax and fiscal system proved much slower in Prussia, where public finances were even less transparent in the nineteenth century. The distinctive characteristic of Prussia, and most other German states, was reliance on extensive public enterprises and property both as sources of revenue and as collateral for public debt. This intermixing of revenue, debt financing, and public enterprises led to practices of hidden subsidies and a host of special accounts, funds, and other fiscal arrangements (Schremmer 1994). Professional concern with 'public' finances grew rapidly in nineteenth-century France, notably under the Inspectorate of Finances, and in Germany, under the influence of Cameralist ideas. However, French and German fiscal practices remained behind those of Britain, the Netherlands, and Sweden. In this sense the idea and the fiscal practices of the European state remained imperfectly matched well into the twentieth century. Claims to the disinterested and impersonal exercise of public power did not always stand up to close inspection.

5

Financial Repression, Debasement, and the Historic Arc of Default

> I think it is dangerous to have the idea go forth that when an Englishman lends his money to a foreign Government he is creating a national obligation, guaranteed by the full weight of the English government.
>
> *The Economist* (14 November 1868: 1301), commenting on the establishment of the Corporation of Foreign Bondholders

The historical contexts within which rulers have sought to secure their creditworthiness have changed in profound ways. Central to these changes have been the evolution of public debt, the professionalization of public finances, the shift from metallic coinage to fiat currencies and electronic money, and the depersonalization and formalization of creditor-debtor state relations. As Chapter 6 shows, the theological, ideological, and social contexts have also altered in ways that have refashioned the relationship of debt to political rule.

Nevertheless, the notion that rulers have a duty to act to protect themselves and their polities from the intolerable demands of creditors retains a firm grip. It resurfaces in calls for 'bail-in' of creditors to reduce costs to taxpayers. Creditor demands are seen as intolerable when they impose deep, potentially protracted tax rises and expenditure cuts on states, leading to a chronic condition of subnormal economic activity and to social and political protest and risks of breakdown. In such circumstances, rulers have an incentive to resort to inflation, devaluation, more or less covert practices of financial repression, and more or less coercive forms of debt default. European history offers insights into the changing use of these various instruments for liquidating debt.

What has been understood as 'normal' practice has changed with different contexts. European history throws light on continuity and change in creditor-debtor state relations. Above all, changing governance structures and mentalities of rule have led to less directly coercive policies against creditors, as well as to less willingness to resort to threats of 'gunboat' diplomacy on behalf of creditor interests. They have also produced a greater concern with balancing social interests, of which creditors are one. More suggestive of continuity is an historic European 'arc of default'. It suggests that certain European states become locked into path-dependent forms of weak state capacity, willingness to avoid or evade payments to creditors, and politically fraught relationships with their official and private creditors.

Currency Debasements

The creditworthiness of rulers in late-medieval and early-modern Europe was intimately associated with their skills in the arts of currency manipulation. Gaining a reputation as trustworthy and constructing and projecting an image of personal glory were bound up with the currency. In the fifteenth century Philip the Good of Burgundy cultivated this reputation and image by differentiating himself from his peers who practised debasements. Another example was King Louis IX of France. In 1262–1270 he sought to strengthen his moral authority and to establish his creditworthiness with a rising merchant class in the cities by a 'hard' currency policy. His reforms instituted a royal monopoly of the currency, increasing his seigniorage income at the expense of the nobility. He made counterfeiting a crime. He also sought to base commercial transactions on two new 'strong' currencies—the silver *gros tournois* and the gold *écu*. Above all, Louis IX used currency policy to increase his credit by allying himself with the new urban merchant social forces in France. He strove to acquire prestige as creditworthy by associating himself with the financial and fiscal practices of the leading commercial powers—Lucca, Genoa, and Florence (Goff 1996: 245–51, 657, 668).

Similarly, the gold *sultani* served as a powerful symbol of the claims of sixteenth-century Ottoman rulers to unify their new Empire from the Balkans, through Egypt, to the Maghreb. Suggestive of the sources of international prestige, it was modelled in weight and fineness on the Venetian ducat. However, Ottoman currency ambitions were frustrated by the lack of centralized state capacity. Pre-Ottoman designs and standards in silver coinage continued in use for daily transactions. Moreover, trade dependency encouraged the circulation of various types of foreign coinage. The problem was compounded by the failure to legally fix exchange rates between the various coins (Pamuk 2009: 11). Weak state capacity meant that the Ottoman Empire was unable to make effective use of currency management to strengthen its creditworthiness.

If re-coinage remained attractive as a tool for securing creditworthiness, the inducements to practise currency debasement proved even powerful. Currency debasement was a central instrument for managing debt problems in the age of metal coinage. It reduced the profits of merchant-financiers on their loans to rulers. Currency debasement gained favour when rulers faced higher than average interest rates in the face of serious external and internal challenges. However, it was only effective once rulers had gained a monopoly of issuance and possessed state capacity to exploit the fiscal and monetary potential of mintage. This dilemma beset the Ottoman Empire.

The competition of European currencies for standing in commercial use was a vital factor in establishing the relative creditworthiness of city states and territorial rulers and their place in the European diplomatic hierarchy. It emerged out of the Carolingian currency system. This system was introduced between 794 and 802, and based on a single denomination, the silver *denarius*. In order to derive historical legitimacy for the new Holy Roman Empire, Charlemagne's system borrowed Roman weight standards. It sought to create a measure of monetary standardization across Carolingian Europe, above all to facilitate trade. Cities competed to claim privilege as imperial mints. By the tenth century, Lucca, Milan, Pavia, and Treviso were the four imperial mints in northern Italy. In the next century their number grew, along with the practice of debasing coinage in weight and fineness. Crucially, the north Italian cities benefited from valuable seigniorage revenues, which played a role in their early emergence as banking centres and sources of pan-European debt financing.

From *c*.1172 the north Italian cities played the pioneering role in building on their role in operating imperial mints to evolving their own 'hard' currency policies and becoming European currency models. They initiated a competition to be part of a new European hierarchy, which was defined by the moral status and financial and commercial advantages that stemmed from superior creditworthiness. By 1200 Venice had introduced larger-denomination, full-bodied silver coins (*grossi*), the first to be used in most of Europe. Other Italian mints emulated Venice. Following Lucca in 1246 and Genoa in 1252, Florence began to issue the gold *florin* in 1253. The designation of the Florentine *florin* as the medium for the accounting of Papal tithes was the key to its establishment as the monetary standard for Christian Europe. It facilitated an extraordinary growth in Florentine banking power, which soon eclipsed that of Pisa and Lucca within Tuscany. Venice caught up in 1284 with its gold *ducat*, which became the standard gold coin in Mediterranean financial transactions. The wide circulation of *denari, ducats*, and *florins* around Europe testified to the enormous prestige of the north Italian city states.

Rulers of larger territorial states sought to endow themselves with moral authority and creditworthiness by emulating the north Italian city states. In 1266 France under Louis IX introduced the *gros tournois*; in 1275 Flanders followed with the *groot*; whilst, more tentatively, in 1279 England issued the *groat* under Edward I. However, these innovations failed to displace the widespread use of the Florentine gold *florin* across western and central Europe. This pattern exemplified the early comparative advantage that smaller city states had over larger territorial states in controlling their public finances, securing creditor interests, and establishing their creditworthiness. Only after the invention and spread of printing from the 1460s did this advantage begin to erode. Financial information and market integration began to circulate more widely and more speedily amongst key European centres (Chilosi and Volckart 2010b).

Scale and Distribution of Debasements

Currency debasements were practised on a grand scale during the late-medieval and early-modern periods (see Table 5.1). The principal English examples date from 1335 under Edward III, 1464 under Edward IV, and 1526 and, above all, 1542–1553 under Henry VIII. The biggest debasement in size occurred in France under Philip IV in 1304, at great cost to his Lombard financiers like the Giudi. The second biggest was that of Henry VIII of England in 1542–1553. In number, the English cases were dwarfed by Flanders/Burgundy. Its eight currency debasements between 1386 and 1434 provided a regular source of income to its rulers. The record was held by the Prussian *mark*, which

Table 5.1 Top Twenty Currency Debasements in Europe, 1258–1799

State/Currency	Largest Debasement (Percentage)	Year	Cumulative Decline in Silver Content (Percentage), 1500–1799
1. France/livre tournois	−56.8	1303	−78.4
2. England/pence	−50.0	1551	−35.5
3. Ottoman Empire/akche	−43.9	1586	−59.3 (1527–1799)
4. Sweden/mar ortug	−41.4	1572	−91.0 (1523–1573)
5. France/livre tournois	−36.2	1718	
6. Belgium/hoet	−34.7	1498	−56.3
6. Flemish/guilder	−34.7	1496	−48.9
8. Bavaria-Augsburg/pfennig	−26.0	1685	−70.9
8. Flemish/grote	−26.0	1488	−12.3 (1500–1575)
10. New Castille/maravedis	−25.3	1642	−62.5 (1501–1799)
11. Bavaria-Augsburg/pfennig	−21.5	1424	
12. Italy/lira	−21.0	1320	−35.6 (fiorentina)
13. England/pence	−20.0	1464	
14. Valencia/dinar	−17.0	1501	−20.4 (1500–1650)
15. Frankfurt/pfennig	−16.4	1500	−12.8 (1500–1798)
16. Belgium/hoet	−15.0	1561	
16. Flemish/guilder	−15.0	1560	
18. Russia/ruble	−14.3	1798	−42.3 (1761–1799)
19. Austria/kreuzer	−12.5	1694	−59.7
20. Austria/kreuzer	−11.1	1463	

(*Source*: Adapted from Reinhart and Rogoff 2008: 42)

was debased eleven times between 1380 and 1455. Eight of these currency debasements, notably the great debasement of 1410, were used to finance the protracted wars of the Teutonic Order against Poland-Lithuania (Chilosi and Volckart 2010b).

The debt burdens of ongoing warfare were the main inducement for territorial rulers to practise punitive currency debasements. Between the 1440s and 1480s under Sultan Mehmet II, the silver content of the Ottoman *akçe* was reduced by 30 per cent (Karaman and Pamuk 2010: 600). Debasement reached its peak between 1808 and 1839 under the centralizing Sultan Mahmud II, under whom the silver content of the *kurush* declined by more than 80 per cent. It was the key instrument in financing protracted wars and the costs of dealing with internal rebellions (Karaman and Pamuk 2010: 620).

The nineteenth-century pattern of currency debasements highlights the devastating effects of the Napoleonic Wars (see Table 5.2). Austria, Prussia, and Russia faced escalating expenditures in the face of collapsing revenues. They resorted to currency manipulation on a major scale, printed paper money promiscuously, and relied heavily on British war subsidies. The biggest single debasements involved Austria (1812) and Russia (1810) and had damaging long-term consequences for their sovereign creditworthiness. Their size was matched only by the Ottoman Empire. Austria and Russia also

Table 5.2 Top Currency Debasements in Europe during the Nineteenth Century

State	Period	Cumulative Decline in Silver Content (Percentage)	Largest Debasement, Year	Share of Years in which there was a Debasement
Austria	1800–1860	–58.3	–55.0 (1812)	37.7
Germany	1800–1830	–2.2	–2.2 (1816)	3.2
Italy	1800–1859	0.0	0.0	0.0
Portugal	1800–1855	–12.8	–18.4 (1800)	57.1
Russia	1800–1899	–56.6	–41.3 (1810)	50.0
Ottoman Empire	1800–1899	–83.1	–51.2 (1829)	7.0
United Kingdom	1800–1899	–6.1	–6.1 (1816)	1.0

(*Source*: Reinhart and Rogoff 2008: 43)

experienced the largest number of years of currency debasement. In contrast, Prussia was affected for a much shorter period.

This distribution of currency debasements matches closely the emerging distribution of power amongst European states in the nineteenth century. It also correlates with the differential growth of *rentier* power, which strengthened political pressure on European states to lock-in sovereign creditworthiness by attaching currencies to a gold or silver standard. There was a symbiosis between the rise of *rentier* power, more states committing to the discipline of an impersonal monetary standard, and greater avoidance of currency debasement.

Aggressive and Defensive Debasements

Currency debasements differed in aim and in motive: aggressive or defensive; and fiscal or monetary (Munro 2010). Rulers used aggressive currency debasements to project power and finance wars by augmenting seigniorage revenues. Up to the sixteenth century, and in some cases beyond, they were the instrument of choice for larger territorial states in offsetting the comparative fiscal advantages that were enjoyed by the smaller, more creditworthy city states (Chilosi and Volckart 2010a). This aggressive, profit-seeking fiscal motive underpinned the debasements under Ottoman Sultan Mehmet II (r. 1451–1481). It featured in early Prussian debasements and in those used by Frederick the Great (r. 1740–1786) to help finance the Seven Years' War. France practised aggressive debasements under Philip IV (r. 1285–1314) and under Louis XIII in 1636. Similarly, the English debasements of 1464–1465 under Edward IV and—on a bigger scale—of 1542–1553 under Henry VIII enabled the use of high mintage fees to increase profits. Faced by the absence of secure, reliable, and buoyant tax revenues, and by weak internal communications, rulers of larger territorial states came to rely on their privilege to set a seigniorage tax on minting. This source of valuable income helped them to pay for wars and to service associated onerous debt payments to Flemish and north Italian merchant-financiers.

The domestic politics of aggressive currency debasement were complex and finely balanced. On the one hand, it risked opposition from the landed nobility and wage-earners. They feared the inflationary consequences and the erosion of their real incomes. On the other, aggressive debasements—above all, at the expense of foreign creditors—could be turned to popular advantage. They were attractive as politically preferable to new onerous loans or taxes.

Defensive currency debasements were also linked to cultivating and above all protecting the image of rulers and governing elites. They were most frequent amongst creditor city states like Basel, Florence, and Hamburg. A key motive was to protect their image of creditworthiness from the continuous deterioration of their coins in circulation. Coins were subject to counterfeiting, 'clipping', 'sweating', and general 'wear-and-tear'. There was a long-term monetary incentive for the city states to pursue this type of debasement in the interests of safeguarding the quality of the currency and confidence in holding and using it.

Defensive debasements had a contagious character. They were used in part in response to aggressive debasements by other territorial rulers and in part to respond to underlying changes in the relative prices of gold and silver. Defensive debasements were designed to protect the money supply from the influx of debased foreign coins and the viability of the royal mint. This aim was typically achieved by restrictions on the circulation of these foreign coins and by lower mintage fees to attract bullion to the mint. The monetary motive and element of contagion were apparent in King Henry VIII's debasement of 1526, which followed those of King Francis I of France in 1519 and the Emperor Charles V for the Low Countries' coinage in 1521. The monetary motive also prevailed in the English debasements of 1351 and 1411.

Control of Precious Metals: Alchemy

In an age of metal coinage, the image of a strong state and ruler was bound up with access to, and control of, silver and gold mines and the ability to take advantage of changes in the relative supply and price of these precious metals. This resource of power was essential in the roles of Athens and later Macedonia in the Hellenic world. Similarly, a key event in helping refashion the image of the Holy Roman Empire was the south German-central European silver mining boom from the 1460s. This boom helped promote the rise of rich merchant-financier families like the Fugger of Augsburg, bankers to the Emperor Charles V. It was a key factor in the emergence of the Hapsburgs as the fulcrum of European diplomacy (Ehrenberg 1963). The even greater silver inflows from Spanish America into Seville from the 1550s were to profit Genoese merchant-financiers, on whom Philip II came to rely.

King Henry VI of England was hugely attracted to exploitation of the gold and silver mines of Cornwall and Devon in the 1440s–1450s. So desperate was his fiscal plight that he placed his faith in alchemy. In 1452 Henry VI licensed an alchemist for life to experiment with the transmutation of base metals. He established a committee of London merchants in 1456 to assess rival claims. In 1457 he appointed a distinguished commission, including bishops, lords, and judges, to examine how the king's debts could be paid off using these new coins (Griffiths 1981: 787).

Similarly, by the sixteenth and seventeenth centuries rulers within the Holy Roman Empire, like the Elector August of Saxony, turned to alchemy in the search for compensation for the lost revenues from mines in central Europe. Their patronage facilitated the emergence of a new breed of entrepreneurial alchemists and fostered the widespread practice of alchemy within the Empire (Nummedal 2007). Alchemy's claims to authority rested both on its status as an ancient, esoteric art and on its promise as a practical technology. However, it lacked the authority of guild status and university recognition and soon succumbed to accusations of fraud.

Rentier Power and the Gold Standard

From the eighteenth century the rise of a *rentier* class to economic and political power in the larger territorial states increased the political costs of currency debasements. Its members sought protection of their savings income through hard-currency policies. They placed their confidence in a new small elite of statesmen-bankers, in central banks, and in an impersonal monetary standard to ensure discipline and the creditworthiness of state finances. Above all, *rentiers* feared the use of inflation as an instrument of financial repression to reduce the value of debts. Amongst the nineteenth-century European powers, the Ottoman Empire represented a notable exception. It failed conspicuously to nurture and develop a politically powerful *rentier* class. The Ottoman Empire's merchant-financier class was concentrated mainly amongst the Jews of Salonika, its main European seaport. Financial and economic reforms were arrested by the interplay of power between the Ottoman central bureaucratic elite, local landed elites, and private bankers and moneylenders. The outcome was frequent currency debasement, financial repression, and default (Pamuk 2009).

The international gold standard stood as testament to the belief in a fixed exchange rate of currency into gold as the central commitment device for ensuring sound money and sovereign creditworthiness. It offered to *rentiers* protection against debasement and other forms of financial repression, like inflation. The size and durability of gold reserves then became a central measure of creditworthiness, one in which France and Russia excelled in 1914. Britain gained enormous prestige from acting as the pioneer and anchor of the international gold system as it gradually emerged in the nineteenth century. Moreover, the discovery of gold in South Africa, part of the British Empire, added credibility to this role. The gold standard—as well as the competitor silver standard—gained authority from the belief in the fundamental superiority of precious metals over paper money.

Leading figures in post-1918 European central banking and finance took it for granted that the return to gold would re-establish the creditworthiness of their states after the financial traumas and losses of world war. For the Bank of England there was no alternative to returning to gold at the pre-1914 rate. Locking-in monetary and fiscal discipline would illustrate British commitment to honouring her debts. However, this *rentier* interest, symbolized in the figure of the Bank's governor Montagu Norman, had become politically more difficult to sustain. It faced opposition from within the ranks of organized labour to the deflation and deep cuts to living standards implicit in the return to gold at the pre-war rate. After the unravelling of the gold standard in 1931, currency debasement was back in fashion. Monetary policy shifted to the management of *fiat* paper currencies. *Rentier* power had been trimmed.

Historical Variations in Sovereign Debt Defaults

Sovereign default is a more specific, targeted instrument than currency debasement. It imposes direct costs on creditors. Its use can be justified as protecting the interests of domestic taxpayers, wage-earners, and social benefit recipients in shouldering the burdens of fiscal adjustments. The burden of existing debts on them is reduced. Default is also often associated with national populist mobilization against 'rapacious' financiers, especially Jews, 'foreigners', and speculators. It is bound up in domestic narratives of victimhood and foreign 'dictatorship'.

As with currency debasement, debt burdens of war were the key inducements to default. The various partial defaults of King Henry IV of France were connected to the protracted and costly domestic wars of religion (1562–1598) and the declaration of war with Spain in 1595. Similarly, defaults occurred in 1648 and 1661 during the regency and early reign of King Louis XIV to help finance anti-Hapsburg wars against Austria and Spain (Bonney 1981). The four defaults of King Philip II of Spain in 1557, 1560, 1575, and 1596 involved payment stops, principally to Genoese merchant-financiers like the

Table 5.3 European States in the World Top Defaults and Reschedulings between Independence and 2006

State	Year of Independence	Share of Years in Default/ Rescheduling since Independence or 1800	Total No. of Defaults/ Rescheduling
1. Honduras	1821	64.0	3
2. Ecuador	1830	58.2	9
3. Greece	1829	50.6	5
4. Nicaragua	1821	45.2	6
5. Mexico	1821	44.6	8
6. Peru	1821	40.3	8
7. Russia/Soviet Union	1457	39.1	5
8. Venezuela	1830	38.4	10
9. Costa Rica	1821	38.2	9
10. Hungary	1918	37.1	7
11. Colombia	1819	36.2	7
12. Guatemala	1821	34.4	7
13. Poland	1918	32.6	3
14. Argentina	1816	32.5	7
15. Dominican Republic	1845	29.0	7
16. Panama	1903	27.9	3
17. Chile	1818	27.5	9
18. El Salvador	1821	26.3	5
19. Brazil	1822	25.4	9
20. Romania	1878	23.3	3

(*Source*: Compiled from Reinhart and Rogoff 2008: 30)

Doria, Grimaldi, and Spinola. The main triggers were costly setbacks in the Dutch wars and the Armada defeat in 1588 (Drelichman and Voth 2007, 2009, 2010).

European states vary greatly in the extent to which they have resorted to default (see Tables 5.3 and 5.4). In number, Spain heads the league table, followed by France and the German states, and then Austria and Hungary (cf. Winkler 1933). Strikingly, Italy sits alongside the Netherlands as a very infrequent defaulter. More telling is the share of years since independence in which states have been in default. Here Greece tops the league table, followed by Russia, Hungary, Poland, Romania, and Spain. The historically 'virtuous' states are Belgium, Denmark, England/Britain, Finland, France, Norway, and Sweden, as well as the United States.

Four factors help explain the historical variations in resort to sovereign debt default. First, its effective use depends on the government having a centralized budget. In the territorial states of late-medieval and early-modern Europe both debt and taxes were typically decentralized to cities. The cities were the conduit through which short-term debts of rulers were converted into long-term debt, through their issue of annuities.

Table 5.4 Number and Periods of Defaults and Rescheduling in Europe and the United States from Independence to 2006

State	Year of Independence	Share of Years in Default or Rescheduling since Independence or 1800	Total No.
Austria	1282	17.4	7
Belgium	1830	0.0	0
Denmark	980	0.0	0
England/UK	1066	0.0	0
Finland	1917	0.0	0
France	943	0.0	8
Germany	1618	13.0	8
Greece	1829	50.6	5
Hungary	1918	37.1	7
Italy	1569	3.4	1
Netherlands	1581	6.3	1
Norway	1905	0.0	0
Poland	1918	32.6	3
Portugal	1139	10.6	6
Romania	1878	23.3	3
Russia	1457	39.1	5
Spain	1476	23.7	13
Sweden	1523	0.0	0
Turkey	1453	15.5	6
United States	1783	0.0	0

(*Source*: Reinhart and Rogoff 2008: 30)

They further ensured the credibility of debt by providing the site for a spatial alignment between debt holders and the people who controlled and enforced the taxes that serviced the debt. Territorial rulers relied on the comparative fiscal advantage of cities in their superior matching of liability and control. Hence, in order to honour payments on short-term debts at times of fiscal pressure, territorial rulers became caught up in complex, parallel negotiations. These negotiations involved not just their bankers but also the representatives of cities, typically in elected assemblies, about tax increases and interest reductions.

This lack of centralized control over taxes and debt in the territorial states of late-medieval and early-modern Europe had complex implications for sovereign defaults. On the one hand, the fragmentation of power over tax and debt reduced the capacity of rulers to resort to default as a deliberate and effective instrument of statecraft. It risked exposing weakness. On the other hand, reliance on the creditworthiness of cities provided rulers, like Philip II of Spain, with a commitment device to reassure creditors, in his case Genoese bankers (Alvarez-Nogal and Chamley 2011). Cities like Burgos, Seville, and Toledo served as guarantors of fiscal capacity and creditworthiness. In consequence, though defaults on short-term debts might be frequent, as under Philip II, the costs to creditors in size of haircuts could be made manageable and their confidence to lend soon restored (Alvarez-Nogal and Chamley 2011). The capacity of European rulers to engage in more deliberate and effective defaults increased in the eighteenth and nineteenth centuries, as they built up more centralized fiscal capacity especially in taxation and in debt issuance.

Secondly, sovereign defaults were less likely in the presence of an economically and politically strong domestic *rentier* class. Its presence was associated with stronger assertion of the legal rights of creditors. Assertion of these rights was linked to narratives about the sanctity of contract; about the parallel between political rule and virtuous households; and about the national humiliation and disgrace that follows from failure to honour debt obligations. Good governments showed their reliability, honesty, and trustworthiness by honouring their contracts. This shift in underlying social forces and in dominant narratives helps explain why the domestic political costs of default rose. Britain did not formally default after 1672. France avoided formal default after 1797. However, *in extremis* both defaulted on US war debts in the 1930s at the onset of the Great Depression. Conversely, the price of default was lower when the domestic *rentier* power base was weak and when debt financing relied heavily on external creditors. This situation applied to the defaults in nineteenth-century and early-twentieth-century Greece, Portugal, and the Ottoman Empire, including Egypt in 1876. Nearly every sovereign debtor in central and eastern Europe defaulted during the 1930s (see Table 5.5).

War debt and reparations constitute a third factor. They increased the incentives to resort to sovereign default, especially when linked to sharp falls in capital inflows, to deep and protracted economic stagnation or recession, and to issues about fair burden-sharing. War debts and reparations were a key factor in late nineteenth-century Greek and Ottoman defaults. Moreover, after 1918 inter-Allied war debts poisoned the relations amongst European states, and above all their relations with the United States. The issue of inter-Allied war debts to the United States was linked with British claims on French war debts, huge French demands for German reparations, and post-war economic crisis. France and Italy delayed agreements on payments of their US war debts till 1926.

Table 5.5 Sovereign Debt Defaults and Rescheduling in Twentieth-Century Europe

State/Year of Independence	Dates			
	1900–1924	1925–1949	1950–1974	1975–2006
Austria		1938, 1940		
Germany		1932, 1939		
Greece		1932		
Hungary, 1918		1932, 1941		
Poland, 1918		1936, 1940		1981
Romania		1933		1981, 1986
Russia/Soviet Union	1918			1991, 1998
Turkey	1915	1931, 1940		1978, 1982

(*Source*: Reinhart and Rogoff 2008: 27)

They settled on much more favourable terms than Britain in 1922, with France not completing domestic ratification till 1929. The onset of the Great Depression in 1931–1933, and the drying up of American capital flows to Europe, further poisoned the politics of debt financing and default. In the end, only Finland paid the Americans in full. Britain ceased to pay US war debts in 1933, after France.

The capacity of a post-war debtor state to escape its creditors was illustrated by Germany. Its government defaulted on reparations in 1931, and Britain and France formally agreed to forgive all German reparations in 1932. Having initially faced Allied demands for $32 billion, Germany settled on $12 billion and eventually paid just $4 billion. Her negotiators were skilful in playing off creditors against each other (Ahamed 2010: 479). The Dawes Plan of 1924 provided an international loan to help Germany pay reparations. It also clarified that Germany would be declared in default only in case of 'flagrant' failure to fulfil its obligations. Allied negotiators sought to avert further German humiliation after her catastrophic hyperinflation of 1923 and the damage to domestic *rentiers*. German negotiators were, in turn, fearful of the consequences of becoming associated with Greece, Turkey, and Egypt in the hierarchy of states.

This history of German war reparations contrasted with France's speedy honouring of its two hefty nineteenth-century war indemnities. After 1815 France was forced to pay a war indemnity equivalent to one year of fiscal revenues, along with the costs of an occupying army of 150,000 men till 1818. It did so and by the 1820s was able to increase its public debt at lower costs, principally through major reforms to its public finances (Oosterlinck, Ureche-Rangau, and Vaslin 2013). After the Franco–Prussian War of 1870 the indemnity amounted to 5 billion francs. The last payment was made in 1873, six months ahead of schedule. The French government borrowed this amount, and more, principally through two big sovereign bond issues and through borrowing from the Banque de France. The result was a large, long-term public debt burden. However, it was not liquidated through big tax increases or spending cuts or defrayed by default. Unlike in Germany after 1918, French compliance with this extraordinarily rapid debt repayment schedule was facilitated by a favourable balance of trade between 1872 and 1875. Moreover, after 1871 France lacked the catastrophic inheritance of domestic debts and inflation that confronted the infant Weimar Republic (cf. Moulton and Lewis 1925: 439–48; Holtfrerich 1980). A favourable balance of trade enabled France to accumulate credits for the discharge of her debts. Germany faced a more daunting structural position after 1918.

Finally, regime transition after war, civil war, and revolution can serve to legitimate default. New governments can resort to the notion of inherited debt as 'odious' to invoke sovereign immunity. On this basis Spain defaulted in 1831 after civil war. In 1898 the US government repudiated debts that had been incurred by Cuba under Spanish rule at the end of the Spanish–American War (Winkler 1933). In 1917 the new Soviet Union repudiated 'odious' Czarist loans, at high cost to French bondholders. French irritation was increased when, in the Treaty of Rapallo of 1922, the German government secured Soviet renunciation of war reparations from Germany in exchange for German recognition of the Soviet debt repudiation. Following the Soviet example, the Czechoslovak communist government repudiated past debts in 1952.

Similarly, Mustafa Atatürk averted ratifying the settlement of Turkey's allotted share of Ottoman debts under the Treaty of Lausanne of 1923. In 1928 he declared as invalid Ottoman arrangements for foreign control of debt servicing and in 1930 defaulted on the Ottoman debts (Wynne 1951). Similarly, in time of war states are highly likely to default on debts to enemy creditors. At the beginning of the First World War, Austria-Hungary, Bulgaria, and Ottoman Turkey defaulted on enemy loans. Italy did the same on entering the Second World War.

Defaults in Late-Medieval and Early-Modern Europe: Historical Myth and Reality

The literature on defaults in late-medieval and early-modern history has tended to perpetuate myths that derive from secondary sources. The most cited myths relate to King Edward I and King Edward III of England and King Philip II of Spain. Edward I is linked with the bankruptcy of the Ricciardi of Lucca (Blomquist 2005; Kaeuper 1973); Edward III with the bankruptcy of the Bardi and the Peruzzi of Florence (Hunt 1994); and Philip II with his four 'serial' defaults, principally to Genoese bankers.

In the cases of Edward I and Edward III, Italian merchant-financiers made rich pickings, independent of the repayment of the principal and interest on their royal loans. They benefitted from gifts, damages, and various highly lucrative trade and financial privileges. Merchant-financiers also practised various forms of concealment and trickery, exploiting the lack of financial sophistication of royal officials. The historical record does not support the view of monarchs and their rudimentary fiscal administrations practising a carefully crafted statecraft of default to punish Italian merchant-financiers (Hunt 1990). These monarchs faced a radical mismatch between liability and control. They lacked centralized fiscal systems, able to link their short-term debts to taxes. They did not have the capacity to operate with a large, floating debt.

The bankruptcy of the Ricciardi had its roots in the wider European economy rather than in royal default. At the basis of the financial relationship between the Ricciardi and Edward I was a complex exchange relationship, of which loans were only a part. The Italian merchant-financiers made loans to the king in exchange for the valuable monopoly of the collection of the new customs duty on wool, the main item in English exports, as well as for other royal favours. They were granted the right to act as managers of Papal tax collections in England. In the early 1290s the Ricciardi were damaged by a combination of factors. The Pope began to call in his taxes urgently. Philip IV of France levied a heavy tax on Italian merchant-financiers. Also, the war of 1294 between England and France disrupted their communications with Italy. Financially squeezed, the Ricciardi rejected the urgent requests of Edward I for loans to finance his simultaneous wars in France, Scotland, and Wales. In response, the king ended their monopoly of the wool custom duty and ordered the seizure of their assets. Edward I gained at the expense of the Ricciardi. However, he was forced to resort to heavy taxation, compulsory purchase of goods, and a less favourable lending arrangement with the Frescobaldi of Florence and with Flemish and German moneylenders. The crisis of the 1290s was significant. It ended in financial ruin for the Ricciardi and in a major constitutional crisis for Edward I in 1297 (Prestwich 1972). However, Edward I did not specifically repudiate his debts to the Ricciardi. His actions were not the most significant factor in their collapse.

A similar myth surrounds the role of Edward III in the collapse of the Bardi and the Peruzzi of Florence in the 1340s. Edward III's promiscuous military campaigns generated a wide circle of creditors in England, Flanders, Germany, and across northern Italy. The two leading creditors were the two Florentine 'super-companies'. By the 1330s, as the Hundred Years' War dawned, the Bardi and the Peruzzi were engaged in joint lending to Edward III. Their scale of operation exceeded that of the later Medici Bank (Hunt 1994). At the heart of the clash between Edward III's officials and the Bardi and the Peruzzi was the issue of how much they were owed. However, Edward III never repudiated these debts. He acknowledged them, disputed their size, and subsequently never paid them. The role of Edward III in this banking collapse has to be seen against the background of the third largest Florentine merchant-financier, Acciaiuouli. It also failed, though it had no loans outstanding to Edward III (Hunt 1990). A far more important factor in the collapse of these three Florentine merchant banks was the tumultuous economic and political events in the city state in the 1340s, including repudiation of the communal debt in 1343 and its restructuring in 1346.

The myth of Spanish King Philip II as a serial defaulter, able to oppress his creditors, has similar roots in the war-like character of his reign. He expended huge resources in the protracted campaigns in the Low Countries after 1566, the Mediterranean campaigns, and the shattering disaster of the Spanish Armada in 1588. The result was expenditure 'shocks' and his dependence on historically unprecedented levels of short-term debt to manage them. War-related expenditure shocks led to four payment stops on short-term debts. The stops in 1557 and 1560 adversely affected the Fugger of Augsburg. Those of 1575 and 1596 damaged the Genoese bankers (Drelichman and Voth 2007, 2009, 2010). This period saw the Genoese merchant-financiers, led by the Doria, Grimaldi, and Spinola families, replace the Fugger in mobilizing vast credits for the Spanish king. They arranged the financing of Spanish troops in Antwerp.

Similar to the Ricciardi and Edward I, the Genoese merchant bankers enjoyed various privileges. Above all, they acted as the linking-pin in exporting the new American treasures of Spain, via Seville, to Italy (Braudel 1984: 164–9). The webs of syndicated lending amongst Genoese merchant-financiers enabled them to ameliorate the costs of Philip II's financial problems through their capacity for coordinated action (Conklin 1998). In this respect the power of the Genoese was akin to that of later nineteenth-century bondholder organizations (Drelichman and Voth 2009).

Despite the myth of Philip II as a serial defaulter, Spanish debt remained sustainable, at least till the late 1580s, because of her strong fiscal position. As under Charles V, the American silver windfall enabled him to command large amounts of credit and pursue an expansionist policy that was not available to his rivals. Expected silver revenues provided the main collateral behind the extension of credit to the Crown (Drelichman 2005: 319). In addition, the eighteen cities of Castile provided an additional source of creditworthiness. They issued long-term annuities (*juros*) at low interest rates, serviced them via assigned taxes, and acted as surety for the king's short-term loans (Alvarez-Nogal and Chamley 2011). The support of the Castilian cities provided a commitment device for Philip II in negotiating with Genoese bankers. Overall, Spain maintained primary fiscal surpluses in every year of Philip's reign. On the basis of secure revenue growth, and the assent of the Cortes to tax increases or interest reductions, he was able to secure the continuing willingness of Genoese bankers to provide short-term loans, despite occasional payment stops. The losses of the bankers were relatively limited and temporary and outweighed by longer-term gains. Fiscal negotiation triumphed over financial repression.

However, the reigns of Philip II, and earlier Charles V, contained the seeds of Spain's long-term decline into a chronic debtor and defaulter. The silver windfall from the Americas generated illusion and hubris in imperial adventures and unsustainable fiscal pressures. Debt servicing problems were compounded when the Spanish Crown established a legal procedure for establishing the legitimacy of claims to the lower nobility title of *hidalguía*. This title was associated with tax and other privileges. Its establishment created an incentive to tax avoidance at a time of rising fiscal pressure and to fabricate evidence and use bribery in pursuit of this claim. By the 1590s some 12 per cent of the Spanish population bore the *hidalguía* title (Drelichman 2005). The tax exemptions with the title meant that a higher tax burden fell on 'commoners'. Spain was characterized by greater social and economic inequalities, social resentment, and political grievance. These problems were further exacerbated by the legal requirement that *hidalguía* must abstain from 'mechanical' tasks and 'bad and vile professions' as incompatible with noble life (Drelichman 2005: 322). The spread of this '*hidalgo* mentality' transformed Spain into a state of rent-seeking.

Chapter 6 highlights the extent of brutal action against creditors, notably Jews and foreigners, during the late-medieval and early-modern periods. However, with the main exceptions of France and Spain, defaults were less frequent instruments than currency debasements (see Table 5.6). Merchant-financiers gained various advantages from their intimate association with rulers and their officials. They charged high interest rates to cover their risks. In addition, they gained from commercial privileges, gifts, claims for damages, and the capacity to use their greater financial expertise to cheat rulers. Conversely, rulers lacked the access to centralized budgets and to consolidated figures

Table 5.6 Early External Defaults in Europe, 1300–1799

State	Years of Defaults	Number of Defaults
Austria	1796	1
England	1340, 1472, 1594*	2*
France	1558, 1624, 1648, 1661, 1701, 1715, 1770, 1788	8
Portugal	1560	1
Prussia	1683	1
Spain	1557, 1575, 1596, 1607	6

Note: * denotes uncertainty about whether the English default was on domestic or external debt.

(*Source*: Reinhart and Rogoff 2008: 20)

for revenue, expenditure, and debt that merchant-financiers possessed in relation to their own financial affairs. Rulers could, however, damage merchant-financiers in ways other than default. They could remove their commercial privileges, seize their assets, and deny them the social status—and thus the financial standing—that came from proximity to royal power.

Patterns of Defaults in Nineteenth- and Twentieth-Century Europe

A central feature of the nineteenth and twentieth centuries was a gradual decline in the importance of egoistic and narcissistic behaviour patterns of rulers in fostering illusion and hubris about debts. This historical model had been represented by King Louis XIV (r. 1643–1715). He had proved a master in raising taxes and securing loans with the aim of establishing French supremacy in Europe through war, diplomacy, and the construction of a court that projected the image of the 'Sun King'. King Ludwig II of Bavaria offered an extreme example of the continuing influence of this model and the illusion and hubris it bred. By 1884–1886 his extravagant castle-building programme led to a major debt crisis for the royal household. Despite repeated protestations of the Bavarian finance minister, Ludwig II refused to economize. When threatened with the prospect of legal action by his creditors, and the possibility that creditors might seek the seizure of his castles, Ludwig variously threatened suicide, going into exile, or use of force to get his way. He even set in motion an unrealized plan to raid the Rothschild bank in Frankfurt in order to acquire the necessary millions to complete his construction programme (Hacker 1966). Such extreme behaviour to safeguard creditworthiness had ceased to be regarded as 'normal'. Notions of fiscal accountability and transparency and of legal redress had begun to take firmer root across Europe. Nevertheless, in subtle, complex, and largely subterranean ways, egoism and narcissism continued to play a role in generating fiscal illusion and hubris.

Table 5.7 External Default and Rescheduling: Europe and Africa in the Nineteenth Century

State/Year of Independence	Dates			
	1800–1824	1825–1849	1850–1874	1875–1899
Austria-Hungary	1802, 1805, 1811, 1816		1868	
France	1812			
Germany				
Hesse	1812			
Prussia Schleswig	1807, 1813			
Holstein			1850	
Westphalia	1812			
Greece, 1829		1826, 1843	1860	1893
Netherlands	1814			
Portugal		1828, 1837, 1841, 1845	1852	1890
Russia		1839		1885
Spain	1809, 1820	1831, 1834	1851, 1867, 1872	1882
Sweden	1812			
Turkey				1876
Egypt, 1831				1876
Tunisia			1868	

(*Source*: Reinhart and Rogoff 2008: 24)

Four patterns are discernible in defaults during the nineteenth and twentieth centuries (see Tables 5.5 and 5.7). However, in focusing on these patterns, one should not forget major structural changes over time that may lead to a much higher future risk of sovereign default in the EU and the euro area. In particular, European states carry a much higher burden of explicit and implicit pension, health, and social care liabilities as well as face existential threats to their banking systems. These liabilities threaten to outstrip the capacity to raise taxes, not least with more opportunities for tax avoidance and evasion with freedom of capital movement and with the growth of the grey or underground economy, particularly in Greece, Italy, Portugal, and Spain. In this context, the efforts of different domestic interests to minimize their share of the burden of domestic fiscal adjustment, combined with the bail-out aversion of taxpayers in creditor states, increases the prospects for sovereign default to become a more frequently used instrument. In the EU and euro area context, with its institutional density and iterative negotiations, default is likely to take the 'soft' form of negotiated restructuring, involving lengthening of maturities and haircuts on coupon payments or interest rates (Buiter and Rahbari 2013).

First, the incentives to default mounted with the rising financial and economic costs of war, reflected in the burdens of war debts and reparations. There was a concentration of defaults during the Napoleonic Wars, notably Austria, the German states, Spain, the Netherlands, and Sweden. A similar pattern was evident during, and after, the First World War, especially Hungary, Ottoman Turkey, Poland, and Russia. The scale and reckless debt financing of the First World War testified to the eclipse of *rentier* power in the context of the exigencies of fight for survival. Contrary to initial expectations, *rentier* power could not ensure that the European war would be short (Ahamed 2010).

In contrast, after the Second World War it proved possible to bring down overall public debt from its historical post-war peak of almost 150 per cent of gross domestic product (GDP) in 1946 without a systemic increase in defaults. Part of the explanation was the lack of hefty post-war reparations and the new provision of international financial support from the International Monetary Fund (IMF) and the World Bank. Governments also benefitted from a combination of rapid economic growth and inflation. In addition, they used their close relations with domestic central banks and financial institutions to bring down public debt/GDP ratios through financial repression. For instance, the British government used a labyrinth of rules and regulations to hold nominal interest rates on debt below inflation. Negative real interest rates, along with 'moral suasion', were instrumental in easing the burden of debt servicing (Reinhart 2012). Dealing with the post-2007 euro area sovereign debt crises was made difficult by the absence of this combination. EU single market rules made use of capital controls and financial repression exceptionally difficult, as the case of Cyprus showed in 2013. The Maastricht monetary constitution ruled out the use of inflation as a debt reduction instrument. The euro area also found itself caught up in declining GDP growth. It became more difficult to avert risks of sovereign default.

Incentives to default also strengthened in the aftermath of internal insurrection, wars of succession, and regime change. They grew with the spread of nationalist, liberal, and socialist revolutions. These domestic revolutionary situations produced severe economic distress and sharply deteriorating financial conditions. The French Revolution initially recognized past royal debts as part of the public debt, viewing them as a 'sacred engagement'. However, in 1797, faced by rampant inflation and a worthless currency, the Directory repudiated the *assignats* and cancelled more than half of the national debt. This was France's last formal default (Grenier 2006). In the nineteenth-century Spain and Portugal experienced wars of succession in which ideological factors led to debt repudiation. The most prominent example of debt repudiation followed the Soviet overthrow of the Russian Czarist regime in 1917. It inflicted considerable damage on creditors in Paris.

A second pattern was the association of higher incidence of defaults with periods of deep and protracted recessions. They led to falling revenues and pressures on social spending, which made high debts unsustainable. The period 1880–1914 was one of fast growth in the European and world economies, helping to lower the overall public debt/GDP ratio. The ratio for the advanced economies fell from 45 per cent in 1880 to an historic low of 23 per cent in 1914 (Ali Abbas, Bellnocine, ElGanainy, and Horton 2010). In sharp contrast, the Great Depression saw the overall public debt/GDP ratio climb to 80 per cent in 1932. This debt platform provided the basis for a sharp increase in defaults. In the post-1945 world high growth and inflation initially acted to bring down the public debt/GDP ratio. However, the aggregate ratio then climbed so that it was 20 per cent higher in 2007 than it had been in 1928 (Ali Abbas et al. 2010). Subsequently, the ratio began to rise faster than during the Great Depression. In this context, inducements to default were likely to increase. The euro area in particular needed the combination of structural reforms with a return to fast economic growth and 'accommodating' inflation to help reduce risks of default.

The third pattern was an historic 'arc of default' across eastern and southern Europe (see Table 5.6). This arc included Bulgaria, Greece, Portugal, Romania, Serbia, Spain, and Ottoman Turkey. It extended into North Africa with European interests in Egypt, Morocco, and Tunisia. In Ottoman Turkey the defaults were fewer in number. However, their scale, duration, and geo-strategic significance preoccupied European financial diplomacy.

The Historic Arc of Default

The historic arc of default in Europe comprised a group of states that shared chronically weak state capacity, limited willingness to pay creditors, and periphery or 'super-periphery' status. They were characterized by either a politically marginal indigenous *rentier* class or one that invested its capital abroad, evaded domestic taxes, and even emigrated. There was widespread exploitation of the state as a valuable resource for rewarding family, friends, and supporters through licenses, jobs, contracts, housing, and tax privileges. In consequence, the public had a profound distrust of the state. People avoided paying taxes, leading to lack of domestic tax capacity to raise revenues to service debts.

External creditors attempted—usually unsuccessfully—to fill the domestic vacuum by seeking out, and trying to empower, a small domestic elite of fiscal reformers to impose domestic discipline. In the pre-1914 period new bondholder organizations endeavoured to coordinate creditor activism and enlist support of their states for this purpose. They were based in the main creditor states which dominated capital exports. A milestone in this process was the establishment of the British Corporation of Foreign Bondholders in 1868, followed by similar bondholder organizations in the Netherlands in 1876 and in Belgium and France in 1898. They were formed in the context of the problems thrown up by Latin American defaults and by the European arc of default (Esteves 2006). They lobbied hard for states to use 'gunboat' diplomacy, but generally in vain. They also pressed for a code of international law governing credit. However, in practice, market power and enforcement capacity rested with the prestigious underwriters, notably the House of Rothschild and Barings. These banks were better able to enforce embargoes on defaulting states (Flandreau and Flores 2010).

Along with Latin American debt crises, the European arc of default was a catalyst for the gradual evolution of more formalized patterns of creditor-debtor state relations in Europe. As in the later euro area sovereign debt crises, states in the arc of default experienced cycles of rapid capital inflows, the loss of creditor confidence, capital exit, and foreign intervention to secure overseas creditor interests. Late nineteenth-century Greece and the Ottoman Empire witnessed the establishment of an international financial commission with the aim of strengthening creditor oversight and maintaining the momentum of domestic reforms.

The creation of the Economic and Financial Organization (EFO) of the League of Nations in 1920 was designed to expedite capital market access for eastern and central European states and reduce their borrowing costs (Flores and Decorzant 2012). The nine League loans between 1923 and 1928 came with stabilization plans and stringent non-negotiable conditions, normally including imposition of a foreign adviser in the central bank. They involved close monitoring of domestic monetary and fiscal reforms and debt servicing by a League 'trustee agent', along with a Commissioner-General. The League Financial Committee insisted on tying foreign loans under its auspices to an independent national central bank, settlement of pre-war loans, and taxes assigned to debt service (Pauly 1996; Silverman 1982). However, these arrangements were short-term. In the 1930s, in the wake of the havoc of the Great Depression, the League Financial Committee's reports on states like Bulgaria and Greece—which together had accounted for four of the nine League loans—were catalogues of failure to deliver on reforms.

The problem was that League power was exercised in a small social world of collusion, involving very few domestic and foreign actors. They attempted to build domestic fiscal capacity to service debts. However, they faced powerful, recalcitrant vested interests, which repeatedly subverted external reforms. In addition, several states sought to avoid the humiliation of League conditionality. Czechoslovakia, Poland, and Romania opted for non-League reconstruction loans, using Barings, Hambros, and Lazard as London underwriters. Albania, Armenia, and Portugal chose to close themselves off from foreign loans altogether rather than accept League conditionality. The establishment of the League Loans Committee in London in 1932 was symptomatic of the overall sense of failure (Wynne 1951: 506). It sought in vain for special protection of the investors in the loans that had been issued under the auspices of the League. Moreover, the League Loan Committee came into conflict with bondholder organizations, which wanted priority for pre-1914 loans. External creditors were weakened by their own problems of collective action vis-à-vis these states.

The two turning points were the Congress of Berlin in 1878, after the Russian–Turkish War and the Ottoman default, and the Greek default of 1893, followed by the Greek–Turkish War of 1897 over Crete and further Greek default. These events exposed a rift amongst European states. On the one hand, the German and Austro-Hungarian governments brought increasing pressure to bear for a more resolute protection of bondholders by foreign intervention. On the other, British policy under Lord Salisbury was guided by the principle of abstention from official interference and hesitation in making 'official demands'. The British position emphasized private negotiations between debtor-state elites and bondholder organizations. Governments should confine themselves to recognizing the 'special' claims of creditors and exerting 'moral suasion' on their behalf.

The French position was much more directly supportive of their bondholder interests. French influence pushed policy towards a new principle of concerted diplomatic intervention by Britain, France, Belgium, the Netherlands, and Germany to settle foreign debt disputes. It was labelled the 'concerted compulsion' doctrine (Levandis 1944). On a scale of foreign intervention, Greece suffered tougher treatment than Ottoman Turkey, becoming the only European equivalent to Egypt's Commission of the Public Debt. The greater systemic significance of the Ottoman Empire helps explain this difference.

Spain

Spain topped the European league table, with eighteen defaults between 1800 and 1941 (Comín 1996). Sovereign defaulting flourished under absolute monarchy. In the wake of the Napoleonic Wars, King Ferdinand VII repudiated debts in 1814, 1823, 1826, and 1828, infuriating Dutch and later French bondholders. Fiscal problems were rooted in weak state capacity and exacerbated by conflicts between monarchists and political liberals, civil war, regime changes, and colonial wars that Spain could ill-afford. The three Carlist Wars and the Spanish–American War of 1898 added enormously to debt legacy.

Despite their ideological commitment to encouragement of externally-financed debt, and to avoidance of debt repudiation, liberal finance ministers were repeatedly forced to engage in debt restructurings because of the high public debt levels. The Bravo Murillo restructuring in 1851 incensed foreign bondholders. As under Ferdinand VII, it led to closure of the Paris stock exchange to Spanish debt. Only in 1867 did foreign bondholders succeed in achieving a debt restructuring to their liking. In 1881 Juan Camacho negotiated a voluntary debt restructuring that reduced the public debt/GDP ratio from 152.5 per cent in 1880 to 71.3 per cent in 1885. In 1900 Fernández Villaverde took radical action to reduce reliance on external debt and thus future vulnerability to default.

Spain's *rentier* class was in an insecure position. Lack of alternative domestic investment opportunities and favourable real interest rates encouraged them to hold Spanish public debt. However, they were made insecure by repeated debt restructurings and in 1900 were penalized by a 20 per cent tax on domestic debt interest. After the Camacho restructuring, and above all the restructuring of Villaverde, Spanish governments ended their dependence on externally-financed public debt. By 1920 it was negligible. It remained so, except for the period 1943–1950 and 2002–2010, when euro-denominated public debt held by non-residents grew. Under General Francisco Franco, default was replaced by a greater reliance on inflation and financial repression, which bore down directly on domestic *rentiers*. The inducement to financial repression increased as real interest rates on public debt became negative and alternative investment opportunities opened (Comín 2012).

Portugal

Portugal was also a serial defaulter. It had affinities with Greece in the scale of venality and corruption in fiscal administration and in the lack of a powerful indigenous *rentier* class. There were also sharp divisions between absolutists and liberals. After a bitter war and succession crisis, the new Portuguese queen repudiated the foreign loan of the exiled king, Dom Miguel (r. 1828–1832), who had been a strong advocate of restoration of absolute monarchy. This repudiation cast a long-term shadow over Portuguese creditworthiness. French bankers waged a public campaign against purchases of new Portuguese bonds (Wynne 1951: 361–89). It mattered because Portuguese governments were dependent on foreign borrowing. Debt defaults followed in 1840, 1845, and 1852, chiefly affecting British bondholders. By 1890 Portugal had the highest public debt per capita ratio of any European state, except France (Wynne 1951: 369).

French lenders returned once the Dom Miguel repudiation had been settled in 1891. A syndicate of French banks, led by Crédit Lyonnais and Société Générale, provided a loan in exchange for acquiring the monopoly of tobacco manufacture. However, financial crisis precipitated further defaults in 1892 and 1893. The French bondholder committee sought international control of Portuguese customs as a guarantee of debt payments and as a safeguard against future defaults. They faced British resistance. Although a debt settlement was agreed in 1902 on the security of Portuguese customs receipts, the Portuguese government refused to give formal diplomatic guarantees.

Portuguese governments were caught up in the paradox between foreign loan dependency and strong domestic resistance to 'humiliating conditions'. This paradox was highlighted after the military coup in 1926, after which the return to the gold standard became a priority. In 1927–1928 Portugal sought support from the League of Nations' Financial Committee to secure a new foreign loan. The Financial Committee agreed subject to conditions. They included fiscal and monetary reforms and the presence in Lisbon of a foreign agent of the League who would receive revenues assigned for the service of the loan. The government dropped its plans for a League loan in the face of what it regarded as national humiliation.

Ottoman Turkey

Ottoman Turkey was a key nodal point in the European arc of default both because of its own size and geo-strategic significance and because its default problems and those of Egypt were closely linked. Before the Crimean War the Ottoman Turk governments had preferred to rely on their own Istanbul-based Galata bankers, many of whom were Greek, as well as on the Jewish bankers of Salonika. Over the centuries, the Ottoman Empire had operated on the basis of granting commercial and tax concessions and privileges, as well as legal immunity, in exchange for credits. The system granted huge power to, and encouraged corruption amongst, moneylenders and private bankers who openly bribed officials (Mazower 2005: 153–8). Revenues became hostage to a complex, inefficient, and venal system of tax farming. The fiscal problem was magnified as the scale of internal insurrections and foreign wars grew, notably in the Balkans and in relations with Russia. Ottoman Turkey had no proper budget or national bank till the reforms of 1862–1863, and efforts to reform the tax system after the Gulhané (Rose Garden) Decree of 1839 were frustrated. Fiscally illiterate and personally extravagant Sultans and Pashas were a key part of the Ottoman problem (Wynne 1951: 395).

The first Ottoman foreign loan in 1854 took place against the background of the Crimean War (1853–1856). It reflected the new active interest of the British and the French governments in strengthening the Ottoman Empire as a bulwark against the spread of Russian power. In the period till 1914 the Ottoman Empire emerged as one of the biggest international capital importers. British and continental European banks began to be excited by the economic prospects that were offered by a new climate of Ottoman reform. Large loans by the House of Rothschild and by the Crédit mobilier were followed by the foundation of the Imperial Ottoman Bank (*Banque impériale ottomane*, BIO) in 1863. Operating as the Anglo-French Ottoman national bank, it was given privileges in exchange for providing credit at favourable rates (Clay 2000). Two subsequent decades of heavy borrowing culminated in the Ottoman defaults of 1875–1876, which triggered the outrage of bondholder organizations. The problems of negotiating a settlement were aggravated by the Balkan uprisings and by the Russo-Turkish War of 1877–1878.

The subsequent Congress of Berlin in 1878 was the site of intensive lobbying by the bondholder organizations to ensure that pre-war debts had priority over the Russian war indemnity. They also proposed that any newly independent Balkan States should take on a proportionate share of the Ottoman debt, according to the principle of state succession in public debts. Furthermore, they pressed the case for an international financial commission to protect the claims of Ottoman creditors. The strategy of the Ottoman government was to minimize the dangers of the international financial commission that was agreed in Berlin. It did so by giving preferential privileges to the Galata bankers over foreign creditors. It also accorded a key role to the Imperial Ottoman Bank in helping negotiate a settlement with the bondholders.

The outcome was the Sultan's Decree of Mouharrem of 1881, which involved a complex, voluntary de facto surrender of Ottoman sovereignty. It had a triple character. The Decree was a law of the Ottoman Empire; a contract between the Ottoman Empire and its creditors; and a treaty between states by virtue of its formal communication to the Great Powers (Wynne 1951). However, given the pivotal geo-strategic significance of Ottoman Turkey, and its chronic weakness, the British and French governments chose to avoid direct engagement in these negotiations and any semblance of coercion.

The Decree of Mouharrem established the Ottoman Public Debt Administration and the Council of the Public Debt as a mechanism for foreign supervision to ensure that revenues were devoted to debt servicing. The Council represented Austro-Hungarian, British, Dutch, French, German, and Ottoman bondholders. Its functions evolved in a more interventionist direction by the 1890s, taking responsibility for the collection of a number of direct taxes. Ottoman Turk creditworthiness improved. However, the Council was not able to curb the Sultan's extravagance, to gain oversight of new foreign loans, or to address the problems of corrupt, inefficient fiscal administration and the lack of accountable and transparent budgeting. There was also a subtle shift in creditor power. It slipped from Britain and France before 1875, to France between 1881 and 1903, and then to Germany, especially via the Deutsche Bank (see Table 5.8). Following British occupation of Egypt in 1882, the Ottoman government sought alternative financial partners (Clark 2013: 335). German strategic interest lay in stabilizing the Ottoman Empire, principally in relation to threats from Russia. German banks helped finance the Anatolian railway from 1888, followed by the ambitious project for a Berlin-to-Baghdad

Table 5.8 Country Distribution of the Outstanding Ottoman Debt, 1881–1914, in Millions of Pounds Sterling, in Percentages

	1881	1914
Britain	33.2	14.0
France	34.3	53.0
Germany	7.5	21.0
Belgium	5.0	8.4
Holland	5.3	3.6

(*Source*: Pamuk 1987: 75)

railway from 1903. These projects were of major symbolic importance, producing strategic anxiety in London and St Petersburg (Clark 2013: 337). Nevertheless, the ownership structure of the Imperial Ottoman Bank and the composition of the Council of the Public Debt reflected the continuing scale of French presence and potential influence.

Bondholders faced further Ottoman Turk default once its government entered the First World War on the side of Germany. The Council of the Public Debt was reduced to just Austrian, German, and Turk bondholders. The Anglo-French Imperial Ottoman Bank was marginalized. Ottoman collapse and the successor state of Mustafa Kemal Atatürk (1881–1938) added to creditor losses. In 1920 the Treaty of Sèvres provided for an international financial commission to take 'complete control' of Turkish financial policies and administration. However, the new nationalist government did not ratify the treaty, and the commission was never established. The Turkish government undermined the Council of Public Debt and declared the Decree of Mouharrem invalid. In 1930 it defaulted on its share of the Ottoman debt, which had been regulated by the Treaty of Lausanne in 1923. Atatürk was determined that his modern Turkey would be free from the forms of foreign control that had marked Ottoman Turkey.

The Balkans: Bulgaria and Serbia

Bulgaria was similar to Greece and Portugal in its weak state capacity, corrupt tax administration, and lack of budgetary control. However, it differed in not being a systematic defaulter. Bulgaria achieved independence from Ottoman rule in 1878 following the Russo–Turkish War. Like Greece earlier, it began life with heavy external debts. Its origins were associated with an understanding that it would be a client state of Russia, above all in pursuing its territorial claims in Macedonia against prospective Serbian rivalry. However, its government soon sought to manoeuvre between Germany and Russia. To the irritation of the Russian government, it defaulted twice temporarily on its occupation debt to Russia.

Bulgaria's victory in the war with Serbia in 1885, and political ambitions to create Greater Bulgaria, led to the domestic empowerment of its officer class. Fulfilment of Bulgarian ambitions rested on seeking out alternative sources of money, both to pay debts and to build military infrastructure (Clark 2013: 276). The outcome of this manoeuvring was mounting mistrust of Bulgaria, above all in St Petersburg. Up to the Balkan Wars of 1912–1913 Bulgaria was caught up in a rearmament competition with its neighbours, principally Serbia, involving large foreign loans to finance expanding military spending. The great powers, notably France, were content to supply these loans, typically tied to lucrative armaments contracts.

Key external and internal interests were satisfied by this cycle of rearmament, external debt, and ambitions for Greater Bulgaria. However, by 1905 Bulgaria was rendered effectively insolvent. Foreign control was the price paid for great-power loans. A bondholders' delegation was established in Sofia to ensure protection of creditor interests. Between 1900 and 1909 Bulgaria contracted four French loans, two Austrian loans, and one Russian loan. Paribas was the lead bank in the four French loans, one of which also involved the State Bank of Russia. As with the Portugal loan of 1891, the French loans were secured on the basis of revenues from tobacco tax (Wynne 1951: 531–74).

Nevertheless, these sovereign debt problems did not inhibit Bulgaria from participating in the Balkan Wars of 1912–1913, which led to further short-term loans from

Paribas and from Austrian and Russian banks. The outcome of the Second Balkan War was disastrous for Bulgaria. By July 1913 the Bulgarian government was seeking massive foreign credits (Clark 2013: 276). The Russian government proved reluctant. French terms were extremely onerous, including the requirement that it must be used only to purchase French military equipment. The final outcome of protracted and diplomatically tense negotiations was a loan, backed by German banks, locking Bulgaria into the policy of the Triple Alliance of Austro-Hungary, Germany, and Italy. Foreign debt proved a key factor in radically shifting Bulgaria's approach to great-power allegiance, from Russia to Germany.

Bulgarian entry into the First World War in 1915 was associated with default and dismantlement of the previous structure of foreign control. Its aftermath was the Treaty of Neuilly in 1919 and the establishment of an Inter-Allied Commission to represent British, French, and Italian creditor interests in Sofia. The Commission was to ensure that customs revenues were used for official reparation payments and, in case of default, to assume 'full control'. Thereafter, Bulgaria was dependent on acquiring loans under the auspices of the League of Nations' Financial Committee in return for domestic stabilization efforts according to principles of conservative monetary liberalism. In 1926, following civil war and severe domestic repression, the League Committee recommended a refugee loan on the security of excise duties and other taxes and in return for settlement of pre-war loans and the establishment of a central bank. A further loan under League auspices in 1928 was secured by customs revenues and tied to further budgetary and monetary reforms. However, in reports of 1933 and 1935 the League's Financial Committee sharply criticized the lack of reforms, weak budgetary controls, and unprofessional tax administration. Bulgaria did, at least, avoid unilateral default till 1940, unlike Greece.

Serbia gained independent statehood in 1882 and, like Bulgaria, lavished funding on its military. The Radicals, led by the populist politician Nikola Pašić, pursued an expansionist pan-Slavic agenda of creating a Greater Serbia, identifying Russia as their natural ally. This agenda brought Serbia into conflict with both the Hapsburg Empire and the Ottoman Empire, as well as with Bulgaria in relation to Macedonian territory. Critically, as with Bulgaria, realizing a Greater Serbia depended on access to foreign loans to build a military infrastructure. Initially, Serbian policy looked to Vienna, in part reflecting Serbian trade and in part as a counterbalance to Bulgaria's privileged relationship with Russia. Austria provided generous loans to Serbia, requiring military orders to be placed with Austrian firms and the pledging of specific revenues that were paid into a special account controlled jointly by the Serbian government and the bondholders. However, Serbian debts continued to accumulate, above all after the defeat by Bulgaria in 1885. With insolvency imminent, a new arrangement was agreed involving a consolidating of debts at a lower rate of interest and control of assigned revenues by a separate administration in which bondholders were represented.

However, in 1905–1906 Austro-Serbian relations experienced a serious crisis. The French government helped orchestrate a major loan to Serbia in 1906, in return for armament orders to the French firm Schneider-Creusot (Clark 2013: 29–30). Soon more than three-quarters of Serbian debt was owned by French bondholders (Feis 1930: 64). A prolonged tariff war ensued between Austria and Serbia. In consequence, Serbia became integrated into the French-based alliance system, in a manner compatible with Pašić's belief in Russia as the natural supporter of pan-Slavism. This policy of military and infrastructure investment based on French loans seemed to be vindicated by Serbian victory and territorial gains in the Second Balkan War of 1913, making it a major regional power. Foreign loans had served as major instruments in the competition to carve out spheres of influence in the Balkans, at the expense of the Hapsburg Empire.

Greece

The two outstanding defaulters were Greece and Portugal. Greece was financially isolated from her independence from the Ottoman Empire in 1829 till 1878. It was born as a 'camouflaged insolvent state' (Levantis 1940: 114). The public debt/GDP ratio was an enormous 213 per cent in 1843 (see Table 5.9). In 1833 the Great Powers had guaranteed a 60 million franc loan to Greece. However, defaults followed as early as 1836 and 1843. They led Lord Palmerston and Robert Peel to assert the right of Britain to interfere to enforce her claims. However, it was not till 1878 that a settlement was negotiated with British bondholders.

Greece's solvency problems stemmed from multiple sources. Heavy foreign debts had been incurred to finance the protracted war of independence. Greece had a crippled economy of debt-ridden peasants, who could not afford to pay taxes. It was burdened by a 'tax-farming' fiscal system that was associated with large-scale extortion and corruption. There was domestic factional competition to control and exploit public finances. Credits disappeared into non-productive uses. In addition, there was repeated reckless resort to a financially unsustainable expansionist Pan-Hellenic policy.

Subsequently, between 1879 and 1890, French banks led a huge expansion of foreign loans to Greece. However, the increase in external debt and public debt burden per capita went along with a continuing huge deficit in Greece's balance of trade (Levantis 1940:73–4). The subsequent default of 1893 took place against a background of a public debt/GDP ratio of 210.8 per cent (see Table 5.9). The outcome was a confrontation between the Greek government, which claimed to act 'under imperious and immediate necessity' and '*force majeure*', and British, French, and German bondholder committees. Their negotiations were made more difficult by a perception that the Greek government was pursuing 'divide-and-rule' diplomacy with creditors. In particular, it exploited British and French fears that a coercive approach would drive Greece closer to Russia. Conversely, the German government favoured unequivocally tough action against Greece.

The Greek–Turkish War of 1897 over Crete and further Greek default left Greece diplomatically isolated, facing a war indemnity. In return for a new internationally guaranteed war indemnity loan, creditors were offered new security. It took the form of the establishment of external foreign control through the new Society for Managing Revenues Assigned to the Service of the Greek Debt. It was set up under Greek law and accountable to an international financial commission, which was to represent bondholders. The commission had powers of appointment and dismissal, as well as inspection powers. Its approval was required for the issue of Treasury bonds. Service of the war indemnity loan and all other national debts were placed under the 'absolute control' of the commission, whilst the Society collected the assigned taxes (Wynne 1951: 283–357).

The international financial commission faced acute domestic distrust. It was seen as a symbol of the 'tyranny' of foreign bondholders over Greece (Mazower 1991). Moreover,

Table 5.9 Greek Domestic Debt, External Debt, and Total Debt, 1843–1914

Year	GDP in Current Prices (Million Drachmas)	Domestic Public Debt in Current Prices (Million Drachmas)[1]	Domestic Public Debt (% of Total Debt)	External Public Debt (Million Drachmas)[2]	External Public Debt (% of Total Debt)	Total Debt in current prices (million drachmas)[3]	Total Debt in current prices (% of GDP)
1843	70,3	0,0	0,0%	150,0	100,0%	150,0	213,4%
1861	150,3	0,9	0,6%	150,0	99,4%	150,9	100,4%
1862	154,5	2,5	1,6%	150,0	98,4%	152,5	98,7%
1863	160,1	4,2	2,7%	150,0	97,3%	154,2	96,3%
1864	187,3	6,2	4,0%	150,0	96,0%	156,2	83,4%
1865	182,3	6,5	4,2%	150,0	95,8%	156,5	85,9%
1866	194,3	8,0	5,1%	150,0	94,9%	158,0	81,3%
1867	227,1	9,5	6,0%	150,0	94,0%	159,5	70,2%
1868	217,6	15,8	9,5%	150,0	90,5%	165,8	76,2%
1869	193,0	19,9	11,7%	150,0	88,3%	169,9	88,0%
1870	230,5	17,7	10,6%	150,0	89,4%	167,7	72,8%
1871	263,5	18,9	11,2%	150,0	88,8%	168,9	64,1%
1872	221,5	18,1	10,8%	150,0	89,2%	168,1	75,9%
1873	239,6	16,3	9,8%	150,0	90,2%	166,3	69,4%
1874	256,5	18,8	11,1%	150,0	88,9%	168,8	65,8%
1875	256,0	18,0	10,7%	150,0	89,3%	168,0	65,6%
1876	246,9	18,7	11,1%	150,0	88,9%	168,7	68,3%
1877	280,2	36,0	19,4%	150,0	80,6%	186,0	66,4%
1881	340,5	101,1	32,5%	210,0	67,5%	311,1	91,4%
1884	409,6	40,1	12,1%	290,0	87,9%	330,1	80,6%
1887	445,6	142,6	21,5%	520,0	78,5%	662,6	148,7%
1889	441,0					698,0	158,3%
1893	550,3					1160,0	210,8%
1911	847,5					1053,0	124,2%
1913	856,7					1216,0	141,9%
1914	1235,8					1424,0	115,2%

[1] The only available data on Domestic Public Debt refer to the debt owed to the National Bank of Greece but this is almost equal to the total domestic public debt.

[2] For the period 1843–1877 External Public Debt refers to an estimated value of the external debt in current prices, using as base the nominal capital of 130.000.000 francs and rounding up towards 150.000.000 to include an estimation of capital and interest, as recognized by the Greek governments (the foreign creditors' claims usually exceeded that sum).

[3] The sum of Domestic Public Debt and External Public Debt is approximately the Total Debt as recognized by the Greek Governments at the time. Debt holders until 1878 were making different calculations and claiming higher amounts.

(*Source*: Professor George Pagoulatos, Athens University of Economics and Business. Data on debt are from Dertilis 2005: 530 (in Greek). Data on GDP are derived from Kostelenos et al. 2007: 137–41 (in Greek))

the commission proved powerless in the face of the effects of Greece's decade of wars in 1912–1922 on debts. The debt burden was exacerbated by the disastrous Smyrna expedition after 1919 and the costs of absorbing the huge influx of refugees from Asia Minor. Throughout the 1920s the commission continued to complain about the lack of reforms and malpractices. In 1932 Greece undertook a further unilateral default, ignoring the commission's protests. In 1937 Greek proposals for a debt settlement included abolition of the international financial commission. They were rejected by bondholders.

Egypt and North Africa

The Egyptian default problem was European in that it was linked to Ottoman Turkey. The large 1854 and 1871 loans to Egypt had been secured on the Egyptian tribute to the Sultan. These monies were remitted to the Sultan via the Bank of England, giving the British government and bondholders a significant leverage in debt negotiations. From the 1850s the Khedive of Egypt engaged in profligate foreign borrowing, culminating with the grand opening of the Suez Canal in 1869, which was financed by British and French capital. He sought to reinvent Egypt as belonging to Europe rather than Africa, though *de jure* a vassal of the Ottoman Sultan. By the 1870s Egyptian bonds had become a favoured investment of the European *rentier* class, notably in London, Paris, and Vienna. William Gladstone, British prime minister during a substantial part of this episode (1880–1885), held 37 per cent of his personal holdings in these bonds (Jenkins 1995: 507).

The Egyptian default of 1876 caused shockwaves across Europe. The subsequent negotiations of the Egyptian Bondholders League with the Ottoman government were bedevilled by changes of Ottoman positions, especially from the outbreak of war with Russia. The outcome was the Khedive's proposal for a permanent, independent Commission of the Public Debt, to which revenues would be assigned for it to service the debt. It would have four commissioners—Austrian, British, French, and Italian. They would be nominated by the respective governments and have the status of Egyptian officials. Moreover, two European controllers-general (British and French) were to supervise the fiscal administration of Egypt on behalf of bondholder interests. This system of dual control was strengthened in 1878 when the two controllers-general were replaced by two European ministers in the Egyptian cabinet, one as finance minister (Wynne 1951: 577–632).

The subsequent coup d'état by the Khedive led to his deposition by the Sultan, despite European government protests, and to the reinstatement of dual control. Sir Evelyn Baring was appointed one of the controllers-general. A further army mutiny in 1881, riots in Alexandria, and the murder of some fifty Europeans led the British government to intervene militarily in 1882 to suppress the revolt. However, it did so with great reluctance, primarily because the Ottoman government was too weak to act. Dual control gave way to a single British financial 'adviser', who was given substantial fiscal authority. The Anglo-French Commission of the Public Debt remained. However, Baring (later Earl Cromer) was appointed 'Minister Plenipotentiary and Consul-General'. As such, he was de facto ruler of Egypt for twenty-four years (1883–1907). His style in implementing a wide range of financial and economic reforms, especially to the punitive land tax system, earned him the nickname 'Over-Baring'.

Throughout the Egyptian debt crisis, British governments sought to sustain an image as a moral influence. Whether intriguing in Constantinople to depose the Khedive in 1879, or directly intervening in 1882, they presented themselves as acting to ensure the principle that foreign debts should be honoured. At the same time they wished to be seen as maintaining a critical distance from bondholder demands. However, this image thinly concealed materialistic geo-strategic and economic calculations. 'Informal' empire, co-opting and working with and through local elites, was viewed as preferable to the high financial costs of occupation and direct rule. Its techniques were best adapted to managing the scale of existing British commitments. At the same time, the new Suez Canal was of vital geo-strategic interest as 'the route to India'. Britain's presence sought to check French power and avoid the unnecessary further weakening of Turkish power to the benefit of Russia. In these ways the nature of British involvement remained consistent with fundamental tenets of British foreign policy. Pursuit of these interests involved continuing disagreements with France. France sought British evacuation for its own geo-strategic reasons, even at risk to French bondholders. Whilst it lasted, Anglo-French control was accompanied by intense suspicion and geo-strategic rivalry, only abated by the 1882 intervention and Baring's appointment.

France had in any case other interests to pursue in North Africa, inviting parallels with Egypt. In Tunisia the problem of securing repayments on mounting debts to European banks led to the establishment of an international financial commission in 1869. French military intervention in 1881 was motivated by a combination of her financial interests with geo-strategic interest in keeping out Italy and securing her position in Algeria. In 1883 Tunisia became an official protectorate of France, which took over responsibility for its fiscal administration. The Bank of Algeria and Tunisia (*Banque d'Algérie et Tunisie*) was established as a key instrument of French colonial policy. It was a privately-owned central bank that financed public works under the military occupation.

Morocco had a different experience. Spain invaded in 1860 and imposed a crippling indemnity that was beyond the country's means. Faced by weak domestic fiscal capacity, and confronted by powerful rural lords, the Moroccan government relied on foreign loans. By 1907, following the German Emperor's declaration of support for Moroccan independence, and subsequent French fury, European governments accepted virtual Franco-Spanish control over Morocco's fiscal administration.

The historic arc of default exerted a profound reverse demonstration effect on the traditional northern and central European powers. Association or comparison with these states risked loss of reputation and position as at the centre or heart of Europe. In inter-war Europe the reparations issue generated a new source of humiliation for Germans. The Dawes Plan of 1924 included provision for a foreign Agent-General for Reparations within the Reichsbank. Seymour Parker Gilbert, a senior US Treasury official, was made responsible for managing German reparation payments (Ahamed 2010: 326–8). German negotiators stressed the risk that this association and comparison with earlier arrangements for Ottoman Turkey would only deepen German resentment.

Inflation, Devaluation, Financial Repression, and the Erosion of Debt

Governing elites can seek to avert the unwelcome choice between politically and economically costly default and politically and economically painful deflation and recession. Inflation, devaluation, and financial repression offer alternative instruments to quickly erode the value of debts. For this reason, creditors have a strong interest in creating institutions that support a low-inflation environment, that tie the hands of governments in exchange-rate policy, and that ensure the non-monetary financing of public debt. For them, the ideal policy regime combines an independent central bank, strictly mandated to deliver price stability, the strict separation of monetary from fiscal policies, and an exchange-rate tie to a 'hard' currency or secure and impersonal monetary standard. Such a regime helps to ensure that inflation, exchange-rate management, and negative real interest rates are not used to liquidate public debt. In the case of external debt, a 'hard' exchange-rate peg helps to both enforce domestic discipline and prevent creditor losses that follow from devaluation. Conversely, states that are faced with big debt overhangs and sharp and persisting economic contraction have incentives to tolerate higher inflation, to pursue currency depreciation, and to resort to various practices of financial repression.

Inflation

Rapid debt liquidation can be achieved by 'inflation tax' on creditors, exploiting the phenomenon of 'money illusion' in which investors, as well as consumers, fail to recognize real cuts in purchasing power (Keynes 1923). However, as after 1918, money illusion is more difficult to maintain in the face of 'surprise' inflation. More subtly, governments and central banks can collude to ensure a persistently sustained increase in inflation rate. In this way high public debt ratios were brought down in Italy and in the United States after 1945, as well as under Franco in Spain (Francese and Pace 2008; Aizenman and Marion 2009; Comín 2012).

However, debt liquidation via inflation carries risks of high social, economic, and political costs, especially if inflation gathers momentum and runs out of control. Revolutionary France and the Weimar Republic offer evidence of how hyperinflation can offer a quick cure for debt problems but entails extremely high costs. Inflation transfers wealth to debtors, at the expense of creditors and savers. Conversely, monetary regimes that lock-in lower inflation can induce debt growth when states have weak governance capacity and limited control over fiscal balances. This phenomenon was discernible in Greece after it joined the euro area.

The incentive to use inflation to liquidate debts increases once governments have monopoly over the printing of paper money without the discipline of gold or firmly entrenched central bank independence. The temptation that it offers to quickly subvert debt burdens is difficult to resist, as in the case of German reparations after 1918. Inflation is all the more likely to follow when there is weak state fiscal and monetary capacity. The French National Assembly in 1789–1790 lacked the capacity to raise taxes to satisfy new popular aspirations and to repay royal debts for which it assumed the obligation. Weimar German governments after 1919 did not possess the central tax powers to pay official creditors. Similarly, high inflation in the Republic of Poland-Lithuania after 1717 followed its reduction to a Russian protectorate, lacking independent fiscal powers (see Table 5.10). Inflation represents the cunning of weak states.

Inflation was less extreme in the late-medieval and early-modern periods, in part because of the metallic basis of coinage. Nevertheless, Poland-Lithuania stands out as having inflation over 20 per cent for more than 40 per cent of the period 1704–1799. France, the German states, and Sweden, which were locked in their early, brutal wars of religion, were also more inflation-prone than the English, Dutch, Norwegians, and Spaniards.

Table 5.10 Debt Erosion through Inflation in Europe, 1500–1799

State	Period	Share of Years Inflation Exceeded 20 per cent	Peak Annual Inflation	Year of Peak
Austria	1501–1799	8.4	99.1	1623
Belgium	1501–1799	25.1	185.1	1708
Denmark	1749–1799	18.8	77.4	1772
France	1501–1799	12.4	121.3	1622
Germany	1501–1799	10.4	140.6	1622
Italy	1501–1799	19.1	173.1	1527
Netherlands	1501–1799	4.0	40	1709
Norway	1666–1799	6.0	44.2	1709
Poland	1704–1799	43.8	92.1	1762
Portugal	1729–1799	19.7	83.1	1757
Spain	1501–1799	4.7	40.5	1521
Sweden	1540–1799	15.5	65.8	1572
Ottoman Turkey	1586–1799	19.2	53.4	1621
United Kingdom	1501–1799	5.0	39.5	1587

(*Source*: Reinhart and Rogoff 2008: 45)

Two of the most important cases of hyperinflation are associated with experiments in paper money in eighteenth-century France: under John Law and under the French Revolution. At the outset of the Revolution, the National Assembly issued *assignats*. This innovation reflected the lack of reliable revenues and the priority to establishing creditworthiness by avoiding default on royal debts. These certificates were supposedly backed by the value of church properties confiscated in 1790. They were also modelled, at least initially, on English exchequer bills, paying an interest rate. The new law required everyone to accept *assignats* in payment of debts. By 1792 their over-issue and the lack of public confidence led to hyperinflation. Those who used *assignats* to pay debts received a windfall. However, inflation generated mounting hardship and social unrest in 1793. It was only rooted out effectively once Napoleon issued the new franc gold coins in 1801.

Inflation figures as a more important instrument for eroding debt once modern European states resort to paper money, especially when lacking the firm anchor of the gold standard. In the early years after the First and the Second World Wars, 1918–1923 and 1944–1946, hyperinflation reaped havoc (see Table 5.11). The two outstanding examples remain Hungary in 1946, when the communist government actively pursued the impoverishment of *rentiers*, and Greece in 1944–1948 when it was mired in brutal civil war. Similarly, Germany, Poland, and Russia suffered hyperinflations in 1923, along with Austria in 1922. The highest recorded inflation rates clustered in 1918–1923: Austria,

Table 5.11 Debt Erosion through Inflation in Europe, 1800–2006

State Period	Start of Years	Share of Years Inflation Exceeded 20 Per Cent	Peak Annual Inflation	Year	Years of Hyperinflation
Austria	1800	20.8	1,733.0 1922	2	
Belgium	1800	10.1	50.6	1812	0
Denmark	1800	2.1	48.3	1800	0
Finland	1861	5.5	242.0	1918	0
France	1800	5.8	74.0	1946	0
Germany	1800	9.7	2.22E+10 1923	2	
Greece	1834	13.3	3.02E+10 1944	4	
Hungary	1924	15.7	9.63E+26 1946	2	
Italy	1800	11.1	491.4	1944	0
Netherlands	1800	1.0	21.0	1918	0
Norway	1800	5.3	152.0	1812	0
Poland	1800	28.0	51,699.4 1923	2	
Portugal	1800	9.7	84.2 1808	0	
Russia/Soviet Union	1854	35.7	13,534.7 1923	8	
Spain	1800	3.9	102.1 1808	0	
Sweden	1800	1.9	35.8	1918	0
Turkey	1800	20.5	115.9	1942	0
United Kingdom	1800	2.4	34.4	1800	0
United States	1800	1.0	24.0	1864	0

(*Source*: Reinhart and Rogoff 2008: 45)

Finland, Germany, the Netherlands, Poland, Russia, and Sweden. The period 1944–1946 saw the highest inflation records for France, Greece, Hungary, and Italy. Similarly, the Napoleonic Wars accounted for the highest recorded inflation rates in Belgium, Britain, Denmark, Norway, Portugal, and Spain. This historical bunching reflected the devastating effects of modernized warfare on public finances and the debt overhang from war. Politically, the incentive to resort to printing money seemed preferable to making taxpayers carry this heavy burden.

Some states stand out because of their historically low inflation rates: Britain, Denmark, the Netherlands, Sweden, and the United States. They were successful for various reasons, whether avoiding participation in big European wars, drawing on the resources of substantial domestic bond markets to finance war, and having substantial tax capacity. The differences are reflected in domestic financing of the First World War. In Britain the currency in circulation doubled, in France it tripled, whilst in Germany it quadrupled (Ahamed 2010: 84, 87). All three resorted to inflationary war financing that hurt bondholders. However, Britain relied more heavily on taxation, whilst France mobilized debt financing through its domestic bond markets and the Banque de France. Lacking such effective instruments, the German government engaged in the most inflationary war financing. Its *rentier* class suffered disproportionately.

Weimar Germany (1919–1933) offers the economically and politically most significant case of hyperinflation as an instrument for reducing the debt burden. The new republican regime faced a war-damaged *rentier* class, internal revolutions, and severe social tensions. Its capacity to act was further undermined by weak governments and by the lack of tax instruments to meet the costs of dealing with acute domestic challenges and with the uncertain, potentially huge, reparation bill from the victorious Allies. The Weimar Republic was born in a climate in which other states sought revenge on Germany. In these threatening conditions, Weimar governments feared resorting to savage deflation to tackle fiscal problems (Feldman 1997). In 1922–1923 tensions over German reparation payments mounted. They led to French complaints that the government was sabotaging agreements, to French and Belgian occupation of the Ruhr, and to German passive resistance. Subsequent German government attempts to finance this passive resistance by printing money increased already high inflation into a spectacular, sharp, hyperinflation.

The surprise 1923 inflation inflicted heavy losses on foreign creditors. Their losses were equivalent to German reparation payments over the period 1919–1923 (Holtfrerich 1980: 330). By means of this 'inflation tax', foreign creditors were drawn into financing German public expenditure. Hyperinflation also helped to substantially reduce income and wealth inequalities in Germany from those in 1914 as war bonds became worthless and savings vanished. In addition, for a limited time, it served German national interests by acting as an incentive for other states to moderate their reparation demands, an outcome achieved with the Dawes Plan. However, the price of hyperinflation was a collapse in capital imports, hoarding of goods, widespread exploitation, and sharp deterioration in living conditions, especially for those dependent on small savings. Faced by this economic dislocation, and threats of radicalization of the electorate, the German government of Gustav Stresemann adopted radical stabilization measures in November 1923.

Devaluation

Devaluation is the key policy instrument for eroding the value of external debt. It serves the broad macroeconomic purpose of restoring lost competitiveness, helping to engineer export-led growth, correcting trade imbalances, encouraging capital imports, and enabling the accumulation of large gold and foreign-exchange reserves. These outcomes help erode external debt burdens and restore creditworthiness in ways that are much less painful to domestic wage-earners than sharp and protracted deflation. They also appear more readily compatible with the political settlement that underpins the notion of socially inclusive entitlements associated with large welfare states and consumer cultures.

The historical record suggests that, despite bearing costs in this way, foreign creditors can be attracted back once economic growth and sovereign creditworthiness are re-established. This scenario played out in France and Germany between 1924 and 1929 after they returned to gold at undervalued exchange rates. By 1929 France had emerged as the top European creditor power, with huge gold reserves. Similarly, once Britain left the gold standard in 1931, followed by the United States in 1933, their economies weathered the Great Depression with less domestic economic, social, and political difficulties than France, which remained on gold.

Financial Repression

Financial repression seeks to reduce the domestic currency debt burden by engineering negative real interest rates and creating captive domestic support for strengthening or safeguarding sovereign creditworthiness. Its effect is to benefit borrowers through lower debt-servicing costs at the expense of creditors. Financial repression takes typically stealthy, opaque forms, using a tightening relationship to the central bank and financial institutions in order to create a 'home bias' in sovereign lending, supported by more stringent regulation of capital requirements and lending activities of financial institutions (Reinhart 2012). Central banks can be drawn into large-scale sovereign bond purchasing, directly or via their liquidity support for the banking system. Financial institutions, like pension funds, can be required to hold a higher share of sovereign bonds in their portfolios to satisfy tougher liquidity standards. Explicit or implicit interest rate ceilings can be placed on bank deposits, akin to former usury laws. Also, as in Cyprus in March 2013, controls on cross-border capital movements can be introduced, including indirectly through new curbs on money laundering and tax evasion. These sorts of measures were an important feature of the enormous rise in public debt of eighteenth-century Britain, whilst avoiding default (Drelichman and Voth 2008). Financial repression was also intense in interwar Europe and in the period from 1945 till the end of the 1970s (Reinhart 2012). Despite the restrictions on capital controls under European single market rules, and its incompatibility with European currency union, financial repression gained new momentum as sovereign debt crises intensified from 2008. By 2012 the 'home bias' in European sovereign debt markets was pronounced, suggesting a rolling back of European financial integration, even within the euro area. Financial fragmentation was given an even more radical form when capital controls were introduced as part of the Cyprus 'bail-out' package in 2013.

Core-Periphery, Empire, and Power

The historical examination of debt and political rule begs questions about the value of concepts like empire and core and periphery in understanding power in European financial diplomacy. The complex, multidimensional relationships of power amongst states are difficult to conceptualize in clear, non-contestable terms. However, the ebb and flow of assets and liabilities creates asymmetries of power that must somehow be defined. Debt is a dimension of power that reveals informal hierarchy. The distinction between rulers and states who are creditworthy and those who are not points to a key differentiator between a European core and periphery.

In late-medieval and early-modern Europe the core comprised a cluster of city states, initially Florence, Genoa, and Venice, and later Antwerp and Amsterdam. They provided or helped organize the debt finance on which territorial rulers depended. To be creditworthy, and thus in the core, territorial rulers depended on branding by the city-state merchant-financiers. The ambition of English Tudor rulers from Henry VII to Elizabeth I was to gain this branding, above all from the Fugger, and to be able to stand alongside the Hapsburgs.

However, the gradual growth of creditworthy territorial states added another attribute to the concept of core: systemic significance. Status as a core state takes on a special character when sovereign creditworthiness is reinforced by large GDP and population size, abundant natural resources, and military power. This combination becomes associated with the notion of empire when rulers or states claim demarcated spheres of extra-territorial influence, through which they can increase their assets and extend their financial and economic control. Examples include Ancient Rome, Charlemagne's Empire, and nineteenth-century Belgium, Britain, France, and the Netherlands. They were able to transfer resources from their colonies to help finance their deficits and reduce their debt. The history of the arc of default across eastern and southern Europe suggested similar relations of domination and subordination, consistent with empire. It went along with a prevailing sense of victimhood, expressed in a discourse of 'humiliation', 'occupation', 'colonialism', and 'resistance'. This language recurred in the post-2010 euro area sovereign debt crises, above all in Cyprus and Greece. It conjured up an image of the euro area as a German 'empire'.

However, on its own terms, creditor-state power is associated with informal rather than formal empire. It involves a preference for defending creditor interests by the exercise of moral suasion over debtor states, combined with economic and financial pressures (Tomz 2007). The classic instruments of creditor-state power rest on 'soft' power, based on 'branding' states as creditworthy or not, and on 'conditionality'. Its agents are financial 'doctors', who prescribe fiscal, monetary, and economic cures for debtor states (Flandreau 2003b). On balance, creditor interests are best served by peace. Although war might bring profits, especially from backing the victor, it places *rentier* power at risk. This risk was appreciated by the Rothschild family in nineteenth-century Europe (Gille 1965; Stern 1978).

The analysis of power over, and within, the politics of creditworthiness illustrates how the shadow of hierarchy has continued to fall over relations between rulers and creditors, sometimes darkly, other times lightly. As Chapter 6 shows, late-medieval and early-modern Europe was littered with examples of the brutal uses of domestic financial power by rulers, not just against Jews and foreign financiers but also against Church, nobility, and cities. Rulers could bestow, and remove, commercial and financial privileges, status, and protection from their creditors. In consequence, financiers often stood in a relationship of awe and fear to their sovereign debtors. Debt financiers had much more to win and to lose than just the interest or principal on their loans. Rulers often resorted to fiscal tyranny over creditors, including the removal of financial and trade privileges, expropriation of assets, and expulsion. They could also use divide-and-rule tactics amongst financiers.

Furthermore, rulers had ultimate power over war and peace. War served as a litmus test of loyalty for financiers. As with Ducci and the Welser, it could break their careers.

The politics of debt financing obsessed ambitious rulers like Francis I of France, the Emperor Charles V, and Philip II of Spain. In the final analysis, as the unexpected length, sheer ferocity, and massive financial cost of the First World War demonstrated, 'hard' power of rulers trumps 'soft' power of financiers. Despite their general aversion to war, the glory of, and gains from, military victory can generate huge new opportunities for financiers. These opportunities were seized by North American bankers after the Civil War of 1861–1865, by German bankers after German unification in 1871, and by American bankers after 1918 and 1945.

Conversely, rulers are more limited in their financial information, knowledge, and understanding than their financiers. They face a pronounced information asymmetry that offers scope for financiers to deceive and cheat rulers. Moreover, the capacity to mobilize debt finance remains vital for the effective deployment of 'hard' power. Credit flows to the creditworthy. As the respective fortunes of the Hapsburg Empire and Prussia after 1815 showed, 'hard' power can be difficult to sustain once investor faith in sovereign creditworthiness erodes.

This symbiotic and incestuous relationship between debt finance and political rule underlines the peculiar, ambiguous character of power in the governance of creditworthiness. Rulers depend on their reputation with lenders. This dependency involves paying a price in their capacity to structure the terms of debate, to set agendas, and to shape outcomes. This price can include heavy collateral damage to the financially innocent outside the small, private social world of rulers and financiers. It can also mean the perpetuation of large economic, social, and political inequalities. Financiers enjoy a privileged role in the process of constructing sovereign creditworthiness.

The history of the arc of default also illuminates a striking parallel between pre-1914 Europe and the character of the post-2010 sovereign debt crises in the euro area periphery. The tough conditionality programmes for Cyprus, Greece, and Portugal echoed the international financial commissions of this earlier period, as well as the League 'trustee agents' after 1918. Their new manifestation was the Troika offices of the European Commission, the European Central Bank, and the IMF in their national capitals to monitor compliance. In the Greek case, the escrow account mechanism, which allows them to make payments directly on Greece's official debts and restructured private debts, looked back to earlier arrangements. This continuity derives from the high concentration of credit risks in the historic European arc of default. It continued to be characterized by weaknesses in state capacity and by types of economic culture that put in question the willingness to pay creditors.

6

Theological Traces and Social Contexts

> It's the need for credit that forces governments to pay attention to public opinion, and, just as trade has civilized nations, credit, which is a consequence, has made necessary constitutional forms to ensure confidence in finances and guarantee contractual commitments.
>
> Madame de Staël (1766–1817), in Girard (1985: 28), translated by the author

Debates about sovereign creditworthiness are deeply embedded in particular, complex, and changing social contexts. Though at any one point in time debate might reflect dominance by one social interest, it resists being reduced to a single abstract model of society. Nevertheless, analytically it is possible to distinguish different conceptions of sovereign creditworthiness on the basis of their distinct set of beliefs about creditors and debtors and their place in the wider society. These differing conceptions gain their coherence and persuasive power from the way in which each can be rationally defended by reference to an abstract model of society. This model serves to support a particular conception of sovereign creditworthiness. It also provides a reference point for critiquing alternative conceptions.

In short, debates about sovereign creditworthiness involve contests that revolve around more general ideological commitments. These commitments are grounded in social and economic interests and in the moral attitudes to creditors and debtors that they engender. Accordingly, complex debates exhibit underlying structure, based around the logically distinct and contending models of society in which they are embedded. For this reason, sovereign creditworthiness remains ideologically contested, even when expressed in technical economic reasoning, quantitative in form, and claiming a de-politicized status.

Historically, debates about sovereign creditworthiness reflect three contending models of society. The model of society as a hierarchy, which is naturally divided into ranks and legitimated theologically, views creditors within a framework of prerogative rights and moral paternalism towards debtors. It contrasts with the market model of society, which takes the creditor as axiom and society as derivative. This social model celebrates the creditor as the basis of social welfare. It treats creditor-debtor relations as essentially a commercial transaction. Financial repression, currency debasement, 'inflation tax', and sovereign default are all stigmatized. The market model underpins conventional economic reasoning about credit and debt.

Both the hierarchical and the market models of society differ from the conception of sovereign creditworthiness that is rooted in the model of society as a cooperative community. In this communitarian model creditors are seen as having one claim amongst other valid claims. The state has a responsibility to foster solidarity, serve social needs and entitlements, and protect taxpayers and the poorest and most needy welfare-state recipients from potentially predatory creditors. Hence creditors should expect negotiated sovereign debt restructurings and 'bail-in' to insolvent banks.

Two historic shifts are discernible. First, the rise of the market and the communitarian social models was identified with the emergence of 'public' opinion as the prime reference point in thinking about sovereign creditworthiness. The question was which notion of 'public' dominates: the public understood as creditors, as taxpayers, or as the most-needy recipients of welfare-state provision. Secondly, the emergence of 'public' debt and the professionalization of public finances were most closely associated with the rise of the new model of market society. In the process, theology retreated from centre ground in framing and constraining ideas about debt. Nevertheless, debates about sovereign creditworthiness continued to bear theological traces of moral paternalism, above all in attitudes of creditors to debtors.

The history of debt and political rule in Europe is a narrative about ongoing contest amongst different social interests about how problems of creditworthiness should be represented and what choices should be made. A particular age or state is not to be defined in terms of a single monolithic social model and supportive social interest. The historical narrative also illustrates how debates about sovereign creditworthiness became more complex and fluid. Different conceptions of creditworthiness came to coexist in uneasy tension. Above all from the late nineteenth century, debates about sovereign creditworthiness took on a more ideologically complex, agonized, and ambivalent character.

Nevertheless, if debate was often confused, the contrasting conceptions of sovereign creditworthiness remained logically distinct in terms of the social models on which they were based. Historical analysis offers insight into how, over time, different social interests helped to reconfigure the politics of creditworthiness. They provided the central reference points not just in framing how problems of creditworthiness were represented and choices debated and made. They also shaped how the history of sovereign debt came to be written. Theology made its own contribution, including an anti-Semitic tendency either to stigmatize Jewish financiers or to write them out of this history.

Theological Traces: New Social Interests, Ideology, and Property Rights

In late-medieval and early-modern Europe, the dominant conception of creditworthiness within territorial states was rooted in a very narrow social world. Theological reference points to the Church were central in thinking about debt. They focused on the special role and duties of kings, and below them nobles, in safeguarding the strict, God-ordained 'great chain of being' (Lovejoy 1964). The notion of prerogative rights dominated debates about debt. Merchants and creditors occupied a lower position in the hierarchy of perfection. Correspondingly, rulers had a responsibility to protect the preordained social hierarchy against their excessive claims. In this hierarchical social model the legal protection of property rights was weak. Rulers were offered justification for engaging in aggressive debasements, coercive defaults, overt financial repression, and brutal anti-Semitism.

A small world of social connections has always counted in debt financing, including the early-twenty-first-century world of Primary Dealers. This intimacy pervaded the late-medieval city states like Florence, Genoa, and Venice with their narrow, patrician, and oligarchic merchant-financier elite. Its members traded perpetual annuities privately, notably through dowries, as a symbol of their social and political standing (Molho 2006). The city states showed that, even when 'public' opinion counted, the 'private governance of public debt' prevailed and deep social and economic inequalities were accepted as normal.

Outside the city states in the late-medieval territorial states, debt financing was bound up in feudal arrangements, which were pictured as anchored in the 'great chain of being'. Debt finance involved convoluted manoeuvrings for status and power between monarchs and their nobles, clergy, and cities. Monarchs borrowed from powerful prelates, nobles, and even their own officials. They borrowed on the credit of their cities. They also used debt as a device to punish rivals. Moreover, monarchs and nobles turned 'outside' the constraints of Christian usury laws to Jews as sources for lending, thereby circumventing religious prohibitions. Theological debates played a constitutive role in the operation of this social world of debt financing. A similar role was to be played by macroeconomic debates about market efficiency and discipline in the operation of twentieth- and twenty-first-century sovereign bond markets.

Usury and its Circumvention

By the thirteenth century theology hung heavily over debates about creditworthiness and debt financing. It took the twin forms of reinvigorated Christian usury doctrine and the notion of the king's 'two bodies'. The enduring weight of usury doctrine stemmed from the later endorsement of Aristotelian scholastic doctrine by the leading Protestant reformer, Martin Luther. It remained a mortal sin for Lutherans, as well as for Roman Catholics, to demand anything above the principal in a loan—never mind 'extortionate' interest. As late as 1745 the Catholic Church reasserted the prohibition of usury in the Papal bull *Vix pervenit*. Money was nothing more than a medium of exchange (Jones 1989). The Florentine Dante Alighieri's *Divine Comedy* (1555) was symptomatic of opinions in the early fourteenth century. He placed usurers in the Inferno, the lower depths of Hell, as 'the last class of sinners that are punished in the burning sands' ('Inferno', Circle 7, Canto 17). The exception was the Swiss Reformation theologian John Calvin, who in his *Letter on Usury* in 1545 permitted interest on commercial loans. His ideas were influential in France, the Low Countries, and England (Hauser 1927; Munro 2011).

Despite theological prohibitions, the notion of creditworthiness gained in significance as Italian merchant-financiers, notably the Genoese and the Lombards, emerged as the masters in creative accounting, identifying and exploiting loopholes in usury doctrine. Before the Reformation, they had evolved credit practices that eclipsed the conservative reliance of Hanseatic League merchants on balancing trade bilaterally. Hanseatic merchants were deeply suspicious of credit, relying on a mixture of barter and silver coin (De Roover 2008). Italian merchants created the conditions for an expansion in the supply of private and public credit. Their justification rested on two principles: that money has time value; and that investors should be compensated for taking risks. However, from the Hanseatic League to the Fugger family in Augsburg, German and other north European merchants continued to distrust the financial intermediation practices of Italian merchants.

By the fourteenth century, new notions of debt financing were taking shape as the social interests supporting a market model of society gained in strength, especially in the cities. Interest on loans to monarchs was disguised as gifts (*dona*) of money in gratitude for good service. These gifts were acceptable under usury doctrine as long as there was no intentional connection to the loan. Claims for interest were also justified as compensation for damages incurred by the lender. A third loophole enabling loans to rulers was creative accounting, in which interest was concealed. For instance, the stated value of a loan could be exaggerated to cover interest payments. Creative accounting emerged as an art form in the dealings of Italian merchant-financiers and exchequer clerks and was made easy by rudimentary single-entry book keeping. In any case, concealed interest was less important to the merchant-financiers than access to privileges like rights of monopoly (for instance in the lucrative alum or wool trades), customs exemptions, or rights of tax collection, including the assignment of customs revenues.

From the thirteenth century, Italian merchants became experts in using new bills of exchange, or letters of credit, to disguise interest payments in commercial lending for long-distance trade. Letters of credit often incorporated elevated exchange rates. However, to comply with usury doctrine, loan contracts had to be non-negotiable and held to maturity (De Roover 1963). Letters of credit came into widespread use by the fifteenth century. Despite Islamic prohibition of usury, they were common within the Ottoman Empire by this time (Pamuk 2009: 18).

As early as the sixteenth century, merchant-financiers had emerged as a powerful social force, pressing for change in inherited notions about debt financing. They sought to draw a distinction between illicit and licit credit practices. Merchant-financiers also pressed for the legalization of interest rates for commercial purposes by appealing to the economic and political interests of monarchs in expanding trade and thus their revenues and credit. In 1540 the Emperor Charles V took the lead in the Low Countries by giving legal force to a maximum interest rate, beyond which rates were 'excessive'. Henry VIII emulated him in 1545 by making interest payments legal up to a maximum. From then on, despite some interruptions, parliaments continued to regulate maximum rates in an increasingly market-friendly direction. Even the liberal economist Adam Smith advocated continuing state regulation of maximum permitted interest rates. On this issue Jeremy Bentham (1748–1832) parted company with Smith in his *Defence of Usury* (1787). Despite their differences, English Utilitarianism and French Saint-Simonism, as represented by Saint-Amand Bazard (1791–1832) and Enfantin, agreed in their opposition to usury. For Bentham it represented state interference with individual liberty. For the Saint-Simonians usury fettered the mobilization of credit for social betterment. It was not until 1854 that the British Parliament finally abolished the usury law. However, more market-friendly usury law continued to remain in place in France.

With respect to debt financing of political rule, late-medieval merchant-financiers seized two opportunities that were deemed consistent with usury doctrine. First, they sought to legitimate loans as serving the Christian purposes of monarchs, notably activities defined as Crusading. The motives of merchant-financiers were not just financial and economic, such as gaining entry into lucrative foreign markets. They were also attracted by access to the tightly restricted social elites, centred on royal courts. It offered the social status, honour, and above all protection to marginalized Jews, who were in desperate need of social recognition. Similar motives influenced newly wealthy Italian merchant-financiers and London goldsmith-bankers. In 1506 Henry VII of England protected the Frescobaldi of Florence from Pope Julius II's ban on the illegal alum trade. He argued that gaining the support of the Frescobaldi for a new Crusade should take priority, whilst making a handsome profit in the process (Penn 2011: 250–2).

Secondly, many merchant-financiers, who feared for their mortal souls, preferred to concentrate on financing city-state governments—or rulers of territorial states through the medium of their cities—by purchasing municipal annuities (*rentes*). In 1250–1251 Pope Innocent IV (r. 1243–1254) ruled that annuities fell outside usury laws because they involved pledging a fixed capital sum to buy a lifetime or perpetual stream of income. They were legitimate 'contracts of sale', not interest-bearing loans or bonds with specific maturity dates. The buyer could not request the return of his capital. Only the issuer had the right to redeem annuities. However, creditors were provided with security by the assignment of excise taxes or property rental incomes to finance the annuities. After this Papal ruling perpetual or life annuities became the debt financing instrument of choice in European public-debt financing up to the end of the eighteenth century. In 1537–1541 the Hapsburg Netherlands took the lead again in establishing the legal principle of full negotiability of annuities. This innovation created the basis for the emergence of Antwerp as the leading European market for annuities (Van Der Wee 1963).

Despite the opportunities that Crusading and annuities offered to debt financing, the rising merchant-financiers and related commercial and professional interests in accountancy and law continued to labour under a handicap. They were seen as outsiders, to be tolerated whilst useful, but expendable when not. They remained subordinate to kings and nobles in the 'great chain of being' (Lovejoy 1964). Thus in 1288–1295 Philip IV of France employed the Giudi bankers of Lombardy to raise enormous loans for his war in Aquitaine. However, in 1309–1310 he introduced a severe squeeze on his Lombard bankers (Strayer 1980). Similarly, in 1294 Edward I cancelled the grant of the custom duties on wool to the Ricciardi of Lucca in return for their loans and ordered their arrest (Morris 2009: 271).

However, hypocrisy lurked beneath the saintly imagery of Christian kings combating usury and encouraging intense and devout theological debates about its sins. Their assumed role in safeguarding a God-ordained hierarchy of perfection offered a thin disguise for pervasive cynicism, subterfuge, corruption, and brutality in debt financing. Coercive financial repression was endemic in late-medieval and early-modern Europe. It was allied to the growth of a new breed of legally trained and financially acute royal officials, who exploited claims to sovereign prerogative. They also used the king's reliance on them to raise debt financing as a means of amassing huge personal fortunes and acquiring social status. Under Louis XIII and Louis XIV, for instance, chief ministers like Cardinal de Richelieu and Cardinal Mazarin, and finance ministers like Fouquet, received money on their private loans to the king and commissions for organizing other secret loans. The *chambre de justice* was employed to serve royal financial interests (Bonney 1981). Earlier the English King Henry VII had used the chamber treasury to rigorously enforce his prerogative rights, notably through penalties in the form of bonds that tied nobles to him (Penn 2011: 34–5).

Incentives for subterfuge and corruption increased as merchant-financiers sought grants of highly profitable commercial privileges in exchange for large loans. This type of exchange characterized the grant of the governorship of the Spanish province Venezuela by Emperor Charles V in 1528 to the Welser. In this way the Welser gained entry into the new highly lucrative American trade (Häberlein and Burckhardt 2002). Similar privileges were sought and gained by Italian merchant-financiers in England, France, Portugal, and other states. Rulers were tempted by the promise of increasing revenues from trade and by gaining new allies, influence, and sources of finance. In 1082 Alexios Comnenus granted Venetian merchants the unrestricted right to trade, free of customs duties, throughout most of the Byzantine Empire. Later, in the eighteenth and nineteenth centuries, the Ottoman Empire expanded the grant of commercial privileges, so-called 'capitulations'. However, the capitulations reflected weakness. They did little at all to address chronic problems of Ottoman creditworthiness. As a result, Ottoman merchants failed to develop a significant presence in European long-distance trade. The rise of a domestic merchant-financier class was frustrated (Pamuk 2009).

The debt financing practices of merchant-financiers often provoked public resentment. In 1456–1458, for instance, riots broke out in London against Florentine, Genoese, Luccan, and Venetian merchants. They threatened further damage to the already impaired borrowing capacity of the financially beleaguered Henry VI (Griffiths 1981: 790–5). For similar reasons of fear about public resentment, the French Kings Philip IV, Francis I, and Henry II sought to shift royal borrowing from south German and Italian merchants to French merchants. Under Elizabeth I of England Thomas Gresham endeavoured to build up domestic sources of borrowing as an alternative to foreign borrowing. However, these manoeuvres were not just or even mainly about containment of public resentment against foreign merchant-financiers. They involved the prudent search to diversify lending sources and to pursue divide-and-rule amongst creditors, who were seen as greedy and ruthless.

By the late-medieval period widespread financial repression and venality brought debt financing into serious discredit, not least amongst nobles, merchants, financiers, and new professional classes. The key problem for these social interests was the weak legal protection of property rights. Territorial states lacked written constitutions, enshrining property rights, and independent courts to ensure their respect. Property rights enjoyed a greater respect in city states and independent cities within larger territorial states because of a self-governing *rentier* oligarchy. The seventeenth- and eighteenth-century revolutions in England, France, and the United States were set in train by new social interests that wished to protect property rights against the exercise of sovereign prerogative. This process took the form of the slow nineteenth-century evolution of the *Rechtsstaat* (state ruled by law); franchise extension; the new empowerment of bondholders and bondholder organizations; and the intellectual shift from a 'chain of being' to a 'chain of becoming', reflecting the widening spread of social aspiration.

The King's Two Bodies

Theology hung heavily over evolving conceptions of creditworthiness and debt financing in the form of the notion of the king's 'two bodies'. New social interests were able to exploit inconsistencies within medieval political theology to reshape attitudes towards the debts of rulers. These inconsistencies proved long-lasting. They also make it difficult to pin down the distinction between 'medieval' and 'modern' Europe in thinking about debt. Theological debates about the nature of Christ spilled over into debates about the financial behaviour appropriate to the monarch in the medieval idea of the 'king's two bodies'. This medieval idea could be used by new social interests to legitimate action to 'protect the King from the king'. In such matters as incurring debts, the Body Politic had to be safeguarded from the irresponsible financial behaviour of the king as a person, not least in incurring debts (Kantorowicz 1997).

The implication of monarchy for debt financing remained unclear in the medieval period. On the one hand, the debts of the king could be seen as attached to his person. They could be interpreted as incurring obligations on all those who had sworn loyalty to him. Monarchs were able to use this notion to legitimate financial repression of those who had shown personal disloyalty, for instance by expropriation of their property. On the other hand, the debts of a monarch could be understood as attached to the Body Politic. In this case the monarch was under an obligation of accountability to those who were being asked to service these debts.

The king 'as person' could ignore property rights. However, the notion of the king as a constituent part of the Body Politic served as the incubator for notions of constitutionally anchored property rights and 'national' or 'public' debt. Consequently, medieval political theology opened space for major political and constitutional conflicts about the notion of creditworthiness and its institutional implications. It offered material that could be used by emerging merchant and *rentier* interests.

The Church, Crusading, and Debt

Rulers manoeuvred with difficulties in establishing their creditworthiness and managing their debts. They saw theology and the Church as variously a source of inspiration, a constraining moral and institutional framework, and a resource that they could exploit and circumvent. Crusading shared all these elements. The onerous burdens of financing Crusades in order to recapture and hold the Holy Land were a key factor in the accumulation of heavy debts. They also provided opportunities for the development of Italian banking, notably in Lucca.

Crusading offered a legitimating device for extraordinary measures of financial repression and the assertion of royal prerogatives. For instance, in 1188, in preparation for the Third Crusade, the French King Philip II Augustus instituted a moratorium on Crusaders' debts (Baldwin 1986: 53). At such times rulers were inclined to seek to secure their superior reputation as Christian rulers by punishing usurers as unchristian. The Crusading mission encouraged them to offer legitimacy to brutal actions to expropriate, punish, expel, and even massacre Jews.

The world of debt financing in the medieval world remains often shocking to later liberal sensibilities. It was also hypocritical. Behind their Christian imagery rulers frequently conspired in the creative use of debt financing by German, Italian, and Dutch merchant-financiers. They sought to avert theological attacks on 'excessive' or 'exorbitant' interest rates by compensating their creditors. Merchant-financiers benefitted from the grant of highly profitable trade monopolies, for instance in the English wool trade or in the Spanish trade with the Americas. Alternatively, interest could be dressed up as gift for services or compensation for damage. Rulers recognized religious constraints and imperatives. However, in varying degrees, they saw debt as a difficult area of private negotiation, involving deception and subterfuge.

Reflecting this powerful theological framing, the connection of debt finance to the Church was significant. Medieval monarchs borrowed from powerful prelates and religious orders, whose economic power rested on land and on bequests. Both King Henry V of England (r. 1413–1422) and King Henry VI (r. 1422–1471) turned to Cardinal-Bishop Henry Beaufort to finance their French wars, especially in the critical period between 1428 and 1445. Beaufort was the most powerful prelate in the kingdom, becoming the privileged and pre-eminent royal creditor. He secured his royal loans on income from taxes on wool (Hariss 2005). In addition, Beaufort—and after 1447 his executors—gained a substantial haul of English crown jewels and benefitted from innumerable royal gifts (Griffiths 1981: 45, 111, 391–3). As chancellor, Beaufort exploited ruthlessly the Crown's indebtedness to him. Similarly, from Philip II Augustus (r. 1180–1223) to Philip IV, French kings relied on the Knights Templar to obtain loans and transfer money (Nicholson 2001).

Conversely, monarchs were not averse to using coercive instruments of fiscal expropriation against clergy as well as nobles. Initially, they sought legitimacy for their financial repression by appealing to the ideas of meeting the financial needs of Crusading and just war and protecting the realm through strengthened military defences. However, the new Renaissance model of kingship, associated with Francis I of France (r. 1515–1548) and with Henry VIII in England, was linked to the use of a new argument for the legitimacy of financial repression. It was justified by reference to the increase of the 'estate, honour, dignity and renown' of the ruler (Schofield 2004).

The price of averting unsustainable debt was often harsh. King Francis I intimidated Italian and south German merchant-financiers in Lyon. King Philip IV of France expropriated the cash and assets of the Knights Templar. King Henry II of France repudiated his debts. Under King Henry VI English troops pillaged France. Henry VIII practised aggressive currency debasement. Before and after the Renaissance glory remained a key legitimating device. The Emperor Napoleon I recognized that the glory of military victories and territorial gains instilled national self-confidence. It also provided access to new sources of finances for his armies and opportunities for pillage (Branda 2007).

King Louis IX (r. 1226–1270), Saint-Louis, is reputedly the first French king to make use of debt financing. In order to pursue his cherished purpose of assuming the leadership of the Crusades, he turned for financial support to his French cities because of their superior creditworthiness. He also established a moratorium on the debts of Crusaders, with the Church as guarantor (Goff 1996: 381). King Francis I played an even more decisive role in shifting royal financing from its reliance on forced loans from subjects to interest-bearing loans raised in Lyon. He turned to Florentines like the Strozzi and south Germans like Hans Kleberg (Hamon 1994). The key defining moments in King Francis I's debt financing were the outbreak of war in 1536 and, above all, in 1542. Reflecting the value of the Church's blessing, a senior prelate, Cardinal de Tournon, acted as the king's agent. Nevertheless, royal intimidation continued to play a role in these loans. It caused great anxiety amongst south German merchant-financiers, who had loyalty to the Emperor and who feared imperial wrath directed against any complicity with Francis I (Ehrenberg 1963: 292–7).

The debt practices of Saint Louis and Francis I paled next to those of the arch exponents of the darker arts of financial repression. King Philip IV, the Fair, of France (r. 1285–1314) was notorious for currency debasement and for extorting money from Lombard bankers and Jews. Above all, he is remembered for expropriating the wealth of the Knights Templar and for their subsequent, infamous, trial in 1308–1312 (Strayer 1980; Hamon 2006). King Henry VII (r. 1485–1509) brought fiscal repression to new heights in England. He employed 'recognizances' to impose onerous, potentially ruinous conditions on debtors, with extortionate fines for non-compliance (Mackie 1972: 215; Richardson 1952: 141–58; Starkey 1987).

His son Henry VIII (r. 1509–1548) gained noble support by desisting from these practices. Instead, he turned to the dissolution of the monasteries (1536–1540) and alienation of their lands in order to further build and reward a constituency of loyalists. However, Henry VIII was soon exacting forced loans on richer subjects and resorting to 'benevolences', which were understood to be free gifts to the monarch. He had the advantage of a compliant Parliament, which in 1529 and again in 1544 relieved the king from his liability to repay certain loans. The law of 1544 provided that lenders who had already been repaid should return the money to the king (Mackie 1972: 438–9). The legacy of Henry VIII's royal extravagance and costly wars was two defaults, three currency debasements, and an onerous debt burden, including large-scale borrowing abroad.

Theology and New Social Interests

As new social interests emerged, theology took on a more complex relationship to changing notions about debt. These new social interests had their economic basis in wealth creation and accumulation. They comprised 'self-made' merchants and associated professionals like lawyers, who based their income on hard work and education and who had savings to invest, and *rentiers*, who could live off investment income without substantial labour and owed their position to having the right ancestors. They formed the backbone of a new market model of society, associated with the rise of financial and consumer capitalism.

Theology continued to help sustain a moral paternalism, which was entrenched in strict usury and bankruptcy laws and expressed in social norms against profligate and improvident borrowing. At the same time, the new social interests were able to exploit gaps and inconsistencies in medieval theological discourse to align their interests with those of territorial rulers whose dynastic ambitions rested on ever-more costly financial requirements. Theology provided both a constraining moral framework and a resource to use.

Gradually, these new social interests, allied to rulers, displaced theology from its central role in sustaining moral paternalism about debt. Notions about debt, and how it should be financed, were no longer confined to the incestuous social world of monarchs, nobility, and clergy. The notion of the 'great chain of being' no longer framed how creditors and debtors were understood. The new social interests were attached to the notion of 'becoming' rather than 'being'.

The rise of new social interests was in part promoted by ambitious centralizing monarchs. They sought new sources of income and new forms of loyalty to evade their overdependence on a fractious aristocracy and on assertive prelates. They looked to new moneyed-men and to the cities as intermediaries to this commercial world. Monarchs sold titles, land, and jobs to raise money. King Richard I of England resorted to these methods to finance his Third Crusade, which cost four years' revenue. Monarchs also promoted new men to key administrative positions as financial reformers. Philip IV of France appointed Biche and Mouche Giudi, Lombard bankers, to organize loans for the war in Aquitaine (Strayer 1980). Henry VIII of England picked out Thomas Cromwell, formerly employed by the Frescobaldi bank in Florence, to enrich himself. King Henry IV of France looked to Maximilien Sully. King Louis XVI placed his hopes of financial salvation on Jacques Necker. King Charles II of England turned to London goldsmith-bankers like Charles Duncombe. These 'new men' were allocated fiscal privileges, including interest rates on loans to the king above the legal limit and positions as receivers of government revenue (Duncombe 2001). Unsurprisingly, they faced the hostility of powerful clergy and nobles, and often paid the price.

Similarly, monarchs came to identify their dynastic interests with the emergence of new professional armies and bureaucracies, including accountants and lawyers. They provided instruments for centralizing and strengthening governing capacity and for reducing the dependence of rulers on independently-minded landed interests. In turn, the new professional groups sought legitimating formulae for their own interests in debt financing and the growth of the fiscal state. These formulae centred on the notion of the distinctive impersonal character of the state as the guardian of the public interest and the repository of moral standards. It required autonomy in order to carry out its specialized functions (Dyson 2010). The status and power of the professional army and bureaucracy prospered in regimes that accorded executives substantial autonomy from parliament. Examples included the France of the Emperor Napoleon Bonaparte (1803–1815) and the Emperor Napoleon III (1852–1870), as well as the German Second Empire (1871–1918).

The notion of sustainable public debt was one around which the interests of the professional army and bureaucracy could converge with those of liberal *rentiers* and 'self-made' wealth. However, this notion was imprecise and open to different interpretations. There was ample scope for friction amongst these new social interests over the proper balance between public expenditure, higher taxes, borrowing, and printing money. Moreover, the interests of the professional bureaucracy and the army were consistent with survival of the notion of the 'private government of public money'. Their dominance ensured that opacity and secretiveness continued to envelop European public debt, perhaps most strikingly in Imperial France and Imperial Germany. This opacity and secretiveness was, in turn, legitimated by the notion that sovereign debt was a world in which discretion was needed to ensure that the state could balance creditor interests against other public interests. The legal rights of creditors were secondary to the ultimate responsibility of rulers to secure the reputation of the state. Its reputation rested on its long-term economic and financial capacity to act on behalf of its citizens, above all in providing external and internal security.

Who Writes Debt History? Jews and Debt Financing

Just as military victors dominate the writing of the history of war, so the virtues of creditors tend to dominate in the history of debt. However, this aphorism begs the question—which creditors are central to narratives about the history of debt? Conversely, which creditors are neglected, and why? The answers to these questions shine a light on unattractive features of the history of states, debt, and power in Europe and the darker aspects of the theological traces that have shaped it.

The historical importance of Jews as financiers of rulers and states is often shrouded in an awkward silence. This silence and neglect reflect the complex and insidious role of anti-Semitism in European history. It was captured in Shakespeare's fictional Shylock, the Jewish creditor who is depicted as cruelly using the law to persecute his Catholic debtor. In the nineteenth and early twentieth centuries debt financing was still caught up in a subtle, subterranean distinction between Gentile bankers, like the Barings and J.P. Morgan, and Jewish bankers, notably the Rothschild, Lazard, Oppenheim, and Warburg families (Ahamed 2010: 9–10; Ziegler 1988). It played a role in attitudes towards the French *hautes banques*. A contrast was drawn between Catholic families, for instance the Mallet, and Jewish families, like the Fould, who moreover attracted suspicion because of links to the Oppenheim banking family in Germany (Stoskopf 2002). These Jewish bankers, including the Rothschild family, were the targets of an aggressive anti-Semitic press campaign.

Writing on German, Russian, and Ottoman Turk debt history illustrates the neglect of Jewish creditors. Strikingly, the German Jewish banker Gersten von Bleichröder disappeared from conventional historical narratives about German unification for decades. In consequence, historians overlooked the central questions of how unification was financed. They also ignored how Chancellor Otto von Bismarck's subsequent policies in Russia, eastern Europe, and above all Ottoman Turkey, were pursued (Stern 1978). Similar neglect surrounds the role of the Jewish Stieglitz family as bankers to successive Russian emperors in financing nineteenth-century imperial expansion. It is also apparent in writing on Ottoman history. Following their expulsion from Catholic Spain in 1492 by Ferdinand and Isabella, Jewish merchant banking families emerged as a powerful presence in Istanbul and Salonica. The Nasi-Mendes family of merchant-financiers were the foremost amongst trusted Jewish advisers to Ottoman Sultans in the sixteenth century. They also made loans to the king of Poland and to King Henry II of France (Epstein 1980; Inalcick 1994: 121–4). In effect, the centre of gravity of the Jewish world shifted eastwards, to the safe haven of the Ottomans. However, Hellenization after Salonica became Greek in 1912, followed by German mass expulsion of Jews in 1943, obliterated traces of this powerful Jewish presence (Mazower 2005).

The brutal face of financial repression of Jews was highly visible in twelfth- and thirteenth-century Europe when Church hostility to usury as a mortal sin took on a more rampant form. Lateran III in 1179 and the Pope's condemnation of usury by Christians were followed by a proliferation of anti-usury laws and the multiplication of theological treaties against usury. They also created a vacuum in which Jewish money-lending could grow. Whilst Christian usurers were tried before the ecclesiastical courts, Jewish and foreign usurers were subject to royal 'justice'. Royal justice proved arbitrary.

In this period it was dispensed on terms that reflected strong resentment towards royal as well as aristocratic indebtedness to Jews and to foreign lenders. Royal justice was also bound up in the attempts of rulers to construct a saintly image. They were tempted to follow the lead of Lateran IV in 1215, which condemned Jewish moneylenders for their 'treachery' and 'cruel oppression' in demanding 'oppressive and excessive interest'. In 1234 a decree of Pope Gregory (r. 1227–1241) commanded Christian rulers to expel all usurers (Munro 2011).

From the 1240s, despite having one of the strongest silver currencies in Europe, the heavily indebted King Henry III of England (r. 1216–1272) pursued rapacious tax repression of Jews, seized their assets, and tolerated their massacring (Huscroft 2006). Following the earlier example of Philip II Augustus in 1182, the saintly King Louis IX of France expelled Jews from the royal demesne in the 1240s, prior to his first Crusade. He then cancelled Christians' debts to Jewish usurers and confiscated Jewish assets in 1258. Earlier, Saint Louis had expressly ruled out these measures to finance his first Crusade as they would 'compromise' its holy aim (Goff 1996: 793–814; Jordan 1979). In 1306 Philip IV of France expelled the Jews and seized their property, as part of a wider campaign to reduce financial dependence on foreign financiers (Strayer 1980). King Edward I of England banned Jewish money lending in 1275 and expelled the Jews in 1290 (Mundill 1998; Morris 2009: 125, 226–8).

In these ways Jews paid a terrible price for the efforts of rulers to rid themselves of heavy debts and to cultivate a saintly image. The damage was accentuated by the creation of opportunities for flagrant abuse by rich individuals who benefitted from these expropriations. They gained title to Jewish debts and then hounded more vulnerable Christian debtors for personal gain (Morris 2009: 87–8). Edward I was repaid by a grateful Parliament and Church with the largest tax collected in England during the medieval period. Anti-Semitism casts a dark shadow over debt financing in the late-medieval period.

The twelfth- and thirteenth-century reinforcement of the prohibition of usury by Christians opened up new opportunities for Jewish lending. By the fifteenth century Jewish moneylending had become a significant activity. It was also encouraged by their exclusion from the fast-expanding merchant and craft guilds in the cities, as well as by the substantial wealth that some Jews had amassed through trade. This development of Jewish moneylending proved to have particular long-term significance in the development of Italian local financial institutions. The Franciscans took the lead in trying to keep Christians away from Jewish moneylending and to drive out this activity by promoting the creation of local, non-profitable, charity lending institutions, the *Monti di Pietà*. Between 1470 and 1570 over 220 *Monti di Pietà* were established in central and northern Italy, for instance in Bologna, Lucca, Milan, Parma, Siena, and Viterbo (Pascali 2013: 10). Jews were often asked to pay taxes or deposit some of their revenues with them, as well as to advise on how to establish them. Nevertheless, Jewish moneylenders remained able to draw on their family networks and accumulated wealth to offer more substantial loans. Hence, in 1515, Pope Leone X sought to offer encouragement by allowing the *Monti di Pietà* to charge interests on loans. By the end of the nineteenth century, some 300 *Monti* were operating. Pascali (2013: 10) shows how the great majority of modern Italian banks trace their origins to the *Monti di Pietà* that were created in the Renaissance. Their presence also helps explain the difference in credit conditions between central and northern Italy and southern Italy. Under Spanish Aragon rule, Jews were expelled from the south. The stimulus of Jewish moneylending presence to the establishment and development of local *Monti di Pietà* was absent there (Pascali 2013).

In the case of the Holy Roman Empire, the huge losses that were suffered by German merchants during the Thirty Years' War (1618–1648) acted as a catalyst for the rise of Jewish moneylending. Jewish court agents (*Hoffaktoren*) provided loans to kings, princes, prince-bishops, and other rulers from their own private capital, as well as from capital borrowed from close relatives and through cross-national financial networks (Stern 1962–1975, 2001; Schnee 1953–1967). The most active Jewish court agents included Leffmann Behrens in Hanover, Nathan Veitel Heine Ephraim in Berlin, Berend Lehmann in Saxony, Joseph Süss Oppenheimer in Württemberg, Samuel Oppenheimer and Sampson Wertheimer in Vienna, and Mayer Amschel Rothschild in Hessen-Kassel. The House of Rothschild and the Sal. Oppenheim & Cie bank originated from Jewish court agents (Gille 1965; Stürmer, Teichmann, and Treue 1989).

The so-called 'court Jews' (*Hofjuden*) formed networks of credit and financial information exchange across the Holy Roman Empire. They used these networks to serve a variety of roles as bankers, currency agents, military suppliers, and unofficial diplomats for their respective rulers. At the same time the fortunes of Jewish court agents became closely bound up with those of particular German rulers in a symbiotic fashion. They gained commercial privileges, connections, status, and influence. In turn, prince-bishops became especially dependent on Jewish court agents because of their reluctance to impose taxes and build strong centralized fiscal administrations.

However, the position of Jewish court agents proved precarious. Their practice of granting credits only against collateral or specific tax assignments was often irksome to rulers. Jewish court agents sought to assimilate in order to counter the risk that rulers might prove susceptible to popular anti-Semitism. However, they continued to face the distrust of estates and of town and city councils because of their association with centralizing, often unpopular, financial measures of rulers. In particular, political succession crises posed a serious danger for Jewish court agents. In 1737 Joseph Süss Oppenheimer, court agent to the Duke of Württemberg, Karl Alexander, was executed for treason after his patron's death. He was the target of popular hostility to what was seen as his excessive privileges, wealth, and influence on public affairs.

Jewish court agents emerged as financiers who made possible the construction of German courtly splendour on the French model. They also provided military financing and served as unofficial diplomats within the Holy Roman Empire. In addition, Jewish court agents helped to reconstitute Jewish cultural and intellectual life across central Europe. Perhaps most importantly of all, they became key figures in the competition amongst German courts for cultural splendour, status, and power.

Issachar Berend Lehmann (1661–1730) drew on his networks, including Leffmann Behrens in Hanover and Samuel Oppenheimer in Vienna, to help finance the hugely costly election of August II 'the Strong' of Saxony (r. 1694–1733) to the Polish throne in 1697. His loans covered the subsequent military and political costs of establishing this new court, as well as Polish participation in the Northern War against Sweden (1700–1704). Behrens served King Frederick I of Prussia and the rulers of Hanover and Braunschweig-Wolfenbüttel (Bürgelt 2007). Veitel Heine Ephraim (1703–1775) was court agent to Frederick the Great of Prussia and the most important financier of his wars. He gained great unpopularity not just because of his wealth but also because of his association with the inflation unleashed by the king's use of covert currency debasement to help finance the Seven Years' War (1756–1763). By 1800 Liepmann Meyer Wulff was court financier to Frederick William II and the richest person in Prussia.

Jewish financiers played a key role in the history of European debt financing. However, they suffered harsh, negative stereotyping and hypocritical persecution that bore a theological imprint. Nineteenth-century anti-Semites depicted Jewish bankers as part of an organized conspiracy—sometimes in association with the Freemasons—to control credit for the purpose of ensnaring good Christians, acquiring their property and wealth, and destroying Christian civilization. The Rothschild and other Jewish families were subjected to vicious assaults by Édouard Drumont in *La France juive* (1886) and, from 1892, his newspaper *La Libre Parole.* These assaults were also echoed within the French Left. Anti-Semitic attacks on Jewish financiers gained further sustenance from the fictitious *Protocols of the Elders of Zion*, which was published in Russia in 1905 by Sergei Nilus. He referred in his introduction to France as the nest of the 'Jewish Masonic Conspiracy'. Adolf Hitler's *Mein Kampf* (1925) used this text as part of his justification for stamping out the 'Jewish peril'. This anti- Semitic narrative of credit and debt proved a central theme in a terrible European tragedy.

The Multilayered Fiscal State: Types of Fiscal Regime

Three ideal types of fiscal regime are discernible in the practice of European state-building: fiscal-military, fiscal-*rentier*, and fiscal-welfare. They reflect differences in dominant social interests and in associated political and institutional developments. However, individual states evade neat historical categorization and tidy temporal sequencing. In terms of types of fiscal regime, states evolved at different paces and in varying ways. The English 'Glorious Revolution' of 1688 and the French Revolution of 1789 symbolize different timings of the coming of age of the fiscal-*rentier* regime (Stasavage 2003). Conversely, traditional features of fiscal-military regimes endured through the history of the Ottoman Empire and in Bulgaria and Greece from post-independence into the twentieth century (Clay 2000; Levandis 1944).

Moreover, states are not to be conflated with a single regime type. Bismarck's Prussia and the post-1871 Second German Empire were characterized by tensions and conflicts between fiscal-military and fiscal-*rentier* regime types. The Prussian executive sought autonomy to unify Germany, whilst the Imperial German executive wanted autonomy to pursue colonies. However, the Prussian parliament and later the Reichstag were deeply reluctant to grant taxes and loans for these purposes (Stern 1978). Similar tensions and conflicts beset the Second French Empire of Napoleon III and, to a lesser extent, the *Belle Époche* period of the Third Republic (*c.*1894–1914). However, *rentier* power had stronger social and political roots in pre-1914 France than Germany (Fontvieille 1976; Théret 1995).

The varied and chequered evolution of European fiscal states exhibited aspects of continuity and change. Substantial historical path-dependence was evident in how early institutional settlements constrained and shaped later fiscal developments. Ottoman Turkey and post-independence Greece were locked into structures of tax farming that supported traditional fiscal-military regimes and enhanced reliance on large-scale foreign debts. The outcome was sovereign debt defaults in the 1870s and 1890s respectively, culminating in external intervention in fiscal sovereignty (Clay 2000; Levandis 1944; Wynne 1951). Conversely, by the eighteenth century, the early establishment of parliamentary control in Britain and the United Provinces locked in place key elements of a fiscal-*rentier* regime. In consequence, their fiscal-military establishments were more publicly accountable.

Change in the balance amongst fiscal regime types was associated with the shift in dominant social interests. The overall pattern was a widening of the stakeholders in the fiscal state and an expansion in the notion of political and social entitlements. It went along with an historic shift away from private, secretive financing, associated with the fiscal-military regime type, and characterized by pervasive cheating, venality, and corruption. This form of financing gave way to institutional arrangements that enshrined the notion of 'public' finances and debt (cf. Bonney 1981; Brewer 1989; Schremmer 1994). The Ottoman Empire remained a notable laggard.

The evolution of a multilayered state, in which fiscal-military, fiscal-welfare, and fiscal-*rentier* regime types coexist, posed difficult challenges to governance. The social interests that supported fiscal-military and fiscal-welfare regime types generated powerful political pressures for high public expenditure. Their dominance was associated with a bias towards reliance on taxation and towards rising sovereign debt. Conversely, the social interests behind the fiscal-*rentier* regime type advocated strong political and market-based fiscal discipline on governments in order to safeguard sovereign creditworthiness. Their rise also coincided with increasing inequality in wealth and incomes and in related economic, social, and political tensions.

Europe evolved complex, multilayered fiscal states, which varied in the ways that they embodied and combined these three ideal-type fiscal regime types. This evolution does not fit with a teleological narrative of state building. The fiscal-military regime type was the product of an era that pre-dated the notion of 'public' finances and debt. Its origins can be traced back to before the age of the so-called 'Renaissance state'. Moreover, the centralizing pressures of the sixteenth-century Renaissance state—as exemplified by the French King Francis I—coexisted with a continuing medieval fragmentation of authority and strong local, regional, and personal loyalties (Molho 2006). As early embodiments of the political power of *rentiers*, cities were often very reluctant to act as financiers of costly new fiscal-military structures of rule.

Already, in the late-medieval period, features of fiscal-*rentier* regime types were evident in north Italian city states, like Bologna, Genoa, Florence, and Venice, as well as in Rome. By the fifteenth century they had consolidated their many floating loans into a sizeable 'public' debt. This debt was funded by their citizens and circulated within a narrow financial oligarchy of leading families (Carboni 1995; Colzi 1991; Molho 2006; Mueller 1997). Also, by the late-medieval period, cities in northern France, Flanders, and the Low Country were issuing permanent annuities (*rentes*) as a means of procuring capital (Van Der Wee 1963). They advanced loans, carrying on a regular banking business (Ehrenberg 1963: 45). Rulers like Philip II of Spain and Francis I of France borrowed the superior creditworthiness of their cities by using them to issue, and to raise taxes to service, their debts. Hence the *rentier* class of the cities became a formal part of debt financing by larger territorial states.

European states evolved in individual ways as distinctive manifestations of how these three types of fiscal regime types can be combined. The following sections show how each regime rests on particular social and institutional supports and exhibits specific forms of statecraft.

Creditors in the Hierarchical Model of Society: Sovereign Immunity and Fiscal-Military Regimes

The notions of prerogative rights and absolute sovereign immunity were at the heart of late-medieval and early-modern conceptions of sovereign creditworthiness, at least in territorial states. No clear distinction was made between government acts and debt financing as a commercial activity. Consistent with 'the great chain of being', loans were understood to be a service to the monarch. They bestowed honour on the creditor. Furthermore, any 'dishonour' that might attach to default was trumped by the greater honour of war, contributing to the dignity of rule, and sharing in their glory.

This hierarchical social model, and the associated conception of debt, found its social support within the nobility, clergy, and wealthy office-holders. They were the chief beneficiaries from the spoils of war, from the sale of financial and other offices, and from revenue farming. Royal borrowing entailed a fusion of private and public gains. The dominant attitude to creditors was summarized by Cardinal Richelieu: 'financiers and contractors comprise a separate party, detrimental to the state, but still necessary' (Bonney 1981: 18). Debt financing took the form of opaque, secretive, and repeated short-term borrowing. It was accompanied by frequent resort to various forms of financial repression of creditors. Under the French *ancien régime*, for instance, financiers had to face the periodic threat of contracts reneged, and penalties imposed, by a special royal commission, the *chambre de justice* (Bonney 1981: 227).

During this period the centralizing, dynastic, and imperial ambitions of territorial rulers, along with Crusading, meant that military expenditures, including funding mercenary armies, were central to debt financing. They provided the incentive to develop a fiscal-military regime (Tilly 1975, 1990). Rulers faced the huge financial challenge of sustaining coordinated, effective military action on an expanding geographic scale. From the fifteenth and sixteenth centuries they resorted to new reliance on the sale of offices and 'revenue farming'. This change was notable under Ottoman Sultan Mehmed II (the Conqueror, r. 1451–1481). Tax farming also spread in France from the mid-sixteenth century. In both cases it created powerful vested interests in resisting fiscal reforms (Inalcik 1994; Bonney 1991). War induced rulers to offer lucrative tax farming to merchant-financiers, in return for debt finance.

These new public office-holders were able to conceal their private interests in the growth of royal borrowing. They also engaged in widespread cheating, venality, corruption, and extortion. As a consequence, France, Spain, and the Ottoman Empire became embroiled in fiscal vice. In France it extended to chief ministers, like Cardinal Richelieu and Cardinal Jules Mazarin, as well as to the unpopular finance minister Nicholas Fouquet (Bonney 1981). In the Ottoman Empire tax collection was privatized to Greeks and to Jews (Inalcick 1994). Tax farming became an integral, entrenched part of the fiscal-military regime in the Ottoman Empire. It remained a part of Bulgarian and Greek public finances into the twentieth century.

Territorial rulers were forced into dependence on debt financing by the limited revenues from the royal demesne, the narrow tax basis, and privatized, inefficient, and corrupt tax administrations. They also encountered recurrent problems of consent when asking for gifts (benevolences), seeking purveyance, imposing levies on the Church and religious orders, and asking for tax increases. Rulers had to cope with unreliable revenues, highly imperfect financial accounts, and widespread financial cheating. There was no fiscal capacity to manage a consolidated floating debt. Instead, territorial rulers relied on short-term loans as instruments for state building and war financing.

The combination of a hierarchical, theologically legitimated social model with the emerging fiscal-military regime defined the nature of the relations between territorial rulers and creditors. Rulers associated financiers with cheating and identified them as inferiors. Hence they felt justified in resorting to financial concealment and trickery, currency debasement, default, and coercive financial repression. Doing so was made easy by opaque and secretive debt financing. Repression included expropriating assets of creditors, most notably of Jewish moneylenders but also on occasion of the Church. It also extended to pillage of conquered territories as war indemnity. These practices rested on belief in absolute sovereign immunity to exercise discretion, the subordinate claims of property rights, and a narrow conception of political entitlements.

However, this type of fiscal-military regime, and the social model on which it rested, fomented a deep distrust of the state and of the cheating and venality of its financial agents. This distrust accelerated with the rise of new social interests, especially in the cities. Between 1648 and 1651 it broke to the surface in France with the failed Fronde revolt and demands for financial reforms. Distrust of the state sowed the seeds of the French Revolution in 1789 and its wide appeal across western Europe. It also fed the recurrent political revolts against nineteenth-century efforts at restoration of traditional fiscal-military monarchical rule. It played a key role in the long spiral of decline into which the Ottoman Empire fell from the 1580s (Inalcik 1994).

The mounting challenges of sustaining creditworthiness in the face of war and the increasing reliance on ad hoc, short-term debt financing were exemplified in the reign of King Edward I of England. His French, Scottish, and Welsh wars, and especially his Crusade, led to huge debts to the Ricciardi of Lucca. The Ricciardi loaned (in 2010 values) the equivalent of £12 million in 1273 and £59 million in 1289. As security, Edward I handed to them the operation of his new customs duties (Prestwich 1972). This practice of matching short-term debts to assigned taxes to creditors, or to trade monopolies and privileges, became a foundation stone of early fiscal-military regimes. Henry VII secured his creditworthiness with the Frescobaldi of Florence by assigning them the monopoly of the illicit and highly profitable alum trade (Penn 2011).

However, wars were notoriously uncertain and perilous and prone to cripple creditworthiness. For this reason, the wars of the Teutonic Knights of Prussia against the Polish-Lithuanian Empire turned them into the European leaders in currency debasements (Chilosi and Volckart 2010a). Similarly, setbacks in the Great Northern War had a negative impact on creditworthiness of the beleaguered Swedish Empire under Charles XII (r. 1697–1718). The war of 1768–1774 exposed the lack of creditworthiness of the Ottoman Empire. The dramatic effects of defeat on creditworthiness haunted Austria, Prussia, and Russia both during and after the Napoleonic Wars. Similarly, war legacies formed the background to the catastrophic defaults of Greece in 1893 and of the Ottoman Empire in 1875–1881 (Cross 2000; Levandis 1944).

The turning point in the reputation of fiscal-military regimes came in the eighteenth century, with the War of the Spanish Succession, the Seven Years' War, and later the Napoleonic Wars. These wars demonstrated the superior character of the new institutional structures and practices of the British fiscal state. Britain seemed to offer a new model of a virtuous circle in debt financing and military success. Her military victories, naval supremacy, and territorial gains were accompanied by a rapid increase in sovereign debt, lower debt servicing costs, and avoidance of default (Brewer 1989). This new type of fiscal regime rested on a very different model of society.

Nevertheless, the legacy of the traditional social model extended into the nineteenth century and beyond. It was enshrined in the prestige of officer corps and bureaucratic elites, which sheltered within constitutional forms that safeguarded executive autonomy. They gained further legitimacy from reforms that sought to strengthen their professionalism. At the same time, military and bureaucratic elites resisted parliamentary accountability. The consequence was a difficult tension between the claims to executive autonomy in matters of war financing and the claims of legislatures in which *rentier* interests were strongly represented (Théret 1995).

This tension ran through the French Second Empire of Napoleon III, the French Third Republic in its post-Dreyfus *Belle Époque* period, and the German Second Empire. It was to some extent mitigated by symbiotic interests. The coercive power of the state could be invoked to secure the interests of bondholders against defaulting debtor states. The governments of the German Second Empire and *Belle Époque* France were disposed to support the principle of armed intervention on behalf of creditors, notably over Greece. Napoleon III came to their defence over Mexico. However, appealing to this symbiosis of interests was often opportunistic rather than the principal motive for advocating intervention. In perhaps the most famous case, British military intervention in Egypt in 1882 and Egypt's subsequent status as a British protectorate, defence of *rentier* interests played a part, but was by no means central. Geo-strategic arguments were decisive as in Napoleon III's earlier intervention in Mexico. Again, during the Ottoman Turk defaults of the 1870s and successive Greek defaults, especially in the 1890s, British governments proved very reluctant to use military intervention on behalf of creditors (Clay 2000; Levandis 1944; Wynne 1951). In any case, *rentiers* had complex interests. They were also taxpayers, who would be asked to pay the bill for intervention. Moreover, those *rentiers* who were unaffected in a given default had an aversion to the moral hazard in paying to bail-out other reckless investors. On the whole, *rentiers* were averse to the lack of caution that characterized fiscal-military regimes.

Creditors in the Market Model of Society: 'Self-Made' Wealth, *Rentiers*, and Professionals

The rise to economic, social, and political power of 'self-made' wealth, inherited wealth, and associated professional groups led to radical change in the conception of creditworthiness. The notions of prerogative rights and sovereign immunity ceded place to the rights of property, the centrality of creditors as the reference point in the operation of fiscal regimes, and deference to the self-governing rights of professions like accountancy, law, and economics. These new notions entailed accountability to 'public' opinion, institutional transparency, and independent mechanisms to ensure compliance with proper standards of behaviour.

Sociologically, the new status and power of creditors rested on merchants, financiers, and the professional classes. Accountants provided the fiscal transparency that creditors sought. Lawyers evolved justifications for limiting sovereign immunity. Economists generated concepts and models of sustainable debt. Economically, new-found creditor status and power had its basis in productivity growth and wealth accumulation. It was associated with the new scale of Euro-Atlantic trade, the agricultural and industrial revolutions, and the enormous rise in the size of financial assets at the disposal of banks. Geographically, the centres of this new type of creditor power were the major European financial centres, notably Amsterdam, London, and Paris. The rising self-confidence of these interests translated into a politics of sovereign creditworthiness that rested on gaining secure returns for those with wealth to invest.

Politically, the new status and power of creditors was bound up with a very different constitutional settlement. Its nature was intimated in the quote which opens this chapter from Madame Germaine de Staël, daughter of the French fiscal reformer Jacques Necker. This new settlement involved a surrender of social and political power by rulers. It involved defining public debt financing as a commercial activity, legitimating legal constraints on sovereign immunity. The principle of parliamentary sovereignty included the assumption of public liability for the national debt. Also, national central banks were required to ensure that sovereign debt was professionally managed on principles of sound money and finance. The balanced-budget principle had a totemic significance. Public finances had to be based on institutional transparency and accountability to public opinion. For this purpose, a professional and centralized fiscal administration was needed to ensure reliable tax collection, efficient public expenditure, and effective control of fiscal balances. Particular importance was attached to low inheritance taxes (cf. Théret 1991). Finally, bondholder organizations spread from Britain. Their aim was to strengthen the collective-action capacity of creditors both in lobbying their own governments and in negotiating directly with distressed debtor states.

The British Model

During the eighteenth century reformers across Europe constructed a narrative of Britain as the model for this new type of fiscal regime. It was dated from the Glorious Revolution of 1688 and the establishment of the Bank of England in 1694. The British

Parliament and the new central bank helped secure the interests of self-made and inherited wealth. They protected these social interests from threats of default and coercive financial repression. The new mechanisms that safeguarded sovereign creditworthiness served also to strengthen incentives to entrust self-made and inherited wealth to new banks and later to investment trusts.

Firm adherence to an impersonal currency standard—gold, silver, or bi-metallic—offered an additional guarantee of sovereign creditworthiness by 'binding fiscal and monetary hands'. It promised to lock-in automatic adjustment to trade, financial, and monetary imbalances. Here again Britain was the nineteenth-century leader. The spread of the gold standard as the international norm from the 1870s was an indicator of British 'soft' power. Imbalances were supposed to be automatically corrected through gold inflows and outflows (Eichengreen 1992). Hence the new constitutional settlement came to rest on three principal foundations: parliamentary sovereignty, central banks, and the gold standard. They secured the interests of self-made and inherited wealth.

Post-1815, emulation of British leadership in evolving a new type of fiscal regime rested on her earlier demonstration of an extraordinary capacity to expand public debt in the eighteenth century and in the Napoleonic Wars without default. This achievement differentiated her from Austria, France, Prussia, and Russia. It had rested on the combination of several innovations: the creation of professional institutions to manage the public debt; the shift of public financing from ad hoc short-term loans to secure long-term borrowing; the spread of public debt amongst a much larger number of creditors; and tough, consensual measures of financial repression that privileged public over private debt (Brewer 1989; Drelichman and Voth 2008). British 'soft' power in European fiscal reforms was bound up with the powerful incentive for other states to emulate this achievement. They wished to combine fast-expanding public debt with lower interest rates. This combination promised increased power for states that could learn and apply the lessons.

The Rise of Statesmen-Bankers

> A court is always a court, and it always leads to something.
> Meyer Amschel Rothschild, letter to James de Rothschild, on 8 February 1816 (Gille 1965)

The Napoleonic Wars and their post-1815 aftermath were decisive in showing that military victory depended on performance on the 'financial battlefield' of debt financing. They also demonstrated that Britain had evolved a superior model of public debt. British sovereign creditworthiness had enabled her to supply subsidies to her allies and to keep her armies in the field, notably in the Iberian Peninsula under Lord Wellington. Debt financing capacity was central to Britain's new place in the informal hierarchy of European states. She sat 'at the high table' of peacetime diplomacy, shaping both its process and the outcomes.

The heavy costs of prolonged, continent-wide war and its deprivations induced European rulers to recognize the importance of fiscal capacity for rapid mobilization of huge syndicated loans. It was vital if they were to regain and retain their position in the European hierarchy. Hence sovereign creditworthiness depended on being able to win the support of the most reputable bankers. Their support was vital in mobilizing the expanding wealth of self-made businessmen and of *rentiers*. Bankers were the intermediaries into this world. They became accordingly the central reference point in newly emerging fiscal regimes. The nineteenth-century evolution of institutional arrangements for public debt financing offered to bankers new opportunities to gain hefty commissions. It also provided them with enhanced social status and recognition through their proximity to state power and their indispensability to its exercise.

Intimate contact with the state endowed them with respectability and social acceptance. It ministered to their vanity. However, this growing significance of inherited wealth and *rentier* power was associated with more pronounced and visible economic and social inequality, above all in wealth distribution. This inequality was most evident in the European financial centres like London and Paris and had a strong relationship to family property ownership. It sowed the seeds for later problems and the rise of a new communitarian social model.

The central characteristic of the spreading fiscal-*rentier* regime in the aftermath of the Napoleonic Wars was a new set of professional bankers. They replaced the traditional merchant-financiers as intimate advisers to senior European statesmen. This new 'statesman-banker' role had been intimated in the rise of Hope and Co. of Amsterdam during the eighteenth century. It involved privileged access to state power, in return for helping to support its geo-strategic and diplomatic objectives. 'Statesman-banker' status was attached to the French *hautes banques*, notably James de Rothschild (1792–1868) under King Louis-Philippe. He raised two large loans to support the new monarch in 1830–1834 and a personal loan in 1840 (Gille 1965). Similarly, the banker Achille Fould (1800–1867) served as finance minister under Emperor Napoleon III (Stoskopf 2002).

Statesmen-bankers were to be found across the European states. An early example was Christian von Rotter, who served as financial adviser to Prussian Chancellor Prince Karl-August von Hardenberg. Rotter prevented Prussian insolvency in the face of the huge war indemnity to France during the Napoleonic Wars. He also negotiated the subsequent French war indemnity to Prussia (Kirchner and Radtke 1987). Later, Rotter was head of the Prussian State Bank (*Preussische Seehandlung*) from 1820 to 1848 and president of the State Debt Administration (*Hauptverwaltung der Staatsschulden*). No less important was the Berlin banker, and Rothschild *intimus*, Gerson von Bleichröder. As personal financial adviser to Chancellor Bismarck, he played a key role in financing German unification and later in relation to Russian, Italian, and Ottoman debt financing (Stern 1978).

A similar role was played by the Stieglitz family in Russia. During the Napoleonic Wars, the German-born St Petersburg court banker Ludwig Stieglitz (1779–1843) was financial adviser to Czar Alexander I. He retained this role under Czar Nicholas I after the Napoleonic Wars. His son, Alexander von Stieglitz (1814–1884), raised big foreign loans for the Crimean War. In 1860 he became the first governor of the State Bank of the Russian Empire.

The ubiquitous Nathan Rothschild was the leading personification of the new breed of European statesman-banker. The Rothschild label became the mark of status in European sovereign lending. Bleichröder was termed the 'German Rothschild'. Ludwig Stieglitz was the 'St Petersburg Rothschild'. After the humiliations and depredations of the long Napoleonic Wars, Prussia, Austria, and Spain led the way in turning to the House of Rothschild. They were attracted by its superior resources, organization, intelligence networks, and reputation. However, they also feared falling too much under the power of the House of Rothschild. This fear was soon exploited by their rivals, who played on emotions of national pride and anti-Semitic sentiments (Gille 1965). From the 1840s, as European governments became increasingly anxious about rising nationalist sentiments, they began to practise divide-and-rule in dealing with the House of Rothschild and other bankers.

Under Bismarck the privileged relationship of statesmen-bankers to state power was institutionalized in the Prussian Consortium. This bank consortium was established after the Austro–Prussian War of 1866 and played a key role in financing the Franco–Prussian War of 1870. The Prussian Consortium served two purposes. It was an instrument for reducing external dependence on the House of Rothschild and for better connecting domestic bank lending to foreign policy aims. The Prussian Consortium was organizationally linked to the Royal Prussian State Bank (*Königliche-Preussische Seehandlung*), which had originally been founded as a maritime trading company by Frederick II in 1772 (Kirchner and Radtke 1987). In its early years the leadership of the Prussian Consortium was provided by Bleichröder and Adolph von Hansemann of the Disconto-Gesellschaft. By 1913 its membership had grown to thirteen Berlin banks and fifteen other banks (Reitmeyer 1999).

Similarly, under Emperor Napoleon III a concerted effort was made to mobilize French credit on behalf of his foreign policy and security objectives. French bankers played a leading role in providing loans for Ottoman Turkey during, and after, the Crimean War. They backed collaborative efforts to buttress Ottoman Turkey through the foundation of the Ottoman Imperial Bank (Banque impériale ottomane, BIO). It began as an Anglo-French venture after the Crimean War but became increasingly a French-influenced Ottoman national bank (Clay 2000). Similarly, under the Second Empire the new Crédit mobilier sought to challenge the House of Rothschild in Austria, Italy, Spain, and Russia. James de Rothschild's leadership of the informal alliance of French bankers in the *Réunion financière* was an attempt to organize the traditional *hautes banques* in the face of this new competition. These initiatives reflected the interest of the Second Empire in returning France to the central position in European diplomacy on the basis of a broad-based, radical financial revolution in French banking and French-centred international bank networking (Stoskopf 2002). Spurred on by the model of the Crédit mobilier, the *hautes banques* became increasingly focused on service to the French state.

Restoration-minded political traditionalists continued to adhere to conservative views of the place of creditors in the social hierarchy. Nevertheless, they too sought to mobilize the growing wealth of self-made businessmen, *rentiers*, and professionals and to gain their loyalty and support. For this reason, the small elite of statesmen-bankers gained a new privileged role in the Congress system of diplomacy, which was promoted by Prince Metternich of Austria after the Congress of Vienna in 1815. His adviser, Friedrich von Geertz, acted as intermediary to the Barings, the House of Rothschild, and various French and German bankers (Gille 1965, 1967; Ziegler 1988). These statesmen-bankers emerged as central players in negotiating war indemnities and in raising loans to pay for them. They greased the wheels of the 'Concert of Europe', from which they benefitted commercially and in social and political status.

After the Napoleonic Wars, Barings was famously termed the 'sixth great power' in Europe for speedily raising the French war indemnity in 1817–1818 (Ziegler 1988: 77–81).

However, Barings was soon eclipsed by the Rothschild family, who were suitably christened the 'financial Bonapartes' of Europe (Ferguson 2009: 86). The Rothschild family emerged as the main players on the stage of European sovereign bond issuance and trading, earning the name 'bankers of the Holy Alliance'. From 1818 their offices in London, Paris, Frankfurt, Vienna, and Naples arranged debt financing for Austria, Belgium, France, the Kingdom of Naples, Prussia, Russia, Spain, and many small German states. In the process, the House of Rothschild built up its own vast portfolio of European sovereign bonds. It gained its reputation by carefully avoiding any connection with default or creditor losses. In particular, the House of Rothschild popularized foreign sovereign debt issues by introducing interest payable in sterling. This innovation made bondholders immune to currency manipulation.

The 'Concert' system suited the Rothschild *modus vivendi* of placing themselves on the side of peace in Europe (Gille 1965, 1967). Its demise after 1848, along with new investment opportunities in railways, initiated a slow shift away from sovereign debt by the Rothschild family. However, this shift was less notable in Paris under James de Rothschild. From the 1860s the French *hautes banques* and, to a lesser extent, German banks assumed a greater significance in European sovereign debt markets. Bleichröder emerged as a central player in negotiating the French war indemnity after the Franco–Prussian War (Stern 1978). He was also a presence behind the scenes at the Berlin Congress of 1878 after the Russo–Turkish War, the final act of the Congress system (Clay 2000; Stern 1978).

As the Congress system unravelled, a few elite bankers became increasingly engaged in financing the political ambitions of European rulers. They became vital to the Emperor Napoleon III's interventions in Italian unification, British imperial policies in Egypt, German unification, Russia's role in the Crimean War, and sustaining the Ottoman Empire. Napoleon III turned to the Parisian, family-based *hautes banques*, like Hottinguer, Mallet, and Sellière. Above all, he relied on the banker Achille Fould, his finance minister from 1861 (Stoskopf 2002). In 1875 Prime Minister Benjamin Disraeli enlisted Baron Rothschild to loan the money (though on expensive terms) to secure British control of the Suez Canal. His aim was to reduce French power over 'the key to India' (Blake 1966: 581–7). Similarly, Bleichröder and von Hansemann were central in raising finance for Prussia's victories of 1866 against Austria and of 1870 against France.

Prominent statesmen-bankers served as 'fiscal' viceroys in financial interventions to prop up the ailing Ottoman Empire and Greece against Russia. They served on the Turkish Public Debt Administration from 1881 and the Society for Managing Revenues Assigned to the Service of the Greek Debt from 1898 (Clay 2000; Levandis 1944). The nineteenth century witnessed the emergence of bankers as 'money doctors' to such states as Spain, Portugal, Italy, and the Ottoman Empire, as well as to new states in south-east Europe like Bulgaria and Serbia (Flandreau 2003b; Wynne 1951). They played a new role as agents in strengthening the financial accountability and transparency of states that lacked a powerful domestic *rentier* class. This role involved new concepts and practices of conditionality (Flandreau 2003b).

Who Were the Creditors, Who the Debtors?

Pre-1914 patterns of cooperation and rivalry between banks in European sovereign debt markets reflected the twin influences of a division of labour and Great Power politics.

From the 1850s a division of labour emerged within the House of Rothschild. The Paris, Frankfurt, and Vienna offices became much more involved in European sovereign debt than the London office (Gille 1967). A division of labour also appeared amongst banks. Barings focused on Russia, its role as official agent making it deeply unpopular with the outbreak of the Crimean War. This embarrassing episode confirmed and strengthened Barings' strategic shift away from Europe towards North and South America (Ziegler 1988). Hambros specialized in Greece. After 1918 Barings, the House of Rothschild, and Schroder divided up their lead roles in the new European sovereign bond markets. Barings led on Czechoslovakia, Rothschild on Hungary (Ziegler 1988: 351).

From the mid-1870s the most striking change was a shift of British sovereign debt financing away from Europe. In 1870–1874 France and Russia had predominated in British sovereign lending, followed by Ottoman Turkey and Austria-Hungary. From then to 1914 British sovereign debt financing focused on colonial and provincial government loans within the British Empire, especially to Australia, India, and South Africa (Stone 1999). Over the whole period 1815–1914, no European state figured in the top five recipients of British sovereign lending (Stone 1999: 383).

In contrast, French sovereign lending was much more Europe-focused. In 1914 Russia was overwhelmingly the top recipient of French lending, followed by Spain and Portugal, Austria-Hungary, Ottoman Turkey, and Romania (Moulton and Lewis 1925: 20). In the 1880s the German Imperial government induced its bankers to shift their sovereign lending away from Russia to Italy and the Ottoman Empire. Displacing French dominance of Italian and Ottoman sovereign debt markets was defined as in Germany's geo-strategic interest (Stern 1978). Similarly, consistent with German foreign policy objectives, Bleichröder, the Berliner Handelsbank, and the Disconto-Gesellschaft played a leadership role in debt financing of the Hapsburg Empire. Conversely, French banks sought to retain their dominant position in sovereign lending to Russia and to the Ottoman Empire. Though Ottoman and Russian debt was risky, it was assessed as sustainable because much of it was used for productive industrial investments that yielded revenue (Flandreau 2003a).

In making sovereign lending decisions, bankers tended to follow political steers with caution and often reluctance, much to the irritation of Bismarck and Napoleon III. They were not prepared to risk their reputations with wealthy investors by being seen as merely the servants of geo-politics. Nevertheless, the role of statesman-banker was difficult to resist. Proximity to state power offered the tempting combination of social honour and status with wider economic opportunities from privileged association with politically powerful figures.

Sovereign debt financing underwent explosive growth after 1815 as new and inherited wealth looked for investment opportunities. The challenge of managing the associated risks led to new, more systematic forms of sovereign credit ratings. Before 1914 the Crédit Lyonnais divided European states into a threefold grouping. The top grouping was occupied by European states that had no recent history of sovereign default and no net debt interest service costs. It included Belgium, Britain, Denmark, Finland, the German Imperial government, Norway, Russia, Sweden, and the Swiss federal government. Russia stands out as the exceptional 'blue-chip' sovereign investment. The second grouping comprised states that had no recent default history and net debt service costs of around 15 per cent of normal revenues. It included Austria, the Netherlands, Hungary,

Italy, and Romania. Strikingly, the Netherlands had lost ground in the European hierarchy, below Belgium. The third grouping was made up of the least creditworthy: Bulgaria, Greece, Ottoman Turkey, Portugal, Serbia, and Spain. They had recent defaults and/or interest service costs over 40 per cent of normal revenues (Flandreau 2003b: 44). Before the establishment of the modern credit rating agencies there was a clear hierarchy of European states.

Tension, Conflict, and Continuity in the Power of Self-Made and Inherited Wealth

This creditor-centred conception of sovereign creditworthiness came under increasing challenge from the late nineteenth century, in a process that was accelerated by the First World War and its aftermath (Théret 1991, 1995). Nevertheless, its longer-term influence remained profound. It continued to structure public debate, shape political agendas, and exert influence within policy processes. Despite sometimes dramatic setbacks, notably in interwar Europe, longer-term wealth accumulation continued to privilege the interests of savers and investors and a restrictive conception of sovereign creditworthiness.

However, there was an inbuilt tension and growing conflict within the market model of society between inherited wealth and new 'self-made' wealth. Wealth acquisition was associated with less risk-averse attitudes to debt financing, with belief in light-touch financial regulation, and with a new collusion between finance capitalism and consumer capitalism. In particular, the combination of wealth accumulation, new debt financing instruments, and rising public expectations of sharing in the new affluence helped to generate a new consumer culture. This consumer culture was essentially hedonistic, establishing new notions of social and economic entitlement, and de-stigmatizing debt. Governments incentivized its growth to keep voters happy by generous deposit guarantees, by taxation that favoured debt, and by trying to keep interest rates low. Consumer culture served to undermine the virtues of thrift and prudence. It also created a dangerous new loop from insolvent consumers to banks and on to sovereign creditworthiness once states chose to assume private-sector liabilities. In short, the market model of society bred a new, more relaxed attitude towards debt.

At the same time, the combination of long-term economic growth with the legacy of new self-made wealth fed, over time, into the resurfacing of inherited wealth as a powerful social force. Inherited wealth remained a defining characteristic of advanced economies. In consequence, the late twentieth century witnessed the re-emergence of major social, economic, and political inequalities in wealth, income, and access to power. Education, hard work, and getting a good job became less important than having the right family inheritance of wealth. Despite universal suffrage, and the new beneficiaries of welfare-state provision, *rentier* interests remained deeply influential in society. They were represented in fast-expanding financial markets, which channelled increasingly high levels of European savings, notably pensions and insurance, into sovereign bonds. Sovereign bonds of the most creditworthy states retained a special status as 'safe havens'. Financial market regulations required holdings of these bonds as balancing elements in pension and insurance risk portfolios. Also, the demographic shift to an ageing population of retired people, who were dependent on fixed incomes, sustained a strong political support for a restrictive conception of sovereign creditworthiness.

Creditors in the Communitarian Model of Society

The underlying political condition for the ascendancy of creditor attitudes to sovereign debt, and the market model of society on which this ascendancy rested, was an electoral franchise that was restricted to property owners. After 1815 a limited franchise made it easier for British governments to pay off heavy public debts. They were able to retain credibility and prestige by imposing heavy, painful costs of adjustment on non-voters (Stasavage 2003). Between 1815 and 1821 the Bank of England almost halved the money supply and drove down prices by 50 per cent. This move paved the way for Britain's return to gold in 1821. Similarly, in 1920 the Bank of England chose the path of deflation, bringing prices down by 50 per cent by the end of 1922 (Ahamed 2010: 61). The aim was to enable Britain to return to the gold standard, at the pre-war parity, at the earliest opportunity.

However, this type of *rentier*-centred argument rested on a restrictive view of 'public' opinion. The deep controversy that accompanied the return to gold at pre-war parity in 1926, and the accompanying protracted and deep recession and unemployment, reflected the new political limits on deflation as a policy instrument. It imposed burdens on employers, workers, and borrowers, who now had the franchise.

From the late nineteenth century onwards the lineaments of a new politics of sovereign creditworthiness began to emerge across west European states. It reflected the widening of the electoral franchise and the extension of education and literacy. These two processes opened opportunities to new social interests, notably to a class-based identity politics and to political radicalism. They helped to restore greater discretion to governing elites in managing public debt by freeing them from the shackles of creditor interests. The most important change was the rise of the labour movement. It took the form of new social democratic parties and trade unions. They reshaped political agendas, party systems, electoral competition, and industrial relations through collective bargaining of employers and workers. The labour movement brought new demands for high employment, welfare benefits, and more progressive taxation onto the political agenda. Above all, the introduction of high inheritance taxation symbolized the erosion of *rentier* power.

The First World War accelerated this shift in social interests. The state was increasingly expected to 'manage' the economy; to develop welfare programmes to tackle problems of unemployment, sickness, old age, and poverty; and to demonstrate social solidarity and a commitment to social justice. In consequence, adjustment processes to external imbalances became increasingly politicized. The notion of automatic reductions in real wages to restore competitiveness lost both market and political credibility (Eichengreen 1992). Hence the gold standard proved more difficult to sustain politically after 1918, other than as a 'managed' system. Flexible adjustment, epitomized in the post-1944 Bretton Woods system, and later in the European 'Snake' and Exchange-Rate Mechanism (ERM), seemed better-adapted to this changing balance of social interests.

The shift to a less restrictive conception of sovereign creditworthiness accompanied demands for a wide range of costly social benefits as 'entitlements'. These entitlements were linked to the emergence of the 'social question' on the political agenda. Citizenship was seen as a matter of economic and social rights, as well as narrow political rights.

The state's function was redefined. It was no longer there just to protect property rights. The state's duty was to promote social peace as a public good and to take an inclusive view of its duty to protect.

This new communitarian social model based on need had several institutional manifestations. It was associated with the spread of 'social partnership' arrangements in welfare-state provision, incorporating employer, trade-union, and professional representation. There was a new reliance on negotiated, neo-corporatist 'social pacts' as a mechanism for managing fiscal policy adjustments and economic reforms. Not least, the parameters of fiscal debates were changed by the growth of public-sector employment and the vested interests in public finances.

In consequence, the conception of sovereign creditworthiness stressed the process of negotiation amongst a much wider range of social interests. The state was expected to balance creditor with wider public interests. These wider public interests included respect for the rights and privileges that attached to an enlarging set of public employees. They involved amelioration of the suffering of the vulnerable, the poor, and the innocent victims of adjustment to external imbalances and banking crises. This reshaped and enlarged context of social interests was also accompanied by demographic shift to an ageing population and associated health and pension costs. Together, they led to the expansion of both public expenditure and sovereign borrowing as shares of gross domestic product (GDP) (Fontvieille 1976).

The Changing Politics of Sovereign Creditworthiness

By the twenty-first century the changing politics of sovereign creditworthiness constituted a mounting challenge for European states. In the first place, states had to find ways of reconciling the interests of self-made and inherited wealth with the growth in new social interests. Governing elites had to contend with a 'public' opinion that included taxpayers and welfare recipients. The increase in welfare-state recipients, and the rise of the bureaucracies that supported them, displaced the political power of *rentiers*. Welfare-state stakeholders emerged as powerful electoral reference groups, promoting a more morally relaxed view about sovereign debt.

At the same time, the rising value of household wealth based on property ownership, the huge growth of financial markets, and the greater dependence of states on these markets, created a context in which *rentier* interests could reassert themselves economically and politically. The financial markets evolved as increasingly important safeguards of a restrictive conception of sovereign creditworthiness. They had insider access through intimate 'relationship' banking to states, along with the branding and disciplinary power of credit ratings and yield spreads in sovereign bond markets. The post-2010 sovereign debt crisis showed that the inclusive, public-interest politics of European states remained underpinned by a private governance of public debt that continued to privilege a restrictive conception of sovereign creditworthiness.

Secondly, the challenge of reconciling the extra demands on public finances, notably from education, health, and pensions, with this restrictive conception of sovereign creditworthiness forced attention on state fiscal capacity. Strengthening state fiscal capacity to service larger-scale public debts required major structural reforms aimed at more effective tax revenue-raising, more productive public spending, and tighter controls on fiscal balances. However, such measures faced powerful vested interests, within and outside the state. The notion of social entitlement often hid self-interested rent-seeking activity and staunch defence of 'insider' privileges. Inability to strengthen state fiscal capacity acted as an inducement to governing elites to resort to 'inflation tax', devaluation, covert financial repression, or default. It begged the question of whether they had the power to punish creditors with impunity.

The challenge to sovereign creditworthiness was ameliorated to some extent by the decline in the relative power of the military as a social and political force in Europe. This decline was associated with widespread cultural aversion to military action after the horrors of two twentieth-century European-centred world wars. The European Union (EU) came to embody a conception of a Europe that specialized in the projection of 'soft' power. Moreover, after 1945 European states were able to shelter under US military protection. They also reaped a 'peace dividend' from the end of the Cold War in Europe. Taking part in the US-led 'military revolution' proved costly but was contained by restrictive security policy commitments. However, new twenty-first-century security challenges had the potential to shift the military back to the centre of the politics of sovereign creditworthiness.

Perhaps the pivotal process in the history of sovereign creditworthiness was the rise of a relatively small but powerful *rentier* class. It strengthened the incentives for governing elites to avoid overt and brutal forms of fiscal repression, currency debasement, and coercive default. The interests of inherited wealth were secured by guarantees of property rights and a more critical legal approach to claims of sovereign immunity. Their institutional legacy was parliamentary assumption of responsibility for 'public' debt, independent central banks, fiscal accountability and transparency, and firm fiscal and monetary rules to ensure sound finances and money. The *rentier* class' hold on power had a strongly path-dependent quality, entrenching deep social and economic inequalities of wealth in an age of universal political suffrage. Its presence was most visible in the main spatial locations of its power: the big European financial centres of Amsterdam, London, Paris, Frankfurt, Munich, and Milan.

More subtly, older cultural attitudes to debt and theological traces found their way into justificatory principles for *rentier* power. They sat alongside the justificatory principles offered by Enlightenment political economists like Hume and Smith, which were grounded more firmly in economic and market-based reasoning. *Rentier* interests took on a 'common-sense' quality, reflecting an enduring moral aversion to debt in traditional pre-market folk belief. They could be seen as consistent with the celebration of simple household virtues of thrift, discipline, and prudence and with their extension to wider society. Living within one's means was the embodiment of moral virtue. Similarly, the concepts of fiscal 'saints' and 'sinners' carried religious overtones into debates about appropriate conduct with respect to debt.

The complex and changing balance of social interests helps in understanding the different ways in which problems of sovereign creditworthiness have been represented across space and over time. They also clarify why different kinds of choices have been made about how best to address these problems. How these problems are represented and which choices are made illustrate differences in moral judgement and in the evaluation of distributive outcomes. The patterns of winners and losers offer insight into continuity and change in who has power in society. From the late-medieval European city states, a key factor of continuity in the politics of sovereign creditworthiness has been the market model of society and *rentier* interests. It is exhibited in a preference for avoiding default and coercive financial repression, for resisting inflation, and for pursuing fiscal consolidation and structural reforms. This set of choices pushes costs away from *rentiers* to others. It remained imprinted in the genetic code of creditor states across European history, from the north Italian city states in the late-medieval period to post-1840s' Britain and post-1940s' Germany.

7

The Dynamics of Public Debt in Historical Perspective: The Limitations of Formal Economic Reasoning

Qui numerare incipit, errare incipit.
Morgenstern (1950: 2)

Historical analysis of European public debt faces many difficulties, not least relating to the availability, accuracy, and comparability of very differently generated long-term data. These difficulties make historical data less suitable for systematic statistical meta-analysis than for narrative synthesis. David Hume and Adam Smith were past masters of narrative synthesis in political economy, treating history as a laboratory that yields a rich assortment of empirical observations. Narrative synthesis starts from the premise that data selection, data errors, and weighting of observations remain problematic in any attempt to think about public debt. The added value in historical analysis lies in revealing the context-specific and contingent character of public debt dynamics and in picking up the significance of low-frequency events. It induces scepticism towards formal economic and probabilistic reasoning about debt sustainability and sovereign creditworthiness. Historical analysis challenges their claims to provide a universal logic, their neglect of 'off-model' developments, their tendency to generalize from temporally limited data, and their proneness to extrapolate from past experience to future prospects.

Longer-term observation of public debt helps puncture the illusion that there can be a single, authoritative, and agreed optimal theory of debt sustainability, from which a simple firm fiscal rule can be derived. Sustainable debt is historically contingent on three factors. It depends on variations in potential gross domestic product (GDP) growth rates and in characteristics of economic structure that affect these rates, including their degree of openness. It varies also with whether states borrow with or without their own currency, the capacity of their banking system to absorb public debt, and the degree of sophistication in debt financing and management techniques. Not least, debt sustainability is a function of political will and state capacity to extract taxes and to translate debt into productive investment in infrastructure and in building social solidarity and political inclusivity. This factor highlights the role of culture. The historical record offers too flimsy an empirical basis for claiming a causal theory that justifies an upper bound of a 90 per cent public debt/GDP ratio or a 3 per cent fiscal deficit/GDP rule. Historical analysis has an additional value. It highlights the precariousness of sovereign creditworthiness. In so doing, it subverts the naïve belief—at the heart of much financial regulation—that sovereign bonds are intrinsically a 'safe' asset.

The analysis of longer-term historical data also puts in question certain conventional beliefs about the accumulation of public debt and sources of threat to debt sustainability. One such belief is that the main source of this threat is to be found in the spread of the notion of social and economic entitlements and its embodiment in fiscally profligate welfare states. In contrast, historical observation shows that what matters is the nature and quality of public expenditure, above all social investment and infrastructure spending, in bolstering long-term economic growth. Political will and state capacity to sustain productive public investment in infrastructure and in building social solidarity have made vitally important contributions to long-term growth-maximizing debt sustainability (Aschauer 1989; Vandebroucke 2012). For this reason, over the period 1960–2010, Denmark, the Netherlands, and Austria, followed in rank order by Germany and France, were able to secure a comparative advantage in debt sustainability over Portugal, Belgium, Spain, Britain, and Greece (Checherita-Westphal, Hughes Hallett, and Rother 2012: 12).

Historically, risks to debt sustainability derived more from the illusion, hubris, and complacency that have been endemic in banking culture and in consumer culture. Financial crises proved a key driver of public debt dynamics, revealing the scale of implicit state guarantees of the largely opaque liabilities of banks. At the political level, the chief source of risks to debt sustainability has come historically from the privileging of the military in constructing external and internal security threats, from engagement in war, and from the prospect and experience of military defeat.

Despite their limitations, formal economic reasoning and formal debt sustainability analysis have an important role to play in enlightening narrative reasoning about what constitutes sustainable public debt. They show that issuing debt is not an alternative to cutting expenditure or raising taxes. Debt accumulation is only a way of deferring these steps. In the long or even short run, it can prove costly—even disastrous—to economic growth. It reduces the fiscal space to deal with emergencies and to absorb the costs of short-term opportunistic political behaviour as well as the capacity to invest productively in infrastructure and in social solidarity (Ghosh, Kim, Mendoza, Ostry, and Qureshi 2011; International Monetary Fund 2009c). Formal economic reasoning helps show how the European Union (EU) and its Member States might define a fiscal 'safe zone' that accommodates future shocks and the temptations of governing elites to self-interested, time-inconsistent behaviour (Checherita-Westphal, Hughes Hallett, and Rother 2012).

Formal debt sustainability analysis contributes enlightenment by showing how public debt dynamics are embedded in the complex interactions amongst a range of macroeconomic variables and by warning of fiscal risks on this basis. However, immersion in formal modelling can produce intellectual amnesia. Many of the key variables that impact on debt sustainability evade precise and reliable measurement or probabilistic reasoning. They are subject to radical uncertainty. Formal economic reasoning and formal debt sustainability analysis neglect vital 'soft' indicators. They ignore governance standards and state capacity; poverty and deprivation; and environmental degradation and resource depletion. Moreover, formal economic reasoning tends to be preoccupied with short-term, not always reliable data; to be caught up in statistical squabbles and in the problems that stem from fiscal data misallocation; and to err towards universal, top-down solutions to context-specific problems of public debt. It is, in consequence, limited in its capacity to produce reliable country-specific estimates about debt sustainability. There is a risk of bias from 'variable omission' in estimation.

The limitations of formal economic reasoning and formal debt sustainability analysis matter because they play a constitutive role in public debt dynamics. They affect how the dynamics work. Their limitations as a camera might be less serious if they did not also function as engines of financial market sentiment (MacKenzie 2006). The formal debt sustainability analyses of the European Central Bank (ECB) and, above all, the International Monetary Fund (IMF) were basic to the design, operation, and redesign of the international bail-outs of Cyprus, Greece, Ireland, and Portugal. The risk was that they could impact negatively by contributing to vicious circles in sovereign creditworthiness (European Central Bank 2012a).

Debate about sovereign risk and creditworthiness is subject to intellectual capture by the formal debt sustainability analyses of official sources. They produce authoritative, technical knowledge about public debt, which is clothed in the mystique of precise measurement and which drives market and political expectations about sovereign creditworthiness. As later chapters show, there are two other engines that drive market and political expectations and mould debate about sovereign risk. Though both are less strictly anchored in formal economic reasoning, they share a fundamental commitment to probabilistic reasoning. Fitch, Moody's, and Standard and Poor's assign formal credit ratings to states and put them on positive or negative outlooks. Disaster risk is signalled once sovereign bonds lose investment grade status and are designated 'junk'. In addition, credit-default-swap (CDS) spreads offer market-based, trading-oriented assessments of propensity to default. Disaster risk is signalled once sovereign CDS spread jumps above 200 basis points.

Credit ratings and CDS market spreads have the additional feature of being internal to the functioning of financial markets, whilst at the same time constructing the reality of fiscal normality that they seek to describe. Formal debt sustainability analysis, credit ratings, and CDS markets are by no means identical types of branding exercises. Credit ratings, for instance, explicitly recognize the role of qualitative variables. Nevertheless, they lean to probabilistic reasoning rather than recognize that radical uncertainty in public debt dynamics makes narrative reasoning about sovereign creditworthiness more intellectually appropriate. They incline to working with a discrete range of variables that can be suitably quantified to provide an objective basis for branding states. A few formal economic assessments of public debt dynamics achieved a seminal importance, notably Aschauer (1989) and Roubini and Sachs (1989). In particular, Reinhardt and Rogoff (2010) gained intellectual status as gurus of fiscal austerity in Europe.

Formal Debt Sustainability Analysis

Conventional formal debt sustainability analysis involves an accounting exercise based on a standard debt accumulation equation. It rests on the implicit assumption that macroeconomic variables are the core drivers of public debt dynamics. Both the ECB and the IMF use similar types of analysis. They identify a set of key determinants of sustainable public debt: the existing public debt level ('debt stock' or 'debt legacy'), the current budget position (the fiscal primary balance, after excluding debt servicing costs), the nominal interest rate, and the nominal GDP growth rate. The key difference is that the ECB adds the 'deficit-debt adjustment'. This measure accounted for changes in the public debt/GDP ratio that are not reflected in the primary balance. Examples include effects from exchange-rate changes or acquisitions of shares in companies by government. Both equations assigned significance to the fiscal primary balance and to the 'interest-growth differential'. High primary surpluses and GDP growth rates in excess of interest rate are identified as the keys to reducing the public debt/GDP ratio. The effects of inflation are incorporated in nominal GDP growth.

The IMF (2003) constructed a simple formula for debt sustainability, in which D^* is the sustainable debt level; PS the primary surplus; r the interest rate; and g the GDP growth rate. Its equation provided an authoritative, technocratic logic of fiscal normality, which could serve as the basis for analysing and critiquing states and their political systems.

$$D^* = PS/(r - g)$$

Using this equation, the IMF concluded that advanced industrial economies—like those at the core of Europe—required primary fiscal surpluses that rise from 2 per cent when public debt is 20 per cent of GDP to around 8 per cent when it climbs to 100 per cent of GDP. As public debt accumulates, primary surpluses need to rise to ensure debt sustainability. On this basis by 2011 Belgium, Greece, Ireland, Italy, and Portugal faced alarming challenges of debt sustainability. The ECB (2012a: 69) calculated that they needed to maintain primary fiscal surpluses of over 4 per cent of GDP for a prolonged period. In contrast, Norway combined a public debt/GDP ratio of 55.4 per cent with a primary fiscal surplus of 9.3 per cent (International Monetary Fund 2011b: 8).

According to the IMF in 2003, the main EU Member States had long-term sustainable public debt levels. However, Greece and Italy seemed much more vulnerable than many central and east European states, like Estonia and Slovakia, which had inherited relatively low public debts and—as 'catch-up' post-communist economies—had relatively high nominal GDP growth. The IMF model also suggested that public debt legacy is decisive in shaping 'fiscal space' or room for manoeuvre in the face of economic shocks. A high debt stock places the political onus of adjustment on the primary fiscal surplus because of the size of debt-servicing costs. It also increases risk of negative effects on nominal GDP growth and a debt/deflation spiral. In formal terms, debt sustainability depends on governments being able to generate future primary fiscal surpluses that are large enough to accommodate the cost of servicing current and future public debt obligations (European Central Bank 2011b: 64).

At the core of formal debt sustainability analysis is the argument that high public debt legacy has negative effects on nominal GDP growth and thus on public debt/GDP ratio. The appropriate policy responses are fiscal consolidation and structural reforms. Given the nature of the general government debt ratio, the central macroeconomic drivers of debt dynamics are seen as nominal GDP growth, variations in unemployment, and the primary fiscal balance. If nominal interest rates exceed nominal GDP growth, a positive primary balance is necessary to prevent rapid debt growth. The higher the inherited public debt ratio, and the greater the difference between the interest rate and growth, the larger the primary surpluses must be. This last scenario faced Greece in an acute form post-2010. In the case of Italy, with its relatively low trend GDP growth rate and inflation rate and its large debt legacy, the 3 per cent fiscal deficit criterion of the Maastricht Treaty made little sense if debt was to be substantially reduced. Hence measures that would raise the trend rate of GDP growth and that would increase primary fiscal balances were central to reducing Italy's public debt and securing creditworthiness. In such cases, the ECB and the IMF argued that the absence of structural reforms to product, services, capital, and labour markets—designed to raise trend growth rate—were a powerful indicator of debt risk.

The Limitations of Formal Debt Sustainability Analysis as Camera and as Engine

Conventional formal debt sustainability analysis suffers from various limitations. They accumulate into its potential to distort perceptions of sovereign risk, by either underestimating or exaggerating risk. Formal economic reasoning may not only fail to accurately picture sovereign risk. It may also destabilize expectations.

Some of the limitations of formal debt sustainability analysis are internal. It is vulnerable to data and calculation errors, particularly due to fiscal data misallocation in official sources (Checherita-Westphal, Hughes Hallett, and Rother 2012: 17). The value of formal debt sustainability analysis also depends on the choice and the realism of its assumptions, notably about GDP growth. In the Greek and Portuguese 'bail-outs', these assumptions proved ill-founded and were the source of later troubles. Moreover, formal debt sustainability deals with 'official' GDP. This measure is extremely narrow. It poses questions about whether national accounting offers a good camera of the economy. As traditionally conceived, official GDP figures were better at capturing tangible than intangible assets, like scientific research, cultural products, design, and branding. They were slow to adapt to the emerging 'knowledge-based' economy, treating research and development as a business cost rather than as investment. Part of the problem was that here were difficult challenges in capturing intangible assets, notably in measuring their productivity. Nevertheless, revision to measures of official GDP offered the inducement of adding to its size. It could also be justified by reference to harmonization with new international accounting standards.

The problems of extreme narrowness in measures of official GDP were more fundamental in that measures of environmental, natural resource, and social accounts were not included. Also, formal debt sustainability analysis captured neither the 'hidden' GDP of the black economy nor the 'criminal' GDP. Hence, in states like Greece and Italy, 'official' GDP offered a poor picture of national wealth. What made debt sustainable was not in the formal analysis.

More generally, formal debt sustainability analysis is highly vulnerable to the radical uncertainties that surround medium-term debt trajectories. The problems are compounded by understatement of contingent and implicit liabilities. Furthermore, the analysis neglects net public debt. It does not account for public assets, in particular more liquid financial assets. Also, insufficient account is taken of short-term liquidity risks from financial market contagion and from refinancing requirements. Finally, and not least, questions arise about the adequacy and reliability of the underlying fiscal and economic statistics, coding errors, and weightings. These various problems can lead to results that prove fragile and potentially dysfunctional.

At a level more fundamental than calculation and data errors, formal debt sustainability analysis is only as persuasive as its core assumption that macroeconomic variables are central. Other factors matter more. This type of formal economic reasoning is intellectually averse to narrative reasoning about sovereign creditworthiness that foregrounds 'softer' indicators of governance standards, poverty and deprivation, environmental degradation, and resource depletion. Formal debt sustainability analysis fails to build in knowledge about state capacity to improve primary fiscal balances, to build an adequate 'safe zone' to manage unexpected shocks, and to enforce fiscal rules on deficits and, above all, debt. It is even less attuned to dealing with the culturally and ideologically conditioned willingness to invest productively in infrastructure and social solidarity. Governance standards, institutional competence and resilience, public trust, and inclusive political processes for managing debt reduction that address poverty and deprivation are 'off-equation'. They are, however, fundamental and political.

Moreover, debt sustainability analysis fails to address two key contextual issues. It is severely limited in historical time period. It is also fails to take adequate account of the interaction of public debt dynamics with developments in the larger European and global economies. This interaction is fundamental in affecting debt sustainability and suggests that appropriate policy prescriptions will differ depending on whether the European and global political economies are experiencing 'good' or 'hard' times. In its enlightenment mission, debt sustainability analysis is dangerously prone to universalize, above all to prescribe fiscal contraction in all cases.

It is difficult to disentangle formal economic reasoning as applied to sovereign creditworthiness from subjective knowledge. Choices about the range of relevant variables, weighting of their individual significance, and interpretation of the available—often incomplete and unreliable—data are ultimately not objective. Other difficult questions arise. How much reliance should be placed on official definitions of the economic cycle in assessing compliance with rules on structural fiscal balance? How accurate are official fiscal data? Are they distorted by statistical manipulation? Credit ratings differ from formal debt sustainability analysis in involving complex, evolving contextual inference and synthesis, which is in part quantitative but ultimately judgemental. More generally, in formal economic reasoning there is a temptation to resort to short cuts and heuristics to resolve uncertainty. This process is a way of trying to elicit the 'real' preferences of governments and their competence to deal with uncertainties and extreme circumstances. Market-based processes of constructing sovereign creditworthiness are conditioned in subtle, often implicit and unconscious ways. They involve subjectively-laden images of state capacity, the honesty and integrity of elites, their governing competence, and their willingness to comply with obligations. These images become more embedded once confirmed by formal debt sustainability analysis and the application of algorithmic skills.

In some respects, context plays a significant role in formal debt sustainability analysis. This type of analysis opens up some difficult and contentious issues of theory and empirical research within formal economics. One such issue is the role of sizeable welfare states in acting as automatic stabilizers during 'hard' times. Neo-Keynesian economists tend to welcome welfare states as mechanisms through which demand is automatically injected into the economy. In their absence, as in the United States, larger-scale use of discretionary fiscal measures can compensate. Hence, EU Member States are less likely to need to resort to discretionary fiscal action. The European Economic Recovery Programme, which was championed by the European Commission in 2008, added no substantial discretionary pan-European fiscal stimulus beyond the limited stimuli (compared to the United States) to which Member States were already making unilateral commitments. Neo-classical economists focused more on regaining fiscal flexibility through deep structural reforms to welfare states, with the adjustment being born on the expenditure side.

However, formal economic arguments of this kind risk overlooking another property of welfare states. They provide social investment in education, training, childcare, health care, and poverty reduction. Social investment remains indispensable to economic growth and, not least, social solidarity in the face of fiscal crisis. From this perspective, the economically and politically difficult challenge is to match short-term fiscal consolidation with strengthening long-term social investment (Vandenbroucke 2012).

Context is also an issue with respect to the role of fiscal multipliers in long-term sustainable debt. Attempts to formally model and give precise value to the effects of fiscal multipliers on economic growth and public debt/GDP ratios generated fragile and contested results. Neo-classical economists tend to argue that these effects are weak so that sharp and rapid fiscal consolidation will have limited, negative short-term impact on economic growth. This impact will be offset by fiscal and structural reform policies that have 'full credibility', lead to a decline in the sovereign risk premium, lower debt servicing costs, and stimulate private-sector investment. The outcome will be an improving public debt/GDP ratio. Conversely, neo-Keynesian economists assess fiscal multiplier effects as substantial and likely to lead to protracted economic stagnation or recession. They are substantial because of credit-constrained households, the decline of productive investment in infrastructure and social solidarity, and loss of credibility as growth proves elusive and the public debt/GDP ratio deteriorates or proves inflexible. In practice, the operation of fiscal multipliers is context-specific. It varies with economic structure and the nature of the growth trajectory, notably the weight of household debt, with exchange rates, and with the effects of non-conventional monetary policy activism.

These internal debates about context-sensitivity within formal debt sustainability are very important and leave a large margin of doubt about results. However, the condition and development of the European and international economies is no less significant for a context-sensitive analysis of debt sustainability. A fast-growing international economy of eager consumers, confident investors, and rising opportunities for exports helps to reduce the costs of short, sharp remedial fiscal consolidation and structural reforms to correct external imbalances and to recover from domestic financial market shocks. GDP growth through exports, investment, and job creation helps fiscal consolidation and reduction of the public debt/GDP ratio by boosting tax revenues and reducing demands on public expenditure. It also facilitates a more politically inclusive agenda that compensates the losers from rapid structural reforms and fiscal consolidation through measures to enhance employability, alleviate poverty, and reduce economic inequalities. In this kind of context, issues of automatic stabilizers, welfare-state retrenchment, and fiscal multipliers are secondary.

After 2002 Brazil succeeded in combining a huge $30 billion IMF rescue with an agenda of economic and social reforms. It averted an Argentinean-style default. Earlier, in the 1990s, after their domestic financial crises, Finland and Sweden constructed the so-called Nordic model out of their benign debt reduction strategy. This model was based on a 'flexi-curity' policy narrative, which linked more flexible labour markets and new firm domestic fiscal rules with stimulus to science-based innovation and growth and with generous social and employment policies to compensate for costs of adjustment. The rapid association of the Nordic model with success—and its projection into the EU Lisbon strategy—was made possible by a supportive international environment of rapid and sustained growth. In contrast, the post-2007 global financial and economic crisis offered a much less benign context for radical fiscal adjustment and structural reforms in Cyprus, Greece, Ireland, Italy, Portugal, and Spain. In a low-growth European environment investors remained sceptical about the continuing political will and state capacity to reduce public debt through harsh and prolonged fiscal consolidation and structural reforms. They were, accordingly, more prone to translate individual pieces of negative news as signals for market alarm and panic. The strategy for dealing with debt sustainability in one context proved less relevant in another where there was a high risk that Europe-wide recession would make debt reduction by individual states elusive, lead to declining confidence, and risk a debt-deflation spiral.

The lack of context-sensitive analysis of debt sustainability was also apparent in an intellectual amnesia that resulted from the lack of an historical and political understanding of public debt dynamics and their social, cultural, and ethical contexts. Historical data on the relationship of default to debt levels show how notions of fiscal 'normality' have changed over time. What was deemed normal and possible for a European state in 1815–1850s or in 1945–1960s did not hold in Europe from the 1870s to 1914 or from the 1970s. The post-1970s period saw the emergence of the notion of public debt/GDP ratios over 60 per cent as 'excessive'. Later, at the turn of the twenty-first century public debt/GDP ratios over 90 per cent were viewed as growth-inhibiting (Reinhart and Rogoff 2010). Sovereign bond yields over 7 per cent were understood as signals of unsustainable public finances.

Crucially, the two periods 1815–1850s and 1945–1960s were located in the protracted, dark fiscal shadows of hugely destructive Europe-wide wars. Also, governing elites in the earlier period lived in fear of liberal and national revolutions. The post-1945 period was associated with the Cold War in Europe till 1989–1991, which pushed up military expenditures, and with increased welfare spending, notably on education, health, and pensions. The return to more restrictive notions of fiscal normality by the 1980s suggests historical parallels with the 1870s–1914 period. The two periods witnessed the renaissance of *rentier* power; rising inequalities of wealth and income; and new and growing social and political movements that began to challenge governing elites.

Based on historically limited data for the period since the 1960s, formal debt sustainability analysis has been helpful in capturing the effects of the demographics of rapid population ageing and welfare-state growth. Post-2007 it has revealed the adverse public debt dynamics spawned by banking liquidity and solvency crises. The value of this analysis derives from data that have been formally compiled on a cross-national, harmonized basis. However, it suffers from its very limited historical time frame. Longer-term historical data have the converse problem. The data is not available on a standardized and harmonized basis. Cross-national variation in the availability and the quality of data limits the value of any attempts at cross-national comparison. Nevertheless, historical data provide an opportunity to capture patterns in public debt dynamics that shorter-term data ignore. It is possible to see changes in notions of fiscal 'normality' over time. Public debt/GDP ratios below the Maastricht 60 per cent emerge as an historical rarity. What emerges is the overriding significance of war and of banking crises for public debt dynamics. Definitions of geo-strategic and external and internal threat trump restrictive notions of fiscal 'normality'. Moreover, what matters is tax capacity to service debt rather than the size of public debt.

US Public Debt

The most salient historical feature of US public debt dynamics is the big impact of wars and their legacies: the War of Independence, the Civil War, and the First and the Second World Wars (see Table 7.1). In the aftermath of Independence, the

Table 7.1 Historical Data on the US Federal Debt, 1790 to 2000, as Percentage of GDP

1790	29.6	1939	43.0
1800	15.1	1942	62.0
1820	8.3	1945	112.7
1840	0.3	1946	102.6
1860	1.9	1950	73.7
1861	16.8	1955	55.5
1866	31.4	1960	44.8
1870	27.9	1965	36.5
1880	18.4	1970	28.2
1890	7.8	1975	26.6
1900	6.6	1980	26.2
1910	3.7	1985	37.1
1916	2.7	1990	42.8
1919	33.4	1995	49.2
1925	21.6	2000	34.5
1929	14.9		
1931	22.3		
1934	44.0		

(*Source*: Congressional Budget Office 2010a)

first Secretary of the Treasury, Alexander Hamilton (1789–1795), was the architect of newly issued Treasury bonds. The United States inherited a huge debt problem from the Revolutionary War, not least the aftermath of the default in March 1780. Many states—mostly in the north—had borrowed heavily by issuing paper notes. Hamilton was faced with the threat of multiple defaults and loss of creditor confidence. However, he encountered strong opposition from southern states to collective debt redemption, as well as populist fears that the winners would be speculators, who had purchased these notes at steep discounts in the hope of redemption at par. Hamilton succeeded in passing a one-off federal assumption of states' debts, with no haircuts for the speculators (Chernow 2005). In order to secure creditor confidence, he introduced new sources of revenue from customs and excise to service the interest costs on the new Treasury bonds. Under Hamilton's leadership, the infant United States showed a capacity to act in supreme emergency that the euro area seemed to lack as its sovereign debt crises spread and mounted after 2007. He served as the architect of a new liquid market in US Treasury bonds.

Public debt problems plagued the new republic. During the 1840s the United States experienced state debt crises. Florida Territory and Mississippi totally repudiated their debts; Arkansas, Louisiana, and Michigan partially defaulted. Barings became involved in managing a number of these crises, principally temporary defaulters like Illinois and Pennsylvania (Flandreau and Flores 2010: 20). However, with respect to these crises, the US federal government and Congress proved unwilling to follow the Hamilton model. The principle of no bail-out was established in relation to US state defaults. Barings' successful involvement proved commercially successful in generating longer-term underwriting business with key US states.

The Civil War of 1861–1865 proved another pivotal event. US public debt, accumulated by the Union, was forty-one times larger, increasing by some 30 per cent of GDP. It was also heavily short-term and chaotically structured (Noll 2012: 2). In 1865–1866 the Republican Party faced the threat that a south-dominated Democratic Party would seek to repudiate this Union debt and to ensure that the United States assumed the huge Confederate debt. It countered this threat by introducing the Fourteenth Amendment to the Constitution, which stated in section 4: 'The validity of the public debt of the United States…shall not be questioned.' The sanctity of the public debt was used as a key campaigning issue in the Republican Congressional victory in 1866 and the Presidential victory in 1868. By the 1870s successive budget surpluses had enabled debt repayment. The political issue of repudiation had lost its momentum (Foner 2002; Noll 2012).

The US public debt remained a manageable financial problem in part because of the lessons learnt from these painful experiences and in part because of sustained and rapid economic expansion after the Civil War. However, in the late nineteenth century the United States remained vulnerable to financial panics. This vulnerability derived from the combination of a fragile, chaotic banking system with the lack of a central bank with a lender-of-last-resort function. Following major bank failures in 1893, the pre-eminent US banker, J.P. Morgan, organized a syndicate to bail out the US federal government in 1895 with $65 million of gold. The federal government faced the imminent risk of a run on the Treasury and humiliating default (Chernow 1990). This vivid demonstration of the power of Wall Street enraged the Democratic Party and generated a populist reaction.

War was the prime driver of public debt dynamics in the twentieth century, followed by domestic financial crises. During the First World War, US public debt climbed by some 30 per cent of GDP. In the Second World War it surged even more dramatically by nearly 80 per cent, reaching its all-time historic high of 112.7 per cent of GDP in 1945. In contrast, the Great Depression of the 1930s, its associated banking crises, and the New Deal of the Roosevelt Administration witnessed a much more modest public debt growth. In terms of impact on public debt, the Great Depression was eclipsed by the post-2007 financial and economic crisis. The US public debt/GDP ratio climbed from 36 per cent in 2007 towards 70 per cent of GDP in 2011. Before then, US public debt had exceeded 60 per cent of GDP only in the Second World War and in its immediate aftermath. After 1945 a combination of inflation and real GDP growth had helped to reduce the ratio rapidly (Aizenman and Marion 2009).

French Public Debt

French public debt data are of immense historical interest because of France's leading role in European sovereign debt markets, pre-1914. They illustrate a fascinating paradox. On the one hand, on the basis of a range of indicators, French sovereign creditworthiness looked highly suspect. France carried the burden of notably high public debt/total revenue ratios. It endured two heavy defeats in 1815 and in 1870 and subsequent foreign occupations; two heavy war indemnities; regime changes in 1815, 1830, 1848, 1852, and 1871; unstable governments, especially under the Third Republic after 1871; and persisting fears of social breakdown, which erupted in 1815–1816, 1848, and 1870–1871 with the Paris Commune.

On the other hand, France managed to avoid sovereign debt default, paid her war indemnities rapidly and in full (unlike post-1918 Germany), and sustained a remarkable stability in her debt interest rates. In the shadow of defeat at Waterloo in 1815, and Allied occupying forces, the Restoration Monarchy undertook major reforms to French public finances, amounting to a structural break after the defaults of the *ancien régime* and the Revolution (Oosterlinck, Ureche-Rangau, and Vaslin 2013). The French state remained creditworthy in the face of domestic political instability, adverse fiscal data, and negative geo-strategic developments after 1815 and again after 1866 when Prussia gained European ascendancy. The efficient secret of this French paradox stemmed from the cohabitation of contending political traditions—Legitimist, Bonapartist, and Republican—and continuity in the political strength of *rentier* power.

Rentier power was the thread that held together monarchical, imperial, and republican regimes: from Restoration France and the so-called July Monarchy of Louis-Philippe to *Belle Époque*, pre-1914 France. It helps explain how the paradox of suspect sovereign creditworthiness and stable debt interest rates was manageable. The institutional base of this power was to be found in the *hautes banques* and in the Banque de France. Its ideological justification drew on historical memories of the destruction of French creditworthiness and external prestige caused by the Law affair in the early eighteenth century and by the Revolutionary *assignats*. *Rentier* power was expressed in an enduring current of conservative liberal thought. It gave primacy to balanced budgets and monetary stability, borrowing the economic principles of Robert Peel and William Gladstone. Conservative liberal thought rested on an aversion to fiscal extravagance and to creative financial practices, above all of the type that grew up in the Second Empire during the 1850s (Plessis 2002).

The Second Empire of Napoleon III (1852–1870) epitomized how this paradox operated. French public debt doubled between 1853 and 1865, excluding Paris, the departments, and the communes (Price 2001). It proved sustainable because of its nature and because French GDP grew by some 30 per cent between 1850 and 1869 (Maddison 2004: 424). The Emperor was attracted by Saint-Simon's principle of using the state to mobilize finance for 'productive' investments in railways, roads, and other public works, typically outside the regular budget. The symbols and instruments of this ambition were the creative financing of Baron Hausmann to rebuild Paris and the new Crédit mobilier investment bank.

However, by 1860–1861 the traditional *hautes banques*, led by Fould and by Rothschild, were publicly backing liberal political campaigns, which exploited growing public fears that this promiscuous attitude to financing public debt would lead to higher taxes and interest rates. The appointment of Achille Fould as finance minister in 1861 symbolized the turning point towards the 'Liberal Empire'. Fould succeeded in getting Napoleon III to formally surrender his power to decree credits for public works programmes outside the regular budget (Maddison 2004: 230). The falling prestige of the Emperor was paralleled by the declining power of the Crédit mobilier in favour of the *hautes banques* and their agenda of balanced budgets and monetary stability.

Tables 7.2 and 7.3 suggest some patterns in the evolution of French public debt. First, the public debt/total revenue ratio between 1820 and 1914 remained remarkably high, compared to the early twenty-first century. It did not fall below the low of 218 per cent in 1855 and hit a high of 760 per cent in 1895. Yet the debt interest rate in 1895 was well under half that in 1820. Intriguingly, the debt interest rate was lower under the Third Republic (1871–1940), despite the legacy of the Franco–Prussian War in 1870, than under either the July Monarchy (1830–1848) or the Second Empire. French GDP had recovered as early as 1874 and grew by over 30 per cent in size between 1894 and 1914.

Secondly, the public debt/total revenue ratio was at its lowest during the July Monarchy, the classic age of *rentier* power. Stendhal wrote of this regime: 'the banks are masters of the state...the bank is the aristocracy of the bourgeoisie' (Price 2001: 42). In 1830 James de Rothschild rallied to the support of the new King Louis-Philippe, offering a loan of 60 million francs. The July Monarchy was least interested in the overseas projection of French power and most focused on balanced budgets (Théret 1995). In a further gesture of his support for the peace policy of Louis-Philippe, and his opposition to the war-like policies of Adolphe Thiers, Rothschild provided him with a personal loan of two million francs in 1840. Conversely, the public debt/total revenue ratio was much higher during the Second Empire. In particular, the public debt data reflect the Crimean War, Napoleon III's intervention in Italian unification, and his military adventurism in Mexico.

Thirdly, the Franco–Prussian War and the subsequent hefty French war indemnity left a long-term debt legacy for the Third Republic. It added some 20 per cent to the public debt/GDP ratio. However, France endured the effects better than Germany after

Table 7.2 French Public Debt/Total Revenues and Debt Interest Rates, 1815–1914, in Millions of Old Francs

	Public Debt	Total Revenue	Public Debt	Interest Rate
1815	1272	876	145%	7.88
1820	3456	939	368%	6.65
1825	3941	978	403%	4.37
1830	4627	1020	418%	4.23
1835	4175	1068	391%	3.75
1840	4458	1234	361%	3.79
1845	5205	1393	374%	3.52
1850	4886	1432	341%	5.32
1855	6083	2309	218%	4.42
1857	8032	1799	446%	4.38
1860	9334	1962	476%	4.33
1863	12020	2265	531%	4.38
1865	13026	2169	600%	4.41
1870	11516	3125	368%	4.76
1875	19918	2870	694%	4.66
1880	20391	3531	577%	3.56
1885	23754	3320	715%	3.78
1890	25153	3376	745%	3.26
1895	25967	3416	760%	2.95
1900	25839	3815	677%	2.97
1905	25934	3766	689%	3.02
1910	25461	4274	596%	3.06
1914	25261	4549	555%	3.77

(*Source*: Bonney 2010; Fontvieille 1976, Table XXXVIII. The public debt to total revenue ratio is calculated by the author from this data)

1918. French debt interest rates were more elevated in 1815–1820 and in 1850 than after 1871. Moreover, post-1890 the so-called *Belle Époque* saw a decline in the public debt/total revenue ratio and in debt interest rates up to 1914, despite being a more militaristic phase of the Third Republic. This decline reflected the recognition within French governing elites that rivalling Germany required a combination of state stimulus to economic growth, creative 'off-balance-sheet' budgeting, and fiscal surpluses. It was a strategy similar to that employed by Napoleon III. The success of this strategy was followed by an inflationary surge between 1901 and 1913, which also helped to reduce the public debt/GDP ratio. Also, during the *Belle Époque*, the Banque de France competed with the German Reichsbank to accumulate the biggest gold reserves in Europe, over $800 million in 1914, to prepare—in its own words—for 'every eventuality' (Ahamed 2010: 70).

Fourthly, the public debt data show a complex association with periods of GDP growth. Between 1896 and 1914, rapid GDP growth generated increased tax revenues,

Table 7.3 French Public Debt as Percentage of Total Revenue, 1815–1914

1815	145
1820	368
1825	403
1830	418
1835	391
1840	361
1845	374
1850	341
1855	218
1860	476
1865	600
1870	368
1875	694
1880	577
1885	715
1890	745
1895	760
1900	677
1905	689
1910	596
1914	555

(*Source*: Bonney 2010)

helping to reduce the burden of debt servicing. It coincided with a fall in the public debt/total revenue ratio. However, this association was less evident between 1850 and 1869. Napoleon III preferred to resort to creative forms of debt financing rather than to higher taxes in pursuit of his foreign policy ambitions and costly public works and urban renewal projects. Similarly, the correlations between macroeconomic stagnation or contraction and public debt dynamics are weak. Public debt/total revenue ratios remained relatively stable between 1815 and 1848 and between 1873 and 1896. Debt servicing as a percentage of public expenditure actually declined in the first period (see Table 7.4). It stayed relatively stable in the second. In 1879 under the Third Republic the Plan Freyssinet sought to stimulate economic growth by means of a public infrastructure investment programme. However, it was kept off-balance-sheet, thereby reducing the public debt/GDP ratio (Keyder 1985: 313). Off-balance sheet activity complicates both the data and makes conclusions about correlations difficult.

Table 7.4 offers additional insights. Debt servicing as a percentage of public expenditure was at its highest at the end of wars: 49 per cent in 1815 and 59 per cent in 1918. It was at its lowest under the July Monarchy (19 per cent in 1845), at the end of the *Belle Époque* (21 per cent in 1914), and on the eve of the Second World War (18 per cent in 1939). Similarly, the biggest increases were associated with wars, notably between 1865 and 1875 and between 1914 and 1918. However, the biggest reductions in debt servicing

Table 7.4 French Debt Interest Payments as Percentage of Public Expenditure, 1815–1869

1815	49%	1918	59%	1949	4%
1820	25%	1920	50%	1950	5%
1825	23%	1925	41%	1955	6%
1830	24%	1930	22%	1960	5%
1835	23%	1935	23%	1965	13%
1840	20%	1939	18%	1969	12%
1845	19%				
1850	25%				
1855	25%				
1860	23%				
1865	22%				
1870	27%				
1875	33%				
1880	34%				
1885	35%				
1890	34%				
1895	30%				
1900	27%				
1905	25%				
1910	22%				
1914	21%				

(*Source*: Fontvieille 1976, Table LVI. The percentage is calculated by the author from this data, rounded off)

as a percentage of public expenditure were achieved in Restoration France, especially in 1815–1820, before the July Monarchy. They were also realized in 1926–1929 during the Third Republic after the consolidation of public finances and stabilization of the franc under Raymond Poincaré. Overall, for most of the period 1815–1939, French debt servicing amounted to 25 per cent or more of public expenditure. It was financed without default.

The post-1918 and the post-1944 periods saw a radical change in the importance of debt servicing in public expenditure. The main factor was inflation, which reduced the value of public debts and undermined the economic power of *rentiers*. By 1949 debt servicing accounted for less than 5 per cent of public expenditure, an outcome radically different from that after 1918. The ratio was still only 5 per cent in 1960, climbing to 12 per cent in 1969. Inflation proved a powerful tool in public debt dynamics. In particular, the period 1947–1970 saw a fall in the public debt/GDP ratio. It reflected the combination of exceptionally rapid economic growth with high inflation. However, this period can be seen as masking nascent fiscal imbalances (Dufrénot and Triki 2012).

From the early 1970s, the adverse effects of declining economic growth rates and falling inflation on the public debt/GDP ratio were not adequately offset by fiscal surpluses. In particular, from the mid-1980s, a policy of competitive disinflation was launched to match German performance as the anchor of the Exchange-Rate Mechanism (ERM).

It underpinned the French policy of playing the lead role in constructing economic and monetary union (EMU) and in sharing in German monetary power. The result of this policy priority was higher real interest rates, a return to pre-1914 levels of debt servicing costs as a percentage of public expenditure, and a rising public debt/GDP ratio (Dufrénot and Triki 2012). The post-2007 crisis added to public debt problems. Doubt about France's sovereign creditworthiness increased for several reasons. The public debt/GDP ratio reached 86 per cent in 2011. Public expenditure rose to a record 56.6 per cent of GDP by 2010. Governments had not produced a single budget surplus since 1974. GDP growth forecasts proved repeatedly overoptimistic. Furthermore, internal problems within the state, particularly the large number dependent on its employment and its pension and other benefits, suggested risks of substantial political inertia. By 2012 France had lost its coveted triple-A credit rating.

Austro-Hungarian Debt

The public debt data of the Austro-Hungarian Dual Monarchy cover the period from its inception with the Compromise of 1867 and its collapse after the First World War. They illustrate the impact of war and its catalytic effect on industrial development (see Table 7.5). The public debt data also show how, within their monetary union, and the apportionment of common historical debt, the two constituent elements of the Hapsburg Empire pursued their independent fiscal policies, each managing its own special debt.

The political background to the Compromise of 1867 was the humiliating defeat of Hapsburg aspirations in central Europe in 1866 and the subsequent war indemnity to Prussia. This profound shock led the governing elites in Austria, and especially Hungary, to develop a common interest in public borrowing to invest aggressively in modernizing their economic infrastructures. Hungary had the additional problem of building a fiscal reputation from scratch (Flandreau 2001). This problem was aggravated by the sovereign debt restructuring in 1868. The debt restructuring owed a great deal to Austrian frustration with the apportionment of the common debt between Austria and Hungary in the 1867 Compromise. It imposed losses on foreign creditors and set back Hungarian

Table 7.5 Debt Burden and Debt Structure in the Austro-Hungarian Dual Monarchy, 1880–1895

	Austria		Hungary	
	Debt Burden	Share of Gold Debt	Debt Burden	Share of Gold Debt
1880	63	11	78	25
1885	70	13	87	33
1890	75	17	99	32
1895	75	19	108	32

(*Source*: Flandreau 2001: 44)

efforts to build reputation in the financial markets. Building this reputation entailed high fiscal costs.

The two key players in helping establish and maintain the reputation of the two sovereign borrowers were the Austrian National Bank and the Vienna branch of the House of Rothschild. The Austrian National Bank gained increased powers in order to help restore the reputation of the florin and financial market discipline. In exchange the House of Rothschild was able to organize lending syndicates (Gille 1967). The outcome was some convergence in sovereign debt financing practices. Austria and Hungary competed to become the benchmark for each other.

Despite gaining reputation through the monetary policies of the Austrian National Bank, Hungary faced greater problems in its public debt financing. Its public debt was over 60 per cent of GDP from 1879 to 1904 and again in 1910–1911. Austrian public debt exceeded 60 per cent between 1875 and 1913. It stood at over 100 per cent for all but three years between 1890 and 1905 (Flandreau 2001). However, these figures hide the fact that Hungary's debt burden was larger than that of Austria. In a marker of the 'original sin' of a new sovereign borrower, it relied on gold-denominated debt, as opposed to debt denominated in florins. Hungary's gold-denominated debt grew rapidly between 1880 and 1995. It imposed a tightening financial market discipline on its sovereign borrowing. Though the Hapsburg Empire regained sovereign creditworthiness after the 1868 debt restructuring, the challenge proved more difficult for Hungary.

Once common public debt burdens were increased by the First World War, the Hapsburg Empire fell victim to destructive fiscal—as well as political—centrifugal pressures. Its collapse, the legacy of high debts and social and political crisis, and the demise of the gold discipline produced a crisis of the 'tax' state in both Austria and in Hungary. The newly independent state of Hungary resorted to 'inflation tax' on debt at the expense of creditors, on a scale not witnessed elsewhere in post-1918 Europe.

Belgian and Dutch Public Debt

The scale of impact of war on European public finances is borne out by Belgian and Dutch public debt data (see Tables 7.6 and 7.7). In 1815 the United Provinces inherited an onerous public debt/GDP ratio of over 150 per cent. It was mainly the product of the War of the Spanish Succession, four Anglo–Dutch wars, the French Revolutionary wars, incorporation into the French Empire in 1810, and British takeover of Dutch interests in Asia and South Africa during the Napoleonic Wars. The ratio remained over 200 per cent from 1821 to 1853 (except 1847) and did not fall below 100 per cent till 1871. In contrast, the Netherlands remained neutral in the First World War, after which in 1918 it had a public debt/GDP ratio of only 70 per cent. Only in the four years before 1914 had it had such a low ratio in the period since 1815. However, German occupation and Allied liberation in the Second World War returned the Dutch public debt/GDP ratio to 223 per cent in 1946. It remained over 100 per cent till 1953. The ratio was above 60 per cent till 1964 and again between 1983 and 2000 (see Table 7.7).

This Dutch capacity to tolerate an elevated public debt/GDP ratio without default reflected its early development of a *rentier* society. In 1820 Dutch per capita GDP was

Table 7.6 Belgian Public Debt/GDP Ratio, 1835–2009

1835	9.81	1946	118.26
1840	17.18	1950	73.69
1845	33.02	1955	69.07
1850	33.72	1960	70.24
1855	22.03	1965	58.07
1860	20.03	1970	47.44
1865	18.08	1975	39.88
1870	15.11	1980	54.94
1875	19.33	1985	99.91
1880	26.19	1990	109.64
1885	35.97	1995	113.76
1890	36.28	2000	99.54
1895	42.12	2005	88.88
1900	42.80	2009	94.76
1905	47.15		
1910	49.64		
1913	49.47		
1920	102.94		
1925	116.26		
1930	59.85		
1935	84.09		
1939	71.72		

(*Source*: Banque Nationale de Belgique, Centre d'études économiques de la KUL, 2010)

higher than British and remained so till the 1850s. Despite higher Belgian GDP growth, Dutch GDP per capita was only slightly below that of Belgium in 1914 (Maddison 2004: 437). Moreover, the Netherlands inherited a banking system with sophisticated debt financing and management techniques. The long struggle for independence against Hapsburg Spain, and with the English and the French, had made Dutch governing and banking elites familiar with the requirements of war financing. Well before 1815, Dutch society had exhibited a high tax capacity. Also, from the 1830s the Dutch proved remarkably successful in raising fiscal tribute from the Indonesian cultivation system, on a much bigger relative scale than the British in India (Maddison 2004: 88–9). In 1844 the Dutch government endowed Indonesia with a fictitious debt of 236 million guilders to cover the costs of liquidating the Dutch East India Company's debts and those incurred during the revolt of 1825–1830. The legacy of these characteristics, along with predominantly liberal governments from 1848, helped make credible Dutch promises of honouring debts.

Nevertheless, pre-1914 data suggest that the Netherlands was much less fiscally virtuous than Belgium. The Netherlands' public debt/GDP ratio did not fall below the Maastricht 60 per cent criterion once between 1815 and 1914. Economic structure and GDP growth played a major role in explaining the differences between Belgian and Dutch public debt dynamics. In addition to big inherited debts, the post-1815 Netherlands had a much weaker, more traditional manufacturing sector than Belgium. It suffered from

Table 7.7 Dutch General Government Debt/GDP Ratio 1815–2005

1815	155.9	1920	59.6
1820	190.7	1925	82.0
1825	219.4	1930	75.6
1830	236.8	1935	117.1
1835	275.6	1939	106.5
1840	243.4	1946	223.0
1845	248.8	1950	141.0
1850	226.1	1955	87.9
1855	180.1	1960	78.7
1860	155.5	1965	57.3
1865	123.7	1970	49.6
1870	107.8	1975	39.6
1875	87.3	1980	45.4
1880	89.6	1985	69.4
1885	91.9	1990	75.8
1890	94.4	1995	76.1
1895	98.9	2000	53.8
1900	85.2	2005	52.7
1905	77.9	2007	47.2
1910	70.1		
1914	61.2		

(*Source*: The Dutch Fiscal Framework: History, Current Practice and the Role of the CPB. CPB Document 150, 2007)

foreign competition, resulting in economic stagnation. Between 1830 and 1910 the gap in GDP size between Belgium and the Netherlands grew, notably in 1850–1870, from a position close to parity in 1830 (Maddison 2004: 424–5).

Belgium's highest public debt/GDP ratio over this period was 50.98 per cent in 1909. Belgian fiscal virtue stemmed in part from the terms of the division of national debt on Belgian independence from the United Netherlands. After much acrimony, and a territorially less advantageous outcome, the split of the national debt was eventually much more favourable to Belgium than the original draft protocol of the London Conference in 1831. Belgians complained that the post-1815 union had penalized them through the punitive taxes that they had to pay to service the high Dutch public debt.

The Belgian public debt/GDP ratio fell from 33.72 per cent in 1850 to the low point of a mere 13.19 per cent in 1872 (see Table 7.6). GDP growth, along with conservative liberal economic policies, were the main factors explaining the trajectory of public debt over this period. Belgium led continental Europe in developing a modern economic structure, based on coal, iron, and engineering. It benefitted to a much greater extent than the Netherlands from export-led growth in the wake of moves towards free trade in Europe in the 1850s and 1860s. Over the period 1820–1913 its annual average GDP growth rate exceeded that of Britain and France (Maddison 2004: 262). Even with rising welfare-state expenditures before 1914, the public debt/GDP ratio remained well below Dutch levels.

After 1918 war and social dislocation changed the relative positions of Belgium and the Netherlands. In 1925, for the first time since the early 1830s, Dutch GDP size overtook that of Belgium (Maddison 2004: 428–9). In contrast to its neutral neighbour, Belgium had a public debt/GDP ratio over 100 per cent from 1920 to 1926. However, from 1929, and the onset of the Great Depression, Belgium returned to its status as fiscally more virtuous than the Netherlands. After exiting the Second World War with higher indebtedness than Belgium, the Dutch public debt/GDP ratio did not converge with that of Belgium till the 1960s. The main shift to a more fiscally virtuous Netherlands began from the mid-1970s. Divergence grew as Belgium's public debt/GDP ratio climbed from 39.17 per cent in 1974, surpassing 100 per cent between 1986 and 1999. This shift reflected the rapid decline in Belgium's traditional heavy industries and rising tensions between her two main linguistic communities.

Seen in this longer historical perspective, Belgium's record as a creditworthy state stands up to comparison with the Netherlands. Its claim to do so is strengthened after the 1970s by its higher domestic savings rate and strong domestic absorption of its sovereign bonds. Above all, the historical data shows an impressive Belgian record in public debt reduction in 1926–1931, 1946–1951, 1968–1975, and 1993–2006.

Prussian and German Public Debt

Prussian and Imperial German public debt data, since 1815 and 1871 respectively, offer insight into the significance of the relationship between the size of debt and tax capacity to service debt. They tell two different stories. Imperial Germany is a story of the difficult domestic politics of sovereign creditworthiness that followed from the mismatch between, on the one hand, assigned taxes and, on the other, a complex combination of expansionary political and geo-strategic ambitions with fears of geographic encirclement by France and Russia within the military under Emperor William II (see Table 7.8). The federal constitution assigned direct tax revenues to the member states rather than the Imperial government. Hence the Imperial government was unable to extract the revenue gains from the historically high GDP growth associated with growing German mastery of the new science-based second industrial revolution. Between 1890 and 1914 German GDP size more than doubled, in contrast to that of France which increased by some 40 per cent (Maddison 2004: 428). German annual average GDP growth in the period 1870–1913 was 2.83 per cent, compared to 1.90 in Britain and 1.63 in France (Maddison 2004: 262). However, Imperial defence expenditure faced fiscal limits that had no direct equivalents in Britain and France (Ferguson 1994).

The Second Empire had the good fortune of being born free of debt in 1871. Till 1876–1877, it covered its military expenditure largely out of the French war indemnity (Schremmer 1994: 181). However, the subsequent rapid growth of Imperial public debt, especially in the 1880s, revealed the fiscal vulnerability of the Imperial government (see Table 7.9). It lacked a sizeable imperial tax base that could match the British and French governments. The political tensions consequent on this weak fiscal position

Table 7.8 Prussia and German Reich Public Debt/GDP Ratios and Per Capita Public Debt in Marken, 1794–1913

	Prussia Debt Ratio	Reich Debt Ratio	Prussia Per Cap.	Reich Per Cap.
1794			16.8	
1807			32.7	
1815	42.49		83.7	
1820	27.95		58.5	
1848	10.84		29.4	
1866	14.69		44.4	
1872	14.18	0.44	50.3	0.95
1882	26.72	4.85	97.0	10.67
1892	48.22	13.96	204.0	35.93
1902	37.99	16.58	189.0	50.79
1913	31.21	16.62	226.0	74.91

(*Source*: Spoerer 2010; Schremmer 1994: 163)

were apparent before 1914. They were sharply exposed by the First World War, when the Imperial government had to rely on debt financing and on the Reichsbank printing money by buying its debt.

Imperial German public debt problems reflected a deep-seated paradox and tension at the heart of the new regime. On the one hand, it was characterized by the entrenched executive power of the military, its immense social prestige after the wars of the 1860s, and the militarization of society. By 1913 key military figures were pressing the case for a preventative war. On the other, the Imperial government faced powerful constitutional and political constraints in gaining agreement for the five-year military budget. One constraint was the lack of significant independent tax capacity. Another was the political desire to appease the German *Länder* after unification in 1871 by costly fiscal equalization measures. A third factor was the deep suspicion of military fiscal profligacy by Chancellor Theobald von Bethmann Hollweg (1856–1921) from 1909. A determined effort was made to rebalance the Imperial budget and cut public debt (Clark 2013: 215–16).

In contrast to Imperial Germany after the Franco–Prussian War of 1870, Prussia had inherited a heavy public debt problem after the Napoleonic Wars (see Table 7.8). Prussian public debt underwent another big increase in the 1880s. This increase was also seen in other German *Länder*. It reflected their large-scale investment in public enterprises, including state guarantees, to support industrialization (Schremmer 1994: 114). The dynamics of public debt mirrored a very different conception of the role of the state in industrialization from that then dominant in Britain. Prussia and other *Länder* sought to mobilize credit to develop infrastructure, extract resources, and develop key industries. The capacity of the *Länder* to service this debt was enhanced, from the 1880s, by the generous fiscal equalization system, at the expense of the Imperial government. By 1913 half of German public debt was attributable to the *Länder*, another third to the municipalities (Schremmer 1994: 116).

Table 7.9 Public Debt of German Empire 1877–1945, in Millions of Marks

	Empire	States (*Länder*)
1877	16	–
1881	308	5244
1886	484	–
1891	1318	9230
1896	2125	–
1901	2503	10797
1906	3818	12495
1911	4910	15571
1914	5202	16841
1915	16715	17608
1916	39496	17981
1917	68877	18242
1918	104945	20582
1920	199728	10455
1921	263543	–
1922	352204	–
1923	6675048	–
1924	1958	–
1926	7141	–
1930	9630	2590
1931	11342	2752
1933	11690	2951
1936	14372	2850
1938	19098	2555
1939	30676	2112
1940	47889	2124
1941	85935	2162
1942	137629	1945
1943	195554	1746
1944	273354	1697
1945	379800	–

Note: Leaving aside both world wars and the period 1919–1927, Leineweber (1988) identified the periods of fastest growth in debt as pre-1914 (especially 1881–1891), 1929–1930, 1939–1940, 1963–1967, 1974–1976, and 1980–1981.

(*Source*: Deutsche Bundesbank 1976)

The First World War and its aftermath led to successive heavy losses raining down on the German *rentier* class. Wartime 'hidden' inflation was followed by post-war uncertainties about the scale of reparations and new pressures to increase social expenditures. Moreover, weak Weimar governments lacked sources of tax revenue. In political terms the debate about reparations was centre-stage. As initially conceived, Allied demands for

Table 7.10 Public Debt of the German Empire, Per Capita of Population in Marks

1877	0.37
1880	4.8
1885	8.8
1890	22.7
1895	40
1900	41
1905	53.1
1910	75
1914	77.6

(*Source*: Schremmer 1994: 110)

German reparations were higher than France's reparations burden after 1871. However, they were not higher than the total burden of outstanding wartime debts on GDP borne by Britain and France in 1920 (Ritschl 2012b: 3). The problem lay at least as much, if not more, in German reluctance to pay rather than capacity to pay. The politics were further poisoned by persistent domestic rumours of new higher reparation demands and by French and Belgian occupation of the Ruhr in 1923. The subsequent catastrophic hyperinflation of 1923 forced a renegotiation of the reparation problem to help stabilize Germany (see Tables 7.9 and 7.10).

During the period of the Dawes Plan (1924–1929), the German government benefitted from a clause that protected German foreign-exchange reserves from reparation transfers. It also benefitted from new incentives to borrow on a massive scale from abroad, principally from the United States, enabling Germany to pay reparations on credit. Moreover, German fiscal policy adopted a neutral stance and failed to generate the surpluses needed to effect reparation transfers. German governments did not heed the criticisms of the Allied Agent-General for Reparations, who was located in the Reichsbank to monitor compliance with the Dawes Plan. However, from 1929 a stop in capital inflows caused a sharp reversion to policies of fiscal consolidation and harsh deflation. These policies were strongly advocated by the Reichsbank. By 1932 short-term foreign debts were being restructured and foreign-exchange controls introduced. In May 1933 Germany announced a unilateral debt default (Ritschl 2012).

An historical examination of public debt data provides little evidence that, before the 1950s, Germany could lay claim to be the European model of sound finances and creditworthiness. Both Imperial and Weimar Germany illustrated the dangers of mismatch between state liability and control. The absence of tax competencies to match commitments, above all externally, led to weak state capacity. After 1918, the Weimar Republic served as the archetypical model of how the attempt to avert the demands of external creditors in a context of weak state capacity could lead to 'hyperinflation'. The outcome was a payments regime under the Dawes Plan, by which reparations were compensated by an inflow of principally US capital. In consequence, in 1929 Germany's relations to its external creditors proved acutely vulnerable to a stop in capital inflows (Ritschl 2012b).

Table 7.11 German Public Debt 1950–2009, as Percentage of GDP and as Debt Per Capita

As Percentage of GDP:

1950	1955	1960	1965	1970	1975	1980	1985	1990	1995	2000
19.3	23.2	18.7	19.0	17.8	23.6	30.3	39.5	41.2	55.1	58.7
2005	2009									
66.4	70.3									

As Debt per Capita (in €):

1950	1955	1960	1965	1970	1975	1980	1985	1990	1995	2000
190	405	520	754	1,053	2,103	3,881	6,366	8,514	12,478	14,734
2005	2009									
18,066	20,701									

(*Source*: Statistisches Bundesamt, *Schulden der öffentlichen Haushalte, Finanzen und Steuern*, Fachserie 14, Reihe 5, 2010: 1.1.1)

The public debt of the Federal Republic after 1950 had a very different trajectory, based on a combination of a stronger tax base for the federal government, debt forgiveness, and export-led GDP growth buttressed by wage moderation. The public debt/GDP ratio was very low in the 1950s and 1960s (see Table 7.11). It rose with the oil crises of the 1970s and early 1980s, and above all with German unification in 1990 after which it topped 50 per cent for the first time. The Bundesbank was the institutional anchor of Germany's post-war self-reinvention as a 'stability culture', averse to inflation. From the 1970s it constructed an historical narrative that bolstered its own institutional independence and status by fixing on the 1923 hyperinflation as the reference point for historical lesson-drawing. This new German cultural model became the basis for constructing European economic and monetary union around fiscal discipline. EMU was built on the credibility of the most creditworthy of European states. Germany's seriousness of commitment to its public debt reputation was reflected in the insertion of the so-called 'debt brake' into its Basic Law in 2009, its export into the euro area fiscal compact treaty of 2012, and a huge correction of Germany's structural fiscal balance of 2.5 per cent between 2010 and 2012. Germany lent a fiscally ascetic nature to the euro area.

British Public Debt

Historical data on British public debt since 1688 suggest three patterns. They illustrate the enormous impact of wars and empire building; the symbiotic relationship between military/imperial ventures and commercial and *rentier* interests; and, not least, the assignment of buoyant tax revenues, based on early industrial and trading supremacy, to debt servicing (see Table 7.12). The fiscal underpinnings of this early, benign public debt dynamics derived from a virtuous circle of agricultural revolution, industrialization, trade expansion, empire building, and success in wars, combined with the professionalization of fiscal administration and the use of financial repression. Between 1700 and 1820

Table 7.12 English/British National Debt 1688–1817

	Debt Per Capita £..s.	Debt as % National Wealth	Average Interest Rate
1688 Revolution	0.4	0.31	
1697 Wars of William III	3.10	5.75	7.18
1714 Wars of Anne	9.7	13.17	6.28
1749 Spanish–Austrian War	13.5	15.99	3.98
1766 Seven Years' War	19. 4	26.62	3.65
1785 American War	29.15	24.42	3.90
1802 Great French War	45.17	28.81	3.83
1817 Great French War	50.0	31.48	3.77

(*Source*: Fisk 1921: 81)

GDP grew nearly 350 per cent, from some 60 per cent of French GDP size to overtake France (Maddison 2004: 424–5).

Hargreaves (1966: 291) highlights the effects of the Seven Years' War. Public debt increased from £77,817,182 in 1757 to £132,120,664 in 1763. It then climbed to £243,206,140 in 1786 with the American War of Independence. The Napoleonic Wars left a huge overhang of public debt. It grew from £244,720,976 in 1793 to £834,262,726 in 1815 (see Table 4.1). Expressed as a percentage of GDP, public debt went up from 50 per cent after the War of the Spanish Succession to 140 per cent after the Seven Years' War. In 1816 it reached 240 per cent, the legacy of over a century of war and empire building. Between 1815 and 1855 debt service costs accounted for almost half British public expenditure (Barro 1987).

There is no evidence that this debt legacy, which stood at over 90 per cent of GDP till the early 1860s, impaired British leadership of the first industrial revolution. It was accompanied by an annual average compound GDP growth rate of 2.05 per cent from 1820 to 1870, surpassed only by Belgium (Maddison 2004: 262). Moreover, the huge growth in British public debt per capita was accompanied by falling debt interest rates (see Table 7.12). This combination was the efficient secret of the eighteenth-century British state. However, this secret depended less on the growth in primary fiscal surpluses than on financial repression. The tightening of usury laws in 1714 privileged government borrowing (Drelichman and Voth 2008). In effect, British governments engineered a stealth subsidy to investors. It ensured that yields on government bonds remained relatively low and attractive (cf. Reinhardt and Sbrancia 2011).

Nineteenth-century British public debt data reflect three factors: Britain's pioneering role in the industrial revolution; its command of vast colonial resources and investments; and the consolidation of the domestic power of the *rentier* class (see Table 7.13). The two fiscal reformers who were central to this consolidation were Robert Peel and, above all, William Gladstone. Their reforms in the budgets of 1842 and 1853 sought to entrench fiscal probity, to establish income tax as a long-term basis for securing the interests of creditors, and to lock in large primary fiscal surpluses. In their wake the Crimean

Table 7.13 UK National Debt since 1855

	% of GDP
1855	107
1860	101
1865	83
1870	73
1875	60
1880	59
1885	58
1890	48
1895	43
1900	33
1905	37
1910	33
1914	26
1916	61
1917	90
1918	114
1920	133
1923	180
1925	167
1930	162
1931	173
1935	168
1939	141
1940	121
1945	232
1946	252
1949	201
1950	197
1955	141
1960	110
1963	101
1964	93
1965	87
1970	67
1975	46
1980	43
1985	46
1990	35
1995	50
1998	50

Note: National debt fell within the later Maastricht 60 per cent rule only from 1880–1915 and 1971 onwards. Between 1918 and 1963 it remained over 100% GDP (over 200% from 1945 to 1949).

(*Source*: Government Statistical Service 1999: 46)

War was financed without the fiscal difficulties that confronted France and Russia. Gladstone's principles of public finance were emulated by liberal fiscal reformers across Europe, from Fould in France to Cavour in Piedmont. By 1875 the public debt/GDP ratio had declined from its post-1815 peak to 60 per cent. It stayed below this level till 1916, reaching its historic low of 26 per cent in 1914 (see Table 7.13). However, David Lloyd George's 1909 budget was the decisive signal of a challenge to *rentier* ascendancy from the 'New Liberalism' of social reforms. The 'People's Chancellor' provoked constitutional as well as political crisis. The 1909 budget set a new differential between earned and unearned income tax, introduced a super-tax, increased death duties, and proposed new land taxes.

The First World War was a turning point in British public debt trajectory. In its aftermath Britain was no longer a massive net creditor state. Foreign assets no longer yielded returns in excess of the interest on debt. The war itself was financed by a combination of debt and taxation. Public debt escalated from £649,770,091 in 1914 to £7,831,744,300 in 1920 (Hargreaves 1966). It remained over 100 per cent of GDP till 1963 and did not return to pre-1914 levels till 1990 (see Table 7.13). Beginning in 1920, British governments responded with large primary fiscal surpluses. The Bank of England raised interest rates. The combination of sharp fiscal contraction with high interest rates led to harsh negative effects on GDP growth. These effects were compounded by British failure to retain a leadership role in the second, science-based industrial revolution. From 1920 to 1939 the public debt/GDP ratio exceeded 140 per cent.

A key feature of the 1920s was the efforts of the political and City establishment, centred on HM Treasury and the Bank of England, to reassure *rentier* interests. This institutional nexus was dominated by belief in the need to pursue deflation and engineer cuts in real wages. It involved the commitment to early return to the gold standard, which occurred in 1926, and willingness to confront organized labour. This priority to re-establishing a pre-war notion of fiscal 'normality' carried a heavy price in social and political bitterness, without reducing the public debt/GDP ratio. However, the 1931 economic and political crisis, with British exit from gold, initiated the use of devaluation and more accommodative monetary policy to restore growth and employment. It also witnessed British default on debt to the United States that had been accumulated in the First World War. In this changed context, the British public debt/GDP ratio fell from 1931 to 1940.

The legacy of the Second World War was a public debt/GDP ratio that exceeded 200 per cent between 1945 and 1949, reaching 252 per cent in 1946. The ratio was brought down in part by rapid economic growth and inflation and in part by financial repression through a host of rules aiming to hold nominal interest rates on debt below inflation. Nevertheless, the public debt/GDP ratio stood above 90 per cent till 1965, for two main reasons. The shadow of empire and aspiration to retain a global power role, not least as a nuclear power, led to continuing high levels of military expenditure. In addition, there was till the 1970s widely-shared agreement on increased welfare-state spending. These two factors helped ensure that the public debt/GDP ratio remained above the 60 per cent level till the 1970s. Nevertheless, despite the relative weakening of British GDP performance from 1950, this period coincided with historically high GDP growth. The background continued to be failure to establish a leadership role in the second industrial revolution.

British historical public debt figures suggest a parallel between the period 1875–1914 and the period after the ending of capital controls and liberalization of credit from the end of the 1970s. Both periods witnessed phenomenal growth in British bank assets. The first period was ended by war; the second, by banking crises. War helped to build British sovereign creditworthiness in the eighteenth century, on the back of empire building and the first industrial revolution. However, war exhausted sovereign creditworthiness in 1914–1918 and 1939–1945. British sovereign creditworthiness reflected the character of its underlying economic structure. Unlike in Germany, it did not rest on a leadership role in the second industrial revolution. It was underpinned by banking assets, financial market liquidity, and innovative debt financing techniques. The post-2007 crisis exposed British fiscal vulnerability to an oversize, risk-prone, and volatile financial sector and—via this sector—to credit risks from any meltdown of the euro area. Its triple-A credit rating rested on shaky foundations, including a double deficit: current account and fiscal. In these circumstances a highly prudent fiscal strategy remained the most rational course.

Debt, Union, and Empire: Ireland and Scotland

The process of unifying the British state was bound up with empire, war, and debt. At the end of the seventeenth century, an impoverished and politically disunited Scotland sought to rebuild a strong national identity by emulating the imperial capacity of England. Its Parliament built on the bold ideas and financial acumen of the businessman William Paterson (1658–1719), a founder of the Bank of England and advocate of Dutch financial practices. In 1695 Paterson helped persuade the Scottish Parliament to establish the Bank of Scotland and the Company of Scotland. They were to provide the groundwork for a worldwide Scottish empire. However, the Company's expedition to Panama in 1698 turned into a human and financial disaster. From the outset the English governing elite had resented this scheme as a threat to its own East India Company. Hence the City of London refused to subscribe to the Company of Scotland. Subsequently, the English king rejected offering any assistance to the Panama expedition. The outcome was huge Scottish debts contracted by the Company of Scotland, which were estimated at £250,000, a deepening of Scottish resentment against what was seen as English bad faith, and a Scotland that was represented as bankrupt.

The context of the Act of Union in 1707 was the combination of this weakened Scottish negotiating position with the English participation in the War of the Spanish Succession against King Louis XIV. The English sense of urgency about sealing the union with Scotland stemmed from fear that the French king would exploit Scottish resentment against England and the mounting and politically divisive costs of a prolonged war. Fifteen of the twenty-five articles in the Act dealt with economic and commercial issues on terms that were designed to suggest English benevolence, including the granting of free trade. Article 15 provided for the 'Equivalent', the sum of compensation to be paid to Scotland in recognition of its future share of the British national debt. However, the Equivalent was less generous than it seemed. Scottish debts on entering the union were calculated to be £710,000, with £250,000 accounted for by the debts of the Company of Scotland. The Equivalent amounted to £398,085. The result was a shortfall of over £300,000 (Scott 2006: chapter 8). Moreover, the Equivalent was financed by introducing the English excise duty of alcohol to Scotland as well as by English borrowing, thus adding to the national debt of which Scots had to bear their share. This debt settlement left a considerable burden to be borne by Scottish taxpayers and the often poor creditors of the Scottish government.

The legacy was a Scottish discourse about English bribery, taken up amongst others by Sir Walter Scott. It was founded on English use of the Equivalent to exploit the self-interest of the many Scottish parliamentarians who were aggrieved creditors of the Company of Scotland. Nevertheless, the narrative of empire, which had driven the foundation of the ill-fared Company of Scotland, could be redeployed as the basis for a new nation building around the British state. Scotland's disproportionately high participation in eighteenth- and nineteenth-century British empire building helped defuse public debt as a basis for reconstructing Scottish national identity.

In the case of Ireland, the narrative of debt and empire was more complex and had different consequences. Ireland retained an independent Exchequer beyond the Act of Union with Great Britain in 1800 up to 1817, when it was assimilated into fiscal union. It also had its own currency till monetary union in 1826. However, eighteenth-century Ireland found itself in a difficult fiscal position. On the one hand, it had its own Parliament, which from 1707 was subservient to the English Parliament. On the other, Ireland was caught up in the English financial revolution of this period and the rapid growth of Irish public debt. The growth of this Irish public debt took place within what could be represented as a colonial context.

As Moore (2010) suggests, Irish public debt played a role in consolidating a new Anglo-Irish identity, whose chief spokesperson was Jonathan Swift. Swift identified the central problem as the incompatibility of English-driven growth in public debt with the limitations on the rights of the Irish Parliament to control tax revenues. There was a serious, politically and economically damaging mismatch between liability and control. In his view, Irish public debt had become excessive as early as the 1730s because of the effects of trade restrictions on Irish revenues, the large remittances to absentee English landlord, and the heavy costs of supporting a standing army that was put in place by England.

The context of this colonial status was the geo-strategic and economic importance of Ireland to England. It was the 'back door to England', a vulnerability that was highlighted by the wars against France in the 1790s and Irish support for French Revolutionary ideas in the May 1798 uprising. Irish trade was also intimately bound up with the English market and English commercial policy. Above all, Ireland was a good place to station a standing army, given its unacceptability at home. It served as a reserve for managing wider imperial contingencies and as a force for order in an area of strategic vulnerability (McGrath 2012). Irish taxation and public debt in the eighteenth century were caught up in supporting the growth in the British military-fiscal state. Notably, the dreadful Irish famine of the 1740s did not register in the Irish public debt data.

The three turning points in Irish public debt were 1716, the 1770s, and the 1790s. In 1716 a small group of Anglo-Irish landowners loaned the Irish Treasury funds for national security, to be paid in perpetuity from future tax revenues. Swift became chief advocate of the interests of this group in a series of pamphlets that sought to mobilize domestic public opinion. According to Moore (2010), the growth of this Irish public debt became bound up with the emergence of an Anglo-Irish national identity. However, the character of that new identity was demonstrated in the trajectory of public debt development.

The two decisive turning points related to the high costs of the English empire and war. The American War of Independence resulted in Irish public debt climbing from £1 million to £1.9 million between 1777 and 1783. It peaked at over £2.2 million in 1788 (Clarendon 1791). By 1782–1783 the fiscal deficit amounted to some 16 per cent of public expenditure. This period coincided with collapsing Irish trade, which affected revenues, two bank failures in 1778, and increased military expenditure.

An even more decisive turning point was the declaration of war against France in 1793. Irish public debt grew from £5.56 million in 1793 to £38.65 million in 1804 (Boyle and Geary 2004: 111). The Irish Exchequer faced mounting public unwillingness to subscribe to the new debt, except at exorbitant borrowing costs. Hence, it sought to finance this debt by looking to two alternative sources. First, it turned to the Bank of Ireland, which by 1796 was already agreeing to a rescheduling of debt repayments. The corollary was huge growth of money in circulation, far in excess of that in Britain, and currency depreciation. Secondly, faced by growing reluctance of the Bank, the Exchequer resorted for the first time to foreign borrowing in the London market. By 1800 some half of Irish public debt was funded through this source (Boyle and Geary 2004: 113).

The Act of Union in 1800 was essentially a political expedient in time of war. It aimed to close England's 'back door' and to counter the political demands of the May 1798 Irish uprising. However, the Act did little to address Ireland's fiscal and economic problems. Its financial provisions required the Irish Exchequer to shoulder a disproportionate share of imperial expenditures, which were mainly military. In consequence, by 1817 the Irish Exchequer was effectively bankrupt and merged into the British Exchequer, with a consolidated debt.

The Irish case illustrates the clash between two very different representations of public debt. In the one case, exemplified by Swift, it is seen as integral to the formation of an Anglo-Irish national identity, albeit a socially narrow one (Moore 2010). In the other, the growth of public debt is represented in Irish nationalist terms as colonial exploitation. Its burdens on Ireland are framed in terms of over-taxation, asymmetrical damage from English-imposed trade restrictions, and neglect of the poor. Public debt becomes integral to the formation of an anti-English Irish national identity, which focused on the disconnection of the poorest part of the population from the monetized economy of public debt (McGrath 2012).

Italian Public Debt

The evolution of Italian public debt after unification in 1860–1861 tells a familiar story of war's impact. In sharp contrast to Imperial Germany, the wars of unification left a heavy debt legacy. Camille de Cavour, prime minister of Piedmont from 1852, displayed formidable financial acumen in employing his liberal economic credentials, especially commitment to a balanced budget, to attract plentiful external credit on favourable terms. He exploited his familiarity with English political economy and with Second Empire France to encourage competition amongst British and French banks. Emperor Napoleon III was sympathetic to Cavour's ideas on using debt financing to develop rail infrastructure, seeing opportunities for French banks. Above all, he was keen to support the bid for Piedmont's hegemony in the Italian peninsula at the cost of the Hapsburg Empire. In pursuing his twin ambitions, Cavour faced the constraints of the small size, relative economic backwardness, and lack of domestic capital of Piedmont. He depended on mobilizing the support of Napoleon III, and British neutrality, to fight Austria.

However, the consequence of Cavour's combination of political audacity, diplomatic cunning, and financial dealings was that the national debt was almost ten times higher in 1860 than in 1847 (Mack Smith 1985: 101). Half of the accumulated debt inherited by Italy in 1861 was accounted for by Piedmont. Alarmingly, the annual deficit in 1861 amounted to almost the total revenue of all the former Italian states put together (Mack Smith 1985: 267). This inherited fiscal burden on unified Italy bore down heavily not just on Piedmont but also on the economically poorer states. It also frustrated the expansionist, imperial policies of successive Italian monarchs, beginning with Victor Emmanuel, and prime ministers, notably Francesco Crispi in 1887–1891 and 1893–1896. They sought to turn Italy into one of the 'great power' European players, alongside Austria, France, Germany, and Russia.

The inherited public debt problem was aggravated from the outset by a weak tax system, the illusory ambitions of King Victor Emmanuel for military action, and the costs of financing potential insurrections against Austrian rule in Hungary and the Balkans (Mack Smith 1971). It was deepened by the financially catastrophic Third Italian War of Independence in 1866 against Austria. Ruinous colonial wars in Africa added to the public debt problem, above all in Eritrea in 1888 and the humiliating defeat at the battle of Adowa in 1896, both associated with Crispi (see Table 7.14). The First World War left a grim public debt legacy. It peaked at close to 160 per cent of GDP in 1920–1921.

However, the interwar period was characterized by a sharp fall in the public debt/GDP ratio. The explanation lies in the combination of external debt forgiveness with the tough fiscal medicine administered by the Fascist governments of Benito Mussolini between 1922 and 1926. The public debt/GDP ratio was cut from 74.8 per cent to 49.7 per cent in this period. The fiscal medicine included de facto default in the form of a forced conversion to extend the maturity of debt in 1926. This medicine was administered again in 1934. In particular, Italy benefited, to a greater extent than Britain and France, from the international relief of pre-war and wartime debts in 1925–1926 with the Washington and the London agreements. Debt to the US government was reduced by some 80 per cent. Credibility was further strengthened by the securing of a large House of Morgan loan in 1926 (Chernow 1990). Along with combating socialism in the north and organized crime and the mafia in the south, public debt reduction was seen as the basis for renewing the image of Italy as a strong state able to claim a seat at the high table of European diplomacy. Strikingly, in contrast to other major European states, Italian public debt remained below 100 per cent during the Great Depression of the 1930s (Francese and Pace 2008: 19). However, Mussolini's final fiscal legacy was ruinous public debt from his foreign policy adventurism and opportunistic entry into the Second World War.

In the post-1945 period, up to the 1970s, the most salient factor in making Italian public debt sustainable was the combination of historically high economic growth,

Table 7.14 Italian Public Debt Since 1861

In Millions of Euros at 2002 Values: All Figures Relate to December of the Year

1861	1.7	1947	914.8
1871	4.9	1950	1,582.0
1881	6.1	1955	2,978.3
1891	7.2	1960	4,032.1
1901	7.9	1965	6,140.0
1911	8.8	1970	13,086.6
1916	15.9	1975	41,899.4
1919	56.4	1980	114,066.0
1921	91.4	1985	347,592.6
1925	92.9	1990	667,847.7
1931	83.1	1995	1,151,488.8
1933	56.5	2000	1,300,340.7
1939	79.4	2005	1,512,779.1
1941	137.2	2007	1,598,971.2
1943	257.3		
1945	566.7		

(*Source*: Francese and Pace 2008). Francese and Pace are only able to compute reliable debt/GDP figures for very limited time periods.

very high inflation, and a high domestic savings rate. The public debt/GDP ratio was kept on a sustainable path by a 'nominal growth dividend' that exceeded the interest cost on public debt. This dividend—and the big reduction in the real value of public debt—was accounted for more by inflation than by real GDP growth (Piergallini and Postigliola 2011).

In addition, domestic savings flowed into Italian sovereign bonds because of the lack of alternatives. Italian public debt dynamics rested on a paradox of trust. The public distrusted the political class, because of its intense factionalism, clientelism, and pervasive corruption. At the same time, it was willing to buy Italian sovereign bonds. Italian fiscal profligacy was possible without debt default or restructuring because it rested on a supportive structure of virtuous households, a cautious and prudent banking sector, and weakly developed equity markets. There was an implicit contract in which the banks, notably Mediobanca, were prepared to underwrite the Italian sovereign bond market and act as bulwarks against external debt dependency. They did so in exchange for being left alone to manage a highly profitable structure of cross-shareholding in Italian business, the so-called *salotto buono*.

External debt relief in the 1920s and high post-1945 inflation provide exceptional factors that help explain the main substantial public debt reductions. Nevertheless, long-term historical data indicate that Italian governing elites have, on significant occasions, demonstrated state capacity to actively use fiscal policies to reduce public debt. Pronounced increases in primary fiscal surpluses were achieved by Cavour's

Piedmont-based conservative liberal successors during the so-called 'Historical Right' period (1868–1876). Prime Minister Giovanni Lanza and Finance Minister Quintino Sella sought—in vain—to present Piedmont as the 'Prussia' of Italy. Increases in primary fiscal surpluses were repeated in the first Fascist period (1921–1927) under Finance Ministers Alberto De Stefani and Giuseppe Volpi.

Similarly, during the first 'Golden Age' period (1951–1957), Finance Ministers Ezio Vanoni, Roberto Tremollini, and Giulio Andreotti delivered significant primary fiscal surpluses. This capacity was again demonstrated during the 'Maastricht' period (1991–1999), especially after the crisis of Italian exit from the ERM in 1992 and the challenge of meeting the Maastricht convergence criteria for euro entry in 1996–1997. In 1992–1993 Italy was saved from imminent default. Primary fiscal surpluses were also achieved by Finance Minister Giulio Tremonti during the second centre-Right government (2001–2004) of Silvio Berlusconi; by Finance Minister Tommaso Padoa-Schioppa during the last centre-Left government (2005–2008) of Romano Prodi; and by Mario Monti during his 2011–2013 technocratic government, when Italy underwent an extreme correction in its structural fiscal balance of some 3.4 per cent of GDP. These historical examples suggest reserves of Italian state capacity in crisis that differentiates her from other southern European states.

Italy managed to avoid association with the south European 'arc of default'. A key factor was the 'other face' of Italy: the quality of a very small Italian technocratic elite and the international and European prestige that its members enjoyed. They were invited to assume the reins of power at times of acute crisis. Examples include 1992–1993, when Italy was at risk of default; 1995–1996, at a time when Italy faced the threat of exclusion from stage three of EMU; and 2011, when Italian bond yields soared and the centre-Right government of Berlusconi was politically paralysed. At such times, Italians could look back to the twelfth-century model of the *podestà*, the impartial magistrate or governor who was above faction and who had been temporarily appointed by the city states to restore order. Technocratic governments were welcomed as a necessary external expedient, enforcing overdue, urgent, and comprehensive fiscal and structural reforms (Monti 2011). The notion of external discipline (*vincolo esterno*) played a key role in legitimating this strand in Italian thinking about public debt.

Italy's triple crises of 1992–1993, which were represented by the end of the Cold War, exit from the ERM, and corruption trials, held the promise of a fiscal transition. The status and power of the Treasury was reinforced. However, the challenges of ERM exit and then joining the final stage of European monetary union in 1999 proved less than radical in strengthening long-term Italian debt sustainability. The Italian political system showed a tendency to revert to inward-looking, highly partisan, and factionalized behaviour, notably under Berlusconi in 2008–2011, and again after the 2013 elections. Ministers continued to behave as feudal lords, protecting their fiscal turf.

Table 7.14 shows that, overall, the period from the 1970s saw an enormous increase in Italian public debt, unprecedented by Italy's own standards. Two factors were at work. The first was an enormous growth in infrastructural investments and welfare spending and their exploitation by party political factions for patronage purposes. There was a failure to use debt productively to build up long-term GDP growth potential and to strengthen sovereign creditworthiness. A fiscal politics of factionalism created conflicting signals that added to market insecurities about Italian public debt. The second factor was the growing economic and political significance of small- and medium-sized enterprises, which had greater opportunities for tax evasion than larger companies. Their owners represented an important part of the electoral base of centre-Right parties, which were in consequence unwilling to engage in major tax reforms.

More seriously, the paradox of trust as an explanation for benign Italian public debt dynamics began to unravel. The European financial market integration that followed monetary union after 1999 induced the big Italian banks and investors to diversify their sovereign bond holdings outside Italy. By 2008 an increasing proportion of Italian sovereign bonds was held outside Italy, one-third by French banks. In consequence, monetary union served to weaken the historic connection of Italian sovereign bonds to the high domestic savings rate. Italy had become more vulnerable to international market pressures.

The post-2011 Italian sovereign debt crisis had paradoxical effects on the structure of financial power that had traditionally underpinned Italian creditworthiness. On the one hand, the risk that the paradox of trust would unravel was diminished by the subsequent financial market fragmentation. The Italian government sought to mobilize domestic financial power. On the other hand, the post-2011 crisis precipitated an unwinding of the *salotto buono*. As Italian bank shares lost as much as 90 per cent of their value, it became clear that the cross-shareholdings served as a vehicle for contagion across the economy. In 2013 the crisis at the venerable Monte dei Paschi bank of Siena cast a negative light on Italy's eighty-six banking foundations. These foundations were deeply locked into local and regional clientelist political networks and came to share in their opprobrium. The Italian state's creditworthiness seemed less well protected by the combination of virtuous households with a domestically-oriented banking system.

Seen over a long time period, Italy's compliance with the Maastricht rule was the exception. Its public debt/GDP ratio was under 60 per cent for only 39 of a 147-year period: 1861–1863, 1926, and 1946–1981. In 1926 it was helped by international debt relief and in 1946–1981 by the combination of relatively high growth with inflation. The ratio was over 100 per cent for fifty-three years.

Spanish Public Debt

In sharp contrast to Italy, the history of Spanish public debt since 1800 is marked by the largest number of defaults in Europe (Comín 1996). In the nineteenth century public debt accounted for almost 100 per cent of Spanish stock-exchange trades and remained over 50 per cent till 1935. Holding this public debt was attractive because of the lack of financial alternatives. Spain remained a relatively backward economy. It was entrapped within the anti-usury doctrines of a powerful Roman Catholic Church and addicted to the aristocratic code of the non-productive *hidalgo*. An additional attraction to holding public debt was that, over the period 1800–1936 (except 1915–1920), real interest rates on public debt were rarely negative (Comín 2012; Prados de la Escosura 2003).

At the same time, defaults on public debt contributed to the uncertainties, turbulence, and lack of confidence that held back Spanish economic development. Avoiding sovereign default was a chief concern of the small professional, liberal middle class.

However, the clashes between liberalism and traditionalism, civil wars, repeated military interventions, and regime changes concealed a striking continuity of monarchical, aristocratic, army, and Church power. Their power frustrated liberal attempts to reform state, society, and economy in ways that would make high public debts sustainable without default. Monarchy, army, and Church stood for 'Eternal Spain'. The corrupt practices that gathered around the political bosses (*caciques*) provided another source of continuity and inertia.

To add to Spain's problems, at least till 1903, public finances were highly vulnerable because of excessive reliance on externally-held central government debt. Over almost all the period 1850–1890 it amounted to over 30 per cent of public debt (see Table 7.15). Defaults led to repeated exclusion of Spanish public debt from trading on European stock exchanges. Symptomatic of its isolation, Spain never belonged to the gold standard. However, sharp reduction in external debt, and later neutrality in the First World War, helped Spain achieve a banking and industrial renaissance between 1903 and 1918. From 1902 to 1965 external debt represented less than 10 per cent of public debt.

Part of the Spanish problem was public debt legacy. Despite the defaults of King Ferdinand VII, the Napoleonic Wars and absolute monarchy bequeathed a huge public debt legacy to nineteenth-century liberal governments. Though liberal governments sought to draw a line under resort to default, the debt legacy combined with domestic constraints and external debt burdens to induce them to repeated debt restructurings. They were constrained by the entrenched power of aristocracy, army, and Church and their devotion to imperial ventures. Liberal governments also faced pervasive corruption and continuous internal political instability and threats of civil war. They had to contend with chronically weak tax capacity, inadequate fiscal controls of the Spanish Treasury, and the mushrooming practice of off-balance-sheet financing. The disruptions that were associated with regime change were further aggravated by a bewildering succession of finance ministers within each regime, none in office long enough to gain mastery of the Treasury. An undeveloped domestic financial system made it difficult, and potentially too costly, to avoid dependence on external financing of public debt.

Spikes in public debt were linked to the three Carlist Wars (1833–1840, 1846–1849, and 1872–1876). They were also caused by disastrous imperial adventures, backed by the monarchy, aristocracy, army, and Church. The Spanish–American War of 1898 led to the loss of Cuba, the Philippines, and Puerto Rico and had a highly negative effect on Spanish public finances. The so-called Rif War in Morocco (1920–1926) was another drain on Spanish finances.

Available figures since 1850 show that between 1867–1882 and 1896–1909 the public debt/GDP ratio was above 90 per cent. It peaked at 169 per cent in 1876—following the Third Carlist War—and at 128 per cent in 1902—in the wake of the 1898 war (see Table 7.15). The scale of the public debt problem was revealed in the debt servicing/public expenditure ratio and in the debt servicing/revenue ratio. The debt servicing/expenditure ratio reached an alarming 52.6 per cent in 1870 and 46.1 per cent in 1903 (Prados de la Escosura 2003). It stood at over 30 per cent between 1880 and 1914. Debt servicing as a percentage of revenue was over 30 per cent in 1856, 1863–1873, 1877–1881, and 1883–1920.

Nevertheless, despite the heavy weight of debt legacy and political inertia, Spanish history is marked by episodes of huge public debt reductions: 1850–1863, 1880–1883,

Table 7.15 Spanish Public Debt Since 1850

	Central Government Public Debt/ GDP Ratio	External Debt/ Sovereign Debt	Debt Servicing/ Spending
1850	91.7	40.2	11.7
1855	62.9	38.5	20.1
1860	59.3	33.6	15.8
1865	70.5	23.7	29.1
1870	122.1	33.9	52.6
1875	150.3	33.2	12.5
1876	169.0	30.5	29.8
1880	152.5	32.1	37.6
1885	71.3	30.1	31.0
1890	77.9	29.2	34.7
1895	86.1	26.8	30.0
1900	124.1	12.9	31.9
1902	128.0	9.5	30.7
1903	114.3	8.2	46.1
1905	110.4	8.3	41.1
1910	89.7	9.9	36.0
1914	76.5	9.9	28.4
1918	50.7	7.9	25.3
1920	44.4	2.5	20.1
1925	56.6	0.6	20.8
1930	58.9	0.4	23.3
1935	65.9	0.3	23.2
1940	71.8	0.2	16.9
1945	69.6	4.9	15.8
1950	46.2	2.5	14.4
1955	38.9	2.4	15.0
1960	29.4	7.7	9.1
1965	18.1	9.3	4.3
1970	19.2	13.2	2.6
1975	11.9	13.7	2.3
1980	10.2	21.9	3.1
1985	31.5	16.6	17.8
1990	40.1	3.8	24.3

Debt Servicing/Public Spending Ratio

1850	11.6
1870	52.6
1875	12.5
1879	33.3
1882	25.4
1883	30.4
1894	40.1

(*Continued*)

Table 7.15 (Continued)

	Central Government Public Debt/ GDP Ratio	External Debt/ Sovereign Debt	Debt Servicing/ Spending
1898	43.0		
1903	46.0		
1914	28.4		
1917	48.6		
1920	20.1		
1923	28.1		
1932	21.4		
1941	19.4		
1975	2.3		
1981	1.9		
1997	47.8		
1999	32.9		
2007	7.3		

(*Source*: Kind permission of Francisco Comín, University of Alcalá, Madrid)

1902–1920, 1945–1975, and 1996–2007. In the nineteenth century the key instrument was debt restructuring. It was used by a succession of liberal, reforming finance ministers, who sought to appease suspicious, often hostile foreign creditors. They included the restructurings of Fernández Gamboa in 1841; Alejandro Mon in 1844; Bravo Murillo in 1851; Garciá de Barzanallana in 1867; Pedro Salaverría in 1876; Juan Camacho in 1881; and Fernández Villaverde in 1900. The bold, coercive debt restructuring by Murillo encountered serious opposition from external creditors, leading to Spanish exclusion from other European exchanges. In contrast, Camacho used a voluntary, negotiated restructuring to radically reduce public debt (Comín 2012).

The key turning point came with the Spanish–American War, including the assumption of the Cuban and Philippine debts issued between 1899 and 1902. Villaverde responded with a radical debt restructuring. He broke new ground by forcing Spanish citizens holding Spanish external public debt to convert it into domestic debt and by imposing a 20 per cent tax on all domestic debt interest. Villaverde achieved fiscal surpluses between 1899 and 1908. Though he failed to get Spain to accept external discipline by adopting the gold standard, his tenure of the finance ministry had long-term effects in changing attitudes to public-debt management.

Strikingly, there was no public debt crisis in the post-1918 period, at least until 2011. Spain had not participated in the First World War. The high point of the interwar public debt/GDP ratio was 67.6 per cent in 1933. The debt servicing/public expenditure ratio did not climb above a high of 28.1 per cent in 1923 and fell to 21.4 per cent in 1932. Finance ministers made occasional use of debt restructuring, but essentially to take advantage of low market interest rates. Their statecraft relied instead on a mixture of inflation, financial repression, and monetary financing by the Bank of Spain.

Following Villaverde's debt restructuring, there had been a sharp decline in reliance on externally-funded public debt. Neither side in the Spanish Civil War (1936–1939) was in a position to resort to large-scale external debt financing. Means other than formal external borrowing were used. The Republican government shipped its huge gold reserves to the Soviet Union in exchange for support. The nationalist authorities handed over control of Spanish mineral wealth to German interests in exchange for German help. The relatively low public debt/GDP and debt servicing/public expenditure ratios after the Spanish Civil War were the result of reliance on monetary financing by the Bank of Spain.

There was also no public debt crisis in the post-1939 Franco period. Under his policy of autarky and harsh financial repression, the public debt/GDP ratio declined from 71.8 per cent in 1940 to a legacy of 8.2 per cent. The debt servicing/public expenditure ratio fell to a mere 2.3 per cent (Prados de la Escosura 2003). Franco used two key instruments to achieve this public debt reduction. He repudiated the debts of the republican governments, following the practice of Ferdinand VII in 1814 and 1823. In addition, José Larraz López undertook a debt restructuring in 1939. Thereafter, the main instruments for achieving the low debt servicing/public expenditure ratio and the low external debt/sovereign debt ratio under Franco were financial repression and inflation (Comín 2012).

The post-Franco transition to democracy and EU entry in 1986 witnessed an escalation in public debt/GDP and debt servicing/public expenditure ratios, lasting till 1996–1997. Equally, the convergence process for euro entry in 1999 and the first decade of the euro saw a striking sharp reduction in both ratios. However, the risks of sovereign debt crisis were not captured in Spanish fiscal statistics, which remained formally strong, boosted by high GDP growth and inflation. The sources of vulnerability proved to be the exceptionally high external debt/GDP ratio, which by 2010 had reached 170 per cent; the asset-price boom in construction and property; overleveraged households; the fragile asset quality of the savings banks (*cajas*); and the sub-national finances of the powerful autonomous communities created after Franco.

Historical Lessons: War, Welfare States, Financial Crisis, and State Capacity

Historical data about the contingencies and vulnerabilities that affect public debt dynamics suggest some general lessons about the limitations of formal debt sustainability analysis. First, war, and threat of war, has the capacity to radically reframe discourse about what is an acceptable level of public debt. Once publics are persuaded of an existential threat and a just cause, their willingness to pay taxes and to purchase 'national' debt is transformed. This willingness was exploited by Napoleon III to issue a national bond to help finance war on behalf of Italian unification and French territorial gains. Jay Cooke followed this example in devising new national bond issues to finance the Union armies in the US Civil War (Oberholtzer 1907). These measures of war financing help reduce dependence on banks and financial institutions and exploit appeals to national identity and exceptionalism.

War also serves as a catalyst in restructuring domestic social interests. Widespread public bondholding makes post-war debt repudiation and resort to hyperinflation politically unattractive instruments. The United States avoided repudiation of the Union debt after 1865. In contrast, the reputation of the Weimar Republic was tarred by the effects of hyperinflation in 1923. The aftermath of war can undermine *rentier* power in other ways. The huge post-1917 debt repudiation by the new Soviet government in Russia produced widespread shock effects, notably in France.

War is important in terms of the huge costs of financing military operations and, above all, in terms of the tendency to underestimate their likely length. As during the US Civil War, expectations of short war can lead to rapid and often chaotically structured public debt expansion (Noll 2012: 3). Three developments in warfare have increased the threat of uncontrollable debt dynamics. First, the growing spatial scale of warfare was signalled by the Seven Years' War in the eighteenth century and its role in the emergence of Britain as a world power. Secondly, from the end of the eighteenth century, war began to involve an increasing scope of societal mobilization. It became 'total' war. Above all, modern war technologies and emulation of war-fighting best practice had direct effects both on military spending and on populations. Thirdly, the devastating aftermath of new mass warfare contributed to political agenda change. It strengthened the rationale for large-scale public welfare-state expenditure as a means of sustaining social consensus.

Another historical feature is that welfare-state development began to play a new role in shaping the dynamics of public debt, especially after 1945. It was associated with a reframing of discourse about acceptable public debt. In particular, the interwar period in Europe served as a chilling lesson about the dangers of neglecting to build and maintain social consensus. From the early twentieth century, the parameters of discourse about public finances and debt changed under the combined impacts of shared experience of 'total' war, franchise extension, and the rising expectations associated with mass education, literacy, media, and exposure to consumer culture. Within a few decades the dynamics of welfare-state development began to increasingly reflect population ageing, notably in health, social care, and pensions spending. This development also substituted for the demise of the 'extended' family as welfare provider.

A third historical lesson is that public debt dynamics have become increasingly vulnerable to the radically new scale of banking and financial institutions. This vulnerability grew as societies became more affluent, as pension provision for longer life expectancy became more critical, and as opportunities for international expansion grew, not least with the digital revolution. Enormous creative energy was employed in creating new esoteric debt instruments; private as well as public debt grew exponentially; and financial institutions became more highly leveraged, with investment bankers operating within more generous credit limits. Cross-nationally active financial institutions often dwarfed the European states that were supervising and regulating them. They were potentially not just 'too big to fail' but also 'too big to save'. This vulnerability was exposed dramatically in the post-2007 crisis. States stepped in to rescue 'systemically-significant' financial institutions from failure and tried to come to grips with the scale of toxic and opaque debt. Public debt levels threatened to explode towards wartime levels. However, they did so in an economic and political context in which the prevailing notion of fiscal normality remained restrictive. 'Rescuing bankers' was a much less attractive just cause than waging war on enemies. Table 7.16 shows just how significant the effects of

Table 7.16 Net Impact of Financial-Sector Support on General Government Gross Debt and Contingent Liabilities in Euro Area Member States, 2008–2012, as Percentage of GDP

	General Government Gross Debt 2008–2012	Contingent Liabilities 2008–2012
Belgium	6.7	15.7
Germany	11.6	2.2
Ireland	31.4	69.8
Greece	14.5	27.9
Spain	5.1	6.5
France	0.2	2.5
Italy	0.2	5.5
Cyprus	10.0	5.6
Luxembourg	6.7	5.0
Netherlands	6.9	3.2
Austria	3.4	3.8
Portugal	10.6	10.0
Slovenia	4.1	0.6
Euro Area	5.7	5.7

(*Source*: European Central Bank, *Monthly Bulletin*, June 2013: 86)

financial-sector support were in euro area Member States in the period 2008–2012. There were major impacts on gross central government debt in Ireland, Greece, Germany, Portugal, and Cyprus. The effects on contingent liabilities through state guarantees were most pronounced in Ireland, Greece, Belgium, and Portugal.

A fourth lesson that emerges, above all from American, British, and Dutch data, is the correlation of the post-1870s classic gold standard period with historically low public debt/GDP ratios. The IMF estimated that the world public debt/GDP ratio fell from 45 per cent in 1880 to 23 per cent in 1914, the lowest ever (Ali Abbas, Belhocine, ElGanainy, and Horton 2010). However, this correlation depended on specific domestic economic and political conditions, notably high GDP growth and the political ascendancy of *rentier* interests. Their ascendancy acted as a disincentive to resort to inflation as an instrument for public debt reduction. It provided the political constituency that supported the combination of the gold standard with disciplined domestic fiscal policy. In this context, British public debt reached its historically lowest level in 1914.

The historical data also highlight the effects of the Great Depression and the demise of the gold standard in 1931–1933, outside a small European 'gold block'. This period saw a rise in the world public debt/GDP ratio to a new peak of 80 per cent in 1932. Strikingly, the ratio for the Group of 20 (G20) states was 20 per cent higher in 2007 than in 1928, on the eve of the Great Depression. It rose at a faster pace post-2007 than post-1931 (Ali Abbas et al. 2010). However, the world public debt/GDP ratio had some way to go to reach its historic peak of almost 150 per cent in 1946.

Longer-term historical data help broaden analysis of debt sustainability and bring out the dynamic effects of war, banking and financial crises, and welfare-state development. In particular, war and banking and financial crises illustrate how extreme, extraneous events can radically shift debt trajectories. Geo-strategic and financial indicators emerge as more powerful indicators of risk to sovereign creditworthiness than conventional economic and fiscal variables. They include the sophistication of diplomacy, the effectiveness of deterrence, the state of banking and household balance sheets, and the quality of financial market supervision and regulation.

Conventional formal debt sustainability analysis has its own problems of dealing with context-specific and time-specific contingencies, as well as with implicit and 'off-budget' liabilities. Uncertainty surrounds the reliability of basic economic data, as well as the precise causal mechanisms at work. It affects what can be realistically expected from efforts to forecast medium-term economic development, to estimate fiscal multipliers, and to specify the nature of the relationship between public debt and GDP growth. Uncertainty pervades attempts to calculate the liabilities associated with population ageing, with the banking sector, and with cross-national financial assistance in the euro area (European Central Bank 2012a: 63–4). The contingent and implicit liabilities associated with foreign, defence, and security policies are even more difficult to capture.

Other core determinants of long-term debt sustainability remain extraneous to this type of formal economic analysis. Welfare-state development—and, in some states, the welfare function of the extended family—provides an insurance mechanism against the personal risks associated with rapid fiscal and structural adjustments to ensure debt sustainability. It also contributes to economic growth through social investment in education, training, labour mobility, health care, and childcare. Social investment and, more broadly, the quality of public finances are not factored into formal debt sustainability analysis. Yet they are essential to compensate and empower losers. Excessive social imbalances endanger debt adjustment strategies (Vandenbroucke, Diris, and Verbist 2013). Hence debt adjustment needs to give priority to social indicators like child poverty, education, and training. On these measures of social investment Romania, Bulgaria, Italy, Latvia, and Spain looked vulnerable.

Similarly, cultural and institutional indicators are excluded from formal debt sustainability analysis. Culturally specific historical path dependencies can be traced in public debt dynamics. They are expressed in various forms of institutional inertia in fiscal, economic, and social policies. In France, for instance, the scale of public-service employment has entrenched defence of entitlements and made debt retrenchment politically very difficult. In Britain, by contrast, the intimate nexus of City of London, Bank of England, and Treasury has helped privilege formal debt sustainability analysis and a discourse of fiscal austerity.

Formal debt sustainability analysis also overlooks two factors that have a profound influence on public debt trajectories: state capacity to tax, to deliver productive investment, to control expenditure, and to maintain financial stability; and political and ideological willingness to prioritize debt reduction. What constitutes sustainable debt emerges as context-specific. It varies with executive autonomy, the professionalization of public administration, the ideological nature of governing parties, the nature of party system competition, and the strength of institutional incentives to veto change and to engage in rent-seeking activity. Sovereign debt does not simply become a problem when it crosses a 'critical' public debt threshold like 90 per cent of GDP. The 'fiscal space' that is enjoyed by a state before it reaches this point is contingent on state capacity. At the time of their defaults in 1998, Russia had a public debt/GDP ratio of 75.4 per cent, the Ukraine of only 39.1 per cent. In the period 1840–1880, the Dutch public debt/GDP ratio was higher than that of chronically defaulting Greece. The crucial factor was not the size of public debt. It was state capacity to service debt through efficient, rigorous tax collection and control of public expenditure, along with political willingness to pay. State capacity is lower in states where clientelism, patronage, and corruption are rife. It is also impaired in states where complex multiparty coalitions preside over a feudalistic government structure, in which ministers safeguard domains of entrenched entitlements.

State capacity and political and ideological willingness to prioritize debt reduction are highly context-specific. They vary across space and over time. This variation is apparent in the use of debt restructuring, structural reforms, inflation, and financial repression. Thus financial repression, which involves creating 'captive audiences' for public debt and manipulating interest rates, was an important tool of statecraft, practised in different ways by British governments in the eighteenth century, by Franco's Spain, and by the United States and Italy after 1945. Financial repression regained attraction as the sovereign debt crisis mounted in Europe after 2008 (Reinhart 2012). In broad terms, opportunities to engage in financial repression narrowed once investors could escape through more globalized markets, once more open democratic politics took root, and once governments were held to account for adverse effects on private-sector investment and credit growth. Nevertheless, scope for financial repression remained (Reinhart and Sbrancia 2011). In some states banks are more vulnerable to pressure from their governments to acquire domestic sovereign debt. They can be induced to do so by changing regulatory requirements. States can also engineer situations where yields on sovereign bonds are kept just below the prevailing rate of inflation for many years, acting as a silent tax on creditors. These forms of financial repression played a key role in bringing down the huge post-1945 public debt levels, alongside growth. Between 1945 and 1970 Italy 'raised' more by wiping out government debt through negative interest rates than it managed to secure from conventional taxes (Reinhart and Sbrancia 2011).

Perhaps most importantly of all, the limited historical time horizon of formal debt sustainability analysis offers no insight into the changing politics of fiscal 'normality'. It fails to show how this politics is embedded in the changing balance amongst social interests. This balance shapes dominant economic cultures and their characteristic ideologies of debt and conceptions of state virtue. Longer-term historical data illustrate how public debt levels well in excess of the conventional notion of fiscal normality from the 1980s to 2010s proved compatible with the avoidance of default and even with reduced debt interest rates. The historical data show that compliance with the Maastricht 60 per cent debt/GDP rule has been the exception, not the rule. Moreover, they do not suggest that compliance with this rule has been a precondition for economic growth. British public debt fell within this rule only from 1880 to 1915 and from 1971 to 2008.

The historical data also indicate that the association between public debt and GDP growth is too context-specific and contingent to be amenable to a simple rule. Sustainable debt is bound up with a range of economic variables like the nature of public expenditure, type of economic structure, the absorptive capacity and sophistication of the banking system, the buoyancy of international economic growth, exchange rates, and real interest rates. More fundamentally, it depends on state capacity to extract tax efficiently and to invest productively in infrastructure and in building social solidarity. In the cases of Italy and Spain—as well as of Greece and the Ottoman Empire, considered in Chapter 5—these context-specific factors suggest an association between high public debt and weak economic growth. However, this association is much less clear in the debt histories of Belgium, Britain, France, the Netherlands, and the United States. The historical lesson is that, in certain conditions, high public debt—potentially well below 90 per cent of GDP in some cases—has costs for economic growth. However, slow GDP growth is always bad for public debt accumulation, and not all debt accumulation is bad for growth.

Despite its many limitations, formal debt sustainability serves an invaluable function in counselling fiscal prudence and arguing for substantial safety margins to cope with unexpected shocks and short-term opportunistic political behaviour. In this sense the lessons from formal economic reasoning and the historical analysis of public debt converge. Long-term historical data highlight the regularity and the significance of extreme events such as war and banking and financial crisis, as well as of longer-term trends in welfare-state development. Their significance in radically transforming public debt trajectories suggests fiscal prudence, potentially more than is allowed for in the EU Stability and Growth Pact ceiling on public debt. Prudence becomes all the more pressing once trend GDP growth declines and tax capacity diminishes, along with the absorptive capacity of the banking system for public debt.

Historical analysis adds the crucial dimension of context-specificity and idiosyncrasy. It draws out the long-term impacts of specific historically formative experiences, like the differences between the legacies of German and Italian unification. Economic structure provides another source of variation through effects on potential GDP growth. Historical analysis also shows the decisive importance of state capacity and political and ideological willingness to extract taxes and to deliver productive infrastructural and social investment that helps generate economic growth and build social solidarity and inclusivity.

Part II

Law, Culture, and Statecraft

8

Law, Public Debt, and the Paradoxes of Power

> For nothing can preserve the integrity of contract between individuals, except a discretionary authority in the State to revise what has become intolerable...[It is] the absolutists of contract, who are the real parents of revolution.
>
> John Maynard Keynes (1923: 56–7)

In stressing the limits of property rights, and arguing that 'in State action, everything is to be considered on its merits', Keynes was not so much arguing from the principle of expediency as recognizing the complex moral judgements at the heart of the politics of sovereign creditworthiness. Excessive emphasis on the rights of investors involved repudiation of 'the right of the State to control vested interest' (1923: 57). Keynes suggested that the social contract was not reducible to legal contract between sovereign states and their creditors. The principle of justice suggested that, in case of conflict, the social contract was pre-eminent. In short, in assessing the claims of property rights, the state had a duty to balance different social and economic interests, of which creditors were one. In this view, negotiated debt restructuring was a legitimate instrument of statecraft.

Sovereign Debt, Social Contract, and Political Rule

Adopting a view about debt based on social contract thought leaves open the question of the nature of the contract. The answers reflect different conceptions of the nature of political rule. Following Thomas Hobbes, the state could restructure or repudiate debts unilaterally for its own individual self-interested reasons of benefit. It is to be guided by prudential concern with its own self-preservation. This position rests on absolutist claims to sovereign immunity. It fits with conceptions of autocratic and charismatic rule, linked to military and populist regimes. Consistent with this claim, states can reject compulsory international arbitration, for instance a statutory sovereign debt restructuring mechanism. Their governing elites argue that their overseas assets are protected from national courts by diplomatic immunity. Similarly, official creditors enjoy a special status over private creditors in any sovereign debt restructuring.

In contrast, one could follow John Locke in stressing the basis of the social contract in property rights. This conception of the social contract fits with a notion of oligarchic rule, wedded to economic liberalism. It provides justification for giving primacy to creditors. It can be invoked to justify the principle of the equal treatment of creditors under the *pari passu* legal clause. This principle would apply whether or not private creditors had signed up to a sovereign debt restructuring agreement. On this basis, on 26 October 2012, the US Appeals Court in New York ruled that Argentina could not discriminate against different groups of its private creditors in making repayments. 'Hold-out' creditors should receive full repayment. Potentially, and most radically, the *pari passu* principle could be extended to include official as well as private creditors, for instance the European Central Bank (ECB) and the International Monetary Fund (IMF). Alongside concerns about its role in the sovereign debt restructuring in Greece, this ruling prompted the IMF to re-examine the process of sovereign debt restructuring in 2012–2013.

However, the outline of a third notion of contract can be discerned in Hugo Grotius' *On the Rights of War and Peace* (1625), Book 2, chapter 10, II (2). He writes: 'No matter what the obligation is, it is more just that the price received through the instrumentality of the debtor should profit him than bring gain to the creditor.' Grotius subscribed to the notion of restitution by creditors. The German philosopher Immanuel Kant offers an additional grounding for a restrictive view of creditor rights. He emphasizes the broad principle of moral equality. On this basis, creditors and other stakeholders, like taxpayers and pensioners, should be treated as moral equals in risk sharing. This position would justify legal provision in bank resolution regimes for 'bail-in' of shareholders and bondholders, potentially even (as in Cyprus) big uninsured depositors. It would also support 'bail-in' of creditors in negotiated sovereign debt restructurings. It surfaced in the ruling of the court of the European Free Trade Association (EFTA) in January 2013. It affirmed that, following the collapse of the Icesave Bank, Iceland—and thus her taxpayers—was not liable for the liabilities of the national deposit insurance scheme. The Kantian view of contract seems closest to the position advocated by Keynes in 1923. It can be appropriated to a democratic conception of rule, wedded to social liberalism or social democracy.

Legal theorists tend to argue that how states use their power in managing their public debt is institutionally anchored. Borrowing takes place within specific institutional frameworks. These frameworks include rules, as well as the principles on which they rest and on the basis of which the use of state power is made justifiable. Legal theoretical perspectives on debt are concerned fundamentally with trust and compliance, with accountability and transparency. Can states be trusted to honour their commitments, and how? To whom do they owe trust? In this respect much of legal theory seems less utilitarian than formal macroeconomic theory, which focuses on the practical problems of gaining the confidence of investors and the technologies for doing so.

However, economic and legal reasoning exist in a more symbiotic relationship. This symbiosis is evident in the terms 'confidence' and 'reputation' in macroeconomics and 'trust' in law. Though macroeconomics may appear utilitarian, it contains a powerful, albeit narrow and often implicit, moral agenda. This agenda is characteristically focused on property rights and highly advantageous to *rentiers*. Moreover, economic and legal technologies converge in designing esoteric forms of debt financing, for instance the use of collateral (Riles 2011). Legal reasoning typically offers utilitarian, technocratic justification for new technologies of credit creation and for creditor protection against risks of state default. The justifications are Lockean.

Paradoxes in the Historical Relationship between Law and Sovereign Debt

At the heart of the legal problems surrounding public debt is an unresolved tension between two logics: the private-property rights of investors and the claims of sovereign states to represent collective interests. The two main historic changes in the law governing public debt have been: first, from the theory of absolute to one of restricted sovereign immunity; and, secondly, from coercive default to the notion of certain normative principles that should govern negotiated 'restructuring' of sovereign debt.

The first change involved a shift from Hobbesian to Lockean contract theory. It took the form of a more active role for domestic courts—notably in London and New York—in better protecting creditor property rights. The period from the late 1980s saw the emergence of so-called 'vulture' funds and an increasing number of litigation cases, peaking in 2005–2007. This change was reflected in the US Appeals Court ruling in 2012, which strengthened the rights of 'hold-outs' in sovereign debt restructurings (Das, Papaioannu, and Trebesch 2012: 51). 'Vulture' funds like Elliott Associates began to specialize in buying sovereign debt claims at a deep discount on secondary markets. Then—as in the case of Argentina—they sued the debtor state for full repayment, including seizing money in the payments system for holders of restructured debt. In general, however, these cases were not primarily related to sovereign debt restructurings (Enderlein, Trebesch, and von Daniels 2010). Another indicator of the shift to restricted sovereign immunity was the emergence of proposals for a state insolvency regime. This regime would not only restrain creditors but also involve 'impartial' institutions 'beyond the state' in determining what level of public debt was sustainable.

The second change involved a Kantian shift. It represented a preference for seeking consensus through 'soft' law and avoiding formal, legalistic, rule-oriented reasoning and the legal codification of state insolvency. Consensus seeking took the form of adaptive learning, tailored to the complexities of individual cases. An example was the new emphasis on principles of 'good faith' negotiation of debt restructuring between states and their private creditors, using a flexible menu of options. It was used in the Greek sovereign debt restructuring of 2012.

Despite these historic changes, the international and European public law governing sovereign debt remained weakly developed. Nevertheless, institutional forms, social norms, and moral sentiments evolved to invest unilateral default and financial repression with guilt and shame. In addition, they helped to tame the potential resentment against creditors turning into disproportionately coercive behaviour. In the process shifts took place in the basis for holding states morally responsible for their debts, especially with respect to default and financial repression.

Pre-1945 Europe operated with a very different set of assumptions about sovereign default and about how states might behave in protecting the interests of adversely affected creditors. This difference was captured in the Drago-Porter Convention of 1907. Reflecting the international context of the time, it called on states to arbitrate disputes arising out of sovereign defaults peacefully, prior to resorting to force for the recovery of contract debts. In so doing, the Convention recognized that state liability for debts threatened international peace and that an alternative was needed to the use of force to secure creditor rights. However, it still assumed that the political 'super-sanction' of foreign armed intervention retained legitimacy in cases where debtor-state elites refused or neglected to reply to offers of arbitration or refused to submit to an arbitration award. Threats of 'gunboat' diplomacy had been frequently used by European states, notably in Latin America. The Convention left open a wide spectrum of possibilities for debtor-state behaviour and for how other states might act to protect creditors.

The post-1945 change was not the product of a new international or European mandatory sovereign debt restructuring mechanism. It was due only marginally to new legal routes for creditors to pursue litigation or arbitration. The main factor was evolving international, and above all European, social norms and moral sentiments, which attached guilt and shame to unilateral sovereign default and to coercive forms of financial repression.

Law highlights two paradoxes at the heart of the politics of sovereign creditworthiness. The first paradox is between formal and informal state power vis-à-vis creditors. The second paradox is between securing creditor rights by abridging state sovereignty and the issue of whether states possess the capacity, and their governing elites the political will, to meet their liabilities. Formally, the distinctive right to claim sovereign immunity, coupled with the weak framework of international and European public law, suggests wide scope for states to exercise power and the limits of creditor enforcement (cf. Eaton, Gersovitz, and Stiglitz 1986). The incentive effects of legal arrangements to secure state compliance tend to be weak. However, informally, the 'soft' law framework of negotiated sovereign debt restructuring, coupled with the 'private governance of public debt', intimates an asymmetry of power that favoured creditors. This same asymmetry is apparent in dominant social norms and moral sentiments about default. The difference in attitudes to restoring sovereign creditworthiness is manifest in terminology. What for the euro area is 'private-sector involvement' is, for the credit rating agencies, 'coercive debt exchange'.

The second paradox reflects the problem of misalignment between liability and control. It arises in the form of the tension between the right to enjoy collective financial assistance through official credits in a transfer union and the responsibility to discharge the attached obligations. This problem is not simply amenable to formal legal solutions, for instance through treaties to create European banking union and fiscal union. State capacity and the political willingness to comply emerge as the key determinants of whether rights and responsibilities can be aligned in managing sovereign debt crises.

Redefining the Boundaries of Sovereign Immunity

Power is inherent in the basic legal principles that define the relationship between states and their official and private creditors. Its complexity derives from the interplay between two contrasting sets of legal principles and the shifts, across space and over time, in their relative weights. On the one hand, the priority to the principles of ownership and the protection of private property rights is linked to *rentier* power. Importance is attached to mechanisms for the enforcement of contractual agreements (Glinavos 2010). The incentive for states to comply with these principles derives from the higher costs and the greater difficulties of raising finance through sovereign bond markets if compliance is uncertain. Economic incentives drive state compliance in a more compelling and urgent way than creditor threats of court action.

On the other hand, states seek to protect their assets from litigation in national courts by claiming sovereign immunity. They also appeal to the principle of international comity (reciprocity) in order to protect their sovereign assets, including assets located within foreign jurisdictions. In the nineteenth and early twentieth centuries courts were prone to accept the doctrine of absolute sovereign immunity. Notably, in its 'gold-clause' ruling of 1935, the US Supreme Court upheld the right of the US administration to refuse to pay its creditors in gold after the devaluation of 1933. There were significant minority dissenting opinions, criticizing the action as expropriation. Nevertheless, the Court ruled that: 'Contracts, however express, cannot fetter the constitutional authority of the Congress.' Ernst Feilchenfeld highlighted the weakness of international law in defining state responsibility:

> (A)s international law stands today, a debtor state commits an international delinquency by annihilating a debt entirely through repudiation, confiscation, or virtual destruction (interference with the substance of the debt), but...international law has not yet reached the point where all lesser acts causing defaults and damage to creditors give rise to legal protests based on international law. (1934: 170)

However, in 1952 the Tate letter, from the US State Department's Acting Legal Adviser, outlined a major shift in US policy towards the restrictive theory of sovereign immunity. Immunity was recognized with regard to governmental or public acts (*jure imperii*) of a state, but not with respect to private acts of a commercial nature (*jure gestionis*). This position was eventually embodied in the US Sovereign Immunities Act of 1976. Its passage reflected the changing economic interests of the United States. It sought to protect its financial institutions against potential defaults. In 1992 the Supreme Court ruled that states can be sued for defaults on debts issued under US law. By 2000 the hedge fund Elliott Management was successfully using the courts to force Peru to repay it in full under the *pari passu* rule.

These developments had an influence across western Europe. In a ruling of April 1963, the German Federal Constitutional Court adopted the restrictive theory of sovereign immunity. The major European promoters of this theory were Austrian, Belgian, Dutch, and German lawyers, reflecting creditor-state perspectives. The shift towards the restrictive theory found expression in the Council of Europe's European Convention on State Immunity in 1972, particularly Article 4, paragraph 1:

Subject to the provisions of Article 5a, a Contracting State cannot claim immunity from the jurisdiction of the courts of another Contracting State if the proceedings relate to an obligation of the State, which, by nature of a contract, fails to be discharged in the territory of the State of the forum.

However, the lack of European legal consensus was shown in the relatively small number of states that had ratified the Convention by 2012: Austria, Belgium, Britain, Cyprus, Germany, Luxembourg, the Netherlands, Portugal, and Switzerland. France, Greece, Italy, and Spain had not signed. Their courts remained reluctant to abandon the restrictive theory of sovereign immunity. In contrast, in a ruling of May 2007, the German Federal Constitutional Court denied that 'a state of necessity', that is extreme economic and financial circumstances, could justify the suspension of payment obligations owed to private creditors holding sovereign bonds (Waibel 2007: 758).

Whilst there was some shift to legal harmonization within the EU, each European state retained the right to delimit for itself the bounds of its immunity. However, the practical scope to exercise discretion by claiming sovereign immunity is narrowed by the economic inducements to gain cheaper, more plentiful credit and thus the need to reassure investors. For this reason, European government bond documentation usually includes waivers of sovereign immunity. As a result, litigation in selected courts is possible if the state should breach its obligations. In this way European states seek both to establish a good reputation with investors and to manage the risk of litigation. These waivers of immunity are designed to make their debt commercially attractive to investors and reduce risk premiums. At the same time, domestic courts have been reluctant to recognize a general exception to the principle of sovereign immunity. They have focused in detail on the scope of the wording in the bond documentation (cf. *NML Capital Ltd v. Argentina*, UK Supreme Court, 2011).

By 2013, despite incentives to caution in its exercise, and shifts in legal doctrine, sovereign immunity was not hedged by an international legal framework governing state responsibility in sovereign defaults. There was no supra-national legal authority to enforce sovereign bond contracts through international arbitration (Waibel 2011). The International Convention on the Settlement of Investment Disputes between States and Nationals of Other States (ICSID Convention) of 1966, under the auspices of the World Bank, sought to formalize conciliation and arbitration rules. However, it appeared to leave sovereign immunity unaffected. States were unable to agree on a common approach to lifting sovereign immunity for commercial transactions (Waibel 2007). There was an indirect link in that sovereign immunity, by design, applies only in domestic courts. Sovereign immunity was irrelevant for the jurisdiction of an international tribunal that had been granted such power by consent of the state parties concerned. Nevertheless, in August 2011, under the ICSID Convention, the Abaclat tribunal decided, by a two-one majority, that it had jurisdiction to examine claims arising out of defaulted Argentinean bonds.

In consequence, the rules of the game governing sovereign debt reflect an inbuilt tension between the right of a state to exercise its sovereign immunity and default and the rights of its official and private creditors to enjoy security of their contractual claims to repayment. The risk that this tension could degenerate into an anarchic Hobbesian state of nature is mitigated by two factors. They provide incentives for states and their creditors to define their relationship as one of negotiation and accommodation. First, a state may be willing, and have the domestic capacity, to abide by rules of the game that constrain its use of default, This constraint can take the form of exogenous enforcement of commitments through a third party. Alternatively, the state may internalize commitment to certain principles that sustain reputation with creditors over time and generate net benefits (cf. Esteves 2007; Kletzer and Wright 2000). State capacity and the willingness to pay creditors are key variables in avoidance of default risk and gaining good reputation with creditors.

Secondly, the empirical record shows that, even with high incidence of defaults, creditors have typically found sovereign lending to be very profitable overall. Hence they tended not to discriminate in general against defaulters (Eichengreen and Lindert 1989; Eichengreen and Portes 1989). Genoese bankers proved willing to lend to Philip II of Spain despite his payment stops. They held shares in sovereign loans in highly diversified portfolios, spreading their risks and insulating themselves from losses from defaults. Similarly, the Fugger of Augsburg continued as the key financiers of the political ambitions of the Holy Roman Emperor Charles V (Alvarez-Nogal and Chamley 2011; Drelichman and Voth 2009, 2010; Ehrenberg 1963).

Whilst sovereign immunity has become more restricted, it endows creditor claims on sovereign debtors with a distinctive character. They lack the security of a common formal international and/or European insolvency law for sovereign states. In the case of companies and individuals they face the problem that individual EU Member States have their own differing insolvency laws. They differ, for instance, in the time it takes for a person to be discharged from bankruptcy; in whether, and how, a person can restructure part of their unsustainable debts, notably associated with home loans; and in notions of what constitutes an acceptable standard of living when attaching conditions to individual debt restructuring. Despite these differences, personal debts are in a very different legal position from sovereign debts. There is no agreed concept of sovereign insolvency that could form a shared reference point for action. The 'Agreed Minutes' of the Paris Club do not constitute a legally binding agreement. They are recommendations to creditor and debtor states to conclude bilateral agreements. In short, the work of the Paris Club achieves legal effect through bilateral sovereign action.

Creditors have had to compensate for the absence of the kind of robust legal framework for investor protection that exists in other creditor-debtor relations. This compensation took the form of 'bottom-up' collective action to ensure that their relations with sovereign debtors were based on the three principles of transparency, predictability, and 'fair dealing'. This agenda was pursued by the bank lobby group, the Institute of International Finance (IIF) (2010). It backed a stronger role for the IMF in managing sovereign debt distress and default based on these principles. The IIF acted as lead player in the negotiated restructuring of Greek public debt in 2011–2012.

There remained a difference between creditor-debtor relationships, where both are party to a legally enforceable contract, and creditor-sovereign state disputes. Only in the limited context of creditor-state arbitration can creditors claim that certain standards of treatment have been violated by reference to international conventions or bilateral investment treaties (BITs). Even when in principle enforceable, the real constraint on arbitration or litigation remains the capacity to claim sovereign immunity from 'attachment' of assets like property in lieu of debt payments (Waibel 2007). With respect to litigation, the most important legal route remains enforcement in domestic courts. In the final analysis, non-legal techniques to obtain repayment are by several orders of magnitude more important than either litigation or arbitration.

Seeking Flexibility: 'Bail-ins', Collective-Action Clauses, and Debt Restructuring

> It is well that defaulting is so terrible. Otherwise we would grow too fond of it.
>
> Lee Buchheit, legal specialist in sovereign debt, Cleary Gottlieb Steen Hamilton, paraphrasing Robert E. Lee, the US Confederate general. (*Financial Times*, 2 August 2010: 7)

Sovereign states have good reason to hesitate before defaulting. Defaulting is associated with radical uncertainty. The threat of it spooks markets and risks both contagion to other states and exclusion from bond markets for an indeterminate period. Nevertheless, whilst sovereign states may recognize and internalize an obligation to their creditors, they have an incentive to retain a measure of flexibility in meeting this obligation. This flexibility can be achieved without incurring the odium of default by seeking out processes of debt restructuring or by financial repression, including moral suasion on their banking systems.

In addition, sovereign states proved more amenable to their domestic courts being market-friendly to creditors than to giving creditor rights 'constitutional' status at the international level. They preferred to avoid the formalized, supra-national limitation of their room for manoeuvre in restructuring debt (Schneiderman 2008; Glinavos 2010; Waibel 2007). Their opposition was based on the legitimacy problems in entrenching creditor rights outside domestic jurisdiction. In the case of low-income states, the Paris Club served as a defender of state flexibility vis-à-vis creditors.

The central legal instrument in the hands of creditors is the pursuit—through the courts—of the doctrinal claim that sovereign debt default is a form of 'indirect' expropriation, for which compensation should be provided. The European Court of Human Rights (ECHR) has been little involved because in recent years very few states subject to this court have defaulted, with the notable exceptions of Russia and Greece. When given the opportunity, it proved somewhat cautious in responding to this claim. Nevertheless, the ECHR ruled that cancellation of a debt that is set in a final and binding arbitration award constitutes an infringement of the right to the peaceful enjoyment of possessions. Furthermore, it clarified that the unilateral termination of a contract does not extend to an arbitration clause (Glinavos 2010: 19). This type of ruling provided an incentive for creditors to ensure that arbitration clauses were included in contracts. In 2013 the Cyprus 'haircut' for unsecured depositors in the two main failed banks raised the prospect of an appeal to the ECHR on grounds of 'expropriation'.

However, highly controversial questions arise about the definition of what constitutes expropriation; how far the concept should be expanded; what degree of interference with property rights is incompatible with Article 1 of Protocol 1 (A1P1) of the European Convention for the Protection of Human Rights and Freedoms; and whether sovereign debt falls within the scope of its application. Sovereign debt default, and especially restructuring, occupies the grey area between the economic rights of creditors and state power to act in the larger public interest. It poses difficult and contentious questions about how this power is, and should be, used.

The language of sovereign debt restructuring adds a further source of uncertainty. Sovereign debt can be restructured in multiple ways so that the term can be understood differently. It can mean coercive restructuring or voluntary restructuring and involve semantic issues of when is a restructuring coercive. Also, voluntary restructuring may or may not involve 'haircuts' for creditors.

To add to complications, restructuring refers to different types of debt: 'official' debt, received as part of European or international bail-outs (e.g. from the EU, the IMF, or other intergovernmental lending dealt with via the Paris Club); and 'market debt', which is all the other debt issued by a state to private investors. Restructuring may involve one or both. Typically, official debt is privileged over market debt, creating another source of grievance. Consistent with IMF practice, Preamble 12–13 of the Treaty Establishing the European Stability Mechanism (ESM) of 2012 gave the ESM preferred creditor status. It stated that: in 'exceptional cases an adequate and proportionate form of private-sector involvement shall be considered in cases where stability support is provided accompanied by conditionality in the form of a macro-economic adjustment programme'.

In sovereign debt restructuring states have a flexible menu of options. Creditor losses can take the form of reduction in the principal amount; cut in coupon/interest or fees; significant extension of maturity date; change from a cash-pay basis to non-cash payment; swap of debt for equity, hybrids, or other instruments; cash tender for less than par; and contractual or structural reduction in seniority. Further losses to creditors can derive from alteration in the currency denomination or indexation of the securities; the de-listing of existing obligations from securities exchanges; regulatory penalties on holders of the original securities; and change in the legal jurisdiction to one less friendly to bondholders, typically a local one. Use of one or more of these instruments may be seen as offering higher net gains and less loss of reputation than the alternatives—a sudden disorderly default, a moratorium on debt servicing, a deposit run in the banking system, politically painful and costly fiscal adjustments, or the imposition of draconian capital controls. Sovereign debt restructuring can also be a way of securing credit facilities from international financial institutions, like the IMF and the World Bank, which may demand matching private-sector burden-sharing.

The central issue is the domestic law under which the sovereign debt is governed. It determines whether, where, and how, redress is sought in domestic courts. Debtor-state elites can seek to shore up sovereign immunity to prosecution by jurisdictional and technical impediments on creditors, preventing them from being able to pursue claims in the domestic courts. Examples include failure to provide for a forum to enforce obligations in cases of default and clauses that limit which entity can sue for recovery of losses (Glinavos 2010: 18). From 2001 a growing proportion of Greek sovereign debt was governed by its domestic law (some 90 per cent by 2010). It provided for the jurisdiction of the Greek courts rather than English or US courts. This change brought Greece into line with most developed European states, which enjoy the privilege of being able to borrow under their own law.

Because international law is minimal in sovereign debt management, states have in principle considerable discretion over how they restructure debts. They can pursue more or less orderly or disorderly processes of sovereign debt restructuring. Disorderly restructuring involves muddling through by ad hoc crisis measures. An example was Ireland in 2007–2011. Its government offered a blanket guarantee to bank creditors and took toxic bank debts onto the public balance sheet. Later, it sought to discriminate between senior and subordinated debt in imposing haircuts on bank creditors.

Orderly mechanisms for debt restructuring take top-down and bottom-up forms. Top-down mechanisms have proved highly problematic to negotiate. Though backed within the IMF and by leading economists, this type of debt restructuring mechanism encounters both sovereignty issues and creditor opposition. It provokes fears that formalizing private-sector involvement may destabilize financial markets by making them nervous about creditor losses, leading to higher risk premiums for states. Additionally, it is claimed that top-down restructuring mechanisms will prove hostage to moral hazard problems as debtor-state elites look to them as a protective umbrella against making overdue fiscal and structural reforms (cf. Meltzer Commission 2000).

Massive sovereign debt defaults and restructurings have served as the spark for calls for a top-down international mechanism. In the wake of the Argentinean default of 2001 economists pressed the case for an international statutory framework, overseen by a supra-national body. The objective was to modify and qualify the rights of private creditors, compelling them to participate in debt relief, and preventing a minority of them blocking a restructuring. Earlier, against the background of Latin American defaults, Kenen (1990) had proposed an International Debt Discount Corporation (IDDC). The IDDC would issue its own marketable obligations, guaranteed by member governments. It would use the proceeds to purchase, at a discount, a portion of the debt owed by a debt-distressed government. The ill-fated Krueger proposal, which emanated from within the IMF, suggested a Sovereign Debt Restructuring Mechanism (SDRM). It was designed to restrain creditors temporarily from litigating before a sovereign debtor had time to negotiate a settlement with bondholders (Krueger 2002). A key aim was to counter the activities of so-called 'vulture funds', which buy distressed debt and then litigate.

Despite broad support from European governments, the IMF proposal foundered on opposition from two main quarters. The United States sought to protect the interests of domestic financial institutions. In addition, key developing states like Brazil feared higher borrowing costs and the new opportunities that would be opened for law firms active in debt restructuring activities.

In default of the Krueger plan, the IMF strongly promoted the insertion of collective-action clauses (CACs) into sovereign bond contracts. On the model of US corporate insolvency law, CACs were designed to allow a super-majority of creditors to bind 'hold-out' creditors to a negotiated restructuring. Their limitation was that they did not apply to existing debt, unless retrofitted to bonds under domestic law. This option was not available when bonds had been issued under foreign jurisdiction.

In 2012–2013 the IMF re-examined how best to deal with sovereign insolvency, seeking to draw lessons from the largest-ever Greek sovereign debt restructuring and from the US court decision to back the claims of 'hold-out' creditors in the Argentinean debt restructuring. It backed away from reviving the statutory approach in favour of reviewing the way in which CACs work. The objectives were to ensure that sovereign debt restructurings were more timely and effective and to make it more difficult for 'hold-out' creditors to interfere with restructurings. The lesson that the IMF drew from the Greek case was that debt restructuring had been too late in the process of crisis management. The IMF proposed that private creditors should be bailed-in before it became involved in a bail-out package. Opposition was loudest from hedge-fund managers and credit rating agencies. The IMF view was that a less creditor-friendly approach to state insolvency was necessary, with more frequent and tougher use of debt restructuring.

The key turning point in the EU and the euro area was the spread and intensification of bank crises, from Britain and Ireland in 2007–2008, through Spain, to Cyprus in 2013. They posed politically challenging questions of fairness and moral hazard. Should taxpayers bear the costs of bank rescues? If so, to what extent should they do so? Do taxpayer bail-outs reinforce incentives to take excessive risks and to disproportionately reward bank executives? On the one hand, unwillingness to impose losses on creditors and other stakeholders in banks had potentially disastrous effects on sovereign debt. Banks and states became locked into a potentially fatal embrace. On the other, it was not clear that bank 'bail-ins' could play a major part in the failure of a huge, systemically significant bank.

Staff in the IMF (2012a), in the ECB, and in the European Commission began to advocate mandatory debt restructuring through 'bail-ins' of systemically important financial institutions. The underlying principle was that sovereign debt crisis management should involve arbitrage between creditor and debtor interests. It should break the fatal embrace of banks and states.

By 2013 mandatory 'bail-ins' were increasingly being seen as essential components of euro area evolution into a banking union and a fiscal union. In February 2013 'bail-in' was applied by the Dutch government to subordinated bondholders in the SNS Reaal Bank. The technique was used with respect to unsecured bondholders by the Irish government in Anglo Irish Bank and as part of the Spanish bank bail-outs. Much more radically and controversially, the Cyprus bank bail-out involved the extension of 'bail-in' to big, uninsured depositors in the two main banks. The question was whether the Cyprus bail-in was a one-off, dictated by the funding structure of its banks and directed at Russian depositors and the problem of money laundering, or a precedent for future bail-out packages. As the IMF and, even more, the European Commission recognized, agreeing mandatory bank bail-ins posed very difficult and contentious issues. In negotiating European banking union German negotiators pressed strongly for bank bail-ins and for clear, firm rules to constrain state flexibility in organizing them.

In October 2010 Chancellor Merkel had used the Franco-German summit at Deauville to push for private-sector involvement in future sovereign bail-outs. However, this proposal faced opposition from the ECB and the European Commission, which feared contagion and volatility across European sovereign bond markets. She backed away, recognizing that it could exacerbate short-term problems of crisis management by making creditors more insecure. Subsequent experience with the failure of the first Greek bail-out led the EU to agree a 'bail-in' mechanism for private-sector involvement in sovereign debt restructuring under the ESM treaty of 2012. However, it was only to be used in 'exceptional circumstances'. This continuing reservation reflected ongoing worries in the ECB and the European Commission about triggering contagion in fragile economic circumstances.

Controversy took on a sharply political form in March 2013, over the question of whether Cypriot bank depositors—and, if so, which—should be bailed-in as a complement to a euro area and IMF bail-out. Within the financial markets there was fear of loss of legal clarity about the hierarchy of shareholders, different bondholders, and depositors in debt restructurings. Insecurity posed a second issue. There was risk that bank bail-ins could provoke contagion effects if bondholders, and worse still depositors, feared losses in prospective restructurings elsewhere in the euro area. The consequences could vary from higher borrowing costs to full-scale depositor panic and 'bank runs'. As the Cyprus case showed, making up rules on a case-by-case basis, and hardening the stance on 'bail-ins', risked damaging the reputation of the euro area for fair and equal treatment of Member States. Cypriots felt aggrieved at being treated differently from the Greeks and the Irish earlier. The temporary solution—pending negotiating a directive—was reliance on the EU state-aid rules as the resolution framework. In 2013 the Netherlands and Spain were benchmarked as best practice in agreeing new state-aid guidelines. According to these guidelines, shareholders and junior bondholders would be bailed-in before taxpayers were asked to contribute.

Historically, state defence of sovereignty and creditor power combined to favour the development of bottom-up mechanisms for sovereign debt restructuring. This type of mechanism was better adapted to the complexity of collective-action problems and to the diversity of interests involved. Bottom-up mechanisms evolved at a relatively early date. As early as the seventeenth century, Genoese sovereign lenders were acting collectively to pursue 'cheat-the-cheater' strategies. They kept at a distance any new lenders to Philip II of Spain in the wake of his defaults (Drelichman and Voth 2009, 2010).

From 1828 the General Purpose Committee of the London Stock Exchange began to establish a system of CACs, which required majority agreement amongst bondholders to sanction a debt restructuring deal and permit market access. Informally, the London Stock Exchange acted as an international court of arbitration (Flandreau 2013). It dealt with the complex problems of Greek and Spanish loans in the 1830s and of Austro-Hungarian loans at the end of the 1860s. The work of the London Stock Exchange was superseded by that of the British Corporation of Foreign Bondholders in 1868. Similar efforts to coordinate creditor activism followed in Belgium, France, and the Netherlands (Esteves 2007). Bondholder organizations sought to play important roles in the Egyptian, Greek, Ottoman, and Portuguese sovereign debt crises. However, they lacked the tools and prestige to compete with the major issuing banks in enforcing terms on defaulting states (Flandreau and Flores 2010).

The post-1970s' shift from syndicated bank loans to much more complex, large-scale sovereign bond markets increased problems of collective action for creditors. There were new opportunities for 'hold-out' litigation, whereby a minority of creditors chooses not to accept a debt restructuring but sues through the courts. In this context bondholder organizations lost credibility and relevance. There was a new emphasis on official support for a 'soft' restructuring approach, which would reassure creditors by not coercing them into taking losses.

A sign of this shift was the so-called Brady Plan of March 1989, which sought to limit private-creditor damage from persisting Latin American debt crises. It recognized that Latin American states were experiencing solvency, not just liquidity crises. They needed to be empowered to kick-start economic growth and structural reforms on the basis of new financial instruments. A key feature of the Brady Plan was official-sector encouragement of outright debt reductions so as to restore the solvency of distressed debtor states.

The process was to involve voluntary agreement with private-sector creditors. They were offered a menu of options, including swapping shorter-dated bonds for longer maturities, thereby avoiding haircuts for investors. Also, bank loans could be exchanged into sovereign bonds. Brady deals were implemented in Bulgaria and Poland, as well as various Latin American states. They were strongly supported by the IMF. By 2012 questions were being asked about whether Brady deals might be applied to Greece and other euro area Member States.

In the case of Greece, the increasing proportion of its sovereign bonds that were held by the official sector changed the nature of the game. Financing substantial debt write-offs would fall on taxpayers. By November 2012 the euro area had embarked on disguised forgiveness of officially-held Greek debt. The Eurosystem agreed to repatriate the profits on its holdings of Greek sovereign bonds. The European Financial Stability Facility (EFSF) also made money available on favourable terms for a Greek buy-back of outstanding debt. If Greece was to stay in the euro area, the question was when the euro area would embrace zero or extremely low interest rates on officially-held Greek debt and an extension of maturity. The answer was bound up in the dynamics of domestic political management in creditor states, above all Germany.

The huge Argentinean default in 2001, and the Greek crisis that unfolded after 2009, stimulated the attempt to address the problem of collective action by creditors through the insertion of CACs in sovereign bond contracts. CACs constituted official recognition that sovereign bonds were not risk-free. They encouraged pre-emptive, negotiated restructuring by preventing a minority of hostile creditors from blocking the process. Soon after the Argentinean default, only 21 per cent of sovereign bonds issued in New York still required unanimity. CAC clauses were adopted by an increasing number of emerging market economies, including the Czech Republic and Poland. They were strongly promoted by the IMF.

Following an initial agreement in November 2010, the ESM treaty of 2012 required the insertion of standardized and identical CACs in all new euro area government bonds, with maturity above one year, from January 2013. The CACs were to have a voting threshold of two-thirds, compared to the 75 per cent threshold that had been standard in emerging markets. The percentage of permissible non-CAC bonds was to diminish over a ten-year period. Full incorporation into a government's sovereign debt stock would take longer. In 2012 Greece showed that CACs could be retrospectively introduced into bonds issued under domestic law. Most euro area sovereign bonds were issued under domestic laws.

CACs offered a number of advantages to states. They avoided the need for formal default and helped reduce risks from legal challenges in the courts. They facilitated a market-based, speedier process of restructuring negotiations, in contrast to the protracted process in Argentina. In addition, it was claimed—though without substantial supporting empirical evidence—that CACs induced investors to more carefully price risk when buying sovereign bonds. On the negative side, there were three risks. States with fragile public finances, like the euro area periphery in 2011–2012, could find that new CAC bonds make older bonds less liquid. There were also potential costs to financial institutions. The exercise of CACs risked triggering a 'credit event', which would lead to payouts under credit default swaps. The negotiated private-sector involvement in a partial restructuring of Greek sovereign debt on 12 March 2012 was based on the CACs introduced into Greek law on 9 March 2012. This action prompted the International Swaps and Derivatives Association (ISDA) to declare a 'credit event'. The payouts to creditors fell to the financial institutions providing the insurance, not to the Greek state. Finally, constitutional lawyers—as in Greece—could challenge the distinction between 'enforced' haircuts on private-sector creditors and the exemption of official creditors, like the ECB. The question arose of how official creditors might react to debt restructuring proposals if they were significant holders of CAC bonds.

Bank insolvency poses a particular risk for sovereign creditworthiness once its liabilities are taken onto public balance sheets. Hence the question arises of whether domestic corporate insolvency law is adequate for dealing with the contagious and systemic risks associated with bank failure. The German bank restructuring law of 2010 sought to mitigate the migration of bank risk to taxpayers. It put in place an orderly, step-by-step procedure for bank 'bail-ins' so that creditors would share in the costs of bank rescues. A key element was a new restructuring fund, financed by the banks. The justification for making banks responsible for their own restructuring was to protect against moral hazard and to reduce the risks to sovereign creditworthiness. In the event of lack of voluntary agreement with creditors, the financial market regulator was empowered to impose transfers of bank assets and liabilities. The German law handed discretion in ranking creditors to regulators. Its aim was to avert the traditional bankruptcy procedure, which involved strict rules and a court-supervised process. However, the question remained whether, when, and how this power would be used in the face of powerful market pressures not to implement a haircut. The German law of 2010 formed the context of formulation of German positions on the design of European banking union.

This approach, which evolved in creditor states like Denmark, Germany, and the Netherlands, was emulated in European Commission documents of 2010–2012, prior to a formal proposal for the 'bail-in' as a debt write-down tool. It was also taken up in a carefully reasoned IMF (2012a) staff document, which outlined the case for a mandatory debt restructuring of systemic financial institutions. The rationale included provision of a more flexible, speedy, and less costly alternative to insolvency law in the case of bank failures. The 'bail-in' would ensure that bondholders shared in the costs of future bank recapitalizations, shifting liabilities away from taxpayers. Not least, harmonizing EU law would help tackle the problem of mismatch between more complex cross-national banking, consequent on single financial market legislation and currency union, and different domestic insolvency regimes. This mismatch offered fertile ground for insolvency lawyers to advise clients on 'jurisdiction shopping' or 'insolvency tourism' in search of domestic defaulting regimes that were more lenient to debtors.

Negotiating Sovereign Debt and Bank Restructuring

Despite continuing international and European legal gaps in the formal rules governing sovereign debt, and the complications of negotiated restructurings, unilateral default has become less credible within the post-1945 framework of European integration and international capital market integration. Bottom-up processes of pre-emptive, negotiated debt restructuring have evolved as the norm, at least in Europe. States have incentives to accept restrictions on the exercise of sovereign immunity. Abiding by principles of transparency, predictability, and 'fair dealing' helps them to build a lasting reputation as creditworthy and to reap the financial and economic gains. Debtor states are more likely to be able to return speedily to the international capital markets and to rebuild their credibility in interlocking European and international negotiating frameworks.

Creditors also have incentives to accept negotiated debt restructurings. This incentive has grown as sovereign bonds have increasingly come to be held by institutional investors, who mark their holdings to market, rather than by banks or retail investors. In consequence, they have already registered most of the losses from falling bond prices. The alternative is the length, complexity, messiness, costs, and uncertainty of litigation. In addition, investment tribunals have a weak record in protecting creditors, given that their jurisdiction over sovereign bond issues remains an open question (Waibel 2011). Furthermore, states can shield their assets from enforcement so that litigants have no real prospect of replacing debt repayments with government property. Given the risks of debtor-state unwillingness to comply with rulings, and of their resort to the extension of sovereign immunity, negotiation offers creditors a promising route.

Nevertheless, negotiating voluntary sovereign debt restructurings is complex, involves a messy and protracted process, and is uncertain in outcome. It involves negotiating terms across different types of bonds held by different kinds of bondholders. Different terms may be negotiated for domestic and external debt and for senior and subordinated debt. External debt is denominated in foreign currency, generally held by non-residents, and governed by foreign law. Traditionally, it features heavily in debt issuance by developing and emerging market economies. Domestic debt is priced in national currency (the euro for euro area Member States), and subject to domestic state law. Matters are further complicated by the fact that external debt can be held by residents, and domestic debt by non-residents.

A further complication derives from the question of how to categorize the euro-denominated sovereign debt of euro area Member States. Because they have pooled monetary sovereignty, but issue sovereign debt separately, this debt appears similar to external debt. Moreover, the high integration of European financial markets, following currency union in 1999, led to its being often held in its majority by non-residents in other euro area Member States (at least prior to the sovereign debt crises). However, the key consideration remains whether the euro-denominated debt is governed by domestic law. This consideration is basic to cases of litigation by creditors before commercial courts. In the large majority of euro area Member States, more than 80 per cent of public bond issuance between 2003 and 2010 was governed by their own laws (Das, Papaioannou, and Trebesch 2012: 42).

The governing law of a sovereign bond is a key factor in debt restructuring. Sovereign bond issuances under English law have traditionally included some form of CACs. Conversely, before 2009 German law gave little explicit encouragement to CACs. Bond issuance under English law was most widespread in the new EU Member States, like the Baltic States, Poland, and Romania, as well as Cyprus and Slovakia that joined the euro. In Greece, Portugal, and Spain, where the large majority of bonds fell under domestic law, their parliaments could legislate to change their terms. Euro area national parliaments may be able in principle to offer different terms for domestic and external debt. However, in practice they are severely constrained by EU norms and pressures and by the international financial markets. Moreover, from 2013 CACs were included in all sovereign bonds issued by euro area Member States, in a manner consistent with English and New York law.

In addition, different terms may be negotiated for senior and junior or subordinated creditors. This distinction was built into the ESM treaty, according to which the ESM was to have senior creditor status. The implication was that private investors would be last in the queue for the recovery of their money. Both the IMF and the ECB made a similar claim. The ESM treaty even defined the IMF as a 'super-senior' creditor, senior to the ESM.

With respect to corporate crises, which can have major implications for sovereign creditworthiness, insolvency law has developed a distinction between types of creditors. For instance, the English 'pre-pack' procedure in corporate insolvency distinguishes a hierarchy of creditors. In bank bail-outs, as in Ireland, subordinated debt is more amenable to radical restructuring. It may, for instance, be converted to equity as a form of 'bail-in' for distressed banks.

Domestic laws offer different kinds of security to bank creditors, most notably in the form of covered bonds. Covered bonds developed in eighteenth-century Germany and entered into widespread use in states like Denmark, France, and Spain. The loans backing covered bonds remain on a bank's books—unlike regular securitizations—and are ring-fenced, protecting these bondholders even in insolvency. Thus the German bank restructuring law of 2010, which forced bondholders to take losses if a bank fails, exempted covered bonds. This extra form of security made covered bonds particularly attractive as a safe haven to investors during the post-2007 crisis. Covered bonds accounted for a third of all European banks' borrowing in 2010. By 2011 the United States was showing interest in introducing covered bonds into its domestic legislation.

There is one big winner from complex debt restructuring negotiations, with their different classes of creditors. They offer fertile ground for big law firms and star insolvency lawyers. They are key stakeholders in negotiated debt restructurings, above all insolvency lawyers in London, New York, and Washington. Law firms gain substantial business and income from helping creditors negotiate their way through the tortuous legal complications and uncertainties and the weak enforcement mechanisms. Firms like Arnold and Porter and Cleary Gottlieb Steen Hamilton were notably active in a series of highly complex debt restructuring negotiations, involving many thousands of private and public creditors. They included Iraq and Uruguay sovereign debt; the long-drawn-out saga of burden-sharing in compensating depositors in Icelandic Icesave; the losses sustained by holders of subordinated debt in Irish banks in 2010–2011; and the biggest ever debt restructuring by Greece in 2011–2012.

The EU, the Euro Area, and State Insolvency

In the three decades before the euro area sovereign debt crises, debate about defaults and restructurings had focused on emerging market economies, whose debt was generally denominated in foreign jurisdictions and foreign currencies. In contrast, the onset of the euro area crises had a different quality. Most Member-State sovereign debt was governed by domestic rather than English or US law. Also, much more was at stake because of the global significance of the EU market, the scale of financial and monetary integration especially with the single currency, and the risk of contagion and systemic collapse. The spreading crises—from Greece, Ireland, and Portugal to the systemically significant Italy and Spain—generated support for a new cross-national legal regime in the form of a euro area banking union and a fiscal union. Sovereign creditworthiness began to be seen as a euro area collective good. Its protection required clearer legal definition of Member-State and euro-area-level responsibilities, as well as new enforcement mechanisms. The ESM treaty was a move in this direction.

As with the Krueger proposal, the problem was that a statutory cross-national insolvency regime had to involve someone other than the debtor state itself deciding what a sustainable level of debt was. Additionally, the intimate connection of bank solvency and sovereign creditworthiness meant that a European single bank supervisory mechanism and a single bank resolution mechanism were needed, alongside cross-national financial assistance mechanisms for sovereign debt. The crisis exposed how far the euro area had to go in developing its legal and institutional framework for banking and fiscal union.

Legal and institutional design of a euro area banking and fiscal union faced many contentious questions that touched on the core of state sovereignty and on political legitimacy. First, who within the euro area was to decide when sovereign debt was unsustainable? Who was to decide when a bank was on the brink of insolvency? Secondly, how much supra-national executive discretion to act should such authorities have? How was their accountability and transparency to be organized? How was the independence of ECB monetary policy to be safeguarded? Thirdly, what was the appropriate balance between enforcing individual responsibility on states for honouring their sovereign debts and assuming collective responsibility for those debts?

On the first question, it was agreed that the ECB should provide the nucleus for the single bank supervisory mechanism and that the ESM should be the permanent collective financial assistance mechanism for states at risk of debt restructuring. However, the ESM fell short of being a 'European Monetary Fund'. Also, the idea of a new European debt management office for euro-bond issuance and/or for debt redemption was vetoed by Germany. The creditor states, led by Germany, were keen to ensure that the Commission would be kept at arms' length in favour of institutional arrangements that would place them in the driving seat, with at least a veto position.

On the second question, creditor-state elites favoured intergovernmental rather than supra-national bodies for both fiscal bail-outs and for bank recapitalization. This type of structure minimized the incentives for the euro area to develop into a transfer union, encouraging moral hazard. It also meant that, in legal terms, the euro area continued to lack full supra-national capacity to act in supreme emergency. The open question was whether, in such circumstances, the ECB would step into the breach unconditionally. In that case the legal principle of central bank independence was breached.

The third question pitted two conceptions of European solidarity against each other. Creditor-state elites favoured the solidarity of effort. Individual Member States should demonstrate solidarity by honouring their fiscal commitments. In contrast, debtor-state elites argued for the solidarity of collective financial assistance. They favoured supra-national bodies for fiscal bail-outs, collective debt management, and collective bank recapitalization. This type of arrangement amounted to an institutionally formalized transfer union.

The problems in agreeing an institutionalized transfer union, matched by external controls on 'responsible' sovereignty in matters of public debt, were not simply rooted in the different material interests of creditor and debtor states. They touched on politically and emotionally sensitive issues of sovereignty and identity. Politically, the enforcement of responsible sovereignty could be interpreted as an abridgement of sovereign rights and identity. It proved easier to agree to insert CACs in future sovereign bond issues than to devise a single European bank resolution mechanism or collective European debt management.

German lawyers in particular saw the mounting scale of euro area crises as an opportunity to press for a treaty-based codification of European banking and fiscal union. They identified four objectives in line with Ordo-liberal principles of stability-oriented economic policy. European solidarity had to be based on clear, firmly enforceable fiscal rules and commitment to structural reforms, giving 'full credibility' to debt sustainability and reducing debt-servicing costs. Secondly, banking and fiscal union had to be organized so as to avert the protracted mutual recriminations, costly delays, and uncertainty that lead to disorderly debt default. Thirdly, it had to prevent protracted creditor lawsuits that might shut debtor states out of international capital markets. Fourthly, a banking and fiscal union must reduce moral hazard by inducing creditors to price risk more accurately. In the intensively integrated financial markets of the EU and the euro area, the risks from a disorderly default seemed too high, above all for creditor states like Germany. German ideas of 'Ordo-liberalism' and disorderly sovereign default were incompatible European bedfellows.

State Insolvency: The Limits of 'Hard' Law

In negotiating the Economic and Monetary Union (EMU) provisions of the Maastricht Treaty in 1990–1991 EU negotiators did not address the problem of state insolvency. It was assumed that the new institutional arrangements would avert such a problem because states would comply with the rules, above all on avoidance of excessive deficits. Hence the foundation of EMU was not accompanied by new EU law dealing with state insolvency. There was no supra-national mechanism to take legally justifiable, discretionary action in supreme emergency to preserve the coherence and integrity of the euro area in the face of financial market contagion. The euro area lacked the basic attributes of a banking union and a fiscal union, with an ultimate lender of last resort. Nevertheless, the formalization of 'private-sector involvement' in sovereign debt restructurings remains a potentially useful instrument for the euro area to reduce the burdens on taxpayers and on welfare-state recipients from bailing-out insolvent states.

Formally, with the ESM treaty of 2012, the euro area lent its support, 'in exceptional circumstances', to private-sector involvement in sovereign bail-outs. However, it backed away from top-down legal codification of the principles and procedures governing state insolvency and debt restructuring. The language of debt restructuring remained very much that of the credit rating agencies. The credit ratings agencies define debt restructurings as 'coercive debt exchange' (CDE). They are deemed to be 'forced' on creditors on an out-of-court basis. CDE is defined as involving a material reduction in terms for bondholders and for lenders as a way of staving off insolvency. The principal instruments are tender offers, exchange offers, and consent solicitations (for details see Fitch Ratings 2009a). In such cases, usually earlier, credit rating agencies rate sovereign bonds as 'junk'. The International Swaps and Derivatives Association (ISDA) regards CDEs as 'credit events'. They trigger payment to creditors who have bought CDS protection.

State solvency issues are bedevilled by this debate about coercion and consent, which prove difficult and slippery concepts to apply in discussions about debt restructuring. The problem is especially acute with respect to the use of financial repression and debt restructuring to liquidate domestic debt. In the case of domestic resident holders of sovereign debt, it is difficult to assess how voluntary their participation can be in debt liquidation. On occasion, courts refer to 'economic coercion', even though there is formally no coercive act. In practice, states can bring various forms of regulatory pressure and moral suasion to bear on domestic bondholders. Residents may find that their economic self-interests are so closely enmeshed with those of their states that they perceive no alternative to participation, making a bond exchange notionally voluntary.

Despite the ESM treaty, EU 'hard' law evolved slowly with respect to Member-State liability in a sovereign debt default. There was a deep-seared reluctance to contemplate the notion that an EU Member State could be the first to default. Member-State liability for damages attaches to acting in violation of EU law, for instance by not implementing a directive or breaching a specific Treaty article. This liability was established in the *Francovich* ruling of the European Court of Justice (ECJ) in 1991 (Craig and de Búrca 2003: 257). However, EU law has been cautious about creating any new obligations of Member States with reference to the treatment of creditors in a sovereign debt rescheduling or to the use of financial repression. The main obligations relate to the Deposit Guarantee Directive (1994, amended 2005), which protects bank customers in the case of a bank default; to breach of the general principle of non-discrimination in EU law, notably with reference to Article 51 of the Charter of Fundamental Rights; and to prohibition of capital controls under single market rules. However, in 2013 Cyprus was enabled to introduce widespread capital controls, as a temporary device, to flank the international 'bail-out' package.

The most constraining formal obligation relates to freedom of capital movement, which impedes the process of exiting the euro area and resorting to devaluation and capital controls to expedite debt liquidation. The non-discrimination principle might also apply in the field of sovereign debt restructuring. However, the fact that till 2012 no EU Member State had restructured its debt meant a continuing lack of clarity about its precise implications. The ECJ had not ruled in this matter. Nevertheless, in 2004, in a case lost by the European Commission, the ECJ rejected Member-State liability for 'defective supervision' (C-222/02). The implication seemed to be that shortcomings in domestic banking supervision that led to bank crisis did not put a Member State's taxpayers at legal risk, for instance in Ireland, or by extension in Iceland as a member of the European Economic Area. The responsibility of domestic taxpayers for banking failures was not established in EU law.

In the absence of 'hard' EU law, issues of Member-State liability came before domestic courts. Here they were adjudicated with reference to three external sources: the Brussels Convention of 1968 on the jurisdiction and the enforcement of judgements in civil and criminal matters, especially relating to insolvent companies and other legal persons; to ECJ rulings; and to the rulings of the ECHR. A key issue for domestic courts was whether domestic debt default violated A1P1 of the European Convention for the Protection of Human Rights and Freedoms. In a ruling of 2010, *Malysch and Others v. the Russian Federation* (30280/03), the ECHR affirmed that a default on domestic debt was in breach of A1P1. Its Grand Chamber declined to examine the case.

A further potential source of Member-State liability derived from the proliferation of BITs since the giant Argentinean sovereign default in 2001. They led to new international arbitration mechanisms, whose decisions were directly enforceable through domestic legal systems and thereby restricted sovereign immunity (Sornarajah 2004; Glinavos 2010). Both the number of BITs and the identity of counterparties matter. Thus, by 2010, Greece had some 40 BITs. However, most of these BITs were with developing states. Greece did not have BITs with Britain and France. Its BIT with Germany dated from the 1960s and lacked a creditor-state arbitration mechanism. Hence, under that treaty, creditors could not bring arbitration against Greece, undermining its effectiveness in protecting them. It remained an open question whether the protection of a BIT would enable creditors to bring treaty-based claims before international arbitration tribunals in a case of sovereign default (Waibel 2007). Nevertheless, the complications of having to face ECHR cases and BIT arbitration tribunals, and losing, acted as a deterrent on sovereign debt default.

State Liability and Corporate Insolvency

Sovereign creditworthiness is inseparable from the legal issues of liability that arise in bank insolvencies and even in certain non-financial corporate insolvencies. In the case of 'systemically important' institutions, 'too significant to fail', corporate insolvencies impact negatively on the public-sector balance sheet. Moreover, the effects spill contagiously across borders, raising difficult issues about cross-national crisis management and burden-sharing in relation to bondholders, bank depositors, and the state.

Just how substantial these effects can be was revealed after the collapse of the Icelandic banking system in October 2008 (Waibel 2010). Management of the crisis over Icesave, the Internet arm of the failed Landsbanki, involved tough negotiations between the Icelandic, British, and Dutch governments over state liability for compensating retail depositors. Because of the massive long-term costs for Icelandic taxpayers, successive negotiated deals were soundly rejected in referenda: first, in May 2010 and again—despite relatively low interest rates and long payment terms—in April 2011. The EU played an essentially passive role in this debt crisis management. The European Commission confirmed that, under the European Economic Area Agreement of 1993 and the Deposit Guarantee Scheme directive (94/19/EC), Iceland had a legal obligation to compensate British and Dutch depositors. More pertinently, the European Free Trade Area (EFTA) Surveillance Authority issued a final warning of intention to take the Icelandic government to court. However, in January 2012 the EFTA court ruled in favour of Iceland. Its government was under no obligation to compensate British and Dutch depositors in Icesave. In practice, they could be paid out of the estate of Landsbanki.

The brake on EU involvement stemmed from legal recognition that, at least prior to 2009, Member-State liability for deficient deposit protection had not been clearly defined. There seemed to be no obligation of the Icelandic government to pick up the bill that its domestic deposit insurance fund could not meet. Alongside this weak EU legal framework, Member States proved reluctant to create a precedent of state liability that could make them vulnerable to future similar creditor claims around the world in the case of a systemic bank crisis. In addition, EU institutions and Member States hesitated to become associated with perceptions of bullying behaviour towards a tiny state like Iceland. There were few attractions in being accused of imposing unfair burden-sharing on hard-hit Icelandic taxpayers.

The problem remained that, even in the EU, insolvencies faced a patchwork of different legal structures. Domestic insolvency regimes varied in the degree of protection that they give to creditors and in the emphasis given to maintaining confidence in credit markets. They also differed in the extent to which they privileged some creditors over other unsecured creditors. In addition, domestic insolvency regimes varied in the emphasis that they placed on preventing a company going into liquidation by keeping it afloat to the benefit of stakeholders like employees. The design of insolvency regimes struck different balances between making it a sufficiently straightforward procedure, so that it was not regarded as a procedure to be avoided at all costs, and avoiding it becoming so attractive that debtors resorted to it with alacrity. The fragmentation of insolvency jurisdictions in Europe reflected the way in which these interests were balanced differently. Some states were seen as more lenient to debt defaulters than others.

By 2013 the EU still lacked the 'top-down' equivalent of the United States' 'one-size-fits-all' Chapter 11 corporate insolvency process. The European Commission-led process of consulting on a bank 'bail-in' mechanism for debt reduction made slow progress. Equally, there was little evidence of a European 'bottom-up' process of devising and enacting the same domestic insolvency laws across EU states. Instead, legal fragmentation provided an incentive for insolvency 'jurisdiction shopping'. Bank and non-bank corporations sought to escape their creditors by moving their 'centre of main interest' to the shelter of legal havens like Britain. 'Jurisdiction shopping' was influenced by the fact that debt restructuring was easier, and discharge from bankruptcy sooner, under British insolvency law than, for instance, under Dutch, German, Greek, or Irish law. British insolvency law allowed senior creditors to sell a company quickly to a new owner through a court process called a 'pre-pack'. It could be done without the permission of lower-ranking creditors like unsecured bondholders, customers, suppliers, or landlords. The main constraint on 'jurisdiction shopping' was risk of negative effect on corporate bond prices once creditors became suspicious that a migrating company was seeking to restructure its debt at their cost. By 2012–2013 pressure was mounting, notably from Ireland, for a new EU debt resolution architecture to reduce 'jurisdiction shopping' as incompatible with the single market.

The evolving sovereign debt crises and their intimate connection to bank solvency issues highlighted the need for a common and credible international and European insolvency regime for restructuring or winding up banks of systemic importance. As the Financial Stability Board (FSB), the Bank for International Settlements (BIS), and the European Commission recognized, an adequate European insolvency regime had to include a single cross-national bank supervisory mechanism, a single bank resolution and recapitalization mechanism (including the 'bail-in' of bondholders), and a cross-national or common deposit guarantee scheme to eliminate fears of 'bank runs'. It would involve burden-sharing mechanisms for central banks in providing bank liquidity and for finance ministries in offering capital support. However, design of these mechanisms raised highly controversial questions about which institutions should be given these powers, how accountability was to be organized, which banks and other financial institutions should be covered, who pays in a transfer union, and how far rights of fiscal sovereignty should be abridged in the interests of banking union.

The alarming implications of the glaring gap between the cross-national reality of corporate debt interconnectedness and legal fragmentation was revealed post-2007. The shock waves from the collapse of Lehman Brothers in September 2008 highlighted just how 'systemically important' financial intermediaries had become. Within Europe, similar cross-national shock waves were created by Royal Bank of Scotland, Fortis, and the Icelandic and Irish banks. These banking crises were handled, first and foremost, on a national basis. The result was new international and European interest in a legal requirement that 'systemically important financial intermediaries' (SIFIs) complete a 'living will', including credible resolution plans. In the case of the euro area it became clear that the logic of a monetary union was banking and fiscal union and a range of treaty and other legal changes to bring them into effect.

Social Norms, Moral Sentiments, and Peer Pressure

In the absence of a 'hard', mandatory, and 'top-down' EU state and bank insolvency law, the politics of sovereign creditworthiness came to be constrained in three 'softer' ways. First, the changed post-1945 international and European institutional context bred new, embedded social norms about what constitutes appropriate behaviour by Member States in managing sovereign debt. Secondly, there was a shift in moral sentiments that attached guilt and shame to sovereign default and other forms of coercive state behaviour towards creditors. Thirdly, the behaviour of Member States became subject to stronger forms of peer pressure, through which they could be held morally responsible for their behaviour.

The origin of these changes resided in vivid historical memory of the catastrophic economic, social, and political breakdown in 1914–1945 Europe and lesson-drawing. Change was reinforced by ever more complex interaction of governing and technical elites within EU Council and committee governance as the policy scope of European integration broadened and forms of integration deepened. In addition, the IMF and the World Bank were new sources of influence as forums for debating principles and practices of sovereign debt management. Reciprocity, reliability, and trust came to be seen as pre-eminent values in conducting creditor-debtor state relations in Europe. This context of social norms, moral sentiments, and peer pressure placed both creditor- and debtor-state elites under great pressure to accept suboptimal outcomes in order to retain trust and influence in ongoing interconnected bargaining games.

The IMF (1999 and 2002) and bank lobbies, notably the Institute of International Finance (2006), sought to take a leading role in shaping social norms and moral sentiments through their principles of 'good faith' and 'fair' debtor behaviour. One major focus of these norms was the IMF's 'lending-into-arrears' policy, which stressed early and continuous dialogue with creditors, transparency, and information-sharing. The IMF and the ECB sought to reinforce these norms with an economic rationale that ruled out sovereign default in the euro area. An IMF staff report referred to sovereign default by an advanced economy as 'unnecessary, undesirable, and unlikely' (Cottarelli, Forni,

Gottschalk, and Mauro 2010). The ECB argued that the structure of bond holding meant that sovereign default would impose harsh domestic costs, not least on vulnerable banks and household and corporate lending. It would threaten dangerous, potentially unmanageable cross-national contagion, undermining general investor confidence in the banks and the sovereign bonds of euro area Member States. In addition, the possibility existed that the ECJ might apply the principle of non-discrimination to sovereign debt restructuring or default.

Precedent and reputation played key roles in constraining EU and euro area Member-State behaviour. The fact that there had been no experience of a sovereign default by an EU Member State (or a state whilst negotiating accession) since the European integration process began in 1950 raised a barrier to its use. No state wished to be branded the first 'sinner'. In addition, prominent voices in the euro area, notably within the ECB, feared that sovereign default would indelibly stain the reputation of the euro. Perhaps more fundamentally, within the EU a set of rules of the game evolved that placed high value on mutual respect and reciprocity. The principle of 'sincere cooperation' and the norm of mutual respect found expression in Article 4(3) of the Consolidated Version of the Treaty on European Union, 2009. These norms and principles can be seen as deeply rooted in the logic of repeated and 'nested' bargaining games that have come to characterize the EU and euro area and to shape how Member States define their interests. This logic was strengthened with the extension of the scope of EU policies, which required complex trade-offs, and with the 'deepening' of the EU, with qualified majority voting emerging as the standard mode of business. It placed a heightened premium on cultivating and retaining sovereign state reputation, over and above that to be found in other world regions or at the international level.

The EU's institutionally entrenched norms and governing principles about how to behave in managing sovereign debt, along with peer pressure, provided an incentive to enlightened self-interest. They encouraged a restrictive definition of sovereign immunity and strengthened support for the notion of responsible sovereignty in managing public debt. However, the search to legally codify state and bank insolvency regimes in a European banking and fiscal union highlighted continuing disagreements about the precise meaning, scope, and content of these norms and governing principles, above all between creditor and debtor states.

Despite the ways in which EU principles and social norms had evolved, a fundamental continuity remained. Other than the ESM treaty, there were by 2013 no formal European or international legal provisions and mechanisms for the speedy and orderly insolvency of states. Neither in Europe nor internationally was there a regulator who was trusted to assess independently and impartially whether a debtor state was behaving appropriately in using its discretion to penalize creditors and to sanction a state. Part of the problem in gaining consensus on the creation of an international regulator was that the IMF was seen as a creditor institution that lacked independence and impartiality. The European Commission was distrusted by the bigger creditor states like Germany as too soft on debtor states and amenable to pressure from them. In consequence, there were no clear, agreed criteria for establishing that a state was insolvent. Until the introduction of CACs, there had been no procedure that reliably subjected a sovereign debtor to the majority vote of its creditors in restructuring its debt. In addition, there was no firm legal protection for the principle that all creditors are to be treated equally so that prior agreements that privilege certain creditors become invalid.

Paradoxes of Power

Legal analysis brings out three paradoxes at the heart of the politics of sovereign creditworthiness in Europe. First, non-legal means of redress are more important for creditors than either litigation or arbitration. They include the capacity to shape the social norms and moral sentiments that attach to sovereign debt in ways that safeguard creditor interests. EU Member States seek to avoid the guilt and shame associated with default and other forms of coercive behaviour, blunting the effectiveness of the claim to sovereign immunity. Standard, narrowly constructed models of rational choice fail to grasp adequately the significance of actors' self-understanding of their roles and their conceptions of proper and acceptable behaviour in particular contexts, like the EU.

Secondly, the politics of sovereign creditworthiness rests on the paradox of formal and informal power. On the one hand, the doctrine of sovereign immunity suggests the discretionary power of the state. Even in its restricted form, sovereign immunity offers a picture of considerable formal power available to states in dealing with their creditors. It points to the deterrent capacity of default and financial repression to coerce creditors into accepting debt restructuring. Negotiation takes place within the 'shadow of hierarchy'. Similarly, creditor-state elites can unilaterally declare that they have senior creditor status, exempt themselves from debt restructuring, and create different kinds of bonds. This picture of state power is suggestive of a residual Hobbesian conception of state sovereignty.

On the other hand, an examination of the informal aspects of power draws out the incentives for EU Member States to avoid default, to embrace flexible forms of negotiated restructuring with creditors, and to practise financial repression through collusion with creditors. State power is exercised within a framework of social norms, stressing reciprocity and fostering moral sentiments of guilt and shame about default and of pride in achieving low debt-servicing costs. Also, as Chapters 11 and 12 show, it is exercised within a particular knowledge structure, provided by dominant macroeconomic theories of market efficiency. The exercise of state power is enmeshed in the private governance of public debt. The state is not powerless. However, its power to act is shaped and hedged by financial markets, those privileged investment banks that act as Primary Dealers in the sovereign bond markets, and the macroeconomic theorists who legitimate market power and define whose confidence matters if a state is to be creditworthy. As the next chapter shows, state power is also exercised within the framework of economic culture.

Finally, legal analysis of the politics of sovereign creditworthiness draws out the paradox that abridging state fiscal sovereignty to secure collective financial assistance serves as an inducement to strengthen state capacity. The politics of sovereign creditworthiness in Europe rests on the complex relationship between rights, responsibility, and state capacity. In formal legal terms, the right to collective financial assistance in a transfer union must be balanced by clear responsibility for complying with the conditions that are attached to enjoying this right. Domestic fiscal accountability and transparency are required. However, in a number of Member States fiscal accountability and transparency are weak. Creative financial accounting and fiscal gimmickry are correspondingly pervasive, for instance in Cyprus, Greece, and Hungary. Achieving the balance between rights and responsibilities depends less on formal legal requirements than on non-legal factors whose roots lie deep within economic and political cultures. They condition political willingness and state capacity to raise revenues, control spending, achieve fiscal balance, invest productively, and effectively supervise financial institutions.

In the case of the euro area, two issues of political will and state capacity arise. The first relates to the willingness and capacity of the euro area itself to ensure the right to collective financial assistance. Meeting this requirement entails giving it a treaty basis and the institutional mechanisms to ensure that there is a lender of last resort in supreme emergency. The second issue relates to the willingness and capacity of Member States to shoulder their own fiscal, financial, and economic reform responsibilities. Political and institutional risks arise when one or more Member States are characterized by predatory, rent-seeking behaviour, whether by political, bureaucratic, or financial elites, and weak institutional structures to hold them to account and make their activities transparent.

The euro area remains highly vulnerable if certain Member States prove congenitally unable to balance rights with responsibility in their sovereign debt management. In these circumstances, legal forms that align mutual liability with control fail on their own to resolve political and institutional problems of compliance. The euro area has a complex, evolving formal structure of mutual liability and control. It includes the Maastricht convergence criteria for euro entry, the restrictive rules on excessive deficits and debt, the excessive imbalances procedure, ESM financial assistance with conditionality, ECB emergency liquidity assistance to banks, and ECB intervention in sovereign bond markets. Ultimately, however, they serve as litmus tests for a more profound problem: the political will and the state capacity to comply with obligations.

9

Economic Cultures, Ideologies of Debt, and State Virtue

> The condition of the monetary being of a people is a symptom of all its conditions. Everything a people wants, does, suffers and is, is reflected in its monetary system.
>
> Joseph Schumpeter (1918: 5–38)

Schumpeter was not only an eminent Austrian economist. He was also briefly finance minister at a time of profound debt crisis for the traumatized post-1918 Austrian state. His understanding of this crisis was grounded in a central European, sociologically-minded approach to public finance dynamics. In contrast to modern formal economic analysis and modelling, Schumpeter attributed a central role to historically-conditioned cultural specificities. In this respect he was close to the late-nineteenth-century German historical and institutional school of economics, notably Stein and Wagner. Schumpeter recognized that the management of the post-war debt crisis was a matter that went beyond what could be captured in formal macroeconomic theories or in analysis of governing structures. It was embedded in mentalities. This approach resonated later amongst some, though by no means all, German Ordo-liberal economists. They believed that 'stability culture' was of primordial importance, rooted in specific German experiences, and not readily exportable. It helped explain the severe reservations within German Ordo-liberal economics towards European monetary union.

The significance of mentalities is most clearly captured in the work of historical sociologists and social anthropologists on how the meanings that are attached to credit and debt are culturally anchored and relative (Graeber 2011; Smith 2012). Credit and debt play a constitutive part in the processes of identity formation through their association with the construction of shared historical memory. For instance, they were a constitutive part of Anglo-Irish identity formation in the eighteenth century (Moore 2010). Similarly, the 'sacred' debt played a major role in Union identity formation during and just after the US Civil War (Foner 2002). The image of onerous debt also helped shape the cultures of resentment that subsequently informed Irish nationalist identity formation and

Indian national identity formation (James 1998). English imperial-contracted debt was identified as the cause of ruinous over-taxation, above all of land, and of the subsequent indebtedness, and acute hardships of the rural poor in India and in Ireland.

Political scientists deal with mentalities and identity construction in the narrower sense of ideology as well as with culture. Ideology draws attention to the interest-group basis of thinking about debt. It focuses on the non-comparability of beliefs about the nature of the debt problem that states face, about what they should do about it, and about how they should act. Grounded in particular economic and social interests, ideologies of debt provide contending formal justifications for self-interested proposals by reference to a mutually consistent set of ideas (cf. Eisenstein 1961). They articulate specific conceptions of distributive justice. At the same time, ideologies of debt have deeper roots in historical changes in economic cultures and the social and political structures in which they are embedded. Economic cultures and social and political structures form part of the background from which ideologies of debt emerge. These ideologies establish certain prevailing standards by which fiscal policies should be judged. This interplay of economic culture and ideology underlines the irreducibly context-bound, subjective, and historical character of thinking about debt, above all in conceptions of social justice.

Economic cultures and ideologies of debt serve to distinguish valid from invalid arguments, virtuous from non-virtuous conduct. They ensure that conceptions of sovereign creditworthiness remain contentious. They help in understanding why thinking about debt continues to be characterized by ambiguity and confusion. In addition, they provide insight into the tense coexistence between intellectual claims to be an 'impersonal moral spectator' of debt and the expression of overt partiality. Not least, they express competing images of what states should do and how. Notions of state virtue are bound up with economic cultures and ideologies of debt. The politics of sovereign creditworthiness is the site of contending representations of state virtue: the dignified state, the ascetic state, the permissive state, the inclusive state, and the protective state.

The principles of justification for the various instruments of statecraft in managing sovereign debt are deeply rooted in economic culture and ideologies of debt and in the images of the state that they carry. Their imprint is accentuated in a context of weak legal enforcement against debtor states. Economic cultures and ideologies of debt share a number of features. They illustrate the partiality and incompleteness of thinking about debt and its susceptibility to dogmatism, hubris, and vanity. Also, their endurance testifies to the tolerance for cognitive dissonance in the face of unfavourable empirical evidence. Economic cultures and ideologies of debt are plagued with contradictions, exposed to contest, and disguise, more or less effectively, self-serving arguments. Given these characteristics, a hegemonic status for a particular economic culture and ideology of debt—as in the euro area—has potentially serious, deleterious implications. It risks fuelling alienation, resentment, and anger on the part of economic cultures that rest on very different values and that share a common monetary space.

Like law, economic cultures and ideologies of debt are not disembodied phenomena, evolving autonomously. The narratives that surround them reflect underlying historical, spatial, and social realities. They are constructed around particular institutional interests. Specificities of space, time, and social and institutional structures help in understanding why particular economic cultures emerge, endure, and fade. They help explain why some experiences and ideas become ascendant and others marginal in shaping the meanings attached to debt. Thinking about sovereign creditworthiness exists within a context of spatial and temporal idiosyncrasies, shared historical memories and identities, and contending interest-based ideologies.

Economic cultures and their distinctive ideologies of debt combine generalizing social norms with idiosyncratic historical legacies. This ambiguous character suggests the value of Aristotle's injunction to proceed on the basis of practical wisdom or prudence when thinking about states and debt. Knowledge of the particular is vital to understanding and working with narratives of sovereign creditworthiness.

Constructing Economic Culture

This context of structural determination evokes an impression that thinking about sovereign creditworthiness is imprisoned within historically conditioned mindsets. In the case of the euro area the dominant mindset seems to reproduce that of the German Bundesbank and its selective construction of German economic culture around historical memory of the 1923 hyperinflation. However, this selective construction—in this case putting the events of 1931–1933 in the shadows—betrays the strategic aspect that gives dynamism to constructions of economic culture. Economic culture serves as a strategic resource (cf. Jabko 2006). From the 1970s the Bundesbank deployed the concept of stability-oriented policy to carve out a central role as guardian of German economic culture. In the 1990s it used the concept of 'stability culture' to justify the 'uploading' of this concept into the design of the euro area and its special role as the guardian of the 'Maastricht constitution'. It was adopted within the political elites, notably by Christian Democrats, to counter sceptics about Economic and Monetary Union (EMU). Later, from 2010, 'stability culture' was to prove central in Bundesbank and federal government legitimating discourse on how best to manage euro area sovereign and banking crises (Howarth and Rommerskirchen 2013).

This strategic dimension in constructing economic culture shows how particular institutions prove successful in crafting and re-crafting a dominant discourse about debt. Historical memory is crafted and used in ways that endow status and prestige on certain elites. In the process it paints a distinctive and recognizable cultural self-portrait of a state and its virtues, as well as an identity that binds together governing elites and the public. A particular image is ascribed to a state and its people, bound up with a dominant notion of shared economic culture and ideology of debt. In the case of creditor states, this image typically distinguishes their elites and people as exceptional in virtue, as possessed of a distinctive dignity and honour. This virtue is expressed in their dedication to a particular type of economic culture and its association with superior governing competence and moral responsibility. The self-portrait of creditor states typically emphasizes discipline with respect to debt, industriousness, frugality in expenditure, honesty in paying taxes and in complying with civic duties, soundness in financial and monetary management, and punctiliousness in honouring contractual obligations.

However, the cultural self-portrait of a state can only bear so much exposure of its illusion and the hypocrisy, vanity, and complacency that it conceals. It has to have a sufficiently close approximation to economic, social, and political experience if it is to remain convincing to the various stakeholders in a state's creditworthiness. The narrative of civic virtues must be plausible enough to induce confidence. Plausibility diminishes once a state deploys policy instruments in ways that put in question its image. For instance, evidence of the spread of rent-seeking, predatory activity by governing elites raises doubts about the image of the virtuous state. A cultural self-portrait as virtuous is difficult to sustain when evidence points to declining state capacity and willingness to pay creditors, when domestic banks become mired in reckless lending and financial malpractice, when its consumers accumulate huge debts to finance hedonistic lifestyles, and when asset price bubbles inflate. For these reasons, by 2011–2012 the sovereign creditworthiness of more and more European states was in question. The image of the euro area as a stability culture lost plausibility.

Economic culture and ideologies of debt matter because narratives about sovereign creditworthiness are a persuasive activity. Elites have to craft narratives and deploy historical memory in ways that foster an image of state virtue. However, virtue is relative to dominant economic culture and ideology of debt. They establish the boundaries of what is judged right and tolerable. The problem that confronts governing elites is how to construct a coherent, integrated narrative and to control that narrative when so many external interests have to be somehow accommodated. The notion of an actor or governing elite who controls the narrative of sovereign creditworthiness appears an illusion.

Economic Culture, Ideologies of Debt, and State Identity: Defining Moments and Historical Memory

Economic culture forms the context within which particular and distinctive sets of attitudes, beliefs, mores, values, and customs relating to credit and debt emerge. It is typically attributed to a state as a mark of its distinctive identity (cf. more broadly Throsby 2001). Thus, above all from the 1970s, Germany was seen as a 'stability culture'. Economic cultures draw selectively on potent and defining historical memories, constructed by influential domestic actors. They are grounded in past critical and painful moments. Unlike Germany, the reference points in Greece and Hungary were not their own past hyperinflations. For Greeks, the most potent reference points in collective memory remained the war for national independence from the Ottoman Empire in the 1820s and its legacy of huge external debts. Later events, like German occupation and brutality in the Second World War and external intervention in the post-1945 civil war, confirmed a powerful national myth of a Greek state that had suffered from foreign intervention. It left a cultural legacy of resentment at victimhood, an economic culture that had strong elements of inward-looking welfare protection, and a self-image of heroic resistance. This legacy shaped how Greeks responded to their post-2009 sovereign debt crisis. For Germans, in contrast, the hyperinflations of 1923 and of the post-1945 periods served as the key reference points in forging historical memory and cultural identity. In contrast, the dramatic financial and economic collapse in 1931, which formed the immediate context of Hitler's rise to power in 1933, had less formative influence on German economic thinking. The emphasis was on the values of stability culture. These wide differences of economic culture are difficult to accommodate within a European monetary union. They are associated with contrasting views about public virtue in managing public finances and debt.

However, the attribution of a single distinctive set of public economic virtues to a state leads readily to illusion. Cultural and ideological fault lines about debt run within, as well as between, states. This phenomenon highlights a problem in analysis of economic culture. Economic culture is a stylized representation of a state, a useful heuristic tool in the hands of governing elites and those who observe them. It serves to reify and even deify the state. In practical terms, narratives about sovereign creditworthiness involve contest about economic cultures and ideologies of debt. This contest reveals domestic as well as international power relationships between dominant and oppressed. It involves evaluations of 'good' and 'bad' economic cultures. Despite their simplistic attribution to states, cultures remain domestically as well as internationally contested. The German centre-Left parties were much less ideologically disposed than the centre-Right to make 'stability culture' a central reference point in debating reforms of the euro area. The domestic contests were much sharper in Greece, Italy, Portugal, and Spain.

Five ideal types of economic culture can be distinguished: the culture of elite magnificence; stability culture; consumer culture; social welfare culture; and welfare protection culture. They differ in the nature and in the range of interests that they encompass and in the motives that shape attitudes to debt. Individual states reflect their presence to different degrees across space and over time. Their cultural configurations are complex and changing. A state may seem to project a coherent image around one type of economic culture and to be identified with a particular ideology of debt. However, detailed examination exposes the underlying realities as more complex, and meanings of debt as more contested, suggestive of the blindness induced by reification of states.

Narratives about economic culture and ideology of debt do not offer a literal record of a state and its society. They express dominant moral beliefs and sensibilities and offer insight into the kind of world with which the collective identity is being associated. They offer insights into how, and why, state identity and social community is being imagined and re-imagined. The economic culture of a state is never as coherent and one-dimensional as a particular narrative might suggest. Greece and Italy have their domestic proponents of stability culture. Sensing the constraints of dominant narratives of economic culture, and their vulnerability to domestic veto politics, they rely on external discipline to anchor and to legitimate change. They challenge a culture of welfare protection, grounded in predatory, rent-seeking activity. Conversely, Germany has attributes of consumer culture and of social welfare culture, within what is seen as a dominant stability culture. The balance of advantage in contests of economic culture is precarious and dynamic. It is not an historical given.

Economic cultures and ideologies of debt have different implications for what is considered appropriate 'sustainable' debt. They map onto different images of the state. Tomz (2007) suggests that sovereign debt markets are central to defining the reputation of states. Reflecting the privileging of creditor power, the image of state virtue is most strongly associated with stability culture. The beneficiaries during the post-2007 crisis were Finland, Germany, the Netherlands, Switzerland, and Norway. Conversely, sustaining an image of state virtue proves more problematic when states are associated with the culture of elite magnificence, consumer culture, social welfare culture, and—most problematic of all—welfare protection culture.

Analysing the particular, dominant economic culture and ideology of debt in a state draws out the distinctive and selective way in which its past formative experiences have been used to shape a shared identity. Relevant negative lesson-drawing may reach back into the more distant past. Thus Dutch narratives about economic culture and debt refer back to the so-called 'Spanish terror' of the sixteenth-century struggle for national independence and the subsequent image of a seventeenth-century 'Golden Age'. The heavy costs of protracted war and high taxes, along with the opportunities and vulnerability that followed from spatial location, formed the basis for an early Dutch attachment to the values of stability culture. In contrast, the German narrative of stability culture is a much more recent, post-1945 phenomenon. Its main development came from the 1970s in the new post-Bretton-Woods world of exchange-rate instability. The Bundesbank used memory of the hyperinflation of 1923 to legitimate an ascendant Ordo-liberalism, which privileged its role as guardian of German stability—and later of euro area stability. Despite these differences in historical anchoring, dominant economic culture in both Germany and the Netherlands was associated with a cautious attitude to debt.

Religion, Economic Culture, and Debt

The process of constructing economic culture out of shared formative and negative experiences draws on and uses varied texts and chronicles, including religious thought and interpretations of tradition. Notable historical reference points in giving meaning to debt have been the teachings of the Swiss John Calvin, the Dutchman Erasmus, and the German Martin Luther, as well as Orthodox and Roman Catholic social teaching. Attitudes to debt have been influenced by efforts to 'moralize materialism', which have been common to Islamic, Orthodox, Protestant, and Roman Catholic societies, as well as to humanist thought. In broad terms, there was a shared focus on the evils of avarice, conspicuous consumption, speculation in 'unsafe' economic activities, imprudent debt, and usury. Religion bequeathed the idea of an impersonal moral spectator as the basis for thinking about economic activity and debt.

However, even in late-medieval and early-modern Europe, when religion was so much more prominent as a moral censor, the precise images and vocabularies of debt differed from city to city and from state to state. Amsterdam, Antwerp, Augsburg, Geneva, Genoa, London, and Venice were united in sharing ambivalence towards capitalism. They expressed it in contrasting ways. Geneva, which—followed by Amsterdam—was in the firmest grip of Calvinism, provided the strongest statements of belief about the moral evils of materialism and debt. Even today, the Netherlands and Switzerland stand out as the epitome of states whose economic cultures and national identities are most deeply historically associated with the moral principles and values of stability culture.

At the same time, caution is needed in following Max Weber's classic thesis which attributes the values of stability culture to the Protestant ethic. In the Pre-Reformation period the economic activities of the Catholic order of Cistercian monastic foundations, as well as those of the Cluny Order, helped spread similar values of hard work, modesty in consumption, and thrift across the European regions in which they had a powerful presence. They seem to have left enduring regional and local imprints, reflected in differences of productivity and employment rates (Andersen, Bentzen, Dalgaard, and Sharp 2013). Moreover, in the Holy Roman Empire during the same period, there is little empirical evidence of differentiation in types of economic values between Catholic and Protestant German cities and regions (Cantoni 2013). In short, stability culture does not seem a distinctly Protestant attribute.

Types of Ideology of Debt: Bad and Good Debt

Economic culture endows debt with different symbolic meanings, which form the context within which ideologies of debt evolve. Ideologies of debt can be grouped into two broad types. One type represents debt as shameful and potentially poisonous to virtue, personal and collective. It provides an inducement to profligacy and to the erosion of discipline and moral responsibility. As Chapter 6 showed, theology played a key role in sustaining a moral paternalism in attitudes to debt. It took two forms. Theology could serve as an impersonal and disinterested moral spectator that arbitrates right and wrong conduct in matters of credit and debt. It could also act as an interest that, at least in principle (perhaps not in practice), stands outside the creditor-debtor nexus, and that therefore is also ideological.

This ambivalence at the heart of moral paternalism towards debt was apparent in constructions of stability culture in the Netherlands, Germany, and Switzerland. At the heart of the argument that debt risked moral hazard and intergenerational injustice was not just the protection of the interests of creditors and of future generations of taxpayers from the burden of servicing and amortizing public debts amassed by past and present generations. Stability culture also rested on the belief that an impersonal moral spectator was required. Central banks, like the German Bundesbank, came to institutionalize this belief, which in turn served to deify their role as guardians of state virtue. The outcome was a strictly, tightly conceived conception of sovereign creditworthiness, one that was exported into the design of the euro area.

The second type of ideology of debt values it for its productive use in endowing public spaces with splendour and dignity, as well as in creating jobs, raising living standards, promoting social mobility, and improving the quality of life. It is seen as benefitting future generations as well as the present generation. This construction of debt as morally neutral or as personally or socially beneficial is grounded in four main types of economic culture: the culture of elite magnificence, consumer culture, social welfare culture, and welfare protection culture. Each type of economic culture was constructed by and around certain distinctive political and institutional interests. Thus European social liberalism and social democracy drove the ideological process of associating debt with social justice and solidarity. Marketing, retail, and property-related interests promoted the association of debt with gaining social status and pleasure through consumption. Powerful patron-client interests across the porous boundaries of state and society fashioned different attitudes to debt, seeing it as a motor of social advancement and a provider of welfare protection.

The Elite-Driven Culture of Magnificence: The Dignified State

In European history constructing the legitimacy of personal rule—whether imperial, monarchical, princely, or priestly—has characteristically been associated with demonstrating the capacity to finance a culture of elite magnificence. Legitimacy is bound up with celebration of the dignity, glory, godliness, as well as the superior taste and wisdom, of a select person or elite. In medieval Europe this elite culture expressed the special rights that attached to hierarchical position in 'the great chain of being'. Elites gained ready access to credit from the collateral provided by possession of property, above all land, and by holding office. Financiers could also be induced by the offer of various commercial and financial privileges by ruling elites.

The culture of elite magnificence is typically associated with authoritarian and charismatic rule. Its attributes can be traced variously in Imperial Rome, the Byzantine Empire, the Renaissance Papacy, First and Second Empire France, and the German Third Reich. It values lavish public expenditure for noble purposes, which include the self-glorification, dignity, and honour of the ruler and the governing and social elites and the promotion of the grandeur and prestige of the state. Debt is invested with positive attributes. It serves to promote the legitimacy of elite rule by securing the admiration and awe of the public, capturing its imagination. In this way it simultaneously helps in keeping creditors respectful and at a distance. Sovereign debt is seen as a special case of private debt. It is special in that the borrower is uniquely powerful and enjoys a superior social status. Debt is a personal service that bestows honour on the creditor. It expresses the special grandeur that attaches to rule.

The new dynamism that this type of economic culture and its characteristic ideology of debt gained from the late twelfth century had its origins in the commercial and governing elites of the wealthy city states of north and central Italy. The so-called Renaissance was closely linked with their merchant-financier interests. Italian merchant-financiers benefitted from the strategic good fortune of their spatial location at the heart of the great trade routes from the East that fed into central and northern Europe. The huge trade surpluses of Florence, Genoa, Lucca and, above all, Venice were ploughed into capital exports. The development of cross-national banking activity became a source of huge, if potentially volatile, external financial income. It could also be converted to domestic use in consolidating the political power of the governing elites of these city states.

The Italian city states had not been bled fiscally dry, like England and France by the so-called Hundred Years' War (1337–1453). Though this war caused substantial losses to two leading Florentine banking houses, strategic location helped Florence to make an early recovery. Hence in central and northern Italy the enormous profits that were yielded by trade expansion meant that financing lavish expenditure on magnificence could be reconciled with sustainable debts. This advantage endured as long as its city states were free from costly wars and foreign invasions. In the fifteenth century per capita income in Venice was vastly higher than in the territorial states. Despite its much smaller size, Venetian fiscal revenues were almost as great as those of England and France and exceeded those of the Spanish kingdoms (Braudel 1984: 119–23). In this benign context, the Italian city states gave birth to the model of the Renaissance court.

The centre of gravity in the process of constructing and emulating this culture of elite magnificence shifted over time between Florence, Genoa, Milan, Naples, Rome, and Venice. The ambition to re-establish Rome as the 'head of the world' (*caput mundi*) drew the Renaissance Papacy into the promotion of this type of elite culture. It resulted in an explosion of Papal debts. Perhaps more importantly in the longer term, this model was emulated by the royal courts in the big territorial states. Examples included the England of Henry VIII, the Burgundy of Duke Philip the Fair, the France of Francis I, and Hapsburg Spain. In the fourteenth and fifteenth centuries it found brief, but influential, expression in the magnificence of the court of Burgundy. Its magnificence derived mostly from the riches of the Flemish cities of Antwerp, Bruges, and Ghent. Luccan and Florentine banks played a key role in constructing and disseminating this type of economic culture. They lent on a large and active scale to English kings and later Popes. Later, in the seventeenth century, Genoese bankers acted as financiers for French and, above all, Spanish Hapsburg kings.

The narrative that grew up to support this culture of elite magnificence drew its inspiration from Classical sources, Athens and Rome in particular. Its authors looked back to Roman ideas of grandeur and to the ambitious civic building programme of Athens at the time of Pericles (*c*.495–429 BC). In his *History of the Peloponnesian War* (Book Two, 41), Thucydides pointed out that this programme, including the Parthenon, began once the Treasury of the Delian League had been transferred to Athens in *c*.454 BC. These Classical examples were taken as models of how to create an image of the virtues and the magnificence of the ruler. They could provide city states like Florence and Venice with moral distinctiveness, grandeur, and dignity. Lavish expenditure was justified as increasing the 'estate, honour, dignity, and renown' of monarchs and republics.

This narrative was legitimated by reference to the Classical theory of magnificence or 'greatness of soul' of the 'superior man', as outlined in Aristotle's fourth book of the *Ethics* and his sixth book of the *Politics*. It justified generosity, liberality, 'magnificence in spending', and the superiority of taste in great public matters as virtues distinctive to the wealthy elite. In the words of Aristotle (*The Ethics*, Book Four, Chapter Two), 'there is something paltry about exact book-keeping'. Exact book-keeping is the activity of 'the shabby man'.

The elite-driven image of magnificence materialized in costly and impressive palace complexes, grandiose squares, monumental cathedrals and churches, exquisite baptisteries, commemorative tombs and monuments, impressive towers, noble civic and guild buildings, exuberant court ceremony and pageantry, and opulent decoration. It was designed to celebrate the virtues of the ruler, city, or state but on terms that marked out certain individuals as exceptional in virtue. Cultivating this image came to depend on secure debt financing. In turn, this dependency created new opportunities for consolidating oligarchic power, mainly through annuity financing in the city states, and for merchant-financiers to gain commercial privileges.

The culture of elite magnificence involved a symbiosis of virtue, lavish expenditure, and a tolerant attitude to debt. It also rested on the foundation of patronage, which served to consolidate dynastic rule when, as often, it rested on fragile social and political foundations. Patronage was a technique for building alliances and for instilling dependencies. It helped rulers to create a reputation for virtue through their generosity in helping embellish and glorify their cities, in supporting religious orders, and in binding artistic and intellectual brilliance to this purpose.

Lavish expenditure and an emollient attitude to debt expressed not just a politics of power and prestige but also social and political status. The culture of elite magnificence found expression in a new European social model of courtly conduct, again Italian in origin. This social model emphasized the cultivated person of refined manners, elegant dress, and cultural accomplishments. It was emulated not just by other rulers and governing elites but also by aristocrats. Also, wealthy private individuals aspired to the superior status of gentleman. Thus the culture of elite magnificence was also promoted by aristocratic, communal, and guild patronage. They competed in setting new and more expensive standards of aesthetic taste.

Defining in this way the distinctiveness of rule, and projecting an image of bold confidence, helped attach key elite power centres in society to dynastic or republican rule and thus to promote social and political stability. The ruler or oligarchy was represented as civic-minded, as the paternal steward of the common good, as pious and Christian, as connoisseur and patron of the arts and intellectual life, as an ardent lover of the virtues, and as possessed of honour. Lavish expenditure aimed to promote confidence and reputation by the admiration and awe that it inspired. It was seen as a means of constructing creditworthiness and inducing lenders to compete to be associated with grandeur and magnificence.

By the eighteenth century the French court was firmly established as the centre from which this image of courtly grandeur and magnificence was disseminated. Imitations of the Versailles palace sprang up all over Europe, from Stockholm to Caserta, from Hampton Court to Peterhof. However, France, as well as many states that emulated her, exhibited the illusion to which this type of economic culture and ideology of debt is prey. They succumbed to problems of creditworthiness as it became clear that their cultures of elite magnificence lacked the solid foundations of creditor-state status. They differed from Imperial Athens and Rome and from the smaller Italian city states at their height. As early as the seventeenth century the French monarchy under the 'Sun King' Louis XIV was heavily indebted to Dutch bankers. Later, in 1788, French debt default deeply damaged them. In the interim the French monarchy had endured the acute financial crisis associated with John Law's experiment.

The problem with this culture of elite magnificence and embellishment was its partiality and incompleteness. It risked forgetting Aristotle's strictures against prodigality and living beyond one's means. Competitive emulation in lavish expenditure induced illusion and its associated negative characteristics of complacency, hubris, and vanity. States that became associated with this type of culture were in danger of forfeiting creditworthiness. The problems of illusion, partiality, and incompleteness manifested themselves in various ways. First, the culture of elite magnificence evolved easily into an imperial style. This process was exemplified in the displacement of Classical Roman republican values by more authoritarian attitudes to dynastic rule. Dynastic ambitions and personal vanity of successive Roman Emperors led to territorial aggrandizement and costly wars. For the same reasons, they cultivated a popular culture of 'bread and circuses'. The debasements of the silver *denarius* reflected the fiscal illusions to which the culture of elite magnificence gave rise. Cultures of elite magnificence had a fatal proclivity to rot from within.

Secondly, this type of elite culture was difficult to reconcile with changing economic, social, and political realities and a more commercial and market-focused society. It fitted uneasily with the new aspirations of self-made wealth, of emerging professional groups, and of a growing employee class. The social interests on which this type of elite culture rested either conceded legitimacy by embracing these new social groups or lost legitimacy in trying to resist them.

Thirdly, the culture of elite magnificence depended for its credibility and viability on retention of creditor-state power. This status could be lost not just through the effects of wars but also through structural historical shifts in world economic power. The gradual, post-fifteenth-century shift from the eastern trade routes towards exploiting the riches of the Atlantic economy created a context in which the city states of north and central Italy began to drift into the illusion of creditworthiness. By the seventeenth century Florence, Genoa, and Venice had begun to lose creditor-power status to Antwerp, Amsterdam, and, to a lesser extent, London. Neither France nor Spain nor Russia matched their opulent courtly cultures of elite magnificence to their underlying macroeconomic realities. As the French *ancien régime* showed, lavish expenditure implied harsh fiscal burdens and strains once gross domestic product (GDP) growth stagnated or declined.

Despite these illusions and the problems to which they gave rise, the model of a culture of elite magnificence retained a powerful hold on European minds. In this sense it remained real. Politically, as post-1789 France illustrated, notably under the legacy of the two Napoleonic Empires, the notion of the republican state proved hospitable to an image of grandeur. Representations of nation and state could be fused in the heroic ideal of public power, which was symbolized in lavish expenditure on public works (*grands projets*). Public works expressed belief in the will and capability of the state, embodying the nation, to take charge of its own destiny. This notion of the state as earning sovereign creditworthiness by its boldness and self-confidence remained a central tenet of French political thinking. In terms of attitudes to public finances, the culture of elite magnificence was associated with a preference for the 'debt state' over the 'tax state'. In addition, the dignified state had its parallel in the wider cultural significance that was attached to 'luxury'. Mirroring Bernard Mandeville, luxury was celebrated as a source of public benefit (Goldsmith 1985). It also functioned as a sign of social status. In short, debt had a functional character.

Stability Culture: The Ascetic State

> The difference between these Lands (and other states) is most singular; glory in other lands reposing in an outward show of flags but here in the manner of thrifty and modest households; elsewhere there is honour in the free spending of money... here there is honour in having no debts.
>
> Romeyn de Hooghe (1706). *Spiegel van Staat der Vereenigde Nederlanden* (Mirror of the State of the United Netherlands), quoted in Schama (1987: 53)

In contrast, stability culture served the interests of a broader set of elite social interests, comprising self-made and inherited wealth. Historically, its origins were associated with oligarchic structures of rule that excluded, or marginalized, the higher nobility and clergy. It generated an ideology of debt that defined the notion of 'sustainable' debt narrowly. Lavish expenditure was seen as ostentatious, vulgar, and wasteful. Debt service was represented as a problem of inter-temporal burden-shifting between present and future taxpayers. It raised issues of intergenerational justice.

Rentiers were central to this culture. They associated debt with moral hazard, abhorred sovereign debt default, and had a high tolerance for short-term welfare costs, borne by wider society, to ensure that sovereign debts were honoured. The characteristic ideology of debt was grounded in the interests of creditors and the sanctity of contract. It stressed the similarity between the virtuous household, which was thrifty and hardworking, and the virtuous state, which guarantees orderly finance through balanced budgets. This type of economic culture and its conception of state virtue are ascetic in nature.

The United Provinces of the Netherlands served as a key historical model. In the wake of the protracted and hugely costly Spanish wars that brought independence, the Dutch constructed a newly confident sense of the distinctiveness of their economic culture. They fashioned an image that was to find support and emulation across Europe. The basis was provided by the emergence of the United Provinces as the dominant creditor power of Europe during the seventeenth century. Its dominance was based on its huge trade surpluses and its borrowing of a range of financial practices that had been pioneered in the banks of the Italian city states of Florence, Genoa, and Venice, like bills of exchange, commercial loans, and various credit notes. Amsterdam overtook Genoa as the centre of European finance. By the eighteenth century its banks financed most of the states of Europe, including the Holy Roman Emperor, the French king, the Danish and the Swedish kings, the electors of Bavaria and of Saxony, Catherine II of Russia, as well as the newly independent states of America. Through their new forms of acceptance trade and bills of exchange, Amsterdam bankers financed the leading merchants and trade across Europe. Dutch credit powered the European economy well into the eighteenth century (Braudel 1984: 235–76).

The evolution of Dutch economic culture within this context offers an insight into how, and in what form, Dutch and foreign writers sought to create an image appropriate to this new and powerful creditor state and its people. The image that was projected by de Hooghe, in the quotation at the start of this section, exemplifies a much broader social and intellectual elite process of constructing a new sense of an inclusive Dutch identity, in which its commercially-minded people could recognize itself. It involved invention of a tradition out of historical chronicles and out of ideas drawn from a native humanism and from Calvinist thought. The process of constructing Dutch economic culture and identity reflected the birth of a sense of shared identity out of historic experience and geographic vulnerability. It took place against the background of the brutal and protracted eighty-year-long Spanish wars and the high costs, above all in taxation, of providing security.

The Dutch model of economic culture was founded on opposition to the royal courtly Renaissance cultures of sixteenth- and seventeenth-century Europe. This opposition focused on their profligate dynastic ambitions, their fiscal tyranny and waste, and their prodigious and wasteful extravagance. The rise of royal courtly cultures and the rigidly stratified social hierarchy around them, above all in France and Spain, were represented by the Dutch as the triumph of leisure and status over hard work and duty. Dutch economic culture came to be defined by reference to common virtuous habits of industriousness and thrift. The reference point was not, in the first instance, economic theory or the notion of the Dutch person as 'economic man'. It was the presumed virtues of the Dutch citizen and his state and the moral obligations that accompany prosperity.

This underlying moral character in Dutch economic culture, and the emotions in which it was expressed, drew inspiration from the Roman Catholic humanism of Desiderius Erasmus, from Calvinism and the Reformed Church, and from the way in which Hugo Grotius celebrated the connection between property and natural sociability. The resemblance to Calvinist Geneva was illustrated in a religious ordinance of 1581 which excluded bankers from communion—alongside actors, brothel keepers, jugglers, and pawnbrokers (Schama 1987: 330). In addition, merchants faced religious censure and potential sanctions for their failure to honour the terms of a loan, for asking for excessive interest (Calvin doubted that rates over 5 per cent were lawful), for the deliberate incurring of ruinous debt, and for the debasement of coin with lead or tin. Such activity was deemed a cardinal commercial sin by the Reformed Church, which in the formative years of the Republic had its own mechanisms of discipline. On the other hand, lending to public institutions at low rates of interest and on long terms was deemed meritorious.

However, as Schama (1987: 330) emphasizes, the beliefs at the heart of Dutch economic culture induced illusion. They lived in an uneasy relationship to a social reality of conspicuous consumption and the enjoyment of luxury goods and worldly pleasures. Mandeville laid bare the hypocrisy (Goldsmith 1985). Prevailing beliefs also sat awkwardly alongside the reckless speculation that was associated with the Amsterdam Bourse and the tulip mania of 1636–1637. The image of the debt-avoiding Dutch was as much a source of personal anxiety and discomfort about hypocrisy and vanity as a source of consolation. It proved morally difficult to reconcile the cunning required to do well in commercial transactions with the dictates of conscience. The Dutch struggled with difficult 'internal dialogues', prompting a sense of shame, even remorse, as weaknesses of character were exposed. To add to these problems, the oligarchic nature of Dutch governance generated an attraction to emulating the model of the dignified state with its culture of elite magnificence.

The Dutch model of economic culture had its critics like Mandeville, who highlighted the hypocrisy and vanity. However, by the eighteenth century it enjoyed enormous prestige. It was carried by Dutch merchants and financiers across Europe. Calvinism spread similar ideas to Scotland, exemplified in the strongly moral dimension of Scottish Enlightenment political economy and its aversion to debt financing. Dutch ideas had similar resonance within German merchant-cities. The aspirations of this German merchant class were brilliantly captured in Gustav Freytag's popular *Soll und Haben* (Debit and Credit) (1855). Freytag celebrated double-entry book-keeping as the sacred text of the German middle-class household. The book-keeper was 'crowned as secret minister of the household…in lonely majesty' (1855: 60). Accounting was praised as providing the principle of objectivity.

Nevertheless, the virtues of stability culture had a less tenacious grip on German public thinking, reflecting the more precarious social and political position of the German middle classes than their Dutch equivalents. Competition for courtly magnificence remained an enduring theme in nineteenth-century Germany. It went along with a focus of German economic thinking on the state as an instrument for mobilizing credit in the service of industrial development. The emphasis was on productive investment in efficient resource extraction, transport infrastructure, and basic industries.

Two defining historical moments helped to inspire German consciousness of the economic, social, and political perils of debt and inflation. These perils were brilliantly outlined in Johann Wolfgang von Goethe's *Faust Part II* (1831). He celebrated the virtues of the ascetic state. As former finance minister at the Court of Weimar, Goethe was very familiar with the hardships that had followed the several currency debasements associated with the wars of Frederick the Great of Prussia. He also drew on his memory of the disastrous French experiment with the *assignats*. Goethe pictured a 'sick' Holy Roman Emperor and court being offered a cure by Mephistopheles, court fool and devil. Mephistopheles suggests that the gold beneath his lands be used as collateral for promissory notes to pay his army, restore order, and return to a life dedicated to pleasure. The temptation to print paper money without restraint leads to hyperinflation and civil chaos. Goethe saw in fiat currency a modern form of alchemy, offering a fatal inducement to tackle debt by creating value from illusion (Krennbauer 1949). Strikingly, in 2012 the president of the German Bundesbank, Jens Weidmann, drew on Goethe's Mephistopheles to underline his fears that the European Central Bank (ECB) was committing to a strategy of printing money without restraint.

However, support for stability culture and the ascetic state did not thrive in a Germany of courtly competition to excel in magnificence. The collapse of this Germany in 1918–1919 left an immediate vacuum in which no single model of economic culture was able to gain clear dominance as the basis for a solid national consensus. It provided the context within which the hyperinflation of 1923 poisoned attitudes to the infant Weimar Republic and within which catastrophic financial and economic collapse in 1931–1933 led to the ascent of a hubristic National Socialism and catastrophic war.

The intellectual basis for constructing post-1945 German stability culture derived from the principles of Ordo-liberalism, which in turn were founded on an analysis of the causes of the German catastrophe in the 1920s–1930s. In the Ordo-liberal view, the function of the virtuous state was to provide the public goods of price stability and competitive markets. The virtuous state was a strong state that based sustainable economic growth on fiscal balance and consolidation and on structural reforms to make product, service, capital, and labour markets competitive. Stability culture was understood within German Ordo-liberal economics as a strict, rule-based approach to sound public finance, with quasi-automatic sanctions for non-compliance. In terms of public finances, Ordo-liberalism exhibited a preference for the 'tax state' over the 'debt state'.

The key institutional author of German stability culture was the Bundesbank, which privileged Ordo-liberal economists in its recruitment and promotions. The main turning point came in the 1970s after the collapse of the Bretton Woods system, which had provided the public good of economic stability, and the oil crises which fuelled inflation. The Bundesbank used Ordo-liberal principles to carve out the privileged role for itself as the guardian of German economic culture. Above all, it drew selectively on the 1923 hyperinflation to provide this cultural model with legitimacy on the basis of historical memory. Stability became a key element in the slow process of new post-war German identity building. In the process the Bundesbank attained enormous status and power within Germany.

European monetary integration served as a vehicle through which this German model of economic culture was exported to the EU. Through the role of the D-Mark as the anchor of the Exchange-Rate Mechanism, the Bundesbank gained the reputation of being 'the bank that rules Europe'. The Maastricht 'constitution' for EMU was designed around Bundesbank principles of strict central bank independence, dedicated to a narrow mandate of price stability, and the separation of monetary policy from fiscal policies. The ECB was born as the Bundesbank 'writ large'. The Bundesbank redefined its role as the guardian of European stability culture.

German attitudes to sovereign debts in the euro area stressed Member-State solidarity in the sense of reliably meeting their fiscal commitments and pursuing structural reforms to enable smooth domestic economic adjustments to imbalances. In this view, establishing reputation as a virtuous Member State rested on a slow, painful 'bottom-up' process. Individual Member States had to demonstrate their reliability by word and by deed. The post-2007 banking and sovereign debt crises exposed the illusory nature of these beliefs. The effects of persistent non-compliance with rules on sustainable debt served to undermine German trust in the euro area as effectively designed to anchor stability culture within Europe. They looked to a model of European fiscal union, based on stricter rules embodied in the fiscal compact treaty.

The problem in seeking to extend stability culture as the organizing framework for European economic and monetary union rested in its partiality and incompleteness. It induced illusion and its counterparts of complacency, hubris, and vanity. First, subscribing to the values of stability culture involved aesthetic as well as moral judgement. Quite simply, the ascetic character of an impersonal moral spectator of fiscal and economic virtue was not to everyone's taste. Toleration could turn to doubts, anger, and rejection when the policy outcomes involved major sacrifice of living standards, quality of life, and hopes for the future. The virtues of the ascetic state are not necessarily more compelling than those of others, like the dignified state, the permissive state, the inclusive state, or even—for some—the protective state. They also raise the question of whether the proper virtues of the household are those of the state. From Aristotle to Keynes, this association has been challenged.

Secondly, the fiscal consolidation and structural reforms that are advocated by proponents of stability culture encounter the contrary empirical claims of those supporting the inclusive state of social welfare culture. These claims question fiscal 'austerity', which is a favoured term of neo-Keynesians and distinguishes them from Ordo-liberals. They point to risks of a self-defeating debt-deflation spiral, in which economic activity declines and debt burdens grow or remain the same. In conjunction with private-sector deleverage, fiscal consolidation leads to falling or negative growth through 'fiscal multipliers', worsens fiscal balances, and locks in problems of sovereign creditworthiness. Other than in the benign contexts of international economic expansion and confidence, and of healthy private-sector balances, the fiscal and structural reform remedies of stability culture risk becoming self-defeating.

Consumer Culture: The Permissive State

Like stability culture, consumer culture was the offspring of a more commercial, market-oriented society. However, its characteristic ideology of debt focused less on wealth producers and inheritors and more on consumption as the measure of social status and belonging. Consumer culture exhibited 'commodity fetishism'. It celebrated the hedonistic life style and induced high levels of personal debt. The drivers included financial institutions, which 'pushed' debt through the creation and promotion of new financial products; individuals, who 'pulled' debt; and retail, advertising, and media industries, which promoted the attractions of the hedonistic life style. State revenues and fiscal balances benefitted, in turn, from the economic activity that was generated by a household economy of high, consumption-fuelled debt. Correspondingly, governing elites evolved self-interest in indulging this process through the liberalization of credit markets and insolvency law and through the tax subsidy of debt. The state's virtue was seen to lie in its permissive character. Given the broad systemic nature of this shift towards consumer culture, and the powerful economic, financial, and media interests bound up with it, all states—creditor as well as debtor—became impregnated with its values.

Stability culture represented a sharp contrast not just with the culture of elite magnificence but also with consumer culture. Strikingly, Berger (1972) argued that the traditional values of the culture of elite magnificence filtered down into the visual imagery of affluent consumer culture. Its function was to lend authority and dignity to this new culture. Retail and promotional sectors celebrated luxury consumption as a sign of status. Consumer culture thrived on the appetites awakened by continual, if often dubiously significant, improvements in the quality of goods, as well as by the seductions of advertising and the exploitation of celebrity role models as consumer models. Heightened awareness of relative deprivation in a media- and image-saturated world served as an incentive to acquire more. In the face of stagnating incomes relative to these consumption opportunities, individuals compensated by taking on higher debt burdens. Consumer culture helped drive and sustain an economy of high household debt.

The problem of personal debt accumulation was aggravated by economic recession and structural adjustment. Individuals faced the falling real value of pensions and social benefits, consequent on fiscal austerity, as well as falling real wages in more open, competitive labour markets and as a consequence of competition from new, lower-cost producers in emerging markets. The challenge of maintaining living standards in a consumer culture drove individuals to pay-day loan companies and 'loan sharks' in increasing numbers.

The state was caught up in this process, above all by the incentive of politicians to pacify electorates, by the power of advertisers and retail giants, and by saturation of the media with consumption images. State permissiveness took the form of banking and credit liberalization and tax privileging of debt. Financial institutions responded with generous and often lax credit provision. They also mis-sold complex and poorly understood financial products. Consumer culture rested on high levels of financial illiteracy amongst consumers, who gave priority to short-term gratification through debt financing over longer-term financial sustainability. A whole edifice of mutually interacting institutions supported this debt-financed consumer culture. They included banks, credit card companies, retail giants, property developers, construction companies, travel companies, media companies, and at their heart advertising and marketing. This structure of 'creative' industries became the major source of employment creation as the twentieth century progressed. Financial services, the retail sector, and marketing evolved whole new specialized languages of product and service promotion that rested on selling the idea of easy credit.

Credit-based booms based on household debt were tolerated by democratic governments in order to please potential voters, with little inducement to attend to the morality of debt. The amplitude of credit booms and busts was accentuated by the growth and spread of economic affluence, the proliferation of channels for mass and segmented communication, and their reliance on advertising finance. In this new commercialized world, the language and ideas of marketing became a central part of everyday discourse: branding, profile, customer focus, penetration. Marketing emerged as a lynchpin of the so-called 'creative industries'. They shared a vested commercial interest in promoting hedonistic consumption and the values of personal display and sensory pleasure. The creative industries were saturated with artistic references to wealth and the opulent life style (Migone 2007). In the age of mass and segmented audiences, and of self-advertising through the Internet, consumption created social status for an increasing range of beneficiaries. The interests within the creative industries identified with the hedonistic life style and subscribed to a value system that was relatively relaxed about personal debt, judging it morally neutral (depending on how credit was used) or socially beneficial. So powerful was the discourse of marketing that it migrated into the public sector where the notion of consumer choice took root.

The problems at the heart of this permissive ideology of consumer debt reflected its high degree of vulnerability to illusion and thus to complacency, hubris, and vanity. It marginalized the public good of financial stability in favour of the public good of price stability, which more directly suited the interests of consumers. The processes at work in affluent consumer culture were underwritten by indulgent governments. They involved heightened risk to personal balance sheets. They created incentives for banks to relax lending standards, exploit financial illiteracy, and mis-sell their products. In consequence, banks became overleveraged, accumulated toxic assets, and put at risk their own creditworthiness. The outcome was a systemic bias to asset-price booms and busts, with subsequent loading of private-sector liabilities onto public balance sheets. The collapse of the sub-prime mortgage market in the United States in 2007, and the subsequent British, Irish, and Spanish banking crises, illustrated the scale of the risks. Consumer culture was saturated with moral hazard. In addition, consumer culture privileged private affluence at the expense of creating public squalor. Longer-term investment in public infrastructure and in building inclusive forms of social capital took second place to more immediate individual consumer gratification. It was inimical to belief in the virtues of the entrepreneurial state supporting bold and high-risk innovation (cf. Mazzucato 2013).

Nevertheless, there were discernible variations in the ways in which consumer culture expressed itself across Europe. In Britain, Ireland, and Spain the interaction between celebration of consumer culture and high household debt, and risks to bank solvency, were graphically illustrated in the post-20007 crisis. Conversely, French, German, and Italian consumers and banks proved, on the whole, more cautious. Their households showed a stronger inclination to save and to avoid debt financing. These differences reflected different attitudes to personal debt. They also revealed a high social valuation of the household family unit, notably in Italy. Moreover, high value was attached to supporting businesses that were based on family units and that relied on retained profits for investment. Not least, the inheritance of the state tradition of independent public authority, dedicated to the public interest, acted as an ideational counterweight to the commercial and financial interests promoting consumer culture (Dyson 2010). Public regulation of social and economic space retained higher social acceptance in some parts of Europe than others.

Social Welfare Culture: The Inclusive State

The rise of the economic culture of social welfare was associated with progressive extension of the electoral franchise and with reactions to the social inequalities and suffering that accompanied rapid agricultural restructuring, industrialization, and urbanization. It was manifested in the rise of social democratic parties and the trade-union movement and by growing aspirations to share in social mobility. Social liberal and social democratic thought focused on the ethical state in conceptions that married classical political ideas of virtue to the new role of the state in promoting social, economic, and cultural, as well as political, inclusion. The reference point became social need rather than personal wants. Its centre of gravity was provided by a notion of social justice that stressed equality of individual moral worth and of opportunity.

Social welfare culture associated debt with social justice, understood as satisfying welfare needs of the population, for instance in education, health, social care, and pensions. Its characteristic ideology of debt justified high public expenditure as essential to the promotion of social peace and solidarity and to strengthening long-term growth potential. Borrowing was justified as a means of ensuring that rich creditors helped to finance state activities of benefit to those with lower incomes and less wealth. Debt service was understood as a transfer payment between bondholders and future taxpayers, rather than inter-temporal burden-shifting between present and future taxpayers. In this conception future generations benefitted from current debt financing through a developmental role for the state in supporting fundamental innovations that were high cost and uncertain and whose fruits lay far in the future (Mazzucato 2013). The state was expected to be inclusive, to balance the interests of creditors with the interests of the poor and vulnerable, and to invest in an infrastructure that encouraged social mobility and future prosperity. This ideology of debt reflected a broad range of social interests, including public employees. In terms of public finances, it exhibited equal preference for the 'tax state' and the 'debt state', as long as they were redistributive in outcome. Social welfare culture was by no means averse to fiscal rules. However, it favoured discretion in their use both for macroeconomic stabilization and for redistributive purposes. The revised Stability and Growth Pact of the EU in 2005 represented a cultural and ideological shift in this direction, away from stability culture.

The Nordic States were the key exemplars of social welfare culture. They combined high taxes and high public expenditure with sound reputations as creditworthy. Keynes (1923) was the seminal figure in the development of its characteristic ideology of debt. He argued that balancing the interests of creditors, employers, and employees was essential in order to avert the risk of becoming captured by the vested interests of creditors. This argument was formulated against the background of post-1918 reparations and inter-Allied war debts. In times of post-1945 crises, Keynesian thought evolved to justify the superiority of neo-corporatist institutional mechanisms, like social pacts, to achieve greater inclusiveness in managing public finances. In addition, Keynes formulated the 'paradox of thrift'. He showed how simultaneous deleverage by households, banks, firms, and governments led to the collapse of aggregate demand and a self-reinforcing debt-deflation spiral. The influence of this argument was seen in opposition within Anglo-American economics to the use of 'austerity' to tackle European sovereign debt problems after 2008. Not least, Keynes used arguments about inclusiveness to propose that adjustment to excessive external imbalances should be borne by creditor as well as debtor states. Social welfare depended on supportive, well-resourced international institutions that would monitor this mutual adjustment. Again, Keynes was seeking to limit creditor power and an excessive reliance on cuts in real wages and social benefits.

A powerful network of interests came to enjoy a vested interest in the social welfare culture and the inclusive state. They included the wide range of beneficiaries from public education, health, pensions, and social care, as well as from employment, labour-market, and environmental policies. Public employees, like teachers, and beneficiaries of state spending provided a formidable constituency of political support that governments could not afford to ignore. This constituency was domestically strong in the Nordic States, France, and Hungary and helped frame the nature of policy and political debates about public finances and debt.

However, social welfare culture, and the ideology of debt that it spawned, harboured its own vulnerabilities to illusion and to complacency, hubris, and vanity. Like other economic cultures, it was characterized by partiality and incompleteness. First, the inclusive state risked creating and becoming captured by rent-seeking activities, in the process losing legitimacy. Social welfare culture could mutate into a welfare protection culture. Secondly, its characteristic ideology of debt focused on the productive use of public debt as a motor of social mobility, innovation, productivity improvement, job creation, and higher living standards. However, this type of ideology faced discredit when evidence associated debt financing with socially wasteful 'vanity' public investment projects that proved cost-ineffective. Thirdly, social welfare culture risked contamination from association with unsustainable debts and lack of intergenerational equity. The state risked becoming identified with moral sentiments of guilt and shame about its debts. By the early twenty-first century a deep-seated tension had emerged between these three challenges to social welfare culture and the powerful structure of interests on which it rested. This tension played a key role in the ongoing crisis of the 'debt state' in the early twenty-first century. Europe faced heightened risks from widespread social unrest, protest, and explosion.

Welfare Protection Culture: The State as Shelter

Welfare protection culture is grounded in the interests of powerful patrons and their clients and justifies the power of these patrons. Their power depends on their capacity to safeguard personal entitlements, through selective tax concessions, restrictions on market access, labour-market regulation, and access to contracts, jobs, and housing. The virtue of the state resides in providing a shelter for this rent-seeking activity, by means of which elites protect their own. Correspondingly, the ideology of debt views public debt in highly accommodating terms. It promotes opacity, gimmickry, and manipulation in public finance statistics. It also takes a sanguine view of debt restructuring and default. In terms of public finances, this type of culture displays a marked preference for the 'debt state' over the 'tax state'.

The culture of elite magnificence and the stability culture were very much the product of states like the north Italian cities, the United Provinces of the Netherlands, and

Germany. They occupied positions at the core of the European and world economies. Even if geographically small, and even if for limited time, they mastered European and world trade and finances and gave rise to cultural models and debt ideologies that were widely admired and emulated. Their characteristic economic cultures and debt ideologies reflected the interests of creditor states. They were the self-assigned signs of the exceptionality and moral worth of the state and its people. Whilst the two cultures and their ideologies differ, they helped define sainthood in the informal hierarchy of European states.

In contrast, the culture of welfare protection came to be associated with the south European 'arc of default'. It was an attribute of the European periphery, of states that identified themselves as victims of exploitation by neo-colonial creditors. This sense of victimhood was associated with an attitude of detachment or alienation from a threatening world of asymmetric power. The culture of welfare protection was a phenomenon of debtor states on the periphery, like Greece, Russia, and many post-communist states. They shared a history of large and/or serial debt defaulting and restructuring. It was a defining feature of *caciquismo* in post-Restoration Spain (1875–1920), the Franco period and beyond, notably in Galicia (Kern 1966). Welfare protection culture characterized the Kingdom of Naples and unified Italy's first republic from 1860, as well as the post-1945 second republic (Allum 1977). It was entrenched in post-independence Greece after 1821 (Featherstone and Papadimitriou 2008). Its attributes were to be found in the role of *notables* in the France of the Third Republic (1871–1940) and the Fourth Republic (1946–1958), for instance in the so-called *Midi* (Tarrow 1977; Williams 1970). A similar kind of welfare protection culture surfaced in post-Soviet Russia (Glinavos 2010).

The culture of welfare protection rested on the paradox of the big but weak state. Distrust of the state because of its complicity in rent-seeking activity led to tax avoidance and evasion on a grand scale, forcing the state to depend on debt financing, often off-balance-sheet. Bloated state size and patronage went along with low productivity and weak state capacity, further reducing incentives to pay tax. At the same time, the state was the main economic actor, offering to the individual benefits like access to secure jobs, commercial and financial exemptions and privileges, along with some collective gains through infrastructure projects like roads and bridges, suitably accompanied by patronage. In this context, states and governing elites were vulnerable to becoming hostages to corrupt practices and entrapped in scandals and scandal-mongering. They were prone to fall into disrepute. Because of weak executive competence and low reform capacity, debt restructuring and default were common instruments of statecraft. They were constrained to pursue debt financing by their chronic inability to raise taxes efficiently, to tackle pervasive rent-seeking activity, and to circumvent political barons with strong territorial power bases and the entrenched factional politics that they represented.

This paradox of state power was expressed in a profound cynicism towards the centralized state. It was seen as both the major provider of a source of living and an object of cynicism and distrust. The culture of welfare protection gave rise to political systems of parasitism and riot and to governmental systems in which powerful political bosses promoted factional politics and produced fragmented, neo-feudal policy-making. The image of the formal contractual arrangements and impersonality of the state, including mechanisms for managing public finances, stood in contrast to a society whose values were rooted in agricultural and rural life and in deeply-ingrained cultural nostalgia, folklore, and myths about this way of life. The culture of welfare protection derived from the coexistence of the material rewards that the big state could offer with the high value that was placed on preserving a rich inheritance of deep communal bonds. These bonds rested on close personal ties of friendship, extended family, and kinship. They embodied respect for tradition, intimacy, and emotional spontaneity over formal rationality.

The paradox of the big but weak state was resolved in the figure of the political patron, notable, or 'boss' and a pattern of relationships that bound together patron and client in a set of reciprocal rights and obligations. Political, economic, and social life was personalized around the figure of the notable or patron, who mediated between the state and the individual and ensured that the welfare of political clients was protected. The power of the patron was based on skill in cultivating personal ties to the state. At its heart was patronage. It took various forms: accessing jobs and benefits for individuals; designing regulation to protect insider interests; shielding clients from the state's demands, for instance in tax assessment; and gaining collective benefits like roads, bridges, and public works. The big—and expensive—state was necessary for this purpose. It provided a source of security against 'intellectual unemployment' for the upwardly mobile and of resources to distribute to clients. For the patron, occupancy of ministerial office, or ready access to it, was indispensable for protecting the welfare of clients. Hence internal party politics and elections were forms of competition amongst rival, often flamboyant patrons. The result was a very high priority to local, parochial, and sectional interests within what appeared a centralized state. More seriously still, patronage elided into the politics of corruption and scandal. In the words of Philip Williams (1970) about French republican politics: 'a chain of intermediaries of diminishing honesty links the politician—often without his knowledge—with the crook'.

The culture of welfare protection derives historical legitimacy from governing elites who construct and use a collective memory of dependency and victimhood. These memories take idiosyncratic forms, for instance in Spain's Galicia and in Greece. Since its birth in 1821 the self-image of the modern Greek state was associated with memories that attributed responsibility for Greek woes to external, neo-colonial intervention by the great powers of Europe. This image of victimhood at the hands of great powers was evoked by historical memories that focused variously on the origins of the Greek state in the War of Independence against the Ottoman Empire; on the series of unpopular foreign monarchs after independence; on the German occupation in the Second World War; on the post-war Greek civil war; and on the short regime of the colonels. The Orthodox Church also played a role in creating and sustaining the image of a beleaguered Greek society. Over centuries of Ottoman rule it had served as the central embodiment of the distinctive and tradition-bound communal bonds of Greeks.

However, caution is required in attributing welfare protection culture to the European periphery. In the first place, this type of economic culture was also to be found within creditor states, amongst those who felt excluded from the advantages that flow from this status. Creditor states have their own peripheries and their own chronic debtors who spawn cultures of welfare protection. Secondly, not all states on the periphery can be simply characterized as welfare protection cultures. Though welfare protection culture had a strong foothold in the post-1922 Irish Republic, it gradually began to lose its ascendancy from the 1950s. Even so, the incestuous relations between governing party, banks, and property developers, which helped fuel Ireland's asset-price bubble before 2007, showed that a culture of political 'cronyism' retained a hold. Welfare protection culture appears more marginal in the three Baltic States, which officially subscribe to the values of stability culture.

Welfare protection culture has its own deep and inbuilt problems of illusion, complacency, hubris, and vanity. As with other types of economic culture, it rests on partiality and incompleteness. In the first place, welfare protection culture conceals an 'insider-outsider' problem. The corollary of powerful patrons is the exclusion from its benefits of those who are not clients. The result is a political culture of intense factionalism and resentment on the part of outsiders. Secondly, once patronage and corruption become endemic, they tarnish the image of the state as untrustworthy. Thirdly, discourses of globalization, Europeanization, and modernization challenge this type of culture, from without and from within. The capacity to sustain this culture of welfare protection rests on the maintenance of a closed, self-referential society. Governing elites have to be able to keep official and private creditors at a distance, circumvent external conditionality and discipline, restructure or default on debts with relative impunity, and ensure public and international tolerance for an exercise of state power that remains opaque.

This capacity is put under pressure once domestic modernizing elites—often educated and trained in creditor-state contexts and values—seek to use external discipline, founded on a valued standard of reference, to legitimate reforms. The purpose is to open up society through a combination of fiscal consolidation, liberalization, and debt reduction. This modernizing agenda involves binding hands through European and international commitments to liberalize markets, including public procurement; to peg the exchange rate; and to join in a currency union. Across southern Europe, European integration and monetary union were instrumentalized by elites to force the culture of welfare protection into retreat. However, the outcome typically involved considerable inertia and active and passive resistance. Welfare protection culture demonstrated a striking capacity to reconsolidate under external pressure.

Historical examples suggest that the displacement or marginalization of welfare protection culture depends on two factors. First, its displacement requires self-confident and skilled modernizing elites. They require the political leadership skills to create a persuasive narrative of reform that mobilizes support in order to overcome powerful entrenched domestic veto players. This challenge eluded Mario Monti's technocratic government in Italy between 2011 and 2013. Secondly, the promise of faster real GDP growth increases the incentives to embrace the types of economic culture associated with creditor states. Characteristically, both factors are central to the process of culture change. Modernizing elites seek self-binding of the state through adopting external discipline and tough conditionality requirements. They use a discourse of globalization and Europeanization to legitimate change as logical. However, the sheer embedded strengths of domestic veto players and the lack of state control over GDP growth illustrate the limits of this strategy. Discourses of globalization and Europeanization have highly conditional traction on cultural change. They may stimulate inertia and resistance rather than transformation. Welfare protection culture has the capacity to provoke narratives of 'de-Europeanization' and retreat from globalization.

European Integration and the Faces of State Virtue: From 'Tax State' to 'Debt State'?

The belief of governing elites and publics that what they regard as their state virtue is compatible with sovereign creditworthiness appears as most at risk of being exposed as illusory when the dominant ideology of debt is defined by the culture of elite magnificence, consumer culture, or welfare protection culture. Social welfare culture promotes both the 'tax state' and the 'debt state' and thus retains an ambiguous character. However, cultures of elite magnificence, mass consumption, and welfare protection serve to shift public finances from the 'tax state' to the 'debt state'. Accordingly, they contain an inbuilt bias to causing anxiety amongst creditors.

One source of challenge to sovereign creditworthiness comes from pervasive tax avoidance and evasion in the 'black economy'. The 'black economy' is most conspicuous in cultures of welfare protection, in which the state is not trusted to spend taxes for social benefit. It is also a by-product of consumer culture. As Eisenstein (1961) argued, tax reflects a continuing struggle among contending interests for the privilege of paying the least. The wider the range of interests that benefit from this privilege, the greater is the weight that falls on debt in public finances and the bigger is the challenge to the inclusive state of social welfare culture. The politics of sovereign creditworthiness is complicated by this shift from 'tax state' to 'debt state' and its cultural and ideological underpinnings.

The problems of sustaining belief in state virtue are further aggravated by globalization and Europeanization. Both processes promote freedom of capital movement and credit liberalization. They help weaken the relationship between state liability and territorial control, notably through growth in external debt, both private and public. They also lead to an erosion of the tax base and profit shifting to low-tax, off-shore havens by the rich and by big transnational corporations. Capital controls are no longer part of the standard-operating policy repertoire of states. These changes threaten the 'tax state' with not just a revenue crisis but also a governance crisis around lack of corporate transparency and a moral crisis around tax justice. In addition, greater opportunities are opened for external debt-financing to support the behaviour associated with consumer culture and the welfare protection culture. External debt-financing is even more volatile than tax financing, further complicating and challenging the politics of sovereign creditworthiness.

In European integration the problems of reconciling the many faces of state virtue are manifested in the tension between the narratives of 'market' Europe and the narratives of 'social' Europe. In turn, narratives of 'market' Europe are torn between the deregulatory agenda associated with promoting consumer culture and the regulatory agenda that is driven by the requirement of safeguarding stability culture. The tension within 'market' Europe narratives is between two faces of state virtue: the permissive and the ascetic. Narratives of 'social' Europe are also marked by tension, in this case between social welfare culture, which inclines to support for negotiated debt restructuring and 'bail-in' of creditors, and welfare protection culture, which is less averse to coercive default and capital controls. Here the tension is between two faces of state virtue: the inclusive and the protective. In this vortex of tensions, the willingness to pay creditors remains an open question.

Spatially, the tensions in economic culture and debt ideology pit north-west against southern Europe. North-west Europe promotes the cultures and ideologies of stability culture and social welfare culture, rooted in the German and the Nordic models. Southern Europe exhibits the tensions between importing stability culture from north-west Europe and defending welfare protection culture.

Examining the complex interplay and coexistence of economic cultures and ideologies of debt helps understand the confusion that surrounds debt in political and policy debates within the EU and the euro area. It suggests that attempts to theorize what is an Optimal Currency Area involve a judgement about which economic cultures and ideologies of debt can plausibly cohabit in an economic and monetary union. In particular, the question arises of whether EU Member States that respectively identify themselves with stability culture and with welfare protection culture are, in the long term, compatible within such a union. In this sense cultural analysis provides an antidote to illusion about who can credibly live together in a monetary union. It suggests that economic identities matter and that they cannot be easily remade. The attempt to do so risks undermining the whole edifice of European economic and financial integration and setting in process disunion.

The question of which economic cultures and ideologies can coexist in economic and monetary union is inseparable from the question of how they are to coexist. Two types of answer are possible. First, one might conclude that the EU is condemned by this cacophony of cultures and ideologies to live with illusion, its debates characterized by their partiality, dogmatism, hubris, and vanity. In this case EMU is at high risk. Secondly, one can believe that it is possible to transcend or to bridge these complex divisions. One solution is Platonic. It involves exploring the potential for agreement on an impersonal moral censor. The Treaty on Stability, Coordination, and Governance in the euro area in 2012 was an attempt to achieve agreement around a censor that would enforce the values of stability culture. It identified the euro area and its Member States with the virtues of the ascetic state. However, compliance with a single authoritative principle, like the balanced budget rule, was highly problematic in such a diversity of economic cultures and ideologies.

The second solution is Aristotelian. It involves reliance on the practical wisdom or prudence of EU governing elites to agree what is necessary to ensure the continuing existence of the union. This type of solution looks to justificatory political and policy narratives that emphasize the common good of Europe. It eschews simple faith in an impersonal moral censor, claiming to deduce proper action from knowledge of general principles. Instead, emphasis is placed on governing elites having intimate knowledge of the particulars of European integration and individual Member States. As Aristotle notes in Book 6, Chapter 5 of *The Ethics*, temperance is required to safeguard prudence. However, the virtue of temperance is difficult to cultivate and sustain once banking and sovereign debt crises intensify and sentiments of resentment, shame, and anger gather force.

10

Space, Time, and Statecraft: Saints, Fallen Angels, False Prophets, Redeemers, and Sinners

If many remedies are prescribed for an illness,
You may be certain that the illness has no cure.
Anton Chekhov (1904: Act 1)

Skill in practising the political arts of statecraft is of pivotal importance in making narratives of sovereign creditworthiness credible. It involves the arts of storytelling, based on insight into cultural and social dynamics, the careful reading and manipulating of sentiments, and capacity to create trust, in part by the sheer power of words and in part by matching deeds to words (Holmes 2013). In 2012 Mario Draghi, the president of the European Central Bank (ECB), provided an example of the power of words. As the euro area crisis threatened to engulf Italy and Spain, he reframed public discourse about the euro by promising to do 'whatever it takes' to protect the euro.

Gaining or retaining sovereign creditworthiness is central to the reputation of governing elites, elected or official, and their preoccupation with gaining and retaining office. As Tomz (2007) argues, reputation is the key to how financial markets price sovereign risk. Skill in the statecraft of sovereign creditworthiness is decisive in achieving the reputation of governing elites in a number of ways. It serves to confirm their governing competence so that, in the minds of their electors, they merit the claim on office. Skill in statecraft also helps ensure that they win the battle of ideas so that holding office is meaningful. It has the additional merit of securing and retaining unity amongst their supporters. Not least, skill in statecraft is the key to leaving an historical legacy of effective leadership.

As previous chapters showed, statecraft is structurally conditioned. Economic culture, law, and institutional context shape how governing elites frame the opportunities and constraints that they face in using the various instruments of statecraft to secure their sovereign creditworthiness. They shape understandings of which instruments are appropriate and how they should be used. Choice and use of instruments of statecraft are bound up with dominant representations of debt, with absolutist or restrictive conceptions of sovereignty, and with the social basis of law, including prevailing norms of conduct that are embedded in institutions. These factors condition whether threats of exit from institutional arrangements and rules, unilateral default, negotiated debt restructuring, trade sanctions, financial repression, or 'gunboat' diplomacy are seen as acceptable.

In other words, statecraft is bound up in hegemonic, and often contested, principles of justification that are expected to govern the relations between creditors and debtors. It is influenced by whether institutional frameworks—as in the EU—enforce high costs on states that renege on their debts or threaten exit from established institutional and policy frameworks. Where states are enmeshed in a dense and complex framework of repeated and nested bargaining games, their governing elites place higher valuation on avoiding reputational loss (Dyson 2000). Worries about spill-over of costs to related issue areas, like trade and financial market activities, induce them to prioritize the reputational benefits of maintaining sovereign creditworthiness.

The arts of statecraft are, in consequence, highly context-specific and historically contingent. Their practice varies across space and over time. Its practitioners—heads of state and government, finance ministers, central bank governors, and their officials—hold historically nuanced, spatially contrasting understandings about which instruments are appropriate, how they are justified, and about how they should be used. Statecraft is practised within powerful structural parameters of space and time. In consequence the search for general theories about sovereign debt, and about why states default, has proved inconclusive (cf. Tomz and Wright 2012).

Statecraft is characterized by synchronic variation. It bears the imprint of highly variable domestic and European institutional configurations of constraint, specific characteristics of economic culture, and changing legal understandings. In addition, statecraft varies with economic size and with the systemic significance of states. Some states have a large gross domestic product (GDP) and financial market size, others small. In political economy terms, some are 'core' to Europe and the international political economy, others 'periphery'. Some states are geo-strategically important, others are not.

Statecraft also exhibits diachronic variation. Time as well as space matter. Its practice depends on whether the context is one of creating foundational institutional arrangements and rules or of reforming these arrangements and rules. In the former creditor-state elites can more credibly threaten exit than in the latter and thus more strongly influence outcomes (Fuchs 2013). Also, the incentive structures in which statecraft is practised alter, depending on whether the European and international political economy is one of 'good' times or 'hard' times. Hard times breed pervasive distrust. They spread insecurity, resentment, anger, fear, and above all humiliation, which in turn infect attitudes to statecraft. Debtor states experience feelings of victimhood, loss of status, and exclusion. Their governing elites draw on the specificities of historical experience and social structures to fashion strategic responses that vary from defiant compliance with creditor demands, through denial, to resistance and outright rejection (Smith 2012). However, default is by no means an inevitable or even common response to hard times (Tomz and Wright 2012: 15).

Broadly speaking, governing elites gain greatest freedom of manoeuvre in statecraft when their states have large GDP and financial market size, are situated in the 'core', are geo-strategically significant, represent creditor states in contexts of negotiating foundational institutional arrangements and rules, and inhabit a political economy of 'good' times.

This context-specific character of statecraft means that what might seem rational state behaviour in one spatial or temporal context of sovereign debt appears misconceived or perverse in another. There is a broad, general structural pattern. Creditor states share strategic interest in limiting their liabilities within European and international financial and monetary cooperation. They understand solidarity as rule-compliance. Their power over outcomes is at its height in the context of negotiating foundational arrangements and rules when their exit provides a credible threat. In contrast, debtor states share strategic interest in strengthening collective financial and monetary support. They understand solidarity as fair burden-sharing to help stimulate economic growth and employment and defray debt burdens. Crucially, when negotiating foundational arrangements and rules in the context of their dissatisfaction with the status quo they cannot credibly threaten exit.

However, this broad and general pattern conceals variation. Neither creditor nor debtor states are unitary actors. Each contains its own structural economic imbalances, which open up domestic variations in attitudes to statecraft. Each has its specific historical experience and generates its own distinctive memories and identities. Also, different domestic incentive structures create contrasting combinations of opportunities and constraints in statecraft. Privileging certain kinds of argument by creditor or debtor state status does not equate to unitary and unproblematic interests.

In particular, the socio-psychological climate within which statecraft is conducted can rapidly turn poisonous under the pressure of negatively experienced events. This climatic turn was evident in the period 1918–1924 when the post-war political economy of hard times coincided with bitterness about German reparations, inter-Allied war debts, and French occupation of the Ruhr to extract payment in kind. It was seen again when the governing elites of a geo-strategically significant state like Germany began to flex its muscles as the Great Depression deepened. The interwar period showed how the governing elites of a big, systemically significant debtor state like Germany could continue to evade its creditors.

Financial Market Scale and Depth and Relative Economic Power

The governing elites of certain debtor states gain a greater degree of freedom of manoeuvre in their statecraft than others from the sheer scale, depth, and liquidity of their domestic financial markets. The United States is a prime example. By 2012 doubts had intensified about its long-term debt sustainability in the face of net external debt and net interest payments. At stake was the US image of state strength, governing competence, and public responsibility. Nevertheless, the United States continued to enjoy the fiscal privileges that are associated with a 'benchmark' borrower status, symbolized by her ten-year Treasury bonds. The US dollar retained its status as the pre-eminent reserve currency.

The United States illustrated in the clearest way how state image is bound up with relative economic power, as measured by GDP and financial market size. Relative economic power bestows status on its currency, encourages investors to purchase its liabilities, and underpins its ability to continue to raise debt easily and cheaply without the apparent need to fear bond 'vigilantes'. It also enables a state to take a leading role in shaping global economic relations, keeping institutions like the International Monetary Fund (IMF) at bay. However, once relative economic power slips away, and painfully high debt legacies are revealed, the messy and politically painful process of transition from image of 'strong' to 'weak' state begins.

Characteristically, relative economic decline is accompanied by illusion and vanity, illustrated in domestic political difficulties in acknowledging its implications. Loss of self-confidence and resentment lead readily to a sense of humiliation, anger, and the search to attribute blame. Illusion is manifested in a more polarized domestic political discourse, which in turn undermines governability. These problems in the political economy of relative decline affected the United Provinces after the seventeenth century. They marked Britain from the 1880s, gathering momentum after 1918. By the early twenty-first century a similar scenario of increasing polarization and weakening governability seemed to unfold within the United States, as relative economic power shifted towards Asia. In August 2011 Standard and Poor's published the first downgrade of US sovereign debt from triple-A. In short, the images of strong and weak states are specific to historical and structural contexts of relative economic power. Narrowly political explanations of strong and weak states remain inadequate.

Words as Weapons: Matching Deeds and Words

The challenge in the statecraft of sovereign creditworthiness is to use words in a culturally nuanced way and to match deeds with words in order to create or re-create trust. Careful choice and use of words by governing elites remain of fundamental importance in gaining and sustaining reputation. Words are embodied in the linguistic context that is provided by economic culture, law, and institutions. However, crafting a persuasive narrative of sovereign creditworthiness has to be matched by appropriate instruments of statecraft. Governing elites must act in a contextually appropriate way if they are to retain the confidence of the public and of creditors.

For this reason, establishing reputation as creditworthy and an image of governing competence and a strong state correlates weakly with domestic constitutional and political structures. Creditworthy states may be centralized or federal. They may have a two- or multi-party system, coalition government or single-party government, and presidential or parliamentary government. German relative economic power within Europe and the unequivocal, consensual commitment of its governing elites to sovereign creditworthiness transformed a 'semi-sovereign' state, with dispersed powers and many powerful institutional veto players, into a 'stronger' state than centralized presidential France. Between the early 1990s and the mid-2000s this confidence in Germany declined, consequent on the huge fiscal burdens of German unification and indicators of relative economic decline. The semi-sovereign state was redefined as weak, its governing elites as incompetent. However, before the post-2007 crisis, this image had been reversed—without significant reforms to German political structures.

Political science has an occupational bias to attribute state strength to a particular type of political structure, typically one that facilitates the centralized or coordinated use of public powers. The capacity to undertake effective statecraft to secure creditworthiness is understood to depend on certain institutional conditions. It requires the centralization of fiscal policy, especially of tax collection, expenditure control, and debt management. It also rests on the monopoly of the mintage of coins and/or of printing paper currency. However, ultimately, state strength is a matter of fitting deeds to words through statecraft in ways that bolster belief in sovereign creditworthiness. It rests on governing elites acting in ways that are consistent with dominant conceptions of economic culture, law, and institutional appropriateness. Statecraft must also be appropriate to a state's size and systemic significance and to the temporality of political economy—good or hard times.

The practice of statecraft is not just about becoming or remaining a creditor state. After all, not all states can be creditors, and gaining this status is a matter of fortune as well as intentional statecraft. Statecraft is, above all, concerned with averting the status of chronic debtor state or with averting being caught out as an illusory creditor state. In short, statecraft is very much driven by averting the limits and thresholds of creditor tolerance for holding 'troubled' sovereign debt. It is about ensuring that sovereign debt does not become 'distressed' debt, acquiring 'junk' status. Statecraft is, in short, very much a crisis prevention and management exercise. Seen in this way, statecraft is pre-eminently about rescuing fiscal states from the threat or reality of collapse of investor and political confidence.

The Aura of Power: Network Capital, Information Delivery and Gathering, and Statecraft

The room for manoeuvre of governing elites in statecraft and their potential to influence outcomes mirror their network capital. Creditor states possess network capital, enabling them to 'punch at, above, or below their weight'. They figure—along with large, systemically significant states—amongst the states with which the governing elites of other states, and the European Commission, most often seek to cooperate. The incentives to do so stem not just from access to their rich and reliable capital markets. They also arise from association with states whose policy positions enjoy credibility and reputation. In the thirteenth to sixteenth centuries this network capital was evident in the Italian city states—Siena, Lucca, Florence, and above all Venice. Later Antwerp and the United

Provinces manifested similar high levels of network capital. They had the capacity to punch far above their weight, expressed in territorial and population size. Network capital is testament to the synchronic variation in statecraft capacity.

The governing elites of creditor states gain better access to information about the negotiating positions of other states, enabling them to identify compromises that are as close as possible to their own positions (Beach 2005; Naurin 2009). Moreover, they have an enhanced capacity to deliver information about what represents 'red lines' for them in negotiations (Fuchs 2013). Network capital makes it possible to make effective use of information as a bargaining resource to exert disproportionate influence over outcomes. Creditor-state status is associated, above all, with high levels of respect and trust, which add enormously to networking capacity. It carries with it 'an aura of power', which became associated above all with German, and to a lesser extent Dutch, negotiating weight in the euro area.

For this reason, governing elites in some small non-euro-area creditor states, like Denmark and Sweden, had greater network capital in the EU than euro insiders like Greece and Portugal. Similarly, within the euro area the Netherlands had more network capital than Italy and Spain, having for instance a major influence on the renegotiation of the Stability and Growth Pact (SGP) in 2004–2005 (Fuchs 2013). Spain's network capital was comparable to that of non-euro-area Poland (Naurin and Lindahl 2009). In the early stages of the post-2007 financial and economic crisis Austria, Finland, Luxembourg, and the Netherlands were able to punch well above their weight within the euro area.

At the same time, network capital is far from being the only, or the most significant, factor in influencing the effective use of statecraft to influence outcomes. In negotiating foundational institutional arrangements and rules—as in the Maastricht Treaty or the SGP—it is secondary to the threat of exit by creditor states. This threat is more credible when the state is characterized by large economic size, systemic significance, and high formal voting weight in the Council. These three last factors matter in strengthening network capital. Britain and France had this advantage over Austria and Denmark. On this basis Italy and Spain were able to add to the influence of France in the EU and the euro area. Similarly, Denmark and Sweden potentially added to that of Britain in the EU (Naurin and Lindahl 2008; Thomson 2009). Moreover, Britain and France retained reputation as former creditor states that had developed commensurate institutional infrastructures. In this they differed from regular debtor states, like Italy, and above all chronic debtors like Greece.

Saints, Fallen Angels, False Prophets, Redeemers, and Sinners: The Dynamics of Power

Before examining how space and time condition statecraft, it is helpful to differentiate amongst types of creditor and debtor states. The language of 'saints' and 'sinners' is inadequate, not just because of its moralizing character but also because it fails to discriminate amongst different creditor and debtor states. At the same time, it is important to remember that individual states do not fit easily and immutably into specific ideal types of creditor and debtor. For instance, Britain was no longer a creditor state after 1914. Thereafter, it exhibited aspects of both 'fallen angel' and 'false prophet'. Over time

Britain displayed variously the attributes of a lapsed creditor state and an illusory creditor state. It proved a false prophet of the gold standard in the 1920s and of fiscal and monetary prudence in the early 2000s. The advantage of a more discriminating typology is the greater insight that it offers into the dynamics of creditor-debtor state relations. States shift along the continuum of creditor-debtor, with implications for their power and for their policy preferences. As individual states move from debtor to creditor, they gain relative power and embrace the narrative of a stability culture. Conversely, the shift from creditor to debtor state status is accompanied by loss of relative power and shift towards narratives of consumer and welfare protection cultures. There is a time lag at work, conditioned by how entrenched are domestic institutional interests.

The dynamics of 'who sits where' on the continuum of creditor-debtor states are determined by two factors: external economic imbalances, often resulting from asymmetric effects of exogenous shocks; and domestic policy mistakes or successes, especially with respect to averting or fuelling credit booms. Exogenous shocks include war, like the Napoleonic Wars, the Franco–Prussian War of 1870–1871, and the world wars of 1914–1918 and 1939–1945. Other examples are commodity price booms, like the oil crises of the 1970s–early 1980s. External imbalances can also build up because of cross-national differences in unit labour cost development, including the effects of wage-setting, skill levels, technology transfer, and fiscal policies.

The second dynamic stems from domestic banking and financial market crises, which impair sovereign creditworthiness asymmetrically. Credit booms and busts leave states with debt liabilities that reduce the fiscal freedom of manoeuvre for their governing elites. They lead to painful and protracted deleveraging and impact adversely on long-term growth potential (Reinhart and Reinhart 2010). Large domestically originated banking shocks can suddenly change long-term indicators of sovereign creditworthiness. They typically occur when financial market liberalization is accompanied by pro-cyclical fiscal and monetary policies and lax credit rules, leading to asset-price booms and busts (Jaeger and Schuknecht 2004). In the period 1970–2002 the main examples of asset-price volatility were Japan, which experienced a spectacular, protracted post-1991 bust; Finland, which had busts in 1974–1979 and 1990–1993; Sweden, with busts in 1977–1985 and 1990–1993; and Ireland and Spain (Jaeger and Schuknecht 2004). Strikingly, during the period 1970–2007 each of these states figured amongst creditor states. They illustrate how the configuration of creditor and debtor states can change rapidly over time.

Table 10.1 offers a framework for the analysis of creditor and debtor states. The typology correlates with different kinds of economic culture and ideologies of debt. Creditor states are associated with stability cultures; illusory creditors with consumer cultures; productive debtors with social welfare cultures; and chronic debtors with welfare

Table 10.1 Typology of Creditor and Debtor States

Creditors			Debtors		
Creditors	Lapsed Creditors	Illusory Creditors	Productive Debtors	Regular Debtors	Chronic Debtors

(*Source*: Author)

protection cultures. The main value of the typology lies in helping to discriminate the different strategic interests, policy preferences, and practices of statecraft, especially in crisis prevention and crisis management. It aids in understanding the distinctive and contrasting approaches of EU Member States to the design and functioning of European and international macroeconomic governance.

However, the limitations of the typology need to be understood. The categories are no more than ideal types. Actual states correspond more or less to individual categories. Their relationship to these categories also changes over time. States cannot be neatly and eternally slotted into a particular category. Creditors become debtors; debtors transform themselves into creditors; complex shifts occur within the broad labels creditor and debtor; and, not least, states are not unitary actors. A state may incorporate features of more than one category, reflecting its complex, variegated, and dynamic character. Moreover, formal analysis faces an even more serious limitation. The self-image and ascribed image of a state is not based purely on objective indicators. It embodies subjective knowledge and unconscious motives and biases. Indicators are selected, synthesized, and interpreted in ways that flatter or undermine the image of a state. Something of the constitutive power of governing elites in flattering their state is captured in the category of 'illusory' creditor state. They are 'false prophets'. However, in general formal analysis has difficulty in capturing the constructed character of states and the illusion that is secreted in state images.

The typology does not rest on a single statistical indicator. It confines its attention to various standard economic and financial indicators that are conventionally judged as relevant to plotting the position of states on the creditor-debtor state continuum. They include current account balance, net external debt, the nature of debt (short or long term, domestic or external), domestic savings rates, inherited public debt, structural fiscal balances, actual and potential GDP growth, and vulnerabilities in economic structure to asymmetric shocks. Consequently, the precise plotting of the position of a state is complicated. A state does not move in neat synchronization with respect to different statistical indicators. Emerging tensions and strains across different indicators suggest dynamic processes of realignment. They preface shifts in the domestic balance of power in debates about strategic interests and policy preferences. Hence, in many instances, states can be expected to exhibit hybrid characters. Moreover, a focus on economic and financial indicators can disguise significant developments across environmental, social, and governance indicators that presage major challenges to statecraft.

Despite these many problems with this type of formal analysis, position on the creditor-debtor state continuum helps to highlight the opportunities and constraints that face governing elites as they attempt to decide what is an appropriate use of statecraft. It shows that the constitutive power of governing elites faces the limitation that claims which they make about state strength, governing competence, and public responsibility must be credible with financial markets.

Saints: Creditor States and the Radiance of Soft Power

Creditors are a superstitious sect, great observers of set days and times.
Benjamin Franklin (1732–1757)

In their ideal typical form, creditor states are paragons of virtue. Their status derives from economic histories of avoiding sovereign debt defaults, restructurings, overt and coercive financial repression, and hyperinflation. The substantial current account surpluses of creditor states are built on persistently low inflation rates, wage moderation, high productivity, and moderate increases in unit labour costs. These current account surpluses typically link to high national saving rates as a percentage of disposable household income. In consequence, their central banks posses substantial reserves, solid reputations, and high resilience. Not least, creditor states have liquid financial markets, export capital, and benefit from large net external interest. Again in their ideal typical form, their banking systems tend to reflect a conservative and cautious savings culture, preferring exposure to more traditional, low-risk forms of wholesale funding and mortgage financing, like covered bonds. Creditor states combine this financial conservatism and fiscal rectitude with competitiveness and with a high-quality infrastructure of education and training, research and development, active state entrepreneurship, and labour markets. Ascetic cultural values of conservatism, frugality, hard work, and discipline are typically attributed to them.

In consequence of the admiration and trust that they enjoy, governing elites in creditor states possess substantial network capital and a 'radiance of soft power'. Other states are keen to associate with them and to seek cooperation with them. Hence they gain a range and depth of information about negotiating positions that is denied other states, along with a capacity to deliver information about their own red lines. Creditor-state elites acquire nodal positions in networks and are in the position to exercise extra influence in creditor-debtor state relations. Their power to secure their strategic interests is expressed in the framing of issues and in agenda-setting and vetoing. It is not a 'power of numbers' but of ideas, shaming and humiliating debtor states.

The strategic interests of creditor-state elites are captured in the priority that they attach to the principle of moral hazard, which justifies the limiting of their collective liability and their attachment to the idea of no bail-outs. They reject monetary financing of fiscal deficits and privileged public-sector access to finance. Creditor-state elites stress individual state responsibility for 'building stability at home' both by debt reduction through fiscal consolidation and by lowering unit labour costs and wage moderation to restore competitiveness. They take a top-down, rules-based approach to policy coordination, stressing solidarity as rule compliance as well as early exit strategies from crisis-related measures (e.g. Deutsche Bundesbank 2009: 79–86). The purpose of cross-national coordination is to provide debtor states with an external anchor for domestic discipline, clear and detailed formal conditionality, close intensive monitoring of compliance, and quasi-automatic sanction mechanisms. Above all, creditor-state elites recognize that they possess the power of credible threat of exit when it comes to negotiating foundational institutional arrangements and rules.

Creditor states come and go, reflecting a combination of whether economic and political fortunes remain benign and whether statecraft is used effectively. In the 1920s Germany was a chronic debtor, above all because of the legacy of the ruinous costs of war, followed by reparations and a fiscally weak Weimar Republic. From the early 1950s, Germany emerged as the paramount European creditor state. It had the EU's biggest current account surpluses, became the EU's largest capital exporter, and had comparatively low household indebtedness. The period 2001–2005 proved problematic. Germany broke the EU's fiscal rules in the wake of the long-term fiscal burdens and competitiveness loss after German unification in 1990. Otherwise, Germany epitomized fiscal rectitude. Its ten-year bonds remained the benchmark for sovereign debt in the euro area. Other examples of creditor states in 2013 included Denmark, Finland, the Netherlands, and Sweden, as well as Norway and Switzerland outside the EU.

Fallen Angels: Lapsed Creditor States and the Legacy of Institutional Capacity

> If thy debtor be honest and capable, though hast thy money again, if not with increase, with praise.
>
> William Penn (1693: 1.48)

Lapsed creditor states represent a special case of recidivist debtor state. They differ from chronic and regular debtors in that they were formerly powerful creditor states. As a consequence, they possess the historical legacy of bureaucratic, taxation, and financial market capabilities that derive from this earlier creditor position. Their governing elites gain credibility from this legacy of institutional capacity. Lapsed creditors possess efficient public administrations that conform to high standards of professional conduct and integrity. Their taxation systems are broad, and their revenue collection is efficient. In particular, lapsed creditors have relatively large and liquid financial markets in relation to their size and thus can avoid excessive levels of external indebtedness. They are less dependent than other debtors on short-term and external debt because of the depth of these markets and because of the preferences of their domestic investors, like pension funds and insurance companies, for assets that match the average duration of their liabilities.

This institutional legacy marks out lapsed creditor states as efficient and as possessing substantial adjustment capacity. For these reasons, stakeholders in their sovereign debt have a high level of confidence that their governing elites will avoid certain instruments of statecraft that damage creditors. Their elites are trusted to avoid sovereign debt defaults, restructuring, coercive financial repression, or hyperinflation as instruments to reduce the value of debt. In consequence of historical legacy, lapsed creditor states have an advantage in retaining credibility with sovereign bond markets. They can benefit from a powerful inbuilt historical path dependency.

The statecraft of lapsed creditor states is often attracted to the mobilization of formal and informal empire to help rebuild their creditor-state status. In this way they gain privileged access to valuable natural resources, investment opportunities, and markets. In such cases as Britain and France, empire formed the context of much of their past institution building. However, empire also contributed to their lapsed creditor-state status. They became burdened with the high costs of over-commitment that managing empire imposed. Britain and France provided the best European examples of this ambivalent imperial legacy. As pre-1914 Britain's creditor-state status was increasingly threatened, imperial preference gained growing domestic political support as an instrument of statecraft. It had even greater success after British exit from the gold standard in 1931. From the 1970s the United States showed characteristics of a lapsed creditor state. Its statecraft became caught up in the ambivalence of empire (Ferguson 2009). Commitments threatened to outstrip capacity.

The strategic interests of elites in lapsed creditor states are less clearly defined than those of either creditor states or chronic and regular debtor states. They exhibit contradictory preferences. Elites in lapsed creditor states favour both collective financial assistance (IMF and/or EU) and clear rules. At the same time, they stress the flexible application of rules in order to protect or enhance their own domestic freedom of manoeuvre. This emphasis characterized British thinking behind the Kindersley Plan of 1931, the Henderson Memorandum, and Keynes' thinking from 1933 to 1944 (Dyson and Quaglia 2010a). It was also evident in French policies towards the EU SGP (Howarth 2007).

On balance, their own history and institutions dispose governing elites in lapsed creditor states to align themselves more closely with those in creditor states than with those in regular debtor states. They are attracted to an economic culture that prizes elite magnificence and display and are strongly attached to the imagery of the dignified state. At the same time, elites in lapsed creditor states retain a strong residual commitment to stability culture. For this reason, they are unreliable 'swing' states for chronic or even regular debtor states. The potential significance of this 'swing' role of lapsed creditor states was evident in the euro area. In 2008, for instance, the creditor states accounted for only 38.3 per cent of euro area GDP, with Germany alone contributing 26.9 per cent (Eurostat figures). Lapsed creditor states were pivotal for creditor states' ability to build majorities in the Council of the EU and overcome their numbers' problem.

False Prophets: Illusory Creditor States

> There is but a step between a proud man's glory and his disgrace.
> Publilius Syrus, *Sentences (Fragments)*: 138

Paradoxically, illusory creditor states represent a special case of debtor state. Their governing elites fall victim to illusion, hubris, complacency, and folly. Persisting external imbalances, lax credit provision, overleveraged banks, and structural fiscal deficits are camouflaged by benign fiscal dynamics. Their positive fiscal balances are contingent on GDP growth levels that prove to be unsustainable, because artificially boosted by the asset-price bubbles in property, housing, construction, finance, or commodity markets. These bubbles generate excessive borrowing and consumption and artificially increase tax revenues from capital gains. In consequence, illusory creditor states harbour disproportionately high private-sector indebtedness. Asset-price bubbles are inflated by over-accommodative monetary policies. Once the bubbles burst, unsustainable private-sector indebtedness leads to massive deleverage by households and companies, banking crises, credit crunch, sharply contracted tax revenues, and the explosion of fiscal deficits and public debt. This type of creditor state punches above its weight for as long as the illusion of creditor status remains.

The characteristic feature of illusory creditor states is structural overdependence on economic sectors that are vulnerable to asset-price bubbles and bursts. They feed economic cultures of elite magnificence and/or of mass consumer culture, which become disembodied from economic and social realities. The result is a bias to complacent self-satisfaction and hubris amongst governing elites and publics. The illusion is easier to sustain when external fiscal surveillance, as in the narrow focus of the original SGP, focuses on the public sector rather than the private sector, ignoring the fiscal implications of private-sector indebtedness.

The strategic interests and policy preferences of governing elites in this type of state can be expected to undergo radical modification once their illusions are exposed. Faced by unanticipated, sudden, and deep fiscal, economic, and political crisis, they are likely to pursue radical domestic reforms in order to restore creditor status. Examples included Finland and Sweden after the burst asset-price boom in 1989–1990 and the banking and financial crisis to which it gave rise (Jonung, Schuknecht, and Tujula 2005). Similarly, the post-2007 exposure of the unsustainable asset-price booms in Ireland, Latvia, and later Spain drove their governing elites to embrace radical reform programmes of fiscal austerity and structural reforms to correct external imbalances and restore structural fiscal balance.

Redeemers: Productive Debtors

O happy fault, which has earned the possession of such and so great a Redeemer
Missal, *Exsultet* on Holy Saturday

Productive debtor states are defined by their institutional capacity to make wise use of their borrowing (cf. Helm 2010). They are associated with the building of long-term assets by sustained investment in public infrastructure and social provision and by developing the attributes of a developmental state willing to take entrepreneurial risks and support fundamental innovation (Mazzucato 2013). Though debtor states, their governing elites construct sophisticated institutional structures in public and private sectors that enable them to increase long-term growth potential and to mobilize and make efficient use of their resources. Productive debtor states are high performers in delivering public goods. They are associated with elites that construct accountable, transparent, and inclusive political and fiscal institutions. The public administrations of productive debtor states are efficient and public-interest-oriented, especially in tax collection and in project management. Their legal systems protect property and other rights. Not least, elites in productive debtor states invest in top-quality education and vocational training provision, high labour-market participation, substantial research and development, technology transfer, modern communication and transport systems, efficient and reliable energy supply, and external and internal security. They believe in the role of governments in driving innovation.

This category identifies states that are making the transition from debtor to creditor state. Late nineteenth-century examples included the Nordic States, which imported large amounts of capital for this purpose. Despite its fatal attraction to the attributes of an illusory creditor state, Ireland showed many of the characteristics of a productive debtor in the 1980s–1990s. Similarly, Slovenia had stood out as a model amongst the post-communist states that entered the EU, at least up to its banking and sovereign debt crisis of 2013. Productive debtor states illustrate that not all debtors are chronic or stuck in this status. In no sense can states that approximate to this type be labelled sinners.

Sinners: Regular and Chronic Debtors

A small loan makes a debtor; a great one, an enemy.
Publilius Syrus, *Sentences (Fragments)*: 12

Regular and chronic debtor states share certain characteristics. They have current account deficits, persistently above-average inflation rates, and comparatively high rates of increase in unit labour costs. Their economic cultures are heavily impregnated with features of welfare protection. Their states shelter rent-seeking behaviour. Typically, both types of 'sinner' have public debt levels in excess of 90/100 per cent of GDP or are moving rapidly in this direction. Reinhard and Rogoff (2008) suggest that such levels depress long-term growth potential and lock states into high public debt/GDP ratios. Regular debtor states tend to differ from chronic debtors in having high domestic saving rates, enabling them to diversify their sources of debt financing. They also lack a serial history of defaulting and rescheduling, in large part because they are less exposed to the build-up of short-term external debt.

The problem of high indebtedness becomes chronic when debtors have low domestic saving rates and over-rely on capital imports to finance trade deficits. Chronic debtor states are unable to adjust to shortfalls in external financing. This high dependency on external debt financing creates serious foreign-exchange risk, especially when short-term. In consequence, chronic debtor states have a strong incentive to resort to new, complex, and often opaque financial instruments—like securitization and currency swaps—to actively manage and conceal (off balance sheet) their liabilities. Above all, chronic debtor states have a history of statecraft in which serial sovereign debt rescheduling and default features prominently and diminishes their credibility in the bond markets. Faced by debt crisis, and outside a monetary union, they are prone to devalue 'to excess'—that is, by enough to change trade and production patterns. They make active use of the right of sovereign states to legislate their own debt terms, for instance converting debt payments into the devalued currency at the cost of creditors. Hence chronic debtor states are the site of the sharpest political fights in creditor-debtor state relations.

In both cases, especially chronic debtor states, their credibility problem is increased by weak domestic political will and institutional capacity for efficient economic adjustment and credible reform programmes. Chronic debtor states are typically concentrated amongst low- and middle-income countries that lack effective tax-raising capacity and possess inefficient administrative systems. Their image of corruption stems from political 'clientelism', in which powerful patrons use office to exploit the resources of a big, but weak state for personal and partisan gains. Chronic debtor states are also limited in their debt management strategies by shallow domestic financial markets. Their elites tend to make poor borrowing choices with regard to the trade-off between debt-interest cost and foreign-exchange risk. These poor choices contribute to the accumulation of unsustainable debt and debt distress (International Monetary Fund and the World Bank 2009).

Governing elites in regular and chronic debtor states share strategic interests and exhibit similar policy preferences. They prioritize the principle of solidarity through large-scale collective financial and economic assistance. Their notion of solidarity involves 'fair' burden-sharing in economic adjustments to external imbalances. Debtor-state elites argue that creditor states must assume part of the responsibility for external imbalances by sustaining aggregate demand through domestic expansion and/or by underwriting debtor states. They take an *ex ante*, discretionary approach to cross-national macroeconomic policy coordination. Its purpose is to enable debtor states to regain domestic autonomy of action. The loosening of external constraints facilitates the pursuit of economic growth and employment.

Over time European states shift their location on the debtor spectrum, between regular and chronic debtors. In 2010–2013 examples of chronic debtors included Greece, Hungary, Portugal, and Romania. Italy was a good example of a regular debtor that had managed to avoid chronic debtor status. The main feature of chronic debtor states was failure to shake off emerging-market characteristics. They were deeply mired in an economic culture of welfare protection. Generally, as with the Baltic States, an inheritance of low public debts meant that those post-communist 'transition' states that became EU members in 2004 were able to avoid chronic debtor-state status.

Who Has Power?

> It is the debtor who has the last word.
> John Maynard Keynes (quoted in Ahamed 2010: 144)

Underlying the continuum of creditor and debtor states is the question of who has power *over* and *in* European macroeconomic governance. The first aspect is power over which ideas and interests prevail in framing negotiations and in agenda-setting. The second aspect is power in shaping negotiated policy outcomes (on this distinction, see Dyson 2009). Framing and agenda-setting power tends to reside with creditor-state governing elites. Negotiations tend to take place around their proposals (e.g. Dyson and Featherstone 1999; Dyson and Quaglia 2010a). Creditor-debtor state relations are fundamentally an ongoing political process, in which the asymmetry of power works against regular and chronic debtor states—the 'sinners'—and in favour of the smaller number of 'virtuous' creditor states. In regular and chronic debtor states domestic consensus building is complicated by a complex mix of emotions, involving shame, remorse, and humiliation. These domestic problems undermine the negotiating credibility of their governing elites.

However, the power of creditor-state elites is far from unlimited. There is the problem of numbers: more debtor states than creditor states. There is also the problem of contagion. Toxic assets pollute the banking and financial systems of creditor states so that providing financial assistance to debtor states can covertly serve their self-interest in supporting their own banks. In addition, there is the problem of the macroeconomic vulnerability of creditor states themselves to meltdown of aggregate demand from painful austerity across debtor states. Moreover, creditor-state status can be undermined by unwise domestic policies of their governing elites.

Not least, there is the problem of the limits of toleration of elites and publics in debtor states. Their compliance with the rules of the game in an asymmetric system of creditor-debtor state relations is ultimately conditional. *In extremis* regular, and above all chronic, debtor-state elites have an extensive and powerful range of instruments of statecraft at their disposal. They may be induced to resort to them when humiliation at loss of control, demotion of status, and exclusion from decision-making turns public and elite opinion from pragmatic conciliation to rage, scapegoat-seeking, and the search for revenge. Creditor-state elites may identify a national interest in averting potentially uncontrollable outcomes that may negatively affect them.

Collectively, these problems add up to the limited capacity for control of creditor-state elites as well as elites in debtor states. Exaggerating this capacity for control can prove a fatal illusion for governing elites in creditor and debtor states alike. It stalked the evolving euro area crises.

Size, Systemic Significance, and Geo-Strategic Centrality: Core and Periphery

Size and systemic significance are important differentiators amongst creditor states and debtor states. Creditor and debtor states are by no means internally the same. They differ in their structural characteristics. They vary in the development, scale, and depth of their domestic financial markets, measured by bank assets relative to GDP (Chitu, Eichengreen, and Mehl 2012: 12–13). Market liquidity, measured by a favourable short-term interest rate differential, is an important attribute in the attractiveness of a currency. It affects the share of the currency in global foreign public-debt markets. Market liquidity helps explain why, by 1929, the US dollar had displaced sterling as the dominant currency of denomination for international bonds. In addition, there is internal variation amongst creditor and debtor states in their exposure to external competition, external debt, and output volatility. They differ in their vulnerability to the political economy of 'hard' times.

Size has a strong claim to be a significant determinant of the resources of power that a state possesses and of significance of the instruments that its governing elites have to deploy. Big states in GDP size are more likely to have large and deep financial markets and abundant liquidity. They are also able to rely on more powerful fiscal and monetary authorities with big balance sheets. Their central banks are able to engage in bold quantitative easing (QE) to buy up large amounts of their own sovereign debt. In this respect, in the early stages of the post-2007 crisis, the ECB did not behave as the central bank of a big 'euro area state'. Its response contrasted with that of the US Federal Reserve Bank's successive, massive QE programmes. A key difference was that there was no market in euro area bonds, as well as an explicit Treaty provision prohibiting the monetary financing of fiscal deficits.

Size also affects the image of the significance of a state in international bond markets. The positive image of creditor states is boosted by their high per capita GDPs, high national savings rates, and capital exports. However, per capita GDP is less important than overall GDP size. Norway and Sweden may be creditor states. However, they cannot claim the power resources of Britain and France, let alone Germany. As Table 10.2 shows, the distinction between large aggregate GDP and small aggregate GDP plays an important role in defining the systemic significance of a state in creditor-debtor state relations. GDP size highlights the core–periphery distinction in creditor-debtor relations. Because of their sheer size, some states matter more than others, whether as creditors or as debtors. The systemic significance of sovereign creditworthiness differs.

Taking the first decade of the euro area as an example, Germany represented the 'core' state. Austria, Finland, Luxembourg, and the Netherlands were 'core-zone'

Table 10.2 Size in Creditor-Debtor State Relations

GDP Size	Large	Small
Creditor State	Core State	Core-Zone State
Debtor State	Systemic-Risk State	Periphery State

(*Source*: Author)

states. Denmark was part of the same group. It was outside the euro area but in the Exchange-Rate Mechanism (ERM) II, with a very narrow band of fluctuation. As creditor states, their policy preferences on design and operation of the euro area rules of the game were broadly the same. However, accounting for 27.5 per cent of euro area GDP in 2011, Germany was the central benchmark. Its participation in setting the rules of the game was more significant than that of any other state. Austria represented a mere 3.2 per cent of euro area GDP, Finland 2.0 per cent, and the Netherlands only 6.4 per cent.

In contrast, Greece, Ireland, and Portugal were periphery states. Though excessively indebted, they were individually small in GDP size: respectively 2.2, 1.7, and 1.8 per cent of euro area GDP in 2011. Their sovereign debt crises could be insulated more readily through 'firebreaks' to prevent systemic contagion to the rest of the euro area. Insulation was similarly easier in the case of Cyprus in 2013, which accounted for only 0.2 per cent of euro area GDP. The transitional European Financial Stability Facility (EFSF) and the permanent European Stability Mechanism (ESM) offered new conditionality-based financial assistance programmes that were appropriate for periphery states. However, Italy and Spain were very different cases. They were debtor states which, because of their GDP size (16.8 per cent and 11.3 per cent of the euro area respectively in 2011), posed much higher risks of unsustainable systemic debt dynamics if they slipped into the chronic debtor-state status. They were only eclipsed by France, which represented 21.2 per cent of euro area GDP. The EFSF/ESM mechanisms could not hope to cope with these cases, without the support of the balance sheet of the ECB.

Both official and private-creditor attitudes towards sovereign creditworthiness and towards appropriate statecraft in cases of sovereign debt crises differed, depending on whether they involved 'periphery' or 'systemic-risk' states. In the case of periphery-state crises, like Greece and Ireland, or Hungary, Latvia, and Romania outside the euro area, Germany adopted a tough crisis-management approach. There were signs of a shift in emphasis towards leniency in German statecraft once sovereign debt crisis began to spread to systemically significant states in 2011–2012. German references to Greek exit from the euro area subsided. There was new German tolerance, if still highly contested, for the proposal that the ECB should, under strict conditions, intervene in secondary sovereign bond markets. The EFSF/ESM was also empowered to recapitalize banks, again on strict conditionality. However, these two developments became hotly contested within Germany, especially by Ordo-liberal economists.

The importance of the liquidity of domestic financial markets is illustrated by the way in which the British and the US sovereign debt markets remained more attractive to investors than the manifestly more creditworthy Danish, Norwegian, and Swedish debt markets. Though debtor states, American and British secondary bond markets were a focus of greater investor interest and activity than smaller creditor states because of the sheer ease of trading in them. Another aspect of size is relative economic strength. The combination of large financial market size and depth with relative economic strength creates the possibility that investors will hold a currency as a reserve asset even though it is a debtor state. In the post-1945 period both the United States and, to a lesser and receding extent, Britain managed to retain reserve-asset status. However, the relative ease with which they could continue to finance fiscal deficits and public debt was placed in question once confidence in their relative economic power diminished. Once this confidence slips away, debtor states can find themselves living dangerously with their large inherited debt.

Geo-strategic importance adds another differentiator amongst creditor and debtor states. It constrains, sometimes very severely, the instruments of statecraft that can be deployed, for instance in dealing with chronic debtor states of geo-strategic significance. British policy in pursuing creditor interests against Ottoman Turkey was inhibited by Turkey's significance in containing Russian ambitions. From the 1850s the notion of the Great Game took hold within British governing elites, endowing Britain with a special responsibility for containing the spread of Russian power through central Asia and threatening India (James 1998: 81–3). This narrative cautioned restraint in opposing Ottoman Turkey. This restraint was only overridden in the case of the invasion of Egypt by the British strategic interest in securing easy, fast access to India to better protect it from Russia. Similarly, geo-strategic calculation played a role in the shift of British policy towards a more lenient approach to German reparations in the early 1920s. It was based on fears of economic collapse in Germany, leading to a crisis in European security.

French policies towards Haiti illustrated a very different, harsher face of statecraft. In 1825, subsequent to Haitian independence, the French government used the threat of military intervention to demand compensation for her slave-owning colonists. Despite protests against this 'odious' debt, remittances continued to be paid till 1947—valued at €170 billion in 2010 prices. In this case, the geo-strategic constraints were much less strong.

The complex relationship between creditor-state and geo-strategic power was evident in Soviet Union-West German relations from the late 1960s. A geo-strategically weaker creditor state, West Germany attempted to use credits as a lever with which to induce wide-ranging economic and political concessions from the militarily powerful Soviet Union. Federal Chancellor Willy Brandt's controversial *Ostpolitik* (Eastern policy) sought to act as a catalyst both for post-war reconciliation and for internal changes in the Soviet bloc. Crucially, it was underpinned by potential German creditor-state power over a range of east European debtor states that fell under the Soviet umbrella. These states and the Soviet Union lacked 'hard' currency with which to finance their imports and borrowing. Credit was a tool to strengthen West German negotiating power over a range of 'linkage' issues, including easing relations between the East and the West German states (Stent 1981). German creditor-state power made plausible the objective of 'change through coming closer' (*Wandel durch Annäherung*).

Instruments of Statecraft: 'Good' and 'Hard' Times

> Pandarus: 'Words pay no debts, give her deeds.'
> William Shakespeare (1602: Act 3, Scene 2)

The arts of statecraft revolve around the matching of deeds to words. Deeds should conform to the 'logic of appropriateness' if they are to be judged legitimate. In the case of sovereign debt this logic derives from the legal framework, the governance structure, and the dominant economic culture and debt ideology that define the mentality of rule. The challenge in managing sovereign debt is to employ instruments of statecraft that match the ascendant narrative of appropriateness. This coherence of words and deeds is decisive for building and sustaining the reputation of political and official elites for governing competence.

Given the underlying asymmetrical power in creditor-debtor state relations, chronic debtor states face particularly serious challenges of political will and institutional capacity in cultivating and sustaining a persuasive image of governing competence in managing debt. Their governing elites can respond to sovereign debt crisis by exhibiting shame and remorse over past profligacy and waste, measuring themselves against the norms of stability culture. In this case, as in Ireland after 2007, statecraft reflects a mentality of conciliation and compliance, however reluctant, with creditor-state norms. However, governing elites may respond very differently when a culture that protects welfare entitlements is perceived to be directly threatened. In this case, statecraft begins to bear the imprint of fear, anger, and humiliation, which spread across elite and public opinion. In these conditions, domestic politics shifts towards greater support for a statecraft that uses more coercive instruments against private and official creditors. Debtor-state cooperation with creditors remains conditional and contingent, underlying how context-specific sovereign debt crises are.

Table 10.3 provides a typology of the large-scale arsenal of instruments of statecraft in creditor-debtor relations. Its limitations stem from binary categorization. We have seen that there is high variability amongst creditor and amongst debtor states, based not just on size and geo-strategic importance but also on legal framework, governance structure, and economic culture. Unsurprisingly, therefore, strong variation is to be found in their use of persuasive and coercive instruments of statecraft. Across the wide range of instruments, persuasion and coercion are matters of 'more or less', involving often gradual and discrete shifts of emphasis. For this reason, the typology is primarily of heuristic value in examining a wide range of cases. It is less useful for examining the political and economic idiosyncrasies of individual states and cases.

How coercively debtor-state elites behave vis-à-vis private creditors depends on a cluster of variables. Domestic political variables are prima facie important, but in ways that are not always clear. For instance, weak executive autonomy may mean that elites become more exposed to public demands that creditors share in the costs of adjustment. However, much depends on precisely to what they are exposed in terms of economic culture. Statecraft is shaped by who occupies the domestic veto points and their policy preferences. In addition, the pressure to resort to coercion of private creditors may be more likely to grow when a state has a high external debt/GDP ratio. However, this type of statecraft may be practised when this ratio is relatively low. The typology in Table 10.3 suggests that a critical variable in the practice of statecraft is whether the state finds itself in the global political economy of 'good' times or 'hard' times.

Table 10.3 Typology of Instruments of Statecraft

	Persuasive Instruments	Coercive Instruments
Creditors	Prevention	Compulsion
Debtors	Assurance	Protection

(*Source*: Author)

The key distinction is between *persuasive* and *coercive* instruments. Creditor states and debtor states are associated with different types of persuasive instruments and different types of coercive instruments. The persuasive instruments of choice for governing elites in creditor states are *preventive*. They seek to engage debtors in specific and firm commitments, whose observance will avert unsustainable debt and sovereign debt crises. Their governing elites aim to create a context of incentives and sanctions in which debtor states will honour their commitments. A typical example is multilateral surveillance and intensive monitoring of fiscal policies and excessive imbalances under EU or IMF auspices.

The persuasive instruments of choice for governing elites in debtor states involve *assurance*. They attempt to assure official and private creditors that their commitments are genuine and credible. One such instrument is 'tying of hands' by voluntarily adopting an external discipline. Examples include ERM membership, euro entry, or a financial assistance programme of the EFSF/ESM or the IMF. Debtor-state instruments for assuring creditors range from fiscal gimmickry—using statistical manipulation, obfuscation, and mendacity—to resolute, transparent structural and fiscal reform measures. The difference between the two boxes of instruments—prevention and assurance—resides in structural and relative power. Assurance is required from debtor states, not creditor states.

When it comes to choice of coercive instruments, creditor-state elites prefer *compulsion*. They emphasize precise, firm commitments to correct external imbalances, to restructure and recapitalize banks, and to tackle excessive debt. The delivery of these commitments is secured by strict conditionality requirements to financial assistance, detailed external surveillance and monitoring, and sanctions—including fines—for non-compliance. Conversely, debtor-state elites prefer to seek *protection* from their creditors in the form of safeguard measures. The relevant coercive instruments include financial repression, in which states resort to capital controls, regulatory requirements on financial institutions, moral suasion, and hidden tax; 'surprise' inflation; and debt restructuring and default.

Statecraft in the Political Economy of 'Good' Times

The shift from persuasive to coercive instruments in statecraft mirrors the transition from the political economy of 'good' times to that of 'hard' times. This shift is signalled by a more pronounced vigilante role of financial markets in policing sovereign debt. The precarious balance that had existed between creditor states, debtor states, and markets dissolves in the face of the threat of disciplinary market power on debtor states. Disciplinary financial market power focuses initially on chronic debtor states and then moves contagiously to illusory creditors and regular debtors, which are perceived as at risk of becoming chronic debtors. This scenario was played out in 2010–2013 as the markets shifted attention from Greece to Portugal, and then on to Italy, Spain, and Cyprus. The shift from persuasive to coercive instruments of statecraft occurs in response to negative macroeconomic data, involving some combination of large inherited public debt, dwindling economic growth, falling tax revenues, toxic bank assets, and escalating fiscal deficits. It is accompanied by financial market signals, principally in bond and foreign exchange markets, that debtor states are losing credibility. Market signals include increasing underwriting fees of Primary Dealers, widening spreads on bond yields and hence higher interest costs on debt, negative swap spreads, failures of debt auctions, and selling the currency of the debtor state, whether its own or a shared currency like the euro. They are the principal triggers for sovereign debt crisis and the shift to a harsher climate of statecraft.

In the political economy of 'good' times, governing elites in creditor states use a variety of instruments to persuade debtor states to behave responsibly. Characteristically, they are consistent with the logic of stability culture. Creditor-state elites press for the firm European and international anchoring of provisions that are designed to avert moral hazard. Examples include a no-bail-out provision or, more realistically, strict limits on creditor-state liability; prohibition on the privileged access of public authorities to financial institutions; and prohibition on monetary financing of deficits. Creditor-state elites seek to entrench the values of stability culture through such devices as clear, specific, and enforceable European and international rules on fiscal deficits and public debt. An example is a balanced budget rule over the economic cycle, as in the euro area fiscal compact treaty. Fiscal rules can be reinforced by harmonized statistical standards to ensure comparability, integrity, and reliability of the data used in fiscal surveillance. They can be accompanied by the requirement to domestically anchor fiscal rules through institutional reforms and judicial oversight.

In addition, creditor-state elites stress improvements in the quality of public finances by reforms that promote more efficient domestic economic adjustment in product, services, financial, and labour markets. These reforms are designed to raise potential GDP growth rate to relieve debt burdens. They are accompanied by measures to mitigate risks of banking crises through anti-cyclical adjustment so that credit is tightened during booms and relaxed during recessions. Particular emphasis is placed on rules to ensure that debtor states take prime responsibility for correcting extreme external imbalances.

The efficacy of these rules on fiscal balance, credit provision, and excessive imbalances is expected to be safeguarded by mutual peer review, surveillance, and sanctions. The Maastricht Treaty of 1993 and the subsequent reforms, like the SGP Pact of 1997, as well as much of the post-2010 package of treaty and legislative changes to EU and euro area macroeconomic governance, bear the firm imprint of these creditor-state preferences. They are, first and foremost, instruments of crisis prevention.

The persuasive instruments of debtor state power during the political economy of 'good' times are different. Their character reflects economic cultures that in various and changing ways combine display of elite magnificence, mass hedonistic consumption, and welfare protection. Reflecting the asymmetry of power between creditor and debtor states, these instruments of statecraft are often more effectively employed domestically than externally. However, size and systemic significance can embolden the governing elites of some debtor states.

Externally, the governing elites of debtor states have an incentive to pursue multilateral action that seeks to persuade creditor states to shoulder the burden of adjustment to excessive external imbalances. Creditor states are called upon to boost domestic consumption and to facilitate a real exchange-rate appreciation of their currencies so as to reduce their excessive surpluses. Debtor-state elites also seek support from collective financial assistance mechanisms to ease and extend their own burden of domestic adjustment. Such mechanisms provide time for them to establish market credibility, including by the use of contingent credit lines through private banks, the IMF, or the ESM. In addition, debtor-state elites have an incentive to argue for 'exceptionality' provisions in fiscal policy rules. Examples include being able to keep certain expenditures off-balance-sheet for the purpose of fiscal surveillance, like bank rescues, defence spending, research and development spending, costly pension reforms, or youth unemployment programmes.

Internally, debtor-state elites can act to reduce their external exposure and assure creditors by developing their domestic bond markets through tax and legal reforms. Pension and insurance sectors can be promoted, with regulatory requirements to hold certain proportions of domestic sovereign debt. Debtor-state elites can also endeavour to shift the composition of their debt towards longer-term issues, even if higher cost, so that roll-over problems are reduced. In addition, they can take measures designed to build up their foreign-exchange reserves relative to short-term external debt and to imports. Vulnerability can be reduced by building up buffer stocks of external assets. However, debtor-state elites have to be able to generate savings for this purpose to substitute for reliance on externally-financed debt.

Many of the difficulties in statecraft stem from the difficulty that creditor-state elites—and those in institutions for multilateral surveillance—have in trusting debtor states, especially chronic debtors. Their conundrum relates to radical uncertainty about what is going on in debtor states; to whether the governing elites of these states are in the grip of self-illusion; and to the risks that creditors also might fall victim to illusions peddled by elites in debtor states. In assessing appropriate statecraft they face the difficulty of distinguishing genuine domestic fiscal, financial, and economic policy regime reforms by debtor-state elites to strengthen compliance and use debt more productively from cynical fiscal gimmickry, obfuscation, and mendacity.

Debtor-state elites can choose a strategy of high-profile structural reforms to budgets and wider economic and social policies that promise to make a difference to long-term growth potential. Such measures include freezing or cutting unsustainable public-sector wages and employment levels, pension reforms, and labour-market reforms. They can seek to build social and political consensus around such reforms. Conversely, debtor-state elites can resort to creative, over-optimistic economic forecasting in order to manipulate expectations about GDP growth, fiscal deficits, and public-debt dynamics. They may also choose to employ creative accounting and statistical manipulation and dissemblance. An example is hiding liabilities off-balance-sheet through the use of derivatives and currency swaps, often at off-market rates. The history of EU and euro area macroeconomic governance during the pre-2007 political economy of 'good' times highlights the difficulties that creditor-state and international financial elites face in making the distinction between domestic regime reform and falling victim to illusion when dealing with debtor states.

Statecraft in the Political Economy of 'Hard' Times

The political economy of 'hard' times provides a different context for the exercise of statecraft. The post-2007 financial and economic crisis showed how poorly designed had been EU macroeconomic governance to manage sovereign debt crisis in such times. An institutional framework for this purpose had been neglected in large part because sovereign default—unlike inflation and payments crises—had not been part of the history of the EU. It was understood—erroneously—as a developing-country or emerging-market problem.

Illusion fed complacency. Too much faith was invested in the efficacy of EU mutual surveillance and the formal compliance with rules. Too many assumptions were made about political will and state capacity to honour commitments, too little attention paid to their capacity to circumvent and subvert commitments, and the significance of economic culture and political mentalities underestimated. Consequently, EU collective crisis-management capacity was primitive, other than in the case of the ECB and its liquidity provision to euro area banks. Moreover, the institutional capacity to address persisting external imbalances and to manage cross-national bank crises was weak, if not non-existent. The interest-rate premium that followed monetary union, with substantially lower real interest rates, induced further complacency about risk. Additionally, complacency was compounded by a benign international context of high, non-inflationary growth that accompanied the first decade of the euro. Illusion and complacency were far from just EU and euro area phenomena.

When credit crisis punctured this complacency, EU and euro area macroeconomic governance had to be redesigned in the most difficult circumstances. Managing interwoven sovereign-debt and bank crises proved an extreme challenge in the absence of both European banking union and fiscal union. In turn, creating European banking union and fiscal union posed acute technical, legal, and political challenges, notably about democratic legitimacy, far exceeding those that had attended European monetary union. These complex challenges could not be met in the market-based time frame of short-term crisis management. The earlier threat from exchange-rate crisis had been removed by monetary union. It was replaced by the shocks in sovereign bond and financial markets and the weight of market discipline. In the absence of this infrastructure the crisis laid bare the risks of reversion to historical patterns of coercive statecraft.

Traditionally, creditor-state elites assume a more coercive approach to statecraft once they face contagious systemic risk, breach of the principle of 'no bail-out', and threat of increasing mismatch between pressures to assume joint liability and the capacity to control outcomes. Their statecraft shifts conventionally towards compulsion. Creditor-state elites advocate principles for mutual assistance that minimize moral hazard and that ensure the matching of any mutual liability with tighter external controls on debtor states. Above all, the burden of adjustment is expected to fall on debtor states on the principle that 'each state must put its own house in order'. They must effect a real 'internal' devaluation through reduced unit labour costs, including wage moderation or cuts and tax and social insurance reforms. Debtor states must also be required to put a stop to unsustainably high domestic demand growth. Mutual assistance had to be based on the 'last-resort' principle, after the domestic political will of debtor-state elites to reform had been demonstrated. There should be no element of interest-rate subsidy in financial assistance. It was to be time-limited and involve tough, detailed conditionality and rigorous, ongoing monitoring of compliance. In the event of non-compliance, sanctions must be progressive, speedy, and automatic. At the extreme, sanctions must include the threat of exclusion from voting or, at the extreme, forced expulsion from European or international arrangements for breach of the rules of the game.

In time of crisis, the framing and agenda-setting power of creditor-state elites becomes most explicit and visible. This power was manifest in successive German finance ministry proposals as the post-2010 sovereign debt crises spread and intensified. Its proposal for a European Monetary Fund in February 2010 included the threat of expulsion from the euro area. The design of the May 2010 Greek bail-out, the new EFSF, and the Irish bail-out of November 2010 reflected German creditor-state principles. The fiscal compact treaty of 2012 uploaded the German 'debt brake' and required it to be entrenched in Member-State law. The ESM Treaty put in place safeguards to limit creditor-state liability and to ensure German veto on any collective financial assistance. Access to the ESM was made dependent on Member-State ratification of the fiscal compact treaty. Both interconnected treaties gave moves to European fiscal union a strong German imprint. Similarly, use of the ESM for bank recapitalization was made dependent on moves towards European banking union, with a Single Supervisory Mechanism. In October 2012 a German memorandum on 'enhanced governance and control mechanisms' called for Greece to be compelled to hire outside experts to help collect taxes, fight corruption, and privatize government assets. It also proposed the transfer of any Greek fiscal surpluses into an internationally-controlled 'trust account' that would be used for debt servicing.

German negotiating power was strengthened by domestic 'binding hands'. Her negotiators pointed to risks of domestic non-ratification of further collective financial assistance measures. In addition to *Länder* elections, and the federal elections of September 2013, the federal government stressed the limits of Bundestag support for further bail-outs. Other constraints included risks from judicial review by the Federal Constitutional Court and from the traditional domestic opinion-leadership role of the Bundesbank. For these reasons the federal government insisted on treaty revision to establish a European banking resolution authority to wind-down banks in solvency crisis.

Governing elites in creditor states also insisted on the principle of the strict separation of fiscal and monetary policy in the interests of safeguarding central bank independence and the mandate of price stability. This principle was consistent with the burden of adjustment lying with debtor states. It implied a tough collateral policy of the central bank on the eligibility of assets in liquidity provision to banks. The sovereign bonds of chronic debtor states should be ineligible in monetary policy operations, or different 'haircuts' should be applied to them. More fundamentally, central bank purchases of sovereign bonds should be prohibited or treated as strictly exceptional and time-limited. Thus German negotiators stressed that the ECB should avoid becoming an instrument for creating a 'transfer union'. They feared that it would succumb to pressure to become a 'bad bank', buying up the asset-backed securities of euro area debtor states, and thereby allowing its expanding balance sheet to become contaminated by toxic assets.

However, the principle of separating monetary from fiscal policy ran into two practical difficulties. First, the balance sheets of sovereign states and banks were caught up in a potentially lethal, mutual embrace. The mandate of protecting financial stability induced central banks to accept that the lender-of-last-resort role in banking was inseparable from being part of a framework of support for state solvency. A monetary union required a discretionary supra-national executive capacity to respond to extreme emergency. Secondly, this lethal, mutual embrace had serious implications for the capacity of the central bank to give effect to its monetary policy. It led to financial fragmentation, with interest rates varying widely within the monetary union.

These practical difficulties formed the background to the ECB announcement of the Outright Monetary Transactions (OMT) Programme in 2012. The ECB would intervene, on certain conditions, in the secondary sovereign bond markets with potentially unlimited firepower. This issue exposed a divide within the informal creditor-state club, isolating the German Bundesbank. On pragmatic grounds, the German Federal Chancellor supported the ECB; on grounds of principle, the Bundesbank voted against the OMT in the ECB Governing Council and led domestic opposition. This episode demonstrated that, when crisis exposes dilemmas, creditor-state positions prove by no means unitary.

Traditionally, the most coercive instruments available to creditor-state elites for enforcing sovereign debt contracts are trade sanctions, other forms of non-military collective retaliation, and so-called 'gunboat' diplomacy. Trade sanctions include tariff and non-tariff barriers against a defaulting state; removal of trade credit; and seizure of a debtor's foreign assets (Tomz 2007). The threat of their use, and the uncertainties it provokes, is likely to function as a deterrent to debtor-state elites. It suggests that costs to reputation from default can spill over into other areas like investment, trade agreements, and other forms of international coalition-building. However, the empirical evidence about the effectiveness of non-military collective retaliation remains weak. In the case of many peripheral debtor states asset seizure is difficult because of their relatively small size in creditor states.

Non-military intervention varies along a spectrum from 'informal' to 'formal' empire. Informal empire takes the form of negotiated agreement with domestic elites with the objective that creditor interests should be institutionally embedded in domestic affairs. Examples include the treatment of Greek and Ottoman debt in the late nineteenth century and, to a lesser extent, of German reparations after the Dawes Plan in 1924. The 'Troika' arrangements in Greece, Ireland, and Portugal bore the hallmarks of 'informal' empire. ECB, European Commission, and IMF officials took up residence in Athens, Dublin, and Lisbon to scrutinize and monitor compliance with financial assistance programmes.

British and Canadian intervention in the British Dominion of Newfoundland in 1932–1933 went much further. Newfoundland was turned from an independent member of the Commonwealth into a protectorate, accepting a voluntary suspension of its elected government. In return for a rescheduling of debts, guaranteed by the British government, an appointed six-member imperial commission of government assumed full responsibility. It governed Newfoundland from 1934 to 1949, when Newfoundland became a province of Canada.

The incentives to resort to 'gunboat' diplomacy to protect bondholders are greater when prospective geo-strategic gains outweigh risks, when the military enjoys a high domestic status and influence within a creditor state, and when a Hobbesian view of international relations prevails within the governing elite. In practice, as Tomz (2007) stresses, historical cases of the use of 'gunboat' diplomacy are few and often complicated by other motives for intervention. However, more important is the threat of its use (Platt 1968; Fishlow 1989). These threats tend to be most likely to be used, and to be most effective, in the case of sovereign defaults by periphery debtor states that are seen as chronically unreliable. Examples include French military intervention in Haiti in 1825 and the French-led attack on Mexico in 1861–1865, initially supported by a joint British, French, and Spanish fleet. However, the results were far from encouraging. The Haiti intervention led to harsh terms and huge long-term economic costs being imposed on the newly independent, poor state. It also caused reputational damage to France, stretching into the twentieth century. The Mexican adventure ended in humiliating defeat for

Napoleon III's ambitions to establish a client state in central America and gain access to Mexican silver to help finance his Second Empire. There is, however, evidence that the threat of 'gunboat' diplomacy produced better deals for creditors in Argentina and Brazil in the nineteenth century than had been originally on offer (Fishlow 1989).

Resort to 'gunboat' diplomacy on behalf of bondholders was a catalyst for British armed intervention in Egypt in 1882, though by no means the main issue in the mind of British policy makers. The case of French intervention in Tunisia in 1881 was even less clear-cut, the main catalyst being threat to established French interests in Algeria. However, Tunisia had defaulted on its big foreign loans, with French creditors the major losers. An international commission had already been established to secure creditor interests. After the French invasion the French Resident assumed powers to guarantee the repayment of debts, turning Tunisia into a French protectorate. The US seizure of Haiti in 1915 was also, in part, to ensure debt payment. Egypt shows that British statecraft, unlike French, preferred to abstain from 'formal' empire. Following its intervention, Britain sought to co-opt local elites. 'Informal' empire had the attraction of being less economically costly and more politically sustainable.

The limits of coercive military intervention were clearly exposed in the case of the Ruhr Occupation by Belgium and France in 1923. It was countered by an effective German campaign of passive resistance and hyperinflation. The Ruhr Occupation failed to secure the change in German reparation payments that it was intended to achieve. Even the interest-free, forced loans that Nazi Germany extracted from occupied states, like Greece, during the Second World War had only very limited successes. There were big costs to both sides (Ritschl 2012b: 5). By 2012 the Greek finance ministry had begun assessing whether Greece still had a legal claim to repayment by Germany.

In the political economy of 'hard' times, the governing elites of distressed debtor states have an incentive to embrace expansive claims to sovereign immunity to protect their assets and to resort to coercive instruments of protection. As Keynes noted, they have a formidable range of instruments to deploy and the potential to inflict heavy collective damage, embracing creditor states. At the same time, these instruments are fraught with high risks because of the underlying asymmetry of power within creditor-debtor state relations. They also invite creditor-state retaliation and mutual losses to both creditor and debtor states. Moreover, sovereign default results in loss of reputation (Tomz 2007; Tomz and Wright 2007, 2012). It leads to the higher pricing of sovereign risk by markets. Defaulting states lose from present and future inability to access financial markets and higher borrowing costs when doing so. However, reputation is context-specific, contingent on legal frameworks, governance structures, and prevailing economic culture and ideology of debt.

As with creditor-state intervention, sovereign debt defaults and restructuring come in various forms (Das, Papaioannou, and Trebesch 2012: 7–8). Defaults occur when states fail to make principal or interest payments in due time. They may be partial or complete. They may discriminate between external and domestic debt. A scale of instruments is available (Standard and Poor's 2007). They range from missed payment; unilateral payment suspension (including interest); freeze on assets of non-residents (linked to capital controls); threats to repudiate outstanding debt; and forced restructuring.

Sovereign debt restructurings involve an exchange of outstanding sovereign bond instruments, like bonds or loans, for new debt instruments through a legal process. They may seek to pre-empt default. More typically, they follow default. Restructuring can be combined with the extension of sovereign immunity to protect the debtor state's assets from litigation. However, the use of this instrument, along with more coercive forms of restructuring, risks the exclusion of a debtor state from international capital markets. Both the IMF and the Institute of International Finance (IIF) advocate pre-emptive negotiated restructurings, based on principles of fair debt restructuring. The Ukraine in 2000 is often seen as a model. However, distressed debtor states may choose to impose hefty coercive debt exchanges, as Russia did in 1993–1995 and 1998 and Argentina in 2001. In short, the line between coercion and negotiation is hard to draw, with many restructurings taking place in the shadow of coercion.

As with intervention in the case of creditor states, sovereign default and restructuring is not necessarily the first instrument of choice for a distressed debtor state in economic 'hard' times. Tomz and Wright (2013) identify four historical periods of 'global default crisis': the 1820s, the 1870s, the 1930s, and the 1980s. However, there is no neat correlation with 'hard' times. Domestic legal frameworks, governance structures, and prevailing economic culture and ideology of debt help shape attitudes to using sovereign debt default or restructuring instruments. The likelihood that default or more coercive restructuring instruments will be selected might be expected to increase when states combine lack of executive autonomy with governance structures that provide incentives to domestic populist mobilization (cf. Enderlein, Trebesch, and von Daniels 2010). However, much depends on the context of economic culture and ideology of debt within which populist mobilization occurs. In particular, public-sector employees, the unemployed, and the poor might be expected to prefer default, which imposes loss on creditors, to creditor-imposed austerity (Tomz and Wright 2013). In states where these groups are electorally pivotal, statecraft has a potential to become coercive and to focus in an emotionally charged way on creditors, especially external creditors.

Financial repression, and more particularly the seizure of private assets, has a long history as a means of staving off sovereign default. Its more coercive use rests on an absolutist conception of sovereign immunity. Classic past examples of asset seizure are topped by repression of Jewish financiers. They also include King Philip IV of France's dissolution of the Knights Templar; Henry VIII's dissolution of English monasteries and confiscation of church lands and property; and the seizure of precious metals and foreign currency under the German Weimar Republic in 1923. Modern forms consist of the 'raiding' of pension funds, sovereign wealth funds, and utilities. More often, financial repression takes hidden forms, ranging from regulatory requirements on financial institutions to hold sovereign bonds to moral suasion and implicit threats. Characteristically, these measures work best when directed at relatively immobile targets. Often, however, private financial institutions can relocate more easily than most other economic institutions, thus blunting the effectiveness of threatening to use this instrument.

Debtor-state elites can also adopt 'safeguard' measures in an effort to rebalance the current account and stave off 'bank runs' by depositors. These measures include tariffs, import quotas, capital and exchange controls, and even 'country-first' publicity campaigns. However, the use of these instruments displaces adjustment pressures not just to creditor states but also to other debtor states. Consequently, their deployment is limited by the risk of retaliation and 'beggar-thy-neighbour' policies that deepen recessionary forces and inflict mutual, contagious damage.

At times of crisis, the governing elites of debtor states are more likely to attempt to put the monetary financing of debt onto the agenda. Money creation is presented as a legitimate tool of economic policy. It can be achieved by an explicit change in the central bank mandate, linked to a focus on growth, employment, and financial stability, as well as on inflation. The central bank is given more flexibility over the time horizon in which inflation is expected to return to target. However, money creation can take a hidden form, pursued indirectly and shrouded in obfuscation, thereby evading potential legal problems. An example was the role of the Irish central bank in the Irish debt restructuring of 2013. More typically, the central bank expands its balance sheet during economic 'hard' times by large-scale purchases of sovereign bonds or even a wider range of asset classes in so-called quantitative easing. Alternatively, it may make generous low-cost, long-term liquidity provision to banks, knowing that they will use this to purchase their government's sovereign bonds. More prosaically, central bank reserves, like gold sales, can be used to pay back sovereign debt. Inevitably, such instruments blur the line between monetary and fiscal policies. The justification is found in the need to prioritize economic growth, employment, and financial stability objectives. Typically, the perceived need to act in this way stems from the interconnections between bank and sovereign state solvency and an impaired credit mechanism. The constraint in using these instruments relates to risks of building up long-term inflation expectations, rewarding speculative position-taking by traders, contributing to asset bubbles, and impairing the balance sheet of the central bank. Both the independence and the credibility of the central bank in securing price stability are in danger of being impaired.

The so-called 'inflation tax' is another traditional instrument that debtor-state elites have employed in the political economy of 'hard' times. It involves the use of fiscal and monetary policies to create higher domestic inflation, which in turn will reduce the real value of government debt and penalize creditors. Inflation detoxifies overleveraged financial systems by eroding the value of fixed debts. In the 1940s to 1960s inflation served to cut the heavy post-war debt legacies that faced European states. Aizenman and Marion (2010) calculate that inflation did almost half the work of cutting the US public debt/GDP ratio from 122 per cent to 25 per cent between 1945 and 1973. The risk of trying to inflate away debt is that wary consumers and creditors might go on strike. This instrument is formally excluded for the euro area under the Maastricht Treaty. It is inconsistent with the prohibition on 'monetizing' debt and the ECB narrow mandate as an independent central bank to secure price stability.

Historically, currency debasement has been a traditional, much-used instrument of distressed debtor states. Rulers added copper to silver coins as a means of financing their wars. Examples abounded from Ancient Rome during the Punic Wars, through King Philip IV of France and King Henry VIII of England, to Philip II of Spain and beyond. King Henry III of England even resorted to alchemists to provide him with a solution to the problem of financing his projected wars to recover lost territory in France. Typically, inflation followed debasement as people demanded more coins for the same amount of goods. Use of currency debasement varied from aggressive to defensive in character. Aggressive debasements, as with Edward III and Henry VIII's last debasement, were fiscal in purpose. Defensive debasements, like the first two under Henry VIII, were monetary in inspiration. They were designed to restore confidence in a currency subjected, for instance, to clipping and sweating. Quantitative easing and liquidity provision to banks can be seen as more modern forms of printing money than currency debasement.

Currency reform is another traditional instrument of statecraft for debtor-state elites. It involves the replacement of a currency, which has been discredited by inflation, debasement, or association with an odious regime. Modern European examples included the German currency reform of 1948, introducing the D-Mark, and the French currency reform of 1959. Brazil made four currency conversions between 1986 and 1994.

The threat of exit from European or international financial and monetary arrangements is an additional instrument to which debtor-state elites can resort. It is allied to the search to set up alternative arrangements. The populist political appeal of this instrument lies in the assertion of sovereign rights and national independence. In the face of international humiliation, and popular anger, governing elites can seek escape by reclaiming the right to act autonomously. However, exit is fraught with multiple risks for debtor states. They include loss of access by both banks and government to international capital markets; costs of protectionist measures, including capital controls; short-term technical problems for the banking and financial system; risk of retaliation; intensification of domestic macroeconomic crisis; and the high costs of rebuilding reputation.

Empire

Empire is an instrument of statecraft but one that is more difficult to situate in a formal analysis of creditor-debtor state relations. Its appeal seems strongest in states where the military has high status and access to power and where there is a high degree of executive autonomy. However, empire also has an important financial and economic dimension, apparent for instance in the autocratic rule of the British East India Company and its merciless exploitation of the Bengal economy (James 1998: 38–9, 59–60). Empire seems to be associated with a certain type of creditor state, but not in a simple causal relationship. Historically, it is exemplified by Macedonia, Ancient Rome, the Spain of Philip II, the Dutch Empire, the French Second Empire, and the British Empire. Its governing elites are attracted, typically opportunistically, by the opportunities to exploit formal or informal empire and to create 'satellite' economies or protectorates. Empire provides a means for gaining privileged access to natural resources, investment opportunities, and markets. It can be used to buttress the domestic financial market.

The problem in talking about empire is distinguishing appearances from reality. The term empire has been attributed to the post-war United States and to Germany within the euro area. For historical reasons, it carries strongly negative emotive connotations, associated with coercive exploitation. Its use associates Germany with neo-colonial attitudes to the euro area and the construction of a German-centric Economic and Monetary Union (EMU). Used in this context, the term empire provokes strong denial, not least with reference to the fact that German policies towards EMU lack the attributes of domestic executive autonomy and military primacy. To the extent that the euro area has attributes of empire, it is informal and based on 'soft' power.

The problem with all empire, formal or informal, 'hard or 'soft', is that a compound of illusion, hubris, and unanticipated consequences can lead governing elites into unsustainable commitments and loss of control. They find themselves locked into path-dependent behaviour that leads to a misplacement of national priorities. Above all, governing elites come to bear heavy and potentially unsupportable fiscal burdens. The use of empire as an effective instrument of statecraft presumes an economic and financial capability to meet commitments that can exhaust the resources of a creditor state. The outcome is typically lapsed creditor states.

Power and Choice in Statecraft

The last two chapters have shown how legal frameworks, governance structures, and economic cultures frame and constrain the choice of policy instruments in practising the statecraft of sovereign creditworthiness. Variations in the legal doctrine of sovereign immunity—from absolutist to restrictive—reflect different conceptions of social contract and their associated types of governance structures. Similarly, states with democratic governance structures and weak executive autonomy are more exposed to populist mobilization and pressures. In these conditions much depends on how dominant economic culture and ideology of debt shapes the nature of populist mobilization. In certain combinations, more coercive forms of statecraft with respect to foreign creditors are to be expected.

This chapter shows how the practice of statecraft varies across space and over time because of two other conditioning factors: geo-strategic location and systemic significance as 'core' or 'periphery'; and whether the international political economy is in a phase of 'good' or 'hard' times. It involves a combination of creative with technical skills. The choice of instruments of statecraft is shaped by the underlying reference point of asymmetric power in framing policy and in agenda-setting. It is about matching the changing parameters of external power with the challenge of opening up strategic room for manoeuvre to pursue domestic priorities.

However, as the earlier historical chapters argued, at a deeper level the character of legal frameworks, governance structures, and economic cultures is conditioned by structures of social interest. The structure of social interests affects whether sovereign default, asset seizure, or 'gunboat' diplomacy are seen as legitimate instruments of statecraft. States in which the poor, the unemployed, and public-sector employees are electorally pivotal have different attitudes to how state power should be exercised, especially vis-à-vis foreign creditors.

The space for exercising creative and technical skills in the statecraft of sovereign creditworthiness opens and closes in complex ways. It requires situational judgements in context-specific situations, making theory-building about sovereign debt a difficult, if not intractable problem. To the extent that all states have sovereign debt, their space for exercising statecraft is ultimately limited. The more that they issue relative to their tax base and their fiscal institutional capacity, the tighter are the limitations that they face. The space in which statecraft is exercised also narrows once legal notions of sovereign immunity become more restrictive. Moreover, within the process of European integration, states find themselves constrained by the 'logic of repeated games', in which reputational costs across a range of negotiated issues, including trade, environment, and social standards, rise for governing elites when they consider unilateral and coercive statecraft over sovereign debt. Statecraft is caught up within more inclusive European as well as international institutions.

The arts of statecraft lie in the carefully calibrated use of words and deeds to increase political room for manoeuvre and to fashion and sustain a credible image of state strength and governing competence. Improving sovereign creditworthiness is understood by governing elites as essential to achieving these objectives. However, in the context of sovereign debt crisis they face the acute political difficulty of matching creditor interests with what domestic political elites, veto players, and publics will tolerate. Debtor-state elites risk becoming entrapped within path-dependent forms of behaviour, in which their choice of discourse and their selection of instruments lock them into a trajectory that is inimical to constructing sovereign creditworthiness.

At the same time, as Keynes stressed, creditor-state power should not be exaggerated. It is diluted by problems of collective action. Private-sector creditors have different attitudes to time and risk. These problems were apparent within and amongst nineteenth-century bondholder associations, which proved weaker than prestigious banks like Barings and Rothschilds in dealing with defaulters (Flandreau and Flores 2010). Similar problems affected later twentieth- and early twenty-first-century ad hoc debt restructurings, which 'hold-out' creditors often refused to accept. Moreover, collective-action problems exist between creditor-state governing elites and private creditors. In the first place, creditor-state elites have to protect the interests of their taxpayers, to whom they are accountable. They face an arbitrage issue of fair burden-sharing between creditors and taxpayers. Secondly, creditor-state elites have an interest in discouraging, rather than rewarding, reckless private creditors, who work on the assumption that, if they misprice market risk, they will be bailed-out. The moral hazard principle distances creditor-state elites from private creditors.

Thirdly, creditor-state elites face a challenge of reconciling private creditor interests with their own geo-strategic foreign, defence, and security interests. Military and non-military interventions in distressed debtor states risked triggering hostile reactions from rival powers and could prove too fiscally, politically, and diplomatically costly (Platt 1968). In turn, prestigious underwriters of sovereign bonds, like the House of Rothschild, Bleichröder, and Barings, feared loss of reputation from being seen as tools of the aggressive foreign policies of governing elites. They were cautious about making themselves too vulnerable to moral suasion and fiscal repression, leading to excessive commercial risks and too much political exposure.

Ultimately, in a world of sovereign states, the limitations on the room for manoeuvre of debtor-state elites should not be exaggerated. Their loyalty to European and international commitments is conditional. The threat of exit can be used as a last resort to regain an image of governing competence through the demonstration of 'heroic' leadership to a humiliated and aggrieved public. Populist mobilization against creditor power offers opportunity to reframe domestic discourse. Its use was evident in the two Greek elections of 2012, in the French elections of May 2012, and in the Italian election of February 2013. Moreover, the negotiating capacity of debtor states with creditor states and creditor institutions, like the IMF, varies. It is stronger in the cases of lapsed creditor states that are systemically significant, like Britain and France. They have inherited effective infrastructures of governance. Negotiating capacity is also stronger when debtor states are economically large and systemically significant, like Italy and Spain. They pose high risks of contagion to creditor states.

By resorting to sovereign immunity doctrine, debtor-state elites can in theory inflict potentially huge damage on official and private creditors through a whole variety of measures. They include coercive debt restructuring, hyperinflation, and seizure of private assets. The damage is all the greater when the debtor states are spatially core to creditor-debtor state relations and thus systemically significant. It mounts further when the global political economy is caught up in 'hard' times. Mutual retaliation operates precariously in creditor-debtor statecraft. It functions both as a persisting threat and as a deterrent. The promise of short-term relative gains for a debtor state is at risk of being cancelled out by long-term, shared absolute losses.

Averting huge systemic damage and retaining the glue of trust within creditor-debtor state relations draws a line under the strict application of the creditor-state principle of moral hazard. However, the question of where, when, and how this line is to be drawn remains an onerous matter of practical, context-specific judgement in the arts of statecraft. No less onerous is the question of how to apply the principle of matching liability with control.

Part III

State Liability and Territorial Control

11

States and Financial Markets: The Imbalance of Power

The main thing about money, Bud: it makes you do things you don't want to do.
Lou Mannheim, a veteran banker, to young Bud Fox in
Oliver Stone's film *Wall Street* (1987)

The mismatch between state liability and territorial control lies at the heart of the politics of sovereign creditworthiness. It highlights the multiple constraints on the exercise of state power and the proclivity to illusion, hubris, and complacency in its use. These constraints relax somewhat with creditor-state status and with relative size and systemic significance. Nevertheless, even for big creditor states, state capacity to match sovereign liability with control is hedged by their vulnerability to contagion. This vulnerability is channelled principally through their banking systems, especially when their banks are highly exposed to other risky sovereigns and have a low share of liquid assets in their balance sheets. States live in a condition of chronic imbalance between the claims of financial markets to be able to accurately assess the creditworthiness of states and the susceptibility of bank supervisors and regulators to 'gaming' when seeking to prudently supervise these markets.

The extent to which European states were particularly exposed was illustrated by how many figured in the top ten international bank bail-outs by size. In 2013 Cyprus was the second biggest, followed by Iceland in 2008 (fourth), Ireland in 2008 (eighth), Macedonia in 1993 (ninth), and Turkey in 2000 (tenth). Moreover, by 2013 the leverage ratio for the big systemically significant European banks, such as Barclays and Deutsche Bank, continued to remain much lower than their US equivalents like Bank of America and Citigroup. All bank host governments remained highly vulnerable, but some were much more so than others. The new international regulatory requirement of a leverage ratio of 3 per cent capital against total assets offered only a tiny measure of protection.

Historically, sovereign debt has continued to represent one of the largest classes of financial assets. Its relative share diminished with industrialization and the corresponding growth of corporate stock. The value of sovereign debt fell from 76 per cent of securities listed on the London Stock Exchange in 1853 to 35 per cent in 1913. The relative share of sovereign debt was also affected by the extent of financial market liberalization and international capital flows. Under the Bretton Woods system its share of world financial assets declined from 22 per cent in 1950 to 11 per cent in 1978. However, by 2010, in the wake of financial liberalization, sovereign debt had risen to some 19 per cent (Tomz and Wright 2012: 3–4). Despite variations in relative share of financial assets, sovereign creditworthiness has continued to have enormous implications for financial markets as a whole. Markets—and above all supervisors and regulators—expect sovereign debt to serve a special function as an anchor of stability and a refuge of security in a world of high financial risks. Its capacity to serve this function is problematic. No sovereign is completely safe.

The problem for states—and the root of the illusion of control—is that they are deeply embedded and imprecated in a global credit-creating financial system. The financial system is often seen as a key part of the solution to the problem of sovereign creditworthiness. It provides the essential external discipline on states. However, the financial system is also part of the problem. Public balance sheets are exposed to banking and financial crises, which are generated by lax credit provision, overleverage, and often grossly inadequate loss-absorbing capacity of banks. Banking is an extremely dangerous activity. Credit creation is lubricated by external imbalances; powered by creative, esoteric financial engineering; and facilitated by the 'gaming' of public regulation. Financial interests penetrate the state itself as privileged interlocutors, directly influencing tax and regulation, and as part of a revolving door in careers.

The challenge of mismatch between state exposure to liability and imperfect control is compounded by the tendency for this complex, opaque financial system to become relatively insulated from critical analysis and pressures for normative justification. It has the capacity to escape the constraints not just of democratic but also of corporate governance. The world of cyber-finance provides an implicit source of cultural identity and attachment for financiers. It is associated with a shared cognitive map, privileged access to information, and the common assumption that only a few highly trained financial technicians understand how governments and markets work and interact. Finance becomes disembodied from the wider society. In this context the state loses credibility. The notion that the state has the will and capacity to act as a buffer between the financially weak and the strong, protecting the vulnerable and marginalized, suffers atrophy. Belief in the state as the balancer between financial, environmental, social, and governance standards ceases to be plausible.

This insulation from sustained critical analysis and pressure for normative justification stems from the notion that banking, like money, is special, sufficiently so for normal market discipline to be suspended when banks are in crisis. Furthermore, the power of financial markets is justified in utilitarian terms. It is made acceptable by faith in their capacity to generate debt-fuelled economic growth, based on rising asset values and improving consumer and investor confidence and well-being. However, the illusion on which this confidence and well-being is based is exposed once excessive bank leverage leads to the accumulation of toxic assets, collapse of confidence in debt sustainability, and credit crunch. The outcome for governing elites and publics is painful, prolonged deleverage and deflation. In this context states experience a sharp reduction in their fiscal and political room for manoeuvre. In these constrained circumstances governing elites face formidable political difficulties in defining and gaining agreement on a new model of economic growth. As after the 2007 crisis, they operate within a prevailing discursive construction of a 'crisis of debt'. The decisive feature of this construction of crisis is that culpability is ascribed, above all, to states.

Financial System Size and State Vulnerability

Vulnerability to oversize, complex, and opaque financial systems was not specifically a feature of debtor states. This factor differentiated creditor states from each other and debtor states from each other: Luxembourg from Finland and Germany; Cyprus from Italy and Portugal. The politics of the Cyprus bail-out of 2013 exposed how, on bank system size, the cleavage line cut across the creditor-debtor state cleavage. France, Germany, Italy, the Netherlands, Portugal, and Spain were all agreed on the need to shrink the Cypriot banking system.

Differences in exposure to derivatives, structured debt, and 'shadow banking' did not correlate with creditor- or debtor-state status. The 'inverted global liquidity pyramid' was constructed before the 2007 crisis, using Bank for International Settlements' (BIS) data (Independent Strategy 2006). Derivatives were estimated to account for a massive 802 per cent of world gross domestic product (GDP), securitized debt for 142 per cent. Derivatives represented 75 per cent of global liquidity, securitized debt 13 per cent. Designed as hedges against risk, derivatives were—in the words of the US investment guru, Warren Buffet—'financial weapons of mass destruction' (Berkshire Hathaway Annual Report 2002).

The Financial Stability Board (FSB) (2012) estimated that in 2011 shadow banking was roughly half the size of the global banking sector. It reached a peak of some 30 per cent of all financial assets in the euro area by 2007, after which it declined sharply. However, the distribution of the shadow banking system did not match the creditor-debtor state cleavage. In late 2012 the Netherlands accounted for 27.2 per cent of shadow banking assets in the euro area; tiny Luxembourg for 22.2 per cent; and Ireland for 12.0 per cent. In contrast, Germany represented only 5.6 per cent; Italy 7.8 per cent; and Spain 6.8 per cent. Shadow banking was largest in relation to GDP in the Netherlands (490 per cent), Britain (370 per cent), and Switzerland (210 per cent). Despite the high risks associated with credit intermediation through this sector, progress in regulating shadow banking proved painfully slow. By 2012 it still escaped liquidity and capital rules.

Economists at the BIS showed just how bad large and fast-growing financial systems could be for state capacity to retain sovereign creditworthiness. A big and booming financial sector could inflict serious costs on the rest of the economy in lost productivity growth and real GDP, above all in research-and-development-intensive sectors (Cecchetti and Kharroubi 2012). These costs became serious once the total private credit/GDP ratio reached 90/100 per cent. The thresholds for the employment share of finance were

3.2 per cent of GDP and for the value-added share of finance 6.5 per cent. States became vulnerable in dealing with shocks once the size of their financial sectors exceeded these three thresholds. Using data for the period 2000–2008, the most vulnerable European states were Ireland, Spain, and Britain, in contrast to Germany.

The problems of the size of the bank sector in economic 'bad' times were highlighted post-2008. In 2012 bank assets in relation to GDP reached some 700 per cent in Cyprus and Ireland, and some 500 per cent in Britain, well above the EU average of 350 per cent. In Austria, Belgium, Finland, Germany, and Italy they were below the EU average. Drawing lessons from the Irish and Cypriot crises, International Monetary Fund (IMF) staff and European Central Bank (ECB) and European Commission officials came round to the view that reducing state exposure to banking crises involved shrinking banking sectors that were above the EU average. This message was unwelcome not just in debtor states like Britain, Cyprus, Ireland, Latvia, and Slovenia but also in Luxembourg, a creditor state. The pro-shrinkage grouping embraced creditor states—led by Germany—and debtor states including France, Italy, Portugal, and Spain. Luxembourg was left defending Cyprus in Euro Group meetings.

The Triad of Power

Sovereign creditworthiness rests on a triad of power, in which financial markets mediate the relationship between creditor and debtor states. Financial markets gain power over states by providing the very language of sovereign creditworthiness. This language frames and constrains the exercise of state power. It shapes what states are understood to be able to do, and how, and their agendas of action and 'non-action'. Financial markets have the power to differentiate states in terms of creditworthiness and to bring sanctions to bear on those perceived as most credit risky. Their resources of power include the powerful disciplinary instruments at their disposal, which they can use to discriminate opportunistically between states. Financial markets contribute to and complicate the asymmetry of power between creditor and debtor states, fomenting tensions, mistrust, and fear in times of debt crisis. They exacerbate the collective-action problems of states.

Financial market power over states expresses itself in three distinctive ways. First, they gain systemic significance from the dependence of the capitalist economy and state finances on credit. Their 'too-systemically-significant-to-fail' character helps evade normal market discipline; whilst belief that losses will be socialized reduces incentives to prudence. The emergence of huge cross-national financial conglomerates has expanded this resource of power. Secondly, to a greater degree than other sectors, financial market players are instantly mobile and can escape territorial control with relative ease. Digitalization has expanded this source of power. Thirdly, financial market power lies in the generation and propagation of an ideology that represents these markets in positivist terms as a natural phenomenon that delivers enhanced social welfare, if kept outside the reach of liberal democratic politics. Financial markets thrive on an ideology of de-politicization, with market liberalization and freedom of capital movement as essential components. This ideology provided them with enormous intellectual self-confidence.

The fundamental weakness of states in taming financial market power derives from the combination of these three characteristics with their own collective-action problems—both domestic and external—and with their dependence on cheap and plentiful liquidity to finance their ambitions. The result is an imbalance of power between two functions: that of the financial markets in 'branding' states as creditworthy (or not); and that of states in 'taming' markets in the public interest. Within the triad of creditor states, debtor states, and financial markets, debtor states are exposed to a dual asymmetry of power. They face creditor states, with which collective action is difficult to organize on other than onerous terms, and the financial markets, which act as vigilantes on behalf of their investors.

Financial Markets in European History

The character of relations between states and financial markets evolved markedly over the centuries: from family-based merchant financiers to global investment banks; from personalized borrowing by rulers, through syndicated loans, to modern sovereign bond markets; from creditworthiness assessed on the basis of personal 'character' to reliance on formalized statistical probability of default; from an absolute to a more restrictive conception of sovereign immunity; and away from the notion that sovereign risk was more threatening than credit risk of leading merchants and private bankers. The one key continuity was that sovereign debt was regarded as exceptional in character. It constituted a specialized, distinctive sector within the financial markets.

The main change from the mid-twentieth century was the notion that sovereign debt is a risk-free asset in a modern European economy. The absence of sovereign default became the new norm (Buiter and Rahbari 2013). This norm justified preferential regulatory treatment for sovereign bonds. Banks were induced to stock up on sovereign bonds by the exemption of these holdings from the large exposure regime. Sovereign exposures were also privileged by low or zero capital requirements. The outcome was an intimate, and potentially lethal, sovereign-bank nexus, whose potentially disastrous character was made apparent by EU and euro area crises.

The growth of sovereign lending reflected the ambitions of territorial rulers. They needed finance for wars, for trade, and to compete for glory and magnificence. More generally, the intermediary role of banking was slow to make headway in the restrictive moral and social context of the theological doctrine of usury. Personal liability attached to debtors, who faced the threat of debtor's prison. Only in the twentieth century, notably in Canada and the United States following the Great Depression, were debtors freed from personal liability beyond collateral property. Debt lost much of its moral and social opprobrium quite late in capitalist development.

As the twentieth century progressed, the United States emerged as the great creditor power. Under the influence of her more assertive competitive individualism, and its global penetration, 'gentlemanly' financial market culture gave way to a new, more abrasive financial market environment. Formal regulation assumed a greater importance as personal and social trust declined in an internationally more mobile financial world whose centre of gravity was no longer just London. Also, the educational and social backgrounds of bankers altered with technological and market changes. Formally trained economists and statisticians played a more central role in complex mathematical modelling of risks and the design of new financial products to spread and mitigate risks.

The language that bound together states and financial markets took on a new formal and technical character. Its mastery became a required right of passage. Marginalization and exclusion from this world was no longer based mainly on social and cultural attributes. Insider status required appropriate professional qualifications as the basis for understanding and using the esoteric discourse of financial markets. However much the world of financial markets had changed in cultural character, it remained a relatively closed one for initiates.

Macroeconomics, Financial Market Hubris, and Asphyxiation of the State

When great men get drunk with a theory, it is the little men who have the headache.
Lord Salisbury, quoted in Roberts (1999: 838)

The power imbalance that evolved at the heart of the construction of sovereign creditworthiness and the functioning of sovereign bond markets since the 1970s proved existentially significant. In the first place, it led to a systematic undervaluation of certain public goods and services, unless they could be justified as infrastructural or social investment. As market-based confidence in sovereign creditworthiness declined, credit rating processes took more intrusive interest in the detail and 'quality' of government tax and spending rather than just in macroeconomic aggregates. Only a select group of creditor states in north-west Europe managed to avoid this asphyxiation of the state. Their 'sound' macroeconomic aggregates served as shield and shelter for more generous and comprehensive public provision. Secondly, the power imbalance opened space for financial markets to engage in reckless and antisocial behaviour and excessive risk-taking and to display exceptional volatility. They were prone to systemically dangerous 'risk-return' trade-offs.

Before the post-2007 crisis, the dominant paradigm in academic macroeconomics contributed both to asphyxiation of the state and to illusion and complacency about systemic risk. It promoted a reassuring image of self-correcting financial market efficiency. Democratic politics was represented as disruptive; central banks as best confined to the narrow function of price stability; and 'better' regulation and supervision as 'light touch'. The 'animal spirits' of financial markets were pictured in a one-sided, virtuous fashion. The dominant paradigm endowed the enormous power of financial market institutions with expert legitimacy. In return, the discipline of macroeconomics acquired enormous intellectual confidence and prestige relative to other social sciences, the humanities, and history.

The belief in market efficiency cloaked, concealed, and neglected a painful history of financial manias, panics, and crashes; whilst intellectual confidence turned into illusion, hubris, and complacency. The dominant paradigm helped justify a prolonged boom based on investor overconfidence, asset-price bubbles, and faith in light-touch and self-regulation. Macroeconomics diverted attention from the systemic risks attendant on the fragile psychology of 'animal spirits'. It neglected the lethal, unstable compound of greed, fear, and contagious herd-like behaviour that drives financial markets. This type of environment was highly attractive to narcissistic personalities and, more worryingly still, to psychopathic types who displayed antisocial, highly manipulative, impulsive, and parasitic behaviour traits. Too many financial market participants were devoid of feelings of guilt and remorse, the usual manifestations of moral conscience. They lacked empathy and a sense of moral restraint (cf. Hare 1993). In this context the failure to embed the precautionary principle in financial market regulation and supervision was a case of double jeopardy.

The durability of the belief in market efficiency illustrated the enormous structural power of financial markets as the lifeblood of capitalist economies. It helped to explain the 'political silence' that shrouded how the financial markets operated during economic 'good' times. Crazy games were played within obscure corners of investment banks, hidden behind the narrow range of discourse about financial markets and the 'non-decisions' about supervision and regulation. The activities within investment banks and shadow banking were labelled esoteric and hidden from sight. States' sovereign creditworthiness was mortgaged through a process of intellectual capture of financial market supervisors, regulators, and sovereign debt managers. Complacent and lax supervision and regulation offered a breeding ground for reckless risk-taking.

The Language of the Financial Markets

> The limits of my language mean the limits of my world.
> Ludwig Wittgenstein (1921: proposition 5.6)

The systemic power of financial markets is exemplified in how much of the language of sovereign creditworthiness is defined by financial markets. As Donald MacKenzie (2006, 2009) reminds us, a limited language means that the world of sovereign debt is dangerously limited. It remains shadowy and opaque because it is held together by an arcane and esoteric language, one that is confined to the initiated. It mixes economic and legal prose, numbers and statistical series, and computerized technical systems that seek to quantify sovereign creditworthiness, 'propensity to default', and 'loss severity' to creditors. Its communication system takes the form of a specialized world of computer terminals that serve the initiates.

Sovereign debt became embroiled in a world of securitization, hedging, and swaps that was of bewildering complexity, even to insiders. Its centre of gravity shifted to quantitative analysts and to software developers, using multiple computer systems to model how risk can best be managed. Its exotic language served to aid consensus building through shared communication amongst a select few financial investors, analysts, and other stakeholders in central banks, debt management offices, and financial market regulation and supervision. Their relations went beyond shared professional interest in gauging investor interest in sovereign bond issues. They formed an epistemic community.

Financial market language raises three problems that compound each other. Only a very few know how to use this language, so that participation is highly restricted and consensus building is extremely narrow. Moreover, not all who must deal professionally with this language fully understand what is actually going on. This problem affects not just those who regulate and supervise markets but also senior bank executives who are responsible for internal corporate compliance.

Finally, and crucially, so much depends on the validity of the underlying assumptions about creditworthiness, reliability of debtors, potentiality to default, and prospective loss severity. Validity claims are made by reference to science and technique. However, the radical uncertainty that pervades sovereign creditworthiness means that subjective knowledge and interpretation are never far from the surface. Subjective beliefs about states, their governing elites, and public opinion continue to play a powerful role in constructing sovereign creditworthiness and the functioning of sovereign bond markets. The problem is that they are camouflaged by a science-based discourse.

Channels of Financial Market Power

States' relative lack of power over their own sovereign creditworthiness derives from their difficulties in correcting underlying external imbalances and in averting domestically-originated banking crises. External imbalances and banking crises expose the vulnerability of their fiscal policies. Their reliance on macroeconomics to address these difficulties is more akin to alchemy than to a scientifically grounded process of control. In the face of radical uncertainty, governing elites depend on confidence management, cultivating belief in their prudence. They rely on favourable contingencies and luck in managing economic growth and employment and in enjoying positive real interest rates. Against this background, states have powerful incentives to conceal the scale of their debt burdens by fiscal gimmickry. Financial market-induced crisis exposes this carefully constructed illusion.

Foreign exchange markets and sovereign bond markets are the principal channels through which financial market power impacts on states. More recently, the much smaller credit default swap (CDS) market has been added. These markets offer opportunities to test the credibility of the commitment of states to sustainable fiscal policies and to compliance with European and international 'rules of the game'. They also test the credibility of the commitment of creditor states to show solidarity with debtor states. Ultimately, sustainability depends on market confidence in the will and capacity of both creditor and debtor states to manage the domestic political costs of cooperation. Signals that electorates in creditor states are not prepared to fund 'feckless' debtor states, or that the political costs of achieving large primary fiscal surpluses in debtor states are too high, increase the probability of market panic. The lower the rate of economic growth, the higher the interest rate, and the longer the period which these conditions endure, the greater is the likelihood that the markets will assess a debtor state's fiscal policy as unsustainable.

The creation of the euro area in 1999 shifted the parameters of power without tackling the problem of external imbalances. It closed down the classic source of market vulnerability for its Member States, the exchange rate. By offering them this shelter, and the early comfort of convergence in sovereign bond market spreads, monetary union induced illusion and complacency. However, as the post-2007 crisis showed, sovereign bond markets continued to offer a disciplinary mechanism through widening spreads between the bonds of debtor states and creditor states, Germany serving as the benchmark. Debtor states faced the prospect of crippling increases in their servicing costs, thereby aggravating their fiscal positions. The new instrument of CDS added a further element of uncertainty. Increases in the costs of taking out this insurance against default offered a further test of market confidence.

Instruments of Financial Market Power

States face enormous challenges in matching their words and deeds with respect to financial markets. Governing elites use the language of 'gaining the confidence of the markets' in order to avoid negative branding. However, they face the domestic political difficulties of gaining support for the kind of fiscal, economic, labour-market, and social policy reform policies that will satisfy creditors. These difficulties relate to ideological commitments, democratic legitimacy, re-election to office, political career prospects, threats of civil disobedience and riot, and the rise of populist extremism. Conversely, once they seek to brand financial markets as 'sinners' and call for 'the moralization of the markets', governing elites encounter the limitations of their instruments of statecraft. They can employ moral suasion, supervision, regulation, taxation, and debt restructuring and insolvency regimes. However, taming financial market power proves an elusive quest. In consequence, states have very limited insurance against financial market crises.

The constraints on statecraft stem from the sheer size, complexity, and opacity of the financial markets—the 'shadow world' of debt. There is a much greater concentration of financial and intellectual resources in investment banking than in regulatory agencies and supervisory institutions. There are often enormous cultural and ideological differences between political elites and investment bankers, creating a cognitive gap and communication difficulties. Problems of statecraft are compounded by differences of view amongst financial market reformers about what is prudent. Moreover, banks have opportunities for 'regulatory arbitrage', for circumventing rules, and for intellectual capture and regulatory capture of states. The instruments of statecraft lack robustness in the face of market instruments to shape and circumvent state power. The emphasis in financial market reforms on the term 'appropriate calibration' of policy instruments reflects this asymmetry of power (cf. European Central Bank 2010f: 136).

Dramatized stories

Storytelling is a powerful instrument in the hands of financial lobbies like the Institute of International Finance (IIF). Financial public relations (PR) consultancies play a key role in helping create and disseminate these stories. Dramatized storytelling constitutes part of the 'animal spirits' of financial markets (Akerlof and Shiller 2009). It is designed to scare central banks, finance ministries, supervisors, and regulators that 'excessive' regulation or tax may force banks to cut lending to companies and households and pull out of certain markets or locations.

During the Basel III negotiations, J.P. Morgan Chase and the 'Project Oak' group of six major British banks produced this type of dramatized story, dressed up as expert reports. They focused on the big negative macroeconomic costs of tougher capital-adequacy regulation. Dramatized stories are also constructed around the impact of tax measures, like the financial transactions tax, proposed by eleven euro area Member States. The International Capital Markets Association warned of a bond market exodus and reduction in market liquidity that would damage the public finances of Member States. Similar dramatized stories arise with respect to any proposals for increasing trading costs through stamp duties or penalty charges, for ending the favourable tax treatment of debt (under which interest is deductible from corporate tax), or for introducing bank levies or higher taxes on big salaries and bonuses. These stories dramatize the size and consequences of the loss of financial competitiveness, emphasizing increased corporate tax costs, the inability to recruit and retain the most talented bankers, and losses to states in revenues and jobs. Dramatized stories also feature once states begin to contemplate bank restructuring and 'down-sizing' to inject more competition and to limit potential taxpayer liability.

Regulatory and Tax Arbitrage

A second powerful financial market instrument involves exploiting the opportunities for regulatory and tax arbitrage amongst different sectors of the financial market and amongst different state jurisdictions. Geographically, the threat of exit from less lenient regulatory, supervisory, and tax systems has credibility because shifting global financial centres, their offices and computer systems, is much easier than shifting manufacturing operations. As the Organization for Economic Cooperation and Development (OECD) (2013) recognized, profit shifting to other jurisdictions puts at serious risk tax revenues, tax sovereignty, and trust in the integrity of tax systems. Within the EU the tax regimes in Austria, Ireland, and Luxembourg—as well as in Switzerland outside—stood out as particularly problematic.

In sector terms, arbitrage involves shifting activities and risks to new, less-regulated or even non-regulated entities. Thus the focus of Basel III on tightening bank minimum capital requirements offered an incentive to push risk into fast-growing 'shadow banks'. Regulation and tax were lighter for hedge funds, private equity firms, money market funds, commodity trading houses, and energy companies. Investors were attracted because of the lower costs of doing business in non-bank firms (Jenkins and Masters 2010). Non-banks became essential sources of credit and means of thwarting tightening bank regulation.

The risks from regulatory arbitrage are increased as Basel III, EU regulation, and domestic regulations evolve into a tangle of fragmented jurisdictions, each with different priorities and individual provisions, and progressing with varying timetables. In the absence of a clear, detailed global regulatory framework the instrument of arbitrage remains powerful. Collective-action problems meant that comprehensive and detailed global regulatory and tax policies, which would enable states to tame financial markets effectively, eluded agreement at Group of 20 (G20) level.

Postponing Deadlines

A third financial market instrument focuses on the politics of time. It involves lobbying to postpone deadlines for as long as possible. The Basel III minimum capital requirements under Pillar 1 were not to be fully implemented till 2019. Interest-rate risks in the banking book were not included in the Pillar 1 requirements. Instead, under Pillar 2, they were based on banks' own internal methods and procedures. The decision about incorporating the 'Basel interest-rate shock' in Pillar 1 minimum capital requirements was deferred. Similarly, the liquidity-coverage ratio remained in 'observational phase' till 2015. Also, crucial decisions on counter-cyclical buffers for systemically important financial institutions were postponed. These timescales offered opportunities for both excessive risk-taking and intellectual and regulatory capture by the financial lobbies.

Opacity

Exploiting opacity offers another type of financial market instrument. Banks can escape effective supervision and regulation by esoteric financial product and process innovations. They include 'over-the-counter' derivatives and high-frequency trading. High-risk strategies can be pursued in a shadow world of special investment vehicles, using swaps and collateralized debt obligations (CDOs). Attempts were made to extend regulation to 'over-the-counter' derivatives after the 2007 crisis. However, regulation was constantly chasing after dimly-understood market innovations. Lawyers were employed to help build loopholes into the design of regulation.

Banks can also resort to technical obfuscation in accountancy practices, creating an illusion of their good health and inducing regulatory complacency. The post-2007 crisis revealed that major banks had not re-valued their illiquid assets ('marked-to-market') in order to avoid registering write-downs in their balance sheets. Thus they looked financially healthier than they actually were (Sorkin 2009: 103–4). The problem of opacity was exacerbated because of the opportunities for collusion in the professional auditing of banks. Accountancy firms faced conflicts of interest between the ill will of not signing off company accounts and retaining income from providing tax advice to companies. Even the calculation of regulatory minimum capital requirements under Pillar 1 of the Basel III framework invited banks to game regulators' risk weighting. They could attempt to categorize assets as lower risk than they actually were, again creating regulatory illusion.

Divide and Rule

The collective-action problems of states provide opportunities for banks to practise divide and rule. They can exploit the lack of agreement amongst financial market reformers about the most appropriate regulatory, tax, and debt-restructuring and insolvency-regime changes. Reformers are not agreed about how best to tame market power. Proposals vary from changes to market structures by breaking banks into smaller entities; the separation of functions between public-utility, deposit-based banking and high-risk investment banking, each with different supervisory, regulatory, and resolution frameworks; radically higher capital adequacy and liquidity ratio requirements; tax measures to increase trading costs in areas of highest risk and to make taxation more equitable; and orderly debt-restructuring and insolvency regimes that involve bail-ins at the cost of creditors. Consensus around these various proposals proves difficult to achieve.

Divide and rule is made easier still because, in assessing which reforms they will support, governing elites are influenced in different ways by the areas of greatest vulnerability in their banking structures. German negotiators acted both as advocates of a tougher global framework of financial market regulation and as an opponent of fast moves to tighter definition of bank capital requirements and to a single euro area bank resolution mechanism. This seeming paradox in taming market power stemmed from Germany being a creditor state, pledged to sound finance, whilst at the same time harbouring some big undercapitalized banks with high exposures to risky markets and fearing financial exposure to banks in crisis across the euro area.

The Limits of Collective Action

Whether acting individually or (as in the EU) collectively, European states are often the authors of their own misfortunes with financial markets. Miscommunication and poor coordination of their actions derive from their collective-action problems. They serve to unnerve markets, stoke investor fears, and cause them to behave in ways that governing elites judge irrational but that markets see as protecting their clients. Taming markets is about ensuring that financial markets function responsibly and according to appropriate moral standards. It requires both disciplined behaviour from states and a capacity for independent action on behalf of the public interest, above all in ensuring systemic stability, avoiding moral hazard, and providing social solidarity and fairness. Both these conditions are exceptionally onerous. They are essential if the instruments of statecraft are to be exercised effectively: moral suasion, supervision, regulation, taxation, and debt-restructuring and insolvency regimes.

Disciplined behaviour means that those who act on behalf of states must communicate coordinated action clearly, coherently, and in a timely way in order to stabilize markets. Governing elites must exhibit sustained commitment to fiscal consolidation and economic reforms in order to reduce their dependence on the markets. They must also find a balance between large-scale liquidity-providing support to banks and debt-restructuring and insolvency mechanisms that enforce responsibility and fairness in bearing adjustment costs. Emergency liquidity provision, from for instance the ECB and the European Stability Mechanism (ESM), enables states in debt distress to buy time for adjustment. A debt-restructuring and insolvency mechanism involves losses for private creditors to provide an incentive for markets to price risk accurately and to deter them from speculating on future bail-outs (Issing 2010b: 14). Not least, in order to keep the toxic liabilities of banks off the public balance sheet, states must coordinate to deliver stringent minimum bank capital requirements and liquidity ratios and to require bail-ins by bank creditors who must share in losses.

Capacity for independent action on behalf of the public interest is even more problematic. Those who act on behalf of states are prone to exhibit cognitive overload and paralysis in the face of the sheer complexity, technicality, and opacity of financial markets. More seriously, governing elites are at risk of intellectual capture by the promotional culture of investment banking. Intellectual capture is reflected in complacency about financial market power and a tendency to share in the illusion and hubris that markets spawn. This process was apparent within Britain's New Labour after the early 1990s.

In short, the conditions for effective statecraft are enormously demanding, even for creditor-state elites. When it comes to arguing for the primacy of politics over markets, creditor states are in a much stronger position than debtor states. In 2010 German Chancellor Angela Merkel took the lead in advocating an EU sovereign debt resolution regime that would involve losses to bondholders as well as taxpayers. However, Greece and Ireland were appalled by the implications of subsequent investor fear for their sovereign bond yields and were backed by other states that faced contagion risks. The outcome was much more measured. The Treaty Establishing the European Stability Mechanism of 2012 stated in Preamble 12: 'In accordance with IMF practice, in exceptional cases an adequate and proportionate form of private-sector involvement shall be considered.' Nevertheless, in 2013 revised EU state-aid guidelines provided for shareholder and junior bondholder bail-ins prior to taxpayer involvement, pending a later EU directive.

State collective-action problems in taming financial market power contribute, in turn, to collective market illusion and complacency about financial risk. In constructing sovereign creditworthiness financial markets have little more of a claim to sainthood than states that indulge in fiscal gimmickry, obfuscation, and misinformation. Their capacity for sin is bound up intimately with the agency problem within the markets, asymmetries of information, and the bias to underestimate risks (Stiglitz 2010). The incentives for investment managers to pursue short-term profits and bonuses are all too often imperfectly aligned with the long-term interests of their financial institutions, with requirements of systemic stability, and with prevailing notions of fairness. Moreover, having underestimated and incorrectly priced sovereign risks, markets are prone to react to their earlier illusion and complacency by panic, leading to sovereign debt crises. Perhaps most seriously of all, the burdens consequent on the banks' failures of self-regulation are shifted to states, which assume bank liabilities and act to fill the gaps in aggregate demand created by credit crunches. Sovereign debt crises alarm financial markets. However, the markets are a part of the very problem that alarms them.

Financial markets produce a series of dilemmas for creditor-debtor state relations. On the one hand, they are judged useful as the vigilantes of fiscal deficits and public debt, above all by creditor states and international financial institutions. On the other hand, financial markets are imperfect barometers of macroeconomic and political conditions and blunt tools for forcing timely, low-cost macroeconomic adjustments.

Again, on the one hand, the capacity of financial markets to innovate instruments enables them to defuse tensions in creditor-debtor state relations by expanding liquidity. On the other hand, they require 'smart' regulation and supervision if their efficient functioning is to prove compatible with the core public good of financial stability as well as with general notions of fairness. The triad of efficiency, regulation, and financial stability remains imperfectly balanced; the precautionary principle is only very weakly rooted with Basel III; and notions of fairness are even less firmly entrenched in the regulatory, tax, and debt-rescheduling and insolvency regimes for banks, not to mention their salary and bonus cultures. In this context a collective illusion, hubris, and complacency continues to thrive across states and markets.

The precariousness of creditor-debtor state relations is grounded in problems of opacity that affect not just public debt but also financial markets. Governments and officials possess weak understanding of how the inner cogs of the financial markets work and how their functioning is affected by their policies and actions. The superficially calm surface of central bank interest-rate decision-making, sovereign bond and related markets, and 'triple-A' credit ratings can hide danger signals in obscure corners and indices, for instance price swings in credit derivatives, asset-backed commercial paper, and swaps markets. These price swings can generate losses and lead to sudden investor panic.

This opacity within financial markets is mirrored in opacity of public debt. The size of public debt, especially implicit liabilities, is all too often hidden from investors in the form of huge, off-balance-sheet guarantees and borrowing. Its exposure by crisis risks setting off self-fulfilling and highly destructive market expectations. It also shows how financial markets have been well disposed to place confidence in illusory creditor states and to be tolerant of some lapsed creditor states. A pervasive technocratic discourse hides the extent to which illusion is pervasive.

Dilemmas in Using State Power: Macro-Prudential Regulation

States face an uncomfortable dilemma in trying to define the appropriate frontiers of regulation and tax. If regulatory instruments focus too narrowly on the banking sector, there will be calls for regulatory extension into the 'shadow banking' areas. However, regulatory extension risks over-reach and subsequent diminution of its quality and effectiveness. The core problem is that regulation is better at form than substance: at observing compliance with prescribed structures and procedures than at assessing whether management of investment banking is prudent. This problem stems from the traditional culture of public regulation, which is bureaucratic and hierarchical. Perversely, once regulation attempts to get closer to the substance, and thus into the culture of investment managers, it risks capture.

Corporate tax policies have also proved highly accommodative to financial markets, reflecting the extent to which tax authorities rely for advice on big accounting companies which, in turn, provide services to investment banks. These policies have been designed in ways that aid profit-shifting to low-tax jurisdictions, so-called 'tax havens'. They have also reduced incentives for banks to internalize losses from risk-taking and to control their leverage. Making debt deductible for tax purposes acts as a disincentive to increase the ratio of equity to debt (Goodhart 2010a; Hellwig 2010). Banks enjoy tax advantages by issuing debt rather than equity. From the perspective of taming market power, corporate tax policy is often perverse.

The conundrum is that, the more effectively a state seeks to tame financial markets through regulation or tax, the more likely it is to create new boundary problems between states or between markets that financial investment operations can exploit. Investors have an incentive to position themselves on the advantageous side of regulatory and tax boundaries (Goodhart 2010a). The unilateral ending of the favourable tax treatment of debt risks adverse effects on location decisions. Putting in place counter-cyclical regulations that require higher capital ratios in 'good' times faces the impediment that, with states at different points in the cycle, the incentive for investors to transfer activities is strong. Tightening regulation of banking creates an incentive to shift activities to lighter-regulated hedge funds or commodity-trading companies.

In the wake of the post-2007 crisis macro-prudential supervision became a new key reference point in EU and international reforms. This concept had been long promoted by the BIS as a means of focusing central banks on their traditional function of limiting systemic risk. It took massive systemic crisis for central banks and supervisors to embrace macro-prudential supervision as an organizing concept. The creation of the European Systemic Risk Board (ESRB) was followed in 2014 by the Euro Area Single Supervisory Mechanism, both under the ECB. However, macro-prudential supervision only highlighted the problem of sources of systemic risk and whether instruments were 'fit for purpose'. Ultimately it is only as powerful as the will and capacity of Member-State authorities to use available regulatory and tax instruments in a timely and decisive fashion. From the perspective of macro-prudential regulation, Basel III was an incomplete and timid framework. Other instruments were needed: tighter limits on loan-to-value (LTV) ratios in property markets, tighter collateral rules in highly-leveraged sectors, capital surcharges in high-risk areas, risk-based deposit insurance schemes, and recovery and resolution plans (including 'living wills') for systemically significant institutions. Words and deeds were not matched.

Proposals for orderly debt restructuring mechanisms to strengthen systemic stability also create problems for creditor-debtor state relations. They are designed to make investors adjust their risk models and thus tame reckless market behaviour in bond markets. At the same time, debt restructuring mechanisms mean that financial market discipline will be increased. The negative effects are felt most by debtor states and their banks. Unsurprisingly, Germany was the principal sponsor of this idea within the EU.

The Distinctiveness of Financial Markets

Contemporary sovereign bond markets are embedded in wider financial markets, which are distinctive in ways that have implications both for how sovereign bond markets function and for how sovereign creditworthiness is constructed. First, financial markets are driven by 'animal spirits', which include greed, fear, and antisocial behaviour (Akerlof and Shiller 2009). They have a non-rational quality (Augar 2010).

Secondly, financial markets are characterized by positive feedback and herd-like behaviour. They are not automatically self-correcting (Cooper 2008). Positive feedback occurs because, under certain conditions, higher asset prices, not just in property but also in 'safe-haven' sovereign bonds, increase the appetite for these assets. Instead of restraining demand, rising prices push up asset inflation. Similarly, in moments of financial market panic, falling prices can trigger further selling. As before the 2007 crisis, governing elites may act in ways that reinforce positive market feedback effects. They do so through accommodative monetary policies; the lack of proactive, anti-cyclical regulation of credit, liquidity, and leverage, like toughening LTV ratios in times of excessive credit growth; and corporate tax policies that encourage debt financing and risk-taking.

Thirdly, financial markets constitute a world of radical uncertainty, randomness, and vulnerability to 'outlier' events. Hence reliance on probability theory and on quantitative modelling of risk as the basis for prediction proves hazardous (Minsky 2008; Taleb 2008). It generates illusion, hubris, and complacency. Financial market regulators and supervisors are encouraged by the ideology of efficient markets to underestimate the scale of macroeconomic, social, and political damage that 'outlier' events in financial markets can cause. An example was the Value at Risk (VAR) metric which measures a bank's risk over a given period at a particular confidence level. Developed by J.P. Morgan in the early 1990s, it was discredited by failing to predict huge losses post-2007. VAR was spawned by the efficient markets' hypothesis. However, it proved inadequate for capturing 'tail-risk', the losses consequent on an extreme event. It proved incompatible with the precautionary principle in financial market regulation.

Fourthly, financial markets are distinctive because of the systemic scale of the damage that is caused by ill-conceived financial innovations, inappropriate risk-return models, and the opaque interconnectedness amongst banks and between banks and the real economy (Authers 2010).

Fifthly, profit-making private banks enjoy the extraordinary privilege of creating new money. Commercial bank money is at the heart of debt problems. It poses an acute problem for central banks not just in performing their core function of price stability but also for ensuring financial stability. Between 1999 and 2006 total financial-sector debt in the euro area doubled to €20 trillion, from 155 to 222 per cent of annual euro area economic output.

These characteristics are accompanied by another factor: the promotional culture that surrounds financial markets. This promotional culture is cultivated by the growth of financial PR. It is disseminated to a small but active audience by specialist financial journalism and media (Davis 2000). In consequence, financial market culture gains a privileged position in the realm of public discourse.

Through sovereign bond markets and foreign exchange markets, states are enmeshed with financial markets, exposing them to the potentially fatal illusion and complacency about risk that pervades these markets. The distinctive characteristics of these markets cast doubt on belief in the rational, self-correcting behaviour of sovereign bond and foreign exchange markets and in market-based credit ratings as measures of sovereign creditworthiness.

Financial markets need taming through high-quality governance because they are not automatically efficient, because they do not automatically produce systemic stability, and because they pose profound questions about fairness and social solidarity. However, their taming proves an elusive quest when markets possess such enormous power, including not just regulatory and tax arbitrage but also intellectual capture of governing elites. States face the challenge of putting in place adequate, cross-nationally coordinated instruments to correct positive feedback mechanisms and herd-like behaviour and to protect against excessive risk-taking and volatility in financial markets. In addition to their collective-action problems, states confront the huge structural challenge of the systemic power of financial markets within capitalist economies. Their discursive constructions frame and constrain debate about sovereign creditworthiness. They create areas of 'political silence' and narrow policy agendas. Regulatory and tax capture is an ever-present threat as regulators and tax authorities come to view issues through the eyes of financial market participants. This conundrum in taming financial markets highlights the asymmetry of power at the heart of narratives about sovereign creditworthiness.

Rules and Discipline: Illusion and Hubris

The history of creditor-debtor state relations is one of precarious, historically-contingent rules of the game, whose purpose is to provide an orderly framework of discipline that will reassure investors. Their precarious and historically-contingent nature results in part from the vulnerability of governing elites to the illusion and hubris about how to finance sovereign debt that, over the centuries, they have been fed by economic and financial gurus. They tend to look with favour on advisers and officials who serve their interest in establishing a reputation for governing competence and thereby help secure their hold on power.

The formalization of creditor-debtor state relations as a set of shared rules, which make discipline automatic, took root with the so-called classic gold standard. Its emergence was tied together with the gradual consolidation of Britain as the centre of the international financial system in the nineteenth century and its sponsorship of the spread of this standard. The idea of automatic discipline was associated with gold flows out of deficit states, which would have to deflate their economies as a corrective. Although in practice the system was 'managed' to ameliorate domestic effects, it helped to introduce a pre-1914 period of increasing discipline into public debt and financial market behaviour. The dissemination of discipline can be dated to the 1840s and 1850s when Robert Peel and William Gladstone, as Chancellors of the Exchequer, sought to address the problem of large-scale inherited British public debt.

However, this formalization of creditor-debtor state relations foundered in the interwar period on the unwillingness of the major creditor state, the United States, to engage actively and on the incapacity of Britain to perform its leadership role, once it had been reduced to a major debtor state. Furthermore, the power of the *rentier* class was undermined by the massive debt legacies of the First World War, franchise extension, and the rise of Left-wing parties. After 1918 the idea of discipline in public debt was more difficult to realize in domestic political practice. The financial and economic turmoil that followed the Wall Street Crash of 1929 and the European banking crisis of 1931, leading to the Great Depression of the 1930s, made coordinated diplomacy even more difficult.

The lessons learned from the 1930s, and that underpinned the post-1944 Bretton Woods system, focused on the illusion that purely domestic-centred policies could generate sustained global economic growth. Emphasis was laid on their costs in retaliatory measures and on the dangers of uncoordinated deflation. The idea of discipline through rules was reborn in the form of a US-dollar-based exchange-rate system, tied ultimately to gold, and backed by the resources of the new IMF and the World Bank. It was accompanied by capital controls and the possibility of agreed devaluations to ease adjustment for debtor states. In practical terms, Bretton Woods had a short life (1958–1973) because the US found the costs of sustaining the system too high. Its abandonment of its anchor role in 1971–1973 ushered in a period of international financial market liberalization and exchange-rate flexibility.

The post-Bretton Woods world evolved to offer a new framework within which financial market illusion and hubris thrived. It gravitated around increasingly powerful international investment banks, whose power was legitimized by the belief that freeing the financial markets would create discipline. The idea of market discipline on states was attractive because this period coincided with exponential growth in international liquidity. It generated a new wave of economic and financial apostles of the efficient market hypothesis. They helped create an international consensus of complacency about securitization, as in US sub-prime mortgages; about derivatives trading, as in swap markets; about 'light-touch' regulation and supervision; and about not 'leaning against the wind' in monetary policy by regulating credit (Rajan 2010; Stiglitz 2010). The power of markets to brand states and the power of states to tame markets were in severe disequilibrium.

There is an underlying historical tension between successive, imperfect efforts to anchor and legitimate discipline in public debt and financial manias, panics, and crashes (cf. Kindleberger and Aliber 2005). When the credibility of the disciplinary devices comes into question, states find themselves at risk of being overwhelmed. They have at their disposal only a limited armoury of regulatory, tax, and bail-out instruments to restore sovereign creditworthiness and belief in their governing competence. There are also limits on their political will and institutional capacity to make use of these instruments.

Extreme, but all-too-regular, events reveal just how much hidden toxic material is strewn across creditor as well as debtor states and how much macroeconomic damage they can do. The financial markets act not just as the conduits through which this toxic material is distributed, and often hidden, from tax, regulation, and supervision. They serve also as its originators through innovative, esoteric forms of financial engineering. Failures of innovations in financial markets are distinctive in having the potential to provoke large-scale macroeconomic meltdowns, the transfer of toxic assets to public balance sheets, and sovereign debt crises.

Digitalization, Globalization, and the De-Synchronization of State and Market Time

From the late twentieth century digitalization was a potent source of change in the social, spatial, and temporal contexts of financial markets (MacKenzie 2006). Digitalization was synonymous with the rise of young quantitative experts, who were intellectually capable of managing complex data sets and handling more anonymous forms of transaction-based banking. They displaced traditionally educated financial elites, whose legitimacy had been grounded in practical experience of markets, intuitive understanding of their operation, and cultivation of long-term personal relationships, founded on judgement and trust. The personalized world of Nathan Rothschild, Gerson von Bleichröder, and J. Pierpont Morgan gave way to the corporate cultures of Barclays, Deutsche Bank, and BNP Paribas. States had to give closer attention to the market-making, organizational, and technical capacity of the Primary Dealers in their bond markets.

Above all, digitalization compressed space and time in financial markets. This process was encapsulated in globally synchronized markets, contagiously bubbling and bursting together, and in new high-frequency electronic trading platforms in secondary bond markets (Authers 2010; Haldane, Brennan, and Madouros 2010; Harvey 1990). 'Modern', bureaucratically organized states were caught up in an unfamiliar 'postmodern' world of financial markets, which many in their governing elites struggled to understand. In a sector that came to rely ever more heavily on data-sets and statistical management of risk, 'space-time compression' was unusually dramatic.

Consequently, there was a progressive de-synchronization of 'state time' and 'market time'. The temporality of the modern democratic state was structured, above all, by domestic electoral and legislative calendars. It produced a politically rational timetable for fiscal consolidation and economic reforms that was weakly matched to intensifying 'space-time' compression in financial markets. The consequence was that governing elites had to give much more attention to instant 'news management' in order to retain some semblance of control over how sovereign creditworthiness was constructed. Not only can market positions be rapidly reversed, catching out both governing elites and investors. Also, markets can stay 'wrong'—seen from a macroeconomic or political perspective—for longer than a state can stay liquid.

In the post-Bretton Woods era, globalization offered a discourse to legitimate increasing financial market power in the construction of sovereign creditworthiness, notably in justifying the logic of market-friendly reforms, above all liberalization. In addition, the discourse of globalization seemed to fit the empirical manifestations of 'space-time compression' in financial markets. It underpinned an image of eroding state autonomy in the face of market logic. Eroding state autonomy was symbolized in the massive growth in size, complexity, and professional self-confidence of the big cross-national financial conglomerates. Mounting floods of speculative money moved, often opaquely, across state borders in seconds.

This new world of digitalization and discursive globalization posed acute challenges for many European states, where bank balance sheets overshadowed GDP and threatened fiscal meltdown in a banking crisis. Moreover, even in normal times, the rising share of the financial sector in employment and in value-added suggested that it surpassed optimal size and risked negative economic effects (Cecchetti, Mohanty, and Zampolli 2011). Particular concerns about optimal size arose with respect to the British, Cypriot, Icelandic, and Irish financial sectors. As insurance, in 2010 Swiss regulators added an extra 'Swiss finish' to Basel III rules on capital adequacy. They could do so with relative ease as a major creditor state.

The Imbalance of Fear and Greed

Given the limited instruments at their disposal, and opportunities for regulatory and tax arbitrage, states had great difficulty in taming markets by putting fear into the hearts of traders. The main instrument was a pledge by the central bank to 'do whatever it takes' and pledge the active use of its balance sheet to deter speculative attacks. The ECB succeeded in taming the markets in 2012 with its Outright Monetary Transaction (OMT) programme. Where financial markets lose fear, the risk is that greed will gain the upper hand. In that case states have more reasons to fear markets than markets have to fear states.

The history of modern banking supervision and regulation bears out of this picture of states trailing behind financial market activities in their efforts to regulate capital, liquidity, and leverage. The Basel Committee on Banking Supervision (BCBS) was not established till 1974–1975. The Basel I Accord on Capital Regulation did not follow till 1988. It was the delayed-action product of the Mexican, Argentinean, and Brazilian (MAB) default crisis of 1982. Essentially, Basel I was an exercise in providing international cover for the US Congress to impose higher capital requirements on US banks, which had been at serious risk of insolvency following the MAB crisis. However, its top-down approach soon gave way to Basel II, which combined a much more relaxed approach to the capital adequacy ratio with reliance on banks to benchmark best practice amongst themselves in their risk management. The genesis of Basel I in the 1980s had been the catalyst for big banks and banking lobbies to engage intensively in the process. The outcome—enshrined in Basel II—was the dangerous idea that supervisors and regulators could trust in the public spiritedness of the banks.

The Distinctiveness of Sovereign Bond Markets: The Primary Dealers

The power of financial markets over states expresses itself in the growing significance of credit within the structure and functioning of capitalism and in the material and visible sanctions that markets can wield. However, at a deeper, less visible level, it takes the form of the disciplinary nature of their discursive constructions. These constructions frame notions of sovereign creditworthiness and representations of the nature and sources of financial and economic crisis. They shape beliefs about state power, public responsibility, and elite competence. This combination of material with cognitive power provides financial markets with a 'framing' role, an agenda-setting role, and the capacity to ensure that issues which relate most directly to their power are confined to 'political silence' (Foucault 1977; Lukes 2005).

However, this picture of the disciplinary power of financial markets needs qualification. First, though this power might be attributed to 'Wall Street' and 'the City of London', or to firms like Goldman Sachs, it does not derive form a single geographic centre or a single powerful bank. The sources of financial market power over states are, above all, systemic rather than agency-based. Secondly, the exercise of this power is widely disseminated across, and takes varying forms in, different market segments. Within the complex, differentiated 'micro-physics' of financial market power, the sovereign bond market has its own distinctive attributes. It has its particular cast of participants, forms of organization, and guiding principles. Power is configured and flows in its own distinctive way in sovereign bond markets.

Thirdly, states vary in their vulnerability to financial market power. Fundamentally, states cannot escape the disciplines of market power. Nevertheless, a small group of creditor states possess the capability to utilize market power for their own purposes (cf. Tobias 2005). This capability derives from a state fulfilling the conditions that markets require to gain confidence in its sovereign creditworthiness. It depends also on knowledge of how to make markets work smoothly on behalf of the state. The capacity to construct an image as 'strong' states with responsible governing elites is not just confined to creditor states like Germany, the Netherlands, and the Nordic States. It is also to be found in lapsed creditor states with large financial sectors, like Britain. Lack of these capabilities makes debtor states much more vulnerable to financial markets. It hollows out the notion of their sovereignty and national independence.

Competition and Coordination in Bond Markets

The operation of sovereign bond markets rests on tension between the principles of competition and coordination. On the one hand, states compete in bond markets over auction size, price, and yields. They seek comparative advantage in order to reduce their fiscal costs. On the other, during 'bad' times, the premium on coordination in sovereign debt issuance grows. Refinancing debt becomes more challenging. There are mounting risks of overcrowding in bond markets once sovereign bonds lose their scarcity value. Sovereign debt managers are forced to pay increased attention to scheduling the timing of issues: when to go to the markets, with what kind of offers, and how. Temporal coordination of debt-issuance calendars promises to mitigate risks of failed auctions.

The escalating and contagious European sovereign debt crises from 2007 strengthened incentives for temporal coordination amongst EU Member States. Article 6 of the Treaty on Stability, Coordination, and Governance in the Economic and Monetary Union requires Member States to report *ex ante* their public debt issuance plans to the European Commission and to the Council. The crises also put on the table proposals for a common euro area bond (E-bond) and for a 'debt redemption pact', as means of securing cheaper and more secure funding. However, these proposals faced powerful opposition from within Germany, notably the Bundesbank, and other creditor states. The criticism focused on the prior need to relinquish national fiscal sovereignty before assuming joint liability for sovereign debts.

The tension between the principles of competition and coordination is also reflected in state attitudes to the role of banks in sovereign bond markets. States pursue two objectives: privileged relationships with certain banks in managing bond sales; and diversification of sources of finance. In building privileged relationships, they count on the interest of banks in establishing their market-leading credibility. Securing Primary Dealer status gives certain banks the right to take part directly in government bond auctions. They can earn fees from government bond syndications and exploit the trading opportunities that come from increased volatility. At least in economic 'good' times, banks can be induced to compete for this privilege.

In 'bad' times of debt distress, banks can make themselves useful to states by helping them to diversify sources of debt finance and to cultivate relationships with new purchasers of debt. For instance, in the post-2009 sovereign debt crises they brought the Greek government together with sovereign-wealth funds. Banks can provide assistance in sales management exercises. States have an interest in using banks to coordinate market behaviour.

Banks also have incentives to coordinate in dealing with recalcitrant debtor states. They can put a stop on lending and cut states off from international capital markets. This type of coordination was evident amongst Genoese bankers in dealing with Philip II of Spain's serial defaults (Drelichman and Voth 2009). It occurred in the nineteenth century with the emergence of bondholder associations (Esteves 2006; Rui 2007; Wynne 1951). Creditors have a strong incentive to coordinate to protect their interests against chronic debtor states. The Paris Club is an example of how creditor states can coordinate to act on their own behalf. A 'cheat-the-cheater' mechanism exists in sovereign debt markets. It serves as an incentive to coordination in cutting off states from borrowing (Kletzer and Wright 2000).

Privileged Insiders

Despite variation in their capability and vulnerability, states have sought to shape sovereign bond markets on terms that, formally at least, safeguard their distinctive sovereignty. Traditionally, sovereign lending has constituted a narrow, elite social world of privileged 'insiders', in which bankers were expected to exemplify 'moral standing' (cf. Ferguson 2010). Governing elites sought out privileged banking intermediaries, who would act on a strictly personal and confidential basis to secure their often ill-administered, opaque, and volatile public finances. These banks became agents for dealing with crisis management and for helping finance longer-term strategic ambitions. Certain banks enjoyed official recognition and a privileged status in making loans to rulers and governments. The appeal of being an 'insider' was that it generated 'moral standing'. Bankers remained strongly attracted to the aura of state power and the honour and reputation that proximity could bestow.

Traditionally, sovereign bonds enjoyed certain privileges within financial markets. These privileges stemmed from the belief that, in contrast to companies and households, states were much less likely to become insolvent. Moreover, lending to them could open other highly lucrative trade and financial opportunities. With respect to advanced market economies in the post-1945 period, the sovereign bond market gained a reputation as relatively safe, staid, and conservative. Its salient characteristic was the absence of collateral. The security of creditors depended on their confidence that they could sell this debt to others at a reasonable price. The bonds of certain creditor states, like Germany, acquired a 'benchmark' role. In consequence, the sovereign bond market had the image of being the less glamorous end of investment banking.

Seeking Special Status

States are attracted to differentiate themselves by issuing ultra-long-dated bonds. Very few are tempted to be part of a tiny elite club of 'century-bond' issuers, mostly US corporations. Much more typically, states seek elite status by getting the markets to accept ultra-long-dated bonds. In 2006 the 'thirty-year-plus' elite club included Austria, Belgium, Britain, Denmark, Finland, France, Greece, Italy, the Netherlands, Spain, and Switzerland. The 'fifty-year-plus' club comprised Belgium, Britain, Denmark, France, Spain, and Switzerland (Blommestein and Wehinger 2007). Most striking was the presence of Greece and Spain, a hangover from the pre-2007 period of illusion and hubris.

In offering ten–thirty year maturities, sovereign bond issuers have the advantage that risk-based regulatory requirements and international accounting standards, like 'mark-to-market' accounting, force insurance companies and pension funds to hold appropriately safe assets to match their long-dated liabilities. Their so-called 'liability-driven' investment strategies push them to invest more heavily in long-dated government bonds and to act as 'buy-and-hold' investors. In 2004, for instance, insurance companies and pension funds accounted for 24 per cent of thirty-year, inflation-linked Italian bonds (Blommestein and Wehinger 2007: 234). Similarly, the collateral policies of central banks make sovereign bonds attractive to banks. By participating in central bank liquidity operations, banks can use these bonds to augment their leverage and extend their credit provision. Sovereign bonds serve as collateral within the repurchase (repo) market. Similarly, until Portugal broke ranks in 2010, the market convention was that governments differed in not needing to post collateral on swaps deals because the risks to counterparties were perceived as negligible.

Principles and Structure: The Team Approach

Sovereign bond markets have a highly distinctive structure. Their distinctiveness derives from the central organizing principle that public debt management offices, or central banks acting in this capacity, grant privileges of access, bidding, and trading in bonds and bills to certain investment banks. In exchange, they serve as market makers or Primary Dealers. These investment banks become pre-approved counterparties for central bank monetary policy operations. Privileges in participating in auctions and placing sovereign bonds are understood as an incentive for Primary Dealers to engage in secondary-market trading and to keep debt management offices informed about market developments. The Primary Dealer system is designed to promote liquidity, predictability, and stability in sovereign bond markets (AFMA/EPDA 2013: 3). Primary Dealer groups exist in most EU Member States, varying in size from just eight in Sweden to thirty-eight in Germany in 2012. They gain official recognition as specialists, based on their long-term commitment to the sovereign bond market and their organizational and financial capacity. In return for their privileges, and the information advantages that accrue, Primary Dealers have contractual obligations laid down in charter. The appropriate balance between these privileges and obligations is determined in discussions between debt management offices and Primary Dealers.

Additionally, most sovereign bond markets are over-the-counter (OTC), dealer-based systems. The Primary Dealers act as principals on most trades. Liquidity derives from their committal of capital to market-making activity. They undertake this activity over the phone or on one of the main European electronic trading platforms, which include BGC Partners, Eurex, ICAP, and EuroMTS. Bond markets are not generally exchange-based. As in Britain, secondary bond markets may provide for Primary Dealers to deal with each other on an anonymous basis through inter-deal broking firms. Hence, despite the emphasis on transparency within the Primary Dealer Group, it remains an exclusive and confidential world.

The distinctiveness of sovereign bond markets is expressed in the importance that debt management offices traditionally place on mutual trust and on proven capacity of market makers to work in a team. This team approach facilitates both bond issuance and trading in the secondary market. To further the team approach, debt management offices across the EU stress similar principles of confidentiality, fairness, predictability, regularity, and transparency in their dealings with Primary Dealers. Official recognition of market makers is seen as vital to governments in providing market intelligence and research and so helping to improve government decisions on its debt financing.

In Britain the team approach is exemplified by the Gilt-Edged Market Makers Association. Similarly, the EU Economic and Financial Committee (EFC) Sub-Committee on Government Bills and Bonds works closely with the European Primary Dealers Association (EPDA) in agreeing 'best-practice' standards and moves to harmonization. In certain cases, a more directive, state-led approach is apparent. In Greece in 2010 the appropriately-named 'Committee of Primary Dealers' Supervision and Control' comprised two central bank and three finance ministry representatives, and one from the Hellenic Banks Association, out of ten members. The context was a traditionally high level of state ownership in Primary Dealer banks, like the National Bank of Greece.

Dealing with a concentrated set of expert counterparties offers debt management offices a number of gains. They save on substantial transaction costs in maintaining due diligence and effective risk management. They secure better access to market research. They strengthen the promotion of the sovereign bond market to new investors. The team approach also supports efficient trading in the secondary market. This type of structure reduces 'search-and-matching' costs for sovereign states, and helps promote smoother adjustment of bond markets to shocks. At the same time, debt managers have an interest in broadening and diversifying the investor base. They believe that liquidity in the sovereign bond market is best promoted by the presence of competing market makers. Dominance by a few big banks risks higher borrowing costs.

A Rule-Based System

The principal means of sovereign bond issuance is a rule-governed auction process, with regular timetabled auctions (e.g. Dutch State Treasury Agency 2010a; UK Debt Management Office 2009). This method is usually preferred over syndications, mini-tenders, and private placements so that debt managers can be seen to issue debt in a transparent and predictable way. However, syndication is used in certain cases, for instance in sales of new instruments like ultra-long-dated bonds. Where demand is uncertain, allocation is more likely to be successful through a formal book-building process. Syndication also increases significantly with sovereign bond market crisis, when the risk of less successful auctions and auction failures rises. Syndication reduces the execution risk. Conversely, it also risks testing the capacity of Primary Dealers to commit capital.

More normally, a chosen set of Primary Dealers (Gilt-Edged Market Makers in Britain) form the Auction Group. They have an exclusive right to participate in trading, promotion, and distribution of sovereign bonds. Primary Dealers have, in consequence, an information advantage over investors, which is reflected in their capacity to charge higher fees for their services. They receive financial compensation in underwriting fees paid by the government. This compensation varies with the amounts bought and rises with the onset of sovereign bond market crisis. Increasing underwriting fees serve as a reliable early-warning indicator of sovereign debt crisis (Parra 2008).

European sovereign bond issuance is best described as a rule-based system that combines some features of a syndicate, like the Primary Dealer system, with the use of auction as a price-discovery mechanism. In the case of syndicated issues of debt, all Primary Dealers are required to participate in the placement syndicate. In these operations, one Primary Dealer takes on the role of lead manager, based on its expertise in the market niche and its place in the Primary Dealer ranking.

Sovereign Bond Markets in the Post-2007 Crisis

In the EU sovereign debt crises after 2008, debt management offices reviewed their operational frameworks and shifted their approach towards greater flexibility at the expense of predictability (Bloomestein, Guzzo, Holland, and Mu 2010: 23–5). Their reassessment was prompted by rising underwriting fees of Primary Dealers (Parra 2009). In addition to greater use of syndication, debt management offices adopted a more opportunist approach to auction scheduling and relied more on short-term bills and notes. They also sought to diversify and expand their investor base, for instance in Italy. More active use was made of 'road shows' to profile themselves to large investors, along with innovative ways of marketing to retail investors.

Debt management offices in states with serious sovereign creditworthiness problems were less able to rely on overseas-based Primary Dealers, who began to disengage. Austrian Primary Dealers were heavily exposed to Hungarian sovereign debt; French and German Primary Dealers to Greek and Italian debt; and German Primary Dealers to Irish, Portuguese, and Spanish debt. These exposures were not made fully transparent in the EU bank stress tests of 2010. The tests focused on trading-book holdings as opposed to banking-book holdings, which are held to maturity (Blundell-Wignall and Slovik 2010: 5). Major cross-national disengagement had occurred by 2012.

This renationalization of Primary Dealer activity was a key indicator of the financial 'fragmentation' of the euro area as banks began to retreat back within their state borders. The process had certain advantages for Member States, above all reduction in the volatility caused by cross-border investment flows. The renationalization of Primary Dealer activity could be explained, in part, by governments resorting to covert financial repression and moral suasion of domestic banks to hold more of their sovereign debt. However, perhaps more significant was the incentive for domestic banks to use cheap, three-year loans made available by the ECB to exploit the interest-rate margin on their government's distressed debt. At the same time domestic Primary Dealers in Greece, Hungary, Ireland, Italy, Portugal, and Spain risked exposure to the sovereign debt of their own state. Examples included the National Bank of Greece and the Banco Espirito Santo in Portugal (details in Blundell-Wignall and Slovik 2010).

Which States Matter in Sovereign Bond Markets?

In 2009 euro area sovereign debt accounted for 34 per cent of the global market, compared to 34 per cent for Japan, 27 per cent for the United States, and only 5 per cent for Britain. This substantial presence of euro area Member States in global sovereign bond markets made their crises of enormous systemic significance.

Within euro area sovereign bond issuance in 2009 Italy occupied first place with 25.5 per cent, followed by France with 19.3 per cent and Germany with 17.6. The 'big three' accounted for 62.4 per cent of issuance. In contrast, Spain represented 13.1 per cent, Greece 7 per cent, the Netherlands 5.5 per cent, Belgium 4 per cent, and Ireland 3.9 per cent (all figures from <www.deutsche-finanzagentur.de/en/institutional>).

Qualitatively, German sovereign debt stood out because of its 'safe-haven' status as the most risk-free and the most liquid market in Europe. Its role as the European benchmark for bond issuance was strengthened by the post-2007 crisis. In 2009 the traded volume in the secondary market for German sovereign bonds was some €4.7 trillion, 57 per cent traded within the EU. There were more than 70 German bonds in circulation across the entire euro yield curve, up to thirty years (<www.deutsche-finanzagentur.de/en/institutional>). The main turnover was in ten-year Bunds. They accounted for the lion's share of the turnover in the international secondary market. They also served as the central benchmark in European sovereign debt markets.

The Eroding Distinctiveness of the Primary Dealer System

Reflecting the displacement of power to financial markets, the distinctiveness of the Primary Dealer system has been reduced, albeit in a limited manner. First, new real-time, electronic trading platforms in sovereign bonds became state-of-the-art. The EuroMTS platform and the domestic MTS platforms in France, Germany, and Italy offered infrastructures in which variations in trading volumes could have significant impacts on price. Secondly, debt management offices began to deal in swaps and derivatives. However, they did so in a conservative manner, principally to hedge against exchange-rate and interest-rate risks. Thirdly, financial innovations emerged within the sovereign bond market. An example was the first STRIPS (separate trading of registered interest and principal securities) market, pioneered in France in 1991. It involved separate selling of the principal and the regular coupon payments. However, they proved relatively modest in number and significance.

The increasing interconnection between the sovereign bond market and other markets was evident in the practice of 'churning' sovereign bonds. Banks used sovereign bonds that they had as collateral for their loans, for instance to hedge funds, to support their own deals. In this way sovereign bonds were caught up in the shadowy banking world of 'rehypothecation', in which banks use a limited asset base to increase hugely their leverage (Singh and Aitken 2010). In addition, banks began to question the special position of states in derivatives markets and to demand similar borrowing standards. In 2010, the Portuguese government led the way in agreeing to post collateral in its derivatives trades. This move was designed to placate banks and make borrowing costs more predictable.

Also, strengthened EU and domestic competition law served to reduce barriers to entry as a Primary Dealer. In particular, the Maastricht Treaty of 1992 symbolized and formalized the erosion of state privilege in financing. Article 104 prohibited governments from privileged access to financial institutions.

The complex interconnections between sovereign bond markets and developments in other financial markets, notably for corporate bonds, swaps, foreign-exchange, and equity, meant that states could not avoid exposure and vulnerability to randomness and to rapid, global contagion. This interconnectedness has been reinforced through the spread of innovative financial instruments like securitization; the dissemination of controversial practices, such as naked short selling; and the importance that has become attached to credit default swaps as benchmarks of sovereign creditworthiness. The common factor that binds together different financial markets is their fiduciary character. They depend on contingency-related confidence and trust. Overall, in the view of the European Central Bank (2010e: 102), the financial markets' contribution to systemic risk in the first stages of the post-2007 crisis substantially outweighed that of the household, non-bank corporate, and public sectors.

Why Creditors Originate Problems

> Speculators may do no harm as bubbles on a steady stream of enterprise. But the position is serious when enterprise becomes the bubble on a whirlpool of speculation.
>
> John Maynard Keynes (1936: 159)

As Keynes suggests, the investment bankers on whom states depend are unlikely saints and there is ample ground for scepticism about their assessments of sovereign creditworthiness. From the 1970s to the post-2007 crisis there were ample incentives for them to sin: extremely low capital requirements; leverage ratios that were inadequately weighted for risk; captive deposits when retail banking operations were not securely ring-fenced; opportunities to spawn a huge 'shadow banking' sector; limited transparency requirements; pay structures linked to short-term returns; and implicit subsidy from governments to investment banking as a systemically significant activity. The effects of these incentives are magnified by the attraction of the sector to psychopaths, individuals who act without conscience behind a mask of sanity (Hare 1993). More prosaically, they are accentuated by the combination of investor overconfidence, stubbornness, and other attributes of 'animal spirits'.

Moral hazard is a greater problem for states in financial markets than in other economic sectors because of the unique way in which they combine a fundamental social utility function with high risk, volatility, and greed. In this context narcissistic and psychopathic behaviour patterns have unrivalled economic opportunities to inflict damage. In the political economy of 'good' times, financial markets can amass extraordinary riches and clothe callous, manipulative behaviour in social virtue. In the political economy of 'bad' times there is widespread denial of responsibility and lack of remorse. This set of attitudes goes along with lack of shame in accepting bail-outs and generous severance packages. The compound of intellectual self-confidence, systemic significance, perverse incentives, and attraction to narcissists and psychopaths makes banking uniquely powerful and dangerous. At the same time, it can be argued that those who govern states have only themselves to blame for failure to dispel financial market illusion and take control. The problem is that they are part of the illusion.

For these reasons, problems of sovereign creditworthiness cannot be seen simply as debtor-state-originated. Elites and publics may justifiably claim that they have been exploited by manipulative creditors and have suffered from market abuse and mis-selling of complex products. The effects of perverse incentives, imprudent investment strategies, and weak internal risk management become shared problems of creditor states and debtor states.

Creditors become a source of systemic problems in sovereign creditworthiness for two main reasons. First, their behaviour is prone to a principal-agent problem. This problem increases as financial market products become more complex and esoteric. The result is a growing asymmetry of information between shareholders, boards of directors, senior management, market technicians, and traders. The effects of this principal-agent problem display themselves in an illusion of corporate control, in an internal banking culture that fosters reckless risk-taking, and in the damage that can be inflicted by narcissistic and psychopathic 'rogue traders'. One symptom is misaligned incentive structures between, on the one hand, traders and management seeking bonuses and commissions and, on the other, shareholders and investors. Asymmetries of information mean that creditor behaviour does not always match up to the standards that are expected.

Secondly, creditors are at risk of investing excessive intellectual confidence in financial models that rest on very fragile assumptions and creating a grandiose sense of their self-worth. In the decade and more before the post-2007 financial crisis, belief in the efficient markets' hypothesis, in its corollary of self-regulation, and in the 'originate-and-distribute' model was associated with group-think, illusion, and hubris. Complacent optimism extended beyond financial investors into the surrounding market infrastructure of central banks, international financial institutions, credit rating agencies, and regulatory and supervisory bodies. Lobbying and self-regulatory bodies like the International Swaps and Derivatives Association (ISDA), dating from the mid-1980s, came to enjoy enormous prestige and political weight. A supporting phalanx of macro- and micro-economists added intellectual weight to this powerful infrastructure.

The Visible Hand of Creditor Power

The structural power of financial markets over states has such firm roots that it soon resurfaces even when, as regularly, their image is battered by crises and scandals. The collapse of Long-Term Capital Management (LTCM) in 1998 did nothing to dent the rapid growth of hedge funds (Mallaby 2010). Seizing the opportunities offered by distortions in sovereign bond supply and demand, hedge funds continued the LTCM investment strategy of relative value arbitrage by exploiting price discrepancies between sovereign bonds. Central bank purchases of sovereign bonds (quantitative easing) in the post-2007 crisis increased these trading opportunities. Though brought into EU and US supervisory and regulatory oversight after the post-2007 crisis, hedge funds went from strength to strength in exploiting relative value arbitrage. They were able to make profits out of distressed debt in states like Greece.

In the early part of the post-2007 crisis the structural power of financial markets was manifested in the willingness of EU Member States like Ireland to make taxpayers bear the harsh burdens of adjustment to unsustainable bank debt. It was seen as preferable to accepting and negotiating debt restructuring, which would entail losses to bank bondholders. The structural power of markets was also apparent in the vehement criticism of the German federal government in 2010 for insisting that the EU must develop a crisis-resolution mechanism with a debt restructuring clause that, post-2013, would entail bank bondholders sharing in the costs of future bail-outs. Market practitioners, backed initially by the ECB, argued that the euro area faced serious loss of face from institutionalizing default, bigger challenges in rebuilding creditor confidence, and higher risk premiums. There were also potential legal hurdles in applying haircuts to bondholders, increasing the risk of damaging defeats in courts of law. However, by reducing the losses imposed on taxpayers, euro area Member States would help protect the agenda of social justice and discourage populist and extremist politics. At least in the short run, 'default phobia' triumphed. The limits of taxpayer acceptance were tested before the limits of bondholder acceptance.

Basel III: 'Recalibrating' Rules in the Shadows of Regulatory Arbitrage and Capture

Language reveals central characteristics of the politics of sovereign creditworthiness. After the 2007 crisis regulators, finance ministries, and central banks spoke of 'recalibrating' regulatory and tax instruments to strengthen financial market supervision and regulation. In order to facilitate cautious recalibration, considerable discretion was left to the regulatory process. This caution was evident in the ways in which the Vickers Commission in Britain and the Liikanen Commission in the EU sought to ring-fence the utility functions of retail banking and payments from trading and investment banking activities. The more radical solution of their separation was rejected. Similarly, caution was reflected in the comprehensive US Dodd-Frank Act of 2010 and in the slow progress of piecemeal EU proposals on derivatives, short selling, market abuse, and bringing hedge funds and credit rating agencies under the supervisory and regulatory umbrellas. The EU Alternative Investment Fund Managers directive took effect in July 2013, amid huge protest from hedge funds and private equity funds.

Following the biggest post-1945 financial market meltdown, the BCBS's Basel III rules of 2010 sought to strengthen bank capacity to weather future crises. The rules introduced tougher and more tightly defined tier-one capital requirements as a percentage of risk-weighted assets (RWA). Capital requirements were to rise from 2 per cent to effectively 7 per cent, and to consist essentially of equity and retained profits. Other innovations were deferred for further discussion because of their complexity. They included a new counter-cyclical capital buffer; a new systemic groups' buffer for super-sized banks; a new 'liquidity-coverage' ratio, which would require banks to hold a minimum of cash and sovereign bonds to survive a thirty-day market crisis; and the requirement that systemically significant financial institutions write 'living wills' to facilitate their restructuring.

This 'recalibration' was far from radical change. The BCBS watered down its initial proposals. It focused on risk-weighted capital ratio rather than leverage ratio or a resolution regime that would put losses that could not be absorbed on to banks' creditors. In part, this lack of radicalism reflected the combination of the innate caution of central bankers, further strengthened by their sense that they had to pick their way carefully through the uncharted waters of major systemic financial and economic crisis. However, it also illustrated bank lobbying power. They retained the capacity to exploit regulatory complexity to create new loopholes.

In addition, the relatively low recalibration of core, tier-one capital, and extended implementation time over almost a decade, owed much to the opposition of German negotiators. They rejected the high burden that the new ratio would place on key undercapitalized and weakly-governed parts of their banking system, especially the deeply troubled public-sector *Landesbanken*. German creditor-state power did not translate into a tough approach to bank capital. The limitations of Basel III reflected a concentration of systemic vulnerability within the euro area *inside* its major creditor state. The outcome was a lack of adequate incentive for banks to price debt in ways that would strengthen discipline and help complement continuingly weak regulation. In consequence, states remained acutely vulnerable to the potent mix of greed and fear in banking, above all in the shadow sector.

The most important questions were left either to the implementation stage or for the Financial Stability Board (FSB) to answer within the framework of G20. Basel III implementation remained vulnerable to regulatory capture. In particular, the question of just how much banks would have to adjust the value of different assets that they hold to account for different levels of risk was open to 'gaming'. The 'too-systemically-significant-to-fail' problem remained unsolved. There was a deep reluctance to pursue the agenda of structural change in banking, including the issues of the optimal size of banks in relation to GDP and of the separation of public-utility from investment banking. By 2012 the EU had still to agree proposals on how to ring-fence, let alone separate, these two functions of banking. This reform was essential if the prospect of public subsidy to high-risk, speculative investment banking was to be removed and moral hazard checked. It would help ensure that a bank resolution regime would impose costs on creditors and shareholders rather than treat taxpayers as risk-bearers of last resort (Kay 2010). Germany took the lead domestically in addressing the issue of orderly resolution and insolvency mechanisms for banks. In 2012 the European Commission produced options. However, investment banks proved reluctant to write 'living wills', which would allow the orderly winding down of banks. They were being asked to identify who would lose out—bondholders, other unsecured creditors, and shareholders—without undue costs for taxpayers.

Perhaps most worryingly of all, the temporal question of how implementation related to cycles of financial crises was left unexamined. The full weight of the new Basel III rules did not apply till 2019, though national and EU regulators could choose to accelerate their introduction. They had long timescales for their full implementation that exceeded normal credit cycles and thus left a high exposure of states to risk when managing past banking crises had already exhausted their fiscal room for manoeuvre.

Finally, the historical context of the Basel III rules was ignored. The capital ratios for British and US banks had been in long-term decline. In Britain they fell from over 10 per cent before 1914—down from over 15 per cent in the 1880s—to around 5 per cent since the early 1980s. In the United States capital ratios declined from over 15 per cent before 1914—down from over 20 per cent in the 1880s–1900s—to well below 10 per cent since the 1940s (Haldane, Brennan, and Madouros 2010). The corollary was heightened risks that banking crises could devour state fiscal capacity.

Useful lessons about the dangers entailed in bank balance sheets can be drawn from historical examination of financial fragility, systemic risk, and counter-cyclical provisions to absorb losses. An examination of previous crises, like 1933, suggested a requirement of a minimum 10–12 per cent core, tier-one capital ratio, in contrast to the 7 per cent ratio in Basel III (Hellwig 2010; Hanson, Kashyap, and Stein 2010). The historic scale of the mismatch between financial risk and loss-absorbing provision had become alarming. Admati and Hellwig (2013) proposed that some 20–30 per cent of the balance sheet of banks should be funded by equity, instead of debt, over seven times the figure in Basel III. The mismatch problem grew in the case of the largest, most complex, and interconnected banks. As 'super-spreaders', they needed to hold higher amounts of loss-absorbing capital (Haldane and May 2010).

By 2013 studies for the Basel Committee cast serious doubt on the reliability of the Basel III 7 per cent capital ratio. Implementation of risk-weightings by banks proved uneven, with European banks taking a less cautious approach than US banks. It was clear that risk-weightings gave too much discretion to banks. By 2013 the Basel Committee had adopted a 3 per cent leverage ratio as a back-stop measure that relates capital to total assets, regardless of risk. The aim was to mitigate the risk of uneven risk-weightings across banks. However, policy solutions to the problem of banks manipulating the core tier-one ratio remained elusive. Once again, the leverage ratio was set low and more weighting benchmarks were needed. Supervisors proved vulnerable to bank lobbying that a high leverage ratio would lead to a contraction in bank lending.

Basel III and EU reforms illustrated that financial market supervisors and regulators were prone to concede to financial lobbies, to vacillate over timetables for implementation, and to create porous and incomplete regulatory frameworks. The shadows of intellectual capture, manipulation and gaming of complex regulation, and 'regulatory arbitrage' hung heavily over the relations of states to financial markets. These shadows were cast by the resources of structural power and by the superior instruments that financial markets possess in dealing with states. In these shadows the notion that banks have a responsibility to serve wider systemic stability rather than their own private interests was very difficult to nurture. Financial markets were better matched to an economic culture of 'hedonistic' consumerism, with its attendant promotional culture of public relations and marketing, than to fostering a stability culture. Banks were part of the problem of illusion, hubris, and complacency that infected public finances. They were not simply the virtuous sovereign bond disciplinarians that act as antidote to public-sector folly. They—or at least their managers and traders—were the chief beneficiaries of the lack of the precautionary principle in public regulation and market discipline.

Systemic Significance

The structural roots of the power of financial markets lie in their systemic significance. Liquidity and credit are the lifeblood of capitalist economies. Their systemic significance stems in part from the way in which they reflect larger global and European imbalances in patterns of trade, savings, and investment. In economic 'good' times, financial markets shift the huge savings of creditor states to debtor states, opening up new opportunities to develop infrastructure, increase growth capacity, and bring more people into the world market (Wolf 2004). Also, through sovereign bond, swap, foreign-exchange and other markets, as well as credit ratings, financial markets define and, if necessary, enforce adjustments to correct external imbalances. In the process they reinforce asymmetric power in creditor-debtor state relations.

However, financial market discipline tends to act with a time lag and in a dramatic, highly disruptive fashion. By not always pricing risk adequately, sovereign bond markets can fail to smooth adjustment pressure over time. They are, in short, imperfect disciplinarians in the absence of effective incentives on risk pricing. This shortcoming provoked the German initiative in 2010 to create an EU orderly debt restructuring mechanism that would impose haircuts on bondholders in case of collective bail-outs.

Above all, the roots of financial market power derive a highly positive narrative that emphasizes their role in providing the infusion of liquidity on which the financial health of governments, non-financial companies, and households depends. They are represented as underwriting the capacity of governments to provide national security and to deliver improved social welfare and infrastructure. Financial markets are seen as essential in providing the ample, cheap credit on which companies rely to make profits and satisfy shareholders, to invest, and to create jobs. Not least, they are pictured as the engine that makes it possible for households to accumulate wealth, to entertain aspirations that had been denied their forbearers, and to make new life-style choices. The more successful financial markets are in mobilizing plentiful credit, in providing it cheaply, and in facilitating efficient arms-length transactions, the more highly they are valued by governments, companies, and households as socially and politically useful.

This narrative of the essential function of credit provision for a capitalist economy privileges financial markets as central to economic growth, to raising material living conditions, to defusing social and political tensions, to easing processes of domestic consensus-building, and to establishing images of governing competence for state elites. They also become identified with the promotion of a political, social, and cultural agenda of optimistic liberalism. It represents financial globalization as a benign process of drawing ever larger sections of the world's population into work and delivering them ever higher standards of living (Wolf 2004). Media outlets like Bloomberg and CNBC, economic commentators, financial analysts, and bankers help construct a narrative of financial markets as indispensable to the effective exercise of state power, to extending economic and social welfare globally, and to wider culture enrichment through more liberal, open societies. This constructed image is central to financial market power within the politics of sovereign creditworthiness.

However, the cultivation of this positive self-image conceals the financial market's vulnerability to illusion, hubris, and complacency. Investment banking has a fatal allure for psychotic and narcissistic personalities, rests on an unstable compound of greed and fear, and carries risks of catastrophic financial meltdown. To make money, financial investors have to use their capital. Depending on their risk aversion and optimism, they have an incentive to seek out the highest returns. Increasing economic affluence, along with saving provision for an ageing population, has placed vastly more capital at their disposal and greater risk of huge systemic damage.

Financial Market Power and Incentives to Excessive Risk-Taking

Several factors increased the incentives to excessive risk-taking, contagion, and systemic instability and meltdown (Authers 2010). The trend to ever larger cross-national financial conglomerates meant greater exposure to risks consequent on principal-agent splits. In a context of lack of market transparency, and internally weak compliance systems, investment managers and traders could more readily escape tight corporate governance. They exhibited less fear in taking risks with other people's money than with their own.

Moreover, investment managers and traders operated in an environment in which reckless banking and market abuse, including insider trading and market manipulation, were easy to perpetrate. The rogue trader was a phenomenon with deep roots in financial market culture. The damage that they could cause was illustrated by Nick Leeson's role in the collapse of Barings and by Jérôme Krievel at Société Générale and John Rusnack at Allied Irish Bank. Part of the problem was weak criminal penalties on reckless banking. Criminal sanctions were notably weak in Austria, Bulgaria, the Czech Republic, Estonia, Finland, Slovakia, and Slovenia. The EU Markets Abuse Directive was an attempt to strengthen sanctions on 'white-collar' crime in the financial sector. In 2013 the British government proposed a new offence of 'reckless misconduct in the management of a bank'.

Three other factors increased risks to systemic stability. First, as financial markets became more complex and large-scale, investment managers were more susceptible to 'following the herd', thereby magnifying market developments into bubbles and bursts. Secondly, the higher status of market practitioners as professionals, with impressive academic qualifications and infectious self-belief, induced excessive trust in their risk models and investment strategies.

Finally, increased corporate size and growing interconnectedness of markets meant a widening range of 'systemically significant institutions', judged 'too big to fail'. The consequence was a growing moral hazard problem in banking that was sharply revealed in the post-2007 crisis and far from resolved by its management. Banks could use cheap plentiful credit, effectively subsidised by the implicit state guarantee that banks will not be allowed to fail in a meltdown, and underpinned by unlimited, emergency, low-cost central bank liquidity provision. Against this background, investment managers could take bold risks for huge returns and create potentially disastrous 'tail-risks' (Haldane, Brennan, and Madouros 2010; Sorkin 2009).

Perhaps the most potent indicator of financial market power in the politics of sovereign creditworthiness is that, in a crisis, the financial sector can depend on vastly bigger public subsidies than would be given to any other sector. The capacity to ensure socialization of losses and privatization of profits is a sign not just of power but also of moral hypocrisy. The hypocrisy stems from loudly advocating 'marketization' of the wider economy, government, culture, and society, whilst escaping market logic—which includes insolvency—in one's own sector. In the process, self-destructive moral hazard is introduced into the heart of the capitalist economy. This costly hypocrisy invites political attack as an outrageous assertion of economic power.

The power of financial markets also expresses itself in their role as originators as well as mirrors of global and European external imbalances. Through instruments like securitization they mis-value assets, build up leverage, and help fuel asset-price booms and busts, which destabilize creditor-debtor state relations. Ready access to wholesale money markets for lower-cost credit, and innovation of new complex financial instruments, offer the means to escape from the constraints of narrow, depositor-based banking and tight LTV credit restrictions. From the 1990s financial market innovations centred on the financial business model of 'originating and distributing' debt, using the expanding technology of swaps and derivatives (Tett 2009). Intellectual confidence in these technologies was buttressed by an ascendant economic paradigm of efficient markets and by a legitimating discourse of globalization (Stiglitz 2010).

With this climate of innovation and intellectual self-confidence, investment banking delivered massive profits alongside a trend growth in credit expansion that far exceeded the trend growth in retail bank deposits (Goodhart 2010a). In return, it produced enormous personal financial rewards for investment managers, traders, and analysts. The rewards were justified as commensurate to the risks that they took. The thrill of this high risk-reward world generated a glamorous image of daring corporate adventurers. However, intellectual confidence in this financial business model proved ill founded. It led to a regulatory and cultural climate that produced powerful incentives to relax risk management standards, resulting in excessive risk-taking and reckless behaviour.

Financial Markets as Cement and Solvent in the Politics of Sovereign Creditworthiness

Financial markets have a paradoxical role in the politics of sovereign creditworthiness. On the one hand, as the next chapter shows, they bind together a large cast of participants. The cement that the financial markets provide is given by a shared esoteric language. A common set of concepts, models, and assumptions delimits the narrow world in which their participants operate. It draws much of its substance from macro- and micro-economic gurus who work on, and often in or close to, financial markets and who offer them the legitimacy of scientific knowledge. A discourse of globalization took firmer root in this sector than in any other. In conjunction with macroeconomic discourse, it legitimated claims that financial markets are disembodied from states, are more cosmopolitan in outlook, and bring greater objectivity and scientific precision to debate about sovereign creditworthiness and optimal debt. From the 1980s this shared language of efficient markets and globalization evolved into a powerful intellectual edifice of market rationality, decorated with numerous Nobel Prizes in Economics.

On the other hand, financial market crises, and the economic 'bad' times that they generate, act as a solvent in the politics of sovereign creditworthiness. They separate the cast of participants into distinct sets, each with its own sharply defined and differing strategic interests. In 'good' times, regulators and supervisors are disposed to trust in the professional competence of banks and their incentives to harmonize around 'best practice'. They become 'hands-off'. For instance, they did not use the discretionary powers available to them under Pillar II of Basel II to assess the professional quality of banking institutions and to intervene if it was lacking. Instead, Basel II was based on the principle of harmonizing around the 'best practice' of the technically most competent institutions, notably their VAR metrics. It relaxed the capital adequacy requirement from a target of 8 per cent under Basel I to a mere 2 per cent. This reduction of capital adequacy requirement ignored the public interest in avoiding systemic risk and the 'tail-risk' of extreme shocks. In so doing, it created the conditions for the post-2007 crisis (Goodhart 2010a; Hellwig 2010).

Financial crisis reveals in sharper form the underlying conflict between the public interest, which is the reference point of legitimacy for regulators and supervisors, and the private interests of bankers. Regulators and supervisors are responsible for preventing systemic risks through negative externalities from bank behaviour. They are also responsible for protecting non-professional consumers by correcting asymmetric information. Banks are, above all, interested in pursuing high profits by making use of their capital in new ways. Avoidance of negative externalities and correction of asymmetric information provide the rationales for regulation and supervision. The difficult negotiation of the Basel III capital adequacy and liquidity requirements in 2009–2010 illustrated this tension and conflict.

Financial markets act as a solvent in the politics of sovereign creditworthiness through their branding of debtor states, which are judged not to have honoured the shared language and to have defied market-based models and assumptions of rational behaviour. Financial markets hold 'sinners' to account by disciplining them with downgrades of credit rating, higher debt-interest costs, and failed sovereign-bond auctions. This capacity to brand states as 'saints' and 'sinners' is the mark of their power. Financial markets assign and entrench images of state strength and weakness, public responsibility and fecklessness, and elite competence and incompetence.

The Cultural, Social, and Political Consequences of Financial Market Power

The cultural, social, and political consequences of the growth of financial market power have been profound (Cetina and Preda 2005). By the 1990s bankers and traders had become cultural icons. The morally corrosive effects of ruthless greed were invested with glamour, heroism, and sophistication (Preda 2005). Despite its critical intent, and its timely release just a few months after the 1987 financial crash, Oliver Stone's film *Wall Street*, and its 'master-of-the-universe' figure Gordon Gekko, achieved cult status on business school campuses. 'The brightest and the best' were attracted to the promise of rapid social and economic advancement by becoming fabulously wealthy in investment banking. There were high social and cultural opportunity costs in foregone talent in other areas of life.

More profoundly, civic and moral values were distorted as the claims of public service were eroded. The virtues of a non-commercial 'gift' culture, which were celebrated in Shakespeare's stress on grace and gratitude as marks of honour, lost resonance. Economic culture was pervaded by the values of individualistic and hedonistic consumption and the 'get-rich-quick' mentality. Its values were promoted by the fast-growing marketing and PR industries and financed by easily available bank credit (Migone 2007). The fast-growing financial and PR sectors became intimately bound together in this promotional culture. It served the purpose of providing positive news stories for the media and communicating crafted messages to investors, regulators, politicians, and other discrete audiences (Davis 2000).

The political effects were equally profound. The image of the 'ascetic' state, devoted to the values of stability culture and morally censorious of debt, gave way to the 'indulgent' state, wedded to a permissive ideology of debt. The ideology of liberal market capitalism, promoted by banks, emerged as cover for 'crony' capitalism, in which privileged insiders were able to exploit self-regulation to gain tax and other privileges. The tests of governing competence were reduced to two: the credibility of the claims to be able to win the confidence of the financial markets; and the capacity to satisfy demands for hedonistic consumption. Financial market activities shaped not just household life and the corporate world outside banking. Their participants and language penetrated into the inner workings and structures of the state itself. Key investment banks enjoyed privileged relationships to prime ministerial offices, finance ministries, revenue and tax-collection agencies, central banks, and debt management offices. Central banks gained new-found independence from the political process. However, in career and intellectual terms, they became more interconnected with the financial markets. The term 'financialization' referred to the use of new financial instruments. It could also serve to describe how pervasive was the depth and reach of financial market power.

As the post-2007 crisis illustrated, this enormous financial market power concealed a capacity for illusion and self-destruction. The greed, one-dimensional thinking, and self-confidence in their own narratives that animated financial market spirits also served to attract personalities with psychopathic and narcissistic attributes. Financial markets proved a force for systemic instability, in substantial part disembodied from the 'real' economy. However, the 'real' economy suffered from the post-crisis drying up of liquidity, with harsh negative effects on consumption, investment, growth and employment, and ultimately on public finances and sovereign debt.

The effect of the post-2007 crisis was to shine a searchlight into some of the darker corners of the financial markets, causing serious damage to their carefully constructed image. This process gathered momentum with the collapse of Lehman Brothers in September 2008, the hugely expensive rescues of the US insurance giant AIG and Royal Bank of Scotland in Britain, the Libor inter-bank lending-rate scandal in 2012, and public outrage at bankers' bonuses (Sorkin 2009). Certain figures came to represent the degeneration of banking ethics and culture. Richard Fuld of Lehman Brothers emerged as the epitome of financial greed and recklessness: he earned $71.9 million in 2007. Bob

Diamond of Barclays presided over the manipulation of the Libor inter-bank lending rate. The US investor Bernard Madoff, as well as rogue traders like Kerviel, were imprisoned for fraudulent behaviour on a huge scale (Ferguson 2009: 2). Narcissistic and psychopathic personalities seemed disproportionately present in financial markets. However, the problems were more systemic than individual. They were rooted in a banking culture of reckless lending. The limitations of state power were clear in the incapacity to tame this recklessness. Effective bank lobbying ensured the failure to enshrine effectively the precautionary principle in financial market supervision and regulation, not least through adequate loss-absorbing bank capital provision.

12

Professional Consensus, Political Silence, and Sovereign Creditworthiness

> [The] enormous preparatory work [for European monetary cooperation]...resembles a hidden treasure: all the papers are written by monetary experts and for the use of monetary experts; they therefore hardly ever have reached the attention of the leaders or heads of state or government; in most cases they have not even been given full attention and full reading by finance ministers.
>
> Former German Chancellor Helmut Schmidt, 1984
> (quoted in Mourlon-Druol 2012: 1)

The politics of sovereign creditworthiness is played out within the framework of the private governance of public debt. This framework rests on a set of formal understandings that continue to privilege state sovereignty as the embodiment of political legitimacy. The institutional characteristics of this market segment remain distinctive in retaining features of a culture of relationship, as opposed to just transactional, banking. Modern Primary Dealers are expected to show some commitment to the welfare of their clients. In this sense, the private governance of public debt can be seen as an attempt to match state liability with control. It enables governing elites to borrow the prestige of elite banks, benefit from their confidential advisory role, secure the confidence of bondholders, and thus ensure market access at favourable interest rates. The corollary of this preference for relationship banking is visible hands at work in this market segment. It was represented by the House of Rothschild and J.P. Morgan in the nineteenth century and by Barclays and Goldman Sachs in the twenty-first. States seek insurance against market power through central banks and debt management offices.

However, the understandings at the heart of the private governance of public debt also include the expectation that states will remain faithful to their undertakings to bondholders. Perception of increasing risk of default puts at stake the market reputation of prestigious banks that have acted as underwriters of a state's sovereign debt. The private governance of public debt functions in the shadow of the fear that these banks will walk away, leading to a denial of market access. Sovereign bond markets come to symbolize the limits of state control and the risk that governing elites will be rendered powerless and international and supra-national institutions left impotent. More generally, the sheer size of banking systems, sometimes a multiple of gross domestic product (GDP), as well as their opacity, above all in the 'shadow' banking sector, underlines just how exposed states are.

Exposures to high risk of systemic collapse in sovereign bond markets, notably in the 1930s and again after 2008, induced lesson-drawing amongst European governing elites. The outcome was an historic process in which the private governance of public debt became enmeshed in an increasingly formalized framework of creditor-debtor state relations. Faced with growing economic and financial interdependence, and with rising public expectations about living standards and social provision, governing elites sought heightened protection and insurance against sovereign risks. These risks were associated with global and European trade and financial imbalances, financial market shocks, deep and protracted economic recession, and their cumulative effects on public finances. Creditor-debtor state relations and the private governance of public debt are worlds that are defined by complex, interweaving strands. Within the EU these strands include bilateral and multilateral intergovernmental bargaining, the delegation of state authority to supra-national actors, transnational learning processes above and beyond states, and manoeuvring for influence by different European and international institutional forums.

The politics of sovereign creditworthiness involves the interaction of various participants across different levels—international, European, and domestic. It is a process of multilevel governance. Despite their claims to special privilege, based on political legitimacy, governing elites share power, externally and internally. Different forums—like the International Monetary Fund (IMF), the European Commission, the European Central Bank (ECB), as well as Member-State heads of state and government in the European Council and in the Euro Summit—compete for influence over policies to secure sovereign creditworthiness. Crucially, this sharing of power extends beyond the narrow technical infrastructure of cross-national policy learning and negotiation to powerful market-based actors. The politics of sovereign creditworthiness is also a process of market-based governance, in which financial elites have privileged, semi-official roles.

Creditor-debtor state relations and the private governance of public debt have experienced considerable formalization. This formalization is most evident within the EU, where supra-national authority has gained a role not seen at the global level. It is evident in European monetary union, moves to banking union, and, more tentatively, to fiscal union. The process of formalization is associated with intensifying intergovernmental bargaining through the European Council and, meeting in the configuration of heads of state and government of the euro area, the Euro Summit. It is also linked to transnational learning processes that operate through a complex technical infrastructure, above all in Brussels and Frankfurt. However, the modus operandi of creditor-debtor state relations and of the private governance of public debt remains principally informal. State claims to sovereignty make difficult the formalization of supra-national rights to intervene in policies to correct external imbalances, reduce fiscal deficits and public debt, and restructure and close failing banks. These types of intervention touch on highly sensitive areas of state sovereignty.

Despite the limitations on formalization, and the opportunities to 'game' rules, creditor-debtor state relations and the private governance of public debt highlight the mismatch between state liability and territorial control. Governments seek to give broad policy directions and to manage and control the temporality of domestic reforms, above all through intergovernmental bargaining at heads of state and government and at finance minister levels. However, as the quote from Helmut Schmidt shows, in pursuing these objectives they remain indebted to the 'hidden treasures' of a world defined by professional consensus and political silence.

Technicalities matter. What were the modalities and limits on central bank intervention to support exchange rates within the European Monetary System? How can excessive fiscal deficits be best avoided? What are the most effective and legal means for the ECB to purchase sovereign bonds in secondary markets? What is the optimal design and operation of a European banking union with a Europe-wide supervisory system? Mastery of these issues is essential to the realization of political ambitions. It is also a signifier of where power lies.

Political Silence and Professional Consensus

Creditor-debtor state relations and the private governance of public debt exhibit a deep underlying paradox and tension. On the one hand, sovereign creditworthiness is of enormous public interest because of its systemic significance not just for state power but also for the functioning of the European and global economies. Hence global and European interest mounts as bank crises become enmeshed with sovereign debt crises and with fears of contagion to systemically significant states. Such crises are not just spectacular in their own right. They may also offer signs of more radical structural shifts in European and global economic and state power. At these times, the world of sovereign creditworthiness gains high political visibility. Bodies such as the European Council, the Euro Summit, the Group of 7 (G7), and the Group of 20 (G20) provide a political superstructure in which in principle it is possible to represent cross-national public interests in financial stability, stable public finances, and economic adjustment consistent with social welfare and notions of fairness.

On the other hand, even in times of intense debt psycho-drama, the world of sovereign creditworthiness remains remarkably opaque, self-contained, and self-referential. Its key participants form an elaborate technical infrastructure, within which they seek to form, sustain, and refashion a professional consensus, to provide an anchor for policy learning in a radically uncertain and uncharted environment, and to define the boundaries of feasibility. They do so by depoliticizing policy issues and processes and by constructing an elaborate edifice of legitimizing and substantiating expert knowledge (cf. Boswell 2009). Other than at moments of high crisis, this technical infrastructure is able to function in political silence. The structural bias to de-politicization of sovereign creditworthiness and debate about optimal debt mirrors the shadowy world of debt in which the private governance of public debt functions. It also attests to the privileged role of macroeconomic knowledge in demonstrating the supposed rationality of technical experts. It offers an empirical crutch to justify their preferences as authoritative with respect to potentially contested policy issues.

Professional consensus serves as a rhetorical device to differentiate the world of sovereign creditworthiness, to unify and mobilize its key participants, and, not least, to legitimate and substantiate its claims to de-politicization. It provides an exclusionary device for insiders, for claiming that those who oppose it are outside 'the community of common sense'. Political silence reflects this distinctive rhetorical characteristic of the world of sovereign creditworthiness. A wide range of issues are judged as too complex and technical, and as sufficiently susceptible to objective determination, for them to be brought into political debate.

However, the boundaries of this political silence remain open to contest. In the first place, professional consensus provides other 'outside' actors with a rhetorical device to attack incestuous elite behaviour, to make claims on behalf of the victims of ideological marginalization, and to promote populist politics in defence of sovereignty and national identity against anonymous forces. The consensus is represented as a problem, resting on technocratic usurpation of democracy, on privileging of rich creditors, and on enforced austerity on the innocent. The professional consensus within the private governance of public debt remains open to rival constructions. Counter-narratives focus variously on strengthening supra-national democratic participation, providing greater fiscal and financial accountability and transparency, and repatriating powers to states to re-establish democratic control. In the EU and euro area contexts, many reformers see 'European economic government' as the antidote to the 'democratic deficit'. It involves a more central role for the European Council and above all the Euro Summit, a directly elected European Commission President, and strengthened accountability to the European Parliament.

Secondly, there is a problem of how to reconcile different sets of interests amongst participants in the world of sovereign creditworthiness. Governing elites face stronger inducements to protect both taxpayers and those dependent on public services from shouldering excessive costs of sovereign and bank bail-outs. Their notion of fairness in burden-sharing, which may be as much ideological as calculative, involves reckless creditors sharing in the pain of insolvency through bail-ins and orderly debt restructuring. Just how hard governing elites push this agenda may be influenced by the relative size of banks in their GDP. Nevertheless, generally speaking, they are likely to complain that creditors should shoulder responsibility for the consequences of their reckless behaviour and that of their agents. In contrast, the interests of official elites, notably central banks, tend to centre more exclusively on placating the sovereign bond markets in order to prevent rising long-term interest rates. They focus on the potential costs in pre-commitment to making creditors bear substantial losses through bail-ins and debt restructurings. Financial market players are, in turn, fearful that revised supervisory, resolution, and regulatory frameworks may diminish their opportunities to make profits.

Thirdly, different institutional forums compete for influence. The post-2007 crisis witnessed a slow, tortuous expansion of roles for the ECB. It began with the establishment of the European Systemic Risk Board (ESRB), the development of unconventional monetary policy operations to ensure bank liquidity, and from May 2010 limited sovereign bond purchasing. In 2012 the ECB Governing Council accepted that it would house the new euro area-wide banking supervisory body. It also indicated that it might drop its insistence on the privileging of its sovereign bonds in any public debt restructuring. Most radically of all, the ECB agreed to flank the European Stability Mechanism's (ESM) financial assistance with more active sovereign bond purchases in secondary markets. The aim was to eliminate 'convertibility risk', which arises when markets fear that the euro might collapse and thus become unwilling to lend to Member States seen as most likely to exit. The ECB adopted a new role as supra-national catalyst for European banking and fiscal union. Similarly, the European Council and the Euro Summit carved out stronger roles in macroeconomic policy coordination.

The private governance of public debt mirrors the distinctiveness of power in sovereign bond markets. It centres on the Primary Dealers and, around them, the central clearing houses, credit rating agencies, financial market lobby organizations, financial journalism, and financial public relations. It is under-researched in part because of the cultivated opacity that surrounds the operation of sovereign bond markets. Yet, alongside taxation and financial management capacity, sovereign bond markets are the key to the realization of political strategies. The actors who shape these markets wield enormous power under cover of political silence.

What Kind of World?

Creditor-debtor state relations takes place at international and European levels. It comprises a thin political superstructure on top of a dense, tightly interconnected technical infrastructure, which is wedded to de-politicization and professional consensus. The key political participants are the sub-group of states that form the G7, the G20, and the complex, differentiated EU. The political level seeks to provide broad general directions, to shape how technical processes are organized, and to insert discipline through setting time rules and deadlines for technical negotiations. However, the combination of collective-action problems of states with the opacity of financial markets and with reliance on transnational learning processes and professional consensus to manage technical complexity suggests that the conditions are ripe for intellectual capture and for inertia at the political level. All too often, in times of crisis, the political infrastructure seems to serve the purpose of persuading others that 'something significant is being done'.

The much thicker technical infrastructure includes international financial institutions—notably the Bank for International Settlements (BIS), the Organization for Economic Cooperation and Development (OECD), the IMF, the World Bank, the Paris Club, and the Financial Stability Board (FSB). The ECB became a more powerful presence as the euro area sovereign debt crises intensified. At the EU level the European Commission, the European Banking Authority (EBA), and the European Securities and Markets Authority (ESMA) also gained new visibility through economic governance reforms. They benefitted respectively from the fiscal compact treaty, bank 'stress-testing', and measures to regulate credit rating agencies and hedge funds. Meanwhile, the ESM was established as the permanent mechanism, replacing the temporary European Financial Stability Facility (EFSF). Its purpose was to grant financial assistance, subject to strict conditionality, 'to safeguard the stability of the euro area as a whole'. At EU, and above all euro area levels, managing crisis expanded the technical infrastructure both in complexity and in flexibility.

Within European states, the key technical participants are national finance ministries, offices of budget responsibility, debt management offices, central clearing houses, and central banks. In some cases, like Ireland and Norway, they include sovereign wealth funds (SWFs), which invest in diverse portfolios including bonds. There are also the financial market lobbying organizations, specialized financial journalists and media, financial public relations (PR) consultancies, and related macroeconomists. They represent a powerful inner world of promotional culture on behalf of investment bank interests.

Financial journalists and media, PR consultancies, and financial lobbying organizations disseminate information and research. They promote particular images of sovereign creditworthiness. Financial journalism is supposed to have a public interest function as a watchdog, holding both states and markets to account. For this reason, it possesses certain privileges. However, like the credit rating agencies, the behaviour of financial journalists cannot be relied upon to be independent of markets. Both credit rating agencies and financial journalism risk becoming part of the problem of positive feedback and pro-cyclical behaviour that bedevils financial markets and leads to wrong judgement calls on sovereign creditworthiness.

The principal technical participants in the private governance of public debt include the credit rating agencies, those investment banks that serve as Primary Dealers, and the central clearing houses. In addition, there are the many hedge funds, mutual funds, pension funds, insurance companies, asset managers, and various non-financial companies that deal in sovereign bonds. These bodies, led by the big, globally active investment banks, have enormous resources of money, political lobbying activity, research capacity, expert knowledge, and intellectual self-confidence to deploy in the private governance of public debt and the world of creditor-debtor state relations. Those investment banks that act as Primary Dealers have the added resource of official status.

The world of creditor-debtor state relations has a number of distinctive characteristics. First, despite having different roles and interests, participants are held together in a network of shared interests, mutual dependence, and cross-sector and cross-national career mobility. Mutual dependence is linked to broad shared interests in maintaining systemic stability and in promoting economic growth. These interests are best secured by keeping a healthy flow of credit through profitable, solvent banks. Credit flows also underline the mutual dependence of creditor states and debtor states. They have a shared interest in ensuring that imbalances do not become 'excessive' and destabilizing. In addition, states and Primary Dealers in sovereign bond markets are bound together by a shared interest in confidentiality and cultivating opacity. There is a common interest in regulated and managed sovereign bond markets and the exchange of privileges and obligations that this interest entails. However, these shared interests are susceptible to very different interpretations and weightings, whilst mutual dependency can prove highly asymmetric.

Secondly, the boundaries between finance ministries, debt management offices, offices of budget responsibility, central banks, financial markets, lobby organizations, financial media, and academia are highly permeable. Specialist financial journalists are deeply embedded in the markets on which they report. They depend heavily on the favourable opinion of banks both for advertising and subscription income and for continuing access to sources of good newsworthy stories. Audience impact is often measured in terms of a very few individual financial market or government readers at whom a news story is directed. Not least, financial market lobbying of international, European, and domestic supervisory and regulatory institutions is intensive, discrete, and confidential. It is backed up by carefully targeted party political donations. Private communications dominate over public posturing.

Thirdly, the central bonding is provided by a shared language and common models and assumptions. This cognitive bonding can be traced to professional macroeconomics and, above all, financial economics. However, it is principally anchored in common practical experience of dealing in and with financial markets. It is associated with shared beliefs about the superior problem-solving quality of efficient markets, about how risk is best conceptualized and managed, and about what constitutes appropriate practices of statecraft. From the 1970s onwards this shared discourse came to focus on the primary requirements of maintaining market confidence, above all on de-politicization. It privileged sovereign bond yields as the key indicator of sovereign creditworthiness.

In consequence, creditor-debtor state relations have the features of a community of shared understandings rather than just a network of loosely interconnected interests. It is strongly self-referential in behaviour. Within this world certain actors possess particular resources of power. Debt management offices or central banks have the legal authority to select—and deselect—Primary Dealers. In turn, the Primary Dealers represent officially privileged banks in sovereign bond markets. They are uniquely positioned at the interface of public and private power. The credit rating agencies provide the financial markets with an anchor for their beliefs about sovereign creditworthiness. This anchoring role is far from new. Earlier it had been played by late-medieval merchant-bankers like the Florentine Bardi and the Peruzzi, who acted as moneylenders to rulers. Later, in early-modern Europe, it passed to the Medici Bank, the Fugger family, and Genoese bankers; and then, in the nineteenth century, to the House of Rothschild, Barings, and Société Générale.

Fourthly, the power dynamics within creditor-debtor state relations reflect differentiated membership, which traditionally favoured the United States and a select group of EU Member States. G7 and G20, in particular, generated resentment on the part of the excluded that their activities rested on a 'self-appointed' group, akin to the nineteenth-century model of the Metternich-inspired Concert of Europe. This resentment was countered by efforts to have certain states attend G20, whilst not being members, like the Netherlands and Spain. Norway remained an outside critic. Other key European creditor states—Austria, Denmark, Finland, and Sweden—were included as part of the EU, which was a member.

Certain European states represented a core in that they were actively represented across a range of international bodies. Britain, France, Germany, and Italy were present in the G7, G20, and the FSB, as well as in the BIS, IMF, and Paris Club. This inner group of European states interacted with the US and Japan, and increasingly with Brazil, China, and India. In 2010 EU Member States were notably overrepresented in the IMF. Their voting power of 32 per cent compared to 17 per cent for the US, 6 per cent for Japan, and 3.7 per cent for China.

Sitting at the High Table: Differentiated Membership of the Political Superstructure

European states participate in differentiated ways in the international and European institutional frameworks of creditor-debtor state relations. Their complex patterns of participation reveal different circles. France, Germany, and Italy formed an inner European core. Britain and Spain were just outside, for different reasons. Britain was outside the euro area and the Exchange-Rate Mechanism II (ERM II), but was in G7 and G20. Spain was not in G7, had a problematic relation to G20, but was in the fast-integrating euro area. However, formal membership does not amount to being a pole of attraction in diplomacy. A state is likely to be sought out as a potential partner and ally on the basis of its net creditor position—like the Netherlands and the Nordic States—or its systemic significance—like Britain.

G7 and G20

European initiatives were central in the foundation of G7 in 1975 and the re-launch of G20 in 2008–2009: in the first case, by French President Valéry Giscard d'Estaing and, in the second, by British Prime Minister Gordon Brown. However, neither G7 nor G20 lived up to the early hopes invested in them as bodies that would deliver global economic and financial governance. The G7 was a marginal player with respect to the Latin American debt crises of the 1980s, which were eventually managed in the wake of the so-called US 'Brady Plan' of March 1989. The IMF was much more central to the management of the East Asia crises of 1998, as it was to the emergence of global imbalances on the international agenda after 2003. The re-launch of G20 revealed similar problems of collective action, as it struggled to deliver globally coordinated financial market regulation and rebalancing.

The post-2007 crisis saw a significant transition in the world of creditor-debtor state relations from G7 to G20. It also saw a newly challenging environment. G20—and the IMF—were less concerned with managing crises in emerging market economies and more with crises in the traditional core of the global economy—the United States and the euro area. The crisis highlighted an accelerating shift in global economic power away from Europe, and especially from the United States, to Brazil, China, and India, as well as some other emerging market powers. This shift made G20 a more relevant forum of coordination than G7.

The G7 meetings of finance ministers and central bank governors dated back to its founding meeting in Paris in November 1975, after which it soon came to embrace the seven largest developed states. Europe claimed four members—Britain, France, Germany, and Italy, with the European Commission as an additional observer—alongside Canada, Japan, and the United States. Its rationale was international economic policy coordination. However, the agenda of G7 had a tendency to extend beyond creditor-debtor state relations. This tendency was reinforced by later Group of 8 (G8) annual meetings of heads of state and government, with Russia present. Over time, it also became less representative of world GDP as the axis of economic development shifted to big emerging market powers like Brazil, China, and India.

G20 in its form as finance ministers and central bank governors can be traced back to a meeting in Berlin in 1999 in the context of the East Asia and Russia crises. However, its rise as the central forum for world economic coordination followed the meeting in the form of heads of state and government in Washington DC in 2008. Essentially, it comprised nineteen states plus the EU, which was represented by the President of the European Council and the ECB. G20 was understood to represent 'the systemically most important states'. In Europe this group comprised Britain, France, the EU,

Germany, Italy, Russia, and Turkey. It excluded Spain (the ninth largest world economy), the Netherlands, Norway, Poland (the largest east central European economy), and Switzerland. Exclusion mattered most for Norway and Switzerland, as—unlike the other three—they were not represented by the EU. G20 also lacked a permanent secretariat. It relied on its rotating chairs and on bodies like the Basel Committee on Banking Supervision (BCBS) and the FSB to provide essential support services. In 2010 the French president proposed a permanent secretariat, but met Italian opposition.

'Sitting at the high table' matters. France, Germany, and Italy occupied the nodal European positions in international creditor-debtor state relations, reinforced by their roles in G7, G20, the European Council and Euro Summits, and the Euro Group. These three EU Member States emerged as privileged interlocutors with international creditor-debtor state relations. However, institutional membership was only part of the story. Despite its voluntary self-exclusion from the evolving architecture of euro area economic governance, Britain was a nodal player because of the size of its financial sector and its roles in G7 and G20.

The European Council, the Economic and Financial Committee (ECOFIN), and the Euro Group

The EU represented potentially the most sophisticated institutional framework for creditor-debtor state relations. However, it continued to face traditional problems of collective action. These problems were manifest in the difficulties in taking fundamental policy measures to reassure investors and publics that the euro area had an effective backstop in cases of acute sovereign debt and banking crises. Issues around state sovereignty and national independence bedevilled attempts to match collective liability with fiscal, financial, and economic controls. Moreover, the EU and the euro area faced the age-old problems of the structural divide between creditor and debtor state interests and policy preferences.

In addition, familiar problems of thin political superstructure/thick technical infrastructure shaped the way in which European creditor-debtor state relations functioned. They ensured that it was firmly embedded in international professional consensus-seeking, a pervasive rhetoric of de-politicization, as well as a counter-discourse of radical critique. EU and euro area mechanisms for addressing economic imbalances were more developed than at G20 level, through the Macroeconomic Imbalance Procedure (MIP) introduced in 2011. However, from a Keynesian perspective, the MIP displayed familiar weaknesses of asymmetrical adjustment pressures. The European Commission worked with a more relaxed indicator for surplus than for debtor states.

Traditionally, ECOFIN was the chief political body at working level, alongside the Euro Group. Being smaller, the Euro Group emerged as the key deliberative body, reinforced by having a fixed-term president since 2005. It gained legal status in the Lisbon Treaty, giving it de facto decision-making powers (Hodson 2011: 42–3). Formal legal authority resided in the larger ECOFIN which included all twenty-eight EU Member States. However, it did not provide an appropriate forum for intensive debates, essentially ratifying agreements reached elsewhere. At this political level the central problem in surveillance and monitoring, and especially in graduated moves to sanctions in the excessive deficit procedure (EDP) and the MIP, was 'sinners voting on sinners'. An attempt was made to address this problem with the so-called 'reverse qualified majority voting' rule. This rule strengthened the role of the European Commission vis-à-vis the Council, which had to collect a qualified majority to block the Commission.

The European Council: Which Member States Matter?

The EU was the core grouping within Europe, which is best visualized as a set of concentric circles of participation in EU arrangements. In the outer ring were states like Iceland, Norway, and Switzerland. They were non-EU members, though Iceland applied following its horrendous 2007 banking crisis. Iceland and Norway participated in the single European market through membership of the European Economic Area (EEA). There was a further group of states with customs union agreements and seeking EU accession, notably Turkey.

Within the EU itself, there were different sets of arrangements. All EU Member States subscribed to core policies like the single European market, competition policy, and external trade policy. However, within the economic and monetary field, differentiated integration prevailed and gathered momentum from 2010. Member States like Britain, the Czech Republic, Hungary, Poland, and Sweden retained both their exchange-rate flexibility and monetary policy independence. Another group, including Denmark, Latvia till 2014, and Lithuania were members of the ERM II, with their monetary policies subordinated to tight exchange-rate pegs with the euro.

By 2014 the inner ring comprised eighteen EU Member States (out of twenty-eight) which formed the euro area, having the euro as their currency and their monetary policy made by the ECB. They had no independent exchange-rate policies. Within the euro area, it was possible to identify an inner core of France, Germany, and Italy, with Spain closest to this core. This core had an unofficial privileged representation in the ECB directorate and thus in the Governing Council. Their national central banks were central to the management of the euro payments and settlement system. Moreover, the post-2007 crisis helped empower the ECB directorate.

Both banking union and fiscal union reinforced differentiated membership. The seventeen euro area Member States ratified the ESM treaty in 2012; twenty-five of the twenty-seven EU Member States ratified the fiscal compact treaty; whilst it was clear that many more than the seventeen euro area members would join in the Single Supervisory Mechanism within banking union. Furthermore, twenty-three EU Member States signed up to the Euro Plus Pact in 2011, with its agenda of reforms to strengthen competitiveness. Britain remained the one consistent outsider.

The post-2007 crisis reinforced the sense of a core within the core. The Franco-German relationship proved once again pivotal in crisis management. The Greek, Irish, and Portuguese sovereign debt crises led to its strengthening by Chancellor Angela Merkel and President Nicolas Sarkozy. After a difficult start under the new French President François Hollande in 2012, the French and German finance ministries intensified the work of the Franco-German Economic Council meetings (held since 1988). They established a new working group on banking union, fiscal union, and competitiveness and growth issues; agreed on twice-monthly meetings of the two ministers; and in May 2013 agreed a joint paper on deepening Economic and Monetary Union (EMU). In addition, the triple-A rated Member States—principally Finland, Germany, and the Netherlands—also intensified their cooperation to forge joint positions. France and Austria had a more problematic relationship to this small creditor-state core within the euro area. Overall, an analysis of cores shows Germany to be the nodal point at European Council level.

Rebalancing Power: A Strengthened European Council

From 2010, the role of the European Council—and later the Euro Summit—in addressing sovereign-debt-related issues was reinforced, at some cost to the European Commission and to the Euro Group. Their new permanent president, who was created by the Lisbon Treaty, became responsible for preparing a succession of crisis meetings. He chaired a working group on economic governance reforms in 2010–2011 and a group that produced a timetable for a 'genuine' EMU in 2012. These reforms led, in turn, to new and strengthened instruments of macroeconomic and fiscal surveillance, with monitoring and sanctioning in the hands of the European Council. The role of the Euro Summit was formally recognized in the fiscal compact treaty (Treaty on Stability, Coordination and Governance in EMU). The Euro Plus Pact provided a further new European Council mechanism of surveillance and monitoring of measures to promote competitiveness and growth.

The Technocratic Infrastructure within the EU and the Euro Area

The distinctive feature of the technocratic infrastructure of the EU and the euro area was the coexistence of intergovernmental bodies like the Economic and Financial Committee and the ESM with supra-national institutions, most significantly the European Commission and the ECB. Both supra-national bodies are also represented in G20 and the BIS.

The European Commission

Despite its marginalization in the process of formulating the post-2008 economic governance reforms, the European Commission emerged with a strengthened position in economic policy coordination. It was better able to coordinate temporally its reinforced surveillance of intra-EU imbalances, structural economic reforms, and fiscal policies in the so-called 'Economic Semester'. The Commission's Annual Growth Survey formed the basis for country-specific recommendations on economic and structural reform policies and for assessing each euro area Member State's national reform programme and stability programme.

The new Troika arrangement illustrated the Commission's relative credibility problems and its capacity to gain extra leverage. This new arrangement started with the Greek crisis in 2010 and was extended to Ireland, Portugal, and in 2013 Cyprus. It involved the Commission working together with the ECB and the IMF in managing the bail-out programmes. A 'Troika office' was located in the Member-State capital to oversee in detail compliance with the tough conditionality requirements of the EU/IMF bail-out. This arrangement enabled the Commission to borrow the stronger inherited credibility of the IMF in enforcing compliance.

The crisis shed light on the credibility problem of the Commission, a problem that owed most to Member-State defence of sovereignty. Member-State compliance with both the EU Stability and Growth Pact (SGP) and the post-2000 Lisbon process of economic reforms had been weak. The Commission had proved reluctant to sacrifice political capital by taking up tough positions in fiscal surveillance and in broader macroeconomic reform. Its tools were limited. The SGP had been narrowly conceived in terms of fiscal deficits and public debts rather than larger macroeconomic balances and indicators of state capacity. Moreover, deficits had received more attention than debt dynamics. In addition, the Commission had not been given independent powers to warn states and initiate sanctions. It faced ECOFIN, in which potential future fiscal 'sinners' had little incentive to punish their fellows. Commission weakness had been revealed in 2003 when the French and the German governments combined to avert the EDP being applied to them. The SGP reform of 2005 further undermined the Commission by creating new scope to claim exceptions and exercise discretion.

Intensive Troika surveillance represented an improvised response in the light of the manifest design weaknesses in European macroeconomic governance. Meanwhile, the EU moved in a slow, piecemeal fashion to create its own institutional frameworks that could provide large-scale collective financial assistance to bail-out sovereign debtors and that could better manage banking crises. The ESM could be seen as an embryonic 'European Monetary Fund'. It was given more flexible instruments, including flexible credit lines to Member States on the IMF model and direct bank recapitalization. Moreover, the ECB's Outright Monetary Transaction (OMT) programme provided a new means to de facto leverage ESM borrowing capacity. The euro area gained an infrastructure for buying sovereign bonds when markets were mispricing risk. In addition, moves to create a euro area banking union began with the Single Supervisory Mechanism under the ECB. However, in all these cases of institutional innovation, the Commission was not a direct beneficiary. In 2013 it made an effort, opposed by Germany, to become the location for a supra-national bank resolution mechanism.

Prior to the post-2007 crisis, the institutional and policy architecture of the EU had not been designed to correct imbalances or deal with state insolvency, for instance by orderly debt restructurings. By 2013 reforms had helped to strengthen the position of the Commission. It had new instruments, including graduated sanctions, in the MIP. The SGP had been strengthened, with a tougher approach to debt levels though few new powers for the Commission. The Commission could also look for domestic support through the fiscal compact treaty.

The new MIP offered an opportunity for the European Commission (2008, 2010) to try to strengthen the case for more coordinated euro area action to identify and correct imbalances in competitiveness and current account developments. However, as it discovered in 2013 with France, highlighting Member-State reform deficits in politically sensitive areas like labour markets and pensions drew out sensitivities about sovereignty. Moreover, the Commission faced difficulties in addressing the sensitive issue of fair balance in adjustment pressure on deficit and on surplus states, notably in relation to rebalancing demand. The European Commission (2010: 3) surveillance report for the Euro Group aligned itself closely with the creditor-state argument that primacy attached to debtor states in taking policy action across fiscal policies, credit markets, labour markets, and product and service markets. The reference value for surpluses was higher than that for deficits and set so that Germany was not defined as a problem.

Financial Market Regulation and Supervision

The same impression of ill-equipped European macroeconomic governance arose with respect to macro- and micro-prudential regulation and supervision of financial markets. Both the post-1986 European single market programme and currency union in 1999 acted as catalysts for closer European financial market integration. Key aspects of this integration were euro-denominated sovereign bond markets and the role of the ECB in the money markets through its liquidity provision. Pan-European banks emerged and posed new regulatory and supervisory challenges. However, the Maastricht Treaty offered limited opportunities for the ECB to extend into the financial stability function. Member States and their domestic regulators and supervisors remained jealous of their competencies, stressing the need to adapt any EU provisions to the distinctiveness of their individual banking structures and cultures. Their governments were intent on ensuring that any cross-national arrangements did not pre-commit them to fiscal policy decisions on bank bail-outs.

In response to deepening financial market integration, the Lamfalussy report led to the creation of a new European architecture for financial market regulation and supervision (Committee of Wise Men 2001). The initial emphasis on enhancing cross-national collaboration in the regulation and supervision of European securities markets was rapidly extended to banking, insurance, and occupational pensions. The three new financial market supervisory bodies provided opportunities for cross-national policy learning. Nevertheless, despite Commission review in 2004, they remained intergovernmental and tightly circumscribed in both legal competences and independent institutional infrastructure.

Following the post-2007 crisis, the de Larosière (2009) High-Level Group on Financial Supervision in the EU proposed a new, two-tier structure for financial market supervision and regulation. The ESRB was created, located at the ECB with its own secretariat, and responsible for macro-prudential supervision. The second tier took the form of micro-prudential supervision, which was reserved for a new European System of Financial Supervisors (ESFS). The three new supervisory authorities covered banking, insurance and occupational pensions, and securities. They could issue binding and non-binding rules, provide binding mediation, and impose specific common action in crises. The EBA took over bank stress tests and capital adequacy issues. The ESMA gained new responsibility for supervising central clearing houses, credit rating agencies, and hedge funds.

However, despite their reinforced competences, the new supervisory authorities continued to lack sizeable independent technical capacity. Their adequacy, and that of the ESRB, depended on the rules and their power to enforce them, above all in capital adequacy, liquidity, and leverage. It was also a matter of whether Member-State governments would prove responsive to their warnings about systemic and corporate risks. Notably, above all at British insistence, they were denied the power to pre-commit governments to fiscal policy measures to support troubled financial institutions. From 2014 the new Single Supervisory Mechanism (SSM) provided further centralization within the euro area. Nevertheless, in the absence of a supra-national Single Resolution Mechanism and Single Deposit Guarantee Mechanism, the SSM was in danger of being blocked by national vested interests.

Central Clearing Houses

Central clearing houses—also known as central counterparties (CCPs)—are systemically important institutions in sovereign-bond and other financial markets. They process trading activities on exchanges. Central clearers use collateral and pooled capital, provided by market participants, to ensure that buyers' and sellers' deals are guaranteed, even if one of them defaults. For this reason central clearers, of which there were thirteen in the EU in 2010, needed adequate capital and robust risk management systems to deal with any default situation. This need increased once financial market regulation shifted processing of over-the-counter (OTC) derivatives through clearers, increasing the volume of trades.

Central clearing houses posed a challenge of regulation in the interests of market safety and security. The post-2007 crisis drew new attention to possible regulatory weaknesses in their capital adequacy and risk management. Not least, experience of sovereign debt crisis revealed to governing elites that this seemingly highly technical activity mattered to states. By varying their thresholds on financial guarantees in the form of margin collateral, central clearing houses signalled sovereign debt distress. Their decisions could reinforce pro-cyclical market behaviour.

The European Market Infrastructure Regulation of 2012 gave the ESMA new powers with respect to central clearing for certain classes of OTC derivatives and to the organization and prudential requirements for central clearing houses. Also, the European Association of CCP Clearing Houses (EACH) strengthened its role, notably in disseminating best practice for CCP stress-testing and in working closely with the ESMA.

However, EACH was dominated by the tensions between two different central clearers, LCH.Clearnet and Eurex Clearing. The debate in Europe about regulation of central clearing houses focused on the two coexisting ownership models. The model of user-owned, not-for-profit, clearing houses entrenched the power of the leading investment banks. It was strongly embedded in Britain and the United States and, as such, invited suspicion of its governance arrangements within continental Europe. LCH. Clearnet was the leading London-based example. In contrast, the preferred French and German model was based on exchanges as a mechanism to maintain a lock on order flow and to make trading more transparent and less internalized to the investment banks, especially in derivatives. The leading example was Eurex Clearing, which was owned by Deutsche Börse/SIX. Determining the governance of the central clearing houses raised once again the issue of the privileged position of the big investment banks, their preference for internalizing trades, and how best to insure against market power.

The Economic and Financial Committee

The technical infrastructure of ECOFIN and the Euro Group in the field of sovereign debt also grew in importance. The approach of monetary union highlighted the need to promote the integration and efficient functioning of the EU sovereign bond markets, especially the euro-denominated bond market. This function was handed to the Economic and Finance Committee (EFC) Sub-Committee on EU Government Bills and Bonds

Markets. In the absence of any provision for euro area sovereign bond (E-bond) issues, as opposed to domestic euro-denominated bond issues, this sub-committee retained a shadowy existence. It comprised officials drawn from the European Commission and the ECB and from the twenty-seven domestic finance ministries, debt management offices, and central banks, depending on their structures for debt management. The sub-committee functioned as an advisory body to the Euro Group and to ECOFIN.

Euro area creditor states like Germany staunchly resisted the proposal for E-bond issues for fear of weakening their own creditworthiness, increasing their debt servicing costs, and undermining fiscal discipline and creating new moral hazard in debtor states. The EFC Sub-Committee explored ways to promote European financial integration within this constraint. Its priorities were greater consultation and transparency in debt-issuing calendars and in risk management techniques and instruments like derivatives. The EFC Sub-Committee also promoted convergence in market conventions like quotation basis, coupon frequency, and settlement days. It sought to make more efficient the functioning of secondary markets and the cross-border 'repo' market. Each quarter it published an indicative calendar for bond and bill issuance. The EFC Sub-Committee also engaged with the issue of orderly restructuring in the event of sovereign debt crisis. Before the post-2007 crisis it took the lead in encouraging the joint insertion of agreed collective-action clauses (CACs) in EU international debt issuance. This initiative was based on the work of the G10 under the auspices of the BIS.

In addition to agreeing best practice, the EFC Sub-Committee attempted to harmonize certain activities. From 2004 it worked with the European Primary Dealers Association (EPDA) to agree a harmonized reporting format for Primary Dealers on their activities in euro-denominated sovereign bonds (Economic and Financial Committee 2007). This work served to upgrade the coordinating role of the EPDA. The EFC Sub-Committee also examined various limited options for E-bonds that might mitigate the risks that German policy makers feared. Again the EPDA was a crucial participant in this process. However, as German reaction to the Commission Green Paper of December 2011 on 'Stability Bonds' showed, E-bonds continued to be seen as a long-term measure, dependent on prior move to fiscal and political union.

The Technocratic Infrastructure at the Global Level

The work of the technocratic infrastructure of creditor-debtor state relations at the European level is closely entwined with that at the global level. This global infrastructure includes the BIS, the OECD, the IMF, the World Bank (with respect to emerging market economies), the FSB, the Paris Club, the International Organization of Securities Commissions (IOSCO), the International Accounting Standards Board (IASB), and the International Public Sector Accounting Standards Board (IPSASB). The East Asia and Russia crises of 1998, and above all the post-2007 global financial and economic crisis, provoked new debates about the adequacy of their mandates and organization. It was unclear whether they were fit for purpose in regulating and supervising global financial markets (macro and micro), in addressing global imbalances, in promoting good practice in fair debt restructuring, and in ensuring transparency and accountability in public and banking finances.

For reasons that reflected the historical balance of economic and political power, five of these bodies were located in Europe: the BIS and FSB in Basel; the OECD and the Paris Club in Paris; and the IASB in London. Though the IMF and the World Bank were based in the United States, the convention was that a European served as IMF managing director. Perhaps most graphically, the IMF quota system had entrenched a disproportionately large role for Europe in its governance.

The International Monetary Fund

Like the OECD, the IMF engaged in work on best practice and on capacity building in public debt management, often jointly with the World Bank (International Monetary Fund and World Bank 2009). In the wake of the East Asian and Russian crises of 1997–1998, and the huge coercive Argentinean default of 2001, it developed a set of key principles to guide sovereign crisis management. In the first instance, any emergency financial assistance should be based on the IMF Debt Sustainability Analysis, with attached conditionality, surveillance, and monitoring. Where it is concluded that a macroeconomic adjustment programme could not restore debt sustainability, debt restructuring should be initiated. However, debt restructuring was only to be used as a last resort, given its potential drastic adverse consequences for banks and other financial institutions, capital flows, trade, and economic growth (International Monetary Fund 1999, 2002). However, in the wake of lesson-drawing from the Greek sovereign debt crisis, the IMF proposed in 2013 that creditor 'bail-in' should precede its involvement in a bail-out.

The IMF formulated principles of 'good faith' negotiations with private creditors, designed to clarify how distressed debtor states should restructure their debts. They included a transparent debt work-out process; early, continuous, and open dialogue on a flexible menu of options; timely information sharing; and preference for voluntary rescheduling over cuts to principal. The IMF also promoted the use of collective-action clauses (CACs) in sovereign bond contracts to clarify terms of restructurings and speed the process of agreement with creditors. However, it noted that CACs had not proved a guarantee for a quick debt exchange with high participation (Das, Papaioannou, and Trebesch 2012). The IMF approach was similar to the principles of fair debt restructuring elaborated by the International Institute of Finance (IIF) (2006). It favoured pre-emptive, negotiated restructurings, on the Ukraine model of 2000, as opposed to the unilateral moratorium by Russia in 1998. In developing an orderly debt restructuring mechanism for Greece in 2011–2012, the EU and euro area institutions sought to remain within this professional consensus.

The IMF's ambitions to extend its role in creditor-debtor state relations were clear when, in the wake of the East Asia and Argentinean debt crises, it floated the idea of a Sovereign Debt Restructuring Mechanism (SDRM) (Krueger 2002). This proposal sought to give the IMF a supervisory role in supra-national insolvency proceedings for states at risk of being pursued in the courts by their creditors. It made no progress for a number of reasons. The SDRM would have required a new treaty and posed serious domestic ratification issues, especially in the United States. There was also suspicion amongst many debtor states that the IMF, as a creditor institution, would not be an impartial authority in the new process.

The IMF is far more powerful than any other international institution in addressing problems of global trade and financial imbalances, including sovereign debt. To a much greater extent than the BIS and the OECD—or the earlier League of Nations' Economic and Financial Organization, it played a systemic role in fashioning a professional technical consensus about how to prevent sovereign debt crises and about how to manage them. The IMF differed from these other institutions in possessing its own capital, with which it could provide large-scale emergency 'balance-of-payments' financial assistance on the basis of tough conditionality and strict monitoring. It had the capacity to extend risk protection to states by substituting for private-sector funding. The IMF acted as a delegated monitor of changes in domestic economic policy behaviour by illiquid and potentially insolvent states. In consequence, it could have a catalysing role in re-attracting capital flows. By 2012 IMF financial commitments amounted to some €190 billion against the background of about €300 billion available liquidity (Deutsche Bundesbank 2012: 68).

However, the IMF faced a number of weaknesses. Its capital was dwarfed by the enormous growth in the scale of international capital flows. Moreover, under its Articles of Agreement, the IMF lacked the instrument of IMF-supported bond issues to underpin the creditworthiness of distressed debtor states. It fell well short of being a bank, able to act as lender-of-last-resort to insolvent states. In addition, the IMF had inadequate instruments to monitor and sanction global imbalances and to enforce symmetrical adjustment between surplus and deficit states. In short, it fell far short of what Keynes (1942) had hoped as chief British negotiator at the Bretton Woods conference of 1944, which gave birth to the IMF. He had envisaged an International Payments Union, which would act as a counterweight to US creditor-state power. The IMF had none of the features of an international central bank. It reflected US aversion to the concept of 'union', fear that the IMF could become entrapped in moral hazard, and worry that its own risk profile and those of its creditors would deteriorate and become a source of systemic risk.

The IMF also faced a legitimacy problem. From its inception, it was seen as 'Atlanticist', as too close to US economic policy thinking, and thus as a barometer of changes in dominant macroeconomic policy beliefs. Moreover, despite limited governance reforms at the G20 Seoul summit in 2010, the IMF remained vulnerable to criticism for overweighting European representation. This legitimacy problem intensified as the balance of economic power shifted towards emerging market economies like Brazil, China, and India and as the IMF's resources became increasingly absorbed in euro area sovereign debt crises from 2010. This changing constellation of pressures meant that the IMF had an incentive to behave more cautiously than it had in the late 1990s.

Creditor states continued to express fears of moral hazard and of weakening of IMF credit conditions and deterioration in its risk profile. These concerns had formed the context of the so-called 'Washington consensus'. From the 1980s the IMF, together with the World Bank, adopted tough conditionality centred on 'structural adjustment programmes' for emerging market economies in crisis. It pursued an agenda of accelerated opening of markets, elimination of capital controls, light-touch regulation, and sound public finances, especially reduction of fiscal deficits and public debt. The potential efficacy of capital controls for managing short-term capital flights was undervalued (Brown 2010). This professional consensus was forged against the background of the challenge to redefine the IMF role in the post-Bretton Woods' world of floating exchange rates and financial market liberalization. The 'Washington consensus' manifested itself in the management of the Latin American default crises, which began with Mexico in August 1982 and spread to Brazil, Argentina, and elsewhere. A key contextual factor in shaping the nature of this consensus was the high exposure of US banks to sovereign-debt risks.

The sharply adverse reaction to this type of IMF intervention in the East Asia crises of 1998–1999 and the experience of the Argentinean default led the IMF once again to redefine its role. It began to stress 'bottom-up', domestic 'ownership' of conditionality requirements in order to strengthen prospects for compliance. The IMF also developed more differentiated strategies of adjustment, recognizing that there were variations in the nature of the debt problems that states faced. The Exceptional Access Framework (EAF) in 2002 provided the IMF with a more flexible instrument in emergencies.

Also, after the East Asia and Russia crises in 1997–1998, the IMF became engaged with the agenda of macro-prudential supervision of markets and financial stability. It established a close working relationship with the new Financial Stability Forum (FSF), later Board (FSB), and the World Bank, notably in the Financial Sector Assessment Programme (FSAP). This interest escalated in the post-2007 crisis. However, the IMF's power was intellectual and persuasive. It lacked specific policy tools in this area.

The biggest changes followed the 2008 global financial crisis and the post-2010 European sovereign debt crises. The IMF gained a substantial increase in its financial resources and a more flexible range of financing facilities. Its financial resources were augmented by a doubling of quota subscriptions by member states, by a multilateral credit line under the New Arrangements to Borrow (NAB), and by new bilateral credit lines, potentially lifting the total to some €660 billion by 2012. These resources were soon deployed in Europe. Early recipients were Hungary, Latvia, and Romania.

Two further financial facilities were added to the IMF repertoire. The Flexible Credit Line (FCL) was a type of insurance facility. Assistance could be provided to states outside the chronic debtor category, without conditionality, based on their sound economic fundamentals and strong economic policy track records. Poland was an early beneficiary, but had not drawn on it by 2012. In addition, the G20 Seoul Summit endorsed the creation of the Precautionary and Liquidity Line (PLL) as a new preventative tool. Focused on states exposed to moderate vulnerabilities, it relied on light-touch, time-limited conditionality. This restructuring of IMF programmes offered a greater element of discrimination in dealing with debtor states. However, in the view of the Deutsche Bundesbank (2012: 68), it exposed the IMF to high financial risks.

The process of IMF redefinition of its role was further accelerated from 2008, as financial crisis permutated into full-scale economic crisis. The IMF (2009) began to advocate fiscal stimulus rather than just fiscal austerity. By 2012 an IMF staff paper argued that: 'There is... no presumption that full liberalization is an appropriate goal for all countries at all times' (International Monetary Fund 2012b: 'Executive Summary'). By 2013 it was advocating creditor bail-in prior to final engagement in bail-outs.

However, this shift towards a neo-Keynesian approach was differentiated. There was concern that too much emphasis on creditor bail-ins could create incentives for domestic governing elites to procrastinate in economic and fiscal reforms. Capital controls were still seen as a last resort rather than a standard instrument. Moreover, fiscal stimulus was seen as dependent on available 'fiscal space', defined by debt legacies and debt sustainability analysis. Fiscal space provided a new unifying concept within the IMF.

It helped bridge the internal divisions about the merits of discretionary fiscal policies, about the size of fiscal multipliers, and about slow versus rapid fiscal adjustment. Above all, fiscal space rested on the belief that there was no 'one-size-fits-all' approach to fiscal policy. Where creditor states had significant fiscal space, they could take a more relaxed view of fiscal deficits (International Monetary Fund 2009). The problem with the peripheral euro area distressed debtor states was that they lacked fiscal space. They could only restore it to deal with future crises by harsh fiscal consolidation, perhaps buttressed by debt restructuring. The German Bundesbank (2012: 64) viewed these developments as a weakening of IMF programme standards.

The IMF evolved two main interconnected roles in creditor-debtor state relations. First, from the early 2000s, global imbalances surfaced on the IMF agenda. This issue was by no means new. Mounting imbalances within the Bretton Woods system had led to the creation of Special Drawing Rights (SDRs) in 1968. However, the combination of increasing capital flows with global imbalances created new pressures, especially from systemically significant deficit states, for the IMF to develop a role as impartial arbiter of global rebalancing.

However, the IMF proved reluctant to act boldly. The strengthening power of emerging market economies like China, with huge surpluses and vast foreign-exchange reserves, forced the IMF to tread a delicate line, especially on exchange-rate policy controversies. The IMF's instruments to help correct external imbalances remained limited. Between June 2006 and April 2007 it sought to mediate a series of multilateral consultation exercises on global imbalances, including the euro area, China, Japan, Saudi Arabia, and the United States, in order to effect a global rebalancing of domestic policies. Though the negotiating parties agreed that a rebalancing of domestic demand growth was desirable, they proved unwilling to commit to new domestic policy changes. Classically, IMF power is greater in dealing with non-systemically significant deficit states, like Greece and Portugal, than with surplus states like China and Germany.

The post-2007 crisis provided the context for the IMF to seek an enhanced role in 'promoting external sustainability' and in 'reducing excessive imbalances'. The instrument was to be a strengthening of the G20 'Mutual Assessment Process' (MAP), in which states submitted country plans that were checked for consistency by the IMF and subject to joint peer review. The G20 Seoul Summit Declaration of 11–12 November 2010 illustrated the successes and limitations of this IMF role. On the one hand, the Declaration represented an advance.

> Persistently large imbalances, assessed against indicative guidelines to be agreed by our Finance Ministers and Central Bank Governors, warrant an assessment of their nature and the root causes of impediments to adjustment as part of the MAP, recognizing the need to take into account national or regional circumstances, including large commodity producers. These indicative guidelines composed of a range of indicators would serve as a mechanism to facilitate timely identification of large imbalances that require preventive and corrective actions to be taken. (<www.g20.utoronto.ca/2010/g20seoul.html>)

On the other hand, the MAP remained firmly 'country-led'. It fell well short of the US proposal for numerical caps on surpluses and deficits. This proposal was designed to force automatic domestic adjustments to correct excessive imbalances and to give the IMF a key enforcement role. The most powerful surplus states—China and Germany—firmly vetoed this proposal. They stressed that the onus must be on debtor-state adjustment, including by the United States.

There was, at least, recognition by G20 that correcting imbalances was a 'shared responsibility'.

> Members with sustained, significant external deficits pledge to undertake policies to support private savings and where appropriate undertake fiscal consolidation while maintaining open markets and strengthening export sectors. Members with sustained, significant external surpluses pledge to strengthen domestic sources of growth. (<www.g20.utoronto.ca/2010/g20seoul.html>)

The open question remained whether G20 states would desist from the earlier practice of relying on other states to change their exchange-rate policies and/or their domestic policies rather than changing their own domestic policies to achieve more balanced global growth.

Secondly, the IMF sought to enhance its economic surveillance role in fiscal policy and in financial stability. However, its role in these areas remained ambiguous because it had been created as a 'monetary' institution. The IMF's Articles of Agreement (V, section 3, (b) (ii)) required its assistance to be provided only if 'the member represents that it has a need to make the purchases because of its balance of payments or its reserve position or developments in its reserves'. Formally, it was entitled to provide balance-of-payments assistance to member states facing temporary foreign-exchange shortages and currency crises. However, informally, over time, the IMF was transformed from a pure monetary towards more of a 'fiscal fund' and towards dealing with the tight nexus between bank insolvency and state insolvency. Its roles and activities were redefined to cope with a changing configuration of crises. They are no longer defined so simply in balance-of-payments terms but more in terms of helping states regain market credibility and manage financial-sector risk. Under the impact of successive crises the IMF extended its agenda of economic surveillance and its financing facilities.

The post-2007 crisis accelerated this development in the direction of IMF lending to promote financial stability. This shift was most evident with its participation in the Irish bail-out of November 2010 and in the 'Early Warning Exercises', conducted with the FSB, since 2009. The changing role definitions with respect to financial stability and fiscal policy were reflected in huge increases in IMF resources in 2010 and again in 2012 and more differentiated financing facilities. The background was provided by deepening financial and economic crisis and by IMF interventions in euro area crisis management operations. The IMF ran large-scale, joint programmes with the European Commission and the ECB. By 2012 the IMF had lent more to Greece than to any other state in its history, including Argentina (1992–2001), Brazil (2002), Mexico (1995), and South Korea (1997). Containing contagion in the euro area was a matter of global systemic significance.

The IMF was prepared to be critical of euro area crisis management. However, its criticisms remained publicly nuanced and cautious up till the publication of its self-evaluation document on the first Greek bail-out of 2010 (IMF 2013). In autumn 2011, the IMF had called for more radical EU action on bank recapitalization and for much bolder and faster reforms to European economic governance. Subsequently, by 2012, some IMF staff expressed their worries about fiscal multipliers. They feared that overly rapid fiscal contraction in Europe would send distressed debtor states into recession and worsen their debt burdens. At staff level, the IMF began to re-examine, in neo-Keynesian fashion, the role of fiscal multipliers in debt adjustment, arguing that fiscal contraction was hitting growth more than forecast.

The self-evaluation document on the first Greek bail-out was much more trenchant in its criticisms, provoking anger within the European Commission. It revealed IMF frustration with its junior partner role in the Troika and with the functioning of the Troika. IMF staff cast doubt on the debt sustainability analyses that had underpinned the design of the bail-out. Their criticisms focused on excessively optimistic growth assumptions, inadequate domestic ownership of the programme, and Greek capacity to deliver on commitments. These inadequacies were seen as the root of illusion about what could be achieved. In particular, the IMF's self-evaluation document suggested that Greece had needed an earlier and a bigger debt write-down than occurred in 2012. The implications of the June 2013 report were pessimistic for Greece's debt sustainability. They were also deeply unwelcome to creditor states, suggesting that a change of policy course was required. A combination of more official financing with further debt restructuring was required if Greek exit from the euro area and default were to be avoided.

However, IMF influence on the euro area fiscal consolidation debate was blunted by two factors. It was the junior financing partner in the Troika. The IMF also faced the institutional and treaty constraints within the euro area, which limited alternative policy options, along with the strength of German insistence on the principle that 'stability begins at home'. In addition, the impact of IMF staff thinking was diluted internally by the presence of powerful European representation in its executive board of shareholder states. More radical positions at IMF staff level were subordinated to an internal culture of consensus that sought to preserve unanimity at executive-board level. The IMF was restrained in 'speaking truth to power', at least as far as many IMF staff—and many more critical emerging market economies like Brazil and Mexico—saw the truth.

The de facto evolution of the IMF as a 'fiscal fund' was recognized in March and May 2010 when the EU agreed a formula for collective financial assistance that would involve a 'substantial' role for the IMF in directly financing government fiscal deficits. After the Irish bail-out of November 2010, IMF assistance found its way indirectly to insolvent banks. For this reason, the Deutsche Bundesbank (2012), and some in the ECB, feared that the IMF was being redeployed to go beyond its mandate and to provide monetary financing of fiscal tasks, a role that was judged to be in contravention of EU treaty law. The Deutsche Bundesbank (2012: 64) viewed the extra credit lines as a shift from short-term liquidity provision towards the role of a bank, contravening the IMF Articles of Agreement. Traditional default risk was being replaced by IMF 'credit-augmentation' risk, namely that 'follow-up' programmes might be necessary. In the process the risk profile of the IMF was deteriorating, creating a new basis for systemic risk. Similarly, the Bundesbank opposed proposals for the IMF to have a more proactive, discretionary role in crisis prevention, especially in capping the size of surpluses.

The Paris Club

The Paris Club provides a forum for ad hoc negotiations between creditor states and debtor states about restructuring bilateral sovereign debt. It dates from 1956 when Argentina sought to avert default by a debt restructuring agreement with its official creditors. The precondition of negotiations within the framework of the Paris Club is that a distressed debtor state must demonstrate its debt payment difficulties and need for debt relief and agree a structural adjustment programme with the IMF. Hence its work can be seen as an extension of the IMF's role in helping low-income states with limited access to sovereign debt markets.

Whereas the IMF is Washington-centred, the Paris Club is Paris-centred and groups together only official creditors. Informal in character, it is chaired by a senior French Treasury official and has its secretariat within the French Treasury. In 2013 the Paris Club comprised nineteen states, which enjoyed official recognition as creditors; fifteen of them were European. They had in common big external lending exposures. They also agreed to abide by a shared set of principles and rules in settling bilateral disputes with debtors by rescheduling or, more recently, cancelling debt. Observers at its monthly meetings included the IMF, the World Bank, the OECD, the European Commission, and the European Bank for Reconstruction and Development (EBRD).

The five operating principles of the Paris Club were consensus amongst creditor states; conditionality (linking debt treatments to IMF programmes); solidarity of creditor states; comparability of treatment; and a case-by-case approach. The comparability-of-treatment principle foresaw equal treatment, including by non-Paris-Club creditor states. This principle constrained negotiations with private creditors. These principles were consolidated in the 'Evian' approach of 2003, which broke new ground in two respects. It offered debt relief to states other than Highly Indebted Poor Countries (HIPCs). It also shifted the focus from short-term debt relief to long-term debt sustainability. Debt treatments were to be better tailored to individual debt sustainability positions and to 'more orderly, timely and predictable' crisis resolution. Debt restructuring was to occur only in cases of imminent default and to ensure long-term debt sustainability.

Though the Paris Club was very much part of an international professional consensus, it sought to refashion this consensus towards a greater sympathy for low-income states. However, the conclusion of a conditionality programme with the IMF remained a precondition for the Paris Club's engagement in negotiations with debtors about 'debt treatments'. Since its foundation in 1956, the Paris Club had—by 2010—concluded 417 agreements with eighty-seven different debtor states, amounting to $543 billion of debt.

The decisive turning point in the development of the Paris Club was the escalating debt crises of the early 1980s in Latin America, especially the Mexican restructuring of 1983. However, during the 1980s developing and emerging market economies in Europe began to absorb more attention, notably Poland, Romania, and Yugoslavia. There were four debt restructuring agreements with Poland, two with Romania, and five with Yugoslavia. Turkey had already negotiated three agreements in 1978, 1979, and 1980. The Paris Club's main engagement within Europe began in the aftermath of the end of the Cold War in 1989–1990 and the collapse of the Soviet Union in 1992. Debt restructuring agreements were concluded with Albania (1993, 1998, 2000), Bosnia and Herzegovina (1998, 2000), Bulgaria (1991, 1992, 1994), Croatia (1995), Georgia (2001, 2004), Macedonia (1995), Moldova (2006), Poland (1990, 1991), and the Ukraine (2001). Russia became a special case, with debt agreements in 1993, 1994, 1995, 1996, and 1999.

Though no European state qualified for the HIPC programme, Georgia and Moldova were beneficiaries of the so-called 'Houston terms' as 'lower middle-income countries'.

Many more qualified under the standard classic debt treatment scheme, principally in the 1980s. They included various republics of Yugoslavia, Poland, and Romania. In 1981 Poland was the first European state to agree a debt treatment with the Paris Club, other than Turkey. By 2010 eight European states were still subject to active debt treatments: Albania, Bosnia and Herzegovina, Macedonia, Georgia, Moldova, Montenegro, the Russian Federation, and the Ukraine. The former Yugoslav republics involved 'exceptional circumstances'. As successor states, they presented difficult issues of how to reallocate inherited debt to them. A similar problem of state succession bedevilled the Russian Federation after the collapse of the Soviet Union. It sought to draw a sharp distinction between external debts that it inherited and those assumed after becoming an independent state. This distinction was insisted on in its management of the 1998 default. The Russian Federation continued to service its post-1992 debt, but fully suspended payments on its restructured Soviet-era debt.

However, the extension of the role of the Paris Club did not involve a change in its legal authority. The 'Agreed Minutes' that formed the outcome of its negotiations did not have direct binding legal effect. They represented recommendations to creditor and debtor states to conclude bilateral agreements that implemented the Agreed Minutes, along with 'guidelines' on applicable interest rates. Bilateral agreements remained the legal foundation for the resolution of creditor-debtor state disputes.

The Organization for Economic Cooperation and Development

With the demise of the European Payments Union (EPU), the OECD emerged—alongside the IMF—as the main institution that engaged with sovereign creditworthiness issues. The epicentre of its work in this area was the OECD Working Party on Public Debt Management (WPDM). Its working methods were similar to those of the BIS. Dating from 1979, the Working Party brought together thirty OECD members. It pursued a 'practical' approach through 'consensus amongst peers', mostly through ad hoc expert groups.

The OECD Working Party sought to establish and develop de facto global standards of best practice in public-debt management, based on fashioning 'common understandings' (Organization for Economic Cooperation and Development 2007). It promoted 'active' debt management and 'state-of-the-art' institutional arrangements in debt management. Also, the Working Party was used by the Italian Treasury as a platform for jointly launching the Public Debt Management (PDM) Network for Emerging Markets. Its twinning projects for disseminating best practice brought together Italian debt managers and experts with those from Bulgaria, the Czech Republic, and Romania.

In its annual 'sovereign borrowing outlook' the WPDM sought to map trends in pressures on debt management, in investor profiles, in size of market issuance, and in strategies and techniques (e.g. Organization for Economic Cooperation and Development 2009). This work formed the background to the annual OECD/World Bank/IMF Global Bond Market Forum, which focused on bond market problems and policy issues. It also informed the annual OECD Global Forum on Public Debt Management, which examined debt management problems and issues. In essence, the OECD attempted to foster professional consensus in approaches to public-debt management.

The Bank for International Settlements

The key weaknesses of the BIS and its Basel Committee on Banking Supervision (BCBS) stem from the limitations of their remits and their lack of access to sanctions. These limitations reflect the problems of democratic legitimacy that are associated with policies to bail-out banks and to restructure or wind them down. The BCBS lacks the competence to apply sanctions for non-compliance with bank capital and liquidity requirements.

The BIS was the first formal institutional development in creditor-debtor state relations, providing a forum within which central bankers could share ideas and experiences and attempt to draw lessons. It was in effect the central bankers' club. Dating from 1930, the BIS continued to have an essentially intellectual and supervisory role, as the prime location for building and sustaining a central banking culture based on cross-national policy learning. The BIS did not develop an interventionist role in correcting international imbalances. Originally, this role had been envisaged by Bank of England and HM Treasury officials in 1931–1933, when—faced by collapse of the gold standard—they advocated that the BIS engage in international note issue and in directing gold flows to debtor states (Bank of England 1931; Henderson 1932). The BCBS, which dated from 1974, had no legal status and could only advise on issues like capital adequacy, liquidity, and leverage rules. It evolved a key role in developing banking regulation standards. Traditionally, the BCBS had been reluctant to be drawn into issues about sanctions for non-compliance. However, the shock of the post-2007 financial crisis led it to take a new approach to implementation of the Basel III regulatory package. It began to issue a scorecard of states, including the EU, in the interests of promoting harmonization and standardization. The scorecard was designed to put pressure on national and EU regulators.

The main function of the BIS was to provide intellectual leadership within central banking. It sought to act as pace-setter in restoring financial stability as the traditional core function of central banks and in promoting the importance of macro-prudential supervision as well as banking regulation. The BIS pioneered the concept of macro-prudential supervision during the period when Alexandre Lamfalussy was its economic adviser (1976–1985) and its general manager (1985–1993). He sought to use the BIS to focus the attention of central bankers on risks to financial stability from external imbalances and debt accumulations and bubbles. Financial market rules were needed to mitigate systemic risk and contagion. Much later, following the financial crisis of 2007, macro-prudential supervision emerged as the organizing concept behind the establishment of the ESRB and the Single Supervisory Mechanism.

In addition, in the wake of the East Asia and Russia crises, the BIS (2002; 2010b) emerged as a major player, alongside the IMF and the World Bank, in making more transparent the scale, nature, and distribution of external debt (World Bank 2010). It has also sought to identify good practice in managing foreign debt and liquidity risks (Bank for International Settlements 2000). Later, the post-2007 bank and sovereign debt crises led the BIS to examine the 'hidden face' of the future of public debt and to establish whether there was an optimal size for financial systems beyond which they had negative effects on GDP growth (Cecchetti, Mohanty, and Zampolli 2010). The BIS continued to lack direct policy levers and the power to use conditionality. However, like the OECD, it played a major role in fashioning professional consensus in the world of creditor-debtor state relations, principally by attempting to critically examine central banking assumptions, above all about financial market efficiency and financial stability.

Financial Stability Board

The origins and trajectory of development of the FSB bore the imprints of financial crises. It was founded as the FSF in 1999 after the Asia/Russia crises under the auspices of the G7 finance ministers and central bank governors. Its organization and mandate followed recommendations from the president of the Bundesbank, Hans Tietmeyer. In its original form the FSF was weakly equipped to carry out the tasks of monitoring financial risks and of providing an early-warning system for systemic risks in the form for which the British Chancellor of the Exchequer, Gordon Brown, had called (Brown 2010).

The post-2007 crisis led to its rebranding as the Financial Stability Board at the November 2008 G20 summit, which also called for a wider membership. The axis of its work shifted from G7 to G20. In April 2009 the G20 summit agreed a broadened mandate, enabling the FSB to address the whole range of systemic risks to the global financial system. It began to examine how best to deal with systemically significant, 'too-big-to-fail' financial institutions, the shadow banking sector, credit rating agencies, and cross-national bank resolution capacity. The FSB focused on extending the regulatory perimeter to internalize sources of systemic risk from financial contagion.

Though its role was upgraded by G20, the FSB continued to be limited to making proposals on regulatory, supervisory, and other financial-sector policies in order to strengthen global financial stability. Like the BCBS, it lacked access to sanctions on banks. The problem for the FSB was the weak collective-action capacity of G20 on issues of global financial stability. Its sizeable technical work lacked firm, sustained political direction.

The BIS retained a strong European character. It was hosted by the BIS in Basel, and two of its first three chairs were Europeans: Andrew Crockett (1999–2003) of the Bank of England; and Mario Draghi of the Banca d'Italia (2006–2011). In addition to the ECB and the European Commission, the FSB had a select group of European states as members: Britain, France, Germany, Italy, the Netherlands, Russia, Spain, and Switzerland. Unlike G20, it gave direct prominence to the Netherlands, Spain, and Switzerland.

The International Organization of Securities Commissions

The IOSCO had extra-European origins, like the International Public Sector Accounting Standards (IPSAS) but in contrast to the BIS and the Paris Club. It grew out of an inter-American regional association, which had been formed in 1974. IOSCO was founded in 1983 against the background of the Latin American crises, with Britain and France playing the leading European roles at the outset. Its mission was to act as the international standard-setter in regulating and supervising securities markets by ensuring open, transparent, and 'fair' markets and by safeguarding systemic stability. IOSCO was, above all, concerned to enhance investor protection. It sought to ensure that investor protection was strongly represented in the professional consensus.

The membership of IOSCO comprised national and European securities regulators. Its work revolved around three main instruments. In 1998 it adopted the IOSCO Objectives and Principles of Securities Regulation as regulatory benchmarks (International Organization of Securities Commissions 2010). Also, the agreement of the IOSCO Principles Assessment Methodology in 2003 provided an objective basis for assessing domestic implementation of these principles. In addition, IOSCO adopted a Multilateral Memorandum of Understanding for the purpose of facilitating greater cross-national exchange of information and ideas and cross-national enforcement by securities regulators. With respect to sovereign bond markets, the key principles dealt with the registration and adequate oversight of credit rating agencies, audit standards, regulation of market intermediaries like brokers and dealers, and the secondary markets, notably transparency of trading and regulation of central counterparties. However, IOSCO remained limited to 'soft' instruments and lacked independent regulatory authority.

Accounting Standards: From Cash-Basis to Accrual Accounting

Harmonization of best practice in international and European accounting was the province of the IASB and the Accounting Regulatory Committee (ARC) of the EU. In public finances work pivoted around the IPSASB and the Statistical Office of the European Union (Eurostat). In its modern form the IASB dated from 2001, under the auspices of the International Financial Reporting Standards (IFRS) Foundation, whose main source of financing was banks and companies with an interest in promoting their accounting standards. In 2011 five of its fifteen board members were from EU Member States. The work of IASB in developing IFRS was pivotal in international and European debates. IFRS was adapted to the EU by the ARC, which included representatives of EU Member-State governments. It was advised by a group of accounting experts who formed the European Financial Reporting Group.

The work of the IPSASB focused on developing IPSAS and was based on the IFRS of the IASB. In the context of escalating sovereign debt crises, it began to take a more active approach to promoting transparency and accountability in public finances. The first result was the IPSASB guidelines on reporting on long-term sustainability of public sector entities' finances, published in 2011. These guidelines advocated a shift from traditional cash-basis accounting to accrual accounting. The aim was to capture more fully liabilities represented by pensions and by financial instruments. Thirty-two accrual standards were published. IPSASB used Britain and Switzerland as European models.

By 2013 Eurostat was backing the development of harmonized accrual accounting for the public sector within the EU European Public Sector Accounting Standards (EPSAS), with support from the ECB and from the president of the European Council. All three saw this development as essential to improving the quality of European economic governance. The central issues were the design of the governance framework for developing and implementing these new accrual accounting standards within the EU and how much flexibility was to be given to Member States in the timetable. There was also some concern about using the work of IPSAS as the benchmark because of what was seen as the underrepresentation of EU Member States on its US-based board.

Insuring Against Market Power

As financial market liberalization gained pace from the 1970s, and the size, sophistication, and complexity of financial markets grew, states came to rely increasingly on public debt management offices and central banks—and, in a few cases, sovereign-wealth funds—as forms of insurance against market power. These institutions became more powerful participants in helping manage sovereign bond markets. Their increased power was legitimated by developments in macroeconomic theory that specified the conditions for establishing market credibility and sovereign creditworthiness. Macroeconomic theory provided vital technical legitimacy for advocates of de-politicization through new forms of institutional independence.

Debt Management Offices and Primary Dealers

Public-debt management has been a classic function of domestic finance ministries and central banks. From the 1990s this function was increasingly professionalized around autonomous debt management offices. Though they work to finance ministry guidelines, they were given more operational independence in their relations with Primary Dealers. The UK Debt Management Office dated from 1998; the *Bundesrepublik Deutschland—Finanzagentur*, from 2000; and the *Agence France Trésor* (AFT), from 2001. Whilst more restricted in form, this shift to independence in debt management paralleled the move to central bank independence. Both shifts reflected strengthened macroeconomic intellectual belief in the virtues of a market-based professional consensus, protected by de-politicization.

Autonomy and professionalization in sovereign debt management was a response to a representation of the problem as one of ensuring greater state efficiency and flexibility in responding to developments within the financial markets. It was based on the belief that financing costs could be reduced, whilst mitigating excessive risks in bond markets. Ideas of more proactive debt management were disseminated as best practice by international financial institutions like the BIS, the IMF, and the World Bank, as well as the OECD. Their proposals focused on building organizational capacity in sovereign debt management and on promoting liquid domestic bond markets. In this way states could more effectively access international capital markets and balance low-cost borrowing with avoidance of excessive risk in financing debt. More active debt management by autonomous debt management offices was also regarded as better compatible with the principle of central bank independence. This principle took firmer root across Europe in the 1990s, especially in preparing for European monetary union. It underlined the separation of fiscal from monetary policies.

Domestic debt management offices varied in their range of functions. For instance, the Swedish National Debt Office (*Riksgälden*) had a central role in supporting financial stability through capital participations in, and loans to, banks. The UK Debt Management Office was involved with loans to local authorities and with the EU emissions trading scheme. Otherwise, European debt management offices converged, in substantial part, in their core activities, strategies, and types of personnel. They dealt in sovereign bond issuance, loan finance, the use of derivative financial instruments, ensuring the smooth functioning of secondary bond markets, cash management operations in money markets, market analysis, and the development of models for optimizing debt portfolio management, including accessing the foreign-exchange and interest-rate swap markets. Debt management offices also provided advice to governments on the sound management of their balance sheets.

These various functions of debt management offices were carried out within a framework of similar principles and guidelines on sound financial management and with similar strategic objectives. The common guiding principles were efficiency, fairness, responsibility, stability, and transparency. There were also similarities in the personnel structures of the debt management offices. They combined traditional civil servants with increasing recruitment from within financial markets in order to extend expertise and contacts. In this way debt management offices became more closely integrated with a market-based professional consensus.

Debt management offices cooperated closely with their Primary Dealers, who were their counterparties on a daily, ad hoc, and regular bilateral basis. They worked together in planning auction procedures in detail. These procedures began with a regularly updated issuance calendar, included the bidding process and allotment decisions, and finished with the settlement of the auction allotment on the value date. In return for the privileges that Primary Dealers enjoyed, debt management offices insisted on obligations (e.g. Dutch State Treasury Agency 2010b). Various conditionality requirements were attached to membership of the issuance Auction Group and were contained in the Primary Dealer contract or charter. Primary Dealers were the subject of on-site as well as off-site controls, which could lead to a Primary Dealer being placed on probation, suspension, or delisted. In the interests of an orderly market, exit procedures for a Primary Dealer were carefully regulated.

The conventions and rules governing Primary Dealers changed in response to the fluidity and volatility of sovereign bond markets. Nevertheless, they remained highly regulated. For instance, the Italian Ministry of Economics and Finance (2010: 7) evaluated its 'Government Bond Specialists' on the qualitative basis of an 'Auction Aggressivity Index', as well on the continuity of their participation in auctions.

The AFT (2009) provided a striking example of tough conditionality, both qualitative and quantitative. It required evidence of long-term commitment. The Primary Dealer had to demonstrate effort to maintain over time the quality of its relationship with the debt management office and the finance ministry. Proximity was also important. A Primary Dealer had to be domiciled in an EU Member State. More importantly, it had to have an active presence in, and commitment to, the territory of the state. Of nineteen Primary Dealers in 2012, only six were located outside France. The Primary Dealer had to have a viable business plan, adequate specialist staff resources, relevant technological infrastructure, and balance-sheet capabilities. In addition, in order to maintain a liquid and orderly market, a Primary Dealer must comply with criteria of creditworthiness, as assessed by financial market supervisors. For instance, it had to have a minimum credit rating. Limits were also imposed on maximum exposure to a single Primary Dealer in order to minimize concentration risk. There was also a 'quotation' obligation: Primary Dealers must participate in designated auctions in order to provide a pool of 'last-resort liquidity' and to share risk. Primary Dealers must subscribe to a defined minimum amount of the total issuance in a calendar year, weighted according to maturity. They must also help to maintain a liquid secondary market and provide monthly reports on their activities in this market. On initial appointment a Primary Dealer was treated as a 'candidate' member, not generally allowed to participate in a syndicate group.

Other debt management offices, like the UK Debt Management Office (2009), tended to be somewhat less prescriptive than the AFT. Nevertheless, they all insisted on a minimum of strict conditionality requirements. Debt management offices ranked members of their Auction Group each year, according to their share of the weighted issuance volume and other performance criteria, including the quality of the service that they provided. Typically, one or two domestic banks figured prominently in the Primary Dealer rankings. Debt management offices recognized that insurance against market expectations of sovereign default could be bought by ensuring a strong domestic investor base of local banks, and of pension and insurance funds, that would buy sovereign debt even in time of sovereign stress. Regulatory requirements could be adjusted to secure this insurance, a form of financial repression. This trend accelerated markedly from 2010 as sovereign debt crises and risks of contagion mounted in the euro area.

Analysis of top-ranked Primary Dealers over time reveals the attention to cultivating a strong domestic base of financial power as a bulwark against external debt dependency. Austria's Primary Dealer list typically included Erste Bank, Österreichische Volksbanken, and Raiffeisen Bank. In France BNP Paribas, Crédit Agricole, and Société Générale continued to have a major presence. Deutsche Bank, Commerzbank, and a cluster of three to five *Landesbanken* were a stable feature of the German Primary Dealer list. Similarly, Alpha Bank, National Bank of Greece, EFG Eurobank-Ergasias, and Piraeus Bank were regular members in the Greek list. In Italy Banca IMI, Intesa Sanpaolo, Mediobanca, and UniCredit featured regularly, as did ABN AMBRO and ING Bank in the Netherlands. Slovenia's Primary Dealer list included Abanka VIPA and Nova Ljubljanska Bank. In Denmark and in Sweden the proportion of domestic banks in the Primary Dealer list varied between one-third and almost half. Finland was the exception with no domestic banks in its Primary Dealer list in 2012. It contrasted with Spain where in 2012 one-third of the twenty-two-member Primary Dealer list were domestic banks. These arrangements acted as a source of continuity and stability for states, as well as facilitating confidentiality and subtle signalling to markets.

This domestic basis was sometimes strengthened through informal corporate governance in banking. In Italy local banking foundations formed the basis for small interlocking core shareholder groups in banking corporate governance. In conjunction with their close political contacts, this ownership structure helped ensure a strong domestic absorptive capacity for Italian public debt.

Before the post-2010 sovereign debt crises certain investment banks figured prominently as Primary Dealers in regional clusters. The Austrian Erste Bank and the Italian UniCredit were present in the Primary Dealer lists of the Czech Republic and Hungary. There was a notable cross-membership of Nordic banks in the Nordic States' Primary Dealers lists. The Danish Danske Bank and Nordea featured in Norway and Sweden. The Swedish SEB appeared in the Primary Dealer lists of Denmark and Norway, whilst Swedbank figured in those of the Baltic States.

However, this element of national distinctiveness and regional clustering was overshadowed by the way in which a few big investment banks dominated the Primary Dealer lists across Europe, measured by number of dealerships held. In 2012 Barclays and Deutsche Bank headed the European list, with sixteen each (AFMA/EPDA 2013: 17.19–17.23). They were followed in descending order by HSBC (fifteen), BNP Paribas (fourteen), RBS (thirteen), Citigroup, J.P. Morgan, Morgan Stanley, and Société Générale (twelve), and Crédit Agricole, Crédit Suisse, Nomura, and Goldman Sachs (eleven). Many of these investment banks gained added weight from their participation in the US Primary Dealer list.

The close symbiotic relationship of European debt management offices to their Primary Dealers was subject to conflicting pressures. On the one hand, before the post-2007 crises, EU single market legislation and monetary union had led big investment banks to diversify their activities across different sovereign bond markets as part of their strategies for becoming European and global players. This trend raised questions about whether a state like Italy could continue to rely on strong domestic absorptive capacity for its public debt. On the other hand, banking and sovereign debt crises led to a process of financial market fragmentation. This process seemed to open up new opportunities to strengthen domestic absorptive capacity, especially when domestic banks were being supplied with large-scale, cheap access to ECB liquidity. Spanish sovereign debt markets benefitted, at least in the short term. However, weak capitalization of many banks and their loads of toxic assets threatened the capacity of debt management offices to rely on their capacity to absorb sovereign debt. In 2012 Ireland had sixteen Primary Dealers, only one of which was domestic; Italy had twenty Primary Dealers, only three of which were domestic (and one of those, Monte Paschi di Siena, soon required a bail-out); and Portugal had only one domestic bank in its Primary Dealer list of eighteen, Banco Espirito Santo.

Central Banks and Sovereign Debt: The ECB

From their inception, management of the public debt was a prime function of central banks. Even more fundamental, however, was their function of promoting financial stability. In particular, central banks engaged in liquidity management, whether to individual banks as lender of last resort, or to the market as a whole through open-market operations (Goodhart 2010b). Liquidity management involved using central bank balance sheets, requiring selected assets as collateral for this purpose. In conditions of financial crisis, as after 2007, central banks were forced to assume—however reluctantly—responsibilities that go beyond the narrow remit of monetary policy directed at price stability.

Financial stability is an existentially significant public good for the functioning of creditor-debtor state relations. Once banking and sovereign debt crises become intertwined in potentially deadly embrace, central banks come under extreme pressure. They experience huge expansion of their balance sheets, difficult challenges in redesigning collateral policy, and later questions about when and how best to exit from 'unconventional' monetary policy measures. At such times central banks are drawn into fiscal policy and consideration of the distributional effects of their liquidity and sovereign bond market operations.

The post-2007 crisis had effects on central banking beyond a return to their role in financial stability. It also pushed central banks to reflect on whether, and how, they might pursue a more active monetary policy. The US Federal Reserve and the Bank of England pioneered quantitative easing. By 2013 the new mantra, also embraced by the ECB, was 'forward guidance', pre-committing to a particular policy in order to stabilize market expectations. 2011–2012 was a tipping point for the ECB. It embraced unlimited, three-year liquidity provision to euro area banks. Then the ECB committed to unlimited, if conditional, intervention in sovereign bond secondary markets, despite the opposition of the German Bundesbank. It also agreed to act as the site for the Single Supervisory Mechanism at the heart of the projected European banking union. The euro area sovereign debt crises catapulted the ECB into a broader role in crisis management.

From the 1980s to the post-2007 crisis, central banks had played a paradoxical role in creditor-debtor state relations. At the heart of this paradox was the withdrawal of central banks from the traditional idea that they had a central role in shaping the structure of the banking and financial system. They retreated to a reactive role. This retreat embodied a paradox. A growth in the prestige and power of central banks went along with a narrowing of their remit to monetary policy.

On the one hand, the growth of financial market power structurally empowered central banks vis-à-vis governments, which came to depend on their high-calibre tactics in managing market expectations. Strategically, the granting of independence to central banks in conducting monetary policy offered states a form of insurance against increasing financial market power. This insurance took the form of independence as a credible pre-commitment to safeguard price stability and to firmly anchor and stabilize market expectations about long-term inflation, consistent with this commitment. After the 1970s central banks experienced a renaissance of intellectual and technocratic authority around their monetary policy expertise in delivering price stability (Dyson and Marcussen 2009). Monetary policy—principally as interest-rate management—became their central rationale, their main instrument for taming markets.

On the other hand, this narrowing of central bank remit was associated with their neglect of the traditional financial stability function. They ceased to give full attention to the conditions for averting being drawn into their 'lender-of-last-resort' role to banks in distress. Across Europe, usually with the exception of small states like Ireland and the Netherlands, financial market supervision and regulation passed to new authorities, as in Britain between 1997 and 2012. Alternatively, with respect to the banks, it was shared between the new authority and the central bank, as in Germany.

Notably, the Maastricht Treaty did not include financial stability and prudential supervision of banks within the definition of the basic tasks of the ECB. Moreover, the ECB was created without a secure fiscal policy umbrella that could shield it if, in extending unlimited emergency liquidity to banks in crisis, it weakened its balance sheet—and thus credibility—through taking on too many toxic assets as collateral. The ECB found itself isolated and exposed in providing liquidity support not just to banks but also, from May 2010, to governments which faced dysfunctional sovereign bond markets. It found a basis for constructing an expanded role in its need to act to secure the monetary policy transmission mechanism by preventing financial fragmentation in the form of widely differing interest rates in Member States.

Monetary policy beliefs exacerbated the effects of this relative neglect of financial stability within the pre-2007 professional consensus. They were founded on the illusion that the financial system was inherently self-stabilizing and that output and trade would always return to equilibrium. This illusion generated a potent mix of hubris and complacency in central banks as well as governments. In addition, belief that central bank monetary policies could not 'lean against the wind' meant that they refrained from seeking to tackle asset-price bubbles in a timely fashion. They ignored the potentially huge damage that could follow their sudden bursting. Central banks retreated from counter-cyclical regulation of credit and the controls that had characterized the period from the 1930s to the 1960s. Tight controls on leverage had been associated with few bank failures. Lax monetary policies became part of the problem of financial market mania, panic, and crashes through the illusion that they spawned.

Professional consensus was refashioned in the wake of the post-2007 crisis around the key lesson that central banks must restore their role, expertise, and intellectual authority in financial stability (Davies and Green 2010; Goodhart 2010b). The concept of macro-prudential supervision, along with proposals for counter-cyclical credit policies, gained a new professional legitimacy. More controversial was the question of the toughness and timing of new rules on leverage ratios and the scale of structural reforms to banking and financial structures. Some in central banking feared that these reforms would exacerbate the credit crunch and make it more difficult to escape from economic crisis.

The counterpart of the entrenchment of the principle of central bank independence was the notion that central banks should not be harnessed to a fiscal policy role. This notion was built into the Maastricht Treaty that governed EMU. Governments were denied privileged access to central banks for financing. Moreover, central bank independence in monetary policy ruled out political pressures to resort to inflation as an instrument for debt reduction. Formally, these ideas narrowed the role of central banks in creditor-debtor state relations. Their views on sovereign debt focused on avoiding measures that might create contagion in sovereign bond markets. Central banks were less concerned than political elites with the costs of bank and sovereign bail-outs to taxpayers and beneficiaries of public services. They were more sensitive to the risks from threats to impose costs on creditors through tough talk about debt restructuring.

However, the post-2007 crisis produced change in central bank thinking (Davies and Green 2010). Fear of catastrophic macroeconomic meltdown from contagious banking and sovereign debt crises qualified the commitment to the no-bail-out principle and to the principle of no privileged access for governments. It drew central banks—directly or indirectly—into 'monetizing' public debt. To avert systemic risk the Bank of England and the US Federal Reserve Bank resorted to 'quantitative easing'. They sought to inject liquidity and to reduce long-term interest rates by purchasing government bonds. By 2009 the Bank of England had acquired holdings of government bonds equivalent to almost 10 per cent of GDP (Bloomestein, Guzzo, Holland, and Mu 2010: 12).

In contrast, the ECB faced stringent EU treaty provisions when faced with the vicious circle of interconnected bank and sovereign debt crises and threats to the coherence and even survival of the euro area. In consequence, it relied on providing liquidity by stealth through enhanced credit provision to banks. In making unlimited liquidity available to banks through its monetary policy operations, and relaxing its collateral requirements, the ECB took onto its balance sheet huge amounts of sovereign bonds. Cheap and plentiful ECB emergency liquidity provision enabled domestic banks to take on larger exposures to their own sovereign debt, notably in Greece, Italy, and Spain. This approach was seen as specifically tailored to the bank-based financial system of the euro area.

In the face of Bundesbank opposition to loss of independence from the monetary financing of sovereign debt, the ECB agreed in May 2010 to limited sovereign bond purchases as part of a larger euro area bail-out package. As the crisis spread, this programme was expanded from Greek to Irish, Portuguese, Italian, and Spanish bonds. However, prompted by the Italian government's failure to comply with domestic reform commitments, the ECB disengaged from this programme in December 2011. This ECB move was intended to act as an incentive for the euro area Member-State governments to assume greater responsibility for collective action to deal with sovereign debt problems. By September 2012 the European Council had committed to provide greater powers and flexibility for the ESM and to pursue European banking union, including a Single Supervisory Mechanism. These commitments provided the opportunity for the new president of the ECB, Mario Draghi, to launch the OMT programme. The ECB would intervene unlimitedly in sovereign bond secondary markets to support euro area Member States that had agreed programmes with the ESM and were complying with them.

As elsewhere, ECB monetary policy operations and support for sovereign bond markets led to an explosion of its balance sheet. It faced two risks. First, the toxic character of some euro area sovereign bonds exposed the ECB to increased risks to its own creditworthiness. Through its covered bond and securities market programmes, the ECB acquired €276 billion in assets between 2009 and 2012, when they were superseded by the OMT programme. This figure included more than 50 per cent of outstanding Greek debt and a quarter of Portuguese debt. Despite the improbability of capital appreciation, net gains could be realized from holding this debt. This net gain could be used to offset some of the costs of a future debt write-down. Net financial costs were likely to be much lower than the alarm triggered by headline figures on ECB exposure.

Secondly, accommodating the liquidity needs of solvent banks had major effects on so-called TARGET balances. These balances derive from the settlement of large cross-border payment flows in a decentralized Eurosystem in which national central banks distribute central bank liquidity. By mid-2012 the total of TARGET claims on the balance sheets of euro area national central banks had climbed to €1 trillion. The risk attached to the Eurosystem operations as a whole, not to one or more national central banks. Nevertheless, there were adverse effects on political debate about the distribution of liabilities, above all within Germany where TARGET balances were seen as burdening the Bundesbank. The Eurosystem was drawn into debates about the de facto creation of a transfer union by stealth and without sufficient accountability and transparency.

Central banks also played a role in creditor-debtor state relations through their management of foreign-exchange reserves. This role made them key players in foreign-exchange and sovereign bond markets. Power gravitated to the central banks that managed reserve currencies, which enjoyed certain privileges. Under the classic gold standard the pound sterling had served as the main reserve currency. From the late 1920s the US dollar began to displace the pound sterling; whilst, from the 1960s the German D-Mark, and post-1999 the euro, gained in importance as a reserve currency, at least up to the euro area crises. The power of the respective central banks in creditor-debtor state relations, above all in forging professional consensus, rose and fell with these larger structural changes.

From the late 1990s China used its fast-growing and soon enormous foreign-exchange reserves to purchase US Treasury bonds. As US fiscal deficits grew, her dependence on Chinese support became a growing vulnerability. The gradual emergence of the off-shore Chinese rembini market offered a further sign of future shift away from the US dollar as the dominant reserve currency. It indicated an additional constraint on the euro's emergence as a reserve currency. This market served initially in financing trade, potentially displacing the Japanese yen as the leading regional currency in East Asia. The longer-term question was whether and when the rembini would emerge as a new world reserve currency, with the associated change in relative central bank power.

Sovereign Wealth Funds

By the twenty-first century sovereign wealth funds (SWFs) represented important new government-owned actors in sovereign debt markets. Their role proved controversial, with allegations about politically motivated investments and accusations of lack of transparency and opaque governance structures (for a rebuttal, see Avendano and Santiso 2009). However, with the post-2007 crisis SWFs were more often welcomed as potential 'white-knights' for debtor states. Their rise reflected in substantial part the widening of global imbalances and efforts to find new ways of managing expanding national wealth. SWF finances are variously sourced from natural-resource wealth, for instance in Norway and Russia; from foreign exchange, notably in Asian states like China and Singapore; or from other sources, typically pension contributions, as in Ireland.

Where SWF portfolio and risk-management strategies focused on long-term savings, they became important buyers of sovereign debt as 'buy-and-hold' investors. In this respect they were akin to pension funds. However, they differed in being less transparent, less constrained by benchmarks and credit rating minimums, and less defined in their investment policies (Avendano and Santiso 2009: 23). On the transparency index used by the Sovereign Wealth Fund Institute, the top scorers were the French, Irish, and Norwegian SWFs. Despite efforts at self-regulation through the Santiago Principles, SWF investment strategies remained controversial because of their opacity. However, opacity was a more general problem, extending to central banks' foreign-reserve management and the activities of hedge funds. They all contributed to the shadowy world of creditor-debtor state relations.

Asia and the Middle East dominated global SWF assets under management, with respectively 40 per cent and 35 per cent in May 2013. European SWFs accounted for only 17 per cent (<www.swfinstitute/org/fund-rankings>). Relatively speaking, France's

Table 12.1 Largest Sovereign Wealth Funds, by Assets under Management, May 2013

Country	Fund Name	Assets (US$bn)
1. Norway (1990)	Government Pension Fund Global	715.9
2. United Arab Emirates	Abu Dhabi Investment Authority	627
3. China	State Administration of Foreign Holdings Investment Company	567.9
4. Saudi Arabia	Monetary Agency Foreign Holdings	532.8
5. China	China Investment Corporation	482
6. Kuwait	Kuwait Investment Authority	342
7. China/Hong Kong	Hong Kong Monetary Authority	298.7
8. Singapore	Govt of Singapore Investment Corporation	247.5
9. Russia	National Welfare Fund	175.5
10. China	National Social Security Fund	160.6
26. France	Strategic Investment Fund	25.5
28. Ireland	National Pensions Reserve Fund	19.4

(*Source*: Sovereign Wealth Fund Institute (<www.swfinstitute.org/fund-rankings/>))

Strategic Investment Fund and Ireland's National Pensions Reserve Fund (NPRF) were small, respectively twenty-sixth and twenty-eighth in the world ranking (see Table 12.1). They were also relatively new, dating from 2001 in the first case and 2008 in the second, and non-commodity based. Under Irish law the government assigned the equivalent of one per cent of GDP to the NPRF every year.

Within Europe, by far the biggest player was the Norwegian Government Pension Fund. It was number one in world rankings in May 2013 (see Table 12.1). Norway made skilful use of the revenues from its new-found natural resources to emerge as a major creditor state, overshadowing its traditionally more powerful neighbour Sweden. Its SWF offered support to the Greek sovereign debt market in 2010. Because of Norway's creditor-state status, its SWF was better able to escape political intervention than the Irish NPRF. In 2009–2010 the Irish government mobilized the NPRF to recapitalize the Bank of Ireland and Allied Irish Bank. It then used it to support its own contribution to the EU/IMF bail-out package.

Anchoring Beliefs: Sovereign Credit Ratings

Three big US credit rating agencies—Fitch, Moody's, and Standard and Poor's—emerged as privileged and semi-official participants in the world of creditor-debtor state relations. In the nineteenth century their role had grown from the provision of financial information about railway companies to benchmarking corporate bond issues. Before 1914 Moody's was the pioneer in expanding credit ratings to the bonds of US government agencies and municipalities. By 1916 Standard Statistics, which merged with Poor's Publishing in 1941, was assigning ratings to corporate bonds, followed shortly by sovereign bonds and, from 1940, municipal bonds. By 1924 Fitch Publishing had introduced the 'AAA' to 'D' credit ratings scale in its 'Fitch Bond Book'.

However, the main historical turning point in the rise of credit rating agencies came in 1975, when the US Securities and Exchange Commission (SEC) gave them official status. It designated Fitch, Moody's, and Standard and Poor's as 'nationally recognized statistical rating organizations' (NRSRO). They gained a new weight in setting and monitoring regulatory standards (Sinclair 2005). Their power was embedded not just in the conduct of financial market regulation and supervision but also in central bank monetary policy operations through the specification of collateral requirements for accessing central bank liquidity in terms of credit ratings.

The power of the credit rating agencies was evident in shaping debate about the nature of sovereign creditworthiness, abut forms of sovereign debt default and restructuring, and about how to assess probability of default (e.g. Standard and Poor's 2007). Their distinction between investment grade and 'junk' bonds constituted a tipping point in terms of access to sovereign bond markets. Similarly, their assignment of 'negative outlook' or a rating downgrade typically acted as a trigger for rising bond yields to cover heightened default risk. However, the embedding of the credit rating agencies in the financial markets created a 'chicken-and-egg' problem. It remained unclear whether they shaped or channelled market sentiments. Either way, they anchored market beliefs.

In consequence of these developments, credit rating agencies were exposed to multiple controversies. There was concern about the imbalance between their disciplinary power over states and their accountability and transparency. Also, because of the way in which credit rating agencies were embedded in financial markets, there was risk of conflicts of interest between charging fees for their services and providing objective ratings. In addition, there were questions about their methodologies, notably the subjective element, and the adequacy of their research capacity for this weighty function. In 2010 the Fitch Ratings Sovereign Group comprised twenty-one analysts dealing with more than 100 states. Political concerns about subjectivity of ratings within Europe were increased by the US-centric character of sovereign credit rating agencies.

These questions about credit rating agency power were put in sharper focus by perceived failures in their credit ratings before the 2007 crisis, both with respect to the US sub-prime mortgage markets and to the sovereign creditworthiness of peripheral euro area Member States after European monetary union. The crisis led to the credit rating agencies being brought under the regulatory umbrella of the ESMA. The European Commission suggested that they provide EU states with advanced warning of changes to sovereign debt ratings. It also supported the idea of an independent European credit rating agency. The ECB also indicated that it no longer wished to rely simply on credit rating agencies to provide the benchmark for its collateral policies.

In particular, questions arose about the independence, neutrality, and objectivity of ratings by agencies. From the 1970s their financing began to rely on charging issuers of securities as well as investors for rating services. The rationale for this development was to capture the gains in market access that issuers secured from their services and to use the extra revenue to pay higher staff wages. However, as both the European Commission and the IMF stressed, this mode of financing credit rating agencies posed conflict-of-interest issues.

Operating under US SEC licence, and taking into account IOSCO Principles, the three credit rating agencies provided anchors in sovereign bond markets and the private governance of public debt. Investors, regulators, and supervisors faced enormous complexity, opacity, and uncertainty when seeking to assess states and the creditworthiness of their public finances. They had an incentive to compensate for their incomplete information, to lower their transaction costs, and to reduce their anxiety by anchoring their behaviour to a credit rating (cf. Kahneman and Tversky 2000). Ratings served as a fixed point of reference, around which to build and anchor beliefs about states.

However, this privileged status and the anchoring role of credit rating agencies depended on the trust and confidence that come from perceived reliability of their ratings. As the period after the launch of the euro in 1999 showed, high ratings could prove illusory, as Ireland and Spain showed. They could even be awarded to chronic debtor states. Credit rating agencies were part of the illusion, shared by the markets and governing elites, about Cypriot, Greek, Irish, Spanish, and Portuguese sovereign debt. This critique needs qualification. Credit ratings began to reflect heightened sovereign risk before 2007. However, they did not do so in a way that exerted timely discipline. The onset of the sovereign debt crisis contributed to a crisis of confidence in the reliability of the agencies.

A triple-A debt rating is *sine qua non* for creditor-state status. However, the ratings failed to adequately anticipate emerging risks, awarding top ratings to lapsed and illusory creditor states, alongside genuine creditor states like Germany and Switzerland. This failure of differentiation highlighted the risk that their disciplinary power would not be used in a responsible and timely fashion to smooth fiscal adjustments. Credit agency ratings could lull bond markets to sleep and make debtor states complacent. Their subsequent, sudden downgrades of sovereign debt could then spread market panic.

The disciplinary power of the credit rating agencies derives from the way in which the ratings that they choose to assign to states provide the signals that prompt bond and foreign exchange markets to discriminate fiscal saints from sinners. They spur bond vigilantes, above all hedge funds, to engage in speculative trades under the ideological cover of behaving as guardians of sound public finances and sustainable debt. Upgrades and downgrades are eagerly anticipated by these market players. They are consequential for yield spreads, costs of sovereign borrowing and insuring against default, and ultimately prospects for sovereign restructuring and default. However, rate changes may fail to smooth the process of discipline. In not discriminating in a timely and nuanced way, credit rating agencies may actually promote fiscal sinning and contribute to sudden, sharp, unanticipated fiscal shocks. They risk accentuating positive feedback processes within sovereign bond markets.

The nodal position of credit rating agencies within the private governance of public debt was reinforced by two developments. First, the credit ratings of Fitch, Moody's, and Standard and Poor's were used by central banks in their definitions of eligible collateral. They affected the access of banks to their liquidity operations. Sovereign debt downgrading heightened the risk that the banks that held sovereign debt of the affected state might lose eligibility to use these bonds in central bank monetary policy operations. Potentially, central bank collateral policy could serve as a coercive instrument in sovereign debt markets, deterring banks from purchasing or holding certain bonds. A central bank could resort to the nuclear device of excluding a state's sovereign debt as eligible and thereby penalize severely the banks that held it. Alternatively, its collateral policy could impose a sliding scale of increasing 'haircuts' (discounts applied to the value of an asset), up to punitive levels for states with serious indebtedness problems. However, even the highly cautious and conservative ECB hesitated to adopt these coercive measures. In 2010, as part of the wider EU rescue package for states in sovereign debt crisis, it announced that it would cease to use the ratings of the agencies in its collateral policies and continue to accept downgraded Greek sovereign bonds.

Secondly, credit ratings were 'hard-wired' into the larger financial system through their use in financial market regulation and supervision. Under Basel II and III rules on capital requirements, regulators and supervisors made use of sovereign credit ratings in their risk assessments of banks. Hence new credit ratings could automatically trigger regulatory calls for remedial action by banks (International Monetary Fund 2010d). In the wake of the post-2007 crisis the FSB called for less reliance on these ratings in financial market regulation, whilst the IMF criticized 'overreliance' on rating agencies.

The semi-official status of sovereign credit ratings, and their use in bond markets, monetary policy operations, and financial market regulation and supervision, raised acute questions about their reliability. The ECB concluded that the credit rating agencies were not giving independent assessments. Their ratings tracked market opinions and behaviour and risked generating pro-cyclical effects. Hence the ECB ceased to depend on them (Bini Smaghi 2009c). The sovereign debt crisis also led to a resurfacing of debate about the need to develop one or more European credit rating agencies as an alternative. In their absence the ECB developed its own broader, more balanced and independent sovereign risk assessment of macroeconomic indicators to guide its monetary policy operation and especially its collateral policy. The Banque de France was especially keen to distance the Eurosystem from using the traditional three US credit rating agencies and thus to avoid giving them official status.

Increased European concerns about the responsible use of power by credit rating agencies were reflected in their incorporation in the regulatory and supervisory framework of the new ESMA from 2011. The ESMA was empowered to issue fines. More controversial was the proposal, which was backed strongly by French and Italian financial market regulators, that an agency in a 'non-equivalent' third country must have standards 'as stringent as' those in the EU and that an agency in the EU must take responsibility for third-country ratings. This proposal was opposed as too restrictive by the European Banking Federation and by regulators in Britain, the Netherlands, and Sweden.

Confidence in the credit rating agencies also suffered a setback within the private sector. The world's biggest investment banks and bond fund managers sought to become more self-reliant. BlackRock and Pimco invested in developing their own internal sovereign bond indices to assess the creditworthiness of states and to provide benchmarks for allocating their funds. Led by the so-called 'sage' of the capital markets, Bill Gross, Pimco had over $1,000 billion assets under its management in 2009. With 1,300 professionals on its staff, it was in a position to develop its own in-house bond rating capability.

Citigroup's World Government Bond Index occupied a privileged position as an elite index in establishing creditworthiness of states and attracting foreign investors to hold their bonds. Entry to this index endowed a state with prestige. Strikingly, by 2010 none of the BRIC states (Brazil, Russia, India, and China) had qualified. However, for the first time, a Latin American state, Mexico, entered the index. The Citigroup index had its origins in Salomon Brothers during the 1980s and its strong role in sovereign bond markets. Subsets that were most relevant to the EU included Citigroup EMU Government Bond Index Euro 1–3 Years and Citigroup EuroBig (Euro).

Private-sector bond indices varied. Some indices gave weight to the size of sovereign bond issuance and the liquidity of markets, identifying scope for trading in assets as an advantage. This method of rating encouraged lending to some indebted issuers, like Britain and the United States, rather than to creditor states like Norway and Sweden, whose markets were much less liquid. Other indices used a GDP-based approach in order to capture overall macroeconomic performance or one that focused on net foreign asset position. This method favoured creditor states like Germany.

Variation in methods of sovereign bond benchmarking mattered in terms of which states benefited from fund allocations. The post-2007 financial and economic crisis witnessed a shift towards GDP- and foreign asset-based approaches by fund managers. These developments in market-based credit ratings exposed the vulnerabilities of creditor-debtor state relations to market-led strategic change. They showed how changes in types of indices shifted who benefitted and who lost amongst states.

Financial Market Lobbies

Financial market lobbying activity, financial public relations, and financial journalism are central to the construction of sovereign creditworthiness and to the dissemination of beliefs about states, their elites, and publics within markets. Above all, the financial lobbies oppose coercive sovereign debt defaults and advocate voluntary, negotiated, and pre-emptive restructurings that protect creditor interest. They stress that access of states to international capital markets is dependent on their adherence to the lobbies' self-defined principles of 'fair' debt restructuring. The Institute of International Finance (IIF) ranks states according to these principles.

At national, European, and international levels the financial sector is able to draw on enormous organizational and technical resources, as well as staff expertise, to underpin its lobbying activity. This activity takes place collectively and by individual investment banks, hedge funds, and other financial market actors. As Chapter 11 showed, the sector has formidable instruments of power at its disposal to deter states from making active use of policy instruments to tame market power. The Essential Information and Consumer Education Foundation (2009) estimated that the US financial sector spent more than $5 billion between 1998 and 2008 funding lobbying activities in Congress, the administration, and the regulatory agencies. Larry Summers (2010) claimed that, during and after the passage of the US Dodd-Frank financial regulatory reform law, the financial sector was funding four lobbyists for every member of the House of Representatives, at a cost of about $1 billion. Lobbying is augmented by the promotional work of financial PR consultancies and by reliance on the services of highly specialist law firms, alongside the banks' own lawyers.

Investment banks provide positive newsworthy stories for financial journalists through their control of access to exclusive bank sources. They finance expensive television advertisement campaigns, make big donations to supportive political parties, sponsor university graduate programmes, and use lucrative consultancy contracts to co-opt leading academic economists. Bank analysts and PR consultants seek to actively promote particular views about sovereign creditworthiness and to act as 'herd leaders', steering markets and wider opinion (Bini Smaghi 2010c).

The public interest is difficult to uphold in this context of financial-sector largess and self-promotion and opaque lobbying activities. Conflicts of interest in constructing and disseminating beliefs about sovereign creditworthiness become enormously difficult to disentangle. The problem extends beyond shaping financial market legislation into the complex and subtle details that have to be worked out by regulatory authorities, not least in giving precision to key concepts like 'conflict of interest', 'hedging', 'proprietary trading', and 'standardized'. On these all-important details the financial lobbyists and their specialist lawyers deploy immense resources. Their resources are directed at shaping the political climate, including media climate, within which regulators work so that they hesitate to become proactive. They are also focused on 'gaming' often less experienced, less well-resourced, and relatively poorly paid regulators whose future career prospects are bound up with the markets. In this context the risk of intellectual capture of regulators and supervisors is high.

The capacity for collective action of the global, European, and national financial market lobby organizations can be exaggerated. It is limited by the sheer scale of the financial, research, and technical resources available to the big international financial conglomerates and by their competitive instincts. These conglomerates possess the capacity for independent lobbying. They use their own extensive and costly government and PR operations and political lobbying staff who are often former public officials. They are able to gain direct personal access through their individually constructed networks into international financial institutions, finance ministries, central banks, debt management offices, and political parties. Banks like Bank of America, Barclays Capital, BNP Paribas, Citigroup, Deutsche Bank, Goldman Sachs, J.P. Morgan Chase, Nomura, RBS, and UBS are close to the centres of domestic, European, and international power (on Wall Street, see Sorkin 2009). Their chairs and chief executives are typically on terms of personal intimacy with national governing elites, political and official. The privileges that these investment banks enjoy through Primary Dealer status adds further to their individual lobbying capacity. Not least, they enjoy the coveted position of being on the Primary Dealer list of the Federal Reserve Bank of New York. They work closely with the US Treasury Market Practices Group to maintain US Treasury securities as the world's benchmark issuance.

Nevertheless, there were strong incentives for collective action. In relation to securities markets the key lobbyists at international level were the IIF, the International Securities Lending Association (ISLA), the International Swaps and Derivatives Association (ISDA), and the Global Financial Markets Association (GFMA). Within Europe, the Association for Financial Markets in Europe (AFME) was a regional member of the GFMA; whilst the EPDA was a division of the AFME. The European Banking Federation (EBF) lobbied on behalf of bank interests, for instance in matters affecting their capital requirements. In addition, there was a wide range of national lobbies representing the capital markets. Consequent on overlapping memberships in these lobby organizations, supervisors and regulators found themselves facing a formidable array of investment banks, pension funds, insurance companies, mutual funds, asset managers, securities dealers, and service providers.

Perhaps the strongest incentive for collective action of these participants lay in their shared preference for promoting self-regulation. They advocated market-based best practice rather than formal regulation, stressing the onerous costs of external compliance mechanisms. In this respect the United States set a global benchmark. The agenda of market-based best practice was pursued by the Government and Federal Agency Securities Division of the Securities Industry and Financial Markets Association (SIFMA). It was also promoted by the Primary Dealers Executive Committee and the Treasury Borrowing Advisory Committee of the SIFMA. These bodies worked with the Treasury Market Practices Group to ensure best market practice, strengthen market liquidity for US debt securities, and reduce the costs of funding over time.

In Europe the financial market lobbies, notably the EPDA, cooperated closely with SIFMA to disseminate best market practice in sovereign bond markets. However, they lacked an equivalent of the US Treasury as a stimulus to collective action. The key stimulus to strengthening collective action in Europe came from common interest in paralleling the gradual growth of EU-wide capacity for collective regulatory action in the wake of the European Single Market Programme, moves to EMU, and above all the post-2007 crisis. The financial lobbies had to interact with a more active European Commission, with new regulatory authorities like the EBA and ESMA, as well as with the EFC Sub-Committee on EU Government Bills and Bonds. In particular, the EPDA sought to contribute technical assistance in harmonization of sovereign bond markets through close cooperation with the EFC Sub-Committee. Collective action also opened up an opportunity for lobby organizations to make a claim to technocratic legitimacy in offering 'objective', market-based research to supervisors and regulators. More generally, the gradual post-1974 development of the BCBS acted as a spur to financial lobbying. Additional catalysts for collective action were provided by the FSB's work on regulation of systemically significant institutions and 'shadow banking', by the work of the BCBS on Basel III, and by the passage, and above all implementation, of the US Dodd-Frank financial reform act and its European equivalents.

International financial market lobbying activities grew to match and reflect the increasing complexity and the global reach of markets and to parallel increasing post-crisis public interest in regulating to strengthen global financial stability. The ISDA was chartered in 1985; ISLA dated from 1989; whilst AFME was formed in 2009 out of a merger of two London- and US-based investment banking associations to strengthen the European dimension in GFMA, alongside SIFMA. Bodies like the AFME, the EBF, the ISDA, and the ISLA sought to collaborate in varying issue-specific configurations to deal with a host of new regulatory initiatives. They included the short selling of securities, especially when uncovered or naked, credit default swaps, OTC derivatives, market-based interest rate benchmarks, and recognition of credit ratings issued in non-EU states, including US ratings. These initiatives aimed to reduce risks associated with deficiencies of transparency, pre- and post-trade reporting regimes, negative price spirals, and settlement failures. Characteristically, in relation to short selling, the financial market lobbies advocated private reporting to regulators in place of public transparency, which they argued would negatively impact on markets, reduce liquidity, and increase sovereign borrowing costs. Similarly they claimed that too strict an interpretation of new rules regulating credit ratings in Europe, especially the use of non-EU-issued ratings, would have negative effects on banks' capital requirements.

The various financial market lobbies shared certain characteristics. They lobbied to promote and protect the interests of creditors by shaping the principles of best practice with which sovereign borrowers were expected to comply. Their lobbying focused on the negative impact of regulatory requirements and poor practice by sovereign borrowers on bank profitability and thus on bank credit provision and macroeconomic growth. Above all, the financial market lobbies had in common a strategic preference for self-regulation through compliance with agreed principles and market-based best practice. By their active engagement in various lobby organizations, individual banks were also able to profile themselves as 'good citizens' in financial markets. They aimed to increase their credibility with governments, helping them to secure and retain coveted Primary Dealer status.

The Institute of International Finance

The IIF promoted itself as the main collective voice of its member banks on matters of prudent management of risk, including sovereign risk, and on regulatory policies for financial stability that had implications for the interests of its members. Its Steering Committee on Regulatory Capital and its Special Committee on Effective Regulation lobbied hard on the Basel III reforms and on the FSB work on systemically significant institutions (details in Institute of International Finance 2010: 16–21). Their arguments for close attention to the macroeconomic impacts of regulatory changes, especially on bank lending, were reflected in longer timetables for implementation and dilution of earlier more ambitious BCBS proposals on capital and liquidity requirements.

Since the early 2000s IIF dialogue with states about best practice in sovereign bond issuance and global financial stability, including 'fair' debt restructuring, centred on its Principles Consultative Group and on emerging market economies. The IIF lobbied for an enhanced role for the IMF and the World Bank in managing sovereign debt issues, including the IMF's new Flexible Credit Line, as means for better protecting creditor interests. It also stressed the need to embed principles of transparency and 'good faith' in sovereign dealings with investors and to pursue pre-emptive negotiated debt restructurings as opposed to coercive defaults. Using the IIF (2006) 'Principles of Fair Debt Restructuring', it scored the performance of different states. The indicators were whether they cooperated closely and on a voluntary basis with creditors, adhered to timely information-sharing, avoided 'unjustified' capital controls, did not discriminate unfairly amongst creditors, and resumed partial or full debt service payments as soon as conditions allowed. Amongst emerging market economies Brazil came top, followed by Turkey and Chile.

The IIF was most controversial in its dealings with low-income, chronic-debtor states. It sought to protect the interests of private creditors and investors through the activities of three working groups. The first was concerned with litigating investors in sovereign debt markets; the second, with reconciliation of past-due sovereign debt; and the third with the role of trustees in bond indentures. The IIF pursued closer cooperation with the Paris Club. It also sought agreed frameworks for debt reconciliation in chronic debtor states. In such cases affected creditors were typically diverse, sovereign records were sketchy after periods of unrest or war, and there had been little constructive contact with creditors over a long period. Finally, the IIF spelt out the principles that should bind trustees acting on behalf of creditors, especially in legal proceedings (details in IIF 2006: 28–32). However, the Paris Club warned the IIF about the risks in pursuing aggressive creditor litigation against low-income states.

The capacity for collective action within the IIF was demonstrated after November 2011, when the Private Creditor/Investor Committee for Greece was established under its auspices. Advised by big law firms, it negotiated a voluntary bond swap as part of a comprehensive deal to bail-out Greece. The committee comprised thirty international banks and insurance companies. However, the key to success was the consensus that was achieved within its steering committee of twelve big financial institutions. They included BNP Paribas, Deutsche Bank, ING, Intesa Sanpaolo, and National Bank of Greece. Their consensus facilitated a very high level of participation in accepting a substantial haircut on Greek sovereign bonds, notably by some more reluctant German financial institutions.

The European Primary Dealers' Association

The main financial lobby in the field of European sovereign debt was the EPDA, a division of the AFME. In 2009 its members traded over 85 per cent of European sovereign bond market volume. EPDA advocacy efforts on behalf of the leading European bond dealers were directed at the integration and efficiency of European sovereign bond markets. In particular, it promoted an active secondary trading of sovereign bonds through a more open and competitive trading environment. At the same time the EPDA sought to sustain traditional regulated markets by protecting the interests of Primary Dealers against third-party access on electronic platforms. The EPDA (2008) lobbied against the disruption of the existing market structure, on the basis that Primary Dealers had market-making obligations that did not apply to third parties.

The EPDA stressed the value of market-based best practices over formal regulation in it dealings with the EFC Sub-Committee, the European Commission, the ECB, national debt management offices, and trading platforms. It drew on the formidable organizational, research, and technical capacity of its members to play an active role in shaping debates about key EU and euro area policy issues. The EDPA's lobbying was influenced by the interest of its members in limiting credit risk and in reducing bond premiums. The main political constraint that it faced was euro area Member-State misgivings about surrendering autonomy in sovereign-debt issuance.

Consistent with its interest in shaping auctioning to its own strategic interests, the EPDA expressed its preference for a single European Auction System procedure. Its concerns about credit risk led it to advocate the six-month Euro Treasury Bill and the possibility of euro area bonds, issued jointly by a group of small-/medium-sized triple-A issuers. The EPDA/SIFMA (2008) recognized that the Common Eurobond was a longer-term possibility, whose merits might first be tested by simpler, less complex products.

The political constraints on building a euro-area-wide integrated sovereign bond market were underlined in December 2011 by German rejection of the European Commission's Green Paper on the Feasibility of Introducing Stability Bonds. Hence the EPDA continued to promote harmonization of auctioning practices on a best-practice basis, with the aim of strengthening market openness, efficiency, and integration. It pursued this aim through a series of position papers with recommendations on a range of technical issues. The EPDA advocated a standard, web-based auctioning system, basic technical requirements for their robust and speedy operation, their functioning in English as the common language, flexible access from various locations, and more caution in the use of the discretion that states have with respect to their issuance calendars. Auctions should not be concentrated on one day or coincide with the release of market-sensitive economic data by Eurostat and other bodies. Above all, as an interim step, the EPDA proposed a Common Euro Area Treasury Bill (T-Bill) instrument. It would provide a highly liquid short-term funding instrument (one year or less) and avoid mutual financial liability. The European T-Bill would require a new independent Euro Debt Agency.

In addition, the EPDA promoted clear rules that would protect Primary Dealers, for instance from trade cancellations across different electronic trading platforms. It also agreed harmonized rules on Primary Dealer reporting formats to national debt management offices, on quotation obligations, and on performance measurement systems.

Through their leadership role within the EPDA, banks like Citigroup, Credit Suisse, ING, RBS, and Sociéte Générale were able to demonstrate their active engagement in, and above all commitment to, the sovereign bond market. In this way they strengthened their long-term credentials as Primary Dealers. However, the big international investment banks saw the EPDA as essentially a component part of their own lobbying, news management, and PR activities.

Financial Journalism, Public Relations, and the Shaping of Sovereign Creditworthiness: Promotional Culture and Public Interest

The financial markets, within which the private governance of public debt is embedded, are served by their own specialized world of financial journalism and media. From small-scale beginnings in the early stages of printing, it grew by the digital age into real-time information, news, and commentary services on a global scale. In addition, the rise of huge cross-national financial conglomerates from the 1970s spawned the rapid development of highly lucrative professional financial PR consultancies. PR consultancies promoted the interests of investment banks by securing prominence in the media for their positive news stories.

Traditionally, because of its association with a public mission of responsibility for the public interest, financial journalism enjoyed certain legal privileges, including confidentiality of sources, as well as privileges of self-regulation (Tambini 2008). These privileges were designed to ensure that financial journalism could act as an effective watchdog, holding sovereign states, investment banks, and other market players to account. Its role was to root out market and political abuse through independent investigative reporting, and to seek truth and accuracy, as well as newsworthy stories.

However, financial journalism had to operate in the context of the fast growth of a professional promotional culture around investment banking. This culture was mirrored in government by the stronger emphasis on 'spinning' positive stories (Gavin 2007). The rise of professionalized promotional culture came to shape how sovereign creditworthiness was constructed. It complicated the ethical issues and dilemmas that confronted financial journalism in seeking to independently construct and present stories about sovereign creditworthiness, investment bank behaviour, and the activities of financial lobbies and credit rating agencies.

Financial journalists operated in a complex world of tension between professional ethics and multiple constituencies, each with its different interests (Tambini 2008). The 'fourth estate' values its professional independence as essential if it is to inform and educate its readers and viewers. However, there are other constituencies. There are bank advertisers and subscribers to online, terminal services, whom financial media owners and editors have a commercial incentive to placate. There are financial PR consultancies, which manage access to newsworthy stories and sources on terms that reflect positively on their investment bank clients. There are central banks, which assess financial journalists on the basis of their responsible, well-informed, cross-checked reporting on states and markets. There are governments, which want positive stories about sound public finances, solid economic fundamentals, and sovereign creditworthiness. There are macroeconomists, who expect a level of professional analysis and commentary that displays knowledge of their own core professional beliefs. Finally, there is a growing host of 'bloggers', who compete in offering rival, online comment. In consequence, the privileged monopoly position of the *Financial Times* and the *Wall Street Journal* disappeared in a new world of fierce media competition. Financial journalism no longer functioned in a protected environment within which independent-minded, investigative reporting could flourish.

Since the onset of rapid financial market liberalization from the late 1970s, two developments affected the character of financial journalism's watchdog function and the problem of balancing its multiple constituencies. First, new financial media like Bloomberg, which was founded in 1981, defined their mission in highly functional terms. Their corporate mission was to promote transparency, increase consumer and investor awareness, and reduce the costs of doing business. In consequence, financial journalism was induced to define its responsibilities more narrowly around 'serving markets'. It was drawn more closely into the world of investment bank analysts and fund managers (Davis 2006).

Secondly, change took place within the constituencies of interest. Investment banks developed their own in-house resources of market intelligence so that they were less dependent on financial journalists. As advertisers, and as subscribers to online financial media services, investment banks grew in importance in the economics of financial media. Their relative power grew with the role of financial PR consultancies as key players in controlling access to newsworthy stories.

In dealing with sovereign debt and other related markets, financial journalism had its own professionally encoded, mainly self-regulated, privileges and obligations. Compliance with principles, rules, and good practice depended primarily on internal editorial control processes and thus was subject to variable interpretations (Tambini 2008). The combination of 'embedding' of journalism in financial markets with relatively lax compliance mechanisms added to ethical risks and dilemmas. It raised questions about whether editors and journalists engaged effectively with these risks and dilemmas, for instance with respect to conflicts of interest. Doubts arose about whether the construction of sovereign creditworthiness was informed by quality, disinterested financial journalism.

The digital age proved another source of serious challenges to ethical standards in financial journalism. Competition in the financial media market increased with the proliferation of new media, the increasing economic importance of online services, and the rise of 'blogs'. They led to a new drive for increased productivity and placed a heightened premium on ultra-fast speed in delivering information, analysis, and comment. These developments reduced both editorial control and the capacity of journalists to cross-check multiple sources in order to establish truth and accuracy. They also raised the difficult question of the boundaries of financial journalism as a profession. Who belongs as its boundaries expand?

Traditionally, the boundaries of financial journalism had been defined by the venerable 'old' specialized financial agencies like Agence France-Press, Associated Press, and Reuters; the traditional financial press, led by the *Financial Times, Handelsblatt*, and the *Wall Street Journal*; the specialist pages of the quality daily and Sunday newspapers, like the *New York Times*; and the specialist editors and commentators of public-service and commercial television and radio. The field of financial journalism grew to include its own specialized cable and satellite television channels like CNBC, round-the-clock web-based news and information services, and personal blogs. Breakingviews and Motley Fool changed the working environment of financial storytelling and of monitoring ethical conduct. Bloomberg and CNBC also transformed journalistic practice. In addition, the field of information, comment, and assessment was occupied by Dow Jones Newswires, Euronews, and specialist subscription services.

This proliferating world of financial media offered a platform on which investment bank analysts could vie to act as 'herd leaders' in signalling messages about sovereign creditworthiness to markets. Their professional commentary on sovereign creditworthiness was based on selecting and interpreting 'favourable' and 'unfavourable' evidence about macroeconomic, financial, political, and government developments. It was saturated with ideologically, culturally, and historically conditioned beliefs about state strength, governing elite competence, and public responsibility. However, this 'herd-leading' role by bank analysts posed serious conflict-of-interest questions (Bini Smaghi 2010c). In commenting on sovereign creditworthiness, to what extent were they promoting the positions that had been staked out by their investment banks?

Financial journalists, bank analysts within the financial media, and the promotional culture around investment banks and financial PR consultancies, are privileged participants in that they share power in constructing sovereign creditworthiness. They contribute to storytelling about state 'character', to determining which states possess news value at a given time, and to the processes by which market credibility is won or lost. In moving markets, they can help create panics. In some cases, financial media companies formally rank performance. Euronews produces annual sovereign bond market awards. Awards are given to the 'most impressive sovereign funding team': the UK Debt Management Office in 2010; the Finnish State Treasury in 2009; and the Italian Treasury in 2007. They also go to the 'most impressive sovereign bank team' and the 'most impressive sovereign euro house': Barclays Capital won both titles in 2010.

The growth of financial PR consultancies, headed by Brunswick and Finsbury, overshadowed that of financial journalism. This phenomenon symbolized the extent to which the watchdog function was caught up in a promotional culture. By working with PR consultancies, investment banks sought to capture the financial news agenda. Financial news reporting became a 'trading game', in which the consultancies offered journalists access to information and stories in exchange for stories being presented in the 'appropriate' form. This process risked the degeneration of financial journalism into an instrumental function. It involved journalists paying more attention to investment banks and PR consultancies than other constituencies. In turn, banks and consultancies valued financial journalism less as an independent source of information and analysis than as a part of their marketing and lobbying strategies.

The Primary Dealer system offered states an entry into this world of promotional culture. Increasingly, Primary Dealers were valued by national debt management offices on the basis of their effectiveness in putting together 'road shows' for sovereign bond issues and in helping build a wider constituency of investors. This development was strengthened as the euro area sovereign debt crises gathered momentum from 2010.

The world of creditor-debtor state relations, and the construction of sovereign creditworthiness, is caught up in this complex, reflexive, and changing relationship between sovereign states, investment banks, financial PR, and financial journalism. This relationship remains opaque and dimly understood, reflecting in part its inherent complexity and multifaceted nature and, in part, the commercially and politically sensitive nature of the interests at stake in sovereign creditworthiness. Crucially, big investment banks relied on building their own specialist capacity on sovereign bond markets both in information and analysis and in investor relations. This capacity building mirrored the increasing size and complexity of sovereign bond markets. In sovereign bond markets, financial journalists and media were less significant as sources of market and political intelligence than as objects of PR activities. The growth of investment bank research capacity and of financial PR, with its own distinctive professional norms, altered the context of financial journalism and marginalized it as insufficiently specialist.

News stories in the financial media could have a strong micro-impact on sovereign-bond prices and yield spreads and a strong macro-impact on market sentiment towards a state's creditworthiness. However, stories about sovereign creditworthiness are not independently and autonomously constructed by the media. The raw material is provided by deeper structural factors: the relative position of states within global and European external imbalances; net external debt to GDP; and larger historical shifts in the world political economy. In turn, this raw material is fed through the promotional culture of investment banking and financial PR. Nevertheless, the processes of selecting and interpreting evidence are shaped by ideology and culture.

In constructing narratives of sovereign creditworthiness, financial journalism relies heavily on the large research capacity of the big financial conglomerates and the niche bond market players. Financial news reporting, for instance in the *Financial Times*, makes much routine use of research materials generated by such banks as Citigroup, Credit Suisse, Goldman Sachs, and J.P. Morgan Chase. Their use raises serious conflict-of-interest issues when reporting and commenting on public debt and sovereign creditworthiness. Banks take up market positions in sovereign bond markets that they wish to justify and to support. Perhaps most worryingly of all, financial journalists are vulnerable to the use of new media and 'blogs' for dissemination of rumours by investors that are self-serving and damaging to reputations.

The tendency for financial journalists to become embedded in financial markets and 'go native' and the pressure to engage with instant commentary on real-time information reduce their capacity to place market-based narratives about sovereign creditworthiness in a larger political, macroeconomic, and historical context. Most importantly, they impair their capacity to engage critically with these narratives. Embedded financial market reporting increases incentives to tell 'positive' stories about financial market players on whom one develops dependence for access and material. 'Negative' stories can invite closure of access and loss of comparative advantage as a financial journalist. Though there may be counter-pressures in scooping big exclusive stories, they are less apparent in the more routine work of financial journalism.

Nevertheless, financial journalists are not ciphers. They play a role in constructing stories about sovereign creditworthiness—about which states figure in the news at any one time, and about whether they are presented as saints or sinners. Financial journalists are aware that 'news' can move financial markets in powerful and often seemingly random ways. Journalistic stories about sovereign creditworthiness are, at best, constructed around a complex and varying compound of professional search for truth, accuracy, and impact on markets and readers. At worst, they are taken up from investment banks and reported with minimal or no cross-checking of sources and without independent, critical reflection. Financial journalism risks cosy and complacent 'herd-thinking'. Critical financial journalism is at a premium in the private governance of public debt.

The watchdog function of financial journalism in offering an independent and critical perspective depends on robust internal professional compliance processes. Enforcement of formal disclosure of conflicts of interest is relatively weak, a factor that can encourage bond 'tipping' (Tambini 2008). There is also a frequent lack of editorial attention to differentiating comment from news reporting. The risks of bad, poor, and complacent professional practice are increased by the digitally-driven incentives to get market-sensitive information to investors faster than competitors. They are compounded by reliance on fast-expanding PR professionals as an information source and by shying away from risk of exclusion from future good stories because of dissent. There are counter-pressures. Stories are filtered against malicious, self-serving rumour-spreading by the professional incentive to retain credibility with the public and with readers as a trusted, authoritative source of information. They are also informed by awareness of the scale of the risks in becoming associated with destroying confidence in a state's creditworthiness.

In consequence of the complex and changing incentive structure, financial journalism has a problematic relationship to sovereign bond markets. It has the capacity to strengthen their efficiency by rooting out malpractice of governments and of investment banks, using various cross-checked sources. However, financial journalism can also contribute to positive feedback effects, herding behaviour, and dysfunctional markets. As we have seen, various developments have reduced the incentives to engage in critical interrogation of sources. In consequence, investigative financial journalism has withered, and financial journalism surrendered its watchdog function and independent-mindedness. It gives momentum to herd-like behaviour through self-fulfilling 'boosterism' and spreading panic in markets. John Kenneth Galbraith (1990: 5–10) wrote eloquently about how individual dissenting voices are drowned out or dismissed as 'alarmist' or 'eccentric' when they question market euphoria and the promotional culture that informs it.

The Weak Link: Democratic Engagement

The coexistence of a 'thin' political superstructure with a 'thick' technocratic infrastructure means that creditor-debtor state relations and the private governance of public debt remain opaque and shadowy worlds. Their key participants operate in a privileged sphere of political silence, legitimated by a discourse that emphasizes de-politicization and professional consensus. This consensus combines intense technical cross-national policy learning processes with market-based processes of constructing sovereign creditworthiness. However, correcting external trade and financial imbalances and anchoring belief in long-term debt sustainability are processes that have enormous political implications. They raise issues about the distribution of adjustment costs across space between creditor and debtor states, across generations, and across different social groups.

Ultimately, tackling basic questions of justice requires democratic engagement and legitimacy. The institutional structures for providing this legitimacy remain undeveloped at the global and the European levels. Moreover, individual states find it increasingly difficult to act as the providers of democratic legitimacy when global and European trade and financial interdependence reduces their capacity for effective autonomous policies. Domestic politics and policy development to address external imbalances and to ensure sustainable debt become disengaged, above all in the context of European monetary union. The consequence is a sense of the powerlessness of states and the 'hollowing out' of democracy amongst electorates. In consequence, creditor-debtor state relations and the private governance of public debt remain highly vulnerable to political shocks, including the rise of national political populism, flash victories for extremist parties, and social protest in its various forms.

The imbalance between the rapid acceleration of financial market liberalization from the late 1970s and the slow evolution of European and global governance structures was a key catalyst in this process of perceived weakening of democratic engagement. The technocratic infrastructure of creditor-debtor state relations grew in complexity and in intellectual self-confidence. Macroeconomics provided a legitimating discourse for market efficiency, light-touch regulation, and de-politicization as instruments for gaining credibility as creditworthy sovereign states. In addition, the enormous growth in the balance sheets and profitability of the big cross-national investment banks served as a catalyst for the emergence of a sophisticated promotional culture centred on financial PR consultancies. Promoting a glamorous image of investment banking took on a newly professional form. It was also articulated through the fast growth in financial market lobby organizations, including the financing of political parties.

Governing elites colluded in this process of de-politicization, for two reasons. First, they sought to insure themselves against growing financial market power through granting independence to their central banks and their debt management offices and, in some cases, through developing SWFs. They bought into the argument that they would be rewarded with lower borrowing costs. Secondly, governing elites had an incentive to cut transaction costs in complex sovereign bond markets and in financial market regulation and supervision. This incentive led them to cultivate the Primary Dealer system. It also gave rise to the privileged role of credit rating agencies in anchoring beliefs about sovereign and bank creditworthiness. Credit rating agencies and Primary Dealers gained semi-official status as nodal points in creditor-debtor state relations and the private governance of public debt.

The increasingly thick technocratic infrastructure of creditor-debtor state relations and the private governance of public debt are deeply embedded in the privileging of market-based processes of constructing sovereign creditworthiness. This privileging takes four forms. Primary Dealers occupy a privileged position. Market-based credit ratings and sovereign bond indices have the key anchoring and signalling roles. Financial market lobbying organizations work to undermine the incentives for collective action by states, using their enormous resources to shape the terms of policy and political debates. Financial journalism and media become immersed in the promotional culture of investment banking and financial PR. These characteristics of creditor-debtor state relations and the private governance of public debt weaken the capacity of governing elites to frame debates and to gain a firm grip on substantive policy issues. Their instruments for taming financial markets and asserting the primacy of politics are less powerful than market-based instruments for branding states. In consequence, creditor-debtor state relations and the private governance of public debt are not conducive to independent, critical thinking and to developing and sustaining public-interest arguments.

Sovereign bond markets are distinctive in their organization and structures of power. They combine privileges with obligations in a unique way within financial markets. Transparency is valued highly. However, transparency is more a question of internal relations between debt managers and Primary Dealers. It is seen as an essential basis so that their teamwork—based on mutual trust and confidence—can be retained. Otherwise, opacity has been cultivated as a means of protecting both state reputation and creditor interests. If internal walls are like glass, external walls are concrete. For this reason, when it comes to revealing bank exposures to sovereign debt, bank stress tests are treated with scepticism. The sovereign bond markets are a striking example of the self-referential character of creditor-debtor state relations and the private governance of public debt.

13

The Dynamics of External Imbalances and Debt

> The evil is not due to being indebted abroad, but to prior unproductive use of credit.
>
> Adolph Wagner (1863: 62)

Gross external debt, public and private debt, features as a key issue in the politics of sovereign creditworthiness and in the management of creditor-debtor state relations. It highlights in the most graphic way the risks posed by the mismatch between sovereign liability and territorial control. The ratios of gross external debt to gross domestic product (GDP), to exports, and to foreign-exchange reserves seem prima facie sensible indicators of default probability and of relative state power. Debt restructuring is, after all, very often associated with a high external debt/GDP ratio. The ratio was 79.4 per cent in Bulgaria in 1994; 68.6 per cent in Moldova in 2004; 49.7 per cent in Russia in 2000; and 54.0 per cent in Ukraine in 2000. However, Turkey restructured in 1982 with an external debt/GDP ratio of 33.0 per cent. Albania restructured in 1995 with a ratio of only 16.3 per cent (Das, Papaioannu and Trebesch 2012: 111–12). Luxembourg did not restructure (it remained triple-A rated) with an external debt/GDP ratio of 4,509.3 per cent in 2012. Clearly external debt is neither the only nor necessarily the most important source of mismatch between sovereign liability and control. It is an unreliable indicator of relative state power. In the nineteenth century Adolph Wagner (1863) noted that the main problem derives from the use of foreign credit for current expenditures that should have been financed from domestic taxation.

Original Sin and External Debt Thresholds

'Original sin' provides one important source of mismatch between sovereign liability and territorial control and thus of state vulnerability. It refers to the inability of a state to borrow abroad in its own currency (Eichengreen, Hausman, and Panizza 2003). Classically, 'original sin' is associated with developing and emerging markets. It arises when domestic lending capacity—public and private—is limited and makes a state dependent on exceedingly short-term and very high-cost borrowing. However, original sin is neither a simple binary matter nor a one-way process of escaping sin by economic development. States may be affected to varying degrees. The practical question is just how much original sin is compatible with debt sustainability. Moreover, a state may revert back to original sin, as in the case of the Austro-Hungarian Empire from the late 1870s (Morys 2010).

Why is original sin a problem? It acts as an incentive for policy makers to keep the exchange rate pegged to the currency or currencies in which debt is denominated. The gain is access to more liquid financial markets and lower borrowing costs. The downside is the incentive for states in original sin to borrow too much in foreign currencies. They face the risk that they will lack sufficient foreign-currency earnings and fail to adequately hedge their exchange-rate exposure. If market confidence evaporates, and the currency peg breaks, foreign-currency-denominated debt is likely to become unsustainable. Central bank reserves will drain away; interest rates will rise to protect the currency; and probability of sovereign default will increase.

Original sin was not a euro area problem. On measures of 'original sin' covering the period 1993–2001, the EU Member States that went on to join the euro area substantially reduced their vulnerability, compared to eastern Europe and developing countries (Eichengreen, Hausman, and Panizza 2003). They took measures to encourage the growth of their domestic bond market, principally by taming inflation and by incentives to strengthen domestic pension and insurance sectors. It was often not a low-cost option.

However, original sin had historically been a big problem within Europe. By 1880–1914 a nucleus of European states were able to issue sovereign bonds in their own currencies, marking them out as core within the European economy. They included Belgium, Britain, Denmark, France, Germany, the Netherlands, and Switzerland, as well as the United States (Bordo and Flandreau 2001). In contrast, with the possible exception of Russia, the states in the European 'arc of default' were mired in original sin.

The Austro-Hungarian Empire was an intermediate case, displaying evidence of reversion to original sin. In the mid-1870s the proportion of total external public debt issued in domestic currency was 39.2 per cent (paper bonds). However, the Austro-Hungarian authorities found greater difficulties in issuing their paper bonds as the gold standard was adopted by an increasing number of European states. Adopting the gold standard became emblematic of the Empire's membership of core Europe. It required mastery of fiscal deficits, above all in Hungary. Hence the financial and political incentives to adopt the gold standard were considerable. Eventually, macroeconomic conditions enabled its adoption in 1892. By 1913 the share of paper debt in total external public debt had fallen to 4.9 per cent (Morys 2010: 3–4). They were replaced by gold bonds, which were protected by foreign-exchange clauses and/or gold clauses. Some 80 per cent of these gold bonds were held externally and, strikingly, at lower yields than previous paper bonds. This development was made possible by a positive trade balance till 1907 and, especially from 1899, by huge and growing remittances from emigrants (Morys 2010: 50).

Nineteenth-century Greece and Spain represented extreme cases of original sin. Greek external public debt accounted for over 200 per cent of GDP in 1843, when statistics are first available. It remained over 100 per cent till 1861, climbing again over 100 per cent in 1887. Further evidence of Greek state weakness was the fact that external debt represented 100 per cent of public debt in 1843. It remained over 90 per cent till 1868 (see Table 5.9).

The external public debt/export ratio of Spain reached historical highs of 10.1 in 1852 and 9.1 in 1876. It stayed above 2.5 till 1883. The debt restructuring of Camacho in 1881–1882 marked the turning point. By 1914 the Spanish external public debt/export ratio had fallen to 0.9; it reached 0.1 in 1920 (see Table 7.15). Except for a brief period in the post-Civil-War period, and during the first decade of the euro, external public debt ceased to be a burden on the Spanish state.

On world and European scales, historical data on total external debt are hard to find. Nevertheless, sufficient data are available for the interwar and post-war periods to offer insights into the changing vulnerability of states to the mismatch between liability and control. By 1929, just before the Great Depression, the amount of external public debt had doubled since 1920. It accounted for some 4 per cent of world GDP, just above the amount of foreign-exchange reserves. By 2010, international debt securities had grown to 17 per cent of world GDP and a huge 114 per cent of world foreign-exchange reserves (Chitu, Eichengreen, and Mehl 2012: 7–8). States could benefit from tapping into this financial liquidity. However, collectively, this comparison of 1929 and 2010 suggests the heightened collective vulnerability of all states to financial markets. In 1929 there were striking differences in exposure to external debt. Sterling-denominated debt represented some 50 per cent of Britain's GDP, whereas dollar-denominated debt was only about 7 per cent of US GDP. Almost 80 per cent of this dollar-denominated debt was owned by Europe, above all by France, which alone accounted for some 60 per cent.

In the late eighteenth century Voltaire had argued that overreliance on external debt exposes the vulnerability of state power. Modern economic research has suggested that, beyond certain thresholds, calculated by reference to GDP or exports, gross external debt has a non-linear, negative impact on economic growth. Most of these estimates derived from emerging market economies. They influenced International Monetary Fund (IMF) and World Bank thinking about debt sustainability. IMF studies suggested an external debt threshold of 35–40 per cent of GDP and 65 per cent of exports. Beyond these thresholds the conditions for debt sustainability deteriorate. A critical turning point is reached at 150 per cent of GDP (Pattillo, Poirson, and Ricci 2004). The threshold is assessed by the IMF as low as 5 per cent of GDP when a state, like nineteenth-century Spain, has a default and inflation history. For emerging economies, the IMF and the World Bank set a threshold of external debt service costs at 15–25 per cent of exports. They pointed out that states need to earn foreign exchange in order to service external debt.

However, an IMF role in developing and applying external debt thresholds proved more contentious and difficult in the case of advanced economies. Some of these economies were major IMF shareholders, represented in the IMF executive board. They feared endorsing thresholds that might put their own private-sector financial institutions at greater risk to states with high external debt exposure, like Greece and Ireland. The vacuum was filled by professional economists. Reinhart, Reinhart, and Rogoff (2012) identified the threshold for advanced economies at gross external debt of 90 per cent of GDP. In 2012 only five EU Member States were within this threshold: the Czech Republic, Lithuania, Poland, Romania, and Slovakia. The euro area as a whole had a gross external debt/GDP ratio of 123.8 per cent. France, Germany, and Italy had respective ratios of 192.6, 163.9, and 120.7 per cent, well below Britain at 415 per cent. Ireland stood out at 1,002.2 per cent but was eclipsed by Luxembourg. Greece and Portugal were far from exceptional with external debt/GDP ratios of 225.6 per cent and 232.9 per cent in 2012, below two triple-A rated euro area Member States: Finland (233.6) and the Netherlands (313.8).

The Challenge to Political Will and State Capacity

The manageability of gross external debt is bound up with domestic political will and state capacity to match sovereign liability with control. This problem has two aspects. First, as external debts mount, governments find themselves positioned precariously between two principals, each with opposed interests and preferences. External creditors—official and private—seek full and timely repayments of interest and principal. They bring external pressure to bear, using tough conditionality requirements to achieve economic stabilization by domestic fiscal consolidation and structural reforms. The implications for governing elites include the politically uncomfortable, potentially humiliating abridgement of state sovereignty.

Conversely, domestic voters tend to reject 'austerity', deflation, and 'intolerable' cuts, especially to real wages and social benefits, when they impact directly and visibly on them. They also resent 'humiliating' externally-imposed conditions. Domestic voters, above all the poor, the unemployed, and public-service employees, prefer debt restructuring and default as instruments for protecting social welfare to what external creditors justify in instrumental terms as necessary and even unavoidable. Governing elites find themselves faced by risk of social and political disintegration and by a vengeful public looking for external scapegoats.

In this precarious position, governing elites have a domestic incentive to play a waiting-game in enforcing fiscal consolidation and economic stabilization and to 'window-dress' public finance figures. As Germany showed in 1931–1933, and Greece post-2010, their great fear is presiding over social and political breakdown. Its indicators are political polarization, national populist radicalization, and violent mass protest against attempts to engineer cuts in real wages and benefits. The problem is compounded when, as in Weimar Germany, political will and state capacity prove weak not just because of fragmentation and ideological polarization in the party system but also because of fragile, instrumental public attachment to liberal democratic norms.

Secondly, the challenge to political will and state capacity to match sovereign liability with control stems from the narrower range of policy instruments that governments possess for reducing external debt than for reducing domestic debt. Financial repression and inflation are less directly useful in the case of external debt than devaluation and debt restructuring and default. Dealing with external debt problems without sacrificing creditor confidence places a premium on strategies for creating external buffers. Governments can seek to mobilize private-sector capacity to reduce unit labour costs and generate export-led growth through encouraging productivity-oriented wage bargaining and skill upgrading. They can undertake financial reforms to develop large, liquid domestic bond markets. Their central banks—or sovereign wealth funds—can accumulate substantial foreign-exchange reserves, like the Banque de France before 1914 and in the late 1920s. Absence of external buffers in Spain between 1814 and 1914 made external debt servicing an onerous fiscal problem. Between 1850 (the first available statistics) and 1885 external debt accounted for over 30 per cent of public debt. Over the nineteenth century Spain held the record for the largest number of debt restructurings.

The euro area presents an additional challenge to political will and state capacity to match sovereign liability and control. The first decade of currency union in Europe was associated with a surge in the external indebtedness of its Member States. This surge derived from the removal of exchange-rate risk, the reduction of transaction costs, and the spur to European financial integration. The consequence was a paradox. On the one hand, Member States of the euro area had lost the classic devaluation policy instrument. Their policy repertoire narrowed to measures for mimicking nominal devaluation through radical fiscal policy and structural economic reforms to reduce unit labour costs.

On the other hand, the treatment of debt across euro area Member States as external was ambiguous. This ambiguity stemmed from the combination of euro-denominated debt issuance by the Member States with the failure to create euro area institutional arrangements for joint liability (debt mutualization). At the same time, cross-border debts assumed a hybrid character once the European Central Bank (ECB) evolved into 'lender-of-last-resort' to the banking sector; once it agreed to undertake unlimited interventions in secondary sovereign bond markets (although on strict conditions); and once the European Stability Mechanism (ESM) was established to provide collective financial assistance, including intervention in sovereign bond markets.

Nevertheless, the ambiguity about sovereign debt in the euro area left its Member States exposed. This exposure mattered to the extent that investors came to believe that there was a threshold of external debt to GDP beyond which massive costs in GDP were incurred. The threshold of 90 per cent of GDP, as formulated by Reinhart, Reinhart, and Rogoff (2012: 7), was far below euro area levels in 2008–2011.

However, the problem with data on external debt as a percentage of GDP is that they focus on gross rather than net external debt. A very high level of gross external debt can conceal the reality that a particular state is a creditor state, whose total external debts are less than the total of the external debts of other states whose ownership is ascribed to it. In particular, small states with large financial sectors—like Luxembourg and Switzerland—have disproportionately large gross external debts. In 2010 Luxembourg had the highest percentage of gross external debt to GDP in the world at 3,443 per cent. However, it was a net creditor (IMF World Economic Outlook Database, <http://www.imf.org/external/pubs/ft/weo/data/changes.htm>, accessed 21 July 2011). In contrast, Greek gross external debt was 174 per cent of GDP, Irish 108 per cent, and Spanish a mere 84 per cent. The figure for the United Kingdom was 360 per cent, and for the Netherlands 344 per cent, again reflecting their large financial sectors. They were well ahead of France at 182 per cent, Germany at 142 per cent, Italy at 108 per cent, the United States at 103 per cent, and the EU as a whole at 85 per cent.

Creditor and Debtor States

The form of debt is a significant factor in the politics of sovereign creditworthiness. Debt takes two forms: internal or external; and short-term or long-term. External debt refers to liabilities that are owed by a resident to a non-resident. Short-term debt, which includes currency, is debt repayable on demand or with an original maturity of one year or less. Long-term debt has an original maturity of over one year or with no stated maturity (Bank for International Settlements 2002). These distinctions matter in terms of where power lies within creditor-debtor state relations. The combination of high external debt with short-term maturities increases the vulnerability of states to 'roll-over' problems. Similarly, rising costs of financing longer-term debt, notably on ten-year bonds, are taken as a leading indicator of emerging crises of sovereign creditworthiness, especially when they exceed domestic GDP growth.

Conventionally, creditor states are much fewer in number than debtor states (Edwards 2004). States are creditors when the value of their gross external assets exceeds, or approximates to, their liabilities. In 2010 Belgium, Finland, Germany, and Norway fitted this definition, along with Japan (International Monetary Fund 2011b: 5). They received net interest payments. In contrast, debtor states have substantial net external debt. Britain, Greece, Hungary, Iceland, Ireland, Latvia, Portugal, and Spain fell into this category. They were characterized by net interest payments. As the post-2007 crisis demonstrated, debtor states risk building up excessive external liabilities, consequent on reckless corporate and household borrowing and supportive pro-cyclical domestic credit expansion. They are all the more vulnerable to volatility when they depend on excessive short-term foreign-currency borrowing, whether by the corporate, household, and/or public sectors.

Creditor-debtor state relations are caught up in a difficult three-way balancing act. The outcome reflects the tension between asymmetric power over ideas and in agenda-setting, which favours creditor states, and the 'power of numbers', which formally favours debtor states. This asymmetric power is most evident when negotiations are about creating new institutional and policy arrangements for cooperation and in the path dependency that follows. When the negotiating context shifts to reforming existing policies and arrangements, the power of numbers becomes more significant. Creditor states are more tightly bound up within institutional and policy frameworks.

Hence three interests contend. Private and official external creditors seek to limit their liabilities. They insist on tough detailed conditionality and prefer to avoid 'write-down' in the value of their assets. The interests of debtor states are in securing bail-outs in order to ease domestic economic and political adjustment costs, not least by buying time, and in spreading costs by bail-in of creditors. However, a third interest emerges once collective institutional and policy arrangements are in place. Collective action can be justified by reference to contagious systemic risks. Thus systemic risks in the euro area adversely affected not just other debtor states, like Italy and Spain in the case of Greece, but also creditor states like Germany. The exit option is a less powerful bargaining resource for creditor states once collective institutional and policy arrangements have been negotiated.

This complex balancing act becomes difficult to sustain once external creditors, public as well as private, are seen not to have economic and political shoulders broad enough, and willing enough, to finance the huge debt loads and to unwind them in an orderly manner. In these circumstances, different ideologies of debt, different cultural understandings of risk, and emotional engagement with these ideologies and understandings become more overt and risk undermining collective action. Building the trust, on which creditor-debtor state relations depend, and avoiding miscommunication prove highly challenging.

How States Behave

Creditor-debtor state relations owe their origins and nature to the challenges of managing external private and public debt for sovereign states and for investors. The central challenges to state liquidity and solvency arise from the external obligations of households, financial and non-financial companies, and governments to pay principal and/or interest to non-resident investors who have acquired a claim on them as debtors. In a national balance sheet perspective, a state faces unsustainable debt when the level of its external debt has made its servicing provision (interest payments and amortization) incompatible with the projection of net capital inflows.

There are various risk indicators to external debt sustainability. They include a sharp drop in exports or an increase in the price of imports, negatively affecting the availability of resources for debt repayments; a rise in interest rates, so that debt costs more; appreciation of the currency or currencies in which external debt is contracted, raising the costs to debtors; attempts by banks to restructure over-the-counter (OTC) derivative contracts denominated in the foreign currency in which debt has been contracted; changes in the maturity structure of external debt, so that the ratio of short-term debt to total outstanding debt rises; and a falling ratio of foreign-exchange reserves to short-term external debt. The policy issues are either liquidity, in which case a state needs to reduce its external debt, or insolvency, in which case it needs to contemplate external debt restructuring and who, if anyone, is to be privileged in such a restructuring (typically, official creditors). Participants in the private governance of public debt select and interpret these indicators in the process of constructing whether and when external debt has become unsustainable.

When states face liquidity and insolvency risk, consequent on excessive public and/or private external debt, their households, corporate sectors, and governments have powerful incentives to shift burdensome liabilities onto someone else's balance sheet. This shift can be achieved by government action to help restructure household debts; the use of complex, often opaque, financial instruments like 'securitization' to spread risk; the transfer of so-called 'toxic' assets into 'bad banks'; securing government guarantees of bank debt; and international and/or European financial assistance for states and banks. Characteristically, this process manifests itself initially in the shift of liabilities from private to public sector. As in Britain and Ireland from 2007, governments resort to bank bail-outs to keep their national financial systems solvent and avert systemic breakdown from contagious banking and corporate failures. The risk of sovereign insolvency arises from the potentially huge implicit liabilities that states acquire in this way. Alternatively, as in Greece, the state engages in reckless external public financing. In one way or the other, excessive external debt manifests itself as problems of sovereign liquidity and/or solvency.

Once burdened in this way, states have an incentive to shift their external liabilities onto the shoulders of creditor states or of international institutions, like the IMF and the World Bank, which act as official creditors. Indirectly, in the post-2007 crisis, the ECB's 'unconventional' monetary policy operations helped relieve states by supporting the liquidity needs of their banking systems and the maintenance of capacity of their banks to purchase their sovereign bonds. In addition, the creation of the temporary European Financial Stability Facility (EFSF) and of the permanent ESM was associated with an increasing range of bail-out instruments for states and banks in debt distress.

The Distinctive Characteristics of Creditor-Debtor State Relations

In the context of the growing dependencies of states on external credit, and their consequent vulnerability, creditor-debtor state relations became gradually more formalized at European and international levels. The catalysts were the economic disasters of the First and the Second World Wars and the Great Depression. The lesson drawn by policy makers was that there were substantial absolute as well as relative gains from European and international cooperation in addressing the build-up and consequences of excessive external trade and financial imbalances and in averting cross-national contagion. The problem was ongoing contention about the normative principles and foundational commitments that can justify creditor-debtor state cooperation.

Structural imbalances in current accounts are reflected in the contrasting differences of strategic economic interests and policy preferences between creditor and debtor states. The causality is complex. In part, states become creditors because they pursue certain policy preferences. In part, because they are creditors, they have an interest in these policy preferences. Either way, there is a powerful symbiotic relationship of structural position and strategic preferences.

Post-1815 Germany offered a striking example of inter-state rivalries that exemplified this divergence of strategic interests and policy preferences and its linkage to chronic external imbalances. One source of these imbalances was the severe dislocations produced by massive increases in cheap British cotton imports. Another was Prussian agrarian restructuring in response to the opportunities offered to the Junker landowners after Britain lifted its corn law in 1846. The city states of Bremen and Hamburg emerged as powerful creditors, based on their dominance of the cotton and the grain trades. The losers were the old-established linen industries of Baden and Württemberg in the south-west. They became chronic debtor states, marked by a large-scale migration to the United States, once again routed largely through Bremen and Hamburg. These structural imbalances within Germany help explain why proud, self-confident governing elites in Bremen and Hamburg advocated free trade. Those in Baden and Württemberg supported policies of protection. Prussian interests proved more divided.

In consequence of external imbalances, creditor-debtor state relations face formidable collective-action problems. 'Rules of the game' matter. Edward I, Henry II, and Henry

VIII of England, and Philip IV of France, were able to practise 'fiscal tyranny', in ways denied to modern European governments (Richardson 1952; Starkey 1987). Since the central banking days of Émile Moreau, Montagu Norman, and Hjalmar Schacht in the 1920s, the rules of the game have changed in ways that suggest a 'new Europe'. At the same time, the rules associated with Economic and Monetary Union (EMU) camouflage an underlying continuity in structural challenges and differences in strategic interests and preferences. The intellectually problematic, culturally sensitive, and politically controversial difficulties in designing and operating European macroeconomic governance, even within a monetary union, were painfully exposed as the post-2007 global financial and economic crisis gathered momentum.

Creditor-debtor state relations have four distinctive characteristics. The number of debtor states always exceeds the number of creditor states, giving the former the numeric advantage. Secondly, power remains asymmetric. Creditor-state elites have strong incentives to act collectively to limit their liabilities in any new collective arrangements. Debtor-state elites have strong incentives to avoid creditor-state defection from negotiations about new collective arrangements, as well as to differentiate themselves from each other. The moral connotations of excessive debt, deeply rooted in folk belief, also place creditor-state elites in a stronger position to frame debates and set agendas of cooperation.

Thirdly, the configuration of creditor states in Europe changes over time. In the first decade of the twenty-first century it included pre-eminently Austria, Denmark, Finland, Germany, Luxembourg, the Netherlands, Norway, Sweden, and Switzerland. From the thirteenth to the seventeenth centuries it was city-based and shifted amongst Amsterdam, Antwerp, Augsburg, Florence, Genoa, Lucca, and Venice. These cities, and later territorial states, had, in consequence, a model character. They possessed 'network capital' and a capacity to exercise 'soft' power that was disproportionate to their size and to their military prowess. Their governing elites evoked admiration. They functioned as economic, cultural, and intellectual magnets, attracting talent in all walks of life.

Creditor-debtor state relations are also distinguished by the participants. By the early twenty-first century they were managed within the context of an increasingly 'thick' technical infrastructure. It included a wide range of institutional investors, such as investment banks, pension funds, insurance companies, mutual funds, sovereign wealth funds, hedge funds, and corporate treasurers; credit rating agencies; international financial institutions like the IMF and the World Bank; supra-national bodies like the European Commission; central banks; creditor-state governments; academic economists; financial market lobbyists; and financial journalists. Publics had an enormous stake in this technocratic esoteric process and its outcomes. They were affected as taxpayers, benefit recipients, and users of public services and infrastructure. Bail-outs imposed costs on publics in both creditor and debtor states.

However, it remains very difficult for the public and its representatives to hold creditor-debtor state relations to account. They face the sheer technical complexity of this world, its shadowy and esoteric character, its susceptibility to manipulation of information, and the myriad ways in which it escapes state boundaries. Moreover, retaining the credibility of the notion of an autonomous and distinctive public interest is formidably difficult. It is placed in question by the nature of the disciplinary power of the sovereign bond markets, the privileges that attach to the investment banks that act as Primary Dealers, the vast resources and sheer scale and intensity of financial market lobbying, the way in which reputedly independent financial journalism is embedded in the markets, and the sheer technicality, opacity, and complexity of markets. Even the most professionally engaged participants—including supervisors, regulators, and heads of financial institutions—encounter formidable difficulties in distinguishing fact from fiction, in avoiding manipulation, and in holding others to account. The world of creditor-debtor state relations connects very imperfectly to liberal democracy and to traditional notions of corporate governance, centred on shareholders.

Constructing Sovereign Creditworthiness

Creditor-debtor state relations are fundamentally concerned with the processes of constructing sovereign creditworthiness. Creditworthiness is given formal expression in the sovereign rating methodologies and the internal peer reviews of credit rating agencies (e.g. Fitch Ratings 2009c). Credit rating agencies have a special place in constructing sovereign bond market preferences. They function simultaneously as 'cameras' and 'engines' of the process (cf. MacKenzie 2006). Out of complex sets of numbers, they simplify, formalize, and construct sovereign creditworthiness into a single set of letters, with 'triple-A' as the top rating and 'negative outlooks' as a danger signal of downgrade. For this purpose, credit rating agencies use a range of formal indicators, including current account balance, external debt and external financing requirement, as well as public finances, economic structure, and macroeconomic performance. These formal indicators serve as important tools in constructing sovereign creditworthiness. They give weighting to external imbalances and debt.

Despite this wide range of 'objective' performance indicators used by credit rating agencies and investment banks, the expectations and fears of investors remain central to the process of constructing sovereign creditworthiness. The centrality of investors derives from the basic fact that the great bulk of public debt is issued on international capital markets, which provide the credit on which states—to a greater or lesser degree—depend. Correspondingly, market preferences serve as the central reference point in processes of constructing sovereign creditworthiness. Credit rating agencies and markets behave in symbiotic, self-reinforcing fashion.

Notwithstanding the power of numbers, imagining how states might behave—and the capacity of their governing elites to deliver 'necessary' changes—is a fragile talent. It requires more than the capacity to calculate and synthesize sets of data. The question remains whether market preferences, as captured in the credit default swap (CDS) market or the assessments of credit rating agencies, are founded on 'sound' images of states, their propensity to default, and the potential severity of loss to their creditors. Unfolding events show that these images prove often illusory. Both CDS spreads and credit ratings of sovereigns failed to adequately capture the risks as the credit-fuelled boom of the early 2000s gathered momentum. Over the post-EMU period 1999–2007, they suggested complacency about the default risks posed by Greece and about Ireland and Spain, which turned out to be 'illusory' creditor states.

Constructing sovereign creditworthiness involves the choice and weighing of indicators and the interpretation and use of complex data. This process goes beyond the limited language and restricted assumptions of formal economic theory, model building, and rigorous statistical analysis. It has an irreducibly qualitative basis in beliefs about the motives and leadership capacities of governing elites; about tolerance of domestic publics; and about institutional capacity to generate export-led growth, to extract taxes, to consolidate fiscal balances, and to speed private-sector deleveraging.

Psychological and sociological studies of human behaviour suggest that processes of constructing sovereign creditworthiness are intimately bound up with images of states, their governing elites, and their publics. Participants in these processes possess often unexamined emotional attachments to these images. They convince themselves that they have correctly branded states as 'saints' or 'sinners', no matter how uncertain, difficult, and contentious the initial choices might have been (cf. Gilbert 2007; Iyengar 2010). The high level of inertia in branding states reflects the depth of emotional attachments to entrenched images of states. Once participants have branded states, their preferences tend to harden in favour of certain 'saints'—which become 'safe havens'—and against various 'sinners'.

Despite this inertia, the behaviour of numbers means that constructing sovereign creditworthiness also has the character of an iterative process. In differentiating states and branding them, investors make use of a wide range of formal indicators that help identify different liquidity and solvency risks. These tools are potentially powerful. Rigorous analysis of patterns and sizes of change across indicators may alter investor choices and rating agency decisions. Formal indicators are an intrinsic part of the construction of sovereign creditworthiness. They are 'engines', not just 'cameras' (cf. MacKenzie 2006, 2009). In reacting to new data, to 'bad' and 'good' news, participants in this process are guided by entrenched images and emotional attachments, which affect their degree of receptivity to news. Credit rating agencies admit to the importance of 'intangible' influences on sovereign creditworthiness, noting that they had traditionally favoured advanced over developing emerging market economies (Fitch Ratings 2009c: 5).

The reaction of participants in processes of constructing sovereign creditworthiness to news betrays the significance of entrenched images of states as 'strong' or 'weak' and of publics as 'industrious' or 'lazy', 'responsible' or 'feckless'. These images reflect beliefs and feelings about the governing competence of elites and the quality of public and private institutions (cf. Boulding 1956; Wallas 2010). In consequence, constructing sovereign creditworthiness is not a purely rational process. Images and emotional attachments are central to the process by which governing and financial elites construct creditworthiness. They affect how investors and analysts choose, interpret, and use formal risk indicators in imagining how states might behave and their propensity to default. This non-rational quality helps us to understand why constructing sovereign creditworthiness is a fragile talent and the process highly contestable.

Creditor-Debtor State Relations: Resting on a Bed of Dynamite

The closely knit, rationalist, and technically sophisticated world of creditor-debtor state relations deals not just with numbers but also with the arts of image formation and confidence and trust building. Its participants are concerned with the reputation of states and their governing elites for fiscal probity and sound money, devotion to good governance, executive capacity, reliability in honouring commitments, and commitment to the principles of fairness, honesty, and transparency in dealings with creditors. The world of creditor-debtor state relations is preoccupied with the branding of sovereign states as creditworthy.

The esoteric nature of the arts of creditor-debtor state relations is bound up with the delimited nature of its social world. In the nineteenth and early twentieth centuries it was defined by the notion of a shared 'gentlemanly' code of conduct (Kynaston 1995; Kynaston and Roberts 1995). Creditor-debtor state relations rested on close personal relations and on personal trust in the integrity of both parties. It was about 'good character'. By the late twentieth century, the world of creditor-debtor state relations had evolved into a more formalized, technocratic world. Standing came from intellectual mastery of economics, statistical modelling, and arcane financial instruments. It meant being at ease in a world of mortgage-backed securities, collateralized debt obligations, swaps, and derivatives. The characteristic cultural models were the coldly calculating quantitative analyst and the aggressive, testosterone-fuelled dealer (Preda 2005).

However, these apparently solid technocratic foundations rested on a bed of dynamite. Despite its outward solidity, creditor-debtor state relations remained precarious. The potential for destruction grew with growth in scale of assets and complexity of products and instruments and with loosening of leverage ratio. The precarious and contingent nature of creditor-debtor state relations derived from its structural parameters and dynamics. Whilst the social forces that sustained it had changed significantly, it remained a socially and intellectually narrow and limited world.

The 'Holy Trinity' of creditor states, debtor states, and financial markets was plagued by asymmetries of power and conflicts of interest that made it irreducibly political. In particular, the quality and character of public debates about sovereign debt sustainability were impaired by the prominent role that the media assigned to the macroeconomic views of bank advisers and investment managers. These views were inevitably identified with the commercial self-interests of their financial institutions. Creditor-debtor state relations were embedded in a deeply promotional culture of market shaping and public-opinion formation. Conflicts of interest were difficult to disentangle and compromised the quality of public debate (Bini Smaghi 2010c).

The quality of public debate was further reduced by the proneness of creditor-debtor state relations to illusion, hubris, and complacency. It was evident in the phenomenon of illusory creditor states. Their 'sound' public finances concealed excessive dependence on domestic asset-price 'bubbles', inward financial flows, private indebtedness, and consumption levels that proved unsustainable. Formally virtuous fiscal behaviour hid the risks from excessive external imbalances and from vulnerability to financial crisis. Illusion was fostered by a narrow, public finance focus on sovereign creditworthiness. Assessments of sovereign creditworthiness gave too little attention to deteriorating current account deficits, to underlying trends in competitiveness indicators like export market share, real effective exchange rates, and unit labour costs, as well as to private credit growth and house prices (Hancké 2103). This neglect stemmed from a failure to anchor assessments of sovereign creditworthiness in broader examinations of macroeconomic developments in national accounts, prior to the EU Macroeconomic Imbalance Procedure (MIP), first used in 2012.

This proneness to illusion becomes even more evident in the context of examination of longer-term historical developments in public debt. They show its vulnerability to the massive exogenous shocks of war, banking failure, and economic depression. Their effect on trend rates of GDP growth and on permanent loss of output changes the dynamics of public debt trajectories radically. They heighten risks of a shift to 'disaster economics' in which spreading fears amongst investors lead them to shift their preferences to protecting asset values (Dow 1998).

The precariousness of creditor-debtor state relations is further accentuated by its vulnerability to a discourse of binary morality and the associated emotional heat that it provokes. It is caught between two threats. The first threat is that creditor-state elites will behave short-sightedly in protecting their taxpayer interests against burdensome financial assistance to debtor states in distress. The second threat is that debtor-state elites will prove feckless and duplicitous in ways that will antagonize their private and their official creditors. Competitive electoral and party politics has limited tolerance either for moral ambiguity or for the long-term and global requirements of collective action to ensure systemic stability. Creditor-debtor state relations embed themselves in a protective narrative of de-politicization and cloak themselves in political silence. However, in the final analysis, this socially and intellectually narrow and technically sophisticated world has its own political roots. Sovereign debt crisis opens up these roots to closer, more critical examination.

Formal indicators of external indebtedness influence how sovereign creditworthiness is constructed by the various participants in creditor-debtor state relations. Statistical analysis is a rationally grounded activity, and sharp and significant changes in data can alter outlooks for sovereign creditworthiness. At the same time, justification in these rational terms conceals underlying psychological, sociological, and political processes involved in processes of (re-)constructing creditworthiness. Gut reactions to changes in data are shaped by images of states as 'strong' or 'weak', of publics as 'responsible' or 'feckless', and feelings about the governing competence of elites. They can be grounded to an extent in qualitative analysis of 'country risk'. However, the underlying images and feelings that shape choice, interpretation, and use of statistics are less susceptible to capture, even in formal qualitative analysis.

Excessive External Imbalances: Asymmetric Power

Creditor-debtor state relations are structurally embedded in global and European imbalances between deficit and surplus states and the asymmetry to which they give rise. Capacity to develop and sustain particular configurations of external assets and liabilities depends on current account balances. In turn, external trade and financial imbalances reflect differences in relative unit labour cost development (the costs in wages of producing a single unit of a good or service), nominal exchange rates (in a currency union, real exchange rates), and thus competitiveness.

Prior to the euro area, the former D-Mark bloc of states had sustained a stable and narrow band of fluctuation over time with Germany within the Exchange-Rate

Mechanism (ERM). They formed a core surplus-state grouping before and after 1999. From the 1980s ERM membership served as an incentive to exercise wage moderation through better-coordinated wage bargaining systems and better-organized labour-market institutions, based on benchmarking German inflation (Dyson 2010b). Within EMU wage negotiators within this former D-Mark block focused on matching German priority to reduction of unit labour costs. They displayed a high capacity for 'bottom-up', private-sector-led adjustment.

On euro entry, the other euro area Member States, which lacked this inheritance of wage bargaining and labour-market institutions, were released from traditional domestic central bank constraints under the ERM. They enjoyed new, historically low real interest rates. More seriously, they experienced rising unit labour costs. The result in Greece, Ireland, Italy, Spain, Portugal, and Slovenia was mounting external imbalances in the first decade of the euro. They became potentially economically and politically unsustainable once large-scale capital inflows ceased. Domestic deflation to avert default was not offset by euro area action to sustain aggregate demand and thus growth or to provide substantial and timely collective financial assistance (Hancké 2013).

External imbalances are reflected in differences in the consumption, saving, and investment behaviour of government, corporate, and household sectors. By definition, the current account balance corresponds to the difference between domestic savings and investment. A surplus means an excess of domestic savings over domestic investment, so that a surplus state must be acquiring foreign assets. A deficit means an excess of domestic investment over savings, net foreign liabilities, and hence greater exposure to international indebtedness.

A rise in the current account deficit is regarded as an indicator of risk when it is attributed to a reduction in domestic savings, when increased investment is being clearly misdirected away from improvement of capital stock (i.e. represents non-productive debt), and when capital inflows comprise volatile short-term portfolio and credit transactions. Conversely, foreign direct investment for the purpose of creating and modernizing the capital stock of the deficit state is treated as an indicator of low risk. It takes the form of productive debt and strengthens asset quality. The tendency for Latvia to attract a higher risk rating than the Czech Republic in the first decade of the twenty-first century owed much to the higher ratio of foreign direct investment to total capital inflows in the Czech case. Similarly, vulnerability is increased when states, like those in the west Balkan 'super-periphery', combine high external debt-service ratios to exports with low international reserves, precarious domestic macroeconomic and political conditions, and weak governance structures.

Imbalances in current accounts have their roots in divergences in relative costs. They threaten systemic crisis in creditor-debtor state relations when domestic policies are persistently inconsistent with sustainable external positions. For instance, a deficit state may experience aggregate demand expansion in excess of potential output growth, consequent on unsustainable increases in asset prices like real estate.

The course of the crisis reflects the channels of external lending. If external lending goes primarily through the banking sector, there will first be a financial crisis. Ireland and Spain offered examples after 2007. The crisis transforms into a sovereign debt crisis if the state chooses to guarantee bank debts rather than impose losses on bank creditors. However, if external lending is channelled through the public sector, as in Greece, the crisis emerges directly as a sovereign debt crisis. It then spreads to the banking sector via bank holdings of domestic sovereign debt. Either way, the intimate nexus of sovereign and bank creditworthiness is exposed. More generally, the speedy development of financial market integration in the early years of European monetary union led to greater dependence on external financing of sovereign debt. For Italy, with its high public debt legacy, this development heightened vulnerability. It went into reverse from 2010 with re-domestication of financial markets.

The scale and depth of the post-2007 global financial and economic crisis led institutions like the IMF (2010a: 1–28), the ECB (2010a: 91–100), and the European Commission (2010) to pay greater attention to the need for policy-correcting rebalancing of the European and world economies. Rebalancing could be achieved by reducing current account surpluses. Surplus states would allow exchange-rate appreciation and/or stimulate domestic demand. Alternatively, deficit states could cut their current account deficits through exchange-rate depreciation, productivity-enhancing supply-side reforms, real wage moderation, and/or fiscal devaluation by using the tax system to mimic a nominal devaluation, notably a shift towards consumption and property taxes.

Policy-induced 'surplus' reversals are less frequent than policy-induced 'deficit' reversals. This observation indicates the underlying asymmetry of power over adjustment processes in creditor-debtor state relations. The IMF (2010a: 1–28) identified only twenty-eight policy-induced surplus reversals over the past 50 years. By 2012–2013 there was evidence that Ireland had made a substantial correction to its unit labour costs, along with Latvia and Lithuania outside the euro area. Greece, Portugal, and Spain were also beginning to show evidence of corrections.

The Challenge of External Imbalances in Creditor-Debtor State Relations

The post-2007 crisis threw up three challenging questions. On what basis were external imbalances to be calculated? How were 'excessive' imbalances to be defined? What was the appropriate action to correct them?

External imbalances are traditionally compiled on measures of trade in gross terms and on a 'country-of-origin' basis, in which exports are attributed to the home state of the company responsible for the final product or service. This basis of attribution and calculation ignores the growing role and complexity of European and international supply chains. It fails to take account of 'value-added' at each stage in these chains and how this varies for different types of goods. Consequently, as the World Bank argued, conventional statistics on external imbalances may offer a distorted picture of economic activity and strength (Lamy 2010). On the basis of position in global value chains, Britain and the United States looked much healthier than measures of trade in gross terms suggested. Germany and, above all, China were less impressive. Conventional state-centric statistical analysis, on the basis of which creditor-debtor state relations has traditionally functioned, does not reflect changes in relative positions within cross-national supply chains.

Characteristically, the political pressure for international and European reforms to define, prevent, and correct excessive external imbalances comes from debtor states. Thus in 1944 the British head negotiator at the Bretton Woods Conference, John Maynard Keynes, highlighted the dangers of deflation and high unemployment if post-war adjustment focused asymmetrically on deficit states. His proposal for an International Clearing Union sought to put in place an automatic, symmetric mechanism that would place pressure on both creditor and debtor states (Skidelsky 2000). At the Group of 20 (G20) summit in Seoul in 2010, the US Treasury Secretary, Timothy Geithner, proposed a 4 per cent numeric value of surplus or deficit to GDP as a threshold that would trigger an obligation to adjust. Both proposals were opposed by creditor powers: the United States in 1944 and China in 2010.

Germany and other EU surplus states, supported by the ECB, played a similar role within debates about European economic governance reforms in 2010–2011. They shaped the new EU MIP for identifying and correcting excessive imbalances on their own terms. The MIP went further than the G20 Mutual Assessment Process (MAP) in having a corrective as well as a preventive arm. In the case of euro area Member States that failed to comply, it required them to submit a corrective action plan. It also provided for financial sanctions, up to 0.1 per cent of GDP. However, the MIP lacked simple, clear criteria to define 'excessive' imbalances. It relied on a complex scoreboard of indicators and benchmarks, including house prices and private credit growth. The aim was to provide an 'alert mechanism', triggering an in-depth European Commission review. The MIP also placed the primary obligation on deficit states to bear the burden of adjustment through structural reforms. Despite pressure from the European Parliament, the MIP failed to address the key question of how the current account surplus states were to recycle their excess domestic savings in order to mitigate risks of financial crisis.

The key indicator of excessive external imbalances is current account deficits and surpluses as a percentage of GDP. Within IMF deliberations the main focus for defining 'excessive' was the 4 per cent criterion. In 2010, using this criterion, the United States, Spain, and Turkey were included in the excessive deficit group. China, Germany, and Russia were in the excessive surplus group. However, Russia would be exempt from adjustment pressure under the Geithner proposals because it was a 'large commodity exporter'. If one factored in the scale of deficits and surpluses, and their systemic significance, the group of excessive deficit states also encompassed Britain and Italy. Italy's systemic significance as a risk state was highlighted in its escalating sovereign debt crisis, post-2011. Within the euro area Germany was the systemically significant excessive surplus state. Italy and Spain were the systemically significant excessive deficit states. On a global level the most systemically significant excessive deficit and surplus states were the United States and China respectively. In any account of systemically significant external imbalances in the euro area, the most prominent states in 2013 were Germany, Italy, and Spain, along with Britain in the wider EU.

Excessive External Imbalances: The Structure of Opportunities and Constraints

What do external imbalances mean for states and their policy instruments? When states run up sustained surpluses from trade in goods and services, and from net income notably from investment, they have policy opportunities that are denied to deficit states. Surplus states amass sizeable external assets relative to gross external liabilities. It provides them with a nest egg for future financial requirements, for instance in Germany and above all Norway to support ageing populations. Surplus states also accumulate substantial foreign-exchange reserves relative to their short-term debt. An example was France in the late 1920s. They can pay down external debt, shift the maturity profile of their debt towards the long term, and finance it at lower interest-servicing costs. Their dynamic export sectors serve as motors of economic growth, act as plentiful sources of profits and tax revenues, and help to keep structural budget deficits low.

In consequence, surplus states have policy opportunities to sustain relatively sound public finances, to serve as capital exporters, and to build up net foreign-asset positions. They gain top triple-A sovereign credit ratings. They enjoy the macroeconomic benefits of low interest rates from which their companies and households as well as their governments benefit. Their currencies function as 'safe havens' especially when, in crisis periods, financial market investors become risk averse. In short, surplus states can exploit a virtuous circle. Germany's role as the pre-eminent power in the EU and euro area was reinforced as sovereign debt crises gathered momentum from 2009.

However, creditor-state status remains precarious. It is contingent on the avoidance of adverse exogenous shocks and on wise policy choices. Maintenance of this status depends on supportive, stability-oriented fiscal and monetary policies, which may be derailed, as for instance by the long-term fiscal shock of German unification in 1990. It requires prudent and effective macro- and micro-prudential supervision and regulation to avert asset-price bubbles and systemic risks from irresponsible corporate or household indebtedness. Sovereign creditworthiness may be undermined if creditor-state banks take on excessive risks in lighter regulated financial environments. It is contingent on sustained investor focus on asset quality in recycling excess domestic savings. Also, the capacity to withstand the sharp adverse effects of global recession on export-led growth depends on domestic collective bargaining that focuses on strengthening corporate competitiveness and skill upgrading. Creditor-state status cannot long survive a process in which unit labour costs become uncompetitive and comparative advantage slips away. Above all, it is put at risk by making strategic commitments that exceed the economic capacity of a state and create unsustainable fiscal burdens. These risks reside, above all, in defence and security, as the debt trajectories of Britain and later the United States revealed, and in taking on unsustainable commitments to bail-out debtor states and their banks within a monetary union, as with Germany post-2010.

States that have current account deficits face a different set of policy opportunities and constraints. They accumulate sizeable net external financial liabilities (private and/or public) relative to GDP, are constrained in capacity to build foreign-exchange reserve buffers, and find that their currencies and sovereign bond yields come under external pressure in times of crisis. Deficit states come to rely more on domestic consumption and investment, on government borrowing, and/or on foreign credit as motors of economic growth. Their public finances face risk from overreliance on tax revenues that flow from the indebtedness of companies and households as they 'over-leverage' in order to consume and invest. Once the private sector starts deleveraging, exemplified in a sharp fall in the private-sector credit/GDP ratio, tax revenues collapse and demands arise for corporate bail-outs. Additional sources of risk include the management of public finances in a short-term and cash-basis manner, with little attention to implicit liabilities, as well as efforts to conceal public liabilities.

The precarious world of debtor states is illustrated by the risks from lower sovereign debt ratings (downgrading ultimately to 'junk' status), rising bond yields, and failures of bond auctions. Credit rating agencies brand them as 'sovereign' risks as well as 'country' risks. Debtor states suffer the macroeconomic and welfare costs of high interest rates and burdensome, potentially unsustainable debt servicing charges. In particular, a shift to overreliance on short-term external borrowing, which is typically motivated by the aim of reducing borrowing costs, exposes them to greater refinancing risks and threats to macroeconomic and financial stability.

External Imbalances: Private-Sector and State Capacity Building

The question of whether a debtor state moves along the continuum to 'chronic-debtor' status, remains trapped within debtor status, or graduates to creditor-state status is contingent on the nature of its policy choices within this constrained framework. Graduation to creditor-state status depends on private-sector capacity building and state capacity building. The difficulties inherent in these policy choices help explain why so many debtor states remain trapped within this category and why creditor states remain at risk.

The challenges of state capacity building to support innovation and reform, to make productive use of debt, to strengthen assets, and thereby to secure creditor-state status are manifold and daunting. The first set of challenges relates to the quality of the governance and economic policies of debtor states. They need prudent, precautionary fiscal policies to create buffers against future adverse shocks. In order to lock in an image as a prudent fiscal state that inspires investor confidence, the budgetary process needs to reflect the principles of independence and impartiality in economic forecasting, in fiscal projections, and in auditing. For the same reason, there also needs to be transparency with respect to liabilities.

Secondly, state capacity building requires clear domestic fiscal rules, targeting both fiscal deficits and public debt, and coordinating different levels of government. They need to be accompanied by broad political consensus about the need for fiscal discipline and by accompanying structural reforms to product, services, labour, and capital markets (European Central Bank 2009a).

Thirdly, fiscal policy needs to build state capacity by focusing on investment in future sources of economic growth rather than by being absorbed by consumption and rent-seeking behaviour (Stein 1885–1886). Priorities include cutting-edge energy, communication, transport, technology transfer, and educational and training infrastructures that build human capital.

Fourthly, public administration has to be professionally competent in order to deliver effective fiscal discipline, to provide quality investment in infrastructure and in public services, and to collect taxes efficiently and reliably. Lack of effective administrative accountability, transparency, and performance management creates a breeding ground for lethargy and corruption.

Last, and fundamentally, state capacity depends on providing investors with legal certainty with respect to property rights and the protection of their interests. Domestic insolvency law must allow for orderly processes for restructuring bank and non-bank companies in ways that preserve their value and maximize benefit to creditors and other interests. The Chapter 11 process of the US bankruptcy code is often seen as a model.

In addition, in order to shift on the continuum towards creditor-state status, debtor states need an appropriate infrastructure for dealing with financial markets. They require effective macro-prudential supervision to identify and prevent excessive, risky lending in the corporate and household sectors. Secondly, domestic financial markets have to be promoted so that they are sufficiently large in size and liquid to absorb government bond issues. They make possible proactive debt management that seeks to lengthen debt maturities, narrow bid/offer spreads, and reduce foreign-exchange risk and risk of currency mismatches (Knight 2006). Thirdly, opportunities need to be seized to build up foreign-exchange reserves as a buffer against external shocks. International financial assistance can be used as a short-term shield behind which to build state capacity in this way.

Last, and perhaps most problematic for sovereign states, use can be made of external expertise in designing and monitoring domestic reforms and gaining market credibility. As with Cyprus, Greece, Ireland, and Portugal, this external expertise can take the form of detailed fiscal surveillance and monitoring by bodies like the IMF, the ECB, and the European Commission (the so-called Troika). It can also involve the drafting in of external experts to help manage domestic structural reforms, for instance to the tax system.

State capacity building provides the supporting infrastructure within which private-sector capacity can grow. In the final analysis, however, correcting external imbalances depends on private-sector leadership in seizing and exploiting comparative advantages that a state possesses.

Stress-Testing States: Indicators of Excessive External Imbalances

There is a lack of consensus within creditor-debtor state relations on one single indicator of 'excessive' external debt. However, a cluster of interrelated indicators act as warning signals of adverse developments. Because of the close relationship between growing external imbalances and external indebtedness, they focus on data relevant to current accounts.

Current Accounts

The nature and evolution of creditor-debtor state relations is shaped by the narrowing and widening in global and European imbalances. Table 13.1 provides a picture of how European current account balances changed over the course of a decade. It places them in a comparative context of selected advanced and emerging market economies. Within Europe there was a clear group of surplus states: the three EU Nordic states of Denmark, Finland, and Sweden; Austria and Germany in central Europe; Luxembourg

Table 13.1 Current Account Balances, as Percentage of GDP, 2009

	2002	2006	2009
United States	−4.3	−6.0	−2.9
Canada	1.7	1.4	−2.7
Asia			
China	2.4	9.5	5.8
Hong Kong SAR	7.6	12.1	11.1
India	1.4	−1.1	−2.1
Japan	2.9	3.9	2.8
Singapore	13.2	24.9	19.1
Middle East and North Africa			
Kuwait	11.2	49.8	25.8
Libya	3.0	44.6	16.9
Saudi Arabia	6.3	27.8	5.5
United Arab Emirates	4.9	22.1	−3.1
Euro Area	0.7	0.4	−0.4
Germany	2.0	6.5	4.8
France	1.4	−0.5	−1.5
Italy	−0.8	−2.6	−3.4
Spain	−3.3	−9.0	−5.1
Netherlands	2.5	9.3	5.2
Belgium	4.6	2.0	−0.3
Greece	−6.5	−11.3	−11.2
Austria	2.7	2.8	1.4
Portugal	−8.1	−10.0	−10.1
Finland	8.8	4.6	1.4
Ireland	−1.0	−3.6	−2.9
Slovakia	−7.9	−7.8	−3.2
Slovenia	1.1	−2.5	−0.3
Luxembourg	10.5	10.3	5.7
Cyprus	−3.7	−7.0	−9.3
Malta	−3.9	2.5	−9.2
EU: Central and Eastern Europe outside Euro Area			
Bulgaria	−2.4	−18.4	−9.5
Czech Republic	−5.7	−2.6	−1.0
Estonia	−10.6	−16.9	4.6
Hungary	−7.0	−7.5	0.4
Latvia	9.4	−6.6	−22.5
Lithuania	−5.2	−10.7	3.8
Poland	−2.5	−2.7	−1.6
Romania	−3.3	−10.4	−4.4
EU: Rest of EU outside Euro Area			
Denmark	2.5	3.0	4.0
Sweden	5.0	8.6	6.4
United Kingdom	−1.7	−3.3	−1.3

(*Continued*)

Table 13.1 (Continued)

	2002	2006	2009
Non-EU Europe			
Iceland	1.6	–25.6	3.8
Norway	12.6	17.2	13.8
Switzerland	8.3	15.2	8.7
Commonwealth of Independent States	6.5	7.4	2.6
Russia	8.4	9.5	3.9
Ukraine	7.5	–1.5	–1.7
South-East Europe			
Albania	–7.2	–5.6	–14.0
Bosnia and Herzegovina	–17.8	–8.4	–7.5
Croatia	–7.3	–6.7	–5.6
Kosovo	–6.7	–6.7	–18.7
Montenegro	...	–24.1	–27.2
Serbia	–5.7	–8.3	–10.1
Turkey	–0.3	–6.0	–2.3

(*Source*: International Monetary Fund 2009: 173)

and the Netherlands, with Belgium also qualifying; and, outside the EU, Norway and Switzerland. Germany, the Netherlands, and Sweden could be labelled as 'chronic' surplus states, based on their wage discipline, high labour productivity, specialization in high-quality products in fast-growing technological niches, and the privileging of their export-oriented industries. The share of the current account surplus in German GDP rose from close to 2 per cent in 2003 to nearly 8 per cent in 2007, overtaking and far exceeding Japan. This surplus state category was exclusively north and west European.

In contrast, central and eastern Europe and south-eastern Europe comprised deficit states. They had the characteristics of emerging market economies, with large net imports in trade in goods and high external dependence in banking and in infrastructure development. In some cases, notably the western Balkans, a high incidence of ethnic enmity, organized crime, and endemic tax evasion further complicated the picture. It reduced the capacity of their states to act as a catalyst for productive investment in infrastructure. The western Balkans represented Europe's 'super-periphery'.

The category of deficit states included the south European states in the euro area: Cyprus, Greece, Italy, Malta, Portugal, and Spain. In their cases deficits were driven by a varying mix of factors: asset-price bubbles notably in Spain, low productivity growth in Italy and Spain, low and declining savings in Greece and Portugal, and general lack of wage discipline. Strikingly, central and east European EU Member States tended to be seen as less at risk than Greece because of the high ratio of foreign direct investment, including equity investment, to total capital flows. This high ratio means that their external debt had increased relatively little despite their large current account deficits.

However, this broad statistical picture needs qualification. Some north and west European states, like Britain, Iceland, and Ireland, were deficit states. In central Europe, Austria and Switzerland were surplus states. In addition, one should delve behind statistics that are compiled on a state basis to look at sub-national differences. Thus north and central Italy had high labour productivity and quality product profiles, giving it a strong competitive industrial sector. The London region stood out as an exceptional performer in the British economy. Within Germany the eastern states (*Bundesländer*) were relatively weak trade performers, with the exception of Saxony.

Overall, the euro area remained broadly in balance in its current account in the first decade after monetary union in 1999, in contrast to the United States. However, Germany was critical to the maintenance of this balance. It was flanked by Austria, Belgium, Luxembourg, and the Netherlands. Without Germany, the euro area would have had current account deficits of 2.6 per cent of GDP in 2006 and 4.7 per cent of GDP in 2008. Germany managed to sustain its real global market share at just under 10 per cent between 1999 and 2008, whilst the rest of the euro area experienced a 4 per cent decline to 18 per cent (Deutsche Bundesbank 2010b: 19–20). Hence Germany was the European state most central to global and European creditor-debtor state relations.

European monetary union fostered the illusion that the internal current account imbalances within the euro area had lost much of their relevance as a policy constraint on Member States (Hancké 2013). Capital inflows could serve to fund current account deficits and thus to empower states. With the elimination of exchange-rate risk, banks were able to allocate the savings of the whole euro area to wherever they found profitable investment opportunities. Following this argument, current account deficits signalled no more than the flow of capital to more profitable, high-yield investments. These flows benefitted savers in creditor states and helped these states to deal with the fiscal problems of population ageing. Conversely, debtor states could invest more than would be possible through their own savings. Through enhanced GDP growth, they were better able to service and repay foreign debt. A surplus could be viewed as indicating the lack of sufficient profitable domestic investment opportunities, leading to the outflow of savings (Collignon 2010). In short, monetary union unleashed a positive-sum economic game for surplus and deficit states.

However, this benign picture proved a source of illusion, hubris, and complacency. Capital inflows from surplus states like Germany did not always equate with effective investor monitoring of asset quality, with their efficient use in deficit states, and with sufficient profitable investments. In Greece these flows were used to finance high, consumption-led budget deficits; in Portugal, to support bank lending for private consumption; and in Ireland and Spain, to feed bank lending to property markets (Deutsche Bundesbank 2010b: 23). The problems of euro area deficit states derived from unsustainably high domestic demand in relation to potential output, high inflation rates, and inefficient use of capital inflows. These problems were exposed by the post-2007 financial and economic crisis. The result was sharp reversal of capital flows, inflicting great pain on deficit states.

Although the euro area was a monetary union, debt issuance and liabilities remained firmly anchored at the domestic level with Member States. Hence the configuration of debtor and creditor states owed most to attributes of domestic political economies in containing unit labour costs. German agenda-setting and negotiating power was articulated in the dominant representation of the euro area problem. It was diagnosed as caused by domestic political, policy, and institutional failures in deficit states, which had led to unsustainably high aggregate demand and loss of competitiveness. The solution was seen as real wage moderation, productivity-enhancing structural reforms, and fiscal devaluations through tax reforms.

On a global scale the category of surplus states included Canada, China, Hong Kong, Japan, Kuwait, Libya, Russia, Saudi Arabia, Singapore, and Taiwan. A notable number in this category were commodity-driven surplus states, with oil and natural gas a major factor. Others—like China—pursued export-led growth strategies, underpinned in some cases by undervalued currencies. In 2009, at this global level, surplus states, which were defined as having surpluses above 3 per cent of their GDP, accounted for 37 per cent of world GDP, at purchasing power parity (International Monetary Fund 2010b). On the same measure, deficit states comprised 32 per cent.

Though widening of external imbalances is enormously important for creditor-debtor state relations, it is important to dig down beneath the figures to examine the question 'deficits and surpluses with whom?' The trade activities of deficit and surplus states within the euro area divide into numerous smaller flows, so that the precise character of trade links between them varies. This variation has serious implications for the potency of 'surplus-state-centred' adjustment policies to alleviate pressures on deficit states. In 2010 the trade links between the main surplus state, Germany, and the main debtor states on the euro area periphery—like Greece, Italy, Spain, and Portugal—were relatively weak. Hence it was possible to question whether there were major external imbalances *within* the euro area. Spill-over effects between Germany and these periphery euro area debtor states proved low. Germany's fast export growth was concentrated on the Organization of Petroleum Exporting Countries (OPEC) states, the Russian Federation, China, and the new EU Member States in east-central Europe. In comparison, export growth to the euro area was negligible. More than half of Germany's current account surplus came from trade with non-EU states, notably China and India. Within the euro area the total German trade surplus was less than €20 billion in the first half of 2010. Hence the 'chronic' trade surplus of Germany did not translate into the same surplus within the EU or the euro area (Deutsche Bundesbank 2010b).

Of particular note in Europe, before the 2007 crisis, was the emergence of double-digit negative external imbalances in some central and east European states, notably Bulgaria, the Baltic States, and Romania. They were followed by sharp corrections. The explanation of the widening external imbalances was not just a 'catch-up' process by emerging market economies. Prior to the 2007 crisis they experienced domestic inflation and real currency appreciation. The contributory factors were unsustainably rapid credit expansion, excessive wage increases, and/or rapid fiscal expansion. Furthermore, a growing share of their current account deficits had been financed by capital inflows that added to external debt levels. They were therefore highly vulnerable to changes in investor sentiments.

Domestic Savings Rates and Net Household Financial Assets

There is prima facie reason to expect a linkage between current account imbalances and variations in domestic saving rates. Differences in savings rates, and as we see later in reserve accumulation, can contribute to external imbalances. States with low saving rates come to rely in part on inflows of external capital to finance spending, notably company investment and government budget deficits. In short, the demand that powers the growth of external imbalances can be underpinned by private-sector and/or public-sector credit needs that cannot be met domestically because of low savings. Conversely, high domestic saving rates in surplus states may contribute to the persistence of external imbalances because they fail to generate fast consumption growth that increases imports. Tables 13.2 and 13.3 highlight the contrast in the period up to 2009 between the low saving rates in deficit states like Britain and the United States, on the one hand, and the high saving rates in surplus states like Austria, Germany, and Japan, on the other.

However, deficit states can offset the potentially negative effects of external imbalances on their debt by high domestic saving rates. Historically, France and Italy had saving rates that were well above the EU average and even further above the average for advanced economies. Because of this important resource, they had the domestic financial capacity to absorb high government debt. Italian sovereign creditworthiness rested on a balance between virtuous households and indebted state. In the context of the historically weak role of equity markets in Italian economic development, domestic savers exhibited a preference for investing in government bonds. They did so usually by way of trusted communal and provincial savings banks. In 2011, 20 per cent of Italian household wealth was invested in sovereign and bank bonds. More typically, this share was below 5 per cent, notably just 1.6 per cent in Britain and 1.5 per cent in France (De Bonis, Fano, and Sbano 2013: 13). Private household affluence not only provided a counterweight to high public debt. It also eased the fiscal burden of unemployment on the state.

Table 13.2 International Patterns of Savings, 1988–2009

	Average 1988–1995	Average 1996–2003	2006	2009
Advanced Economies	22.2	21.1	21.0	17.1
Euro Area	...	21.4	22.1	18.7
France	20.2	21.0	20.6	17.7
Germany	23.1	20.1	24.1	21.8
Italy	20.4	20.9	19.0	15.5
Central and Eastern Europe	22.1	18.2	16.9	16.5
United Kingdom	15.8	16.0	14.2	12.3
United States	15.9	17.0	16.2	10.8
Japan	33.1	28.1	27.7	23.0
Canada	16.7	20.8	24.4	18.5
Fuel Exporters	25.6	28.1	40.1	27.8
Net Debtors	15.7	15.0	23.0	19.7

(*Source*: International Monetary Fund 2010b: 182)

Table 13.3 Gross Household Savings Rate, Selected EU States, 1999–2008

	1999	2002	2006	2008
EU (27 States)	12.1	12.22	11.06	11.09
Euro Area				
Austria	12.93	15.45	16.70	
Belgium	17.40	17.34	15.78	16.65
Finland		7.92	6.81	7.89
France	15.06	16.67	14.81	15.12
Germany	15.31	15.71	16.36	17.23
Greece	–	–	–	–
Ireland	–	9.02	9.95	9.96
Italy	15.77	16.82	15.23	15.o7
Netherlands		13.69	12.17	12.98
Spain		11.36	11.15	12.91
Outside Euro Area				
Czech Republic	8.55	8.05	9.45	10.17
Denmark	2.98	9.51	5.45	5.48
Estonia	2.57	0.46	–	–
Hungary		11.35	12.18	8.25
Latvia	–0.16	1.07	–3.60	5.03
Lithuania	3.83	4.74	1.08	–1.28
Sweden		10.79	9.42	13.92
United Kingdom		4.80	2.87	1.75

(*Source*: Eurostat 2010; http://epp.eurostat.ec.europa.eu/tgm/table.do?tab=table&init=1&language=en&pcode)

In the first decade of the euro, European monetary union and financial market integration widened investment opportunities for Italian households and banks. Till then, high domestic savings helped lower exposure of the Italian state to external financial markets, relative to other euro area states. However, the paradox of trust—a public that distrusted its political class trusted the sovereign debt—began to unravel with European financial integration. By 2011 some 43 per cent of Italian public debt was held externally, making the Italian state potentially much more vulnerable. In the face of mounting sovereign debt crisis in 2011, the Italian government resorted to 'national bond-buying days'. They were supported by the banks, which waived their commissions. The Italian sovereign bond market underwent a re-domestication.

High domestic private savings meant that Belgium was in a similar benign position of being able to combine high public debt with resilience. Also, Austria and Germany exhibited high precautionary saving rates. However, Denmark, Finland, and the Netherlands showed that not all surplus states had high domestic saving rates. This lack of clear correlation is evident in central and eastern Europe. Though sharing current account deficits, the Czech Republic and Hungary had much higher domestic saving rates than the three Baltic States. At the same time, as Latvia and Spain demonstrated, global financial and economic crisis can lead to higher domestic saving rates once governing elites dramatize the issue of whether external imbalances are sustainable.

Net household financial assets as a percentage of GDP provide an additional indicator of whether a state possesses a buffer against external imbalances. They offer a measure of capacity to rapidly correct structural budget imbalances and to reduce public-debt levels, though not of the will to do so. On this measure, the best-placed European states in 2007 were Switzerland (375 per cent of GDP), followed by Belgium, Britain, Denmark, the Netherlands, and Italy, all with over 200 per cent. In contrast, the figure for Slovakia was a mere 48 per cent. The figures for net financial wealth of households as a percentage of GDP showed a similar result. However, the wealth of the average German household (median wealth) was comparatively low. One factor was the relatively low German home ownership rate, which was linked to the availability of a broad and efficient market for rented accommodation. In addition, unlike in Greece or Italy, German households could depend on high standards of social provision in unemployment, education, health, and pensions. Moreover, even those German households with debt tended to have matching or higher-value assets (Deutsche Bundesbank 2013: 35).

Given the high public-debt levels in Belgium and Italy, and their debt-servicing costs, the size of their net household financial assets pointed to their potential resilience (Sachverständigenrat 2011a). The lower percentage of net household financial assets to GDP in Germany served as a disincentive for Germans to see the solution to Belgian and Italian public-debt problems in a 'transfer union'. In German eyes, the solution lay in domestic measures to tap into household financial assets, notably through property taxes. The technocratic government of Mario Monti pursued this policy option to address the Italian sovereign debt problem. However, it ran into major domestic opposition, led by Silvio Berlusconi.

Unit Labour Costs

Tables 13.4 and 13.5 illustrate the strong correlation between external imbalances and development in relative unit labour costs. By measuring levels of nominal wages relative to productivity, unit labour costs offer insight into the competitiveness of national economies. They are consequent on wage setting, work organization, and working time, which—with some exceptions in the last case—are negotiated domestically. However, as the United States shows, the connection between external imbalances and unit labour costs is complex. It is mediated by other factors like the rate of growth of domestic consumption, investment and fiscal deficits, as well as by the size and liquidity of financial markets. The strong US performance in unit labour costs was not reflected in its shift from a deficit to a surplus state.

Inside the EU the growth in external imbalances was more clearly related to unit labour cost developments. In the decade up to 2009 the increases in Dutch, German, and Swedish surpluses and in British, Cypriot, Irish, Italian, Portuguese, and Spanish deficits mirrored different unit labour cost developments. In central and eastern Europe the 'catch-up' processes in emerging market economies were reflected in high increases in unit labour costs. Bulgaria, Hungary, Latvia, and Romania stood out as above trend.

Table 13.4 Unit Labour Cost Development, in Manufacturing, 1992–2011

	Average 1992–2001	Average 2002–2011
Advanced Economies	0.6	0.6
United States	–0.2	0.1
Japan	0.3	0.5
Euro Area	0.8	1.3
France	–0.7	0.8
Germany	1.1	0.2
Italy	2.0	3.2
Spain	0.5	2.9

(*Source*: International Monetary Fund 2010b: 4)

Table 13.5 Unit Labour Cost Development in EU and Euro Area, Average Annual Percentage Changes, 1996–2012

	Average 1996–2000	Average 2001–2005	Average 2001–2010	Average 2010–2012
EU	1.7	1.9	2.0	
Euro Area	0.9	1.7	1.8	
Austria	–0.4	0.9	1.4	4.2
Belgium	0.7	1.7	2.0	6.2
Cyprus	2.2	3.8	2.9	4.2
Estonia	7.3	3.7	5.7	–2.3
Finland	0.4	1.5	2.2	3.8
France	0.7	2.0	2.1	4.1
Germany	0.0	0.2	0.4	3.2
Greece	...	3.1	3.0	–8.1
Ireland	1.5	3.4	2.3	–9.4
Italy	1.5	3.1	2.7	3.0
Luxembourg	1.0	2.7	3.4	8.3
Malta	...	3.1	3.0	5.1
Netherlands	1.7	2.4	2.2	2.4
Portugal	3.8	3.0	2.3	–5.8
Slovakia	7.3	3.7	2.9	–1.2
Slovenia	5.2	4.9	4.3	0.5
Spain	2.4	3.0	2.7	–6.7
Rest of EU: Central and Eastern Europe				
Bulgaria	94.9	3.2	6.1	9.0
Czech Rep.	6.8	3.3	2.4	3.3
Hungary	13.4	5.6	4.6	7.4
Latvia	5.7	4.7	6.4	–5.9
Lithuania	7.9	1.7	2.6	–5.2
Poland	12.0	–2.8	...	4.1
Romania	...	17.1	12.4	4.7
Rest of EU: Others				
Demark	1.9	2.5	3.0	0.0
Sweden	1.9	1.0	1.4	0.2
United Kingdom	2.5	2.5	2.5	8.0

(*Source*: European Central Bank, *Statistics*, June 2013: 37, 49)

Table 13.6 EU and Euro Area Inflation Differentials, Annual Percentage Changes in Harmonized Index of Consumer Prices (HICP), 1996–2012

	Average 1996–2000	Average 2001–2010	2012
EU	1.7	2.2	2.6
Euro Area	1.6	2.0	2.5
Austria	1.2	1.9	2.6
Belgium	1.6	2.1	2.6
Cyprus	2.9	2.4	3.1
Estonia	8.8	4.2	4.2
Finland	1.6	1.7	3.2
France	1.3	1.9	2.2
Germany	1.1	1.6	2.1
Greece	4.6	3.4	1.0
Ireland	2.6	2.2	1.9
Italy	2.4	2.2	3.3
Luxembourg	1.7	2.6	2.9
Malta	3.2	2.4	3.2
Netherlands	1.9	2.1	2.8
Portugal	2.4	2.4	2.8
Slovakia	8.2	4.1	3.7
Slovenia	8.2	4.2	2.8
Spain	2.6	2.8	2.4
Rest of EU: Central and Eastern Europe			
Bulgaria	10.3	6.0	2.4
Czech Rep.	5.8	2.3	3.5
Hungary	15.1	5.6	5.7
Latvia	4.3	5.4	2.3
Lithuania	8.2	3.0	3.2
Poland	11.0	2.8	3.7
Romania	64.2	12.1	3.4
Rest of EU: Others			
Demark	2.0	2.0	2.4
Sweden	1.1	1.9	0.9
United Kingdom	1.4	2.1	2.8

(*Source*: European Central Bank, *Statistics*, June 2013: 38)

Inflation Rate Differentials

Differentials in domestic inflation rates provide an additional indicator of external imbalances. Persisting inflation differentials emerged as a distinctive and troubling feature within the euro area and contributed to rising external imbalances. Inflation differentials matter less when they are temporary and corrected through fiscal and wage policies and product, services, and labour market measures. As Table 13.6 shows, the low inflation performers in the euro area over its first decade were Austria, Finland, France, and Germany, along with Britain and Sweden in the wider EU. However, the list of those with persistently above-average inflation rates was long. It included Greece, Ireland, Italy, Malta, Portugal, Slovakia, Slovenia, and Spain in the euro area. In the wider EU Bulgaria, Hungary, and Romania had the same problem.

Stress-Testing States: Indicators of Excessive External Debt

Asymmetries of power in creditor-debtor state relations are related to contrasting external debt exposures and vulnerabilities. They are captured in different indicators of external private and public debt. These indicators variously examine gross external debt, net external debt, net interest payments, external debt relative to exports, debt-service payments relative to exports, and foreign-exchange reserves relative to imports (European Central Bank 2010d; World Bank 2010). Characteristically, three buffers against external vulnerability are identified as important. They are private-sector capacity for export-led growth; the size and liquidity of domestic bond markets; and foreign-exchange reserves. Through its various databases, the IMF (2009b: 182; 2011b: 5) highlighted outstanding amounts of, and net issues of, international debt securities and gross and net external liabilities. It also attempted to consolidate various external debt indicators into a 'heat map' of highly vulnerable states (International Monetary Fund 2009b: 23). The Bank for International Settlements (BIS) (2010a) generated huge amounts of data on different types of external debt exposure by banks.

Each of these indicators offered its own insights into risks to debt (re)financing and external debt sustainability. However, the process of constructing and using these indicators within international financial institutions proved acutely politically sensitive. Governing elites in systemically significant states resented potentially negative representations of their states. Hence the idea of developing 'heat maps' placed strains on public unity within the IMF, where there is a search for unanimity within the IMF executive board. The result was a bias to analytical risk aversion within the IMF. The IMF is caught up in the conflicting interests of its shareholder states in the executive board. They are often creditors or political allies of debtor states in difficulties. Hence 'speaking truth to power' about external debt proves exceedingly difficult, often to the irritation of IMF staff.

The IMF sought to stress-test states by constructing a composite 'heat map' of the most vulnerable emerging market economies in Europe (see Table 13.7). The 'heat map' focused on a limited set of indicators, four of the six relating to external debt. However, it was unclear, and contentious, what weighting should be assigned to individual indicators and thus how to score vulnerability. In 2009–2010 Bulgaria, Latvia, and Lithuania seemed to fall into the most vulnerable category simply because they had negative scores on all indicators. However, a state might have a high vulnerability score on only one or two indicators, which turn out to be systemically contagious. The 'heat map' leaves

Table 13.7 IMF Heat Map of Macro and Financial Indicators: The Most Vulnerable European Emerging Market Economies, 2010

	Current Account Balance (% GDP)	External Debt Refinancing Needs, 2010 (% Reserves)	Net External Position vis-à-vis BIS-Reporting Banks Years (% Year on Year)	Average Real Credit Growth Over Last Five (% Year on Year)	Loan/Deposit (Ratio)	Forex Share of Total Loans (% Total Loans)
Bulgaria	X	X	X	X	X	X
Croatia	X	X	X			X
Czech Republic						
Estonia		X	X		X	X
Hungary			X		X	X
Latvia		X	X	X	X	X
Lithuania		X	X	X	X	X
Poland		X	X			
Romania	X	X	X	X	X	
Russia				X	X	
Serbia	X		X			X
Turkey		X				
Ukraine				X	X	

Note: X denotes highest vulnerability.
(*Source*: International Monetary Fund 2010b: 23)

issues of choice, weighting, and interpretation unresolved. Its extension to advanced economies proved even more contentious.

Europe's Relative Position in Global Financial Flows

The significance of Europe in creditor-debtor state relations, not least within the power structures of the IMF, owes much to the position of different European currencies in global financial flows. Table 13.8 shows that by 2009 European currencies, led by the euro, played the leading role in international debt securities, both in amounts outstanding and in net issues. The eclipsing of the US dollar by the euro in these markets reflected the large-scale debt issuance by the individual euro area governments. In 2009 euro-denominated debt securities accounted for some 45 per cent of outstanding international debt securities and nearly 40 per cent of net issues. The position of other European currencies in this market, including both the pound sterling and the Swiss franc, was dwarfed by the euro.

However, two factors combined to ensure that the size of euro-denominated debt issuance did not translate into euro area agenda-setting power and negotiating advantage in creditor-debtor state relations (Dyson and Quaglia 2010b: Section 6). First, the euro area did not speak with a single unified voice. Its Member States proved unwilling to pool authority and resources, notably in common euro area bond issuance. They continued to stress their individual profiles within international financial institutions like the IMF. Secondly, the deepening debt crisis in Europe, especially from 2010, exposed the

Table 13.8 Global Financial Flows: Amounts Outstanding and Net Issues of International Debt Securities, in Billions of US Dollars, 2004–2008

	2004	2006	2008
Amounts Outstanding by Currency of Issue			
Euro	6,211.4	8,303.8	10,875.1
Pound Sterling	979.8	1,446.2	1,701.9
Swiss Franc	227.9	253.3	331.6
Swedish Krona	21.0	34.3	48.4
US Dollar	4,905.7	6,390.3	8,225.5
Japanese Yen	529.8	486.6	750.2
	2004	2006	2008
Net Issues by Currency of Issue			
Euro	918.2	1,200.2	954.3
Pound Sterling	132.2	221.1	564.3
Swiss Franc	12.7	27.9	13.4
Swedish Krona	3.4	7.0	11.7
US Dollar	369.0	1,011.5	690.3
Japanese Yen	26.9	19.3	20.9

(*Source*: International Monetary Fund 2009b: 182)

institutional vulnerabilities of the euro area. A growing gap emerged between market expectations about what the euro area should be doing collectively, and when, especially in mutualizing debt, and the speed and difficulties of consensus building within the euro area. The IMF, the World Bank, and G20 were thrown into the difficult position of criticizing the lack of urgency and ambition in reforms of European economic governance. Invidious comparisons were made between the speed of private-sector deleveraging in the United States and within the euro area and between Finnish and Swedish deleveraging in the 1990s and euro area crisis management (McKinsey Global Institute 2012).

Gross External Debt as Percentage of GDP

Gross external debt provides a broad picture of debt in national accounts. It includes cross-border bank deposits and loans, international debt securities, portfolio investments, official bilateral loans and trade credits, and international reserves. The ratio of gross external debt to GDP provides an indication of the capacity to service external debt by switching resources from the production of domestic goods to exports.

This indicator highlights two features of creditor-debtor state relations in Europe (see Table 13.9). First, in 2006–2009, Britain and Switzerland stood out because of the large role that their financial sectors played in international lending. In both cases, cross-border bank deposits and loans and liabilities to banks were by far the biggest components in their gross external debt. Secondly, the post-2007 financial and economic crisis led to an immediate major increase in the gross external debt positions of the euro

Table 13.9 Gross and Net External Debt Indicators for Key States, Percentage of GDP, 2006 and 2009

	2006	2009
Gross External Debt		
Canada	54.3	70.4
Japan	34.7	42
Switzerland	266.2	245
United Kingdom	378.2	419.2
United States	83.6	96.6
Euro Area	101.5	116.5
	2006	2009
Gross External Public Debt		
Canada	11.3	15.3
Japan	9.5	13.3
Switzerland	7.1	3.9
United Kingdom	11.5	18.4
United States	16.5	26.0
Euro Area	13.0	21.3
	2006	2008
Net External Debt		
Canada	21.4	18.2
Japan	–50.6	–48.4
Switzerland	–130.1	–115.8
United Kingdom	70.3	44.4
United States	42.6	52.5
Euro Area	6.4	14.6
	2006	2008
Net Interest Payments		
Canada	1.4	1.2
Japan	–1.9	–2.2
Switzerland	–2.7	–3
United Kingdom	1.7	1.6
United States	1.3	1.5
Euro Area	0	0.2

Notes: (1) Net external debt is derived from subtracting gross external debt assets from liabilities; (2) net interest is interest payments minus interest receipts originated by the debt position.
(*Source*: European Central Bank 2010d: 82)

area, Britain, and the United States, though not Switzerland. Ireland's gross external debt relative to GDP was more than twice that of Britain. In consequence, these states became much more vulnerable.

Table 13.10 offers a broad regional picture of central, eastern, and west Balkan Europe in a comparative context for the period 2002–2009. Their states, like Croatia and

Table 13.10 Ratio of External Debt to GDP, as Percentage, 2002–2009

	2002	2006	2009
Emerging and Developing Economies	36.6	27.4	26.9
Central and Eastern Europe	50.7	52.8	68.6
Commonwealth of Independent States	45.8	35.7	43.0
Developing Asia	25.7	19.3	15.0
Middle East and North Africa	33.1	32.0	34.4
Sub-Saharan Africa	62.0	25.5	24.2
Western Hemisphere	42.2	23.8	23.3

(*Source*: International Monetary Fund 2010b: Table B24)

Serbia, were particularly vulnerable because of their relatively high ratio of external debt to GDP. The external dependency of these states remained high or grew. In contrast, the gross external debt/GDP ratio of other emerging and developing economies tended to fall, often sharply, assisted often by international debt relief.

A key factor in this high and increasing ratio of external debt to GDP was the ever-tightening financial integration of central, east European and western Balkan economies into the EU. They experienced increased and high levels of foreign (EU/euro area-based) ownership of their banks. Additionally, their consumers and investors were attracted to euro- and Swiss-franc-denominated foreign-currency debt by lower interest rates. In consequence, their private sectors were vulnerable once home supervisors of foreign-owned banks tightened bank credit rules, as the Austrian central bank did in 2011. They were also exposed to euro and Swiss franc appreciation. Unlike some other world regions, these emerging market economies did not benefit from debt relief as a device for tackling world poverty. In addition, Asian and Commonwealth of Independent States' economies had drawn lessons from their debt crises of 1997–1998 about reducing external debt dependency.

Gross external debt as a percentage of GDP can be used to identify a league table of the world's top twenty debtor states (see Table 13.11). In 2009 the list revealed an overwhelming European predominance. The top ten were European states. Only three non-European states appeared in the top twenty. The list consisted, above all, of small European states. Ireland—at 1,312.0 per cent—was far ahead of any other state, followed by Switzerland, the Netherlands, Belgium, and Denmark. There was also a striking distance between Britain, in second place (425.9 per cent), and Germany, in fifteenth (182.5 per cent), and Italy, in seventeenth (147.4 per cent). Amongst central and east European states, only Hungary appeared in the list. States that have a very high gross external debt to GDP ratio have a big stake in creditor-debtor state relations. Their debt service costs are potentially high-risk because of reduced scope to switch resources to export production. They have an increased incentive to embrace fiscal discipline.

Composition and Sources of Gross External Debt

World Bank/JEDH (2010) statistics bring out more detailed cross-national differences in the total size of gross external debt, including its composition by instrument, its sources

Table 13.11 The World's Top Twenty Biggest Debtor States: Gross External Debt to GDP, 2009

	External Debt to GDP
Ireland	1,312%
United Kingdom	425.9%
Switzerland	382.2%
Netherlands	376.6%
Belgium	328.7%
Denmark	316.0%
Sweden	264.3%
Austria	256.2%
France	248.0%
Portugal	235.9%
Hong Kong	223.1%
Finland	220.2%
Norway	202.6%
Spain	186.1%
Germany	182.5%
Greece	170.5%
Italy	147.4%
Australia	124.3%
Hungary	121.9%
United States	96.5%

(*Source*: CNBC.com)

by sector, and its original maturity (short- and long-term). As Table 13.12 shows, in the third quarter of 2009, the European league table of gross external debt was headed by Britain ($9,294,051 millions), followed by Germany ($5,278,654 millions), France ($5,222,413 millions), Italy ($2,714,792 millions), the Netherlands ($2,587,402 millions), and Spain ($2,538,610 millions). These EU Member States, above all Britain, had a particularly strong stake and engagement in creditor-debtor state relations.

The figures indicate the different sources of vulnerability to EU Member States. The proportion of international debt securities to gross external debt was notably high in Austria, Greece, Italy, Portugal, and Spain (as well as the United States), at well over 50 per cent. Cross-border loans were a significant factor in Ireland, Latvia, Lithuania, Romania, and Switzerland. Foreign currency and cross-border deposits played a central role for Britain. However, the figures represented a quarterly snapshot and change sharply over time.

Table 13.13 illustrates the high proportion of bank debt relative to other sectors in gross external debt. This observation applies to the large majority of EU Member States, notably Britain, Denmark, Ireland, Latvia, Luxembourg, Portugal, and Spain. Further details can be extracted from the Joint External Debt HUB (World Bank 2010) and from the Bank for International Settlements (2010a). In the third quarter of 2009, short-term

Table 13.12 Gross External Debt by Instrument: Selected States, US Dollar Millions, 2009 Third Quarter

	Debt Securities	Loans	Currency and Deposits	DI/IC	Total
UK	2,467,796	1,237,456	4,836,362	730,093	9,294,051
Germany	2,618,956	1,840,901	0	661,440	5,278,654
France	2,415,968	300,656	1,896,506	482,436	5,222,413
Italy	1,669,274	384,451	489,763	100,832	2,714,792
Netherlands	1,103,053	293,758	753,731	338,824	2,587,402
Spain	1,193,058	274,296	798,171	265,126	2,538,610
Ireland	778,360	1,144,324	0	292,337	2,397,435
Luxembourg	434,072	1,308,378	1,825	218,744	2,017,819
Belgium	403,016	402,668	329,444	96,133	1,323,152
Switzerland	55,534	680,372	263,332	157,499	1,230,838
Sweden	383,527	266,306	0	220,619	898,742
Austria	475,613	57,420	256,153	59,026	869,225
Greece	327,861	48,404	213,394	3,448	594,598
Finland	174,407	40,071	86,171	65,074	381,766
Central and Eastern Europe/EU					
Poland	76,364	92,214	31,235	56,194	276,110
Hungary	50,085	71,400	28,114	81,992	240,085
Romania	4,784	66,802	18,367	23,930	117,935
Czech Rep.	21,301	31,374	14,403	11,137	85,274
Latvia	1,536	30,414	4,222	4,645	42,960
US	7,991,935	2,306,338	2,035,795	1,109,355	13,671,606
Japan	764,754	931,915	112,833	43,177	2,215,128

Note: DI/IC refers to direct investment/intercompany lending.
(*Source*: World Bank 2010: Table C4: note some columns have been omitted)

bank debts, mainly foreign currency and cross-border deposits, represented over 50 per cent of Britain's gross external debt. In Germany banks accounted for nearly 50 per cent of gross external debt, compared to about 40 per cent in France. However, in contrast to Britain, only just over 20 per cent of German bank debt was short-term. German government external debt was mostly in the form of long-term bonds and notes. Austria was similar in having a very high proportion of government external debt in long-term bonds and having banks with almost 50 per cent of gross external debt, again mostly long-term. The contribution of general government debt to gross external debt was tiny in Switzerland compared to the banks, especially short-term cross-border bank loans, foreign currency, and deposits. Norway was similar to Switzerland. Ireland's gross external debt was dominated by three items: short-term bank loans, long-term corporate borrowing, and direct investment and inter-company lending. In Belgium nearly half of gross external debt was accounted for by short-term bank debt.

Greece, and to a lesser extent Italy, were exceptions in their greater external exposure through sovereign debt. In Italy long-term government bonds represented some 40 per cent of gross external debt in 2009. Other important sources of external debt were

Table 13.13 Gross External Debt by Sector: Selected States, US Dollar Millions, 2009 Third Quarter

	General Government	Monetary Authorities	Banks	Other Sectors	DI/IC
US	3,527,468	373,070	2,842,177	5,819,536	1,109,355
Japan	709,391	1,749	1,028,027	432,784	43,177
Euro Area	2,832,585	387,052	6,869,791	3,171,840	2,056,784
UK	389,907	35,845	5,865,788	2,272,418	730,093
Germany	12,653	2,559,688	697,158	661,440	1,347,715
France	264,808	2,373,805	798,574	482,436	1,302,791
Italy	1,195,135	688	922,720	495,417	100,832
Netherlands	10,029	1,420,131	451,515	338,824	366,902
Spain	402,780	69,611	1,125,249	675,845	265,126
Ireland	107,465	81,523	1,011,519	904,590	292,337
Lux'bourg	1,589	1,825	685,300	1,110,361	218,744
Belgium	305,213	82,592	691,441	147,773	96,133
Switzerland	18,574	14,820	718,125	321,819	157,499
Sweden	7,674	489,770	102,377	220,619	78,302
Austria	222,468	36,337	445,929	105,466	59,026
Greece	327,524	56,601	168,865	38,160	3,448
Finland	87,946	1,171	162,411	65,164	65,074
Central and Eastern Europe/EU					
Poland	83,282	5,228	61,197	70,209	56,194
Hungary	65,163	4,909	58,272	29,749	81,992
Romania	18,562	9,751	32,824	32,867	23,930
Czech Rep.	18,648	110	23,010	32,368	11,137
Latvia	6,583	29	23,012	8,691	4,645

Note: DI/IC refers to direct investment/intercompany lending.
(*Source*: World Bank 2010: Table C2)

the non-bank corporate sector, especially in the Czech Republic, Ireland, and the United States, and inward investment/inter-company lending, notably in Hungary. In Bulgaria, for example, nearly 40 per cent of gross external debt took the form of direct investment and inter-company lending. It amounted to some one-third of gross external debt in Hungary, higher than the contribution of either banks or general government. Monetary authority debt captures foreign-exchange reserves. Here France had a source of gross external debt that dwarfed Germany, Italy, Spain, and Britain. It was exceeded only by the United States in the World Bank statistics.

World Bank statistics on the domestic and foreign-currency proportions of external debt were less complete by 2009. Table 13.14 reflects the importance of the size and liquidity of domestic financial markets, the presence of foreign-owned banks, and differentials on loans in domestic and foreign currencies. There was a strong bias to foreign-currency loans in parts of central and east Europe, notably Bulgaria and the Ukraine. In the period 2005–2008 they averaged around 80 per cent in Estonia and Latvia, over 60 per cent in Lithuania, and some 50 per cent in Hungary (European Central Bank 2010e: 87).

Table 13.14 Gross External Debt: Domestic and Foreign Currency Debt, Selected States, US Dollar Millions, 2009 Third Quarter

	Total Foreign Currency Debt	Total Domestic Currency Debt
United States	1,118,844	10,669,337
Argentina	112,873	7,940
Bulgaria	52,507	2,578
Germany	1,131,590	4,147,064
Hungary	200,653	37,265
Romania	104,330	13,604
Slovakia	668	10,959
Switzerland	928,699	302,139
Ukraine	103,697	1,098

(*Source*: World Bank 2010: Table C5)

In contrast, over the same period, the share of foreign-currency loans was 10 per cent and 25 per cent respectively in the Czech Republic and in Poland. Expectations regarding euro entry were a factor. In addition, private-sector, foreign-denominated debt facilitated a strong credit expansion. However, it also made households and companies very vulnerable to depreciation of their currencies against the euro and the Swiss franc, notably in Hungary, and against the Swedish krona if Latvia had left the ERM II. Their household and corporate sectors were highly exposed to exchange-rate volatility.

External Debt, Debt Service Payments, and Exports

A key risk indicator for sovereign creditworthiness is the capacity of a state to earn the foreign exchange to service its external debt. This capacity is assessed by reference to external debt as a percentage of exports of goods and services and debt service payments as a percentage of exports (see Tables 13.15 and 13.16). Solvency risk heightens with an increasing external debt-to-exports ratio and with a greater share of export revenue having to be used to service external debt. These indicators were first developed by the IMF and the World Bank to deal with highly indebted and emerging economies. Hence they shed most light on central and eastern Europe in a comparative context. Both indicators suggested that in 2009 central and eastern Europe was at greater risk than other emerging market regions, in substantial part because Africa and Latin America had benefitted from large-scale debt relief. On IMF figures it breached the IMF and World Bank threshold of external debt as 150 per cent of exports.

However, according to the UN Millennium Development Goal Indicators (2012), EU Member States like Bulgaria, Latvia, and Romania had by 2010 debt service payment ratios to exports well within the IMF/World Bank threshold of 15–25 per cent: respectively, 1.5 per cent, 5.0 per cent, and 5.1 per cent. On the basis of IMF/World Bank benchmarks for debt service costs (both as percentage of the value of exports of goods and services and as percentage of GDP), on entering the EU none of the central and

Table 13.15 External Debt as Percentage of Exports of Goods and Services, 2002–2009

	2002	2006	2009
Emerging and Developing Economies	121.8	73.2	89.7
Central and Eastern Europe	154.6	143.0	191.9
Commonwealth of Independent States	118.9	95.7	133.0
Developing Asia	86.3	48.5	51.6
Middle East and North Africa	83.5	56.5	75.0
Sub-Saharan Africa	181.7	67.6	77.8
Western Hemisphere	187.2	95.6	116.3

(*Source*: International Monetary Fund 2010b: Table B21)

Table 13.16 Debt Service Payments as Percentage of Exports of Goods and Services, 2002–2009

	2002	2006	2009
Emerging and Developing Economies	32.8	22.1	21.2
Central and Eastern Europe	45.9	44.5	69.9
Commonwealth of Independent States	36.8	34.9	46.9
Developing Asia	20.5	10.0	11.4
Middle East and North Africa	19.8	12.7	14.5
Sub-Saharan Africa	22.7	22.6	15.0
Western Hemisphere	60.5	39.6	39.4

(*Source*: International Monetary Fund 2010b: Table B21)

east European states had been 'severely indebted'. Bulgaria, Estonia, and Hungary had been classified as 'moderately indebted' (Deutsche Bundesbank 2002: 59). Outside the EU, Turkey, Russia, and the Ukraine had reduced their debt service payments ratios to exports radically since 2006: respectively to 8.1 per cent, 5.2 per cent, and 2.5 per cent. In the period 1999–2010, Romania and Turkey had been notable success stories. In 1999 they had been within the IMF/World Bank danger zone, with debt service payments ratios to exports of 20.6 and 18.4 per cent respectively (UN Millennium Development Goal Indicators 2012). Greece, Ireland, and Latvia told a very different story. In Greece, external debt servicing payments were over 80 per cent of exports by 2010; in Ireland 77.6 per cent; and in Latvia 50 per cent (IMF Press Release 10/4961, 16 December 2010). They were 'severely indebted'.

Net External Debt and Net Interest Payments

Gross external debt neglects assets. In consequence, it is open to abuse and misuse by partisan economic commentators. A more nuanced picture emerges from the indicators of net external debt and net interest payments (see Table 13.9). Net external debt reflects the effects of a large financial sector when it holds a large amount of assets in the form of cross-border debt securities, loans, and deposits. In consequence, in 2011 the net external debt position of Britain was very much lower than the gross position. Belgium, Germany, and Switzerland emerged as creditor states with net external asset positions (International Monetary Fund 2011b: 5). By 2007 German net external assets represented a huge 26.5 per cent of GDP. They were the product of the accumulation of current account surpluses since 2001, nearly twenty times higher than in 1999, and were largely attributable to the activities of German financial institutions. By 2007 German external assets and liabilities were mainly concentrated within the euro area, at 50 per cent and 51.5 per cent respectively. Strikingly, Germany was more closely integrated financially than by trade within the euro area. In 2007, 31 per cent of German debt securities were held by non-residents in the rest of the euro area (Deutsche Bundesbank 2008). In part assisted by this German performance, the euro area as a whole had a net external debt position similar to those of Britain and the United States (International Monetary Fund 2011b: 5).

Net interest payments offer an even more important insight. They show how much of national income in any one year has to be allocated to servicing the costs of net external debt. In 2006–2008 the euro area emerged as almost in credit, whilst Britain and the United States were clear debtor states (see Table 13.9).

Bank Exposure to External Debt

Given the significance of bank debt, a key indicator of risk for states is the exposure of their banks through their external positions in foreign currencies vis-à-vis all sectors (see Table 13.17). The BIS (2010a) provides detailed figures, showing that in 2009 the list was headed by Britain. The very limited exposure of US banks—lower, for instance, than the Swedish banks—owed much to the ascendant role of the US dollar in foreign-exchange transactions. Strikingly, the second-placed state, Japan, had below 50 per cent of the British banks' exposure. German, Swiss, and French banks occupied fourth, fifth, and sixth places respectively, with Irish and Dutch banks in ninth and tenth positions. The low exposure of Italian banks was especially striking, below that of Danish, Finnish, and Norwegian banks, and one-third that of Belgian banks.

From BIS figures it is possible to derive net external positions by subtracting bank liabilities from assets (see Table 13.18). German banks emerged as having strong net external positions, alongside Swiss banks. Austrian, Belgian, and French banks appeared in positive balance, unlike the Danish, Dutch, Irish, and Swedish banks. More problematic were the external positions of the British and Italian banks. Again, these figures were liable to change rapidly, especially as banks sought to reduce external exposures during the mounting sovereign debt crisis.

The foreign claims of banks on individual European countries, including their sovereign bonds, provide a key indicator of exposure to risk through interdependence and contagion. The establishment of the euro area, its effects in deepening financial market integration, and the emerging sovereign debt crisis from 2009 onwards gave added significance to this indicator. European states found it more difficult to conceal these exposures, especially to the sovereign bonds of the peripheral economies of the euro area. Both the BIS and the European Banking Authority (EBA) brought new data to light, with the EBA using stress-testing of EU banks to secure compliance.

Table 13.17 External Positions of Banks in Foreign Currencies vis-à-vis All Sectors, in Billions of US Dollars, December 2009

	December 2009
United Kingdom	4,859.4
Japan	1,876.2
Cayman Islands	1,755.8
Germany	872.6
Switzerland	808.2
France	755.2
Singapore	746.8
Hong Kong SAR	675.2
Ireland	495.2
Netherlands	414.8
Sweden	289.4
Luxembourg	255.9
Belgium	239.6
Spain	195.1
Denmark	172.4
Norway	91.1
Finland	80.7
Italy	70.5
Greece	51.2
Portugal	23.8
United States	259.0

(*Source*: Bank for International Settlements 2010a: A12)

Table 13.19 highlights the scale of this exposure in December 2010. With respect to the euro area Member States at highest risk from sovereign default, the exposure of European banks was greatest in scale to Italy and Spain. French, followed by German, banks were most exposed to Italy. In the case of Spain, German banks were most exposed, followed by French. British banks had very considerable exposures, above all to Ireland and Spain. Strikingly, Italian banks were much less exposed, with the exception of Spain. Foreign claims by European banks on Greece were on a lower order of magnitude, but made more serious by the Greek sovereign debt restructuring negotiated in 2011–2012. French and German banks were, once again, most exposed, along with Cypriot banks. Austrian banks were especially exposed to central and east Europe. These figures highlighted the risk that small shocks in terms of order of magnitude could be amplified through feedback loops within and between banking systems. This risk helps explain the reluctance of EU institutions to consider a Greek sovereign debt restructuring in 2010.

At the end of 2010, 96 per cent of Greek sovereign bonds held abroad had been owned by European banks: $22.7 billion by German, and $15 billion by French (Committee on the Global Financial System 2011: 18). Contagion risks were highest for Cypriot, French, and German banks (see Table 13.20). A key purpose of the European collective financial assistance mechanisms negotiated in 2010–2012 was to offer opportunity and time for

Table 13.18 Net External Positions of Banks in all Currencies vis-à-vis all Sectors, in Billions of US Dollars, December 2007 and December 2009

	Amounts Outstanding	
	December 2007	December 2009
Austria	160.8	183.7
Belgium	191.4	184.5
Finland	−18.7	−40.5
France	8.3	178.7
Germany	1,568.3	1,408.7
Greece	−19.7	78.5
Ireland	−122.1	9.0
Italy	−294.4	−260.5
Luxembourg	334.5	277.4
Netherlands	−110.2	−176.9
Portugal	−103.0	−42.1
Spain	−88.5	−194.6
Denmark	−120.7	−132.8
Sweden	−66.1	−113.1
United Kingdom	−539.4	−466.2
United States	−754.4	−278.1
Japan	1,689.7	1,484.5
Norway	−90.9	−102.9
Switzerland	145.9	16.1

Note: This table is constructed from the BIS data by subtracting bank liabilities from assets.
(*Source*: Bank for International Settlements 2010a: A8 and A9)

French, German, and British banks to sharply reduce their foreign claims on Greece, Ireland, Portugal, and Spain. Banks sought to protect themselves against losses in any future sovereign debt restructurings or in a euro exit. They were able to strengthen their own capital positions and to respond to domestic regulatory pressures to reduce risk of cross-border contagion. However, Cypriot banks remained highly exposed, contributing to the Cypriot crisis of 2013.

With respect to Greece, Ireland, Portugal and Spain, and above all Italy, the French banking sector stood out as most exposed in relation to Tier 1 capital (see Table 13.21). The Danish and the Swiss banking sectors were least exposed to the euro area periphery states. Italian banks were also less exposed. However, the Achilles' heel of the Italian banks was their high exposure to their own sovereign debt, at 29 per cent of the total in 2010. At the end of 2009, the consolidated claims of the French and the German banks on Greece, Ireland, Spain, and Portugal had been 16 per cent and 15 per cent of their GDP, respectively. Austrian banks' exposure to central and east Europe amounted to almost 80 per cent of Austrian GDP (Bank for International Settlements 2011). Reducing this vulnerability to cross-national banking contagion became a key domestic priority in managing systemic risk.

Table 13.19 Foreign Claims of Banks on Individual European Countries, in Millions of US Dollars, End December 2010 and End December 2012

	European Banks	Belgium	France	Germany	Italy	UK
End December 2010						
Greece	136,317	1,909	56,740	33,074	4,085	14,061
Ireland	377,636	25,411	29,623	118,154	13,519	135,240
Italy	783,867	25,807	392,577	162,285	–	66,387
Portugal	194,605	3,542	26,923	36,421	4,052	24,345
Spain	632,189	21,512	140,628	181,895	29,657	107,157

(*Source*: Bank for International Settlements, *Quarterly Review*, June 2011: Table 9E)

	European Banks	Belgium	France	Germany	Italy	UK
End December 2012						
Greece	29,177	32	2,801	5,293	902	5,631
Ireland	327,063	20,000	37,207	81,581	10,207	135,821
Italy	632,526	10,339	340,621	129,200	–	49,227
Portugal	143,833	716	16,932	21,670	1,725	17,337
Spain	447,529	9,471	105,068	120,717	22,977	82,863

(*Source*: Bank for International Settlements, *Quarterly Review*, June 2013: Table 9E)

Table 13.20 EU Banks' Exposure to Greek Institutions, 2010

Cyprus	12%
Germany	10%
France	5%
UK	2%
Belgium	1%
Portugal	1%

Note: Compared to Tier 1 capital.
(*Source*: European Banking Authority, *EU-Wide Stress Test Aggregate Report*, 8 July 2011: 14)

Buffers against External Debt Crisis

Governing elites have three key strategies for shielding their states against risks of external debt crisis. The Finnish and Swedish financial crises of 1990–1994 and those of Asia and Russia in 1997–1998 proved a catalyst for their governing elites to pursue these strategies, if with different emphases. The euro area crises represented a similar challenge to its governing elites to consider how best to shield it from future external shocks.

Table 13.21 Exposure of Banks Headquartered in Euro Area to Sovereign Debt of Greece, Ireland, Portugal, and Spain, Totals and Compared to Tier 1 Capital

Total, of which:	$254 billion			
	Total	Spain	Greece	Portugal
French banks	$106bn	$48bn	$31bn	$21bn
German banks	$68bn	$33bn	$23bn	$10bn
Cf. UK	$22bn			
Compared to Tier 1 Capital				
Germany	12.1%			
France	8.3%			
Belgium	5.0%			
Italy	2.8%			
Netherlands	2.7%			
Switzerland	2.0%			

(*Source*: Bank for International Settlements, *Quarterly Review*, June 2010: 20–1)

Promoting Export-Led Growth: Private-Sector Capacity

Radical action to reduce unit labour costs and to invest in human capital was a common feature of crisis management in Finland and Sweden and in Asia. The main instruments were nominal devaluation to restore lost competitiveness; changes to collective bargaining towards longer-term, productivity-oriented framework agreements that gave greater autonomy to companies; and 'fiscal devaluation' through a shift in taxes from labour and employers to consumption and property. Export-led growth offered a protective shield by making it easier to service external debt payments and to build external assets.

Nominal devaluation is closed as an instrument for correcting intra-euro-area trade imbalances. However, euro devaluation can serve to boost extra-euro-area exports, potentially to the benefit of periphery economies like Ireland and Portugal. Otherwise, euro area Member States depend on correcting their mutual imbalances by some combination of fiscal devaluation, differential inflation rates, wage moderation, flexible labour markets, and skill upgrading. This strategy is slow and painful, above all in the short term. It is slow to generate results and tests political will and state capacity to the limit especially when it bears down heavily on the unemployed. The main advocates of the strategy were the ECB and the EU creditor states. Its success depends in substantial part on the level of political tolerance for the unemployment that accompanies structural adjustment. It also depends on private-sector capacity to respond, notably by investing in the upgrading of skills, in innovation, and in research and development.

The Size and Liquidity of Domestic Bond Markets: Home Bias

Promoting larger and more liquid domestic bond markets offers a second strategy for building buffers against external debt vulnerability. Power within creditor-debtor state relations is closely related to the size and liquidity of domestic bond markets. They offer an indicator of state capacity to finance itself and thus of sovereign creditworthiness. When states can 'internalize' debt by tapping into high national savings, they reduce exposure to foreign-exchange risks. For instance, Italy could draw on the size of its net household assets to help reduce reliance on external debt.

In 2010, some 53 per cent of total government debt in the euro area was held by non-residents, including those in other euro area states (European Central Bank 2010b: 31). However, the share of domestically held government debt varied from around 20 per cent to as much as 90 per cent (European Central Bank 2010b: 31). For this reason, despite their high public debt to GDP ratios, Belgium and Italy were better protected against adverse debt developments than Greece and Portugal.

The IMF and the World Bank (2009) attach great importance to the development of resilient sources of domestic savings as a means of absorbing shortfalls in external financing and, more generally, of diversifying risk. However, there are limits to how much debt a domestic bond market can absorb without a state having to pay exorbitant costs or revert to financial repression. Most graphically, this limit is highlighted by war. During the First World War, Germany could no longer access liquidity through the financial markets of London, Paris, and New York to help finance the huge costs of war. The German external debt crisis after 1918 was exacerbated by the succession of reparation arrangements, including the period under the Dawes Plan (1924–1929) when reparations were paid out of inflows of foreign credit rather than fiscal surpluses. By early 1931 the ratio of German external debt to GDP approached 100 per cent (Ritschl 2012). The limit of reliance on domestic debt is also illustrated by adverse current and prospective demographic developments. In the case of Japan, with its fast-ageing population, doubts surfaced in the early twenty-first century about whether 'internalization' of its huge debt could continue to work as a successful strategy.

States with developed bond markets exhibit differences in 'home bias' to holding debt. The decreased home bias within the euro area over the period 1997–2007 was in line with the increasing integration of financial markets. Overall, however, the home bias remained greater in Belgium, Italy, and Spain than in France and especially Germany, where the decrease in home bias was sharp. In 2008 the debt home bias for euro area investors was considerably lower than in Japan and the United States, reflecting the scale and speed of financial integration within the euro area since the currency union.

Changes in the risks associated with holding foreign assets, notably during financial crisis, lead to differences over time in debt home bias. Home bias increased considerably in Spain in 2008, followed by France and Italy, but only to a limited extent in Germany. Foreign holdings of Italian sovereign bonds fell from 52 per cent of the total in 2010 to 36 per cent in 2012. The situation was even more pronounced in Britain, where the Bank of England embarked on a massive quantitative easing programme, buying domestic bonds. The percentage of British public debt held abroad fell to 18.7 per cent in 2011 (International Monetary Fund 2011c: 8). Cross-border integration of both private and public debt markets proved highly vulnerable to financial instability, receding substantially after 2010 (European Central Bank 2010c: 36–9).

Foreign-Exchange Reserves

Foreign-exchange reserves offer a third buffer against external debt vulnerability. Under the gold standard and the Bretton Woods regimes, foreign-exchange reserves were understood as linked to global and European imbalances. States 'earned' their reserves by operating current account surpluses and thereby increasing their net foreign asset position. Foreign-exchange reserves were a by-product of global imbalances, their accumulation deriving from current account surpluses. However, the shift away from an international fixed-exchange-rate regime after the collapse of the Bretton Woods system in 1971–1973 broke the direct causal link between current account surpluses and reserves. The link to external imbalances matters most when governments determine to peg their currencies or seek to enter into currency union, as in the EU. It also matters when central banks choose to intervene in foreign exchange markets to stabilize their currencies, like the Swiss National Bank post-2009.

In the context of exchange-rate flexibility, reserve accumulation reflects government and central bank policies. Their growth can be the product of deliberately targeting rapid export-led growth, supported by a managed, perhaps undervalued exchange rate. This type of policy was pursued after the external debt crises of the late 1990s by several Asian states, notably China. A second driver of reserve accumulation is policy decisions to create buffers as a form of unilateral self-insurance against future financial crises. Substantial reserves are a means of guarding against sudden stops in capital flows, more proactively managing the exchange rate, and gaining financial independence, above all from onerous IMF conditionality in extending credits. A third driver of reserve accumulation is the underdeveloped financial structure of many emerging market economies, including the difficulties of channelling private savings into investment. In this case reserves are not 'earned'. They are 'borrowed', either officially by issuing sovereign bonds internationally or by the private sector generating financial surpluses through attracting foreign direct investment (FDI), portfolio, or banking inflows.

This type of strategy reflects lesson-drawing from crises. It was evident in many central and east European states, not least in pursuing entry to the Exchange Rate Mechanism II (ERM II) and euro area entry. The Swiss National Bank sought to build up a shield around its financial sector during the post-2007 financial crisis. It sought to mitigate risks from foreign-held household and corporate debt denominated in Swiss francs.

The importance of foreign-currency reserves lies in enabling central banks to manage external debt and to inject foreign currency liquidity in times of crisis. This capacity can be augmented in three ways. Central banks can pool foreign reserves. They can arrange inter-central-bank swap lines and repo agreements. Alternatively, international institutions, notably the IMF, can create monetary units or loan facilities. However, reserve accumulation, and external support for it, also entails risks. There are economic opportunity costs in foregone alternative investments, as well as credit and foreign-exchange risks. Not least, moral hazard arises if external liquidity provision reduces the incentive to conduct sound domestic fiscal and monetary policies.

Creditor-debtor state relations face two important challenges. The first is whether reserve accumulation contributes to external imbalances and systemic instability. The second challenge is to define what is an 'adequate', and what an 'excessive', level of foreign-exchange reserves. The existence of a reserve-issuing state and of reserve-accumulating states creates a potentially tense and unstable interdependence. The systemic risk was identified in the so-called 'Triffin dilemma'. This dilemma stems from the need for a reserve currency that—like the US dollar after 1945—can provide a secure anchor of price stability and a shared global store of value. However, the accumulation of reserves depends on the reserve-issuing state running persisting current account deficits. These deficits raise, in turn, issues about the security of the anchor, and risk fuelling global imbalances and destabilizing creditor-debtor state relations (Triffin 1960).

An influential BIS paper claimed that a strategy of self-insurance tended to lead to 'adequate' reserve accumulation. However, the pursuit of export-led growth, with managed exchange rates, risked aggravating external imbalances and inviting retaliation by other states (De Beaufort Wijnholds and Sondergaard 2007). The Asian and Russian crises of 1997–1998, and the subsequent Argentinean and Turkish crises in 2001–2003, pushed the issue of reserve adequacy higher up national and international agendas, especially in relation to emerging market economies, including central and east Europe. The traditional benchmark focused on current accounts and the need for adequate reserves for at least three months of imports (one year for emerging market economies). Given the importance of imports in emerging market economies, foreign-exchange reserves played a key role as an indicator of creditworthiness. The 'reserves-to-imports' ratio provided a benchmark for assessing reserve adequacy (see Table 13.22).

However, in the post-Bretton Woods world of intense financial volatility, the emphasis in assessing vulnerability to liquidity crisis shifted to the 'reserves-to-short-term-external-debt' ratio. States needed an adequate level of reserves to cover potential capital flight ('external drain'). Attempts to construct technical formulas to determine reserve adequacy (like De Beaufort Wijnholds and Kapteyn 2001) recognized that the level should cover short-term external debt. However, the level should rise when the context was one of high roll-over rates of short-term debt, of operating a managed exchange-rate regime, and of indicators suggesting increasing 'country risk'. After the 1997–1998 crises governing elites in emerging market economies dramatized external risks, opting for an active strategy of reserve accumulation. They redefined their notions of reserve adequacy differently from advanced market economies. They also lengthened the maturity structure of their debt to reduce their exposure to refinancing risk and to changes in monetary-policy rates.

In advanced economies like the EU, the post-Bretton Woods world of liberalized, fast-growing financial markets severed the link between external imbalances and reserve accumulation. Their governing elites had the opportunity to access international financial markets rather than remain reliant on current account surpluses to increase their reserves. Advanced economies could also reduce the macroeconomic and central bank balance-sheet costs of holding large reserves. These costs included overheating and inflation, foregone fixed investment, sterilization costs for the central bank, and exposure of the central bank to exchange-rate risk. Hence their governing elites opted to define reserve adequacy more tightly. They retained relatively modest foreign-exchange levels. European central banks were the major sellers of gold reserves between 2000 and 2006.

Table 13.22 Ratio of Reserves to Imports of Goods and Services, 2002–2009

	2002	2006	2009
Central and Eastern Europe	39.5	37.4	47.3
Brazil	60.8	70.7	136.5
China	89.0	125.4	211.6
India	90.0	75.5	88.1
Russia	52.9	141.7	166.9
States with Debt Arrears and/or Rescheduling, 2004–2008	30.4	35.0	43.0
Heavily Indebted Poor States	31.0	30.8	35.1

(*Source*: International Monetary Fund 2010b: 181)

EU Member States operated on the basis of a low ratio of reserves to imports of goods and services.

Table 13.23 puts European central banks in perspective. In 2009–2010 the top-ten holders of foreign-exchange reserves included Japan, Russia, India, Korea, Brazil, Singapore, and Thailand, but not the British and US central banks. However, on the basis of the size of reserves, the Eurosystem and the Swiss National Bank emerged as significant players in creditor-debtor state relations. The Eurosystem was second only to Japan, and third if China had been included in the IMF figures. The French, German, and Italian central banks had individually larger reserves than the US Federal Reserve and the Bank of England. Also striking was the inclusion of the Swiss National Bank in the top ten. Its reserve accumulation served to inhibit appreciation of the Swiss franc once it came under pressure as a safe haven during the post-2007 crisis. Appreciation of the Swiss franc threatened not just Swiss exporters, especially to the euro area. It also increased risks of defaults on franc-denominated loans in central and east Europe, notably Hungary, with potentially serious negative effects on the solvency of Swiss banks. Denmark's relatively large reserve holdings reflected the strong official commitment to maintaining its tight fluctuation band within the ERM II. In addition, there seemed to be a divide between central and east European EU Member States and longer-serving EU Member States. In the early period of the crisis, the reserves of Poland, Romania, Hungary, and the Czech Republic exceeded those of Spain, Belgium, and the Netherlands. There were clear gains in economic security from euro area membership.

This broad picture of modest reserve accumulation in Europe and the United States was repeated in the oil-based surplus states of the Middle East. However, most of their foreign-exchange revenue was channelled into sovereign wealth funds. They tended to pursue high, long-term returns and were not counted as part of the international reserves held by central banks. In terms of currency composition, the Norway Pension Fund, the Russia Oil Stabilization Fund, and the Qatar Investment Authority had the highest (declared) sovereign wealth fund exposures in euros (Mohi-uddin 2008: 7). This process of channelling reserves into sovereign wealth funds was a factor in severing the link between current account surpluses and reserve accumulation.

Table 13.23 Time Series Data on Key International Reserves and Foreign Currency Liquidity Official Reserve Assets, in Millions of US Dollars at End of Month, 2009–2010

	June 2009	March 2010
Japan	1,019,175	1,042,715
Russia	412,590	447,004
India	265,142	278,357 (Feb.)
Korea	231,735	272,331
Brazil	201,467	243,762
Singapore	173,191	196,361
Switzerland	107,847	161,823
Thailand	120,811	144,094
United States	82,194	127,505
United Kingdom	74,624	95,358
Denmark	63,473	76,098
Norway	47,907	49,223 (Feb.)
Sweden	40,402	46,492
Eurosystem including:	539,219	672,110
Germany	147,970	181,732
France	103,034	134,958
Italy	111,259	133,105
Netherlands	30,291	40,311
Spain	21,401	28,196
Belgium	16,811	24,278
Greece	3,779	5,503
Ireland	1,126	2,039
Poland	67,119	85,232
Romania	40,550	46,886
Hungary	38,091	44,591 (Feb.)
Czech Republic	38,448	40,151 (Feb.)
Latvia	3,943	7,513
Iceland	3,024	3,824

Notes: (1) The Eurosystem includes the ECB and the national central banks of the EU Member States that have adopted the euro; (2) China is not included.
(*Source*: International Monetary Fund 2010b)

The severed link between external imbalances and reserves meant that financing public debt through a reduction of borrowing costs became more reliant on other mechanisms for gaining the confidence of the financial markets, for instance favourable tax and regulatory policies. Currency swaps could be used to cushion foreign-exchange reserves and to provide foreign-currency liquidity, especially short-term US dollar funding, to the private sector, notably to banks. Nevertheless, this severed link facilitated the growth in power of financial markets vis-à-vis states.

Table 13.23 illustrates the extraordinary reserve accumulation process in states like Brazil, China, and Russia, alongside the more modest growth in central and eastern

Europe. In 2005 China accounted for a massive 54 per cent of total reserve accumulation (Dorrucci 2006: 3). In consequence, the reserves of these emerging market economies were large relative to the size of their domestic financial systems. This observation applied above all in China, where reserves dwarfed bank credit (Bank for International Settlements 2010: 53).

In contrast, the euro area experienced a substantial reduction in foreign-exchange reserves after 2000, as the size of their financial systems grew. In 2009 no EU state appeared in the top-ten largest holders of gold and foreign-exchange reserves; eight were Asian. However, gold continued to hold attraction for European central banks. Its attraction stemmed from perceptions of contingency risk, diversification risk, economic security, and confidence. Germany was the second largest holder of gold reserves after the United States in 2009, whilst the Eurosystem held 34 percent of total gold reserves (Wainstein 2010: 10).

This distribution of reserves meant that states like China and Japan came to play a central role in financing global imbalances, especially purchasing US-dollar denominated assets like US Treasury bonds. In 2009 the US dollar accounted for 59.8 per cent of central bank foreign-exchange reserves in emerging market economies. The euro represented 31.1 per cent (Analistas Financieros Internacionales 2009: 9). Because of the size and distribution of their reserves, a few emerging market economies surfaced in a short period as pivotal players in creditor-debtor state relations. However, by helping to make it easier to finance current account deficits at relatively low long-term interest rates, they also lessened policy discipline in deficit states and delayed adjustment to external imbalances (Dorrucci 2006). The United States benefited from reductions in its government bond yields, whilst being shielded from external discipline. In this context, illusion and complacency were fostered.

The rise of the emerging market economies testified to the continuing significance of foreign-exchange reserve accumulation and foreign-exchange intervention by central banks in creditor-debtor state relations. The post-2007 crisis served to reinforce the post-1997 crisis lesson that large reserve holdings are useful insurance mechanisms against external shocks. They could be used both to support the exchange rate and to provide foreign-currency funding to domestic banks. Characteristic of financial crisis situations, China, India, and Russia increased their gold reserves significantly (Wainstein 2010: 11). At the same time, large-scale reserve accumulation created inflationary risks from loose monetary and financial conditions and potentially high sterilization costs.

Table 13.24 reveals a number of factors that influence reserve accumulation in EU states outside the euro area. First, entry into, and membership of, the ERM II is associated with an incentive to build relatively large foreign-exchange reserves. For instance, in 2009 Denmark had larger reserves than Britain, a non-ERM II member. Although on a much smaller scale, the three Baltic States strengthened their foreign-exchange reserves for ERM II entry. Conversely, Slovakia had much smaller reserves after euro area entry. Anticipation of ERM II entry also influenced Polish reserves. Secondly, the financial and economic crisis led to a pronounced growth of foreign-exchange reserves in Hungary, Poland, and Romania. The costs of self-insurance against external exchange-rate shocks had risen. In 2009 Poland had larger foreign-exchange reserves than Britain.

The experiences of Hungary, Latvia, and Romania, which in 2009–2010 had to turn to the IMF and the EU for balance-of-payments assistance, showed that existing reserves

Table 13.24 Foreign Official Reserves: Annual Data for Selected EU States Outside the Euro Area, 2002–2009. Total Reserves Including Gold in Millions of Euro

	2002	2006	2008	2009
Bulgaria	4,577.4	8,926.8	12,713.5	-
Czech Republic	22,630.8	23,704.1		27,890.6
Denmark	26,700.5	23,704.1		44,536.1
Estonia	957.7	2,119.2		2,607.9
Latvia	1,283.4	3,466.7		3,915.1
Lithuania	2,314.3	4,397.6		4,535.4
Hungary	9,904.0	16,431.3		29,336.7
Poland	28,444.2	36,834.5		53,669.2
Romania	6,966.0	22,923.0		29,336.3
Slovakia	12,220.4	11,642.6		1,264.0
Sweden	18,441.6	21,217.6		28,003.9
United Kingdom	39,153.0-	34,148.9		40,627.3

(*Source*: Eurostat, 3 August 2010: http://appsso.eurostat.ec.europa.eu/nui/show.do?dataset=mny`for`a&lang=en)

proved insufficient to provide self-insurance. Poland sought to differentiate itself as a state with stronger economic fundamentals and domestic policy frameworks by gaining IMF assistance through its new Flexible Credit Line (FCL). This IMF instrument offered upfront and automatic access to its resources for a privileged set of emerging market economies.

In contrast, the euro area was sheltered from the need to rapidly build reserves by the capacity of the Eurosystem to provide unlimited liquidity to the banking system through its money-market operations. Given this capacity, unlike in Iceland, Ireland could avert some of the worst effects of its external-debt exposure, without the costs of rebuilding foreign-exchange reserves. This capacity to use unconventional ECB monetary policy operations meant that the crisis did not lead the Eurosystem to draw the lesson that reserve accumulation was necessary. Monetary policy tools offered insurance within a currency union, alongside greater new financial assistance mechanisms tied to toughened euro area conditionality and surveillance.

External Debt as Political Differentiator: Private-Sector and State Will and Capacity

External debt serves as a great political differentiator amongst states. The various indicators of gross and net external debt serve both as cameras and engines in the structures and dynamics of power in creditor-debtor state relations. They provide material with which to construct an informal hierarchy of European states, with contrasting vulnerabilities. Strikingly, this process of differentiation appears to be independent of the political and institutional features of European states: their degree of centralization; their extent of executive autonomy; and whether they are majority- or consensus-based in government formation. Political science examinations of 'strong' and 'weak' states tend to neglect external debt dynamics and their implications for the construction of state image.

External debt indicators can be used to construct different types of states, from creditors to chronic debtors. Two groups sit atop the hierarchy. First, there is a group of 'big' European players in creditor-debtor state relations, alongside the United States and China on the global stage. This group comprises Germany (a creditor state), Britain (a debtor state), and Switzerland (a creditor state). These states are defined by the sheer size and nature of their international financial assets and liabilities.

The systemic significance of Britain and Switzerland stems from their structural dependence on banking and financial services. Both are disposed, from economic self-interest, to articulate the institutional and policy preferences of this sector in creditor-debtor state relations. Assisted by the lobbying power of its financial sector, British negotiators were able to exert substantial influence on the contents of European banking union and the EU Markets in Financial Instruments Directive. They were able to secure prohibition of any policy or regulation that discriminated, directly or indirectly, against any Member State as a venue for conducting financial market activities. However, the counterpart to structural dependency was vulnerability to the shadowy world of debt inside banking and financial services and to bank lobbying activity.

Secondly, as a consequence of their net external debt positions, some European states possess an arguing and a negotiating power well above their relative demographic and economic size. They include Denmark, Finland, Luxembourg, the Netherlands, and Sweden. They punch above their weight.

The two groups at the top of the European hierarchy possess certain attributes. Their private-sector elites have the will and the capacity to make possible current account surpluses by building on comparative advantage. Alternatively, or in addition, they exhibit the political will and the state capacity to manage fiscal and structural reforms on terms that satisfy investors.

Conversely, at the foot of the hierarchy is a clear category of European chronic debtor states. They share limited political will and state capacity to pay debts, above all by effective fiscal and structural reforms, and weak private-sector will and capacity to build on comparative advantage. Chronic debtors lack strong fiscal institutions and the presence of a powerful export sector. Their low state reform capacity is reflected in limited strategic planning and management, weak institutional adjustment and learning, and inadequate involvement of wider civil society and political actors. The Bertelsmann Stiftung (2009) study placed Greece, Italy, Hungary, and Turkey into the category of weak reform capacity. Chronic debtor states exhibit preferences for large but weak public sectors: large because they offer access to resources, with which political parties can reward their political clients and supporters; and weak because of deficient central authority to mobilize and make effective independent use of state resources.

The sense of an underlying pattern in creditor-debtor state relations derives from its structural context of current account imbalances and the external assets and liabilities that they create. Constructing sovereign creditworthiness is bound up with the evolution of external imbalances. However, the causal links are complex. As the central and east European EU Member States with their large current account deficits showed, a large share of direct investment in total capital imports means a relatively low growth in external debt. Similarly, high domestic savings rates, as in France and Italy, and very large and liquid domestic financial markets, as in Britain, reduce risks of external debt crisis. They help to explain why some debtor states avoid 'chronic' status. At the same time, in the post-Bretton Woods' world of liberalized, large-scale capital flows, European debtor states altered their definitions of foreign-exchange adequacy. They relied less on self-insurance through reserve accumulation and more on building market confidence.

As external imbalances change, so does the configuration of creditor and debtor states, the location of the pressure points, and the strength of the pressures. The majority of states shift between these two polar types of creditor and chronic debtor state. As Chapter 10 shows, they approximate variously over time to regular debtors, lapsed creditors, and illusory creditors. There is no simple binary picture of creditor and debtor state and much flux over time within the European hierarchy. Creditor-state status remains precarious. Creditor states become debtors, classically and dramatically Britain after 1914. Debtor states become creditors, classically and dramatically Germany from the early 1950s.

External debt data reveal the vulnerability of creditor states to contagion. In 1999, when European monetary union was launched, a few states figured prominently in the scale of their banks' short-term exposure to foreign debtors. They were, in descending order, Germany, the Netherlands, Switzerland, Belgium, and Italy (Bank for International Settlements 2002: 23). The post-2010 sovereign debt crisis highlighted the exposure of German banks to Greece and Spain. In a Europe of monetary union and highly integrated financial markets, implied liabilities of creditor states are endemic to the extent that the self-interests of states are shared and common identities acknowledged. Post-2010, German governing elites had to face the deeply uncomfortable question of whether they had constructed European monetary union on the basis of the illusion that shared pooling of risks could be avoided when financial integration had created webs of interdependent interests through which contagion could flow.

The precarious nature of external debt dynamics is illustrated by the way in which the comparative advantages on which the current account surpluses of a creditor state are based may atrophy. This process exposes the degree of illusion, hubris, and complacency that follows from self-characterization as 'exceptional'. It was seen in the effects of the explosive influx of Spanish gold and silver in the sixteenth century. It was also evident in the British corporate sector's failures to adapt efficiently to changing patterns of demand and costs and proactively embrace new technologies and skills from the late nineteenth century. Complacency is a potent danger.

External Risk Management as an Imprecise Science: The 'Debt Trap' as 'Image Trap'

External risk management remains an imprecise science, given the radical uncertainty affecting debt dynamics and its implication for efforts to assign mathematical probability to default. In these circumstances, external risk management is an exercise in plausibility, in constructing persuasive narratives that reflect certain beliefs about states, their banks and companies, and their household sector. These beliefs relate to the normative and professional quality of their governing, banking, and corporate elites. They rest on certain understandings about whether these elites function in a benign and accountable manner or in a malign, capricious, and dangerous way. They include assessments of private-sector will and capacity to build on comparative advantage and of political will and state capacity to manage liquidity problems and avert insolvency.

Transparency remains an acute problem in external debt. In authoritarian states, which lack accountability, problems of debt opacity, elite collusion, and fiscal gimmickry make it unclear, even to the most careful analyst, to what extent notional creditor status conceals extensive financial repression, conflicts of interest in audit processes, and reckless lending. For these reasons, alongside ideological aversion, external investors were hyper-cautious about lending to Franco's Spain. China too was vulnerable to reckless lending by its banks, at the behest of government. However, as financial crises have shown, democratic states are not immune from the risk that what seems a creditor state may turn out to be an illusion. Illusion is not just the preserve of authoritarian states.

The Asian crises of the late 1990s, the Argentinean crisis, and the post-2007 global financial and economic crisis served as catalysts in spurring recognition of the need for strengthened official monitoring and surveillance of external debt, especially short-term debt. The result was a proliferation of indicators, reporting systems, and spreadsheets, as well as new tensions between states and international financial institutions like the IMF about their use. There was a deep-seated reluctance to see systems, evolved for emerging market economies, applied to advanced economies when the latter were key IMF shareholders.

Assessing the dynamics of external debt continued to be shrouded in problems of definition, opacity, uncertainty, and comparability. These problems added to the uncertainty facing investors, credit rating agencies, international financial institutions, and EU and domestic policy makers. Incomplete, deficient, and potentially unreliable official statistics on types, location, and scale of external debt bedevilled creditor-debtor state relations. They made the accurate pricing of risk notoriously difficult and the risks from illusion commensurately high. Weighing indicators and interpreting data remained deeply contentious.

External risk management was complicated by two particular problems. First, calculations of net external debt remained more difficult than gross debt, with often negative implications for the quality and the balance of public debate. Secondly, monitoring and surveillance of bank external liabilities and public-sector external debt were made difficult by 'off-balance-sheet' and implied obligations. By 2013 accrual accounting remained weakly developed within EU Member-State governments, let alone those of emerging market economies. Conventional cash-based accounting opened up opportunities for financial obfuscation and manipulation. Furthermore, the liberalization of external accounts made borrowing by the 'shadow' banking sector and by publicly-owned enterprises difficult to record. This context of radical uncertainty was one in which illusion and complacency about sustainable debt could breed.

Despite their limitations, external debt indicators and data matter in constructing sovereign creditworthiness and legitimating ratings. States are most at risk of sovereign debt crisis when various factors combine: mounting current account deficits, large and growing net external debt, intractable fiscal deficits, weakening economic growth rates, low and falling domestic saving rates, foreign investment that is misdirected away from strengthening domestic capital stock, greater reliance on short-term and volatile capital flows, and increasing borrowing costs. This toxic combination entrenches their image as 'weak' states, with 'feckless' and 'irresponsible' publics and elites that lack governing competence. These images are associated with rising expectations of default and potentially severe losses for external creditors. The 'debt trap' is an 'image trap'. The challenge to statecraft is to cultivate image change by creating buffers against excessive external debt and by reframing what is considered sustainable external debt. As Adolph Wagner noted in 1863, the key lies in providing evidence that external credit has been productively used.

14

Which Truth? The Power of Numeric Indicators and Probabilistic Reasoning about Public Debt

> The driest argument has its hallucinations, too hastily concluding that its net will now at last be large enough to hold the universe...No formulas for thinking will save us mortals from mistake in our imperfect apprehension of the matter to be thought about...We must be patient with the inevitable makeshift of our human thinking, whether in its sum total or in the separate minds that have made the sum.
>
> George Eliot, *Daniel Deronda* (1876: 572)

The political controversies about the mismatch of liability and control in public finances reflect a cognitive problem. It is about what kind of discourse about public debt prevails and about who masters this discourse. From the perspective of political legitimacy, the problem lies in the difficulties and uncertainties that face governing elites in mastering the discourse about public debt. This discourse is embedded in the structural power of financial markets and is focused on numeric financial indicators. Correspondingly, governing elites appear at risk of being imprisoned by financial market mentalities. Political legitimacy seems to be 'hollowed-out'. The solution lies in reasserting control. It involves shifting discourse beyond financial variables towards concern with broader environmental, social, and governance factors. It means engaging with the challenges of sustaining long-term social and infrastructural investment in raising productivity, in providing collective insurance, and in securing social integration.

From the perspective of financial markets, the problem lies in the difficulties and the uncertainties that derive from the irresponsible accumulation of liabilities by governing elites. They are viewed as prone to indulge in illusion, hubris, and hypocrisy; in short-term political opportunism; and in fiscal gimmickry, deception, and mendacity.

The solution lies in reasserting control through fiscal transparency, strict limits on liabilities, and firm fiscal rules to discipline governing elites. At the heart of ongoing controversy about the mismatch between liability and control is the question of which truth prevails in defining the problem and the solution.

Whatever the claims made for the superiority of political legitimacy, debate about public debt has been dominated by widespread faith in formal reasoning and mathematical skills. This cognitive shift was discernible from the 1930s as economics changed from being a discipline of words to one of models (Morgan 2012). Economists began to inhabit and to manipulate artificial worlds that were understood to represent how economies functioned. Their models took on a life of their own, configuring the domain of debt and constituting its nature. Reflecting this cognitive shift, policy makers, analysts, and markets began to represent debt as a problem of numeric financial indicators. They acquired faith in the possibility of estimating the objective probability of debt default. This faith in modelling, measurement, and probabilistic reasoning derived from the power of investors and their aversion to ambiguity and uncertainty. It offered intellectual security. They also had an interest in saving on the big transaction costs of gaining sufficiently detailed and intimate knowledge about states to have confidence in their own narratives about debt. More fundamentally, the power that was assigned to objective indicators stemmed from widely shared belief in the superior knowledge provided by science. This belief had deep roots in Enlightenment thought. In consequence of this marriage of self-interest with science, investors had an incentive to embrace simple numeric probability statements as the basis for their decisions. The 'hard-wiring' of credit ratings into financial market regulation further enhanced this discursive power over states.

Narrative Reasoning, Probabilistic Reasoning, and State Power

The implications of faith in modelling, measurement, and probabilistic reasoning for state power are profound. Power attaches to those in, and close to, financial markets who provide, manipulate, and use measurable risk indicators and the relevant data. They help define how states come to be perceived and hedge how their power is used. Numeric indicators can be employed to differentiate state character in terms of virtues and vices. They offer 'objective' evidence in terms of which the rhetorical use of otherwise intellectually lazy, simplifying labels, like fiscal 'saints' and 'sinners' can be justified. States lose power when particular market-based probability assessments provide 'unfavourable' evidence. They undermine the credibility of governing elites in their efforts to craft a distinctive narrative about sovereign creditworthiness.

Numeric indicators create 'good' or 'bad' news, which states struggle to respond to, let alone shape. Governing elites have an incentive to seek to establish credibility on their terms. In this sense, risk indicators act as engines, and not simply cameras, of sovereign debt markets. They configure these markets, constitute their nature, and shape how they evolve (cf. MacKenzie 2006; Morgan 2012). Indicators define what investors need to know when extending credit. They become as important, if not more so, than material collateral like money or property. Faced by this structural power, governing elites have strong inducements to respond by resorting, as expedient, to illusory debt arithmetic and fiscal gimmickry. They make heroic assumptions, for instance about gross domestic product (GDP) growth. They use concealment, mendacity, and trickery in compiling national accounts and public finance balance sheets (Morgenstern 1950). In one sense, risk indicators help to clarify certain underlying realities. In another, they induce new forms of illusion and hubris.

Despite the discursive power of probabilistic reasoning, governing elites are not helpless. They can attempt to reframe how the state is perceived by telling a 'good' story about sovereign creditworthiness. A good story is founded on narrative reasoning. It offers a historically grounded vision of common purpose, mobilizes moral sentiments around a notion of shared identity, captures the public imagination, and synthesizes relevant 'favourable' evidence. Typically, it includes reference to the intangible as well as the tangible non-financial assets of the state. A good story draws on vivid historical memory to establish the virtues in state and public character. An example was the Bundesbank's post-1970s use of the hyperinflation of 1923 to construct a narrative of German commitment to stability culture. Narrative reasoning is persuasive to the extent that it creates the conviction that the preponderance of evidence supports long-term debt sustainability.

The challenge in constructing narrative reasoning about sovereign creditworthiness is to trump the discursive power of probabilistic reasoning. However, governing elites face a dilemma. Success in telling a 'good' story risks being short-lived unless they can position the state in a fiscal safe zone so that it can manage unexpected shocks and risks from opportunistic political behaviour. Narrative reasoning that fails to centralize prudence as a shared moral value will not prove persuasive for long in the face of the structural realities of financial market power.

Crafting a narrative reasoning involves the arts of political communication and persuasion in building consensus about the legitimacy of measures that have been taken to ensure future solvency. It is a process of mobilizing moral sentiments, manipulating public imagination, and managing expectations. The German Bundesbank proved a master of these arts in establishing a hugely influential mythology of Germany as inflation-averse and in embedding this mythology in the design of the European Central Bank (ECB). Similarly, Mario Draghi displayed mastery of the arts of communication in attempting to position the ECB as master of the integrity of the euro area with his statement in 2012 that the ECB stood 'ready to do whatever it takes to preserve the euro. And believe me it will be enough.' The problem was that the ECB president alone could not provide the fully persuasive narrative that euro area Member States needed if they were to be deemed creditworthy. This narrative had to combine clear pre-commitment to banking and to fiscal union, a growth-maximizing debt sustainability strategy, and unequivocal signalling that there was a lender-of-last-resort to Member-State governments.

Serious risks arise from the discursive power of probabilistic reasoning. The belief in objective indicators of default probability, and the technocratic legitimacy that they enjoy, rests on fragile epistemic foundations. First, historically, dominant ideologies of debt change, along with the social interests that underpin them. The corollary is that there is no one authoritative construction of what is fiscally 'normal', against which to measure debt sustainability. Sovereign creditworthiness is a domain of subjective, historically contingent knowledge. It involves contest about which indicators matter most and how to weigh different indicators, not just economic but also environmental, social, and governmental indicators. At a deeper level, sovereign creditworthiness is about who matters most and about how gains and losses should be spread over time.

Secondly, sovereign creditworthiness is a domain of radical uncertainty and ambiguous, incomplete, and often unreliable information. It involves an intuitive understanding of what drives formal models, contest about how economies and particular states work, and, not least, the tension between universalistic and context-specific approaches to how they work. Radical uncertainty is bound up with the complex interactions between public-debt and private-debt dynamics and with the exposure of public balance sheets to domestic credit conditions and to external imbalances. Moreover, there is lack of clarity about when a sovereign debt crisis mutates from one of liquidity to one of solvency. These features render implausible precise numeric attributions of default probability. Sovereign creditworthiness is associated with multiple probabilities.

Thirdly, as Chapter 7 shows, the value of the evidence that is provided by probabilistic reasoning is diminished by its reliance on extrapolation from relatively short-run historical data. It tends to underestimate the risks of huge economic, social, and political costs from low-probability, catastrophic crises, notably in banking but also in external and internal security. In social welfare terms, the preponderance of historical evidence supports the crafting of narrative reasoning that argues for the superiority of a precautionary strategy in fiscal policy and in financial market supervision and regulation. A single numeric indicator and probabilistic reasoning offer a less reliable guide than a preponderance of evidence drawn from multiple indicators, in particular suggesting that governing and banking elites are firmly attached to the virtue of prudence. This virtue is most persuasively displayed in 'good' times. It involves building fiscal 'buffers' or safe zones and well-capitalized banks, able to withstand the large economic shocks that highly complex and opaque financial systems regularly deliver.

Faith in numeric probability reasoning is ill-suited to a world of sovereign creditworthiness that is characterized by subjectivity and contest between core normative beliefs; by ambiguous, questionable, and incomplete information; by its context-specific character; and by radical uncertainty, multiple probabilities, and very high stakes. The evidence that risk indicators provide does not become valueless. However, it has to be weighed within a context of non-comparable beliefs about what states should do, and how. In consequence, it is impossible to assign objective mathematical probabilities to risk of sovereign default. Nevertheless, numeric indicators populate narrative reasoning about public debt in ways that can distort judgement.

Public Debt and National Balance Sheets

The limitations of numeric probability reasoning stem in part from the way in which public debt dynamics are embedded in national balance sheets. This embedding of public debt underlines its complexity and the radical uncertainty that surrounds its dynamics.

Debate about debt sustainability poses fundamental issues of definition and composition. In its broadest sense, debt is defined by the national balance sheet of assets and liabilities. It includes direct investment, including inter-company lending; loans and currency deposits; money market instruments; bonds and notes; trade credits; and advances due to non-residents (cf. European Central Bank 2010c). Aggregate debt includes household, financial, and non-financial corporate debt, and public-sector debt. The linkages amongst them are critical, especially the potentially lethal embrace between bank liabilities and sovereign debt.

As the post-2007 crisis illustrated, liabilities can shift dramatically when bank liabilities are transferred to the public sector. Britain, Cyprus, Iceland, Ireland, and Spain provided graphic examples. A wave of banking crises is typically followed, after a time lag, by heightened risk of sovereign debt default. Moreover, this process of cross-contamination of balance sheets can go into reverse once sovereign debt crisis affects the liquidity position of banks that hold their state's debt. The result is credit contraction and further pressures on sovereign creditworthiness through falling tax revenues and higher welfare-state spending. Given the systemic importance of the banking sector, aggregate public and financial debt is an important indicator of risk.

The linkages within national balance sheets are also demonstrated when high public debt is offset by low household debt. This linkage was evident in Italy, where in 2010—because of low household debt—aggregate debt was lower (319 per cent of GDP) than Britain (413 per cent), Spain, and the United States. Italy stood out in Europe because of the relatively big size of household assets, notably through property ownership. Another linkage takes the form of the corporate sector using bank debt to invest in foreign assets in fast-growing emerging markets in eastern Europe, Latin America, or Asia. By 2012 Spain's high levels of household debt were offset, in part, both by the positive external balance of Spanish companies and by relatively low public debt. In short, the importance and nature of aggregate debt is often poorly understood, leading financial markets to misprice sovereign risk.

The irresponsible financial behaviour of banks and households in creating credit and in accumulating debt is often fundamental to problems of sovereign creditworthiness. Characteristically, the roots of these problems lie in property credit booms and inflated construction sectors. Between 1999 and 2007 financial institutions in the euro area increased their debt from less than 200 per cent of GDP to more than 250 per cent. Strikingly, over the same period, the government debt ratio fell from 72 per cent to 67 per cent (De Grauwe 2010). This irresponsibility was recorded in the International Monetary Fund (IMF) surveillance reports that accompanied its concerted bail-outs with the EU of Hungary and Latvia in 2008–2009. In a survey that included European financial crises, the Bank for International Settlements (BIS) (2010: 33) pointed out that the ratio of private-sector credit to GDP dropped by as much as 44 percent in Finland (1992–1998) and 35 percent in Sweden (1990–1996). Before these Nordic crises, the ratio had climbed, trough to peak, a dramatic 51 per cent in Finland and 46 percent in Sweden.

In its narrower sense, debate about sovereign creditworthiness focuses on sovereign debt in the context of public-sector accounts. The Maastricht definition of debt, in contrast to the European System of Integrated Economic Accounts (ESA) 95 definition, followed this restricted approach. It included two main types of debt instruments: marketable debt securities (i.e. government bonds and bills) and bank loans. In the euro area at the end of 2009, about 82 per cent of government debt took the form of debt securities. The 15 per cent share of bank loans was mainly accounted for by local governments and municipalities and by long-term investment projects (European Central Bank 2010b: 30–3).

The importance of the linkages between public finances and the broader national accounts is thrown into relief in two ways. First, liquidity and solvency problems in the private sector have systemic implications that lead to implicit (and ultimately explicit) liabilities of government. For these reasons, the collapse of an asset-price bubble in financial markets, property markets, or commodity prices (like oil) increases risks of sovereign debt default. The increased risk stems from prospective or actual expensive public bail-outs of 'systemically significant' institutions, from sharply falling tax revenues, from unemployment-related effects on public finances, and from widening structural budget deficits. The corollary of private-sector deleverage is heightened public indebtedness. In 2009 alone government debt-to-GDP ratios rose by over 10 per cent in Greece, Ireland, Spain, and Slovakia. This increase was especially problematic in Greece where (like Italy) the ratio stood at over 100 per cent. Between 2007 and 2010 government borrowing rose from 17 per cent to an estimated 26 per cent of euro area GDP (European Central Bank 2010b: 30).

Secondly, government bonds tend to serve as benchmarks for interest rates in the wider economy because, traditionally, they represent the safest assets to hold. Rising risk premiums have broader macroeconomic effects on the costs of corporate borrowing, including for banks. They pose a special challenge to the monetary transmission mechanism in the euro area, consequent on differential borrowing costs in Member States. Rapidly increasing sovereign debt issues also 'crowd out' private-sector investment by reducing liquidity in the corporate bond markets. Fund managers become reluctant to buy even high-quality corporate bonds in states that have weak fiscal positions. In time of sovereign debt crisis, the biggest differentiator in returns on corporate bonds becomes the location in which the issuer is domiciled. Hence sovereign debt crisis is transmitted into corporate bond markets. Not least, confidence in banks, their capacity to recapitalize themselves and to borrow in the money markets, is closely tied to government bond markets. The consequence is a transmission channel from sovereign debt crisis, through bank lending capacity, to the financial health of the corporate and household sectors.

What Debt? Gross and Net Public Debt

The limitations of numeric probability reasoning about public debt dynamics also stem from disagreement about what should be measured. Traditionally, risk indicators of probability of sovereign default focused on gross public debt. It had the advantage over net debt of greater consistency across states in its definition (International Monetary Fund 2010c: 15). Hence gross public debt remained the principal indicator of roll-over risk and risks to medium-term GDP growth. Net public debt was seen as a less reliable comparator.

Despite measurement and comparability problems, it can be argued that net public debt provides a clearer picture of debt sustainability. Available comparative data on net public debt for 2011 showed a notable gap between net public debt (57.2 per cent) and gross public debt (83 per cent) in Germany. The corresponding figures for the Netherlands were even more striking: 30.6 per cent net public debt and 65.5 per cent gross public debt. In Finland, Sweden and, above all, Norway the value of financial assets corresponding to debt instruments meant that net public debt was negative (International Monetary Fund 2011b: 8). This data highlighted the robustness of these states' creditworthiness. In contrast, net public debt in Italy was the highest in the EU at 100.4 per cent, followed by Ireland at 98.8 per cent. France and Britain were also high net public debtors at 81 per cent and 72.9 per cent respectively. However, figures on net public debt could prove volatile. The pre-2007 'sound' net public debt positions of Estonia, Ireland, and Latvia vanished with banking and financial crises.

What Debt? The Limitations of Official Fiscal Balance Sheets

The problem of what should be measured arises with respect to official fiscal balance sheets. The narrow official fiscal balance sheet ('Maastricht debt') has to be seen alongside two other balance sheets. The 'off-balance-sheet' balance sheet comprises hidden, legally contracted liabilities. The 'phantom' balance sheet represents implied obligations and risks that confront the public sector. They arise from reckless private-sector financial behaviour or from exposure through bail-outs to the reckless fiscal behaviour of other governments (Rothkopf 2010). Implicit transfers to the euro area periphery states raised questions about risks to German sovereign creditworthiness.

The 'off-balance-sheet' balance sheet is similar to the official balance sheet. In both cases the obligation on the debtor involves the outstanding amount of the current legally contracted liabilities that require payment of principal on maturity and the interest payable at regular times till maturity. In national accounts it appears in the form of debt instruments like debt securities, loans, currency and deposits, trade credits, and other liabilities. In contrast, the 'phantom' balance sheet refers to implied, and as yet not legally contracted, obligations. These obligations are elastic and open. They refer to the risk that governments will assume liabilities by bailing-out banks, non-financial corporations (as in the automobile sector), other sovereign states, or their own sub-national governments. Bail-outs are justified because these institutions are too 'systemically significant' to be allowed to default and fail. In short, the 'phantom' balance sheet takes account of the risk that governments will multiply their liabilities by becoming engaged in moral hazard. The scale of this phenomenon was highlighted by the big increases in government support for banks after 2007, notably in Cyprus, Greece, Ireland, and Spain (Committee on the Global Financial System 2011: 23).

The Elusive Public-Debt 'Overhang'

The sheer complexity and gathering momentum of European sovereign debt crises provided a context within which governing and technical elites and financial markets became more receptive to new measurable risk indicators. Their receptivity was conditioned by whether intellectual prescriptions buttressed the political choices that they wished to make. Official reports began to base their recommendations on academically-generated targets for optimal, growth-maximizing public debt (cf. Champsaur and Cotis 2010; International Monetary Fund 2010c). They were attractive because they identified the crises as a 'debt problem' and provided clearly specified triggers for fiscal consolidation and structural reforms. Academic research helped frame the direction and the parameters of debate about public debt, providing a technocratic legitimacy to the political priority of debt reduction.

Reinhard and Rogoff (2010) provided the most influential benchmark in the early phase of the European sovereign debt crises. They analysed gross public debt and GDP growth across twenty advanced economies over more than a century. The conclusion was that gross debt in excess of 90 per cent of GDP, over at least a five-year period, represented a public-debt 'overhang'. It produced negative effects on GDP growth relative to states below that level. Exceeding this level limited state capacity for anti-cyclical macroeconomic stabilization, 'crowded-out' private investment, and heightened vulnerability to a rise in real interest rates. As public debt grew beyond this 90 per cent level, it became more difficult for states to grow out of debt. The implication was the need for tough adjustments in the primary budget balance. Reinhart, Reinhart, and Rogoff (2012) calculated the cumulative GDP losses as massive, typically lasting well over a decade, even when states were able to retain access to capital markets.

These empirical findings received substantial confirmation. In an influential BIS paper, based on eighteen Organization for Economic Cooperation and Development (OECD) states between 1980 and 2010, Cecchetti, Mohanty, and Zampolli (2011) identified a threshold of about 85 per cent of GDP, beyond which public debt was a drag on GDP. Similarly, an ECB staff paper looked at twelve euro area states over the period 1970–2008. It concluded that, beyond a threshold of about 90–100 per cent of GDP, public debt had, on average, a negative effect on long-term GDP growth (Checherita and Rother 2012). This finding was supported in a second ECB staff paper for the same euro area states, covering the period 1990–2010 (Baum, Checherita, and Rother 2013).

Using the 90 per cent benchmark, the euro area crossed the 'dangerous' trigger point by the third quarter of 2012. Greece and Italy stood out as particularly at risk from public-debt overhang because of its longevity in their cases. Greece's public-debt overhang began in 1993, Italy's in 1988. The record was held by Greece, which had been in a public-debt overhang for 56 per cent of the time since 1848 (Reinhart, Reinhart, and Rogoff 2012: 12). It had a public debt/GDP ratio of 170.6 per cent in 2011. In contrast, Finland (49.0 per cent), Luxembourg (20.9 per cent), Slovakia (43.3 per cent), and Slovenia (46.9 per cent) could achieve much higher rates of GDP growth. Strikingly, over the period since the early 1980s four euro area states had no episode of a public-debt overhang of five years or more: Austria, Finland, Germany, and (till 2010) Portugal (Reinhart, Reinhart, and Rogoff 2012: 11).

In 2011 the worrying cases outside the euro area were Hungary (81.4 per cent) and Britain (85.0 per cent). However, states like Bulgaria (16.3 per cent), the Czech Republic (40.8 per cent), Denmark (46.6 per cent), Estonia (6.1 per cent), and Sweden (38.4 per cent) faced much lower risks of negative effects on GDP growth. At the same time, some central and east European states had seen a sharp rise in public debt/GDP ratios between 2006 and 2011: in Latvia from 10.7 to 42.2 per cent, and in Romania from 12.4 to 33.4 per cent (for these figures see European Central Bank, Statistics, March 2013: 46). The United States was also at risk by 2011. The Congressional Budget Office (2010) suggested that its public debt/GDP ratio could grow rapidly to Greek proportions.

Despite its academic pedigree, supportive empirical evidence, and early influence in structuring debate, the notion of a 'one-size-fits-all' public debt/GDP target of 90 per cent was shown to be highly questionable. Chapter 7 details the historical counter-evidence and the weaknesses of causal argument. Looking just at the post-1945 period, the 90 per cent rule seemed a poor fit with empirical evidence. The 1950–1960 decades witnessed public debt over 90 per cent during a 'golden age' of GDP growth. High GDP growth helped to make that debt sustainable and to facilitate its reduction. Governing elites could also use financial repression and rely on domestic banks to absorb public debt. There was also ample scope to invest productively in post-war reconstruction, leading in turn to growing tax revenues to service debt (Stein 1885–1886). Moreover, from the 1980s rising public debt/GDP ratios went along with historically low debt servicing costs. From 1999, European monetary union opened up new debt financing possibilities that enabled low-cost servicing of high levels of public debt and reduced crowding-out effects. Governments, banks, and companies could much more readily raise capital outside the constraints of their domestic financial markets. However, the euro area sovereign debt crises and the subsequent fragmentation of financial markets showed the limits of risk-sharing in monetary union.

Furthermore, certain sovereign bonds—like US Treasuries and German Bunds—come to be viewed by investors as a store of value. The 'safe-haven' status of its bonds enables a state to enjoy a public-debt threshold higher than what is the average for other states. Acquiring this status is easier when a state lacks a history of serial default. Historical reputation alters what markets assess as sustainable debt.

The search for a public debt/GDP target overlooks the contingencies that stem from differences in economic structure and GDP growth potential; in the absorptive capacity of the banking system and sophistication of debt financing techniques; and in political will and state capacity to extract taxes and spend productively. Much depends on what public debt is used for (Stein 1885–1886). Public debt that feeds rent-seeking activity, including state patronage, clientelism, and corruption, is clearly highly detrimental to GDP growth. However, public debt has positive effects on long-term GDP growth when it finances bold structural reforms, improvements in infrastructure, and social investment, above all in human capital and social inclusion (Aizenman, Kletzer, and Pinto 2007; Vandenbroucke 2012). Political will requires governments that are ideologically inclined to implement structural reforms and to master fiscal deficits and public debt. It depends on a domestic logic of electoral and party competition that supports these preferences. Not least, debt sustainability is enhanced by a persuasive narrative that the public authorities are in control and prepared to take fundamental policy measures in a crisis.

State capacity building requires institutional arrangements that are able to mobilize the necessary resources for effective implementation of structural reforms and efficient delivery of infrastructure spending and social investment. Above all, states must avoid bureaucratic 'capture' by special interests. A notable feature of post-2007 crisis management was the privileging of the discourse of 'new public management'. It stressed performance indicators, new fiscal instruments, and tighter sub-national financial controls. The aim was to strengthen state productivity.

Public Debt Reduction

Persuasive narrative reasoning about debt sustainability could draw evidential support from the 'proven' political will and state capacity for reduction of public debt. However,

Table 14.1 The Development of Debt in Selected Euro Area States and Sizeable Government Debt Reduction, as Percentage of GDP

	Change in Debt Ratio, Peak to Trough
Belgium (1994–2007)	–50.2
Ireland (1994–2006)	–69.2
Spain (1997–2007)	–30.6
Netherlands (1994–2007)	–32.9
Finland (1995–2008)	–24.4

(*Source*: European Central Bank, 'Experience with Government Debt Reduction in euro area Countries', *Monthly Bulletin*, September 2009: 87)

the nature of this evidence was contestable. Table 14.1 illustrates how, over a period of a decade and more, five out of twelve euro area states were able to achieve significant reductions—Belgium, Ireland, Spain, the Netherlands, and Finland. The decline of the Irish public debt/GDP ratio by 69.2 per cent between 1994 and 2006 was most striking. In contrast, French and German public debt/GDP ratios rose over this period.

Two features of this public debt reduction process were notable (European Central Bank 2009b: 86–9). The first had little to do with political will and state capacity. After European monetary union, at least four of the five states gained from a substantial reduction in the real interest rate. Monetary policy acted as a spur to GDP growth and helped flatter the public debt/GDP ratio. The second feature had more to do with political will and state capacity. Belgium, Finland, and Ireland—and, to a lesser extent, the Netherlands and Spain—ran primary fiscal surpluses.

However, the post-2007 financial and economic crises exposed the extent to which the Irish and Spanish primary fiscal surpluses and public debt reductions had been based on the fiscal illusion of asset-price bubbles in property and construction. They did not reflect political will and state capacity to pursue fiscal prudence, extract taxes, and invest productively. The post-2007 public debt reductions proved to be much more substantial challenges to Irish and Spanish political will and state capacity. These challenges had to be met in the much tougher conditions of 'hard' times in the European political economy.

Fiscal Deficits and Debt Dynamics

From the 1980s the most influential numeric risk indicator in European narrative reasoning about debt sustainability was fiscal deficit in relation to GDP. In a given year, the public debt is equal to the sum of the debt inherited from the previous year and of the budget deficit in the current year. Hence persistently high budget deficits lead, over a period of time, to accumulating public debt. They spread alarm amongst investors unless there is substantial offsetting GDP growth. The Maastricht Treaty of 1993 enshrined the 3 per cent fiscal deficit/GDP rule as the basis for debt sustainability.

The relationship of fiscal deficits to public debt is complicated by so-called deficit-debt adjustments (DDAs). Annual increases in public debt/GDP ratios may prove higher or lower than can be explained solely by fiscal deficit figures (European Central Bank 2007: 87–9). These changes reflect financial investments of governments and accounting practices and rules. Over the period 1999–2006 significant debt-increasing DDAs were apparent in Finland (an average of 4.5 per cent per annum), as well as in Greece and Luxembourg (both an average of 3 per cent). Germany had a moderately debt-reducing DDA, whilst the DDA in Italy averaged zero. In Finland, Luxembourg, Austria, and Spain the debt-increasing DDAs were explained by increases in the assets of social security funds to pay for future pensions. Also, the European Commission's statistical office, Eurostat, influenced DDAs through its decisions on accounting of financial transactions, like injections of equity into public enterprises, recording of social security accounts, and military expenditures (Savage 2005). Hence both regulatory and policy decisions affect the relationship between fiscal deficits and public debt.

Despite these qualifications, fiscal deficit–public debt dynamics remain a central risk indicator in public debate. Tables 14.2 and 14.3 provide an overview of EU and euro area fiscal deficits and surpluses and set them in a wider international context. Using the Maastricht benchmarks of fiscal deficit and public debt, respectively 3 per cent and 60 per cent of GDP, fiscal sainthood and sinning appear highly contingent. Germany was a fiscal sinner between 2001 and 2004. However, from 2005 it regained its image as fiscal saint. Germany reaped fiscal gains from export-led growth after long years of unit labour cost containment, wage moderation, and corporate restructuring. Its fiscal balance also benefitted from new forms of flexible employment through labour-market and welfare-state reforms and from restructured taxation to yield increased revenues.

Conversely, Britain, Ireland, and Spain—and Iceland outside the EU—shifted from being saints on fiscal deficits to double-digit deficits by 2009. Greece remained an unrepentant fiscal deficit sinner, along with Hungary. The principal fiscal deficit saints were two EU 'outsiders': Norway and Switzerland. Up to 2007 they included Austria, Belgium, Finland, Ireland, Luxembourg, the Netherlands, and Spain within the euro area. With

Table 14.2 IMF Statistics on General Government Deficits/Surpluses, Selected States, as Percentage of GDP, 2002–2009

	2002	2006	2009
Advanced Economies	−3.3	−1.4	−8.7
United States	−3.9	−2.0	−12.5
Euro Area	−2.5	−1.3	−6.3
Japan	−8.1	−4.0	−10.3
Canada	−0.1	1.6	−2.8
Hong Kong SAR	−4.8	4.3	0.8
Iceland	−2.5	6.3	−12.4
Norway	9.2	18.5	9.7
Switzerland	−1.1	1.4	1.4

(*Source*: International Monetary Fund 2010b: Table B6)

Table 14.3 General Government Deficits/Surpluses in EU, as Percentage of GDP, 2002–2012

	Share (% in 2012)	2002	2006	2009	2012
Euro Area	–3.7	–2.6	–1.3	–6.4	–3.7
EU	–4.0	–2.3	–1.4	–6.9	–4.0
Euro Area					
Austria	–0.1	–0.5	–1.5	–4.1	–2.5
Belgium	–0.2	0.0	0.3	–5.6	–3.9
Cyprus	0.0	...	–1.2	–6.1	–6.3
Estonia	0.0	1.0	2.5	–2.2	–0.3
Finland	0.0	4.1	4.0	–2.5	–1.9
France	–1.0	–3.2	–2.3	–7.5	–4.8
Germany	0.0	–3.7	–1.6	–3.1	0.2
Greece	–0.2	–4.9	–3.6	–15.6	–10.0
Ireland	–0.1	–0.4	3.0	–13.9	–7.6
Italy	–0.5	–2.9	–3.3	–5.5	–3.0
Luxembourg	0.0	2.0	1.4	–0.8	–0.8
Malta	0.0	...	–2.6	–3.7	–3.3
Netherlands	–0.3	–2.0	0.5	–5.6	–4.1
Portugal	–0.1	–2.9	–3.9	–10.2	–6.4
Slovakia	0.0	...	–3.5	–7.7	–4.3
Slovenia	0.0	...	–1.3	–5.9	–4.0
Spain	–1.2	–0.3	2.0	–11.2	–10.6
EU Outside Euro Area					
Bulgaria	0.0	...	3.0	–4.3	–0.8
Czech Republic	–6.8	–2.6	–5.8	–4.4	–0.1
Denmark	–0.1	1.2	5.2	–2.7	–4.0
Hungary	0.0	–8.4	–9.3	–4.6	–1.9
Latvia	–1.2	0.0	–2.3	–0.5	–9.8
Lithuania	0.0	–1.4	–0.4	–9.4	–3.2
Poland	–0.1	–3.2	–3.6	–7.4	–3.9
Romania	0.0	...	–2.2	–9.0	–2.9
Sweden	0.0	–0.2	2.5	–0.7	–0.5
United Kingdom	–0.9	–1.6	–2.7	–11.5	–6.3

(*Source*: European Central Bank, *Statistics*, June 2013: 45, with added 2002 figures from same publication, May 2006: 43)

the exception of Spain, they were all small states, characterized by high external exposure. Amongst EU Member States outside the euro area the fiscal deficit saints were Britain, Estonia, Latvia, Lithuania, and Sweden. However, the post-2007 crisis was to cast a range of previously model states into the category of sinners, headed by Britain, Ireland, Latvia, and Spain. Structural dependency on economic sectors that were vulnerable to asset-price inflation was a significant factor in this fiscal reversal.

At the same time, there was a measure of continuity on the indicator of fiscal deficit sainthood and sinning. Looked at over a longer time scale, France had been in permanent fiscal deficit since 1974. There were periods of improvement in 1976–1980, 1994–2000, and 2004–2006. However, they were followed by regression. The outcome was that overall, from a comparatively low base (compared to Germany) of some 20 per cent in 1980, the French public debt/GDP ratio continued to climb without interruption. France had fiscal deficits of 3 per cent of GDP and over for more than half the years between 1990 and 2010 (Champsaur and Cotis 2010: 2). For the shorter period covered in Table 14.3, Greece remained the most unrepentant fiscal deficit sinner, followed by Hungary.

However, from the revision of the Stability and Growth Pact (SGP) in 2005 to the so-called fiscal compact treaty of 2012, the EU shifted away from simple belief in a 'one-size-fits-all' 3 per cent fiscal deficit rule. This shift had two components. It involved a new emphasis on structural fiscal balance over the economic cycle and on commitment to a public-debt reduction target when Member States exceeded the 60 per cent public debt/GDP ratio. Moving towards structural fiscal balance became the central tenet of euro area policies, giving them a less flexible character. For states like Italy it implied large structural surpluses for a decade and more. At the same time, the European Commission showed greater flexibility about the 3 per cent fiscal deficit rule, giving more attention to creating scope for structural reforms that enhanced long-term debt sustainability. Narrative reasoning about fiscal deficits became more differentiated.

Also, from 2006 the European Commission began a regular assessment of the sustainability of public finances in EU Member States covering the period till 2060. It developed a wide range of indicators which were designed to capture short-term fiscal stress risks, medium-term debt compliance risks, and long-term ageing-induced fiscal risks. The key measure was the so-called sustainability gap indicator. It identified the requited adjustment in the structural primary balance to: (1) stabilize the debt ratio given the initial budgetary position and (2) address long-term changes in the primary balance due to ageing. A component of qualitative assessment was added to capture additional sources of fiscal pressure.

The result was an overall sustainability risk assessment, grouping Member States into three categories (European Commission 2012). In 2012 the Member States at high risk comprised Belgium, Cyprus, Luxembourg, Slovenia, and Slovakia. The category at medium risk included Austria, Denmark, Finland, and the Netherlands, as well as Britain, Romania, Spain, and others. Strikingly, Hungary and Italy were at low risk, alongside such Member States as France, Germany, and Sweden. Cyprus and Slovenia had been at high risk in 2006 and 2009; Belgium and Luxembourg graduated from medium risk to high risk in 2012; whilst France and Italy dropped from medium risk to low risk in 2012. The Commission sustainability reports highlighted the often huge scale of the adjustment in structural primary balances needed to address projected increases in age-related expenditures on pensions, health, and social care and ensure debt sustainability. They also subverted the picture of 'saints' and 'sinners' based on conventional fiscal deficit/GDP ratio. Austria, Britain, Denmark, and Finland were in the same category of risk as Bulgaria and Romania.

Public Expenditure and Taxation Reform Capacity

The public expenditure/GDP ratio served as an influential numeric risk indicator in narrative reasoning about debt sustainability (Table 14.4). Its influence was based on

Table 14.4 Total General Government Expenditure, Percentages of GDP, 1960–2012

	1960	1980	1998	2004	2008	2012
Euro Area	30.4	45.0	49.0	47.7	46.9	50.0
Belgium	33.2	56.1	51.2	50.2	50.0	54.8
Germany	31.8	47.1	48.7	47.5	43.7	45.0
Greece	20.6	29.0	49.5	49.9	46.8	54.8
Spain	20.3	31.5	41.0	39.0	41.1	47.0
France	33.4	45.7	53.5	54.0	52.8	56.6
Ireland	26.0	46.1	34.8	34.2	42.0	42.1
Italy	28.1	43.0	49.6	48.6	48.8	50.6
Luxembourg	25.4	48.4	42.1	45.6	37.2	43.0
Netherlands	29.3	53.3	46.0	47.1	45.9	50.4
Austria	34.1	46.8	53.9	50.4	49.0	51.2
Portugal	14.7	34.8	42.3	46.5	46.1	47.4
Finland	26.3	39.1	52.8	51.5	49.5	56.0
United Kingdom	36.1	43.2	40.0	44.1	47.3	48.5
Japan	16.6	31.5	42.5	38.6		
United States	28.2	33.8	33.0	34.3		

(*Source*: European Central Bank 2006: 62; European Central Bank, *Statistics*, July 2013: 47)

the argument that, where the long-term trend was rising, and increasing tax capacity was problematic, there was a risk that fiscal deficits would escape control. Hence public expenditure and tax reforms were identified as indicators of the political will and state capacity to ensure long-term debt sustainability. The European Central Bank (2006) identified a virtuous circle of public expenditure reform, higher GDP growth, and improved debt sustainability.

However, numeric indicators of public expenditure and tax reforms provide only a partial picture. Governing elites face tough, contentious, and context-specific choices about the balance between public expenditure and tax reforms. In the case of Finland, for instance, a sharp rise in public expenditure did not inexorably lead to higher fiscal deficits and public debt. Greece and Portugal tell a different story in which high growth in public expenditure, from a very low base (as in Finland), leads to negative deficit-debt dynamics. Two factors helped explain this difference: tax capacity and the content and quality of public expenditure. Greece and Portugal had unbalanced fiscal structures. They spent far more than the Nordic states on consumption relative to taxes and, where they spent on infrastructure, were more likely to embrace political 'vanity' projects. High infrastructure and social investment expenditure meant that Nordic states balanced their liabilities with asset accumulation in areas like higher education, vocational training, and research and development.

Tax reform became a key indicator of state capacity both to secure structural fiscal balance and to mimic a nominal devaluation of the exchange rate by increasing taxes on imports and reducing them on exports. The ECB advocated a combination of fiscal devaluation with structural reform by a shift in tax burden from payroll and corporate income taxes to value-added tax (VAT) or sales tax and property taxes. However, tax reform that shifted the burden from production costs to consumption ran into political barriers. Governing elites feared the electoral implications of challenging economic cultures that were dedicated to conspicuous consumption. They also feared ideological opposition to less progressive forms of taxation as incompatible with economic cultures that prioritized social solidarity. Nevertheless, European monetary union, allied to sovereign debt crises, created a strong systemic pressure for this kind of politically difficult tax reform.

Some EU Member States demonstrated evidence of political will and capacity to reverse the trend of long-term growth in public expenditure/GDP ratio. In the 1980s Belgium, Ireland, Luxembourg, and the Netherlands were the leading public expenditure reformers (European Central Bank 2006). In Ireland the main phase of expenditure reform began in 1987, with substantial reductions in transfers and subsidies and in civil service employment, as well as wage restraint. In the 1990s Ireland and the Netherlands continued to excel as major public expenditure reformers, along with Austria, Finland, and Spain. A major catalyst for these reforms was political priority to meeting the entry criteria for European monetary union in 1999, including compliance with the requirements of the SGP. The key public expenditure reformers were Austria, Belgium, Finland, Ireland, and the Netherlands. Finland and Spain strengthened budgetary control mechanisms. Austria, Belgium, and the Netherlands introduced tougher fiscal rules. Dutch governments agreed ambitious coalition fiscal contracts and shifted to multi-annual budgeting. Belgium established independent monitoring through a fiscal council. Ireland delegated fiscal powers to its finance ministry. Public expenditure reforms were more modest in France, Germany, Greece, Italy, and Portugal.

The post-2010 sovereign debt crisis acted as a further spur to public expenditure reforms. In particular, EU Member States established new independent domestic fiscal councils to strengthen accountability and transparency, to sharpen policy debate about debt sustainability, and to make more transparent the choices in fiscal policy strategy and their implications for GDP growth. Once again Ireland was at the forefront in deep-seated public expenditure reforms.

Generational Accountancy

An official consensus emerged that the costs of population ageing were a key long-term risk indicator in public finances, requiring additional and substantial adjustments to primary fiscal balances that politicians were reluctant to embrace. The associated costs rose as electoral competition led to political promises in pensions, health, and social care whose outcome was accumulating unfunded liabilities. The scenario was one of increasing demands in these three policy sectors (Table 14.5). They represented implicit liabilities and suggested a continuing upward momentum in public expenditure. This momentum derived from longer life-expectancy, the rising costs of new medical treatments, and the demise of the extended family as a support structure for ageing parents and grandparents. Diminishing labour-force participation added to the fiscal problems because of falls in contributions.

Attempts at generational accountancy in order to estimate sustainability risk are fraught with difficulties, above all the plausibility of the assumptions on which they are based. Though they generate different results, they agree in putting almost all EU

Table 14.5 Projected Changes in Selected Age-Related Expenditure-to-GDP Ratios between 2004 and 2050

	Pensions	Health	Long-Term Care	Total
Euro Area	2.6	1.5	0.5	4.6
Belgium	5.1	1.4	1.0	7.5
Germany	1.7	1.2	1.0	3.9
Greece	na	1.7	na	na
Spain	7.1	2.2	0.2	9.5
France	2.0	1.8	na	na
Ireland	6.4	2.0	0.6	9.0
Italy	0.4	1.3	0.7	2.4
Luxembourg	7.4	1.2	0.6	9.2
Netherlands	3.5	1.3	0.6	5.4
Austria	-1.2	1,6	0.0	0.4
Portugal	9.7	0.5	na	na
Finland	3.1	1.4	1.8	6.3

Note: Na = not available.
(*Source*: European Central Bank 2006: 64, from Economic Policy Committee, Ageing Working Group, January 2006)

Member States at risk. The European Commission (2012: 33) identified the fiscal challenges as greatest in Belgium, Cyprus, Luxembourg, Malta, Slovakia, and Slovenia. In contrast, the fiscal challenges were less in Britain, Denmark, France, Greece, Hungary, Italy, and Portugal. Conversely, the Forschungszentrum Generationsverträge at Freiburg University identified the sustainability gap as widest—in rank order—for Ireland, Luxembourg, Greece, Spain, Cyprus, Slovenia, Belgium, Britain, the Netherlands, and Slovakia. It was narrowest—again in rank order—for Italy, Latvia, Estonia, Poland, Germany, Bulgaria, Sweden, Portugal, Hungary, and Romania (Moog and Raffelhüschen 2013). Despite their differences, these estimates suggested that some creditor states—like Luxembourg and the Netherlands—faced acute adjustment pressures, whilst some debtor states—notably Italy—were less vulnerable. Ultimately, much depended on how birth rates, death rates, immigration levels, and economic growth and employment rates evolved over time. Generational accountancy was also bound up in the complex cumulative effects of changes to family, childcare, and tax policies, to labour-market participation, and to eligibility criteria for benefits. Constructing and using risk indicators was deeply problematic in a context beset by such uncertainty.

Structural Fiscal Balances

Conventional fiscal deficit figures suffer from the limitation that they do not allow for the effects of cyclical changes in revenues and expenditures. For this reason, the concept of structural fiscal balances gained support, not least within the reformed SGP and in

Table 14.6 General Government Structural Balances, Selected States, as Percentage of Potential GDP, 2002–2009

	2002	2006	2009
Advanced Economies	–2.9	–1.9	–5.8
United States	–2.8	–2.5	–7.9
Canada	–0.5	1.2	–2.0
Japan	–7.0	–3.9	–7.4
Norway	–2.6	–3.6	–6.8
Euro Area	–2.8	–2.0	–4.3
Germany	–2.8	–1.4	–1.1
France	–3.5	–2.6	–4.9
Italy	–4.2	–3.3	–3.9
Spain	–1.1	–1.3	–8.4
Netherlands	–2.2	0.3	–4.5
Belgium	–0.3	–0.8	–4.8
Greece	–4.0	–3.9	–13.1
Austria	–0.8	–2.4	–3.0
Portugal	–5.1	–4.0	–7.8
Finland	3.9	2.5	–0.1
Ireland	–5.0	–6.2	–10.0
Slovakia	–8.2	–3.8	–4.9
Slovenia	–1.0	–1.9	–4.9
Cyprus	–5.1	–1.3	–5.5
Malta	...	–3.4	–3.1
EU: Rest of EU outside Euro Area			
Denmark	...	...	0.0
Sweden	–1.3	0.8	–0.6
United Kingdom	–1.9	–2.7	–7.8

(*Source*: International Monetary Fund 2010b: Table B7)

the fiscal compact treaty. It promised a superior indicator both of the underlying risks to sustainable public finances and of the scale of the fiscal adjustments that were required to meet the Maastricht excessive deficit criteria (European Commission 2009). On this measure, compared with a euro area average fiscal adjustment of 4.3 per cent in 2009, Greece faced an adjustment of 13.1 per cent; Ireland, 10.0 per cent; and Spain, 8.4 per cent. Structural fiscal balance was much healthier in Italy, as well as in Germany and Finland. Outside the euro area, Denmark and Sweden were best performers on the indicator. Britain performed badly (see Table 14.6).

Gross Financing Requirement, Sovereign Bond Yield, and Public Debt Maturity Profile

The euro area sovereign debt crises gave added salience to three related risk indicators: gross financing requirement, sovereign bond yield, and public debt maturity

Table 14.7 Gross Financing Requirements, Gross Public Debt, and Average Public Debt Maturity, 2010, as Percentage of GDP

	Gross Financing Requirement, 2012	Gross Debt, 2011	Average Maturity (Years)
United States	30.4	100.0	4.4
Japan	58.6	233.1	5.2
Canada	18.6	84.1	5.6
Norway	–1.0	55.4	
Euro Area			
Belgium	22.2	94.6	5.4
France	20.8	86.9	6.5
Germany	10.5	82.6	6.0
Greece	16.5	165.6	7.4
Ireland	13.9	109.3	6.7
Italy	23.5	121.1	6.7
Portugal	22.3	106.0	6.2
Spain	20.6	67.4	6.7
EU outside Euro Area			
Sweden	3.6	36.0	6.0
United Kingdom	14.7	80.8	12.8

(*Source*: International Monetary Fund 2010c: 21 for average maturity; International Monetary Fund 2011b: 8 for gross debt and gross financing requirement)

profile. The International Monetary Fund (2011b: 8) sought to capture the interaction between fiscal deficits and public debt in its concept of gross financing requirement (see Table 14.7). Gross financing requirement is defined as the new overall borrowing requirement (fiscal deficit), plus gross government debt maturing during the year.

On the gross-financing-requirement indicator, applied to 2012, Japan appeared an alarming case, followed by the United States. Within the EU, the 'most-at-risk' states were (in descending order) Italy, Portugal, Belgium, France, Spain, and Britain. Their gross financing requirements stood at, or above, 20 per cent of GDP. In contrast, Austria, Finland, Germany, Slovenia, Sweden and, above all, Norway had low gross financing requirements. EU Member States in central and eastern Europe had limited problems because of their relatively low levels of maturing debt. Hungary was an exception because by 2009 its gross debt level had climbed to 78.3 per cent. Latvia and Lithuania were also experiencing significant increases in gross financing requirements.

As Japan showed, gross financing requirement does not translate neatly into a sovereign debt crisis. Investors take account of the liquidity and resilience of domestic financial markets, the capacity of domestic banks, pension funds, and insurance companies to absorb public debt, and the public debt maturity profile. These factors helped Japan to retain its sovereign creditworthiness. Conversely, by late 2011 investors became alarmed about the gross financing requirements of Italy and Spain.

The market-based risk indicator of sovereign bond yield needs to be seen in the context of the gross financing requirement. By 2011 financial markets had begun to regard euro area 7 per cent sovereign bond yields as a threshold beyond which public debt was becoming unsustainable in the absence of radical action. However, whilst painful, yields above 7 per cent were sustainable—at least for a period—as long as the impact on the average interest rate on the outstanding debt remained low. In the mid-1990s German yields had been over 7 per cent; those of Ireland, Spain, and Portugal some 12 per cent; whilst Greece had yields of around 20 per cent. Despite these elevated yields, investors regarded their debt as sustainable. Nevertheless, the danger remained that panic might ensue if financial markets mispriced sovereign risk by not contextualizing the sovereign bond yield indicator.

The gross financing requirement is intimately related to the public debt maturity profile. The amount of public debt maturing within one to two years is taken as an indicator because of vulnerability to financial market tensions as well as to variable interest rates. At the end of March 2010, 32.8 per cent of total euro area government debt securities was two years or under, compared to 48.8 per cent between two and ten years (European Central Bank 2010b: 32). In contrast, on the indicator of average maturity of public debt, Britain scored notably highly at 12.8 years (see Table 14.7). This maturity profile could be explained by the size of its financial system, including the role and investment preferences of the large pension and insurance companies located in Britain. BIS (2010b: 68) figures for May 2010 showed average French, Italian, and Spanish public debt maturity at about nine years, compared to some six to seven years in Greece and Ireland. Medium- and long-term public debt maturities accounted for 96 per cent of German debt and 86 per cent of French debt. However, the US case was different. Its average debt maturity was a mere 4.4 years (the lowest in Table 14.7), and the share of medium- and long-term debt only 59 per cent (in 2008).

Two factors play a role in shortening public debt maturity profile. First, as in the United States, domestic public debt management strategies may prioritize the reduction of interest costs. Secondly, financial market crisis creates additional incentives to shorten the terms of bond issues. This incentive increases where there is a flight to certain bonds as a 'safe haven', and thus strong demand for them, and where difficulties are anticipated in placing long-term bonds. Thus, as the sovereign debt crisis intensified, the percentage share of short-term government debt securities (up to twelve months) in euro area GDP rose from just over 10 per cent in 2008 towards 20 per cent in early 2010 (European Central Bank 2010b: 31–2).

States become vulnerable once average maturities start to fall to one to two years (Bank for International Settlements 2010b: 67). The average life of Italian government debt in December 1982 had fallen to a mere 1.13 years, climbing to 3.88 in December 1986. By the start of monetary union it had risen to 5.64 years (December 1999) (Dipartimento del Tesoro 2010). Spain and Portugal followed a similar pattern. Average maturity of Spanish central government debt was 2.05 years in 1990. By 2000 it was 5.63 years, climbing to 6.84 years in 2007 (Tesoro Publico 2010). This strengthening of public debt maturity profile did not survive the euro area sovereign debt crises.

Sovereign CDS Market Spreads

Market-implied indicators of sovereign creditworthiness played a new but controversial role in narrative reasoning about public debt. Credit default swap (CDS) markets are forms of insurance against sovereign default and hence serve as indicators of sovereign debt risk. However, the IMF noted that CDS market data needs to be treated with caution (on which Singh and Youssef 2010). Their value as indicators of medium-term sovereign creditworthiness is diminished because they reflect position-taking by market players as they hedge against various risks. Spreads are affected by factors like the leverage inherent in CDS trading, liquidity conditions, counterparty risk, and the overall risk aversion of market participants. They tend to overstate default risk and to prove highly volatile. Nevertheless, this kind of market-based sovereign debt risk data is influential in branding states. In crisis conditions it may assume a price leadership role. During the European sovereign debt crises the notion gained ground that the 'tipping point' in sovereign CDS market spreads was 200 basis points with reference to the key market reference, Germany. Beyond that point, it was argued that bond and equity prices moved downwards together in a negative spiral.

Table 14.8 offers snapshots of sovereign credit risks as assessed by CDS market participants in 2010 and 2012. It can be used to compile a top-ten list of fiscal 'saints' and 'sinners'. Once again, the 'saints' were geographically concentrated in northern and western Europe, especially the Nordic region, which functioned as a safe haven. Denmark, Finland, Norway, and Sweden all featured in the world top ten, along with Switzerland. Belgium and France were just outside the top ten in 2010, but by 2012 Belgium was ranked thirty-first and France thirty-fourth, both just below Bulgaria. In east central Europe, the Czech Republic and Estonia were top performers.

The 'sinners' were above all in southern Europe. Greece was in a category of its own amongst euro area Member States, followed by Cyprus, Portugal, and Spain, each of which figured in the top ten in 2012, with Italy in eleventh position. In 2010 the highest risk in east central Europe attached to Lithuania and Romania, followed by Bulgaria and Hungary. By 2012 Latvia and Lithuania had strengthened their position. One of the biggest improvers was Britain. In 2010 it was only twenty-first amongst the safest sovereign debtors, measured by cumulative probability of default (CPD). It counted as more risky than Austria (thirteenth), Slovenia (fifteenth), Slovakia (sixteenth), China (seventeenth), Japan (eighteenth), and the Czech Republic (nineteenth). By 2012 it was in the top-ten saints in sixth position, just ahead of Germany.

These figures are a snapshot. They do not capture the precariousness that attaches to sainthood and sinning. States shift their rankings as markets respond to 'bad' and 'good' news. Thus Belgium (fourteenth in 2010) and France (twelfth) had been in the top-ten 'saints' during the previous quarter. They were replaced by Sweden and Hong Kong. Lithuania and Romania had been in the top-ten 'sinners' during the previous quarter, but had moved to fourteenth and fifteenth positions respectively with CPDs of 15.0 per cent and 13.3 per cent. Hungary was eighteenth in 2010 with a CPD of 12.2 per cent. Greece was in a different situation from all other euro area Member States, with Portugal showing the fastest deterioration globally. They compared unfavourably with Estonia, which in 2010 showed the greatest improvement globally to 91.4 CDS.

Over 2010 other key EU states suffered falls, indicative of the contagious nature of the sovereign debt crisis in the euro area. Germany dropped from fourth to ninth position; Austria to thirty-fifth; and France to thirty-eighth, just ahead of Turkey, Poland, and Russia. Ominously, Italy stood at twelfth in the 'sinner' list, followed by Belgium at sixteenth, both serious deteriorations. Conversely, Switzerland remained a clear 'saint'. Within the list of 'saints', in central and east Europe the Czech Republic (sixteenth),

Table 14.8 World's Saints and Sinners, Credit Default Swap Spreads, 2010 and 2012

The Saints: The World's Safest Sovereign Debt

2010			2012		
Rank	State	5-Year CPD (%)	Rank	State	5-Year CPD
1	Norway	2.1	1	Sweden	1.64
2	Finland	3.0	2	Norway	1.72
3	Sweden	3.0	3	Finland	2.64
4	Switzerland	3.6	4	Denmark	2.94
5	United States	3.6	5	United States	3.30
6	Hong Kong	3.9	6	UK	3.66
7	Denmark	4.0	7	Germany	3.66
8	Australia	4.4	8	Switzerland	3.77
9	Germany	5.2	9	Austria	3.96
10	Saudi Arabia	5.2	10	Netherlands	4.04

The Sinners: The World's Riskiest Sovereign Debt

2010			2012		
Rank	State	5-Year CPD (%)	Rank	State	5-Year CPD
1	Greece	58.0	1	Argentina	61.4
2	Venezuela	51.4	2	Cyprus	60.5
3	Ireland	41.2	3	Pakistan	42.8
4	Portugal	35.9	4	Venezuela	37.4
5	Argentina	35.4	5	Ukraine	36.3
6	Ukraine	30.6	6	Portugal	32.6
7	Spain	26.7	7	Egypt	30.4
8	Dubai	25.5	8	Iraq	28.1
9	Hungary	23.6	9	Lebanon	27.5
10	Iraq	23.1	10	Spain	23.5

Note: The data are provided by swap market participants. CPD refers to cumulative probability of default. Greece was excluded from the 2012 ranking.

(*Source*: Credit Market Analysis, 'Global Sovereign Credit Risk Report', fourth quarter 2010 and fourth quarter 2012)

Estonia (twenty-first), Slovenia (twenty-second), and Slovakia (twenty-third) were top performers, and Latvia had significantly improved its position. The highest risk in this region attached to Hungary, followed by Romania, Latvia, and Lithuania. The chief 'sinners' were in southern Europe. Over 2010 Britain improved its position slightly from twenty-first to nineteenth in the ranking of safest sovereign debt. It counted as slightly more risky than the Czech Republic.

Overall, data for the final quarter of 2010 indicated that the sovereign debt crisis was spreading from the periphery to the core of the euro area. EU states accounted for five out of the ten 'worst sinners' in the global league table, three of which rated worse than Argentina and the Ukraine. Conversely, they had four states in the top-ten 'saints', three of which were Nordic and topped the list. However, Germany, France, Belgium, and the Netherlands fell in the rankings during 2010, the Netherlands from sixth to twelfth position in the list of 'saints'.

Sovereign CDS market data need to be treated with caution. States can shift position quite rapidly as markets respond to 'bad' or 'good' news. The CDS market proves a relatively poor indicator of longer-term sovereign risk because it is driven by changes in the mark-to-market value of the position over a relatively short-time frame. Nevertheless, despite an uneven predictive performance, this kind of sovereign debt risk data provided a new and potentially influential indicator in branding states.

Externally-Held Public Debt

Prima facie, issuing public debt in another currency exposes a state to risk, raises questions about its threshold of sustainable debt, and helps shape how governing elites construct narratives about public debt. Externally-held public debt can be assessed as an indicator of sovereign risk in two forms: data on marketable public debt, held by non-residents, as a percentage of total marketable debt and as a percentage of GDP. The higher these percentages, the more important it is for a state to manage public finances with reference to global financial market confidence. A debt management strategy that seeks to increase non-resident ownership of public debt is typically based on one or more objectives. It aims to diversify away from dependence on narrow, illiquid domestic bond markets; to lower public debt interest rates; and to impose an external market discipline on domestic fiscal politics and policies.

European monetary union acted as a major catalyst for closer financial market integration. The promise of high rates of return from enhanced GDP growth in the euro area periphery states, along with the greater protection offered by elimination of currency risk, endowed these sovereigns with 'safe' status. Hence banks that were headquartered in euro area creditor states increased their exposures to the sovereign debt of other member states, relative to their Tier 1 capital. The post-2009 sovereign debt crises altered this dynamic. Fearing euro area exits and introductions of capital controls, and facing regulatory pressures to match their local lending much more closely to their local deposits, Dutch, French, and German banks radically reduced their exposures to Greece, Ireland, Italy, Portugal, and Spain.

Traditionally, and again from 2010–2011 onwards, European banks had been most exposed to their own domestic sovereign bonds. For this reason, Belgian, Greek, Italian, Spanish, and Portuguese banks were at highest risk from their domestic bond holdings (European Banking Authority 2011: 14; International Monetary Fund 2011b: 21–3). However, by December 2009 the exposure of Belgian, Cypriot, French, and German banks to sovereign debt in the euro area periphery states had climbed to some 20 per cent of their Tier 1 capital (European Banking Authority 2011: 14). They faced major losses, initially on Greek bonds, sharp falls in their share prices, and consequent urgent needs for recapitalization, potentially at cost to public finances. Similar risks faced large insurance companies in France and Italy (International Monetary Fund 2011b: 22–3).

Canadian public debt offered a striking contrast to developments within the EU in the years before 2007. The percentage of non-resident debt in total marketable debt fell from just under 30 per cent in 1992 to below 20 per cent in 2000 and continued to decline to under 15 per cent in 2007. It accompanied a fall in Canadian total central government debt to GDP from over 55 per cent in 1995 to 25 per cent in 2006–2007. The United States provided a very different picture. US marketable public debt held by non-residents climbed from just over 30 per cent of total marketable debt in 1999 to over 50 per cent in 2005–2007 (<www.FT.com>, accessed in 2011).

Within the euro area, despite considerable variations, there was a marked tendency for the percentage of non-resident debt to increase between 1999 and 2007, reaching some 53 per cent of total government debt. This rise was in substantial part driven by the effects of monetary union in integrating euro area financial markets so that much non-resident debt was accounted for by other euro area states. Non-resident Spanish public debt was held chiefly by central banks (34.5 per cent), household and non-financial companies (26.88 per cent), and mutual and pension funds (16.34 per cent). French investors topped the list (2009 figures in Tesoro Público 2010). The steepest climbs in non-resident share in marketable public debt were in Greece (from close to 20 per cent in 1998 to nearly 40 per cent in 2007) and in Italy (from about 20 per cent in 1998–2004, rising to nearly 40 per cent in 2007). In France the share was below 30 per cent in the mid-1980s, then rose to just over 58 per cent in 2007, climbing to some 65 per cent in 2009 (L'Agence France Trésor 2010; Champsaur and Cotis 2010, Annex 3: 13).

More typically, as in Britain, Ireland, and Portugal, the rise in non-resident share of marketable public debt was from about 20 per cent to just over 35 per cent between 1999 and 2007. In Germany it increased from some 20 per cent in 1999–2003 to over 35 per cent in 2007 (German Federal Finance Ministry 2010: 124). This marked increase in external dependence, especially between 2004 and 2007, was followed by decline from 2007 onwards. In Britain, Germany, Greece, and Ireland, for instance, non-resident public debt fell to below 30 per cent in 2009.

By 2011, the percentage of sovereign debt held abroad, relative to GDP, climbed over 50 per cent in seven euro area states: Greece (91.3 per cent), Ireland (60.8 per cent), Belgium (58.2 per cent), Austria (55.5 per cent), Portugal (53.3 per cent), Italy (51.4 per cent), and France (50.3 per cent). In contrast, this percentage was only 12.6 per cent in Sweden, 18.7 per cent in Britain, and 23.9 per cent in Norway (International Monetary Fund 2011: 8). There were, in short, major differences in external vulnerability and in challenges to political will and state capacity.

Illusion, Hubris, and Hypocrisy: Telling Truth to Power?

The maxim 'telling truth to power' raises difficult questions about which truth and whose truth. It poses issues about the indicators being used, including environmental, social, and governance as well as fiscal indicators; how to weigh different observations; and, even if using just numeric financial indicators, what constitutes the preponderance of evidence. Reliance on individual numeric indicators is problematic because of their vulnerability to data errors, to extrapolation from past experience, and to misappropriation for partisan uses and commercial gain. 'Whose truth' is determined by the source of probabilistic reasoning about the sustainability of public debt. It is a matter of who controls narrative reasoning about the nature of the problem of mismatch between liability and control. The truth is different for environmental activists, anti-poverty campaigners, political reformers, and investors.

In constructing narrative reasoning, governing elites have an interest in selecting and synthesizing a set of financial and non-financial indicators that offers a preponderance of favourable evidence about sovereign creditworthiness. This narrative seeks to draw out the idiosyncratic qualities of their states and to reconcile investor confidence with domestic political legitimacy. However, the structural power of financial markets privileges discourse that centres on numeric indicators and probabilistic reasoning. To complicate matters for governing elites, some indicators—like widening yield spreads, rising credit default swap rates, and growth in debt servicing costs—are endogenous to crisis. They gain significance only once crisis has begun and as general perception of the probability of default evolves (Parra 2009). Bond-market sentiment becomes a powerful contagious factor as crisis gathers momentum. This sentiment enhances the power of the investment banks that act as Primary Dealers in sovereign bond markets, as well as the power of the clearing houses. As market makers, Primary Dealers have a uniquely privileged relationship with states. They act as central players in the confidence game with investors and as potentially active stewards of states. The underwriting fees of Primary Dealers—the compensation that they receive for their services within the primary bond market—provide an 'insider' early-warning indicator of sovereign debt crisis. In addition, clearing houses, like LCH.Clearnet, reflect and channel bond-market sentiment by changing margin (deposit) requirements on banks using sovereign debt as collateral to secure short-term funding in repurchase deals. These margins are typically raised when yield spreads between a state's ten-year bonds and a basket of triple-A rated debt rise above 450 basis points.

Despite the idiosyncrasies that can be claimed for European states, it is possible to identify some patterns by applying a narrative reasoning that is grounded in various numeric financial indicators. In the first decade of the twenty-first century there was a distinct group of creditor states in Europe. Its members could claim sustainable public debt dynamics: the Nordic states, Germany, the Netherlands, and Switzerland. There was another group of states—led by France—whose public debt dynamics could, on balance, be constructed as positive, if controversially so. They were seen as emulating, with mixed success, this first group. However, some of its members could be defined as at risk of slipping into the category of 'fair-weather' debt performers. Finally, there were the European states that formed part of the historic 'arc of default'.

A more enduring historical pattern is that there are many fewer creditor states than debtor states at any one time. Creditor states possess strong political will and high state reform capacity, measured by the quality of their strategic planning and management, institutional adaptation and learning, and wide involvement of political and civil society actors. Strikingly, the Bertelsmann Stiftung (2009) study of governance indicators put in its top-ten states for executive capacity the European creditors: in descending order, Norway, Finland, Sweden, the Netherlands, Denmark, Switzerland, and Germany (though Iceland appeared in ninth place).

Despite these insights, the question at the heart of controversy about the mismatch of liability and control remains the balance of risks. On the one hand, there are the risks to political legitimacy and to long-term asset building through social and infrastructural investment that follow from relying on the discipline that is promised by narrowly conceived and highly problematic numeric risk indicators. Technical elites—the quantitative analysts, investors, and their macroeconomically trained advisers and staff—add their own toxic element of intellectual vanity. Their thinking tends to be formed by taken-for-granted axioms, notably about market efficiency and about what can be learned through extrapolation from retrospective statistical analysis. These types of axiom help shape an illusory world, composed of an apparently impregnable edifice of concepts and theory, around which formulaic policy-making can be based. They conceal a mixture of intellectual vanity and self-deception that risks compounding rather than solving problems of mismatch between liability and control and makes public debt dynamics highly vulnerable.

On the other, there is the risk to long-term debt sustainability from the tenacious grip of illusion, hubris, and hypocrisy and of short-term political opportunism on the way in which governing elites construct narratives about sovereign creditworthiness. This problem is compounded by illusion, hubris, and hypocrisy in the corporate and household sectors. Governing elites face powerful incentives to tolerate wider social illusions about sustainable debts and to refrain from questioning 'feel-good' factors. They are prone to claim credit for successes that prove contingent epiphenomena; to promise more than they can deliver; to place faith in optimistic forecasts; and to be captured by their own illusions. These various behaviour patterns, rooted in both public and private sectors, and in temptations to collusion, feed into and infect public debt dynamics. They provide unfavourable evidence about the credibility of governing elites and strengthen the rationale for privileging numeric indicators and probabilistic reasoning as controls on states.

Narrative reasoning, which is grounded in requirements of political legitimacy, and probabilistic reasoning, which is based on numeric financial indicators, share weaknesses. They tend to under-appreciate the nature of the structural context of political action and the limits that it places on political agency. They are prone to underestimate the role of historical contingency and uncertainty. These two factors are reflected, in the one case, by exaggeration of political will and state capacity and, in the other, by overestimation of intellectual capacity to assign 'true' objective probability to default risk. Both structure and contingency are imperfectly grasped by governing and by technical and financial elites. Probabilistic reasoning tends to underestimate the risks from 'fat tails' and from simple data errors. Similarly, hubris infects the narrative reasoning of governing elites. It is a by-product of the self-delusion that is fostered by the politician's own carefully constructed image of political success. Self-belief is vital to political success. It can, however, turn into a political cage that breeds vainglory.

In consequence of these weaknesses, neither narrative reasoning nor even probabilistic reasoning with its numeric indicators is able to offer an adequate cognitive solution to the problem of mismatch of liability and control. The cultivation of illusion remains pervasive in public finances. It pervades the assumptions built into modelling debt sustainability, notably about projected economic growth. Banks' own risk models and their obscure, high-risk funding structures carve out an illusory world. In public finances statistics can be manipulated, and international financial reporting standards subverted (Morgenstern 1950). Greece was not an outlier. International institutions like the IMF are pressurized by systemically significant debtor states to alter their reports, as in the case of Britain (Peretz 2010). Commitments can be hidden off-balance-sheet, whether in complex funding structures like the private finance initiative (PFI) or in 'shadow' banking. International financial institutions like the IMF, as well as the European Commission, can fall victim to the same illusions about risks to public finances as domestic central banks and finance ministries (Independent Evaluation Office of the IMF 2011).

Illusion is present, above all, in fiscal forecasting, which is characteristically shaped by unrealistic expectations of future economic growth. These expectations are driven by a mixture of hope and desire to generate economic and political optimism. Political massaging of fiscal assessments is notably apparent in relation to whether the budget has been balanced over the economic cycle. Assessments of structural fiscal balances depend on estimating the length of the cycle, the level of peaks and troughs, and the exact point in the cycle at which the assessment is being made. The consequence is a tendency to subvert the aim of structural fiscal balances, which is to encourage adequate safety margins by building fiscal surpluses in good times. Political incentives to sacrifice the precautionary principle are strong.

In monetary policy central bank independence has provided some insulation from political illusion and hubris. Independent central banks, like the ECB during the euro area sovereign debt crises and debates about European economic governance reform, seem to possess a unique capacity to speak truth to power. They are less likely to be politically pressured to use higher inflation as an instrument for defraying public debt or to relax monetary policy prior to elections. Even so, central banks have been prone to intellectual illusion and hubris, reflecting their much lesser degree of independence from financial markets than from politics. They inhabit a world of financial indicators and probabilistic reasoning. Before the post-2007 financial and economic crisis central banks became fascinated by, and ensnared within, their own macroeconomic inflation forecasting models. They underestimated the serious implications of asset-price inflation. Their models paid too little attention to the dynamics of debt accumulation in the private sector, especially within the banking system.

In this world of intellectual and political vanities, 'speaking truth to power' about public debt is difficult without becoming caught up in these same vanities. The shadowy, illusory, and fragile world of debt has a tendency to ensnare those who come close to its limited and esoteric language and its shared assumptions. The illusion, hubris, and hypocrisy that infect public debt dynamics beg two questions: 'who is prepared and able to speak truth?' and 'which truth is being spoken?' The politically difficult nature of the first of these questions is reflected in a paradox. How is it possible to increase the scope for independent and structured enquiry into public debt sustainability outside government, whilst ensuring that it is endowed with the kind of authority that only official status, and thus proximity to power, can confer? Moreover, the search for truth means raising the level of debate about creditworthiness not just in the public sector but also in the corporate and household sectors. It touches on larger questions about economic culture and financial literacy.

Given the inherent political difficulties, probably the best that can be secured is to develop and sustain international and domestic institutions that can help to ensure that a range of financial, environmental, social, and governance indicators are fully considered and that asset-building as well as liability limitation are taken into account. The political challenge is to make transparent the different interests behind contending ideologies of debt and to mediate some sort of consensus. The Group of 20 (G20) and the IMF have this task at the international level. The European Council, the European Commission, and the ECB have a similar role at the EU and euro area level. European states must rely, to varying degrees, on their domestic central banks, auditors, economic think tanks, and fiscal councils or offices for budgetary responsibility. The fiscal compact treaty also brings national courts into the framework for ensuring some match between liability and control. However, the post-2007 metamorphosis of banking into sovereign debt crisis suggested that European states remained resistant to antidotes to illusion, hubris, and vanity.

The question of 'whose truth?' highlights the enormous structural power of international financial markets—investors, credit rating agencies, and academic economics, which offers intellectual support. Their representations of the problem of mismatch between liability and control have dominated discourse, defining notions of fiscal normality and what constitutes state fiscal virtue and good governance. Moreover, history suggests that alterations between Left and Right in government are far less significant in redefining these notions than wars, external imbalances, and financial shocks. War suspends conventional notions of fiscal normality by making national security, and the financing requirements of military victory, the touchstone of public finances. External imbalances, financial shocks, and subsequent protracted economic recession serve to change creditor views about the future. What was previously prudent public debt is redefined as reckless. What was an appropriate level of debt becomes 'over-indebtedness'. The expectations and fears of creditors, their risk appetite, act as the key catalysts for shifts in notions of fiscal normality and in states' reputations.

15

Public Debt Dynamics: Political Will and State Capacity

It is part of probability that many improbable things will happen.
Aristotle, *Poetics*, Book XXV

The political will and the state capacity to manage public debt dynamics are hedged by a complexity of factors that readily escape governmental control and that are typically incompletely and imperfectly understood, not least by professional economists to whom governing elites turn for guidance. Governing elites face the size of the inherited stock of public debt; the maturity profile of this debt; the gross financing requirement; and borrowing costs in financial markets. Their problems of control are compounded by uncertainty about current and prospective GDP growth rates and about the precise connections between fiscal consolidation and structural reforms, on the one hand, and economic growth and social and political stability, on the other. Moreover, the room for manoeuvre of governing elites is constrained by the state of, and dynamics within, national financial balance sheets, including those of the bank, corporate, and household sectors. In particular, they are acutely limited in their capacity to tame financial market credit-creation and make self-interest compatible with public virtue.

These control problems are exacerbated by two further problems. The first is the often poor quality of statistical knowledge. This quality issue is a matter not just of timeliness of data and margins of error. It is also bound up with concealment, mendacity, and trickery in data compilation and with the competence of those using available data (Morgenstern 1950; Alt, Lassen, and Wehner 2012). More fundamentally still, governing elites are prone to become entrapped within dominant 'mentalities'. During the period before the 2007 financial crisis many had bought into the belief in self-equilibrating processes of demand and supply of credit. This belief justified the withdrawal of state control. It also induced illusion, hubris, and complacency about private credit-creation that were shared across public and private sectors.

Above all, in justifying their debt as sustainable, governing elites depend on GDP growth, whose sources and dynamics are complex and elude control. Gross domestic product (GDP) growth is vital in generating supportive tax revenues and in reducing demands on public expenditure. In addition, the nature of GDP growth matters. GDP growth based on productivity-driven exports and investment opens up the prospect of a virtuous circle in public debt management (Stein 1885–1886). However, when GDP growth is concentrated around 'asset-price-bubble-prone' sectors, like finance, construction, and real estate, it is too easily associated with an illusory sense of safety. The result is the accumulation of hidden, unsustainable debts, painful deleveraging, and long confinement in a fiscal straitjacket with radically uncertain outcomes.

Managing public debt depends on political and institutional capacity to influence a range of financial, macroeconomic, and fiscal factors. Their behaviour illustrates the mismatch between liability and control at the heart of government. The narrow problem of fiscal factors is framed within the bigger framework of the will and capacity of states to extract taxes, control expenditures, and limit budget deficits on behalf of wider public interests. This problem is bound up with the strength, resilience, and inclusiveness of public institutions, with public trust in their honesty and integrity, with the availability of appropriate policy instruments, and with the ideologically-conditioned willingness to make active and effective use of these instruments.

Sovereign creditworthiness is an integral part of the process by which the identity of a state is (re-)constructed. Once the perception gains ground that a state cannot control its public debt dynamics, its image of strength and virtue suffers adverse effects. This fate befell the Byzantine Empire and the Ottoman Empire and, for much of their modern history, Greece, Hungary, Portugal, and Spain. *Ceteris paribus*, once states lose their creditworthiness, their governing elites have less freedom of manoeuvre than those of creditor states. In order to retrieve power they are caught between two contending incentives. They can embrace the policy solutions pressed on them by their creditors and relinquish formal sovereignty. Alternatively, they can resort to a mixture of protection, deception, and playing-off of their creditors. They may attempt to do both.

However, not all states that suffer credit downgrades are treated equally. Despite a downgrade by Standard and Poor's in August 2011, the United States remained a 'benchmark' borrower, continuing to enjoy the benefits of 'reserve-currency' status. It benefitted from its entrenched image as the strongest state in the international system, as well as from its financial 'depth' as the most liquid global market. By 2013 sharpening domestic partisanship about raising the US debt ceiling had not destroyed the belief that the United States had a capacity to manage its difficulties by printing money that was denied to other debtor states. The United States was a privileged borrower.

Central governments can suffer further indignities. As Chapter 16 shows, some of their sub-national governments may enjoy higher credit ratings. More alarmingly, governments may find that their ratings are lower than those of their leading corporations. By August 2011 the credit derivatives market implied that seventy large US corporations—including AT&T, Coca-Cola, Google, and McDonald's—were less likely to default than the US federal government. Standard and Poor's rated ExxonMobil and Microsoft higher than the US federal government. Similarly, Italy's and Spain's central governments were judged less safe than some of their sub-national governments and corporations. This judgement was based on evidence that government balance sheets were less easy to understand; their assets and liabilities more difficult to track; their revenues less clear and less easily identified; their cash on hand less plentiful; and their climate of decision-making less conducive to reliable and steady cash flows.

The Limitations of Fiscal Policies in Controlling Public Debt

Public finances cannot be understood simply in narrow terms of internal fiscal measures, deficit-debt adjustments, public-sector liquidity management, or even the quality of the taxation system and the public administration. More fundamentally, public finances are affected by financial factors. They include the structural characteristics of the private sector, notably its wealth and its propensities to save and to invest; the extent of prudent and trusted stewardship of private savings and public taxes; the risk of shift of liabilities from private to public sector consequent on banking crises; and the degree of exposure to external debt. Public finances are damaged by an excessive overhang of debt that finances worthless investment or vanishes into consumption, whether in private or public sectors. Their vulnerability is exposed by excessive reliance on debt-fuelled consumption. At some point, liabilities have to be liquidated, potentially in economically and politically painful ways. The result is sharpening debates about social justice, enflamed populist passions, the search for scapegoats, and social unrest in its various forms: riots, demonstrations, general strikes, even political assassinations and attempts at revolutionary overthrow. Loss of sovereign creditworthiness has its origins well beyond fiscal factors.

As Chapter 14 shows, sovereign creditworthiness revolves around contested concepts of 'excessive' and 'sustainable' public debt that have been largely colonized by professional economists. They are expressed in the formula of the public debt/GDP ratio and complex, technical, and mathematical statements of the relevant factors and their relationships to each other. The public debt ratio measures changes over time in the relationship between government debt and nominal GDP. Its value depends on whether public debt grows more quickly or more slowly than nominal GDP (Deutsche Bundesbank 2010).

This ratio informs the design of the Excessive Deficit Procedure (EDP) of the Maastricht Treaty and of its operational form, the Stability and Growth Pact (SGP). Taking average potential GDP growth of 3 per cent and inflation of 2 per cent for EU Member States as conditions, the 3 per cent of GDP fiscal deficit rule was consistent with stabilizing public debt at 60 per cent of GDP. The 60 per cent rule was defined by the EU as 'sustainable' debt. However, it was only as sustainable as the political will and capacity of a state to secure these conditions, to comply with the rule in relation to its debt legacy and long-term GDP growth capacity, and to avoid contagion from private to public liabilities. Moreover, as early as 1886, Lorenz von Stein had questioned the significance of the public debt/GDP ratio. He argued that far more relevant was the relation between public debt and state revenue. The use of public debt for productivity-raising investment would generate extra tax revenues that would make debt servicing easier (Stein 1886: 230).

Despite the critiques of Dietzel, Stein, and Wagner, the dominant approach to debt sustainability within professional economics has drawn on the British classical school of economics, including the works of David Hume, Adam Smith, and Ricardo. This approach points to the need for a long-term, inter-temporal budget constraint, with which public finances must comply. Otherwise, public finances risk higher debt servicing costs, consequent on rising interest rates as investors seek increased risk premiums. Large public debt is associated with negative macroeconomic effects from the 'crowding-out' of private investment. The dominant approach to debt sustainability has also appealed to the so-called Ricardian equivalence principle. It argues that increasing public debt provides households with an incentive to engage in hoarding to build up precautionary savings against future anticipated tax increases, again with negative macroeconomic effects. Falling rates of GDP growth will in turn impact negatively on the primary budget balance. Short-term fiscal autonomy of action will be reduced, at both economic and political cost to governments and to their image of governing competence.

However, key figures in the late-nineteenth-century German historical school of economics opposed the limited and negative conception of the state in British classical conceptions of debt sustainability. They saw it as grounded in the idiosyncrasies of Britain's early industrial revolution (Holtfrerich 2013). Karl Dietzel, Lorenz von Stein, and Adolph Wagner argued that credit was vital in enabling the state to invest productively in the economy, enhancing GDP growth potential. Their work reflected the very different historical context of German economic development from that in Britain. Mobilizing credit for investment in infrastructure and skills, above all in the emerging science-based manufacturing world of the second industrial revolution, meant that debt took on a more positive role.

Traditionally, as we have seen, public debt sustainability has been most severely tested by the association between states and warfare and by banking and financial crises. Over the course of the twentieth century, the growth of welfare states has put new additional strains on debt sustainability. Economists in the classical tradition argue that the implicit liabilities in pension, health, and long-term care expenditures, associated with population ageing, are tightening the inter-temporal budget constraint. They emphasize the close connection between debt sustainability and intergenerational equity. In particular, intergenerational burden-sharing is influenced by the temporal distribution of the primary fiscal balances. A rise in age-related public expenditure shifts the necessary primary surpluses into the future. In so doing, it raises not just debt sustainability but also intergenerational equity issues. Current debt may be regarded as sustainable only if it is covered by the sum of all discounted future primary surpluses.

By the early twenty-first century the risks of excessive and unsustainable public debt had been catapulted to the top of European political agendas. A crisis of public debt was seen as threatening both EU Member-State solvency and the post-1945 European integration project. The long-term increases in public expenditure and rise in implicit liabilities with population ageing were only part of the story. Public debt had also proved acutely vulnerable to banking shocks and subsequent financial sector stabilization operations. Protracted economic stagnation and recession in the wake of these shocks had further heightened susceptibility to fiscal shocks. Default risk was suddenly no longer an emerging-market issue. So parlous was the fiscal situation that the Bank for International Settlements (BIS) calculated that, in most advanced economies, the fiscal budget (excluding interest payments) would need twenty consecutive years of surpluses exceeding 2 per cent of GDP just to bring the public debt/GDP ratio back to pre-2007 levels (Cecchetti, Mohanty, and Zampolli 2010). The challenge of rebuilding fiscal buffers or safety margins was acute.

How Sustainable? Size of Public Debt and Public Expenditure

Debt sustainability has no clear relationship to the value of the public debt, to public debt per capita, or to the size of public expenditure in relation to GDP. According to The Economist Global Debt Clock in August 2011, the league table of European states by value of public debts was headed by Germany, followed in order by Italy, France, and Britain. At a considerable distance, they were followed by Spain, the Netherlands, Belgium, Greece, and Turkey. On the measure of public debt per capita, Iceland was top of the league after its catastrophic banking collapse. It was followed in order by Belgium, Norway, Italy, Ireland, France, Greece, the Netherlands, Germany, Britain, and Switzerland. These rankings do not help in differentiating creditor and debtor states. The figures were huge: for instance, German public debt of $2,348,799,726,027 and Belgian public debt per capita of $41,028.76. However, they tell us nothing about political will and state capacity to service public debt or about whether public debt is used to invest productively in enhanced GDP growth and hence generate higher tax revenues.

Whether one takes 1950 or 1960 as the base line, or just the period since 1980, the key EU Member States experienced a huge long-term growth in public expenditure and in public debt (on France, Champsaur and Cotis 2010 and L'économie française 2004–2005; on Germany, German Federal Finance Ministry 2009 and Deutsche Bundesbank 2010). Table 14.4 shows that, within this general pattern, some EU states like Britain and Ireland had relatively low public expenditure growth. Other states had above average growth: Finland, France, Greece, Italy, and Portugal.

One of the components of public expenditure is debt servicing costs. From the mid-1990s up to the post-2007 crisis, a combination of low inflation, belief in convergence consequent on commitment to European monetary union, and powerful credit-creation processes in fast-expanding global financial markets reduced market interest rates. This gain in reduced debt servicing costs benefited those EU Member States that joined with Germany in European monetary union. They experienced a sharp reduction in yield spreads on their government bonds. Hence, over this period, fiscal pressure was relaxed, inducing complacency about risks in expanding public debt financing. Sovereign debt could be increased without a proportionate growth in debt servicing costs. This complacency induced fiscal hubris and a failure to build fiscal buffers as insurance against 'bad times'. In consequence, euro area states were vulnerable to financing risks from the combination of high debt legacies with rising interest rates once financial markets began to entertain doubts about their creditworthiness.

Compared to the public debt/GDP ratio, the level of public expenditure was much less significant in sovereign debt sustainability. Images of the appropriate size of the fiscal state are associated with different political judgements about the purposes of government and how it can best promote welfare. In any case, public expenditure is not an indicator of the extent to which states choose to intervene by regulation and monitoring for compliance. Also, it does not tell us whether debt finances productive investment. There is no simple correlation between public expenditure levels and sovereign creditworthiness.

The Nordic states combine creditworthiness with high, progressive taxation and generous spending on advanced welfare states in the interests of social cohesion. Their fiscal arrangements complement dynamic private sectors. In contrast, Switzerland is a creditworthy state with much lower taxation levels, less progressive taxation, and a residual—if important—welfare state. In the case of debtor states the key variable is the quality of public expenditure. As in the case of Sweden, high expenditure in the form of sustained investment in human and social capital, the research base, and infrastructure can lever a state from debtor to creditor status. In contrast, high public expenditure associated with 'rent-seeking' behaviour by elites is a typical indicator of a chronic debtor state. Once credit rating agencies and markets identify default risk, they begin to take a greater interest in state capacity to control public expenditure growth and in the extent to which its various components contribute to GDP growth and competitiveness.

Patterns in Public Debt Accumulation

Tables 15.1 and 15.2 show that few EU Member States had public debt/GDP ratios in 2007 at, or below, their levels in 1980: only Britain, Denmark, Ireland, Luxembourg, the Netherlands, and Sweden. The bigger story was of growing public debt levels. Table 15.3 provides a picture of public debt accumulation in euro area Member States from monetary union in 1999 to the 2007 crisis and then during 2008–2012.

Several patterns are notable. First, public debt accumulation reflected developments endogenous to particular states. A striking example was rent-seeking behaviour. It included the use of state resources to reward supporters through new and improved benefits, public sector jobs, and access to contracts. Rent-seeking behaviour fuelled the expansion of the Greek public sector. The Greek public debt/GDP ratio exploded from 22.3 per cent in 1980 to 103.4 per cent in 2000. Greek debt accumulated by 11 per cent between 1999 and 2007, second only to Portugal. This growth was symptomatic of the use of the improved image of sovereign creditworthiness, consequent on association with European monetary integration, to further embed a system of political clientelism and patronage. This process served the electoral purposes of governing parties. However, it was at the expense of institutional capacity to generate collective goods like fiscal discipline and productivity-enhancing investment. The casualty was public trust in political and state institutions. Even Denmark, a much more inclusive and institutionally robust state, experienced an increase of some 35 per cent in public debt/GDP ratio between 1980 and 1985.

Secondly, public debt accumulation illustrated the impact of economic, financial, and geo-strategic shocks. An example was the short-term surge in public debt/GDP ratios in Finland and in Sweden in 1990–1995, consequent on their financial crises. Better known was the fiscal shock of German unification. Germany's public debt/GDP ratio changed

Table 15.1 Public Debt in EU, as a Percentage of GDP, 1980–2000

	1980	1985	1990	1995	2000
USA	43.9	56.1	64.3	71.5	55.0
Japan	51.4	67.7	68.4	92.5	142.1
Euro Area	33.4	50.3	56.5	72.5	69.5
EU	...	...	...	69.6	63.2
Euro Area:					
Austria	35.3	48.0	56.1	68.3	66.5
Belgium	74.1	115.2	125.7	129.9	107.9
Cyprus	...	...	...	40.6	48.7
Finland	11.3	16.0	14.1	56.6	43.8
France	20.7	30.6	35.2	55.5	57.3
Germany	30.3	39.5	41.3	55.6	59.7
Greece	22.3	47.9	71.0	97.0	103.4
Ireland	69.0	100.6	93.1	82.1	37.8
Italy	56.9	80.5	94.7	121.5	109.2
Luxembourg	9.9	10.3	4.7	7.4	6.2
Malta	...	...	...	35.3	55.9
Netherlands	45.3	69.7	76.8	76.1	53.8
Portugal	30.5	58.3	55.0	61.0	50.5
Slovakia	...	...	...	22.1	50.3
Slovenia	...	...	...	...	...
Spain	16.4	41.4	42.6	63.3	59.3
Rest of EU					
Bulgaria	...	...	...	...	74.3
Czech Republic	...	...	...	14.6	18.5
Denmark	39.1	74.7	62.0	72.5	51.5
Estonia	...	...	...	9.0	5.1
Hungary	...	...	...	86.2	55.0
Latvia	...	...	...	15.1	12.3
Lithuania	...	...	...	11.5	23.7
Poland	...	...	...	49.0	36.8
Romania	...	...	...	7.0	22.5
Sweden	39.3	60.9	41.2	72.2	53.6
UK	52.7	51.8	33.3	50.8	41.0

(*Source*: German Federal Finance Ministry, *Monatsbericht*, July 2010: Table 14, p. 124)

from 41.3 per cent in 1990 to 55.6 per cent in 1995. More fundamentally, the post-2007 financial and economic crisis administered the biggest single shock to European public debt dynamics since 1945. The subsequent rapid rise in public debt/GDP ratios, alongside stagnant or declining GDP growth and evidence of falling GDP trend growth rates, induced a heightened investor risk aversion in sovereign debt markets. Between 2007 and 2012 Irish public debt exploded by 70 per cent; Greek by 45.7 per cent; Spanish by 33.2 per cent; and Portuguese by 27.1 per cent.

Table 15.2 Public Debt in EU, as a Percentage of GDP, 2002–2012

	Share (% in 2012)	2002	2006	2009	2012
Euro Area	100.0	68.1	68.2	80.0	90.7
EU	100.0	60.5	61.4	74.0	85.4
Euro Area					
Austria	2.6	66.0	62.2	69.2	73.4
Belgium	4.3	103.2	88.1	95.7	99.6
Cyprus	0.2	...	64.6	58.5	85.8
Estonia	0.0	5.5	4.5	7.2	10.1
Finland	1.2	41.3	39.7	43.5	53.0
France	20.9	58.2	63.7	79.2	90.2
Germany	24.6	60.3	67.6	74.5	81.9
Greece	3.5	110.7	97.8	129.7	156.9
Ireland	2.2	32.1	24.9	64.8	117.6
Italy	22.6	105.5	106.5	116.4	127.0
Luxembourg	6.5	6.5	15.3	20.8	0.1
Malta	0.1	...	63.7	66.4	72.1
Netherlands	4.9	50.5	47.4	60.8	71.2
Portugal	2.3	55.5	64.7	83.7	123.6
Slovakia	0.4	...	30.5	35.6	52.1
Slovenia	0.2	...	26.7	35.0	54.1
Spain	10.1	52.5	39.6	53.9	84.2
EU outside Euro Area					
Bulgaria	0.1	...	22.7	14.6	18.5
Czech Republic	28.8	29.4	34.2	45.8	0.6
Denmark	1.0	46.8	32.1	40.7	45.8
Hungary	0.7	55.0	65.6	79.8	79.2
Latvia	0.1	13.5	10.7	36.9	40.7
Lithuania	0.1	22.3	18.0	29.3	40.7
Poland	1.9	39.8	47.7	50.9	55.6
Romania	0.4	...	12.4	23.6	37.8
Sweden	1.4	52.0	45.7	42.6	38.2
UK	15.2	37.6	43.5	67.8	90.0

(*Source*: European Central Bank, *Statistics*, June 2010: 46, with added 2002 figures from same publication, May 2006: 43)

Thirdly, various European states proved capable of implementing sharp reductions in public debt. Examples included Belgium (1995–2007), Bulgaria (2000–2007), Denmark (1995–2007), Estonia (1995–2007), Finland (1995–2007), Hungary (1995–2000), Ireland (1995–2007), Latvia (1995–2007), the Netherlands (1995–2007), Romania (2000–2007), Slovakia (2000–2007), Spain (1995–2007), and Sweden (1995–2007). Bulgaria slashed its public debt/GDP ratio from 74.3 per cent in 2000 to 22.7 in 2006; Denmark nearly halved its ratio between 2000 and 2007; Ireland brought its ratio down about 45 per cent between 1995 and 2000; Romania down from 22.5 per cent in 2000 to 12.4 in 2006; and

Table 15.3 Public Debt Accumulation in Euro Area Member States, as Percentage of GDP, 1999–2007 and 2008–2012

	Debt Accumulation 1999–2007	Debt Accumulation 2008–2012
Belgium	–29.5	12.5
Germany	4.0	9.0
Estonia	–2.8	7.1
Ireland	–23.5	70.0
Greece	11.0	45.7
Spain	–26.2	33.2
France	5.0	22.3
Italy	–10.1	13.6
Cyprus	–0.6	20.1
Luxembourg	0.2	7.3
Malta	4.5	7.7
Netherlands	–15.8	9.1
Austria	–7.9	10.8
Portugal	13.2	27.1
Slovenia	–	25.1
Slovakia	–18.3	19.6
Finland	–10.5	18.9
Euro Area	–5.8	18.2

(*Source*: European Central Bank, *Monthly Bulletin*, April 2011: 67)

Slovakia from 50.3 per cent in 2000 to 29.3 per cent in 2007 (European Central Bank 2009b). Table 15.3 shows that between 1999 and 2007 the biggest public debt reductions were achieved in Belgium (29.5 per cent), Spain (26.2 per cent), and Ireland (23.5 per cent).

These examples of vigorous fiscal consolidation suggest that narratives of the EU, and of the EU accession process, as lacking significant structural reforms is not completely accurate. During the post-2007 crisis governing elites in Britain, Estonia, Ireland, and Latvia sought to mobilize popular consensus behind fundamental shifts in fiscal policy strategy to make tax and spending more conducive to economic growth and thus to debt sustainability. However, managing fiscal austerity without provoking social protests and disorder proved much more difficult once European states lacked the cushion of an expanding European and international economy that provided growth impulses.

Fourthly, the process of meeting the Maastricht convergence criteria for euro entry and complying with the EDP seemed to correlate closely with intensified efforts at public debt reduction. However, one must assess this correlation with caution. Sharp debt reduction also reflected other factors. They included exit from financial crisis, as in Finland and Sweden; contingent gains from asset-price bubbles, seen in Ireland and

Spain; an element of fiscal window-dressing, notably in France, Greece, and Italy; and priority to EU accession, for instance in Bulgaria, Hungary, and Romania.

Nevertheless, underpinning these variations in public debt levels and trajectories at any one time, the broad picture is of steady rise in public debt/GDP ratios. France had a public debt/GDP ratio of 20.7 per cent in 1980, rising to 63.8 per cent in 2007. Over the same period the German ratio climbed from 30.3 to 65.0 per cent, and the Italian ratio from 56.9 to 103.5 per cent. Across the EU as a whole, the ratio changed from 43.9 per cent in 1980 to 62.2 per cent in 2007, and 82.5 per cent in 2011. In the euro area it increased from 33.4 per cent in 1980 to 66.0 in 2007 and 87.3 in 2011. Central banks (led by the European Central Bank (ECB)), finance ministries, international financial institutions, financial market players, and academic economists began to ask questions about whether public debts in the EU were excessive and sustainable. These questions were asked before the post-2007 crisis and led to the institutionalization of EU-level fiscal rules and an excessive deficit procedure. After 2007 the German 'debt brake' and its export into the euro area fiscal compact treaty represented a tightening of both rules and procedure. The implications for the space for democratic politics and the exercise of state power were potentially profound.

The Questionable Assumptions of Linearity and 'One-Size-Fits-All'

There is no particular reason why the Maastricht 60 per cent public debt/GDP ratio should serve as the level beyond which public debt becomes excessive. Equally, there is no consensus around an alternative level. The economics literature developed the concepts of 'strong' and 'weak' sustainability, based on different assumptions about the relationship between public expenditure and revenue and about fiscal deficit dynamics (Hakkio and Rush 1991; Quintos 1995). In both cases the relationship between public expenditure and revenue is understood as linear. They move in the same direction. In the 'strong' sustainability argument, changes in public expenditure translate into similar adjustments of magnitude in revenues, implying a stationary fiscal deficit and public debt/GDP ratio. Clearly much depends on the nature and effects of public expenditure, as Karl Dietzel (1855) and Lorenz von Stein (1885–1886) had recognized.

Empirical evidence seems more consistent with the 'weak' sustainability concept. It sees the public debt/GDP ratio evolving in a dynamic fashion, with variation in the degree and speed of change in public expenditure and revenues (e.g. L'économie française 2004–2005). The 'weak' sustainability concept highlights the precariousness of sovereign creditworthiness and the need for high insurance through fiscal buffers.

The gap at the heart of this debate stems from the assumptions of linearity and of 'one-size-fits-all'. These assumptions encourage a systematic underestimation of the precariousness of sovereign creditworthiness. Neither sustainability concept captures fully the complex interaction between the evolution of the public debt/GDP ratio and market interest rates. In particular, both concepts underestimate the impact of exogenous shocks, like banking and financial crisis, and of deficiencies in political will and state capacity. Their impact is demonstrated in GDP losses, declining revenues, and increased risk aversion amongst investors. As the evolving post-2007 financial and economic crises illustrated, trajectories of public debt/GDP evolution prove much more transitory than concepts of 'strong' and 'weak' sustainability allow. Faith in extrapolating from present into the future and in the continuity of underlying trends can breed illusion and blind rather then enlighten public policy.

Moreover, differences in the characteristics of economic and financial structures and in political will and state capacity make the notion of a 'one-size-fits-all' public debt/GDP rule questionable. States like Britain, France, and Germany are very much less at risk of being deemed as potential defaulters than Greece and Portugal because of the size, depth, and liquidity of their financial markets, their efficient public administrations, and their tax-raising capacity. They have, in consequence, greater autonomy of fiscal action. A 'one-size-fits-all' public debt/GDP ratio fails to take account of differences in political will and state capacity. Some states can maintain higher public debt ratios for longer and be less susceptible to market contagion.

Public Debt Dynamics: Structural Drivers

At first glance, structural drivers of public debt dynamics might seem less significant than macroeconomic drivers. Population size and trade openness are weakly correlated with strong and weak public debt positions. Finland and Greece are both small in population size but very different in public debt dynamics. Estonia and Hungary are very open economies but again have very different public debt dynamics.

Nevertheless, public debt dynamics are powerfully bound up with economic structure. The precariousness of sovereign creditworthiness increases when states are particularly vulnerable through structural dependence for buoyant tax revenues on economic sectors that are prone to asset-price bubbles and bursts—like construction, housing, property, and finance. Bursting bubbles produce radical collapse in tax revenues, shifts of debt liabilities from the private sector to the state, and hence the rapid explosion of public debt. The effects of this kind of structural vulnerability were apparent post-2007 in Britain, Ireland, and Spain, as well as in Iceland. Their status as fiscally virtuous states vanished dramatically. They emerged with enormous fiscal adjustment problems. Similar problems arise when a state is excessively dependent on a particular commodity sector, like oil and natural gas. Russia was a fiscally virtuous state in the first decade of the twenty-first century. However, it enjoyed a precarious sovereign creditworthiness.

Structural dependency derives from the way in which public debt dynamics are embedded in national balance sheets. The accumulation of excessive indebtedness by companies (financial and non-financial) and/or by households impacts on public debt dynamics once private liabilities are shifted onto public sector balance sheets. These linkages within national balance sheets were largely ignored in the Maastricht Treaty and the SGP definitions and analyses of public debt dynamics. Public debt dynamics are haunted by contingent liabilities, implicit as well as explicit. For this reason, credible stress tests of banks under scenarios of abnormal macroeconomic conditions are an essential component in estimating the potential scale of these liabilities. The first EU bank stress tests of 2010 were judged weak in this respect. They did little to clarify the likely impacts of sovereign defaults on banks or the contingent liabilities facing public finances. The objective of reassuring markets was not achieved.

Public Debt Dynamics: Cultural, Ideological, and Institutional Drivers

Formal public debt sustainability analysis has produced even less agreement on the relative significance of cultural, ideological, and institutional drivers. Being pre-eminently qualitative, they are much more difficult to operationalize as exogenous factors for the determination of public debt dynamics and to measure in a satisfactory way. There is accordingly a bias within formal economics to marginalize or ignore their significance. Cultural, ideological, and institutional factors are best seen as playing a constitutive part in public debt dynamics. They help shape elite and public attitudes to public debt through the self-image of a state that its governing elites project and that the public, or at least part of it, share (Boulding 1956).

Some states evolve reputations for managing public debt dynamics because of their political leadership and institutional capacity. In this way France is differentiated from Italy and Britain from Greece. Some governing elites are seen as ideologically united around primacy to sound finances, others as too factionalized and polarized to behave in a fiscally competent way. Here Britain might be compared with Italy. Some publics have an image as industrious, thrifty, and prudent; others as feckless and lazy. This image is used to contrast Dutch with Greek economic culture.

However, once one treats cultural, ideological, and institutional factors as exogenous, their connection to public debt dynamics seems far from clear-cut. Public debt dynamics may prove benign in contexts of minority party government, ideologically incoherent coalition government, caretaker government, or unpopular government. Greece had one-party majority governments till 2012, a hallmark of strong government. Nevertheless, its public debt dynamics proved unsustainable. Its governing elites proved to be corrupt, venal, and mendacious. Italian governments were hyper-factionalized, and prey to clientelism. Nevertheless, despite a huge public debt legacy, they avoided debt restructuring.

In broad terms, the different public debt dynamics in north and west European states from those of southern European states can be attributed to cultural, ideological, and institutional factors. North and west European states can be seen as sharing certain characteristics. They have strong state capacity based on the professionalism and integrity of their institutions. They seem to possess civic-minded governing elites, as well as publics who take their public obligations seriously. In consequence, states in north and west Europe are more likely to be labelled creditworthy than states in Europe's historic 'arc of default'.

This reputation for institutional capacity, for governing competence, and for civic-minded elites and publics is important in providing a shield when confronted by sudden negative public debt dynamics. It provides a context in which it is easier to appeal to self-image as justification for speeding through large-scale, painful fiscal adjustments in the face of high, short-term social and economic costs. However, the endogenous character of this process makes the causal direction far from clear. Making large-scale fiscal adjustment can serve as a way of building and differentiating state reputation. In dealing with the Troika, Irish governing elites were highly motivated to distinguish themselves from Greek elites and construct an image of a very different kind of state. Deep crisis offers an opportunity to remake images. It may also lead to confirmation of the negative image of a state. In short, cultural, ideological, and institutional factors play complex constitutive parts in public debt dynamics.

Ideology: Party-Based and Culture-Based

The ideological factor of 'Left/Right' in party government composition seems to correlate weakly with public debt dynamics. There is a presumption that Left-wing governments are likely to be less averse to higher public debt than Right-wing governments. They see it as the hallmark of a benign state that provides high social welfare. Public debt can be viewed as the expression of ideological priority to social solidarity and peace. In the summer of 2010, there seemed to be a correlation between the only four centre-Left governments in the EU—in Cyprus, Greece, Spain, and Portugal—and adverse public debt dynamics. However, Hungary and Italy had adverse public debt dynamics with centre-Right governments. In a longer-term perspective, the sovereign debt problems of some of these south European states owed at least as much to centre-Right governments. Conversely, the Nordic states combined strong, deep-rooted social democratic traditions, and high levels of public expenditure, with a status amongst the top world fiscal 'saints' in managing public debt.

Public debt dynamics in Belgium, Britain, France, Germany, Italy, and the Netherlands corroborate this weak correlation between the political Right and low debt and the political Left and high debt (Sadeh 2006). To take one example, British public debt fell under the Labour governments of 1964–1970 from its previous levels under Conservative governments. Political partisanship seems to express itself more in the detailed content of tax and spending decisions than in aggregate fiscal deficit and public debt dynamics.

In coalition government, ideological coherence functions as a test of durability and effectiveness in securing sustainable debt. Prima facie competence in managing public debt dynamics should be higher in an 'ideologically connected' government in which the 'ideological space' between the coalition parties is narrow. Ideological connectedness has tended to elude successive centre-Left and centre-Right governments in Italy since the early 1990s. They have shown a tendency to implode. Conversely, the German centre-Left/centre-Right Grand Coalition of Christian Democrats and Social Democrats between 2005 and 2009 showed much more cohesion. Its Social Democratic (SPD) Federal Finance Minister, Peer Steinbrück, was the agenda-setter who pushed through the tough German constitutional 'debt brake'. The subsequent German centre-Right coalition of Christian Democrats and Free Democrats proved, if anything, more deeply divided on fiscal policies and debt reduction strategy.

In practice, ideological coherence is difficult to assess. Few governments seem to possess it. They become embroiled in issues that relate to the personal ambitions, rivalries, vanities, and chemistry of coalition leaders and to complex factional politics. The interplay of these internal, often highly personalized political factors is hard to disentangle from ideological position-taking. Together they form a combustible compound that readily translates into a negative image of capacity to manage public debt dynamics. This negative imagery is reinforced when—as in Greece and Italy—parties contain powerful internal factions and 'barons'. They protect their electoral clients and treat their ministries as fiefdoms to be protected against budgetary cuts.

Culturally-anchored ideologies of debt seem to count for more than party-anchored ideologies in shaping public debt dynamics. The German SPD was ideologically ill disposed to emphasize 'stability culture' in its official discourse about public debt. Nevertheless, the strong support for these cultural values within German public opinion induced the SPD to embrace stability-oriented policies. The image of the ascetic state triumphed over alterations of party power.

Cabinet Duration and Party Government

Cabinet duration seems a useful political indicator of debt sustainability. Using data from the period 1992–1998, Sadeh (2006: 79–89) identifies Italy and Romania as having the lowest scores on cabinet duration. Britain, Germany, and the Netherlands had the highest scores. These findings seem to support the hypothesis that cabinet duration affects public debt dynamics. However, although the three Baltic States and Poland featured as having low-duration cabinets, they scored well on public debt dynamics over this period. Portugal, which provided the first case of excessive deficit problems after the creation of the euro area, fitted into the high-duration category.

Beliefs about capacity to manage public debt dynamics are also bound up with the notion of the superior governing competence of single-party governments. Does coalition or single-party government correlate more strongly with this capacity? Taking the period 1945–1999 in western Europe, and using the cut-off point of 50 per cent of time in office, the model of coalition government was most entrenched (in descending order) in the Netherlands, Luxembourg, Germany, Belgium, Finland, France, Italy, Austria, and Denmark (Müller and Strøm 2000). In descending order, the model of single-party government was most strongly represented in Britain, Spain, Greece, Norway, Sweden, Portugal, and Ireland. Only three states had no significant experience of coalition government in this period: Britain, Spain, and Greece. These rankings had no clear correlation with public debt dynamics. They do, however, discredit the prevalent notion—above all, in Britain—that single-party government is a necessary condition for sustainable public finances.

Some of the most striking cases of benign public debt dynamics occur where single-party government has had no, or only a short, appearance. Examples include Austria, Finland, Germany, the Netherlands, and Switzerland. The first coalition government in Britain since 1945 under David Cameron, post-2010, was noticeable for the priority that it attached to massive public debt reduction, exceeding in scale anything attempted by any single-party Conservative government in this period. In a study of thirty-six modern democracies, Lijphart (1999) concluded that coalition governments were as good as single-party governments in limiting fiscal deficits. Coalition governments tended to have higher levels of public expenditure, but without translating into elevated public debt/GDP ratios. They were notably better than single-party governments at achieving a close alignment between voter preferences and government policies.

Domestic Fiscal Institutions

Domestic fiscal institutions and rules seem more relevant than party ideology, ideological coherence, cabinet duration, and type of party government in explaining public debt dynamics. State fiscal governance capacity can be measured in three main ways. One measure is whether, and how far, majority-party, minority-party, and coalition governments delegate fiscal powers to the finance minister. A second measure is whether, and how far, coalition governments take office with pre-commitments to fiscal contracts that outline detailed spending and deficit/debt targets for the legislative period. A third measure is whether, and how far, individual ministers are able to shelter within their own fiscal fiefdoms.

Both the fiscal delegation and the fiscal contract regimes featured more strongly in the EU after Economic and Monetary Union (EMU) was agreed in 1991, suggesting a general strengthening of institutional capacity (Hallerberg, Strauch, and von Hagen 2009). Some states were laggards, notably Italy and Spain. The problem of weak fiscal institutional capacity went beyond the role of ministers as 'feudal overlords'. As the cases of Greece and Italy demonstrated, even 'feudal' ministers who were committed to enforcing fiscal control could be frustrated by powerful bailiffs and troublesome peasants within their ministries.

However, institutional forms of fiscal governance are not a reliable indicator of public debt dynamics. On both the delegation and the fiscal contract measures, Greece scored more strongly than Finland, the Netherlands, and Spain. The fiscal governance measures tell us about executive capacity. However, they ignore the character of elite and public preferences towards fiscal deficits and public debt. They tell us nothing about willingness to engage in fiscal reforms and to pay creditors. Fiscal power might be formally centralized but decision-making fragmented and dispersed. Hungary scored more highly on fiscal centralization than the Czech Republic (Dimitrov 2006). This score did not translate into better performance in public debt dynamics.

The weakness of fiscal governance measures is that they deflect attention from the character, distribution, and intensity of domestic elite and public preferences towards fiscal deficits and public debt. They overlook the nature of domestic veto players. Fiscal governance measures also ignore the governing competence of party and official elites, above all in building and sustaining an inclusive approach to public debt dynamics. These factors are central to political will and state capacity. They play a central role in shaping the domestic politics of public debt dynamics. Strength in terms of fiscal governance measures can deceive.

Economic Culture and Ideologies of Debt

As we saw in Chapter 9, state capacity to manage public debt dynamics is framed and constrained by economic culture and ideologies of debt. Governing elites must take account of the beliefs and attitudes of those they seek to persuade, including the public. Economic cultures incorporate different beliefs about, and attitudes to, public debt. They reflect different constructions of its political and moral significance with respect to social welfare and national identity. The meanings attached to public debt vary from, at one extreme, stability cultures, which tolerate short-term welfare losses for longer-term gains from debt reduction, to 'welfare protection' cultures, which stress entitlements.

However, again, causal direction is far from clear. Public debt dynamics and economic culture and debt ideology are bound together in an endogenous process.

The complex relationship between public debt dynamics and economic culture was evident in east central Europe (Greskovits 2008). From 1998 onwards Hungary's problems in managing public debt dynamics were bound up with two-party competition to consolidate the legacy of decades of buying social peace after the 1955 uprising through building a generous welfare protection culture. In Slovakia, by contrast, there was a clear political break with the first post-independence governments under Vladimir Meciar (1993–1998). They had constructed an economic culture of welfare protection, buttressed by political authoritarianism and isolation within Europe. The political break took the form of refashioning economic culture around sound finances as part of the construction of a new European identity. This refashioning could also look back to the former Czechoslovakia, which during the interwar period and after 1945 had pursued more stability-oriented policies than Hungary. The legacy of public debt dynamics in Slovakia was more favourable to the construction of an economic culture of stability than in Hungary.

Veto Players

Public debt dynamics are also affected by the existence of domestic veto players, whose preferences become critical reference points in fiscal consolidation and structural reforms. They include formal institutional veto points, such as upper chambers in bicameral legislatures, federal systems, constitutional courts, systems of collective bargaining, and social partnership in welfare-state arrangements. However, there is again no clear correlation between scale of problems in managing public debt dynamics and formal veto points in 'semi-sovereign' political systems. Germany remained a fiscal saint despite having a very high dispersion of domestic power.

The relationship between public debt dynamics and domestic veto points is mediated by economic culture and the public prestige and intellectual self-confidence of the institutions that become identified with safeguarding that culture. From the early 1990s the constituency of support for stability culture was strengthened as central banks were granted independence across the EU. National central banks, for instance in France and Italy, promoted the agenda of fiscal consolidation and structural reforms on often reluctant governments. One factor in the different public debt dynamics in Slovakia from Hungary was the greater independence that Slovak central bank governors enjoyed. Characteristically, the classically independent Bundesbank defined its role as the self-appointed guardian of German (and now euro area) stability culture.

Moreover, the key veto points may be informal. They are most typically found in 'party states' in which extensive patronage and clientelism flourish. A putatively 'strong' state like Greece—with its formally centralized powers and single-party government—was emasculated by entrenched networks of privileges and protection. These networks extended from leaders of party factions to groups like civil engineers, doctors, pharmacists, lawyers, lorry drivers, seamen, as well as to civil-service unions, which enjoyed generous public-sector wages, pensions, and working conditions. Vested interests reached into the political parties and through them into the state, producing institutional inertia and weakness and the spread of tax exemptions and evasion. Consequently, the institutional capacity of the core executive to deliver on fiscal commitments was very low.

Governing Competence

Public debt dynamics can also be attributed to the governing competence of elites. In the first place, political elites need to be skilful in crafting a persuasive national narrative of creditworthiness that mobilizes broad support for fiscal consolidation and structural reforms. They have to be able to build a sustainable domestic consensus around reforms. These skills are often difficult to practise. In 2010 George Papandreou, the Greek prime minister, sought to devise a new domestic narrative that painted opponents of reform as 'leeches' on society, who had evaded taxes whilst imposing their own levy on society. However, by 2012 his party had been decimated in the elections. An inclusive approach continued to elude Greek elites. They faced a combination of multiple powerful veto points with a deep commitment to protecting privileges and entitlements.

Secondly, governing elites must possess the competence to translate words into actions, if they are not to appear rhetorical dissimulators who lack character. However, the legacy of nepotism and patronage can prove a powerful constraint on managing public debt dynamics. Clientelism diminishes capacity for collective action on behalf of public goods. Its effects were discernible not just in Greece but also in Hungary, Italy, and Spain, each in its own idiosyncratic way.

Fiscal Rules

The willingness of states to bind themselves by tough, numeric domestic fiscal rules and incentives for sound public finances, including independent fiscal councils, provides another potential explanation for differential state capacity to control public debt dynamics. By December 2012 numeric public debt rules remained the exception. They were to be found only in six out of twenty-seven EU Member States: Hungary, Ireland, Poland, Slovakia, Spain, and Sweden. These Member States were, however, not always paragons of fiscal virtue.

The two main European role models were Germany and Sweden. Sweden possessed the most comprehensive and tough domestic fiscal framework. Following the Swiss example, Germany pioneered the introduction of a domestic constitutional 'debt brake' in 2009. It rested on the 'balanced-budget' rule and created new punishment mechanisms through the courts and through public opinion for failure to comply. By December 2012 eleven of the twenty-seven EU Member States had taken the lead in implementing the balanced-budget rule in compliance with the new Treaty on Stability, Coordination, and Governance in the Economic and Monetary Union. They included France, Italy, and Spain. The treaty required the incorporation of the balanced-budget rule into national laws through 'provisions of binding force and permanent character, preferably constitutional'.

Sweden was the leader in introducing a strictly enforced numeric public expenditure rule. It did so from 1997 in the wake of its banking and fiscal crisis of the early 1990s. The budget surplus law stipulated that governments should set expenditure ceilings three years in advance and should run a surplus equivalent to 1 per cent of GDP over the business cycle. The key budgetary principle became: 'Each minister is his own finance minister.' Subsequent success in reducing the public debt/GDP ratio from 78 per cent in 2000 to 34 per cent in 2011 led the OECD to praise Sweden as a model. With reference to the Swedish model, the ECB (2009b: 73) noted that across the EU debt sustainability had been seriously compromised before the post-2007 crisis by public expenditure growth exceeding nominal GDP growth. This excessive growth of public expenditure had too often been financed by large windfall revenues from asset and housing market booms. The ECB argued that EU Member States lacked prudent public expenditure growth rules. Prudent rules would combine limits on expenditure growth, defined by potential GDP growth, with a margin of safety. However, as with domestic debt rules, numeric expenditure rules remained the exception. By December 2012 only seven of twenty-seven EU Member States had them: the three Nordic States, Austria, Ireland, the Netherlands, and Spain.

Despite their numeric character, domestic fiscal rules to strengthen financial market confidence left significant scope for various forms of circumvention. There was, for instance, provision for 'exceptional circumstances' in both the German debt brake and the euro area fiscal compact treaty. Governments retained discretion to respond to emergencies or natural disasters or when, in the German law, 'market developments deviate from normal conditions'. In addition, the problem of 'off-balance-sheet' provisions remained.

The main instrument of compliance remained public pressure and the construction of a supportive stability culture. In this respect independent domestic fiscal councils could play a useful supportive role. They could verify government projections and highlight risks to long-term debt sustainability. The leading role in establishing independent fiscal councils was played by Austria, Belgium, and Sweden. By December 2012 independent fiscal councils were established in twelve out of the twenty-seven EU Member States.

The Electoral Cycle

Political will and state capacity to control public debt dynamics can be seen as a function of the electoral cycle (Alesina 1989). According to traditional political business cycle theory, competition for office is instrumental in triggering party political bidding contests over lower taxes and higher public spending. As elections approach, governments seek to stimulate the economy, raise incomes, and create jobs on terms that defy fiscal sustainability (Nordhaus 1975). In other versions, politicians seek to increase benefits for favoured clients. The resulting negative effects on public debt sustainability surface with a time lag and, over the longer term, generate concerns about the governing competence of political elites. They provide the rationale for clear, precise, and 'quasi-automatic' fiscal rules to bind governing elites.

However, the political business cycle is endogenous to particular domestic politics. Domestic structural context matters. Electoral bidding wars are more likely in states with very large public sector employment and with many dependent for income on social benefits than in states in which large numbers depend on fixed incomes. In some circumstances promises of higher wages, better pensions, and improved social protection seem electorally rational. As Hungary demonstrated, the political risk resides in post-election public debt crisis, embarrassing reversal of policies, and a domestic as well as international image of governing incompetence that can become a future electoral liability. Once rising public debt is perceived to threaten the image of governing competence of party elites, electoral contest focuses on the details of the timing and the pace of fiscal consolidation. In consequence, political business cycles do not have a strong correlation with public debt dynamics. However, they may—as in Hungary—be important in fashioning a particular negative image of the state and its public and of the governing competence of party elites.

Public Opinion

At a more fundamental level political will and state capacity to control public debt dynamics can be attributed to public opinion. The problem is to specify what is significant in public opinion and how it affects public debt. Three dimensions of public opinion seem relevant: the legacy of traditional folk beliefs and religious ideas about debt; the degree of social and political fragmentation; and public trust in institutions.

As we have seen, attitudes to debt have deep roots in traditional beliefs about virtuous households and citizens. They are also religiously anchored, even if in an indirect, implicit fashion as societies become more secularized and commercialized. There is a traditional association of Roman Catholicism and Lutheran Protestantism with hostility to usury. Hence one would expect public opinion in societies that have been shaped by these religions to penalize governments that built up high debt levels. To the extent that this is true in Italy, it seems to apply to personal and corporate debt rather than to public debt and to express itself in a critical attitude to the weak governing competence of party elites. However, taking three major Roman Catholic states—France, Italy, and Spain—the relationship of religion to public debt dynamics seems unclear. Calvinism and Lutheranism seem to have a closer association in northern and western Europe with public mistrust of public debt.

On closer examination, public opinion poses contradictory challenges to public debt reduction strategies. On the one hand, there is no evidence that advocacy of public debt reduction leads to electoral punishment (Alesina, Carloni, and Lecce 2010). On the other, historical evidence since 1919 suggests that implementation of public debt retrenchment generates various forms of social unrest: riots, demonstrations, general strikes, assassinations, and even attempts at revolutionary overthrow (Ponticelli and Voth 2011). The conclusions seem contradictory. From the perspective of avoiding social unrest and political instability, avoidance of public debt retrenchment seems a rational political strategy. From the perspective of public attitudes to excessive debt, it is not rational.

Political will and state capacity to control public debt dynamics might also be attributed to the degree of ethnic, religious, and linguistic fragmentation. Social fragmentation creates incentives for the proliferation of political parties and problems of majority formation. In these ways it might be expected to hinder political consensus building to deal with major public debt adjustment. However, again the evidence is mixed. The most homogenous societies in the EU correlate very weakly with fiscal 'saints'. They include Greece, Ireland, and Portugal, as well as Denmark, Malta, and Poland. The most ethnically, religiously, and linguistically divided states are Belgium, Estonia, Latvia, and Switzerland, followed by the Netherlands (Sadeh 2006: 97). They correlate better with political will and state capacity to pay creditors than with fiscal sinning. Much depends on the nature of social fragmentation and its endogenous aspects. Difficulties in managing public debt dynamics increase with the intensity of the social cleavages. They are influenced by whether, and how, party elites choose to mobilize cleavages, in particular whether this mobilization supports public debt stabilization. Reputation for governing competence turns positive in divided societies like Switzerland when party elites commit to devices, like grand coalition and proportionality in office-holding, that achieve accommodation across cleavages in support of fiscal stability.

Public trust in institutions has a complex relationship to the political will and state capacity to manage public debt dynamics. On the one hand, perceptions of fiscal performance affect levels of trust. On the other hand, public trust is a condition for sustaining the political will and state capacity to control public debt dynamics. Public trust can prove resilient when, as in Latvia, governing elites are able to draw on historical memories of past successes in mastering crises to strengthen resolve. However, it has a tendency to decline when faced with adverse macroeconomic developments, notably sharp GDP decline, and structural developments, like asset-price and property busts and banking crises. Financial and economic evidence alters images of governing competence and serves to change trust in institutional arrangements. Mobilizing and sustaining public trust is critical to political will and state capacity. It is also fraught with difficulties.

The State Tradition

Political will and state capacity to manage public debt dynamics is about more than party and political elites (Dyson 2010). It is also bound up with the creation and maintenance of a professional, efficient administrative system that demonstrates evidence of executive autonomy from both civil society and the market. Managing public debt dynamics is easier when the state is perceived to serve public interests and purposes rather than to exist as an arena within which financial, business, and party elites extract and exploit resources from state and society for their own rent-seeking purposes. The image of the state as the servant of 'crony' capitalism erodes public trust.

Political will and state capacity is about the embedding of strong norms of moral integrity and dedication to service in public life, the careful and sustained nurturing of these norms, and their credibility with public opinion and markets. It is about sustaining a broad political consensus that values civic obligations in paying taxes and honouring debts, in investing in productivity-enhancing infrastructure and social investment, and in exercising prudence in public finances. In short, sovereign creditworthiness can outlive adverse developments in party political and electoral factors. It does so when confidence in the autonomy and moral integrity of the state remains intact and supports an ongoing image of governing competence.

Managing public debt dynamics is caught up in the complex relationship between political will and state capacity. Both matter. However, they can combine in different ways. Political will to manage public debt dynamics may be present, but without state capacity to deliver. State capacity may exist, but without the political will. Where both political will and state capacity to manage public debt dynamics are absent, serial sovereign debt crises follow. Where both are present, public debt dynamics are more likely to prove benign and sovereign creditworthiness more secure.

The Context-Specific, Contingent, and Constructed Nature of Public Debt Dynamics

The range of exogenous and endogenous factors that influence public debt dynamics underlines the acute problems in matching liability with control. Public debt dynamics is both context-specific and constructed. It is affected by particular configurations of macroeconomic, financial, and structural factors that are imperfectly controlled by governing elites. It is vulnerable to events, whether single exogenous shocks or an accumulation of mini-shocks. The effects spread contagiously within financial systems and onto public balance sheets. In addition, changes in institutional, political, and ideological factors flash red warning signals about sovereign creditworthiness. Examples include fiscally irresponsible electoral competition, ideological warfare about public debt within government, shortening cabinet duration of minority or unpopular governments, recalcitrant fiscal behaviour of ministerial fiefdoms, and indicators of declining social trust.

Evidential changes across any of these indicators can serve as engines, redefining whether a state is perceived as creditworthy. However, what matters in the last analysis is whether a state—or more precisely its governing elite—is seen as possessing the political will and having the state capacity to master public debt dynamics. This perception is again context-specific and potentially fragile. It is not reducible to a single, measurable indicator. It also correlates weakly with such factors as party ideology, single-party or coalition government, or type of fiscal institution.

16

Public Debt and Multilevel Statehood: Sub-National Fiscal Governance, Structural Imbalances, and 'Stand-Alone' Fiscal Capacity

Examining the conundrum of matching liability with control requires looking into the 'black box' of the state. As other chapters show, this black box includes the nature of fiscal governance at the level of central executives; the cultural attributes and political behaviour of governing elites; and the state's capacity for managing banking and financial crises. The structure and dynamics of sub-national fiscal governance represent another aspect of the black box of the state. The problematic of matching liability with control touches on the formal and the material fiscal capacity of cities and regions. It also highlights ongoing controversy about the purpose of sub-national fiscal capacity building. Is it about compliance with firm nominal fiscal rules to ensure sustainable debt and fiscal transparency and accountability? Is it about sub-national capacity to invest productively in asset building and social provision in order to strengthen long-term gross domestic product (GDP) growth potential and future tax capacity?

Controversy about public debt in Europe is situated within a great variety of complex frameworks of multilevel fiscal governance. Sovereign debt crises highlight the seriousness of the problem of sub-national fiscal capacity, the high degree of historical path dependency in sub-national fiscal governance, and the difficult trade-offs in seeking to build sub-national fiscal capacity. At one extreme states can re-centralize in ways that erode sub-national fiscal capacity for productive investment; at another, they can become caught up in sub-national bail-outs that threaten their sovereign creditworthiness. Most attempt to negotiate sub-national fiscal bargains that, in very variable ways, combine hierarchical controls; political and legal sanctions through direct sub-national fiscal accountability to voters and courts; and market-based discipline on sub-national borrowing.

Why Does Sub-National Fiscal Capacity Matter?

As we have seen, cities and regions played a formative role in the history of European public debt. The phenomenon of spatial differentiation within an informal hierarchy of European regions and cities predated the modern European state. It was evident amongst the city states of Ancient Greece. Later, in early-modern Europe, dynastically ambitious, centralizing territorial rulers emulated the borrowing practices of the most successful European regions and cities. Cities like Amsterdam, Antwerp, Augsburg, Florence, Lucca, Lyon, and Venice served as the major historic pioneers of public-debt financing. The historic relationship of cities and regions to English state-building was very different. Moreover, this spatial differentiation in late-medieval and early-modern Europe had its roots in external economic imbalances and the territorial agglomeration of finance. This phenomenon continues to remain fundamentally important in structuring the opportunities for, and constraints on, sub-national fiscal capacity building. Structural economic imbalances and financial agglomeration empower a few European cities and regions over the many others.

Formal and material sub-national fiscal capacity matters for the reputation of cities and regions. It affects their ability to provide the conditions for sustainable real GDP growth and to effectively deliver infrastructural and social investment. Fiscal capacity affects their position in the informal hierarchy of European cities and regions and their ability to compete in leading on best practice. It is also a vital component in sub-national identity formation and in securing their political legitimacy. Moreover, sub-national fiscal capacity means having access to a wide tax base, some freedom in setting tax rates, and, not least, borrowing capacity. It is essential for sub-national governments to have access to, and secure confidence in, international bond markets. Their prize is ample liquidity and lower interest rates for borrowing than has been traditionally available through domestic banks. Fiscal capacity is essential for sub-national credit ratings, which in turn define the relative positions of cities and regions. They provide sub-national governments with status and with symbolic affirmation. In short, sub-national image and reputation for governing competence is bound up with fiscal capacity.

Also, sub-national fiscal capacity matters to central and federal governments. It has implications for sovereign creditworthiness. It affects capacity to comply with EU fiscal rules and commitments and to avoid financial sanctions under the excessive deficit procedure. Moreover, failures of sub-national fiscal capacity building and compliance heighten risks of territorial bail-outs, with the result that sub-national liabilities are added to national liabilities. These fears were elevated post-2007 by banking and sovereign debt crises, actual and potential.

At times of financial and economic crisis, heightening risks to sovereign creditworthiness and to compliance with EU fiscal commitments create incentives for national governments to re-centralize through the 'hardening' of fiscal constraints. These incentives also increased during the process of meeting the Maastricht fiscal convergence criteria for euro entry. They continued in the form of the Stability and Growth Pact (SGP). However, the key factor in changing the dynamic of sub-national fiscal governance was the post-2007 sovereign debt crises and the European economic governance reforms that followed, notably the fiscal compact treaty of 2012. This dynamic was reinforced when, as in Belgium and Germany, the bulk of fiscal deficit reduction had been achieved at the federal level (Organization for Economic Cooperation and Development 2010: 61).

Variations in domestic sub-national fiscal capacity matter in their own right. They shed light on domestic power relations, notably territorial asymmetry of power. They also expose vulnerability to the mismatch between liability and control in public finances. In addition, they reveal differences of view about the normative principles on which sub-national fiscal governance should be based. Economic and Monetary Union (EMU), and above all the post-2007 sovereign debt crises, highlighted the problems associated with variations in sub-national fiscal capacity. They also served to empower cities and regions with high fiscal capacity in defining the terms on which the problems of sub-national fiscal governance were debated and addressed. There was a gradual shift of domestic territorial power away from cities and regions with weak fiscal capacity.

This shift in the axis of territorial power was reflected in the new saliency of two types of discourse about sub-national fiscal governance reform. The discourse of 'too much regions' represented the problem as threat to national identity and solidarity; as sub-national inefficiency and the misallocation of resources to 'vanity' projects of sub-national elites; and as sub-national 'crony' politics and corruption, typically associated with licenses, public tenders, and undue influence over local and regional banks. The solution was a new national priority to strengthening hierarchical fiscal discipline on regions and to protecting national integrity. The second discourse represented the problem as the lack of sub-national fiscal autonomy and clear fiscal transparency and accountability. The solution lay in a shift away from horizontal and vertical fiscal transfers to stronger direct political accountability to sub-national voters for tax and spending decisions and greater discipline through financial market sanctions. This discourse was strongly promoted by cities and regions with high fiscal capacity, reinforced where this capacity coincided with strong sub-national cultural identity.

The outcome of these discursive shifts was a more abrasive sub-national politics. Sub-national relations became infected with distrust and mutual suspicion. There was a reopening of contest about the normative principles that should govern territorial politics. Regions like Flanders in Belgium, Bavaria in Germany, Lombardy in Italy, and Catalonia in Spain took a tougher line on fiscal transfers. They demanded greater fiscal autonomy, above all in taxation. In turn, disciplinary pressures on cities and regions with weak fiscal capacity mounted.

By 2010–2012 there were powerful political and market-based pressures to renegotiate sub-national fiscal governance across Europe. They stemmed from contagious sovereign debt and banking crises, the heightened risk of negative spill-over from sub-national liabilities, and more abrasive sub-national political relations. Pressures to strengthen hierarchical controls took the form of 'top-down' Europeanization. The EU excessive deficit procedure was strengthened, with particular reference to targets for debt reduction. The fiscal compact treaty 'locked-in' national 'balanced-budget' rules to ensure sound public finances, including the possibility of domestic legal challenge. In addition, direct market pressures increased on sub-national governments that had earlier been beneficiaries of moves towards fiscal federalism. They experienced the new intrusiveness of sub-national credit ratings and the associated risk of being shut out of bond markets and losing their capacity to finance infrastructural and social investment.

These developments acted as catalysts for new debates about territorial justice. They altered prevailing conceptions of what constitutes fiscal fairness, empowering supporters of greater fiscal autonomy or even independence in regions with strong fiscal capacity, like Flanders and Lombardy. Sub-national bail-outs in regions like Andalusia and Sicily were accompanied by specific, detailed, and tight central government conditionality. Debate about reforms to sub-national fiscal governance illustrated a changing trade-off: away from traditional concerns with territorial equity and solidarity towards a new stress on promoting national economic efficiency and strengthening sub-national fiscal accountability and transparency. Regions with weak fiscal capacity were subjected to reinforced hierarchical and market-based budgetary constraints. The chief domestic political driver was a rebalancing in the relative power of regions with strong and weak fiscal capacity. Catalonia represented a paradox. It had strong fiscal capacity, transferring substantial taxes. At the same time, Catalonia's fiscal position deteriorated, forcing it in 2012 to request financial support from the Madrid government. Fiscal autonomy or independence was seen as a means of strengthening fiscal capacity.

The Distinctive Characteristics of Sub-National Fiscal Governance

Central problems in sub-national fiscal governance mirror those in European creditor-debtor state relations. Normatively, sub-national fiscal governance involves difficult and contentious political trade-offs between allowing fiscal autonomy and choice to regions, promoting efficiency in resource allocation, ensuring equity across regions, and providing accountability to taxpayers (cf. Commission on Scottish Devolution 2009). To this list can be added support for sub-national fiscal capacity building to invest productively and to strengthen fiscal discipline. In making these trade-offs, the balances are struck differently across space and over time. Broadly speaking, receiving regions from fiscal transfers favour the principle of territorial justice and support for sub-national capacity building based on central funding according to need. Contributing regions promote the principle of fiscal autonomy, efficiency in resource allocation, and support for building sub-national fiscal discipline. Outcomes depend on what can be politically agreed in the context of these opposed interests and on the way in which certain kinds of argument about trade-offs are privileged by economic structure. Sub-national fiscal governance bears the imprint of structural imbalances and asymmetric territorial power.

At the same time, sub-national fiscal governance is distinguished from state fiscal governance in various ways. First, and most obviously, sub-national governments lack the common denominator of sovereignty that attaches to states. They are deeply embedded in the complex institutional and policy residues of protracted historical European state-building and national-identity building processes. Typically, these historical processes led to a dominant notion of European states as economic and social unions, which express the collective commitment to shared values of solidarity and to principles of equity, equalization, and uniformity. However, some sub-national regions, like Catalonia and Scotland, retain powerful historical memories of statehood that can be evoked and mobilized to claim sovereign status.

The historical processes of state-building have made territorial justice and hierarchy key issues in sub-national fiscal governance. They become even more important when, as in the Nordic states and Spain, sub-national governments have responsibility for the delivery of major aspects of welfare-state provision, like education, health, and social protection. Their delivery requires elaborate fiscal transfer systems to support notions of need and of equalization of sub-national fiscal capacity. In addition, it poses questions about state capacity to develop mechanisms of hierarchical control over costly sub-national budgets. The incentives to strengthen this capacity were increased by EU treaty change in 2011–2012.

Secondly, sub-national borrowing is principally about managing short-term cash balances, which arise from temporal variation in the flows of revenues and expenditures, and about financing infrastructural investments. Despite the ambitions of some German *Länder*, Spanish autonomous communities, and Swiss cantons, sub-national borrowing has less to do with macroeconomic stabilization through counter-cyclical fiscal policies. Even federal systems offer little scope for sub-national governments to engage in counter-cyclical borrowing. Moreover, sub-national borrowing for capital investment is subject to national prudential rules to prevent negative externalities. These rules remained notably tight in Britain, the Nordic states, and east central Europe. In the context of EMU, and above all the post-2007 crisis, they were 'hardened' in federal and federalizing states like Belgium, Germany, Italy, and Spain.

Thirdly, sub-national fiscal governance exemplifies the strength of the political economy constraints on the exit options—full fiscal autonomy and independence. Typically, the main alternatives in negotiating sub-national fiscal governance are loyalty and voice (cf. Hirschman 1970). Exit may have strong cultural, institutional, and political attractions (Keating, Loughlin, and Deschouwer 2003). However, in political economy terms, fiscal autonomy is a less attractive option for regions that lack 'stand-alone' fiscal capacity. Exit is less attractive to Bremen than Bavaria; to Galicia than Catalonia; to Sicily than Lombardy; or to Wallonia than Flanders. It involves high risk of lower operating revenues, higher taxes and/or expenditure cuts, and incapacity to access international capital markets. Regions that lack 'stand-alone' fiscal capacity have a vested political-economy interest in emphasizing the ideological importance of 'social union' in designing sub-national fiscal governance. Its governing principles should be common standards of social welfare, equal living conditions, and collective support for sub-national capacity building.

Regions with 'stand-alone' fiscal capacity are also constrained from exercising the exit option. They function in a context in which the power of regions that lack this capacity is firmly entrenched within national institutional frameworks. Their power is expressed in second chambers of federal systems (like Germany), national party systems (like France and Spain), and clientelist networks (as in Greece and Russia) (Wibbels 2003). Regions that possess 'stand-alone' fiscal capacity lack the power of numbers. The political consent of other regions for 'hard' budgetary constraints has to be won. Gaining this consent involves complex coalition building, use of the disciplinary power of national party systems, changing national legislative rules to reduce veto power, and regional reforms to strengthen political competition and hence electoral threat to incumbent sub-national governments.

More pertinently, regions that have 'stand-alone' fiscal capacity benefit from the intricate, opaque web of domestic and international trade and financial flows in which they are embedded. There is an incentive for them to accept fiscal transfer systems as a side-payment for these benefits (Rodden 2009). In exchange, costly sub-national fiscal transfers provide compensation to other regions for the beneficial structural imbalances enjoyed by regions with 'stand-alone' fiscal capacity. These imbalances follow from the 'agglomeration effects' that are associated with an internal economic union. Moreover, constitutional provisions, institutional arrangements, and veto points, like territorially-based upper chambers, serve to lock-in fiscal transfer commitments. They take on a path-dependent character.

This combination of institutionally enshrined side-payments with historical path dependency constrains the power of regions with 'stand-alone' fiscal capacity. Within this framework, discourse about sub-national fiscal governance assumes the form of counter-claims about loyalty to the principle of solidarity and about dangers of moral hazard. It involves mutual accusations of exploitation: the language of resentment in regions with 'stand-alone' fiscal capacity about 'robbery' and that of 'victimhood' in regions which lack this capacity. Regional political leaders in Baden-Württemberg, Catalonia, Flanders, Lombardy, and potentially London and southern England, complain that they are forced to live 'beneath their means' because regions like Berlin, Andalusia, Wallonia, Sicily, and Scotland and Wales live 'above their means'.

Despite this often highly emotive language, the exit option loses attraction for both types of region because they benefit, if asymmetrically, from 'risk-pooling' by tax-sharing. Exit would deny them the incentive of being able to mitigate the impact of regionally specific shocks on their budgets. This incentive proved important not just for the new German *Bundesländer* like Saxony-Anhalt but also for North-Rhine Westphalia. Fiscal transfer systems are a form of collective insurance.

Finally, in the face of mobile factors of production, sub-national governments have even more limited scope for fiscal autonomy in setting tax rates than states. In federal as well as decentralized fiscal systems, sub-national governments tend to have greater autonomy over public expenditure than over tax revenues. They fear internal 'harmful' tax competition as a threat to the principle of progressive taxation. It risks stimulating a territorial 'race to the bottom' in which the main casualty would be sub-national social welfare (cf. Commission on Scottish Devolution 2009). Fear of a 'race to the bottom' was accentuated by interregional competition for investment as a result of the European single market. It was also increased by the erosion of belief in the effectiveness of central transfer-based regional policy and by the rise of new theories of endogenous regional development.

The risks from tax competition take on extra significance when regions have tax powers over mobile factors like business and labour. For this reason, regions that lack 'stand-alone' fiscal capacity tend to be more attracted to formula-based, block-grant funding systems, based on the principle of need, than to fiscal tax autonomy. Tax autonomy threatens to expose their weak fiscal capacity, generate fiscal inequity, and make them vulnerable to less predictable revenues (cf. Independent Commission on Funding and Finance for Wales 2009).

Moreover, tax-varying powers, for instance in corporation tax, face the hurdle of the conditions set out in the Azores, Gibraltar, and Rioja rulings of the European Court of Justice (ECJ). In order to avoid infringement of EU state-aid rules, tax-varying powers would have to be accompanied by institutional and procedural changes that gave greater fiscal autonomy to the sub-national government. Otherwise, differential taxation would constitute selective regional subsidy in contravention of the European single market. Hence it remained unclear whether selective corporation-tax-varying powers for the Northern Ireland Executive could be used to compete with the Irish government's lower corporation tax rate. The Executive would have to accept responsibility for the full fiscal consequences, including the commensurate reduction of the UK block grant (Her Majesty's Treasury 2011).

Grand Bargains and National Cohesion

Living in a state and sharing a collective identity imply the willingness, if conditional, to equalize living conditions, to provide common insurance, and to share burdens through tax transfers. In short, states internalize collective assistance from cities and regions with 'stand-alone' fiscal capacity to those that lack this capacity. The scale and implications of this collective assistance constitute a potentially explosive issue area in domestic politics. For this reason, this issue area is not amenable to a purely dispassionate economic analysis. Emotionally-laden moral arguments are never far from the surface in sub-national fiscal governance. By 2012 German politicians were singling out Bremen and Berlin as domestic variants of Greece. Andalusia in Spain and Sicily in Italy were stereotyped in the same way. Managing sovereign debt crisis draws emotional language to the surface. The resulting tensions and conflicts could threaten the very cohesion of states.

National cohesion is premised on often implicit grand bargains. Bargains can take different forms. They may involve a trade-off in which regions that lack 'stand-alone' fiscal capacity give loyalty to the centre in exchange for costly tax and spending programmes that offer a public sector corrective for private sector economic imbalances. This corrective characterizes the relationship of Northern Ireland, Scotland, and Wales to England. Within England itself, it distinguishes the relationship of London and the south-east to the north, the north-west, and the south-west. In terms of taxes and public spending, London and the south-east can be pictured as paying a fiscal price for the broader economic benefits they derive from the union. Conversely, in Italy and Spain, the grand bargain takes a different form. It involves a trade-off in which sub-national entities which possess 'stand-alone' fiscal capacity, like Bolzano and Trento, and the Basque Country and Navarre, pledge loyalty to the centre in exchange for substantial fiscal autonomy, limiting their liability for regions like Sicily and Andalusia.

These two types of grand bargain illustrate different ways in which sub-national 'stand-alone' fiscal capacity interacts with sub-national identity politics. The key is whether the national and history-based minorities that represent a threat to national cohesion have sub-national 'stand-alone' fiscal capacity. Those that have this capacity can argue that they are being asked to pay 'too high a price' for the union. Those that lack this capacity resent the absence of fiscal support from a union which is seen as economically exploiting them. The post-2007 sovereign debt crises, and associated central fiscal tightening and conditionality, helped to unmask the nature of these grand bargains, with unpredictable consequences.

Historical Path Dependence in Sub-National Fiscal Governance

The ways in which shared pressures are refracted into sub-national fiscal governance are shaped by domestic legacies of ideas and practices of political rule and by specificities of territorial economic structure. Governing elites at domestic and European levels are embedded in very different worlds of sub-national fiscal governance. These worlds involve multi-actor and multi-level coordination through complex and varying mixes of hierarchy and negotiation, involving contextually specific rules and codes of behaviour. There is no standard European model of sub-national fiscal governance (Wyn Jones and Scully 2010: 7).

Sub-national fiscal governance is variously 'top-down' or 'bottom-up' in its historical origins and dynamics. In France ideas and practices of sub-national fiscal governance were constrained by the value attached to the 'unity' of the state in the Republican and Bonapartist traditions (Dyson 2010). The main shaping influence was top-down: central government efficiency, state-led economic development, and statistical convenience. In post-Franco Spain, by contrast, the strength and importance of sub-national cultural identities was recognized in the constitution. Similarly, the price of German unification in 1871 was substantial fiscal powers for the *Länder*. Post-1945, the process of German constitution building was essentially a bottom-up affair. In historical contexts in which sub-national fiscal governance has emerged in a top-down fashion, their elites are more likely to see themselves as fiscal policy 'takers' rather than 'makers'. In historical contexts in which sub-national fiscal governance has emerged in a bottom-up fashion, their elites possess more opportunity to build and sustain high domestic and international profile by mobilizing resources to boost city or regional image.

However, factors of institutional and political path dependence are far from decisive in building sub-national fiscal capacity, in establishing a leadership role in sub-national emulation processes, and in gaining reputation for policy delivery and best practice. Sub-national fiscal capacity building is closely associated with economic structure, in particular with a strong sub-national presence of industries representing the second, science-based industrial revolution and the 'knowledge-based' economy. Fiscal capacity building is linked to the domestic political economy of structural imbalances. Cities and regions are embedded in complex trade and financial flows, which either empower or disempower them. These flows shape both tax capacity and endogenous credit creation. They help explain why Baden-Württemberg and Bavaria have much greater fiscal capacity than Bremen and the Saarland or why the fiscal capacity of Northern Ireland and Wales lags far behind that of England.

The Formal Index and Material Reality of Sub-National Fiscal Capacity: Autonomy and 'Stand-Alone' Capacity

Formal sub-national fiscal governance relationships help shape the resources of power that are available to sub-national governments in exercising their authority and in gaining status and significance in the informal hierarchy of European cities and regions. However, in examining sub-national fiscal capacity, three points must be borne in mind. First, it is important to distinguish the criteria that help formally measure sub-national fiscal capacity from the material reality of sub-national fiscal capacity. Secondly, one must not forget that sub-national fiscal capacity is bound up with that of the sovereign state. There are exceptions: the Basque Country and Navarre have higher credit ratings than Spanish debt. Generally speaking, however, sub-national fiscal capacity is more secure when the sovereign has a triple-A credit rating. Sovereign creditworthiness has the attributes of a public good in sub-national fiscal governance.

Thirdly, the key and controversial question is: sub-national fiscal capacity to do what? For the EU and for Member-State governments, the answer has principally been the capacity to comply with firm fiscal rules in order to secure long-term debt sustainability. However, for many city and regional elites the answer has involved building the capacity for productive investment in infrastructure and in social provision. Sub-national fiscal capacity has been about strengthening city and regional balance sheets through asset building.

Formally, sub-national fiscal capacity in the form sought by city and regional elites is to be measured by the extent of their fiscal autonomy in setting rates across a range of taxes, including business rates, property taxes, environmental taxes, and even some part of income tax. On this basis, London lagged far behind Berlin and Paris; Scotland and Wales were far behind French departments, German *Länder*, Spanish autonomous communities, and Danish, Norwegian, and Swedish local authorities. Sub-national fiscal capacity can also be measured by how much, if any, fiscal co-determination cities and regions have in the distribution of national tax revenues. On this measure, London, Northern Ireland, Scotland, and Wales lacked formal fiscal capacity. In addition, sub-national fiscal capacity can be measured by the extent to which cities and regions are vertically dependent on central grants, on the conditionality that is attached, and on how 'hard' or 'soft' budgetary constraints are. Here, the British model of choice for the devolved regions within centrally transferred resources provides them with some fiscal autonomy. Using the above three criteria, Denmark and Sweden emerge as notably high in sub-national fiscal capacity (Loughlin and Martin 2005: 25).

Tax autonomy relates to another measure of formal sub-national fiscal capacity: whether cities and regions have freedom to borrow, above all for productive investment in infrastructure and for investing in education, training, and research and development. The main indicators of borrowing autonomy are legal powers to borrow; central limits on the purposes for which debt may be used; requirements for central authorization to borrow; external rules that constrain borrowing; and access to sub-national public banks and public enterprises for debt financing (Rodden 2002). Generally, federal or federalizing states provide greater borrowing autonomy. In 2012 borrowing autonomy was highest for Swiss cantons, followed in descending order by Spanish autonomous communities, German *Länder*, and Italian regions. Austria was something of an anomaly: a federal state that had much lower borrowing autonomy than other European federal states. There was even greater variation amongst traditionally centralized states. France scored highly on the borrowing autonomy index, whereas Britain had one of the lowest scores (Rodden 2002).

Another key measure of formal sub-national fiscal capacity is the degree of generosity of horizontal and vertical fiscal transfer systems in supporting cities and regions. Fiscal transfer systems provide 'system strength' and predictability to sub-national public finances. One element of system strength is the credibility of expectations of sub-national bail-outs. These expectations tend to be higher with large and systemically significant sub-national governments, like Berlin and Lazio. System strength helps boost international credit ratings. The German *Länder* score well on the formal fiscal capacity index with respect both to freedom to borrow for productive investment and to system strength through fiscal equalization.

In contrast, cities and regions in east central Europe perform much less well in the formal fiscal capacity index. Traditionally, states like Bulgaria and Hungary have been highly centralist. Moreover, attitudes to sub-national fiscal governance were negative after sub-national fiscal and financial crises in the early post-communist transition period. The expectation that EU accession would facilitate regionalization, notably for Structural Fund purposes, was frustrated by the preference of east European central governments for 'hard' hierarchical budgetary constraints in managing both transition and Europeanization. This preference was reinforced by the post-2007 crisis and by reforms to European economic governance in 2011–2012. Sub-national governments had to be brought firmly within the framework of the revised SGP. Moreover, 'hardening' sub-national budgetary constraints was an instrument by which governing elites in states like Hungary could seek to distinguish themselves from those in the Ukraine (Rodden and Eskeland 2000).

One particular area of risk in sub-national fiscal governance stems from the 'common resource pool' problem. It arises when low sub-national fiscal autonomy and high dependency on central grants are accompanied by sub-national freedom to borrow. This combination of features creates incentives for sub-national fiscal indiscipline. It fosters high expectations that national governments will take on responsibility for expenditures that are of local or regional benefit (Rodden 2002 and 2009; Rodden and Wibbels 2002). This type of sub-national fiscal governance promotes a lack of transparency about the relationship between tax and spending and weakens political accountability.

The different formal criteria of sub-national fiscal capacity provide a highly differentiated picture of sub-national power. They also highlight the paradoxes at work. For central and federal governments, sub-national fiscal capacity tends to be represented as a problem of compliance with nominal fiscal rules. For sub-national governments it is above all a matter of capacity to invest in building assets and to build social solidarity and identity. High system strength also has paradoxical effects. On the one hand, it strengthens sub-national fiscal capacity in those many cases, like Galicia or Wales, where 'stand-alone' fiscal capacity is weak or non-existent. On the other hand, system strength creates risks of moral hazard. Fiscal transfers potentially weaken the creditworthiness of federal or central governments and of those sub-national governments that are net losers of tax revenues, like Catalonia. They also undermine sub-national incentives to put in place the conditions for strengthening 'stand-alone' fiscal capacity. The political effects are increased by resentment within net contributor cities and regions.

However, the formal criteria for measuring sub-national fiscal capacity are not to be confused with its material reality. Doing so generates illusion. The material reality relates to economic capacity to generate own tax revenues; to influence fiscal co-determination; to shape the terms of fiscal equalization; and to access ample, low-cost market credit. For instance, Berlin benefits in terms of its credit ratings from system strength through generous fiscal equalization. However, it lacks the 'stand-alone' fiscal capacity of Bavaria. The critical material factor is 'stand-alone' fiscal capacity. 'Stand-alone' fiscal capacity problems were highlighted in the ongoing debt problems of Calabria, Lazio, Sicily, Rome, and Naples; in the sub-national problems across the Russian Federation, the Ukraine, and the Balkan States; in the highly indebted German *Länder* of Berlin, Bremen, Saarland, Saxony-Anhalt, and Schleswig-Holstein; and in Northern Ireland and Wales. Sub-national status and power within the informal hierarchy of European cities and regions are deeply conditioned by 'stand-alone' fiscal capacity.

'Stand-alone' fiscal capacity reflects underlying structural imbalances within domestic, European, and international economies. It is associated with buoyant and predictable 'own-tax' revenues, along with efficient tax collection. It reflects a high ratio of investment to revenue, strengthening sub-national balance sheets through better-quality asset building and improving future tax capacity. It is linked to high sub-national administrative capacity in managing infrastructure and social investment. It is underpinned by sub-national political and administrative capacity in networking skills, both in intergovernmental relations and in accessing financial and business elites. Sub-national political and administrative capacity also takes the forms of sound public finances with accurate and timely fiscal data, fiscal transparency, careful efficiency auditing, and inclusive political processes that sustain solidarity and identity building. Moreover, 'stand-alone' sub-national fiscal capacity is characteristically associated with sound balance sheets in the household and corporate sectors. It stems from the strength, diversity, and resilience of the sub-national economic structure to asymmetric shocks. Characteristically, it correlates with a strong presence in science-based manufacturing and in the 'knowledge-based' economy and with the headquarters of leading companies in these sectors.

Combining the formal and material dimensions of sub-national fiscal capacity yields a second, differentiated picture of power relationships. Table 16.1 captures the more

Table 16.1: Sub-National Fiscal Power

	The Formal Dimension	
	Low	High
High	London	Basque Country Bavaria
The Material Dimension		
Low	Wales Northern Ireland	Berlin Galicia

(*Source*: Author)

extreme cases. It points to the weak fiscal power and negotiating positions of Northern Ireland and Wales; to London as underperforming in relation to potential sub-national fiscal power; to the paradox of Berlin and Galicia, both of whose fiscal capacity is bolstered by system strength; and to the power optimizers like the Basque Country and Bavaria. The vast majority of Europe's cities and regions occupy more complex, intermediate positions of relative fiscal power.

The problem for central or federal governments is how to address the mismatch of liability and control by preventing negative fiscal externalities. One method is to impose hierarchical controls on sub-national taxes, spending, and borrowing. Another is to establish clear sub-national fiscal transparency and accountability and then rely on political and legal sanctions by regional and local voters and by courts. Finally, they can rely on the combination of financial market sanctions with a firm and credible 'no-bail-out' principle to discipline sub-national fiscal policies. The risks from opportunistic sub-national fiscal behaviour and negative fiscal externalities increase when sub-national budgetary constraints are 'soft'; fiscal transparency and accountability are weak; and central governments cannot credibly commit to the no-bail-out principle (Rodden and Eskeland 2003). The outcome is mismatch between liability and control and mounting risks to sovereign creditworthiness.

The unfolding post-2007 financial and economic crisis threw into bold relief the significance for sub-national power of combining formal fiscal autonomy with fiscal capacity building, above all 'stand-alone' capacity. It also highlighted its close association with economic structure. The lack of 'stand-alone' sub-national fiscal capacity was a key source of mismatch between liability and control. Addressing this problem of mismatch generated two sets of mutually incompatible argument. One argument stressed matching sub-national fiscal governance with new, tough, 'hard' budgetary constraints to reinforce compliance with fiscal rules by sanctions. The problem of 'soft' budgetary constraints had long been manifest within the sub-national fiscal governance of the key European creditor state, Germany (cf. Scharpf, Reissert, and Schnabel 1976).

The second argument favoured giving greater tax autonomy to the sub-national level in order to clarify fiscal accountability to local electorates and to prevent sub-national elites engaging in politically motivated blame-shifting. This argument rested on the claim that decentralization and federalization since the 1980s had gone along with a weak stake of sub-national governments in taking action to strengthen their 'stand-alone' fiscal capacity and to impose fiscal discipline on themselves (Rodden and Eskeland 2000; Organization for Economic Cooperation and Development 2009b).

The post-2007 crisis period saw a 'hardening' of budgetary constraints across Europe. Sub-national fiscal governance was more firmly nested in, and reframed around, reforms to EU and domestic macroeconomic governance. Tightening of fiscal rules in the EU SGP and the fiscal compact treaty had clear implications for sub-national fiscal governance. This 'hardening' of sub-national fiscal constraints represented a new stage in 'top-down' Europeanization. Threats of non-compliance acted as a trigger for politically and constitutionally contentious renegotiations of sub-national fiscal governance, notably in Spain. In addition, and more urgently, those sub-national governments that were empowered to access international capital markets were subjected to greater market-based discipline through differentiation in sub-national credit ratings and in sub-national bond spreads. Sub-national fiscal governance was embroiled in vortex of forces for change: top-down pressures to strengthen hierarchical, state-centred steering of sub-national fiscal governance; market-based pressures from international bond markets and credit ratings; and bottom-up political pressures for greater sub-national fiscal autonomy, even—as in Catalonia and Scotland—for independence. The tensions were played out within the larger framework of the relative empowerment of creditor over debtor regions in the battlefield of ideas about reshaping sub-national fiscal governance in Europe.

Structural Imbalances, Regional Balance Sheets, and 'Stand-Alone' Fiscal Capacity: Indicators and Ratings

Identifying creditor and debtor regions is made difficult because macroeconomic statistics have been traditionally state-centric. Moreover, regional public finances have often been opaque, and sub-national borrowing powers have been often narrow or non-existent. More fundamentally, broader regional balance sheets of private sector assets and liabilities are difficult to compile. State-centric national accounts are poor at capturing service, trade, and financial flows across regions and hence internal structural imbalances. It is impossible to gain a clear, systematic, and comparative overview of the assets and liabilities of regional governments, regional banking and non-banking corporate sectors, and regional household sectors. Notwithstanding these difficulties, the broader, hidden sub-national balance sheets matter for territorial governance.

Despite the lack of regional balance sheets, cataloguing and valuing assets and liabilities, there are some indicators of sub-national creditworthiness. They are used by credit rating agencies in assigning risk ratings to regions. They help differentiate Lombardy from Sicily and the Basque Country from Andalusia. These indicators tend to be financial. They focus on sub-national public debt sustainability with reference to the ratio of net direct debt to operating revenue and the ratio of debt servicing costs to operating revenue. More broadly, macroeconomic figures are available for regional GDP size and GDP per capita, as well as for regional gross value-added (GVA). They offer a picture of relative strengths and weaknesses. For instance, they showed the widening disparity in GVA per capita between Scotland and Wales from the mid-1990s.

Sub-national credit ratings have been less good at capturing the underlying strengths and weaknesses in private sector balance sheets, which remain fundamental to sub-national, 'stand-alone' fiscal capacity. Various indicators offer insights into the condition of regional household and corporate sector balance sheets. They include rates of house repossessions, as well as welfare benefit and housing benefit claimants. Other indicators are the number and quality of company headquarters, new company formation rates, bankruptcy rates, and shop vacancy rates. Further insight is gained from labour migration; from the excellence ratings of regional universities; and from the proportion of professional, university-trained employees in the labour force, as well as in regional, elected assemblies.

Sub-national governments may be fiscally constrained by structural economic imbalances and weak regional balance sheets. However, they can offset these disadvantages by their financial and macroeconomic sophistication. Regions that lack 'stand-alone' fiscal capacity can increase the share of investment in infrastructure and social support in relation to their revenues. Debt can be used to invest productively in asset building. Conversely, sub-national governments can undermine strong regional balance sheets by profligate fiscal policies. In short, there is no clear-cut, one-to-one relationship between sub-national public debt and the broader regional balance sheet. Sub-national governments may prove smart or inept in managing their own tax revenues and receipts from fiscal equalization and in investing in infrastructure and building social solidarity.

Variations in sub-national financial sophistication were illustrated by the increasing use of complex derivatives contracts by city and regional governments in Austria, Belgium, France, Italy, and Portugal. Derivatives offered the attraction of borrowing at rates below prevailing market rates and thereby helping to flatter balance sheets. They were also useful as a hedge against foreign-currency exposure. Between 2001 and 2008, 525 Italian sub-national governments entered into some 1,000 interest-rate swaps, with an aggregate value of €35 billion. This figure equated to almost one-third of the total debt of Italy's regions, provinces, and municipalities (Banca d'Italia 2009). However, some sub-national governments—in France as well as Italy—faced substantial losses once the bet on interest rates turned sour with the economic and financial crises. Numerous Italian local authorities successfully took investment banks like UniCredit to court to nullify swap contracts on the basis of mis-selling. Improving financial sophistication was clearly a key aspect of sub-national fiscal capacity building.

In the absence of comprehensive regional balance sheets, the key differentiator of sub-national 'stand-alone' fiscal capacity was between net contributors to, and net recipients from, fiscal equalization systems. Characteristically, net contributors to fiscal transfers share most or all of the other features of 'stand-alone' fiscal capacity. They have high GDP per capita and low GDP volatility. They perform highly on competitiveness indicators. They have either a diversified economic structure or a particular valued natural resource. They score well on indicators of strength of their civil societies and on the World Bank 'government effectiveness' index. They have large, buoyant, and resilient tax revenues, which reflect vibrant, fast-growing economic sectors, profitable enterprises, high saving rates, and a strong regional financial sector. They are likely to contain the headquarters of major banks and non-bank firms and/or major savings banks. Net contributor regions tend to perform well on indicators that measure 'knowledge-based' economies, including research and development spending, patent activity, level of qualifications of the workforce, and internationally recognized higher education institutions. They have high labour-market participation, low unemployment, and net immigration. There is a high degree of civic engagement by professional and self-confident middle-class groups. There is potential for mobilization around defence of regional culture and promotion of autonomy or establishing a reputation for acting as the pace-setter for modernization of the larger state.

In terms of sub-national 'stand-alone' fiscal capacity, the EU hierarchy is topped by London and the south-east of England; Paris and the Île de France; Amsterdam and the west Netherlands; Milan and Lombardy; Munich and Bavaria; Stockholm and southern Sweden. At the national level, Brussels and Flanders lead within Belgium; Madrid, the Balearic Islands, the Basque Country, and Catalonia top the regional league table within Spain; whilst Britain and France are dominated respectively by the south-east of England and by the Île de France. In contrast, in Europe's biggest creditor power, the city state of Berlin trails towards the bottom of the German hierarchy, along with the other eastern *Länder*. The German hierarchy is led by the south-west *Länder* (Bavaria and Baden-Württemberg) and the city state of Hamburg. Characteristically, cities and regions with 'stand-alone' fiscal capacity resent fiscal equalization mechanisms as 'confiscatory' or as 'robbery'.

Structural economic imbalances differentiate 'strong' from 'weak' regions within European states. They also create cross-national spatial affinities of economic interest and policy preference. In political economy terms, Bavaria in Germany has more in common with Emilia-Romagna and Lombardy in Italy than with Berlin, the Saarland, and Mecklenburg-Vorpommern. Rhône-Alpes in France has greater similarities with Baden-Württemberg in Germany than with Limousin, Lorraine, and Nord-Pas de Calais. The Basque Country and Navarre have closer affinities of economic interest and policy preference with Lombardy and Rhône-Alpes than with Asturias, Extremadura, and Murcia. Governing elites in Lombardy situate themselves in a different pan-Alpine and pan-European world of political economy from those of Lazio in central Italy and Calabria and Sicily in the south.

Cities and regions with 'stand-alone' fiscal capacity tend to be more self-confident and outward-looking in economic development policies. Their governing elites seek out leadership roles in developing para-diplomacy and in cross-national network building. They stress their role in facilitating a vibrant private sector, especially through infrastructural and social investments. Regions like Bavaria, Catalonia, Flanders, and Lombardy promote their fiscal autonomy, resent how much of their GDP is being transferred upwards and horizontally, and stress the efficiency costs of fiscal equalization. Cities and regions that lack 'stand-alone' fiscal capacity—like Galicia, the Saarland, Sicily, and Wallonia—emphasize national fiscal solidarity through active lobbying for interregional equalization of per capita tax revenue and equal standards of social provision in order to support their interventionist policies. They argue the case for a positive role for the state in ensuring equity and narrowing differences in living standards.

Contextualizing Structural Imbalances: Decentralization and Sub-National Empowerment

The effects of structural imbalances in GDP size and in trade and financial flows on sub-national fiscal governance are complex and variable. They are mediated by historic and invented sub-national identity building; by the specifics of sub-national institutional arrangements; and by the nature and quality of sub-national leadership. As in Catalonia and Scotland, cultural identity serves as an instrument for sub-national leaders to justify claims to, and mobilize popular support for, fiscal autonomy or independence (cf. Keating, Loughlin, and Deschouwer 2003). Sub-national leaders can use sovereign debt crisis, and the political and policy responses of central governments, to define historical turning points for sub-national governance.

However, the incentive to make claims to fiscal autonomy depends on the coincidence of cultural identity with credible sub-national 'stand-alone' fiscal capacity. In

Flanders, the Basque Country, and Catalonia, claims to fiscal autonomy are bound up with national identity building, based on shared historical institutions and language. The Lega Nord's promotion of a fiscally autonomous 'Padania' in north Italy takes the form of the construction of a mythology of historic identity.

In contrast, the main tendency within the governing elites of Galicia and Wales is to detach issues of language and culture promotion from fiscal issues. They prefer to retain and strengthen fiscal equalization through nationally-organized transfers. Linguistic autonomy is not so powerfully matched by claims to sub-national fiscal autonomy. Hence the cleavage based on the political economy of structural economic imbalances cuts across the cleavage based on cultural identity. Cultural identity serves to differentiate some regions from others as 'special' in character. However, it justifies different arguments about appropriate institutional and policy arrangements for sub-national fiscal governance.

In consequence of this complex interplay of structural economic imbalances and internal cultural differentiation, European states evolved different, often asymmetrical and ambiguous, forms of institutional arrangements for sub-national fiscal governance. Territorial asymmetry and ambiguity are reflected in differences in sub-national tax and expenditure assignment and harmonization. They are evident in contrasting approaches to the principle of equalization of living standards, to the scale and form of horizontal and vertical fiscal transfers, and to the conditionality attached to transfers. Varying institutional arrangements for sub-national fiscal governance embody pragmatic adaptation to cultural differences, to structural economic imbalances, and to challenges to sovereign creditworthiness. This adaptation is also influenced by the national leverage of regionally-based political parties.

From the 1980s, up to the post-2007 sovereign debt crises, the broad direction of change in institutional arrangements for sub-national fiscal governance was away from the centralized state. This process was driven by the pace-setting role of cities and regions with 'stand-alone' fiscal capacity in pressing the case for fiscal autonomy and for limiting their liability to bail-out other regions. The overall picture was one of intensifying normative conflicts about sub-national fiscal governance, increasingly complex asymmetry in territorial governance, and the evolution of transnational spaces and networks below the level of states. These developments complicated creditor-debtor state relations within the EU and the euro area, especially in the context of monetary union. They highlighted the scale of the mismatch between state liability and territorial control.

In one account the source of this trend away from the centralized state was cultural. It stemmed from the need to recognize historic stateless nations and, more broadly, regional identities and the historical symbols on which they drew. On this basis the Basque Country, Bavaria, Brittany, Flanders, northern Italy, and Scotland laid claim to fiscal autonomy. Other accounts of the trend from centralization stressed institutional and political factors. One such factor was the dynamic unleashed by failures of central governments' regional policies to deliver prosperity. These failures opened space for regional mobilization and the radicalization of nationalist into separatist movements. Another factor was ideational change. This change involved a new European model of competitive regionalism. It was embedded in a broader discursive shift to 'globalization' and 'Europeanization', which provided mobilizing themes for sub-national collective action. An alternative factor was regional leadership, especially where—as in

Belgium, Germany, Italy, and Spain—it acquires political leverage through a pivotal role in national coalition politics.

In these various ways, cultural, institutional, and political factors empowered sub-national governments. However, with respect to sub-national fiscal governance, the key structural determinant remained imbalances in GDP strength and in trade and financial flows. The gainers were the cities and regions with 'stand-alone' fiscal capacity. They advocated a new, decentralized economic development model based on building and supporting 'endogenous' regional growth potential through competition rather than fiscal transfers. The language of 'moral hazard' entered into the pressures for redesign of sub-national fiscal governance. Other cities and regions were to be encouraged to take greater fiscal responsibility.

International Credit Ratings, Bond Markets, and Fiscal Surveillance under Monetary Union

From the 1990s onwards international credit rating agencies, global bond markets, and EU processes of fiscal policy monitoring and threats of sanctions began to exert a wider and more intrusive scope of influence on sub-national fiscal governance. These three factors reshaped its functioning and altered the room for manoeuvre of sub-national governments.

Classically, sub-national governments with borrowing powers relied on bank credit. However, from the 1980s as financial market deregulation gathered pace, the incentive to access much more liquid and cheaper bond markets led many sub-national governments to reduce this traditional reliance. The result was wide variations in dependence on international bond markets. In 2011, for instance, bonds accounted for some 70 per cent of debt of the German *Land* Hesse, compared to only 13 per cent in Saxony. From 2013 the joint federal-*Land* issue of 'Germany bonds' provided an additional incentive to access international bond markets, above all for the financially weaker *Länder*. Sub-national governments also had a new incentive to recruit financial market consultants to more proactively manage their debts. More pertinently, official credit rating agencies began to focus on the details of sub-national tax and spending and on sub-national 'stand-alone' fiscal capacity.

The market leaders in the explosion of the supply of sub-national credit ratings were Moody's and, especially in Europe, Standard and Poor's (Gaillard 2006). More differentiated sub-national ratings, above all at times of sovereign debt crisis, increased status anxieties amongst German *Länder*, Italian regions, and Spanish autonomous communities. Shifts in their relative creditworthiness had implications for the reputation of their governing elites for competence. They also made transparent the illusory nature of past claims to sub-national fiscal health, on the basis of which governing elites, for instance in Valencia, had sought to boost the relative position of their region. Credit ratings exposed 'vanity' infrastructure projects and the hollow claims of cities and regions to be engines of productive investment. More immediately, credit downgrades generated higher borrowing costs, exclusion from international capital markets, and resort to the humiliation of seeking collective financial assistance. Catalonia suffered this fate in 2012. The effects were also felt in the inability to access bank loans to provide liquidity. Sub-national governments faced new pressures for fiscal transparency, notably about their complex off-balance-sheet financing, their contingent liabilities, and their use of complex derivatives instruments. In the case of regions based around historic nationalities, doubts arose about the credibility of carefully constructed narratives of independence.

The combination of more differentiated sub-national credit ratings with the EU SGP rules and the fiscal compact treaty induced central and federal governments to pay greater attention to the risks to their own sovereign credit ratings from free-riding sub-national fiscal behaviour. In consequence, they sought to 'correct' federalization and decentralization processes by a 'hardening' of budgetary constraints. The aims were to minimize central or federal governments' exposure to negative externalities; to provide stronger incentives for sub-national fiscal adjustment; and to reduce both market and political expectations of sub-national bail-outs (Liu 2009; Rodden and Eskeland 2003).

Central or federal governments turned to one or more of three instruments. First, they toughened direct hierarchical controls on sub-national borrowing and placed stronger emphasis on earmarked central funding based, for instance, on the 'standard costs' of providing centrally defined 'essential levels' of services. Secondly, central or federal governments negotiated cooperative, rules-based approaches to monitoring fiscal deficit and public debt ratios and to expenditure growth. Thirdly, following the US model, they relied on the combination of credible commitment to the principle of no bail-outs with market discipline through credit ratings and bond spreads to enforce sub-national fiscal discipline.

The first instrument appealed to states with strong traditions of centralization, like Britain and France. The second instrument was characteristic of federal or federalizing systems like Austria, Belgium, Germany, and Spain. The third instrument was attractive to states whose governing elites were ideologically committed to market efficiency. It also appealed when states lacked the capacity to impose 'hard' budget constraints on sub-national governments. In whichever combination used, these instruments provided a 'technology of commitment'. It could take the form of constitutional rules on sub-national balanced budgets, as in the US states, Germany, and across euro area Member States under the fiscal compact treaty. Constitutional rules could also enshrine the principle of no sub-national bail-outs, as in Italy from 2001. Other technologies of commitment included sanctions on excessive deficits and debt, as in Spain, and the temporary suspension of local self-government, as in Italy. However, such rules could be flouted in practice, for instance the no-bail-out principle in Italy.

The new saliency of the sub-national dimension of sovereign creditworthiness came from more than the greater willingness of credit rating agencies to differentiate in their ratings. It stemmed also from the 'sound finances' arrangements that accompanied monetary union in Europe. By 2003 recommendations under the EU excessive deficit procedure began to recognize the importance of domestic fiscal stability plans, including in Germany. They were essential to align sub-national fiscal arrangements with EU fiscal rules and to ensure Member-State compliance with EU commitments. In consequence, sub-national fiscal governance acquired a stronger EU dimension. The shadows of credit ratings, bond markets, and the SGP darkened, with significant institutional, policy, and political implications. Cumulatively, they sharpened status anxieties about relative positioning in domestic and European hierarchies of cities and regions. At stake were the 'brand' images, characters, and identities of cities and regions in both financial markets and within the EU.

The demand for sub-national credit ratings increased with fiscal decentralization, which was a component part of the rise of municipal and regional authority in Europe. Its significance grew when two criteria of sub-national fiscal capacity were present: the authority to raise tax revenue; and fiscal co-determination of the distribution of national tax revenues (cf. Hooghe, Marks, and Schakel 2010). When sub-national governments had these attributes, they became increasingly important fiscal actors in economic development, especially infrastructure provision. They were also able to play a major role in social investment, notably in education and training and in child care. The ratios of sub-national investment and of consumption spending to revenue became important indicators of long-term fiscal capacity.

Sometimes, as with the Bassanini reforms in Italy in the late 1990s, the sub-national governments' own revenue base grew. After the Bassanini reforms it increased from 27 to 43 per cent. However, more problematically, transfers of competences in social policies were often not matched by corresponding delegation of revenue-raising powers. This phenomenon was apparent in France in 2004, Germany in 2005, and Italy from 2001. It was inconsistent with the recognition that investment in infrastructure was essential if cities and regions were to escape from having net liabilities to having net assets and thus to strengthen their fiscal capacity.

For these reasons, sub-national governments sought to borrow more extensively in international markets. Traditionally, this inducement had been lower for sub-national governments in France, Italy, and Spain. They had access to favourable loans from, respectively, the *Caisse des depôts et consignations*, the *Cassa depositi e prestititi*, and the *cajas*. The National Loan Board and the Public Works Loan Board offered similar facilities for British local authorities, deterring the development of the municipal bond market, at least till the cost of loans rose from 2010. Similarly, German sub-national governments could rely on their state banks (*Landesbanken*) and local public savings banks (*Sparkassen*). However, as long-term interest rates fell from the 1990s, the international capital markets became more financially attractive, and sub-national bond markets grew across Europe.

Fiscal federalism and devolution from the 1980s, monetary union, and then the unfolding post-2007 financial and economic crisis, meant that sovereign credit ratings became more closely bound up with the ratings of their cities and regions. Their ratings tended to move in tandem. Sovereign downgrades triggered sub-national downgrades. On average, the ratings of sub-national governments were lower than those of their sovereigns (Gaillard 2006). However, as sovereign ratings were downgraded, for instance in Spain, some autonomous provinces, like the Basque Country and Navarre, were able to outrank the sovereign in creditworthiness. Bolzano, Friuli Venezia Guilia, and Trento were rated above Italy (Fitch 2009c: 5). Other autonomous communities, like Catalonia and Valencia, lost status as their credit ratings slipped below the sovereign. They converged towards those of traditionally poor autonomous communities like Galicia. Some cities enjoyed a better credit rating than their sovereign, including Zagreb in Croatia, Krakow, Lodz, and Poznan in Poland, and Moscow in Russia. Conversely, Naples had the worst rating in Italy (Fitch 2009c: 5).

The growing significance of international credit ratings within sub-national fiscal governance stemmed from a variety of long-term factors. They included fiscal decentralization; the development of market-based borrowing policies by sub-national governments; and their increased incentive to strengthen market credibility in the search for better borrowing conditions. After 2007 credit ratings became even more important. Sub-national governments faced serious and deepening structural economic imbalances; collapsing local and regional tax revenues; and the debt legacies from showpiece infrastructural investments in regions like Andalusia, Catalonia, Madrid, and Valencia. The political sensitivities were acute where sub-national governments had secured responsibility for social expenditure, with its inbuilt rigidities.

As fiscal crisis and default risk grew from 2007, both international credit ratings and EU policies began to extend their interest beyond broad sub-national macro-fiscal balances to the details of the composition of sub-national budgets, including infrastructural investment financing and the investment/consumption elements in social expenditures (cf. Mosley 2003). This new intrusiveness reduced the room for manoeuvre of sub-national governments in their economic, infrastructural, and social policies. Concerns about the creditworthiness of sub-national governments affected not just problematic Italian local authorities, like Naples and Rome. They extended to regions like Lazio and Sicily, as well as to once-seemingly creditworthy regions like Catalonia and Valencia in Spain. Even though they remained 'AAA', Baden-Württemberg and Bavaria were put on 'negative outlook'. In Italy and Spain credit rating agencies began to have doubts about the implicit bail-out guarantees of central governments. Doubts about creditworthiness increased where sub-national governments had weak influence with their central government or within the federal system. They also grew against a background of heightening sovereign credit risk.

Determinants of Sub-National Credit Ratings

One of the most important determinants of sub-national credit ratings was the historical creditworthiness of the sovereign. Sovereign creditworthiness provided evidence to credit rating agencies that the central government had the requisite fiscal will and capacity to support sub-national governments. Will and capacity to offer large *ex ante* vertical fiscal transfers reduced the probability of sub-national defaults. Alternatively, the central government could bail-out *ex post* a debt-distressed sub-national government.

A second determinant was 'system strength'. Solidarity was made credible by large-scale horizontal intergovernmental fiscal transfer systems, notably in Germany and Spain. System strength involved regions with 'stand-alone' fiscal capacity providing support to fiscally weaker regions.

A third determinant was sub-national 'stand-alone' fiscal capacity. 'Stand-alone' fiscal capacity was assessed by the ratio of net direct sub-national debt to operating revenue; by the ratio of sub-national interest payments to operating revenue; and by sub-national GDP per capita. These ratios indicated the probability of needing external support. Credit rating agencies weighed sub-national 'stand-alone' fiscal capacity against the quality of the protective umbrella, which was determined by the sovereign's credit history and by 'system strength'. Standard and Poor's classified European sub-national governments into five groups, based on the strength and predictability of their institutional frameworks. In 2009 Group One included Austrian and German *Länder*, Swiss cantons, and British sub-national governments. Turkish and Ukrainian sub-national governments were in Group Five. Greek and Lithuanian sub-national governments were withdrawn from system scoring.

In the case of the German *Länder*, the ratios of both debt and debt servicing costs to operating revenue were very high in comparison with Belgian, Italian, and Spanish regions. However, this weakness was compensated by the quality of the protective umbrella in Germany, based on the sovereign credit rating history and on the fiscal equalization mechanism. Consequently, the differentiation of sub-national credit ratings in Germany was low. In 2009 the city state of Berlin was able to achieve a credit rating of Aa1 from Moody's. This rating was given despite a per capita *Land* debt of €17,695; a ratio of net debt to operating revenue of 503 per cent; and a ratio of debt service to total revenue of 54.2 per cent. Brandenburg and Saxony-Anhalt enjoyed a similar credit boost. In contrast, in 2009 the Italian region of Lazio had a ratio of net debt to operating revenue of 77.5 per cent and a ratio of debt service costs to total revenue of a mere 4.9 per cent. However, it managed a credit rating of A2. Abruzzo was rated at A2 with respective ratios of 6.2 per cent and 5.8 per cent. Rome and its city region of Lazio gained higher system-strength scores (groups one and two respectively) than other Italian regions (group three) because of their high economic and political significance and their history of extraordinary fiscal support from the Italian central government.

Why the Territorial Dimension Matters

Territorial disaggregation of creditor-debtor state relations is important for a number of reasons. In the first place, European states comprise different levels of government: national, regional, and local/municipal. Typically, complex territorial structures coexist with unclear assignments of competences, exacerbating the mismatch between liability and control. This mismatch is reflected in ongoing controversies about whether transferred or 'own' revenues compensate for assigned competences. The politics of sovereign creditworthiness is embedded in these convoluted domestic problems of multilevel governance. It is caught up in institutionally and politically complex and variegated patterns of sub-national creditor-debtor relations. They affect the capacity of national governments to honour European and international commitments in fiscal policy and to pacify bond markets. The mismatch of liability and control is further exacerbated by domestic asymmetries in sub-national arrangements, as well as by the complex interactions between national and sub-national party systems.

This cross-national variety in the basic design of sub-national fiscal governance reflects different historical processes of nation- and state-building in Europe. It expresses, in particular, the cultural and historical distinctiveness and/or the geographic insularity of particular regions. Germany has its Bavaria. Italy has its Val d'Aosta, Trentino Alto Adige, and Sicily. Spain has its Basque Country, Catalonia, and Galicia. France has its Corsica. Britain has its Northern Ireland, Scotland, and Wales. German and Swiss fiscal federalism and federalizing processes in Belgium, Italy, and Spain stand out as representing (modified) domestic forms of creditor-debtor state relations. They also suggest lessons about the value and limitations of fiscal transfer systems in securing sovereign and sub-national creditworthiness.

There is also great variety in the political leverage of sub-national governments in national politics. During the Italian Second Republic electoral volatility was a characteristic of the fiscally weak regions of the south. In consequence, they often had the capacity to determine who wins nationally. In some European states, notably Germany, sub-national governmental power is entrenched in federal upper chambers, along with the requirement of a special majority for constitutional amendments and treaty ratification. This type of constitutional arrangement strengthens the opportunity to make federal governments pay a political price for reforms that affect sub-national fiscal governance.

Thus in 2012 the German *Länder* used the leverage of ratification of the euro area fiscal compact treaty—and the constraints that it would impose—to get the federal government to accept future joint federal-state 'Germany bonds'. By borrowing the superior creditworthiness of the federal government, all *Länder* could reduce their borrowing costs, including Bavaria and Baden-Württemberg. However, the major beneficiaries were the *Länder* that lacked 'stand-alone' fiscal capacity, notably Bremen, Berlin, and Schleswig-Holstein. The new 'Germany bonds' offered lower borrowing costs than previous joint *Länder* bonds.

Centre–periphery cleavages are sometimes mirrored in the structure of party systems. Examples include the Christian Social Union (CSU) in Bavaria; the different party systems in Flanders and Wallonia; the Lega Nord in northern Italy; the Catalan *Convergència i Unió* (CiU) in Spain; the Scottish National Party (SNP) in Scotland; and Plaid Cymru in Wales. There is an important, if complex, relationship between party-system development and developments in sub-national fiscal governance. The leverage of a regional party grows if two conditions are met. It must be able to establish its position as a major coalition player at the national level and also project an image as effective in mobilizing support and getting things done. In these circumstances a regional party is in a position to extract not just new sub-national competences but also *ex ante* fiscal support to avert sub-national bail-outs. This capacity was demonstrated by the Flemish Liberal Party (VLD) in pressing within the Belgian national government for greater fiscal autonomy. Similarly, in 2010 the Lega Nord gained an Italian fiscal federalism reform that endowed municipalities with greater tax-raising powers.

Secondly, central or federal governments face potential challenge to their sovereign creditworthiness from debt distress and default at the sub-national level. Systemic risks from contagion mount with the size, economic significance, and symbolic importance of sub-national governments. Examples include Detroit and New York City in the United States, Berlin in Germany, and Rome, Naples, and Lazio in Italy. These cases raise in a vivid fashion the tensions between heightened incentive to sub-national bail-out and the avoidance of moral hazard. New York was granted special federal loans in 1975; Rome and Lazio benefited from special central government transfers after 2001; whilst Berlin is embedded in a generous fiscal equalization system. All posed serious moral hazard problems.

Thirdly, from the 1980s European cities and regions accounted for larger and increasing proportions of public sector employment and public expenditure and investment. The proportions were especially high in federal states and grew in federalizing states. Sub-national governments accounted for some 40 per cent of Belgium's public expenditure (Organization for Economic Cooperation and Development 2009b: 63). In Spain regional governments accounted for more public expenditure than the central government, chiefly in education and health, with a spending share amongst the highest in countries within the Organization for Economic Cooperation and Development (OECD) (Organization for Economic Cooperation and Development 2010: 79). Their share of public expenditure increased from 14.4 per cent in 1984 to 53.2 per cent in 1997. In 2008 Spanish regional governments received 50 per cent of personal income tax and value-added tax (VAT) revenues, 58 per cent of excise duties, and all revenues from their own taxes on fuel, inheritance, and vehicle registration (Organization for Economic Cooperation and Development 2010: 79). In France sub-national governments were responsible for some 75 per cent of public investment by 2008. Against this background, the attempts of central government to strengthen hierarchical controls over fiscal policy proved highly controversial.

'Hard' budgetary constraints took different forms. Federal states like Austria, Germany, and Switzerland resorted to national stability pacts, negotiated 'in the shadow of hierarchy'. Traditionally centralized states, like France, tightened finance ministry controls. Federalizing states like Italy and Spain used more hybrid approaches, combining negotiation with assertion of central controls. The technocratic rationale for 'hard' budgetary constraints stressed sovereign creditworthiness as a public good, which required constraints on sub-national fiscal free-riding. Sub-national fiscal autonomy was represented as a problem of negative externalities, involving spill-over to other regions and to the centre. The solution was to reduce political pressures on central or federal governments to engage in costly sub-national bail-outs. These pressures were strongest in the case of party-politically friendly sub-national governments. Central or federal governments faced the risk of highly negative effects on party image for governing competence, especially in key electoral battlegrounds. Political risk for central or federal governments was compounded when voters were confused about who was responsible for sub-national fiscal crisis. Risk could be reduced if sub-national governments lacked their own tax resources and were the beneficiary of generous fiscal equalization arrangements. They could continue to support high levels of public expenditure per capita through transfers of tax income from wealthier regions and thus were cushioned against sub-national bail-outs.

Fourthly, sovereign creditworthiness typically conceals a much more complex sub-national reality of fiscally 'strong' and 'weak' regions. It also does not take into account cross-national spaces in which cities and regions share interests and policy preferences across borders that they do not have with other domestic regions. Sub-national creditworthiness can be very different from national images. In 2012 California, Illinois, Ohio, and New Jersey were less creditworthy than the United States; Calabria, Lazio, and Sicily than Italy; Nord-Pas de Calais than France; and Catalonia and Valencia than Spain. Conversely, Flanders was more creditworthy than Belgium; Emilia-Romagna, Lombardy, and Veneto than Italy; and the Balearic Islands, the Basque Country, and Navarre than Spain. These differences between sub-national and national creditworthiness have major implications for party-system development. They affect the capacity of city and regional elites to project their profile of governing competence at domestic and European levels. They bear on the image for virtue of regional and local populations.

A powerful creditor state like Germany can harbour fiscally weak *Länder*, like Bremen, the Saarland, and Schleswig-Holstein in the west and the six new federal states in the east, including Berlin. Equally, Rhône-Alpes in France, Baden-Württemberg in Germany, Lombardy in Italy, and—more problematically—Catalonia in Spain represented a cross-national European cluster of powerful regions with 'stand-alone' fiscal capacity. Their high status roles as models for emulation and agenda-setting power were symbolized in their collectively defined image as the 'Four Motors of Europe'. These variations in fiscal capacity to engage in cross-national leadership have implications for sub-national fiscal governance.

Fifthly, sub-national regions can possess larger GDP size than many EU Member States. In 2009 Catalonia had a GDP larger than those of Portugal and Ireland and only surpassed by twelve of the EU twenty-seven Member States. Lombardy had a GDP roughly equivalent to Sweden and larger than Denmark's. Only six EU Member States exceeded the GDP size of Bavaria. The GDP of North-Rhine Westphalia far exceeded those of Austria, Belgium, Greece, Ireland, Poland, and Sweden. Rhône-Alpes' GDP eclipsed those of the Czech Republic, Finland, Ireland, and Portugal. That of Nord-Pas de Calais was larger than that of the three Baltic States combined or of Hungary. The combination of GDP size with 'stand-alone' fiscal capacity gives enormous political leverage at the national level.

Sixthly, creditworthiness and political leverage at national level is even greater where cities and regions possess substantial banking and financial systems. Financial strength derives from the presence of the headquarters of major nationally and cross-nationally active commercial banks. Examples include Frankfurt in the state of Hesse, Milan in Lombardy, and Madrid in Spain. Financial strength also stems from large state banks, like the German *Landesbanken*, notably those in Baden-Württemberg, Bavaria, and North-Rhine Westphalia. Other examples include big public savings banks, as in the German, Italian, and Spanish regions, as well as local banking foundations with mandates to invest locally, as in Italy. Though their roles have changed, public sector banks traditionally played a central role in regional and local economic development and in buying sub-national government bonds. In some cases they served as symbols of distinctive sub-national cultural identity. Examples included the regionally-based savings bank La Caixa in Catalonia, the Leuven-based commercial bank KBC in Flanders, and the Banca Popolare di Milano in Lombardy. In Italy local banking foundations acted as core shareholders in Italy's biggest banks, helping to reinforce their regional and local identities. Their boards became prime targets for Lega Nord powers of patronage.

However, the post-2007 financial crisis transformed these banking symbols of regional identity, status, and power into bail-out risks. They became negative indicators of sub-national creditworthiness. The crisis exposed problems of political cronyism and corruption that followed from sub-national political control, notably in Italy and Spain. The scale of toxic debts and the weakness of capitalization became evident in the German *Landesbanken*. Their problems led credit ratings agencies to put even the most creditworthy *Länder* like Baden-Württemberg, Bavaria, and North-Rhine Westphalia on 'negative outlooks'. In 2009 the Bavarian *Landesbank* held €1.6 billion of Greek, Italian, Portuguese, and Spanish sovereign debt. Acute problems of toxic assets affected the Spanish *cajas*, including Caja Madrid in the capital and La Caixa in Catalonia. *Cajas* and *Landesbanken* emerged as the European banks least able to withstand the EU stress tests. They segregated out 'bad banks' to ring fence their toxic loans and to become more attractive for recapitalization.

The serious fiscal consequences of banking crisis had been foreshadowed in Berlin in 2002, when the city-state government had mounted a costly bail-out of Bankgesellschaft Berlin. By 2008 debt servicing amounted to some 50 per cent of Berlin's operating revenue. Flanders provided a different example. In 2010 the Flemish regional government faced an acute crisis over the undisclosed toxic assets at the commercial bank KBC. Aware that Walloon politicians would block federal aid without offsetting fiscal compensation, it decided to bail-out KBC amidst great acrimony. Flanders could afford to do so because it carried no debt legacy. Moreover, it had been able to bail-out the debt burden of the region's municipalities.

The post-2007 restructuring of *cajas* and *Landesbanken*, and the broadening of their capital participation, weakened a key aspect of sub-national fiscal capacity. It also had sub-national political implications. 'Defending "our" *cajas*' offered a new mobilizing theme for nationalism in Spanish autonomous communities. In Galicia, for instance, it took the form of a sub-national narrative of 'robbing' regional savings. Galician nationalism underwent a discursive shift from inward focus on Galician history to resentment towards, and resistance to, 'outside forces'. Conversely, a narrative of re-centralization evolved. *Cajas* were represented as part of sub-national political cronyism that had led to credit malpractice and corruption. The beneficiaries were sub-national party elites and factions. Their self-interested activities had inflicted damage on the public goods of financial stability and fiscal discipline.

Defensive nationalist narratives were less apparent in Germany. Nevertheless, from 2008–2009 the governments of Bavaria, Baden-Württemberg, and North-Rhine Westphalia were engaged in costly bail-outs of their *Landesbanken*. They took on large-scale contingent liabilities and experienced a sharp rise in their ratios of net debt to operating revenue. By 2010 this ratio was over 310 per cent in North-Rhine Westphalia, 156 per cent in Baden-Württemberg, and some 110 per cent in Bavaria. Moreover, the effects of the banking crisis posed serious electoral risks for traditionally strong regional parties, like the CSU in Bavaria. They also raised new questions about the credibility of political claims for independence, notably in Scotland. It was unclear whether Scotland could claim 'stand-alone' fiscal capacity to strengthen economic development. More generally, banking bail-outs increased risks of sub-national credit rating downgrades, leading to exclusion from international credit markets and loss of reputation for governing competence. The credit rating agencies indicated that they would monitor debt developments in German *Länder* 'very closely', even in those that had traditionally possessed 'stand-alone' fiscal capacity.

Spatial Differentiation: Status Anxieties and Structural Economic Imbalances

The politics of sovereign creditworthiness functions within the context of the high degree of spatial differentiation within Europe (cf. Keating 2010). Spatial differentiation takes two forms. First, the complex webs of trade and financial transactions amongst European regions escape the confines of state-based political space. Catalonia in Spain, Flanders in Belgium, and Lombardy in Italy are at least as much economically integrated into EU and international as into domestic space. Less than half Catalan exports go to the rest of Spain, whilst small- and medium-sized firms in northern Italy are closely integrated into German-centred supply chains. High cross-national trade and financial interdependencies open up spaces for narratives about sub-national distinctiveness and claims for fiscal autonomy or independence. Catalonia prioritized the Mediterranean arc over its relations with Madrid and harboured a strong independence movement. Leading north Italian bankers and industrialists differentiated themselves as more closely tied to Germany than to the south.

Hence, in territorial terms, creditor and debtor states are not homogenous spaces with single, unified strategic interests and policy preferences. The idea of the unitary state conceals complex status anxieties at city and regional levels about changing relative positions in national and European hierarchies. These status anxieties stem from structural economic imbalances in sub-national trade and financial flows. Structural imbalances either privilege and empower, or enfeeble, sub-national fiscal capacity.

Complex patterns emerge from structural economic imbalances. Cities and regions with 'stand-alone' fiscal capacity exist in debtor states, like London and the south-east in Britain, Paris and the Île de France, and Milan and Lombardy in Italy. Their net assets mean that they enjoy a high status relative to their states. Conversely, cities and regions that lack 'stand-alone' fiscal capacity are the rule rather than exception in creditor states. Examples include Berlin, Brandenburg, and the Saarland in Germany and the rural hinterland of Finland with its declining industries. Structural economic imbalances have negative implications for their relative status. However, the most enfeebled and disempowered of all are cities and regions that lack 'stand-alone' fiscal capacity in debtor states. Examples include Extremadura in Spain and Wales in Britain. In contrast, the cities and regions with the top 'stand-alone' fiscal capacity in creditor states are the most privileged and empowered. Examples include Baden-Württemberg and Bavaria in Germany and the cantons of Basel and Zürich in Switzerland.

Variations of position in national and European regional and municipal hierarchies over time reflect in part changes in underlying structural economic imbalances. They are also the product of the policy choices of sub-national elites, for instance in prioritizing fiscal consolidation and asset-building through infrastructural and social investments. Both changes in structural imbalances and policy choices help to explain why, since the 1960s, there was a pronounced shift in the relative positions of Flemish-speaking Flanders and Francophone Wallonia within Belgium. From 1965 to 2006 the gap in their per capita GDPs widened (Organization for Economic Cooperation and Development 2009: 61). In Spain in the 1980–1990s some regions, like Andalusia, Catalonia, Madrid, and Valencia, improved their relative position through ambitious infrastructural developments. Others, like Asturias, Extremadura, and Murcia exhibited relative decline.

Greater Madrid strengthened its relative economic position vis-à-vis Catalonia. It invested in a superior infrastructure to that of Barcelona. More seriously, from the late 1990s, Catalonia also evolved a negative trade balance. It also accounted for a falling share of national GDP and of Spanish inward investment. These developments helped fuel the radicalization of Catalan nationalism, expressed in a more assertive civic mobilization, including mass demonstrations. At the same time they raised questions about indigenous governing capacity. By October 2010 Catalonia was selling bonds directly to its own citizens at yields far higher than on Spanish debt. This humiliating move followed credit rating downgrades and a large-scale placement of bonds with La Caixa. Catalonia's credit rating had fallen below that of its traditional counter-model, Andalusia.

Shifts in structural economic imbalances lead sub-national governments to differentiate themselves in new ways. Since German unification in 1990, Saxony differentiated itself from the other new eastern *Bundesländer* on the basis of its trade and fiscal performance and on the quality of its infrastructure. Similarly, from the 1990s, Puglia attempted to differentiate itself from the Italian south. Shifts in relative positioning provoke, in turn, intense status anxieties within, as well as across, regions. Examples include resentment towards Seville within Andalusia and Lille within Nord-Pas de Calais.

Structural economic imbalances are not historical 'givens'. Moreover, as in Brittany, Saxony, Andalusia, and Valencia, regional reform coalitions can emerge and seek to reinvent regional cultures. There is no logic of functional determinism at work. Nevertheless, structural imbalances are important in opening up opportunities for, and posing constraints on, a city's or region's capacity to translate the mobilization of a distinctive culture into credible claims for fiscal autonomy. They affect policy and political strategies. The politics of sub-national fiscal governance is caught up in the two competing narratives of cities and regions with and without 'stand-alone' fiscal capacity.

The political economy of structural economic imbalances helps explain why sub-national elites advocate different domestic fiscal arrangements and different models of economic development. The model of endogenous growth capacity, in which regional government serves as facilitator, has been most actively supported and propagated by cities and regions with 'stand-alone' fiscal capacity. Other regions favoured state-led intervention, backed by large-scale fiscal transfers. This political economy cleavage cuts across historic cultural cleavage. It distinguishes the city state of Bremen from Bavaria, Galicia from the Basque Country, and Sicily from Lombardy. Shifts in relative political economy position challenge ruling parties to adapt their ideologies at sub-national level.

Fiscal Rules in Sub-National Governance

There is an underlying commonality that distinguishes all forms of sub-national fiscal governance from that within the EU and the euro area. As in the Maastricht and the Lisbon Treaties, sub-national bail-outs may be ruled out by national constitutions. The new article 119.5 of the Italian constitution since 2001 is an example, though without much practical effect. Sub-national governments can be allowed to default. Nevertheless, there is a strong residual political belief that factors of national integrity and domestic solidarity, combined with electoral and political calculation, mean that national government is likely to play the role of lender of last resort. It may do so by *ex ante* shoring up of the revenues of debt-strapped sub-national governments or by *ex post* bail-outs. This role is not ruled out by provisions at EU level. In turn, the regional government plays the 'lender-of-last-resort' role for local authorities in cases where it has direct responsibility for them.

The availability of a lender of last resort makes sub-national bonds a traditionally safe haven, at least to the extent that generous fiscal equalization arrangements are in place and sovereign creditworthiness makes a sub-national bail-out credible. In Germany two legal principles reinforce this sub-national safe-haven status: the concept of federal loyalty (*Bundestreuekonzept*) and the principle of common liability (Germany as a *Haftungsverbund*). They are understood to require *Länder* to financially assist local authorities and to require the federal government and other *Länder* to financially assist a debt-distressed *Land*. The effect is to create incentives for convergence of credit ratings for *Länder* governments and the federal government. The city-region of Berlin is a chief beneficiary.

Whether explicit or implicit, the 'lender-of-last-resort' role means that central and federal governments and cities and regions with 'stand-alone' fiscal capacity have a powerful incentive to limit their liability and avert negative externalities. They have a vested interest in 'hard' hierarchical budgetary constraints, along with strengthening political incentives for voters and financial markets to discipline profligate sub-national fiscal behaviour. Clear fiscal rules with attached sanctions diminish sub-national bail-out expectations. They also provide benchmarks for the public and for markets to assess the fiscal performance and competence of sub-national governments.

The problem for central and federal governments and for cities and regions with 'stand-alone' fiscal capacity stems from the strength of domestic political pressures for costly sub-national bail-outs. These pressures are increased because of the tendency for the number of cities and regions without this fiscal capacity to exceed the number with this capacity. The numerical factor is potent in federal systems like Germany, where the federal upper chamber, the Bundesrat, is composed of the *Länder* governments. The federal government is often induced to 'buy' votes in order to pass its legislation. Hence it ended up bailing-out the debts of Bremen and the Saarland in the 1990s. The bail-out pressures also mount when a city or region that lacks 'stand-alone' fiscal capacity plays a pivotal role within a governing political party. Examples include Nord-Pas de Calais in the French Socialist Party and North-Rhine Westphalia within the German Social Democratic Party. Pressure also grows when a regionally-based party is central to national coalition formation, as with Wallonia in Belgian centre-Left governments.

Domestic economic culture plays a role as an intervening variable. In states with dominant stability cultures, like Germany and Switzerland, virtuous fiscal behaviour by cities and regions that lack 'stand-alone' fiscal capacity is likely to prove electorally rewarding. Conversely, in states like Greece and Russia, whose economic cultures are characterized by welfare protectionism, clientelism, and patronage, cities and regions that lack fiscal capacity are more likely to be tolerated.

Overall, fiscal stability rules on deficits and public debt across all levels of government became more central and contentious issues in sub-national governance from the 1990s, above all since 2007. Sub-national governments were subjected to tightening external discipline. It took the forms of growing structural economic imbalances; the revisions to the EU SGP since 1997 and the euro area fiscal compact treaty; EU and International Monetary Fund (IMF) conditionality requirements associated with national bail-outs from 2010; and the vigilante role of increasingly large-scale sovereign bond markets in branding sub-national governments. These external dynamics privileged the arguments of cities and regions with 'stand-alone' fiscal capacity for firm fiscal rules that limit liability and strengthen territorial control. In backing fiscal stability rules, these cities and regions could identify themselves with European pace-setting in fiscal virtue. They could further differentiate themselves from fiscally weaker cities and regions.

The Alternatives to Hierarchy and Bail-Outs: The Historic Example of the United States

The United States offers an important historical example of how the challenge of sub-national fiscal crises has been managed in a federal state. The US model relies on internal political mechanisms of accountability to state voters and on market-based 'hard' budgetary constraints. In the 1840s nine, mainly southern, US federal states defaulted. They were led by Louisiana, but included Michigan and Pennsylvania. The defaults were the product of reckless state-bank-financed infrastructure investments and strong state-level anti-tax attitudes. A majority of fiscally prudent states, led by New York, prevented a federal bail-out. This episode provided a strong federal pre-commitment to avoid becoming lender of last resort. It established the precedent that hierarchical, 'hard' budgetary constraints were to be avoided. The default crises of the 1840s had two other consequences. They led the large majority of federal states to impose self-binding constraints on sub-national debt. Constitutional amendments required balanced budgets and strengthened state-level fiscal accountability (Wibbels 2003). The crises of the 1840s also induced financial markets to begin at a very early stage to assess the 'stand-alone' creditworthiness of US federal states and thus their capacity to comply with fiscal discipline.

Despite these political and market 'hard' constraints, US municipal debt crises and defaults proved a periodic problem. Following the 1873 Depression, more than 24 per cent of municipal debt was in default, mostly in the post-Civil-War south. The 1930s Great Depression led New York City close to bankruptcy. However, over the post-1945 period, defaults were relatively rare, in relation to the huge size of the US municipal bond market (some $3,000 billion in 2010) and the number of diverse issuers (over 50,000). Between 1970 and 2009 there were only fifty-four defaults by issuers, mostly in health-care and public-housing bonds and involving debt mismanagement (Moody's 2011). Default risks at the state level were to some extent offset by the scale of federal assistance to states in times of macroeconomic crisis. However, the availability of this assistance depended on the political composition of Congress.

The most celebrated case of systemic risk was the protracted New York City fiscal crisis, including near default in 1975. In this case the federal government had great difficulties in sustaining the 'no-bail-out' principle. The escalating bail-out involved a range of actors: federal government loans, the state government, the city pension fund, and the Wall Street banks that had served as underwriters. The federal government's involvement was widely seen as a dangerous precedent. Nevertheless, it involved tough terms.

The post-2007 financial and economic crisis led to escalating state and local government budget deficits and to fears of multiple, contagious US municipal bond defaults. New questions arose about whether investors were correctly pricing credit risks in a complex and diverse US municipal debt market that was more than half the size of total euro area sovereign debt markets. Nineteen out of fifty states had estimated budget gaps over 10 per cent for 2012. They were led by Alabama (33.7 per cent), Nevada (31 per cent), and California (28 per cent). Eleven states had between 2.3 per cent and 9.6 per cent (National Conference of State Legislatures 2011). State budgets were under pressure from big falls in tax revenue and the uncovering of huge underfunded pension liabilities. In consequence, municipal debt ceased to be viewed as a safe-haven investment. In 2012 three Californian cities filed for bankruptcy because of financial commitments based on over-optimistic revenue assumptions. Jefferson County, Alabama, had already filed for bankruptcy, followed in 2013 by the biggest municipal bankruptcy in US history—Detroit, with debts at $18 billion.

Traditionally the municipal debt market had been used to finance infrastructural investments, for instance in transportation. Otherwise, state and local governments, which, unlike the federal government, were required to operate balanced budgets, could not fund them. Municipal debt had been seen as a safe haven because many bond payments had been a priority obligation on state and local governments and because of balanced budget requirements. Moreover, the municipal bond market was privileged by tax incentives, thereby attracting millions of individual investors through specialized mutual funds. However, by 2011 states like Illinois were leading the way in issuing bonds not just to help pay huge underfunded pension liabilities but also to cover a backlog of unpaid bills. Accounting rules had enabled state and local governments to hide the true economic value of their unfunded pension and healthcare liabilities. These liabilities put states like Illinois, New Jersey, Kansas, Kentucky, and Oklahoma at high risk. Illinois' pension liabilities were funded at just 50.7 per cent. Fears mounted that, without drastic state-level fiscal reforms, US sovereign debt distress could be deepened by municipal bond defaults and calls for bail-outs. The politics centred on who would bear the pain: taxpayers, public service users from heavy spending cuts, public sector pensions, or bondholders?

High System Strength and Sub-National State Capacity: The Case of Germany

Germany represented the traditional model of cooperative, stable, and predictable European fiscal federalism. Its status as a model of high sub-national fiscal capacity rested on three elements: the triple-A credit rating of the sovereign; the existence of a set of *Länder* with notably high 'stand-alone' fiscal capacity; and 'system strength'. System strength was provided by 'cooperative' fiscal federalism. It took the form of joint federal-*Land* decision-making in fiscal policy. In addition, system strength was reinforced by large-scale, formula-based, horizontal fiscal transfers amongst the sixteen *Länder*. It was supplemented by vertical transfers from the federal government, as well as by voluntary cash-sharing to ease short-term borrowing requirements (Renzsch 1991). The aim of this elaborate and generous fiscal transfer system was to promote the constitutionally-guaranteed equalization of living conditions in the Federal Republic, whilst protecting *Land* sovereignty. It resulted in the seeming paradox of a creditor state that combined high sub-national fiscal capacity with 'soft' hierarchical budgetary constraints.

The guiding principles of German fiscal federalism are laid down in Articles 104a, 106, 107, 109, and 115 of the Basic Law, as amended in 1969 and 2009. Articles 104a and 106 apportion public expenditure and tax revenue between federation and *Länder*. Article 107 deals with financial equalization and makes provision for *Länder* to receive a share of corporation and income taxes and VAT. Not least, it requires 'a reasonable equalization of the disparate financial capacities of the *Länder*, with due regard for the financial capacities and needs of municipalities'. Article 107 also allows the federal government to make grants to financially weak *Länder* 'to assist them in meeting their general financial needs'. Article 109 enshrines the principle that the federation and the *Länder* are 'autonomous and independent' of one another in the management of their respective budgets. At the same time, in managing their budgets, they 'shall take due account of the requirements of the overall economic equilibrium'. This article suggests a cooperative element in taking into account macroeconomic requirements. Finally, Article 115 enshrines the 'golden rule' in public debt: 'Revenue obtained by borrowing shall not exceed the total of investment expenditures provided for in the budget; exceptions shall be permissible only to avert a disturbance of the overall economic equilibrium.'

However, there was in-built gridlock in translating these constitutional provisions into legislation and in debating constitutional amendments on fiscal federalism. It stemmed from the authority of the *Länder*. Their authority at the federal level derives from their co-determination of constitutional change and national legislation through the Bundesrat. It is augmented by their co-determination of the distribution of the major national tax revenues and, to a much smaller extent, by their tax autonomy.

This gridlock is reinforced by the different political economy interests of the federal government, *Land* governments with 'stand-alone' fiscal capacity, and those without this capacity. The federal government was interested in ensuring Germany's sovereign creditworthiness and in reducing its transfer payments to the *Länder*. At the same time, it was concerned not to penalize party-politically aligned *Land* governments. *Länder* with 'stand-alone' fiscal capacity sought greater fiscal autonomy and lower contributions to financial equalization. *Länder* without this capacity pursued more burden-sharing.

In consequence, it proved extremely difficult to achieve internal party-political unity on federalism reforms, to mobilize party positions, and to arouse public interest in reforms to German sub-national fiscal governance. Hence fiscal federalism remained essentially an issue in executive politics and in elite accommodation within, as much as across, parties. Moreover, the requirement of special two-third majorities for constitutional reforms in the Bundesrat—as well as in the Bundestag—added to gridlock. The combination of voting rules with a complex constellation of political economy interests meant that there was a strong element of path dependency in fiscal federalism reforms. The cooperative element retreated but retained a firm foothold.

The Basic Law left scope for very different interpretations of 'reasonable' fiscal equalization through horizontal and vertical transfers and of how to strike the balance between strengthening fiscal autonomy for the *Länder* and strengthening coordination around macroeconomic objectives. As the *Länder* had only very limited fiscal autonomy in setting their own taxes, the central issues arose over co-determination in agreeing the distribution of the major national tax revenues. Also, the qualified 'golden rule' on public debt in Article 115 was too imprecise to serve as an instrument of fiscal discipline. It left to the *Länder* considerable flexibility in expenditure. However, it did not fit with the EU fiscal rules that Germany insisted on as the basis for the SGP in 1997.

From 1997, as the third stage of EMU approached, the federal finance ministry began to call for a national stability pact. The aim was to achieve a better match between domestic fiscal federalism and the SGP through more precise fiscal rules, strengthened monitoring, and sanctions. It sought also to commit the *Länder* to share the burden of any future EU sanctions. The *Finanzplanungsrat* (Financial Planning Council), which was composed of the federal and the *Länder* finance ministers, was the venue in which these issues were debated and negotiated. However, little progress was made on a national stability pact before Germany was threatened with the EU excessive deficit procedure in November 2003.

The most striking underlying shift was from the paradigm of cooperative to one of competitive fiscal federalism. The earlier rationale of 'equality of living conditions' in the Federal Republic gave way to one of incentives to 'sound finances', fiscal efficiency, and 'stand-alone' fiscal capacity. This shift reflected a combination of factors. Many were domestic. First, there was mounting criticism of the growing fiscal opacity and lack of clear accountability to voters after the 1969 constitutional reforms had created joint federal-*Land* tasks for large expenditure sectors (Scharpf, Reissert, and Schnabel 1976). Secondly, the fiscal shock of German unification in 1990 led to an increasingly assertive attitude of the key *Länder* with 'stand-alone' fiscal capacity, led by Bavaria, Baden-Württemberg, and Hesse, towards more deeply indebted *Länder*. Thirdly, for the same reason, the post-unification fiscally burdened federal government had a stronger interest in reducing its exposure to making supplementary vertical fiscal transfers to bail-out the *Länder*.

In addition, the shift to a paradigm of competitive federalism had European and international roots. There was mounting political interest at *Land* level in attracting more mobile investment and qualified workers within the increasingly competitive environment that was being created by the European single market, European currency union, and EU enlargement to east central Europe. *Länder* were caught up in so-called *Standortwettbewerb* (competition to attract investment). Also, the *Landesbanken* redefined their strategic interests away from regional economic development, increasing the incentive to shift the financing of *Länder* debt to international bond markets.

The process of paradigm change had begun pre-unification as from the 1970s structural economic imbalance within the 'old' Federal Republic grew. *Länder* like Bremen and the Saarland suffered asymmetric shocks from the demise of traditional industries like shipbuilding and steel. They became bigger claimants in fiscal equalization. However, momentum was added to paradigm shift by German unification in 1990, EMU in 1999, EU eastern enlargement in 2004, new discourses of Europeanization and globalization, and the evolving post-2007 crisis.

German unification added six new chronically fiscally weak *Länder*. From 1995 the Solidarity Pact placed onerous transfer obligations on the few western *Länder* with 'stand-alone' fiscal capacity, above all Bavaria, Baden-Württemberg, and Hesse. By 1997–1998 these three *Länder* were complaining about a 'confiscatory' fiscal equalization scheme. In 1999 they succeeded in gaining a favourable Federal Constitutional Court ruling. It required a different system of financial equalization from the Solidarity Pact.

Solidarity Pact II of 2003, which fixed transfers to the East till 2019, was a victory for the federal government and the *Länder* with 'stand-alone' fiscal capacity. It created incentives for the *Länder* to increase their tax income by exempting parts of a disproportionate growth of revenues from fiscal equalization. Solidarity Pact II also replaced guaranteed minimum standards of equalization by a sliding scale for recipient *Länder*, thereby reducing their gains. Their one gain was that fiscal equalization was increased in scope by taking a bigger proportion of local taxes into account. Overall, however, the net winners were the *Länder* with 'stand-alone' fiscal capacity and the federal government, which used the opportunity to cut federal supplementary grants.

The shift in attitudes towards fiscal federalism was evident in judicial rulings. In a ruling of 1992 the German Federal Constitutional Court concluded that, in respect of their high debt levels, Bremen and Saarland were facing a situation of 'extreme' fiscal hardship. In consequence, the federal government had an obligation to provide additional special-need financial assistance, which was made available from 1994 to 2004. However, in a comparable case in 2006—following the costly rescue of Bankgesellschaft Berlin—the Constitutional Court ruled that Berlin was not in the same situation because inter alia it had not yet exhausted all its fiscal options. This ruling argued that a *Land* had to use all its own revenue-raising flexibility and expenditure-cutting options before it could be categorized as a fiscal 'emergency' and receive extraordinary federal financial support. An emergency was defined as a threat that a *Land* would not be able to carry out its constitutional duties. The ruling was based on the danger of moral hazard that followed from the federal government having no instrument to control the indebtedness of *Länder*.

The constitutional amendment of 2006, which followed from the first Commission on Modernizing the Federal Order, took a first small step towards more fiscal autonomy for the *Länder* with respect to 'their' taxes. It also modified voting rules so that the veto powers of the Bundesrat were reduced and the federal government could more easily avoid being held hostage by a few *Länder*. Not least, the 2006 federalism reform reduced federal government obligations to help finance public investments of *Land* and local governments. These changes were symptomatic of a shift towards a competitive federalism, based on more assertive projection of creditor-state power within Germany. Otherwise, the 2006 reform did little to strengthen fiscal autonomy of the *Länder* or to align tax revenue powers with clear assignment of competences (Baus, Eppler, and Wintermann 2008). It failed to strengthen political mechanisms for hardening sub-national budgetary constraints.

After unification, the second main catalyst for change was the SGP and German violation of the EU 3 per cent fiscal deficit rule in 2001–2004. The result was deepening concern within the federal government that Germany risked losing its shaping influence ('soft' power) within the EU and euro area. Domestic institutional reforms were necessary to ensure its number-one place as the most creditworthy state in Europe. Against this background, a second Commission on Modernizing the Federal Order set to work to design fiscal federal arrangements. The aim was to mirror the SGP arrangements on which the German federal government had insisted at EU level.

The challenge went beyond reputational loss. Historical data suggested that the *Länder* had borne a relatively smaller share in public debt consolidation than the federal government, compared to their US equivalents (Claeys, Ramos, and Surinach 2008). The data showed a rise in the *Länder* and local authority share in public debt to GDP from 14.3 per cent in 1979 to 26.6 per cent in 2009 (Statistisches Bundesamt 2010: 1A4). By 2003–2005 per capita debt service costs varied from €736 in Bremen, €665 in Berlin, €348 in the Saarland, and €344 in Saxony-Anhalt, to €83 in Bavaria, €137 in Saxony, and €171 in Baden-Württemberg (Bertelsmann Stiftung 2007: 315). The per capita debt service costs in Berlin increased six-fold between 1990 and 2003. Along with Bremen, Berlin's fiscal position was labelled 'catastrophic' by the Bertelsmann Foundation.

The so-called 'debt brake' (*Schuldenbremse*) of 2009 formed the centrepiece of the second fiscal federalism reform under the Christian Democrat/Social Democrat Grand Coalition of Chancellor Angela Merkel (Renzsch 2010). This new, tough hierarchical mechanism for hardening budgetary constraints amended Articles 109 and 115 of the

Basic Law. It established that: 'The budgets of the federation and the *Länder* have in principle to be balanced without income from credits.' In addition, burden-sharing in case of sanctions under the EU excessive deficit procedure was regulated on a ratio of 65:35 between federal and *Land* governments (Hrbek and Bussjäger 2011).

The 2009 constitutional reform placed tightened constitutional and political constraints on *Länder* to balance their budgets. It empowered their finance ministers vis-à-vis colleagues and parties and provided a new reference point for future *Land* political debates, electoral contests, and court rulings. The main concession was that, in recognition of their significant ratios of net debt and of debt service costs to operating revenue, the *Länder* were given a longer time scale than the federal government in which to achieve fiscal balance—2020 instead of 2016. In addition, the federal government offered transitional financial assistance to chronic debtor *Länder* to help them meet their extremely tough fiscal consolidation targets.

The new borrowing limits were accompanied by the creation of the federal-*Land* Stability Council (Article 109a Basic Law). The Stability Council had the power to declare that a budgetary emergency was imminent, based on four key fiscal ratios and threshold values. In that case it was empowered to stipulate restructuring programmes and to publish its decisions and the relevant data. Its decisions required a majority of at least eleven of the sixteen *Länder* and the approval of the federal government, with individual governments abstaining on votes relating to themselves.

The political and legal implications of sub-national fiscal hardening were soon made clear. Given the limited tax autonomy of the *Länder*, the burden of sub-national fiscal consolidation fell heavily on expenditure. In May 2011 the Stability Council classified Berlin, Bremen, Saarland, and Schleswig-Holstein as at risk of a budgetary emergency. It began to monitor their restructuring reports, criticizing the lack of detailed information. Moreover, these four *Länder*, plus Saxony-Anhalt, were already in receipt of special transitional assistance so that they could meet the 2020 target for balanced budgets. In its justification the chair of the Stability Council referred to the risks of an internal Greek-style debt crisis. He noted that Bremen's debt per capita was close to that of Greece.

Additionally, in a landmark ruling of March 2011, the Constitutional Court of North-Rhine Westphalia declared unconstitutional the supplementary budget of the *Land* government because of increased borrowing. The Court questioned whether there was a 'severe' disruption of the macroeconomic equilibrium that justified the supplementary budget. It argued that, in any case, the government had failed to demonstrate how this measure was supposed to avert macroeconomic disruption. The supplementary budget was also incompatible with the principle of cost-effectiveness, which required that public debt must be kept in check. The clear implication was that more precise analysis and arguments would be required to justify recourse to the exemption clause for the ceiling on new borrowing.

Nevertheless, sub-national fiscal 'hardening' took a different and weaker form within Germany than German negotiators required within either the SGP of 1997 or the euro area fiscal compact treaty of 2012. The Stability Council lacked sanctions. It was also weakened by its lack of access to timely, up-to-date, and detailed fiscal data. The *Länder* retained and sought to use their room for manoeuvre under the reform. Significantly, the 'debt brake' allowed additional new borrowing when the business cycle deviates from the 'normal course' (*Normallage*) and there is a 'severe disruption' of the macroeconomic equilibrium. Many *Länder* proved slow to act to insert debt brakes in their constitutions and introduce implementing legislation (Deutsche Bundesbank 2011b: 20–3). When they did so, requirements for minimum debt reduction were often imprecise and lacked ambition, leaving little fiscal safety margin. Moreover, questions remained about the scope of the 'debt brake' and whether it would embrace all off-budget entities and fully factor in public–private partnerships.

The reforms of 2003, 2006, and 2009 represented an ongoing process of shift in power within German sub-national fiscal governance. The net gainers were the federal government and the *Länder* with 'stand-alone' fiscal capacity. At the same time, reforms retained a path-dependent character. Their trajectory was shaped by continuity in constitutional principle, including the Federal Constitutional Court's ban on mutual liability and special voting rules on constitutional reform. It was also influenced by the numerical advantage that debtor *Länder* enjoyed, by the complexities of multilevel governance, and by the consequent lack of internal party unity. In consequence, messy and shifting compromises and ambiguity triumphed over the strict application of basic creditor-state principles like the balanced-budget requirement and the clear alignment of liability and control.

An example was the federal government's concession of joint federal-*Land* 'Germany bonds' in 2012 as the price for *Länder* ratification of the fiscal compact treaty. The *Länder* stood to gain by lower borrowing costs. On the one hand, it served as a reminder that the political infrastructure of cooperative federalism was strikingly resilient. On the other, it fell well short of a step towards mutual liability. The 'Germany bonds' involved the federal government and each *Land* being individually responsible for their share of the borrowing.

Sub-National Fiscal Capacity Building in a Context of Federalization

A number of other European states had witnessed a powerful dynamic of federalization since the 1980s. However, none of them had achieved the high sub-national fiscal capacity building of Germany, in part because of the historic record of their sovereigns. Moreover, their sub-national fiscal governance was, if anything, even more messy and characterized by shifting compromises and ambiguity than in Germany.

At different paces, and in different ways, Belgium, Italy, and Spain created and/or strengthened regional governments and gave birth to strong regional political elites. In the process they embraced a new discourse of fiscal federalism (Conversi 2007). Much of this dynamism was internal. It sprang from pace-setting by politically confident regions with 'stand-alone' fiscal capacity and from emulation by other regions, which sought to protect their relative positions. The pace-setter in Belgium was Flanders; in Italy, Lombardy; and, in Spain, the Basque Country, Navarre, and Catalonia. Each region saw in Bavaria and Baden-Württemberg its models in defining a national leadership role.

Sub-National Fiscal Capacity in a Federalized State: The Case of Belgium

Belgium had the most advanced federalization process and, in Flanders, a region with high 'stand-alone' fiscal capacity. It was the only one of the three European states to explicitly characterize itself as federal in its revised constitution of 1993. The political and social roots of federalization rested on a movement against the 'French-speaking bourgeoisie', which had dominated the Belgian state after its foundation in 1830 (Gérard 2001). Federalization became intertwined in a powerful mix of conflicts over language boundaries and over economic interests as defined by structural imbalances. A key driver was the shift in the axis of economic development from the 1960s, away from French-speaking Wallonia to Flemish-speaking Flanders. Brussels stood out as a focus of contention between both. This shift in structural imbalance sparked new politically contentious questions about the long-term future of Belgium's generous system of social security, which fell mainly under federal jurisdiction. Flemish politicians lobbied strongly for decentralization of unemployment benefit and health insurance, thereby limiting the liabilities of Flanders with respect to Wallonia. Walloons feared that fiscal competition would drive down taxes and enforce social hardship.

The 1993 Constitution established Belgium as a complex and distinctive 'dual' federalism. On the one hand, it comprised three linguistically organized communities, dealing with education, health, and culture. On the other, it represented three territorially organized regions—Brussels, Flanders, and Wallonia, each of which was responsible for economic development, key infrastructure, employment, and foreign trade. Dating back to 1970, the regions were given enhanced competences. Between 1995 and 2006 the sub-national share in total public expenditure rose from around 33 to around 38 per cent. Moreover, sub-national governments had considerable blocking powers in any renegotiation of competences and fiscal arrangements. Reforms required either constitutional amendment or, in the case of fiscal policy reforms, 'special laws' with two-third legislative majorities (Deschouwer 2005).

A key landmark in building sub-national fiscal capacity was a law of 1988, which gave the regions a share in national income tax. Gradually, by 2000 the basis of sharing shifted to favour Flanders. It was offset by the National Solidarity Measure of interregional equalization, from which Brussels and Wallonia were beneficiaries (Gérard 2001: 20–2). Subsequently, the OECD (2009b: 70–1) criticized the negative effects of the progressive nature of the fiscal equalization on incentives for Brussels and Wallonia to develop their own tax base. This international critique helped bolster Flemish arguments.

A second and more decisive landmark was the Lambermont Agreements and special law of 2001. Regional fiscal capacity was strengthened by new powers of fiscal co-determination over the distribution of major national tax revenues. It also gained from enhanced fiscal autonomy over property, inheritance, and eco-taxes, vehicle registration, and a range of special taxes (including on any activity where there was not a federal tax). The regions could also increase or offer reductions on income tax, within specified limits designed to limit tax competition (Gérard 2001: 35–6). This power was used by Flanders to reduce tax. However, the degree of tax autonomy continued to be limited. Notably, the regions lacked fiscal autonomy with respect to corporation tax and VAT. Their revenues continued to be dominated by central transfers, principally shared taxes (Van der Stichele and Verdonck 2002).

Because of the decline of its once prosperous industries, Wallonia stood out as the 'problem' region. It suffered from structural economic imbalances and from lack of 'stand-alone' fiscal capacity. Wallonia's strategic interests crystallized around defence of the principle of fiscal solidarity in the face of more strident Flemish demands for fiscal autonomy. Conversely, Flanders succeeded in freezing its transfers to Wallonia at about 3 per cent of 1999 revenue. This change enhanced Flanders' fiscal autonomy. However, the divergence of territorial interests at the heart of the Belgian state heightened complications of national coalition-building. It paralleled a political bifurcation, in which centre-Right politics gained ground in Flanders, and centre-Left politics in Wallonia. The subsequent problems in national coalition-building put in question the viability of this traditionally leading state in European integration.

Despite these difficulties, the overriding Belgian national interest in remaining at the heart of European economic and monetary integration led it to be a pace-setter in agreeing a national stability pact. The 'Cooperation Agreement' of 1996 paralleled the Maastricht 'convergence' process for euro entry. It bound the increasingly empowered communities and regions into a framework of voluntary fiscal discipline, centred on a commitment to achieve balanced budgets. They were expected to comply with medium-term guidelines, including annual deficit and debt levels, which were jointly set in the High Council of Finance. The federal government was empowered to impose restrictions on sub-national borrowing if it interfered with macroeconomic objectives or if there was risk of structural slippage in the budgetary position of a sub-national government (Organization for Economic Cooperation and Development 2009b: 61).

Sub-national compliance was facilitated by an established stability culture and by a shared process of learning the lessons from the big sovereign debt accumulation of the 1970s–1980s. Despite its high public debt/GDP ratio on euro entry, Belgium had a long history of avoiding excessive deficits and debt. It sought to align itself with the Dutch and the German models of economic stability and sound finances, all the more so as Flemish power grew. Factors of Flemish power, economic history, and strategic positioning within the European integration process—not least within Benelux—facilitated regional compliance with fiscal policies that reduced Belgian public debt not just before but also after euro entry. Flanders prided itself in not needing to resort to debt financing.

Belgium provided an example of how sub-national fiscal capacity could exceed sovereign fiscal capacity. The scale of fiscal autonomy accorded to Belgian regions, especially in taxation, meant that they were less challenged by fiscal consolidation than the federal government. The greater dynamism of their revenues contrasted with the continuing responsibility of the federal government for social security, with its considerable contingent liabilities. Moreover, the special Finance Act of 1989 had entrusted the existing debt burden, with debt service charges, to the federal government.

Sub-National Fiscal Capacity in a State of Asymmetrical Autonomies: The Case of Spain

Though characterized as 'the state of the autonomies', Spain avoided federal language within its 1978 Constitution in favour of ambiguous formulations. Invoking Article 2, which describes the Spanish nation as 'indivisible', the Constitutional Court continued to act as a brake on sub-national ambitions for independence. At the same time, to mark a radical shift from the authoritarian, centralizing Franco period, the new state was identified officially as a state of autonomous communities. Each was to have its own statute of autonomy, generating an open, flexible process of asymmetric federalization. Article 2 'recognizes and guarantees the right to autonomy of the nationalities and regions of which it is composed, and the solidarity amongst them'. The resulting ambiguity was reflected in an evolving 'semi-federal' political system.

Sub-national fiscal governance contained elements of high and low fiscal capacity. On the one hand, it provided system strength. The principle of solidarity in Article 2, reinforced in Articles 130 and 138, legitimated a large-scale fiscal equalization system to ensure a minimum level of services across Spain, as well as 'economic balance'. On the other hand, the Senate remained a weak, territorially based upper chamber, unlike the German Bundesrat. The autonomous communities lacked fiscal co-determination powers over the distribution of national taxes.

Title VIII of the 1978 Constitution formed the basis for an open, flexible process of decentralization. Its effects on sub-national fiscal governance and capacity building were messy and complex. They were shaped by various factors: the political will of nationalities and regions, emulation processes at regional level, the degree of compliance of national governments (the centre-Right Popular Party was less enthusiastic), and the hurdle of the Constitutional Court. The three historic nationalities—the Basque Country, Catalonia, and Galicia—were recognized in the Constitution as having prior and distinct claims to autonomy. This status followed from pre-Civil War recognition. They could build on a legitimating discourse of cultural distinctiveness and 'victimhood' under Franco. The result was asymmetry in arrangements for sub-national governance, in which the Basque Country and Navarre gained a fiscal autonomy that was denied to others, even to Catalonia.

The post-Franco history of Spain was characterized by mounting claims for autonomy from the historic nationalities, led by Catalonia, alongside emulation by other Spanish regions, led by Andalusia and Valencia, which also began to build their own cultural identities. The political dynamism behind federalization was sustained by the continuous and active presence of Basque and Catalan nationalist parties in the Spanish Parliament, sometimes in a pivotal position with respect to government formation. It was reinforced more broadly by the regionalization of national party organizations and the emergence of strong regional political elites. Catalan nationalism saw itself traditionally as a force for the modernization of Spain, identifying Andalusia as its counter-model.

On an individual basis each autonomous community negotiated its own arrangements. Nevertheless, the Basque Country and Navarre remained exceptional in their high fiscal capacity. Their fiscal autonomy was exceeded only by the Swiss cantons and was matched by the provinces of Bolzano and Trentino in Italy. In all these cases fiscal autonomy was matched by the top international credit ratings. Though subject to the national budgetary stability law, the Basque Country and Navarre set most of the taxes originated in their territories. They stood outside the national fiscal equalization system and made an independently negotiated, small contribution to national revenues. This high fiscal capacity was much envied in Catalonia.

A discourse of fiscal federalism emerged within this complex, disaggregated process of ongoing renegotiated regionalization. The autonomous communities had a measure of fiscal autonomy with respect to fuel, housing, inheritance, and vehicle registration taxes. However, the central support of sub-national fiscal capacity was a highly developed system of fiscal equalization, which transferred tax revenues from some autonomous communities, like Catalonia and Madrid, to others like Andalusia, Extremadura, and Galicia. This system was modified in 1997, 2002, 2009, and 2011. The autonomous communities' fiscal capacity was further demonstrated in their co-determination of the distribution of major national taxes, notably income tax and VAT (rising to 50 per cent by 2009) and excise duties (58 per cent) (Organization for Economic Cooperation and Development 2010: 80). Their share was increased from 2002 to reflect their enhanced responsibilities, especially in education and health, which accounted respectively for 28 and 37 per cent of their expenditure (Organization for Economic Cooperation and Development 2010: 80).

In 2009 the autonomous communities were given greater fiscal autonomy with respect to setting rates of income tax. Also, reflecting the priorities of the Socialist government, three new elements in fiscal equalization were created: a convergence fund to assist regions with low per capita GDP; a guarantee fund to adjust for demographic developments; and a sufficiency fund for non-social expenditures. At a time of fiscal crisis, they were designed to provide greater system strength for autonomous communities that lacked 'stand-alone' fiscal capacity.

However, even before the post-2007 crisis, emerging structural economic imbalances introduced new tensions. From the late 1990s Catalonia experienced negative trade balances, in contrast to the Basque Country and Navarre. Its governments, parties, and public became more resentful of being 'robbed' by Spain, notably by the 'feckless' people of Andalusia, and of being 'starved' of investment by Madrid. Territorial status anxieties were further increased by asymmetries in the relative benefits from large-scale EU structural funds and, from the 1990s, cohesion fund expenditure on infrastructure. The relative gains to the autonomous region of Madrid, compared to Catalonia and Barcelona in particular, sparked new tensions about relative position.

In the wake of the 2007 financial crisis, Catalonian frustration with fiscal 'robbery' mounted. A discursive shift from fiscal autonomy to independence followed a succession of major public protests in Barcelona in 2011–2012. This development was accelerated by a Constitutional Court ruling of 2010 that declared invalid a carefully negotiated decentralization reform. It gained further momentum in 2012 when the Catalan government took the humiliating step of following Andalusia and Valencia in seeking a national bail-out, despite its big net contribution to fiscal equalization. Catalan resentment was fuelled by the belief that fiscal equalization was generating inequitable outcomes and that its 'stand-alone' fiscal capacity was being exploited.

The key catalysts for fiscal re-centralization pressures were, first, the mounting Spanish sovereign debt crisis, credit rating downgrades, and increasing borrowing costs; and, secondly, the majorities secured by the Popular Party in the national election in 2011 and in eight of thirteen autonomous communities. The previous Socialist government had faced growing problems of sub-national compliance with macroeconomic stabilization objectives and sought to avert more intrusive credit rating and bond market influence. Its ideological, party-political, and electoral problems in tackling this issue stemmed from the large role of the autonomous communities in social expenditure and in public sector employment. Nevertheless, if belatedly, the Spanish Socialist government agreed tough new fiscal rules and compliance mechanisms with the autonomous communities. The incentive for the autonomous communities was fear that Spanish sovereign credit downgrading would have disproportionately negative effects on their own ratings and borrowing costs. Also, they faced deepening fiscal problems with a huge collapse in their own real-estate and other tax revenues.

The process of fiscal re-centralization began in 2007. In 2006 the revised budgetary stability law, which dated from 2001, had relaxed discipline, requiring a balanced budget over the economic cycle rather than annually. Minor fiscal deficits were permitted if national GDP growth fell below 2 per cent. *In extremis* the central government could—by decree—block sub-national borrowing. The Budgetary Stability Law of 2007 clarified that, in the absence of a national bail-out mechanism, early warning indicators and strengthened fiscal surveillance were required. Autonomous communities had to remain within fiscal deficit limits of 0.25 per cent of GDP if national GDP growth fell below 2 per cent. They had to run surpluses if GDP growth was over 3 per cent. However, these surpluses could be minimal and thus, in counter-cyclical terms, inadequate.

The 2007 law constrained sub-national fiscal autonomy in other ways. Fiscal deficit targets, and deficit-reduction plans in case of non-compliance, were to be agreed within the Fiscal and Financial Policy Council (*Consejo de Política Fiscal y Financiera*), in which the central government held 50 per cent of the votes. Also, debt issuance was tightened. Autonomous communities could only issue debt of maturity in excess of one year to finance investment spending. Long-term debt issuance required approval by central government. Where there was non-compliance with fiscal targets, central government approval was required for all debt issuance (Organization for Economic Cooperation and Development 2010: 82). Moreover, debt servicing was not to exceed 25 per cent of operating revenues. These provisions represented a reduction of borrowing autonomy. The 2007 law also provided for special central government monitoring of local authorities whose debt to operating revenue ratio exceeded 110 per cent. In September 2011 this reform was reinforced by a controversial reform that inserted the budgetary 'golden rule' in the Spanish constitution. Both main parties agreed to introduce a cap on the budget deficits of all state administrations, including the autonomous communities. In 2012 a new institutional structure was created to 'bail-out' Spanish autonomous communities.

Catalonia presented a special problem in applying these new rules. By 2010 it was caught up in serious fiscal crisis, excluded from international capital markets, and raising loans from La Caixa and, like Valencia, from its own citizens. It also became increasingly clear that autonomous communities had been hiding liabilities off-balance-sheet in various private entities. In consequence, the scale of sub-national debt problems had been underestimated. By 2013 autonomous communities were divided on the future of sub-national governance. Catalonia was determined to seek fiscal independence; Castile-La Mancha, Madrid, and Murcia sought re-centralization; whilst others, like Andalusia, preferred to wait and see.

Politically Contingent Sub-National Fiscal Capacity: The Case of Italy

Complex, asymmetric sub-national fiscal capacity was built into the constitutional arrangements of post-war Italy. It comprised 'special-status' regions and 'ordinary' regions. With the exception of one region, the special-status regions dated back to Article 5 of the 1948 Constitution and the perceived threat of secession. They comprised a set of geographically peripheral and/or linguistically distinctive regions—Friuli-Venezia Giulia (since 1963), Sardinia, Sicily, and Val d'Aosta, as well as Trentino Alto Adige with its two provinces of Bolzano and Trento. These provinces and regions were accorded a high degree of fiscal autonomy, closer to that later enjoyed by their Belgian and Spanish equivalents. Unlike the 'ordinary' Italian regions, they were responsible for the finances of their municipalities and communes. Moreover, the 'special-status' regions did not take part in the national fiscal equalization scheme.

Otherwise, the fifteen ordinary regions remained limited both in fiscal autonomy and in fiscal co-determination of the distribution of national taxes. Their main leverage in enhancing their fiscal capacity derived from the power to extract fiscal transfers from politically friendly central governments, especially in election years, or on the basis, like Lazio, that they were 'too significant to fail'. System strength was available but too politically contingent to ensure sustained high sub-national fiscal capacity.

The emergence of ordinary regions, and of the discourse of fiscal federalism, proved a protracted, hesitant, and politicized process. The State-Region Conference (*Conferenza Stato-Regioni*) was strengthened in 1997. However, it was a purely consultative organ that could not bind governments. Although the 1948 Constitution provided for regions, the creation of directly elected ordinary regions had to wait till 1970. Their detailed shape only emerged in 1972–1977. Major functional and fiscal decentralization reforms followed in the 1990s. After the 2001 constitutional reform, federalization provoked mounting conflicts before the Italian Constitutional Court.

Continuing uncertainty pervaded Italian sub-national fiscal governance, and posed questions about sub-national fiscal capacity. It reflected complex cross-cutting party-political and factional currents at the national level. Central government proved vulnerable to clientelist pressures from cities and regions for special fiscal transfers and bail-outs. Not least, during the Cold War years, this vulnerability was increased by the fear of the political capture of several regions by a powerful Communist Party. In addition, as in France, the municipalities and communes were able to use channels of party-political influence to prevent the 'ordinary' regional governments from gaining hierarchical authority over their finances. This constraint was relaxed in 2009 when the regions were given a stronger intermediary role in the implementation of the national stability pact.

The main growth in regional competences took place in 1997 when—in addition to health, which had been allocated to them in 1978—they gained functions in economic development, infrastructure, labour markets, and education. However, strengthening the fiscal autonomy of regions was a slow, progressive process with laws in 1992, 1995, 1997, 2000, and 2009. It did not proceed in parallel with political federalism and was accompanied by serious implementation deficits (Buratti 2011). Central transfers were changed from earmarked to block grants. On the one hand, there were moves to strengthen regional fiscal capacity through increased tax autonomy. The 1997 reform assigned to regions a new tax on productive activities (Imposta Regionale sulle Attivita Produttive (IRAP)). In 1995 a new fiscal equalization fund on German lines was established. However, despite its reform in 2001, it proved ineffective in reducing ad hoc political deals between central governments and regions (Ambrosianio, Bordignon, and Cerniglia 2008). On the other hand, there were signs of erosion of sub-national fiscal capacity. After the 2006 national elections, the centre-Right Berlusconi government abolished the local property tax, replacing it with central transfers.

The key formal changes were the 2001 constitutional amendments (especially Articles 116 and 119) and the framework law 42/2009. If they had been fully implemented in letter and spirit, the 2001 constitutional changes would have moved Italy closer to Spain (Ambrosianio, Bordignon, and Cerniglia 2008: 11). They formally recognized municipalities, regions, provinces, and 'the state' as components of the Republic. The constitutional reform also established regions' competence on all matters not reserved expressly for the state. In addition, in response to pressure from Lombardy and Veneto, it created the possibility of greater asymmetry on Spanish lines by enabling individual regions to negotiate greater autonomy. Finally, the 2001 reform provided the constitutional basis for sub-national fiscal autonomy and a revamped fiscal equalization system. However, it also empowered the state to set 'standard levels of service' (SLS) for all citizens. This provision opened up new opportunities to shape sub-national governments' expenditure decisions.

The framework law 42/2009 aimed to implement the fiscal federalism commitment of the Constitution (Article 116-3). It required 'standard levels of service' in education, health, and social services, accounting for some 80 per cent of regional expenditure. In order to meet the SLS for the region, the law provided for future detailed legislation on fiscal autonomy so that the regions would receive (unspecified) shares in income tax, VAT, and the new horizontal fiscal equalization fund, the latter to be funded out of VAT revenues. Against strong opposition from southern regions, the law sought to promote greater sub-national fiscal responsibility and efficiency and more transparency in fiscal transfers. At the same time, in making 'expenditure need' central to the reform, it aimed to shore up system strength through a more cooperative fiscal federalism that favoured the south. The system was to be monitored, from 2011, by the Permanent Commission for the Coordination of Public Finances, with support from the Joint Technical Commission for the Implementation of Fiscal Federalism. Past experience with reforms to sub-national fiscal governance suggested that implementation was likely to prove a disappointment (Buratti 2011).

The political economy of sub-national fiscal governance in Italy is shaped by two factors: the enduring north–south structural imbalance and the relative shares of national and sub-national debts. Though seen as historically rooted, the north–south structural economic imbalance only emerged out of a previously economically diversified southern Italy during the first half of the twentieth century. After a period of some convergence from the 1940s to 1970s, it grew again in significance (Felice 2011). The north–south imbalance was compensated by large-scale fiscal transfers, borne by the north, where they were seen as a source of inefficiency, as a cause of national decline, and as unsustainable.

In consequence, Italy was characterized by sharp differences in sub-national fiscal capacity. By the first decade of the twenty-first century, using the measure of the richest regions in per capita tax revenues, the regions with highest fiscal capacity were Val d'Aosta, Lombardy, Trentino Alto Adige, and Emilia-Romagna. The poorest were Calabria, Campania, Puglia, and Sicily (Ambrosianio, Bordignon, and Cerniglia 2008: 18). On the measure of the biggest net contributor to fiscal transfers (excluding capital expenditure) the region with the highest fiscal capacity was Lombardy, followed by Veneto. The biggest net recipient was Calabria, followed by Sicily (Ambrosianio, Bordignon, and Cerniglia 2008: 20, 23). On the measure of the highest levels of indebtedness to regional GDP, the lowest fiscal capacity in 2007–2008 was in southern regions, notably Campania, Sicily, as well as the province and city of Naples, Rome, Lazio, and Abruzzo in the centre. The highest sub-national fiscal capacity was in Emilia-Romagna,

Lombardy, Trentino Alto Adige, and Veneto (Banca d'Italia 2009: 6). A striking exception was Val d'Aosta, a special-status region with fiscal autonomy, high per capita GDP, and yet one of the highest debt levels in Italy. The sustainability of fiscal transfers became increasingly controversial as north–south structural economic imbalances grew from the 1970s and again with the post-2007 crisis.

Sub-national governments in the south were characterized by lower GDP per capita and less buoyant tax revenues. They suffered from weak administrative capacity and weak political capacity, reflected in the quality of their administrations, their personalized clientelist political practices, and the pervasive influence of organized crime. They operated in a context of weak social capital and the relative lack of an active civic society. These characteristics were manifested in sub-national fiscal governance in an ingrained habit of southern dependency on large-scale central transfers. Sub-national governments in the south were chronic debtors, with huge health service debts and a lower-quality service provision, despite higher per capita health expenditure than in the north. At the same time, reforms to sub-national fiscal governance were constrained by the politically pivotal electoral position of the south at the central level. Southern power was also apparent within the State-Regions-Local Government Conference (*Conferenza unificata*), where formal agreement was required before the implementation of fiscal federalism reforms. In consequence, the effects of commitments in 2000 and 2009 to strengthen sub-national fiscal responsibility, especially in debt management, were diluted.

The problems of sub-national debt were overshadowed by the huge debts of the central government. In 2008 sub-national debt amounted to only 6.4 per cent of total public debt and 6.8 per cent of national GDP. Moreover, the highest debt levels were accounted for by the communes rather than by the regions or provinces. As a percentage of geographic GDP, they varied from 8.7 per cent in the south to 5.8 per cent in the north (Banca d'Italia 2009: 6). However, these figures hid high levels of off-balance-sheet debt in quasi-private corporations.

There were several catalysts for 'hardening' budgetary constraints in Italian sub-national fiscal governance. They included the inflationary and fiscal crisis of the 1970s; the fall of the Communist Party; the rise of the Lega Nord; the crisis of Exchange-Rate Mechanism (ERM) exit in 1992; the Maastricht convergence process for euro entry; and the post-2007 crisis. The so-called Stammati decrees (law 62/1977 and law 43/1978) provided a massive bail-out for Italian cities, as well as increased central grants, in exchange for stricter rules on sub-national budgets. These rules represented a turning point in the sub-national use of debt to finance recurrent expenditure. They were in place before Italian sub-national governments began, from the mid-1990s, to issue regional and local bonds on a significant scale.

The rise of the Lega Nord was a central feature of the new party-political landscape of the so-called 'Second Republic' from the early 1990s. It formed a key part of the new centre-Right within a bipolarized, though still highly fragmented and factionalized, party system. At the same time, the 'brake' of fear of the Communist Party was removed. The Lega Nord created a new mythology of the 'three Italies'—Padanian, Etruscan, and Mediterranean—and promoted an agenda of independence from the south. Padania was represented as fiscally virtuous, thrifty, hardworking, and possessing high civic engagement. The Lega Nord used its pivotal position in centre-Right governments under Silvio Berlusconi to campaign for fiscal federalism, above all for fiscal autonomy for the north. By extension, the aim was greater fiscal responsibility on the part of sub-national governments in central and southern Italy. The Lega Nord's models of fiscal 'sinners' were Rome and Lazio, Naples and Campania, and Palermo and Sicily.

Italy's forced exit from the ERM in 1992, the race for euro entry in the period 1996–1999, and euro area membership (above all, with the post-2007 crisis) induced a spate of reforms to strengthen sub-national fiscal discipline. They formed the background to the 1992, 1995, and 1997 reforms. With monetary union, procedures were put in place to regulate central government intervention in case of sub-national default (*dissesto*). In exchange for assuming responsibility for sub-national debt restructuring, the state was empowered to dismiss the local authority and to establish a national commission of state and regional officials to restore sound finances. However, in practice this instrument was rarely used because it was politically costly. The default by the city of Taranto in Puglia in 2006–2007 was a rare case. Earlier, in 1996–1999, the region of Puglia had rescheduled its debts (Fitch 2009c). From 2007 the debt default procedure of national commissions was extended to the regions with respect to health finances. It was used in the case of Campania in 2009. By 2010 all southern regions, Lazio in the centre, and Liguria in the north, were governed by national commissions in health expenditure. Campania, Lazio, and Sicily accounted for more than 80 per cent of huge regional government health debts (some €30 billion).

Article 119, Title V, of the constitutional reform of 2001 clarified that the central government was not responsible for sub-national debt: in effect, a no-bail-out clause. Sub-national governments could borrow only for capital expenditures. Under law 267/2000 the total amounts of borrowing were strictly regulated. Various financial rules were introduced to ensure balanced budgets, including rules to limit debt service payments as a proportion of operating revenues. The framework law 42/2009 also envisaged new incentives and sanctions in case of non-compliance with the centrally-determined public finance targets. They included the requirement to draft 'convergence plans' on standard levels of service and on sub-national fiscal deficits and debt. These measures sought to reinforce the national stability pact through a form of 'controlled' fiscal federalism.

The national stability pact was introduced in 1999 as a complement to the EU SGP. However, it had mixed results. On the one hand, the annual approval of the stability pact has been used, especially post-2007, to strengthen control on capital as well as recurrent expenditures of sub-national governments. It has also been used to require and increase budget surpluses. Fiscal autonomy was tightly constrained by spending limits and by limits on capacity to adjust regional tax rates.

On the other hand, regions, provinces, and cities sought to evade these restrictions by creating private-law corporations, partly or in whole owned by the sub-national government. These bodies could raise debt and also served as a source of income for sub-national governments. In this way, as in Rome, the sub-national budget could be effectively 'emptied'. The national stability pact had the further effect of inducing sub-national governments—led by the regions of Campania, Lazio, Piedmont, and Sicily—to make use of financial derivatives, notably interest-rate swaps, to reduce interest payments (Banca d'Italia 2009: 22). The resulting debt scandals, notably in Lazio, led the central government to ban their use.

Despite the formal constitutional prohibition, expectations of sub-national bail-outs remained high. Typically, Italian governments intervened by making special *ex ante* central grants to head-off defaults. Sub-national financial rescues were influenced by size and systemic significance, including presence in the public bond markets. Rome and Lazio were understood to be most likely candidates for rescue. Sub-national financial rescues were also affected by the political sensitivities that attached to healthcare. In addition, they were more likely when the sub-national government was party-politically friendly with the central government. These factors helped explain the rescues of Catania, Palermo, and Rome under the third Berlusconi government. *Ex ante* grants to politically-friendly governments sought to avert the political embarrassment of their being declared in default and having to be replaced by a national commission of state and regional officials. Thus, in 2009, Campania, which was governed by the centre-Left, was put under commission by the Berlusconi government. Sicily, which was governed by a Right coalition, was not. However, Sicily was less fortunate under the Monti government. In 2012 it imposed a binding financial recovery plan on Sicily to pre-empt the threat of default on its €5.3 billion debt. Sicily earned the sobriquet of 'Italy's Greece'.

Sub-National Fiscal Capacity in the Centralized State: France

In contrast to Britain, France was characterized by a growing discourse about sub-national fiscal autonomy and capacity building. However, unlike in Belgium, Italy, and Spain, this discourse was not legitimated by the notion of fiscal federalism. Political elites on both Left and Right retained a strong historical commitment to the idea of the unitary state as the basis of nation building, territorial integrity, and fiscal justice. This commitment was shared within the traditional administrative corps, notably the powerful Inspectorate of Finance. The Jacobin principle of 'the one and indivisible republic' supported belief in a vertically focused state (Dyson 2010). This belief was inhospitable to asymmetrical forms of sub-national regionalization, based on historic identities. Hence Alsace, Brittany, Corsica, and Normandy did not evolve forms of sub-national fiscal governance like the Basque Country and Navarre, let alone Catalonia or the special Italian regions and provinces.

Decentralization was predominantly seen as an instrument to strengthen 'central steering at a distance'. It was part of wider state reforms, in which the central tension was about whether France was to be a 'state of regions' or a 'state of departments' (Cole 2008: 62–8). This vertical focus stemmed from deep-seated fears that decentralization could lead to fiscal 'neo-feudalism', territorial fiscal competition, and fiscal inequity with an increasing reliance on non-progressive local taxation. The pre-democratic prefects remained key nodal points in sub-national relations, representing the central state, coordinating its field services, and supervising sub-national governments.

Within this formally constraining context, the centralized state had always operated in a flexible manner as a form of 'tamed' Jacobinism. It was reflected in the way in which the prefects, who were the traditional symbols of state executive power at the departmental level, accommodated to the power of local *notables*, who often held multiple elected offices at central and local levels (Grémion 1976). Flexibility was also apparent in the rivalries amongst the key administrative corps of the state. There was ongoing tension between the efforts of prefects to strengthen horizontal coordination of field services and vertical control through centralized ministries like finance. Hence the practice of sub-national fiscal governance typically fell short of the theory of hierarchical, 'hard' budgetary controls.

Moreover, beginning in 1982 under the Presidency of François Mitterrand and lasting till 2004, major decentralization reforms increased the traditionally flexible operation of the centralized state. Twenty-two directly elected regions were established with new economic development powers in 1982. Also, the competences of the ninety-six departments were reinforced. The constitutional amendment of 2003 enshrined the principle of the 'decentralized organization of the state'. It gave new constitutional status to the regions and established the formal principle of the 'fiscal autonomy' of sub-national governments. The 2004 laws sought to give clarity to these principles and to provide new opportunities for experimentation with 'asymmetric' decentralization (Hertzog 2010).

However, by the 1990s, and especially after the 2007 crisis, the discourse about sub-national fiscal governance began to be increasingly associated with the notion of negative externalities for the central state. Budgetary controls were seen as in practice too 'soft'. The French state encountered two major sources of problem in delivering on its new fiscal commitments under the Maastricht Treaty and the SGP. One source was the social security funds, under the control of employers and employees; the other was sub-national governments, especially the departments. The consequence was reinforcement of the French state's traditional tendency to conceive of decentralization as 'steering at a distance' (Cole 2008).

A first stage in this process was a law in 2004 which increased fiscal pressure on sub-national governments by transferring difficult social policies to them, without compensating revenues. The result was twofold: sharp increases in local taxation, and stronger incentives to access international capital markets, including use of complex interest-rate swaps. By 2009 local fiscal crises were increasing. This period ushered in new centralized fiscal constraints on sub-national governments, allied to an agenda of raising state productivity through public administration reforms. The shift to stronger macroeconomic steering of sub-national fiscal governance was prefigured in 2006 with the establishment of the National Council for Public Finances and the Council for Guidelines on Public Finances. They were designed to promote dialogue and consensus about responsible public finances between the state, sub-national governments, and the social security funds.

In contrast to Belgium, Germany, Italy, and Spain, the regional level in France remained the relatively weak link in decentralization reforms (Dupéron 2010). French regions possessed limited formal fiscal autonomy. They lacked co-determination rights, let alone veto power, over the distribution of national tax revenues. They also had very limited 'own' revenue sources, only some 10 per cent after the 2009 reform. French regions had limited policy competences and scope and remained executively dependent on regional prefects, who were appointed by the central state. They accounted for a much smaller proportion of total sub-national expenditures (11.2 per cent in 2009) than departments.

The main work of the French regions centred on negotiating state-region plans and complex co-financing with the state (Dupéron 2010: 268–9). However, even in regional economic development, infrastructure, and vocational education, they lacked exclusive competence vis-à-vis the central state and the departments. After the 2009 reform, the regions shared economic development with the new urban authorities. In contrast, the departments had the main social expenditure responsibilities, including minimum income. Their expenditures rose sharply in 2003–2008. Regions were less favoured than departments in both the 1982 and the 2004 reforms, in part reflecting the power of the departments in the French Senate. The Senate reflected departmental more than regional political interests.

Also, the French regions lacked the hierarchical authority over departments and communes that was enjoyed by their German and Spanish equivalents. They did not possess the historical legitimacy of departments and communes as the basic units of territorial governance in France. Like the departments in Revolutionary France, the regions were created in 1964 as instruments of the centralized state to strengthen regional economic development. The centre of gravity was provided by the regional prefects. In 2009 the role of the regional prefects was strengthened in coordinating the field administration of the central state, at the expense of the departmental prefects. However, this development paralleled rather than reinforced the elected regional councils. In particular, the regional prefects gained new instruments of financial monitoring and budgetary oversight. In short, the technocratic character of the regional level was strengthened. In sub-national fiscal governance the vertical face of the state was reinforced.

Progressive, piecemeal decentralization accentuated the multilevel structural complexity of French territorial governance. It included 22 regions, 96 departments, over 36,000 communes, and—after 1999—an increasing number of inter-communal public corporations, all under direct control of the central state. The inter-communal public corporations, some 2,500 in 2008, proved problematic from the perspective of system strength and predictability in sub-national fiscal governance. Ultimately, communes with 'stand-alone' fiscal capacity could decide to dissolve the structure, in which case their own assets and liabilities reverted to them.

The problem of mismatch between liability and control was compounded by the lack of a clear assignment of competences and of formal fiscal autonomy to discharge competences in a transparent and accountable manner. Between 2004 and 2007 'own' resources—as a proportion of operating revenues—rose appreciably for departments and regions. However, they complained about lack of progress in granting the fiscal autonomy that had been promised in the 2004 law. The complaints stemmed from the failure to match transfer of increased social expenditure responsibilities with commensurate revenues. France evolved a labyrinth of co-financing. It fostered a politicization of sub-national fiscal governance as regional and local bodies sought to negotiate special deals with the central state (Leroy 2010: 305). The result was a proliferation of politically shaped *ex ante* fiscal transfers to debt-distressed sub-national governments.

Risks of sub-national fiscal crisis were increased by the combination of high dependence on vertical fiscal transfers with lack of fiscal transparency and clear fiscal accountability to local electors and taxpayers. Sub-national governments were freer to borrow than their British counterparts and did not need authorization. However, they faced the legal requirement to balance their budgets and to cover compulsory expenditures—including debt service costs—out of 'own resource' revenues. If a sub-national government ran a deficit in excess of 5 per cent of its operating revenues, it was placed under the tutelage of the prefect and the regional audit board, with restrictions on further borrowing. In this way a 'hard', hierarchical budgetary constraint was introduced.

Traditionally, the risk of sub-national fiscal crisis through bond market discipline had been diminished by the capacity to rely on state loans, principally through the *Caisse des depôts et consignations*. However, sub-national governments began to resort increasingly to international capital markets and to solicit, and pay for, credit ratings. By 2010 a few departments and communes were in serious difficulties with complex derivatives contracts. There was renewed caution about accessing international capital markets. Overall, French regions and departments sought fewer credit ratings than the German *Länder*, Italian regions, and Spanish autonomous communities. Hence international financial markets remained a less significant instrument of 'hard' budgetary constraints than hierarchical mechanisms.

A key difference from Belgium, Germany, and Spain was the relative weakness of the horizontal fiscal equalization system as a protective umbrella. Though there was an equalization component in central grants, all sub-national governments remained in a direct fiscal relationship with the central state. The state was there either to provide *ex ante* fiscal support, as to departments in 2010, or to offer bail-outs. Sub-national fiscal governance was heavily reliant on the discretionary action of the state and on complex and constantly evolving rules for vertical fiscal transfers. In consequence, it was strongly politicized, with great scope for multilevel bargaining, focused on the finance and the interior ministries.

Above all, the French central government had a strong inducement to anticipate risks to its own sovereign credit rating. The main aim behind the reforms of 2009–2011 was containment of the risk from irresponsible sub-national fiscal behaviour. These reforms hardened sub-national budgetary constraints by strengthening hierarchical controls. In 2009 the business tax, which accounted for some 50 per cent of sub-national revenues, was taken out of the hands of sub-national governments. It was replaced by a new, complex funding formula, which reduced formal fiscal autonomy. Moreover, in 2012, to comply with Franco-German agreement to back the euro area fiscal compact treaty, the French government introduced constitutional reform proposals for a 'debt brake' akin to Germany.

Fiscally 'Hardened' Devolution and Weak Sub-National Fiscal Capacity in an Asymmetric Unitary State: The Case of Britain

Sub-national fiscal governance in Britain reflected an overriding, historically entrenched constitutional principle of Crown-in-Parliament as the fount of legislative authority. This centralizing principle applied to the evolving post-1998 devolution settlement, which remained open to revision at Westminster. It also shaped sub-national fiscal governance, creating little space to develop sub-national fiscal capacity. The devolved regions were not given a fiscal co-determination role. Scotland was enabled to introduce land transaction and landfill taxes in 2015 and a locally determined income tax in 2016. However, despite various commission recommendations, the devolved regions—including London—lacked any substantial tax or borrowing autonomy. Even more stringently than the French 'unitary state', they were subject to tight hierarchical controls that provided the main 'hard' budget constraint.

The distinctive character of British sub-national governance stemmed from the complex, protracted, and contested process of English-centred state-building. It also reflected the stark structural economic imbalance between England, above all London and the south-east, which had high 'stand-alone' fiscal capacity, and the rest. The legacy of

English state-building was a multinational state, with a periphery of imperfectly assimilated nationalities: Irish, Scottish, and Welsh. In consequence of the power relationships at the heart of the difficult process of state-building, sub-national fiscal governance evolved as a delicate centralizing arrangement. It was founded on extension of centralizing English constitutional principle in parallel with the effort to construct political legitimacy based on the principle of territorial justice and economic and social union. Fiscal transfers compensated the economically weaker periphery. They were, effectively, a side-payment for the benefits of Anglo-centric union. The delicacy of this settlement became apparent in the deeply contested process of devolution, going back to the bitter controversies over Home Rule for Ireland from the 1880s. Devolution suffered political defeats in the late 1970s, before being realized under the Labour government after 1997.

Territorial asymmetry involved individual devolution arrangements for Northern Ireland, Scotland, and Wales. Wales gained more primary legislative powers in defined areas, following the 2006 Government of Wales Act. However, Scotland could legislate in any areas not explicitly reserved to the British Parliament. It also had limited tax-varying powers over income tax. By 2010–2011 Scotland was offered an extension of tax powers. Strikingly, the most populous and the richest part of Britain, England, had no devolved powers either in its own right or to its regions, other than a special arrangement for London. The result was a complex and contentious set of sub-national governance relationships under the constitutional umbrella of Crown-in-Parliament. Nationalist parties in Scotland and Wales threatened exit, a reminder of the difficult and sensitive legacy of English state-building. Any direct English challenge to continuing to bear the fiscal cost of union would put that union in jeopardy.

In addition to sharp territorial asymmetry, there was a paradox at the heart of devolution. On the one hand, devolution to Northern Ireland, Scotland, and Wales endowed them with wide-ranging regional authority over expenditure decisions, across such sectors as education and health. In this respect their authority was notably greater than French or even Belgian regions. British devolution approximated to a 'choice' model with respect to fiscal control over transferred resources (cf. Loughlin and Martin 2003, 2005). London benefitted in a similar way, though its formal competences were fewer and its funding arrangements different (London Finance Commission 2013).

On the other hand, in tax and borrowing powers, the devolved governments lacked the degree of formal fiscal capacity enjoyed by cities and regions in Belgium, Germany, Italy, the Nordic states (notably Norway), Spain, and Switzerland. In the absence of their 'own resources', and given high dependence on vertical transfers, they were in a 'principal-agent' relationship to central government (London Finance Commission 2013). Constitutional principle was, in any case, inhospitable to the language of fiscal federalism. The devolved governments had only extremely limited fiscal autonomy in relation to assigned taxes or to tax-varying powers. The 3 per cent for income tax in the Scotland Act 1998 remained unused. The Finance Ministers' Quadrilateral Meeting remained a weakly developed venue, especially in relation to macroeconomic dialogue. It played no role in co-determination over national taxes. In the early years the devolved governments in Scotland and Wales had even less borrowing freedom than local authorities, other than a facility for short-term borrowing. Northern Ireland was an exception because it had functions carried out by local authorities elsewhere.

With respect to the devolved governments, HM Treasury kept a tight central grip on taxation, on borrowing for capital investment, and on the central block grant in the interests of macroeconomic policy management. This grip can be traced back to the Napoleonic Wars. It was reinforced when the first major devolution debates in the 1970s coincided with severe economic crisis. The grip of HM Treasury formed the central historical fiscal context of devolution.

Northern Ireland, Scotland, and Wales depended on block-grant funding, which was based on the historic 'Barnett Formula' from 1978. The block grant was financed from British taxes and borrowing and contained an element for capital expenditure. The Barnett Formula was designed to determine how devolution was to be financed and so did not apply later to London. It took expenditure per head in the devolved regions as its baseline. The Barnett Formula was adjusted to take account of changes in population share and in spending in England, with reference to comparability in relation to the policies devolved. Its virtues were predictability and an element of equity. Over time, the Barnett Formula generated a convergence in expenditure per head with England. However, it invited criticism because it did not focus explicitly on relative need. Also, the Barnett Formula did little to promote fiscal transparency and fiscal accountability to taxpayers.

The combination of these limitations of the Barnett Formula with threats of cuts to block grant, consequent on sovereign debt crisis, sparked growing debate in Scotland and Wales about reforms to sub-national fiscal governance. Another factor was sub-national political ambitions. The Mayor of London established the London Finance Commission (2013), which called for expanded formal fiscal autonomy for London, including property, business, tourism, and environmental taxes, as well as borrowing powers. The aims were to enable major infrastructural investment and to make London able to compete with Paris, Berlin, Tokyo, and New York. Earlier, the Calman and Holtham Commissions had reported respectively on Scotland and on Wales. They had argued that the block grant should be made fairer by being more 'need-based'. This argument was rejected by the British government. Both commissions also argued for greater fiscal accountability through extension of powers to vary income tax and some assignment of specialized taxes. This change in the balance between a lower block grant and higher own-tax revenue was seen as justifying greater borrowing powers for capital expenditure (Commission on Scottish Devolution 2009; Independent Commission on Funding and Finance for Wales 2009, 2010). The SNP government in Edinburgh went further in calling for borrowing powers to engage in counter-cyclical economic policy management.

Like the previous Labour governments (1997–2010), the Conservative/Liberal Democrat coalition government accepted the Calman principle of income-tax variation. There was to be a new Scottish rate of income tax, though one involving a complex, lengthy transitional process. However, the Cameron government added an extra element to debate about sub-national fiscal governance with the suggestion that Northern Ireland might be given powers to vary corporation tax (Her Majesty's Treasury 2011). The rationale was economic efficiency. It would help rebalance the Northern Irish economy towards the private sector. It would also help Northern Ireland to deal with the special circumstance of competing for inward investment against the territorially adjacent Irish Republic. This proposal generated new support for the extension of this power over corporation tax to Scotland and to Wales. It also raised concerns about the wider implications for territorial justice within Britain, as well as about compatibility with the Azores ruling of the ECJ on state aid. To meet these concerns, the British government stressed that devolved governments would have to bear the fiscal risks that would follow from combining increased tax-varying powers with a reduced block grant. Similarly, any enhancement of borrowing powers for capital expenditure would involve consequent fiscal risks being born by the devolved governments through their own tax revenues.

As a result of the very tough hierarchical borrowing constraints, credit ratings of devolved governments did not play the same role as in France, let alone Germany, Italy, and Spain. Their governments were not exposed to the differentiating effects of international credit ratings, notably on their room for manoeuvre in public expenditure decisions. The long-standing lack of 'stand-alone' fiscal capacity in Northern Ireland, Scotland, and Wales had not been exposed to sanction by the international capital markets. Notably, when advocating limited borrowing powers for Scotland and Wales for capital expenditure, the Calman and the Holtham Commissions stressed that lending should come from the National Loans Fund and the Public Works Loan Board rather than capital markets. Dependence on central government was preferred to exposure to the disciplinary power of international capital markets.

British debate about reforms of sub-national fiscal governance and sub-national fiscal capacity highlighted a central tension between claims for national independence and 'stand-alone' fiscal capacity. The electoral appeal of the SNP, compared to its Welsh equivalent Plaid Cymru, depended on the persuasiveness of the narrative that Scotland had the potential to achieve this 'stand-alone' fiscal capacity. The credibility of this narrative depended on Scottish exports, natural resources, and the tax revenues generated by oil and by the financial sector. Before the 2007–2008 banking crisis, the SNP government had sought to situate Scotland within the narrative of an 'arc of prosperity' stretching from Ireland, through Iceland, to Norway. This narrative had some credibility problems because of the ongoing scale of fiscal transfers to Scotland from England. However, it lost traction with the exposure of the vulnerability of Scottish banks, like Royal Bank of Scotland, and their rescue by the British government. The 'stand-alone' small-state narrative also foundered with the demise of the Celtic tiger image of Ireland and with the collapse of the Icelandic banks. By 2013 HM Treasury was warning that an independent Scotland would lack the fiscal capacity to rescue its banks, which accounted for well over 100 per cent of its GDP. Wales had even less potential to evolve a credible narrative of independence. It lacked 'stand-alone' fiscal capacity. Scotland and Wales had to renegotiate sub-national fiscal governance from a position of relative political-economy weakness. Also, since the late 1970s, they had lacked national political leverage in forming majorities at Westminster.

Reframing Sub-National Fiscal Governance: Vulnerability to Illusion

The intertwined and contagious banking and sovereign debt crises that engulfed the EU from 2007 led to a major reframing of sub-national fiscal governance. Governing elites at state level began to view the gathering pace of decentralization and federalization across European states from the 1980s as a source of risk to sovereign creditworthiness. Debate about sub-national fiscal governance was reframed around the problem of sovereign creditworthiness. In the process, this debate represented sub-national fiscal capacity increasingly narrowly as a problem of compliance with firm nominal fiscal rules. Its other dimensions were given less attention. Virtue attached to those who could comply. The corollary was that questions were ignored about the deeper roots of fiscal compliance problems in structural economic imbalances and in differences of sub-national 'stand-alone' fiscal capacity. There was less debate about how sub-national fiscal governance might be reformed to address these two problems and the social and economic inequalities with which they were associated.

The debate about how best to ensure long-term debt sustainability became embroiled in a paradox. On the one hand, central or federal governments, and cities and regions with 'stand-alone' fiscal capacity, used technocratic arguments to justify the hardening of fiscal rules. These arguments found support from the euro area fiscal compact treaty. On the other hand, cities and regions that lacked 'stand-alone' fiscal capacity resorted to arguments about fiscal justice and territorial equity. They also sought to re-politicize sub-national fiscal governance by pressing their individual cases for *ex ante* financial assistance or for 'bail-outs', using where available privileged political access to the centre. However, capacity to apply effective political pressure in this way and territorial equity were not necessarily aligned. The playing-out of this paradox involved highly contested, difficult, and often grubby compromises in sub-national fiscal governance. However, a broad pattern could be discerned, based on the use of Europeanization and globalization by central and federal governments and by cities and regions with 'stand-alone' fiscal capacity to empower their positions.

The secular growth in public debt across the EU placed a long-term question mark over the design and sustainability of sub-national governance. Questions about sub-national fiscal governance shifted to the centre of the political agenda. Decentralization to cities and regions was not necessarily the main causal mechanism in the trajectory of rising public debt across European states. Nevertheless, the two phenomena could be readily politically associated with each other. Moreover, pressures for re-centralization in sub-national fiscal governance were created by the process of making EMU sustainable, by new incentives to borrow from international capital markets, and, above all, by the post-2007 banking and sovereign debt crises. The role of hierarchy in hardening sub-national budgetary constraints was strengthened by the fiscal compact treaty. Financial markets had also shown that they could directly discipline sub-national governments through bond yields and credit ratings. In addition, the banking and sovereign debt crises brought to light the fiscal opacity and weak fiscal accountability, within which crony capitalism, inefficiency, and waste, political corruption, and fiscal gimmickry had thrived at sub-national levels. Together, these various factors empowered the arguments of cities and regions with 'stand-alone' fiscal capacity that they should have higher fiscal autonomy and that sub-national fiscal transparency and accountability should be strengthened. The corollary was that other cities and regions should be more tightly disciplined.

Illusion, hubris, and complacency are endemic in the history of private and public debt. Sub-national fiscal governance is especially vulnerable. One reason is that sub-national structural economic imbalances represent a shadowy world of trade and financial flows. These flows cut across state boundaries in highly complex and largely opaque ways. They are only very partially captured in statistics, which remain mainly state-centric. An example is increasingly intricate cross-national supply chains. They make it exceedingly difficult to trace value-added by particular cities and regions. Weak financial and economic intelligence provides fertile ground for illusory debate about sub-national fiscal capacity. Moreover, vulnerability to illusion, hubris, and complacency about fiscal capacity is heightened by the opacity of sub-national household net assets/liabilities and corporate net assets/liabilities, coupled with the uncertainties that surround forecasts of potential 'own-tax' revenues. Illusion is further compounded by the incentive of sub-national governments to 'game' state fiscal surveillance and monitoring by hiding debts off-balance-sheet. Fiscal gimmickry is used to help protect the positive image of cities and regions. Regional and local 'boosterism' leads all too readily to 'vanity' infrastructural investments and loss of touch with economic fundamentals. Sub-national governments are all the more prone to underestimate their fiscal vulnerability when they lack the financial expertise to manage highly esoteric debt instruments.

The re-centralizing agenda of states, above all after 2007, was reinforced by the greater intrusiveness of international credit markets and of EU and international macroeconomic and fiscal surveillance and monitoring. Both international credit rating agencies and peer reviews of states by international institutions like the OECD gave more attention to sub-national fiscal governance. They examined not just numeric economic and financial indicators but also the quality of sub-national public finances. Thus in its Economic Survey, the OECD (2009: 70) stressed the adverse economic effects of fiscal equalization mechanisms in Belgium. In its view, they diminished the incentives for Wallonia to develop its own growth potential and fostered a vested interest in retention of large-scale transfers. The OECD Economic Survey of Spain (2010: 81–5) called for tougher fiscal rules to ensure that regional governments were required to build up substantial surpluses in periods when GDP growth was above national potential. This international reframing process had potentially powerful domestic ramifications in shifting the domestic battlefield of ideas about sub-national fiscal governance.

A key feature of the reframing of sub-national fiscal governance was strengthening narratives about globalization and Europeanization. These narratives focused on the need for new sub-national fiscal arrangements to lock-in discipline. One factor was the EU SGP. It precipitated domestic debates about who assumes responsibility for tackling excessive deficits, as defined by the EU, and, in the case of sanctions, about who pays. More intrusive EU monitoring induced sub-national governments to shift their attention to compliance with macroeconomic stabilization objectives.

However, pressure from global financial markets proved far more potent than EU and international peer pressure and politically agreed sanctions, which lacked much credibility. Financial markets could inflict more direct and immediate pain by sapping investor confidence through widening yield spreads on sub-national bonds and through credit rating downgrades. In consequence, attention shifted to regaining market credibility by sub-national fiscal governance reforms that would bind the hands of regional and local governments to rectitude. The German 'debt brake' served as the European pace-setter, uploaded into the fiscal compact treaty. By 2012, long-term rising public debt, and sovereign debt crises, had subsumed debate about sub-national fiscal governance within the larger narrative about sovereign creditworthiness. Its outcome was a shift towards formalized, hierarchically enforced fiscal rules, constraining fiscal autonomy. Debate also moved in the direction of strengthening sub-national fiscal discipline through clearer accountability to voters and taxpayers. In addition, credit ratings and bond yields had assumed a greater significance in sub-national fiscal governance.

Two broad patterns were discernible in reforms to sub-national fiscal governance. Reforms were designed to enable states to better deliver on the 'virtuous' fiscal policies that were required of them by financial markets. Sub-national fiscal capacity building was about compliance with both hierarchical fiscal rules and market expectations. Secondly, fiscal transfer systems were redesigned to strengthen incentives to pursue sub-national 'stand-alone' fiscal capacity. As evident in OECD thinking, predominant narratives shifted away from a needs-based conception to an incentive-based conception of fiscal transfers. Established principles of fiscal justice and territorial equity were under assault. The umbrella of system strength seemed to offer less reliable protection in a context of heightened concern with moral hazard within political economy.

The shift within European federal and federalizing states towards a more competitive fiscal federalism seemed to offer once again in European history a possible sub-national model for EU and Member-State elites in building a 'genuine' EMU. However, such a model was only likely to gain 'hearts and minds' and secure a sense of solidarity and shared identity if it articulated the principles of fiscal justice and territorial equity. Fiscal federalism needed more than compliance with nominal fiscal rules. It had to address underlying structural economic imbalances by building fiscal capacity to productively invest in infrastructure and in social provision. Whatever the outcome, once again, as in late-medieval and early-modern European state-building, Britain—or perhaps, longer-term, England—looked like being an outsider.

Part IV

Sovereign Creditworthiness and European Integration

17

Still the 'Old' Europe? Historical Legacies and Long-Term Political Challenges

> Germany is the economic motor and the stability anchor in Europe, but even Germany's strength is not infinite ... Germany's powers must not be overestimated ... it would be clear that Germany was overcommitted and that in turn would have unanticipated consequences for Germany and Europe. We will not permit that.
>
> Angela Merkel, German Chancellor, Government Declaration to the German Bundestag on the European Council of 28/29 June 2012, 27 June 2012 (<www.bundestag.de/dokumente/textarchiv/2012/index.html>)

The post-1945 evolution of European economic governance and policies suggested an historic shift away from what, in 1931, the Bank of England governor Montagu Norman had called the 'old' Europe (Dyson and Quaglia 2010a: 49). He referred in a tone of pessimism to a post-1918 pattern of intense inter-state rivalries. As the post-1931 Great Depression gathered pace, even highly conditional and limited cooperation proved deeply problematic. Norman's 'new' Europe was, in his view, one in which an international question could be addressed 'on its merits', not as an individual matter for each state. It was far out of reach, as a disastrous succession of economic and political events in the 1930s seemed to confirm. Europe drifted into bank and sovereign defaults, fragmentation into different currency blocs, retreat into trade protection and exchange controls, and negotiation of bilateral arrangements. These developments were symptomatic of an absence of collective political will and institutional capacity to pursue synchronized policies that offered a perspective of return to coordinated international economic expansion.

As post-war European elites pondered the challenge of economic and political reconstruction, memories of this interwar period evoked general remorse at the collective damage that had been inflicted by the politics of resentment and humiliation after 1918.

There was a particular sense of shame and desire for atonement within the governing elites of the state that was to emerge as the leading creditor power in Europe—Germany. Despite the embrace of 'ever closer union' as the leitmotif of post-war European institution building, the question remains whether the EU, and above all the euro area, had made Norman's historic shift to a 'new' Europe.

A 'new' Europe would involve formalizing creditor-debtor state relations on the basis of collective institutional structures to support banking, fiscal, and monetary union. These structures would embody the normative criteria of accountability, transparency, and inclusivity. They would have the capacity to deliver positive policy outcomes for Member-State governing elites and voters, in particular sustainable debt trajectories. They would have to be compatible with—rather than corrosive of—meaningful citizen participation and trust in representative democracy. The challenge was to create institutional structures that were both robust and flexible enough to prevent the return to the politics of resentment and humiliation in times of acute financial and economic crisis that had scarred interwar Europe. By 2013 it was by no means clear that the EU and the euro area were meeting this challenge (European Social Survey 2013).

The Limits and Fragility of the Formalization in Creditor-Debtor State Relations: Britain and the Gold Standard

A major historical lesson from the period from the mid-nineteenth century till the Second World War is that the formalization of creditor-debtor state relations, around agreed institutional arrangements and rules of the game, is not necessarily a one-way, irreversible process. Its formalization is made difficult not just by the high consensus requirements of intergovernmental negotiations but also by the concessions that debtor-state elites have to make in order to keep creditor states in the negotiating game. These difficulties dispose governments to move by stealth in designing foundational institutional arrangements and rules. In the case of debtor-state elites, the key motive for embracing this strategy is to prevent creditor-state exit from negotiations. In the case of creditor-state elites, the motive is to minimize risks of failure in domestic ratification by binding-in opposition.

When formalized institutional arrangements are in place, their fragility is exposed once the exercise of power by intergovernmental or supra-national arrangements intrudes into core state powers in ways that challenge domestic norms of political acceptability (Genschel and Jachtenfuchs 2013). Risks of reversibility increase as sensitive, often emotionally laden issues of democratic legitimacy, state sovereignty, and identity come into play. These issues arise with European banking, fiscal, and economic union because of their overt redistributive implications in terms of who gains and who loses.

The fragility of formalized creditor-debtor state relations is further exposed once the creditor state or the informal creditor-state club that serves as its anchor loses credibility. As the quotation from Chancellor Merkel suggests, one or just a few creditor states lend credibility to the institutional arrangements and rules. This credibility endures only as long as investors believe that the anchor has both the political will and the state capacity to shoulder the liabilities of other states and to ensure compliance with the rules.

Credibility depends on two conditions. It requires retention of the sovereign creditworthiness of the anchor state. It also hangs on the will and the capacity of debtor states to comply with the rules of the game as politically acceptable. Mounting evidence of a mismatch between liability and control reinforces perceptions of an emerging political vacuum at the core of formalized creditor-debtor state relations. This sense of a vacuum increases risks of growing mistrust, the poisoning of relationships, and an increase in geo-strategic rivalry. Containment of risks of systemic breakdown requires supra-national institutions with adequate authority and policy instruments to take discretionary executive action. However, the creation of such institutions depends on a framework of political legitimacy that continued to be absent in post-1945 Europe. It was shown to be incomplete as the post-2007 financial and economic crisis gathered momentum. Hence reversibility of the process of formalization in creditor-debtor state relations could not be discounted.

A second historical lesson is that efforts to formalize creditor-debtor state relations depend on the geo-strategic priorities of the leading European creditor state. Despite an enormous increase in intra-European trade and investment in pre-1914 Europe, there was little growth in formalized European creditor-debtor state relations. This lack of formalization reflected, in part, the increasing focus of the capital exports of the major European creditor state—Britain—on its extra-European empire from the 1870s. British governments had a stronger incentive to attach and mobilize the Empire to the defence of Britain's role as the anchor of the international gold standard than to lead any efforts to formalize European creditor-debtor state relations.

Instead, efforts to formalize creditor-debtor state relations focused on Second Empire France under Napoleon III. However, the French attempt to lead this process through the Latin Monetary Union soon proved abortive. The Latin Monetary Union of 1865 brought together France, Belgium, Italy, and Switzerland, with other states joining later (Dyson and Quaglia 2010a). Its ambitions as a currency union were undermined at the outset by the absence of a joint central bank able to conduct a single monetary policy. They were soon fatally compromised by the humiliating French defeat in the Franco–Prussian War of 1870 and the harsh burden of war reparations (Dyson 1994). French ambitions to lead European creditor-debtor state relations foundered on the hard rock of German unification.

A third historical lesson relates to an intellectual problem at the heart of formalizing creditor-debtor state relations in Europe. The mythology of 'automatic' adjustment within the pre-1914 and interwar gold standard downplayed the relevance and importance of formalized central bank cooperation, not just in a routine technical sense. Similarly, the mythology of efficient financial markets during the period of creating a single European market in financial services and designing European monetary union reduced incentives to take financial stability and European banking union seriously. These mythologies generated elite complacency, with adverse consequences. They distracted attention from the question of whether technical logics of adjustment would prove politically acceptable, above all when they involved sharp deflation, job cuts, and reductions in wages and social benefits. The intellectual problem in formalizing creditor-debtor state relations remained political. It was about citizen participation;

about basing the quality of economic governance on normative criteria of accountability, transparency, and inclusivity; and about policies to deliver politically acceptable outcomes, ones that offered a perspective of hope.

An additional historical lesson is that central bank competition and cooperation formed the institutional axis around which formalized creditor-debtor state relations in Europe evolved. Strategic rivalries and intense mistrust in an age of assertive nationalism ensured that pre-1914 Europe continued to lack any substantial cross-national institutional arrangements. These rivalries found expression in political contest about the appropriate monetary standard. The French governing elite included advocates of the merits of a bi-metallic standard over those of gold (Flandreau 2004).

Pre-1914 Europe was, above all, a world of central bank competition for spheres of monetary and financial influence. This competition reflected different national strategic priorities and alliance building. The competitive drive of French elites was apparent in the Latin Monetary Union, French debates about reinstating a bi-metallic standard after the 1870s, and the subsequent hoarding of gold reserves by the Banque de France. External credits and holdings of sovereign debt were used to carve out spheres of influence in Mediterranean and eastern Europe (Dyson 1994; Flandreau 2004; Ahamed 2010). French policy makers sought to challenge both British monetary and financial ascendancy and German economic and military power. The scale and implications of the post-1871 war indemnity to Germany cast a long-lasting, deep shadow over French policies in pre-1914 Europe.

The gold standard was the foremost material and symbolic expression of British claims to monetary and financial dominance in pre-1914 central bank cooperation. It endowed the Bank of England and the City of London with pre-eminent status and power. The period of most intensive British engagement with the gold standard as an instrument and a symbol of her international power and status extended from the 1870s to her departure from gold in September 1931. The dominant narrative about this period focused on the post-1914 decline of British monetary and financial power. Because of her huge wartime liabilities and loss of export markets, Britain was no longer able to act as the benign hegemonic power, organizing and sustaining the interwar gold standard (Kindleberger 1973).

However, the precariousness of Britain's position as the anchor creditor state was signalled before 1914. It faced assertions of French and German financial power, notably in central, southern, and eastern Europe, where Britain's relative power declined. There were also threats of contagion from banking and sovereign debt crises, above all in Latin America. The coordinated rescue of Barings Bank in 1891 illustrated the degree of British vulnerability. In addition, the heavy debt burden of the Boer War led to a rise in British external borrowing. These developments created a pre-1914 climate of growing British uncertainty. They ignited new domestic debates, including the 'National Efficiency' movement and proposals for imperial preference. A domestic tension emerged between internationalist and imperialist restructuring agendas (Michie 2004). The structural context was increasing British disengagement from a leadership role in European sovereign debt markets from the mid-1870s in favour of the Empire.

In addition, the claim to pre-1914 British hegemony, based on automatic adjustment under the gold standard, is undermined by evidence of discretionary central bank management to cushion the sharp, adverse domestic effects of deflation (Dutton 1984; Eichengreen and Flandreau 1997). Extensions of the electoral franchise and the emergence of working-class-based political parties and trade unions led to new domestic challenges to *rentier* power. A new agenda of social reforms reflected the rise of new social interests and changing norms of political acceptability. Against this background, the gold standard did not respond in an automatic fashion to market signals. There was a gap between central banking practice and British-based theory, which suggested—in line with the classic creditor-state view—that the burden of adjustment must fall exclusively on debtor states.

The iconoclastic Swedish economist Knut Wicksell was one of the first to capture theoretically these changes in central bank practice. He was to influence later economists, like Ralph Hawtrey (1879–1975), the long-serving HM Treasury official and friend of John Maynard Keynes (Deutscher 1990). Wicksell argued that central banks, including the Bank of England, did not follow the script of an automatic gold standard. According to this script, external imbalances would generate offsetting gold flows and consequent changes in domestic interest rates, thereby creating deflation in debtor states. Instead, according to Wicksell, central banks played a more active role. They used monetary policy anti-cyclically to smooth adjustments and thus cushion their domestic economies. At the same time, central banks exercised this discretion cautiously, based on their unwillingness to undermine the credibility of the gold standard. Hawtrey (1927, 1932) continued to believe in the gold standard but absorbed Wicksell's insights.

The pre-1914 gold standard can be pictured as decentralized and multi-polar, with different 'monetary spheres of influence', not least within Europe (Balachandran 2008; Eichengreen 1992). Influential voices in France, Germany, and the United States continued to call for a different bi-metal regime (Balachandran 2008: 316–18; Flandreau 2004). Britain was faced by the emergence of these three powers as rival international lenders in the late nineteenth century. France was the major investor in European sovereign bond markets.

Despite these important qualifications to the dominant narrative about pre-1914 Europe, the First World War proved the watershed. Britain shifted from being a 'regime-shaping' creditor state to a beleaguered debtor state. Key banking, financial, and official elites were committed to restoring pre-war 'normality'. However, they lacked the economic, financial, and political capacity to realize this objective. The period 1918–1931 was a painful lesson in illusion and hubris to British elites. The costs of savage domestic deflation in lost output and unemployment proved too high to support the return to the gold standard at the pre-war parity in a sustainable manner. As Keynes noted, norms of political acceptability had changed. Fundamentally, Britain was a debtor state, unable to play a credible leadership role.

Any prospects for European central bank cooperation in the 1920s were undermined by different choices of national economic and monetary policy strategies for managing post-war sovereign debt problems. The Bank of England opted for deflation, at least till early 1932; the German central bank chose inflation; and the French central bank pursued devaluation (Ahamed 2010). The mythology of the automaticity of the gold standard, even that of a managed gold standard on terms of tightly constrained discretion, lost credibility in this context of diverse and conflicting national policy preferences. It was further undermined by illusion and hubris about British leadership capacity and by changing domestic electoral and party dynamics. The problem of chronic imbalances in the distribution and flows of gold became more acute. Britain was confronted by huge debt burdens, current account deficits, and difficulties in building up gold reserves to sustain an early return to gold. The intertwined embittered politics of German reparations and inter-Allied war debts burdened economic reconstruction. They ensured that trade and capital flows no longer enjoyed the same pre-1914 dynamic growth.

The power vacuum at the heart of the uncoordinated return to gold encouraged disruptive geo-strategic competition. By the late 1920s France and the United States were serious rivals in the competitive struggle to accumulate gold and strengthen their domestic financial centres. The new states in central and eastern Europe offered newly fertile ground for competition. Both the British and the French central banks sought to establish their own 'monetary spheres of influence' within Europe, creating a dynamic of mistrust. In preparing for the Genoa Conference in 1922, the British Prime Minister David Lloyd George pushed the political case for focusing the agenda on eastern Europe and Russia rather than the narrow monetary issue of returning to gold (Toye 2007: 228–9). However, neither he nor Keynes could divert British policy from pursuing a pre-1914 path that was firmly anchored in the interrelated requirements of preserving British leadership of her Empire and of the City of London's dominance of international financial markets.

Before 1914, and especially after 1918, the Bank of England began to look for external, coordinated support for itself and the City against threats from external imbalances and systemic risks from financial shocks. British policies reflected an increased strategic interest in using the imperial role to attach Australia, Canada, India, and South Africa more closely to the monetary and financial embrace of the Bank of England and the City of London. The aim was to strengthen British credibility within the gold standard system (Balachandran 2008; Cain and Hopkins 2001; De Cecco 1984). South Africa also offered access to new gold supplies, which addressed a critical supply shortage problem. This imperial dimension of harnessing colonial resources was central to the timing of Chancellor Winston Churchill's decision to return to gold (Hansard 1925). He feared that otherwise Australia and South Africa might choose to enter the gold standard first. They would then gravitate towards US monetary and financial leadership, seriously eroding British status and power and jeopardizing London's future as a financial centre. British policy on the gold standard became, in short, embedded in imperial associations. However, imperial associations became a burden once colonial states began to question the costs of supporting British ambitions (Balachandran 2008).

In 1918 the Cunliffe Committee outlined an orthodox British account of the functioning of the gold standard and of the rationale for Britain's leadership of an early post-war return. Despite radically changed conditions, this classic British creditor-state view was embodied in the report of the Genoa Financial Commission (1922). It argued that European reconstruction depended on the Bank of England leading central bank cooperation in the return to gold. This return was to be based on individual states taking responsibility for the stability of their own currencies, notably by balanced budgets.

Hawtrey (1927), who was the senior HM Treasury official working on the Genoa Financial Commission report, adopted an approach to return that was much more consistent with a managed gold standard. His approach was better adapted to the changing strategic interests of post-1918 Britain as a debtor state. However, given the scale of external imbalances, the Bank of England was unable to manage the gold standard in a way that reconciled the conflict between external and internal stability, consistent with high growth and employment. British policies represented the triumph of illusion and hubris.

The interwar period was characterized by the failure to formalize cooperation in European creditor-debtor state relations. The British return to gold in 1925 reflected unilateral action, more closely aligned with the imperial dimension than the European. Neither the choice of parity rate nor the timing of return was coordinated with Britain's main European counterparts, each of which responded by trying to make relative gains, ultimately at collective cost (Dyson and Quaglia 2010a). The British authorities looked to mobilize the imperial dimension to offset the costs of return to gold.

There was a lack of European political solidarity about refashioning the terms of cooperation around a conception of a 'new' Europe. The consequence was tight constraints on ambitions for developing the League of Nations to mobilize credits for European reconstruction. Similarly, little progress was made in formalizing central bank cooperation on an apolitical basis. Plans to use the new Bank for International Settlements (BIS) to stabilize exchange rates and to provide collective financial assistance were aborted (Toninio 2005). Instead, the vacuum of political leadership on behalf of a 'new' Europe fed into assertive position-taking by central bankers like Émile Moreau in France and Hjalmar Schacht in Germany. Neither of the two grand conferences—the Genoa Economic Conference in 1922 and the London World Economic Conference in 1933—produced substantial results. The Tripartite Monetary Agreement of 1936 between the British, French, and US governments offered minimalist commitments to exchange-rate stability. It also bypassed the BIS (Dyson and Quaglia 2010a: 54).

A series of conferences and committees on German reparations, including the Dawes Plan and the Young Plan, failed to produce a final, agreed settlement. Mutual bitterness continued, leading to the final cancellation of reparation payments at Lausanne in July 1932. The issue pitted Germany against her official creditors—Belgium, Britain, France, Italy, and (indirectly via inter-Allied debts) the United States. Agreements on the settlement of inter-Allied war debts were also bilateral and uncoordinated. They took place at different times, on very different terms, and generated great rancour. With the exception of Finland, these agreements were not honoured.

The weaknesses in post-1918 European economic governance mechanisms were paralleled by a failure to coordinate policies for reducing the overhang of huge debts. France opted for devaluation; Germany, for hyperinflation; and Britain, for deflation. In the period before the onset of the Great Depression, policies had accentuated intra-European imbalances rather than reduced them. Gold became concentrated in France and the United States, making them pivotal for any formalized international coordination. The return to gold, which was agreed in principle at the Genoa conference, was conducted in a way that involved no coordination in timing or on terms. This failure undermined the stability of the standard. Even the departure from gold took place at different times: Britain and Germany left in 1931, and France and Poland in 1936.

The League of Nations and the Bank for International Settlements

The interwar period presents a paradox. On the one hand, the creation of the Economic and Financial Organization (EFO) of the League of Nations in 1920 and of the BIS in 1930 represented historic innovations. These new Europe-centric international financial institutions—based respectively in Geneva and Basel—collected and disseminated economic and financial information, offered policy advice, and provided forums for collective deliberation of problems of access to credit. In particular, the League loans were a mechanism for mobilizing international credit. The League pioneered the use of conditionality at one remove from borrowers and lenders and directly monitored compliance. The BIS and the EFO represented the beginnings of formalized creditor-debtor state relations.

On the other hand, the powers of the BIS and the League's EFO were fundamentally disproportionate to the scale of interwar problems in international lending. The newly configured post-1918 European states, above all in the wake of the collapse of the Hapsburg and Romanov Empires, faced a toxic combination of wartime destruction—human and physical, inter-Allied war debts, reparations, and trade disruption. Pervasive feelings of resentment and humiliation poisoned relationships. They sustained a climate of distrust that made it impossible to develop the functions of the League and the BIS, especially in the face of the post-1931 Great Depression.

The stimulus for the establishment of the EFO was the urgent need to mobilize loans for reconstruction in central and eastern Europe. However, its activities fell short of the original ambitious plans that had been developed by Gerard Vissering, the president of the Dutch central bank, and by Carel Eliza ter Meulen, a director of the Dutch bank Hope and Cie and later a key member of the League's Financial Committee (Pauly 1996). The 'ter Meulen' international credit scheme had envisaged a League role in assisting companies to obtain credits for essential imports in order to facilitate reconstruction. However, European governments proved reluctant to contemplate such interference in their affairs or to be designated as 'impoverished'. The eventual outcome was agreement that the League should be able to raise loans on request from central and east European states. The process for gaining League support began with agreement on a reconstruction and currency stabilization plan. It was followed by the appointment of League trustees and agents to monitor compliance, above all prompt debt-service payments. Then, the League and the requesting state sought expressions of support from central banks and underwriters before market placement.

The first—and by far the biggest—League loan was to Austria in 1923 and had highly prestigious underwriters, the Bank of England and J.P. Morgan. The nine loans secured for six European states between 1923 and 1928 demonstrated the capacity of the League to lower borrowing costs by building its reputation as a trusted intermediary (Flores and Decorzant 2012). However, the League's resources of power and room for manoeuvre were constrained. Critically, it lacked its own capital. Also, some European states proved unwilling to accept its tough conditionality requirements, judging them politically humiliating. In addition, once the League trustees' and agents' roles were finished, there was a risk that a state would revert to patterns of behaviour at odds with its creditors. Against the background of these constraints, the EFO was overwhelmed by events as the post-1931 Great Depression gathered momentum (Pauly 1996). Creditor willingness to be mobilized by the League evaporated.

The BIS embodied the powerful myth—propagated by Montagu Norman—of an apolitical central bankers' club. Its functions were to build mutual trust through regular confidential interaction in its monthly weekend meetings; to provide independent financial and monetary intelligence; and to serve as the brains' trust for financial and monetary diplomacy. However, in order to serve these functions effectively, it depended—like the League—on a protective political umbrella of European and global solidarity. This umbrella was absent in the 1930s, nullifying efforts of British and German central bankers to extend its functions into credit mobilization. Illustrative of this absence was the reaction within the French central bank and government to the request of the Austrian government for an international loan to help resolve the deepening crisis of the Creditanstalt bank in May 1931. They demanded a renunciation of the recent preliminary agreement to form an Austrian-German customs union. By the time the politics was resolved, the international loan was too little and too late. The BIS was also lucky to survive the Second World War. US policy makers were angered at the BIS role in the infamous wartime transfer of Czechoslovak gold to Nazi Germany (Toniolo 2005: 204–12).

The BIS was shaped by the difficult conditions of its birth in 1930 and its early life. It emerged out of discussions within the Young Committee about how best to enforce German reparations' obligations and to secure investor confidence by 'commercializing' reparations. The central banks of the official creditor states, led by France, wanted an international bank that could act as trustee for these transactions. This essentially technical function continued up to, and beyond, the 1953 London Agreement on German External Debts, which provided for the continuation of servicing the Young and the earlier Dawes loans.

In the negotiations about its establishment, some central bankers had envisaged a much more ambitious function for the BIS. Schacht, the president of the German Reichsbank, proposed a new international bank that would act as a 'clearing house' or 'settlements bank'. It was to be backed by government guarantees and to provide long-term credits (Toniolo 2005: 33–48). This idea of the BIS as an instrument for credit creation was understood as a quid pro quo for Germany's compliance with the Young Plan on reparations. However, the French and Italian central banks firmly rejected the proposal as inflationary. Moreau, the governor of the Banque de France, was concerned to defend his autonomy—and protect French gold reserves—in the face of pressures to formalize and strengthen central bank cooperation. Schacht's proposal had more traction within the Bank of England, which sought to use the BIS to mobilize international support for the embattled gold standard. Through the 1920s Montagu Norman had proved a tireless advocate of closer, more formalized central bank cooperation.

Even in the post-1945 period, the BIS evolved no more than a limited role as provider of short-term credits, mainly to small European states. The technical role of the BIS grew in significance once it became the agent for the first European multilateral payments systems from 1947 and for the European Payments Union (EPU) in the period 1950–1958. During the 1950s the BIS offered help to central banks with their gold operations. Post-1961, it helped manage the US Federal Reserve's complex swap lines to help supply liquidity to European states with balance-of-payment difficulties. The BIS also monitored gold-market transactions of members of the Gold Pool between 1961 and 1968. In these ways the BIS sought to instil confidence in post-war exchange-rate structures and to prevent US Treasury gold losses under the Bretton Woods system. However, it had initial reservations about the US-inspired effort to enlist European surplus states like Germany in burden-sharing through the Gold Pool. The BIS feared that the Gold Pool and the expanding use of swap lines would disguise fundamental disequilibria. In consequence, it would undermine the incentive for deficit states to adjust and encourage them to concede to domestic electoral and party obstacles (Toniolo 2005: 375–81).

The technical role of the BIS remained important in the background of post-1945 European integration. It provided the European Coal and Steel Community (ECSC) with additional security in raising loans on favourable terms (Toniolo 2005: 318–19). From 1971 the BIS acted as the agent for the European Economic Community (EEC) agreement on short-term credit assistance. It performed the same function with respect to intra-Community exchange rate stabilization in the case of the European Monetary Cooperation Fund (EMCF) between 1973 and 1993 and of the European Monetary System (EMS) from 1979 to 1993 (Dyson and Quaglia 2010a: 236–42). Not least, the BIS offered the location and secretariat of the Committee of EEC Central Bank Governors from 1964 to 1994. It also hosted the meetings of the Delors Committee on Economic and Monetary Union (EMU) in 1988–1989. In short, the BIS was an indispensable element in the technical infrastructure of pre-European Central Bank (ECB) European creditor-debtor state relations. It represented a neutral location that helped secure the reputation of independent professionalism in central banking. As managing director, Alexandre Lamfalussy helped turn the BIS into an early advocate of macro-prudential financial market supervision.

Supporting Supra-National Integration in the Great Depression: The Bank of England and HM Treasury versus France and the US

As early as May–August 1931 the limitations of the BIS as a crisis manager were exposed. The collapse of the Austrian Creditanstalt was followed by a wave of contagious banking crises across Austria, Danzig, Germany, Hungary, and Yugoslavia. Collective emergency credit was made available. However, it was impeded in scale and timing by the mounting constraints on the Bank of England's freedom of manoeuvre. British exit from the gold standard in September followed the exhaustion of the Bank's reserves. As early as May, a second BIS syndicated loan to Austria was torpedoed when the French government insisted on extremely tough, politically motivated conditions that involved the surrender of sovereignty (Dyson and Quaglia 2010a: 96–7). Once the crisis spread to Germany, French negotiators insisted on German disarmament and renunciation of German claims to the 'Danzig corridor' as preconditions for increasing emergency credits (Dyson and Quaglia 2010a: 104).

Constrained by this lack of political solidarity, and by its legal mandate, the BIS offered largely ineffectual, often ill-advised advice that risked deflationary spirals. This advice was tacitly supported by leading German economists, including Walter Eucken and Wilhelm Röpke, at a meeting convened by the German central bank in September 1931. They warned against expansionary German fiscal and monetary policies in the absence of international support (Ritschl 2002: 172–6). The evidence was that this support was not forthcoming. In June the French government had rejected the request of the German government of Heinrich Brüning, backed by the US administration, for a moratorium on war debts and reparations. It called for further fiscal tightening. Gradually, however, the Austrian and German governments became more assertive towards their foreign creditors. By September they had resorted to exchange controls.

Before German reparations were cancelled at Lausanne in July 1932, Brüning had been forced to resign.

At this critical moment in European history, the BIS lacked the legal powers, financial resources, and intellectual rationale to mobilize collective financial assistance and act as an effective multilateral crisis manager. Intellectually, it remained 'fettered by gold'. The BIS gave priority to defending foreign private creditor interests in central Europe, advocating balanced budgets and higher interest rates (Eichengreen 1992). Politically, it lacked a protective umbrella of solidarity provided by European governments, above all the largest creditor states. The two major creditor states—France and the United States—stood aloof. The French government pursued narrowly conceived strategic interests. The US administration would not engage with the BIS.

From the outset the Bank of England had been in favour of using the BIS to give a more formal dimension to central bank cooperation. It proved less hostile to Schacht's proposal on long-term credit than the Banque de France. However, the Bank's declining influence was reflected in its failure to transform the BIS from its trustee role in routine central bank transactions, including short-term credits, to a more active role in correcting external imbalances and insulating European states from financial market pressures. The broader shift in British thinking in 1930–1933 indicated both its changed interests as a debtor state and growing recognition of the limits of British power. It was at this time that Norman, the Bank's governor, lamented the failure to transform the BIS into a body that could 'regard an international question on its merits' (Dyson and Quaglia 2010a: 49).

British policy initiatives lacked the traction of 'framing' power over debates, agenda-setting power, or negotiating power. Their failure reflected the slippage of power *over* ideas and power *in* shaping outcomes away from Britain. Changing British attitudes to international cooperation reflected underlying structural shifts in trade and financial imbalances. This shift in strategic interests was exemplified in three key documents: the Kindersley-Norman Plan of February 1931; the Henderson Memorandum on Bank for International Settlement Note Issue of June 1932; and the Keynes Plan of 1933. The history of these initiatives puts in question conventional interpretations of how Britain and France have related to supra-national European integration.

In 1931–1933 both the Bank of England and HM Treasury developed radical new policy proposals to strengthen supra-national coordination in crisis management. The Bank is an institution not normally associated with support for the ideas of Keynes. This source suggests that the chain of causation in new ideas about formalizing supra-national integration in creditor-debtor state relations was not simply traceable back to Keynes. These ideas had their origins in the Bank's own internal strategic appreciation of a profoundly altered structural context of trade and financial imbalances and their associated risks. Leading Bank and HM Treasury officials came to appreciate that the return to gold in 1925 had imposed burdens on British policy that were proving difficult, if not impossible, to sustain economically and politically (Skidelsky 1992). In this sense Keynes had been right in his earlier strategic assessment of the return to gold. The imminent threat—and then reality—of exit from the gold standard signalled the collapse of the central post-war objective of British economic policy. It made fully visible the failure of Britain's claims to hegemonic status. It also made clear the high risks of a slippage of monetary and financial power from London to New York. The Bank was alert to the profound long-term strategic implications for British interests.

Bank and HM Treasury officials identified the strategic choice as between passive ceding of financial and monetary power to the United States and actively seeking to share financial and monetary power in new and strengthened forms of supra-national integration. British leadership in promoting the foundation of the BIS offered a new platform to pursue the second alternative. The BIS became the site for British ambitions to share power rather than cede it to the United States. This aim involved extending its role beyond narrow, technical central banking functions.

Equally, the failure of these bold British proposals triggered deepening pessimism about prospects for international and European policy coordination, not least within the Bank and HM Treasury. This pessimism was reinforced by the World Economic Conference in London in 1933, which was undermined by President Roosevelt's sudden, explicit endorsement of an approach founded on domestic stabilization. The Keynes Plan of 1933, which tried to set out an agenda for the World Economic Conference, can be seen as the end of a British-based phase of radical proposals (on which Dyson and Quaglia 2010a: 51–3). Thereafter, British policy retreated further into a domestic-led approach, aimed at retrieving national autonomy of action and exploiting imperial trading ties.

The short, four-page 'Kindersley-Norman Plan' of February 1931 represented the central problem as imbalance in the distribution of gold. The solution involved mobilizing French and US gold to support debtor states (Bank of England 1931). In light of the scale of the crisis, 'extraordinary measures' were required to restore confidence. These measures involved the creation of a new international corporation, 'probably linked' to the BIS. It would have a subscribed capital of between £25 and £50 million (£1.3–2.6 trillion in 2010 value, using the Bank of England's inflation calculator). On this basis it could issue bonds in the creditor states—France, the United States, and perhaps the Netherlands and Switzerland—up to three times the amount of this capital. The purpose of this bold and ambitious plan was to divert the flow of gold and shore up the creditworthiness of debtor states, to which the money would be lent. A key beneficiary would be Germany, which faced severe difficulties. As a symbolic gesture, the Kindersley-Norman Plan hinted that Britain might make a modest contribution by buying these new bonds.

By March 1931 it was clear that Norman had failed to persuade the Banque de France to support this long-term credit proposal within the BIS. The French central bank resisted the idea that a new supra-national institution should gain power over its gold (Dyson and Quaglia 2010a: 48). It wanted much stronger French oversight and control, commensurate with its official creditor status and with the size of its gold reserves. The Banque de France went on to argue that debtor states had 'only themselves to blame' (Toniolo 2005: 76). This failure—and the contagious banking crises that rapidly followed—contributed to Norman's famously downbeat performance in his hearing before the Macmillan Committee on Finance and Industry in 1931 (Dyson and Quaglia 2010a: 49). He commented that 'a new Europe' would be necessary before the BIS could function beyond narrowly technical and routine central bank cooperation. The Bretton Woods institutions, the EPU, and later the evolving arrangements for EMU opened up the prospects for such a 'new Europe'.

The Henderson Memorandum and the Keynes Plan were closely associated, reflecting the close social and intellectual interaction between these two economists. Both were active Liberals and members of the Economic Advisory Council. Hubert Henderson served for a time as its Secretary and adviser to HM Treasury. Unlike the Kindersley-Norman Plan, their proposals emerged after the British exit from gold. In its various drafts, the

Henderson Memorandum proposed that the BIS should be empowered to issue notes (international certificates) in order to support debtor states with interest-free advances, up to an aggregate of about £1,000 millions worth of gold. Governments were to be free to use them at their own discretion. Notably, there was very little conditionality and intrusion into sovereignty. The proposal encountered once again French and US resistance. Faced by this failure, Henderson began to shift towards a domestic-focused approach to 'national self-sufficiency' and bilateral economic coordination, which differed from that of Keynes (Skidelsky 2000).

Keynes sought to address the same problem of imbalance in the distribution of gold reserves. His proposal to the World Economic Conference sought to bypass French and US reluctance to share out their gold reserves with debtor states (Dyson and Quaglia 2010a: 51–2). Keynes suggested the creation of a greater absolute amount of gold reserves by means of a new international authority that would be empowered to issue gold notes up to a maximum of $5,000,000,000. The proposal involved a de facto qualified return to the gold standard. Like the Henderson Memorandum, Keynes stressed lack of conditionality for debtor states. The twin aims were to harness French and US gold reserves to support world economic expansion and to strengthen national autonomy of action of debtor states. This lack of conditionality—compared to earlier League loans and later International Monetary Fund (IMF) and EU and euro area credits—reflected the origins of the proposal. It served to support a debtor state whose elites were deeply attached to sovereignty and feared French and US interventions in the highly symbolic area of their financial and economic affairs.

The phase of British innovatory proposals for formalizing creditor-debtor state relations was effectively brought to an end by President Roosevelt's 'bombshell' message of July 1933 to the World Economic Conference. Roosevelt pursued the classic creditor-state argument that 'the sound internal economic system of a nation is a greater factor in its well-being than the price of its currency' (Dyson and Quaglia 2010a: 53). As the main creditor power, the United States declined to share in the radical kind of schemes for international collaboration that were being proposed in London. This reluctance was maintained in the Tripartite Monetary Agreement between Britain, France, and the United States in 1936 (Dyson and Quaglia 2010a: 54–5). The French government had been encouraged to the negotiating table by its slippage into debtor-state status. It could no longer credibly hold to the hubristic vision of leading the residual European 'gold block'. The French government needed international cover for devaluation of the franc. However, the new good intentions on exchange-rate cooperation and on convertibility of their three currencies to gold were offset by continuing US insistence that internal equilibrium had precedence.

Keynes and the Reconstruction of International Economic Policy Cooperation

The sharp disparity in the economic costs and gains of waging the Second World War produced acute, crippling trade and financial imbalances and massive debt burdens in Europe. European states lacked the credibility to raise loans for the reconstruction of their war-ravaged economies. External imbalances and problems of financing a massive debt overhang and reconstruction provided a context within which the arguments of 1931–1933 had an opportunity to resurface.

Between 1941 and 1944 American and British officials began to examine the terms of post-war economic reconstruction and burden-sharing. British gold and hard-currency reserves were depleted. Her debts to sterling creditors were huge in relation to her capacity to export. Hence there were major differences of strategic interest between Britain as a major debtor state and the United States as the overwhelming creditor state. European governments faced an acute external imbalance challenge. The challenge involved dollar shortage in Europe, huge wartime debts to the United States, and dependence on the US economy for European reconstruction. To a much greater extent than in 1931–1933, Keynes was the clear intellectual leader in developing British policy positions in HM Treasury during 1941–1944 and in the Bretton Woods negotiations (Gardner 1980; Skidelsky 2000). His proposals echoed his ideas of 1933 (Newton 2000).

Keynes' evolving arguments in 1941–1944 reflected the underlying strategic reality of a chronic debtor state. The British government's interests lay in protecting its large international financial services sector. It also sought to secure its autonomy of national action in order to pursue sustainable post-war economic expansion, to provide jobs, and to finance both improved welfare-state provision and a global military capability. Keynes looked to a formalized system of international creditor-debtor state relations that would safeguard British interests by reducing its crippling external financial burdens and those of its major trading partners in Europe.

In line with underlying structural realities, Keynes prioritized Anglo-American partnership. However, neither he nor Henderson was an unconditional supporter of this partnership. Henderson was more sceptical. He veered closest towards the so-called 'Schacht' solution, named after the German Third Reich's minister of economics. According to Schacht, international cooperation in pursuit of growth and employment was best constructed through a network of bilateral policies. Keynes stressed the risk that this approach, which Henderson promoted, might strengthen US power. It might also incline the United States towards isolation. In contrast, multilateralism, grounded in Anglo-American partnership, provided an opportunity to mobilize and empower US New Dealers behind new arrangements for global economic expansion. It would simultaneously disempower US fiscal conservatives.

Keynes' priority was to devise an international approach that would mobilize US resources as the overwhelming creditor state to support the European debtor states in their arduous and costly tasks of post-war economic reconstruction. Anglo-American partnership in devising this approach could enable Britain to recover its privileged role and help defend the interests of the City of London against New York (Skidelsky 2000). However, like Henderson, Keynes was never an unconditional supporter of multilateralism and Anglo-American partnership. After the bitter disappointment of the Bretton Woods negotiations, he flirted with dissociating himself from the outcome (Newton 2000).

The difficult negotiations at the Bretton Woods Conference in 1944, and the Articles of Agreement of the IMF, were a manifestation of the enormous structural power of the United States (Dyson and Quaglia 2010a: 61–7). The relationship between Britain and the United States was one of extreme imbalance. The United States owned two-thirds of the world's monetary gold. Faced by American power to script the negotiations from start to finish, Keynes was reduced to 'the status of articulate annoyance' (Steil 2013).

Earlier in February 1942, Article VII of the UK-US Mutual Aid Agreement, which regulated the terms of the Lend-Lease system, had made very visible the overwhelming power of US interests as the pre-eminent creditor state. For Henderson and Keynes, it reflected the dangerous risks that had to be avoided or mitigated in building post-war international cooperation. Article VII made clear that Anglo-American cooperation in constructing post-war international cooperation was to be based on the central principle of non-discrimination in currency and trade policies (Gardner 1980). Keynes' evolving plans were a bold attempt to replace this thinking.

Keynes' initial proposal in November 1941 centred on the creation of a set of currency unions rather than on the design of a wider international economic order (Dyson and Quaglia 2010a: 55–60). He suggested possible currency unions based on the sterling area, the 'Germanic' states, the 'Latin Union', central Europe, the Balkan states, the Scandinavian states, and North America. However, by February 1942 Keynes was proposing a supra-national International Clearing or Currency Union, founded on Anglo-American leadership. This idea was to be revived later with the EPU. In one version of this proposal, he suggested the creation of the 'bancor', a new international bank money fixed in terms of gold. The International Clearing Union would address external imbalances, offering overdrafts to debtor states so that they could engage in expansionary economic policies.

The central bone of contention was Keynes' argument that responsibility for part of the burden of adjustment must fall on creditor states. In Keynes' view, they could not remain passive. The International Clearing Union would enhance national autonomy of action for debtor states, like Britain. Moreover, Keynes sought to use it to promote a privileged role for Britain, with London potentially becoming the location of its headquarters. These ideas were watered down in successive drafts to anticipate US misgivings. Nevertheless, later versions continued to encounter stiff resistance from within the US administration. US fiscal conservatives were to prove more influential than New Dealers on questions of US external obligations. Keynes was extremely disillusioned with the final outcome. Neither the IMF nor the World Bank came close to measuring up to his plans.

At the core of Keynes' thinking was an intellectual challenge to the asymmetric power of both private creditors and creditor states. He sought to restore balance or symmetry in their relations with debtor states. There should be burden-sharing. Politically, the roots of Keynes' thinking were in his social liberalism. It did not reject the principle that 'stability begins at home' or close a blind eye to moral hazard. However, it was inimical to Hobbesian forms of unilateral sovereign default. Keynes' thinking was also at odds with Montagu Norman's version of Lockean contract culture, in which creditor power reigned supreme. It continues to provide material for an intellectual counter to the process of asymmetric design of foundational institutional arrangements in the design of European banking and fiscal union.

The Role of Creditor-Debtor State Relations in European Integration

The centrality of creditor-debtor state relations within post-1945 European integration reflected the continuing difficulties of managing both external imbalances and 'home-grown' problems of excessive credit expansion. Excessive external imbalances and excessive liquidity growth posed threats to exchange-rate stabilization, trade, and investment. The European integration process was marked by the importance attached to exchange-rate stabilization. The result was political contestation about the proper assignment of responsibility for correcting external imbalances and for tackling banking crises. European integration proved deeply problematic in the context of asymmetrical power in framing debates and in agenda-setting about European (and global) economic governance and policies.

Despite increasing formalization, above all with EMU, pervasive distrust remained an attribute of the European integration process. A key factor was the strict eligibility and conditionality criteria, on which creditor states insisted as the precondition for their participation in collective European arrangements for banking and fiscal union. The principles of moral hazard and of matching liability with control served as cloaks for their mistrust of debtor states. Creditor-state elites sought to limit their liabilities, to ensure that the prime responsibility for adjustment to external imbalances lay with debtor states, to put in place strict eligibility criteria for accessing financial assistance for bank recapitalization, to minimize flexibility in bank bail-ins, to secure 'hard' terms and strict conditionality for credit provision, and to establish close external surveillance, monitoring, and sanctioning in case of non-compliance by debtor states.

The European integration process risked becoming embroiled in potentially toxic sentiments of creditor-state resentment at financing bail-outs and debtor-state shame and humiliation at the conditions being imposed on them. The risk was that the passions aroused could subvert the founding principle of solidarity on which European integration depended (Smith 2012). The sense of humiliation at public and elite levels in debtor states opened up three strategic choices as alternatives to compliance: evasion or subversion of creditor-state requirements under the veil of loyalty; demand for revision of terms; and threat of exit.

In 1944–1945 European governing elites were in the grip of huge post-war debt liabilities. The challenge was meeting these liabilities, whilst managing crises of economic and political reconstruction. The challenge was heightened by external threat as the Cold War in Europe gathered momentum. In addressing this challenge, governing elites drew lessons from the post-1918 failures of international and European cooperation, above all in averting and managing the Great Depression of the 1930s. They became gradually more open to economic arguments based on the principle of mutual gains from trade liberalization, exchange-rate stabilization, and ultimately monetary union. European integration on this basis seemed to make compatible new claims on collective solidarity with old attachments to sovereignty. It offered a mechanism to rescue European states from their debt burdens and from external and internal threats to stability through sustained economic growth and employment. The period from the late 1940s witnessed the slow, complex evolution of new institutional arrangements and rules of the game. Creditor-debtor state relations became more formalized within a new historical context of repeated bargaining within common European institutions.

This changing context had two consequences for thinking about debt. Norms of European cooperation were strengthened vis-à-vis incentives to unilateral state action. Both coercive financial repression and sovereign default were seen as neither practical nor desirable. They would inflict heavy collateral damage, leading to collective welfare losses through credit and trade channels. Until 2011–2012 sovereign debt restructuring was not understood to be a policy instrument that had any part in European integration.

The veil of this more formalized diplomacy concealed historical continuity. This continuity was evident in problems of reconciling the interests of creditor and debtor states. They coexisted in asymmetrical power relationships, with their contending economic preferences and appeals to different moral principles. Even the shared principle of European solidarity proved susceptible to very differing interpretations. For creditor states, solidarity entailed 'effort-sharing'. States were responsible for rebalancing their own economies, for curbing their excessive fiscal deficits, for recapitalizing their banks, and for securing their sovereign creditworthiness. The post-2007 crises were represented as 'home-grown'. They were the product of faulty financial and economic policies in debtor states that undermined their competitiveness and/or that led to unsustainable credit booms. For debtor states, solidarity was about 'burden-sharing'. It was about mutual support through collective financial assistance, including fiscal transfers, joint bond issuance, banking resolution mechanisms, and collective deposit guarantees. The post-2007 crises were represented as stemming from trade and financial imbalances, from reckless lending from creditor states, and from the lack of symmetrical adjustment by creditor states.

The enduring controversial political question in organizing European solidarity was: 'who pays?' It bedevilled efforts to organize consensus around a set of organizing principles that would secure the long-term sustainability of the euro area and the sovereign creditworthiness of the Member States. As the core creditor power, Germany faced the often lonely role of safeguarding long-term collective sustainability of the euro area. However, fulfilling this role proved difficult. It was hostage to the fiscal and financial policies of Member States. It was also complicated by the short-term exigencies and expediencies of domestically focused crisis management. Crisis management was fixated on different Member State electoral calendars and on changing configurations of domestic party competition. There were powerful inducements to procrastinate and 'muddle through', evading long-term strategic choices.

The Historic Priority to Central Bank Cooperation

The features of asymmetrical power and conditional political cooperation in formalizing creditor-debtor state relations in Europe were supplemented by the historic comparative advantage that central bankers had in designing the road maps and the operational arrangements (Dyson and Featherstone 1999; James 2012). Central banks possessed a 'first-mover' advantage in formalizing creditor-debtor state relations within European integration. A thread of continuity connected the post-1930 BIS, through the post-1964 Committee of EEC Central Bank Governors, to the post-1994 European Monetary Institute (EMI) in preparing the final stage three of EMU and the post-1999 ECB. The euro area was essentially ECB-centric in its foundational design (Dyson 2000).

The comparative advantage of central bankers stemmed from a combination of factors. Central banks had a relatively narrow mandate. They were united in a high level of consensus about core principles and about the causal mechanisms at work in fulfilling their mandate. Their policy beliefs tended to evolve in tandem. There was a shared professional commitment to independence. Also, central banks benefitted from the dependence of states on their expertise about financial markets, giving them a privileged role in establishing state reputation and government credibility. In sum, they existed within a well-defined, 'club-like' professional milieu of shared knowledge and benefitted from a certain mystique (Dyson 2009).

However, EMU also showed that central bank power was circumscribed. First, its limits were defined by the agenda-setting power of European governments, above all French and German. This agenda-setting power remained conditional on changing dynamics of domestic political acceptability and thus variable. Nevertheless, European governments had the legitimate right to drive the process of integration on the basis of their views of fundamental national interest, above all in their foreign and security policies. They could define European integration as an historical responsibility. On this basis Chancellor Helmut Kohl pursued an effective political strategy of 'binding-in' the Bundesbank to the process of monetary union. He did so initially by ensuring that its president was one of the European Community (EC) central bank governors in the Delors Committee for the Study of EMU (Dyson and Featherstone 1999: 334–42).

Secondly, the post-2007 financial crisis was a reminder to central banks that their monetary policies, focused on price stability, could not be divorced from wider determinants of economic stability, including the operation of financial markets and the credit-creation process. They were drawn back to their historic responsibilities for financial stability and, through their responsibility for the efficient transmission of monetary policy, for the functioning of debt markets. These responsibilities led them to cross the boundary between monetary and fiscal policy.

More broadly, central banks could not ignore their self-interest in the adequacy of the larger macroeconomic governance mechanisms, especially when there was a political vacuum in leadership on fiscal and economic reform policies. The ECB was drawn reluctantly to cross the boundary of its narrowly defined monetary policy mandate by fear of the vicious feedback loop between bank balance sheets and sovereign debt and consequent financial meltdown. Its capacity to conduct monetary policy was threatened with damage. Hence the ECB adopted a more visible political advocacy role on behalf of Member-State action to establish European banking and fiscal union, not least to reduce the pressures to which it was subjected. In 2012 ECB President Mario Draghi took the lead in stressing the need for a long-term political vision for the euro area, with a clear road map to a genuine EMU. It was difficult for the ECB to resist pressures to become proactive in crisis management and to engage in European Council package deals. Central banks could not ignore changing expectations of their role, including responsibility for safeguarding European integration and for the currency that they managed. The ECB was the closest, if incomplete, approximation to a supra-national authority with the discretionary power to act in supreme emergency. The Outright Monetary Transactions (OMT) programme and the establishment of the Single Supervisory Mechanism reflected the role expansion of the ECB. It committed to purchase euro area sovereign bonds in the secondary market, based on strict and effective conditionality, and to assume responsibility for one of the three pillars of European banking union.

Perils of Sleepwalking: Three Historic Political Challenges to Providing a New Europe with Legitimacy

Both Keynes and Norman had failed to fully address the long-term political challenges that the creation of a 'new' Europe would entail. However, Keynes had a social liberal, less technocratic perspective on 'output' legitimacy. His conception of output legitimacy envisaged economic and financial policies that would deliver governmental performance that met the aspirations not just of *rentiers* but also of wider social groups. Keynes (1923) was sensitive to the more complex underlying ideological choices that had to be made to ensure political inclusivity in managing difficult sovereign debt crises and in delivering a sustainable growth model for Europe. These choices involved burden-sharing in making adjustments to external imbalances and scepticism about the functioning of financial markets (Keynes 1932).

Keynes understood that the 'merits' of coordinated European policies were politically contentious. They embodied different views about what constituted effective policies. He was aware how much legitimacy depended on the quality of outputs and whether they were seen as the 'right' medicine. Keynes' model of sustainable growth focused on counter-cyclical fiscal policies and on political willingness to embrace debt forgiveness. Sustainability depended on fairness in ensuring benefit to those on lower incomes and the jobless, on sustained aggregate demand, and on mitigating risks of social unrest and populist political mobilization. Later, those who identified themselves with the Keynesian tradition held a critical view of the Ordo-liberal foundations on which European macroeconomic governance was being constructed. They took a positive view of the contribution to economic growth and debt sustainability from welfare-state provision and from public infrastructure expenditure on education, transport, communications, and a low-carbon economy (cf. Hay and Wincott 2012).

Deflationary economic policies were associated historically with Norman in the 1920s, as well as with German Chancellor Brüning between June 1931 and May 1932. They were justified very differently. Deflation sought to drain excessive liquidity, correct private and public balance sheets as a precondition for restoring confidence, and refocus investment away from sectors prone to asset-price 'boom and bust' (Ritschl 2012a). Welfare states were seen as a burden on competitiveness and a drain on economic performance. Similarly, consumer culture and toleration of asset-price inflation risked subverting the principle of 'living within one's means'. This model of sustainable growth prioritized the interests of *rentiers* over other social interests and external constraints over domestic expansion. Keynes was acutely aware of the political implications of pursuing this model of sustainable growth for Europe. In his view, it lacked political inclusiveness and openness to interest consultation. It undermined political legitimacy and was doomed to fail.

Norman, and to a lesser extent Keynes, did not adequately address two fundamental, long-term political challenges that confronted a 'new' Europe, additional to output legitimacy. These challenges related to the appropriate normative and institutional framework for cross-national economic governance in an increasingly interdependent Europe in finance and trade. They derived from the widening gap between, on the one hand, cooperative policies to deal with ever-more complex cross-national problems stemming from financial and economic integration and, on the other, democratic participation within states. The problem was how to reconcile the growing policy-led scope, depth, and pace of financial and economic integration with political requirements of accountability, transparency, and inclusiveness. The sense that democracy was being 'hollowed-out' and emptied of meaning contributed to the spread of public disquiet, disaffection, and disenchantment with democracy (European Social Survey 2013). In periods of crisis, like the 1930s and post-2007 Europe, bold new political thinking became more urgent. However, such periods risked breeding political drift, confusion, and retreat into either the search for elusive technocratic solutions or populist mobilization around delusional political alternatives.

From 2007 the euro area—and the wider EU—faced political risk from a combination of ineffective economic policy performance, locking in economic stagnation or worse still deflation, with minimal citizen participation and a deepening sense of the erosion of democracy. The first long-term political challenge in mitigating this risk was the design of a European economic governance process that could combine efficacy in pursuit of collective European interests with accountability, transparency, and inclusiveness (Schmidt 2013). These normative criteria were relevant to the design of European banking union, especially its pillars of a Single Supervisory Mechanism and of a Single Resolution Mechanism. The criteria of accountability, transparency, and inclusiveness were indispensable for reconciling the interests of creditor and debtor states in negotiating an acceptable balance between mutual liability and external control. Mutual liability required the design of accountable, transparent, and inclusive European governance arrangements for direct bank recapitalization, for bailing-in banks, for fiscal insurance against shocks, and for structural reform policies. Institutionalization on the basis of these normative criteria would help ensure that creditor states had the requisite incentives to contribute, whilst debtor states had the requisite incentives to comply. Meeting this challenge of improving the quality of European economic governance structures was also one of political timing and sequencing. Was stricter external control on European states to come before, in parallel, or after mutual liability?

The second long-term political challenge was to embed contests about the appropriate model for sustainable debt, and about the quality of European economic governance processes for this purpose, within a framework of European political institutions that increased citizen participation and engagement. 'Input' legitimacy for European economic governance depended on creating a pan-European deliberative space. Within this new deliberative space, fundamental political choices could be made about European collective interests, about the policy instruments to be deployed, and about accountability for their use. The creation of a pan-European deliberative space in European economic governance required an enhanced role for the European Parliament and national parliaments, for cross-national parties and social movements, as well as for the European Council and the Council of Ministers.

European economic governance required an institutional framework that provided input legitimacy for difficult and contentious political choices. It was the essential precondition for the euro area to develop a credible supra-national institutional capacity to take bold, decisive, and discretionary executive action in times of supreme emergency, when its coherence and integrity were threatened by financial markets. Inherent imperfections in the quality of *any* governance process, and persisting risks of failures in policy performance, made this supra-national institutional capacity indispensable. On input legitimacy grounds, the ECB alone could not undertake this function (Dyson 2013). A qualitative leap in European political union was required.

With respect to all three long-term political challenges, EMU remained an incomplete project. The prospects for a 'new' Europe became brighter in the post-1945 period, above all with EMU and its formalization of creditor-debtor state relations. However, the post-2007 financial and economic crises showed that the longer-term political challenges had been woefully neglected in the design and operation of the euro area. European political leadership was marked by illusion, hubris, and complacency in negotiating EMU and in the first decade of the euro. An unwillingness of those in leadership positions to reflect self-critically on the process was induced by a combination of factors. They shared in a widespread intellectual faith in the efficiency of financial markets. They adhered to a model of economic growth that rested on belief in central bankers' technocratic mastery of monetary policy and the capacity of financial markets to deliver continuing credit expansion without major risks to financial stability. They overlooked the question of whether banks had provided themselves with adequate capital in relation to their credit risks. They also gained from the initially benign, disinflationary effects of competition from the newly emerging economies. The sense of sleepwalking into crisis was compounded by the illusion that states could be expected to comply with fiscal rules and structural reform commitments.

European monetary union seemed able to accommodate large and persisting trade and financial imbalances. They led to large-scale capital inflows to debtor states under the new protective umbrella of a single currency, which—in the absence of exchange-rate risk—lowered long-term interest rates. The ECB could focus on a narrow price stability function, which—in the context of such a benign set of circumstances—was relatively easy to deliver. Like other central banks, it tended to neglect the problems that financial markets could pose for monetary policy and the traditional financial stability function of central banks. Once debts were shown to be unsustainable, capital flows went into sharp reverse, bank liquidity dried up, sovereign risks mounted, financial integration was jeopardized, and financial fragmentation and harsh economic contraction followed.

The euro area was caught up in a paradox. In the absence of an institutional infrastructure of banking, fiscal, and economic union, the euro area was extremely vulnerable to shocks. At the same time, creating this infrastructure proved seriously challenging in the face of the urgent temporal pressures of crises and of high consensus requirements amongst Member-State governments. On the one hand, European banking, fiscal, and economic union was inextricably bound up with the long-term political challenges facing European macroeconomic governance. These challenges included the creation of deliberative space and citizen participation; incorporating accountability, transparency, and inclusivity into governance structures that achieved an acceptable balance between mutual liability and external control; and strengthening policy performance, above all in promoting consensus around a new sustainable growth model. On the other hand, the long-term political challenges of building this 'new' Europe had to be met in inhospitable circumstances of crisis, which heightened mutual mistrust and induced powerful emotions of resentment, shame, and humiliation (European Social Survey 2013). The euro area and the wider EU lacked a cross-national political structure within which strategic choices could be deliberated and endowed with supra-national democratic legitimacy. The concept of the European 'public good' was weakly anchored in macroeconomic discourse.

Between Old and New Europe

Creditor-debtor state relations and post-1945 European integration coexisted in a symbiotic relationship. On the one hand, domestic constraints on the formalization of creditor-debtor state relations continued to shape the structure and dynamics of European integration. Asymmetric and conditional cooperation suggested a substantial continuity of 'old' Europe. European political elites remained protective of state sovereignty. In the face of domestic party competition and electoral calendars, they were disposed to prove cautious and short-term in outlook and to procrastinate over matters of cross-national institutional design. They also viewed their European counterparts with varying degrees of personal and ideological distrust and through the distorting lens of national stereotyping. In particular, elites and publics in creditor states held highly restrictive attitudes to 'burden-sharing', notably financial transfers, justified by reference to the principle of moral hazard. Creditor states retained disproportionate power over framing the integration process and in shaping its agenda, above all in the negotiating context of foundational institutional design and in its path-dependent legacy. Their priorities were to limit contingent liability and to insist on strict conditionality and rigorous monitoring as the prior price for mutual liability. Conversely, elites and publics in debtor states resented deeper interventions in their sovereignty as reversion to historic and demeaning 'colonial' attitudes. They viewed highly restrictive collective financial assistance as lack of European solidarity.

On the other hand, European integration attained a dynamics of its own that helped reshape creditor-debtor state relations. Economic and financial integration deepened under the cumulative impacts of customs union, progress towards a single market in goods, services, capital, and labour, exchange-rate stabilization, monetary union, and—not least—technological changes. In turn, the economic rationale and benefits imputed to this process—ensuring sustained growth, prosperity, and stable prices—supported the strategic choices of key European political elites in prioritizing European political union as central to their foreign policy and security interests. These choices were embedded in refashioned historical memories that attributed the catastrophic economic and political failures of the interwar period to lack of timely and decisive international cooperation. They help sustain a powerful political drive, above all from France and Germany, for European political union and for using monetary union to make European integration irreversible (Dyson and Featherstone 1999).

This changed historical context suggested a powerful momentum towards a 'new' Europe. Creditor-debtor state relations were reframed around the construction of post-war historical memory that stressed the symbiosis of economic prosperity and national security. It also became embedded in evolving, increasingly complex governing structures of European integration and cooperation around a widening scope of policy sectors. The resulting pattern of repeated bargains provided incentives for cooperative social norms. Governing elites prioritized cultivation of their reputation for reliability as a bargaining resource. They were prepared to accept sub-optimal outcomes in particular negotiations as the price for present and future gains in other related negotiations. This structure of cooperative social norms raised the costs of resorting to such instruments as unilateral sovereign default, competitive devaluation, and overt financial repression. A powerful symbol of the political dynamic behind this 'new' Europe was the binding-in of central banks into the process of EMU from 1988, a major strategic contribution of Chancellor Helmut Kohl (Dyson and Featherstone 1999).

The post-2007 economic and financial crises threw into starker relief the unresolved tensions between the old and new elements in European economic governance. They were manifest in the contradictions between debtor-state emphasis on simultaneously protecting state sovereignty from external controls and appeal to European solidarity in assuming mutual liability. They were also apparent in creditor-state emphasis on limiting their own liability, above all that of their taxpayers, whilst demanding closer economic and political union through conceding sovereignty. This vortex of political pressures meant that formalizing creditor-debtor state relations in Europe faced acute long-term strategic political challenges. Sovereignty had to be transferred in order to create the four pillars of a 'genuine' EMU: a banking union, a fiscal union, and an economic union, to parallel a monetary union. It involved the assumption of mutual liabilities, in exchange for tighter controls on states, including sound domestic budgetary policies and contractual arrangements to address external imbalances through structural reforms. It also meant financial transfers, including a bank resolution mechanism, common bank deposit guarantees, a fiscal capacity for the euro area to absorb shocks, and Eurobonds (Van Rompuy, Barroso, Juncker, and Draghi 2012). The euro area required an automatic insurance mechanism (De Grauwe 2011). It also needed the supra-national executive capacity to act in supreme emergency (Dyson 2013).

However, a 'genuine' EMU with these characteristics directly engaged taxpayer interests. Hence it required a supportive political infrastructure, based on democratic legitimacy, accountability, and transparency at the European level. Europe had to create a shared public space, in which discourse focused on European collective interests and public goods. This embedding of the euro area in political union involved upgrading the authority of the European Parliament and the role of cross-national parties and political movements. 'Democracy across borders' was, above all, a process of moving the institutional balance away from intergovernmental negotiating arrangements to supra-national political arrangements. This dynamic in refashioning creditor-debtor state relations in Europe depended, ultimately, on two conditions. The first was the will and the capability of the major creditor power to engage with mutual liability; the second was debtor-state compliance with the terms of creditor-state assumption of mutual liability. The challenge for German political leadership was how to support the larger project of European economic and political unification, whilst at the same time lending credibility to EMU by maintaining its own sovereign creditworthiness and keeping its own public opinion onside.

This precarious balance between 'old' and 'new' Europe suggested that the formalization of creditor-debtor state relations might not necessarily prove a one-way process. Its continuing fragility stemmed from dependence on changing domestic norms of political acceptability and thus on domestic political dynamics. It remained unclear whether key debtor states would comply with fiscal rules and commitments to structural reforms.

A further question mark was whether creditor states would allow supra-national institutions to act in timely and decisive ways in bank and sovereign debt crises that represented supreme emergencies.

Enormous faith was invested in the domestic political skills—and good fortune—of governing parties in creditor states and debtor states. The one had to contain public fears and resentment about bailing-out debtor states. The other had to contain the public sense of humiliation and anger about the harsh terms that they had to endure, not least those innocent of responsibility. Lack of domestic political acceptance for the terms on which a balance was being struck between mutual liability and supra-national control threatened to send formalization of creditor-debtor state relations into reverse. A particular constraint was the fear that assumption of mutual liability without adequate external controls could prove the catalyst for the decline of creditor states. German elites were anxious that huge implicit liabilities for rescuing European banks and sovereigns could drag down Germany's own creditworthiness and that of the euro area as a whole.

The subsequent hesitancy and procrastination in formalizing creditor-debtor state relations had negative effects. It created a power vacuum at the heart of the euro area, institutional and political rivalry to fill the vacuum, reluctant ECB entry into this vacuum, and mounting mutual political mistrust, resentment, and humiliation. It led to increasing investor uncertainty about the credibility of formalized arrangements that lacked clear and decisive leadership, above all in times of supreme emergency. The risk was that key political figures and market players would diagnose regression to 'old' Europe and draw historic parallels with the gold standard and the Bretton Woods system, both of which had proved reversible processes. A key difference was that the ECB proved ready to step into the vacuum in order to change market and political sentiments. In July 2012 its president, Mario Draghi, promised 'to do whatever it takes to preserve the euro... And believe me it will be enough.'

Despite ECB activism, the credibility of the euro area continued to suffer from the political vacillation over creating appropriate supra-national institutions. They were required for financial stability. However, direct bank recapitalization by the European Stability Mechanism (ESM) required co-financing by the Member States, only partially breaking the link between bank bail-outs and sovereign debt. Also, German negotiators argued that the creation of a Single Bank Resolution Mechanism depended on prior treaty change. In addition, as Van Rompuy, Barroso, Juncker, and Draghi (2012) noted, the euro area needed a fiscal shock absorption mechanism, joint debt issuance, and contractual arrangements to secure coordinated fiscal and structural policies.

Vacillation over these issues of banking, fiscal, and economic policy union left open the question whether the euro area would fall victim to previous historical failings. By 2012–2013 the euro area was seeking to address its failings by introducing a substantially enlarged and more flexible repertoire of policy instruments. They included private sector involvement (in 'exceptional cases', according to the ESM Treaty), debt buy-backs for Greece, direct bank recapitalization, and bail-in of bank creditors. The ESM's range of instruments to provide collective financial assistance was widened to include purchases of sovereign bonds in primary and secondary markets, precautionary financial assistance, and loans, as well as direct bank recapitalization.

The ECB commitment to buy sovereign bonds under the OMT Programme suggested that it was evolving into a supra-national authority, possessed of executive discretion to act in supreme emergency, even if on a conditional basis. The effective discharge of its duty to ensure efficient implementation of its monetary policy led it to have an interest in preventing the financial fragmentation within the euro area, which resulted from heightened sovereign risk. It gave the ECB an interest in warding-off the effects of threat of a euro break-up on sovereign bond yields. The ECB emerged as a pivotal player in European banking union through its role as the institutional host for the Single Supervisory Mechanism. However, this mechanism was still in pursuit of instruments, above all for restructuring and bailing-out failing banks.

The problems that beset the ECB as a prime site and catalyst for the 'new' Europe stemmed from the way in which the post-2007 crises drew attention to major gaps in institutional design of EMU, above all in fiscal and banking union. Its design failed to address the acute economic and political vulnerability of a Europe that had become ever more dependent on efficiently functioning cross-national financial markets (Jones 2014). Closing this gap depended on intergovernmental agreement, above all in ceding sovereignty in fiscal, financial, and economic policies. By arguing that its hands were bound by the monetary financing prohibition in the treaty (Article 123.1), the ECB sought to encourage Member-State governments to move more decisively to complete the design of EMU. However, this ECB strategy for institutional reform encountered the problems of collective action that had beset the formalization of creditor-debtor state relations since the beginning of EMU.

The architects of European integration repeatedly tried, and failed, to create durable and effective mechanisms for addressing and correcting excessive external imbalances amongst Member States. Before the euro area, external imbalances manifested themselves in risks to European integration from disruptive exchange-rate shocks and realignments. European monetary union served to rescue its Member States from shocks to nominal exchange rates. In the process it induced complacency about unit labour costs. The post-2007 crisis showed that the monetary union had shifted the sources of vulnerability to three sources: real exchange rates, more closely integrated financial systems, and sovereign bond markets. Member States were exposed to sudden reversals of capital flows, to the potentially deadly mutual embrace of banks and states, and to rising costs of debt servicing (on sudden stops as shocks see Caballero, Cowan, and Kearns 2004). Risks had not been eliminated. They had been displaced.

The question was whether, and to what extent, European economic governance should be reformed to help rescue Member States from these three sources of shock. The consensus remained that Member States remained responsible for adjustments to changes in real exchange rates. However, the disagreements related to whether the burden should fall principally on deficit states or whether surplus states must also share responsibility. The ECB and the informal creditor-state club argued that deficit states should give priority to 'fiscal devaluation' by means of tax reforms and welfare-state reforms that lowered employment costs. They also stressed structural reforms, above all to labour markets and wage-setting. Member States with deficits were under increased pressure to enhance competitiveness, defined in terms of reducing unit labour cost developments. They were expected to take responsibility for their own rescue. This ethos permeated the new EU Macroeconomic Imbalance Procedure (MIP) and the European Commission's alert mechanism reports and in-depth reviews. With respect to fiscal union, the linkage of the ESM treaty with the fiscal compact treaty indicated that access to any conditionality-bound collective financial assistance was premised on legal self-binding to the balanced-budget rule. Similarly, European banking union was premised on any future access to a Bank Resolution Mechanism being conditional on membership of the Single Supervisory Mechanism. In short, rescuing European states from their vulnerabilities within monetary union involved a substantial loss of sovereignty.

By the time of the post-2007 crisis, the stakes in creditor-debtor state relations had escalated. In the 1960s–1970s fears of European disunion and the unravelling of the *acquis communautaire* had been bound up with risks to the customs union and the Common Agricultural Policy (CAP). By the first decade of the twenty-first century they had grown to include disorderly disintegration of monetary union, the single market, and competition policies. The stakes rose as the EU broadened in policy scope. They also grew as the EU deepened in institutional terms, notably through increasing resort to qualified majority voting in Council and greater powers to the European Parliament. Moreover, the stakes took on a wider geographic scale through successive rounds of enlargement. The EU grew from six Member States between 1957 and 1973 to twenty-eight by 2013. The resulting increase in stakes was apparent in dependence of euro area banks on an integrated money market or on the ECB to support credit provision. It was also manifest in the enormous complex of euro-denominated contracts. In this high-stakes' context, intertwined banking and sovereign debt crises assumed systemic proportions. They put at risk financial stability across Europe and threatened seismic shocks to the real economy of output and jobs.

The perception of shift in the location of risks and the scale of the stakes began with the Irish government unilaterally guaranteeing the liabilities of its banks on 30 September 2008. It reached a new post-war historic high point during November–December 2009 as the dimensions of the Greek sovereign debt crisis unfolded. The initial institutional winners were the ECB and the European Council. The spreading crises led to the rising number of, and sense of drama surrounding, meetings of the European Council. Heads of state and government also began to meet in the new format of the Euro Summit, which comprised the euro area heads of state and government. It was given treaty expression in the so-called fiscal compact treaty of 2012. The Franco-German document of 30 May 2013 looked forward to more regular Euro Summits. They would review key euro area indicators and policy areas; enter into contractual arrangements for competitiveness and growth with euro area Member States; and task work to euro area finance and other ministers.

In this fast-moving political context, the European Commission risked being overshadowed. The focus for designing new crisis prevention and management measures moved to the President of the European Council. In addition, the work of the euro area finance ministers in the Euro Group took on a more formalized character, with its technical content being hammered out in the Economic and Financial Committee and its sub-committees. The Euro Group's work fell increasingly under the shadow of the Euro Summit. The new ambitions of the European Council were first manifest in the Euro Plus Pact, a coordinating and surveillance mechanism for structural reforms to boost competitiveness and growth. The ESM remained firmly intergovernmental in design, whilst the Franco-German document of May 2013 seemed to suggest a strong presence of relevant Member-State officials in the future Single Resolution Mechanism. The supra-national principle was not extended to collective financial assistance.

At the same time there were signs of a shift towards the supra-national principle. Following the report of the de Larosière Group (2009), macro-prudential oversight of the EU financial system was strengthened by the creation of the European Systemic Risk Board (ESRB). It operated under the auspices of the ECB, developing an EU-wide systemic risk dashboard and, as necessary, issuing warnings and recommendations for remedial action. In 2013–2014 the ECB became the location for the Single Supervisory Mechanism. In another sign of supra-national authority, under Article 8 of the fiscal compact treaty the European Court of Justice (ECJ) could be asked to rule on compliance of domestic budget laws with the treaty and was empowered to impose financial sanctions. Also, under the so-called 'Six-Pack' legislation governing reform of European economic governance, the European Commission gained additional powers in the excessive deficit procedure (EDP) and in the newly introduced MIP procedure. More generally, as the crises evolved, the ECB began to take on a broader, more visible role in pressing for a long-term political vision for a 'complete' EMU.

This complex combination of intergovernmental and supra-national features, of ever more complex structures and procedures, and of wrestling with short-term crisis management, often under conditions of high drama, led to a problem of coherence in formalizing creditor-debtor state relations. Heads of state and government, ministers, and officials had to manage crises on terms that were consistent with the long-term, coherent design of strengthened European economic governance if they were to secure confidence in the sustainability of the euro area. In turn, these terms had to be compatible with the interests of the core creditor power, Germany, and its smaller allied creditor states like Austria, Finland, and the Netherlands. German officials defined Germany's central role within this process as the 'stability anchor', ensuring principle-based coherence around avoidance of moral hazard, calibrating mutual liability with external control, and retaining the separation of fiscal and monetary policies. This role involved opposition to the monetization of sovereign debt by the ECB assuming collective responsibility as 'lender of last resort' to governments (Weidmann 2011). It also meant resisting Eurobonds, except as the final stage in a 'complete' EMU.

Despite a degree of formalization not seen before, by 2013 European creditor-debtor state relations remained primarily intergovernmental. Only the ECB possessed significant supra-national authority. However, the ECB was preoccupied with protecting its monetary policy credibility, with staying within restrictive treaty law, and with avoiding being dragged into a direct fiscal role as 'lender of last resort' to governments. The evolving crisis exposed an institutional framework of European economic governance that was not fit for purpose, above all in economic, fiscal, and banking union. The corollary of its intergovernmental design was enduring doubts about the credibility of mechanisms to monitor and correct excessive external imbalances; to enforce fiscal discipline on governments; to stem contagious banking and sovereign debt crises; and to secure efficiently functioning cross-national financial markets.

The fragility of domestic (including sub-national) ownership of EU and euro area policy commitments had been exposed before 2007. Member States had weak records of compliance with the rules on fiscal deficits and public debt of the Stability and Growth Pact (SGP), as well as with the structural reform ambitions of the Lisbon process. The subsequent reforms to European economic governance sought to address some of the problems. They tried to make it more difficult for fiscal 'sinners' to conspire with fellow 'sinners' by forming blocking minorities in Council. They attempted to strengthen independent domestic sanctioning of breach of fiscal rules. They also provided for intensified surveillance of euro area Member States that were subject to, or threatened with, international bail-out programmes. However, the missing link remained supra-national authority to sanction non-compliance. For this reason, the German federal government made treaty change the heart of its crisis response. It envisaged a 'Maastricht plus', a stability-oriented fiscal union of treaty rules that would empower the Commission and the ECJ to ensure compliance (Weidmann 2011).

Ultimately, the most existentially significant missing link in the 'new' Europe remained the lack of collective executive capacity to act decisively in extreme emergency. Vulnerability to banking and sovereign debt crises is an inherent condition in a credit-based capitalist economy whose functioning regularly imperils financial stability. Deficiencies in euro area crisis prevention and management mechanisms placed at risk the very existence of European monetary union and the wider EU. The euro area lacked the ultimate sovereign, capable of securing market credibility at moments of clear and imminent danger by assuming collective responsibility for debts and by demonstrating that it could match the assumption of liability with control. Ultimately, crisis management required an 'extreme emergency exemption' from standard stability-oriented policies (Dyson 2013). In its absence, the euro area remained acutely vulnerable to investor fear that sovereign and bank debts would not be honoured. This vacuum at the core of monetary union heightened the risk of disorderly defaults, exits, and financial and economic meltdown. The euro area lacked the attributes of a 'new' Europe in that it did not possess ultimate sovereignty over its own money.

18

The Achilles Heel of Post-War European Integration: Endogenous Preference Formation and the Boundaries of Creditor-State Power

> I was unable to imagine at the time [1990–1991] that the Treaty would not be honoured...It was clear that an optimal currency area must endure shocks. By that, I imagined oil price shocks...whatever. But not that suddenly there are states which are actually insolvent. We had put in place every provision so that it would not arise...It was naïve not to have thought of such an eventuality. I have to accept that.
>
> Helmut Schlesinger, former President of the German Bundesbank. Interview in *Capital*, 19 April 2012 (translation by author)

Professor Schlesinger's comments arose in the context of the embittered negotiations over how best to manage the euro area's sovereign debt crises. The two principal protagonists were Germany and Greece. They represented the archetypal creditor state and the archetypal debtor state. Greece's sovereign debt restructuring in 2012 was the largest in history, at present value, eclipsing Argentina in 2001 and Russia in 1918 (Tomz and Wright 2012: 9). Schlesinger was reflecting back on the negotiations that had led to the Maastricht Treaty provisions on Economic and Monetary Union (EMU), and to later additions, notably the fiscal rules in the Stability and Growth Pact (SGP). His remarks reveal a number of enduring and contentious themes in the formalization of creditor-debtor state diplomacy in Europe. They also offer insight into the limitations of creditor-state power.

First, since the early 1950s, Germany had been at the heart of an informal creditor-state club in Europe. In a long-term perspective, the process of formalizing creditor-debtor state diplomacy embodied the triumph of the power of creditor-state ideas over the numerical advantage enjoyed by debtor states within European negotiating processes. Creditor states sought to build in assurances that moral hazard would be averted; that liability of their taxpayers would be strictly limited; and that any mutual liability would be matched by the precondition of tough external control over state sovereignty. The triumph of their ideas stemmed in part from their superior policy performance, notably in securing competitive advantage and sustained, non-inflationary economic growth. Creditor states possessed 'soft' power, reflected in the power to persuade others of the merits of their proposals. Moreover, the numerically few creditor states stressed that the credibility of any cross-national arrangements depended on their continued dedication to pursue stability-oriented domestic policies. Collective credibility rested on the will and capacity of a few creditor states to retain—and export to others—the benefits of their sovereign creditworthiness. The triumph of creditor-state ideas was also based on the fewer collective-action problems that they confront. Debtor states had stronger incentives to differentiate themselves from each other in order to strengthen their individual external economic and political leverage. Spain was keen to demonstrate that it was not Portugal, Ireland that it was not Greece. In consequence, negotiations tended to rest on agenda-setting by Germany, as the leading member of an informal creditor-state club. They gravitated typically around German-tabled documents. This process was evident in the Delors Committee for the Study of EMU in 1988–1989, the process of agreeing the SGP in 1995–1997, and the reforms to EU economic governance and policies in 2010–2011, notably the so-called 'Six-Pack' and later 'Two-Pack' legislation (Dyson and Featherstone 1999; Dyson 2013).

Secondly, Schlesinger's comments illustrate that honouring commitments is regarded as a core virtue by creditor states. Nevertheless, the issue of what constitutes 'good' and 'bad' creditor-state and debtor-state policies has remained contentious. In Schlesinger's view, 'good' debtor states honour their commitments. They do not go insolvent and default; they take individual responsibility for their own liabilities. Schlesinger was similarly clear what represented 'good' creditor-state policies. They ensured that Germany would provide the 'stability anchor' of the euro area by sustaining its own sovereign creditworthiness. In contrast, those who spoke on behalf of debtor states were more inclined to understand 'good' creditor-state policies as sharing in the burden of adjustment to external trade and financial imbalances. Creditor-state solidarity should take the form of domestic expansion of demand and generous provision of collective financial assistance to help rebalance the euro area.

Finally, Schlesinger admits that creditor states can prove naïve, the victims of illusion. The Greek sovereign debt crisis showed the limitations of the thinking behind the Maastricht Treaty about what constitutes an Optimum Currency Area (OCA). Since 1961 OCA theory had evolved as a multi-stranded, internally conflicted body of thinking about the conditions for establishing a sustainable currency union, in particular absorbing asymmetric shocks efficiently (Dyson 2000). These conflicts reflected changing assessments of the costs and benefits of currency union. Theorists have variously stressed exogenous conditions such as economic openness, diversification, structural similarity, capital mobility, labour mobility, and fiscal transfers. Subsequently, examining the prospects for European monetary union, they have examined its trade-creation effects as evidence of endogenous effects. From 1988 EMU negotiators were faced with the mounting political drive behind EMU, the problems of misfit between much OCA theory and a likely monetary union, and the internal contentions and the lack of clear detailed guidance from OCA theory. Faced with the difficulties of drawing clear, politically realizable lessons from OCA theory, German negotiators focused on inserting into Treaty law numerical nominal fiscal deficit, public debt and long-term interest-rate and exchange-rate criteria of convergence to assess readiness for euro entry (Dyson and Featherstone 1999). Subsequently, they reinforced the nominal fiscal rules for euro area Member States in the SGP in order to avert excessive deficits.

However, neither the Maastricht convergence criteria nor the SGP—nor OCA theory—addressed the complex, elusive but crucial factors of economic culture and ideologies of debt that shaped whether preference formation was homogenous. They also neglected state institutional capacity—inclusivity, accountability, transparency, and professionalism—to sustain compliance. This naïvety reflected the formalistic legal understanding of compliance on the part of German negotiators. Its roots lay in the specifically Germanic compound of principle-based, Ordo-liberal economic thinking with *Rechtsstaat* ideology. German negotiators were driven by faith in law as the basis of economic governance. There was a presumption that debtor states would possess the will and the capacity to comply with principle-based economic policies and with stability-oriented rules, like the SGP. This presumption was shown to be false by the fast-evolving sovereign debt crisis in Greece from late 2009.

More generally, creditor states were inclined to exhibit a naïve faith in responsible external lending by their own private creditors. In the context of rapidly integrating financial markets within a monetary union, their own financial systems became infected by bad debts, with risks of cross-national contagion. The upside of currency union was risk insurance; the downside proved to be 'risk contagion'. In short, the crisis contained lessons about the weak relevance of traditional OCA theory. Sustainable currency union depended on both European-level governance structures and shared mentalities of economic culture and ideology of debt. Both were indispensable for homogenous preference formation. It required EU, euro area, and Member State political will and institutional capacity to manage fiscal transfers, deliver fiscal discipline, deal with banking crises, and—in supreme emergency—take discretionary executive action (Dyson 2013).

Germany and Greece Compared

The enduring and contentious themes in post-war European creditor-debtor diplomacy contain an element of paradox. Prior to the Greek debt restructuring in 2012, the young Federal Republic of Germany had provided the only example of a debt restructuring by any of the twelve EU states that negotiated the Maastricht Treaty in 1990–1991 or by any of the Member States that formed the euro area during its first decade. In the period 1950–1953 the United States underpinned Europe's post-war economic growth through the Marshall Plan. Within this framework, the European Payments Union (EPU) offered adjustment assistance to a Germany that had been struggling with large current account deficits.

Negotiated by the veteran German banker Hermann Abs, the London Debt Agreement of April 1953 reduced the value of the external pre-war and post-war debts of Germany from some DM 30 billion to DM 14 billion (Abelshauser 1983: 158; Stolper et al. 1967: 282–3). The huge scale of this reduction becomes apparent when set against a German federal budget of DM 24 billion in 1952. The United States wrote off two-thirds of its post-war foreign aid debts to Germany. German gold and foreign-currency reserves were left at a sustainable level. Moreover, the London Agreement stipulated that Germany's financial obligations were dependent on her economic performance. This debt restructuring put in place a central pillar of the German 'economic miracle'. By 1956–1957 the Federal Republic had emerged as a major creditor state.

This episode puts in historical perspective the attitudes of creditor states towards the morality of debtors. In the early 1950s the United States combined self-interest with generosity towards Germany, having learnt lessons from her benign neglect of Europe in the interwar period. In December 2012 the Greek radical Left party Syriza called for a similar debt restructuring conference to prevent south European states falling into a debt trap, including a stipulation that debt repayments over a thirty-year period would be premised on economic growth. The London Debt Agreement was presented as a model that was much more effective and fair than the Greek sovereign debt restructuring, which had omitted official creditors, and had been followed by a debt buy-back programme in 2012, from which some hedge funds had earned huge profits.

German attitudes to Greece proved complex. On the one hand, German elite and public opinion was alarmed by the scale of their liabilities for Greek debts, which took two forms. First, insolvent Greek banks benefitted from the generous, ultimately unlimited liquidity support of the Eurosystem (which comprised the European Central Bank (ECB) and the national central banks of the euro area). The Greek government was also assisted through the ECB Securities Markets Programme (2010–2012), which led the Eurosystem to buy a big portfolio of Greek, as well as Italian, Spanish, Portuguese, and Irish sovereign debt (in total €208 billion). The subsequent huge imbalances in the euro payment and settlement system (TARGET2) unleashed deep anxieties about German implicit liabilities. Secondly, German guarantees to the European Financial Stability Facility (EFSF), and then her capital contribution to the European Stability Mechanism (ESM), became the key to euro area financial assistance. German attitudes were shaped by fears about moral hazard and about the risks of mortgaging future German sovereign creditworthiness to profligate, self-serving Greek politicians. They also reflected the lessons drawn about the future of European unification from the experience of the fiscal legacy of German unification in 1990.

Conversely, in the early 1950s Germany had not faced the tough conditionality requirements and the intrusive external monitoring on which German negotiators insisted in 2010–2012. Also, Greek debt payments were not subject to a growth stipulation, on the lines of the 1953 Agreement. These differences reflected the great international confidence in German Federal Economics Minister Ludwig Erhard and his previous post-1948 currency and economic liberalization reforms. Such confidence was lacking in Greek finance ministers and their governments. In addition, the fiscal outlook of US 'New Deal' reformers in the late 1940s and 1950s differed from that of German elite opinion leaders over the euro area sovereign debt crises. German elite opinion was, on the whole, deeply attached to Ordo-liberal notions of 'sound money' and 'sound finances' and to compliance with rules. Rules were deemed essential in order to pre-commit to disciplined behaviour, to avoid moral hazard, and to match mutual liability with external control. German public as well as elite opinion was deeply shocked by Greek fiscal behaviour, especially evidence of duplicity and obfuscation in providing official data. It cast Greek governing elites and Greek state capacity in a highly negative light.

Assuming Liability for Europe: Britain and Germany Compared

The configuration of European creditor and debtor states changed rapidly in the chaotic aftermath of the Second World War. In intra-European payment terms, the main creditor states in 1950–1951 were Belgium, Britain, and France. Germany and the Netherlands were debtors. However, by 1951–1952, Germany and the Netherlands had emerged as creditor states, alongside Belgium. Britain and France had already been transformed into debtor states (Kaplan and Schleiminger 1989: 128–9). Similarly, the post-2007 financial and economic crisis witnessed a reconfiguration of the informal creditor-state club within the euro area. Its composition was by then defined in terms of tripe-A ratings of sovereign bonds. By late 2012 Austria and France had lost this cherished status. The German finance minister and officials sustained an intensified relationship in negotiations with Finland, Luxembourg, and the Netherlands in a smaller inner club. They ensured that the presidency of the Euro Group of euro area finance ministers remained within this informal creditor-state club.

External trade and financial imbalances continued to serve as a barometer of shifting power relationships in European creditor-debtor state diplomacy. Not least, they affected the core Franco-German relationship, which assigned itself the role of the 'motor' of European integration. In the late 1950s Franco-German imbalances widened. Their narrowing by the mid-1960s followed President Charles de Gaulle's domestic measures to stabilize the new, devalued franc and formed the background to a more assertive French diplomacy within the European Economic Community (EEC). A subsequent widening of Franco-German imbalances in the late 1960s induced the new president, Georges Pompidou, to support priority to EMU at The Hague Summit of EEC heads of state and government in December 1969.

One of the most significant long-term developments was the eclipse of Britain's role in post-war European creditor-debtor state diplomacy. The willingness and the capacity of British governments to assume liability were from the outset bound up in ambivalence. In British discourse engagement with European economic governance was just an aspect of a more profound commitment to a world role and global ambitions. These ambitions focused on ensuring the continuing strength of the City of London as Europe's pre-eminent financial centre, not least in the context of European monetary union. Additionally, British governments were inhibited from engagement by Britain's post-war problems as a debtor state. They had to defend the pound sterling and sovereign creditworthiness if global ambitions were to be realized. However, the priority to the defence of sterling as a world reserve currency lost credibility as exchange-rate crises mounted, especially with devaluation in November 1967 (Cairncross and Eichengreen 1983). Following the demise of the Bretton Woods system in 1971–1973, sterling was no longer the 'domino' which the United States had to defend (Schenk 2010). The incentive was to manage a floating currency on terms consistent with triple-A sovereign creditworthiness.

The decline of sterling as an international currency was important because it unfettered British policy from the high domestic costs of prioritizing exchange-rate stability. Its effects on Britain's role within the evolution of more formalized European creditor-debtor state diplomacy were more complex. On the one hand, sterling's decline encouraged a new strategic refocusing on European integration, reflected in EEC entry in 1973. On the other, British policy acquired a bias towards avoidance of exchange-rate commitments. The preference was for freedom of manoeuvre to deal with asymmetric shocks, to which Britain was judged susceptible because of the size of its financial sector. This bias did not preclude occasional short-term flirtations with exchange-rate anchors: the European Snake in 1974 and the Exchange-Rate Mechanism (ERM) in 1990–1992.

However, the humiliation of the 1992 ERM exit helped reinforce a deep British scepticism about fixed exchange-rate regimes. This scepticism was further legitimated by references to the crises of 1931, 1947, and 1967. Notably, Britain had secured a relatively early recovery from the depths of the Great Depression following the combined effects of a managed float and devaluation in 1931 with a monetary expansion that started in early 1932. Scepticism about fixed exchange-rate regimes was reinforced by the post-2010 euro area crisis. British governments defined their willingness to assume liabilities in European creditor-debtor state diplomacy extremely tightly. They played the role of—often unwelcome—outside critical observer in the unfolding post-2010 crisis.

In contrast, from 1951–1952 onwards, the central and enduring feature in the evolution of creditor-debtor state diplomacy in Europe was the rising structural power of Germany. It was based on German export prowess in manufactured goods, increasing current-account surpluses, and distinctively favourable macroeconomic indicators for inflation, economic growth, job creation, and competitiveness. This structural power formed the basis for the emergence of German intellectual leadership in the evolving process of formalizing European creditor-debtor state diplomacy. It also gave this aspect of German leadership a distinctively robust character at a very early date, an attribute long predating German unification in 1990. German Ordo-liberalism provided a coherent set of principles to justify the assertive exercise of creditor-state power, based on trade openness, a competitive market economy, and a stable currency.

The key, existentially significant question—posed most starkly after 2007—was how much liability Germany was prepared to assume in order to underwrite the 'new' Europe in whose creation its elites and public opinion so believed. Its construction was mandated in the preamble to the Basic Law of 1949, becoming part of the genetic structure of German politics. Initially, this question had been sidelined. Germany—and European creditor-debtor state diplomacy—had been able to free-ride on US leadership of the Bretton Woods system. German negotiators regarded the Bank for International Settlements (BIS), the Organization for Economic Cooperation and Development (OECD), and the International Monetary Fund (IMF) as more relevant and important forums for macroeconomic policy coordination than the EEC. During the 1960s the collective good of European economic stability—indispensible for growth of trade and investment—was secured by US liability as the 'benign' hegemon.

However, this strategy for sidelining German responsibility lost credibility once the Bretton Woods system became mired in deep crises from 1967. UK devaluation was followed in 1968–1969 by economic and political crisis in France. The Bretton Woods system broke down in 1971–1973 as the US administration refused to underwrite its mounting costs. In its wake the question was: who could organize the collective good of European economic stability, and at what cost to itself? The power vacuum of leadership was filled by Germany in the context of the EEC.

German political leaders had to determine how much liability they were prepared to shoulder for the economic and political benefits of European integration in this post-Bretton Woods' world. As the scale of economic and financial interdependence grew with moves towards EMU, the challenge of limiting liability became more difficult to manage politically. Under Bretton Woods, this challenge had taken the form of external pressures for D-Mark revaluation in order to ease the burden of adjustment on debtor states like France and Italy. Despite humiliation of French elites, German policy makers proved deeply reluctant to revalue. German willingness to underwrite the foundations for EMU had been tested at the outset of the 1960s by the Belgian/French proposal for a European Reserve Fund (ERF) for collective intervention to support EEC exchange rates. It was further exposed by proposals for new EEC short- and medium-term credit support mechanisms.

The challenge of limiting liability was central in defining German negotiating positions on the new European Exchange-Rate Mechanism (ERM) in 1978–1979. Domestic stability-oriented policies were secured by anchoring exchange rates on the D-Mark and by exempting the Bundesbank from unlimited foreign-exchange interventions in order to give primacy to a stable D-Mark. In ERM crises, notably involving the French franc in 1983, 1987, and 1993, German negotiating positions placed the onus of adjustment on debtor states and safeguarded the independence of the Bundesbank in monetary policy.

Similarly, the focus on stability-oriented policies underpinned German negotiating positions on EMU in 1988–1991 (Dyson and Featherstone 1999). However, the interconnected banking and sovereign debt crises that surfaced from 2007 challenged Germany in a more fundamental form because of the scale of financial integration in a currency union and vulnerability to contagion. The economic, financial and political trade-offs in German policy grew in complexity and in their existential significance for German national interests in the European integration process.

Institutional Catalysts for Post-War Integration

At the heart of the slow post-1945 evolution of European economic integration was the gradual formalization of creditor-debtor state diplomacy around a complex, evolving set of institutions. Each was concerned to act as a catalyst for the integration process; each sought to protect its own jurisdiction; and each was a venue within which an informal creditor-state club was active in promoting its own policy ideas and agenda-setting. They included the Organization for European Economic Cooperation (OEEC), the EPU, the BIS, the European Commission, the EEC Monetary Committee, and the Committee of EEC Central Bank Governors. Two institutional catalysts were added later: the ECB in 1999 and the European Stability Mechanism (ESM) in 2012.

Over time the respective roles and significance of these institutions altered. In the 1950s the OEEC and the EPU were central to the evolving formalization of European creditor-debtor state diplomacy. The US government sought to use them as catalysts. In this context the BIS took on the function of a European clearing house. By the 1960s the European Commission, the EEC Monetary Committee, and, from 1964, the Committee of EEC Central Bank Governors had become leading if competitive players. From 1994 the European Monetary Institute (EMI) replaced the Committee of EEC Central Bank Governors, giving way in turn to the ECB in 1998. As the post-2007 financial and economic crisis intensified, the ECB evolved into a major supra-national institutional catalyst for completing EMU in terms of banking, fiscal, economic, and political union. Despite its status as an intergovernmental institution, the ESM seemed to provide the institutional nucleus for a future European Monetary Fund. Its governance did, however, entrench the power of an informal creditor-state club, with de facto veto power for Germany.

Complications arose from the efforts of these institutions to protect their own jurisdictions; from contests about which had the right to exercise leadership; and from institutions escaping the control of creditor-state principals. Scope for agency escape from creditor-state control increased when institutions were endowed with supra-national authority, like the European Commission and the ECB. It was also associated with creditor-state expectations and fears that these institutions would 'go native', get too close to debtor-state interests, and hesitate to apply tough conditionality requirements. German policy makers were regularly opposed to European Commission efforts to advance EMU rapidly on the basis of proposals that bore the imprint of debtor states. Clashes occurred over the Triffin-inspired European Reserve Fund proposal in 1959–1960; over the Commission Action Programme of 1962; and, in 1964, over the establishment, location, functions, and working of the Committee of EEC Central Bank Governors (Dyson and Quaglia 2010b; Toniolo 2005: 439–52).

Similar difficulties arose over the pace, timing, and conditions for European monetary union. Creditor-state elites, led by Germany and the Netherlands, held to the view that it should follow economic and political union. They supported the 'economist' conception of EMU, in which economic convergence would precede a sustainable monetary union, and the 'coronation' theory, in which monetary union would be the final stage after political union (Dyson 1994). In contrast, debtor-state elites were inclined to adopt the 'monetarist' conception of EMU. The process of monetary integration should precede, or at least parallel economic union, in order to drive economic convergence (Dyson 1994). This conflict of views was manifest in the negotiations about the Werner Report on EMU in 1970, about the proposed second stage of the European Monetary System (EMS) with its European monetary fund in 1982, and about the significance that political and fiscal union should have in the negotiations of the Maastricht Treaty on EMU in 1990–1991 (Dyson and Featherstone 1999).

The European Commission had problems in establishing a leadership role with respect to monetary policies and economic and fiscal policy surveillance. From its first meetings in 1964, the Committee of EEC Central Bank Governors signalled its independence of the European Commission—symbolized by its location in the BIS in Basel. It intended to conduct its business in an atmosphere of privacy and confidentiality (James 2012). Moreover, the status of the BIS as 'the central bankers' bank'—with direct experience in financial market operations, if limited in available resources—gave it a leverage that the European Commission lacked. Similarly, the EEC Monetary Committee of Member-State central bankers and finance ministry officials also stressed its independence from the Commission (Dyson and Featherstone 1999: 699–700). The European Commission lagged behind the other institutions in intellectual authority. Despite reform efforts in the early 1980s and beyond, the Commission Directorate-General for Economic and Financial Affairs operated in the shadow of the vastly greater intellectual resources of the IMF and later the ECB.

As one of the two main institutions at the heart of the Bretton Woods system, the relationship of the IMF to these European institutional developments was unclear and often difficult. On the one hand, the IMF played an enabling role. However, it did so on creditor-state terms of pressing for accelerated moves to economic liberalization, in particular to non-European multilateral trade and investment and current account convertibility. In the 1950s these terms, as the price of standby IMF credits, were far from welcome in some leading European states, where gold and foreign-exchange reserves were exhausted. In common with the BIS, the IMF feared that European institutional arrangements, like the EPU, would soften external pressures to embrace fiscal and structural reforms. It was already developing its conditionality agenda on creditor-state terms in a tougher form than the European Commission later. It stood ready to apply it once the EPU was dissolved and the Bretton Woods' system fully operational.

Additionally, by 1960–1961 the IMF recognized that the priority to stabilize exchange rates required new, much more intensive central bank cooperation, above all to stabilize the US dollar price of gold. Here the IMF followed US pressure as its main shareholder. The main role fell to the BIS in helping to organize a vast and growing network of standby loans, currency swaps, and credit support, notably through the Gold Pool during 1961–1968. The BIS demonstrated an initial reluctance based on the creditor-state argument that slowing US gold losses through burden-sharing by surplus states, like Germany, Belgium, and Switzerland, would reduce pressure on the United States to make domestic adjustments (Toniolo 2005: 377).

On the other hand, the Bretton Woods' system proved a constraining influence on European institutional developments. It reduced the incentives for formalization of independent European creditor-debtor state diplomacy and for the BIS and for German central bankers to take EMU seriously. Bretton Woods acted as a globally organized provider of the public good of economic stability for Europe. Only with the end of the Bretton Woods' system in 1971–1973 was the incentive to pursue EMU in Europe strengthened. The EMS, which was negotiated in 1978–1979, was seen as a first stage in EMU with the objective of stabilizing EEC exchange rates through the Exchange-Rate Mechanism (ERM) and thereby underpinning economic integration. In the view of French President Valéry Giscard d'Éstaing, the EMS was a 'Bretton Woods for Europe'. The motivation for President François Mitterrand to choose to stay in the ERM in March 1983 was that he preferred German conditions for stabilizing the French franc to IMF conditions following a franc exit (Dyson and Featherstone 1999: 142–6).

This same sense that European institutional arrangements would be less tough on conditionality requirements for collective financial assistance continued to complicate the IMF role in the management of the European sovereign debts crises from 2010. In the view of euro area creditor states, bringing in the IMF to create a 'troika' with the European Commission and the ECB had the merit of 'outsourcing' the tough conditionality requirements in domestic fiscal and structural reform policies that were sought for Greece, Ireland, and Portugal. The merit of this course was not lost on German politicians, who wished to avoid charges of humiliating, amongst others, Greece and awakening historically-conditioned resentments. Nevertheless, the IMF proved a complex, often difficult, partner when it came to creditor state interests. It favoured earlier and more radical EU and euro area action in bank recapitalization, as well as in Greek debt restructuring. However, the IMF was in financial terms the junior partner. Hence it proved difficult for it to occupy the 'driving seat'. Given this limitation on its leverage, the IMF feared being drawn into the compromising position of being seen by newly powerful emerging market economies as Euro-centric, softer on European states than it had been earlier on East Asian and Latin American states.

The EPU: The Informal Creditor-State Club and the Emerging Discourse of 'Good' and 'Bad' Creditor States and Debtor States

The negotiators at the Bretton Woods Conference in 1944 had given little attention to whether Europe might need separate institutional arrangements to manage adjustment problems to post-war external trade and financial imbalances and ensure the flow of credit. However, it soon became clear that exhaustion of European gold and foreign currency reserves made early transition to multilateral trade and free currency convertibility impossible. US export potential to post-war Europe was diminished. Hence the US had a strong interest in transitional bilateral arrangements, outside the multilateral IMF framework, to address the external imbalance problem and to speed the shift to multilateral trade and free convertibility. This interest was strengthened as the Cold War in Europe gathered momentum, along with fears that in states like France and Italy communist parties could come to power.

European states were confronted with acute material devastation and human distress, following the second European-centred world war in thirty years. Their political elites had an interest in discouraging the flight to extremist, populist politics on Left and Right, seen after the First World War. They drew the lesson from the interwar period that multilateral cooperation and integration were of paramount importance for sustained European reconstruction. This lesson was reinforced by the negative example of the Third Reich's bilateral and crudely exploitative approach under Schacht. Geo-strategic arguments provided further momentum behind multilateral cooperation and integration. European elites shared the core belief that it was essential to contain Soviet ambitions in Europe and protect fragile liberal democracies.

The key factor was the new engagement of the United States in providing the financial underpinning for this process of multilateral cooperation and integration. It took the form of Marshall Aid and the coordination of Marshall Aid budgets through the new OEEC. In the period 1947–1949 the new US Economic Cooperation Administration (ECA) used the OEEC as a platform for developing the idea of a European multilateral clearing union to provide temporary credits into concrete proposals, using US aid as an incentive to cooperate. US, rather than IMF, conditionality was an instrument for helping to speed European states towards trade and financial integration on a multilateral basis.

Formalized European creditor-debtor state diplomacy evolved within the interlinked frameworks of the BIS in Basel and of the new OEEC in Paris. The OEEC was established to coordinate the distribution of US aid in Europe. It offered an opportunity for US officials in the ECA to press for an agenda of European economic integration, of which the EPU became the central pillar. Some key US officials saw tighter coordination of national economic policies, a single market, and even monetary policy coordination, as essential components of this strategy. However, they met the formidable constraints of scepticism within European political elites about ceding sovereignty and frequent reluctance to abandon a preference for more controllable bilateral agreements.

During this early post-1945 period the central European states in this process were Britain, France, and the Benelux states, notably Belgium. They were at the core of the initial proliferation of bilateral payment agreements. Then they were leaders in the first steps towards mutual aid through the first and the second multilateral payments agreements in 1948–1949 and 1949–1950. Both multilateral agreements rested on an intricate network of drawing rights, based on US dollar aid, for the purpose of financing deficits. They provided a superstructure that rested on existing bilateral agreements. Their purpose was to provide new financial resources to enable debtor states to settle with their creditors, without resort to precious scarce gold or US dollars. The biggest net contributors of drawing rights were Britain and Belgium, followed by Sweden, Italy, and Turkey. The main recipients were France, followed by Greece, the Netherlands, Austria, Norway, Germany, and Denmark. In 1948–1949 Belgium was the major creditor state, making the Belgian franc a hard currency. France was the heavy debtor (Diebold 1952: 38–45).

The revised payments agreement of 1949–1950 sought—under US pressure—to correct some of the weaknesses of the first. It made some progress towards a multilateral payments system by making a proportion of drawing rights transferable. However, this change, which benefitted France, encountered the opposition of creditor states. The second payments agreement introduced more flexibility in revising drawing rights in order to help reflect the speed of change consequent on currency realignments. However, the central criticism remained that the agreement still offered no financial incentive for debtor states to reduce their deficits (for fear of losing aid) or for creditor states to increase imports from debtor states. Moreover, drawing rights were calculated primarily on a bilateral basis (Diebold 1952: 64–86).

The EPU of 1950 represented a new, more radical step towards formalizing multilateral creditor-debtor state diplomacy in Europe. It also saw the early formation of an informal creditor-state club, as well as a discourse of what constituted good and bad creditor and debtor state policies. The birth of the EPU was facilitated by the combination of US pressure and financial incentives with a shift to greater trade balance within Europe, which induced a new climate of optimism (Kaplan and Schleiminger 1989). The United States assisted by supplying $350 million of working capital for the EPU. It would not, however, allow IMF credits to member states as long as the US provided

Marshall Plan aid, so as not to blunt the ability of the US to attach conditionality. However, the United States used its dominant shareholder position in the IMF to gain its support for a much faster transition to current-account convertibility than the EPU planned. In addition to US help, both Britain and France proved more cooperative about addressing the weaknesses of the first two payments agreements. Britain was less concerned than formerly that intra-European payments would drain US dollars from, and thus would weaken, the sterling area.

However, more radical ambitions were pre-empted by the tough positions adopted by the two main European creditor states, Belgium and Switzerland. As a condition of participation, they insisted that the EPU agreement should limit obligations on them to extend credits to their trading partners. It should also provide for some liquidation of existing debts. They were, above all, concerned to limit their liabilities within the EPU. The side-payment to Belgium for participation was the provision for automatic repayment of existing debts within two years in the absence of bilateral agreement. Belgium was identified by EPU officials as a problem of 'chronic' surplus.

The EPU differed from the agreements of 1948–1949 and 1949–1950. It was a closed European clearing union and was more automatic and more flexible in operation. It was no longer based on drawing rights. Each state's deficits and surpluses with other OEEC states were set off against each other, resulting in a single net deficit or surplus within the EPU. An automatic grant of credit was provided for debts less than a specific amount of the quota assigned to each state in the agreement. In case of higher debts, a combination of credits with gold and dollar payments was to be used. A sliding scale of gold and dollar payments provided debtor states with a new incentive to reduce their deficits. Crises arose once states exhausted their EPU quotas.

The OEEC was the governing framework of the EPU, with the BIS acting as its agent. Once the BIS had calculated each state's net creditor or debtor position, the balance was settled between its government and the EPU, not bilaterally. This book-keeping arrangement encouraged cooperation in two ways. First, it enabled European states to economize on US dollars in their mutual transactions. In this way, the EPU helped to bring about a liberalization of some 85 per cent of intra-European trade by 1955 (Toniolo 2005: 311). Secondly, it made member states acutely aware of external imbalances and of their implications for each other. It pushed the contentious issue of who takes responsibility for correcting them to the top of the European agenda (Kaplan and Schleiminger 1989: 342–55).

The EPU had its own seven-person managing board, with a member of the ECA as an additional US observer. The board comprised a high-profile group of financial experts, who developed an *esprit de corps* during lengthy periods of office. Despite the reluctance of the OEEC governments to cede powers to the board, it rapidly established a formidable reputation as a crisis manager under Guido Carli and Hans Karl von Mangoldt as its chairs. The EPU managing board pioneered the use of conditionality in enforcing compliance with the terms of the EPU agreement. By 1952 it was recommending to the OEEC Council that France pursue 'a strong budgeting policy, designed to eliminate the present total deficit' (Kaplan and Schleiminger 1989: 143). From the outset, it was clear that mounting external imbalances threatened the operational capacity of the EPU. Hence the OEEC and the managing board shared an interest in making recommendations to both 'extreme' creditors and 'extreme' debtors. In the words of

Wilhelm Vocke, president of the Bank deutscher Länder: 'The EPU is above all a valuable means of overcoming nationalism in currency matters, and of educating people to think in international terms' (Kaplan and Schleiminger 1989: 117).

Notably, in the light of later developments, the first major crises that the EPU had to manage in 1950–1951 focused on Germany and the Netherlands. Both states faced serious deterioration in their payments positions (Kaplan and Schleiminger 1989: 91–153). However, by spring 1953, Germany was already the largest creditor of the EPU, accelerating its liberalization of EPU imports. The long-term pattern was soon evident in the polarization between Germany as the creditor power and France as the debtor power. This polarization culminated in the crisis of 1957–1958. France undertook a harsh stabilization programme, involving devaluation and liberalization in return for EPU credits (see Table 18.1). From 1955–1956 Britain too settled down as an EPU debtor state. By the time of the EEC in 1957, the pattern of Germany as creditor and France as debtor was established. It was to prove a persisting theme at the heart of European integration.

By 1954 an informal creditor-state club had emerged within the EPU managing board, led by Belgium, Germany, the Netherlands, and Switzerland. They sought a 'harder' system as the appropriate path to full convertibility of currencies. Their arguments centred on the right of persistent creditor states to earn more convertible currency and give less credit and on the systematic repayment of all future debts. It was even intimated that the German federal economics minister, Ludwig Erhard, might force a withdrawal from the EPU if creditor state demands were not met (Kaplan and Schleiminger 1989: 199). In order to exert more external discipline on their 'home' governments, the French and Italian members of the managing board aligned themselves with creditor-state positions (Kaplan and Schleiminger 1989: 159–60). In line with creditor-state views, the 1954

Table 18.1 Annual Net Deficits or Surpluses under the European Payments Union: 1 July 1950 to 27 December 1958, in Millions of US Dollars

	1950/1	1951/2	1952/3	1953/4	1954/5	1955/6	1956/7	1957/8	1958
Austria	−104	−38	+42	+106	103	−6	+23	−4	+24
Belgium-Luxembourg	+236	+509	−33	−55	+80	+222	+14	+153	+66
Denmark	−68	+46	−17	−92	−94	+4	−43	+10	−1
France	+194	−602	−417	−149	+115	−180	−969	−576	−317
Germany	−281	+584	+260	+518	+296	+584	+1,336	+826	+350
Greece	−140	−83	−28	−40	−27	+40	+5	+7	−49
Iceland	−7	−6	−4	−5	−2	−4	−3	−3	−9
Italy	30	+194	−223	−210	−225	−125	−94	+219	+73
Netherlands	−270	+477	+139	−42	+84	−62	−36	+86	+181
Norway	−80	+21	−59	−61	−70	−27	+41	−78	−30
Portugal	+59	+28	−23	−19	−59	−33	−38	−54	−37
Sweden	−59	+284	−44	−37	−104	+6	+111	−30	+11
Switzerland	+11	+158	+85	+73	+10	−66	−83	−189	+20
Turkey	−64	−96	−50	−94	−38	−27	−36	−50	−14
UK	+604	−1,476	+371	+107	+136	−327	−225	−317	−267

(*Source*: European Payments Union Board (1959), *Final Report*: 36)

reform package 'hardened' the EPU by the repayment of old debts and by increasing the use of gold relative to credit in settling external imbalances.

However, crisis management within the EPU defined not just who were the problem creditors and debtors. It also highlighted the limits of the capacity of the EPU to tackle issues of excessive external imbalances. The managing board evolved a discourse of 'extreme' creditors and of what constituted 'good' creditor policies. Correspondingly, it recommended that Germany increase imports, reduce export promotion, and increase capital exports (Kaplan and Schleiminger 1989: 248–51). At the same time, the EPU managing board hesitated to intervene too closely in German debates on how best to tackle the external imbalance issue. It advocated 'good' creditor policies, like import liberalization, encouragement of capital exports, and faster domestic economic growth. However, these steps did not reduce German surpluses and the accumulation of its foreign-exchange reserves. The board stepped aside from pushing for a softening of EPU credit arrangements in face of opposition from the informal creditor-state club. It also hesitated to engage in the debate about D-Mark revaluation, preferring to avoid jurisdictional conflict with the IMF. The informal creditor-state club stressed that the OEEC was not the venue within which currency realignments should be decided.

Nevertheless, by 1955–1956 the EPU managing board expressed its opposition to increasing German interest rates as evidence of neglect of external considerations. At the same time, the German federal government opposed 'untied' German special credits to deficit states. The problem of German surpluses and its accumulation of foreign-exchange reserves proved one that the EPU managing board was unable to resolve. It was bequeathed to the EEC and to its new Monetary Committee of Member-State central bankers and finance ministry officials.

As originally intended, the EPU was no more than a temporary bridge to full convertibility of its member states' currencies. Thereafter, European states were expected to prove capable of honouring their commitment at Bretton Woods to make their currencies convertible at a fixed rate. The IMF then became the central forum for formal creditor-debtor state diplomacy. The divisive questions on convertibility in the 1950s were about how and when. Leading figures in Britain exhibited a stronger preference for an early and, if necessary, unilateral move. Leading figures in most continental European states were much more cautious about the adequacy of foreign-exchange reserves and about the risks of leaving some trading partners behind in the rush to convertibility. Eventually, in 1959 free convertibility of European currencies—into each other and into the US dollar—was declared. Just one year after the foundation of the EEC, the EPU dissolved. However, many of the creditor-debtor state arguments in the EPU resurfaced inside the EEC, notably its Monetary Committee, where Dutch and German central bank and finance ministry officials proved highly influential and resistant to peer pressure.

The First Decade of the EEC

The demise of the EPU shifted the location of European creditor-debtor state diplomacy to the IMF and to the new EEC. Over the 1960s the IMF remained the privileged forum.

With free currency convertibility, the IMF's role in the Bretton Woods' system of fixed but adjustable exchange rates provided the essential European public good of economic stability. Within this framework, the benefits of the EEC's first work programme after 1958—the new customs union and the Common Agricultural Policy (CAP)—could be captured. In effect, the IMF acted as the backstop for the EEC's work. It deterred Member States from resorting to safeguard measures. After the collapse of the Bretton Woods' system, and the post-1973 oil crises, the IMF continued to play a role in providing financial assistance, notably to the British and Italian governments.

However, from 1960 mounting recognition of the limitations of the Bretton Woods' system opened up space for the European Commission and pro-integration groups and individuals to develop a case for EMU. The intellectual case was founded on the so-called 'Triffin dilemma'. The Bretton Woods' system depended on US current account deficits to supply dollars and ensure liquidity. The dilemma stemmed from the problem of how the United States was to eliminate its external deficits, given the appetite of other states for dollar reserves (Triffin 1960). Continuing US deficits eroded confidence in the US capacity to sustain its anchor role. The eventual collapse of the Bretton Woods' system in 1971–1973, once the US withdrew from its anchor role, left a vacuum for the EEC to fill by proposals to restore the public good of economic stability in Europe.

In this evolving context the European Commission, the EEC Monetary Committee, and the Committee of EEC Central Bank Governors emerged as the institutional context that both enabled and constrained the formalization of creditor-debtor state diplomacy within Europe. By 1964–1965 the nature of their respective roles became clearer. The European Commission and the EEC Monetary Committee focused on the internal dynamics of the European integration process. As a supra-national bureaucracy, with an ambitious Treaty mandate of promoting 'ever closer union', the Commission was the boldest in agenda-setting (Maes 2006). At the same time, it lacked a clear mandate for EMU in the Treaty of Rome.

The EEC Monetary Committee rapidly built up its own *esprit de corps*. However, it comprised national finance ministry and central bank officials. The Monetary Committee remained intergovernmental in character and retained an organizational distance from the Commission. In consequence, it served as a forum in which officials and central bankers from creditor states could more directly articulate their interests. They sought to persuade their counterparts from debtor states, like France and Italy, to argue domestically for the merits of stability-oriented policies. The Monetary Committee proved cautious in reacting to Commission initiatives.

The post-1964 Committee of EEC Central Bank Governors was even more circumspect. It focused less on the internal dynamics of European integration. Reflecting its home in the BIS in Basel, the Committee of Central Bank Governors concentrated its attention on the international monetary system (James 2012). It retained the cautious outlook of a central bankers' club. Above all, the Committee sought to safeguard its prerogatives and to retain independence from the European Commission.

In developing its agenda-setting role on behalf of EMU in the 1960s—and beyond—the European Commission faced the central problem of Franco-German imbalances. In 1958–1959 and in 1968–1969 these imbalances became alarming. They generated mounting mutual distrust and irritation between French politicians and officials and their German counterparts. The problem of external imbalances testified to a lack of economic convergence, which in turn reduced the credibility of any Commission proposals for EMU, above all to German officials. Moreover, the lack of firm legal legitimacy for EMU in the Treaty of Rome was not lost on legally-minded German officials.

Proposals for EMU faced an additional intellectual difficulty. They depended on an agreed, clearly articulated theory about the process for realizing EMU. It had to be persuasive both to Gaullist, sovereignty-minded, French policy makers and to the creditor interests of German policy makers and, more generally, of central bankers and financial markets. However, there were radically different conceptions of EMU. French policy makers were attracted to collective monetary support mechanisms, drawing creditor states into accepting responsibility for managing adjustment problems. In their 'monetarist' conception of EMU, the early creation of these mechanisms would promote economic convergence. Conversely, German policy makers stressed priority to economic convergence around stability-oriented policies and fiscal and monetary policy performance. EMU had to be founded on credible commitments of debtor states—demonstrated by deed as well as word—to put their own houses in order. The principle was 'stability begins at home'. Coordination had to be built in a 'bottom-up' fashion. In arbitrating these conflicting views, the European Commission lacked the authority that the EPU managing board had possessed consequent on its clearing house function. It was also less able to develop conditionality as a policy tool than either the EPU or the IMF.

For these reasons, not least the lack of a policy vacuum consequent on the Bretton Woods' system, the first decade of the EEC was a story of frustrated ambitions for the European Commission. Its proposal for the ERF in 1958–1959 made no headway (Maes 2006). The Commission Action Programme in 1962 produced only gradual role expansion, including a set of new committees and a right of initiative in the monetary area (Dyson 1994). However, this right was highly circumscribed in practice by the new Committee of EEC Central Bank Governors. In part drawing lessons from this experience, the Barre Plan of 1969 reflected a new realism within the Commission. There was a stronger strategic appreciation of the need to adapt to German creditor-state power and to carry the support of the EEC central banks (Dyson 1994; Maes 2006).

External imbalances remained the central problem that drove the timing of European Commission initiatives in the 1960s. It was clear to Commission officials that disparities in price and cost developments led to balance of payments' disequilibria. They posed risks to the emerging *acquis communautaire* from exchange-rate realignments under the Bretton Woods' system and from Member State resort to safeguard measures under the Treaty of Rome. The unilateral Dutch and German revaluations of 1961 exposed at an early stage the inadequacies of formalized creditor-debtor state diplomacy within the EEC, even at the rudimentary level of prior consultation.

The scale of Franco-German imbalances varied over time. It narrowed in 1960–1962 after President Charles de Gaulle's devaluation of the franc and domestic stabilization programme. By 1965 it was temporarily eliminated. This process of convergence offered some support for the partial implementation of the Commission Action Programme. However, Franco-German imbalances widened sharply again in 1967–1969, inducing France to resort to safeguard measures. It persuaded the European Commissioner for Economic and Financial Affairs, Raymond Barre, that the time was not ripe for major initiatives on EMU.

Chronic external imbalances in 1958–1959 and 1968–1969 had paradoxical effects. On the one hand, they offered justification for Commission initiatives to protect the customs union and the CAP by new forms of economic policy coordination. On the other, external imbalances testified to lack of economic convergence and reduced the credibility of EMU to German negotiators. German resistance was a continuing problem for the Commission. Its most radical proposal, the ERF in 1958–1959, involved pooling 10 per cent of the international reserves of the Member-State central banks. The ERF would intervene to support states in balance of payments' difficulties. However, the proposal met stern German and central bank resistance. It lost momentum once President Charles de Gaulle opted for domestic stabilization in December 1958, with the aim of rebalancing Franco-German relations at the heart of the EEC.

The less ambitious Commission Action Programme of 1962 was also emasculated by German resistance, led by Federal Economics Minister Ludwig Erhard. It rested on the idea of common short- and long-term economic policies, with the European Commission setting long-term objectives. German officials viewed the document as too receptive to the *dirigiste* thinking of debtor states. They viewed France as seeking to use the EEC to erect a protective umbrella around a 'little' Europe. For the same reason, distrust of French motives, Erhard kept economic affairs out of the Franco-German Elysée Treaty of 1963. The main innovation after the Action Programme was a modest redesign of the technical committee structure of EEC economic governance. However, the final form taken by the new Committee of EEC Central Bank Governors fell well short of Commission ambitions.

EEC central bankers became only reluctantly involved in the internal dynamics of European integration. Their primary focus remained the BIS, which in turn looked to the Group of 10 (G10) level. The BIS gained new significance once the Bretton Woods' system became fully operational after full currency convertibility. During the 1960s it began to carve out a more active role in banking and financial market supervision. The catalyst was increasing worries of European central banks about the implications of the rapid growth of the new euro-currency market for domestic monetary stability. The central axis of BIS institutional development shifted to global financial stability and prudential regulation. This shift was formalized once the Basel Committee on Banking Supervision was established in the 1970s (Toniolo 2005: 442–55).

From the outset, opinion formation within the Committee of EEC Central Bank Governors was led by the central banks of the major creditor states, above all the German and the Dutch. The European Commission was seen as a monetary policy amateur, its institutional self-interest centred on developing collective financial assistance mechanisms. It was kept at a distance. Consistent with their commitment to preserving the identity of the BIS as the central bankers' club, the EEC central banks rejected the location of the new Committee in Brussels. They stressed both the broader international G10 outlook of the BIS and Basel as a symbol of their independence. The EEC central bankers also limited the European Commission to a right to attend the Committee meetings, well short of the Commission's original aim of chairing its meetings in Brussels and providing its secretariat.

Above all, the Committee of EEC Central Bank Governors ruled out any notion of prior consultation on important domestic monetary policy decisions. It rejected the idea of defining a common EEC position in international monetary affairs (Toniolo 2005: 441–2). Similar positions were adopted with respect to technical proposals for a common unit of account, for a progressive reduction of fluctuation margins amongst

EEC currencies, and for an EEC pool of central bank reserves for joint currency intervention. They were judged as premature, pending an EEC commitment to full political and economic union. Such proposals were also seen as reducing the incentive for debtor states to put their own houses in order. The Committee limited itself to the exchange of views and to promoting enhanced understanding. It did so on the terms of a club that was wedded to creditor interests.

The Process and the Substance of EMU

The history of the formalization of creditor-debtor state diplomacy in EMU, including the moves towards banking, fiscal, and economic-policy union after 2007, revealed a common pattern. Member-State governments—through the heads of state and government in the European Council—sought mastery of the process. They provided political leadership in three ways: declaratory commitment, shrouded in historical symbolism and providing legitimacy; road maps, with attached timetables of action; and the design of new institutional venues to bypass or bind-in potential opposition. These tools served to motivate, drive, and structure the process (Dyson and Featherstone 1999).

However, the substance of reforms was negotiated within, and amongst, a range of other, essentially technical institutional forums. From the 1970s to 1994, the start of stage two of EMU, they included the European Commission, the Committee of EEC Central Bank Governors, the EEC Monetary Committee, and the Council of Economic and Finance Ministers (ECOFIN). Between 1994 and 1998 the European Monetary Institute (EMI) served as successor to the Committee of EEC Central Bank Governors, mandated to prepare the final stage of monetary union. From 1998–1999 onwards the institutional structures changed again. The ECB managed the single monetary policy; the Euro Group provided a new informal body, institutionalizing dialogue amongst the euro area finance ministers; and the Economic and Financial Committee took over the responsibilities of the Monetary Committee. Subsequently, following and expanding on the recommendations of the Lamfalussy Committee, three new EU technical committees were created to coordinate regulation of banking, securities, and insurance markets. With the start of EMU the technical infrastructure took on a new complexity.

Leadership was decisive in both driving and managing the process of EMU and in defining its substantive content, including its institutional arrangements. The importance of political leadership for the process was manifested in The Hague Summit of the EEC heads of states and government in December 1969. On German initiative, it was agreed to make the political commitment to EMU into the basis of the second work programme of the EEC. The Werner Committee was established to study how EMU was to be designed and realized. This political commitment was re-established at the Paris Summit in 1972. Similarly, the launch of the EMS in 1978–1979 was steered by European Council meetings, beginning in Brussels and ending in Bremen, with close synchronization by the French president and the German federal chancellor (Dyson 1994).

In historical terms, the pivotal European Council was in Hanover in June 1988. It appointed a committee, mainly of EEC central bank governors, chaired by European Commission President Jacques Delors, to report on *how* EMU was to be designed. The

Council stressed that political decisions of principle had already been made. The period between the Strasbourg European Council in 1989 and the Rome European Councils in 1990 provided the political mandate for an EMU treaty negotiation, with dates. At the Maastricht European Council of December 1991 a fixed date for the final transition to EMU was agreed and inserted in treaty form. Political steering of this transition was completed at the Madrid European Council in June 1995, the Dublin European Council of December 1996 (when the main outlines of the SGP were agreed), and the Amsterdam European Council of June 1997 (when an employment chapter was added). Later, from autumn 2007, an intensive series of European Council crisis meetings—and new meetings of the euro area heads of state and government—began to provide political momentum for the construction of banking, fiscal, and economic-policy union.

In each case political leadership depended on the will and the capacity of French presidents and German federal chancellors to agree the broad direction of change and to establish parameters for negotiations, including timetables. This will and capacity related in turn to a favourable conjunction of a policy threat with a policy vacuum and with domestic opportunity structures to take initiatives in constructing Europe. Above all, German federal chancellors had to be prepared to make political commitments to EMU. This favourable constellation of events with policy threats, emerging policy vacuum, and opening domestic political opportunities was seized by Willy Brandt at The Hague Summit in 1969. It underpinned Helmut Schmidt in pushing for the EMS in 1978–1979 and Helmut Kohl pushing for EMU in 1988 and again—emboldened by German unification—in 1989–1991.

The scale of the liabilities that Germany was being asked to assume with banking, fiscal, and economic-policy union after 2007 made Chancellor Angela Merkel more cautious about managing the domestic politics of such a high degree of formalization of creditor-debtor state diplomacy. Her problem was how to respond to acute financial and economic—and increasingly political—threats and to a manifest policy vacuum whilst retaining vital support from domestic Ordo-liberal opinion. Rethinking Ordo-liberal principles involved a shift beyond moral hazard arguments to the principle of matching liabilities with control. The outcome was a strategy that stressed careful, detailed attention to negotiating 'quality' banking, fiscal, and economic-policy union. The immense political challenge for Merkel was to attach German creditor-state power to European monetary, banking, fiscal, and economic-policy union on terms that would prove acceptable to her party, coalition, and electorate, as well as to debtor states, their fractious publics, and the financial markets.

If the process was politically driven and managed, leadership in defining the substantive content of EMU rested principally with the informal creditor-state club. The attraction of membership of this club to small states like Luxembourg and the Netherlands, and later also Austria and Finland, as well as Denmark within the ERM, lay in being close to Germany and punching above one's weight. Negotiating EMU was characterized by Germany tabling the main technical documents, around which other Member States negotiated. This process was less obviously true of the Werner Committee and the EMS negotiations. The gap between the proposals in the successive Schiller Papers from the federal economics ministry and the Werner Report was a factor in German 'distancing' in subsequent negotiations (Dyson and Quaglia 2010a). It soon became clear that the French government was hostile to ceding fiscal sovereignty.

Similarly, in the face of strong political leadership on the EMS, above all from the French president and the German chancellor, the German Bundesbank had to mount a tough, rearguard action. It succeeded in ensuring that the EMS would not create an obligation for its unlimited intervention to support the Exchange-Rate Mechanism (ERM). Any intervention was to be consistent with the Bundesbank's domestic statutory responsibility to 'safeguard the currency'. It also ensured that the 'anchor' currency was not the artificial European Currency Unit (ECU) but the D-Mark as the strongest currency in the system. In these ways, German liabilities were strictly limited. The onus of adjustment was placed on debtor states and the path set towards a 'hard' ERM that would enforce external discipline through the D-Mark anchor.

Capacity to remain within the 'hard' ERM became a litmus test of Member-State virtue. The ERM served as the vehicle through which Germany emerged as the 'stability anchor' of Europe. The Bundesbank gained its reputation as 'the bank that rules Europe'. The ERM was seen as an instrument for raising domestic policy standards towards the level of the top creditor state, epitomized in the French 'hard franc' (*franc fort*) policy after 1983. Also, German negotiators kept off the agenda European Commission proposals for a second stage of the ERM, involving a new European Monetary Fund (Dyson and Quaglia 2010a: 311–13). Creditor-state 'hardening' had priority over collective monetary support for debtor states. The evolution of this body of thought around the ERM—picturing it as a de facto D-Mark zone—created a very different context within which EMU was debated from the 1980s. The ERM followed a path-dependent logic.

The Delors Report of 1989 bore the imprint of the Bundesbank. Several papers were presented. However, negotiations took place around the Pöhl Paper, which was written within the Bundesbank and carefully cleared with the Danish and Dutch central banks (Dyson and Featherstone 1999: 342–9). The reference point of EMU was to be a Treaty commitment to a single currency, managed by an independent ECB which was to have a narrow mandate of price stability. Economic stability was to be reinforced by a commitment to avoid moral hazard. There were to be fiscal rules on deficits and public debt and no monetary financing of fiscal deficits. By creating the Delors Committee, Chancellor Kohl secured the essential political gain of the 'binding-in' of the Bundesbank to the process of EMU. In exchange the Bundesbank could shape the design principles. This required major political concessions from the French Socialist government, above all on central bank independence.

Kohl's political leadership on the process of EMU involved domestic concessions, principally by the federal economics and finance ministries and by the Bundesbank. Since at least the time of the Werner Committee negotiations, they had been committed to the 'coronation' theory of EMU. This theory had also become the dominant narrative of the Committee of EEC Central Bank Governors. Monetary union had been seen as the final step in a long process of political and economic union, involving 'a hard and rocky road' (Dyson 1994). The 'coronation' theory counselled caution in relation to any timetable for EMU. In line with this theory, the Committee of EEC Central Bank Governors had reacted coolly to earlier European Commission proposals for strengthening EEC monetary cooperation. It had agreed to Commissioner Barre's proposal for a new Community Mechanism for Short-Term Monetary Assistance. However, its agreement was premised on continuity. The BIS had experience of this type of support mechanism. In addition, the new mechanism involved a much more limited and conditional provision of short-term credits than the European Commission had envisaged. Moreover, the quid pro quo was EEC Council of Ministers' acceptance of the principle of prior consultation on all important short-term economic policy decisions. The Committee of EEC Central Bank Governors sought to strengthen mutual surveillance. A modest increase in liabilities was to be balanced by more opportunity to exert external control.

Subsequent lack of compliance with the principle of prior consultation, notably by the French government, fortified the belief of the Committee of Central Bank Governors that the EEC was not ready to commit credibly to the degree of political and economic union required for monetary union. Shortly after the publication of the Werner Report, it became clear that the French Gaullist government was not prepared to share, let alone delegate, fiscal sovereignty in parallel with the proposed shift to monetary union. Hence the Committee of EEC Central Bank Governors emptied most of the substantive content out of the Werner Committee's proposal for a new medium-term credit mechanism, the European Monetary Cooperation Fund (EMCF). Its approach to EMU enshrined a cautious strategy of small steps, guided by the protection of long-term principles. The Committee of EEC Central Bank Governors rejected resort to political expediency in pursuit of EMU. It sought clear evidence of parallel moves to merge fiscal sovereignty so that the assumption of liability by creditor states was matched by external control of debtor states.

Kohl's leadership was exemplified in three ways. He provided historical legitimacy, including the principles of binding Germany to Europe and making European union 'irreversible'. By means of asserting the primacy of these principles, and by designing institutional venues like the Delors Committee, Kohl 'bound-in' the Bundesbank to the process of EMU. Perhaps most strikingly of all, he encouraged the insertion of a fixed, final date for the transition to stage three of EMU in the Maastricht Treaty. Both Kohl and Mitterrand were pre-committing their successors. The timetable device was already part of the genetic structure of European integration. It had been used with the so-called '1992' timetable, which was seen as having been successful in delivering faster progress towards a single European market in goods, services, capital, and labour.

Two other elements were essential in marginalizing the 'coronation' theory inside Germany. First, progress towards a 'hard' ERM and adherence to the *franc fort* policy suggested that France had become wedded to stability-oriented policies. Secondly, and more importantly, the shock of German unification in 1989–1990 changed the domestic and European parameters. Kohl gained enormously in domestic political status and power from his domestic mastery of this process. He also needed to appease the fears of European Community (EC) partners, notably France. The Delors Report on EMU offered a 'ready-made' project on which Kohl could base an accelerated commitment to European unification as the counterpart to German unification. He stressed that German unification required a new urgency in pursuing European unification. Kohl's preference was parallel progress in two intergovernmental conferences (IGCs), one on political union and one on EMU. However, faced with unresolved problems of trade-off, he opted for a firm timetable for EMU and use of EMU as a tool to speed further political union in future IGCs and treaty revision.

Completing the Circle: The Rise and Eclipse of the 'Stand-Alone' Model of Monetary Union

The history of EMU illustrates that German creditor-state interests were not simply exogenous 'givens'. They were subject to redefinition, at least twice. In 1988–1991 the 'coronation' theory of European monetary union gave way to the 'stand-alone' model of monetary union. Then, in 2011–2012, under the impact of protracted problems of financial and economic crisis management, there was a shift from the 'stand-alone' monetary union model to a model of European banking, fiscal, and economic-policy union, which required an even larger framework of political union. This dynamic character of creditor-state interests reflected endogenous preference formation. Nevertheless, the concepts of banking, fiscal, and economic-policy union that were pursued by German negotiators continued to be based on Ordo-liberal, stability-oriented principles. The key negotiating principle became the requirement that mutual liability had to be matched by European-level control to ensure the responsible exercise of Member-State sovereignty. It remained logically consistent with the principle of moral hazard.

The first catalyst for German Ordo-liberal negotiators in the federal finance ministry and the Bundesbank to redefine their approach to EMU occurred in 1989–1990. It came from their emerging recognition that Chancellor Kohl's political commitment to pursue European monetary union was not matched by the willingness of other EU Member States, led by France, to concede European political union or fiscal union in parallel. There was a mismatch between the new political momentum and urgency behind European monetary union and the 'coronation' theory.

The conclusion was that European monetary union had to be constructed as a 'stand-alone' project. It had to be based on an institutional and policy framework that was consistent with the institutionalization of a 'stability culture' in Europe. This approach rested on two pillars. First, EMU required a strictly independent ECB, dedicated to ensuring price stability in the euro area as a whole. The foremost political requirement was to reassure German public opinion that the new currency would be 'at least as strong as the D-Mark'. Hence ECB independence had to be founded on treaty-based safeguards that were stronger than those applying to the German Bundesbank. Secondly, fiscal, economic, and collective bargaining policies were to remain matters of national responsibility. They were to be based on stability-oriented rules that flanked and supported ECB monetary policy (Issing 2008). This framework respected the principle of avoiding moral hazard by limiting creditor-state liability.

The 'stand-alone' model of EMU meant treaty provisions that would rule out 'bail-outs' of fiscally incontinent Member-State governments and prevent monetary financing of fiscal deficits by the ECB (Issing 2010a). It also required clear and detailed fiscal rules, along with quasi-automatic and draconian sanctions, in cases of non-compliance. They were needed to ensure no excessive deficits and to safeguard against unsustainable public debts. In addition, the price stability mandate of the ECB had to be shielded against any attempts by the European Council to use exchange-rate policy to boost growth and employment. Ultimately, responsibility for growth and employment rested with Member-State governments, employers, and trade unions. It required responsible wage bargaining, labour-market flexibility, free and open financial markets, and policies consistent with low market interest rates. The success of ECB monetary policy depended on clear assignment to the one objective of price stability, facilitating sustainable growth. Consistent with this model of a 'stand-alone' monetary union, the imprint of creditor-state power was apparent in the ECB-centric character of the institutional design of the euro area.

Centre-Left governments, including those headed by the German Social Democratic Party (SPD) between 1998 and 2005, were, in general, more open to Keynesian ideas of coordinated economic policy management, focused on aggregate demand. However, in debtor states Centre-Right as well as Centre-Left governments had stronger inducements to flesh out and 'add on' institutional arrangements that would strengthen economic union. They sought to frame monetary union within *ex ante* coordinated policies to promote economic growth and job creation. German Ordo-liberal negotiators frustrated these ambitions in the Delors Committee, where they received scant attention. They also successfully promoted their model of a 'stand-alone' monetary union in subsequent negotiations in the EC Monetary Committee and in the IGC on EMU, where Commission ideas on collective financial assistance mechanisms made little headway (Dyson and Featherstone 1999). The attempts of Oskar Lafontaine, SPD chair and federal finance minister in 1998–1999, to bind the ECB into new frameworks of macroeconomic coordination also failed. He resigned from both offices, after just six months as finance minister. The French-inspired idea of 'economic government' remained both formless and content-less in the Maastricht Treaty and on the birth of the euro area in 1998–1999.

Two factors strengthened demands for strengthened economic policy coordination in the late 1990s. First, the insistence of German negotiators on the SGP in 1995–1997 in order to strengthen the excessive deficit procedure (EDP) created a political counter-pressure to rebalance the treaty, especially on growth and employment. Secondly, Centre-Left governments came to power in France (1997) and Germany (1998), just as the final stage three of EMU neared. The euro area was launched in the context of Centre-Left dominance of the European Council. In the period 1997–2001 new EU coordinating processes proliferated. They included the Luxembourg process for employment policies, the Cologne process for macroeconomic policy 'dialogue', and the Lisbon process for structural economic reforms. The EU Employment Pact was to be the counterpart to the SGP. However, the EC Monetary Committee (later Economic and Financial Committee) and ECOFIN ensured that the new coordinating mechanisms were framed in Ordo-liberal terms. They remained 'flanking' processes to monetary union.

Even before the post-2007 financial and economic crisis, the notion of a 'stand-alone' monetary union had begun to lose credibility. By 2003 it was already clear that the Lisbon process for creating 'the most advanced knowledge-based economy in the world' was failing. In 2005 it was reformed to simplify its objectives, to strengthen domestic ownership of structural reforms, and to encourage 'naming and shaming' of Member States for poor compliance. Nevertheless, Member States proved unwilling to make firm and detailed commitments to structural reforms. Their domestic ownership of the Lisbon process continued to be weak. Similar problems beset multilateral surveillance of economic policies within the framework of the Broad Economic Policy Guidelines (BEPGs), which were provided for in the Maastricht Treaty. As early as 2001, the Irish government firmly rejected the recommendation of the European Commission that its budget was in breach of the BEPGs. This experience highlighted the political weakness of the European Commission, which was forced to placate the Irish government.

A similar loss of credibility affected the SGP. The SGP had been negotiated before the start of stage three of EMU in order to detail and strengthen the treaty provisions on the EDP. It sought to reassure German elite and public opinion by putting in place a tougher fiscal policy framework at the EU and euro area level than Germany's own. However, the SGP fell short of the quasi-automaticity and the avoidance of provisions for exceptionality that German negotiators had originally wanted.

As Schlesinger came to realize, German Ordo-liberal negotiators were naïve in assuming state will and capacity to comply with the fiscal rules. The rules were persistently flouted by EU Member States. The European Commission was shown to be relatively powerless in the face of ECOFIN, where fiscal 'sinners' and prospective sinners were being asked to vote on fellow sinners. Worse still, the SGP crisis of November 2003, and the subsequent reform of the SGP in 2005, showed that German Ordo-liberals were naïve in thinking that their own federal government would wish to comply. The Red/Green government of Chancellor Gerhard Schröder colluded with the French and Italian governments to reject the European Commission proposal that the EDP be applied to Germany. Instead, it supported reform of the SGP to make it less 'mechanistic'. The SGP crisis exposed again the weakness of the European Commission in processes of policy coordination that were intergovernmental in nature and depended on peer pressure for their effectiveness.

The 2005 SGP reform placed more emphasis on the 'preventive' pillar in exchange for a less mechanistic 'corrective' pillar. The SGP was to be applied more flexibly. Greater fiscal policy discretion was permitted to Member-State governments to make it more counter-cyclical in functioning. In consequence, the 2005 reform faced strong criticism from Ordo-liberals in the Bundesbank—led by Jürgen Stark—and in the ECB—led by Otmar Issing. It reflected a weakening of creditor-state arguments within Germany and across the EU. This weakening stemmed from the coincidence of the traditionally stronger Keynesian element in SPD thinking with the effects of the long-drawn-out, heavy fiscal burdens and the loss of competitiveness that followed German unification in 1990. The Schröder government sought greater domestic fiscal room for manoeuvre to ameliorate the economic and political impacts of its radical Agenda 2010 reforms, especially to labour markets. Not least, it faced internal dissent within the SPD and critical *Länder* and federal elections.

From 2005, the new Christian Democratic (CDU/CSU)/SPD federal government of Chancellor Merkel returned to the discourse of 'stability culture' and Germany's 'stability anchor' role that had marked the Kohl chancellorship. This discursive shift under the Grand Coalition was supported by strong improvement in indicators of German competitiveness and fiscal performance. By 2009 the Merkel government had inserted the 'debt brake' in the German constitution. This formalized commitment to balanced budgets over the economic cycle signalled a strategy to return Germany to the pinnacle of fiscal virtue as 'stability anchor' of the euro area. Germany had fully returned to its creditor-state principles.

Nevertheless, the combination of the 2003 SGP crisis, the 2005 SGP reform, and persistent 'sinning' by Member-State governments had undermined the 'stand-alone' monetary union model. The will and capacity of Member-State governments to liberalize goods and services markets, as well as of employers and trade unions to reform wage bargaining and labour markets, had proved weak. There had been an unwillingness to make clear and detailed reform commitments within the Lisbon Process and to demonstrate 'ownership' of the implications of a monetary union. The evidence of mounting problems was apparent in the depressing statistics on unit labour cost developments and in the resulting large and growing external trade and financial imbalances within the euro area. Member-State governments seemed oblivious to the warnings from both the ECB and from the European Commission. Complacency reigned as Member States reaped the large benefits of historically low real interest rates and sovereign bond yields. These gains helped disguise the scale of fiscal vulnerability, not least in those Member States that were successful in complying with the SGP.

The post-2007 crisis forced a gradual rethink of the 'stand-alone' approach to monetary union. It became clear that the euro area faced a choice. It could return to, and reinforce, stricter compliance with the Maastricht Treaty provisions, consistent with the principle of enforcing national responsibility. This position was strongly advocated by the Bundesbank, especially its president Axel Weber, as well as by many in the ECB. They included the ECB chief economist Jürgen Stark (2010), who had negotiated the original SGP, and his ECB predecessor, Otmar Issing (2008). Strict compliance with the Maastricht Treaty meant 'no bail-outs', no monetary financing of fiscal deficits, greater authority for the European Commission in EU policy coordinating processes, and strict automaticity in enforcing the SGP. It involved rejection in principle of ECB sovereign bond purchases, which began in May 2010. Advocates of the 'stand-alone' approach to monetary union were also suspicious of proposals to formalize the Euro Group and meetings of the heads of state and government of the euro area (Puetter 2006). They risked both subverting the independence of ECB monetary policy and transferring authority from the more 'technical' Euro Group to the more 'political' heads of state and government (Hodson 2011). Their preference was for informal governance as a better means of protecting creditor-state interests.

The reforms in the architecture of EU financial market regulation and supervision in the wake of the 2007 crisis were consistent with the logic of the 'stand-alone' monetary policy model. Revelation of the scale of cross-national exposure of banking and financial systems led to the de Larosière High-Level Group report on financial supervision in 2009. Its outcome was the creation of the European Systemic Risk Board (ESRB), located at the ECB and mandated to provide macro-prudential supervision of risks to financial stability. In addition, the three technical committees for harmonizing financial market regulation were upgraded into authorities with enhanced powers. The European Banking Authority began to concern itself with bank stress-testing and bank recapitalization requirements. Following EU legislation, the European Securities and Markets Authority took regulation of credit rating agencies and hedge funds under its wing.

The so-called 'Six-Pack' legislation of 2010, followed by the 'Two-Pack', was also consistent with this logic. The aim was to reinforce European economic governance and strengthen the role of the European Commission in processes designed to provide more comprehensive crisis prevention. The European Commission's Annual Growth Survey was to form the basis for the new European Semester. Processes of fiscal-policy, structural-policy, and macroeconomic surveillance were to be temporally synchronized. The conclusions were embodied in National Reform Programmes and Stability Programmes for each Member State (Convergence Programmes for non-Euro Area Members). Also, as part of the 'Two-Pack', Member-State draft budgets were to be submitted to Brussels for review before they were debated in national parliaments. The Commission's role in the EDP was strengthened through 'reverse' qualified majority voting in ECOFIN, making it more difficult to construct blocking coalitions. It was also empowered to issue early warnings to Member States. The SGP was reformed to focus on rules on public debt reduction rather than fiscal deficits; to stress measures to strengthen longer-term structural sustainability of fiscal positions; and to introduce graduated, speedier fines for non-compliance. In addition, a new Macroeconomic Imbalances Procedure (MIP) was introduced, broadening the agenda of surveillance and monitoring. The MIP was based on a scoreboard of indicators, including competitiveness and current account balance. It also provided for fines. These economic governance reforms left essentially untouched the creditor-state, 'stand-alone' model of monetary union. They attempted to embed Member States in much more rigorous and comprehensive peer-review processes. Notably, the MIP was asymmetrical in design, placing the main onus on deficit-state rather then surplus-state adjustment.

By summer/autumn 2011 it became clear to German negotiators that the euro area faced an alternative choice. This choice involved moving away from the 'stand-alone' model of monetary union. The euro area could pursue treaty changes that would 'complete' EMU through banking, fiscal, and economic-policy union. In that case any assumption of mutual liability had to be not just balanced but also preceded by strengthening of external control on Member States. Ordo-liberal principles required a ceding of sovereignty. The European Commission would possess greater authority in fiscal and economic-policy union. The European Court of Justice (ECJ) would gain a new treaty-based role in enforcing the German-inspired 'debt brake' on Member States. The ECB would develop a new presence in the Single Supervisory Mechanism within banking union, notably through its asset quality review, and in triggering bank resolution processes. It would also flank fiscal union by sovereign bond purchases on the basis of strict conditionality. As the implications of this choice for the ECB became apparent, Stark resigned from its executive board. Earlier in 2011 Weber had resigned as Bundesbank president. Both cited disagreements over ECB policy in purchasing sovereign bonds.

The new ECB president, Mario Draghi, seized on this discursive shift during 2012 to promote a new, active ECB role in designing a road map and timetable for 'completing' EMU. In particular, he sought to break the dangerous link between banking crisis and sovereign debt crisis, which risked seriously overexposing the ECB to risk. The ECB commitment to unlimited long-term liquidity provision as lender of last resort enabled euro area banks to purchase their home-state sovereign bonds. Its sovereign bond programme of May 2010 lacked conditionality. Neither addressed the potentially fatal link of banking and sovereign debt crises.

The solution was twofold. First, the ESM should be empowered to directly recapitalize euro area banks. However, this empowerment of the ESM was made dependent on commitment to European banking union, beginning with a Single Supervisory Mechanism under the auspices of the ECB.

Secondly, against the opposition of the Bundesbank, the Governing Council of the ECB launched the Outright Monetary Transactions (OMT) programme. This programme committed the ECB to purchasing shorter-dated sovereign bonds in secondary markets. Unlike with the former sovereign bond programme, this commitment was conditional on the Member State having agreed a fiscal consolidation and structural reform programme with the ESM and on its compliance with that programme. The OMT programme was justified on the grounds of ensuring the efficient transmission of ECB monetary policy and counteracting risks of financial fragmentation within the euro area. By commitment to unlimited support in specified circumstances, the ECB aimed to eliminate the higher yields that markets might require because of perceived fears of euro exit. The consequent shock within the German Ordo-liberal economics community was articulated by the Bundesbank. It reflected the eclipse of the 'stand-alone' model of monetary union. The ECB had not become lender of last resort in sovereign bond markets. However, the principle of separation of fiscal and monetary policies had been breached.

Despite this discursive shift, the approach to fiscal union continued to rest on creditor-state interests. Fiscal discipline on Member States was given a clearer supra-national character through the role of the ECJ in enforcing the 'debt brake'. In contrast, the new collective financial assistance mechanism, the ESM, possessed an intergovernmental character. Member States had no access to the ESM unless they had ratified the Treaty on Stability, Coordination, and Governance in EMU (the so-called fiscal compact treaty). They had first to enshrine the 'debt brake' in their constitution or a higher law. Germany also ensured that it retained a de facto veto power in the ESM. The principle of avoiding moral hazard had been redefined as one of matching mutual liability with tight external controls on Member State sovereignty.

The Post-2007 Financial and Economic Crisis

The road to European monetary union proved hard and rocky. However, it was not as hard and rocky as that to banking, fiscal, and economic-policy union. It took the sheer scale, magnitude, and longevity of the post-2007 crisis to set the EU and the euro area on this path, above all the whip-hand of financial market discipline. Even then, the approach was hesitant.

By its very nature, formalizing creditor-debtor state diplomacy in banking, fiscal, and economic-policy union was more difficult than in monetary union. The policy scope of delegation or sharing of sovereignty was much broader. It touched more directly and visibly on politically sensitive issues of the distribution of costs and benefits. In addition, the depth of institutional effects was far greater. It affected working methods within the European Council, the European Parliament, the European Commission, and the ECB, as well as their relationships to each other and to national parliaments. Banking, fiscal, and economic-policy union posed complex normative issues about how to build criteria of accountability, transparency, inclusivity, and efficiency into institutional design. The challenges of creating governance structures were more far-reaching and less tractable than in the case of monetary union. The ECB, for instance, could not expect to operate in the same way as the Single Supervisory Mechanism in banking as it did in monetary policy. The creation of a bank resolution authority raised issues about legitimacy and efficiency that touched on its relationship with both the Single Supervisory Mechanism and the European Council and ECOFIN. However, there remained an unwillingness of creditor states to see the ECB become lender of last resort in sovereign debt crises or to envisage Eurobonds as other than the culmination of a long process of fiscal union. Eurobonds were in effect the 'coronation' of fiscal union.

Creating banking, fiscal, and economic-policy union had profound implications for power structures within the EU as a whole. Already European monetary union had led to three categories of membership: 'ins', 'pre-ins', and semi-permanent 'outs'. The new expanded agenda of EMU helped drive a deeper political wedge through the EU, one that had major implications for the balance between the unitary model of integration and differentiated integration. The EU became more visibly divided. Member States chose to define themselves as 'ins' or 'outs' no longer just on the basis of monetary union. New lines were drawn around membership of banking union, the ESM treaty, the fiscal compact treaty, the Euro Plus Pact, and any future provisions for 'contractual arrangements' in structural reforms to enhance competitiveness. In particular, the British government stood aloof from this process of formalization. The evolving new infrastructure of EMU heightened political sensitivities. 'Outs' by conviction wished to defend the integrity of the 'unitary' single European market as a 'level playing field'. They sought to secure safeguards against measures that the new group of banking union 'ins' might propose and that might have implications for the single market. The British government saw agreement on double-majority voting for euro area and non-euro area Member States as a victory for this position. However, 'ins' by conviction argued that constructing banking, fiscal, and economic-policy union required new, closer forms of coordination that affected the single market policies. The requirements of a sustainable EMU had to have priority within the single market. They ensured that the blocking minority for euro area outsiders would end once a lower threshold of number of opt-outs from the banking union was crossed. They also proposed euro area residency requirements for specific types of financial transaction.

It took 'clear and present danger' to the euro area, and the tightly interconnected risks facing both its creditor and debtor states, its banks and its sovereigns, to push the euro area, and those Member States which saw their future as bound up with the euro, to face up to these political challenges. Three developments accelerated this process. First, the British government's exercise of a veto on EU treaty change at the December 2011 European Council meeting confirmed that Britain was a permanent outsider in fiscal as well as monetary union. This message was underlined in January 2013 when the British prime minister committed a future Conservative government to seek renegotiation of EU membership and hold a referendum in 2017. The British government's aloofness from euro area crisis management led the German as well as French and other Member-State governments to conclude that moves to macroeconomic union would give a more formalized and clear-cut character to differentiated integration in the EU.

Secondly, during 2011–2012 the euro area sovereign debt crisis intensified and spread to two systemically significant states—Italy as well as Spain. Fears of a Greek euro exit increased as political protest and violence mounted, Troika implementation deadlines were missed, and electoral uncertainty grew in early 2012. Between November 2011 and July 2012 senior German ministers speculated openly about a so-called 'Grexit'. France lost its triple-A credit rating in January 2012. In the face of contagion, the euro area had to look at the size, flexibility, and instruments of its collective financial assistance mechanisms. It had to decide whether and how it would provide a credible backstop for Member States.

Thirdly, international pressures for urgent and bold action mounted, from the IMF and from the Group of 20 (G20), notably its meeting of November 2011 in Cannes. Already, in June 2011, after the crises of Ireland and Portugal intensified, Germany had bowed to these pressures to increase the size of the EFSF. There was a new recognition that European monetary union was unsustainable without rapid moves to formalize banking, fiscal, and economic-policy union. Previous European Council crisis packages had proved too little, too late.

Creditor States and the Strategic Management of Crisis

As the financial and economic crisis gathered momentum from 2007, the European Council opted for a strategy of buying time and reform by stealth. This strategic choice reflected German views about the nature of the crisis. It was a crisis of unsustainable debts, requiring a long and painful process of public- and private-sector deleverage and deep-seated political, institutional, and structural reforms. Elite and public opinion in Germany and other creditor states was deeply shocked by the duplicitous fiscal misbehaviour of political elites in Greece, whose euro entry seemed to be based on falsified data. They were similarly appalled by the financial misbehaviour of banking elites.

Before committing to collective financial assistance aspects of European banking union, German negotiators sought clear, unambiguous evidence that banking elites were willing to comply with reformed supervisory and regulatory arrangements. In backing the ESM and the OMT programme, they sought similar evidence that Member States' elites were committed and able to embrace radical domestic reforms to boost competitiveness, reduce public debt, and recapitalize banks. New control, intervention, and sanction instruments were to be firmly anchored in EU law, including contractual arrangements to boost compliance with structural reforms. German negotiators stressed that 'putting their own houses in order' would be a long and painful process for debtor states. The search for short cuts and magic bullets would only delay or derail this adjustment. The onus was on debtor states to demonstrate European solidarity through their sustained efforts to comply with tough external conditionality. Conditionality was to be reinforced by an active role for the IMF, alongside the ECB and the European Commission. For this reason, proposals for Eurobonds and for collective debt redemption were firmly rejected. The emphasis was on convergence through domestic discipline.

Disagreement centred on whether reforms to European economic governance should lead to a 'transfer union'. This term took on a negative connotation in creditor states. Their elites and publics viewed collective financial assistance, mutual liability for domestically generated public debts, and a lender-of-last-resort role with respect to Member-State governments as incentives to evade fiscal discipline. Creditor states also feared that a 'transfer union' would provoke a populist politics of resentment towards the EU on the part of their taxpayers, a phenomenon apparent in Finland and the Netherlands. In contrast, debtor-state elites and publics were receptive to the notion of a transfer union. They saw it as reflecting the contribution of reckless private creditors to their banking and public debt problems. Debtor states also stressed the risk of political alienation from a euro area that failed to show solidarity in sharing the burden of adjustment. They feared a legitimacy crisis as populist, euro-sceptic political parties exploited sentiments of humiliation by creating external negative stereotypes. This disagreement was managed by trying to ensure that policy measures were consistent with keeping the term 'transfer union' off the political agenda.

Secondly, the strategy of buying time and reform by stealth reflected the unwillingness, notably in Germany, to deepen the divide between euro area 'ins' and 'outs'. Developing the single European market and continuing structural reforms on an EU-wide basis had been seen as essential German interests. A key ally was the European Commission, within which leading officials stressed its role as guardian of the single market, where its authority was strongest. Proposals to strengthen European economic governance by intergovernmental treaty amongst the euro area Member States—outside EU treaty law—threatened to undermine the position of the European Commission. For this reason the European Commission was concerned about the Euro Plus Pact. This Franco-German initiative sought to strengthen the role of the European Council in agreeing and monitoring structural reforms to promote convergence and competitiveness. The European Commission feared that the Euro Plus Pact would tip the balance away from the Community method to the intergovernmental method.

German officials were sensitive to the risk that strengthening banking, fiscal, and economic-policy union, in parallel with monetary union, would create a serious dilemma for the British government. On the one hand, the British government saw European banking and fiscal union as part of the economic logic of monetary union. It was also recognized in London that banking and fiscal union was the precondition for ensuring that a euro crisis did not spill-over into severe damage to the British economy. On the other hand, European banking and fiscal union opened up fundamental and domestically difficult debates about Britain's future place in Europe. It strengthened domestic demands for treaty renegotiation and for a subsequent referendum that could lead to EU exit. The risks became manifest with British isolation at the December 2011 European Council meeting. Its government forced the other Member States to use intergovernmental treaty when it became clear that they would not accept British conditions for safeguarding the interests of the City of London as the price for accepting EU treaty change.

Thirdly, the strategic choice to buy time and reform by stealth reflected the strength of disagreements about what reforms to European economic governance meant for 'who has power over policies'. There was a protracted contest about institutional beneficiaries and losers. The leading supra-national institutions—the European Commission, the European Parliament, and the ECB—favoured strengthening the Community method. They wanted Community-level fiscal 'shock absorbers', an independent European banking resolution authority, and a shared bank deposit protection scheme. The ECB was in many ways the model. It had taken financial markets by surprise with its generous, unlimited liquidity to euro area banks, Draghi's commitment to do 'whatever it takes' to save the euro, and the OMT programme.

However, crisis management had been mainly in the hands of the European Council, which represented the slow-moving intergovernmental method in economic and fiscal policies. In 2008–2009 it proved reluctant to embrace coordinated fiscal stimulus or to consider a common bank rescue facility. The European Council hesitated from December 2009 till May 2010, following a key German *Land* election, before it agreed a rescue package for Greece and a collective financial assistance mechanism. It reacted late and defensively to crises in Ireland and in Portugal. Crisis meetings of the European Council, and in the new formation of the heads of state and government of the euro area, increased in frequency. However, their declarations and resolutions failed repeatedly to calm the financial markets for other than very brief periods.

Above all, there was an 'inter-temporal' consistency problem. The time frames of financial markets and of intergovernmental decision-making were radically different. Members of the European Council were repeatedly looking over their shoulders to domestic electoral calendars. Chancellor Merkel wished to wait till after the North-Rhine Westphalia *Land* election in May 2010 before finalizing the euro area crisis response. In 2013 she sought to defer decisions on a European bank resolution authority or a shared bank deposit protection scheme till after the September federal elections.

By late 2011 it was clear that the intergovernmental method was wholly unsuited to the existential requirement for the euro area to have an actor with the authority and the capability to do all necessary in a supreme emergency (Dyson 2013). The deadlocks and hesitations in the European Council were a central part of the credibility problem of the euro area. Market investors lacked confidence that the euro area could ensure that the sovereign debt commitments of its Member States would be honoured. The absence of the decisive 'lender of last resort' in fiscal policy meant that euro area Member States had to pay elevated risk premiums in sovereign bond markets. They were forced by the markets into disproportionately harsh fiscal retrenchment and deflationary spirals at great human cost. The lack of a supra-national authority with executive discretion to act in supreme emergency also showed that the euro area had—through monetary union—only imperfectly escaped from the 'old' Europe of Montagu Norman. The strategy of buying time and reform by stealth reflected the tenacity of the intergovernmental method. Creditor states were reluctant to give supra-national bodies the executive discretion to act boldly and decisively.

The Exercise of Creditor-State Power in a Shrinking Hard Core: Retaining Control, Averting Isolation

The mounting financial and economic crisis from 2007 exposed the underlying power realities at the heart of the EU and the euro area. It became more difficult to conceal German hegemonic power in the governance of crisis management. This transparency of power opened up the German chancellor to negative and uncomfortable political stereotyping as 'imposing' harsh austerity on other Member States. At the same time, the evolving crisis revealed the limits of German power in safeguarding its interests as a creditor state. Germany had high stakes in EU and euro area negotiation processes, and her negotiators were caught up in their momentum. The problem was to balance retaining control with averting isolation.

By 2012 a divide had emerged within the euro area. There was a shrinking 'hard' core of triple-A-rated Member States, a growing 'soft' core, and a distressed periphery whose sovereign bonds were relegated to, or threatened with, 'junk' status. Moreover, leading states in the 'soft' core—led by Italy and Spain—were at risk of becoming distressed sovereign debtors. The traditional 'motors' of European unification, France and Germany, had shared the coveted triple-A rating from the start of the Maastricht Treaty negotiations, through the launch and first decade of the euro. However, in 2012 France lost this rating. It was relegated to the 'soft' core. By 2013 its sovereign creditworthiness was looking even more fragile. The euro area 'hard' core was reduced to Finland, Germany, Luxembourg, and the Netherlands.

In consequence, as the crisis intensified, German negotiators experienced growing European and international isolation. The 'hard' core was diminishing. Exposure to European and international pressure to cross its 'red lines' was politically unwelcome within Germany. On the one hand, firmly resisting this pressure was seen as a necessary price if Germany was to retain its role as stability anchor for the euro area. Germany's own sovereign creditworthiness was seen as a primordial interest of both Germany and the euro area. On the other hand, German elites and publics were sensitive to the risks of negative historical stereotyping of Germany, the poisoning of external relations, and loss of political legitimacy for the euro and the wider EU. Populist forces could mobilize the emotions aroused by the sense of humiliation and resentment within Member States suffering austerity programmes and direct them against German hegemony. The Greek elections of 2012 and the Italian election of February 2013 testified to this danger. French President François Hollande was offered the opportunity to capitalize on spreading resentment and to translate it into demands for a new model of growth within the EU.

The challenge for German statecraft was how to avert isolation and to soften the face of creditor-state power, whilst ensuring its 'red lines' were not crossed. The sheer pressure of events forced Germany to play an increasingly assertive role in crisis management as the centre of the embattled 'hard' core. Its self-assigned role as 'stability anchor', as the ultimate guarantor of the creditworthiness of the euro area, required German negotiating success in exporting fiscal discipline through the 'debt brake' and policies to promote competiveness to the EU and euro area level. The German leadership role in reforming European crisis management and prevention mechanisms took the forms of framer of ideas, agenda-setter, and veto player.

The German chancellor gained negotiating advantage by combining a disciplinarian narrative of creditor-state power with a strategy of 'tied hands'. The disciplinarian narrative rested on the dependence of euro area credibility on Germany's long-term creditworthiness and its role as the guarantor of stability-oriented policies. Germany's assertive exercise of creditor-state power was conditioned by, and framed around, three powerful domestic institutions. The Bundesbank continued to enjoy intellectual power and institutional prestige, based on its post-war record as 'stability guardian' and on its role as the architect of the 'stand-alone' model of European monetary union. It acted as the central linkage point within the German Ordo-liberal economics establishment, as the protector of market-based, 'stability-oriented' economic principles. This role gave to the voice of the Bundesbank a highly didactic character in EMU negotiations. Bundesbank support was seen as essential for the ECB's credibility. Consequently, German negotiators sought to resolutely defend the economic 'stability-oriented' principles enshrined in the Maastricht 'monetary' constitution.

The Federal Constitutional Court had delivered successive major rulings on European economic governance. They included the Maastricht Treaty ruling in October 1993, the Lisbon Treaty ruling in September 2009, and the ruling on the ESM treaty and the fiscal compact treaty in September 2012. The Lisbon Treaty ruling in particular provided a restrictive interpretation of the German government's room for manoeuvre. Fiscal sovereignty was not to be relinquished without treaty-based political union, based on democratic principles. The Court also ruled that there was to be no increase in German liabilities within the ESM without express agreement of the Bundestag. It carved out a role as the safeguard of the democratic legitimacy of reforms to European economic governance. The Court's rulings stressed the restricted legal basis for reforms and served as powerful inducements for the federal government to emphasize treaty-based changes, for instance to create the ESM.

The Bundestag was the key beneficiary from these rulings. It gained a central role in decision-making about German engagement in 'bail-outs', limiting the flexibility in use of the EFSF and the ESM. The Court's rulings empowered the Bundestag to exercise detailed scrutiny and monitoring of German negotiating positions. In EMU negotiations the federal government could stress the Bundestag's veto power over infringements of fiscal sovereignty.

These three domestic institutional constraints served as a source of external negotiating strength. German negotiators could claim that their hands were tied, notably in assuming greater liabilities. They could variously highlight their narrow room for manoeuvre consequent on Federal Constitutional Court rulings, political problems with the Bundestag, and intellectual opposition from the Bundesbank. In this way German negotiators could fend off strong international pressures, principally from the United States and Britain, for Germany to finance a 'big bazooka' and assume collective responsibility for euro area sovereign debts. They pointed to the constitutional issues raised by proposals for Eurobonds and for bolstering the size and the discretion of the ESM.

Narrow domestic constraints induced the federal government to adopt clear and tough 'red lines' in negotiations and to ensure that German documents on this basis were tabled early. The economics' establishment, political elites within the coalition government, and public opinion were hostile to German financing of a 'transfer union'. It was seen as rewarding reckless, improvident debtor states, at heavy cost to German taxpayers. The experience of the enduring high costs of German unification helped shape public and political attitudes. Opposition to the shift of financial risks to German taxpayers formed the context to German government rejection of Eurobonds. Germany would pay higher debt servicing costs. It also influenced attitudes to sovereign bond purchases by the ECB. They were seen as transferring risk to Germany through the balance sheet of the Eurosystem. Instead, the German federal finance ministry pushed for the suspension of sovereign voting rights when debtor states seriously violated the principles of EMU. It proposed a 'super-Commissioner' with the right to veto draft national budgets.

At the same time, German negotiators were concerned that this domestic 'tying of hands' risked excessively narrowing their freedom of manoeuvre, especially in managing a severe crisis in the euro area. By 2012 there was some sense of a wider freedom of manoeuvre. The Federal Constitutional Court ruling on the ESM treaty and on the fiscal compact treaty recognized the prior role of the ECJ in interpreting the European treaties. In addition, the Bundesbank had begun to move beyond the 'stand-alone' model of

European monetary union. It was central in putting stability-oriented fiscal union at the centre of German negotiating strategy. However, the concept of fiscal union rested on the Ordo-liberal principle that increased joint liability must be matched by tighter and tougher European-level control.

Despite these formidable sources of negotiating power, German leadership was complicated by anxiety about being in a shrinking 'hard' core, concerns about becoming the lonely creditor-state power, and fear of provoking negative historical stereotyping of Germany. The empirical reality that the number of euro area debtor states increasingly exceeded creditor states promoted the sense of a lonely, potentially exposed leadership position. German negotiators were conscious of the potentially high political and economic costs in over-assertively pursuing creditor-state interests. Blame of Germany for imposing deflationary policies, job losses, cuts in real income, and growing economic and social insecurity took on a poisonous character when linked with historical images of wartime Germany, notably in Greece. Germany faced the political threat of deterioration in her relationships within the euro area and the wider EU. German negotiators feared that their motives were being misunderstood. They worried that Germany might serve as the scapegoat in the spread of national political populism and extremism, which would distract attention from the culpability of domestic elites. The outcome could undermine democratic support for European integration. Germany had in the past prized her association—through the European integration process—with democratization, especially in Greece, Spain, and Portugal. The risk that Germany could become the target for popular anger and frustration across southern Europe seemed heightened by the electoral campaigns of Syriza in Greece in 2012, the 55 percentage of the vote attracted by Berlusconi and by the Five Star Movement in the Italian election of February 2013, and the *indignado* movement in Spain.

German negotiators sought to reduce their isolation in a shrinking 'hard' core by pursuing coordinated action in three forms: the traditional reliance on the Franco-German relationship as the 'motor' of reforms; the informal creditor-state club; and working closely with the ECB. The rationale for reliance on the Franco-German relationship came from several sources. It had a uniquely treaty-based, institutionalized, and regularized form, going back to the Elysée Treaty of 1963. Since 1987 meetings of the Franco-German Economic and Financial Council had been paralleled by informal meetings both for crisis management and for preparing Franco-German initiatives in EMU. In addition, the Franco-German relationship was clothed in the historical symbolism of reconciliation between the two states at the heart of successive ruinous wars in Europe. More specifically with reference to EMU, it had justification in the material reality that France and Germany accounted for nearly 50 per cent of euro area GDP. Together, they provided 47.5 per cent of the subscribed capital of the EMS. They could also claim to internalize and represent the larger creditor-debtor state divide.

The strange combination of mutual need and mutual distrust and suspicion within the Franco-German special relationship had its source in its value as a cloak over French weakness and over German power. It disguised a power asymmetry. French presidents could claim to be at the highest table, enjoying equal status and influence. German chancellors were offered the opportunity to exercise power through France.

By 2011 the term 'Merkozy' was being used to characterize the nature of European Council crisis management. Chancellor Merkel and President Nicolas Sarkozy sought to closely integrate French and German positions, similar to the processes used during the ERM crises of the 1980s and 1990s and during the negotiation of EMU in 1989–1991 (Dyson and Featherstone 1999). An additional stimulus was the more overt distancing of the post-2010 British coalition government under David Cameron from euro area crisis management. This British disengagement helped change the position of the German government, above all on supervision and regulation of financial markets. The French and German governments found common ground against the British government over a financial transaction tax and over strict limits on bankers' bonuses.

However, French concessions were more evident than German. An early instance was the Franco-German Declaration at Deauville in October 2010. Sarkozy accepted strengthened sanction mechanisms in both the preventive and the corrective arms of the SGP. Merkel insisted on treaty change as the basis for the future permanent collective financial assistance mechanism (later ESM). She also gained French acceptance that there should be provision for private-creditor participation and for suspension of voting rights in Council when a Member State had seriously violated the principles of EMU. Similarly, the Franco-German Communiqué on the euro area of August 2011 involved French acceptance of a fiscal compact treaty, with its German-style 'debt brake'. It was the price for German ratification of the ESM treaty.

The asymmetry of power was difficult to disguise. Key German 'red lines' remained firm and intact, despite French pressure. There was to be no bank licence for the ESM so that it could leverage its lending capacity through the ECB. The ESM was to be strictly intergovernmental in design, with German veto on increase in its capital and on use of instruments. Eurobonds were off the agenda, at least till full fiscal and political union. German veto power was all too evident.

President Sarkozy was to some extent able to exploit German fear of isolation. He positioned himself as balancing creditor-state and debtor-state interests by pushing the agenda of collective financial assistance, especially a lender-of-last-resort role for the ECB. However, Sarkozy's seemingly greater domestic freedom of manoeuvre than that of Merkel proved illusory. His main domestic constraint was opposition within his neo-Gaullist party to loss of fiscal sovereignty. Leading party figures feared that too close identification with the German narrative of the crisis would create vulnerability on the Right to electoral threat from the anti-euro National Front. Accordingly, Sarkozy distanced himself from the German idea of 'fiscal union'. However, adverse public reaction to the austerity policies of Germany, symbolized by Sarkozy's agreement to write the 'debt brake' into French law, made 'Merkozy' an electoral liability in the presidential elections of May 2012.

French agenda-setting power remained severely inhibited both by German veto power and by the financial markets. By 2011 French leaders began to fear loss of her triple-A credit rating, without which French relative power would be further diminished. The French government supported the principle of strengthening collective financial assistance. However, it was constrained in pushing this agenda by the risk to its own sovereign creditworthiness from assuming additional liabilities through strengthening guarantees to the EFSF or bolstering the capital of the ESM. French frustrations at their relative weakness focused on the credit rating agencies, the sovereign bond markets, and the ECB for reluctance to assume a fiscal lender-of-last-resort role.

After May 2012 the new Socialist government under President François Hollande adopted a much more openly critical position vis-à-vis Germany. Hollande was more open than Sarkozy had been to the concept of fiscal union. However, he was opposed to the idea of a fiscal union founded on the 'debt brake' as too narrow and restrictive. Fiscal union required an agenda that would promote economic growth and employment. Hollande sought to balance Germany by looking to Italy and Spain as allies in advocating a strategy of coordinated economic expansion to help tackle Europe's debt problems. His first European Council meeting in June 2012 was preceded by a summit in Rome, involving Hollande, Merkel, Italian Prime Minister Mario Monti, and Spanish Prime Minister Mariano Rajoy. This development helped push the German federal government to agree a joint paper with the Bundestag parliamentary parties on a Pact for Sustainable Growth and Employment. This paper endorsed an increase in the capital of the European Investment Bank and new EU 'project loans', both designed to boost infrastructure expenditure. Hollande sought to reframe debate by widening pre-European Council agreements beyond Germany. The key outcome was agreement that the ESM could be used for direct bank recapitalization. However, the German government insisted once again on tough conditions in the form of commitment to a banking union. Like Sarkozy, Hollande sought to play a balancing role within the euro area. He did so on terms that more explicitly isolated Germany.

The second mechanism through which German negotiators sought to reduce their isolation was the mobilization of an informal creditor-state club. Germany's leading role in organizing creditor-state coordination went back to the EPU in the 1950s and derived from the high incentive of numeric disadvantage vis-à-vis debtor states. The informal creditor-state club was defined by triple-A-rated Member States. Initially activated by the Greek sovereign debt crisis, this group contained Austria, Finland, France, Luxembourg, and the Netherlands, as well as Germany. It accounted for 60.8 per cent of euro area GDP and 58 per cent of the subscribed capital of the ESM. However, by 2013 Austria and France had lost their triple-A rating. The informal creditor-state club was reduced from six to four Member States. It accounted for only 36.4 per cent of euro area GDP and 35 per cent of the subscribed capital of the ESM. Consequently, the political cover that coordinating an informal creditor-state club provided for German negotiators was reduced.

In the search to strengthen their influence, creditor states sought to ensure retention of the presidency of the Euro Group, which in 2013 passed from Luxembourg to the Netherlands. They were also flexible, as for instance in the so-called 'Frankfurt Group' that convened in October 2011. This group of seven was not exclusively official creditors. It included the European Commissioner for Economic and Financial Affairs, the president of the European Commission, and the president of the European Council. Each had a wider mediating role. However, there was no member who could be said to directly represent the interests of debtor states, other than the French president. The managing director of the IMF, the president of the ECB, and the German chancellor represented official creditor positions. The 'Frankfurt Group' brought together the 'troika' of ECB, European Commission, and IMF, which was involved in detailed surveillance and monitoring of the bail-outs to Greece, Ireland, and Portugal.

The third mechanism through which German negotiators sought to avert isolation was by working closely with the ECB. By 2011–2012, the ECB was pushing strongly for banking, fiscal, and political union in the euro area. Similarly, the German chancellor had recognized that the traditional 'stand-alone' model of monetary union had lost credibility. The ECB understood that a clear road map and timetable for 'complete' EMU depended on German political support and that this support was highly problematic, especially given opposition within and from the Bundesbank. Hence the opportunity emerged for German-ECB partnership in agreeing a path to 'complete' EMU that would write creditor-state principles into banking and fiscal union. The ECB had emerged as the major player in euro area crisis management. As the most powerful credit institution, it was a natural partner for the German government. However, this partnership provoked intra-German tensions, above all with the Bundesbank, where opposition was strongest to any abridgement of the principle of the separation of fiscal and monetary policies.

The Boundaries of Creditor-State Power

Ambitious proposals for urgent reforms to EU and euro area crisis prevention and crisis management capacity were frustrated by the way in which the evolving post-2007 crisis simultaneously increased power asymmetries in Germany's favour and tightened domestic constraints on German leadership. This frustration was evident with respect to German prevarication on a European bank resolution capacity, common deposit guarantees, Eurobonds, and a fiscal lender of last resort to Member States. German political strategy focused on buying time and integrating, where possible, by stealth.

The political strategy of buying time was justified by the German Ordo-liberal emphasis on a principle-based approach. It was fixated on the risk that short-term expediency in crisis management would compromise the construction of European crisis prevention and management capacity on the basis of their long-term quality, consistency, and credibility with respect to stability-oriented economic principles. German negotiators retained the negotiating advantage that the solidarity amongst the fewer creditor states was greater than that between debtor states. Debtor states were more disposed to differentiate themselves from each other. Their governing elites sought to avoid association with the worst 'sinners' and to identify themselves with virtuous insiders. Creditor states defined norms of appropriate behaviour, departure from which involved loss of reputation and status, higher borrowing costs, and heightened risk of unsustainable debt.

To counter the risks from short-term expediency in crisis management, German negotiators erected 'red lines'. These 'red lines' were drawn in the protracted negotiations between December 2009 and May 2010 that led to financial assistance to Greece and the creation of the EFSF. The EFSF had to be temporary in order to comply with the Treaty and its economic principles. Its interventions had to be 'last-resort' and designed to buy time for painful domestic structural adjustments and fiscal consolidation. EFSF conditionality had to be much tougher than pre-existing EU procedures. Its lending terms were to be based on existing market interest rates rather than subsidized. Hence German negotiators insisted that financing, monitoring, and surveillance were to involve the IMF and the ECB as well as the European Commission. The EFSF was to have preferred creditor status. The aim was to limit German liability in the face of the shocking evidence that Greece had misled its partners about its fiscal position and evaded compliance with EU fiscal rules. In the German view, crisis management was a long-term process. It had to combine harsh structural adjustments to establish competitiveness and to reduce debts with tough new fiscal rules at the EU level with quasi-automatic sanctions. Any liability had to be matched by adequate and proportionate control.

However, as the crisis evolved, original German 'red lines' were crossed, and sub-optimal outcomes accepted. German negotiators revised their positions as they drew lessons from experience with crisis management. They learnt from the Greek crisis management between December 2009 and May 2010 how hesitation increased the cost of calming financial markets. The endogenous learning process was most evident in the eclipse of the 'stand-alone' model of monetary union in 2011–2012. By autumn 2012 key German negotiators, including Chancellor Merkel, had discovered that they had an interest in eliminating investor fears of redenomination risk. They saw the ECB as central to this task.

Secondly, German negotiators were caught up in the distinctive incentive structures and the momentum of EU negotiating processes. Initially EMU and then the post-2007 crisis intensified the negotiating pressures under which German negotiators worked. One element was the negotiating logic of package deals. States outside the informal creditor-state club could seek out issue-linkages and side-payments. For instance, French President Hollande mobilized the Italian and Spanish governments to pursue a new European growth programme at the June 2012 European Council. Another element was the way in which previous moves in response to urgent crises constrained later German negotiating discretion. Chancellor Merkel was confronted by mounting domestic resistance after she agreed to the EFSF in May 2010. At the same time, she was under increasing international pressure to hugely increase its resource and instruments and those of the ESM to create a so-called 'big bazooka'.

From German perspectives, the outcomes were sub-optimal. Many in the Bundesbank and the stricter Ordo-liberal economists viewed the concessions as excessive. German concessions were typically made when domestic elections did not pose a threat, for instance after the North-Rhine Westphalia election in May 2010. From May 2010 the ECB began to purchase sovereign bonds in the secondary market, ostensibly to smooth the transmission of its monetary policy. In October 2011 it decided to buy Italian and Spanish bonds. The two Germans on the ECB Governing Council—Axel Weber, president of the Bundesbank, and later Jürgen Stark, ECB chief economist—opposed this policy change on the basis that it crossed the boundary into fiscal policy. They argued that it compromised the independence of the ECB, at cost to its long-term credibility in anchoring expectations of stable inflation. It would also create disincentives for Member States with excessive debts to make the necessary structural adjustments. Both were to resign.

A third motive for crossing red lines was German fears that the sheer scale and opacity of financial market integration in the euro area and the wider EU created high risks of contagion from the euro-area periphery. The risks centred not just on the German banking system and public finances but also on other members of the informal creditor-state club. The most likely transmission mechanism was through creditor-state banks' holdings of peripheral-state sovereign debt. Germany's sovereign credit rating risked downgrading if these German bank holdings were seen in the markets as inducing the German federal government to protect its banks by taking on increasing liabilities through a progressively enlarged ESM. Additionally, German policy makers feared that ECB sovereign bond purchases could negatively affect the balance sheet of the Eurosystem, both in size and in quality. Indirectly, and principally through changed perceptions of risk, German sovereign creditworthiness could be placed in question.

Hence creditor-debtor state diplomacy within the EU and euro area had its own dynamics, which constrained creditor-state power. There was an awkward imbalance between German cognitive and agenda-setting power and the power of numbers. Germany found itself one of a declining few creditor states in an EU and euro area with many more debtor states. Side-payments and issue-linkages were unavoidable and meant accepting various sub-optimal outcomes. In the final stages of negotiating the Maastricht Treaty in 1991, concessions had been made on creating a cohesion fund to satisfy periphery states like Greece, Ireland, and Spain. The SGP of 1997 had more scope for exceptions and discretion and less automaticity than German negotiators had wanted. ECOFIN retained discretion over the EDP, creating a process of fiscal policy surveillance in which 'sinners voted on sinners'. Hence enforcement and compliance proved weak. The management of the post-2007 crisis led to a blurring of the boundaries between monetary and fiscal policies, in part through the indirect effects of ECB liquidity provision to the banks, and in part due to ECB sovereign bond purchases in secondary markets.

In addition, German creditor power was not a given. It had its own dynamics, suffering decline and loss of confidence in the period 2001–2004. German governments confronted the burdensome fiscal legacy of German unification, the associated loss of competitiveness, protracted economic stagnation, and budget deficits rising over the 3 per cent limit. The architect of the SGP was in breach of the rules. In the same period other EU states emerged with the self-confidence of illusory creditors, led by Britain, Ireland, and Spain, each powered by domestic asset-price booms that helped drive consumer-based growth. They enjoyed historically low interest rates (in the cases of Ireland and Spain consequent on euro area membership), increased capital inflows, high growth, and fiscal good times. This combination of weakening German creditor power with illusory creditor states altered the political economy within which the SGP functioned. The renegotiated SGP of 2005 represented a laxer fiscal framework, providing even more exceptions and discretion to states. This weakening of the SGP, along with its narrow focus on nominal fiscal criteria, contributed to the limited fiscal room for manoeuvre in most euro area states in the face of the post-2007 crisis. In contrast, Germany's return to large trade surpluses, economic growth, and a sound fiscal position after 2004 encouraged the government to call for a new, much tougher SGP. By 2012 its own new constitutional 'debt brake' was being anchored in treaty form for EMU.

Ultimately, however, the strong structural basis for the tendency of creditor and debtor states to hold different policy preferences does not translate into each having and pursuing unitary interests. German policy makers face difficult and contentious trade-offs that they strike differently according to institutional location and political identification. Ordo-liberals, notably in the Bundesbank, focus on limiting liability in order to secure German creditworthiness and economic stability. This position is defended in more flexible political terms within the federal finance ministry.

In contrast, the German foreign ministry is more inclined to prioritize support for a European integration process, in which Germany is seen as engaged from profound strategic interest, as well as from a sense of historic and moral responsibility to secure peace in Europe. Strategic interests are defined in terms of the painful historical lessons learnt about the value of German 'calculability' and 'reliability', stemming from her exposed position at the centre of Europe with multiple borders. They are also bound up with German trade dependence on the euro area and the wider EU, including reliance on extensive cross-national supply chains. This sense of strategic interest is reinforced by sensitivity to the risks to Germany from contagious banking and sovereign debt crises and from economic downturn in Europe. The sense of historic and moral responsibility after decades of catastrophic war had been captured in Chancellor Kohl's justification for EMU in 1991 as 'making European union irreversible' (Dyson and Featherstone 1999). The sense of what was at stake for Germany was summed up by Chancellor Merkel to the German Bundestag on 26 October 2011: 'If the euro fails, Europe fails.' This message had powerful political resonance in Germany. It served to constrain the naked exercise of creditor-state power. The German chancellor had the difficult task of balancing these different assessments of Germany's complex interests when making crisis management package deals in the EU and the euro area.

Similarly, debtor states contain powerful interests committed to modernization and conformity to European and international norms of appropriate behaviour. These interests readily embrace technocratic European and international intervention as correctives to irresponsible conduct by the political class, especially when it is discredited by cronyism, corruption, and scandal. They look to apolitical mechanisms for addressing critical long-term threats to sovereign creditworthiness: independent central banks, constitutionally anchored fiscal rules, independent fiscal councils, even interim technocratic governments. National central banks of debtor states tend to adopt a critical distance from their domestic political elites, a process accentuated with the creation of the Eurosystem.

The constraints on both creditor and debtor states were highlighted by their increasingly high and shared stakes in the wake of the creation of European monetary union in 1999 and, above all, of the sheer magnitude and momentum of the post-2007 crisis. By eliminating exchange-rate transaction costs, the euro area acted as a catalyst for rapid financial market integration. In consequence, the banking and financial systems of Member States became much more closely integrated and exposed to each other's debt problems. Financial market integration meant increasing vulnerability to contagious banking and sovereign debt crises. By June 2011 the German banks held €28 billion of Greek debt and €118 billion of Italian debt. Risk mitigation led a reverse shift towards financial fragmentation, as banks retreated into their home markets. The consequence was further reduction of liquidity and higher borrowing costs in the euro-area periphery. The ECB identified a new risk to the single monetary policy, above all its efficient transmission, and played a more central role in getting creditor as well as debtor states to address this risk.

The Achilles Heel of European Integration: From Regulatory Union to Macroeconomic Union?

> We all know what to do, we just don't know how to get re-elected after we've done it.
>
> Attributed to Jean-Claude Juncker, Luxembourg prime minister and president of the Euro Group

The shock of the post-2007 financial and economic crisis, and the permanent state of emergency in which the euro area operated from 2009, exposed the Achilles heel of post-war European integration. European monetary union lacked an adequately formalized, balanced, and supportive structure of creditor-debtor state relations. Both governance structures and crisis prevention and crisis management policy instruments were inadequate for this purpose. The euro area possessed neither the governance structures nor the policies that credibly embodied criteria of impartiality, fairness, and effectiveness in managing the costs of adjustment. It required a combination of euro area fiscal transfer arrangements; encouragement of sustained public investment; tough fiscal discipline; country-specific contractual arrangements for structural reforms in both creditor and debtor states; and independent supra-national institutions with the discretionary authority to act in a speedy, decisive, and bold manner in banking and sovereign debt crises, with generous credit lines at their disposal.

Monetary union could not survive in the context of a regulatory union. It required the EU to become a macroeconomic union. Flanking fiscal rules were not enough. European macroeconomic union needed to be founded on a new, inclusive model of economic growth. This model would focus on shifting priority to productivity-enhancing infrastructure and social investment. It would combine implementation of structural and fiscal reforms, for instance to labour markets, with active measures to compensate losers through fiscal transfers and to prioritize investments. In the absence of this type of growth model, the euro area faced a serious and potentially widening legitimacy gap with dangerous social, economic, and political consequences.

However, becoming a macroeconomic union required voter consent. Voter consent was made problematic by the perceived weaknesses in performance of the former model of economic growth, on which European integration had rested. Falling living standards, rising unemployment, and mounting social deprivation and poverty were acutely threatening to a European polity that had rested its claims on output rather than input legitimacy. Moreover, in the discursive and structural context of a crisis that was attributed to debt, it proved problematic to build consensus and re-launch European integration around a new model of economic growth that entertained a notion of 'good' debt. Fear, anger, and resentment provided fertile ground for populist mobilization of distrust against Member-State governing elites, the EU, and creditor states, above all Germany (European Social Survey 2013). Domestic governing elites became targets not just when—as in Greece, Ireland, Italy, and Spain—they were perceived as self-serving and corrupt. The dismal performance of Mario Monti's party in the Italian elections of February 2013 showed that it was enough that they were seen as out of touch with people's concerns about economic security.

Seen in a long-term historical perspective, the euro area reflected general characteristics of the relationship between states, debt, and power. From the outset it had been beset by illusion, hubris, and complacency and by the mismatch of liability and control. The euro area's banking and sovereign debt crises revealed the illusion that was at the heart of the 'stand-alone' model of monetary union. However, it took some four years of crisis management before there was clear political recognition that European monetary union could not survive without major steps towards banking, fiscal, and political union. The post-2007 crisis also showed the naïvety in believing that Member States could be relied on to comply with fiscal rules or that the Council could be expected to act against fiscal 'sinners'. Domestic elites and publics were not always prepared to tolerate the sacrifices required. By 2013 the hubris of governing elites was exposed. They had been shown to be wrong in their tacit assumption that Member-State governments and their voters would make the sacrifices required for a 'stand-alone' model of monetary union. Moreover, as this assumption was undermined, it was evident that voters were unlikely to be willing to back new treaty moves to a European 'transfer' union unless a clear, persuasive narrative of mutual gains from 'good' debt could be crafted.

The only escape route out of this 'austerity-democratic deficit' trap was to restore popular faith in European integration by a new model of sustainable economic growth that could deliver practical benefits to voters. However, more than 'output' legitimacy was required. Macroeconomic union had to be designed on principles of accountability, transparency, inclusivity, and fairness. It had to inhabit a European public space where the public could engage in debates, see how these debates connected to policies, and establish that burden-sharing was fair.

The euro area's crises of sovereign creditworthiness became poisonous in the absence of collective agreement on a new model of growth that could transcend the divide between creditor- and debtor-state diagnoses and preferences. The model of consumer-led growth, powered by rising asset price values, oversize banking sectors, and cheap, plentiful credit, had lost credibility. Furthermore, by 2013 it was clear that there were sharp limits to voter tolerance for macroeconomic policies that offered no clear and early exit from deflation and stagnation. The financial and economic crisis had mutated into a serious political crisis for key Member States, including France and Spain but above all Greece, and for the euro area as a whole (European Social Survey 2013).

The underlying problem in gaining agreement on a new model of economic growth was the lack of a lender of last resort to Member-State governments. The euro area did not possess the supra-national discretionary capacity to act boldly and decisively in supreme emergency (Dyson 2013). This institutional capacity would reduce the elevated bond spreads that sparked the drive to harsh fiscal contraction and deflation. It would provide time to adjust through structural reforms without the massive economic losses, social shock, and political pain endured by Cypriots, Greeks, Irish, Portuguese, and Spaniards. Within this macroeconomic shelter, Member States would be enabled to construct a new model of growth around anti-cyclical adjustment and strengthening public and private sector assets through productivity-enhancing investment. Retrieving state power rests on regaining capacity to provide higher public investment in infrastructure; to incentivize private sector investment; to detoxify bank assets and recapitalize and restructure banks; and to make fiscal retrenchment and sovereign debt reduction contingent on economic growth. The rescue of Member States in the euro area—and its own legitimacy—depends on putting in place the central pillar of macroeconomic union, a lender of last resort.

A sustainable euro area needs the indispensable foundation of shared identity, of belonging together. Nurturing and retaining mutual trust places bounds on asymmetric adjustment to crises. It circumscribes the application of the moral hazard principle, which—dogmatically applied—risks creating a vicious circle of resentment within creditor states and humiliation, victim mentality, and anger in debtor states. Mutual concessions are required in creating European banking and fiscal union. Creditor states will only be satisfied with a conception of European fiscal union that gives priority to institutionalized fiscal discipline at both EU and domestic levels through treaty and constitutional reforms. In their view, trust has to be earned through domestic commitment to, and compliance with, policies that promote stability and competitiveness. At the same time, the concept of fiscal union has to offer shelter, within which distressed debtor states can pursue politically difficult structural reforms and fiscal consolidation. They have to regain a capacity to compensate losers. Fiscal union requires an element of collective insurance against extreme events that might inflict excessive economic, social, and political pain on Member States and jeopardize the integrity and survival of the euro area.

Mutual trust is premised on recognizing that creditor and debtor states are caught up in distributional rather than merely regulative conflicts. Their conflicts are pre-programmed, ongoing, and indeterminate. A regulative approach has limitations. 'Firm' fiscal rules are built on slippery concepts like structural balance. They leave scope for interpretation, including evasion. Moreover, the application of 'universal', principle-based policies by creditor states risks showing intolerance for cultural and structural specificities. Creditor states are, in any case, rarely free from guilt and easily tainted by hypocrisy through association with reckless lending. Trust is hard to sustain in the absence of a symmetrical definition of 'good' and 'bad' creditor states, as well as 'good' and 'bad' debtor states. It requires a foundation of stability-oriented economic policies that promote reciprocal adjustment. Disciplining errant debtor states is not an adequate basis for building mutual trust. It requires the collective good of insurance for the euro area as a whole, including the supra-national capacity to act in supreme emergency.

Mutual trust is premised on a symmetrical definition of 'good' and 'bad' creditor states, as well as 'good' and 'bad' debtor states. It forms the basis for policies to promote reciprocal adjustment. Making the quantum leap to a 'new' Europe requires a process of trust-building. This quantum leap has to be undertaken in the less-than-promising context of multiple crises. Their management revealed a moral vacuum and opened a serious legitimacy gap. There was a failure to balance the stress on painful fiscal and structural reforms with demonstrable political will and institutional capacity to underwrite the coherence and integrity of the euro area, to admit a narrative of 'good' debt around productivity-enhancing investment, and to compensate often innocent losers. This failure bred mutual suspicion, misunderstandings, fear, resentment, humiliation, and anger. In the absence of a fiscal lender of last resort, regression to the 'old' Europe of coercive statecraft remained an existential threat.

Epilogue: History as Oracle

A Man says yes without knowing
How to decide even what the question is,
And is caught up, and then is carried along
And never again escapes from his own cocoon.
Pablo Neruda, 'Emerging', in Astley (2011: 417)

If, as Nietzsche suggested, history serves as an oracle, then it seems condemned to be a Cassandra. It offers warnings but seems doomed to be ignored. An historical perspective on the unfolding financial and economic crises in Europe, especially in the euro area, is no exception. History provides a sense of recurrent patterns and changes, so that patterns manifest themselves very differently over time. It also suggests lessons, many of which are unwelcome to governing elites, technical elites, and publics. It is a cautionary tale in the dangers to thinking about debt in terms of the ideal of Platonic ethics and the belief in universal and timeless rules. In the world of debt the prudential wisdom of Aristotelian ethics appears in short supply and imperfectly secured by democratic rule. In thinking about fiscal and other rules relevant to sustainable debt one needs to have a sense of their contingency on what occurred before. History offers our best intellectual protection against illusion, hubris, and complacency and against subconsciously absorbing certain habits of mind common to one's own time.

This Cassandra-like character of history is hardly surprising. It has a critical function in holding up conventional wisdom to inspection. History punctures the illusion, hubris, and complacency that bedevil problems of credit and debt, including in the design and operation of the euro area. It also highlights its corollary: the transience of creditor-state power. This book has shown how, in dealing with debt, governing elites have continued to live on the edge of failure, having far less control over events than they—and the economic theories and models to which they turn—suppose. The structures of power that they inhabit rest on fragile foundations, subject to external vulnerability, structural economic dependency, and internal dissent. Characteristically, they make too little good use of credit and lack sufficient prudence in managing debts. There is too little good debt and too much bad debt, albeit contingent on governance standards. Governing elites are far from alone in this respect. Their advisers, academically trained analysts, financial elites, and households are caught up in their own forms of illusion, hubris, and complacency. Saints are at a premium in the history of debt.

History's messages are unwelcome in various ways. It uncovers the routine practices of fiscal gimmickry and balance-sheet manipulation and the greed, deception, and naïvety that infect supposedly rule-based conduct in both states and markets. It shows how each and every economic culture and ideology of debt, including those associated with creditor states, has its own distinctive bias to illusion, hubris, and complacency. It reveals the slipperiness of seemingly precise, technical concepts like gross domestic product (GDP), structural fiscal balance, and risk-weighted capital adequacy of banks. They are open to interpretation and evasion. Debt itself emerges as a slippery concept with its contingent and implicit components, its secreting off-balance-sheet. Not least, history teaches that one needs time to change a country through structural reforms. The power of vested interests takes time to overcome, whilst in crisis situations both elites and publics need time to learn in the absence of a clear script. In terms of the politics of time, a policy of small steps has much to commend it. In these circumstances it is hardly surprising that the mismatch between liability and control emerges as an enduring theme. It suggests the limits of state power and of international and European surveillance and monitoring.

History also poses the question of how well financial and economic data represent a country. How well do they capture the resilience and adaptability of its polity and its social structures? As in much of southern Europe, family structure may display high absorptive capacity as a buffer against external shocks. As in parts of central and northern Europe, collective bargaining systems may prove highly adaptive to external imbalances in the absence of formal institutional reforms. Bottom-up change, often corporate-sector led, is a vital aspect of effective crisis management that is less readily captured by international and European institutions than formal top-down reform measures.

The discomfort that history provokes amongst elites and publics is bound up with its capacity to provide critique of established power structures and to uncover areas of silence. Thus it looks at the structures of interest that underpin the scientific garb of professional, often esoteric financial, economic, and legal knowledge. *Rentier* interests are protected by various forms of economic theory and modelling, as well as by contract theory in ways that support rising inequalities in wealth and income. Moreover, governing elites are not just users of economic theories and models as justification. They are also readily seduced, their thinking entrapped within the terms of these theories and models. History draws out the mismatch between the promise of free markets, opening up and spreading economic and social opportunities, and the grubby reality of 'crony' capitalism. The reality is one in which states and regulators succumb to intellectual capture by financial elites, and morally offensive inequalities of wealth and income grow. History shows how the ideal of the autonomous and impersonal state, acting to secure public interest, is besmirched by evidence of the sordid reality of clientelistic relationships and weak state capacity.

History also has the capacity to peer behind dominant historical memories to rescue from silence the role of Jewish financiers in central and northern Italy and later in the Holy Roman Empire and the Ottoman Empire. It shows how key financial institutions can be traced back to their impact as well as the deleterious consequences for Spain of the expulsion of the Jews. In addition, history helps rescue the role of cities and city states in late-medieval and early-modern Europe in pioneering public debt through annuity financing. In this way established narratives of the Anglo-American financial revolution can be contextualized.

Perhaps more importantly, history has the capacity to critique the way in which established structures of power lead governing elites to morally dubious policies of crisis management. Their effectiveness depends on the political silence of those disproportionately affected. Creditworthiness emerges as an inescapably moral question, in which what is seen as at stake is the representation of the character of the state, its virtues, and the extent to which it exercises sovereignty in a responsible manner. In seeking to retain or regain creditworthiness, governing elites face difficult moral trade-offs. They also face living with morally odious outcomes to the extent that the reckless and the feckless bear a lesser share of the burden of adjustment costs than the innocent. For governing elites creditworthiness is a complex exercise in risk management, within parameters that are not those that they might choose. Moreover, this risk management is not simply a matter of dealing with rational expectations. Panic and extreme volatility are latent in financial markets. Financial markets are driven by fear and greed. History enables us to look behind the rational expectations of economic modelling to deeper phenomena of social psychology.

Continuity and Change

The history of states, debt, and power reveals continuities over long historical periods. At any one time the number of debtor states exceeds that of creditor states, posing enduring questions about the capacity of the few creditors—or the sole creditor—to act as an effective stability anchor. Germany did not have the relative economic size or buffer of creditworthiness to bail-out a growing number of euro area Member States in sovereign debt and banking crises. It was, at best, a semi-hegemonic power.

However, this numerical disadvantage of creditor states is offset in two ways. First, they have a strong incentive to coordinate so that the design and operation of creditor-debtor state relations is characterized by an informal creditor-state club. Secondly, creditor states benefit from their 'soft' power and 'network' capital. Against this background, debtor states have an incentive to differentiate themselves from each other. In consequence, they have a lower collective-action capacity than creditor states. The ability of creditor states to gain disproportionate influence over the outcome of international and European negotiations is grounded in their aura of power. Their elites have arguing power and bargaining power. They possess power over how policy issues, like coordination and liquidity, are framed in discussions. This arguing power is expressed in what others come to regard as appropriate normative standards by which agreed negotiated outcomes will be evaluated and policies assessed. It is expressed in agenda-setting so that others negotiate around their proposals. Creditor-state elites have negotiating power in that their policy positions are more likely to be reflected in agreed outcomes. Other negotiators look to them as the key source of information on the most relevant policy positions for agreement. Creditor-state elites have an advantage in claiming to be the main source of substantive policy expertise in designing policies. They also have disproportionate influence over decisions about the best timing and the appropriate institutional setting for negotiation. In short, their bargaining resources tend to exceed those of debtor states.

We can observe how creditor- and debtor-state status gives rise to asymmetries of power, especially in the case of chronic debtor states that lack systemic significance. It shapes various forms of hierarchy in relations amongst European states, from informal hierarchy through hegemonic power to empire. We can see how a few creditor states are able to imprint themselves on the larger world through trade and finance. This pattern was evident from the city state of Athens, through Rome, to Lucca, Venice, and Antwerp in late-medieval Europe, to the United States from the 1920s, and to Germany in the late twentieth and early twenty-first centuries. The asymmetry of power becomes clear once debtor states seek to entice creditor states into creating new formalized and supportive European and international structures of policy coordination and liquidity creation and management. Creditor states' participation is essential for the credibility and thus sustainability of such structures, endowing them with the capacity to threaten exit as a bargaining resource. However, the parameters of creditor-state power change once structures of policy coordination and liquidity creation and management are in place and states begin to share belief in the need for their reform to correct deficiencies of performance (Zartmann and Rubin 2000). Creditor-state power is blunted by fears of vulnerability to contagion and the diminished power of the exit threat. Creditor-debtor state relations take on a less asymmetric form of bargaining power once creditor states are locked into structures that promote close trade and financial integration, like the euro area. In short, the context of negotiations matters (Fuchs 2013).

Similarly, patterns can be discerned in the moral sentiments that characterize creditor-debtor state relations, above all in times of crisis. Creditor-state elites and publics resent the behaviour of debtor states, attributing negative qualities of fecklessness and laziness to their elites and publics. Debtor-state elites and publics ventilate feelings of humiliation, anger, and victimhood with respect to creditor states, attributing to the latter arrogance and bullying. At the same time, we can note the transience of creditor-state status, in part due to external structural developments and in part to domestic factors. Creditor-state elites and publics readily fall victim to illusion, hubris, and complacency. These characteristics are bred by their belief in their own exceptional virtues and wisdom and by underestimation of their vulnerability, especially to external dynamics.

Historical continuities in creditor-debtor state relations cannot disguise change over time. These continuities are played out in changing contexts of technology, social and professional interests, legal understanding, political ideologies, and social dynamics. In the first place, technological changes have created an experience of space-time compression. The barriers of distance have been overcome. There is a sense that time has speeded up. This phenomenon is most apparent in financial markets. Their geographic scale and their timetables have become radically dissociated from those in EU, euro area, and Member-State politics and policy-making, where structural reforms and fiscal consolidation move at a different pace. In addition, the context and the substance of state action have been changed by new financial technologies like derivatives, formalized credit ratings, and the rise of contract law, academic economics, and macroeconomic modelling. They have been associated with the emergence of new, highly articulate and self-confident professional groups, with their own interests and logical constructs of state action. In particular, the evolution of contract law has led to more restrictive conceptions of sovereign immunity, privileging creditors.

This process of professionalization is part of a wider process of greater social and political inclusion. Its defining features have been electoral reforms, extension of educational opportunities, welfare-state provision, and emerging consumer cultures. Governing elites have to consider and appease a wider range of interests. The outcome has been new dilemmas in state action, caused by rising expectations of social provision, hostility to tax increases that undermine individual consumption and the status it confers, and the gradual emergence of interlinked tax crisis and debt crisis in European states. Private sector and public debt evolved in complex interaction with each other. Public finances became vulnerable to the effects of increasing corporate and household debts, to the excessive exposure of banks and financial institutions to all this debt, and to subsequent large-scale financial crises. The contingent liabilities of states rise as financial institutions become systemically significant and 'too big to fail', as well as too large and opaque for prudential supervision and regulation, even for effective internal corporate governance.

Moreover, profound demographic changes, above all population ageing, mean states face huge and growing implicit liabilities in pensions, health, and social care. Governing elites become caught up in processes that lead to accumulating debt, much of it contingent and implicit. Across much of Europe family structure has ceased to provide an adequate support mechanism for an ageing population. No less significantly, states face social breakdown in their midst once families fail to rear responsible adults with financial literacy and the capacity for economic self-sufficiency.

Another distinctive and important change has been the post-1945 engagement of governing and expert elites in the project of European economic and monetary integration and union. This engagement was linked to lesson-drawing from the horrendous experience of two world wars and their association with the destructive power of forms of nationalism that demonized foreigners and outsiders. By the beginning of the twenty-first century, a majority of EU Member States, led by France and Germany, had joined into a radically new form of monetary union. Creditor-debtor state relations in Europe were formalized and institutionalized in a new way, shifting the framework within which Member-State elites need to consider and promote their self-interests. Mutual dependence through a shared currency, trade and financial flows, and euro-denominated contracts exposed Member States to contagion and altered the parameters of risk management. Thus by 2013 German policy makers were redefining euro crisis management as about the stabilization of the euro area, in its political as well as its economic aspects. It was about combating the association of euro crisis management with institutionalized and enduring austerity and with the rise of national populism.

Lessons from History

History offers no privileged insight into how the financial and economic crisis in Europe will unfold and into when, how, and with what consequences it will end. We lack the historical perspective, and the opportunity to inject objectivity, that will arise 'after' the euro area crises. Given the radical uncertainty in such a period, the historian can aspire to be little more than a 'possibilist'. Only those—and there are many—who believe tenaciously in a particular theory, and see the crisis as an unfolding of its logic, will deny that we are living in times of radical uncertainty. Otherwise, views about the balance of probabilities will change with events and with new evidence. What history teaches us about financial and economic crises of this magnitude is that they endure a decade and possibly much more. Moreover, they take on their own dynamics. These characteristics place a premium on public and private virtues of enormous endurance, adaptability, and capacity to learn as we go along. The euro area can survive. But it is far from clear that it will do so in its present configuration of Member States and without major institutional changes to create European banking union and fiscal union.

Secondly, history shows how crisis management is endangered by negative national stereotyping. Germans are 'arrogant' and 'bullying'; Greeks are 'work-shy' and feckless. Neither stereotype survives examination of the evidence. Greeks are hardworking and thrifty and have a long history of entrepreneurial energy and acumen. Like other southern Europeans, they benefit from relatively supportive family structures that help cushion against austerity and structural change. For historical reasons, Germans are 'reluctant hegemons', fearful of becoming isolated in post-war Europe. In giving oxygen to claims about fecklessness, bullying, and victimhood, the euro area crisis has been ill-served by its media, which has too readily pandered to national populist sentiments.

Thirdly, history makes clear that the euro is fundamentally a political project (Dyson and Featherstone 1999; Dyson 2000). It was created as a political project. EU central bankers and finance ministry officials were asked to focus on how it could be realized technically as a sustainable Economic and Monetary Union (EMU); they were not asked whether it should be created. As the crisis progresses, the euro area will either come together and prosper within the new architecture of banking, fiscal, and political union; or it will limp along precariously from crisis to crisis; or it will fail as a political project. The euro area crisis is not in the first instance a test of whether it meets the stringent economic conditions of an optimum currency area. As elaborated by economists, these conditions place in question most currency unions. The crisis is, above all, a test of political solidarity and shared identity within a heterogeneous economic area. It is about whether Member States and their publics wish to continue living together in a union with this degree of heterogeneity. It is a test of whether they are prepared to take the economic, financial, and political risks of European disunion. In this sense the crisis is a high-stakes exercise in risk management. The key question is whether politicians remember the basics of negotiation, namely that elites need to focus on the outcomes for themselves if they fail to reach agreement. This becomes harder, the more Member States are negotiating and the greater the range of domestic disagreements and difficulties of ratification. However, the bias to negotiate to agreement increases when—as in the euro area—the same Member States are negotiating time and again on different issues. Negotiations take on a different dynamic in an institutional setting that creates repeated games.

Fourthly, the euro area crisis is an existentially significant challenge, posing some core, normatively laden political questions. What kind of state do we want? What kind of EU do we want? What is the proper balance between the market and social policies? What do we understand by solidarity? Is it the solidarity of effort, expressed in compliance with one's commitments, for instance those in the euro area financial compact treaty or in future contractual arrangements for structural reforms? Is it the solidarity of mutual liability and risk-sharing, expressed in collective and conditional financial assistance through the European Stability Mechanism (ESM), unlimited and unconditional liquidity provision to banks by the European Central Bank (ECB), some arrangement for a euro area single bank resolution mechanism, Eurobonds, or collective debt redemption? What is understood by responsibility? Is it enforcing policies in ways that avoid moral hazard by making Member-State policy makers take domestic ownership of problems that they have created? Is it about sharing the costs of adjustment to excessive imbalances, so that pain is born in part by creditor states through domestic economic expansion and liquidity creation as part of coordinated policies?

These questions are ultimately moral and highly controversial. They are about fairness and do not admit of a single answer that will command universal consent. The outcome will depend on how they are politically negotiated. They can be answered didactically by the logic of some principle, like moral hazard. Alternatively, they can be answered in ways that sustain and restore mutual trust by recognizing reciprocal interests of creditor states and debtor states. Ultimately, trust is at the heart of creditor-debtor state relations in Europe. It is so easily lost and so difficult to regain. If the management of the euro area crises does not seek to build trust, and leads to outcomes that undermine trust, it will not be seen as consistent with norms of reciprocity. By 2013 German economic crisis management faced the issue of whether it would abide by the fundamental economic logic of principle-driven Ordo-liberal theory or would adapt to the new realities of coexistence in the euro area.

Fifthly, insight into the hard and difficult moral and political choices in euro area crisis management should deter us from a too simplistic analysis in terms of 'saints' and 'sinners'. This type of analysis induces the very illusion, hubris, and complacency that helped to bring about the crisis and that stand in the way of effective crisis management. The crisis is more complex and morally more odious than the easy categorization into euro area saints and sinners allows. It is a story about the reckless—above all, bankers and financiers; about the feckless—many households, companies, and governments; and about the innocent—those whose financial illiteracy has been exploited by the mis-selling of products and those who have played no part in causing this crisis. The crisis takes on a morally odious character to the extent that the reckless and the feckless have escaped being held to account, whilst the innocent have born disproportionately the costs of acutely painful adjustment. In this context it is hardly surprising that there is widespread political alienation from what people see not as free markets that offer opportunities to all but as 'crony' capitalism, in which the state is exploited by insiders to gain regulatory and tax privileges. Governing elites are perceived as lacking the political will and not having available state capacity to protect and further public interests. In this sense crisis management requires urgent political renewal and reconstruction to re-establish the social prestige of public service ethics and to reopen channels of social mobility. Relying on the political silence of the disadvantaged is a morally bankrupt strategy.

Sixthly, we should cease to think that the problem of 'failing' states is just a developing-world problem. It is with us in Europe. The problem of 'crony' capitalism and state incapacity is pronounced in states like Greece. But the crisis is far from being just a Greek case. Its roots are both wider and deeper. It reflects the way in which esoteric, opaque forms of global financial 'casino' capitalism, notably 'shadow' banking, have become disembodied from prudential state supervision and regulation. They fail to underpin the kind of productive long-term investment that societies need in infrastructure, modern industries, and social provision.

Seventhly, the euro area crises have been associated with a growth of far-Right national populism and Euro-scepticism across Europe. A return to economic growth might be seen as the main route both to exit from the crisis and to reverse this shift. There is much to be said for this view. However, two notes of caution are necessary. First, and critically, everything depends on just how sustainable this economic growth is. Credit-fuelled, consumption-led growth, and measures that encourage asset-price inflation, lay the ground for future financial crises. Above all, sustainable economic growth needs to be underpinned by political reforms that help strengthen state capacity to represent public interests and face down vested interests. Robust institutional structures are needed to secure financial stability and to promote infrastructural investment. A return to economic growth without strong economic, financial, and political foundations will offer only temporary reprieve from further, potentially worse, crisis and from further shifts towards far-Right national populism and Euro-scepticism. Deep-seated, painful, and protracted structural reforms will be needed to help unlock the potential for sustainable economic growth.

Moreover, Europe was becoming more controversial before the crisis and will remain so afterwards. The controversies revolve around more or less Europe—solidarity or sovereignty—and which type of Europe—more market or more social. In an increasing number of fields the EU has become more intrusive, impacting on individual lives: whether environmental regulation, health and safety, or fishing quotas. This will not change with an end to the crisis. European economic governance will intrude more actively into fiscal sovereignty, structural reforms, and national banking supervision and regulation. The issue of sovereignty—above all, responsible sovereignty—remains fundamental and will not go away, least of all in Britain.

Eighthly, the creation of the euro area, and its reforms under the conditions of crisis, is having major effects on the balance between the principles of unitary and differentiated integration (Dyson and Sepos 2010). The euro area is the most advanced exercise in differentiated integration. Managing its crises has generated institutional and policy reforms that have radically changed the nature of the EU. The outcome is three circles within the EU. There are the insider Member States, which use the euro as their currency and which sign up to European banking union, fiscal union, and enhanced economic-policy coordination. Then there are the many 'outsider-insider' Member States, like Poland, that remain politically committed to join the euro area and keen to sign up to enhanced economic-policy coordination and to banking and fiscal union. Finally, there are the permanent 'outsiders', which are led by Britain and which disengage from all these mechanisms. By 2013 the British Conservative Party had committed to seek renegotiation of the terms of EU membership and to put this to a referendum in 2017. This commitment posed the question of whether a Member State can seek exemptions from current policies that fall under the principle of unitary integration. For instance, can a British government gain exemption for the City of London from key aspects of EU financial market supervision and regulation? Does this open the way to a general unravelling of the treaty as each Member State seeks to protect its own position? European banking union was a policy that drove the British Conservative Party further towards disengagement. In analysing this development one should note the structural dependency of British governments on financial services, their version of 'crony' capitalism.

Lessons from the Crisis

In the first decade of the euro, governing elites across the euro area, and by implication the financial markets that failed to sanction them, fell victim to illusion, hubris, and complacency. They failed to grasp the logic of entering into a monetary union, to educate their electorates into this logic, and to take responsibility for dealing with the implications. In particular, they believed wrongly that the removal of their historic vulnerability to exchange-rate crisis gave them freedom to practise indulgence in their economic policies. This illusion was compounded by a more general belief, for which economists must remain culpable, that financial markets were perfectly efficient and would smoothly adjust to any imbalances. This belief ran counter to what we know historically about financial market behaviour. The first decade of the euro was one of extreme optimism that the historic problems of financial capitalism had been resolved. This was erroneous. In the case of the euro area, vulnerability had shifted from the exchange rate to the sovereign bond markets, expressed in bond yield spreads, and to credit ratings and what they both communicated about default risks. The crisis was about a bursting of illusions and complacency. It initiated a traumatic and fitful learning process.

The first lesson is that the logic of a monetary union is that neither the exchange rate nor monetary policy offer Member States independent policy instruments of adjustment. Neither devaluation nor inflation provides an answer to problems of external imbalance and excessive debt. Hence the weight of adjustment falls on so-called 'internal' devaluation through policy changes and wage-setting formulas that target unit labour costs. Here Germany led the way from the late 1990s through wage moderation and then structural reforms to labour markets and to social policies. Member States have to reform collective bargaining, corporate governance, taxes, and social benefit systems in ways that keep unit labour costs under control and crucially gain political consensus for these reforms.

The second lesson is that, for the same reason, monetary union disciplines domestic political choices in fiscal policies, initially with the Stability and Growth Pact (SGP) and later the euro area fiscal compact treaty, and in structural reforms to strengthen competitiveness through contractual arrangements. In a monetary union there is a need to consider the interdependence of fiscal policies, especially to prevent fiscal 'free-riding' by a Member State, and to link any fiscal leniency in meeting rules to agreed structural reforms. In times of crisis, fiscal surveillance becomes even more intrusive.

In this sense monetary union is fraught with political consequences. It poses political choices about the basis of legitimacy, each choice raising serious difficulties and a source of contention. On the one hand, it can be argued that the logic of the euro area is the 'hollowing out' of democracy in the Member States. It reduces the domestic scope for political choice and for fruitful and meaningful political discourse, leading to a democratic deficit. The European state risks asphyxiation once its elites become associated with a fixation on institutionalizing fiscal austerity. The EU and the euro face the nightmare scenario of European electorates turning against the project of European integration (Heisbourg 2013).

Seen in terms of this 'hollowing-out' narrative and a dysfunctional euro area, the search for solutions can range between two poles. One solution is to re-establish political democracy and accountability at the EU level, where relevant decisions can be made about economic policy coordination, fiscal rules, and structural reform priorities. For this purpose, monetary union requires a European political demos, focused on the reinvigoration of the European Parliament and of transnational political parties (Schmidt 2013). It involves the construction of a macroeconomic union, with both liability and control concentrated at the European level. It would require a fiscal transfer mechanism, a banking union firmly anchored at the European level, joint liability for future debt, a framework for the resolution of existing debt, and, not least, ceding sovereignty in banking, fiscal, and economic policies. The question is whether this option remains politically and institutionally feasible. Its feasibility is diminished in a crisis context of widespread disillusionment with policy outcomes associated with the EU and the euro area. Electorates would be unlikely to endorse the necessary treaty changes, suggesting that the EU is caught in a vicious circle. European political union in this sense seems beyond immediate reach.

A very different solution to this democratic deficit problem is abandonment of the euro in its existing form. The EU could opt to reverse back to 1998 and recreate a 'Bretton Woods for Europe' in the form of a stable, managed exchange-rate system, with the euro as a residual competing currency (Streeck 2013). This choice poses the challenge of how to unwind the euro area without unleashing potentially uncontrollable financial and economic consequences. Moreover, without a single currency, the risk is increased that the EU would roll back the single European market. It is an option that governing elites are likely to resist because of the huge financial, economic, and political sunk costs that have been invested in the euro project and in the single market.

On the other hand, one can argue that democracy in Member States is not being 'hollowed out' and that the euro area is being designed in ways that are functional for Member States. In this narrative, the EU and the euro area are being reformed in ways that address serious deficiencies in the practice of democracy, namely its spatially and temporally bounded character. Competitive, partisan democratic politics has serious difficulties in factoring in negative externalities for other states and future generations. Robust institutional arrangements are needed to constrain the bias to short-term and inward-looking indulgence in economic, financial, and social policies; to secure financial as well as monetary stability; and to address population ageing. The euro area can be seen as engaged in reforms to make for more sustainable policy and political choices that look to the long term beyond conventional electoral horizons. The aim is to anchor both liability and control more firmly at national level through stricter rules. However, this promise of an EU 'sustainability union' leaves open the political question of whether it can acquire and retain legitimacy. Are Member-State electorates prepared to pay the price?

The third lesson is that between Germany in 1953 and Greece in 2012 no euro area Member State used sovereign debt restructuring as a policy instrument. Sovereign debt restructuring was seen as a developing-market phenomenon. Although EU institutions and Member States are reluctant to recognize it, sovereign debt restructuring is likely to become more than just confined to Greece and a one-off. After the Argentinean default, the International Monetary Fund (IMF) proposed a Sovereign Debt Restructuring Mechanism. It fell victim to US opposition. Such a proposal in the euro area is likely to fall victim to German opposition.

Nevertheless, the alternatives raise serious problems. The safety valve of reliance on domestic banks and financial institutions to buy up the sovereign debt of their state has limits. It reflects a reversal of the logic of monetary union, which is supposed to generate extra liquidity through private sector cross-border financial flows. Moreover, it exposes domestic banks to risky sovereign debt, undermining their own creditworthiness, leading to problematic bank asset quality reviews and stress-testing, and creating a potentially fatal embrace of sovereign debt and banking crisis. Enhanced liquidity provision, backed by creditor states, also faces political and economic constraints, especially once domestic adjustment in 'bail-out' states is seen to fall behind schedule.

It is also important to be clear about the difficulties of sovereign debt restructuring. In the EU and euro area context we are looking at negotiated sovereign debt restructuring, not coercive treatment of creditors, Argentina-style. Such processes will be painful and slow. Moreover, sovereign debt restructuring is contingent on its likely outcomes, which vary with who owns the debt. Where domestic institutions and households are highly exposed, the effects could be negative for the domestic economy and thus counterproductive. Finally, there is the issue of the privileged position of official creditors like the ECB and the IMF. This will be a politically difficult red line to cross in any negotiated sovereign debt restructuring. Despite these constraints, sovereign debt restructuring is likely to feature in future euro area crisis management in a way it did not earlier, for instance in the Irish rescue programme.

The fourth lesson is that the logic of a monetary union requires a systemically significant creditor state at its centre. If the monetary union is to survive, this state must act in a decisive and precautionary manner to preserve its own sovereign creditworthiness in the interests of the union as a whole. This is what is meant when policy makers refer to Germany as 'the stability anchor' of the euro area. Taking on more and more implicit and contingent liabilities through euro area rescue programmes is inconsistent with the systemically significant creditor state retaining the creditworthiness that it exports to the rest of the euro area. It would pose the question—'who will rescue the rescuer?' There are, in short, limitations to what Germany can be expected to do if it is to act in the interests of the union as a whole.

The fifth lesson is that in a monetary union the gain for a Member State that derives from others supporting it by assuming mutual liability is offset by the loss in the form of tightened external surveillance and accountability. This is consistent with the principle that liability must be matched by control. German negotiators have insisted on this principle. In doing so, they are only behaving as creditors always do. Notably, reflecting the importance of systemic significance, external surveillance and accountability is more marked in a case like Greece than that of Spain. This phenomenon is discernible in the history of IMF as well as EU interventions.

The sixth lesson is that the logic of a monetary union that wishes to survive in its current configuration is that it must have a credible supra-national executive capacity to act with discretion in a supreme emergency to its coherence and survival (Dyson 2013).

The ESM is not such an institution. It is intergovernmental, subject to German veto, and limited in firepower to what would be needed to help rescue small Member States, not Italy or Spain. This leaves the ECB. Its Outright Monetary Transactions (OMT) programme of autumn 2012 was the embodiment of Mario Draghi's commitment that the ECB would do 'whatever it takes'. However, it remains conditional on a Member State having a structural reform programme with the EMS; on its continuing compliance with that programme; and on German political support for the use of the OMT. Ultimately, the balance sheet of the ECB remains the backstop of the euro area. The survival of both is bound up together.

The Challenge of Sustainable Debt: What Kind of European State? What Kind of Europe?

The stress in this book on contextualized thinking about states and debt suggests that the test for the EU, the euro area, and their Member States will be what proves institutionally and politically possible. Nevertheless, it is important to try to tease out what this historically-informed review of the EU and euro area crises implies for the design of a European state structure compatible with sustainable debt. Doing so has to contend with the problems of complexity and radical uncertainty that bedevil thinking about states and debt. What emerges is a view of the European state and of the EU and the euro area that defies simple ideological categorization. As such, it is unlikely to be welcome to vested political and economic interests. The seeming contradictions that beset its design are united by the importance that is attached to high tax capacity, effective public management, and a strong ethic of public service—characteristics of the state that have been unfashionable since the late twentieth century. In addressing the problems of sustainable debt the state matters. However, it appears ill-fitted both ideologically and institutionally for this purpose. There are problems of political will and of institutional capacity.

The EU matters in various ways. First, the capacity of the European state to fulfil its key functions in a manner consistent with sustainable debt stands to benefit from its embedding in a framework of European integration. However, this framework needs to offer equal support to binding state to fiscal prudence and to fostering the developmental and entrepreneurial state, dedicated to strengthening productive long-term investment in infrastructure and social provision. The fiscal compact treaty is not enough. Secondly, it must not be forgotten that any credible and enduring structure of European economic integration and monetary union requires a systemically significant creditor state. The creditworthiness of that state is a European public good and must be safeguarded. Thirdly, policies on EU and euro area enlargement, and for European economic governance, need to give much more attention to political will and state capacity. It is naïve to assume compliance with rules. In this respect euro area crises suggest that the genie is already out of the bottle. Finally, the EU is a form of insurance, above all represented by the balance sheet of the ECB. However, no insurance comes without conditions and the willingness to abide by these conditions. Otherwise the insurer would be broken.

If European states are to compete—collectively and individually—in a world of global competition and new and rising economic and political powers, they need to rediscover the virtues of the developmental or entrepreneurial state for raising long-term GDP growth potential and thus tax capacity. This rediscovery depends on cultivating a high social prestige for public service ethics. It means gaining public confidence in state capacity for public sector management of large-scale infrastructure projects and of social policies that support structural adjustment. EU and domestic fiscal rules that target infrastructure spending as a proportion of GDP have value in incentivizing political support for the developmental state.

However, efforts to lend political support to the developmental state face two challenges. First, it is hard to pin down what the 'correct' level of public investment should be. There are big variations in the return on public investment, depending on when, where, and to what the money flows. Secondly, confidence in state capacity for this purpose is variable across space and over time. This confidence remains historically weak in southern Europe. Moreover, in northern and central Europe belief in the developmental state had eroded from the 1970s. The lack of public confidence in the developmental state carries heavy economic and social costs because of the inability of the private sector to shoulder the long-term and risky nature of investments in education, energy, innovation, and transport. It matters for debt sustainability.

At the same time, the European state needs to commit in a self-binding fashion to tough EU and domestic fiscal rules. Crucially, these rules need to take account of contingent and implicit liabilities. They need to focus political attention on state vulnerability to financial crisis, to population ageing, and to external and internal security threats. Seen in this way, the Maastricht fiscal rules may seem too relaxed. The more structurally dependent a state is on the financial sector, the more it is demographically challenged, and the more it is embroiled in discourse of external and internal security threat, the greater is its need for fiscal prudence. In such circumstances the potential for sustainable social democratic politics is diminished.

The size and structure of the financial sector is a key determinant of the scale of the challenge to debt sustainability. In order to reduce state vulnerability to contingent liabilities, a strong coordinated system of international, European, and domestic supervision and regulation of banking and financial institutions is essential. It needs to address structural issues like 'too big to fail' and the existential risk of 'too big to save'. If supervision and regulation is to tackle debt sustainability, it needs to focus on the optimal size of a banking system before it begins to have negative effects on GDP growth rates. It needs to mitigate the dangers to economic stability from structural overdependence on a financial sector liable to bouts of panic and extreme volatility. It needs to link bank lending to value-added in supporting production of goods and services. Not least, the underlying politics of financial sector supervision and regulation needs to address the association of growing financial sector size with rising wealth and income inequality.

Too much bank lending has found its way into property and other asset markets rather than into productive investment in infrastructure and in smaller businesses that create the largest employment gains. It has fed volatility and debt accumulation. The public interest resides in a downsizing of finance to its key productive economic functions; in a clear ring-fencing of retail banking from investment banking; in bringing shadow banking within supervisory and regulatory systems; in ensuring adequate capitalization of banks; in ensuring leverage ratios are more consistent with prudential principles; in lower risk weightings in capital adequacy ratios for loans to small businesses; in providing for bail-in of bank creditors in any rescues so that taxpayers are better protected and principles of fairness respected; and in establishing clear professional and legal sanctions against bankers who fail in their duty of care for the resources that are put in their trust. Above all, states must act to safeguard the public-utility aspect of banking as the essential plumbing of the economy.

Finally, the European state cannot hope to reconcile these demands without a high tax capacity. This capacity is vital to support the developmental state, to safeguard social policies that support structural economic adjustment and protect those who risk being caught in a spiral of deprivation and poverty, and to bolster the credibility of prudent fiscal rules. It means shifting the burden to the wealthy through taxes that fall on immobile factors like land values and property and to consumption rather than production. Politically, this shift is frustrated by underlying structures of power that favour the wealthy and by practices of tax arbitrage by leading companies and wealthy individuals. Political collective-action problems have triumphed over efforts to build strong international and European policy frameworks that combat tax competition and evasion.

The gap between what is needed and what is do-able to make debt sustainable is sufficiently great to induce pessimism. Political rule is bound up in the complex interaction and co-evolution of public and private sector debts. European states find themselves highly exposed to debt crises. This exposure reflects in part path-dependent growth in public debts, driven by inherited social entitlements and by population ageing. However, state exposure to debt also derives from private sector credit booms and the structure of financial and economic interests that supports the credit-growth engine in property and other asset markets. After the financial crisis, this structure of financial and economic interests is politically on the defensive but, in policy terms, remains largely intact. It is able to ensure that, despite the combination of bail-out costs to the financial sector with falling tax revenues, the political problem is represented as one of reducing excessive public debts. Public-debt reduction then tends to exacerbate the effects of private sector deleveraging. The resultant prolonged economic stagnation or recession creates the political risk that governing elites will be seduced by a return to reliance on bank lending to property and other asset markets, to credit-fuelled consumption, and to a more relaxed approach to prudential standards in banking. This type of strategy induces moral hazard. It leaves unresolved the fundamental structural problem of how to ensure that debt is compatible with sustainable GDP growth.

Glossary

In compiling this glossary the author has used several sources. However, he would like to express a particular debt of gratitude to Moles and Terry (1999), Mackenzie (2009), and the European Central Bank, *Monthly Bulletin* (various).

Arbitrage= is trading that seeks to make low-risk profits from price discrepancies, as between the prices of similar assets.

Automatic stabilizers= refer to changes in the cyclical fiscal balance over time.

Bad bank= is a publicly initiated institution that holds non-performing loans and impaired assets of other troubled financial institutions, typically until they are amortized or sold.

Basel II= is an accord negotiated within the Basel Committee on Banking Supervision. It covers minimum *capital adequacy* standards for banks (Pillar I); the supervisory review process (Pillar II); and disclosure of banks' financial positions (Pillar III). To be replaced by Basel III.

Benchmark= The mix of debt instruments, currencies, and duration that reflects an investment manager's tolerance for exposure to credit, liquidity, and market risks. Investment benchmarks are defined as good practice to ensure discipline in reserve management.

Bond= is a tradeable form of debt. It commits the issuer (usually a government or company) to repay a fixed sum (the principal) on a given date and to make periodic interest payments (coupons) of fixed amounts until that date. The owner can sell the bond to another investor.

Bond market= is the market in which longer-term debt securities are issued and traded.

Borrowing requirement= is the net incurrence of debt by the general government.

Capital adequacy ratio= describes the percentage of a bank's capital to its assets, generally risk-weighted.

CDS spread= refers to the annual amount that the protection buyer must pay the seller of a *credit default swap* (CDS) over the length of the contract to protect the underlying asset against a credit event.

Central government debt= differs from public sector debt in that it mostly relates to debt issued by states to plug the holes that budget deficits have left in their balance sheets. It ignores the debt that relates to such items as social security funds.

Coercive debt exchange (CDE)= results when an issuer is forced to restructure its debt obligations in an effort to avert a liquidity crunch or insolvency, and thereby causes a reduction in contractual terms at the cost of creditors. See *liability management.*

Collateral= is assets pledged or transferred in some form as a guarantee for the repayment of loans.

Collateralized debt obligation= is an investment vehicle that acquires pools of debt instruments like *bonds* and sells on to investors, repackaged in structured form, the cash flow from the instruments, along with the risk that their issuers will default.

Contingent liabilities= refer to possible future increases in government debt and payment obligations that could emerge from explicit guarantees (e.g. in case of crop failures or natural disasters) and from implicit, non-contractual government guarantees (e.g. bailing out the banking sector, state-owned enterprises or sub-national governments). They are uncertain but potentially very large.

Counter-cyclical capital buffer= is an additional capital add-on applied contingent on the economic cycle.

Covered bonds= are favoured instruments of capital-market-based refinancing of mortgages and public projects in Denmark (*særligt dækkede obligationer*, or SDOs), France (*obligations foncières*), Germany (*Pfandbriefe*, 'letter of pledge'), and Spain (*cédulas*), where they are regulated under special covered bond laws. The bond is collateralized by a 'cover pool' of assets (typically mortgages and public debt) that are legally ring-fenced on the issuer's balance sheet. Bondholders have a priority claim on the collateral, and they rank at or above all the issuer's other creditors. Hence, because investors are substantially protected against default, covered bonds are assessed as less risky and typically given a rating 'uplift' to AAA, often beyond the stand-alone rating of the issuer.

Credit default swap (CDS)= is a credit derivative that is used to hedge against a debt default. CDSs are designed to transfer the credit exposure between parties. The buyer of a CDS receives credit protection, whilst the seller guarantees the creditworthiness of the product. In this way the risk of default is transferred from creditor to debtor.

Credit risk= arises in sovereign debt management and refers to the risk of non-performance or default by borrowers on loans or other financial assets, or by a counterparty on financial contracts.

Cumulative probability of default= quantifies the probability of a state being unable to honour its debt obligations over a given period of time, for instance five years.

Currency risk= refers to the risk of adverse movements in exchange rates that reduce the domestic currency value of international assets. It also results from an appreciation of the domestic currency.

Currency swap= occurs when the parties to a swap exchange debt denominated in different types of currencies, agreeing flows of interest and repayment.

Current account balance= covers all transactions in goods and services, income, and current transfers between residents and non-residents of a state.

Cyclical fiscal balance= is the cyclical component of the overall fiscal balance, typically computed as the difference between cyclical revenues and cyclical expenditures.

Debt= refers to the loans taken out by public authorities (including debt securities and currency and deposits); by non-financial corporations (including debt securities and pension fund reserves); and by households.

Debt overhang= an hypothesis that predicts a negative impact of debt on economic growth: beyond a certain point the debt overhang will start to exert negative pressure on investors' willingness to provide capital.

Debt ratio= is the ratio between general public debt and nominal GDP. It changes over time if debt grows more quickly or more slowly than nominal GDP and depending on the interest rate and the primary fiscal balance (excluding interest payments).

Debt securities= are a promise on the part of the borrower to make one or more payment(s) to the lender at a specified future date or dates. Debt securities are negotiable and can be traded on secondary markets. They do not grant the lender any ownership rights in the borrowing unit. The lender's income consists of any coupon payments received plus the difference between the purchase price of the bond and its market value on sale or maturity.

Deficit= is the general government's net borrowing i.e. the difference between total government revenue and total government expenditure.

Deflation= is a significant and persistent decline in the prices of a very broad set of consumer goods and prices that becomes entrenched in expectations.

Derivative= is a contract or security (like a *swap*) the value of which depends on the price of an underlying asset (like bonds, residential mortgages, or some other future income stream) or on other parameters such as the probability of default by a bond issuer. It is a financial instrument to facilitate borrowing by expanding liquidity.

ESA debt= is a definition of gross public debt that derives from the national accounts in line with the European System of Accounts (ESA 95). It covers all government liabilities (excluding equity), including some financial derivatives, and is recorded at market value. Because its instrument coverage is broader than Maastricht debt and it is recorded at market value as opposed to nominal value, it is on average some 12 per cent of GDP higher.

EURIBOR= is the Euro Interbank Offered Rate, which refers to the interest rate at which a prime bank is prepared to lend funds to another prime bank in euros. EURIBOR is calculated daily for interbank deposits as the average of the daily offer rates of a representative panel of prime banks. See also *LIBOR*.

Euro Area= comprises those EU Member States that have adopted the euro as the single currency.

Eurosystem= is the central banking system comprising the European Central Bank and the national central banks of those EU Member States that have adopted the euro.

Exchange Rate Mechanism II (ERM II)= is the mechanism that provides the framework for exchange-rate policy cooperation between the euro area states and EU Member States not participating in stage three of EMU. It replaced the ERM (1979–1999), which had the German D-Mark as its de facto anchor currency.

Fiscal stimulus= is provided by discretionary fiscal policy action taken in response to financial and economic shocks that affect the fiscal balance.

Foreign-exchange reserves= are external assets that are readily available to, and controlled by monetary authorities, for direct financing of payments imbalances, for indirectly regulating the magnitude of these imbalances through intervention in exchange markets to affect the exchange rate, and for other purposes. They need to be liquid or marketable foreign currency assets in the form of convertible foreign currency claims of the authorities on non-residents. They include gold, foreign-currency denominated claims on non-residents, special drawing rights (SDRs), and the reserve positions held in the IMF.

Gross external debt= represents the outstanding amount of its actual (i.e. non-contingent) current liabilities that require payment of principal or interest to foreign investors. These liabilities are incurred by the corporate, financial, household, and public sectors. They include debt assets, such as bonds and notes, money market instruments, loans and currency deposits, as well as trade credits, inter-company lending, and advances due to non-residents. Gross debt is a better indicator of roll-over risk than net debt. Usefully, the definition of gross debt is fairly consistent across countries.

Gross financing needs= are the overall new government borrowing requirement plus debt maturing during the year.

Gross public debt= encompasses all debt liabilities that require future payment of interest and/or principal to the creditor and that are owed by the public sector as a whole (i.e. central, state, and local governments and all non-market, non-profit bodies that are controlled and mainly financed by these governments). It is useful for analysing short-term refinancing risks. See *Maastricht or EDP debt* and *ESA debt.*

Haircut= is a deduction in the face value of their bonds that is suffered by bondholders in the event of a debt rescheduling.

Hedge fund= is a special type of investment vehicle, often registered overseas, and exempt from various regulatory requirements on banks and insurance companies and thus free to engage in speculative activities like *short selling* that are prohibited to other institutions.

Imbalances= refer to the pattern of current account deficits and surpluses that build up in international and/or regional economies.

Institutional investor= is a bank, insurance company, pension fund, mutual fund, hedge fund, brokerage, or other financial group that takes investments from clients or invests on its own behalf.

Interest-rate risk= involves the adverse effects of increases in market yields that reduce the present value of fixed-interest investments. It increases with the duration of the investment.

Interest-rate swap= occurs when the parties to a swap exchange the flows of different types of interest payments on debt, such as various combinations of floating and fixed exchange rates, to reflect the risk of the swap.

Leverage= is the ratio of tier-one equity capital to overall assets, regardless of risk. High leverage means increased reliance on debt financing and thus a greater share of total earnings absorbed by paying debt interest. Leverage can be built up by borrowing on balance sheet or by using off-balance sheet transactions.

Liability management= or so-called soft restructuring is not technically a sovereign debt default as it involves creditors in voluntary rather than coercive changes to terms on their bonds. Typically, it takes the form of swapping shorter-dated bonds for longer maturities, allowing a government longer to pay off its debt and to deal with a lump in future payments and providing investors with additional yield. See *coercive debt exchange*.

LIBOR= is the London Interbank Offered Rate, which is the average rate of interest at which a panel of major banks report that other banks are prepared to lend them funds in a particular currency for a particular period. See also *EURIBOR*.

Liquidity risk= arises in sovereign debt management and refers to the possible difficulties in selling large amounts of assets quickly or raising cash quickly, because the confidence and thus number of market participants declines and/or because of the lack of depth of a particular market.

Maastricht or EDP debt= applies within the framework of the EU excessive deficit procedure to assess whether the criterion of a public debt ratio below 60 per cent of GDP is met. It excludes certain financial instruments like financial derivatives and trade credits.

Market risk= arises in sovereign debt management and is associated with changes in market prices, such as exchange rates and interest rates. Shorter-duration securities are less at risk than long-term, fixed-rate securities.

'Naked' short selling= is selling a debt security short without first having borrowed, or arranged to borrow, the security in time to deliver it for settling the trade. Naked shorts are used to provide default protection without ownership of the underlying debt security.

National accounts= comprise the assets and liabilities of the government, the central bank, the commercial banks and financial institutions, the corporate sector, and households.

Net external debt= derives from subtracting gross external debt assets from the liabilities. This figure tends to be much lower than gross external debt in states with large financial sectors that play an international role. Their banks and financial institutions tend to hold a large amount of assets in the form of cross-border debt securities. Definitions of net debt are less uniform than of gross debt, due to different treatment of assets.

Net interest payments= derive from interest payments minus interest receipts originated by the debt position. They show how much of the income generated by an economy in one year is to be allocated to servicing the costs of net external debt.

Net public debt= is gross debt minus financial assets, including those held within the broad public sector, for example social security funds. These assets include gold and special drawing rights (SDRs), currency and deposits, debt securities, loans, shares and other equity, insurance, pensions, and standardized guarantee schemes. It is relevant to assessing longer-term solvency because governments need an adequate buffer of liquid financial assets.

Off-balance-sheet entity= allows a financial institution to transfer risk off its balance sheet, improve the liquidity of loans through securitization, generate fee income, and gain relief from regulatory capital requirements.

Originate-to-distribute model= describes how financial institutions originate loans like mortgages, repackage them into securitized products, and then sell them to investors.

Output gap= is the deviation of actual from potential GDP, in percentage of potential GDP.

Overall fiscal balance= refers to net lending/borrowing, defined as the difference between revenue and total expenditure.

Primary fiscal balance= is the overall balance minus interest revenue plus interest expenditure.

Public debt= is a legal obligation on the part of a government to make interest and/ or amortization payments to holders of designated claims in accordance with a defined temporal schedule (Eatwell, Milgate, and Newman 2007).

Public debt management = involves the process of establishing a strategy for managing the government's debt in order to raise the required amount of funding, achieve its risk and its cost objectives, and to meet any other debt management goals that the government may set, notably minimizing cost and stabilizing the economy.

Public sector= refers to central, state, and local governments plus government-controlled bodies whose primary activity is commercial.

Quantitative easing= involves the expansion of a central bank's balance sheet through its purchases of assets from the financial sector. Its effect is to boost asset prices.

Recognizance= is the bond by which a person commits before a court or magistrate to pay a debt; a sum pledged as surety for this commitment.

Regulatory arbitrage= arises when institutional investors exploit differences in regulation across states or across financial sectors to reduce capital requirements.

Repurchase (repo) agreement= is an arrangement to sell an asset and to repurchase it at a specified price on a predetermined future date or on demand.

Repurchase (repo) market= involves banks raising cash in the market through exchanging mainly sovereign bonds as collateral. It is the most widely used way for banks to raise money to fund their daily operations, make loans, and balance their books. Hence it is regarded as the plumbing system of the financial system.

Reserve management= is the process by which public sector assets are managed in order to ensure the ready availability of funds, the prudent management of risks, and the generation of a reasonable return on the funds invested. It includes managing external debt for the purpose of reducing external vulnerability, notably an adequate level of reserves to provide liquidity as needed and to allow time to absorb shocks.

Ricardian equivalence= arises when a debt-financed fiscal stimulus induces consumers to save the proceeds in anticipation of future tax increases that will be required to repay the extra public debt. Also, an increased risk of sovereign default and the potential rise in interest rates will dampen or offset the fiscal stimulus. In these circumstances budget deficits have no or limited short-term effects. This theory contrasts with the conventional Keynesian view that higher fiscal deficits will stimulate demand in the short run.

Risk-weighted asset= is an asset weighted by factors representing its riskiness and potential for default.

Roll-over risk= arises in sovereign debt management and refers to risk that debt will have to be rolled over at an unusually high cost or, in extreme cases, cannot be rolled over at all.

Safe asset= provides a reliable store of value, serves as collateral in financial transactions, and functions as a pricing benchmark.

Securitization= is designed to reduce risk and increase liquidity by issuing new negotiable securities backed by existing assets like loans, mortgages, credit card debt, and accounts receivable. In this way risk is spread amongst dozens, even hundreds of parties.

Shadow banking= covers credit extension by means of 'conduits' and 'structured investment vehicles' that remove assets from banks' balance sheets, typically incorporated offshore. They take in relatively illiquid, long-term assets and in return issue shorter-term assets. A key incentive for growth of this sector was avoidance of regulation.

Short selling= is a process in which a trader sells a security that they do not own or own only temporarily. It often takes the form of finding an owner who is prepared, for a fee, to lend the security to the trader.

Sinking fund= moneys set aside for the purpose of sinking or wiping out a state's debt by degrees.

Sovereign credit ratings= measure creditworthiness of states in terms of the risk of a sovereign government defaulting on its debt obligations, by assessing willingness and financial capacity to pay (by reference to criteria like macroeconomic performance and prospects, structural strengths and weaknesses, political risk, public finances, and external finances).

Sovereign debt default= occurs when a sovereign state is unable to meet its debt obligations.

Sovereign debt management= See *public debt management.*

Sovereign debt rescheduling= involves a material reduction in terms for creditors, like reduction in principal amount, cut in interest, extension of maturity date, change from cash to no-cash payment, swap of debt for equity, cash tender for less than par or contractual or structural reduction in seniority. See *coercive debt exchange (CDE).*

Sovereign risk= is the risk that a government will restrict the ability of a holder to gain access to their assets or the proceeds from the sale of these assets.

Sovereign wealth fund (SWF)= is a special investment fund created and/or owned by a government to hold assets for long-term purposes. Typically funded from reserves or other foreign-currency sources like commodity export revenues (e.g. oil), it has significant foreign-currency claims on non-residents.

Sterilization= is used by central banks to offset the unintended inflationary effects of foreign-reserve accumulation. Typically, it entails the central bank exchanging (at cost) high-yield domestic assets for low-yield reserves. It leads to an expansion in the balance sheet of the banking system and transfers foreign-exchange risk from the private to the public sector.

Stress-testing= is the estimation of credit and market valuation losses that would result from the realization of certain extreme scenarios (like sharp GDP downturn and sovereign default), in order to determine the stability of the company or of the financial system.

Structural fiscal balance= is defined as the actual budget deficit (or surplus) minus the effects of cyclical fluctuations in potential output. Changes in structural balances may reflect policy changes or the built-in momentum of existing policy commitments. Structural balances should be interpreted as broad orders of magnitude because of the uncertainties that attach to estimates of cyclical gaps and to changes in revenues and expenditures related to national income.

Sub-prime borrower= is a borrower with a poor credit history and/or insufficient collateral who, consequently, does not qualify for a conventional loan and is charged a risk premium.

Swap= is a financial tool for public debt management. A swap occurs when two parties contractually agree to exchange the streams of payments on equivalent amounts of debt. There are two forms: interest rate and currency swaps, which can be used to extend the time periods for payments on interest and on principal.

Tier 1 capital= is a measure of the capital adequacy of a bank, which is calculated as the ratio of a bank's core equity capital to its total risk-weighted assets. Equity capital includes ordinary shares and retained profits and earnings.

Unit labour costs= a measure of total labour costs per unit of output.

Value at risk= measures a portfolio's maximum loss during a specific time period at a given level of probability.

Write-down= occurs when a loan is recognized as having become partly unrecoverable and its value on the balance sheets of financial institutions is reduced accordingly.

Write-off= occurs when a loan is recognized as having become totally unrecoverable and is removed from the balance sheet.

Yield= is the term used in bond markets to refer to the interest paid on a bond over its lifetime at current market price. The yield has an inverse relationship to the price of the bond: the higher the price, the lower the yield.

Yield curve= is a graphical representation of the relationship between the interest rate or yield and the residual maturity at a given point in time for sufficiently homogenous debt securities with different maturity dates. The slope of the yield curve can be measured as the difference between the interest rates or yield at two selected maturities.

References

Abelshauser, W. (1983). *Wirtschaftsgeschichte der Bundesrepublik Deutschland 1945–1980.* Frankfurt am Main: Suhrkamp.

Abraham, J. and Lemineur-Toumson, C. (1981). *Les Choix Monétaires Européens 1950–1980.* Namur: Cahiers de la Faculté des Sciences Économiques et Sociales de Namur.

Acemoglu, D., Johnson, S., and Robinson, J. (2005). 'The Rise of Europe: Atlantic Trade, Institutional Change and Economic Growth', *American Economic Review,* 95: 546–79.

Admati, A. and Hellwig, M. (2013). *The Bankers' New Clothes: What's Wrong with Banking and What to Do About It.* Princeton, NJ: Princeton University Press.

AFME/EPDA (2013). *European Primary Dealerships Handbook.* London: AFME.

L'Agence France Trésor (2009). *STV Charter* (17 July), <http://www.aft.gouv.fr/>

L'Agence France Trésor (2010). *Bulletin mensuel,* No. 242 (July), <http://www.aft.gouv.fr/rubriques/bulletins-mensuels˙202.html>

Ahamed, L. (2010). *Lords of Finance: 1929, The Great Depression, and the Bankers Who Broke the World.* London: Windmill Books.

Aizenman, J., Kletzer, K., and Pinto, B. (2007). 'Economic Growth with Constraints on Tax Revenues and Public Debt: Implications for Fiscal Policy and Cross-Country Differences', *NBER Working Paper,* No. 12750. <http://www.econstor.eu/bitstream/10419/64089/1/604579217.pdf>

Aizenman, J. and Marion, N. (2009). 'Using Inflation to Erode the US Public Debt', *NBER Working Paper,* No. 15562. <http://www.voxeu.org/article/using-inflation-erode-us-public-debt>

Akerlof, G. and Shiller, R. (2009). *Animal Spirits.* Princeton, NJ: Princeton University Press.

Alesina, A. (1989). 'Politics and Business Cycles in Industrial Democracies', *Economic Policy,* 8: 55–98.

Alesina, A., Carloni, D., and Lecce, G. (2010). 'The Electoral Consequences of Large Fiscal Adjustments', Harvard University, mimeo.

Alesina, A. and Perotti, R. (1995). 'The Political Economy of Budget Deficits', *IMF Staff Papers*, 42 (1): 1–31. Washington, DC: International Monetary Fund.

Alesina, A. and Perotti, R. (1996). 'Fiscal Adjustments in OECD Countries: Composition and Macro-Economic Effects', *NBER Working Paper*, No. 5730. <http://www1.worldbank.org/publicsector/pe/pfma07/alesinaperotti1996.pdf>

Alesina, A. and Spolaore, E. (2003). *The Size of Nations*. Cambridge, MA: MIT Press.

Ali Abbas, S., Belhocine, N., ElGanainy, A., and Horton, M. (2010). 'A Historical Public Debt Data Base', *IMF Working Paper*, 10/245 (November). Washington, DC: International Monetary Fund. < http://www.imf.org/external/pubs/ft/wp/2010/wp10245.pdf>

Allum, P. (1973). *Politics and Society in Post-War Naples*. Cambridge: Cambridge University Press.

Alt, J., Lassen, D., and Wehner, J. (2012). 'Moral Hazard in an Economic Union: Politics, Economics and Fiscal Gimmickry in Europe', *Working Paper*, 5/2012. London: London School of Economics, Department of Government.

Alvarez-Nogal, C. and Chamley, C. (2011). 'Debt Policy under Constraints between Philip II, the Cortes and Genoese Bankers', *Working Papers in Economic History* 11–06 (June). Madrid: Universidad Carlos III de Madrid.

Ambrosianio, M., Bordignon, M., and Cerniglia, F. (2008). 'Constitutional Reforms, Fiscal Decentralization and Regional Fiscal Flows in Italy', *Working Paper*, No. 84 (December), DISCE. Milan: Universita' Cattolica del Sacro Cuore, Milan.

Analistas Financieros Internacionales (2009). 'FX Reserves' (8 September). Foreign Exchange Contact Group, European Central Bank.

Andersen, T., Bentzen, J., Dalgaard, C.-J., and Sharp, P. (2013). 'Pre-Reformation Roots of the Protestant Ethic', *Working Paper*, No. 137, Centre for Comparative Advantage in the Global Economy, University of Warwick.

Andreau, J. (2006). 'Existait-il une dette publique dans l'Antiquité romaine?', in J. Andreau, G. Béaurd, and J.-Y. Grenier (eds), *La Dette Publique dans l'Histoire*. Paris: Comité pour l'histoire économique et financière de la France, pp. 101–14.

Aristotle. *The Ethics*. Harmondsworth: Penguin, 1955.

Aristotle. *Poetics*. London: Penguin, 1996.

Aschauer, D. (1989). 'Is Public Expenditure Productive?', *Journal of Monetary Economics*, 23: 177–200.

Aspinwall, M. and Schneider, G. (eds) (2001). *The Rules of Integration: Institutionalist Approaches to the Study of Europe*. Manchester: Manchester University Press.

Astley, N. (2011). *Being Human*. Tarset: Bloodaxe Books.

Augar, P. (2000). *The Death of Gentlemanly Capitalism: The Rise and Fall of London's Investment Banks*. London: Penguin.

Augar, P. (2010). *Reckless: The Rise and Fall of the City.* London: Vintage Books.

Authers, J. (2010). *The Fearful Rise of Markets: Short View of Globalized Bubbles and Synchronized Meltdowns.* Harlow: Pearson.

Avendano, R. and Santiso, J. (2009). 'Are Sovereign Wealth Funds' Investments Politically Biased? A Comparison with Mutual Funds', *OECD Development Centre Working Paper*, No. 283 (December). Paris: OECD.

Axelrod, R. (1984). *The Evolution of Cooperation.* New York: Basic Books.

Balachandran, G. (2008). 'Power and Markets in Global Finance: The Gold Standard, 1890–1926', *Journal of Global History*, 3: 313–35.

Baldwin, J. (1986). *The Government of Philip Augustus.* Berkeley: University of California Press.

Balladur, E. (2010). 'Mieux gouverner l'Europe', *Le Figaro*, 17 February.

Balzac, H. de (1843). *Lost Illusions.* London: Penguin, 1976.

Banca d'Italia (2009). *Supplementi al Bollettino Statistico: Debito delle amministrazioni locali*, No. 36 (30 October).

Bank of England (1931). 'The Kindersley-Norman Plan' (2 February). Bank of England Archive Ref: OV4/23 (marked 'private and confidential').

Bank for International Settlements (2000). *Managing Foreign Debt and Liquidity Risks.* Basel: BIS.

Bank for International Settlements (2002). 'Comparison of Creditor and Debtor Data on Short-Term External Debt', *BIS Papers*, No. 13 (December).

Bank for International Settlements (2010a). *Detailed Tables on Provisional Locational and Consolidated Banking Statistics at end-December 2009.* Basel: BIS.

Bank for International Settlements (2010b). *80th Annual Report, 1 April 2009–31 March 2010.* Basel: BIS.

Bank for International Settlements (2011). *Quarterly Review* (June). Basel: BIS.

Barbour, V. (1950). *Capitalism in Amsterdam in the 17th Century.* Baltimore, MD: Johns Hopkins Press.

Barro, R. (1979). 'The Determinants of the Public Debt', *Journal of Political Economy*, 87 (5): 940–71.

Barro, R. (1987). 'Government Spending, Interest Rates, Prices, and Budget Deficits in the United Kingdom, 1701–1918', *Journal of Monetary Economics*, 20: 221–47.

Baum, A., Checherita-Westphal, C., and Rother, P. (2013). 'Debt and Growth: New Evidence for the Euro Area', *Journal of International Money and Finance*, 32: 809–21.

Baus, R., Eppler, A., and Wintermann, O. (eds) (2008). *Zur Reform der föderalen Finanzverfassung in Deutschland.* Baden-Baden: Nomos.

Beach, D. (2005). *The Dynamics of European Integration: Why and When EU Institutions Matter*. Basingstoke: Palgrave Macmillan.

Beaulac, S. (2004). *The Power of Language in the Making of International Law: The Word Sovereignty in Bodin and Vattel and the Myth of Westphalia*. Leiden: Martinus Nijhoff.

Beckert, J. and Streeck, W. (2012). 'Die Fiskalkrise und die Einheit Europas', *Aus Politik und Zeitgeschichte, 4*: 7–16.

Bell, A., Brooks, C., and Moore, T. (2009). *Accounts of the English Crown with Italian Merchant Societies, 1272–1345*. Kew: List and Index Society.

Berger, J. (1972). *Ways of Seeing*. London: Penguin.

Bertelsmann Stiftung (ed.) (2007). *Die Bundesländer im Standortwettbewerb*. Gütersloh: Bertelsmann Stiftung.

Bertelsmann Stiftung (2009). *Policy Performance and Executive Capacity in the OECD: Sustainable Governance Indicators 2009*. Paris: OECD.

Besley, T. and Persson, T. (2011). *The Pillars of Prosperity*. Princeton, NJ: Princeton University Press.

Betzold, C. (2010). '"Borrowing" Power to Influence International Negotiations: AOSIS in the Climate Change Regime, 1990–1997', *Politics*, 30 (3): 131–48.

Bini Smaghi, L. (2010a). 'It is Better to Have Explicit Rules for Bail Outs', *Financial Times*, 16 March.

Bini Smaghi, L. (2010b). 'Lessons of the Crisis: Ethics, Markets, Democracy', speech at the Unione Cristiana Imprenditori Dirigenti (UCID), Milan, 13 May.

Bini Smaghi, L. (2010c). 'Challenges for the Euro Area, and the World Economy', speech at 'The Group of Thirty', sixty-third Plenary Session, Rabat, 28 May.

Blake, R. (1966). *Disraeli*. London: Eyre and Spottiswoode.

Blanchard, O. (1985). 'Debt, Deficits, and Finite Horizons', *Journal of Political Economy*, 93 (2): 223–47.

Blanchard, O. (2008). 'The State of Macro', *Working Paper*, No. 08-17. Cambridge, MA: MIT Press.

Blanchard, O. (2009). 'The Crisis: Basic Mechanism and Appropriate Policies', *Working Paper Series*, No. 09-01. Cambridge, MA: MIT Press.

Blomquist, T. (2005). *Merchant Families, Banking and Money in Medieval Lucca*. Abingdon: Ashgate.

Bloomestein, H., Guzzo, V., Holland, A., and Mu, Y. (2010). 'Debt Markets: Policy Challenges in the Post-Crisis Landscape', *Financial Market Trends*, 1: 1–27.

Bloomestein, H. and Wehinger, G. (2007). *Public Debt Management and the Evolving Market for (Ultra-)Long Government Bonds*. Paris: OECD.

Blundell-Wignall, A. and Slovik, P. (2010). 'The EU Stress Test and Sovereign Debt Exposures', *OECD Working Papers on Finance, Insurance and Private Pensions*, No. 4 (August). Paris: OECD Financial Affairs Division.

Blyth, M. (2002). *Great Transformations: Economic Ideas and Institutional Change in the Twentieth Century*. Cambridge: Cambridge University Press.

Bodin, J. (1577). *Six Books of the Commonwealth (Les Six livres de la République)*, trans. M. Tooley. Oxford: Blackwell, 1955.

Bonney, R. (1981). *King's Debts: Finance and Politics in France 1589–1661*. Oxford: Clarendon Press.

Bonney, R. (2010). 'The Apogee and Fall of the French Rentier Regime, 1801–1914', in J. Cardoso and P. Lains (eds), *Paying for the Liberal State: The Rise of Public Finance in Nineteenth-Century Europe*. Cambridge: Cambridge University Press, pp. 81–102.

Bonney, R. (ed.) (1999). *The Rise of the Fiscal State in Europe, c. 1200–1815*. Oxford: Oxford University Press.

Boone, M., Davids, K., and Jannsens, P. (eds) (2003). *Urban Public Debts: Urban Government and the Market for Annuities in Western Europe (14th–18th Centuries)*. Turnhout: Brepols.

Bordignon, M. and Turati, G. (2003). 'Bailing Out Expectations and Health Expenditure in Italy', *CESIFO Working Paper*, No. 1026 (December).

Bordo, M. and Flandreau, M. (2001). 'Core, Periphery, Exchange Rate Regimes and Globalization', *CEPR Discussion Paper*, No. 3077. London: Centre for Economic Policy Research.

Bordo, M. and Meissner, C. (2006). 'The Role of Foreign Currency Debt in Financial Crises, 1818–1913 versus 1972–1997', *Journal of Banking and Finance*, 30: 3299–329.

Bordo, M. and Schwartz, A. (eds) (1984). *A Retrospective on the Classical Gold Standard, 1821–1931*. London: University of Chicago Press.

Borio, C. and White, W. (2004). 'Whither Monetary Stability? The Implications of Evolving Policy Regimes', *BIS Working Papers*, No. 147 (February). Basel: Bank for International Settlements.

Boswell, C. (2009). *The Political Uses of Expert Knowledge: Immigration Policy and Social Research*. Cambridge: Cambridge University Press.

Boulding, K. (1956). *The Image: Knowledge in Life and Society*. Ann Arbor: University of Michigan Press.

Bourdieu, P. (1991). *Language and Symbolic Power*. Cambridge: Polity Press.

Boyle, G. and Geary, P. (2004). 'The Irish Currency Report of 1804', *Central Bank of Ireland Quarterly Bulletin*, Spring: 107–27.

Braddick, M. (1996). *The Nerves of State: Taxation and the Financing of the English State, 1558–1714*. Manchester: Manchester University Press.

Branda, P. (2007). *Le prix de la gloire: Napoléon et l'argent.* Paris: Fayard.

Braudel, F. (1984). *Civilization and Capitalism 15th–18th Century: Volume III—The Perspective of the World.* London: William Collins.

Breslau, D. (2003). 'Economics Invents the Economy: Mathematics, Statistics, and Models in the Work of Irving Fisher and Wesley Mitchell', *Theory and Society*, 32 (3): 379–411.

Brewer, J. (1989). *The Sinews of Power. War, Money and the English State 1688–1783.* London: Unwin and Hymans.

Broner, F., Lorenzoni, G., and Schmukler, S. (2007). 'Why Do Emerging Economies Borrow Short Term?', *NBER Working Paper*, No. W13076. Cambridge, MA: National Bureau of Economic Research.

Brown, G. (2010). *Beyond the Crash: Overcoming the First Crisis of Globalisation.* New York: Simon and Schuster.

Buchheit, L., Gulati, G., and Thompson, R. (2007). 'The Dilemma of Odious Debts', *Duke Law Journal*, 56 (5): 1201–62.

Buiter, W. and Rahbari, E. (2013). 'Why Do Governments Default, and Why Don't They Default More Often', *CEPR Discussion Paper*, No. 9492. London: Centre for Economic Policy Research.

Buratti, C. (2011). 'The Federalizing Process in Italy', workshop on financing devolution, Wales Governance Centre, Cardiff University, January 2011.

Bürgelt, C. (2007). 'Der jüdische Hoffaktor Berend Lehmann und die Finanzierung der polnischen Königskrone für August den Starken', *Medaon*, <www.medaon.de>

Caballero, R., Cowan, K., and Kearns, J. (2004). 'Fear of Sudden Stops: Lessons from Australia and Chile', *NBER Working Paper*, No. 10519. Cambridge, MA: National Bureau of Economic Research.

Cain, P. and Hopkins, A. (2002). *British Imperialism, 1688–2000.* London: Longman.

Cairncross, A. and Eichengreen, B. (1983). *Sterling in Decline: The Devaluations of 1931, 1949 and 1967.* Oxford: Blackwell.

Calvo, G. (1988). 'Servicing the Public Debt—The Role of Expectations', *American Economic Review*, 78 (4): 647–61.

Cantoni, D. (2013). 'The Economic Effects of the Protestant Reformation: Testing the Weber Hypothesis in the German Lands', *Munich Discussion Paper*, No. 2013-4. München: Volkswirtschafliche Fakultät, Ludwig-Maximilians-Universität.

Carande, R. (1987). *Carlos V y sus banqueros*, 3 vols. Barcelona: Critica.

Carboni, M. (1995). *Il debito della città. Mercato del credito, fisco et società a Bologna fra Cinque e Seicento.* Bologna: Il Mulino.

Carboni, M. (2012). 'From Communal to State Finance: A New Fiscal Pact in the Early Modern Papal States', *Quaderni—Working Paper*, 850. Bologna: Department of Economics, University of Bologna.

Carlos, A. and Neal, L. (2011). 'Amsterdam and London as Financial Centres in the Eighteenth Century', *Financial History Review*, 18 (1): 21–46.

Cecchetti, S. and Kharroubi, E. (2012). 'Reassessing the Impact of Finance on Growth', Conference Paper (January). Basel: Bank for International Settlements.

Cecchetti, S., Mohanty, M., and Zampolli, F. (2010). 'The Future of Public Debt: Prospects and Implications', *BIS Working Paper*, No. 300 (March). Basel: Bank for International Settlements.

Cecchetti, S., Mohanty, M., and Zampolli, F. (2011). 'The Real Effects of Debt', *BIS Working Paper*, No. 352 (September). Basel: Bank for International Settlements.

Cervantes, M. (1605/1615). *Don Quixote*. London: Penguin, 2003.

Cetina, K. and Preda, A. (eds) (2005). *The Sociology of Financial Markets*. Oxford: Oxford University Press.

Champsaur, P. and Cotis, J.-P. (2010). *Rapport sur la Situation des Finances Publiques* (April). Paris: République Française.

Chankowski, V. (2008). *Athènes et Délos à l'époque classique. Recherches sur l'administration du sanctuaire d'Apollon délien*. Athens: École Française d'Athènes.

Checherita, C. and Rother, P. (2012). 'The Impact of High and Growing Government Debt on Economic Growth: An Empirical Investigation in the Euro Area', *European Economic Review*, 56: 1392–405.

Checherita-Westphal, C., Hughes Hallett, A., and Rother, P. (2012). 'Fiscal Sustainability Using Growth-Maximizing Debt Targets', *Working Paper*, No. 1472. Frankfurt am Main: European Central Bank.

Chekhov, A. (1887). 'A Problem', in *Short Stories 1887: 3*. Createspace Independent Publishing Platform, 2013, pp. 309–16.

Chekhov, A. (1889). 'The Bet' in *Short Stories 1888–1895 (The Complete Short Stories of Anton Chekhov)*. Createspace Independent Publishing Platform, 2013, pp. 134–7.

Chekhov, A. (1904). *The Cherry Orchard*. London: Methuen, 1995.

Chekhov, A and Senelick, L. (1888). 'The Bear', in A. Chekhov and L. Senelick, *The Complete Plays*. New York: W.W. Norton, 2007, pp. 415–33.

Chernow, R. (1990). *House of Morgan: An American Banking Dynasty and the Rise of Modern Finance*. New York: Simon and Schuster.

Chernow, R. (2005). *Alexander Hamilton*. London: Penguin.

Chilosi, D. and Volckart, O. (2010a). 'Good or Bad Money? Debasement, Society and the State in the Late Middle Ages', *Working Paper*, 140/10. London: Department of Economic History, London School of Economics.

Chilosi, D. and Volckart, O. (2010b). 'Books or Bullion? Printing, Mining and Financial Integration in Central Europe from the 1460s', *Working Paper*, 144/10. London: Department of Economic History, London School of Economics.

Chitu, L., Eichengreen, B., and Mehl, A. (2012). 'When Did the Dollar Overtake Sterling as the Leading International Currency? Evidence from the Bond Markets', *NBER Working Paper*, No. 18097. Cambridge, MA: National Bureau of Economic Research.

Claeys, P., Ramos, R., and Surinach, J. (2008). 'Fiscal Sustainability across Government Tiers', *International Economics and Economic Policy*, 5 (1–2): 139–63.

Clarendon, R. (1791). *A Sketch of the Revenue and Finances of Ireland.* London: Lowndes and Debrett.

Clark, C. (2013). *The Sleepwalkers: How Europe Went to War in 1914.* London: Penguin.

Clay, C.G.A. (2000). *Gold for the Sultan: Western Bankers and Ottoman Finance 1856–1881: A Contribution to Ottoman and International Financial History.* London and New York: I.B. Taurus/St. Martin's Press.

Clegg, L. (2010). 'Our Dream is a World Full of Poverty Indicators: The US, the World Bank, and the Power of Numbers', *New Political Economy*, 15 (4): 473–92.

Clement, P. (2010). 'The Term "Macroprudential": Origins and Evolution', *BIS Quarterly Review*, March: 59–67.

Cohen, E. (2008). 'Elasticity of the Money Supply at Athens', in W. Harris (ed.), *The Monetary Systems of the Greeks and Romans.* Oxford: Oxford University Press, pp. 66–83.

Cole, A. (2008). *Governing and Governance in France.* Cambridge: Cambridge University Press.

Collignon, S. (2010). 'Who Is Reforming Europe's Economic Governance?' *Social Europe*, <http://www.social-europe.eu/2010/08/who-is-reforming-europes-economic-governance/>

Colzi, F. (1999). *Il debbito pubblico del Campidoglio: Finanza communale e circolazione dei titoli a Roma fra Cinque e Seicento.* Napoli: Edizioni Scientifiche Italiane.

Comín, F. (1996). *Historia de la Hacienda pública, II, España (1808–1995).* Barcelona: Critica.

Comín, F. (2012). 'Default, Rescheduling, and Inflation: Debt Crisis in Spain during the 19th and 20th Centuries', *Working Papers in Economic History*, 12-06. Madrid: Universidad Carlos III de Madrid.

Commission on Scottish Devolution (2009). *Serving Scotland Better: Scotland and the United Kingdom in the 21st Century.* The Calman Commission. <www.commissiononscottishdevolution.org.uk>

Committee on the Global Financial System (2011). *The Impact of Sovereign Credit Risk on Bank Funding Conditions.* Basel: Bank for International Settlements.

Committee of Wise Men (2001). *Final Report on the Regulation of European Securities Markets.* Brussels: European Commission.

Congressional Budget Office (2010a). *Historical Data on the Federal Debt Held by the Public, 1790 to 2000* (July). Washington, DC: CBO.

Congressional Budget Office (2010b). *Federal Debt and the Risk of a Fiscal Crisis.* Washington, DC: CBO.

Conklin, J. (1998). 'The Theory of Sovereign Debt: Spain under Philip II', *Journal of Political Economy*, 106 (3): 483–513.

Conversi, D. (2007). 'Asymmetrical Federalism and Consociational Practice: Spain, Italy and Beyond', ECPR Conference, Pisa, Italy, September.

Cooper, G. (2008). *The Origins of Financial Crises: Central Banks, Credit Bubbles and the Efficient Markets Fallacy.* Petersfield: Harriman House Publishing.

Cottarelli, C., Forni, L., Gottschalk, J., and Mauro, P. (2010). 'Default in Today's Advanced Economies: Unnecessary, Undesirable, and Unlikely', *IMF Staff Position Note*, 2012/12 (1 September). Washington, DC: International Monetary Fund.

Craig, P. and de Búrca, G. (2003). *EU Law. Text, Cases, and Materials*, 3rd edn. Oxford: Oxford University Press.

Crosthwaite, P. (2010). 'Blood on the Trading Floor: Waste, Sacrifice and Death in Financial Crises', *Angelaki: Journal of Theoretical Humanities*, 15 (2): 3–18.

Cunich, P. (1999). 'Revolution and Crisis in English State Finance, 1534–47', in R. Bonney (ed.), *The Rise of the Fiscal State in Europe, c. 1200–1815.* Oxford: Oxford University Press, pp.118–39.

Cyr, P. (2010). 'Réalité financière de la reconstruction de l'armée', *Revue historique des armées*, 260: 90–102.

Daniel, K., Hirschleifer, D., and Subramanyam, A. (1998). 'Investor Psychology and Security Market Under- and Overreactions', *Journal of Finance*, 53–6: 1839–85.

Dante, A. (1555). *The Divine Comedy.* Oxford: Oxford University Press, 2008.

Das, S. (2011). *Extreme Money: The Masters of the Universe and the Cult of Risk.* Pearson: Australia.

Das, U., Papaioannou, M., and Trebesch, C. (2012). 'Sovereign Debt Restructurings 1950-2010: Literature Survey, Data, and Stylized Facts', *IMF Working Paper*, WP/12/203. Washington, DC: International Monetary Fund.

Davies, H. and Green, D. (2010). *Banking on the Future: The Fall and Rise of Central Banking.* Princeton, NJ: Princeton University Press.

Davis, A. (2000). 'Public Relations, Business News and the Reproduction of Corporate Elite Power', *Journalism*, 1 (3): 282–304.

Davis, A. (2006). 'The Role of the Mass Media in Investor Relations', *Journal of Communication Management*, 10 (1): 7–17.

De Beaufort Wijnholds, J.O. and Kapteyn, A. (2001). 'Reserve Adequacy in Emerging Market Economies', *IMF Working Paper*, 01/143. Washington, DC: International Monetary Fund.

De Beaufort Wijnholds, J.O. and Sondergaard, L. (2007). 'Reserve Accumulation: Objective or By-Product?', *ECB Occasional Paper*, No. 73 (September). Frankfurt am Main: European Central Bank.

De Bondt, W. (2005). 'The Values and Beliefs of European Investors', in K. Cetina and A. Preda (eds), *The Sociology of Financial Markets*. Oxford: Oxford University Press, pp. 163–86.

De Bonis, R., Fano, D., and Sbano, T. (2013). 'Household Aggregate Wealth in the Main OECD Countries from 1980 to 2011: What Do the Data Tell Us ?', *Working Paper*, No. 82 (May). Money and Finance Research Group.

De Cecco, M. (1984). *International Gold Standard: Money and Empire*. London: Pinter.

Defoe, D. (1710). *An Essay upon Publick Credit*. London: W. Baynes and J. Jordan, 1797.

De Grauwe, P. (2011). 'The Governance of a Fragile Eurozone', *Discussion Paper*, <http://www.econ.kuleuven.be>

de Larosière Group (2009). *The High Level Group on Financial Supervision in the EU*. Brussels: European Commission.

della Paolera, G. and Taylor, A. (2012). 'Sovereign Debt in Latin America, 1820–1913', *NBER Working Paper*, No. 18363. Cambridge, MA: National Bureau of Economic Research.

Dennett, D. (1991). *Consciousness Explained*. Boston, MA: Little, Brown and Co.

Den Uyl, D. (1991). *The Virtue of Prudence*. New York: Peter Lang.

De Roover, R. (1963). *The Rise and Decline of the Medici Bank*. Cambridge, MA: Harvard University Press.

De Roover, R. (2008). *Money, Banking and Credit in Medieval Bruges—Italian Merchant Bankers, Lombards and Money Changers—A Study in the Origins of Banking*. Washington, DC: Rinsland Press.

Dertilis, G.B. (2005). *History of the Greek State, 1830–1920*, Vol. B, 3rd edn. Athens: Estia.

Deschouwer, K. (2005). 'The Kingdom of Belgium', in J. Kincaid and G. Tarr (eds), *Constitutional Origins, Structure and Change in Federal Countries*. Montreal: McGill-Queen's University Press, pp. 48–75.

Deutsche Bundesbank (ed.) (1976). *Deutsches Geld- und Bankwesen in Zahlen 1876–1975*. Frankfurt am Main: Fritz Knapp.

Deutsche Bundesbank (2002). 'Developments in the External Economic Relations of the EU Accession Countries in Central and Eastern Europe', *Monthly Report*, December: 49–68.

Deutsche Bundesbank (2008). 'Germany's International Investment Position since the Beginning of Monetary Union: Developments and Structure', *Monthly Report*, October: 15–32.

Deutsche Bundesbank (2009). *Annual Report.* Frankfurt am Main: Bundesbank.

Deutsche Bundesbank (2010a). 'Government Debt and Interest Payment Burden in Germany', *Monthly Report*, March: 15–33.

Deutsche Bundesbank (2010b). 'On the Problems of Macro-economic Imbalances in the Euro Area', *Monthly Report*, July: 17–33.

Deutsche Bundesbank (2011a). 'The Transmission and Regional Distribution of the German Economy's Cyclical Impulses within Europe', *Monthly Report*, March: 22–3.

Deutsche Bundesbank (2011b). 'The Role of the Stability Council', *Monthly Report*, October: 20–3.

Deutsche Bundesbank (2012). 'The International Monetary Fund in a Changed Global Environment', *Monthly Report*, September: 61–74.

Deutsche Bundesbank (2013). 'Household Wealth and Finances in Germany: Results of the Bundesbank Survey', *Monthly Report*, June: 23–49.

Deutscher, P. (1990). *R.G. Hawtrey and the Development of Macroeconomics.* London: Macmillan.

Dickens, C. (1837). *Pickwick Papers.* Oxford: Oxford University Press, 2008.

Dickens, C. (1850). *David Copperfield.* Oxford: Oxford University Press, 2008.

Dickens, C. (1857). *Little Dorrit.* Oxford: Oxford University Press, 2012.

Dickson, P.G.M. (1967). *The Financial Revolution in England: A Study in the Development of Public Credit, 1688–1756.* London: Macmillan.

Diebold, W. (1952). *Trade and Payments in Western Europe: A Study of Economic Cooperation, 1947–1951.* New York: Harper.

Dietzel, K. (1855). *Das System der Staatsanleihen im Zusammenhang der Volkswirtschaft betrachtet.* Heidelberg: Mohr.

Dimitrov, V. (2006). 'EMU and Fiscal Policy', in K. Dyson (ed.), *Enlarging the Euro Area: External Empowerment and Domestic Transformation in East Central Europe.* Oxford: Oxford University Press, pp. 261–78.

Dincecco, M. and Katz, G. (2012). 'State Capacity and Long-Term Performance', *MPRA Paper*, No. 38299 (23 April), <http://ub.uni-muenchen.de/39299/>

Dipartimento del Tesoro (2010). *Historical Database on Government Debt Breakdown 1982–2000.* Rome: Treasury Ministry.

Dorrucci, E. (2006). 'The Accumulation of Foreign Exchange Reserves', European Central Bank, 31 May.

Dow, C. (1998). *Major Recessions: Britain and the World, 1920–1995.* Oxford: Oxford University Press.

Drelichman, M. (2005). 'All That Glitters: Precious Metals, Rent Seeking and the Decline of Spain', *European Review of Economic History*, 9 (3): 313–36.

Drelichman, M. and Voth, H.-J. (2007). 'The Sustainable Debts of Philip II: A Reconstruction of Spain's Fiscal Position, 1560–1598', *CEPR Discussion Papers*, 6611. London: Centre for Economic Policy Research.

Drelichman, M. and Voth, H.-J. (2008). 'Debt Sustainability in Historical Perspective: The Role of Fiscal Repression', *Journal of the European Economic Association*, 6 (2/3): 657–67.

Drelichman, M. and Voth, H.-J. (2009). 'Lending to the Borrower from Hell: Debt and Default in the Age of Philip II, 1566–1598', *CEPR Discussion Papers*, 7276. London: Centre for Economic Policy Research.

Drelichman, M. and Voth, H.-J. (2010). 'Serial Defaults, Serial Profits: Returns to Sovereign Lending in Hapsburg Spain, 1566–1600'. Department of Economics paper. British Columbia: University of British Columbia.

Drumont. E. (1886). *La France juive: Essai d'Histoire Contemporaine.* Hardpress. net, 2013.

Dufrénot, G. and Triki, K. (2012). 'Public Debt Ratio: Its Determinants in France since 1890. Does Econometrics Support the Historical Evidence?', *Document du Travail*, no. 385 (July). Paris: Banque de France.

Duncombe, P. (2001). *Great Goldsmith: The Life of Sir Charles Duncombe (1648–1711).* Rockville, MD: Leonard Communications.

Dupéron, O. (2010). 'Quelle conception de la regionalization dans la nouvelle organization territoriale?', in J.-C. Nemery (ed.), *Quelle nouvelle réforme pour les collectivités territoriales françaises?* Paris: L'Harmattan, pp. 263–72.

Dutch State Treasury Agency (2010a). *DDA—The Dutch Way of Auctioning* (29 March), <http://www.dsta.nl/english/Subjects/Dutch˙Direct˙Auction>

Dutch State Treasury Agency (2010b). *DDA Rules—May 2010* (I June), <http://www.dsta.nl/english/Subjects/Dutch˙Direct˙Auction>

Dutton, J. (1984). 'The Bank of England and the Rules of the Game under the International Gold Standard: New Evidence', in M. Bordo and A. Schwartz (eds), *A Retrospective on the Classical Gold Standard, 1821–1931.* Chicago: University of Chicago Press, pp. 173–95.

Duval, R. and Elmeskov, J. (2005). 'The Effects of EMU on Structural Reforms in Labour and Product Markets', *OECD Economics Department Working Papers*, 438. Paris: OECD.

Dyson, K. (1994). *Elusive Union.* London: Longman.

Dyson, K. (2000). *The Politics of the Euro-Zone: Stability or Breakdown?* Oxford: Oxford University Press.

Dyson, K. (2008a). 'The First Decade: Credibility, Identity, and Institutional "Fuzziness"', in K. Dyson (ed.), *The Euro at 10: Europeanization, Convergence, and Power*. Oxford: Oxford University Press, pp. 1–34.

Dyson, K. (2008b). 'European States and the Euro Area: Clustering and Covariance in Patterns of Change', in K. Dyson (ed.), *The Euro at 10: Europeanization, Convergence, and Power*. Oxford: Oxford University Press, pp. 378–413.

Dyson, K. (2009). 'The Age of the Euro: A Structural Break? Europeanization, Convergence, and Power in Central Banking', in K. Dyson and M. Marcussen (eds), *Central Banks in the Age of the Euro: Europeanization, Power and Convergence*. Oxford: Oxford University Press, pp. 1–51.

Dyson, K. (2010). *The State Tradition in Western Europe*. Essex University: European Consortium for Political Science Research Classics Series.

Dyson, K. (2013). 'Sworn to Grim Necessity? Imperfections of European Economic Governance, Normative Political Theory, and Supreme Emergency', *Journal of European Integration*, 35 (3): 207–22.

Dyson, K. and Featherstone, K. (1999). *The Road to Maastricht: Negotiating Economic and Monetary Union*. Oxford: Oxford University Press.

Dyson, K. and Marcussen, M. (2010). 'Transverse Integration in European Macro-economic Governance: Between Unitary and Differentiated Integration', *Journal of European Integration*, 32 (1): 17–39.

Dyson, K. and Quaglia, L. (2010a). *European Economic Governance: Commentary and Documents, Volume I—History and Institutions*. Oxford: Oxford University Press.

Dyson, K. and Quaglia, L. (2010b). *European Economic Governance: Commentary and Documents, Volume II—Policies*. Oxford: Oxford University Press.

Eaton, J., Gersovitz, M., and Stigler, J. (1986). 'The Pure Theory of Country Risk', *European Economic Review*, 30: 481–513.

Eatwell, J., Milgate, M., and Newman, P. (eds) (2007). *The New Palgrave: A Dictionary of Economics*. London: Macmillan.

Economic and Financial Committee: Sub-Committee on EU Government Bonds and Bills Markets (2007). *Harmonization of Primary Dealers' Activity Reports*. Brussels: ECFIN/CEFCPE(2005)REP/50677—Rev 5, 26 January.

Economist Intelligence Unit (2011). 'Sovereign Ratings' (January–February), <www.eiu.com/site˙info.asp?info˙name=sovereign˙ratings&rf=0>

Edwards, S. (2004). 'Thirty Years of Current Account Imbalances, Current Account Reversals and Sudden Stops', *NBER Working Paper*, No. 10276. Cambridge, MA: National Bureau of Economic Research.

Ehrenberg, R. (1963). *Capital and Finance in the Age of the Renaissance: A Study of the Fuggers and their Connections*. New York: Kelley.

Eichengreen, B. (1992). *Golden Fetters: The Gold Standard and the Great Depression 1919–1939*. Oxford: Oxford University Press.

Eichengreen, B. (2010). *Global Imbalances and the Lessons of Bretton Woods.* Cambridge, MA: MIT Press.

Eichengreen, B. and Fishlow, A. (1996). *Contending with Capital Flows: What Is Different about the 1990s?* New York: Council on Foreign Relations.

Eichengreen, B. and Flandreau, M. (1997). *The Gold Standard in Theory and History.* London: Routledge.

Eichengreen, B. and Flandreau, M. (2008). 'The Rise and Fall of the Dollar, or When Did the Dollar Replace Sterling as the Leading Reserve Currency?', *CEPR Discussion Paper*, 6869. London: Centre for Economic Policy Research.

Eichengreen, B., Hausman, R., and Panizza, U. (2003). 'Currency Mismatches, Debt Intolerance and Original Sin: Why They Are Not the Same and Why It Matters', *NBER Working Paper*, No. 10036. Cambridge, MA: National Bureau of Economic Research.

Eichengreen, B. and Lindert, P. (eds) (1989). *International Debt Crisis in Historical Perspective.* Cambridge, MA: MIT Press.

Eichengreen, B. and Portes, R. (1989). 'Settling Defaults in the Era of Bond Finance', *World Bank Economic Review*, 3 (2): 211–39.

Eliot, G. (1874). *Middlemarch.* Harmondsworth: Penguin, 1965.

Eliot, G. (1876). *Daniel Deronda.* London: Penguin, 1967.

Emminger, O. (1958). 'Les aspects monétaire du Marché Commun', *Bulletin d'Information et de Documentation*, No. 2 (August). Belgium: National Bank of Belgium, pp. 93–103.

Emminger, O. (1977). 'The D-Mark in the Conflict between Internal and External Equilibrium, 1948–75', *Essays in International Finance*, No. 122. Princeton, NJ: Princeton University Press.

Enderlein, H., Trebesch, C., and von Daniels, L. (2010). *Sovereign Debt Disputes.* Berlin: Hertie School of Management.

Epstein, M. (1980). *The Ottoman Jewish Communities and their Role in the Fifteenth and Sixteenth Centuries.* Freiburg: Klaus Schwarz Verlag.

Essential Information and Consumer Education Foundation (2009). 'Sold Out: How Wall Street and Washington Betrayed America' (March), <www.wallstreetwatch.org>

Esteves, R. (2007). 'Quis custodiet quem? Sovereign Debt and Bondholders' Protection before 1914', *Department of Economics Discussion Paper*, No. 323. Oxford: University of Oxford.

European Central Bank (2007). 'From Government Deficit to Debt: Bridging the Gap', *Monthly Bulletin*, April: 87–93.

European Central Bank (2009a). 'Domestic Fiscal Rules and Institutions as a Complement to the EU Fiscal Framework', *Monthly Bulletin*, September: 84–6.

European Central Bank (2009b). 'Experience with Government Debt Reduction in Euro Area Countries', *Monthly Bulletin*, September: 86–9.

European Central Bank (2010a). 'Prospects for Real and Financial Imbalances and a Global Rebalancing', *Monthly Bulletin*, April: 91–100.

European Central Bank (2010b). 'The Size and Composition of Government Borrowing in the Euro Area', *Monthly Bulletin*, May: 30–3.

European Central Bank (2010c). 'Recent Developments in the Gross External Debt of the Euro Area, *Monthly Bulletin*, May: 36–9.

European Central Bank (2010d). 'Recent Developments in the Gross External Debt of the Euro Area, *Monthly Bulletin*, May: 81–3.

European Central Bank (2010e). 'Measuring the Contribution of Individual Sectors to Systemic Risk during the Recent Financial Crisis', *Financial Stability Review*, June: 101–3.

European Central Bank (2010f). 'Macro-Prudential Policy Objectives and Tools', *Financial Stability Review*, June: 129–37.

European Central Bank (2010g). 'The Impact of the Financial Crisis on the Central and Eastern European Countries', *Monthly Bulletin*, July: 85–96.

European Central Bank (2011a). 'Government Debt Dynamics and Primary Budget Balance Developments in the EU Member States', *Monthly Bulletin*, March: 95–7.

European Central Bank (2011b). 'Measuring Fiscal Sustainability in the Euro Area', *Monthly Bulletin*, April: 61–77.

European Central Bank (2012a). 'Analyzing Government Debt Sustainability in the Euro Area', *Monthly Bulletin*, April: 55–70.

European Central Bank (2012b). 'Government Financial Assets and Liabilities in the Euro Area', *Annual Report 2011*, 63–5.

European Commission (2008). 'EMU@10: Successes and Challenges after Ten Years of Economic and Monetary Union', *European Economy*, 2. Luxembourg: Office for Official Publications of the European Communities.

European Commission (2009). 'Sustainability Report', *European Economy*, 9. Luxembourg: Office for Official Publications of the European Communities.

European Commission (2010). 'Surveillance of Intra-Euro-Area Competitiveness and Imbalances', *European Economy*, 1. Luxembourg: Publications Office of the European Union.

European Commission (2012). 'Fiscal Sustainability Report 2012', *European Economy*, 8 (December). Luxembourg: Publications Office of the European Union.

European Primary Dealers Association (2008). 'A Common European Government Bond' (September). London: European Primary Dealers Association.

European Social Survey (2013). 'Economic Crisis, Quality of Work and Social Integration: Topline Results from Rounds 2 and 5 of the European Social Survey', *European Social Survey*, 3, <www.europeansocialsurvey.org>

Fairclough, N. (1989). *Language and Power.* London: Longman.

Featherstone, K. and Papadimitriou, D. (2008). *The Limits of Europeanization: Reform Capacity and Policy Conflict in Greece.* Houndmills: Palgrave Macmillan.

Feilchenfeld, E. (1934). 'Rights and Remedies of Holders of Foreign Bonds' in S.E. Quindry (ed.), *Bonds and Bondholders, Rights and Remedies*, vol. 2. Chicago: Burdette J. Smith and Co, pp. 3–21.

Feis, H. (1930). *Europe, the World's Banker 1870–1914.* New Haven, CT: Yale University Press.

Feldman, G. (1997). *The Great Disorder. Politics, Economics, and Society in the German Inflation, 1914–1924.* Oxford: Oxford University Press.

Felice, E. (2011). 'Regional Value Added in Italy (1891–2001) and the Foundation of a Long-Term Picture', *The Economic History Review*, 64: 929–50.

Ferguson, N. (1994). 'Public Finance and National Security: The Domestic Origins of the First World War Revisited', *Past and Present*, 142: 141–68.

Ferguson, N. (2009). *The Ascent of Money: A Financial History of the World.* London: Penguin.

Ferguson, N. (2010). *High Financier: The Lives and Time of Siegmund Warburg.* London: Penguin.

Fielding, H. (1742). *Joseph Andrews.* Oxford: Oxford University Press, 2008.

Financial Stability Board (2012). *Global Shadow Banking Monitoring Report 2012.* Basel: Bank for International Settlements.

Financial Times (2010). 'Berlin Urged to Aid Eurozone', interview with Christine Lagarde, 15 March, p. 1.

Finn, M. (2003). *The Character of Credit: Personal Debt in English Culture, 1740–1914.* Cambridge: Cambridge University Press.

Fisher, I. (1933). 'The Debt-Deflation Theory of Great Depressions', *Econometrica*, October: 337–57.

Fishlow, A. (1989). 'Conditionality and Willingness to Pay: Parallels from the 1890s', in B. Eichengreen and P. Lindert (eds), *The International Debt Crisis in Historical Perspective.* Cambridge, MA: MIT Press, pp. 86–98.

Fisk, H. (1921). *English Public Finance: From the Revolution of 1688 with Chapters on the Bank of England.* London: Sir Isaac Pitman.

Fitch Ratings (2009a). 'Coercive Debt Exchange Criteria' (3 March), <www.fitchratings.com>

Fitch Ratings (2009b). 'Rating Subnationals above the Sovereign in the Euro Area' (25 June), <www.fitchratings.com>

Fitch Ratings (2009c). 'Sovereign Rating Methodology' (16 October), www.fitchratings.com>

Flandreau, M. (2001). 'The Bank, the States, and the Market: An Austro-Hungarian Tale for Euroland, 1867–1914', *Working Paper*, 43. Vienna: Österreichische Nationalbank.

Flandreau, M. (2003a). 'Caveat Emptor: Coping with Sovereign Risk under the International Gold Standard, 1871–1913', in M. Flandreau, C.-L. Holtfrerich, and H. James (eds), *The International Financial History in the Twentieth Century: System and Anarchy*. Cambridge: Cambridge University Press, pp. 17–50.

Flandreau, M. (ed.) (2003b). *Money Doctors: The Experience of International Financial Advising 1850–2000*. London: Routledge.

Flandreau, M. (2003c). 'Crises and Punishment: Moral Hazard and the Pre-1914 International Financial Architecture', *CEPR Discussion Papers*, No. 3742. London: Centre for Economic Policy Research.

Flandreau, M. (2004). *The Glitter of Gold: France, Bimetallism and the Emergence of the International Gold Standard, 1848–1873*. Oxford: Oxford University Press.

Flandreau, M. (2013). 'Collective Action Clauses before they had Airplanes: Bondholder Committees and the London Stock Exchange in the 19th Century', *Working Paper*, 01/2013. Geneva: Graduate Institute of International and Development Studies.

Flandreau, M. and Flores, J. (2008). 'Bonds and Brands: Foundations of Sovereign Debt Markets, 1820–1830', <http:ssrn.com/abstract=1534169>

Flandreau, M. and Flores, J. (2010). 'Hamlet Without the Prince of Denmark: Relationship Banking and Conditionality Lending in the London Market for Foreign Government Debt, 1815–1913', *CEPR Discussion Paper*, No. 7915. London: Centre for Economic Policy Research.

Flandreau, M., Flores, J., Gaillard, N., and Nieto-Parra, S. (2009). 'The End of Gatekeeping: Underwriters and the Quality of Sovereign Bond Markets, 1815–2007', *CEPR Discussion Paper*, No. 7347. London: Centre for Economic Policy Research.

Flandreau, M., Gaillard, N., and Packer, F. (2009). 'Ratings Performance, Regulation and the Great Depression: Lessons from Foreign Government Securities', *CEPR Discussion Papers*, DP7328. London: Centre for Economic Policy Research.

Flandreau, M., Galimard, C., Jobst, C., and Nogués-Marco, P. (2009). 'Monetary Geography Before the Industrial Revolution', *Cambridge Journal of Regions, Economy and Society*, 2: 149–71.

Flandreau, M., Holtfrerich, C.-L., and James, H. (eds) (2010). *International Financial History in the Twentieth Century: System and Anarchy*. Cambridge: Cambridge University Press.

Flandreau, M., Huitzilihuiti, J., Zendejas, F., and Gaillard, N. (2009). 'The End of Gatekeeping: Underwriters and the Quality of Sovereign Bond Markets, 1815–2007', *CEPR Discussion Papers*, 7347. London: Centre for Economic Policy Research.

Flandreau, M. and Jobst, C. (2005). 'The Ties that Divide: A Network Analysis of the International Monetary System', *CEPR Discussion Paper*, 5129. London: Centre for Economic Policy Research.

Flandreau, M. and Sussman, N. (2004). 'Old Sins: Exchange Clauses and European Foreign Lending in the 19th Century', *CEPR Discussion Papers*, No. 4248. London: Centre for Economic Policy Research.

Flandreau, M. and Zumer, F. (2004). *The Making of Global Finance*. Paris: Organization for Economic Cooperation and Development.

Flaubert, G. (1856). *Madame Bovary*. Harmondsworth: Penguin, 1950.

Flores, J. and Decorzant, Y. (2012). 'Public Borrowing in Harsh Times: The League of Nations Loans Revisited', *WPS*, 12091. Faculty of Economic and Social Sciences, University of Geneva.

Foner, E. (2002). *Reconstruction: America's Unfinished Revolution, 1863–1877*. New York: Harper Collins.

Fontvieille, L. (1976). *Evolution et croissance de l'Etat Français: 1815–1969*. Paris: Institut de Sciences Mathematiques et Economiques Appliquees.

Foucault, M. (1977). *Discipline and Punish: The Power of the Prison*. Paris: Gallimard.

Francese, M. and Pace, A. (2008). 'Italian Public Debt Since National Unification: A Reconstruction of the Time Series', *Occasional Paper, Banca d'Italia*, 31 (October).

Franklin, B. (1732–1757). *Poor Richard's Almanack*. Elibron Classics, 2007.

Freud, S. (1927). *The Future of an Illusion*. London: Hogarth Press.

Freytag, G. (1855). *Debit and Credit*. Minneapolis, MN: Filiquarian, 2010.

Fryde, E. (2004). 'Pole, Sir William de la (d. 1366)', *Oxford Dictionary of National Biography*. Oxford: Oxford University Press.

FT.com/debt (2010). *Interactive: Sovereign Debt Levels by Country*, updated 23 June at 16.44.

Fuchs, S. (2013). *'Member-State Performance in Intergovernmental Negotiations: The Case of the European Union Stability and Growth Pact'*. PhD thesis. University College London, University of London.

Gaillard, N. (2006). *Determinants of Moody's and S&P's Subsovereign Credit Ratings* (April). Paris: Fondation Nationale des Sciences Politiques.

Galbraith, J.K. (1990). *A Short History of Financial Euphoria*. London: Penguin.

Galdós, B.P. (1889–1895). *Torquemada en la hoguera*. Hamburg: Tredition Classics, 2013.

Gardner, R. (1980). *Sterling-Dollar Diplomacy in Current Perspective: The Origins and Prospects of our International Economic Order.* New York: Columbia University Press.

Gavin, N. (2007). *Press and Television in British Politics: Media, Money and Mediated Democracy.* Basingstoke: Palgrave Macmillan.

Genoa Financial Commission Report, 20 April (1922). *Federal Reserve Bulletin*, June 1922, pp. 678–80.

Genschel, P. and Jachtenfuchs, M. (eds) (2013). *Beyond the Regulatory Polity. The European Integration of Core State Powers.* Oxford: Oxford University Press.

Gérard, M. (2001). 'Fiscal Federalism in Belgium'. Conference on Fiscal Imbalance, Quebec City, 13–14 September.

German Federal Finance Ministry (2009). 'Reforming the Constitutional Budget Rules in Germany'. Deficit Rule Reform Team: Economic Department, http://www.kas.de/wf/doc/kas˙21127-1522-4-30.pdf?101116013053>

German Federal Finance Ministry (2010). *Monatsbericht* (July), < http://www.bundesfinanzministerium.de/Content/EN/Standardartikel/Service/Publications/Monthly˙Report/Abstract/2010-07-abstract.html>

Ghosh, A., Kim, J., Mendoza, E., Ostry, J., and Qureshi, M. (2011). 'Fiscal Fatigue, Fiscal Space and Debt Sustainability in Advanced Economies', *NBER Working Paper*, No. 16782. Cambridge, MA: National Bureau for Economic Research.

Gilbert, D. (2007). *Stumbling on Happiness.* New York: Random House.

Gille, B. (1965). *Histoire de la Maison Rothschild, Vol I: Des origins à 1848.* Geneva: Droz.

Gille, B. (1967). *Histoire de la Maison Rothschild, Vol II: 1848–1870.* Geneva: Droz.

Girard, L. (1985). *Les libéraux français—1814–1875.* Paris: Aubier.

Glinavos, I. (2010). 'Pro-Market Reform Sustainability and the Tool of 'Constitutionalization': Economic Rights as Fundamental Rights?', *Hart Workshop 2010* (8 June), http://papers.ssrn.com/sol3/papers.cfm?abstract˙id=1622683>

Goethe, J.W. von (1809). *Elective Affinities*, ed. R. Hollingdale. London: Penguin, 1978.

Goethe, J.W. von (1831). *Faust Part Two.* Oxford: Oxford University Press, 2008.

Goff, J. de (1996). *Saint Louis.* Paris: Gallimard.

Goldsmith, M. (1985). *Private Vices, Public Benefits: Bernard Mandeville's Social and Political Thought.* Cambridge: Cambridge University Press.

Goodhart, C. (1999). 'Monetary Policy and Debt Management in the United Kingdom: Some Historical Viewpoints', in K. Alec Chrystal (ed.), *Government Debt Structure and Monetary Conditions.* London: Bank of England, pp. 43–97.

Goodhart, C. (2010a). 'How Should We Regulate the Financial Sector?', in *The Future of Finance: The LSE Report* (July). The London School of Economics, pp. 165–86.

Goodhart, C. (2010b). 'The Changing Role of Central Banks', BIS Working Papers, No. 326 (November). Basel: Bank for International Settlements.

Government Statistical Service (1999). *Monthly Statistics on Public Sector Finances: A Methodological Guide*. London: Office for National Statistics.

Graeber, D. (2011). *Debt: The First 5,000 Years*. New York: Melville House Publishing.

Grémion, C. (1976). *Le Pouvoir péripherique: bureaucrates et notables dans le régime politiques français*. Paris: Seuil.

Grenier, J.-Y. (2006). 'Introduction: dettes d'État, dette publique', in J. Andreau, G. Béaurd, and J.-Y. Grenier (eds), *La Dette Publique dans l'Histoire*. Paris: Comité pour l'histoire économique et financière de la France, pp. 1–19.

Greskovits, B. (2008). 'Hungary and Slovakia: Compliance and its Discontents', in K. Dyson (ed.), *The Euro at 10: Europeanization, Power and Convergence*. Oxford: Oxford University Press, pp. 274–291.

Griffiths, R. (1981). *The Reign of King Henry VI*. Stroud: Sutton.

Gros, D. and Mayer, T. (2010). 'Towards a Euro(pean) Monetary Fund', *CEPS Economic Policy Briefs* (17 May, update on February paper). Brussels: Centre for European Policy Studies.

Grotius, H. (1625). *On the Rights of War and Peace*. Central, Hong Kong: Forgotten Books, 2010.

Güran, T. (2003). *Ottoman Financial Statistics, Budgets 1841-1918*. Ankara: State Institute of Statistics.

Häberlein, M. and Burckhardt, J. (2002). *Die Welser. Neue Forschung zur Geschichte der Kultur des oberdeutschen Handelshauses*. Berlin: Akademie Verlag.

Hacker, R. (1966). *Ludwig II von Bayern in Augenzeugenberichten*. Munich: DTV.

Hakkio, C. and Rush, M. (1991). 'Is the Budget Deficit "Too Large"?' *Economic Inquiry*, 29 (3): 104–118.

Haldane, A., Brennan, S. and Madouros, V. (2010). 'The Contribution of the Financial Sector: Miracle or Mirage?', in *The Future of Finance: The LSE Report*. The London School of Economics, July.

Haldane, A. and May, R. (2011). 'The Birds and the Bees, and the Big Banks', *Financial Times*, 21 February: 11.

Hallerberg, M. and Stolfi, F. (2008). 'Partisanship, Social Capital, and Fiscal Federalism in the Italian Regions', Hertie School of Governance Working Papers No. 32, Berlin, May.

Hallerberg, M., Strauch, R. and von Hagen, J. (2010). *Fiscal Governance in Europe*. Cambridge: Cambridge University Press.

Hamon, P. (1994). *L'Argent du roi. Les finances sous François Ier*. Paris: Comité pour l'histoire économique et financière de la France.

Hamon, P. (2006). 'Les dettes du roi de France (fin du Moyen Âge-XVI siècle): une dette publique?', in J. Andreau, G. Béaurd, and J.-Y. Grenier (eds), *La Dette Publique dans l'Histoire*. Paris: Comité pour l'histoire économique et financière de la France, pp. 85–99.

Hancké, B. (2013). *Unions, Central Banks and EMU: Labour Market Institutions and Monetary Integration in Europe*. Oxford: Oxford University Press.

Hansard (1925). 'Gold Standard', *House of Commons Debate*, vol. 187, cc1457-71 (5 August). House of Commons Hansard Debates, <http://hansard.millbanksystems.com/>

Hanson, S., Kashyap, A., and Stein, J. (2010). 'A Macroprudential Approach to Financial Regulation', *Chicago Booth Research Paper*, No. 58, < http://faculty.chicagobooth.edu/brian.barry/igm/58KashyapMacroprudentialApproach.pdf>

Hare, R. (1993). *Without Conscience: The Disturbing World of the Psychopaths Among Us*. New York: Guilford.

Hargreaves, E. (1966). *The National Debt*. London: Routledge.

Harris, W. (2008). 'The Nature of Roman Money', in W. Harris (ed.), *The Monetary Systems of the Greeks and Romans*. Oxford: Oxford University Press, pp. 174–207.

Harriss, G. (2005). *Shaping the Nation: England 1360–1461*. Oxford: Oxford University Press.

Hart, M. (1999). 'The United Provinces, 1579–1806', in R. Bonney (ed.), *The Rise of the Fiscal State in Europe, c. 1200–1815*. Oxford: Oxford University Press, pp. 309–26.

Harvey, D. (1990). *The Condition of Postmodernity: An Enquiry into the Origins of Cultural Change*. Oxford: Blackwell.

Hauser, H. (1927). *Les débuts du capitalisme*. Paris: F. Alcan.

Hawtrey, R. (1927). *The Gold Standard in Theory and Practice*. London: Longman.

Hawtrey, R. (1932). *The Art of Central Banking*. London: Longman.

Hay, C. and Wincott, D. (2012). *The Political Economy of European Welfare Capitalism*. Houndmills: Palgrave Macmillan.

Haynes, C. (2010). *Lost Illusions: The Politics of Publishing in Nineteenth-Century France*. Cambridge, MA: Harvard University Press.

Hegel, G.W.F. (1807). *Hegel's Phenomenology of Spirit: A Critical Guide*, <http://www.Digireads.com>, 2009.

Heisbourg, F. (2013). *La fin du rêve européen*. Paris: Stock.

Hellwig, M. (2010). 'Capital Regulation after the Crisis: Business as Usual?', *Working Paper*, 31. Bonn: Max Planck Institute for Research on Collective Goods.

Helm, D. (2010). 'Rethinking the Economic Boundaries of the State', Social Market Foundation, <http://www.smf.co.uk>

Hemmings, F. (1965). *Émile Zola*. Oxford: Clarendon Press.

Her Majesty's Treasury (2011). *Rebalancing the Northern Ireland Economy*. London: HMT.

Hertzog, R. (2010). 'Collectivités territoriales: La réforme sans l'argent, impossible ou indispensable?', in J.-C. Nemery (ed.), *Quelle nouvelle réforme pour les collectivités territoriales françaises?* Paris: L'Harmattan, pp. 91–106.

Hildebrand, P. and Weber, A. (2010). 'Die Preisstabilität verteidigen', *Neue Zürcher Zeitung*, 5 March.

Hirschman, A. (1970). *Exit, Voice, and Loyalty*. Cambridge, MA: Harvard University Press.

Hirst, P., Thompson, G., and Bromley, S. (2009). *Globalization in Question*. Cambridge: Polity.

Hitler, A. (1925). *Mein Kampf: Volumes 1 and 2: The Official 1939 Reich English Edition*. Createspace Independent Publishing Platform, 2013.

Hodson, D. (2011). *Governing the Euro Area in Good Times and Bad*. Oxford: Oxford University Press.

Holmes, D. (2013). 'Communicative Imperative in Central Banks', *Cornell Law Review* Symposium on the Changing Politics of Central Banks, New York, 9 March.

Holtfrerich, C.-L. (1980). *Die Deutsche Inflation 1914–1923: Ursachen und Folgen in internationaler Perspektive*. Berlin: de Gruyter.

Holtfrerich, C.-L. (1999). *Finanzplatz Frankfurt. Von der mittelaltischen Messestadt zum europäischen Bankenzentrum*. München: Beck.

Holtfrerich, C.-L. (2013). 'Government Debt in Economic Thought of the Long 19th Century', *Working Paper*, 2013/4. Berlin: School of Business and Economics, Freie Universität Berlin.

Hooghe, L., Marks, G., and Schakel, A. (2010). *The Rise of Regional Authority: A Comparative Study of 42 Democracies*. London: Routledge.

Howarth, D. (2007). 'Making and Breaking the Rules: French Policy on EU "Gouvernement Économique"', *Journal of European Public Policy*, 14 (7): 1061–78.

Howarth, D. and Rommerskirchen, C. (2013). 'A Panacea for all Times? The German Stability Culture as Strategic Political Resource', *West European Politics*, 36 (4): 750–70.

Hrbek, R. and Bussjäger, P. (eds) (2011). *Finanzkrise, Staatsschulden und Föderalismus—Wege der Krisenbewältigung*. Schriftenreihe des EZFF. Tübingen: Europäisches Zentrum für Föderalismus-Forschung.

Hume, D. (1739). *A Treatise of Human Nature*. London: Penguin, 1985.

Hume, D (1759). *On Public Credit*. In E. Miller (ed.), *Essays, Moral, Political and Literary*. Indianapolis, IN: Liberty Fund, 1987, pp. 249–301.

Hunt, E. (1990). 'A New Look at the Dealings of the Bardi and Peruzzi with Edward III', *The Journal of Economic History*, 50 (1): 149–62.

Hunt, E. (1994). *The Medieval Super-Companies: A Study of the Peruzzi Company of Florence*. Cambridge: Cambridge University Press.

Huscroft, R. (2006). *Expulsion: England's Jewish Solution*. Stroud: Sutton.

Ibsen, H. (1879). *A Doll's House*. London: Methuen, 2013.

Inalcik, H. (1990). *An Economic History of the Ottoman Empire, 1300–1914*. Cambridge: Cambridge University Press.

Independent Commission on Funding and Finance for Wales (2009). *Funding Devolved Government in Wales: Barnett and Beyond*. The Holtham Report.

Independent Commission on Funding and Finance for Wales (2010). *Fairness and Accountability: A New Funding Settlement for Wales: Final Report*. The Holtham Report.

Independent Evaluation Office of the IMF (2011). *IMF Performance in the Run-Up to the Financial and Economic Crisis: IMF Surveillance in 2004–07*. Washington, DC: IMF Independent Evaluation Office.

Independent Strategy (2006). *Inverted Pyramid* (10 April). London: Independent Strategy.

Innis, H. (1950). *Empire and Communications*. Toronto: Dundurn Press.

Institute of International Finance (2006). 'Principles for Stable Capital Flows and Fair Debt Restructuring in Emerging Markets: Report on Implementation by the Principles Consultative Group'. Unpublished.

Institute of International Finance (2010). *IIF 2009 Annual Report: Advancing Toward a More Stable Global Financial System*, <http://www.iif.com>

International Monetary Fund (1999). *IMF Policy on Lending into Arrears to Private Creditors*, <http://www.imf.org/external/pubs/ftprivcred/lending.pdf>

International Monetary Fund (2002). *Fund Policy on Lending into Arrears to Private Creditors: Further Consideration of the Good Faith Criterion*, <http://www.imf.org/external/pubs/ftprivcred/073002.pdf>

International Monetary Fund (2003). *IMF World Economic Outlook*. Washington, DC: International Monetary Fund.

International Monetary Fund (2009a). *World Economic Outlook: Crisis and Recovery*, April. Washington, DC: International Monetary Fund.

International Monetary Fund (2009b). *Global Financial Stability Report: Navigating the Financial Challenges Ahead* (October). Washington, DC: International Monetary Fund.

International Monetary Fund (2009c). 'The State of Public Finances Cross-Country Fiscal Monitor: November 2009', *Staff Position Note*, SPN/09/25 (3 November). Washington, DC: International Monetary Fund.

International Monetary Fund (2010a). 'Getting the Balance Right: Transitioning Out of Sustained Current Account Surpluses', *World Economic Outlook: Rebalancing Growth* (April). Washington, DC: International Monetary Fund.

International Monetary Fund (2010b). 'Statistical Appendix', *World Economic Outlook: Rebalancing Growth* (April). Washington, DC: International Monetary Fund.

International Monetary Fund (2010c). *Fiscal Monitor: Navigating the Fiscal Challenges Ahead.* World Economic and Financial Surveys (May). Washington, DC: International Monetary Fund.

International Monetary Fund (2010d). *Global Financial Stability Report: Sovereigns, Funding, and Systemic Liquidity* (October). Washington, DC: International Monetary Fund.

International Monetary Fund (2011a). *Global Financial Stability Report: Durable Financial Stability* (April). Washington, DC: International Monetary Fund.

International Monetary Fund (2011b). *Global Financial Stability Report: Grappling with Crisis Legacies* (September). Washington, DC: International Monetary Fund.

International Monetary Fund (2012a). *From Bail-Out to Bail-In: Mandatory Debt Restructuring of Systemic Financial Institutions.* SDN/12/03 (24 April). Washington, DC: International Monetary Fund.

International Monetary Fund (2012b). *The Liberalization and Management of Capital Flows* (14 November). Washington, DC: International Monetary Fund.

International Monetary Fund (2013). 'Greece: Ex Post Evaluation of Exceptional Access under the 2010 Stand-By Arrangement', *IMF Country Report*, No. 13/156. Washington, DC: International Monetary Fund.

International Monetary Fund and the World Bank (2009). 'Managing Public Debt: Formulating Strategies and Strengthening Institutional Capacity', *Staff Paper* (3 March). Washington, DC: International Monetary Fund.

International Organization of Securities Commissions (2010). *Objectives and Principles of Securities Regulation* (June), < http://www.compliance-exchange.com/governance/library/ioscoprinciples2010.pdf >

Isaacs, A. and Prak, M. (1996). 'Les villes, la bourgeoisie et l'État', in W. Reinhard (ed.), *Les elites du pouvoir et la construction de l'État en Europe.* Paris: PUF.

Issing, O. (2008). *The Birth of the Euro.* Cambridge: Cambridge University Press.

Issing, O. (2010a). 'A Greek Bail-Out Would Be a Disaster for Europe', *Financial Times*, 16 February.

Issing, O. (2010b). 'Germany is Right: Bondholders Must Pay', *Financial Times*, 2 December: 14.

Italian Ministry of Economy and Finance (2010). *Italian Government Bond Specialists: Evaluation Criteria for the Period Year 2010.* Department of the Treasury—Directorate II.

Iyengar, S. (2010). *The Art of Choosing: The Decisions We Make Everyday.* New York: Little, Brown.

Jabko, N. (2012). *Playing the Market: A Political Strategy for Uniting Europe, 1985–2005.* Princeton, NJ: Princeton University Press.

Jaeger, A. and Schuknecht, L. (2004). 'Boom-Bust Phases in Asset Prices and Fiscal Policy Behaviour', *IMF Working Paper*, No. 54. Washington, DC: International Monetary Fund.

James, H. (2012). *Making the European Monetary Union. The Role of the Committee of Central Bank Governors and the Origins of the European Central Bank.* Cambridge, MA: Harvard University Press.

James, L. (1998). *Raj: The Making and Unmaking of British India.* London: Abacus.

Jefferson, T. *The Papers of Thomas Jefferson: Retirement Series.* The Jefferson Monticello, <http://www.monticello.org/site/research-and-collections>

Jenkins, P. and Masters, B. (2010). 'The Money Moves On', *Financial Times*, 15 September: 11.

Jenkins, R. (1995). *William Gladstone.* London: Macmillan.

Johnson, C. (1997). *France, Gold and the Great Depression.* New Haven, CT: Yale University Press.

Jones, E. (2014). *Europe's Systemic Crisis.* Oxford: Oxford University Press.

Jones, M. (2010). 'Sources of Power and Infrastructural Conditions in Medieval Governmental Accounting', *Accounting, Organizations and Society*, 35 (1): 81–94.

Jones, N. (1989). *God and the Moneylenders: Usury and Law in Early Modern England.* Oxford: Basil Blackwell.

Jonung, L. (1984). 'Swedish Experience under the Classical Gold Standard, 1973–1914', in M. Bordo and A. Schwartz (eds), *A Retrospective on the Classical Gold Standard, 1821–1931.* Chicago: University of Chicago Press, pp. 361–404.

Jonung, L., Schuknecht, L., and Tujula, M. (2005). 'The Boom-Bust Cycle in Finland and Sweden 1984–1995 in an International Perspective', *European Economy*, No. 237. Brussels: European Commission.

Jordan, W. (1979). *Louis IX and the Challenge of the Crusade.* Princeton, NJ: Princeton University Press.

Jouganatos, G. (1992). *The Development of the Greek Economy, 1950–1991.* Westport: Greenwood Press.

Junkernheinrich, M., Korioth, S., Lenk, T., Scheller, H., and Woisen, M. (eds) (2010). *Jahrbuch für öffentliche Finanzen 2010.* Berlin: Berliner Wissenschafts-Verlag.

Kaeuper, R. (1973). *Bankers to the Crown: the Riccardi of Lucca and Edward I.* Princeton, NJ: Princeton University Press.

Kahneman, D. and Tversky, A. (eds) (2000). *Choices, Values, and Frames.* Cambridge: Cambridge University Press.

Kantorowicz, E. (1997). *The King's Two Bodies: A Study in Medieval Political Theology.* Princeton, NJ: Princeton University Press.

Kaplan, J. and Schleiminger, G. (1989). *The European Payments Union.* Oxford: Clarendon Press.

Karaman, K. and Pamuk, S. (2010). 'Ottoman State Finances in European Perspective, 1500–1914', *The Journal of Economic History,* 70 (3): 593–629.

Kay, J. (2010). 'We Must Press On with Breaking Up Banks', *Financial Times,* 15 September: 13.

Keating, M. (2010). 'The Spatial Dimension', in K. Dyson and A. Sepos (eds), *Which Europe? The Politics of Differentiated Integration.* Basingstoke: Palgrave Macmillan, pp. 54–66.

Keating, M., Loughlin, J., and Deschouwer, K. (2003). *Culture, Institutions and Economic Development: A Study of Eight European Regions.* Cheltenham: Edward Elgar.

Kenen, P. (1990). 'Organizing Debt Relief: The Need for a New Institution', *Journal of Economic Perspectives,* 4 (1): 7–18.

Kern, R. (1966). *Caciquismo versus Self-Government: The Crisis of Liberalism and Local Government in Spain.* Chicago: University of Chicago Press.

Keyder, C. (1985). 'State and Industry in France, 1750–1914', *The American Economic Review,* 75 (2): 308–14.

Keynes, J.M. (1923). *A Tract on Monetary Reform,* in D. Moggridge (ed.), *The Collected Writings of John Maynard Keynes: Volume IV.* London: Macmillan, 1971.

Keynes, J.M. (1932). 'The Consequences to the Banks of the Collapse of Money Values', in J.M. Keynes, *Essays in Persuasion.* New York: Harcourt, Brace and Company, pp. 244–270.

Keynes, J.M. (1933). *The Means to Prosperity.* London: Macmillan.

Keynes, J.M. (1936). *The General Theory of Employment, Interest and Money,* in D. Moggridge (ed.), *The Collected Writings of John Maynard Keynes: Volume VII.* London: Macmillan, 1974.

Keynes, J.M. (1942). *Plan for an International Currency (or Clearing) Union,* 24–25 January, in D. Moggridge (ed.), *The Collected Writings of John Maynard Keynes: Volume XXV.* London: Macmillan, 1980.

Kiander, J. and Vartia, P. (1998). 'The Depression of the 1990s in Finland: A Nordic Financial Crisis or a Result of the Collapse of the Soviet Union?', in T. Myllyntaus (ed.), *Economic Crises and Restructuring in History: Experiences of Small Countries.* St. Katharinen: Scripta Mercaturae Verlag.

Kindleberger, C. (1973). *The World Depression 1929–1939.* London: Allen Lane.

Kindleberger, C. and Aliber, R. (2005). *Manias, Panics and Crashes: A History of Financial Crises*. Basingstoke: Palgrave Macmillan.

Kipling, R. (1897). *Recessional*, in *London Times*, 17 July, issue 1 of Critic leaflet.

Kirchner, W. and Radtke, W. (1987). *Bankier für Preussen: Christian (von) Rotter und die Königlich-Preussische Seehandlung*. Berlin: Nicolaische Verlagsbuchhandlung.

Kletzer, K. and Wright, B. (2000). 'Sovereign Debt as Intertemporal Barter', *American Economic Review*, 90 (3): 621–39.

Knight, M. (2006). 'Promoting Liquidity in Domestic Bond Markets', speech at the Government Borrowers' Forum, St. Petersburg, 23–25 May.

Kostelenos, G., Vasileiou, D., Kounaris, E., Petmezas, S., and Sfakianakis, M. (2007). *Gross Domestic Product, 1830–1939*. Greece: Centre of Planning and Economic Research—Historical Archives of the National Bank of Greece.

Kózmiński, L. (1929). *Voltaire financier*. Paris: Presses Universitaires de France.

Krasner, S. (1999). *Sovereignty: Organized Hypocrisy*. Princeton, NJ: Princeton University Press.

Krennbauer, F. (1949). *Goethe und der Staat: Die Staatsidee des Unpolitischen*. Hamburg: Springer.

Krueger, A. (2002). *A New Approach to Sovereign Debt Restructuring*. Washington, DC: International Monetary Fund.

Kydland, F. and Prescott, E. (1977). 'Rules Rather Than Discretion: The Inconsistency of Optimal Plans', *Journal of Political Economy*, 85 (3): 473–91.

Kynaston, D. (1995). *The City of London: A World of its Own 1815–1890, Volume 1*. London: Pimlico.

Kynaston, D. (2000). *The City of London: Illusions of Gold, 1914–45, Volume 3*. London: Pimlico.

Kynaston, D. and Roberts, R. (eds) (1995). *The Bank of England: Money, Power and Influence, 1694–1994*. Oxford: Clarendon Press.

Kynaston, D. and Sulkin, W. (2002). *The City of London: A Club No More, 1945–2000, Volume 4*. London: Pimlico.

Lake, D. (2011). *Hierarchy in International Relations*. Ithaca, NY: Cornell University Press.

Lamy, P. (2011). '"Made in China" Tells Us Little About Global Trade', *Financial Times*, 24 January, p. 12.

L'économie française (2004–2005). *Dossiers—La dette publique en France: La tendance des vingt dernières années est-elle soutenable?* Paris: INSEE.

Le Galès, P. (2002). *European Cities: Social Conflicts and Governance*. Oxford: Oxford University Press.

Leineweber, N. (1988). *Das säkulare Wachstum der Staatsausgaben. Eine kritische Analayse*. Göttingen: Vandenhoeck and Ruprecht.

Lemarchand, Y. (2010). 'Accounting, the State and Democracy: A Long-Term Perspective on the French Experiment, 1716-1967', *LEMNA, Working Paper*, 43. Pays de la Loire: University of Nantes.

Leroy-Beaulieu, P. (1888). *Traité de la science des finances*, 4th edn. Paris: Alcan.

Levandis, J. (1944). *The Greek Foreign Debt and the Great Powers, 1821–1898.* New York: Columbia University Press.

Lewis, M. (2010). *The Big Short: Inside the Doomsday Machine.* London: Allen Lane.

Lijphart, A. (1999). *Patterns of Democracy: Government Forms and Performance in Thirty-Six Countries.* New Haven, CT: Yale University Press.

Liu, L. (2009). 'Subnational Credit Ratings: A Comparative Review', *World Bank Working Paper*, 5013. Washington, DC: World Bank.

London Finance Commission (2013). *Raising the Capital.* London: City Hall.

Longford, E. (1972). *Wellington: Pillar of the State.* London: Weidenfeld and Nicholson.

Loughlin, J. and Martin, S. (2003). 'International Lessons on Balance of Funding Issues: Initial Paper' (November). Cardiff University: School of European Studies.

Loughlin, J. and Martin, S. (2005). 'Options for Reforming Local Government Funding to Increase Local Streams of Funding: International Comparisons'. Prepared for the Lyon Inquiry into Local Government Funding. Cardiff University: School of European Studies.

Lovejoy, A. (1964). *The Great Chain of Being. A Study of the History of an Idea.* Cambridge, MA: Harvard University Press.

Lukes, S. (2005). *Power: A Radical View*, 2nd edn. Basingstoke: Palgrave Macmillan.

MacKenzie, D. (2006). *An Engine, Not a Camera: How Financial Models Shape Markets.* Cambridge, MA: MIT Press.

MacKenzie, D. (2009). *Material Markets: How Economic Agents Are Constructed.* Oxford: Oxford University Press.

MacKenzie, D., Muniesa, F., and Siu, L. (eds) (2007). *Do Economists Make Markets? On the Performativity of Economics.* Princeton, NJ: Princeton University Press.

Mackie, J. (1972). *The Earlier Tudors 1485–1558.* Oxford: Oxford University Press.

Mack Smith, D. (1971). *Victor Emmanuel, Cavour, and the Risorgimento.* London: Oxford University Press.

Mack Smith, D. (1985). *Cavour.* London: Weidenfeld and Nicolson.

Maddison, A. (2004). *Historical Statistics for the World Economy: 1–2003 AD.* Paris: Organization for Economic Cooperation and Development, <http://www.ggdc.net/maddison/>

Maddison, A. (2006). *The World Economy.* Paris: Organisation for Economic Cooperation and Development.

Maes, I. (2006). 'The Ascent of the European Commission as an Actor in the Monetary Integration Process in the 1960s', *Scottish Journal of Political Economy*, 53 (2): 222–41.

Makinen, G. and Woodward, G. (1990). 'Funding Crises in the Aftermath of World War 1', in R. Dornbusch and M. Draghi (eds), *Public Debt Management: Theory and History*. Cambridge: Cambridge University Press, pp. 153–82.

Mallaby, S. (2010). *More Money than God: Hedge Funds and the Making of a New Elite*. London: Bloomsbury Publishing.

Mandeville, B. de (1714). *The Fable of the Bees*. London: Penguin, 1989.

Mann, T. (1901). *Buddenbrooks*. London: Penguin, 1957.

Masson, P. and Mussa, M. (1995). 'Long-Term Tendencies in Budget Deficits and Debt', *Proceedings*, 0: 5–55. Kansas City, MO: Federal Reserve Bank of Kansas City.

Mazower, M. (1991). *Greece and the Inter-War Economic Crisis*. Oxford: Oxford University Press.

Mazower, M. (2005). *Salonica: City of Ghosts*. London: Harper Perennial.

Mazzucato, M. (2013). *The Entrepreneurial State: Debunking Public versus Private Sector Myths*. London: Anthern Press.

McGrath, C. (2012). *Ireland and Empire, 1692–1770*. London: Pickering and Chatto.

McKinsey Global Institute (2012). 'Debt and Deleveraging. Uneven Progress on the Path to Growth' (January), <http://www.mckinsey.com/insights/global˙capital˙markets/uneven˙progress˙on˙the˙path˙to˙growth>

Melon, J.-F. (1738). *A Political Essay Upon Commerce*. Dublin: Philip Crampton.

Meltzer Commission (2000). *Report of the International Financial Institutions Advisory Commission*. Washington, DC, < http://repository.cmu.edu/cgi/viewcontent.cgi?article=1029&context=tepper>

Michie, R. (2004). 'The City of London and the British Government: The Changing Relationship', in R. Michie and P. Williamson (eds), *The British Government and the City of London in the Twentieth Century*. Cambridge: Cambridge University Press, pp. 31–56.

Migeotte, L. (1984). *L'Emprunt public dans les cités grecques. Recueil des documents et analyse critique*. Paris: Québec-Les Belles Lettres.

Migeotte, L. (2006). 'L'endettement des cités grecques dans l'Antiquité', in J. Andreau, G. Béaurd, and J.-Y. Grenier (eds), *La Dette Publique dans l'Histoire*. Paris: Comité pour l'histoire économique et financière de la France, pp. 115–28.

Migone, A. (2007). 'Hedonistic Consumerism: Patterns of Consumption in Contemporary Capitalism', *Review of Radical Political Economics*, 39 (2): 173–200.

Mill, J.S. (1848). *Principles of Political Economy*. London: Longman. <http://www.econlib.org/library/Mill/mlP69.html>

Miller, P. (1990). 'On the Interrelations between Accounting and the State', *Accounting, Organizations and Society*, 15 (4): 315–38.

Minsky, H. (1982). 'Debt Deflation Processes in Today's Institutional Environment', *Banca Nazionale Del Lavoro Quarterly Review*, December: 375–95.

Minsky, H. (2008). *Stabilizing an Unstable Economy*. New York: McGraw-Hill.

Mitchener, K.M. and Weidenmier, M.D. (2005). 'Supersanctions and Sovereign Debt Repayment', *NBER Working Paper*, No. 11472. Cambridge, MA: National Bureau of Economic Research.

Mohi-uddin, M. (2008). 'UBS FX Strategy: Sovereign Wealth Funds', Foreign Exchange Strategy Group, UBS Investment Bank.

Moles, P. and Terry, N. (1999). *The Handbook of International Financial Terms*. Oxford: Oxford University Press.

Molho, A. (1971). *Florentine Public Finances in the Early Renaissance, 1400–1433*. Cambridge, MA: Harvard University Press.

Molho, A. (2006). 'La dette publique en Italie aux XIVe et XVe siècles', in J. Andreau, G. Béaurd, and J.-Y. Grenier (eds), *La Dette Publique dans l'Histoire*. Paris: Comité pour l'histoire économique et financière de la France, pp. 37–61.

Montesquieu, C. de (1751). *The Spirit of the Laws*, ed. A. Cohler, B. Miller, and H. Stone. Cambridge: Cambridge University Press, 1989.

Monti, M. (2011). 'Il podestà forestiero', *Corriere della Sera*, 7 August.

Moody's (2011). 'Sub-Sovereign Ratings List', 25 February, https://www.moodys.com/Pages/rr005˙0.aspx?bd=4294966358&ed=4294966623&rd=4294966358&tb=0&po=0&lang=en&cy=global&kw=>

Moog, S. and Raffelhüschen, B. (2013). 'Ehrbarer Staat? Die Generationenbilanz Update 2013: Nachhaltigkeitsbilanz der Wahlprogramme', *Argumente zu Marktwirtschaft und Politik*, 121. Freiburg : Forschungszentrum Generationsverträge, Albert-Ludwigs-Universität Freiburg.

Moore, S. (2010). *Swift, the Book, and the Irish Financial Revolution: Satire and Sovereignty in Colonial Ireland*. Baltimore, MD: John Hopkins University Press.

Moran, M. (1991). *The Politics of the Financial Services Revolution*. London: Macmillan.

Moravcsik, A. (1998). *The Choice for Europe*. Ithaca, NY: Cornell University Press.

Morgan, M. (2012). *The World in the Model: How Economists Work and Think*. Cambridge: Cambridge University Press.

Morgenstern, O. (1950). *On the Accuracy of Economic Observations*. Princeton, NJ: Princeton University Press.

Morris, M. (2009). *A Great and Terrible King: Edward I and the Forging of Britain*. London: Random House.

Morys, M. (2010). '*The Original Sin that Started Only Later: How Austria-Hungary's Paper Debt Turned Golden, 1870s–1913*', Cherry DP 02/10. Centre for Historical Economics and Related Research. York: University of York.

Mosley, L. (2003). *Global Capital and National Governments.* Cambridge: Cambridge University Press.

Moulton, H. and Lewis, C. (1925). *The French Debt Problem.* New York: Macmillan.

Mourlon-Druol, E. (2012). *A Europe Made of Money: The Emergence of the European Monetary System.* Ithaca, NY: Cornell University Press.

Mueller, R. (1997). *The Venetian Money Market: Banks, Panics, and the Public Debt, 1200–1500.* Baltimore, MD: The John Hopkins University Press.

Müller, W. and Strøm, K. (eds) (2000). *Coalition Governments in Western Europe.* Oxford: Oxford University Press.

Mundill, R. (1998). *England's Jewish Solution: Experiment and Expulsion, 1262–1290.* Cambridge: Cambridge University Press.

Munro, J. (2010). 'The Coinage and Monetary Policies of Henry VIII (r.1509–1547): Contrasts between Defensive and Aggressive Debasements', *New Economic Papers*, 26 November, <http://ideas.repec.org/p/tor/tecipa/tecipa-417.html>

Munro, J. (2011). 'Usury, Calvinism, and Credit in Protestant England: From the Sixteenth Century to the Industrial Revolution', *Department of Economics Working Paper*, 439 (28 June). Toronto: University of Toronto.

Murphy, A. (2006). 'John Law et la gestion de la dette publique', in J. Andreau, G. Béaurd, and J.-Y. Grenier (eds), *La Dette Publique dans l'Histoire.* Paris: Comité pour l'histoire économique et financière de la France, pp. 269–96.

National Conference of State Legislatures (2011). *State Budget Update: March 2011.* Washington, DC: NCSL.

Naurin, D. (2009). 'Most Common When Least Important: Deliberation in the European Council of Ministers', *British Journal of Political Science*, 40: 31–50.

Naurin, D. and Lindahl, R. (2008). 'East-North-South. Coalition-Building in the Council Before and After Enlargement', in D. Naurin and H. Wallace (eds), *Unveiling the Council of the EU: Games Governments Play in Brussels.* Basingstoke: Palgrave, pp. 64–80.

Naurin, D. and Lindahl, R. (2009). 'Out in the Cold? Flexible Integration and the Political Status of Euro-Outsiders', *European Policy Analysis*, 13 (December). Stockholm: Swedish Institute for European Policy Studies.

Newton, S. (2000). 'A "Visionary Hope" Frustrated: J.M. Keynes and the Origins of the Post-War International Monetary Order', *Diplomacy and Statecraft*, 11 (1): 189–210.

Nicholson, H. (2001). *The Knights Templar. A New History.* Stroud: Sutton.

Nietzsche, F. (1876). *Untimely Meditations*, ed. D. Breazeale. Cambridge: Cambridge University Press, 1997.

Nietzsche, F. (1879). *Human, All Too Human*, ed. Hollingdale. Cambridge: Cambridge University Press, 1996.

Nietzsche, F. (1887). *On the Genealogy of Morals*, in A. Tille (ed.), *The Works of Friedrich Nietzsche, Volume X: A Genealogy of Morals.* New York: Macmillan, 1897.

Nietzsche, F. (1895). *Twilight of the Idols.* In A. Ridley and J. Norman (eds), *The Anti-Christ, Ecce Homo, Twilight of the Idols and other Essays.* Cambridge: Cambridge University Press, 2005.

Nilus. (1905). *The Jewish Peril: Protocols of the Learned Elders of Zion.* London: Eyre and Spottiswoode, 1920.

Noll, F. (2012). *Repudiation! The Crisis of United States Civil War Debt, 1865–1870.* Geneva: Graduate Institute of International and Development Studies.

Nordhaus, W. (1975). 'The Political Business Cycle', *Review of Economic Studies*, 42 (2): 169–90.

Norman, M. (1931a). 'Letter to George Harrison (Governor of Federal Reserve Bank of New York), 3 March', in S.V.O. Clarke, *Central Bank Cooperation 1924–31.* New York: Federal Reserve Bank of New York, pp. 179.

Norman, M. (1931b). 'Minutes of Evidence, Committee on Finance and Industry' (so-called Macmillan Committee), in S.V.O. Clarke, *Central Bank Cooperation 1924–31.* New York: Federal Reserve Bank of New York, pp. 32.

Nummedal, T. (2007). *Alchemy and Authority in the Holy Roman Empire.* Chicago: Chicago University Press.

Oates, W. (1993). *Fiscal Federalism.* Aldershot: Gregg Revivals.

Oberholtzer, E. (1907). *Jay Cooke: Financier of the Civil War.* Philadelphia: George W. Jacobs.

Office for National Statistics (1999). *Monthly Statistics on Public Sector Finances: A Methodological Guide.* Government Statistical Service Methodology Series, No. 12. London: Office for National Statistics.

Oosterlinck, K., Ureche-Rangau, L., and Vaslin, J.-M. (2013). 'Waterloo: A Godsend for French Public Finances?', EHES Working Papers in Economic History, No. 41, <http://www.ehes.org/EHES˙No41.pdf>

Organization for Economic Cooperation and Development (2007). *Objectives, Strategy and Operations of the OECD Working Party on Public Debt Management* (14 November). Paris: OECD.

Organization for Economic Cooperation and Development (2009a). 'OECD Sovereign Borrowing Outlook 2009', *Financial Market Trends* 1: 1–10.

Organization for Economic Cooperation and Development (2009b). *OECD Economic Surveys: Belgium.* Paris: OECD.

Organization for Economic Cooperation and Development (2010). *OECD Economic Surveys: Spain*. Paris: OECD.

Organization for Economic Cooperation and Development (2013). 'Declaration on Base Erosion and Profit Shifting', Meeting of the Council at Ministerial Level. Paris: OECD, < http://www.oecd.org/mcm/>

Packer, F. (2003). 'Mind the Gap: Domestic Versus Foreign Currency Sovereign Ratings', *BIS Quarterly Review*, September: 55–64.

Padoa-Schioppa, T. (2010). 'Europe Cannot Leave Athens On Its Own', *Financial Times*, 18 February.

Pamuk, S. (1987). *The Ottoman Empire and European Capitalism*. Cambridge: Cambridge University Press.

Pamuk, S. (2000). *A Monetary History of the Ottoman Empire*. Cambridge: Cambridge University Press.

Pamuk, S. (2009). 'Changes in Factor Markets in the Ottoman Empire, 1500–1800', *Continuity and Change*, 24 (1): 1–30.

Parra, S. (2008). 'Who Saw Sovereign Debt Crises Coming?', *Working Paper*, No. 274 (November). Paris: OECD Development Centre.

Parra, S. (2009). 'Sovereign Debt Crises and Early Warning Indicators: The Role of the Primary Bond Market', *Policy Insights*, 89 (February). Paris: OECD Development Centre.

Partnoy, F. (2009). *The Match King: Ivar Kreuger, the Financial Genius Behind a Century of Wall Street Scandals*. London: Profile Books.

Pascali, L. (2013). 'Banks and Development: Jewish Communities in the Italian Renaissance and Current Economic Performance', *Warwick Economic Research Papers*, No. 1026. Warwick: University of Warwick, Department of Economics.

Pattillo, C., Poirson, H., and Ricci, L. (2004). 'What Are the Channels through which External Debt Affects Growth?', *IMF Working Paper*, WP/04/15. Washington, DC: International Monetary Fund.

Pauly, L. (1996). 'The League of Nations and the Foreshadowing of the International Monetary Fund', *Essays in International Finance*, No. 201. Princeton, NJ: Princeton University Press.

Penn, T. (2011). *Winter King: The Dawn of Tudor England*. London: Penguin.

Penn, W. (1693). *Some Fruits of Solitude*. Central, Hong Kong: Forgotten Books, 2012.

Peretz, D. (2010). 'Bilateral Surveillance of the United Kingdom', *IEO Background Paper*, No. BP/10/05. Washington, DC: International Monetary Fund.

Pfetsch, F. and Landau, A. (2000). 'Symmetry and Asymmetry in International Negotiations', *International Negotiation*, 5 (1): 21–42.

Piergallini, A. and Postigliola, M. (2011). 'Fiscal Policy and Public Debt Dynamics in Italy', *MPRA Paper*, No. 28200, < http://mpra.ub.uni-muenchen.de/28200/>

Pierson, P. (2001). 'From Expansion to Austerity: The New Politics of Taxing and Spending', in M. Levin, M.K. Landy, M.M. Shapiro (eds), *Seeking the Center: Politics and Policymaking at the New Century*. Washington, DC: Georgetown University Press, pp. 54–80.

Pinto, I. de (1771). *Traité de la Circulation et du Crédit*. Amsterdam: Rey.

Pirenne, H. (1971). *Les villes de Moyen Âge*. Paris: PUF.

Platt, D. (1968). *Finance, Trade and Politics in British Foreign Policy, 1815–1914*. Oxford: Clarendon Press.

Plessis, A. (2002). *Histoires de la Banque de France*. Paris: Albin Michel.

Pocock, J.G.A. (1985). *Virtue, Commerce and History: Essays on Political Thought and History Chiefly in the Eighteenth Century*. Cambridge: Cambridge University Press.

Ponticelli, J. and Voth, H.-J. (2011). 'Austerity and Anarchy: Budget Cuts and Social Unrest in Europe, 1919-2009', *CEPR Discussion Paper*, No. 8513. London: Centre for Economic Policy Research.

Prados de la Escosura (2003). *El progreso económico de España (1850–2000)*. Bilbao: Fundación BBVA.

Preda, A. (2005). 'The Investor as a Cultural Figure of Global Capitalism', in K. Cetina and A. Preda (eds), *The Sociology of Financial Markets*. Oxford: Oxford University Press, pp. 141–62.

Prestwich, M. (1972). *War, Politics and Finance under Edward I*. London: Faber and Faber.

Price, R. (2001). *The French Second Empire: An Anatomy of Political Power*. Cambridge: Cambridge University Press.

Publilius Syrus. *Sentences (Fragments)*. Paris: Les Belles Lettres, 2011.

Puetter, U. (2006). *The Eurogroup: How a Secretive Circle of Finance Ministers Shapes European Economic Governance*. Manchester: Manchester University Press.

Purcell, J. and Kaufman, J. (1993). *The Risks of Sovereign Lending: Lessons from History*. New York: Salomon Brothers.

Quintos, C. (1995). 'Sustainability of the Deficit Process with Structural Shifts', *Journal of Business and Economic Statistics*, 13 (4): 409–17.

Rabelais, F. (1653). *Gargantua and Pantagruel*. London: Penguin, 2006.

Rajan, R. (2010). *Fault Lines: How Hidden Fractures Still Threaten the World Economy*. Princeton, NJ: Princeton University Press.

Reinhart, C. (2012). 'The Return of Financial Repression', *Discussion Paper*, No. 8947. London: Centre for Economic Policy Research, April.

Reinhart, C. and Reinhart, V. (2010). 'Beware Those Who Think the Worst Is Past', *Financial Times*, 31 August, p. 11.

Reinhart, C., Reinhart, V., and Rogoff, K. (2012). 'Debt Overhangs: Past and Present', *NBER Working Paper*, No. 18015 (April). Cambridge, MA: National Bureau of Economic Research.

Reinhart, C. and Rogoff, K. (2008). 'The Forgotten History of Domestic Debt', *NBER Working Paper*, No. W13946. Cambridge, MA: National Bureau of Economic Research.

Reinhart, C. and Rogoff, K. (2009). *This Time is Different: Eight Centuries of Financial Folly*. Princeton, NJ: Princeton University Press.

Reinhart, C. and Rogoff, K. (2010). 'Growth in a Time of Debt', *NBER Working Paper*, No. 15639. Cambridge, MA: National Bureau of Economic Research.

Reinhart, C., Rogoff, K., and Savastano, M. (2003). 'Debt Intolerance', *Brookings Papers on Economic Activity*, 1 (Spring): 1–74.

Reinhart, C. and Sbrancia, M. (2011). 'The Liquidation of Government Debt', *BIS Working Paper*, No. 363. Basel: Bank for International Settlements.

Reitmeyer, M. (1999). *Bankiers im Kaiserreich. Sozialprofil und Habitus der deutschen Hochfinanz*. Göttingen: Vandenhoeck and Ruprecht.

Renzsch, W. (1991). *Finanzverfassung und Finanzausglech*. Bonn: Verlag J.H.W. Dietz Nachf.

Renzsch, W. (2010). 'Federal Reform under the Grand Coalition', *German Politics*, 19 (3–4): 382–92.

Ricardo, D. (1817). *The Principles of Political Economy and Taxation*. London: J. Dent, 1911.

Richardson, S. (1740). *Pamela*. Oxford: Oxford University Press, 2008.

Richardson, W. (1952). *Tudor Chamber Administration, 1485–1547*. Baton Rouge: Louisiana State University Press.

Richardson, W. (1953). *Stephen Vaughan: Financial Agent of Henry VIII. A Study of Financial Relations with the Low Countries*. Baton Rouge: Louisiana State University Press.

Riles, A. (2011). *Collateral Knowledge: Legal Reasoning in the Global Financial Markets*. Chicago: Chicago University Press.

Riley, J. (1980). *International Government Finance and the Amsterdam Capital Market, 1740–1815*. Cambridge: Cambridge University Press.

Ritschl, A. (2002). *Deutschlandskrise und Konjunktur 1924–1934. Binnenkonjunktur, Auslandsverschuldung und Reparationsproblem zwischen Dawes-Plan und Transfersperre*. Berlin: Akademie Verlag.

Ritschl, A. (2012a). 'Reparations, Deficits, and Debt Default: the Great Depression in Germany', *CEP Discussion Paper*, No. 1149. London: London School of Economics, Centre for Economic Performance.

Ritschl, A. (2012b). 'The German Transfer Problem, 1920–1933: A Sovereign Debt Perspective', *CEP Discussion Paper*, No. 1155. London: London School of Economics, Centre for Economic Performance.

Robb, G. (1994). *Balzac*. London: Picador.

Roberts, A. (1999). *Salisbury: Victorian Titan*. London: Weidenfeld & Nicholson.

Rodden, J. (2002). 'The Dilemma of Fiscal Federalism: Grants and Fiscal Performance around the World', *American Journal of Political Science*, 46 (3): 670–85.

Rodden, J. (2003). 'Reviving Leviathan: Fiscal Federalism and the Growth of Government', *International Organization*, 57: 695–729.

Rodden, J. (2009). *Federalism and Inter-Regional Redistribution*. Barcelona: Institut d'Economia de Barcelona.

Rodden, J. and Eskeland, G. (2000). 'Lessons and Conclusions', in J. Rodden, G. Eskeland, and J. Littvack (eds), *Fiscal Decentralization and the Challenge of Hard Budget Constraints*. Washington, DC: World Bank, pp. 431–66.

Rodden, J. and Eskeland, G. (eds) (2003). *Fiscal Federalism and the Challenge of the Hard Budget Constraint*. Cambridge, MA: MIT Press.

Rodden, J. and Wibbels, E. (2002). 'Beyond the Fiction of Federalism', *World Politics*, 54: 494–531.

Roseveare, H. (1991). *The Financial Revolution 1660–1760*. London: Longman.

Rossel, F. (1909). *Voltaire, créancier du Württemberg, correspondance inedite*. Paris: Champion.

Roth, J. (1932). *The Radetzsky March*. London: Granta, 2003.

Rothkopf, D. (2010). 'The All-Too-Real Phantom Balance Sheet', *Financial Times*, 14 June.

Roubini, N. and Sachs, J. (1989). 'Government Spending and Budget Deficits in the Industrial Countries', *Economic Policy*, 11: 100–32.

Rowlands, G. (2012). *The Financial Decline of a Great Power: War, Influence, and Money in Louis XIV's France*. Oxford: Oxford University Press.

Sachverständigenrat (2011a). *Deutschland und die europäische Ungleichgewichte*. Auszug aus dem Jahresgutachten 2010/11. Wiesbaden: Statistisches Bundesamt.

Sachverständigenrat (2011b). *Ein Schuldentilgungspakt für Europa*. Auszug aus dem Jahresgutachten 2010/11. Wiesbaden: Statistisches Bundesamt.

Sadeh, T. (2006). *Sustaining European Monetary Union: Confronting the Cost of Diversity*. Boulder, CO: Lynne Rienner.

Saint-Simon, H. (1760–1825). *Selected Writings on Science, Industry and Social Organization*, trans. with introduction by K. Taylor. London: Croom Helm, 1975.

Sassen, S (2005). 'The Embeddedness of Electronic Markets: The Case of Global Financial Markets', in K. Cetina and A. Preda (eds), *The Sociology of Financial Markets*. Oxford: Oxford University Press, pp. 17–37.

Savage, J. (2005). *Making the EMU: The Politics of Budgetary Surveillance and the Enforcement of Maastricht*. Oxford: Oxford University Press.

Schama, S. (1987). *The Embarrassment of Riches: An Interpretation of Dutch Culture in the Golden Age*. London: Collins.

Scharpf, F., Reissert, B., and Schnabel, F. (1976). *Politikverflechtung: Theorie und Empirie des kooperativen Föderalismus in der Bundesrepublik*. Kronberg: Scriptor.

Schäuble, W. (2010). 'Liebäugeln mit einem EU-Währungsfond', interview with Jan Dams, *Welt am Sonntag*, 7 March, <http://www.welt.de/politik/deutschland/article6668719/Schaeuble>

Schenk, C. (2010). *The Decline of Sterling. Managing the Retreat of an International Currency, 1945–1992*. Cambridge: Cambridge University Press.

Schmidt, H. (1996). 'Die Bundesbank—Kein Staat im Staate', *Die Zeit*, 46, 8 November.

Schmidt, V. (2013). 'Democracy and Legitimacy in the European Union Revisited: Input, Output and "Throughput"', *Political Studies*, 61 (1): 2–22.

Schnee, H. (1953–1957). *Die Hoffinanz und der moderne Staat. Geschichte und System der Hoffaktoren an deutschen Fürstenhöfen im Zeitalter des Absolutismus*, six vols. Berlin: Duncker and Humblot.

Schneiderman, D. (2008). *Constitutionalizing Economic Globalization: Investment Rules and Democracy's Promise*. Cambridge: Cambridge University Press.

Schofield, R. (2004). *Taxation under the Early Tudors 1485–1547*. Oxford: Blackwell.

Schremmer, E. (1994). *Steuern und Staatsfinanzen während der Industrialisierung Europas. England, Frankreich, Preussen und das Deutsche Reich 1800 bis 1914*. Berlin: Springer.

Schumpeter, J. (1918). 'The Crisis of the Tax State', in R. Swedberg (ed.), *The Economics and Sociology of Capitalism*. Princeton, NJ: Princeton University Press, 1991.

Scott, J. (1998). *Seeing Like a State: How Certain Schemes to Improve the Human Condition Have Failed*. New Haven, CT: Yale University Press.

Scott, P. (2006). *The Union of 1707: Why and How*. Edinburgh: Saltire Society.

Sen, A. (1989). *On Ethics and Economics*. Oxford: Wiley Blackwell.

Sen, A. (1993). 'Capability and Well-Being', in M. Nussbaum and A. Sen (eds), *The Quality of Life*. Oxford: Clarendon Press, pp. 30–53.

Shakespeare, W. (1596). *The Merchant of Venice*. Oxford: Oxford University Press, 2010.

Shakespeare, W. (1602). *Troilus and Cressida.* Oxford: Oxford University Press, 2008.

Shakespeare, W. (1605–1606). *Timon of Athens.* Oxford: Oxford University Press, 2008.

Shiller, R. (2003). 'From Efficient Markets Theory to Behavioral Finance', *The Journal of Economic Perspectives*, 17 (1): 83–104.

Silverman, D. (1982). *Reconstructing Europe after the Great War.* Cambridge, MA: Harvard University Press.

Sinclair, T. (2005). *The New Masters of Capital: American Bond Rating Agencies and the Politics of Creditworthiness.* Ithaca, NY: Cornell University Press.

Singh, M. and Aitken, J. (2010). 'The (Sizeable) Role of Rehypothecation in the Shadow Banking System', *IMF Working Paper*, No. 10/172. Washington, DC: International Monetary Fund.

Singh, M. and Youssef, K. (2010). 'Price of Risk—Recent Evidence from Large Financials', *IMF Working Paper*, No. 10/90. Washington, DC: International Monetary Fund.

Skidelsky, R. (1992). *John Maynard Keynes. Volume Two: The Economist as Saviour 1920–1937.* London: Macmillan.

Skidelsky, R. (2000). *John Maynard Keynes. Volume Three: Fighting for Britain 1937–1946.* London: Macmillan.

Smith, A. (1759). *The Theory of Moral Sentiments.* London: Penguin, 2010.

Smith, A. (1776). *An Inquiry into the Nature and Causes of the Wealth of Nations*, eds R. Campbell and A. Skinner. Oxford: Clarendon Press, 1976.

Smith, D. (2012). 'Coping with the Threat of Humiliation: Contrasting Responses to the Eurozone Crisis in Greece and Ireland', conference on 'The Debt Crisis in the Eurozone: Social Impacts', Lesvos Chamber of Commerce, Greece, September.

Sokol, M. (2001). 'Central and Eastern Europe a Decade after the Fall of State-Socialism: Regional Dimensions of Transition Processes', *Regional Studies*, 35 (7): 645–55.

Solomon, R. (1976). *The Passions: Emotions and the Meaning of Life.* Indianapolis, IN: Hackett.

Sorkin, A. (2009). *Too Big to Fail: Inside the Battle to Save Wall Street.* London: Allen Lane.

Sornarajah M. (2004). *The International Law of Foreign Investment.* Cambridge: Cambridge University Press.

Spence, M. (1973). 'Job Market Signaling', *Quarterly Journal of Economics*, 87 (3): 355–74.

Spoerer, M. (2010). 'The Evolution of Public Finances in Nineteenth-Century Germany', in J. Cardoso and P. Lains (eds), *Paying for the Liberal State: The Rise of Public Finance in Nineteenth Century Europe.* Cambridge: Cambridge University Press, pp. 103–31.

Standard and Poor's (2007). *Sovereign Defaults and Rating Transition Data: 2006 Update*, <http://www2.standardandpoors.com/spf/pdf/fixedincome/KR˙sovereign˙SovDefaultsTransitionData2006.pdf>

Stark, J, (2010). 'Der Euro am Scheideweg', *Handelsblatt Wirtschafts- und Finanzzeitung*, 9 March.

Stark, J. (2013). 'Es gibt keine rote Linie mehr', *Handelsblatt Wirtschafts- und Finanzzeitung*, 26 July.

Starkey, D. et al. (ed.) (1987). *The English Court: From the Wars of the Roses to the Civil War*. London: Longman.

Stasavage, D. (2003). *Public Debt and the Birth of the Democratic State: France and Great Britain, 1688–1789*. Cambridge: Cambridge University Press.

Stasavage, D. (2010). 'When Distance Mattered: Geographic Scale and the Development of European Representative Assemblies', *American Political Science Review*, 104 (4): 625–43.

Stasavage, D. (2011). *States of Credit: Size, Power, and the Development of European Politics*. Princeton, NJ: Princeton University Press.

Statistisches Bundesamt (2010). *Finanzen und Steuern: Schulden der öffentlichen Haushalte*. Wiesbaden: Statistisches Bundesamt.

Steil, B. (2013). *The Battle of Bretton Woods: John Maynard Keynes, Harry Dexter White and the Making of a New World Order*. Princeton, NJ: Princeton University Press.

Stein, L. von (1885–1886). *Lehrbuch der Finanzwissenschaft*, 4 vols. Leipzig: Brockhaus.

Stent, A. (1981). *From Embargo to Ostpolitik: The Political Economy of West German-Soviet Relations, 1955–1980*. Cambridge: Cambridge University Press.

Stern, F. (1978). *Gold und Eisen. Bismarck und sein Bankier Bleichröder*. Frankfurt am Main: Ullstein.

Stern, S. (1962–1975). *Der Preussische Staat und die Juden*, 7 vols. Tübingen: Mohr Siebeck.

Stern, S. (2001). *Der Hofjude im Zeitalter des Absolutismus. Ein Beitrag zur europäischen Geschichte im 17. und 18. Jahrhundert*. Tübingen: Mohr Siebeck.

Stiglitz, J. (2010). *Freefall: Free Markets and the Sinking of the Global Economy*. London: Penguin.

Stolper, G., Häuser, K., and Borchardt, K. (1967). *The German Economy 1870 to the Present*. London: Weidenfeld and Nicolson.

Stone, I. (1999). *The Global Export of Capital from Great Britain, 1865–1914*. New York: St. Martin's Press.

Stoskopf, N. (2002). *Les patrons du Second Empire: Banquiers et financiers parisiens, Vol. 7*. Paris: Picard-Céromane.

Strayer, J. (1980). *The Reign of Philip the Fair.* Princeton, NJ: Princeton University Press.

Streeck, W. (2013). *Gekaufte Zeit: Die vertagte Krise des demokratischen Kapitalismus.* Berlin: Suhrkamp.

Streider, J. (1931). *Jakob Fugger the Rich: Merchant and Banker of Augsburg, 1459–1525.* Washington, DC: Beard Books.

Stürmer, M., Teichmann, G., and Treue, W. (1989). *Wägen und Wagen. Sal. Oppenheim jr. & Cie.: Geschichte einer Bank und einer Familie.* Piper: München.

Sturzenegger, F. and Zettelmeyer, J. (2007). *Debt Defaults and Lessons from a Decade of Crises.* Cambridge, MA: MIT Press.

Summers, L. (2010). 'Keynote Address', *FT Future of Finance Conference*, New York, 7 October.

Suter, C. (1992). *Debt Cycles in the World Economy: Foreign Loans, Financial Crises, and Debt Settlements, 1820–1990.* Boulder, CO: Westview Press.

Swift, J. (1732). *'A Proposal to Pay Off the Debt of the Nation'.* University College Cork: CELT, 2010.

Swift, J. (1812). *The Works of the Rev. Jonathan Swift D.D. with Notes, Volume 2*, ed. T. Sheridan. New York: William Durell.

Sylla, R. and Roussea, P. (2001). 'Financial Systems, Economic Growth and Globalization', *NBER Working Paper*, No. 8323. Cambridge, MA: National Bureau of Economic Research.

Taleb, N. (2008). *The Black Swan: The Impact of the Highly Improbable.* London: Penguin.

Tallberg, J. (2008). 'Bargaining Power in the European Council', *Journal of Common Market Studies*, 46 (3): 685–708.

Tambini, D. (2008). *What Is Financial Journalism For? Ethics and Responsibility in a Time of Crisis and Change.* London: LSE, Polis.

Tarrow, S. (1977). *Between Center and Periphery.* New Haven, CT: Yale University Press.

Taylor, C. (1994). 'The Politics of Recognition', in A. Gutman (ed.), *Multiculturalism: Examining the Politics of Recognition.* Princeton, NJ: Princeton University Press, pp. 25–74.

Tesoro Publico (2010). *Composition of Government Debt.* Madrid: Ministry of Finance.

Tett, G. (2009). *Fool's Gold: How Unrestrained Greed Corrupted a Dream, Shattered Global Markets and Unleashed a Catastrophe.* London: Little, Brown.

Théret, B. (1991). 'Apogée et declin du rentier de la dette publique dans le "Grand" XIX siècle libéral 1815–1935', *Economies et Sociétés*, Série Economia, PE no. 14: 87–136.

Théret, B. (1995). 'Régulation du deficit budgétaire et croissance des dépenses de l'Etat en France de 1815 à 1939. Une modélisation économétrique simple des régimes fisco-financiers libéraux', *Revue économique*, 46 (1): 57–90.

Thomson, R. (2009). 'Actor Alignments in the European Union Before and After Enlargement', *European Journal of Political Research*, 48: 756–81.

Throsby, D. (2001). *Economics and Culture*. Cambridge: Cambridge University Press.

Thucydides. *History of the Peloponnesian War*. London: Penguin, 2010.

Tilly, C. (ed.) (1975). *Formation of National States in Western Europe*. Princeton, NJ: Princeton University Press.

Tilly, C. (1990). *Coercion, Capital and European States: AD 990–1990*. Oxford: Blackwell.

Tobias, S. (2005). 'Foucault on Freedom and Capabilities', *Theory, Culture and Society*, 22: 65–85.

Tobin, J. (1980). 'Real Balance Effects Reconsidered', in J. Tobin, *Asset Accumulation and Economic Activity*. Chicago: Chicago University Press, pp. 1–19.

Tommaso Padoa-Schioppa Group (2012). *Completing the Euro. A Road Map towards a Fiscal Union in Europe* (June). Paris: Notre Europe.

Tomz, M. (2007). *Reputation and International Cooperation: Sovereign Debt across Three Centuries*. Princeton, NJ: Princeton University Press.

Tomz, M. and Wright, M. (2007). 'Do Countries Default in "Bad Times"?', *Journal of the European Economics Association*, 5 (2–3): 352–60.

Tomz, M. and Wright, M. (2012). 'Empirical Research on Sovereign Debt and Default', *Federal Reserve Bank of Chicago Working Papers*, No. 2012-06, <http://ideas.repec.org/p/fip/fedhwp/wp-2012-06.html>

Toniolo, G., with Piet Clement (2005). *Central Bank Cooperation at the Bank for International Settlements, 1930–1973*. Cambridge: Cambridge University Press.

Torre, I. de la (2010). 'The Monetary Fluctuations in Philip IV's Kingdom of France and their Relevance to the Arrest of the Templars', in J. Burgtorf, P. Crawford, and H. Nicholson (eds), *The Debate on the Trial of the Templars (1307–1314)*. Abingdon: Ashgate, pp. 57–69.

Toye, R. (2007). *Lloyd George and Churchill: Rivals for Greatness*. London: Macmillan.

Triffin, R. (1960). *Gold and the Dollar Crisis: The Future of Convertibility*. New Haven, CT: Yale University Press.

Trivers, R. (2011). *Deceit and Self-Deception*. London: Allen Lane.

Trollope, A. (1875). *The Way We Live Now*. Oxford: Oxford University Press, 1982.

UK Debt Management Office (2005). *Executive Agency Framework Document* (April). London: UK Debt Management Office.

UK Debt Management Office (2009). *A Guide to the Roles of the DMO and Primary Dealers in the UK Government Bond Market*. London: UK Debt Management Office.

Vandenbroucke, F. (2012). 'The Social Challenge: Defining the Union's Social Objective is a Necessity rather than a Luxury', *OSE Opinion Paper*, No. 11. Brussels: European Social Observatory.

Vandenbroucke, F., Diris, R., and Verbist, G. (2013). 'Excessive Social Imbalances and the Performance of Welfare States in the EU', *Euroforum Policy Paper*, No. 3. Leuven: KU Leuven.

Van Der Stichele, G. and Verdonck, M. (2002). 'The Lambermont Agreement: Why and How?' Conference on Fiscal Imbalance, Quebec City, 13–14 September.

Van Der Wee, H. (1963). *The Growth of the Antwerp Market and the European Economy (Fourteenth–Sixteenth Centuries)*. The Hague: Nijhoff.

Van Rompuy, H., Barroso, J., Juncker, J.-C., and Draghi, M. (2012). 'Towards a Genuine Economic and Monetary Union'. Brussels: European Council, < http://www.consilium.europa.eu/uedocs/cms˙Data/docs/pressdata/en/ec/134069.pdf>

Von Justi, J.H.G. (1760). *Des Herrn Von Justi Natur und Wesen der Staaten als die Quelle aller Regierungswissenschaften und Gesetze*, ed. J. Gott. Charleston, SC: Nabu Press, 2012.

Wagner, A. (1863). *Die Ordnung des österreichischen Staatshaushaltes mit besonderer Rücksicht auf den Ausgabe-Etat und die Staatsschuld.* Wien: Carl Gerold's Sohn.

Waibel, M. (2007). 'Opening Pandora's Box: Sovereign Bonds in International Arbitration', *American Journal of International Law*, 101: 711–59.

Waibel, M. (2010). 'Iceland's Financial Crisis—Quo Vadis International Law', *Insights, The American Society of International Law*, 14 (5), 1 March.

Waibel, M. (2011). *Sovereign Defaults before International Courts and Tribunals.* Cambridge: Cambridge University Press.

Wainstein, B. (2010). 'The Role of Gold in Global Markets', < http://www.scotiabank.com/gls/en/index.html>

Wallace, R. (1994). *Responsibility and the Moral Sentiments.* Cambridge, MA: Harvard University Press.

Wallas, G. (2010). *Human Nature in Politics*, 3rd edn. Minneapolis: Filiquarian Publishing.

Weatherford, J. (1997). *The History of Money.* New York: Three Rivers Press.

Weber, A. (2010). 'Der IWF spielt mit dem Feuer', *Financial Times Deutschland*, 25 February.

Wee, H. van der (1963). *The Growth of the Antwerp Market and the European Economy: Fourteenth–Sixteenth Centuries.* The Hague: Nijhoff.

Weidmann, J. (2011). 'Die Krise als Herausforderung für die Währungsunion', *Auszüge aus Presseartikeln*, Deutsche Bundesbank, 14 September, pp. 3–8.

Weill, G. (1896). *L'école saint-simonienne, son histoire et son influence jusqu'à nos jours*. Paris: Alcan.

White, L. (2011). 'Markets: The Credit Rating Agencies', *Journal of Economic Perspectives*, 24 (2): 211–26.

Wibbels, E. (2003). 'Bailouts, Budget Constraints, and Leviathans', *Comparative Political Studies*, 36 (5): 475–508.

Williams, P. (1970). *Wars, Plots and Scandals in Post-War France*. Cambridge: Cambridge University Press.

Winkler, M. (1933). *Foreign Bonds, An Autopsy. A Study of Defaults and Repudiations of Government Obligations*. Philadelphia: Swain.

Wittgenstein, L. (1921). *Tractatus Logico-Philosophicus*. London: Routledge, 1961.

Wolf, M. (2004). *Why Globalization Works*. New Haven, CT: Yale University Press.

Wolf, M. (2011). 'The Eurozone's Journey to Defaults', *Financial Times*, 11 May, p. 15.

World Bank (2010). Joint External Debt Hub (JEDH), joint BIS-IMF-WB Statistics on External Debt, <http://jedh.org/>

Wyn Jones, R. and Scully, R. (2010). 'Introduction: Europe, Regions and Regionalism', in R. Wyn Jones and R. Scully (eds), *Europe, Regions and Regionalism*. Basingstoke: Palgrave Macmillan, pp. 1–15.

Wynne, W. (1951). *State Insolvency and Foreign Bondholders: Selected Case Histories of Governmental Foreign Bond Defaults and Debt Readjustments Volume II*. London: Oxford University Press.

Zartmann, I. and Rubin, J. (eds) (2000). *Power and Negotiation*. Ann Arbor: The University of Michigan Press.

Ziegler, P. (1988). *The Sixth Great Power: Barings 1762–1929*. London: Collins.

Zola, E. (1871). *The Kill*. Oxford: Oxford University Press, 2008.

Zola, E. (1885). *Germinal*. Oxford: Oxford University Press, 2008.

Zola, E. (1891). *L'Argent*. Paris: Editions Flammarion, 1980.

Name Index

Subject Index

Please see under entries for individual countries/regions for specific topics relating to that country